TPI New Testament Commentaries

General Editors
Howard Clark Kee   Dennis Nineham

★

Saint Luke

TPI New Testament Commentaries

These paragraph-by-paragraph commentaries have
been written by modern scholars who are in touch
with contemporary biblical study and also with the
interests of the general reader. They interpret the
words of the New Testament for the twentieth
century in the light of the latest archaeological,
historical and linguistic research and are neither
over-simplified nor abstruse and academic.

TPI New Testament Commentaries

Saint Luke

C. F. EVANS

SCM PRESS
London

TRINITY PRESS INTERNATIONAL
Philadelphia

First published 1990

SCM Press
26–30 Tottenham Road
London N1 4BZ

Trinity Press International
3725 Chestnut Street
Philadelphia, Pa. 19104

British Library Cataloguing in Publication Data

Evans, C. F. (Christopher Francis, *1909*)
Saint Luke.
1. Bible. N.T. Luke—Critical studies
I. Title
226′. 406

Library of Congress Cataloging-in-Publication Data

Evans, Christopher Francis.
Saint Luke / C.F. Evans.
p. cm. — (TPI New Testament commentaries)
ISBN 0–334–00951–0.—ISBN 0–334–00950–2 (pbk.)
1. Bible. N.T. Luke—Commentaries. I. Title. II. Series.
BS2595.3.E82 1990   89–78459
226.4′06—dc20

334 00951 0 (cased)
334 00950 2 (paper)

Typeset by Gloucester Typesetting Services
and printed in Great Britain by
Richard Clay Ltd, Bungay, Suffolk

Contents

CONTENTS

memorans conjugem dilectam et patientem

Acknowledgements

Any commentator on the Gospel is aware of a profound indebtedness to a long line of predecessors, as well as to a host of writers on the matters involved. I am most immediately and personally indebted to one of the General Editors, Dr Dennis Nineham, for his invitation to contribute to the series, and for the time and care he has given to reading the manuscript. There are few of its pages which do not bear the marks of his concern for precision of statement and clarity of expression. I am also much indebted to Miss Jean Cunningham, formerly of the SCM Press, for all her work in preparing the manuscript for printing, in reading the proofs and in compiling the index.

References, Abbreviations and Technical Terms

The English text of Luke's Gospel used in the Commentary, as of the Bible as a whole apart from the Old Testament Apocrypha, is that of the Revised Standard Version (RSV), 2nd edition, 1971. Reference is sometimes made to the text of the Authorized Version (AV), the Revised Version (RV) and the New English Bible (NEB).

Where a Greek word or phrase is mentioned it is transliterated into an English equivalent. The letters *ng* (e.g. in *angelos* = messenger) represent a double G in Greek.

The books of the Bible are cited by their customary abbreviations. The modern designation Luke–Acts (L–A) is used for the Gospel and Acts considered as a single work, and because of the frequency with which it has to be cited Acts is often abbreviated as A.

Luke can denote both the author of the Gospel and the Gospel itself, as can also Matthew, Mark and John.

Q is the symbol for the source which some believe Matthew and Luke to have possessed in common in addition to Mark, and L is the symbol for material found only in Luke's Gospel.

Frequent reference is made to the text and language of the Septuagint (LXX), so called because of a legend that it was the work of seventy translators. This was the earliest rendering into Greek of the Hebrew scriptures along with certain books now in the Old Testament Apocrypha. It was standard by the first century AD, and was commonly, though not invariably, used by the New Testament authors. It differs at times from the Hebrew text, upon which English versions of the Old Testament are based.

Other Jewish writings referred to are:

i. Pseudepigrapha – as collected in *The Apocrypha and Pseudepigrapha of the Old Testament in English*, Vol. 2, ed. R. H. Charles, Oxford 1913 (abbreviated as *AP*).

ii. Mishnah – an authoritative collection of Jewish Oral Law in the form of sixty-three treatises or tractates. It is cited from the edition of H. Danby, Oxford 1933.

xi

iii. Rabbinical – generally cited from *Kommentar zum Neuen Testament aus Talmud und Midrasch*, ed. H. L. Strack and P. Billerbeck, 4 Vols., Munich 1922–28 (abbreviated as SB).

iv. Qumran Scrolls – in the edition of G. Vermes, *The Dead Sea Scrolls in English*, Harmondsworth 1962 (Vermes, *Scrolls*).

References to the Jewish historian Josephus, and to the Jewish theologian Philo, are to the Loeb edition of their works.

The text of the Gospel was transmitted over centuries in hand-written copies. This inevitably resulted in differences in the text, called 'variant readings' or 'variants' (abbreviated as v.l.); and of the hundreds of manuscripts (mss) now available no two are in exact agreement. The Greek text behind AV was that of a few comparatively late mss; that behind RV depended on a consensus of a comparatively few fourth-century mss. The majority of variants concern minor matters of spelling, style, accidental omission, etc. Some, however, are substantial, such as those reproduced in the margin of RSV introduced by 'Some ancient authorities read . . .' The object of textual criticism is to assess these variants, and to determine, if possible, which is primary and which secondary. The evidence for such an assessment is generally set out by reference to the earliest mss and those judged more reliable, in the following form:

i. Papyri – for Luke esp. p^{75} (early third cent.) and p^{45} (third cent.).

ii. Uncials – i.e. Greek mss written in larger and separate letters, denoted by capital letters. The chief of these are:

א	Codex Sinaiticus (fourth cent.)
B	Codex Vaticanus (fourth cent.)
A	Codex Alexandrinus (fifth cent.)
D	Codex Bezae (fifth-sixth cent.).
L	Codex Regius (eighth cent.)
W	Washington Codex (fifth cent.)
M	Codex Koridethi (ninth cent.)

iii. Minuscules – i.e. Greek mss written in smaller and running hand, denoted by numbers. Chief among these are:

28 (eleventh cent.), 33 (ninth–tenth cent.), 157 (twelfth cent.), 565 (ninth cent.), 579 (thirteenth cent.), 700 (eleventh-twelfth cent.).

iv. Versions – i.e. translations of the Greek text into a native tongue. The principal versions are:

(a) Old Latin – sometimes called Itala (it.), denoted by the letters a–z. These witness to the Latin text from the second to the fourth century. Vulgate (vulg) denotes witnesses to the Latin text as standardized by Jerome in the fourth century.

(b) Syriac – esp. the Sinaitic (syr^s or syr^{sin}, fourth–fifth cent.), the Curetonian (syr^c or syr^{cur}, fifth cent.) and the Peshitta (syr^p, the standardized Syriac text, fifth cent.).

(c) Coptic – in two forms, the Sahidic (co^{sah} third to fourth cent.) and the Bohairic (co^{boh}, sixth to seventh cent.).

v. The text as quoted by Christian writers – e.g. Origen, Tertullian (Tert.).

The textual evidence can also be set out in terms of 'families' or text-types. Such are the Alexandrian, represented by p^{75}, ℵ , B, and sometimes A; the Western, represented by D, it. syr^s; and in the view of some 'fam 1' (= a consensus of 1, 118, 131, 209) and 'fam 13' (= a consensus of 13, 69, 124, 346, 543).

In choosing between variants the evidence of earlier mss, and those judged more reliable, is to be preferred, though this is not always conclusive, as all texts are to some extent mixed texts, and a correct reading could be preserved in a late ms which had been copied from an earlier ms no longer extant. That reading is to be preferred which is judged more likely to have given rise to the other(s), but this cannot always be established with certainty. Knowledge of the author's mind and style can assist in deciding what he would have written, though this may be qualified in the case of an evangelist, who derived some of his material from the writings of others.

(See further, B. M. Metzger, *The Text of the New Testament*, Oxford and New York 1964; J. N. Birdsall, 'The New Testament Text' in *The Cambridge History of the Bible*, Vol. 1, ed. P. R. Ackroyd and C. F. Evans, Cambridge 1970, pp. 308ff., and R. V. G. Tasker, *The Greek New Testament, being the text translated in The New English Bible*, Oxford and Cambridge 1964, pp. vii–xiii, and for Luke pp. 417–24.)

A.	The Book of Acts
ad loc.	on the passage under discussion
AP	R. H. Charles, *The Apocrypha and Pseudepigrapha of the Old Testament*, 2 vols., Oxford 1913
BJRL	*Bulletin of the John Rylands Library*, Manchester
BZNW	Beiträge zur *Zeitschrift für die Neutestamentliche Wissenschaft*, Berlin

Beginnings   *The Beginnings of Christianity*, ed. F. J. Foakes-Jackson and
K. Lake, 5 vols., London and New York 1920–33

c.   circa (about)

ConjNeot   Conjectanea Neotestamentica, Lund

CR   Community Rule (= 1QS, Dead Sea Scrolls)

DR   Damascus Rule (= CD, Dead Sea Scrolls)

ET   English translation

Eus. *HE*   Eusebius, *Historia Ecclesiastica*

ExpT   *Expository Times*, Edinburgh

HTR   *Harvard Theological Review*

ICC   International Critical Commentary, Edinburgh and New York

ILS   *Inscriptiones Latinae Selectae*, ed. H. Dessau, Berlin 1892–1916

JB   Jerusalem Bible, 1966

JBL   *Journal of Biblical Literature*, Philadelphia

JE   *Jewish Encyclopaedia*, 12 vols, New York and London 1901–06

Jos. *BJ*   Josephus, *Bellum Judaicum (Jewish War)*

Jos. *Ant.*   Josephus, *Antiquities of the Jews*

JSNT(S)   *Journal for the Study of the New Testament* (Supplement), Sheffield

JTS   *Journal of Theological Studies*, Oxford

L–A   Luke–Acts

LXX   The Septuagint, the Greek translation of the Old Testament

MM   J. H. Moulton and G. Milligan, *The Vocabulary of the Greek Testament*, London 1914–29

ms(s)   manuscript(s)

NovTest   *Novum Testamentum*, Leiden

ns   new series

NT   New Testament

NTRJ   D. Daube, *The New Testament and Rabbinic Judaism*, London and New York 1956

NTS   *New Testament Studies*, Cambridge

op. cit.   the work just cited

OT   Old Testament

p   papyrus

par(s).   parallel(s) (in the synoptic gospels)

1QH   Qumran Cave 1, Hodayoth, the Thanksgiving Hymns

1QM   Qumran Cave 1, Milhamah, the War Rule

1QS   Qumran Cave 1, Serekh, the Community Rule

SB   H. L. Strack and P. Billerbeck, *Kommentar zum Neuen Testament aus Talmud und Midrasch*, 4 vols., Munich 1922–1928

SBT   Studies in Biblical Theology, London and Naperville, Ill.

SNTSM   Society for New Testament Studies. Monograph Series, Cambridge

s.v.   sub verbo (i.e. under the word in question in dictionaries)

TDNT   *A Theological Dictionary of the New Testament*, ed. G. Kittel and G. Friedrich, ET by G. W. Bromiley, 10 vols., Grand Rapids and London 1964–76

Test.   Testament (of the Twelve Patriarchs)

v.l.   varia lectio (i.e. variant reading in ms; see p. xii)

ZNW   *Zeitschrift für die Neutestamentliche Wissenschaft*, Berlin

+   the references following list all the NT instances of the word under discussion

++   this is the only NT instance of the word under discussion

Bibliography

COMMENTARIES

(normally cited by author's name only)

Caird, G. B., *The Gospel of St Luke*, Pelican Gospel Commentaries, Penguin Books 1963, reissued, SCM Press and Westminster Press 1977

Creed, J. M., *The Gospel According to St Luke*, Macmillan 1930

Easton, B. S., *The Gospel According to St Luke*, T. & T. Clark and Scribner 1926

Ellis, E. E., *The Gospel of Luke*, New Century Bible, Nelson 1966

Fitzmyer, J. A., *The Gospel According to Luke*, 2 vols., Anchor Bible, Doubleday 1981, 1985

Grundmann, W., *Das Evangelium nach Lukas*, Theologischer Handkommentar sum Neuen Testament 3, Berlin 1962

Klostermann, E., *Das Lukasevangelium*, Handbuch zum Neuen Testament, Tübingen 1929

Lagrange, M.-J., *Évangile selon Saint Luc*, Études bibliques, Paris 1927

Leaney, A. R. C., *The Gospel According to St Luke*, Black's/Harper's New Testament Commentary 1958

Loisy, A., *L'Évangile selon Luc*, Paris 1924

Manson, W., *The Gospel of Luke*, Moffatt New Testament Commentaries, Hodder and Stoughton 1930

Marshall, I. H., *The Gospel of Luke*, New International Greek Testament Commentary, Paternoster Press and Eerdmans 1978

Plummer, A., *A Critical and Exegetical Commentary on the Gospel According to St Luke*, ICC 1896

Rengstorf, K. H., *Das Evangelium nach Lukas*, Das Neue Testament Deutsch, Göttingen 1949

Schlatter, A., *Das Evangelium des Lukas*, Stuttgart 1931

Schürmann, H., *Das Lukasevangelium*, Herders theologischer Kommentar zum Neuen Testament, Freiburg 1969

Wellhausen, J., *Das Evangelium Lucae übersetzt und erklart*, Berlin 1904

Other Works

(Books which appear most often are usually cited by the
short title shown in bold type.)

Abrahams, I., **Studies** *in Pharisaism and the Gospels*, 2 vols., Cambridge
and New York 1917, 1924

Alsup, J. E., **The Post-Resurrection Appearance Stories** *in the
Gospel Tradition*, Stuttgart 1975

Barrett, C. K., *The* **Holy Spirit** *in the Gospel Tradition*, new ed.
London 1966

Bauer, W., *A Greek–English Lexicon of the New Testament and Other
Early Christian Literature*, ET by W. F. Arndt and F. W. Gingrich,
Cambridge and Chicago 1957 (**Bauer**)

Black, M., *An* **Aramaic Approach** *to the Gospels and Acts*, 3rd ed.,
London and New York 1967

Blass, F. W., and **Debrunner,** A., *A Greek Grammar of the New
Testament and Other Early Christian Literature*, ET of ed. 9–10 by
R. W. Funk, Cambridge and Chicago 1961

Brown, R. E., *The* **Birth** *of the Messiah: a Commentary on the Infancy
Narratives in Matthew and Luke*, London 1977

Bultmann, R., *The* **History** *of the Synoptic Tradition*, ET Oxford and
New York 1963

Cadbury, H. J. *The Making of* **Luke–Acts**, 2nd ed., London and
Naperville, Ill. 1958 (See also **Beginnings** in Abbreviations)

Catchpole, D. R., *The* **Trial** *of Jesus*, Studia post-biblica 18, Leiden
1971

Cullmann, O., *The* **Christology** *of the New Testament*, ET, 2nd ed.,
London 1963

Conzelmann, H., *The* **Theology** *of St Luke*, ET London 1960, New
York 1961

Dalman, G., *The* **Words of Jesus** *considered in the light of post-Biblical
Jewish Writings and the Aramaic Language*, ET Edinburgh and New
York 1902

Daube, D., *The New Testament and Rabbinic Judaism*, London and New
York 1956 (**NTRJ**)

Derrett, J. D. M., *Law in the New Testament*, London 1970 (**Law in the
NT**)

Dibelius, M., *From* **Tradition** *to Gospel*, ET London 1934, New York 1935
— **Studies** *in the Acts of the Apostles*, ET London and New York 1956

Dodd, C. H., *The* **Parables** *of the Kingdom*, London 1935, New York 1936
— *According to the Scriptures: the Sub-structure of New Testament Theology*, London and New York 1952
— *More New Testament Studies*, Manchester 1968 (**More NT Studies**)

Drury, J. H., **Tradition** *and Design in Luke's Gospel*, London 1976

Dupont, J., *The* **Sources of Acts:** *the Present Position*, ET London and New York 1964

Evans, C. F., **Resurrection** *and the New Testament*, SBT 2.12, 1970

Field, F., **Notes** *on Select Passages of the Greek Testament*, Cambridge 1899

Fuller, R. H., *The* **Foundations** *of New Testament Christology*, London and New York 1965

Haenchen, E., *The* **Acts** *of the Apostles*, Oxford 1971

Harnack, A. von, *The* **Sayings** *of Jesus*, ET London and New York 1908

Huck, A., **Synopsis** *of the First Three Gospels*, 9th ed. revised by H. Lietzmann, ET Tübingen 1936, reissued Oxford 1949

Hull, J., **Hellenistic Magic** *and the Synoptic Tradition*, SBT 2.28, 1974

Interpreter's Bible, 12 vols., New York 1951–57

Jeremias, J., *The* **Parables** *of Jesus*, 2nd ed., ET London and New York 1966
— *The* **Eucharistic Words** *of Jesus*, ET, rev. ed., London and New York 1966
— **Jerusalem** *in the Time of Jesus*, ET London and Philadelphia 1969
— *New Testament* **Theology**, vol. I, ET London and New York 1971

Keck, L. E., and Martyn, J. L., *Studies in Luke–Acts*, New York 1966, London 1968

Klausner, J., *Jesus of Nazareth*, ET London and New York 1926

Knox, W. L., *The* **Acts** *of the Apostles*, Cambridge and New York 1948
— *Some* **Hellenistic Elements** *in Primitive Christianity*, London and New York 1944

— The **Sources** of the Synoptic Gospels, 2 vols., Cambridge and New York 1953, 1957

Kümmel, W. G., **Introduction** to the New Testament, ET London and New York 1965

— Promise and Fulfilment, SBT 23, 1957

Laurentin, R., **Structure** et Théologie de Luc I–II, Études bibliques, Paris 1957

Maddox, R., The Purpose of Luke-Acts, Edinburgh 1982

Manson, T. W., The **Sayings** of Jesus, London and Toronto 1949

Marxsen, W., **Mark** the Evangelist, New York 1969

Montefiore, C. G., The Synoptic Gospels, 2 vols., London 1909, New York 1910

Moulton, J. H., A Grammar of New Testament Greek: I, Prolegomena, Edinburgh 1906; II, Accidence, with W. F. Howard, 1929; III, Syntax, by N. Turner, 1963; IV, Style, by N. Turner, 1976

Moulton, J. H., and Milligan, G., The Vocabulary of the Greek Testament illustrated from the papyri and other non-literary sources, London 1914–29 (**MM**)

Nineham, D. E., St Mark (Pelican Gospel Commentaries), Harmondsworth 1963, reissued London and Philadelphia 1977

— ed., Studies in the Gospels: Essays in Memory of R. H. Lightfoot, Oxford 1955

O'Neill, J. C., The Theology of Acts, 2nd ed., London 1970

Otto, R., The Kingdom of God and the Son of Man, ET London and Grand Rapids 1938

Perry, A. M., The Sources of St Luke's **Passion-Narrative**, Chicago 1920

Sahlin, H., Der **Messias** und das Gottesvolk, Uppsala 1945

Sanders, E. P., Jesus and Judaism, London and Philadelphia 1985

Sanders, J. T., The Jews in Luke-Acts, London and Philadelphia 1987

Schürer, E., The History of the **Jewish People** in the Age of Jesus Christ (175 BC–AD 135), new English version ed. G. Vermes and F. Millar, Edinburgh 1973ff.

Sherwin-White, A. N., Roman Society and **Roman Law** in the New Testament, Oxford and New York 1963

Streeter, B. H., The **Four Gospels:** a Study of Origins, London and New York 1924

Stauffer, E., New Testament Theology, ET London 1955

Taylor, V., *Behind the* **Third Gospel**, Oxford 1926

— *The* **Formation** *of the Gospel Tradition*, London 1933

— *The* **Passion Narrative** *of St Luke*, ed. O. E. Evans, SNTSM 19, 1972

Turner, N., see Moulton

Van Unnik, W. C., *Sparsa Collecta, Nov Test* Suppl. 29, 1973

Vermes, G., *The Dead Sea* **Scrolls** *in English*, Harmondsworth 1962

— *Jesus the Jew*, London 1973, New York 1974

Williams, C. S. C., *The Acts of the Apostles*, London 1957, New York 1948

Winter, P., 'The Treatment of his Sources by the Third Evangelist', *Studia Theologica* 8, 1955, pp. 138–72

L. A. C. Alexander's thesis, 'Luke-Acts in its Contemporary Setting with special Reference to the Prefaces', is to be published shortly as an SNTS Monograph, *Luke to Theophilus: The Lucan Preface in Context*.

Introduction

The origins of Luke's Gospel, like those of the other gospels, are obscure. understanding of the separate sections or units of the Gospel, and of individual statements in them. The intention of the Introduction is to consider the Gospel as a whole, and in its relation to its historical setting. This will be attempted under the headings of its origins, its composition and its character.

A. ORIGINS

The origins of Luke's Gospel, like those of the other gospels, are obscure. This is due partly to the paucity of reliable external evidence about them surviving from the first or second centuries AD. It is also due to their involvement in what was to be one of the most decisive actions of the early Christian churches, which put them to a use which was not necessarily on all fours with the original intentions of their authors. This was the process of creating a body of authoritative Christian 'scripture', the Canon, eventually to be called 'The New Testament', alongside what had hitherto been for Christians 'the scriptures', which was now in consequence to be called 'The Old Testament'.[a] In this process, which appears to have been gradual, and to have proceeded in different ways, and at a different pace, in individual churches, the gospels came to play a special part. For the NT emerged, for reasons that are not entirely clear (but see on Marcion below), as a Canon in two parts, called 'The Gospel' (or 'The Lord') and 'The Apostle'. The first came to consist of four accredited gospels, or, in an earlier period, of a (single) Gospel 'according to' four named authors. This in itself created a theological problem.[b] For how could the Gospel (of God), which in Christian usage was by definition singular (as always in Paul, and cf. Mark 1[14f.]), come to have a plurality of differing written versions? So Irenaeus (*Against Heresies* III, 11.8), in establishing the four gospels as alone

_a_ On this crucial and highly complex matter, see esp. H. von Campenhausen, *The Formation of the Christian Bible*, ET London and Philadelphia 1972, chs. II–VI, and R. M. Grant, 'The New Testament Canon', in *The Cambridge History of the Bible*, Vol. 1, edd. P. R. Ackroyd and C. F. Evans, 1970, pp. 284ff.

_b_ See O. Cullmann, *The Early Church*, ET London and Philadelphia 1956, pp. 39ff.

I

authoritative scripture in face of the Gnostics and their writings, felt
compelled to argue on both natural and supernatural grounds for the
propriety and excellence of fourfoldness. The Christian scholar Tatian
attempted (*c*. 170?) to undo this by scrambling the four gospels into a
single narrative in his *Diatessaron*, the only form of the gospels in his
church of Assyria until the fifth century. His arrangement was not,
however, successful, and elsewhere it was as components of a fourfold
gospel that the individual accredited gospels continued. Even so, it was
of prime concern to show that, though separate, they told a single
harmonious story, and in this their individual characteristics, and the
circumstances of their origin, tended to be lost to view. Thus, 'The
Gospel according to Luke' appears in the various canonical lists that
have survived, and generally in the third place, whether the list was
compiled on a supposed chronological order of writing (Matthew,
Mark, Luke, John), or by placing first those supposedly written by
apostles (Matthew, John, Luke, Mark – Codex Claromontanus has
the order Matthew, John, Mark, Luke). In the earliest of such lists, the
Muratorian Canon, it is introduced in more primitive fashion with the
words 'The third book of the Gospel, according to Luke'.

In one respect Luke's Gospel is deficient in external attestation in
comparison with those of Mark and Matthew. For statements about
their authorship and composition had been made by Papias, bishop of
Hierapolis (*c*. 120?), and were preserved by Eusebius in his *Church
History* (3. 39.15f.; for the former of these see Nineham's Pelican
Commentary *Saint Mark*, pp. 26f., 39). Eusebius does not reproduce
any such statement on Luke's Gospel. Whether this was because he did
not have occasion to do so, or because Papias's statement had been
hostile and he suppressed it, or because Papias had not made any statement about Luke's Gospel and had not known of its existence, cannot
be determined. In another respect Luke's Gospel has superior attestation
through its association with Marcion. This churchman, reputedly the
son of the bishop of Sinope in Pontus, promulgated (*c*. 140?) a distinctive form of Christianity, and on his excommunication by the church
in Rome founded a church that was to be universal in scope, in some
places rivalling the 'orthodox' churches. His Christianity was derived
entirely from Paul, and was a kind of ultra-Pauline dualism. The gospel
was one of the total love and grace of God in Christ, and stood in
antithesis to all law; so that the Father of Jesus Christ was not identical
with the just (or evil) God of the OT. In thus breaking with what had

been so far a cardinal tenet of Christian theology, that the Gospel was 'according to the scriptures', i.e. in fulfilment of the OT, he was compelled to supply some other written foundation for his version of it. This he did by issuing a corpus of the Pauline epistles (without the Pastorals), though with the text purged of any Jewish sentiments, which, he claimed, were corruptions introduced by the 'orthodox'. To this he added Luke's Gospel, also suitably purged, perhaps as representative of what Paul had referred to as 'the (my) gospel' (Gal. 1$^{7-9}$). Whether he did this by selecting Luke's from among a number of already existing gospels (the canonical four?) as the most (or only one) suitable for his purposes, or because it was already current on its own as the written gospel in his home church in Pontus, or because it had Luke's name attached to it and he knew a tradition of a personal relationship between Luke and Paul, cannot be determined.[c]

There are two further distinctive features of Luke's Gospel which are not unrelated to its origins and its involvement in the making of the Canon, and which could be of importance for its interpretation. The

[c] On this crucial area of church history see von Campenhausen, op. cit., pp. 147ff., E. C. Blackman, *Marcion and His Influence*, London and New York 1948, and J. Knox, *Marcion and the New Testament*, Chicago 1942. Some scholars have deduced from Marcion's actions that he was the originator of the idea of a NT Canon and of its bipartite form of Gospel and Apostle, and that the churches reacted to him with a gospel section containing other gospels than Luke's and an apostle section with other epistles besides Paul's. Others prefer the view that Marcion served to accelerate a process of Canon-making that was already under way in the churches. The matter is complicated, not least by the fact that all our knowledge of Marcion comes from those who feared, hated and bitterly opposed him as a deadly rival and the most dangerous of heretics. Tertullian wrote his longest treatise, the five books *Against Marcion*, to controvert him. In books IV and V he works through Marcion's text of Luke's Gospel and the Pauline Epistles. He does this in Latin, which was the language of his own Bible, and it is not clear whether he had before him Marcion's text in Greek, or that Greek text already rendered into Latin, either by Marcion himself or by later Marcionites. A particular problem arises when Tertullian fails to comment on passages that are in the canonical text of Luke. Some of these omissions are explicable as due to abridgements made by Marcion himself in accordance with his theological standpoint – e.g. the absence of Luke 1–2. which present John and Jesus as having a Jewish origin – but others such as the absence of the Parable of the Prodigal Son (Luke 15$^{11-32}$) are not. This forms the basis of Knox's hypothesis that the gospel Marcion edited was shorter than the canonical Luke, which was an expanded version issued c. 150 along with Acts as an anti-Marcionite work aimed at showing, amongst other things, that Paul was not the only true apostle.

first is the form of its first appearance. Whereas the other gospels are self-contained works that permit no sequel, Luke's appears to have been the first half of what the author had conceived from the first as a two-volume work (not as a single volume with a supplement).[d] Had it come down in the ordinary secular literary tradition it would have been in the form '(Luke) To Theophilus I, To Theophilus II'. Since it ultimately came down in the Christian literary tradition, a certain violence will have been done to it in that the two volumes were separated from each other. The first volume (called such in A. 1^1), since it conformed to the gospel pattern already set by Mark (and perhaps others), came eventually, but later than the gospels of Mark and Matthew, to be included as a self-contained work in the gospel section of the Canon, thereafter to function as such in the church. The second volume, now also regarded as a self-contained work, and under a fresh title of its own, 'The Acts of the Apostles', which only partly corresponded to its contents, was eventually, though later still, to be included in the second part of the Canon. Since it did not conform to the pattern of any other writings there, it could occupy different positions; in some lists it is placed last (Marcion shows no knowledge of it). It now performed the task of validating the early church and the apostles, as also Paul and his epistles. The cumbersome modern designation Luke–Acts aims to restore the two volumes to a single whole with a single subject matter, which then constitutes a distinctive strand within the NT. Even so, as previously, they are generally treated apart, and commentaries continue to be written on them in isolation and never together.

The second feature is the mechanics of the Gospel's first appearance. The other gospels are anonymous works, each, it is supposed, originally written to and for a particular community (or communities) to give instruction and guidance in Christian faith and life, perhaps to correct false teaching, in the opinion of some for liturgical use. Luke's Gospel

---

d This has been denied, e.g. by A. C. Clark, *The Acts of the Apostles*, Oxford and New York 1933, pp. 393ff. (and see A. W. Argyle, 'The Greek of Luke and Acts', *NTS* 20, 1973–74, pp. 441–5) on the grounds of discrepancies in vocabulary and style of such a kind as to preclude a common authorship of the two books. Some of these are certainly striking, but they could be accounted for by a literary versatility on Luke's part and a command of more than one style of Greek, together with the probability that in the Gospel and the first half of Acts he will not have been writing from scratch, and in his native manner throughout, but will have been dictated to in some measure by the vocabulary and style of the sources he uses, and which he only sporadically revises (see W. L. Knox, *Acts*, pp. 2ff.).

is also anonymous, but it is personally addressed to an individual, Theophilus, by means of a preface probably intended to cover the whole work. Even if Theophilus was a Christian acquaintance of the author, and an influential member of a Christian group, who was expected as the dedicatee to secure knowledge of the work amongst his friends for their further instruction in the Christian faith, the question arises of how this book in his private library gained a wider circulation, and did so at some stage in the form of two separate volumes, so that the first was available for e.g. Marcion (in Pontus? Rome?), and for adoption into the Canon. If Theophilus was not a Christian, and the work was intended to give a reliable picture of the Christian movement to an influential and sympathetic outsider, and to allay his suspicions about it, the question becomes more acute by what route such a work passed into the Christian bloodstream, and ended up in the Canon. Some have spoken in this connection of the work's publication on the book market for a wider literary public, the dedication being then fairly conventional.[e]

Although Luke's preface is not of the epistolary kind, where the author was bound to give his name – 'Luke to Theophilus greeting' – it is considered likely that his name was attached to the work somehow (it is not known whether or not it had a title), or was attached to it by Theophilus.[f] If so, it would presumably have remained attached when the work gained wider currency, and had found its way into the growing Canon of Christian churches. There, at some stage, it would have been given the specifically Christian denomination '(The) Gospel according to Luke', as in the earliest known text p[75] (dated 175–225). Tertullian (*Against Marcion*, IV.2), rightly or wrongly, accuses Marcion of deception in that he 'attaches to his gospel no author's name'. Since the motive of a Canon was to have a body of 'scripture' that was authoritatively Christian, which at the time meant 'apostolic', it became necessary to identify this 'Luke', and to establish his apostolic

---

e So M. Dibelius, *Studies in Acts*, p. 135. For this, see the note on 1³.

f According to Dibelius, *Studies*, p. 136, this is to be taken for granted. 'It would have been strange indeed if the person to whom the book was dedicated had been named, but not the dedicator.' The few exceptions to this in ancient literature are dismissed, perhaps too easily, by von Campenhausen, op. cit., p. 126 n. 92. The names attached to the other gospels will have had a different origin, as these had not been 'published' in the same way, and in the opinion of some they are of questionable value.

credentials. This can be seen happening in the earliest statements on authorship to have survived, which are from the last decades of the second century, some eighty years, perhaps, after the date of writing.[g]

Probably the earliest is that in the Muratorian Canon.[h]

The third Gospel book, that according to Luke.
This physician Luke after Christ's ascension (resurrection?)
since Paul had taken him with him as an expert of the way (of the teaching)
composed it in his own name
according to (his thinking). Yet neither did he himself see
the Lord in the flesh; and therefore as he was able to ascertain it,
    so he began
to tell the story from the birth of John.

Then, after twenty-four lines on John's Gospel:

But the acts of all the apostles
are written in one book. For the 'most excellent Theophilus' Luke
summarizes the several things that in his own presence
have come to pass, as also by the omission of the passion of Peter
he makes quite clear, and equally by (the omission of) the journey
    of Paul, who from the
city of Rome proceeded to Spain.

Irenaeus, writing _c._ 180 against heresy and appealing to an authoritative scripture, first makes the brief statement (_Against Heresies_ III, 1.1), 'Luke, the follower of Paul, recorded in a book the gospel that was preached by him (sc. Paul).' Later (_Against Heresies_ III, 14.1) he elaborates this in opposing the heretical view that Paul was the only source of Christian truth. 'But that Luke was inseparable from Paul and was his fellow-worker in the gospel he himself makes clear.' As proof he then cites the so-called 'we' sections in Acts, where the narrative suddenly changes to the first person plural, viz. A. 16[8] ('we came to Troas', so in Irenaeus's text) – 16[17]; 20[5-15]; 21[1-18]; 27[1]-28[16]. He then proceeds,

---

g For these in full in English, see _Beginnings_ II, pp. 209ff.

h So called because discovered by L. A. Muratori in a codex in the Ambrosian Library at Milan. This document, fragmented at both ends, is generally dated between 170 and 200, and is thought to be a statement of the church in Rome about its NT Canon. It is a translation of a Greek (verse?) original into barbarous Latin, which, together with evident corruptions in the text, make it at times almost unintelligible, and translation guess work. The translation above is that in E. Hennecke, _New Testament Apocrypha_ I, ET London 1963, reissued 1974, pp. 43ff.

'That he was not only a follower but also a fellow-labourer of the apostles (cf. III, 10.1, 'Luke the follower and disciple of the apostles'), but especially of Paul, Paul himself declared also in his epistles, saying "Only Luke is with me" (II Tim. 4¹¹). From this he shows that he was always attached to him and inseparable from him. And again he says in the Epistle to the Colossians, "Luke, the beloved physician, greets you" (Col. 4¹⁴).' Tertullian (c. 200), in pursuance of his argument that Paul and Luke cannot stand as sole authorities, states (*Against Marcion* IV.2), 'Luke, not an apostle but an apostolic man, not a master but a disciple, at any rate inferior to a master, and so far later than the others as he was a follower of a later apostle, Paul of course.' Often cited in this connection is the so-called anti-Marcionite prologue, found along with prologues to Mark and John in thirty-eight Latin mss, and the only one to be found in Greek (in a single ms). This begins with 'Luke is a Syrian from Antioch, a doctor by profession, who was a disciple of apostles, and later accompanied Paul until his martyrdom, having followed the Lord without distraction, being unmarried and without child. He fell asleep in Boeotia at the age of eighty-four full of the Holy Spirit.' It continues that after the composition of Matthew's Gospel in Judaea and Mark's in Italy, Luke composed his in the regions of Achaea for Gentiles to preserve them from Jewish myths and heretical fancies; and that it properly begins from the birth of John since John is the beginning of the gospel (cf. the reference to this in the Muratorian Canon, where it is related to the affirmation that though the gospels have different beginnings they all teach the same thing). Both the supposed second-century date and the anti-Marcionite character of this prologue have been questioned. Its hagiographical tone and the character of some of its information, e.g. the stress on Luke's ascetical piety, could point to a fourth-century origin.[i] Later statements on Lukan authorship appear to be either repetitions of those already cited, or legendary.

The question at issue is whether these statements, which may not be entirely independent of one another, preserve, and rest upon, a reliable tradition that goes back nearer to the period of the Gospel's origins. Or are they, like other such statements (e.g. perhaps those by Papias on Mark and Matthew), no more than conjectures arising from the exigencies of the contexts in which they are made, especially the need to

---

i For the full text in translation and a discussion of it see R. G. Heard, 'The Old Gospel Prologues', *JTS* ns 6, 1955, pp. 1–16. See also Haenchen, *Acts*, p. 10 n. 1.

establish the Gospel's authority, which meant its apostolic character, and the fundamental unity of apostolic testimony. Thus the statement that Luke wrote as a follower of all the apostles – Irenaeus may have got that by taking *pāsin* = 'all things' in Luke 1³ as masculine – is made in order to ground the Gospel and the first part of Acts on the firmest possible basis; but it is plainly false. The Gospel is based largely on Mark's and on other anonymous traditions, written or oral, while the first part of Acts would seem to depend on local traditions about events that are already a long way back. The statement that because he was an inseparable companion of Paul Luke's Gospel is a written version of the gospel Paul preached is also plainly false. There is no indication from Paul's epistles, or indeed from Acts, that Paul preached by means of the kind of materials that make up Luke's Gospel. It has been maintained that that Gospel reflects Pauline theology in some of its features, such as the emphasis on salvation and faith, on God's love for sinners, and its universalism; but these are common Christian teaching without any distinctive Pauline flavour (see Plummer, p. xliv); while Luke's presentation of the passion as that of an innocent martyr, and of the resurrection as the transition to ascension and to a new epoch, is very different from Paul's. The question then at issue is whether any reliable tradition remains in such statements once the reasons for making them, and the false inferences they contain, are of necessity discounted.

Cadbury argued (*Beginnings* II, pp. 260ff.) that Irenaeus could have arrived at the conclusion that Luke was the author purely from an investigation of NT texts, and by a process of elimination. He took the statement in II Tim. 4¹¹ 'Only Luke is with me' to refer to the time of Paul's imprisonment in A. 28, and used it along with the greeting from Luke in Col. 4¹¹ to identify Luke as the close and constant companion of Paul who is implied in the 'we' in A. 16–28 (cf. the deduction in the Muratorian Canon from Rom. 15²⁸ that the author of Acts deliberately omitted Paul's journey to Spain because he was not present at it). Cadbury's argument would have to be modified if the Gospel (and Acts?) had had the name 'Luke' attached to it from the first and had retained it along whatever route it had travelled to become authoritative in the churches (did Marcion suppress it for reasons of his own?); for then the identification would have had a clear starting point, and would have been more immediate.

Both the bases of Irenaeus' conclusions have been questioned. Firstly, the Pastoral Epistles are widely held to be later pseudonymous writings, and, though far less widely, the Pauline authorship of Colossians has been disputed. In that case the references to Luke, apart from Philemon 24, which Irenaeus does not refer to, would stem not from Paul direct, but from traditions current in the Pauline wing of the church, the date and historical value of which can be variously assessed.

Secondly, the puzzling phenomenon of the 'we' sections has been for a century or more, and continues to be, a vexed question.[j] On this scholars have been led to adopt one of two positions, neither of which can be said to have established itself against the other. (i) Some have held to, or have eventually returned to, the position of Irenaeus in some form. The use of 'we' is a deliberate device, not without parallels in ancient literature, by which the author indicated his own presence at the events then being recorded, though whether at the events also recorded in the third person between the uses of 'we' is uncertain. At these points he was writing either from memory, or by transcribing, or excerpting from, what is variously described as his memoirs, his (travel) diary (stretching over an indefinite number of years), or for chs. 16–21 his missionary report, or his record of an itinerary. Some have seen this procedure as already prepared for by the author's statement in his preface (1³) that he had 'followed' all things for some time past, taking 'followed' in the sense of 'being personally present at'. This associate of Paul is best identified with Luke. (ii) Others have postulated the incorporation by the author of another's (Luke's) memoirs, (travel) diary or itinerary, of which he for some reason retained (at times) the first person plural, but which he so worked over as to make its style indistinguishable from his own. The bases for this view have been the abruptness with which the 'we' sections are introduced, and the contrast between their detailed character and that of the surrounding narrative; cf. the cautious judgment of C. K. Barrett,[k] 'This means, not necessarily that the author was an eyewitness but that he had some sort of access to some sort of eyewitness material for this part of his narrative.' An additional basis has been the discrepancies of fact and theological outlook between Acts and the Pauline epistles, which are held to preclude that Acts was written by a companion of Paul. Chief amongst these are the contradictions between Paul's account of his visit to Jerusalem in Gal. 2 and the account in A. 15; the lack of

---

[j] How vexed can be seen in the detailed and judicious review of the discussion up to 1964 in J. Dupont, *The Sources of Acts*, II.

[k] *Luke the Historian in Recent Study*, London 1961, p. 22.

reference in Acts to events in Paul's life, e.g. in his relations with the
church at Corinth, and to his motives, e.g. in the collection for the
saints, which we know from his epistles; the contrast between Paul's
emphasis on his apostleship and the refusal of the title of apostle to him
in Acts (except along with Barnabas in A. 14⁴, ¹⁴, and possibly in the
reduced sense of envoys of the church in Antioch); and the theological
differences between what Paul says in his epistles and his utterances in
Acts.[1] There are, to be sure, imponderables here. How far is it possible
to make this kind of comparison between two types of writing
which, even if they cover some of the same ground, are as diverse as
the sequential narrative of Acts, where Paul appears in the second half
as a heroic illustration of one of its major themes, and the passionate,
personal, pastoral and polemical letters of Paul himself? Do the epistles
in fact yield a single consistent theology of Paul? Does it have to be
required of an associate of Paul that he must never have misunderstood
him, or insufficiently appreciated what he stood for, or shown any
measure of independence of him? Nevertheless, the same arguments as
are used to mitigate the differences, or to explain them by Luke's
limited acquaintance with, or comparative independence of, Paul, also
serve to lessen the force of any appeal to the 'we' sections to account for
distinctive features of Luke–Acts as due to its composition by an associate of Paul. An individual view, which bypasses most of the discussion,
is that of Haenchen (*Acts*, pp. 489ff., 581f.). He also sees the 'we' as a
deliberate literary device; which is employed, however, not to indicate
the author's presence as an eyewitness, but to bring the reader at this
point into a more intimate relation with the events then being recorded.
If the reader identified the 'we' at all, it would have to be with persons
already mentioned in the adjacent narrative, as is generally the case in
the parallels cited of this use of 'we' in ancient literature. Thus at 16¹¹
he would have identified the 'we' with Timothy and Silas, who are
mentioned along with Paul in 15⁴⁰; 16³, and not with a previously
unnamed author of the whole work.

Auxiliary to this discussion have been the attempts to establish the
author of Luke–Acts as a physician by examination of its vocabulary,
notably that of W. K. Hobart.[m] The evidence was re-examined by

---

l See J. Knox, *Chapters in a Life of Paul*, New York and London 1954, reissued
1989, chs. I–VI; Kümmel, *Introduction to the New Testament*, pp. 128ff.

m In a work entitled *The Medical Language of St Luke* and subtitled *A Proof from*

Cadbury, who showed, not only that the language adduced as evidence of Luke's medical background was to be found equally distributed in writers without any such background, but also that writers without any such background could illuminate the language of Luke–Acts.[n] His conclusion was that 'if it be believed that the writer of Acts was a physician the language of Acts offers no obstacles; but neither does it forbid the view that he was nothing of the kind'.[o]

Finally, it may be noted that even if the author of Luke–Acts was Luke, a physician and companion of Paul, this throws no light at all on the character and circumstances of the first volume, which owes nothing to it; and might throw comparatively little light on the second volume, despite the prominence of Paul in it. Related to this is the further vexed question of the ending of Acts with the statement that Paul 'remained for a whole two-year period on his own earnings, and welcomed all who came to him, preaching the kingdom of God and teaching the story of the Lord Jesus Christ quite openly, without hindrance.' This, which reads like a postscript, though of a studied kind, has appeared a lame conclusion, especially of the dramatic narrative from ch. 21 onwards, and if written by one who was with Paul at the time. Various hypotheses have been put forward to account for it. (i) Luke planned, but did not write, a third volume, in which he would have recounted what happened to Paul, and other matters;[p] but this would not redeem the poor ending of the second volume. (ii) Luke laid down his pen here because his narrative had caught up with events, when Paul's trial

---

Internal Evidence that 'The Gospel according to St Luke' and 'The Acts of the Apostles, were written by the same Person and that the writer was a Medical Man. See also A. Harnack, *Luke the Physician,* ET London and New York 1907, Appendix I.

n *The Style and Literary Method of Luke,* I, Harvard Theological Studies VI 1920; also 'Lexical Notes on Luke–Acts II: Recent Arguments for Medical Language', *JBL* 45, 1926, pp. 190–209.

o *Beginnings* II, p. 166. So L. A. C. Alexander, 'Luke–Acts in its Contemporary Setting with Special Reference to the Prefaces' (unpublished Ph.D. thesis, Oxford 1977), concludes from an analysis that Luke's preface is of the 'scientific 'type that this 'would be consistent with the tradition, but it would not prove that the tradition is correct. On our evidence, the author of Luke–Acts could as well have been an engineer as a doctor; the value of that particular tradition must still be assessed on other grounds.'

p See W. M. Ramsay, *St Paul the Traveller and the Roman Citizen,* London and New York 1895, pp. 27ff., and others.

had not yet come to an end,q and consequently Acts was written first and before the Gospel in its present form (C. S. C. Williams, *Acts*, pp. 12ff., and others), or, more specifically, was written as a document in Paul's defence (Sahlin, *Der Messias und das Gottesvolk*, pp. 34ff., and others mentioned there). These latter suggestsions all require an early date; the last is given its *coup de grace* in the comment of C. K. Barrettr that 'No Roman official would ever have filtered out so much of what to him would be theological and ecclesiastical rubbish in order to reach so tiny a grain of relevant apology.' There is one hypothesis which, if it could be established, could transform the last sentence of Acts into a very telling conclusion. It concerns the appeal to Caesar from the provinces and the procedural rules belonging to it. From the evidence, which is astonishingly scanty and obscure, it is possible to derive a rule that if the prosecution did not turn up to press the charges within a specified (two-year?) period the case was held to go by default.s If so, the concluding sentence could be capping a thesis which has been developed since the entry of Paul into the narrative. The Jewish case against him, and so against Christianity as represented in him, that he was engaged in criminal activity in preaching the gospel, fell because the prosecution failed to press it throughout the statutory two-year period (*dietia*, A. 28[30]). This proves that there had never been a case. If this is the perspective of Luke–Acts it could have been written in retrospect long after the events, and by one for whom, whether companion of Paul or not, Paul was not a subject of biography, nor even the missionary to the Gentile world and the pastor of individual churches (he appears to make no use of Paul's letters), but was the supreme paradigm and exemplar of the Christian movement as he understands it, and as he has so structured his work, including the gospel of 'the things concerning Jesus' (A. 1[1]; 28[31]), to present it.

That Luke was a Gentile Christian is generally held to be established by Col. 4[10-14], where the greeting from him and Demas is separated off from that of Aristarchus, Mark and Jesus Justus, who are specified as 'the only men of the circumcision' among Paul's fellow-workers for the kingdom of God, by an intervening greeting from Epaphras

q A. Harnack, *The Date of the Acts and the Synoptic Gospels*, London and New York 1911, pp. 90ff.

r Luke the Historian in Recent Study, London 1961, p. 63.

s See the detailed discussion by Cadbury in 'Roman Law and the Trial of Paul', *Beginnings* V, note XXVI.

as 'one of yourselves', presumably a Gentile. But in this somewhat obscurely expressed passage it is not altogether clear (i) what is meant by 'of the circumcision' – Ellis argues that it means a certain kind of Jewish Christian who was ritually strict as opposed to Paul who was ritually lax, (ii) whether 'these only . . .' means that they were the only Jewish Christians ever to have been Paul's fellow-workers or the only ones left, and (iii) whether the contrast is between them and Epaphras as a Gentile, leaving Luke and Demas undifferentiated. If the author is not Luke the question remains open. For the interpenetration of Judaism and Hellenism in the first century AD, especially as that had been augmented by the Christian movement itself, was of such a kind that it does not permit of a definite answer. Thus it cannot be affirmed dogmatically that no Gentile could have acquired the knowledge of Judaism and of the phraseology of the LXX as is evidenced in Luke–Acts; it was perfectly possible for an intelligent and literary-minded Gentile, perhaps already interested in Judaism before his conversion and then embracing Christianity with its Jewish scriptural foundation, to have done so. Nor could it be said that it was impossible for a Jew to have attained the standard of Greek and the concern for the world of the Greco-Roman empire as is evidenced in Luke–Acts; it was perfectly possible for an intelligent Diaspora Jew to have done so, and Josephus, Philo, the author of Hebrews (Apollos?) and Paul himself are examples.

Date and Place

Here we can only guess. There are few firm dates for any of the events in the New Testament, and none at all for its writings apart from some Pauline epistles. The latest date of composition is supplied by the date of the earliest writing that can be shown to quote words from the book in question; this is complicated, especially with a gospel, by uncertainty whether these words are in fact a quotation, or a parallel statement to them taken from a still fluid oral tradition or from common Christian language. This is so with all those passages (sometimes a few words only) in the Apostolic Fathers from I Clement (c. 90?) to the *Shepherd of Hermas* (c. 130?) which have been held to echo something in Luke's Gospel (Haenchen, *Acts*, pp. 1–8, shows the same to be the case with Acts). The composite version of the passion in the surviving fragment of the Gospel of Peter has phraseology that could have been derived from Luke's, and the Gospel of Thomas has more sayings in a Lukan than in a Matthaean or Markan form; but the date of both these works is disputed. If the gospel Marcion edited was what was to become, or had already become, the canonical Luke, then the latest date has to be pushed back sufficiently far for the Gospel to have been in circulation and use for Marcion (c. 130?). The earliest date has become for modern scholarship, as it was not previously, Luke's use of Mark's Gospel, and the time required for that to have been in circulation and to have become authoritative. But the date of Mark's Gospel is also guess-work. Important here is the interpretation of Luke 21$^{20-24}$. Some have seen the passage as a prophecy of a general kind couched in LXX language (Harnack, *Date of Acts*, pp. 116ff.), and C. H. Dodd (*More NT Studies*, pp. 69ff.) argued that at this point Luke was not using Mark but an alternative version of the discourse. If this is not the case (see Commentary ad loc.), and Luke deliberately altered Mark's 'When you see the desolating sacrilege set up where it ought not to be . . .' into 'But when you see Jerusalem surrounded by armies . . .', it is difficult to resist the conclusion that he did so in knowledge of the destruction of Jerusalem in AD 70 as an already accomplished fact. The objection that if Luke was writing after that event 'it is almost incomprehensible why he did not refer to it' in Acts (Williams, *Acts*, p. 15, and others) is singularly unconvincing. It is difficult to imagine how or where such a reference would have been germane to the narrative in Acts, or could have been made with any semblance of verisimilitude. All that can be suggested, therefore, as a date for Luke–Acts is between AD 75 and 130. Attempts have been made to plot a more precise date by establishing affinities of theological outlook between Luke–Acts and some Christian writer at a particular point of theological development or milieu within this period. While such attempts can contribute to the understanding of Luke–Acts, they inevitably suffer from the comparative paucity, and the heterogeneity, of Christian writing in the period from which to construct such a development. Thus, J. C. O'Neill† arrives at a date 115–130 on the grounds that Luke–Acts breathes the same air, and has the same theological concerns, as the writings of Justin Martyr; but he is only able to do so by explaining verbal similarities between them as due, not to Justin's use of Luke, but to their use of a common source, and

---

† *The Theology of Acts in its Historical Setting*, 2nd ed., London 1970.

by assigning Justin to an earlier date than is usual. H. Conzelmann[u] arrives at a date 90–100 through an analysis of Luke–Acts as shaped by a concept of 'the third generation', i.e. those Christians who are the recipients and guardians of a tradition about the Lord from the apostles in the past, which he finds most clearly expressed in I Clement (ch. 42), which is probably to be dated at this time.

Identifications of the place of writing are also guess-work. The tradition that Luke was an Antiochene does not appear before Eusebius (HE 3.4.6), unless the anti-Marcionite prologue antedates Eusebius. It could have been an inference from the prominence of Antioch in the narrative of A. 11–13 (18[22f.]), and the Western reading 'we' in A. 11[28] could have been a product of, rather than a further basis for, the inference. While it might indicate the source of some of Luke's information, it says nothing about where the work was written, or for whom (the prologue says vaguely 'in the districts around Achaea' and 'for Gentiles').

B. COMPOSITION

(i) Sources

The external evidence above throws no light on the questions of the origins, composition and purpose of the Gospel. In theory such questions should be capable of being answered internally from the preface which Luke has provided, with its references to the antecedents, methods and intentions of his work. In fact the preface is so compressed and so ambiguously worded that it leaves them largely unanswered. Thus, even if the mention of the 'many' who had previously written accounts of the Christian events is more than simply conventional, Luke does not indicate whether he had read or used them. Had he done so he was not bound to say so. Some ancient authors did not; some did, though this was contrary to the convention. Nor is it clear whether Luke intended to contrast these with his own personal 'following' of the events from a long way back. And the final clause in 1[4] expressing his purpose is open to more than one interpretation. Further, in the case of Luke there are additional preliminary questions. Did he first write a book on the model of a 'gospel' as a literary genre already current among Christians, and then later a sequel on some different

_u_ 'Luke's Place in the Development of Early Christianity', in _Studies in Luke–Acts_, ed. Keck and Martyn, pp. 298ff.

model? Or did he conceive and execute from the first a two-volume work? If so, was the first volume shaped so as to be able to lead to a second? Was the first even written for the sake of the second? For Luke's writing is unique in the NT in this respect, that whereas the other two synoptic gospels narrate the deeds and words, the passion and resurrection, of Jesus without direct reference to the consequences to which they gave rise, and epistles are concerned with these consequences with little or no reference to the deeds and words of Jesus, and the circumstances of his death and resurrection, Luke alone brings the two together and treats them seriatim (John may be said to treat the first in terms of the second). Scholarship has been driven, therefore, to internal analysis of the Gospel itself, and to attempts to detect its character and purpose from the evangelist's selection of what to record and his manner of recording it.

From the beginnings of historical criticism the point of departure for this has been the synoptic problem, where the Gospel was considered apart from Acts. This is the problem presented by the following phenomena:

(i) the first three gospels, though markedly distinct as finished works, are yet sufficiently similar in general structure to be placed alongside one another in a 'synopsis', and so viewed together;

(ii) over considerable stretches their stories are told in the same order, although they have the appearance of having once been separate units of tradition, and there is nothing obvious or inevitable about this order; and

(iii) in some passages the wording, including the order and construction of whole sentences, is very similar, occasionally identical, in all three gospels. Such phenomena require explanation, which would throw light on how these gospels came to be composed. In the nature of the case such an explanation has been difficult to arrive at, especially in relation to Luke.[v]

The first explanation to be put forward was the Oral Tradition Theory. This accounted for the phenomena on the supposition that each of the three evangelists relied on, and reproduced independently, an oral tradition of events and sayings, which, while still fluid, was also to a large extent stereotyped. When this was abandoned as inadequate

---

[v] For a history of the investigation of the synoptic problem, see Kümmel, *Introduction*, pp. 33–60. The most detailed discussion of it in a commentary on Luke is now that of Fitzmyer, Introduction III.

to account for the degree of similarity of order and wording, the only alternative was that one or other of the evangelists had used the written work of another or others of them. Eventually there came to be a wide consensus that the evidence was most satisfactorily accounted for on the hypothesis that Matthew and Luke had, independently of each other, made use of Mark's Gospel.[w]

On this analysis Luke will have been dependent on Mark for the following (brackets round a passage indicate that the dependence is subject to some doubt):

$(3^{1-7a}$	$= \text{Mark } 1^{1-6}$	The Baptist)
$(3^{19-20}$	$= \text{Mark } 6^{17-18}$	The Baptist imprisoned)
$(3^{21-22}$	$= \text{Mark } 1^{9-11}$	Baptism of Jesus)
$(4^{1-2a}$	$= \text{Mark } 1^{12-13a}$	Jesus tempted)
4^{14-15}	$= \text{Mark } 1^{14-15}$	Preaching in Galilee
4^{31-44}	$= \text{Mark } 1^{21-39}$	Exorcism, Healing, Many Healings, Withdrawal, Preaching Tour
$5^{12}-6^{19}$	$= \text{Mark } 1^{40}-3^{19}$	Leper, Paralytic, Levi, Fasting, Sabbath Work, Sabbath Healing, Choice of Twelve, Healing of Multitudes
8^4-9^{17}	$= \text{Mark } 3^{31}-4^{25};$ $4^{35}-5^{43};$ $6^{6-16, \, 30-44}$	Parabolic Teaching, Jesus' Family, Stilling of Storm, Gerasene Demoniac, Jairus' Daughter and Woman with Issue, Mission of Twelve, Herod, Feeding of Five Thousand
$9^{18-50} (51)$	$= \text{Mark } 8^{27}-9^8;$ $9^{14-41} (10^1)$	Peter's Confession, Discipleship, Transfiguration, Epileptic Child, Prediction of Passion, Dispute on Greatness, Anonymous Exorcist, (Journey to Judaea)

w The position maintained in this Commentary. An alternative has been the view, first adumbrated by Augustine in *On the Agreement of the Evangelists* I, and developed critically by B. C. Butler in *The Originality of St Matthew*, Cambridge and New York 1951, that Mark copied and abbreviated Matthew (and both were used by Luke?). Apart from detailed considerations, the weakness of this has been that in the common passages it is Mark, the supposed abbreviator, who generally has the lengthier version. A further alternative has been the hypothesis of J. J. Griesbach, the author of the first 'synopsis' (1789). This is in the course of repristination in the form that Matthew's was the first gospel, which was then used by Luke, Mark composing his from the other two. For this see W. R. Farmer, *The Synoptic Problem*, Dilsboro, N.C., 1976. For the current debate see *Synoptic Studies*, ed. C. M. Tuckett, *JSNT(S)* 7, 1984, pp. 67ff., 75ff., 99ff., 197ff. For this view in the context of synoptic criticism as a whole and of Luke's Gospel in particular, see J. B. Tyson, 'Source Criticism of the Gospel of Luke' in *Perspectives on Luke-Acts*, ed. C. H. Talbert, Edinburgh 1978, pp. 24ff., and Fitzmyer, ch. III.

18^{15-43}	= Mark $10^{13-34,\ 46-52}$	Blessing of Children, Rich Young Man, Prediction of Passion, Blind Man
19^{28-38}	= Mark 11^{1-10}	Entry into Jerusalem
19^{45}–21^{33} (21^{37})	= Mark $11^{11,\ 15-18}$; 11^{27}–12^{27}; 12^{35}–13^{32}; (11^{18b-19})	Cleansing of Temple, Authority, Parable of Wicked Husbandmen, Tribute, Resurrection, David's Son, Woes, Widow's Mite, Apocalyptic Discourse (Jesus in Temple)
22^{1-13}	= Mark $14^{1-2,\ 10-16}$	Plot, Judas' Betrayal, Preparation for Passover
(22^{14-23}	= Mark 14^{17-25}	Last Supper, Prophecy of Betrayal)
(22^{39-53}	= Mark 14^{26-52}	Gethsemane, Arrest)
(22^{54-71}	= Mark 15^{53-72}	Trial before Sanhedrin, Denial of Peter)
($23^{1-5,\ 18-25}$	= Mark 15^{1-15}	Trial before Pilate and Condemnation)
($23^{26,\ 33-38}$	= Mark 15^{21-32}	Crucifixion)
23^{44-49}	= Mark 15^{33-41}	Death
23^{50-56}	= Mark 15^{42-47}	Burial
24^{1-11}	= Mark 16^{1-8}	Empty Tomb

Luke will then have reproduced the greater part of Mark's Gospel, and, with a few exceptions, in the same order. His single large omission is that of the self-contained section Mark 6^{45}–8^{26}, so that his narrative passes straight from the Feeding of the Five Thousand to the Confession of Peter, which is now located at Bethsaida, the place which stands at the beginning and the end of this section in Mark. More than one reason can be suggested for this omission, such as economy of space for the inclusion of non-Markan material in 9^{51}–18^{14}, the inconsequential meanderings of Jesus in the section, and the avoidance of the Feeding of the Four Thousand, on the grounds that it is a doublet, together with the obscure dialogue that follows. But the primary reason could be that the section is predominantly Gentile, entirely so if the second feeding is symbolic of the nourishment of the Gentiles. For Luke the mission to the Gentiles does not belong to the earthly ministry of Jesus. It will be described historically in Acts as the consequence of his exaltation. And it is noteworthy that a lengthy and important portion of the omitted section, the controversy over clean and unclean (foods, Mark 7^{1-23}), contains precisely the issue over which the first Gentiles are admitted as Christian converts through the agency of Peter (A. 10^1–11^{18}; 15^{6-14}). Luke, along with Matthew, probably fails to appreciate the connection in Mark between the two-stage healing of the blind man (Mark 8^{22-26}) and the two-stage confession to follow, and omits it. Other alterations or omissions are: the advancement of the imprisonment of the Baptist from Mark 6:17-18 to round off the Baptist section 3:1-20, his death, narrated in Mark 6:14-29, being omitted so that he can ask the question in 7:18ff.; the advancement of the visit to Nazareth from Mark 6:1-6 and its rewriting to provide a dramatic and programmatic opening to a preaching ministry that is otherwise referred to only in general terms; the replacement of the excessively compressed call of the first disciples in Mark 1:16-20 by a longer and more personal account in 5:1-11. The section on parabolic teaching, 8:4-18, is concentrated on the single parable of the Sower, that of the Secret Seed (as in Matthew) and of the Mustard Seed being omitted, to be compensated for later by twin parables of Mustard Seed and Leaven (13:18-21); and the story of Jesus' family is moved from before the parabolic section to after it, so as to make them exemplars of the true hearer (8:19-21). The identification of the Baptist with the returning Elijah (Mark 9:9-13) is dropped, perhaps as too specifically Jewish. In the section beginning at 18:15 Luke rejoins Mark in such a way as to pass over the question about divorce (Mark 10:1-12), being content with the single equivalent saying in 16:18, and he omits the teaching on greatness (Mark 10:35-45) in favour of a shorter equivalent at the Last Supper (22:24-27). It is hardly surprising that he should omit the cursing of the fig tree (Mark 11:12-14, 20-25), especially when he has an equivalent parable of a fig tree (13:6-9). For Mark's somewhat obscure story of a woman's anointing of Jesus (as messiah? Mark 14:3-9) he was able to substitute a similar story, which emphasizes his favourite theme of repentance and forgiveness (7:36-50).

On this analysis Mark will have supplied him not only with a great deal of material, but also with the general framework of a gospel composed as a narrative into which to integrate materials from other sources. Such a filling out of the Markan framework could be seen in:

(i) the introductory section 3:1-4:13, where the opening of the Gospel proper with the Baptist, as the fulfilment of prophecy, preaching a baptism of repentance for the forgiveness of sins, Jesus' baptism and temptation (from Mark), are filled out with eschatological and practical teaching of John, the actual temptations of Jesus as Son of God, and his genealogy as such;

(ii) the first part of the Galilean ministry as far as the choice of the Twelve and the healing of the multitudes (from Mark), which supply the occasion of the sermon addressed to disciples in 6:20-49, and the events and teaching to follow in 7:1-8:3;

(iii) the latter part of the Galilean ministry as far as the departure to Judaea and Jerusalem via Jericho (from Mark), which provides the setting for the long section of teaching on a journey in 9^{51}–18^{14} (19^{27});

(iv) the entry into Jerusalem and the teaching there, the apocalyptic discourse, and the main sequence of the passion narrative.

An alternative analysis of the relation of Luke's Gospel to Mark's has been advanced in the Proto-Luke hypothesis.[x] This begins from the contention that when the passages taken from Mark are removed from the Gospel, what remains is not a collection of disconnected units, but a continuous narrative recognizable as that of a gospel. It would consist of 3^{1}–4^{30}; 5^{1-11}; 6^{12}–8^{3}; 9^{51}–18^{14}; $19^{1-28,\ 37-44,\ 47-48}$; $21^{20,\ 21b,\ 22,\ 23b-26a,\ 28,}$ 21^{34-36}; 22–24 (minus additions from Mark in $22^{1-13,\ 19a,\ 22,\ 50b,\ 52-53a,}$ 22^{54b-61}; $23^{3,\ 26,\ 34b?,\ 38?,\ 44-45,\ 50-54}$). This could have been Luke's first draft of a gospel, the gaps in which he filled at a later stage from Mark. Such a procedure would explain why for the most part the Markan materials occur in the Gospel in blocks (4^{31-44}; 5^{12}–6^{11}; 8^{4}–9^{50}; 18^{15-43}; 19^{28}–21^{4}), and why Luke omitted such passages as Mark 1^{16-20}; 6^{1-6}; 4^{30-32}; 10^{35-45}; 12^{28-34}; 14^{3-9} because his first draft already contained equivalents of them. Mark's Gospel will then have been a secondary and not a primary authority for Luke, and will not have provided him with a framework for his Gospel but only with supplements to it.

Acceptance or rejection of this hypothesis depend in the end on decisions reached in answer to the following questions:

(i) whether certain passages, which must have been in Proto-Luke if it was a continuous narrative, are or are not derived from Mark. Examples here are the introduction of the Baptist as preaching a baptism of repentance for the forgiveness of sins and the baptism of Jesus in 3^{1-20}, the setting of the sermon on the plain and what follows in 6^{12-19}, and the relation of the journey in $9^{51ff.}$ to that in Mark $10^{1ff.}$

(ii) whether certain striking passages in Proto-Luke show evidence of having been written by Luke with knowledge of equivalent passages in Mark already to hand. Examples here are the Nazareth scene in 4^{16-30} (cf. Mark 6^{1-6}), the call of the disciples in 5^{1-11} (cf. Mark 1^{16-20}), the anointing scene in 7^{36-50} (cf. Mark 14^{3-9}).

x First outlined by B. H. Streeter, *The Four Gospels*, ch. VIII, and developed in detail by V. Taylor, *Behind the Third Gospel*; see also his *Passion Narrative of St Luke*. For a critique of the hypothesis, see Kümmel, *Introduction*, pp. 92ff., and the literature cited there.

(iii) whether in ch. 21 and chs. 22–23 the combination of similarities and differences is better explained by the supplementation of a non-Markan apocalypse and passion narrative by Markan words and phrases, or the supplementation and elucidation of obscure Markan materials by non-Markan material. It is noteworthy that the non-Markan material concerns matters of special importance to Luke in determining future history and in establishing the innocence of Jesus. These questions are addressed in greater detail in the Commentary, and reasons are given for rejecting the hypothesis.

This resolution of the relation between Luke's and Mark's Gospels still leaves as part of the synoptic problem those passages in Luke's and Matthew's Gospels which have no equivalent in Mark's, but which show a varying but sometimes extensive degree of similarity of wording, such as goes beyond the use of a common oral tradition, and requires some literary relationship.

In their Lukan sequence these comprise:

$3^{7-9,\ 16-17}$	= Matt. 3^{7-12}	John's preaching
4^{2-12}	= Matt. 4^{2-10}	Jesus' temptations
$6^{20-23,\ 27-30,\ 31,\ 32-36,\ 37-40,\ 41-46,\ 47-49}$	= Matt. $5^{2-4,\ 6-7,\ 11-12}$; $5^{39-40,\ 42}$; (7^{12}), 5^{44-46}; 5^{48}; 7^{1-2} $(15^{14}$; $10^{24-25})$ $7^{3-5,\ 16-21}$ (12^{33-35}); 7^{24-27}	Sermon
7^{1-10}	= Matt. 8^{5-13}	Centurion's servant
7^{18-23}	= Matt. 11^{2-6}	Baptist's question
7^{24-35}	= Matt. 11^{7-19}	The Baptist
9^{57-60}	= Matt. 8^{19-22}	Discipleship
10^{2-16}	= Matt. 9^{37-38}; $10^{16,\ 9-10a,\ 11-13,\ 10b,\ 7-8,\ 14-15}$; 11^{21-23}; 10^{40}	Mission
10^{21-22}	= Matt. 11^{25-27}	Jesus' Praise
10^{23-24}	= Matt. 13^{16-17}	Disciples blessed
$(11^{1-4}$	= Matt. $6^{9-13})$	Lord's Prayer
11^{9-13}	= Matt. 7^{7-11}	Prayer
11^{14-23}	= Matt. 12^{22-30}	Beelzebub
11^{24-26}	= Matt. 12^{43-45}	The evil spirit
11^{29-32}	= Matt. 12^{38-42}	Evil generation
11^{33-35}	= Matt. 5^{15}; 6^{22-23}	Sayings on light
11^{39-52}	= Matt. $23^{25-26,\ 23,\ 6-7}$; $23^{27,\ 4,\ 29-31,\ 34-36,\ 13}$	Woes on Pharisees

12^{2-12}	= Matt. 10^{26-33}; 12^{32}; 10^{19-20}	Confession, Denial
12^{22-34}	= Matt. $6^{25-33,\ 19-21}$	Earthly cares
12^{39-46}	= Matt. 24^{43-51}	Watchfulness
13^{18-21}	= Matt. 13^{31-33}	Twin parables
13^{24-30}	= Matt. 7^{13-14}; 25^{10-12}; 7^{22-23}; 8^{11-12}; 19^{30}	Condemnation
13^{34-35}	= Matt. 23^{37-39}	Lament over Jerusalem
$(14^{15-24}$	= Matt. 22^{1-10}	Parable of Supper)
14^{26-27}	= Matt. 10^{37-38}	Discipleship
$(15^{1-7}$	= Matt. 18^{12-14}	Parable of Lost Sheep)
$(16^{16}$	= Matt. 11^{12-13}	Law and prophets)
(16^{17})	=(Matt. 5^{18})	The Law
$(16^{18}$	= Matt. 5^{32}	Divorce)
$(17^{1-4}$	= Matt. $18^{6-7,\ 15,\ 21-22}$	Offences, Forgiveness)
17^{22-37}	= Matt. $24^{26-28,\ 37-41,\ 40,\ 28}$	Eschatology
$(19^{11-27}$	= Matt. 25^{14-30}	Parable of Pounds)

A natural conclusion to be drawn from the above could be that Luke, on the assumption that his is the later Gospel, has taken such passages from Matthew's Gospel, and has used them in his own way and for his own purposes.[y] It was not drawn because it was judged that such an extraction of materials from their often excellent arrangement in Matthew, and their redistribution in other contexts that were not compelling, would have been a very unlikely editorial procedure. The conclusion that was therefore drawn was that Matthew and Luke, independently of each other, and each in his own way, has made use of a common written source, designated Q, which was composed almost entirely of sayings of Jesus. Luke will have used it in blocks, sometimes alongside his special material, at points suggested by the Markan framework, $3^{7-9,\ 16-17}$ filling out the Baptist section, 4^{2-12} the temptations, 6^{20}–7^{35} providing teaching in the context of the choice of

---

[y] It is this assumption that Luke's is the later Gospel which has secured that the contrary, and in some ways more natural, hypothesis, that Matthew used Luke has not been given serious consideration.

the Twelve in Mark 3^{7-19}, and the remainder articulating the long teaching journey from $9^{51}-18^{14}$. Matthew will have used it differently in conflating it with other material to produce the five discourses of his Gospel.

The reconstruction of this hypothetical document has always and inevitably been subject to difficulties. With respect to its contents, if either Matthew or Luke failed to reproduce a passage from Q then it can no longer be known whether it stood in Q; and when the level of verbal agreement is sufficiently low in a common passage there is doubt whether it should be assigned to Q.[z] An original order of the contents proves difficult to establish in view of the widely different contexts in which they appears in the two gospels, though V. Taylor[a] argued that the order in which the common material is found in blocks in Luke is the original, since it is substantially that in which it is found even when conflated with other material in Matthew's more composite discourses. Whether an original wording is better preserved in any one instance by Matthew or by Luke is also difficult to determine; and variations of wording which have been judged to go beyond the limits of editorial revision by one or the other evangelist have led to a modification of the hypothesis in the form of two recensions of Q – Q^{Mt} and Q^{Lk}.

The hypothesis has come under attack in the last thirty or forty years, and Q has been declared redundant, notably by A. M. Farrer.[b] He argues negatively that a document made up only of teaching of Jesus and lacking a passion narrative would have been inconceivable in the church; and positively that Luke is to be seen as taking over Mark for narrative and as quarrying Matthew for teaching, and that the manner of this quarrying becomes intelligible once it is recognized that he is, like Matthew, though in a different way from Matthew, constructing his Gospel on a hexateuchal pattern. But the first argument is a dogmatic *a priori*, which could leave unexplained why and how any teaching of Jesus came to be preserved at all in the context of the preaching

[z] See the reconstructions of Streeter, *Four Gospels*, ch. X, A. Harnack, *The Sayings of Jesus*, T. W. Manson, *The Sayings of Jesus*, pp. 39ff.; also Fitzmyer, pp. 75ff., and his bibliography, pp. 101f. It has been proposed by some that only those passages with a high percentage of verbal agreement should be assigned to Q, the rest to be accounted for along other lines; see C. K. Barrett, 'Q: a Re-examination', *ExpT* 54, 1942–43, pp. 320–3; C. J. A. Hickling, 'The Plurality of "Q" ' in *Logia: les paroles de Jésus*, ed. J. Delobel, Louvain 1982, pp. 425ff.

[a] 'The Order of Q', *JTS* ns 4, 1953, pp. 27–31.

[b] 'On Dispensing with Q' in *Studies in the Gospels*, ed. Nineham, pp. 55–88.

of the crucified and risen Christ. The second is only partly true, as on occasions Luke takes teaching directly from Mark (as in 8[4-18]; 9[2-6, 46-49]; 20[1-47]). The third, which is crucial, detects a pattern in Luke which is by no means evident to others.

A more detailed and nuanced presentation of the case for Luke's use of Matthew is made by J. H. Drury and H. B. Green.[c] Here frequent appeal is made to *midrash* as a major, and hitherto neglected, phenomenon for the understanding of much Christian, as it is of much Jewish, writing. *midrash* was a standard term for a wide-ranging activity of interpretation (the word means 'interpretation'). It took the form of a reworking of an authoritative text, generally by retelling the stories in it with a greater or less freedom of invention and embellishment (sometimes by adding a story to the text). The object was to apply the text to the writer's own time, and to make it a vehicle of his own viewpoint. A classic example is that of the books of Chronicles, where the stories of the books of Samuel and Kings, while still showing through, are radically rewritten to express the Chronicler's own theology. The term, however, is a slippery one, and is to be used with caution.[d] When applied as a heuristic device for showing Luke's text to have been derived from Matthew's it would seem that either too much or too little is being required of it. On the one hand, if the Lukan birth stories are to be adjudged a retelling of those in Matthew (as by Drury, op. cit., pp. 46ff., 122ff., and by Green, op. cit., pp. 143ff.), this is hardly to be termed *midrash*; for it will have involved, not the revision of Matthew's stories but their disappearance without trace and their total replacement, the only basis for Luke's *midrash* in Matthew's text being the bare statement that Jesus was born in Bethlehem of a virgin through the agency of the Spirit. On the other hand, for Luke to have broken

---

c Drury, *Tradition and Design in Luke's Gospel*, esp. ch. 6; Green, 'The Credibility of Luke's Transformation of Matthew' in *Synoptic Studies*, ed. Tuckett, pp. 131ff.

d Thus Drury (*Tradition*, pp. 54ff.) shows clearly, as have others, that Luke's birth stories are shot through with OT motifs and the appropriate LXX language; but this in itself does not argue for *midrash*, since the motifs are taken from various parts of the OT, and do not together constitute the retelling of a significantly long sequence of OT narrative. Fitzmyer (pp. 308f.) observes that the term *midrash* 'would be more accurately used of the Matthean text than the Lucan, because Matthew at least quotes the OT, and a starting-point in an OT text is an essential of midrash. Even then it would have to be used in the broadest of senses. The term is better avoided, and is in any case quite unsuitable for the Lucan form.'

up Matthew's discourses and redistributed them would not have involved a midrashic expansion of Matthew's text (*midrash*, it would seem, operates by expansion and not by abbreviation), but either a transcription with a few stylistic alterations, as in 3^{7-9}, $^{16-17}$; 7^{18-35}; 11^{24-26}, or an actual reduction of it (a de-midrashing of it?). This would be the case in the sermon and the sayings on cares (6^{20-49}; 12^{22-31}) compared with Matt. 5^1-7^{27}, in the mission (10^{1-22}) compared with Matt. $9^{35}-10^{42}$, in the attacks on the Pharisees (11^{37-54}) compared with Matt. 23^{1-36}, and in the teaching on readiness (12^{35-46}; 17^{22-37}) compared with Matt. $24^{37}-25^{46}$.

M. D. Goulder combines the midrashic with the calendrical.[e] He finds the main clue to Luke's construction, including his extraction and use of material from Matthew, in an intention to provide his church of Gentile Christians with a lectionary of gospel readings (sermons?) for the liturgical year. The passion and resurrection narratives were designed for reading at the festival of Passover/Easter, while the order and contents of the rest of the Gospel are parallel to, and determined by, the order and content of the *sidrôt*, i.e. the passages from the Law prescribed for sabbath reading in the synagogue, and also from the order and content of the *haphtarôt*, i.e. the further passages prescribed in the Jewish lectionary from the OT Histories, Prophecies and Writings. That the latter part of the Gospel, $9^{51}-21^4$, has an overplus of material for this purpose is to be accounted for by a further intention of Luke to intercalate here lectionary readings for a series of thrice weekly catechetical instructions.

If these and similar analyses fail to carry conviction, recourse must be had to the Q hypothesis in some form. As generally reconstructed, Q exhibits something of the shape and character of a prophetic book, beginning with the vocation of the prophet, who is here also the Son of God and the Son of man, and ending with eschatological teaching. While there is much teaching in Mark's Gospel, it is for the most part in the form of separate units of debate, and not of continuous didactic discourse. Luke will then have used the Q material at suitable points to fill out such themes as those of the Baptist and his relation to Jesus, the victorious conflict of Jesus and the kingdom of God over Satan and his

e In *The Evangelist's Calendar*, London 1978. For a more detailed account and critique of this, see my article, 'Goulder and the Gospels', *Theology* 82, 1979, pp. 425ff. The theory is less likely to the extent that the Gospel and Acts are a unity, as the latter is less amenable to division for lectionary purposes.

kingdom, the demands made by Jesus, the Son of man and by the kingdom for discipleship, the judgment upon Israel, Jerusalem and the Pharisees, and the eschatological future.

With the removal of what is taken from Mark and of the non-Markan material that is common with Matthew, the following remains as peculiar to the Gospel (L):

1.	1^{5}–2^{52}	The births of John and Jesus
2.	3^{10-14}	John's teaching
3.	3^{23-38}	Jesus' genealogy
4.	(4^{16-30})	Jesus at Nazareth
5	5^{1-11}	Call of disciples
6.	(5^{39})	Saying
7.	7^{11-17}	Raising of widow's son
8.	(7^{36-50})	Penitent woman
9.	(8^{1-3})	Ministering women
10.	9^{51-55}	Samaria
11.	9^{61-62}	Discipleship
12.	$10^{1,17-20}$	The Seventy
13.	(10^{25-28})	The commandments
14.	10^{29-37}	Parable of Good Samaritan
15.	10^{38-42}	Martha and Mary
16.	11^{5-8}	Parable of Importunate Friend
17.	11^{27-28}	The truly blessed
18.	(12^{1})	Saying on leaven
19.	12^{13-21}	Greed and parable of Rich Fool
20.	(12^{35-38})	Sayings on readiness
21.	12^{47-48}	Servants
22.	12^{49-50}	Fire and baptism
23.	12^{54-56}	Signs of the age
24.	13^{1-9}	Repentance
25.	13^{10-17}	Healing of woman
26.	13^{31-33}	Herod
27.	14^{1-6}	Healing of man
28.	14^{7-14}	Teaching on humility
29.	$14^{28-35\ (33?)}$	Discipleship
30.	15^{1-10}	Twin parables of Lost Sheep and Lost Coin
31.	15^{11-32}	Parable of Prodigal Son
32.	16^{1-15}	Parable of Steward, interpretation, response

The L material comprises more than a third of the Gospel's contents, and is responsible for some of its distinctive features. Its origin(s), and the form(s) in which it was available to Luke, are necessarily conjectural. Easton (pp. xxiiiff.) saw it as constituting a single homogeneous written source, and from a statistical analysis of a number of words and expressions concluded that it exhibited a vocabulary and style distinct both from Luke's own and from those of his other sources. But while linguistic evidence undoubtedly points to a common style and milieu for some of the material, it cannot do so for all, as insufficient test words and expressions occur in all the L passages to prove that they belong together; and one or two of Easton's examples should perhaps be ascribed to Luke's hand (e.g. the construction of *egeneto* with *kai* and a verb in the indicative = 'it came to pass that . . .', and the use of 'the Lord' for Jesus). In one form of the Proto-Luke hypothesis L is also a single written source providing the sequential narrative into which the Q material is inserted.[f] This is unlikely. The date in 3^{1-2a} (not listed above) is, as it stands, framed by Luke as an opening, not only to the Gospel proper, but the section 3^{1-20}, which may be judged to have been influenced by Mark. The Galilean ministry, $4^{14}-9^{50}$, is articulated from Mark (as in 4^{14-44}; $5^{12}-6^9$; and 8^4-9^{50}), while its two distinctive

---

[f] So, with one or two exceptions, Taylor, *Third Gospel*, ch. VII. Streeter in *Four Gospels* did not speculate on the form of L.

opening events (nos. 4 and 5 above) may exhibit influence from Markan parallels. The long journey to Jerusalem, 9^{51}–19^{44}, within which most of the L material is located (10–41), would be more, and not less, artificial if it stood in L, where it would follow a very brief Galilean ministry. That L contained an alternative version of the apocalyptic discourse, discernible in ch. 21, and a continuous passion narrative of its own discernible in chs. 22–23, is highly disputable (see the Commentary ad loc., where it is rejected), and without a passion narrative it is unlikely to have contained continuous resurrection narratives.

Thus the L material may have reached Luke from more than one source, and as separate units of tradition, though some measure of collection cannot be ruled out.[g] While the form of some of the units is recognizably the same as that of units in other sources, that is not so of all of them; and distinctions need to be made. The birth stories (no. 1 above) are self-contained, are *sui generis* in subject-matter and manner, and may be of distinct origin. So also, for similar reasons, are the resurrection narratives (no. 47). There are four miracle stories, two being of cures on the sabbath (nos. 7, 25, 27, 35); but while the third is brief, and almost a replica of that in 6^{6-11} (= Mark 3^{1-6}), the others are more expansive, and contain a certain dramatic and affective personal element – 'the only son of a widow', 'Do not weep' ($7^{12f.}$), a woman completely bent, 'a daughter of Abraham' ($13^{11, 16}$), the only leper to give thanks an alien Samaritan (17^{18}). This same affective element can be seen in 4, 5 and 8 when compared with their briefer Markan counterparts, as also in 4^{40} and the resurrection narratives (cf. also Luke's addition of 'The Lord turned and looked at Peter', in 22^{61}, and of the healing of the ear in 22^{51}). It is also to be found in some of the parables, in which L is particularly rich (nos. 8, 14, 16, 19, 20, 24, 29, 30, 31, 32, 33, 34, 38, 39). Compared with parables in the other sources, these are often, though not always, of a distinctive tale type, sometimes of considerable length, and can be introduced by a rhetorical question, or contain a soliloquy from a principal character. There are also independent units of teaching of a more straightforward didactic kind, but others of a strikingly original or circumstantial nature (nos. 2, 15, 22, 24, 26, (22^{35-38}), 44, 45, 46). Sometimes Luke's hand is fairly evident (nos. 6, 9, 12, 37, 42). The suggestion that Luke composed a good deal of this

g See W. L. Knox, *Sources* II, ch. xvi for a collection of parables. His suggestions of other collections of teaching on special themes are not so convincing.

material himself out of oral tradition fails to account for the not infrequent incongruities both within individual pericopes (4, 5, 12) and between parables and the introductions and conclusions provided for them (14, 31, 32, 33, 38). These indicate rather that Luke was working with, and adapting to his own purposes, materials that had already been shaped. There is evidence of compilation of various kinds, either by Luke himself or before him, e.g. in the weaving of separate sayings to form a connected whole (28), or in the combination of parables on a common theme (30–31, 32–33), with two parables followed by a longer (30–31), two parables enclosed within exhortations (29), a parable following a *chria*[h] type saying (19) or following a double saying (24).

In content the L material could be said to exhibit a positive emphasis on the salvation and redemption available to Israel, and ultimately beyond Israel, through the words and actions of Jesus (1, 4, 7, 10, 17, 22, 25, 26, 27, 30, 31, 36, 38, 40, 46, 47), and on the sacrifice, devotion, generosity, perseverance and preparedness involved in becoming and remaining a disciple of Jesus (11, 13, 14, 15, 16, 19, 20, 21, 23, 28, 29, 34, 37, 42). It has a negative tone in the condemnation of Israel (4, 14, 23, 24), especially of Pharisees (8, 30, 31, 32, 33, 39) and of a doomed Jerusalem (26, 41, 45); on Samaritans it pronounces both a favourable and an unfavourable verdict (14, 35, 10). In some of this it overlapped with emphases in the Q material, and was able to be combined with it to form larger sections. In this it would appear that L material is used to introduce a theme, and Q material added to develop it, as in the sections 9^{51-62}; 10^{1-24}; 11^{27-36}; $12^{13-34, 35-48, 49-59}$; $13^{1-21, 31-35}$; 14^{1-24}; 17^{20-37}; 19^{1-27}. The opposite would appear to be the case in 11^{1-13}; 14^{25-35} and 17^{1-10}.

Thus Luke's writing will have entailed a considerable degree of search for, and investigation of, Christian traditions. This would be so even if his Gospel were the product of a simple dovetailing of three documentary sources – Mark, Q (or Matthew) and L. It would be much more so if the Q material was not single, and if the L material was not unified and documentary but heterogeneous and largely oral. It would be more so still if Luke was engaged from the outset in composing a single two-volume work, and therefore occupied with whatever sources or traditions were available for the narrative of Acts.

---

h See note on 17^{20}, p. 628 below.

(ii) *Redaction*

Luke's methods and habits in redacting his sources can be observed at first hand only in those sections where he is clearly dependent on Mark. These methods may be classified as literary, stylistic and theological. The first two are sometimes hardly separable, and both can be connected to the third, which involves an assessment of the Gospel, or Luke–Acts, as a whole, and of parts in relation to that whole.[i]

(i) Literary. As specimen examples the two sections 4^{31-44} and 5^{12-39} may be briefly analysed. The first section reproduces without addition and in the same order the four incidents of Mark 1^{21-39}. The extent of agreement with Mark's wording varies between 68% in the first, 58% in the second, 36% in the third and 38% in the fourth (so Taylor, *Third Gospel*, p. 78). The differences tend to come at the beginnings and endings of the stories. Thus in vv. 31–37 *went down* links to the previous episode in Nazareth, and *a city of Galilee* marks the first mention of Capernaum in narrative (that in v. 23 is in speech), with the consequent omission of Mark's 'of Galilee' at the end of v. 37. In vv. 38–39 is the regular Lukan copula *arose*, repeated in *she rose*, and James and John are omitted from a story about Simon, and because, like Simon, they have not yet been called. In vv. 40–41 a single time reference replaces Mark's tautology, and the door of Simon's house is omitted as an improbable location for such a large and generalized crowd. *with various diseases* is advanced to the beginning to mark a class of the sick, whose cure, *he laid his hands on every one of them and healed them*, is described in language probably taken from Mark 6^5. This is in distinction from demoniacs, whose knowledge of Jesus, which in Mark they are forbidden to express, is explicated as *crying, 'You are the Son of God'* by advancing words from a similar passage in Mark 3^{11}, and as *that he was the Christ*. In v. 42 there is again a single time reference, and instead of Simon and his companions (already omitted in v. 38) seeking Jesus to tell him that all are looking for him, it is (improbably) the crowds themselves who arrive in the desert places, and, anticipating what he is to say, importune him not to leave. That he must preach elsewhere is then taken to

---

i Classical here remain the works of H. J. Cadbury, *The Making of Luke–Acts* and *The Style and Literary Method of Luke*. In the latter (p. 75) he protests against the facility with which recourse is had to non-literary and theological tendencies to explain a writer's procedure before his literary habits have been adequately examined.

indicate a preaching tour beyond Galilee and in Judaea.

Thus Luke's reproduction of Mark here is not a mechanical transcription. He recasts Mark's stories so as to assimilate them to one another and to secure a better sequence, gaining in smoothness what may be lost in circumstantial detail. He aims to treat subjects seriatim, and this is perhaps what is chiefly meant by writing in an orderly fashion (*kathexēs*, 1³). In doing this he appears to have mastered Mark's section as a whole (perhaps Mark's Gospel as a whole), and to manipulate it with confidence. Hence Taylor's explanation of the gradual decrease in faithfulness to the Markan text – 'the impression made on the Evangelist's mind by the reading of Mark 1²¹⁻³⁹ is fading as he comes to the closing incident, and failure to consult his source afresh accounts for the freer rendering' (*Third Gospel*, p. 79) – appears to be the opposite of the case. It is precisely where Luke departs furthest from Mark that his editorial faculties are seen to be most alert.

The same redactional features may be seen in the six passages of the next section, 5¹²⁻6¹¹. These are taken *en bloc* from Mark 1⁴⁰⁻3⁶ with the single addition of 5³⁹. They show a similar range of agreement with the Markan text – 77% in the episode in the cornfields and 43% in the synagogue healing. In Mark the connecting links show a mixture of vagueness and precision. The cleansing of the leper, and the question about fasting introduced by impersonal verbs, have no particular context; while the cure of the paralytic is prepared for by a return to Capernaum and thronging crowds, the call of Levi by teaching on the sea shore, and the healing of the man with a withered hand by attendance at the synagogue. Luke treats the section as a whole. He has no additional information enabling him to provide more precise settings, but he relates the episodes more closely, so that each follows from its predecessor. Thus, *in one of the cities* (5¹²) links to the tour of Judaea (4⁴⁴); *when he saw Jesus* replaces Mark's vague 'came to him'; 5²⁹⁻³² now follows the call of Levi since it is in his house that the feast takes place; the sayings in 5³⁶⁻³⁹ are provided with an introduction *he told them a parable also*; and the two sabbaths are correlated by *another* (6⁶). The scribes of the Pharisees, mentioned incidentally in Mark 2¹⁶, are expanded into a huge audience of *Pharisees and teachers of the law . . . from every village of Galilee and Judea and from Jerusalem*, which is placed at the beginning (5¹⁷); and they provide a thread of continuity, as it is now they who ask the question about fasting (5³³, even though now referring awkwardly to their own disciples as *the disciples of the Pharisees*), and they are still there to dispute over the sabbath (6^2) and in the synagogue (6^7).

Similar features may be detected in the other 'Markan' portions of the Gospel. Thus 8^4–9^{50} appears to be conceived as a single section, beginning after the widespread preaching tour in 8^1 and ending before the new departure of the journey to Jerusalem in $9^{51ff.}$. It is highly concentrated on a threefold subject matter, which involves more drastic editing of Mark than previously. The first matter, in 8^{4-21}, is Jesus' parabolic teaching. This is stripped down to the single parable of the sower, its interpretation and attached sayings; its setting is a vast audience from far beyond the confines of the sea of Galilee; and by means of one of Luke's rare transpositions is concluded by the incident of Jesus' mother and brethren, so that *those who hear the word of God* now refers to the audience listening to the parable. The second matter, in 8^{22}–9^{17}, is Jesus' miraculous actions. Five of these are narrated in connection with a journey across the lake and back and an eventual arrival at Bethsaida (as in Mark 8^{22}), together with the mission of the Twelve to perform similar actions and their effect on Herod. Everything in Mark which interrupts this sequence is jettisoned – the visit to Nazareth (Mark 6^{1-6}, for which 4^{16-30} has been an equivalent), the 'flashback' account of the death of the Baptist (Mark 6^{17-29}), and the whole of Mark 6^{45}–8^{26}, where, in a diffuse section with an itinerary impossible to trace, Jesus operates on Gentile soil and raises Gentile issues that are for Luke to be raised later in Acts. The third matter, in 9^{18-50}, concerns, by deliberate juxtaposition with his miraculous actions (cf. $9^{28-36, \ 43}$), his person and passion, and their consequence for his disciples. Connected here chronologically and thematically are the confession of Jesus' messiahship and his declaration to all of the necessity of his passion (the rebuke to Peter alone is omitted) and of the law of triumph through suffering; the Transfiguration eight days later interpreted with reference to his destiny in Jerusalem; the cure next day of the epileptic boy in the midst of a faithless generation including his disciples (the conversation about Elijah being omitted); and a second prophecy of the passion to them in the face of wonder at his mighty works, and their instruction on true greatness.

The final Markan section begins at 18^{15}, and arguably extends to 23^{56}. At times verbal agreement is close, as in the four units in 18^{15-43} (the teaching on greatness is omitted in favour of an equivalent in 22^{24-27}). These are assimilated to one another as belonging in the journey to Jerusalem, which has been in progress since 9$^{51ff.}$, but which is reiterated from Mark (18$^{31-34}$, though awkwardly, as Mark 10$^{32-34}$ refers to the beginning of a journey), and by the Markan mention of Jericho (18^{35} = Mark 10^{46}), where Luke places the episode of Zacchaeus and the parable of the Pounds. After the entry into Jerusalem and the lament over it (19$^{28-44}$) agreement is again close in the cleansing of the temple and the polemical passages that follow – on tribute, the parable of the Wicked Husbandmen, on resurrection (that on the chief commandment being omitted as already used in 10$^{25-28}$), on David's Son, the denunciation of the Pharisees and the widow's mite. These are also assimilated to one another as forming a continuous sequence of instances of a regular teaching ministry in the temple in the presence of a favourable audience of the people and a hostile audience of the authorities (19$^{47-48}$; cf. 21^{37}; and 20$^{1, 9, 26, 27, 39-40, 45}$; 21^1). The following discourse, 21$^{5-36}$, exhibits both close agreement with Mark in sequence of thought and in language and also considerable divergence from him. The question at issue is whether the latter stems from Luke, who, as the author of L-A, is compelled to freer editing here than elsewhere by the subject matter, viz. the divinely ordained pattern of history between the departure of Jesus and the end of all things. The passion narrative, 22^1–23^{56}, similarly exhibits close agreement with Mark at the beginning and the end (22$^{1-13, 47-65}$; 23$^{26-56}$) along with considerable divergence in between. The issue is the same. Is this due primarily to Luke's possession of an alternative passion narrative or of a large quantity of additional material, or to the constraints upon him to produce, on the basis of Mark's account, a convincing sequence of events showing Jesus to have been innocent in Roman eyes of the political charges brought against him falsely by the Jews?

Luke's compositional methods with his other sources cannot be so directly observed (unless his use of Matthew be granted), but such features as a smoother sequential narrative and the treatment of subjects seriatim may be detected here and there in his presentation of the non-Markan material. In 3^1–4$^{15 (30)}$, as the initial section of the Gospel proper, Luke's editing might be expected to be freer, and it can be debated whether what is taken from Mark, though much smaller in quantity, is nevertheless still determinative here. The arrangement is clearly seriatim. Thus in 3$^{1-20}$ various traditions are brought together and articulated into a miniature picture of the prophetic career of the Baptist, who is then removed from the scene even at the expense of his not being there to baptize Jesus. In 3^{21}–$4^{15(30)}$ the 'beginnings' of Jesus (3^{23}) are governed by his plenary inspiration as the Son of God at baptism, in virtue of which he both repels Satan and proclaims God's salvation ($3^{22,\ 23,\ 38}$; $4^{1,\ 14,\ 22}$).

In the section 6^{20}–8^3 the sermon addressed to the double audience of disciples and people supplied from Mark (6^{17-20a} = Mark 3^{7-12}) is further articulated by *I say to you who hear* (6^{27}) and *He also told them a parable* (6^{39}). What follows in 7^{1-30} is made into something of a unity by pairing the miracle at Capernaum (Q) with that at Nain (L), both of which, together with the further, somewhat awkward specification of miracles in 7^{21}, are then the basis both of the Baptist's question – the disciples of John *told him all these things* (7^{18}) – and of Jesus' reply (7^{22}). Between Jesus' observations on John and the parable of the children in the market place Luke inserts a statement of the contrasted attitudes to John of Pharisees and people and tax collectors (7^{29-30}), which paves the way for the following story of a contrast between a penitent sinner and a grudging Pharisee (7^{36-50}).

The lengthy section 9^{51}–18^{14} is entirely made up of non-Markan material and is likely to have involved considerable editorial activity. Luke has cast it into the mould of a journey, a not infrequent literary device, though here it is a specific journey, possibly already suggested by Mark, from activity in Galilee to rejection and passion in a doom-laden Jerusalem. This framework, which is artificial, and has to be reiterated (9^{57}; 10^{38}; $13^{22\ (33)}$; 17^{11}), is made a repository of a large amount of heterogeneous material. Most of this is didactic, and one principle of its selection and organization could have been supplied by the book of Deuteronomy, also a book of teaching set in the context of a journey, as the following correspondences suggest.[j]

Deut. 1. Israel journeys from Horeb to Canaan under Moses, who sends twelve men in advance.	*Luke* $10^{1-3,\ 17-30}$. Jesus journeys from the Mount to Jerusalem, and appoints seventy to be sent in advance.
Deut. 2–3²². Moses sends messengers of peace to Sihon and Og, who on rejecting are destroyed.	*Luke* 10^{4-16}. The seventy sent with a message of peace; destruction on those who reject.

[j] For a more detailed presentation of these correspondences see C. F. Evans, 'The Central Section of St Luke's Gospel' in *Studies in the Gospels*, ed. Nineham, pp. 42ff., though not as part of an overall pentateuchal structure of the Gospel postulated by A. M. Farrer (ibid., pp. 66ff.). Evidence that 1^5–9^{50} is arranged on the basis of Genesis – Numbers is tenuous in the extreme.

INTRODUCTION

Deut. 3²³–4⁴⁰. Moses urges Israel as having heard God's voice and seen his presence to keep his statutes, which is their wisdom.

Luke 10²¹–²⁴. Jesus thanks God for his disclosure to disciples of what is hid from the wise, and blesses their eyes and ears.

Deut. 5–6. The decalogue summarized in the *shema*. Observance brings inheritance of the land and life.

Luke 10²⁵–²⁷. The *shema* with love of the neighbour brings inheritance of eternal life.

Deut. 7. Have no mercy on the foreigner lest he corrupt from true worship.

Luke 10²⁹–³⁷. Parable of the Good Samaritan. The corrupt foreigner shows mercy.

Deut. 8¹–²⁰. Man does not live by bread alone; God has dealt with Israel as a father, given food and put her to the test.

Luke 10³⁸–11¹³. Mary and Martha. The Our Father.

Deut. 9¹–10¹¹. Israel to take possession of impious nations stronger than her, though neglecting tables written with the finger of God.

Luke 11¹⁴–²⁶. Jesus by the finger of God casts out demons, taking the possessions of the stronger one.

Deut. 10¹²–11. The Lord, who is no respecter of persons, requires total obedience to his words in the heart and before the eyes.

Luke 11²⁷–³⁶. Blessed those who keep the word of God. Aliens will condemn this evil generation. The eye the lamp of the body.

Deut. 12¹–¹⁶. Clean and unclean.

Luke 11³⁷–12¹². Clean and unclean.

Deut. 12¹⁷–³². Rejoice with your wealth before the Lord. Beware of serving other gods.

Luke 12¹³–³⁴. Be rich towards God. Life is more than possessions. Seek first God's kingdom.

Deut. 13¹–¹¹. Judgment on any who lead Israel astray, including members of the family.

Luke 12³⁵–⁵³. Reward and punishment for faithfulness and unfaithfulness in stewards. Jesus divides the family.

Deut. 13¹²–¹⁸. Communal destruction for communal apostasy.

Luke 12⁵⁴–13⁵. Communal judgment and repentance.

Deut. 14²⁸. Tithe every third year.

Luke 13⁶–⁹. A vineyard unfruitful for three years.

Deut. 15¹–¹⁸. Release from debt and slavery every seventh year.

Luke 13¹⁰–²¹. Release on the sabbath of a woman from bondage to Satan.

Deut. 16¹–17⁷. Israel keeps the three feasts with sacrifice and joy in the place where God chooses his name to dwell. The apostate to be killed.

Luke 13²²–³⁵. Jesus journeys to Jerusalem, the city which kills God's prophets, and warns that aliens will take Israel's place in the feast of the kingdom.

Deut. 17⁸–18²². Appoint judges and officers to give righteous judgment; the ruler must not be lifted up above his brethren.

Luke 14¹–¹⁴. Jesus in the house of a ruler of the Pharisees pronounces on the sabbath; he exhorts to humility and the lower place.

35

Deut. 20. Exemption from battle for those who have built a house, planted a vineyard or married. Offer peace before destroying an enemy.

Luke 14$^{15-35}$. Parable of the Great Feast; those who give excuses excluded. Counting the cost in building a tower or waging war.

Deut. 21^{15}–22^4. Father and son. In the division of inheritance the first-born to be given his right. The rebellious son to be stoned. Restoration of anything the brother has lost.

Luke 15$^{1-32}$. Parables of Lost Sheep and Lost Coin teaching joy over repentant sinners. Parable of two sons, first-born and rebellious, the latter received back with joy.

Deut. 23^{15}–24^4. A slave escaping shall live among you. Filthy money an abomination to the Lord. No usury. A vow is binding. Law of divorce.

Luke 16$^{1-18}$. Parable of Unjust Steward, who acts to live among the debtors. Pharisees as lovers of money an abomination. The Law abides. Law of divorce.

Deut. 24^6–25^3. Injunctions against oppressive treatment of the poor. Take heed of leprosy. In harvest leave a sheaf for the alien. Judges to justify the righteous.

Luke 16^{19}–18^8. Vindication of the poor in the judgment. Parable of Rich Man and Lazarus. Healing of lepers. The kingdom of God amongst you. Parable of Unjust Judge.

Deut. 26$^{1-19}$. Go to the sanctuary with first fruits and profess that you have given tithes and kept the commandments.

Luke 18$^{9-14}$. Parable of Pharisee and Publican in the temple.

Within this framework are sequences with various measures of coherence, which could be Luke's work, or could be antecedent to him. Thus, 10$^{1-24}$ depicts what oscillates between a mission *en route* and one which proceeds from, and returns to, a headquarters. Into it is incorporated, somewhat awkwardly, a condemnation of towns which have rejected in the past (10$^{13-16}$), and at the end a general thanksgiving is applied to the disciples' success (10$^{21-24}$). In 11$^{1-13}$ Jesus, after prayer, teaches the Lord's Prayer, and this is developed by sayings introduced by *And he said to them* (11^5), and by *And I tell you* (11^9). In 11^{14}–12^{12} the connections are very loose. An exorcism provides a setting for teaching on the subject, which leads to an expostulation and reply (11$^{27-28}$). Then, for no apparent reason, large crowds are assembled to be taught about signs, and disciples are taught about faithful confession (11^{29}; 12^2), while in between these there is a meal with a Pharisee as the occasion for denunciation of Pharisees and lawyers. 12$^{13-48}$ has a general theme of possessions and the cost of discipleship, introduced by a request from one in the crowd, and articulated by *And he told them a parable* (12¹⁶), by *And he said to his disciples* (12²²) and by a question from Peter (12⁴¹). The pregnant personal statements in 12⁴⁹⁻⁵³ lead by a loose association of ideas to sayings on the necessity of true judgment. 13¹⁻³⁵ is something of a unity on the theme of destruction and deliverance. It is initiated by a report of the slaughter of Galileans, is punctuated by *And he told this parable* (13⁶), and is continued with the release of a woman from Satan as evidence of the power of the kingdom and with teaching on the saved and the lost in the context of a necessary journey to the doomed Jerusalem (13²²⁻³⁵). 14¹⁻²⁴ is the most carefully articulated section. A sabbath meal with a Pharisee is the occasion for a cure, and for teaching on humility to the guests, on generosity to the host and on the feast of the kingdom in reply to one of the guests. In 15–16 five parables are assembled (with sayings between the fourth and fifth), the first three on repentance, the fourth on wealth and the fifth on both, as rejoinders to the Pharisees (and scribes), as those who both oppose Jesus' treatment of sinners, and are lovers of money (15²; 16¹⁴). It is difficult to detect any rationale in the concluding sequence of the sayings in 17¹⁻¹⁰, the healing of the lepers, the eschatological teaching in 17²²⁻³⁷ and the two parables in 18¹⁻¹⁴, except perhaps concern with 'faith' and 'the Son of man' (17⁶, ¹⁹, ²²; 18⁸).

(ii) *Stylistic.* A second element in Luke's redaction is his style and diction. This can be fully appreciated only in the Greek, though even in the English translation a sensitive reader is aware that in the Gospel, and even more in L–A, he is concerned with more polished writing than elsewhere in the NT. Even in the Greek, however, this is a complex matter.ᵏ This is because the vocabulary is more extensive, and the possible sources of it more diverse, than elsewhere in the NT (or even

---

k The most detailed treatment remains that of H. J. Cadbury, *Style . . . of Luke*; the most recent is that of Fitzmyer, Introduction IV, where the Greek is both transliterated and translated; see also the works referred to in his bibliography, pp. 125ff., esp. N. Turner, 'The Style of Luke-Acts' in *A Grammar of the Greek New Testament*, Vol. IV, pp. 45ff. See also Plummer, pp. xliff. Creed, pp. lxxviff. and W. L. Knox, *Some Hellenistic Elements in Primitive Christianity*, pp. 7ff. A limited attempt is made in the Commentary to indicate some aspects of Luke's diction by the use of + + to denote *hapax legomena* in the NT, of + followed by reference to the only other instances in the NT in the case of a word or expression which is comparatively rare there, and by adducing parallels in the LXX. Notice, however, Cadbury's warning, reiterated in 'Four Features of Lucan Style' (*Studies in Luke–Acts*, ed. Keck and Martyn, p. 90), that the value of such lexical observations can be greatly overestimated.

outside it). Thus, as already noted, it has been possible for scholars to reach the conclusion that the Gospel and Acts are not by the same hand on the score of striking differences between them in vocabulary and syntax; and this conclusion has generally been resisted only by taking account of the differences of subject-matter in the two volumes, and of the possible influence on Luke of the language and style of his sources, whatever those may have been. There are also considerable stylistic differences between A. 1–15 and A. 16–28, which are also normally accounted for by differences of subject-matter, and by the supposition that in A. 16–28 Luke is now writing without sources and in his native manner. There are also differentiations of style within the Gospel itself, as between the birth narratives in chs. 1–2, the Markan and Q sections, and the material generally ascribed to L. Hence, Easton, in his enquiry whether the L material constituted a written source with its own peculiar vocabulary and style (pp. xxiiiff.), considered that statistical lists of words could furnish reliable evidence only if the words were listed according as they occurred in (i) the Gospel as a whole, (ii) passages taken from Mark, (iii) passages taken from Q, (iv) Luke's editing of Mark or Q, (v) A. 1–12, (vi) the 'we' passages in A., and (vii) the rest of A.

Apart probably from the second part of A., the only clear evidence of Luke's style, albeit of his revising style, is in his redaction of Mark. To take a single example, in the passage examined above for its composition, 4³¹⁻⁴⁴, Luke omits *euthus* = 'immediately' in Mark 1²¹, ²⁸, ²⁹ ³⁰; alters to the aorist the historic presents in Mark 1²¹ ('they come'), 1³⁰ ('they say') and 1³⁸ ('he says'); changes Mark's 'with (lit. 'in') an unclean spirit' to 'who had the spirit (for Luke 'in spirit' means 'inspired') of an unclean demon'; adds the literary interjection *ea* = 'see!' (v. 34); replaces Mark's 'they were all amazed' with 'there was amazement (the noun only here in the NT) upon all'; *said to one another* stands for Mark's 'questioned among (lit. 'to') themselves' (v. 36); *reports* (v. 37) is *ēchos* in place of Mark's *akoē* (= 'hearing'), which is used in a different sense from elsewhere in L-A, where it means 'sound'; *was ill with* translates *sunechein*, a word found in this sense in literary authors; the forceful *stood over* (*ephistasthai*) is confined to Luke in the NT (v. 39); in v. 40 Mark's 'were sick' (lit. 'were badly') is replaced by the normal *asthenein*; and in vv. 42–43 Luke rewrites more drastically, with *when it was day, departed* (his favourite *poreuesthai*), *kept* (*katechein*), *said to* (*eipen pros*), *from leaving* (the genitive of the infinitive with article); all of which are more refined expressions, and are peculiar to Luke in the NT.

In the following Markan section, 5^{12}–6^{11}, Luke's more fluent and polished style is evident. This has a wide coverage, from such literary and semi-technical terms as *charged* (*parangellein*, 5^{14}), *went abroad* (*dierchesthai*, 5^{15}), *withdrew* (*hupochōrein*, 5^{16}) and *are well* (*hugiainein*, 5^{31}), to the thoroughly biblical *the power of the Lord was with him to heal* (5^{17}) and the LXX *behold* (5^{18}). This diversity may be illustrated by the two constructions with *egeneto* = 'it happened' (AV 'it came to pass'). In $5^{12, 17}$ it is coupled by 'and' with a verb in the indicative, a LXX idiom appearing frequently in the more Semitic type Q material in the Gospel, but only once in A., while in $6^{1, 6}$ it is followed by the normal Greek construction of an accusative and infinitive.

Thus, it should be possible to compile from Luke's revision of Mark a list of words and constructions that he favours and of those he avoids, and perhaps from this to detect his characteristic style in his non-Markan material. But caution would be necessary here, as Luke is not systematic or consistent in his revision. Thus, Mark's *euthus* (immediately), so often omitted by Luke, is retained in 5^{13}; unclean spirit, altered in 4^{33}, is retained in 8^{29}; and 'were sick' (*kakōs echein* = 'were badly'), emended in 4^{40}, is taken over in 5^{31}. As H. J. Cabury observes, 'The author will sometimes correct his source in a certain way, and sometimes leave the same expression or thought in his source unchanged. The many exceptions we shall find to what is plainly the usual literary practice of Luke will abundantly illustrate this point. Not infrequently in a single passage Luke will leave unchanged at its second occurrence a word or expression in his source that he has just modified.'[1] Further, Luke's revision of Mark is evidence of his reaction to a certain type of predominantly narrative text, and it may be noted that, in the two sections examined above, it is the narrative introductions and conclusions to a story that he tends to revise, leaving the inside of the story and the words of Jesus relatively untouched. It does not follow that he would have reacted in identical fashion to a different type of text.

The complexity of the situation appears to arise from Luke's moving in at least three worlds at once. The first, perhaps hinted at in 1^{1-2}, is the world of the gospel tradition. In Mark and in other sources this tradition is found at some stage of its development (whether as the

1 *Style . . . of Luke*, p. 76. For Luke as a slipshod reviser of his sources, see Knox, *Hellenistic Elements*, pp. 7ff., 17, and *Acts*, pp. 5ff.

result of direct translation from Aramaic or not can be a matter of dispute) couched in the language of the Koinē, or the vernacular, a colloquial non-literary lingua franca of the empire, for which the papyri furnish the primary evidence. This will have provided the means of expression for such as miracle stories, controversial dialogues or parables, for which there was little by way of models in the OT or in such Jewish literary tradition as was available.[m] But the Koinē was itself subject to regional variation in vocabulary and syntax, and was nowhere more likely to be so than in the strongly 'biblical' culture of Palestine as it became bilingual, with the result that its Greek was a dialect impregnated with Semitic idiom – parataxis of sentences, the verb at the beginning of the sentence, the redundant pronoun, pleonasms such as 'answered and said', prepositions such as 'in the face of'. As well as revising this in his Markan source – and perhaps in his non-Markan sources, including any sources for Acts – Luke is also prepared to take it over. He may even be prepared to write in it himself – e.g. such a passage as the summary in A. 5^{12-16}, which resembles the language of Mark 6^{56}, includes the colloquial word for 'bed' (*krabbatos*), which Luke alters elsewhere, and A. 28^8 'putting his hands on him he healed him' is poor Greek with a redundant pronoun, but is conventional 'Christian' language in healing stories.

The second world is that of the LXX, the Greek literary form of sacred scripture. This translation had already produced a type of Greek strongly moulded by the idiom of the Hebrew original, and would overlap, and itself be a source of, written or spoken Jewish Greek. It was, however, more self-consciously religious, and established itself as a style proper to religious narrative and speech. Its influence can be traced throughout the NT writings, and nowhere more than in Luke-Acts.[n] Thus in his revision of the cure of the paralytic referred to above (5^{17-26} = Mark 2^{1-10}) he rewrites the opening sentence with the LXX construction of *egeneto* followed by 'and' and a verb in the indicative, adds the dramatic *behold*, which is found in Koinē Greek but is characteristic of LXX narrative, inserts *and the power of the Lord was with him to heal*, which recalls language such as that of Isa. 61^1, and concludes with *they glorified God*, a LXX expression, which is here taken from its

---

m For this see N. Turner, *Grammatical Insights into the New Testament*, Edinburgh 1966, ch. 7.

n For Acts see W. K. Lowther Clarke, 'The Use of the Septuagint in Acts' in *Beginnings* II, pp. 66ff.

only occurrence in Mark, but which becomes in Luke a stereotyped reaction, especially to miracle. Analysis of L–A from this angle suggests that Luke was soaked in the language of scripture, whether as a Jewish Christian or as a Gentile (proselyte?) turned Christian, and that this is to be reckoned an important factor in his presentation of the Christian movement as rooted in, and the fulfilment of, the Jewish religion. It does not necessarily follow, however, that he was either inclined, or able, to compose whole pericopes or sections himself in this style, as has been suggested for, e.g., the birth narratives, and for certain passages peculiar to his Gospel.[o]

The third world is that of Greco-Roman civilization, with which Luke shows himself more conversant than any other NT writer. Cadbury concludes from an examination of Luke's vocabulary and style that they are comparable with those of some Hellenistic authors, and include a similar proportion of classical Greek expressions. Of the LXX books he is closest to the historical work II Maccabees.[p] In the second part of A., where he would appear to be less dependent on sources, written or oral, and is freer to compose in the manner that was natural to him, he can write in a more fluent Greek style, with periodic sentences containing participle and verb instead of two verbs in parataxis, the genitive absolute, and other marks of a Greek that is freely composed and not the product of translation, though even here there are lapses. This appears in the Gospel only in flashes – e.g. in 1^{1-4}; 2^{1-7}; 3^{1-2}; 7^{2-8}; $23^{1-5,\ 6-12}$. It can operate in different directions. On the one hand it can impart an impersonal and generalizing character, as in the addition of 'all' or 'everyone' in summary statements. On the other hand it can impart an individualizing character, as in the various vignettes in A. 16–28, and in such stories as the visit to Nazareth (4^{16-30}), the call of Peter (5^{1-11}), the penitent woman (7^{36-50}), Zacchaeus (19^{1-10}) and the larger tale type parables.

o For the first see Turner, *Grammar* IV, p. 56, and for both Drury, *Tradition*, ch. 4. Decision here may be affected by the judgment whether such passages contain not only Septuagintalisms (i.e. the passages were written from the first in Greek, which at times imitated the hallowed language of the LXX translation of the OT), but also Semitisms (i.e. expressions which betray that they are translations of what had originally circulated, in oral or written form, in Aramaic) – the two could, of course, overlap. For both in ch. 15, see Turner, *Grammar*, pp. 60f. Knox, *Hellenistic Elements*, p. 1, judges 7^{11-18} 'a typical bit of bad translation Greek, even worse than the average'.

p *Style . . . of Luke*, pp. 4–39.

These linguistic phenomena of L–A remain puzzling, and permit of differing judgments and explanations. If the style of the latter part of A. was his native style why did not Luke use it for the whole work? Variations of style according to subject-matter might apply in some cases (e.g. a LXX style for the pious birth narratives in 1–2, and a more Hellenistic style for the Areopagus speech in A. 17^{22-31}); but this criterion cannot be applied throughout, and would not account for abrupt transitions from one style to another in a single passage (e.g. 3^{1-3}). What for some is judged versatility is for others evidence of inconsistency and patchwork.[q] It has been accounted for as the work of a Jewish Christian who had come to appreciate the Gentile world, and to familiarize himself to some extent with its diction; or, of 'one who may have come as a raw Gentile to Christianity', and in the period of his companionship with Paul 'had not quite succumbed to the full influence of Jewish Greek, as he did later'.[r]

The finished product of Luke's selection, redaction and stylistic revision of his materials displays at times considerable artistry.[s] This is neither to be ignored, as by those who hold theology to be incompatible with art and psychology, nor to be exaggerated, as in E. Renan's verdict on the Gospel as 'the most beautiful book there is'. Not infrequently in L–A religious truth is conveyed by word-pictures of such liveliness and vigour, suspense and pathos, as to establish the author as a superb story-teller, not only in comparison with other NT writers, but in his own right. It is not altogether surprising that there should have arisen a Byzantine tradition that Luke had been a painter. As such, however, he might have to be classified as an impressionist. For in too many cases for it to be accidental his word-pictures, which are so impressive and winning when viewed at a distance, tend on closer inspection to become blurred and confused. This occurs not only in such well-known instances as the story of Pentecost (A. 2^{1-16}) or the Appointment of the Seven (A. 6^{1-6}), where the problem for the commentator is to determine what precisely is being described, but also in some of the most distinctive passages in the Gospel, where an otherwise telling account is marred by discordant features – e.g. in the visit

---

q Thus Creed, pp. lxxviff., refers to Luke's literary versatility, while Knox, *Acts*, pp. 5ff., refers to his carelessness.

r So Turner, *Grammar* IV, p. 61.

s See S. C. Carpenter, *Christianity according to S. Luke*, London and New York 1919, ch. xiii, 'S. Luke the Psychologist', ch. xiv, 'S. Luke the Artist'.

to Nazareth (4^{16-30}), the call of Peter (5^{1-11}), the penitent woman
(7^{36-50}), the mission of the Seventy (10^{1-24}), and the parable of the Good
Samaritan (10^{25-37}).

Attempts have been made to explore this artistry further as a clue to
Luke's composition, and even to his theology. Cadbury (*Luke–Acts*,
ch. xvi) drew attention to duplication as a, perhaps unconscious, habit
in Luke's diction (e.g. in the expression 'power and authority', or the
double appellation 'Saul, Saul', 'Martha, Martha'), and to a pairing in
parallel, as in the accounts of the births of John and Jesus, and, possibly,
in the journeys of Jesus and Paul to Jerusalem. R. Morgenthaler carried
this to extremes, and assembled from L–A multiple and lengthy lists of
expressions and arrangements to illustrate Luke's predilection for 'twofoldness', in almost every conceivable meaning of the word. This, it is
maintained, is the form that Luke's artistry took; but it stemmed from
his theological intention to write history as 'witness' to God and Christ
on the principle of Deut. 19^{15} that 'only on the evidence of two witnesses, or three witnesses, shall a charge be sustained'.[t]

Talbert seeks to establish 'twofoldness' of a different kind in a series
of correspondences in subject-matter and order between larger units of
material.[u] These can be between sections of the Gospel and A., or
between sections within the Gospel itself or within A. itself. Such, it is
maintained, are deliberate, and show Luke's work to have an architec-
tonic design based on the principle of balance, which may be detected
in other writings of the period. From this design conclusions may be
drawn as to the genre of Luke's work – it is biography of a certain type
– and as to his understanding of the course and meaning of the story he
narrates.[v]

t Hence the title of Morgenthaler's book *Die lukanische Geschichtsschreibung als
Zeugnis* (Zurich 1949), and its sub-title *Gestalt und Gehalt der Kunst des Lukas*.
u *Literary Patterns, Theological Themes, and the Genre of Luke–Acts* (Studies in
Biblical Literature: monograph 20), 1974.
v The issue here is often whether such correspondences are genuine, and can
bear the weight put upon them, or are fancied and contrived. Thus the correspondences set out by Talbert (p. 16) between Luke 1^1–8^{56} and A. 1^1–12^{17} are selected
from a large amount of material in each case which does not correspond. And it
may be questioned whether the correspondences between the journeys of Jesus
and Paul to Jerusalem (p. 17) are not outweighed by the differences between them,
the first, covering nine chapters, being Jesus' journey to his passion in Jerusalem,
and the second, covering two chapters, being not primarily to Jerusalem but to
Rome (A. 19^{21}). To what lengths such correspondence may be driven when pur-

H. Flender also takes the phenomena of parallelism in L–A as a starting-point, distinguishing various types of it, and deducing from it a dialectical structure for Luke's theology.[w] Complementary parallelism, as in twin stories about a man and a woman, two versions of the ascension, or two eschatological discourses, aims to present the same truth from different angles, the individual and personal and the cosmic and universal. Climatic parallelism as in twin birth stories or the missions of the Twelve and Seventy, aims to point the connection of old and new, of earthly and heavenly, and the superiority of the latter. Antithetical parallelism, as in woes set over against beatitudes, aims to set God and the sinful world over against each other. Artistry of this kind will not be a starting-point, but an accidental by-product, for those analyses which trace the grand design of the Gospel to its being modelled on the OT Hexateuch, or constructed as a Christian lectionary based on the Jewish.[x]

C. CHARACTER

(i) *History*

In modern critical study Luke's work has generally been placed in the category of ancient history writing, and has been assessed as such.[y] There are strong pointers to this. There is first the very existence of a preface (1^{1-4}), picked up by a secondary preface in A. 1^1 with its reference back to the first *logos* (book, volume) as concerned with what Jesus did and taught. Within the preface is the description, by implication, of the work as a *diēgēsis*, which in itself need mean no more than an 'account', but when followed by 'of the things which have been accomplished' is likely to denote a historical narrative (cf. Dionysius of

---

sued through typology (which Talbert repudiates) may be seen in M. D. Goulder's *Type and History in Acts*, London 1964, pp. 36ff., where Paul's survival of the shipwreck is deemed to be Luke's presentation of the death and resurrection of Paul in parallel to those of Jesus.

w St *Luke Theologian of Redemptive History*, ET London and Philadelphia 1967.

x For the first, see A. M. Farrer, 'On Dispensing with Q', in *Studies in the Gospels*, ed. Nineham, pp. 55ff., and for the second Goulder, *The Evangelists' Calendar*. J. Drury, *Tradition*, illuminates many features of Luke's style and method without being committed to a single theory of the Gospel's composition.

y See Cadbury, 'The Greek and Jewish Traditions of Writing History', *Beginnings* II, pp. 7ff.; C. K. Barrett, *Luke the Historian in Recent Study*.

Halicarnassus, *Roman Antiquities*, 17.4, 'of which things I am making a narrative'). There is also the claim there to give an orderly account and to supply the true facts (1^{3-4}), – standard claims in ancient historians (e.g. Polybius, *Histories* II, 56.11–12). In the work itself there are sporadic attempts to bring the narrative into connection with the history of the civilized world (*hē oikoumenē*, a word almost confined to Luke in the NT). Such are the dating of Jesus' birth in relation to a supposed universal taxation ($2^{1ff.}$), of his ministry in relation to contemporary rulers; the reference to the destruction of Jerusalem and to subsequent periods of Gentile rule (21^{20-34}); the prophecy of Agabus of a supposed world-wide famine in the reign of Claudius (A. $11^{27f.}$); the description of Christians as a threat to civilization (A. $17^{6f.}$; 19^{27}; 24^5); and the association of Paul with imperial authorities (A. $18^{12ff.}$; 21–28). The use of a journey as a setting for events and teaching ($9^{51ff.}$), and 'speeches' put into the mouth of principal characters (A. passim), may also reflect conventions of Greco-Roman historiography. This itself was not uniform, even in the outstanding examplars that have survived.[z] As T. R. Glover observed, 'Every fresh movement in literature affected the writing of History. Whether the historian realized it or not, all the traditions played upon him; – character-drawing, scene painting, tragic effects, marvels, self-revelation, general essay writing, temptation beset him on every side.'[a] And for a Christian there would be additional influences peculiar to his subject-matter and its origins. W. L. Knox's refusal to Luke of any claim to be a scientific historian on the ground that he was simply a compiler of a number of sources at his disposal is hardly warranted; indeed Knox himself admits that '*like many other ancient writers* he (Luke) is mainly concerned with the amalgamation of pre-existing materials'.[b] Nor would the wholly religious content and character of his narrative necessarily exclude a claim to be a historian. The purpose of history writing, which was a frequent subject of discussion, was generally held to be in some way didactic. Others had written history paradigmatically with a religious or moral thesis – e.g. that the Roman polity was the product of divine providence, or a reflection of the commonwealth of God, mirroring in

z F. Jacoby's monumental edition of *Die Fragmente der griechischen Historiker* (Berlin/Leiden 1923ff.) is a reminder that a considerable part of ancient historiography has perished.

a *Cambridge Ancient History* VIII, 1930, p. 18.

b *Hellenistic Elements*, pp. 7–8 (italics mine).

its unity the unity of all history (so Polybius, Posidonius). Such authors painted on a vastly wider canvas than did Luke. Nevertheless, the claims they were wont to make for their subject, that it was the greatest of all time (so Polybius, I, 1; cf. Jos. *BJ*, 1.1, 'the greatest not only of the wars of our time, but well nigh of all that ever broke out between cities and nations'), could in principle be made for Luke–Acts, which was concerned with nothing less than the ultimate purpose of the one God for the whole of mankind.

H. Conzelmann has proposed a more specific model, the historical monograph. This covered a particular and restricted area, as in the work of Diodorus Siculus, in Sallust's *Cataline* or *Jugurtha*, or, in the Jewish sphere, in I, II and III Maccabees. He proposed the model, however, only for Acts when taken on its own, believing Luke's first volume to have been based on the 'gospel' form as a genre of writing already established in the church.[c] In view of its contents, a specifically Jewish kind of history writing has been suggested as a background for L-A.[d] There is, however, little resemblance to the actual history books of the OT, while later Jewish historians such as the authors of the Maccabean books (and Josephus?), with whom parallels might be drawn, were themselves to a greater or less extent influenced by Hellenistic historiography.[e] C. H. Talbert has proposed, as a model for the gospels as a whole, ancient biography, maintaining that the dismissal of this genre by scholars in the past has been made on mistaken grounds. Biography was concerned with historical events only in so far as they revealed a person's character, and set him forth as an object of imitation. Talbert sees in L-A a mixture of two types of biography, the type which aimed to give a true picture of the person involved over against false ones, and the type, popular in the philosophical schools, in which the life and teaching of the founder were followed by an account of those in whom the true tradition of his teaching was to be found.[f] But

c *The Acts of the Apostles*, ET Philadelphia 1987, pp. xl, 3.

d As by B. Gärtner, *The Areopagus Speech and Natural Revelation*, Uppsala 1955.

e See the comment of M. Hengel (*Judaism and Hellenism* I, ET London and Philadelphia 1974, pp. 95ff.) on Jason of Cyrene, whose work was epitomized in II Maccabees, that he was 'profoundly influenced by the spirit of solemn Hellenistic historiography . . . He does not set out to write an 'objective' historical report, but to give a 'theological' interpretation of the events of the most recent past . . . The fact that he could attempt this in what is externally a completely Hellenistic, highly rhetorical form, is a sign of the flexibility of the Jewish religion.'

f *What is a Gospel?*, Philadelphia 1977, London 1978, esp. pp. 94f., 134.

while Luke's organization of the traditions undoubtedly makes his Gospel approximate more than the others to a Life of Jesus, it can hardly be said to be governed by an intention to depict his personality, nor, except within very restricted limits, by a requirement to imitate him. And while Luke is certainly responsible for the portrait of the Twelve as the officially commissioned apostles of Jesus, the to and fro of the missionary narrative in A., where the Twelve play a relatively minor part, and its eventual concentration on the vicissitudes of the missionary career of Paul, hardly qualify it as being primarily an account of where the true succession of Jesus was to be found. Also proposed as a background is the biographical novel or historical romance, which belonged to the popular culture of the time.[g] Here the historical elements, largely if not entirely fictitious, were included in the service of depicting the career, adventures, trials, misfortunes and ultimate triumph of some heroic figure. Elements of romance can be seen incorporated into Jewish writing in such books as Tobit and Esther, and into its historiography in Josephus's retelling of biblical narratives. The story of Joseph in Genesis was a kind of archetype, and a full-scale example of this genre may be seen in the story of Joseph and Asenath.[h] But while there may be motifs of romance in individual stories in L–A, the gospel narrative as a whole is too pronouncedly theological and didactic, and that of A. too much distributed between a plurality of persons, to have been determined by this genre, as some later apocryphal gospels and Acts of individual apostles were.[i]

To be 'history', however, a narrative has to be the history of something. Of what is Luke to be adjudged the historian? If 'the things which have been accomplished among us . . . the things of which you have been informed' (1^{1-4}) refer to the contents of both volumes, how

g On these, see M. Braun, *History and Romance in Greco-Oriental Literature*, Oxford 1938, and B. E. Perry, *The Ancient Romances. A Literary-historical Account of their Origins*, Berkeley, Calif. 1967.

h See Drury, *Tradition*, pp. 5–9, 31, 51–5.

i For these, see E. Hennecke, *New Testament Apocrypha* II, ET London 1965, reissued 1974, pp. 174ff., 428f. Note should be taken, however, of the observation of H. J. Cadbury (*The Book of Acts in History*, London and New York 1955, p. 8), 'It is astonishing how out of the way writers sometimes give insight into the Book of Acts . . . Sometimes the fictitious romances offer the best parallel. I do not know where one can get so many illustrations of the idiom and ideas of the author of Acts in 150 pages as in the love story of his near contemporary, Chariton of Aphrodisias.'

is this single subject-matter to be understood? Luke is sometimes called the first historian of the church, to be followed in the fourth century by Eusebius as the second; but this is hardly accurate. The single universal church, which is the subject of Eusebius's history, is not present in L–A, where *church* (*ekklēsia*) is used only of local Christian communities. The term 'Christianity' does not appear to have been an option for Luke, as it was for Ignatius – cf. his *Letter to the Magnesians* 10.3, where *Christianismos* = 'Christianity' is contrasted with *Ioudaismos* = 'Judaism', a word which is also absent from L–A, though Paul uses it. This is, perhaps, because, to judge from A. 11²⁶, *Christiānos* = 'Christian' was an outsider's term, the -*ānos* ending, a Latinism, denoting the adherent of a party or group (cf. -*ist* in English, e.g. Marxist). Luke did not think of himself as writing about one religious group amongst others. An insider's term was, perhaps, 'the Way'; but this is found only in A., where it is introduced suddenly and without explanation at 9² (18²⁵ᶠ?, called 'the way of God' or 'of the Lord'); 19⁹, ²³; 22⁴ (24¹⁴, called by opponents a *hairesis* = 'party'); 24²². Occasionally the subject-matter of the whole work is alluded to in general terms. Thus, in A. 5³⁸ Gamaliel refers to *this plan or this undertaking*, meaning thereby the apostles' missionary activity as proceeding from the divine action of raising Jesus from the dead to be the saviour of Israel through forgiveness and the Spirit. In A. 10³⁷ Peter speaks of 'the thing that has happened', which is then explicated as Jesus' anointing with spirit and power for a healing ministry in Judaea, his death and resurrection, and the carrying out thus far of his command to preach him as the divinely appointed judge. In A. 26²⁶ Paul refers to 'this thing' as not having been done in a corner, meaning thereby God's fulfilment of his promise to Israel through the death and resurrection of Jesus. In modern terms Luke might then be called the historian of the Christian movement, as that had emerged into the world from within Judaism, of which the birth, ministry, death and resurrection of Jesus were the unique and indispensable *fons et origo*.

This, however, would still be inadequate in two respects. Firstly it would hardly account for the shape of the work. Why is it orientated upon Jerusalem, with nothing about the Christian movement in Galilee, where, according to some traditions, the risen Lord had appeared? How did there come to be Christians in Damascus and in Rome before Paul went there? Why, in view of A. 1⁸, do first 'the apostles', and then Peter, fall out of the story, which is then focused almost entirely on Paul, and ends with his arrival in Rome? Secondly, it would fail to place the emphasis where Luke himself places it, i.e. on God. For if there is any one term which covers the subject-matter of the whole work, it would seem to be 'the word', or more specifically 'the word of God' (or 'of the Lord'; the text often varies between the two, and it is not always possible to determine whether by 'the Lord' God or the exalted Jesus is meant). Thus, what underlies previous accounts is said to be the tradition from those who had been eyewitnesses and servants of the word (1^2). In a careful revision of Mark 1^{16-39} Jesus' synagogue preaching is specified as his word, which is effective (4^{31-36}). This consists in gospelling God's kingdom, and it must reach all the towns of Judaea, since it is for this that he has been sent by God (4^{42-44}). What crowds hear in the open air is the word of God (5^1, a term found only once in Mark/Matthew, and then in a different sense – see Mark 7^{13} = Matt. 15^6). In a further revision and rearrangement of Mark the sower's seed is expressly identified as the word of God, and Jesus' family are those around him who listen to, and carry out, the word of God (8^{4-21}; reinforced on the teaching journey to Jerusalem by 11^{27-28}). In A., what apostles, missionaries or preachers utter or distribute, and what believers, Jewish or Gentile, hear and receive, is the word, the word of God (A. $4^{4, 31}$; $6^{2, 4}$; $8^{4, 14}$; $11^{1, 19}$; 14^{25}; 17^{13}; 18^{11}), or the word of the Lord (A. 15^{36}; 16^{32}). It is further specified as 'the word of this salvation', i.e. the salvation intended by God (cf. A. 13^{23}). God confirms it as his by miracle (A. 14^3) and by the Spirit (A. 4^{29-31}; $10^{36ff.}$). It can be a synonym for God himself, so that Paul can commit believers to it, as that which is able to establish them in Christian living, and to bring them to ultimate salvation (A. 20^{32}); and it can be glorified along with God (A. 13^{48}). Since, as often in the OT, it expresses God's activity in the world, it can be spoken of as an entity which grows and increases in strength and numbers (A. 6^7; 12^{24}; 19^{20}). On the last passage Haenchen comments (*Acts*, p. 568), 'The Word "of the Lord" is none other than the mission church itself, for which an abstraction like "Christianity" had not yet been invented.' Finally, it is irresistible precisely because it is God's (A. 13^{46-49}; $5^{29, 39}$).

(ii) *History and Theology*

The beginnings of NT criticism coincided, and were in some measure connected, with the beginnings of the modern study of history; and Luke's work has been the object of special scrutiny. This can be at more than one level. There is, first, the question of historical accuracy. This was given a special twist by scholars of the Tübingen school in the nineteenth century, with their thesis that early Christianity was deeply divided into two factions, the Jewish and the Gentile, the Petrine and the Pauline; and that Luke's writing, especially his second volume, was a tendentious work, composed long after the events, to represent these factions as having been in harmony from the first. Here notable contributions have been made by professional scholars in the fields of Greek and Roman history.[j] These have tended on the whole to vindicate Luke's historical trustworthiness, sometimes in conscious correction of what they regarded as the unwarranted scepticism of theologians. Where he can be tested he is held to be accurate in respect of such matters as the Roman organization and jurisdiction in the period, the geography of Asia Minor, its local institutions and practices, and the ethos of the communities he describes. Nevertheless, some historical statements remain in dispute – e.g. the reference to a universal census (2^1) or to Theudas (A. $5^{36f.}$) – while it can remain an open question whether Luke's revisions and supplementations of Mark, as in the eschatological discourse (21^{5-36}), or the examinations before Pilate and Herod (23^{1-25}), and some of the episodes in A. (e.g. Pentecost), rest on trustworthy historical traditions, or are primarily theological constructions, as also whether his picture of Paul is historically reliable.

There is, however, a deeper level of discussion arising from the nature of Luke's undertaking as a whole, and from the character and background of his materials. For there are grounds in the NT for the view that early Christian belief was governed, at least in some quarters, by a passionate eschatology, that is, the belief that in what had taken place in the life, death and resurrection of Jesus the final events of history had begun to take place. For that reason they would be speedily brought to completion, and be seen for what they were, in the parousia, the coming and presence of Jesus in his exalted state, and in the gather-

j See the writings of W. M. Ramsay, *The Bearing of Recent Discoveries on the Trustworthiness of the New Testament*, London and New York 1915, *Luke the Physician*, London and New York 1908, *Was Christ Born at Bethlehem?*, London and New York 1898, *St Paul the Traveller and the Roman Citizen*, London and New York 1895; and more recently and circumspectly A. N. Sherwin-White, *Roman Society and Roman Law in the New Testament*. See also Arnold Ehrhardt, *The Acts of the Apostles*, Manchester 1969, and many observations by Cadbury in *The Book of Acts in History*.

ing of the elect to God (cf. I Thess. 1[9–10]; 4[13–17]; Gal. 4[4]; I Cor. 7[29ff.]; 10[11]; 11[26]; 16[22]). How far this was related to, or was a restatement of, a previous proclamation by Jesus of the kingdom of God as imminent (e.g. Mark 1[14f.]; 9[1]; 13[4ff.]) remains a matter of debate.[k] Individual gospel units may originally have been cradled in this belief and shaped to serve this message, confronting the hearer with this situation, and demanding the appropriate response. The earliest presentation of such traditions in a consecutive narrative, Mark's Gospel, could still reflect such a belief.[l] But eschatology and history are awkward bedfellows. The former is concerned with the end of history; and when it expresses this in terms of events, these are depicted in supernaturalistic fashion and highly symbolic language as a single sequence unfolding according to a predetermined pattern (cf. Revelation). The latter requires that attention is paid to the contingent factors in events, to the temporal circumstances and human conditions of their happening. The former, when it proclaims the end-events to be 'at hand', almost dissolves the distinction between present and future; the latter has to take account of the period of time between them. It was thus a problem for a Christian author how to write historically and eschatologically at the same time, i.e. how to narrate actual events so as to convey their ultimate character in the present. This was so for all the evangelists, and each deals with it in his own way. It was especially so for Luke, since he deliberately extends his story beyond the unique life, death and resurrection of Jesus, into the protracted period of time which had seen the advance and growth of the Christian mission, but had not seen the consummation of all things. In doing this he was more than simply a preserver and transmitter of early Christian traditions. He was both a historian in his selection and arrangement of those traditions of past events which he judged appropriate for the continuous story he had to tell, and also a creative theologian in his moulding and presentation of those traditions so as to indicate, in the telling, their uniqueness and divine significance.

It is this aspect of Luke's work that has especially engaged attention in recent times, and that has made it a 'storm centre in contemporary scholarship'.[m] This may be illustrated by a summary of H. Conzel-

k See W. G. Kümmel, *Promise and Fulfilment*.

l So W. Marxsen, *Mark the Evangelist*.

m The expression is taken from the title of W. C. van Unnik's contribution to *Studies in Luke–Acts*, ed. Keck and Martyn, p. 15.

mann's highly influential study, *The Theology of St Luke*.[n] Though primarily concerned with the Gospel, Conzelmann takes the Gospel and Acts together. Both are to be regarded as history. Indeed, the very idea of writing two volumes arises from the continued delay of the parousia, and from the fading of the picture in which the two eras, the present and the future final era, overlapped. What now replaces it is a different overall conception, that of the history of salvation, which is divided into successive periods. This, in Conzelmann's view, governs both Luke's selection of the components of tradition at his disposal, even if some are recalcitrant to it, and also his presentation of them. This presentation consists in the division of time into three epochs. The first epoch is that of Israel, the law and the prophets, an epoch of past promise. The key text here is 16^{16}, where *until* is to be taken as inclusive, and means that John the Baptist belongs to this epoch as its conclusion. Hence Luke does not, along with Mark and Matthew, depict him as the direct forerunner of the kingdom, and as the Elijah heralding the eschatological age, but as the last preacher of repentance, his ministry being over before that of Jesus begins (3^{20}). The second epoch is that of fulfilment in the ministry of Jesus (3^{21}–19^{27}). This also belongs to the past, though some of it, e.g. the teaching in the sermon on the plain, has present force. As 'the centre of time' this epoch is paradisal in character, being marked by the temporary banishment of Satan (4^{13}, where 'for a time' means 'until an appointed time', i.e. the time of his return to tempt Judas, 22^3), by the consequent absence of temptation, and by the presence, in anticipation of the end, of salvation in the form of healings, conversion, peace and truth ($4^{16ff.}$). The third epoch is that from the Ascension onwards (it is not entirely clear where 19^{28}–24^{53} fits into this scheme). This is partly past, but is also present and future. It is the epoch of the church, which now stands in the place of Israel, and through the Spirit brings salvation to mankind. Though now subject to temptation and persecution, it lives in confident hope of a future consummation. The second of these three epochs is itself divided by Conzelmann into three stages. The first (3^{21}–9^{50}) is the Galilean ministry, beginning with Jesus' appointment as the Son of God at his baptism, and marked by saving acts and teaching, through which disciples are gathered. The second (9^{51}–19^{27}) is cast in the form of a journey to Jerusalem, the place of rejection (13^{33}), so as to teach the way of suffer-

n The German title of this book is *Die Mitte der Zeit* = The Centre of Time, which indicates its main thesis.

ing necessary for Jesus himself and for his disciples in the future. The third (19^{28}–24^{53}) comprises Jesus' entry into Jerusalem, and into the temple, which he makes his own, his martyrdom at the hands of the Jews, and his vindication as the suffering and glorified messiah.

This reconstruction is open to criticism as over-schematized, and as vulnerable at important points. Thus, it is not certain that in 16^{16}, which itself suggests a twofold rather than a threefold division of time, *until* has an inclusive sense, or that Luke's removal of John from the scene before the ministry of Jesus begins is evidence of anything more than his desire to write in an orderly fashion, i.e. seriatim. In the birth stories, which Conzelmann virtually ignores, John and Jesus are more intimately related (cf. $1^{17, 76}$), while elsewhere parallels rather than distinctions are made between them (e.g. 3^{7-18}; 7^{18-35}; 11^1; cf. A. 1^{22}; 13^{24}). Nor is it clear that Jesus' ministry is marked by a complete absence of Satan; some statements could imply an ongoing conflict with Satan (cf. $8^{12, 26ff.}$; 9^1; 10^{17-20}; 11^{14-26}; 13^{16}), and Conzelmann's restriction of the 'temptations' in 22^{28} to those which have occurred since Satan had been allowed back (22^3) is forced. Further, the contents of the journey to Jerusalem are too heterogeneous to be brought under a single heading. What is convincing is that the concept of a history of a salvation, which has God as its author, is dominant in the construction of L–A. Thus, in the prelude (chs. 1–2) both the principal figures are hailed as harbingers or bearers of divine salvation. John is so as the prophet of a salvation related to the divine promises concerning David's house (1^{67-79}). Jesus is so as expressly called a saviour in the city of David, who is to be given the throne of David for ever (2^{9-19}; $1^{32f.}$). Nowhere else in the NT are the Davidic promises and salvation brought together in this way. Nor can it be accidental that, after the prelude, the whole two-volume work is bracketed between two references to what is called, in the distinctive wording of Isa. 40^5 LXX, *to sōtērion tou theou* = 'the saving (thing, action) of God', which is seen as embracing the Gentiles. The first is in the opening words of the Gospel proper, when an Isaiah quotation, already applied to the Baptist in tradition (Mark 1^3), is continued until the words are reached 'and all flesh shall see the salvation of God' (3^{4-6}). The second is in the closing words of A., when Paul affirms that 'this salvation of God has been sent to the Gentiles: they will listen' (A. 28^{28}). Elsewhere in L–A salvation appears as the goal of human existence (13^{23}; A. $2^{21, 47}$), and as the purpose of the Son of man's mission (19^{9-10}; 8^{12}); while the burden of the Christian message can be that God has supplied in Jesus a saviour for Israel (A. 5³¹; 13²³), the only one so supplied (A. 4¹²), and the message itself can be called 'the word of this salvation' sent by God (A. 13²⁶), or the announcement of salvation by servants of the most high God (A. 16¹⁷). Such statements show Luke's thought to be profoundly theological in the sense of concentrated upon God. His task as an evangelist was to give effect to this in the form of narrative. This meant that in composing *theological* history he had to write about events in such a way as to make clear that they were the work of God, and had their origin in his effective will; though in writing theological *history* it was difficult to avoid the impression that God's saving actions were now in the past, or to convey their significance for the present.

This theological emphasis can take other forms. Thus in A. it is the God who alone controls events and knows all hearts (A. 1⁷, ²⁴), who, either directly, or indirectly through the exalted Christ, the Spirit or angels, stands behind, and effects, all the major decisions, experiences and activities of the Christian movement: the choice of the twelfth apostle (A. 1²⁴ᶠ·), the effusion of the Spirit (A. 2¹¹, ¹⁷, ³³; 5³²; 11¹⁷ᶠ·; 20²⁸), the inspiration of apostles and their deliverance from their enemies (A. 5¹⁹ᶠᶠ·; 12⁶ᶠᶠ·, ²³; 27²³), Paul's conversion (A. 22¹⁴ᶠ·), and the direction of the mission, especially to the Gentiles (A. 8²⁶ᶠᶠ·; 10³ᶠᶠ·; 11¹⁷⁻¹⁹; 13⁴⁵⁻⁴⁸; 15⁷⁻¹⁹; 16⁶⁻¹⁰; 21¹⁹).ᵒ The same emphasis is to be seen, in the nature of the case somewhat differently expressed, in the Gospel. In the birth stories the conceptions of John and Jesus are announced as effected by God's power and spirit. John, as prophet of the Most High, will be the agent of God's salvation of Israel (1⁶⁹, ⁷⁷ᶠ·), and Jesus, as God's Christ and God's Son, will be a saviour from God for Israel and the Gentiles (1³²⁻³⁵; 2²⁶⁻³²). In effecting this the word of God summons John to be the prophet of a salvation that is to be universal (3²⁻⁶), and the Spirit and the voice of God endow and appoint Jesus as God's Son. Under the control of this Spirit he is subjected to temptation as God's Son, is victorious over Satan, and announces the good news of deliverance (4¹⁻³⁰). This is the good news of God's kingdom, which he has been sent by God to proclaim, and is the word of God (4⁴²⁻⁵¹). The healing of the paralytic is prefaced by the statement that *the power of*

ᵒ It may be noted that the so-called 'apostolic preaching' in A. 2¹⁷⁻⁴⁰; 3¹²⁻²⁶; 4⁸⁻¹²; 5²⁹⁻³²; 7¹⁻⁵³; 10³⁴⁻⁴³; 13¹⁶⁻⁴¹, whether rightly regarded as sermons or as 'speeches' commenting on the situation, set what is said about Jesus firmly in the context of the action of the God of Israel in pursuance of his purposes.

the Lord was with him to heal (5¹⁷), which is probably intended to apply to all Jesus' healing acts in the Gospel (cf. 8³⁹); and it is concluded by the statement that both the healed man and the audience *glorified God*, which is a characteristic ending of healing stories in Luke. When Jesus takes the step of selecting the Twelve he spends the night in prayer to God (6¹²), and Luke underlines that it is God's Christ that Peter confesses Jesus to be (9²⁰). Peculiar to Luke among the evangelists is the expression of divine prevenience by means of the noun *boulē* = 'plan', as in 7²⁹⁻³⁰; A. 2²³, and the verb *horizein* = 'to determine', as in 22²², of the Son of man's rejection, and A. 10⁴²; 17³¹ of his appointment by God as universal judge.

Two further features of L–A may be seen as proceeding from Luke's emphasis on God as the author of a salvation that is historically describable in the life of Jesus and of the first Christians.

(*a*) *The Supernatural.* A predilection for the supernatural in objective physical form is apparent in Luke's version of some major episodes in the Gospel. Thus, while Matthew is content with the bare statement that Mary was found with child by the Holy Spirit (Matt. 1¹⁸), Luke spells out a miraculous conception in more detail, and in language that comes as near as possible to that of physical divine paternity (1³⁵). At Jesus' baptism any idea that the descent of the Spirit 'as a dove' was symbolic is ruled out by the addition of *in bodily form* (3²²). At the Transfiguration what is underlined in Luke's version is the physical nature of the transformation into glory which the disciples observe to have taken place when they wake from sleep, and of the cloud into which they themselves enter; as also the objective character of Moses and Elijah, the subject of whose conversation is recorded (9²⁸⁻³⁶). The darkness accompanying Jesus' death is that of physical eclipse (23⁴⁵), while the appearances of the risen Lord in 24¹³⁻⁵³ are of the most concrete kind possible (cf. also A. 1³⁻⁶). This continues in A., where what is elsewhere in the NT referred to as Jesus' exaltation to the right hand of God is depicted as elevation in space as far as a cloud in the sky, on which he is to return (A 1⁹⁻¹¹; cf. 21²⁷ = Mark 13²⁶); and where what is elsewhere referred to as possession of, or by, the Spirit is depicted in terms of wind filling a house, individual flames of fire, and the ability to speak in foreign tongues (A. 2¹⁻¹¹; 4³¹; 10⁴⁶; cf. also A. 8³⁹, Philip transported by the Spirit, and 9⁷; 22⁹, Paul converted by a light and voice visible or audible to bystanders). Similar is Luke's predilection for angels as agents of divine purpose on earth or of divine intervention in conflict. The background here was current Jewish belief, where the OT angel of the Lord as Yahweh's representative or *alter ego* had been expanded into a company or army of angels, sometimes hierarchically ordered, as his entourage. These are generally found in an eschatological scenario, though a book such as Tobit shows that they could become a naturalistic element in a folklore Judaism as agents of divine succour and protection for the individual. In the body of the Gospel angels are eschatological – as in 9^{26} (from Mark), 12^9 (from Q?), 15^{10}; 16^{22}. But in the birth stories a self-identified angel of the Lord, Gabriel, makes an appearance, not in a vision or dream (contrast Matt. 1^{20}; $2^{13, \ 19}$), but concretely at a precise location to engage in dialogue, and to communicate the divine intentions of salvation ($1^{11-20, \ 26-38}$), while an angel of the Lord, supported by an angelic host, secures the knowledge of those intentions among men before returning to heaven (2^{9-15}). A like supernatural realism attaches to incidents in Acts: cf. A. $1^{10f.}$; $5^{19f.}$; 8^{26}; 10^3; 12^{3-11}; 12^{23}; 27^{23}).

(b) *The Old Testament*. Here Luke stood in an already established tradition of speech and writing. To speak or write about an action, event or utterance theologically is to present it as having God for its cause, and as being the outcome of his will. For the first Christians this meant relating it in some way to the OT, since for them it was there, principally, that God, his will and purpose, were to be found. The appeal to 'scripture', to 'what has been written', was theological in intention, being an appeal to the authority of God.[p]

The OT could be used for this purpose in a variety of ways. One way was to employ tell-tale words or phrases, either simply to create a verbal parallel (e.g. 'it came to pass'), or to evoke a whole background (mention of 'the new covenant' could recall what is said in Jer. $31^{31ff.}$). Or an extended statement in the OT about a significant action of God promised for the future may be quoted, together with an indication that what was now taking place constituted God's 'fulfilment' of it. This schema of promise/fulfilment is so ubiquitous as to suggest that the OT as a whole had come to be seen as a book of prophecies awaiting realization. It could even be extended to the use of statements in which God's action was spoken about, not in the future, but in the present or past tenses (cf. John 10^{34} = Ps. 82^6; Matt. 8^{17} = Isa. 53^4). It might then

p For investigations of this see C. H. Dodd, *According to the Scriptures, The Sub-Structure of New Testament Theology*, and B. Lindars, *New Testament Apologetic. The Doctrinal Significance of the Old Testament*, London 1961, Philadelphia 1962.

be called fulfilment-prophecy, if the starting-point was the event that was being described, and the OT citation was applied to give it the quality of being God's work. Or, an OT passage may have been reflected upon in such a way as to produce an event corresponding to it (e.g. Matt. 2$^{13-15}$, based on Hos. 11^1). Or a passage might be used in a more limited manner as a proof text, to show something to be true because it is contained in scripture (e.g. resurrection, as by the quotation of Exod. 3^6 in Mark 12^{26}). Or, in what is called the *pesher* type of exegesis, now abundantly illustrated in the Qumran scrolls, an OT passage may be quoted *in extenso*, and its individual statements interpreted as referring to the present with some such formula as 'What this means is . . .' (cf. Heb. 2$^{5-9}$).[q] Or, typological exegesis regarded the OT as furnishing theologically significant figures or patterns of behaviour, which are then said to be recurring, as when the Baptist is depicted as the (returning) Elijah (Mark 1^6; 9$^{11-13}$).

Luke can be seen employing most of these usages. Firstly, as already noted, he shows amongst his various literary styles a marked fondness for that of the LXX, i.e. for the hallowed idiom of sacred scripture. This is most evident in chs. 1–2, which, while containing very little by way of citation of the OT text, are nevertheless soaked with this idiom. How far this comes from Luke's own pen, or from his inclusion of materials already composed in this way, is a matter of debate. It serves to create the impression that the Christian movement had its origin in pious 'biblical' circles, where the God of Israel was personally at work, as he had been in the days of old. There are further touches of the LXX, though in less concentrated form, throughout the Gospel, and in the first part of Acts; they impart a 'biblical' flavour to the story, and so anchor it in the plan and foreknowledge of God (A. 2^{23}).

Secondly, Luke utilizes OT texts, of greater or less length, in a variety of ways. This is especially evident in Acts in those 'sermons' or 'speeches' which expound, or argue for, the Christian message, generally before Jewish audiences, and which thus form the chief theological comment on events. These may be placed within the framework of God's intentions as declared through the prophets (A. 3$^{18, 24}$; 10^{43}; 13^{27}), or as revealed by his previous actions (A. 13$^{17-23}$). Within this general framework individual items may be established by reference to individual passages, as in A. 13$^{26-37}$, where, in the context of Jesus as a Davidic

q For this, see Lindars, op. cit., pp. 15ff.

type saviour, David's statements in Ps. 2⁷ and Ps. 16¹⁰ are taken as prophetic of God's bringing Jesus upon the scene and his raising Jesus from the dead (cf. the same argumentation from Ps. 16⁸⁻¹¹ and Ps. 110¹ in A. 2²⁵⁻³⁵). In A. 2¹⁵⁻³³ there is exegesis which approximates to a *pesher* kind, when Joel 2²⁸⁻³² is cited *in extenso* as what *God declares*, and is used to identify the experiences at Pentecost with the promised eschatological gift of Spirit and prophecy (A. 2³³). In the prayer in A. 4²⁴⁻²⁷ the inspired words of David in Ps. 2¹⁻² are the words of God, and are applied directly to the passion of Jesus according to Luke's version of it (Pilate and Herod). The same principle is at work in A. 8³²⁻³⁵, when Philip is said to preach Jesus from the 'passage of scripture' quoted, i.e. Isa. 53⁷⁻⁸ LXX, though no details are given of the exegesis used.

In the Gospel by comparison quotation from the OT, explicit or implicit, is relatively infrequent, and is largely due to Luke's sources, which he generally reproduces without much alteration. Thus in the section 3¹⁻9⁵⁰, the citations in 3⁴⁻⁶ and 8¹⁰ are from Mark; those in 4¹⁻¹² and 7²⁷ are from Q. In the section 9⁵¹⁻19²⁷, the rehearsal of the commandments in 18²⁰ is from Mark, and that in 10²⁷ may be; the biblical language in 10¹⁵ and 13³⁵ is from Q. In the section 19²⁸⁻24⁵³, the OT references in 19³⁸, ⁴⁶; 20¹⁷ ⁽¹⁸?⁾, ³⁷, ⁴²⁻⁴³; 21²⁷; 22⁶⁹; 23³⁴ are all from Mark, occasionally with alterations which may be significant.

There are, however, three passages peculiar to Luke of particular importance in this connexion. The first, 4¹⁶⁻³⁰, is one of the most telling stories in the gospels, and Luke may have had a considerable hand in its composition. It gains added force from being both the opening scene of the ministry, and also programmatic of that ministry. It hangs on the public reading by Jesus of a particular passage of scripture (in fact a composite of Isa. 61¹⁻²ᵃ and Isa. 58⁶), in which someone (the prophet?) speaks of himself as endowed with God's Spirit, and as thereby commissioned by God to proclaim God's jubilee year of freedom, with its tidings of victory for the poor, of release for the captives and those who are shattered, and of sight for the blind. Then, by a forceful application of the schema fulfilment-prophecy (*Today this scripture has been fulfilled in your hearing*), Jesus appropriates these words as the correct theological statement of his person and mission. The other two passages – 24²⁶⁻²⁷, ³² and 24⁴⁴⁻⁴⁷ – are at the end of the Gospel, where the risen Jesus is depicted as conducting private Bible instruction with his intimate disciples. Here it is not a matter of individual texts from scripture, but of scripture as such ([all] the scriptures – 24²⁷, ³², ⁴⁵), which is spelt out as Moses and all the prophets (24²⁷), and as the law of Moses and the prophets and the psalms (24⁴⁴). It is said, first, in a comprehensive way, that latent in the scriptures were the things concerning himself (24²⁷; cf. 24¹⁹; A. 18²⁵), i.e. the total history of Jesus, however that may be conceived; and then, more particularly, that the scriptures, properly understood, taught the divine truth that the messiah enters into his glory (his messianic status) only by way of suffering, and that a proclamation of repentance and forgiveness was to be made to all nations in his name (24⁴⁵⁻⁴⁷). While no details are given of any exegetical procedures he may have employed, a powerful picture is painted of the risen Jesus as the supreme and only true interpreter of scripture; and it is suggested that the interpretation of the OT which effectively turned it into a Christian book, of which A., and other NT books, provide numerous examples, had had its source in him. In 22³⁷ one aspect of this is illuminated. At the conclusion of his instruction at the supper Jesus affirms that 'what is about me' is coming to completion, and in confirmation quotes Isa. 53¹², 'he was counted with transgressors'. This is peculiar to Luke, and is the only express citation of the OT in his passion narrative. Its immediate purpose is to set the imminent arrest of Jesus as a criminal within the divine plan, but it extends beyond this to cover the whole passion as Luke understands it. The paradox of the innocent one among the guilty, and of the royal Christ who saves others but not himself, pervades the accounts of Jesus' examination by Pilate and Herod, and comes to a head in the dialogue of the two (fellow) criminals (23³⁹⁻⁴¹). It is resolved when, from a position of apparent helplessness and criminality, but in confidence that he will be rescued by God, Jesus secures the salvation of the penitent criminal along with himself (23⁴²⁻⁴³). Luke then replaces the cry of dereliction from Ps. 22¹, the last words of Jesus in Mark 15³⁴, by different words from Ps. 31⁵, expressive of Jesus' total trust in, and dependence on, God. (The comparative scarcity of typology in L–A may be due to its tendency to focus attention on the typical figures presented (Moses, Elijah, etc.), and less on the God who stands behind them.)

(iii) Eschatology

There is a natural, indeed inevitable, progression in Jewish and Christian thought from theology, i.e. speech about God as the author of, and prime mover in, saving historical events, to eschatology. For the latter, as speech about the last or ultimate things, intends to affirm that God is in truth the God he is said, or claims, to be. This it does by statements about, or pictures of, a divine judgment, through which God destroys evil and establishes the good. He is thereby shown carrying his purposes to their goal, and as bringing to its consummation what he had had in mind in the creation of the world, and in the choice, guidance and succour of his people. This can approximate to a philosophy of history, as in the influential book of Daniel, where God's gift of his eternal rule to his saints follows on the destruction of the four previous earthly empires (Dan. 7).

As a theological historian Luke will have needed to come to terms with eschatology, particularly as one who wrote in a Christian milieu. For there the language of eschatology no longer expressed simply a hope for a more or less distant future. In a variety of ways, and beginning with Jesus himself, it had been pressed into service to convey the final and ultimate quality of what had taken place in the earthly career of Jesus, and what therefore required to be completed, and to be manifested for what it was, through the parousia (the presence through return) of the exalted Lord, and the end of all things. This matter has moved into the centre of the study of L–A since Conzelmann postulated that a supposed crisis for Christian faith, brought about by the delay of this parousia, was a, or the, principal factor, which led Luke to write two volumes at all, and to write them in the way he did. In his view – and in this he has been followed, if with modifications, by a number of scholars – Luke set out to eliminate from the tradition any expectation of an imminent parousia, which is now deferred indefinitely, and to make room for a further extended period of history, the present possession of the Spirit being a substitute for the life of the last days (see *Theology*, Part Two).

The subject may be briefly investigated in three areas: (*a*) Acts, (*b*) the material in the Gospel derived from Mark, and (*c*) the material in the Gospel derived from elsewhere.[r]

(*a*) Eschatology appears as part of the exordium to A., though in a curiously oblique and inconclusive manner. In A. 1[6–8] the rebuke of the risen Lord – 'It is not for you to know times or seasons (technical

---

[r] For detailed investigations of this complex subject, and reviews of previous discussions of it, see E. E. Ellis, *Eschatology in Luke*, Philadelphia 1972 (he postulates a revival of apocalyptic fervour in Luke's own time, *c.* AD 90, which he wrote to counteract), and R. Maddox, *The Purpose of Luke–Acts*, ch. 5.

eschatological terms) which the Father has fixed in his own authority' – may be a revised version of Mark 13^{32}, which Luke omits in that context. It rules out human speculation about the final consummation, though about that consummation conceived in the restricted form of the restoration of the kingdom to Israel. And it does so almost parenthetically, as the main weight falls on the positive assertion of a universal mission through the Spirit. This serves to replace a temporal eschatology ('to the end of time') by a spatial one ('to the end of the earth' – Matt. 28$^{16-20}$ combines both). The angelic rebuke in A. 1^{11} is also obscure. It assures the disciples that a future return of the Lord is certain, and will be recognizable by them, since it will be the ascension in reverse ('in the same way as', i.e. on a cloud); but they are forbidden to remain there gazing, as if to behold an immediate reverse movement from heaven to earth there and then – but had the parousia ever been thought of in this way? The 'speeches' in A. are notably uneschatological. Their rehearsal of the facts about Jesus stops short with his resurrection or exaltation, or, when delivered to Gentiles, with his appointment as the future universal judge (A. 10^{42}; 17^{31}). Nothing is said about what he is doing in his exalted state, or about any return from it. The single exception, in A. 3$^{19-21}$, is remarkably expressed, and is difficult to evaluate. It refers to the parousia in the form that God will (or may – the language is somewhat tentative) send Jesus from heaven, where until then he resides by God's will, to be the Christ appointed for Israel (still appointed despite its previous rejection of him?). This is conditional on the repentance and forgiveness of Israel (for the previous rejection of the Christ?), and will take the form of *times* (*kairoi* = 'periods') *of refreshing* and *the time* (*chronoi* = 'times') *for establishing* . . . Whether these expressions refer to two occurrences in succession, or are synonyms denoting the subjective and objective sides of the same occurrence, is not clear. Both are unique in the Greek Bible, and it is not evident whence Luke derived them, nor what they are intended to convey. The first, *refreshing* (*anapsuxis*), generally means '(temporary) breathing space', which is hardly appropriate for the eschatological age. The second, *establishing* (*apokatastasis*) would be at home either in the Stoic doctrine of the periodic restitution of the cosmos, or in Polybius, who uses it in connection with his doctrine of historical recurrence through the reconstitution of a political order. For the rest, the eschatology of A. is conventional. There will be a final judgment and a resurrection of the righteous and the unrighteous (A. 23^6; 24^{15}; 26$^{6f.}$). There may be, however, two qualifications of this. In A. 7^{54-60}, according to a possible interpretation, Stephen is received into heaven at death by Jesus as the Son of man. In A. 2^{14-36} the interpretation of the Pentecost events by way of the citation of Joel 2^{28-32} (whether 'in the last days' is the correct reading in 2^{17} or not), could be taken to indicate that Luke saw the coming of the Spirit, here as elsewhere (e.g. A. 4^{31}; $10^{44\text{ff.}}$), not as a substitute for the life of the coming age, but as in some sense an inauguration into it. This could also be the significance of the designation of believers as 'those being saved', or as having life (A. 2^{47}; 11^{18}), and of their mode of life as marked by awesome signs and wonders, the community of possessions and festival joy (A. 2^{43-47}; 4^{23-31}, 4^{32-37}; $5^{1-16, \ 32}$; 13^{52}).

(*b*) Here two passages stand out. Firstly, Mark 9^1 closes a christological section with a solemn asseveration that some of those present will not die before they have seen the kingdom of God come with power, i.e. the eschatological consummation. Luke excises 'come with power' (9^{27}), and so renders the statement opaque. For it is not evident what is meant by the promise that they will 'see the kingdom of God', nor by the assurance that they will do this before death. Secondly, in ch. 21, where he incorporates and edits Mark 13, the 'problem' of eschatology for Luke was inescapable. For there eschatological language of a heightened, and sometimes technical, kind was used for the disclosure, through authoritative and imperishable words of Jesus, of a sustained programme of all future history as determined by God. The aim of his redaction here (for the details of which see the Commentary ad loc.) seems to be to establish more clearly than in Mark, as the background of Christian existence, a succession of periods of time in the context of, or as components of, the end. A period of apocalyptic error and deception is followed by one of internecine strife between nations; then the fall of Jerusalem gives way to 'times of the Gentiles'; upon the chaotic conditions of which times, and upon cosmic disorders, there will supervene the coming of the Son of man. This is then expressed differently as a universal visitation, the sudden coming of which *you* (the disciples? the audience?) are to pray to evade, so as to be able to stand approved before the Son of man in the judgment (cf. 22^{69}, Luke's alteration of Mark 14^{62} to 'From now on the Son of man shall be seated at the right hand of the power of God'). Here is a bold attempt to rationalize some of Mark's bizarre language, and to extrapolate from past and present events to the future. It does not appear, however, that it was motivated by a special concern with the delay of the parousia; nor does it defer the end indefinitely, for it retains the emphatic assertion that all things will happen before this generation passes away (21^{32}). Its purpose may then not have been, as is sometimes alleged, to distinguish certain events as historical from the events of the end, and so to secularize them, but rather to underline their ultimate significance by bringing them within a now protracted series of end events. Thus the fall of Jerusalem is not a secular event, however tragic. It is the destruction for ever of God's own city, already prophesied with tears as the consequence of failure to recognize divine visitation (19^{41-44}), and is the reverse side of God's final salvation. Luke would here seem to be engaged, not in eliminating or historicizing eschatology, but in eschatologizing, i.e. theologizing, history.

(c) Luke chose to supplement his Gospel with further eschatological teaching from other sources than Mark. In 17^{22-37} he has incorporated a miniature eschatological discourse, which is only partly paralleled in Matthew. It proceeds from what is enigmatically called a desire to see one of the days of the Son of man. This is rebuked, not because they will not live to see the end, but because calculation about it is futile, since it belongs to the day(s) of the Son of man to come instantaneously and unpredictably. In 12^{35-46}, which has more parallels with Matthew, the same theme is handled in terms of master and slaves, but in order to enjoin constant readiness. In 12^{54-56} the rebuke is for failure to discern from its signs the crucial nature of the present time. Some of the teaching in Luke, such as the beatitudes and woes and the remainder of the sermon on the plain (6^{20-46}), has a more pronounced eschatological accent in affirming a future reversal by God of a present condition, rather than, as in Matthew, the future consequences of a present disposition. Some of the parables peculiar to Luke are given an orientation to an eschatological future of various kinds – to the finality and judgment of death (the Rich Fool, 12^{16-21}), to a final judgment on unfruitfulness (the Fig Tree, 13^{6-9}), to an irrevocable judgment and salvation at death (the Rich Man and Lazarus, 16^{19-31}), to God's ultimate succour of the oppressed elect (the Unjust Judge, 18^{1-8}); while the parable of the Pounds (19^{11-27}) is applied, in contrast to its parallel in Matthew, to counter a specific expectation that the kingdom of God would appear on Jesus' arrival in Jerusalem. Luke also includes explicit statements of a 'realized' eschatology. In 4^{16-30} the promises of God's jubilee year are said emphatically to be fulfilled in the present. In $17^{20f.}$, according to the most likely interpretation, 'observation', a technical term for apocalyptic calculation of the future, is ruled out on the ground that the expected kingdom of God is already present among men. In 10[17-20] the success of the disciples in exorcism is interpreted as evidence of the fall of Satan and of their enrolment already in God's elect. Finally, in 22[28-30] and 23[42-43] occur two of the rare references in the NT to a kingdom of Jesus. In the first the apostles are promised, in conventional imagery of corporate eschatology, presence at the messianic banquet, and thrones for the exercise of final judgment on Israel. In the second, in a unique expression of individual eschatology, the penitent criminal is promised presence with Jesus in paradise immediately upon death.

Luke would appear to have been open to a wide variety of traditions here, and hardly to have been occupied in eliminating, or even reducing, the eschatological element in Christian teaching. The kingdom to come and the kingdom come, the last days here and the last days not yet, the parousia still distant but to be seen by the present generation, the judgment certain and in some ways already visible, but also in the future and incalculable, eternal life as a corporate possession at a general resurrection and as the possession of an individual spirit at death – these declarations stand side by side and jostle one another. Each enunciates in its own way the divine determination of the world's history and destiny, and the central role in them of Jesus and his disciples. None absolutely demands for its understanding that Luke was expressly concerned with the delay of the parousia, or, indeed, with any particular internal problem of Christian faith and life. In the context of L–A they could well be directed to demonstrating to non-Christians that the Christian movement was irresistible because it had God on its side, stood at the centre of his ultimate purposes for mankind, and had in Jesus the only one privy to the divine secrets. They cannot, however, be brought together to form a single coherent system of thought. They made a considerable contribution to the amalgam which Christian eschatology was to become in the second and third centuries, and which it was to remain.

(iv) *Christology*

The unity and continuity of the Gospel and A. are secured by Luke in the first instance theologically, i.e. by reference to the operation of the God of Israel, who is also God of the world, and of his word. Closely bound up with this is his christology, i.e. his presentation of

Jesus as God's unique agent in the two modes of his existence. For the earthly Jesus, who is the subject of the Gospel, does not depart at his ascension into a heavenly sphere of inactivity until his return, but continues to be active in one way or another in the decisions, actions and lives of his disciples. This is stated in a number of ways, and Luke's christology may be said to be the most variegated in the NT. This may be the result of his use of a greater diversity of sources and traditions, with their different emphases; but it may also reflect a desire to give as powerful an impression as possible of the place of Jesus in the divine work, and of the combination in him of the natural and the supernatural, by means of a multiplicity of available appellations and images. None of these is dominant, either in the two volumes taken together or in each one taken separately. Nor is any one worked out in detail, as is the relationship of the Father to the Son in John's Gospel. And while in A. 2^{36} the two basic titles of Christian confession, Lord and Christ, are singled out, Luke's account is not articulated by them, as Mark's Gospel may be said to be by a careful disposition of the terms 'the Son of man' and 'the Son of God'. Since he was writing two volumes and not one, Luke did not need to the same extent as the other evangelists to write the doctrine of Jesus' person into his gospel narrative. He could let it appear by stages, and on the whole his account of the earthly Jesus is less doctrinal than theirs. This is not always the case, however. For Luke can use the post-resurrection title 'the Lord' of Jesus in the pre-resurrection period; and the identity between the messiahship which is predicated of him at his birth ($2^{11, 30}$), which is confessed by his disciples (9^{20}) and which is constituted by his resurrection (A. 2^{36}), is simply presumed, and nowhere explained. Nor is the christology 'advanced'. There is no reference to any pre-existence of Jesus, nor any exposition of his lordship over the created order, over the church, or over the individual Christian. This may be due less to ignorance or incomprehension of such conceptions, than to the destination and purpose of his work. For if it was addressed to outsiders to advance their knowledge, and not to Christians to aid their understanding and piety, it required a christology which would account for the Christian movement as a public phenomenon, which was at one and the same time human and divine, historical and supernatural.

(a) *Man.* More clearly than that of the other evangelists Luke's portrait of Jesus is that of a man. This impression can be conveyed by the historical framework provided for his life (e.g. 2^{1-52}; 4^{16-23}), or by notices with a historical anchorage (e.g. 8^{1-3}; 13^{31}); but it is chiefly a literary creation. Luke can be seen rewriting a Markan story so as to make it humanly more intelligible. Throughout the Gospel there are touches, too many to enumerate, in which the theological concentration already inherent in the traditions, and retained or increased in the use of them made by Mark and Matthew, is relaxed. In its place can be introduced human features, and elements of drama, pathos and irony. There is no evidence that in this Luke was combating docetism, i.e. the theological viewpoint that Jesus' humanity was apparent only (the stress on his humanity in 24^{39} is peculiar to the circumstances of resurrection, which specially raised the possibility of being mistaken for a ghost). If Luke avoids associating Jesus with violent emotions (cf. 5^{12-16} with Mark 1^{40-45}), that may reflect the Greek ideal of equanimity in great men. The human and the more than human are set side by side without reflection. Though miraculously conceived, Jesus as a child grows physically and mentally, with human as well as divine approval. As an adult he is both son of Adam and son of God, son of Joseph and anointed with divine spirit; and as the Son of man he can incur the charge of being a glutton and drunkard. Even when raised from the dead he remains a man, who consorts with human companions under human conditions. This is carried over into the doctrinal statements in A., where the central figure of Christian proclamation is Jesus of, or from, Nazareth. If appointed by God as Lord and Christ, it is as a man previously accredited to men by God through the works God did by him (A. 2^{22-36}). If now Lord of all, it is as one whose earthly activity had consisted in the philanthropic work of healing (A. 10^{36-38}); and the resurrection is evidence of the intention of the universal God to conduct a universal judgment through the agency of a man (A. 17^{31}). This confidence in the capacity of humanity in the person of Jesus for the task of a universal divine salvation, could reflect both the high Jewish estimate of human nature when it is subject to God, and also trends of theological humanism in Hellenistic thought, as seen, for example, in the cult of Heracles as philanthropic saviour.

(b) *Teacher*. Mark makes more frequent reference to Jesus' activity as a teacher than might at first sight appear, though the amount of teaching he reproduces, mostly in the form of disputes, is limited. Luke underlines this activity, and incorporates into the Markan framework from other sources a large amount of material of a didactic kind. Already in youth Jesus is depicted as an expert among teachers. (2^{41-50}).

The ministry in Galilee can be summarized as teaching, both in the synagogue ($4^{15, 31}$; 6^6) and elsewhere (5^{17}), and it now includes the sermon on the plain. The journey to Jerusalem, which provides the framework for a variety of discourse, none of it expressly called 'teaching', is summarized as 'going through towns and villages teaching' (13^{22}); and one instance of synagogue teaching is recorded (13^{10}). And distinctive of Luke's picture of Jesus' last days in Jerusalem is his placing of the individual units in Mark, mostly disputes, within the context of a daily instruction, for an unspecified period, of the people in the temple, which evokes immense enthusiasm (19^{47}; 20^1; 21^{37}).

All this, however, proves difficult to bring into focus, because of uncertainty concerning the precise meaning of the terms used, ignorance of the conditions of the period, and the character of the gospel traditions, where the contours are often sharp with respect to the content of the teaching, but seldom with respect to its circumstances, occasions or audiences. Thus, it so happens that the account of synagogue ritual in 4^{16-20} is the earliest we possess. Evidence of synagogue practice, of the character and status of rabbis, and of scribal methods of OT interpretation, comes for the most part from sources, chiefly rabbinic, that belong to a time after AD 70, when Jewish faith and practice were in a process of considerable transformation.

With his customary avoidance of Semitic terms, Luke does not use the word 'rabbi' of Jesus. He has its Greek equivalent *didaskalos* = 'teacher' (cf. John 1^{38}) eleven times in address to Jesus, always on the lips of persons other than disciples (though in 22^{11} disciples refer to him as 'the teacher'). In 9^{33} he translates Mark's 'rabbi' by *epistatēs* (not found elsewhere in the NT) which, with the exception of 17^{13}, is always on the lips of disciples. This word is used in Greek sources for a wide variety of persons (though never for a teacher), the common denominator of which seems to be 'ruler' or 'master'. It may then express Jesus' position of authority over his disciples rather than his status as their teacher. It remains a matter of debate whether in this period 'rabbi' was still simply a title of respect, with the basic meaning of '(my) great one' (hence rendered by *kurie* = 'Sir', 'my Lord' – cf. John 13^{13}), and had not yet become a designation of a trained, accredited and officially ordained scribe or exegete.[s] It is also uncertain whether teaching in the synagogue was at this time restricted to the latter, or was open to any

---

s See the different conclusions on this reached by Daube, *NTRJ*, pp. 205ff., and M. Hengel, *The Charismatic Leader and His Followers*, Edinburgh 1981, ch. III.

pious Israelite. Luke does not indicate, any more than the other evangelists, in what capacity Jesus 'taught' in the synagogue, whether as accredited rabbi, or as one who had already gained elsewhere a reputation as a spiritual teacher. Nor does he give any content to this teaching – the single sentence in 4^{21} hardly counts as such. While certain units in the tradition could be taken as evidence of Jesus' use of scribal method in argument (e.g. $20^{34-40, \ 41-44}$), the impression recorded in Mark 1^{22} is that his teaching was quite different from that of the scribes, presumably in being directly authoritative, introduced by 'Amen, I say to you', and not the outcome of learned exegesis of the authoritative OT text. And while certain features of the gospel picture of Jesus as teacher accompanied by groups of disciples (*mathētai* = 'pupils'), whom he can instruct in private, could accord with that of the (later?) rabbi and his pupils or school, other features do not, such as the peremptory manner in which he 'calls' his disciples, and the fact that they 'follow' an itinerant preacher wherever he goes, so as to share his destiny. Nor does the freedom in wording with which even such teaching as the Lord's Prayer was handed down suggest that it had been learnt by heart as by a rabbi's pupils.

Where, what and in what capacity Jesus teaches outside the synagogue is also unclear (e.g. 5^{17}; 8^4). Individual units of teaching may have been handed down in oral tradition for the sake of their content as authoritative guidance for Christian faith and life, and irrespective of any original setting (in the case of Luke's lengthier parables literary composition at some stage may have to be posited). In some cases Luke is content to reproduce them in this form (e.g. $17^{20f.}$; 13^{23}). In other cases he has supplied a minimum setting, revealing by his choice of audience how he understood, or perhaps misunderstood, the content (e.g. 12^{22-48}, and the introduction to parables in 18^1; 19^{11}). The sermon on the plain is provided with a double audience taken from Mark, and this double audience appears again in $12^{1-12, \ 13-34}$; 15^1-16^{13}. Sometimes the situation is more circumstantial and the teaching *ad hoc* (e.g. $10^{38ff.}$; $13^{1ff., \ 31ff.}$). Sometimes a meal is provided as a setting, not for table talk, but for authoritative instruction of, or judgment upon, those present ($11^{37ff.}$; 14^{1-24}).

None of this is carried over into A., where there is no reference to Jesus as teacher, nor to his teaching, unless it is to be presupposed in the teaching of 'the things concerning Jesus' (A. 18^{25}), or in the Christian teaching about the kingdom of God (A. 19^8; 20^{25}; 28^{31}; cf. 1^3). Nor is there reference to anything he had ever said, except, strangely, the saying in A. 20³⁵, which is not to be found in any of the gospels. The reason for this may be that Luke's design in L–A was to provide a literary and historical account of the origins of the Christian movement, in which Jesus' teaching of necessity belonged in the first volume. But it raises acute questions for the understanding of early Christianity as a whole, and of Luke's Gospel in particular. For if the general assumption is correct that Jesus' teaching was passed down in tradition because it was required by the first Christians for practical purposes of instruction and guidance, it is strange that the only written account of those Christians nowhere shows them using the teaching in this way. It therefore remains uncertain whether Luke gave literary form to Jesus' teaching in the Gospel so that it should be authoritative and valid for the future, or because it had once been responsible, along with other things, for bringing into being Christian faith and Christian communities, which were then to live by other criteria.

(c) *Prophet.* In 3¹² the word 'teacher' is applied to the Baptist, certainly not as a scribe, but as one who voiced God's judgment more immediately, and who is elsewhere called 'a prophet' and 'more than a prophet' (7²⁶). Words are also applied to his teaching which are used of Jesus – *euangelizesthai* = 'to preach good tidings' (3¹⁸) and *kērussein* = 'to proclaim' (A. 10³⁷). This suggests that, while teaching and prophecy were distinct (cf. A. 13¹, teachers and prophets), they were not rigidly so. In virtue both of its matter and its manner Luke may have subsumed much of Jesus' teaching under prophecy.[t] A marked feature of his account of the births of John and Jesus is that they were the occasion of an outburst, or rebirth, of prophecy through the Spirit in Israel. The birth of specifically Christian faith in Israel was occasioned by the Spirit at Pentecost, and the utterance the Spirit brought about is identified by Luke with prophecy (cf. A. 19⁶, and the insertion into the Joel citation of the words 'and shall prophesy', A. 2¹⁸). Jesus can be designated by disciples 'a prophetic man mighty in deed and word before God and all the people' (24¹⁹; i.e. of the Mosaic type, cf. A. 7²²); and while such a designation is not adequate, and is overtaken and corrected by other terms such as 'the Christ' (24²⁶), it is not thereby cancelled. For he can also refer to himself as a prophet in 4²⁴, and this may go

---

t See C. H. Dodd, 'Jesus as Teacher and Prophet', in *Mysterium Christi*, ed. G. K. A. Bell and A. Deissmann, London and New York 1930, pp. 53ff.

beyond the simple use of a proverb to illuminate his situation at that moment, and extend to his whole mission as summarized in the prophetic words he has read, and has applied to himself (4^{18-21}). It is *qua* prophet that he continues on his way to death in Jerusalem (13^{32-33}). Luke possibly saw many of Jesus' utterances as prophecy, not only those which were plainly predictive (e.g. 21^{5-36}), or exposed the sin of 'this generation' ($11^{29ff.}$), or pronounced judgment on Jerusalem (13^{34-35}; 19^{41-44}), but much else that is introduced by 'to teach', 'to preach good tidings' or 'to proclaim'. If the view is correct that the contents of the journey in 9^{51}–18^{14} are ordered in a Deuteronomic sequence (see pp. 34ff.), Luke will have placed a great deal of Jesus' teaching in a Mosaic, i.e. prophetic setting. This is given forceful expression at one point in A., where the repentance required in response to the death and resurrection of Jesus, the Christ, which is the burden of several speeches in A., is explicated, by the citation of Deut. 18^{15-19}, as listening to all the words of Jesus as the prophet like Moses, whom God had promised to raise up; upon which listening now depends membership of Israel (A. 3^{22-23}; cf. A. 7^{37}).

This is a proper context in which to consider the place of *miracle* in the Gospel. For it is in response to miracle that Jesus is popularly acclaimed as 'a great prophet' raised up by God, through whom God has visited his people (7^{16}; cf. $9^{7-8,\ 18-19}$). He can be characterized by disciples as 'a prophet mighty in deed and word' (in that order, 24^{19}), and he can himself summarize his prophetic vocation in terms of healing and exorcism (13^{32-33}; only demons hail him as 'the Son of God' in response to exorcism, 4^{41}; 8^{28}). Miracles constitute a dominant component of the Gospel both in number and importance. While Luke loses five from among the Markan miracles by his omission of Mark 7^{1}–8^{26}, he makes this good by the inclusion of seven from other sources: in the Galilean (Judaean) ministry 5^{1-11}; $7^{1-10,\ 11-17}$; in the journey 11^{14}; 13^{10-17}; 14^{1-6}; 17^{11-19}, with one in Jerusalem, 22^{51}. He not only takes over from Mark summary statements of widespread healings (4^{40-41}; 6^{17-19}), but also supplies one himself (7^{21}; cf. 9^{43b}). If the expressions in the lection from Isa. 61 – release for captives, sight for blind, liberty for oppressed – are to be taken literally and not metaphorically, they serve, along with 'gospelling the poor', to mark from the outset the dual character of Jesus' activity (4^{16-30}); and this is reiterated in the reply to John (7^{22}). In 13^{32} this activity is described in terms of miracle alone. The miraculous element is also brought into relation with discipleship. Luke alone has Peter called through miracle (5^{1-11}), duplicates the healing mission of the Twelve with that of the Seventy (10^{1-20}), inserts a notice that Jesus and the Twelve were accompanied by women who had been healed or exorcised (8^{1-3}), and restricts the acclamation at the entry into Jerusalem to disciples, and attributes it to 'all the mighty works they had seen' (19^{37}).

In form Luke's account of a miracle will be found to be literary and artistic. The scene is neatly set, the illness and cure clearly described with the use of a wide vocabulary; and Jesus is in the centre of the picture. In content two features already present in the miracle tradition are stressed. The first is the explanation of miracle in terms of *dunamis* = 'power', sometimes reduplicated as *dunamis* and *exousia*, i.e. power, and authority over the rival which gives the power effect (cf. 10^{19}). This power is conceived realistically as a substance or energy emanating from the healer. It 'comes upon' Jesus (5^{17}, added by Luke); it can reside in him and be released by the touch of an individual (8^{46}; in Luke's version Jesus announces this to have occurred); or it can go out from him repeatedly (6^{19}, added by Luke). It can be extended by transference from the healer to others for their use (9^{1}; Luke adds 'power'), though it is not said how this was done, nor what was involved in the use of this power in Jesus' name (10^{17}). All this accords both with Luke's predilection for the supernatural in physical form, and with the preconceptions of contemporary thaumaturgy. The second feature is a tendency to approximate illness to demonic possession, and healing to exorcism. Thus, a fever is addressed as a demon (4^{38-39}), curvature of the spine is the work of Satan (13^{11-16}), an exorcism is called a healing (9^{42}), and the authoritative word of Jesus is not his teaching but his exorcistic command (4^{36}). In 7^{21} exorcism is added to the list of cures being performed, though it was not mentioned in the reply to John, and in 10^{17} the Seventy report success in terms of exorcism alone, though no healing of any kind had been included in the charge to them. Luke appears more at home than the other synoptists in the world of demonology and its diagnoses (cf. the seven devils in 8^{2}). Hence, while he presents miracles, as they do, as signs of the presence of the time of salvation and its wholeness, he depicts the ministry of Jesus more than they do as a sustained conflict between two rival supernatural powers, God and Satan, each with his own kingdom or sphere of power. The latter is active, not only in the plainly possessed, but in other sick people also (13^{16}). He assaults Jesus as the Son of God, but is worsted by 'the power of the Spirit', which Jesus has received at baptism, and by which he has been impelled into the desert (4^{1-14}). He assaults the Twelve, and is successful in occupying Judas (22^3, peculiar to Luke in the synoptists), but fails in the case of Peter in face of the countervailing intercession of Jesus (22^{31-32}, peculiar to Luke). The successful exorcisms performed by disciples spell his demise (10^{17-20}). Luke's theocentric emphasis may be seen here also. The source of Jesus' miraculous power is God (5^{17}), and a standard feature of Luke's miracle stories is the chorus glorifying not Jesus but God.

This aspect of the gospel, and its importance for Luke, are immediately recognizable in Acts. Firstly, in relation to the apostolic message. The proclamation at Pentecost of the exalted Lord as the source of the Spirit begins from Jesus of Nazareth, a man who, as a matter of common knowledge, had been accredited to Israel by the mighty works, wonders and signs which God had done through him (A. 2^{22}). In the speech to Cornelius (A. 10^{34-43}) this is expanded into a miniature of the gospel story as Luke saw it. God's word to Israel through Jesus Christ, the Lord of all, is spelt out in the form that, as a matter of common knowledge covering the whole of Judaea, Jesus from Nazareth had been anointed by God with holy spirit and power so as to go about 'doing good' (*euergetein* $++$ a characteristically Hellenistic word, with ethical and philanthropic overtones of benefactors, human or semi-divine); which benefaction had consisted in the healing of all who were under the tyranny of the devil (*katadunasteuein* $+$ James 2^6, a forceful word), and had been effected through the accompanying assistance of God. Secondly, in relation to apostolic practice, it is said in summary form that the apostles performed many wonders and signs (A. 2^{43}). This is repeated in A. 5^{12} as a hallmark of their life, with details of multitudes in and around Jerusalem bringing sick and possessed for healing at their hands. Their first conflict with the Jerusalem authorities does not arise out of their preaching or over doctrine, but out of Peter's cure of a man 'in the name of Jesus Christ' and over the nature of the power involved (A. 3^1-4^{30}). In Lydda Peter heals a man with the direct address, 'Jesus Christ heals you', showing that 'the name of Jesus Christ' is Jesus Christ himself operating through his apostle (A. 9^{32-35}). Nor is this confined to apostles. Stephen is not only a powerful speaker, but also performs signs and wonders (A. 6^8); Philip in Samaria makes converts not only by preaching but by extensive healing and exorcism (A. 8^{4-8}); and when Paul enters the story it is not only as an evangelist but as a healer, and as one who is known for his use of the name of Jesus Christ in exorcism (A. 14$^{8-10}$; 16$^{16-18}$; 19$^{11-17}$). The force of this was captured by A. Harnack, when, after showing the extent to which the demonic had penetrated Greco-Roman society, he concluded, 'It was as exorcists that Christians went out into the great world, and exorcism formed one very powerful method of their mission and propaganda. It was a question not simply of exorcising and vanquishing the demons that dwelt in individuals, but also of purifying all public life from them.'[u]

(*d*) *The Christ.* There are considerable problems in connection with this appellation (see on 2^{11}). These arise, on the one hand, from a dearth of contemporary evidence outside the NT that 'the anointed (one)' was an already established term in Judaism for a (the) expected royal deliverer (as in 20^{41}), and, on the other hand, from established Christian usage, where it is unclear what force, if any, it still had when it became an alternative name for Jesus (e.g. I Cor. 15^3), or in the combinations 'Jesus Christ' (A. 4^{10}) and 'Christ Jesus' (A. 24^{24}). For Luke it was perhaps the most important appellation of all. While not frequent in the Gospel, it appears at crucial points, and carries much weight. At his birth Jesus is proclaimed by angels 'Christ Lord', and is recognized by Simeon as 'the Lord's Christ' (2$^{11, 26}$). In contrast to public speculation whether John might be the Christ, Jesus is explicitly acknowledged as such by demons (4^{41}), and by Peter (9^{20}), and, perhaps, implicitly acknowledges himself to be such (22$^{67f.}$); while his interpretation of the OT with reference to himself concerns the character and destiny of the Christ (24$^{26f.}$). In A., where it is rather more frequent, it can be used to cover the past, present and future status of Jesus, without articulation of the relation between them (A. 4^{26}; 2$^{31, 36}$; A. 3$^{18-20}$ has all three at once). The Christian message can be defined as teaching, preaching, witnessing to, or proving from scripture the messiah, or Jesus as (to be) the Christ (A. 5^{42}; 8^5; 9^{22}; 18$^{5, 28}$).

Luke shows considerable theological sensitivity in his use of the term. He appears to be aware that the original had been 'the Lord's Christ', i.e. the one appointed and empowered for his work by God, which is

---

u *The Expansion of Christianity in the First Three Centuries*, ET London and New York 1904–5, p. 160. There is, however, a certain ambivalence when Luke demonstrates the triumph of Christianity over magic (A. 8$^{9-24}$; 19$^{8-41}$), but also describes activities of apostles which are themselves magical (A. 5^{15}; 19$^{11-12}$).

the form found in the latest extant pre-Christian attestation (Ps. Sol. 17^{36}; 18^{8}). He has it in this form in 2^{26} and A. 3^{18}, and, through the citation of Ps. 2^{2}, in A. 4^{26}; and lest it should be thought that the messiah was an autonomous figure he alters Peter's confession from 'the Christ' to 'the Christ of God' (9^{20} = Mark 8^{29}; cf. 23^{35}). The same theological point is made by the use of the verb 'to anoint', of which 'Christ' = 'anointed' is a verbal adjective. Thus, 'his anointed' in Ps. 2^{2} is explicated by 'your holy child (son) Jesus, whom you anointed' (A. 4^{27}), and Jesus' ministry is said to follow from the fact that God had anointed him with spirit and power (A. 10^{38}; cf. 4^{18}, where Isaiah's words, 'The spirit of the Lord is upon me, because he has anointed me . . .' refer to the empowering of Jesus for his mission by the gift of the spirit and the voice of God at his baptism). Once Luke uses the word without article and adjectivally, when he formulates the charge against Jesus that he called himself *christon basilea* = either 'an anointed one, a king', or 'an anointed king' (23^{2}). This unique expression suggests that for Luke the messiahship of Jesus involved the attribution to him of (Davidic) kingship. This is certainly so in the birth of the Lord's Christ in the city of David, and the comment upon it, expressed in the language of Israel's national hope, that God intended to give him the rule of his father David (1$^{32f.}$); to which 'the horn of salvation' already raised by God in the house of his servant David (1$^{68f.}$) may also refer. This theme is not picked up in the Gospel until, in the proximity of Jerusalem, Jesus is hailed as 'Son of David' by the blind man (18$^{38f.}$ from Mark), and, at the entry into it, is acclaimed 'the king (coming) in the name of the Lord' (19^{38}, with the suppression of Mark's 'Blessed be the coming kingdom of our father David'). The scene is thus set for Jesus, who has privately claimed an eschatological kingship, but as a ministering servant (22$^{27-30}$), to be publicly and falsely accused of political offences (23$^{1-2}$), and to be condemned as 'the king of the Jews' (23$^{37f.}$, mockingly identified with 'the Christ of God', 23^{35} = Mark 15^{32}, 'the Christ, the king of Israel'). This theme is not continued in A., where the question about the restoration by Jesus of the kingdom to Israel is simply ignored (A. 1^{6}), where the argument in terms of Davidic kingship concerns Jesus as saviour (A. 13$^{16-23}$), and where the preaching of the kingdom of God and of Jesus as the Christ simply lie alongside each other. At one point, however, it comes alive, namely when Paul and Silas are charged with raising revolt over the whole empire, and with committing high treason, in speaking of Jesus as 'another king', the word 'king' being increasingly reserved by Rome for the emperor alone (A. 17⁶⁻⁷).

This is a proper context in which to consider Luke's presentation of the *death* of Jesus. For while he takes over Mark's three predictions of his death as the Son of man (9²², ⁴⁴; 18³¹⁻³³), and adds one of his own (17²⁵), it is his death as the Christ that is crucial. Two passages strikingly illustrate this. In the first the risen Lord himself enunciates it as a dogmatic conclusion from the sum total of scripture that the messiah enters his glory by way of suffering (24²⁵⁻²⁶, ⁴⁶). In the second Paul affirms his own witness and the content of scripture to be in agreement in coming down on one side of what sounds like a topic of theological debate – *ei pathētos ho Christos* = lit. 'Is the Christ passible?' (A. 26²³; cf. A. 17³, and A. 3¹⁷⁻¹⁸, where the suffering of the Christ, though brought about by (culpable?) human ignorance, is nevertheless the work of God, who thus fulfils the words of his own prophets). No individual passages of scripture are adduced as the grounds of this conclusion. The words from Isa. 53 quoted in 22³⁷ and A. 8³²⁻³³ do not include those which interpret the Servant's lot as vicarious suffering or as an offering for sin, but are limited to illustrating particular aspects, that he was counted as a criminal, and was patient in the face of unjust treatment. It is not said in Luke, as in Mark 10⁴⁵, that Jesus' death was a ransom (price), nor, if the shorter text in 22¹⁹⁻²⁰ is read, that it was a covenant sacrifice (the verb in A. 20²⁸ should be translated 'obtained', and not, as in AV, 'purchased'). The significance of the death of Jesus in L–A comes to depend almost entirely on the meaning to be given to the verb *paschein* = 'to suffer'. The absolute use of this verb is peculiar to Luke among the evangelists (it is found in Heb. 2¹⁸; 9²⁶; 13¹²; I Peter 2²¹, ²³; 3¹⁸; 4¹). In 22¹⁵ 'before my suffering' and A. 1³ 'after his suffering', both with the infinitive of the verb used as a noun, it clearly denotes Jesus' death, but does so as a general and abstract expression for what is elsewhere referred to more specifically and concretely as 'to be killed' (9²²; 18³³; A. 3¹⁵), 'to be crucified' (24⁷; A. 2³⁶), 'to be destroyed' (23³²; A. 2²³), or 'to be murdered' (A. 5³⁰). The verb is very rare in the LXX, having no corresponding Hebrew original. Its particular nuance is probably to be found in ordinary linguistic usage, where it functioned as the passive of the verb 'to do', 'to act', with the primary meaning of 'to be done to', 'to be the patient', i.e. to be subject to the action of others. If so, that the Christ (of God) must, by divine will, suffer, and only so enter his glory, constitutes, quite apart from any concrete occasion or circumstantial details of his death, a contradiction in terms. For the Christ of God is by definition the supreme agent of God's activity, and, as (messianic) king is the vice-gerent of God's rule and power; and his glory is his heavenly status and effective power. That Jesus must suffer, not despite his being the Christ, but because he is the Christ or in order to be the Christ, is for Luke a paradox potent for the transformation of the concepts of messiahship, royalty, rule and power. The same thought is conveyed by the statement that Jesus is, or must be, handed over (9^{44}; 18^{32} (by God?); A. 3^{13}). This means essentially that he is transferred from the sphere where he is his own agent, and the free agent of the will and purpose of God, into the sphere where he is subject to the will and purpose of others (20^{20}; A. 8^{32-33}). Behind, and responsible for, this is the adverse judgment upon him of the leaders of Israel, and their repudiation of him and his claims. Anticipated in Simeon's pregnant statement (2^{34}), and beginning with the murderous reaction in Nazareth (4^{29}), this runs like a thread through the Gospel. Because of it Jesus' ministry is an area of division, constraint and constant trial (12^{49-53}; 22^{28}, peculiar to Luke); and it moulds what in Luke's case is properly called a *passion* narrative. Hailed as God's king by disciples, and defining his rule as that of a serving man, Jesus is arraigned by Israel's leaders on false revolutionary charges, and is condemned as king of the Jews to be the king who is no king. Into this theme of power and powerlessness Luke introduces, not without a certain irony, the issue of guilt and innocence, over which the protagonists, the Jews and the Romans, are almost on opposite sides. In the company of disciples with enough swords between them to give the semblance of being political criminals, Jesus is arrested and treated as such, though Pilate repeatedly, albeit in vain, bears witness to his innocence (cf. A. 3^{13}). These intertwined themes reach a dramatic climax in the final scene, when one of the two criminals taunts Jesus to the effect that if he were in fact the Christ he could save them all, while the other counters that they are guilty but Jesus innocent, and discerns that, despite his powerlessness, Jesus has a kingdom; and at Jesus' expiry the centurion attests his innocence. That Jesus was wrongfully *crucified*, i.e. put to death as an insurrectionary, is of great importance for Luke, since it bore directly on the relations of the Christian movement to the empire, which figure prominently in the second part of A. It was more important, however, that as the Christ he *suffered*. For this established the sequence suffering-glory, passion-action, dishonour-honour, powerlessness-power, as belonging to the divine order of things; cf. 24²⁶, 'Behoved it not . . .?', Heb. 2¹⁰, 'It fitted God's nature that . . .'. It was, therefore, the true way of life for man. Hence Luke adds 'daily' to the command to take up the cross (9²³), thus making it cover the whole life of the disciple, who is instructed that 'through many tribulations we must enter the kingdom of God' (A. 14²²; cf. A. 5⁴¹, the joy of the apostles at being counted worthy to suffer for the name).

(e) *The Lord.* In the angelic announcement at the beginning of the Gospel (2¹¹), and in the speech at Pentecost at the beginning of A. (A. 2³⁶), 'Christ' and 'Lord' (*kurios*) are juxtaposed as appellations of Jesus. Both are without the article, and could be primarily adjectival in force. In 2¹¹ they are in apposition in the order *Christos Kurios* = 'Christ, Lord', or 'Christ, who is Lord'; in A. 2³⁶ they are in conjunction in the order 'Lord and Christ'. As a noun, and in some cases as an adjective, *kurios* requires a following genitive, because the corresponding verb *kurieuein* means to be the lord of, because the owner of, property or persons. A regular correlative of *kurios* is *doulos* (slave), who is the property of his master (cf. the genitives in 12⁴²⁻⁴⁷, and 10² 'the lord of the harvest', 20¹³ 'the owner of the vineyard'). At a human level, especially in the vocative *kurie*, it could be a term of respect without special stress on ownership or dependence ('my lord', 'sir', 5¹²; 7⁶). As an address on the lips of disciples it could reflect the relationship of pupil and teacher (cf. John 13¹³, 'You call me Teacher and Lord', developed in John 13¹⁶ in terms of master and slave). The origins of 'the Lord' as an appellation of Jesus at a more than human level are obscure. The most likely explanation is that it began as 'our Lord', to express in Christian communities their trust in, reliance upon, ownership by and devotion to, Jesus as the one through whom, uniquely, they had been brought into relation with God, and the ultimate things of God; which relation would be maintained to the end (cf. I Cor. 16²²⁻²³; Rev. 22²⁰⁻²¹; A. 15²⁶). Parallel to, it was also distinct from, (the) Christ. The Christ (of God, never 'our Christ') had a more external and official flavour, denoting Jesus' place in God's plan, and needing to be proved from scripture. 'The Lord' was more personal and intimate, an expression used internally amongst believers for the object of their common faith and experience; though A. 10³⁶⁻⁴² shows its extension to cover Jesus' lordship over all (men) in his appointment as judge of living and dead. In the form 'the Lord Jesus' or 'the Lord Jesus Christ' it displaced 'the Christ', perhaps because it conveyed what 'Christ', a word never readily intelligible to Greeks because of its connection with the Semitic custom of the anointing of kings, no longer conveyed once it became a personal name or part of a name. In A., where it is frequent, it is somewhat stereotyped. Preaching or gospelling the Lord Jesus (A. 11[20]) is an equivalent for preaching the word of God, no particular content of the message being given. To believe on the Lord (Jesus) is to become a Christian (A. 5[14]; 9[42]; 14[23]; 16[31]: 18[8], etc.).

Its use raised profound theological questions. For 'the Lord' was in the OT a designation of God, and 'to call upon the name of the Lord' was one way of expressing Jewish monotheistic belief and worship (cf. Joel 2[32]). It had now become a way of expressing belief in, and worship of, Jesus (A. 9[14, 21]; 22[16]) and other OT statements referring to God as Lord could now be applied to Jesus (cf. 3[4]). An important text here was Ps. 110[1], where God as the Lord is shown addressing a figure called 'my lord', and inviting him to share his throne. Applied to Jesus this text both assimilated him to God and distinguished him from God, and in A. 2[34f.] it is used so as to lead to the conclusion that God had made Jesus Lord. This identity and distinction are maintained by Luke in A., where, for the most part, he reserves 'the Lord' for the exalted Jesus and 'Lord' for God. The title also raised problems outside the sphere of Judaism by reason of its widespread use in Hellenistic religions for a cult divinity – 'my Lord Mithras', 'my Lady Isis' – who existed in his or her own right as the object of total devotion, and without any relation to a God who was creator, ruler and judge of the world. On its own 'the Lord Jesus' could convey the impression that 'Christianity' was another such cult. Paul shows (I Cor. 8[4ff.]) that he was aware of this, and that it was necessary to affirm that Jesus was the only Lord, and that he was such in relation to the one creator Father God. There is nothing in L–A to indicate that Luke was aware of it (A. 11[26] might indicate that he saw a similar danger in relation to the title 'Christ'). On the other hand, his phrasing of the conversation in A. 25[25–26] could show that he was aware that the title had been appropriated by the emperor to himself as the sole object of total loyalty, as was increasingly the case from Nero onwards.

Luke alone of the synoptists introduces this post-resurrectional and exaltational title into his Gospel. This he does, however, relatively infrequently (fourteen times), and apparently in a haphazard and comparatively superficial manner. It is nowhere inserted into Markan material, and may have been derived from another source or sources;

though it is likely to be due to his editing. Elizabeth, in hailing Mary as 'the mother of my Lord' (1^{43}) is made to speak as a Christian in advance. In the angelic announcement (2^{11}) 'Lord' stands alongside 'Christ' to identify further who and what Jesus will be as saviour (it is not said when). The rest of the occurrences of 'the Lord' are in narrative. Those in $7^{13,\ 19}$ and 13^{15} might be to underline the saving character of the miracles. Those in $10^{1,\ 39-41}$; 12^{42} and 17^{5-6} are in dialogue with disciples (apostles), and perhaps mark Jesus' complete authority over them. If so, the vocative *kurie* in these contexts ($10^{17,\ 40}$; 12^{41}; 17^{37}) may go beyond the honorific address 'Sir', and contain something of later Christian devotion. This is probably the case in 5^8, and may be an indication that that story was originally of a resurrection appearance, and may be the case in 22^{61}.

This is a proper context in which to consider Luke's presentation of the *resurrection* of Jesus, which can be intimately connected with his lordship (cf. Rom. 10^9). Its crucial character for him is suggested by the following considerations:

(i) In gospel testimony to the resurrection ch. 24 is pre-eminent. Without it synoptic testimony would be jejune indeed, and even the highly symbolic narratives of John 20–21 do not displace it.

(ii) The apostolic message in A. is predominantly one of the resurrection of Jesus. It passes fairly briefly over his death, which remains uninterpreted, to its reversal by resurrection, which is interpreted with the aid of scripture as God's action (A. 2^{24-36}; $3^{13-21,\ 22-26}$; 4^{10-12}; 5^{30-31}; 10^{36-42}). In conflict with Sadducees it can be summed up as 'proclaiming in Jesus the resurrection' (A. $4^{2,\ 33}$). It has this character also for Paul, whether before Jewish or pagan audiences (A. 13^{26-41}; $17^{18,\ 31f.}$; 23^{6-8}; $24^{15,\ 21}$; 26^{23}).

(ii) For Luke the resurrection (exaltation) is the bridge between the mission and message of Jesus and the mission and message of the apostles ($24^{44-49,\ 50-53}$; A. $1^{1-5,\ 6-11,\ 21f.}$; 2^{32}; 3^{15}; 5^{32}; $10^{40f.}$; 13^{31}).

Mark's three predictions of the suffering of the Son of man, to which his resurrection is somewhat formally attached, are taken over by Luke (9^{22}; 9^{44} – with the reference to resurrection removed; $18^{31ff.}$). His concern with resurrection is, however, far from formal. For he organizes his narrative from 9^{51} onwards under the sign manual of Jesus' 'assumption' (i.e. his elevation to heavenly existence). This is prepared for in Luke's redaction of the story of the Transfiguration, where, in the context of glory (heavenly existence), the conversation of the heavenly figures is said to be about the exodus Jesus was going to accomplish in Jerusalem. Within the journey itself are included mysterious statements (peculiar to Luke) in which Jesus refers to his *telos* (goal, completion), towards which he moves, and short of which he remains under constraint (12⁴⁹⁻⁵⁰; 13³²⁻³³; cf. 22³⁷). Luke's supplementation of the only gospel pericope to deal with the subject of resurrection as such, shows how it engaged his attention. It is there emphasized that those who participate in the resurrection from the dead are those judged worthy of the age to come; that they are immortal; and that it is as 'sons of the resurrection' that they are sons of God, in relation to whom all live (20²⁷⁻⁴⁰ = Mark 12¹⁸⁻²⁷). This theme of life is continued in Luke's version of the words of the angels at the tomb, 'Why do you seek the living among the dead?' (24⁵), and in the two massive accounts of the 'appearance' (from Paradise?, cf. 23⁴³) of Jesus alive after death (24²³). In these two themes are intertwined. The first is that Jesus is alive beyond death as a man, 'appearing' under the human conditions of a protracted journey, a conversational dialogue, and common meals over a period of forty days; and he is recognizable as the one he had been by reason of his physical body and his actions (24¹³⁻³⁵, ³⁶⁻⁴³; A. 1³⁻⁴; 10⁴¹). The second is that he is now successfully, what previously, in the face of human dullness, he had been unsuccessfully, the master of spiritual intelligence. He is the supreme exegete of scripture, now at last enabling the minds of disciples to comprehend there the purposes of God as culminating in his life and death, and in the universal mission in his name that was to be their consequence. For Luke, as the sole evangelist to narrate this consequence, the language of resurrection takes on a certain ambivalence. On the one hand, it speaks by definition of what is ultimate, as in 'proclaimed in Jesus the resurrection of the dead' (A. 4²; cf. A. 26²³). On the other hand, with respect to Jesus himself, it speaks of what is still penultimate, a stage on the way to his exaltation to God's right hand, from where he will exercise his lordship and dispense heavenly gifts (A. 2³³⁻³⁶). This exaltation has then to be given a separate description (contrast Matt. 28¹⁶⁻²⁰; John 20–21), in the form of his elevation, also as a man, to 'a cloud' which receives him, and with which he is to return (A. 1⁶⁻¹¹).

In this emphasis on resurrection Luke was conscious of carrying over into Christianity, and making central there, an important strand of belief in Judaism of the Pharisaic kind (A. 4²; 23⁶ᶠᶠ·; 26⁴ᶠᶠ·). He may also have been conscious of writing for a Greco-Roman world, in which, as the mystery cults amongst other things testified, there was an increasing preoccupation with death, and with the possibility of life beyond it.

(*f*) *The Son of man*. This enigmatic self-designation on the lips of Jesus was evidently still a living and important term for Luke. He reproduces, relatively unchanged, Mark's instances of it, with the exception of those in Mark 9[9,12]; 10[45], in pericopes he omits, and in Mark 14[21,41], where he abbreviates. And he reproduces all three types of statement – those referring to: (i) the eschatological Son of man of the future, (ii) the Son of man who is present and active on earth, and (iii) the Son of man who is destined to suffer. He has supplemented these with statements from Q, both of the first type (11[30]?; 12[8,40]; 17[24,26]), and of the second type (6[22]; 7[34]; 9[58]; 11[30]?; 12[10]), where it is often a question whether he or Matthew has more nearly an original form. All three types are also represented in material, either from his own sources, or from his own hand (17[24,30]; 18[8]; 21[36]; 17[22]?; 22[48]; 17[25]; 24[7]). He is also the only NT writer to give any example of the use of the term outside the gospels (A. 7[56]). Thus its use and meaning for Luke are closely bound up with its use and meaning in the synoptic gospels and their sources (for modern discussion of this, see on 5[24]). There are instances where Luke may have made modifications expressing a distinctive theology. Thus statements of the first type present the future heavenly Son of man in a variety of stances. His future coming to execute the divine judgment (in 18[8], peculiar to Luke, to succour the elect) is certain, and will be instantaneous and unanticipated (12[40]; 17[24-30]). It will be, however, 'on (in) a cloud' rather than 'on (in) clouds', perhaps as his descent as a heavenly man, or his ascension in reverse (21[27] = Mark 13[26]; A. 1[11]). As the advocate of the one who confesses him in the world he stands facing God (12[8]), and it is perhaps as such (sc. as the inspirer of the disciple's confession, 21[15]) that he is represented as standing at God's right hand in Stephen's vision (A. 7[56]). It is, however, as sitting alongside God as judge that men are to appear before him (21[36]; cf. 22[69], correcting Mark 14[62]). Significant here could be Luke's version of the discourse in 17[22-37]. Like the parallel sayings in Matt. 24[26-28,37-41], it is primarily concerned with the eschatological manifestation of the Son of man 'in his day'. Incorporated into it, somewhat awkwardly, and probably from Luke's hand, is a prophecy of the rejection of the Son of man by the present generation (17[25]). But it is also introduced by a reference to 'the days of the Son of man', for one of which disciples will come to yearn. This is an unparalleled expression, also possibly from Luke's hand. In 17²⁶ it appears to be a synonym for 'the day' of the Son of man; but this is difficult, as an unspecified number of days, or period of time, does not lend itself to being specified as coming suddenly or instantaneously. It may, then, refer to the past, and designate the earthly ministry of Jesus – cf. 19¹⁰, where his mission can be summed up by 'The Son of man came to seek and to save the lost', and 7³⁴; 6²²; 22⁴⁸, where the Son of man is Jesus in his human activity. The special value of this title may, then, have been for Luke, that, more than any other, it had the capacity to span heaven and earth, and to encompass the whole career of Jesus as a man – his earthly ministry, his rejection by men, and his vindication by, and co-operation with, God. For, on the one hand, in the synoptic tradition, it was 'the Son of man' rather than, as later, 'the Son of God', which conveyed Jesus' 'divinity', if by that is meant that he belonged on the other side of the dividing line betwen men and God, and shared uniquely in certain divine functions and prerogatives. On the other hand, however much the term had been inflated in order to depict a transcendent figure, it could not but retain, and could always return to, its basic meaning of 'man'. Luke may also have been aware of a tendency in Hellenistic religious thought towards apotheosis, whereby a human benefactor or saviour was exalted to the gods, as with Heracles (see W. L. Knox, *Hellenistic Elements*, pp. 38ff.), or Romulus (Plutarch, *Life of Romulus*, ch. xxviii).

(*g*) *The Son of God*. In the previous title 'son of' denoted membership through generation of the human species. Here it functions differently. With respect to God it expresses his choice and appointment of someone to a position of special intimacy, honour and responsibility. A synonym is 'the elect' or 'the chosen' one (9³⁵). In this sense God can call Israel 'my (only) son' (Exod. 4²; Hos. 11¹), or likewise the (Davidic) king (II Sam. 7¹⁴). The language of generation in 'You are my son, today I have begotten you' (Ps. 2⁷) is simply a forceful way of saying this. In A. 13³³ it is applied to the historical appearance (or resurrection?) of Jesus as a saviour-king of the Davidic line. With respect to men 'son of' expresses their reproduction of the character of the father – in this case God – by obedience to his will (cf. 6³⁵). In contrast to the Fourth Gospel and later theology, where it is central, the confession of Jesus as the Son of God is found only once in A. (9²⁰). There it is an equivalent for the more common term 'the Christ', as it is in the confession of the demons (4⁴¹), and, possibly, at Jesus' trial, where the single question in Mark 14[61] about the Christ, the Son of the Blessed, is divided into two – 'If you are the Christ tell us' (22[67]), and 'Are you the Son of God then?' (22[70]) – with non-committal replies in both cases. At focal points in the Gospel, however, Luke reproduces from his sources scenes where 'the Son of God' stands alone and at the centre – the baptism, the temptation and the transfiguration. These have two characteristics in common. The first is that they all stress the humanity of Jesus, and his obedience in conditions of lowliness and humiliation. At baptism he participates in a communal act of penitence with a view to the forgiveness of sins; in the temptations he is subjected to the testing of his obedience at the hands of Satan; and the transfiguration follows after, and in Luke is closely connected with, his acceptance of a necessary rejection and suffering. The second is that in these circumstances his divine sonship is known to, and attested by, supernatural agencies alone, the voice of God or Satan (cf. also the demons in 4[41]; 8[28]). Something of the same duality may be reflected in the thanksgiving in 10[21–22], where God is praised as Father because he has revealed his secrets, paradoxically, to 'babes', and has done so through the medium of a supernatural communication between himself and one who is 'the Son'. In the scene of Jesus' death Luke replaces the human confession of his divine sonship at the moment of dereliction by a confession of his innocence as that of the trustful martyr (23[46–47]). In the birth narratives divine sonship and divine paternity may be thought of more realistically, though the precise force of the language is difficult to assess. The angel promises to Mary the conception and birth of a son who 'will be called the Son of the Most High'. This will come about because 'the Holy Spirit will come upon' her, and the power of the Most High will 'overshadow' her; therefore 'the child to be begotten' will be called holy, the Son of God'. Here 'therefore' makes a causal connection of some kind between Jesus' divine sonship and his begetting by God, though of what kind is not clear. If 'will be called' means 'will be called by God', it may refer in advance to those occasions, such as baptism, transfiguration (and resurrection?), when God will appoint, and re-appoint, Jesus to his office and work; and the miraculous conception would then be of the one who, when the time came, was capable of being so appointed. If it means 'will be called by men', it could suggest that the divine begetting was of one who possessed from the beginning a divine (holy) nature, though this thought does not appear elsewhere in L–A. Luke's intention in juxtaposing Jesus' baptism, where the voice of God appoints him his Son (possibly with the words 'Today I have begotten you' – see Commentary ad loc.), with a genealogy which, somewhat awkwardly, traces his physical ancestry back to Adam as son of God, remains puzzling. Nowhere else in Jewish tradition does a genealogy come to a conclusion with God; nor is Adam called, as a result of his creation (not generation), 'son of God'. Logically the genealogy in this form would imply the divine sonship of the whole human race up to that point (cf. A. 17$^{27-29}$). For Jesus as 'Saviour', see note on 2^{11}.

(v) *The Spirit*

Theology and christology do not cover the whole of Luke's presentation of Jesus and the Christian movement. For these are sometimes explicated, and related to each other, in terms of the (holy) Spirit. In L–A links are made between Christian experience of the Spirit and the operation of God in and through Jesus. This is in contrast to Mark and Matthew, where reference to the Spirit, at least on the lips of Jesus, is surprisingly rare.[v]

The Greek word *pneuma* meant in common usage 'wind', 'breath', and by extension 'life' or 'the principle of life'. It had these meanings in the LXX as a translation of the Hebrew word *ruach*, with the important addition that it frequently referred to the 'spirit' of God. In contrast to Stoicism, where 'spirit' is found for the 'divine' principle of order immanent in the world, this God is transcendent. Hence, like God himself, the Spirit can be called 'holy', or separate from the world. Associated with power and strength, the Spirit of God was to be seen in his creation of the world and in his presence to it (Gen. 1^2; Ps. 33^6; Wisd. 1^7; II Bar. 21^4, etc.). It was also to be seen in his control of events through empowering certain special persons to carry out his purposes (Judg. 3^{10}; I Sam. 16^{13}, etc.). The Spirit was thought of both impersonally, as a force or energy proceeding from God and producing the desired effects, and also, more personally, as a circumlocution for God himself, like Wisdom a personification, but not a separate being. In Jewish thought it came to be closely associated with prophecy, though not generally in the canonical prophets themselves. It was by inspiration that prophets had discerned and declared the mind and will of

v On this see C. K. Barrett, *Holy Spirit*, where it is argued that the Spirit did not belong to the thought and vocabulary of Jesus. See also for the whole subject Marie E. Isaacs, *The Concept of Spirit*, Heythrop Monographs, London 1976.

God. When the belief grew up that prophecy had ceased in Israel, inspiration was connected rather with Wisdom and the interpretation of the Law (Wisd. 9¹⁷; Ecclus 24²³). Important for the future, however, was that in some prophets the eschatological hope of Israel had been envisaged in terms of an invasion or outpouring of the Spirit, whereby Israel would be recreated and renewed, and would experience the fullness and reality of life in relation to God (Isa. 44³; 61¹; Ezek. 11¹⁹; 37¹ᶠᶠ·; Joel 2²⁸ᶠ·; cf. Ps. Sol. 17³⁷).

Some NT writers express, each in his own way, the conviction that the eschatological age has dawned, with the presence and activity of the Spirit as primary evidence of this. Thus, Paul, for whom the end of the ages has come (I Cor. 10¹¹), sees the hallmark of Christian life, and its governing principle, in the reception and operations of the Spirit (Gal. 3²ᶠᶠ·; 5¹⁶⁻²⁵). It is the present pledge of ultimate heavenly existence (Rom. 8¹⁻²⁷), and its (his) gifts are productive of holiness, and of all the virtues (I Cor. 12–13). John, for whom eternal life is already the possession of the believer, sees the Spirit as both imparting to all the words and actions of Jesus their divine quality, and also as the *alter ego* of the glorified Christ, who leads men into the fullness of truth and life (John 4²³ᶠ·; 6⁶³; 7³⁹; 14¹⁵⁻¹⁷; 16⁷⁻¹⁵). By comparison Luke's treatment of the Spirit is at once more limited and more extensive. There is little in L–A by way of the Spirit's interior working in Christian communities or individuals to reproduce there supernatural qualities of life. On the other hand, the Spirit occupies a crucial position in the structure of the two volumes. In the exordium to the second volume the dramatic story of Pentecost locates the supernatural source and origins of the Christian movement and message in an unprecedented outpouring of the eschatological Spirit in the visible symbols of wind and fire. And at the conclusion of the first volume the risen Lord interprets his resurrection as having its goal, not in itself, but in his ability thereby to clothe the disciples for the purpose of their mission with the promise of the Father, the heavenly power, for which they are to wait in Jerusalem (24⁴⁸ᶠ·). This is reiterated in A. 1⁴⁻⁸. In being called here 'the promise of the (my) Father', to which the only NT parallel is in Eph. 1¹³, the Spirit is represented as the quintessence of all the previously promised gifts of God to men. In Peter's speech (A. 2¹⁴⁻⁴⁰) the career of Jesus under God is rehearsed as having for its object that he might receive from, and at, God's right hand 'the promise of the Holy Spirit', and to be the agent of its communication to men in visible and audible form. In this respect

Luke's first volume could be said to have been written for the sake of the second.

From Pentecost onwards the story in A. is to a considerable extent the story of the operation of the Spirit. The theological concentration in L–A, already noted, whereby God himself is the principal actor in events, is often conveyed in terms of the activity of the Spirit, who is therefore sometimes spoken of more personally. The Pentecost experience is renewed in the Jerusalem church at prayer under persecution (A. 4²³⁻³¹). The supernatural illapse of the Spirit forces Peter's hand to extend the mission to the Gentiles (A. 10¹⁻⁴⁷; 11¹²⁻¹⁸), and the Spirit stands behind the church's decision on this crucial issue (A. 15²⁸). The Spirit is responsible for appointing missionaries and equipping them for their task, and can direct their strategy and movements (A. 8²⁹, ³⁹; 10¹⁹; 11¹²f.; 13²⁻⁴, ⁹; 16⁶; 19²¹; 20²²f., ²⁸; 21⁴). The christology, whereby the exalted Jesus is shown as still active, can also be expressed in terms of the (his) Spirit (A. 1²; 16⁷). All this has some counterpart in the Gospel in the initial stages of Jesus' ministry, as Luke chose to shape them in the redaction of his sources (3¹–4³⁰). There, John, called by the word of God to be a prophet in the power and spirit of Elijah, prophesies the coming one who will baptize with spirit and fire. Jesus is himself baptized by the Spirit in visible and plenary form as the Son of God. He returns from this baptism full of the Spirit, under whose control he is subjected to testing as the Son of God by engagement with the prince of evil. From this he returns to Galilee in the power of the same Spirit to teach in the synagogues with universal approbation, and in the Nazareth synagogue this teaching, as indeed his whole mission, is placed under the aegis of the Spirit by means of the words of Isa. 61¹⁻² (cf. A. 10³⁸).

The principal gift of the Spirit in A. is that of prophetic utterance; indeed, unless healing and community of goods are to be reckoned such, it is the only gift. This is established at the outset when the promised baptism with the holy Spirit is fulfilled at Pentecost in ecstatic speech. This Luke regards both as some kind of universal vernacular for the proclamation of a world-wide gospel, and also as prophecy (cf. the citation of Joel 2²⁸ff., with 'and they shall prophesy' inserted). Apparently this gift is given to all believers in connection with baptism (A. 2³⁸; 9¹⁷; 19⁵⁻⁷), despite the puzzling exception in A. 8¹⁴⁻¹⁷, and the existence in the church of particular persons known as prophets (A. 11²⁷; 21⁹⁻¹¹). This prophesying appears to cover both the initial ecstatic praise of God in response to his salvation through Jesus, and also the capacity to expound and elucidate this, to defend and apply it, and to recognize its anticipation in the OT. It is as 'filled with the Holy Spirit' that Peter addresses the Sanhedrin (A. 4^8), and this is probably to be presupposed for all the speeches in A. (cf. A. 5^{32}; $6^{3, 10}$). To this there is also some counterpart in the Gospel. The narratives in 1–2 celebrate the coming of the era of salvation in the miraculous conception of John, to be filled with the Spirit from his mother's womb, and that of Jesus by the direct agency of the Spirit. They also celebrate it as accompanied, and interpreted, by a rebirth through the Spirit of prophecy in Israel. Some of the principal figures are inspired to prophesy, i.e. to have the insight to recognize the significance of what is happening, and to place it in the context of God's ultimate purposes. This is so of Zechariah with respect to John ($1^{67ff.}$), of Elizabeth with respect to Mary and her unborn child ($1^{41-45, 46-55}$), and of Simeon with respect to the child Jesus and his mother (2^{25-35}; cf. Anna in 2^{36-38}). And, as noted above, Luke places much of Jesus' teaching in the category of prophecy.

Luke, like John, was concerned with the relation between the holy Spirit resident in, and active through, Jesus, and the holy Spirit resident in, and active through, Christians. Each deals with this in his own way, Luke largely by dramatic narrative, and John largely by theological discourse. Their answers are not altogether dissimilar. To say that Jesus possessed, or was possessed by, the Spirit fully was to say that his life and work were wholly effective, as being grounded in the will and ultimate purposes of God, and as governed by God's power throughout. This was not transmitted as an efluence or influence from him to disciples in the course of his earthly ministry, though his power to proclaim God's kingdom and to exorcise and heal was so transmitted, at least temporarily (9^{1-6}; 10^{1-20}). For disciples at this time the holy Spirit remains a supreme object of prayer to God (11^{13}; and cf. the variant reading in Luke's version of the Lord's Prayer, 'Let thy holy Spirit come upon us and cleanse us'). It was first necessary that this life and work should be brought to completion in the world by way of suffering and death ($12^{49f.}$; $13^{32f.}$), and in such a way that God would acknowledge them for his own, and give them permanence and ultimacy. In Luke this is by Jesus' assumption by God (9^{51}; 24^{26}; A. 1^{1-11}), in John by his glorification (John 17^{1-5}). It was the 'Spirit' involved in the life and work so completed and so consummated that was transmitted from God through the exalted Christ (A. 2^{33}; John 7^{37}). By it the disciples were enabled to apprehend these things for what they were, and to proclaim them as divine salvation for the world.

(vi) *The Church*

In composing two volumes, with a narrative of the activity of the God of Israel through Jesus, succeeded by a narrative of his activity through the risen Christ and the Spirit, Luke was bound to be more evidently concerned with what came to be called 'the church' than were the other evangelists; and his work has been often regarded as supplying the opening chapters of church history. The matter is, however, far from straightforward. Thus, while the parousia and consummation of all things are deferred longer than they are in some other NT writings, they are not deferred indefinitely. The return of the Lord in the same manner as he had been seen to depart (A. 1^{11}) would still be in the lifetime of those who are addressed in $21^{27ff.}$ (cf. A. $3^{19f.}$), and this hardly envisages a lengthy period of church history. Nor is there in L–A a clear doctrine of a single universal church, which is the body of Christ, as in Eph. $1^{22f.}$; Col. 1^{18}. The word *ecclēsia* = 'church' is absent from the Gospel (contrast Matt. 16^{18}), and in A., where it is introduced without explanation at 5^{11}, it is used throughout, possibly in the secular sense of 'assembly', for local or regional congregations of believers. This suggests that Luke is less a historian of the church as such, than of it as the product and accompaniment of what is his principal concern, viz. the mission of the God of Israel to his people and to the world. On the evidence of the NT quite apart from L–A, this had taken a circuitous route, and had involved a combination of continuity and discontinuity, of the old and the new, of affirmation and negation and of acceptance and rejection. It had emerged within the religious community of Israel as a (messianic?) announcement by Jesus of the imminent realization of its eschatological hopes. As such it had gained many adherents; but it had been officially repudiated, and condemned to extinction, by the religious authorities. Nevertheless, it had been miraculously revived by divine power in a fresh form, which was still the fulfilment of scriptural promises. It had again, in the face of opposition, official and otherwise, gained many adherents, including Gentiles, who participated in its salvation with some measure of detachment from the tenets and practices of Judaism.

More than once stance was possible towards such a complex and controversial phenomenon, according as different aspects of it were stressed, or passed over, by different people in different circumstances. The NT contains examples of acute theological wrestling with it – e.g. Rom. 9–11; Eph. 1–2; I Peter 1^3–2^{10}; the Gospel of John passim – where the thought, and the situation that is being addressed, can be obscure on account of the use of blanket terms such as 'Israel', '(the) people', 'the Jews', 'the Gentiles'. In L–A alone it is presented *in extenso* by means of materials put together to make up a continuous historical and theological narrative. This is, however, of such an episodic kind as to allow two divergent conclusions (with variations) to be drawn from it. [w]

(i) Luke is essentially a universalist. The mission to the Gentiles, and their acceptance of God's message of a salvation that is independent of the Mosaic law, which is the main concern from A. 9 onwards, was the goal of the divine purpose in scripture (A. $15^{14\text{ff.}}$). This message had indeed originated in Judaism as the fulfilment of its expectations, but that fulfilment belonged to the past. Its outcome had now superseded Judaism, for which, by reason of the persistent opposition of 'the Jews' to Jesus, and then to his followers, there remained in the future only divine retribution and destruction ($13^{34\text{f.}}$; 19^{41-44}; 21^{20-24}; A. 6^8–7^{53}; 18^6; 21^{27}–22^{21}; 28^{25-28}). A possible reason for Luke's writing in this way was to counter in his area Jewish or Jewish-Christian propaganda aimed at showing that Gentile Christianity was inauthentic.

(ii) Luke's intention was to depict the emergence through God's actions in Jesus of a reformed Judaism, an Israel or people of God that was no longer constituted by reference to Jerusalem and the temple, but by virtue of response to Jesus (A. 3^{22-26}). A vast number of Jews had made that response (6^{17}; 12^1; $19^{47\text{f.}}$; A. 2^{41}; 4^4; 6^7; 21^{20}); and even the rejection of Jesus and his followers was pardonable as done in ignorance ($23^{34\text{v.l.}}$; A. 3^{17}; 7^{60}; 13^{27}). And now through the Spirit and faith God had removed the impurity of Gentiles in order to add them to believing Israel as his people, with the requirement only of obedience to laws binding on sojourners in Israel (A. 10^1–11^{18}; 15^{6-21}). A possible reason for Luke's writing in this way was to counter some form of the Marcionite view that Christianity was an entirely new phenomenon, without any pedigree in Judaism.

---

w For detailed surveys and discussions of this question, which has become one of the most vexed in NT study, see J. T. Sanders, *The Jews in Luke–Acts*, esp. ch. 3, R. Maddox, *The Purpose of Luke–Acts*, esp. ch. 2, J. L. Houlden, 'The Purpose of Luke', *JSNT* 21, 1984, pp. 53ff., and J. Jervell, *Luke and the People of God*, Minneapolis 1972.

The matter mainly concerns the story in A.; but the evidence of the Gospel is not irrelevant, if also inconclusive. There the story is, to a greater extent than in the other gospels, one of Jesus' journeyings on a mission ($4^{14, 43f.}$; 8^1; $9^{51ff.}$); but the mission is to Israel, for salvation or judgment. Gentiles will participate in these only in the eschatological future with the final coming of the kingdom (10^{12-15}; 11^{29-32}; 13^{22-30}).[x] There are occasional hints of something beyond this. In 3^{4-6} the traditional citation of Isaiah is extended to include the words 'all flesh shall see the salvation of God', which do not of themselves entail a mission to the Gentiles, though the equivalent in A.28^{28} does so. In 4^{16-30} Jesus' responds to the hostility of compatriots by a reference to OT examples of non-Jews receiving assistance from a prophet. In 7^{1-10}, a particular instance of this, the picture of the pious centurion, who is vouched for by Jews and exhibits greater faith than that found in Israel, undoubtedly prepares for that of Cornelius, the first Gentile convert, in A. $10^{1ff.}$. In 14^{23-24} the third class of guests, apparently introduced by Luke into the parable, probably refers to Gentiles, but to them as invited to a (messianic?) banquet, and not necessarily as the objects of a mission. Two passages are more explicit. In the birth narratives, with their inspired interpretations of coming events, the emphasis is on the salvation of Israel ($1^{16f., 54f., 68f.}$; $2^{10, 25, 38}$). In Simeon's prophecy (2^{29-35}, for the difficulties of which, see Commentary ad loc.), there is reference, not only to a division within Israel to be brought about by Jesus, but also to a salvation prepared by God 'in the presence of' all peoples (it is not said how this is to be); which is then broken down into an illumination of Gentiles and glory for his people Israel (in that order). Finally, as the closing words of the risen Lord ($24^{45ff.}$), there is an explicit command to a universal mission as the will of God in scripture.

A number of terms are used in A. to establish the identity of the members of 'the churches'. One such is 'the believers' (A. 2^{44}; $4^{4, 32}$, etc.), 'to believe' being used absolutely for response to the Christian message of salvation. This usage Luke introduces into his revision of the Markan interpretation of the parable of the Sower (8^{12-13}), and he may have intended to present Mary proleptically as the archetypal believer (1^{45}). Otherwise it is found in the gospel tradition only in the formula in healing stories, 'Your faith has saved you' (7^{50}; 8^{48}; 17^{19};

x See S. G. Wilson, *The Gentiles and the Gentile Mission in Luke–Acts*, SNTSM 23, 1973, esp. ch. 2. He argues that these elements are reproduced by Luke from tradition, and represent Jesus' own view.

18^{42}; cf. 8^{50}). Another term is 'the brethren' (A. 1^{15}; 9^{30}, etc.), who can even be addressed in Hellenistic oratorical fashion as *andres adelphoi* = 'Men, who are brethren' (A. 1^{16}; 2^{29}, etc.). This had its origin in the Jewish use of 'brother' for a fellow Israelite, a co-religionist who is also a compatriot (so frequently in the OT, and cf. A. 7^2). It is found occasionally in the gospel tradition in the formulation of Jesus' teaching (e.g. 6$^{41ff.}$; 17^3; 22^{32}), where it seems to mean a fellow member of the religious group around Jesus. It may have been given a certain intensity by Jesus' statement that his brothers are those who hear the word of God (uttered by him) and do it (8^{21}). Another term is 'the disciples', used absolutely (in A. 9^1 'the disciples of the Lord'). This is puzzling in two respects. Firstly, in A. it is introduced abruptly, and without explanation, at 6^1, and is not found after A. 21^{16}. Haenchen (*Acts*, p. 260) judges it to have been a self-designation of Jewish Christians, which came to Luke in a particular body of tradition (but with what meaning?), and that he himself used it to include Gentile Christians. Secondly, it is absent from the LXX, where it would not have expressed the relationship between the Israelite and Yahweh, or Yahweh's prophets or teachers of wisdom. Its only background in Judaism was in the personal pupils of a rabbinic teacher. The somewhat generalized and undefined usage in A. corresponds with the frequent appearance in all the gospels of 'the (his) disciples' for an undifferentiated body, which is variously represented as the companions, or entourage, of Jesus in his ministry or travels, and sometimes as the sole, or inner, audience of his teaching. Luke is unable to be more specific about what he once calls 'the whole multitude of the disciples' (19^{37}). They can hardly have all received a personal summons to followers, like Peter and his companions (5$^{10f.}$), or Levi (5^{27}; cf. 9^{59}; 18^{22}). At one point they are a large crowd (6^{17}), at another they all get into one boat (8^{22}). Luke can introduce them as the audience for teaching which he judges to have been intended for such (e.g. 12^1; 16^1), though this is hardly as the personal pupils grouped around a teacher, as perhaps they are intended to be in 8$^{9ff.}$. He alone records a saying about them, in which they are addressed as 'little flock' (12^{32}), and are bidden not to be afraid (because they are so few and powerless?), because God has decreed that it is they who are to exercise his (eschatological) rule over the world (cf. Dan. 7$^{22, 27}$).

The only differentiation among the disciples in the Gospel is supplied by the Twelve. Here Luke is certainly more specific, and in comparison with Mark (or Matthew and John) could be said to have written up the

Twelve. In his revised version of Mark 3$^{13ff.}$, they are solemnly chosen from among 'the disciples', and the official title 'the apostles', by which they came to be known (cf. Matt. 10^2; Rev. 21^{14}), is said to have been conferred on them by Jesus himself (6$^{12ff.}$). From then on it is 'the apostles' who, from among the disciples, can ask a question about what concerns them (17^5), who are Jesus' companions at the supper, where they are instructed in detail about the future (22$^{14-38}$), and to whom, as if to a headquarters, the women report from the empty tomb (24^{10}). In A. they come to occupy a central position, being pivotal in the transition from Jesus' ministry, death and resurrection, to what follows from these. They are the sole recipients of visions of the risen Lord over a period of forty days, are commanded to await the gift of the Spirit, are commissioned as his witnesses and the sole spectators of his ascension (A. 1$^{1-11}$). For the purpose of their witness their number is solemnly made up (by God or Christ) to the required twelve (though this is not repeated with the death of James). They then constitute an authoritative core of the brethren (believers, disciples) in Jerusalem by their preaching and healing, their teaching and manner of life (A. 2$^{37, 42-43}$; 4$^{33, 35}$; 5$^{2, 12}$), and by their engagement with the religious authorities (A. 5$^{18-42}$). They make the vital decisions in matters of spiritual life and of organization (A. 6$^{1ff.}$; 8$^{14f.}$) and of mission and faith (A. 11^1–16^4; from this point they disappear from the story).

Luke may then be said to have painted, at least in outline, the later picture of a unique and golden 'apostolic age', when all had gone according to the divine plan; and of a single, organized and universal church, emerging from Judaism as the authoritative bearer of the divine truth for mankind, and guaranteed as such by its origins in the apostles, and, through the apostles, in Christ and God. This is not to be exaggerated, however. Here, as elsewhere, Luke appears to be impressionistic rather than systematic, and L–A may be searched in vain for a single, coherent doctrine of 'the church', as also of some of its major practices (e.g. baptism). Thus, while Luke goes some way towards placing the contents of the Gospel under the aegis of the appointed twelve apostles, he gives no hint of who the 'seventy (two) others' were (10^1: other apostles?), whose appointment and mission are described even more impressively than those of the Twelve; nor whether they had any permanent place in the Christian community. And while he places the contents of A. under the aegis of the risen Lord's commands to the apostles to be his witnesses to the end of the earth (A. 1^8), he makes no attempt to conceal the fact that they did nothing of the sort; so that it was left to later Christian romancers to write fictitious Acts of individual apostles, in which they are made to do what they were supposed to have done. There is no account in A. of how the multitudes of Jesus' disciples in Galilee, referred to in the Gospel, became 'the church in Galilee' (A. 9³¹), nor how there came to be believers in Damascus or Rome. Nor is there any concern with an apostolic succession of bishops in the principal churches, which was of such importance for later Christian writers, from Hegesippus onwards, as providing the title deeds of the church. Also, while Luke includes materials which could have been used to support the primacy of Peter (5¹ff.; 22³¹f.; 24³⁴; A. 1¹⁵ff.; 2¹⁴; 10¹ff.), he is quite content to remove Peter casually from the story (A. 12¹⁷, 'he went to another place'), and for him to reappear only once more at the apostolic council (A. 15); where, however, it is not he who presides, but James, no explanation being given of how this momentous change had come about. Indeed, this council is incorrectly called 'apostolic', since it is a gathering of 'the apostles and elders' (A. 15⁶), again with no explanation of who 'the elders', introduced suddenly at A. 11³⁰, might be, how they had been appointed, and why they should be conjoined with the apostles. The second half of A. concentrates almost entirely on Paul, an apostolic rogue elephant, more closely connected with the church in Antioch than with that in Jerusalem, but the one divinely directed to reach Rome. Luke may have written in this way because he was not addressing a church or churches, or the internal problems of Christians, Jewish or Gentile; but was commending to outsiders a movement, which, with a noble pedigree in Judaism, had shown its capacity to reach, and answer, the needs of the Gentile world.

(vii) *Ethics*

Here the relation between Luke's two volumes is somewhat puzzling. In the Gospel he reproduces most of Mark's account of Jesus as preacher and teacher in Galilee and Jerusalem, occasionally reinforcing it; and, like Matthew, though in a different way from him, he supplements this with a great deal of ethical instruction, sometimes of a systematic, but more often of an episodic kind. This is especially so in 9⁵¹–19²⁷, which is largely the journey of an itinerant teacher. In A., on the other hand, although Christianity is there called 'the Way', and apostles are said to teach in the name of Jesus and about the kingdom of God, there is scarcely any ethics at all. Apart from references to community of goods, what conversion entailed in terms of the moral life is not described. The reason for this may be that Luke intended it to be understood that the believers referred to in the second volume lived in accordance with the teaching already set forth in the first volume; though this is not stated, except, perhaps, in A. 3²²⁻²⁶, where listening to Jesus as the prophet like Moses is now the condition of belonging under the covenant to the people of God. Or, the reason may be that Luke, unlike Matthew, does not aim to write prescriptively, i.e. to provide a series of moral injunctions, which were to be carried over as applicable to Christians in all circumstances, but descriptively, i.e. to give an account of a particular and unique manifestation of the will of God in the teaching of Jesus, which had brought into being communities of believers, who were then to discover in the light of it, and through the Spirit, the true way of life in particular circumstances.

(a) *Repentance*. In a measure this binds the two volumes together. Repentance, whether of sinners in Israel, or of Israel as a whole, in the sense of turning, or returning, to God, to life within the covenant, and to the observance of his law and commandments, was a fundamental concept in Judaism. It is less frequent in the NT than might be supposed. Mark has the verb twice for the object of the teaching of Jesus and the Twelve (Mark 1¹⁴ᶠ·; 6¹²), and the noun once, of John's baptism for forgiveness (Mark 1⁴). The situation in Matthew is not very different; the concept has little place in the Pauline letters (Rom. 2¹¹), and it is absent from the Johannine Gospel and epistles. Luke makes it prominent. He retains it in connection with John's baptism (3³, for forgiveness; A. 13²⁴; 19⁴); but he also adds it at 5³² to define (mistakenly?) the object of Jesus' invitation to sinners and his behaviour towards them, which are then defended against attack by parables, interpreted by Luke (mistakenly?) as teaching about repentance (15¹⁻³²; cf. 18⁹⁻¹⁴; 16³⁰). To secure repentance is the object of the preaching and healing of Jesus and his apostles (10¹³⁻¹⁶; 11²⁹⁻³²); and unless repentant Israel will perish (13¹⁻⁵). In Jewish teaching repentance involved in some cases sacrifice, in others restitution, and was to be demonstrated in action by appropriate fruits. There is no instance in the gospels of the first, but Luke alone of the evangelists provides an instance of the second in the case of Zacchaeus (19⁸), and of the third in the Baptist's specification of fruits appropriate to individual groups (3¹⁰⁻¹⁴). Further, repentance with a

view to forgiveness is, for Luke, the sole content of the universal proclamation to be made in Jesus' name (24⁴⁷). This is taken up in A. in
apostolic preaching to Jews (A. 2³⁸; 3¹⁹; 5³¹), and to Gentiles (A. 11¹⁸;
17³⁰), or to both on the same level (A. 20²¹; 26²⁰). It is not clear whether
in the first the repentance demanded, implicitly of all Israel, is specifically for the act of having rejected Jesus as God's emissary, even if it
was done in ignorance (A. 3¹⁷), or also meant a return to God, his
covenant and commandments, as those were now represented by Jesus,
whom God had raised and exalted (cf. A. 20²¹, where repentance towards God and faith in Jesus Christ may be two sides of the same coin).
With reference to Gentiles, repentance meant in Judaism primarily the
renunciation of idolatry, and the worship of the one true God of the
Jews (A. 14¹⁵; 17²²⁻³¹; I Thess. 1⁹). In the test case in A. 10¹–11¹⁸, however, this is blurred, when the revolutionary conclusion that God
through the Spirit had granted 'repentance unto life' to Gentiles is
drawn from the conversion of one who was not a pagan idolater, but
was already a devout worshipper of the true God (A. 10², ³⁵; cf. 7¹⁻¹⁰).

This pregnant expression 'repentance unto life' for the saving gift of
God to Jews and Gentiles alike, raises issues of the connection of the old
and new in Christianity, of the continuity and discontinuity between
Christianity and Judaism, and specifically of the relation of the Law to
the teaching of Jesus and the apostles. From the diversity of Luke's
materials, and the largely episodic manner of their presentation, it is
difficult to derive a single, coherent and consistent view on these
matters.

(*b*) *The Law*. Here the issue is present from the outset. For in chs. 1–2
the principal figures are all Jews pious in their observance of the Law,
but also prophetically inspired to hail a coming salvation, which, while
it accorded with scriptural promises, was not the outcome of such a
piety, but was to be God's gracious gift to the poor and oppressed, and
was eventually to reach Gentiles. A dominant theme in A. is that this
salvation has become, on the basis of faith and repentance, the common
possession of Jew and Gentile. On that basis the latter are dispensed,
through an inspired judgment, from the major requirement of the
Law – circumcision, and the obligations it entailed – and are bound
only by the minimum requirements of the Law for sojourners in Israel
(A. 15¹⁻³⁵). Nevertheless, they co-exist with a large number of Jewish
Christians, for whom the Law remains binding in its entirety (A.

21[17–26]). In L–A various viewpoints on the matter are represented, and it is debated whether this was the result of Luke's incorporation of divergent traditions without any sustained attempt to harmonize them, or was conscious and deliberate on his part.[y]

In Luke's use of the expression for the OT dispensation, 'the law and the prophets', the former tends to be subsumed under the latter. The Law is given a prophetic role, and it is Moses as a prophet rather than as a lawgiver that is stressed. Together Law and prophets foresee, and proclaim in advance, the messiahship of Jesus, his suffering and resurrection (24[27, 44]; A. 3[18–26]; 26[22f.]; 28[23]). It is Jesus as the prophet like Moses who is to be listened to (9[51ff.?]; A. 3[22f.]). In 16[29–31] the opposite may be the case, the prophets being like the Law in inducing repentance. The question then is whether Law and prophets have exhausted their function in pointing to Jesus, or have a continuing status. Generally speaking, the teaching of Jesus in Luke's version of it is much less connected with the Mosaic Law than is the case in Matthew and Mark. The systematic ethical teaching in A. 6[20–49] is not set, like much of Matt. 5–7, in antithetical or dialectical relationship with the Law or Jewish religious practice. And Luke passes over some Markan passages where religious or ethical truth emerges from debate over the validity, or relative authority, of particular commandments (e.g. Mark 7[1–23]; 10[2–12]; 12[28–34]; the omission of the first is especially striking, since it bore closely on the crucial issue of social intercourse between Jew and Gentile, A. 10[1]–11[18]). The Law remained, however, as a large collection of moral injunctions to Israel, called by Stephen 'living oracles' (A. 7[38]). The question of its quintessence, and therefore for Luke of its wider

γ As in three recent studies. S. G. Wilson, *Luke and the Law*, SNTSM 50, 1983, concludes that Luke is inconsistent on the matter, and was able to be so, because, by the time he wrote, the Law had ceased to be a burning issue. He was thus free to use divergent statements to illustrate different aspects of the truth. P. F. Esler, *Community and Gospel in Luke–Acts*, SNTSM 57, 1987, pp. 110ff., concludes that Luke held consistently to a conservative view that Christianity involved no breach of the Law; that he did so in face of the facts for the sake of Jewish Christians in his community; and that he avoided technical discussions of the matter for the sake of Gentile Christians in the same community. Sanders, *The Jews in Luke–Acts*, concludes that Luke held consistently a radical view of the Law. 'Luke is at pains to show how the early church, like the early Jesus, sought a home of piety and devotion in Judaism, but it would not. And so Jesus and the church turned from Judaism and the Jews to the Gentiles, and Christianity became a Gentile religion, and all the Jewish laws in the Torah were rendered null and void, and Torah-observant Jewish Christians became hypocrites' (p. 128).

applicability, was important.[z] This quintessence is established as the double commandment to love God totally and the neighbour as the self. But in distinction from Mark/Matthew, where this emerges from technical theological discussion over greater or less commandments in the Law (Mark 12^{28-34} = Matt. 22^{34-40}), it emerges in Luke in connection with the urgent practical quest for what is to be done so as to obtain eternal life ($10^{25f.}$, 'What is written in the Law? How do you read [interpret]?'). In Luke's version of the polemic against the teaching and practice of the Pharisees, it is not the weightier matters of the law, defined in Matt. 23^{23} as 'justice, mercy and faith', that they are accused of neglecting, but 'justice and the love of God', which is possibly a Lukan rendering of the two commandments in reverse order (11^{42}; cf. A. 10^{35}, anyone who fears God and does what is right is acceptable to him). In $10^{29ff.}$ it is the second commandment that is explicated in a parable, where it is the despised Samaritan, in contrast to the Jewish priest and levite, who actually practises the love of the neighbour, and does so in relation to his traditional enemy. The love of the enemy in its extreme form has pride of place in the sermon on the plain (6^{27-36}), and then not, as in Matt. 5^{43-48}, in antithesis to the Law. In the polemic against the Pharisees it is their rules of tithing deduced from the Law that are attacked, and then only because they are accompanied by a neglect of the Law's essentials (11^{42}); and the complaint against the lawyers is that they bind on men burdens 'hard to bear' (11^{46}), which is the word used by Peter about the Law itself (A. 15^{10}). In all this Luke appears as a person of wide sympathies, and as engaged in extracting from Judaism a broad and humane ethic. Nevertheless he chose, for no evident reason, to follow an isolated statement of the cessation of the Law and prophets in face of the preaching of the kingdom, with another isolated statement, of the most emphatic kind possible, of the permanent validity of the Law to the letter (16^{16-17}).[a]

z Wilson, *Luke and the Law*, pp. 3ff., draws attention to Luke's use, unique in the NT, of *ethos*, the ordinary word for 'custom', in connection with the Law (19; $2^{27, 42}$; A. 6^{14}; 15^1; 16^{21}; 21^{21}; 26^3; 28^{17}); and he compares Josephus's frequent employment of this word with the apologetic purpose of describing the Jewish Law in cultural terms which would be recognizable by moralists in the Roman world. This might suggest that Luke was writing for the outside world rather than to, and for, Christians.

a To the despair of the commentator. Cf. Wilson, *Luke and the Law*, p. 43, 'In terms of both content and context these words must surely be as obscure as anything in the synoptic tradition.' Sanders, *The Jews in Luke–Acts*, p. 202, takes

(c) *The Kingdom of God*. Whatever Luke may have intended by the inclusion of 16¹⁷, his version of the saying in 16¹⁶ (cf. Matt. 11¹²⁻¹³) clearly demarcates the period of the ministry of Jesus onwards as that of the preaching of the good tidings of the kingdom, or sovereignty, of God. It is this which is now to determine the moral and spiritual response required of men by God. Luke reproduces the term 'the kingdom of God' from all his sources, and has it in editorial statements of his own (e.g. 8¹). Moreover, he alone of the evangelists uses it as the object of verbs of speaking – *euangelizesthai* = 'to preach the good tidings of' (4⁴³; 16¹⁶), *kērussein* = 'to proclaim' (9²), *lalein* = 'to speak (about)' (9¹¹). This is continued in A., first in connection with the risen Lord (A. 1³), and then in connection with Christian preachers (A. 19⁸; 20²⁵), whose preaching of the kingdom of God can be combined with (or be a synonym for?) speaking in the name of, or the things concerning, Jesus (A. 8¹²; 28²³, ³¹). From his sources Luke inherited a double strand of teaching about the kingdom – that it was to come in the future, and that it was already operative in the activity of Jesus. On the whole he tends to stress the latter – cf. 10²³ᶠ·; 11²⁰; 17²⁰ᶠ·, and the aorist tenses in the canticles, 1⁵¹ᶠᶠ·, ⁶⁸ᶠᶠ·; 2³⁰. Particularly significant here is the programmatic scene in 4¹⁶⁻³⁰, especially if it is intended as a substitute for Mark's terse announcement of the message of the gospel as 'The time is fulfilled, and the kingdom of God is at hand' (Mark 1¹⁵); and if there is a reference back to it in 4⁴³, 'I must preach the good news of the kingdom of God to the other cities also; for I was sent for this purpose.' For in 4¹⁶⁻³⁰ the good news (of the kingdom), which is preached through the 'gracious words' of Isa. 61¹, and which is said already to be taking effect, is of the divine gift of succour to the poor, of liberation of captives, of sight for the blind and freedom for the oppressed (cf. A. 20²⁴, the gospel of the grace of God). Luke appears to have regarded the whole healing activity of Jesus as belonging in this context (cf. his summary of it in A. 10³⁸ as *euergetein* = 'to exercise

---

them as referring to Jews. 'That the Law and the Prophets are being fulfilled, however, does not mean that the Torah has been summarily set aside, for God still expects the Jews to keep all the laws and the Gentiles some of the laws.' J. L. Houlden, *Ethics and the New Testament*, Harmondsworth 1973, p. 63, judges that they can only make sense if taken as ironical: 'though the Law, in the full sense, has now had its day, heaven and earth might disappear for all the notice the Pharisees take of the fact, so distorted is their perception of God's ways.'

beneficence', and as healing those under the oppression of the devil). In the disputes over sabbath healing, where Jesus is attacked for contravening the Law, it is this positive aspect of healing which is stressed – it gives life (6^9), it is to release from the bonds of Satan (13^{14-17}), it is to rescue from a pit (14^{1-6}).

In Luke the ethical response proper to such a message of the kingdom is primarily generosity of mind and heart and action. Thus, in the systematic instruction in 6^{20-49}, which opens with a recapitulation of this message in beatitudes upon the poor, hungry, sorrowful and persecuted, and which concludes with the affirmation of the words of Jesus as the sole foundation of the true life, the focal point is the command to imitate the beneficence of God (6^{35-36}, rather than, as in Matt. 5^{48}, his perfection). This is spelt out in the requirements of a love which goes beyond all bounds of circumspection in a love of the enemy and of the persecutor (an instance of this is given in A. 7^{60}, the behaviour of Stephen), of a giving which is without stint or expectation of return, and of a refusal to judge or condemn. These are the natural products of the heart which is good, and they will procure a heavenly reward and satisfaction (6^{27-45}). The same accent is seen in the teaching on true prayer (11^{5-13}), on true hospitality (14^{12-14}), and on readiness to forgive (17^{1-4}), and in such a formulation as that in 12^{48}. It is, perhaps, not accidental that the only saying of Jesus recorded in A. is the statement – perhaps a Christianized version of a secular maxim – that 'It is blessed to give rather than to receive' (A. 20^{35}), upon which Paul bases his conduct as a pastor, and his injunction to others to support the weak.

(*d*) *Discipleship*. The response proper to Jesus' message of the kingdom is also specified in terms of actions and attitudes required of disciples.

(*i*) *Poverty and Wealth*. That this was a special concern of Luke is suggested by the amount of teaching bearing on it that he has incorporated in the Gospel from his sources. There are different motifs in it, which, while not unrelated, are distinct. There is, firstly, the commendation of the poor and the condemnation of the rich, because of their present and future relation to God. In 6^{20} the disciples are blessed as being materially poor, and not, as in Matt. 5^3, poor in spirit, because they are open to, and will therefore be given, the satisfaction provided by possession of the kingdom of God, as also the satisfaction of their physical hunger and the solace of their human grief. The corresponding woe (6^{24}) is on the materially wealthy, who are condemned because they are not open in this way, believing themselves to be already in possession of what is needful. For such entry into the kingdom of God is as good as impossible apart from divine miracle. This contrast is reproduced in the parable of the Rich Man and Lazarus in Abraham's statement (16^{25}; cf. also 1^{52-53}). One side of it is stated in the judgment appended to the parable of the Rich Fool, that he was rich towards himself and not towards God (12^{21}), and the other side of it in the exhortation to seek first God's kingdom, since that brings with it all that is needful (12^{22-31}). Such teaching could be seen as reproducing, in concentrated form, a motif which is already present in the OT, especially in the prophets and psalms, and which is epitomized in Isa. 61. It is not continued in A., where belief and unbelief are not related to economic and social status.

There is, secondly, the commendation of almsgiving to the poor as evidence of a godly disposition, as in Zacchaeus's promise (19^8), and in the demands made of the rich ruler (18^{22}) and of disciples (12^{33-34}). It secures the possession of a treasure that is permanent and heavenly. Corresponding to this is the condemnation of wealth as prime evidence of an evil disposition. It has the character of an idol, claiming a total allegiance, and is by definition unjust (16^{9-13}, the unrighteous mammon). It breeds covetousness (12^{13-15}), self-sufficiency, arrogance and self-display, and is the source of corruption (11^{39}, which can be redeemed by almsgiving). It is one of the chief enemies of the soul (8^{14}). The strength of Luke's detestation of wealth is evident from his own comment upon (libel of?) the Pharisees, as opponents of Jesus, that they were money-lovers to a man (16^{14-15}; cf. 20^{47} of the scribes). This motif could also have a background in Judaism; clearly so in the commendation of almsgiving, which was one of the three official duties of Jewish religion, and possibly so in a sectarian Judaism of the type represented by I Enoch 92–105, with its blanket judgment on the rich as unrighteous.[b] It is continued in A., in the commendation of the first Gentile convert as one who gave alms, and on that account was approved by God (A. $10^{2, 4, 31}$; cf. A. 9^{36}), and in the curious description by Paul of what, in his letters, appears as relief from Gentile churches for the poor Christians in Jerusalem, as bringing 'to my nation alms and offerings' (A. 24^{17}). It may also lie behind the much debated practice of the first Christians in Jerusalem (Luke does not say how long it continued there, nor whether it obtained elsewhere), when possessions were regarded as

b See G. W. E. Nickelsburg, 'Riches, the Rich and God's Judgment in I Enoch 92–105 and the Gospel according to Luke', NTS 25, 1978–79, pp. 324–44.

held in common, and owners of property and goods sold them for the relief of any in need (A. 2$^{44f.}$; 4$^{32ff.}$). Luke's purpose in reproducing in this connection the macabre story of Ananias and Sapphira (A. 5$^{1-11}$), may have been to illustrate the power of wealth to corrupt even this piety.

There is, thirdly, the specific demand made by Jesus of those who would follow him, and be like him, to make a complete break with all worldly ties. This involves renunciation of family ties and those of filial piety (9$^{57-58, 59-62}$, peculiar to Luke), and even of the family itself (18^{29}; 14^{26}; Luke alone includes in this the wife). It also involves the abandonment of possessions. Luke makes this abandonment total by adding, in all three cases where he is dependent on Mark, the word *panta* = 'everything' – so in the case of Peter and his companions (5^{11}), of Levi (5$^{27f.}$) and of the rich ruler (18$^{22, 28}$). Luke alone has this demand in absolute form, 'Whoever of you does not renounce all that he has cannot be my disciple' (14^{33}). This has no continuation in A., except where Peter replies to the request for alms with 'I have no silver or gold' (A. 3^{6}). Nor does it appear to have any parallel in Judaism. If there is any parallel to the figure of Jesus in poverty, surrounded by disciples in poverty (albeit ministered to by adherents with possessions, 8$^{1-3}$), and teaching in a highly authoritative, even abrasive manner, it might be that of the Cynic philosopher in the Hellenistic world.

(ii) Lowliness and Greatness. The character of the disciple is also conveyed by the paradox of lowliness as the means to, or as itself constituting, true greatness. This could also pertain to the message of the kingdom, since 'kingdom', in the sense of sovereignty or rule, was naturally associated with ideas of greatness, power and authority as those were normally understood. The paradox is present in all the gospels; what is distinctive of Luke is the variety of ways in which it is expressed. It is voiced in hymnal form by Mary, the one whose own lowliness (*tapeinophrosunē*) is being overturned, in celebration of the power of God as exercised, both in enriching the poor and depriving the rich, and also in deposing the powerful and exalting the lowly (*tapeinoi*, 1$^{51-52}$). The corresponding verb, *tapeinoun* = 'to make lowly', appears in two general formulations of the paradox, both peculiar to Luke. The first is a piece of worldly wisdom about social behaviour, given at a meal with Pharisees and in criticism of their behaviour (14$^{7-11}$; cf. 11^{43}). The second is the conclusion drawn from the contrasted spiritual attitudes in the parable of the Pharisee and the Tax Collector (18^{14}; cf. the

comment on the loftiness of the Pharisees, which goes along with their avarice, and is an abomination with God, 16^{14-15}). The paradox was possibly already present in what may have been a designation of Jesus for his disciples, 'the little ones' (17^2), and in his choice of the child as a figure of the disciple. Thus, only by receiving it 'as a child' can the kingdom of God be entered (18^{15-17}), and this is to determine the attitude of disciples to one another; it is the little one among them who is great (9^{46-48}). The 'littlest one' in the kingdom is greater than any outside (7^{28}), and it is the body of disciples addressed as 'little flock' to whom God intends to commit his rule (12^{32}). In 22^{24-30} the question of greatness is raised as an issue in itself, in relation to the Twelve as the destined judges of Israel in the coming kingdom. In contrast to the customary manner of exercising rule, and of earning thereby the reputation of benefactor, the governing principle among them is that the senior becomes as the junior, and the leader as the one who serves. The paradox is then anchored to the person of Jesus, who exercises his lordship over them as the one who performs the menial tasks.

(*iii*) *Endurance and Achievement.* This characteristic of discipleship is also related to the message of the kingdom as Luke conceives it. For, while he lays stress on the presence of the kingdom in the activity of Jesus, he is also bound to be concerned, by virtue of the sources he incorporates, with its future consummation, and, by virtue of his own historical undertaking, with the time in between. This consummation is certain, and will take place in the lifetime of the present generation (21^{25-32}; 9^{27}; A. 1^{11}; 3^{19-21}); but speculation about it is proscribed, and attention is directed instead to the present ($17^{20f.}$), and to the immediate future tasks of a universal mission (A. 1^{4-8}; cf. the parable in 14^{15-24}, which in Luke's version commands such a mission). What is required here is faithfulness in the allotted tasks to the end – from the apostle in providing for the community, with the result that he will be set over the whole of God's estate (12^{42-48}), and from the disciple in exercising his capacities, with the result that he will be served by the Lord himself (12^{35-40}; cf. 19^{17}; 16^{10-11}). This emphasis may be seen in Luke's handling of specifically eschatological teaching. Thus, in Mark 13 the consummation is presented as a single series of critical events, and the prime requirement of the disciple is watchfulness, i.e. he is to be constantly on the alert, so as not to be overtaken unawares by what may come at any time (Mark 13^{32-37}). It is the one who continues (the verb *hupomenein*) to the end in such a state of alertness who will attain salvation

(Mark 13¹³). In Luke's revision these events become a protracted sequence; and while watchfulness is still a prime requirement, it is now a moral term for the circumspection which will preserve the disciples from being overwhelmed by worldliness and dissipation, and which, with prayer, will enable them to escape the troubles, and stand morally approved by the Son of man at the judgment (21³⁴⁻³⁶). And it is by his endurance (the noun *hupomonē*) that he will attain salvation (gain his life, 21¹⁹). In Luke's other eschatological discourse, 17²²⁻³⁷, the familiar eschatological motif of the suddenness and unexpectedness of the end, here the coming of the Son of man in his day, is crossed by the moral motif that judgment comes upon those engrossed in worldly occupations; and the eschatological warning, that there will not even be time to pick up any of one's possessions, is crossed by the moral truth that to attempt to preserve one's life is to lose it, and vice versa. It may be noted also that in the interpretation of the parable of the Sower, Luke replaces Mark's more eschatological terminology of 'tribulation' and 'persecution' as the occasion of apostasy by the more ordinary moral word 'temptations', and adds that those who produce good fruit do it through endurance (*hupomonē*; 8¹³, ¹⁵ = Mark 4¹⁷, ²⁰).

This endurance is also christologically based. It is for allegiance to Jesus as the Son of man and the Christ that disciples will encounter opposition and suffer persecution and trial, where they will also be sustained by him (12⁸⁻¹²; 21¹²⁻¹⁹); and it is as those who have participated in his own trials, arising from the opposition of Israel, that they will share in his sovereignty over Israel (22²⁸⁻³⁰). This is corroborated by Christian experience in general (A. 8¹⁻⁴), and by that of Christian leaders in particular – of the Twelve, who rejoice to be found worthy to suffer for the name of Jesus (A. 3¹–5⁴¹), of Stephen, the first martyr (A. 6⁸–7⁶⁰; 11¹⁹), and of Paul, who is warned in advance of how much he is to suffer for the name (A. 9¹⁶). This is not, however, fortuitous. For the messiahship intended by God, and exemplified in Jesus, is defined as the entry into glory (achievement) by way of suffering (24²⁶); and the Son of man, when identified with Jesus, is one who is manifested in power over this generation only after suffering and rejection at its hands (17²⁵, ³⁰). This gives rise in L–A to two formulations for the disciple. In 9²³ the taking up of the cross of rejection and suffering, which marks the disciple as a disciple of Jesus, becomes by Luke's addition of *kath' hēmeran* a daily necessity; and in A. 14²² the rule is laid down for believers that only through many tribulations can they enter the kingdom of God (for a similar christologically based ethic, cf. Heb. 5^{1-14}; 12^{1-11}).

(viii) *Destination and Purpose*

Whatever conclusions are reached about the sources used by Luke, and about the extent and character of his editing and composition, the resultant work has to be judged remarkable.[c]

This is shown, firstly, by its inclusion in the NT Canon, where it makes up rather more than a quarter of the whole, and is the largest contribution from a single author. While this may have involved the division of the work into two separate books, and their use in a manner not contemplated by the author, they proved adequate for this use. The first volume, the Gospel – for Marcion possibly the only one of its kind – was included among the four gospel accounts; and while its presentation could be said to be the least profound in comparison with the mysterious dynamic and tragic quality of Mark, with the systematic and didactic character of Matthew, or with the theological penetration of John, it has periodically come to the fore by virtue of its attractive style, its narrative power, both as a whole and in its parts, and by its emphasis on the human factors in the story of Jesus. The second volume, Acts, has from early times provided a historical matrix for the theological message of salvation for Israel and the Gentile world, the consequences of which are reflected in the NT epistles.

It is shown, secondly, in the relation of the work to emergent Christianity. In so far as that became an independent religion in the world, with divine origins in the past in the OT and Judaism, but with a divinely authoritative message for the present and future marked by a saving sequence of events in the birth, ministry, passion, resurrection and ascension of the messiah and Son of God, and by the presence of the Spirit, it corresponded more closely to Luke's picture of things than to that of any other NT writer. His version of the birth and the resurrection of Jesus was to be the most influential in the church, while he is alone in the NT in furnishing an account of the ascension and of the descent of the Spirit. And since L–A as a whole had the character of a narrative of divine triumph through suffering, both for Christ himself and for Christians, it was possible for the first church historian

---

[c] See the appreciation of Luke's work in A. by A. Harnack, *The Acts of the Apostles*, ET London and New York 1909, pp. xiiiff., and of his achievement in L–A by Cadbury, *Luke–Acts*, esp. ch. xxii.

Eusebius, writing at a time when persecution at the hands of the empire had given way to imperial patronage, to carry on where Luke had left off.

For whom, and with what purpose, did Luke write? These are questions that historical analysis has to ask of any NT book, if it is no longer regarded as conveying divine truth of a general and timeless kind, or as having immediate and ultimate authority simply as a constituent part of the Canon. In default of trustworthy contemporary information the attempt has to be made to answer such questions from the book itself. This is inevitably a hazardous undertaking. There is plenty of room for error in the critic's assessment of the shape and scope of the book as a whole; and it cannot be assumed in advance that everything the author included was written with a conscious and detectable purpose as a part of that whole. Further, our knowledge of the Christian communities in the period concerned – probably the closing decades of the first century AD and the opening decades of the second – and of their circumstances and needs, is too sparse and fragmentary for the book to be located there with confidence. Nevertheless, the aim of the most recent phase of historical criticism of the synoptic gospels, redaction criticism, has been to arrive at answers to these questions by uncovering an evangelist's theological attitudes and intentions by noting, where possible, the ways in which he has arranged and moulded the traditional materials available to him. An important work here has been Conzelmann's *Theology of St Luke*. Its central thesis, based on a detailed treatment of certain emphases in the Gospel and much of its text (with some attention to Acts), is that Luke reordered and refashioned traditional materials from Mark and elsewhere, so as to present through them a theological history of salvation in three periods or stages, the last of which was still in progress. The primary reason for this is held to be Luke's need to grapple with the acute problem for Christian faith resulting from the fact that expectation of an imminent parousia, which had previously governed those materials (e.g. in Mark), was fading, or had faded. Conzelmann does not suggest a date at which, nor a community for which, Luke felt this to be necessary; and those passages which do not fit the thesis are deemed to have been included by him simply because they were there in the tradition. While some of Conzelmann's observations have permanently influenced Lukan studies, his thesis as a whole has been challenged as being based on only a few governing texts, which are overpressed, and as misjudging Luke's eschatology. Other redactional critical assessments have been put forward.[d]

In theory such questions should be more readily answerable in Luke's case, since he has provided a preface, which concludes with a statement of his purpose in writing. In fact, however, the preface is so brief and compressed, and its wording so ambiguous, as to provide no definite contours for the work; and the statement of purpose in 1^4 is open to different translations, which can lead to directly opposite conclusions.

(i) 'that thou mightest know the certainty of those things, wherein thou hast been instructed' (AV); 'concerning those things wherein thou wast instructed' (RV); 'which thou wast taught by word of mouth' (RV margin). The almost universal interpretation of these words has been that Theophilus was a (recent? upper class?) convert, presumably of Luke's acquaintance; and that Luke writes to him (and possibly through him to other Christians in the same milieu) to supplement (reinforce? authenticate?) such instruction as he had received on becoming a Christian. A great deal can be said in favour of this. There is the ultimate reception of Luke's work into, and its tradition as part of, the churches' Canon; the nature of its contents, which stem from traditions already current among Christians for their use; the mixture of the 'biblical' and the secular in the language and style in which it is largely written; and the assumptions it makes that the readers will be familiar with certain religious terms and ideas, and particularly with the OT as an authoritative basis of belief. These all suggest powerfully that the work was an internal one, written by a Christian for Christians somewhere, and to meet specifically Christian requirements. Difficulties arise, however, with attempts to be more precise. For we know too little of the circumstances of Christian churches or groups at the time to be able to envisage clearly an individual Christian's being written to in this way. Nor do we know sufficient about the forms taken by catechetical instruction, before or after baptism (if that is what is referred to in 1^4), to be able to recognize Luke's work as closely related to it. So far no

---

[d] E.g. that of Flender, *St Luke, Theologian of Redemptive History*. For a review of some of these, see J. Rohde, *Rediscovering the Teaching of the Evangelists*, ET London and Philadelphia 1968, ch. V. The whole question, and the complexities attached to it, may be studied in *The Purpose of Luke–Acts*, by Maddox. Cf. also Houlden's article 'The Purpose of Luke' in *JSNT* 21, 1984, pp. 53ff., where he reaches different conclusions from those of Maddox on one aspect, viz. Luke's attitude to Judaism.

commentary has been written with the consistent aim of showing how Luke's Gospel is best explained, both as a whole and in its parts, as a supplementation of catechetical instruction. Ellis (p. 64) judges that 'the emphasis upon the "truth" or "certainty" of the teaching pre-supposes denials or heretical perversions of it. In some considerable measure Luke's purpose is to counter heretical misinformation as well as to verify and supplement fragmentary Christian teaching.' The only instance he quotes of this, however, is Luke's stress on the bodily nature of the risen Christ, which he interprets as countering Gnostic docetism, but which is open to other explanations. In the view of Cadbury (*Luke-Acts*, p. 302), 'No passages seem worded as though the writer were removing religious doubt with iteration of fact and presentation of new evidence, or were anxious to substitute one Christian viewpoint for another.' These difficulties are compounded if 1^{1-4} are to be taken as a preface not simply to the Gospel, but to Luke–Acts. For then it has to be asked whether it was ever thought necessary for a Christian convert, in order to have a satisfactory faith, to be acquainted with, for example, the missionary career of Paul, and the procedures and events (including a shipwreck) by which he arrived as a prisoner at Rome. It may be noted that some of the principal commentators have tended to speak somewhat hesitantly and hypothetically at this point.

Creed (p. 5): 'It is more probable ... that Theophilus was a professed Christian of good standing ... On the other hand, he may have been an interested out-sider, in which case *katēchēthēs* will refer to information received, not to instruc-tion in the faith.'

Lagrange (p. 7): '*katēchēthēs* could certainly be understood of a first and in-complete knowledge of Christianity ... or even simply of information. One cannot determine from this word whether Theophilus was completely a Christian ... whether Theophilus had been baptized.'

Marshall (pp. 43f.): 'It is possible that Theophilus had learned about Jesus from hearsay, but more probable that he received formal Christian instruction ... At the same time Luke will have included in his intended audience those who had a minimal or defective knowledge of Christianity ... There may be a polemical reference to heretics who disputed the truth of the message, as it had been told to them. If many accounts of Jesus were circulating, Luke may have wished to enable his readers to sift out what was reliable from what was doubtful.'

Fitzmyer (p. 300): 'Was Theophilus a Christian, an influential non-Christian, or a God-fearer? It is almost impossible to answer this question with certainty

... Theophilus is best regarded not as an interested non-Christian, but as a catachumen or a neophyte. Because Luke dedicates the two volumes to Theophilus, it means that his opus is not a private writing; Theophilus stands for the Christian readers of Luke's own day and thereafter.'

In a number of special studies W. C. van Unnik insisted that the concluding word of the preface, *asphaleia*, was the vital clue to Luke's purpose, and was to be given the meaning of 'exactitude'. Luke wrote for Christians, to bring to the faith already expounded by others the certainty of historical fact. He then interpreted Acts as written to supply 'confirmation of what God did in Christ as told in the first book'.[e] This would appear to make the preface apply primarily to the second volume, leaving the place and function of the first unclear.

(ii) 'And so I in my turn, your Excellency ... have decided to write a connected narrative for you, so as to give you authentic knowledge about the matters of which you have been informed' (NEB). According to this rendering (and possibly that of RSV) Luke's two-volume work was planned and executed for a non-Christian readership, and was basically an apologia for Christianity.[f] As well as being a possible, even a more likely, translation of the Greek, this has a number of advantages. It could account better for (*a*) the shape and scope of the whole work as a continuous descriptive narrative of the emergence of the Christian movement in the world; (*b*) the impression it conveys of a certain detachment of the historical observer of past events, with the consequent difficulty of detecting how Luke saw those events in relation to the Christianity of his own time; and (*c*) the element of apologia in the work, provided that the word is not given too narrow a meaning. For the apologist generally had two aims, as may be seen in the professional Christian apologists of a later time, such as Justin and Tertullian. The first aim, a negative one, was to rebut current charges against Christianity in the Greco-Roman world. The second, a positive one, was to commend Christianity to that world as answering its needs. The first aim may be seen in the Gospel in Luke's version of the crucifixion

e See 'Remarks on the Purpose of Luke's Historical Writings' and 'The "Book of Acts" – The Confirmation of the Gospel', reprinted in *Sparsa Collecta* I, *Nov Test* Suppl. 29, 1973, pp. 6–15 and 340–73; and 'Once More St Luke's Prologue', *Neotestamentica* 7, 1973, pp. 7–26. He complained that commentators generally disregarded any conclusions they had reached from the preface when it came to the writing of the commentary.

f See Manson, p. 3, Caird, p. 44, Cadbury in *Beginnings* II, pp. 489ff.

of Jesus at the hands of the Romans (always an acute embarrassment for a Christian apologist at the time), and in A. in the prominence given to charges of sedition (always the primary question about any religion in the eyes of the Roman authorities) brought against Christianity in connection with Paul, their rebuttal as due to Jewish calumny, and the declarations of Paul's innocence, even by Roman officials themselves. This aim does not have to be made more specific, as in the contention of B. S. Easton[g] and others, that L–A was an official appeal to the authorities to grant Christianity the position of a *religio licita*, or that of Harnack and others, that it was written to be used in Paul's defence.[h] The second aim could be seen in what may be judged to run through the work, viz. the claim that Christianity, with its roots in the noble religion of Judaism, of which it was the residuary legatee, and with its branches spreading over the Gentile world, was the religion for mankind. These two aims together may be said to be more at home in a work directed outwards to the Gentile world, than inwards to a Christian individual, church or churches.[i]

It is not a decisive objection to this view that L–A was not written, like later Christian apologies, as a treatise, but as a historical narrative, composed out of the traditions of the churches, sometimes in a more Grecized form. Luke may not have been incapable of writing a treatise, but his powers clearly lay in historical narrative; and he may have shared the belief of some of his contemporaries, Jewish and Gentile, that history had a didactic, moral and religious force, and was a means of establishing the identity of a group or nation, as in the vastly larger apologetic enterprises of Josephus and Dionysius of Halicarnassus, with their respective *Antiquities*. Nor is it a decisive objection that Luke assumes in his readers an acknowledgment of, and familiarity with, the

g Early Christianity, Greenwich, Conn., 1954, pp. 41ff.

h It is these which merit the dismissive judgment of C. K. Barrett quoted on p. 12 above.

i Though with respect to the first, it may be noted that Dibelius suggested Luke's purpose to have been to instruct Christians in how they should regard, and behave towards, the Roman power, a view worked out in detail by P. W. Walasky in '*And So We Came To Rome*': *the Political Perspective of St Luke*, SNTSM 49, 1983. With respect to the second, the question of how the contents of L–A were related to the (supposed) development of, and conflicts within, the early church has dominated study, since F. C. Baur put forward his hypothesis that the work was written to reconcile Jewish and Gentile Christianity; see the survey by Haenchen, *Acts*, pp. 14ff.

OT and Judaism. There is not lacking evidence that in the Greco-Roman world at the time there was, along with anti-Semitism, and contempt for, and persecution of, Jews, a marked interest in Judaism, sometimes to the point of embracing it, even in the upper classes.ʲ In such circumstances it would not have been an inconceivable undertaking to produce an account of a religious movement, which had a pedigree in Judaism, its monotheism and its ethic, but which was stripped of the racial and religious exclusivism of Judaism, and had a saviour figure to boot.

It is in order to do justice to the diverse aspects of L–A that some have postulated for it a dual readership, Christian and non-Christian. Dibelius (*Studies*, p. 147) concluded that 'Luke's Gospel had from the beginning (speaking in a modern idiom) two market outlets; it was intended as a book to be read by the Christian community ... but also, at the same time, intended for the private reading of people of literary education.' There are difficulties in the hypothesis in this, or perhaps in any form.ᵏ Was it possible for an author to address two such audiences at the same time? What would be the mechanics of his reaching both? Our knowledge of publishing at the time is too limited to be able to say with precision what would be meant by the 'book market', and how it might have operated for Christians. And it is probably illegitimate to speak of 'the Christian community' or 'the Church' in this

j See M. E. Smallwood, *The Jews under Roman Rule: from Pompey to Diocletian*, Leiden 1976, esp. pp. 205ff. Cf. Josephus, *Against Apion* II, 284, 'As God permeates the universe, so the Law found its way among all mankind. Let each man reflect for himself on his own country and his own household, and he will not disbelieve what I say.' The statement is doubtless greatly exaggerated for apologetic purposes, but can hardly have been entirely without foundation.

k E.g. in that of Easton, *Early Christianity*, p. 33, 'Luke wrote for two audiences; audiences, moreover, whose capacities were very unequal'; or of O'Neill, *The Theology of Acts*, p. 181, 'In drawing the attention of educated Romans to the magnitude of what God had done in Jesus' death and resurrection, he was at the same time reminding the Church of the power to which it owed its existence, and warning it not to betray its trust'; or of von Campenhausen, *Formation of the Christian Bible*, pp. 123f., 'Luke writes not, or at any rate not only for the Christian community but for a wider public. His work is to appear on the open market, and therefore calls for an introduction. The dedication to the "most excellent Theophilus" is to commend it to the heathen public, and to catch their interest'; or of Williams, *Acts*, p. 17, 'He addressed cultivated folk on the theme of what God had done, and he relied on Theophilus to disseminate the work even among non-Christians.'

connection, as if it were a single entity, for which an evangelist could contemplate writing, and to which he could despatch his work. The two readerships are likely to have been still too distinct, and too widely separated from each other, to have been reached at one and the same time by the same book. If Luke designed his work in the first instance with Christians in mind, and sent it to Christians, or a church, in a particular place, it is difficult to envisage that he could have secured in advance that it would also be read by non-Christians somewhere, whom he had also had in mind. Contrariwise, if he had designed the work in the first instance for a non-Christian readership, and had sent it to a group of non-Christians somewhere, he can hardly have secured in advance that it would pass into Christian hands. With so many unknown factors decision is difficult; but a more likely hypothesis could be that Luke wrote an apologia, in the fullest sense of the word, for a non-Christian readership, and that, like Justin's *Apology*, it became by some route part of Christian literature, and indeed of canonical Christian literature.

1^1-4^{13}

Birth and Preparation for the Ministry

1^{1-4} The Preface

1 *Inasmuch as many have undertaken to compile a narrative of the things which have been accomplished among us,* ²*just as they were delivered to us by those who from the beginning were eyewitnesses and ministers of the word,* ³*it seemed good to me also, having followed all things closely* for some time past, to write an orderly account for you, most excellent Theophilus,* ⁴*that you may know the truth concerning the things of which you have been informed.*

* Or *accurately*

This single sentence, preserved as such in RSV but broken up in NEB, articulated in periods and idiomatic in expression, self-conscious yet formal, is unique in the gospels, the anonymous authors of which do not refer to themselves or their works (John 20³⁰⁻³¹; 21²⁴ are partial exceptions). It is also unique in the Bible, and the LXX will not have provided Luke with any model here; the prologue to Ecclesiasticus and the 'preface' in II Macc. 1¹⁻⁹ are not real parallels. Nor is there anything like it in Jewish apocryphal, pseudepigraphical or rabbinic writings. In style and content it is in marked contrast to the gospel it introduces and to much of Acts. It is almost entirely secular and sounds oddly when read in church. In the modern search for the origins of the gospels and their contents it has naturally been the object of special scrutiny. Unfortunately, by reason of its extreme compression, its conventional character and its high-flown vocabulary it proves ambiguous at several points, and singularly uninformative as a whole.[a]

a The classic treatment remains that of H. J. Cadbury in *Beginnings* II, pp. 489ff. See also his articles 'The Knowledge claimed in Luke's Preface' in *The Expositor*, 8th series, vol. 14, Dec. 1922, pp. 410ff., and ' "We" and "I" Passages in Luke–Acts' in *NTS* 3, 1956–57, pp. 128–32. W. C. van Unnik returned more than once to the subject; see his *Sparsa Collecta* I, pp. 6ff., 92ff. and *Neotestamentica* 7, pp. 7ff. More recent is the important study by L. C. A. Alexander, 'Luke–Acts in its Contemporary Setting'.

Its uniqueness lies in its being the only instance in the Bible of what had become an established Greek literary convention (adopted also in Roman literature), and it may be taken as at least some indication that Luke, probably alone of NT writers, understood his work as literature. But of what kind, and written for what purpose? The convention by which the author of a prose work addressed his readers in a preface that was part of the text, and informed them in advance of its character and purpose, had developed from the fifth century BC onwards. This development had not been unaffected by the rhetoric which was the basis of all Greek (and Roman) education, and by the prefaces to speeches for the law court and the political assembly, rules for the composition of which were part of the school curriculum. It was felt necessary even for writers on non-literary and technical subjects, if they were to be regarded as educated, to show somewhere in their writing a knowledge of rhetoric.[b]

Such prefaces came to be made up of certain stock constituents. These were (i) the author's name, (ii) a dedication, (iii) a statement of the subject matter and of its importance and value, and (iv) a transition to the work itself; while reference might also be made to (v) the author's predecessors or sources of information, and (vi) his reliance on 'eyewitness'. Not all of these were present in any one, or in any one type of, preface, and there was variety in the form and order in which they were presented, as also in the length with which this was done. Something of this common pattern may be seen from the following examples.

A Josephus, *Against Apion*, 1.1–3 (*c.* AD 100; historical).

In my history of our *Antiquities*, most excellent Epaphroditus, I have, I think, made sufficiently clear to any who may peruse that work the extreme antiquity of our Jewish race, the purity of the original stock, and the manner in which it established itself in the country which we occupy today. That history embraces a period of five thousand years, and was written by me in Greek on

---

b See H. I. Marrou, *A History of Education in Antiquity*, London and New York 1956, pp. 194ff. It is hardly possible to reach firm conclusions from the preface concerning Luke's educational and cultural standing. Luke–Acts is not the work of one thoroughly versed in rhetoric, i.e. one educated in the strict sense of being trained in the Greek literary tradition. Such elements of rhetoric as it contains would not require more than familiarity with the oratory available in the marketplace. He is thus unlikely to have learnt about prefaces from school text books. He might, however, have come across them in his reading, not necessarily of the classics of the past, but of more contemporary works at a lower literary level.

the basis of our sacred books. Since, however, I observe that a considerable number of persons, influenced by the malicious calumnies of certain individuals, discredit the statements in my history concerning our antiquity, and adduce as proof of the comparative modernity of our race the fact that it has not been thought worthy of mention by the best known Greek historians, I consider it my duty to devote a brief treatise to all these points; in order at once to convict our detractors of malignity and deliberate falsehood, to correct the ignorance of others, and to instruct all who desire to know the truth concerning the antiquity of our race.

B Hero of Alexandria, *Pneumatica* I, lines 1–17 (1st cent. AD?; engineering).

Since the subject of air has been considered worthy of attention by ancient philosophers and engineers, the former expounding its power theoretically and the latter by reference to its observable effects, I have myself thought it necessary both to make an orderly presentation of the traditions of the ancients, and also to introduce my own discoveries; for in this way those wishing subsequently to engage in the science will be assisted. And judging it to follow on from the properties of water-clocks, which I have already treated in four books, I am writing about this also, as I have said, for it to be a continuation. For it is through the combination of air, fire, water and earth, and of the three or rather four elements, that a variety of conditions is brought about, some of which answer to the most important needs of this life, while others display marvels of a striking kind.

C Dioscorides, *De Materia Medica* I, lines 1–51 (1st cent. AD, medical).

Since there have been many not only ancient but also recent writers who have compiled works on the preparation, action and testing of medicines, most beloved Areius, I shall attempt to show you that my own preoccupation with the subject has not been vain or foolish; for of these some have not given a complete account, while others have written for the most part at secondhand . . . [Here follow twenty-six lines in criticism of named authors as to omissions and defects of method.] But I so to say from early manhood have had an incessant desire for knowledge of the subject, and after travelling widely (you know that I have led a soldier's life) have systematized the subject in five books at your instigation; to whom also I dedicate the treatise in expression of the feeling of gratitude for your disposition towards me, you who are by nature so well disposed towards the learned, and especially to those of the same profession, and more particularly to myself . . . And I beg you, and any who may read the treatise, to have regard not to any force of my language but to my attention to the empirical facts. For it is with knowledge gained for the most part from personal observation, and after a thorough investigation of accounts arising from the common tradition and examination of the inhabitants in their native lands, that I shall attempt with the greatest possible accuracy both to employ a different arrangement, and to describe the species according to the effective properties of each.

D   Vitruvius, *De Architectura* IV, preface (*c.* 10 BC).

I have observed, Emperor, that many in their treatises and volumes of commentaries on architecture have not presented the subject with well ordered completeness, but have made a beginning and left, as it were, desultory fragments. I have therefore thought that it would be a worthy and very useful thing to reduce the whole of this great art to a complete and orderly form of presentation, and then in different books to lay down and explain the required characteristics of different departments.

The earliest Greek prose writing to emerge as literature had been historiography. There Thucydides had established the convention of a preface setting out the subject matter of the work, its usefulness for the present, and the historian's need for accurate investigation and truthful presentation (I, 1–23, later discussed by Lucian, *On the Writing of History*, 42–53 and Dionysius of Halicarnassus, *On Thucydides*, 19). In this he had been followed by a succession of historians down to the first century AD, with some stressing history's educational value (e.g. Polybius, Dionysius, Diodorus Siculus) and others its value as record of the past (e.g. Dio Cassius, Tacitus; Josephus, *BJ*, 1.1–6 combines both). In view of Luke's reference to his own work, at least by implication, as *narrative* (*diēgēsis*, 1^1), of the character of Luke–Acts as a sequence of events, and of his possible use of other historiographical conventions (e.g. 'speeches' in Acts), his preface has generally been taken to belong to the historiographical genre, and to indicate that he regarded his work as primarily historical. Against this, however, may be reckoned its extreme brevity. Thucydides' twenty-three chapters of preface had been, indeed, far too long (and was criticized on this score, see Dionysius, *On Thucydides*, 20), but no Greek or Roman historian had ever produced a preface like Luke's, with the stock constituents compressed into a single sentence. The shortest historical preface consisted of seven or eight sentences (cf. A above). Further, with few exceptions, historical prefaces did not have a dedication, the personal style of which did not fit the impersonal manner of history writing (Josephus, *Life*, 430, which has his *Antiquities* belatedly dedicated to his patron Epaphroditus, hardly constitutes an exception, being an appendix to a second edition of a work that was antiquarian rather than historical). There were, however, other types of writings, not judged to be literature in the strict sense, in which prefaces had also become standard, and L. C. A. Alexander proposes as a more immediate background to Luke's those found in 'scientific' works, i.e. technical treatises on 'crafts' such as medicine, engineering, architecture, etc. (including philosophy). Generally these were briefer, occasionally of one or two sentences (as in B and D above), and with few exceptions contained a dedication. And while these again did not conform to a single pattern, they tended to include by convention a reference to the work of predecessors, to the tradition of the subject and to 'eyewitness' (cf. B and C above). Further they were generally written in structured periodic sentences, and were couched in elevated and somewhat ponderous phraseology (e.g. periphrasis and compound words) affected for the purpose by those otherwise unaccustomed to writing 'literature'. 'The content of Luke's preface is classic for the scientific tradition. A single sentence announces in its main verb the author's decision to write; this decision is related to the dedicatee by means of an address in the vocative and the insertion of *soi* (*to you*), and by the final clause 'so that you . . .', the basis of the decision is given in the opening subordinate clause, 'since many . . .'; information about the author is subjoined in a participial phrase agreeing with *emoi* (*to me*). The author does not give his name, as is normal where the address is of this kind . . . Note the oblique form of these remarks: the 'decision' itself appears in the middle of a lengthy sentence, and although it is the grammatical centre of that sentence, it is rather overshadowed by the opening clause. It is this subordinate clause which introduces the subject matter of the book (*the things which have been accomplished among us*) in a grammatically indirect fashion typical of scientific prefaces. The subject appears again, equally obliquely, in the final 'so that you . . .' clause; the author's 'decision' to write has no direct object. Neither of these phrases is very informative as to the actual contents of the book; Luke carries the normal obliquity of the scientific prefaces to extremes.'[c]

Luke could then have written in imitation of such models, with perhaps modifications due to the character of the subject matter (e.g. *narrative, ministers of the word*), albeit as something of an amateur. For in his single conventional but curiously constructed sentence, *it seemed good to me also* with difficulty escapes being a *non sequitur*, the clause

[c] Alexander, 'Luke–Acts', p. 85.

introduced by *just as* hangs in the air, and the final clause allows of more than one translation; while of the vocabulary Cadbury observes (*Luke–Acts*, p. 198) that 'in some of his language the writer has overshot the mark, and sacrificed clearness to sonorous style'. Hence, as the history of interpretation shows, the meaning is hardly anywhere clear and incontrovertible.^d

Two questions concerning the preface as a whole arise from its specifically Christian context. Firstly, to what is it a preface? As it stands it gives the impression of being a preface to the Gospel only. This, however, could be a false impression created by the exigencies of the formation of the Canon, which, since it was framed in two parts, the Gospel (or the Lord) and the Apostle, could have involved the division of a two-volume work, Luke–Acts, into two independent volumes, the one to be included in the first part as a constituent of the fourfold gospel, and the other to stand on its own in the second part. Originally I¹⁻⁴ could have been a preface to the two-volume work, to be picked up by a recapitulation or secondary preface in A. I^{1ff.}. This is the case in A above, Book II beginning with 'In the first volume of this work, my most esteemed Epaphroditus, I demonstrated the antiquity of our race, corroborating my statements by the writings of Phoenicians, Chaldaeans and Egyptians . . . I shall now proceed to refute the rest of the authors who have attacked us.' In B above, Book II begins with 'In the previous volume, beloved Areius, which is the first of those I have compiled on medicine, I have given an account of spices, oil, unguents and trees . . .; in this second one I shall continue on the subject of animals, honey, milk and so-called cereals . . .' In I¹ *the things which have been accomplished among us* could most naturally be interpreted as including a reference to events narrated in Acts, as could

---

d See the remarks of van Unnik ('Once More St Luke's Prologue', *Neotestamentica* 7, p. 9) who deems it a serious consideration whether the preface, in which Luke did his best, is to be judged a tragic failure. Also Alexander, op.cit., pp. 84f., 'It may be remarked a bad sign in itself that so much effort has been expended in trying to understand a text whose content is essentially simple. . . . The obscurity of the preface . . . may be ascribed to two factors: (i) Its allusiveness is convincingly explained if we accept that, like the prefaces of the later scientific writers it comes at the end of a long period of development, during which the expression of stock ideas has become compressed through familiarity. (ii) Like many of the scientific writers, Luke gives the impression that he is not fully in control of this formal style, particularly of the periodic method of composition.'

1^4 on one interpretation (see notes ad loc). E. Haenchen maintains[e] that the opening words of the preface make it clear that 'the prologue is intended only for the gospel; there were several gospels, in the sense in which we use the word today, but not acts of the apostles.' But this begs the question, for it is far from clear what compilations Luke was referring to here, nor what his relation to them was, nor whether he may not have used written compilations of tradition for the first part of Acts.[f]

Secondly, for whom is it a preface? It has generally been assumed (though it cannot be proved) that each of the other gospels was written to and for a Christian community (or communities) by some person who stood in an authoritative relationship to it, and to meet the spiritual needs of that community as the author envisaged them; and that this determined that gospel's contents and shape. As such it eventually became a natural candidate for inclusion in an emerging canon. Luke, however, wrote his work for a private individual, his relationship to whom is unclear, and communicated it to him by way of a preface containing a dedication. This was a secular procedure, and amounted to some form of 'publication'. And while it generally aimed beyond the addressee to gain a hearing for the work among his friends and those he might influence, it is questionable whether these would have constituted a Christian community or 'church', even if Theophilus was a Christian and Luke–Acts was designed to supplement his Christian instruction; while the language of 1^{3-4} leaves it open that he was not a Christian, and that Luke–Acts was so shaped as to supply a reliable account of the Christian movement for outsiders. In either case, and particularly in the latter, its path from this private sphere to the more

e *The Bultmann School of Interpretation*, ed. J. M. Robinson, New York 1965, p. 96.

f The matter is complicated by the poor quality of the secondary preface in A. 1^{1ff}. The first clause – literally 'The first volume on the one hand (*men*) I wrote . . .' requires a corresponding 'Now (or, in this second volume) on the other hand (*de*) I shall . . .'. In fact it proceeds with an anacolouthon in an ill-constructed sentence difficult to translate. This, and other features, have led to conjectures that originally Luke–Acts was a single book, and that when divided into two for the purposes of the Canon the first part was given an ending of its own ('he was carried up into heaven'), and the second a beginning of its own (A. 1^{1f}.). See the discussion of such hypotheses by J. Dupont (*The Sources of Acts*, p. 24, no. 22) and Kümmel (*Introduction to the NT*, pp. 109ff.), who, while admitting the awkwardness of A. 1^{1-2}, gives reasons for rejecting them.

public Christian sphere of the canon could have been less obvious and immediate – was it due in some way to Marcion's selection, on whatever grounds, of Luke's Gospel as the only gospel in his canon? It is perhaps perhaps significant that in Tatian's attempt in his Diatessaron to reduce the four gospels to a single narrative Luke 1$^{1-4}$ was omitted, presumably as being too individual and private for a gospel which was by its nature general and universal.

ҁҁ

1

The preface, as not uncommonly, begins with a subordinate clause. This serves to indicate as early as possible in the sentence the subject matter of the work, but in an oblique manner – here by implication from the subject matter of the work's predecessors. It is phrased in a rotund style, and with marked rhetorical assonance with the letter *pi* - *epeidēper* (*inasmuch as*), *polloi* (*many*), *epecheirēsan* (*undertaken*), *peri* (*of*), *peplērophorēmenōn* (*accomplished*), *pragmatōn* (*things*) – cf. Heb. 1$^{1-3}$.

Inasmuch as: This reproduces in English the tone of the opening word in the Greek, *epeidēper* + +. This was a lengthened form of *epeidē* = 'whereas', itself a strengthening of *epei* in its causal sense ('since') and especially common in introducing decrees (cf. A. 15$^{24-25}$, where it is also followed by 'it seemed good to . . .'). By classical standards *epeidēper* is incorrect here, the additional *per* being an enclitic particle which may not stand first in the sentence; the word should properly introduce a subordinate clause following the main clause. But contemporary Greek was less exact, and Luke strikes a formal note from the beginning by choosing the longest possible causal conjunction. For this causal basis of his work, see next two notes.

many: Luke begins to give the reason for his writing. It consists in the existence, at whatever date, of many predecessors in the field. Such a reference to predecessors was a not uncommon feature in all types of preface, and especially in those of a scientific type (see B and C above), and could take the place in the opening sometimes occupied by a reference to the dedicatee. There are, however, difficulties here. (i) Luke does not state his relation to the works of his predecessors, e.g. whether he did not simply know of them but relied on, or used, some of them. Hence the logic of 'Inasmuch as many . . . it seemed good to me also' is not evident; the opposite conclusion could be drawn, 'Since many . . . there was no need for me . . .' If *have undertaken* expresses criticism of all these previous attempts (see next note), then the purpose of the reference to the *many* could be to claim that his own work was to be an improvement on theirs. If it does not, then the argument would seem to be a somewhat stilted version of a feature of some prefaces, whereby the importance of a subject is indicated by noting the frequency and variety of its treatment. (ii) It is not clear what is denoted by *a narrative of the things which have been accomplished among us*, nor why Luke refers not simply to 'others' but to *many* (others). If the reference is to works in the gospel form as parallels to his first volume, then there is firm evidence only for one such, Mark's Gospel (two if the use of either Matthew's Gospel or a Proto-Luke is granted). If, as standing in a preface to the two-volume work, the reference is to works of the type of Luke–Acts, then there is no surviving evidence for any predecessors of this kind. The word *polus* = 'much', and its plural *polloi* = 'many', was an established rhetorical cliché for catching the attention at the beginning of a speech (cf. A.24^2), and had spread to other forms of expression (cf. Heb. 1^1), including prefaces. In view of Luke's fondness for the word in A. and his exaggerated use of *pās* = 'all' throughout L–A, it cannot be pressed here for exact information about the state of gospel writing in Luke's time. It may refer to no more than one (or two). The preface thus gets off to an uncertain start.

have undertaken to compile: A heavy periphrasis for 'have compiled', another example of what has been called 'office prose' used for sonorous effect. In this context it raises a question. *undertaken* renders *epicheirein* = 'to put one's hand to'. This can have the meaning 'to attempt without succeeding' (cf. A. 9^{29}, one of the two other NT instances), and commentators from Origen and Jerome have taken it in that sense here, judging that Luke is criticizing his predecessors, and is basing his work on the fact that they had failed; cf. Origen, *Homily on Luke*, 1; 'The expression "they have taken in hand" involves a covert accusation of those who precipitately and without the gift of grace have set about the writing of gospels. Matthew, to be sure, did not "take in hand" to write but wrote from the Holy Spirit; so also Mark and John, and equally Luke.' So also H. Conzelmann (*Studies in Luke–Acts*, ed. Keck and Martyn, p. 305), 'He does not merely want to complement but to replace his predecessors. He offers not a contribution to the tradition but *the* tradition.' While this could be supported by one interpretation of the concluding clause in v. 4, 'that you might have a reliable account ...', it appears to be contradicted by *it seemed good to me also*, where he seems to be aligning himself with them. The verb could have a neutral sense and be used almost as an auxiliary. It was fairly conventional with another verb for the deferential statement by an author, sometimes in a preface, of his intentions – 'I shall attempt to write' (see *Beginnings* II, p. 494 for examples). *to compile* is *anatassesthai* + +, a compound verb in the middle voice, which was a rare and late equivalent for the more normal *suntassesthai*. Alexander ('Luke–Acts', p. 93) sees it as an example of the fondness of scientific writers 'for creating endless variations by changing the compound elements in verbs of composition'. It is thus not clear whether the two parts of the compound may be pressed to indicate the method of composition (= 'to arrange existing material in an orderly sequence'), or the verb is simply a flowery way of saying 'to compose'.

a narrative: diēgēsis + +. This is important as indicating how Luke understood the works of his predecessors, and by implication his own. Compared with the corresponding verb, which was common (eight times in the NT) and had the general meaning 'to tell', 'to record', the noun was comparatively rare. In rhetoric it could have the semi-technical meaning of the statement of the case which followed the preface in a speech (Aristotle, *Rhetoric* 1416, 29), but it was also used for 'narrative'; cf. Plato, *Republic* 392d, 'All mythology and poetry is narrative of events, past present and future.' The instances in II Macc. 2^32, *Epistle of Aristeas* 8 show the one meaning passing over to the other. Historians could use the word of their work (e.g. Dionysius of Halicarnassus, 1.7.4), but so could other kinds of writers of theirs as being 'accounts' of a subject.[g]

of the things which have been accomplished among us: A well balanced clause – lit. 'of the things among us having been accomplished' – but the language florid and vague.

the things: ta pragmata = 'things (done)', i.e. events, a very common Greek word, though comparatively rare in the NT (once again in L–A at A. 5^4), is the most general word possible. It was not particularly used of 'history', though the Latin word for this was *res gestae* = 'things done'. Cf. Josephus, *Life* 40, 'undertook to write a history of these events (*pragmatōn*)'.

accomplished: Another instance in the preface of a longer and high sounding word, *plērophorein* = 'completely fill', 'fully accomplish', for the shorter and simpler *plēroun*, which is the word used in A. 19^21 for 'after these events'. It is frequent in the papyri, where M.-J. Lagrange[h] sees it as an instance of decadence in the language in the use of a lengthier word for the sake of intensity. It is not said by whom the things were accomplished (contrast A. 1^1 'all that Jesus began to do and teach' as a summary of the Gospel), and the meaning could be simply 'which have come about'. The word certainly does not here contain the Christian idea of events as the 'fulfilment' of prophecy.

among us: This shows Luke writing as a member of an identifiable group, and presumes that Theophilus and the reader will know who *us* here and in v. 2 refers to; cf. Josephus' frequent use of 'us' of the Jewish nation, of which he was a member, and which he is describing. It raises questions of when, where and how 'the believers' came to think of themselves as a single entity, and were so identified by others, perhaps as 'the Christians' (A. 11^26). It may also indicate that the preface is to L–A as a whole, as *the things which have been accomplished among us* could refer as well, perhaps even better, to the events recorded in Acts as to those recorded in the Gospel.

g See W. K. Hobart, *The Medical Language of St Luke*, Dublin 1882, p. 87.
h *Bulletin d'ancienne Litterature et Archéologie Chrétienne* 2, 1912, pp. 96ff.

I^{1–4}

2

In this verse the structure of the preface is elongated by an appended clause somewhat loosely attached to the previous statement about the predecessors, and qualifying it – see C above. It possibly contains the only religious (Christian) element in an otherwise secular preface, but is so expressed as to make precise interpretation difficult.

just as: kathōs, a more precise form of *hōs* = 'as' by the addition of *kata* = 'according (to)', common in the NT, though disapproved of by Greek stylists. Luke uses it imprecisely. For it can hardly refer to the whole of v. 1, to say that the many had compiled narratives just like (i.e. reproducing) what the eye-witnesses of the word had done, as this would deprive *compiled* of its force. Probably a loose connection is intended with *the things which have been accomplished among us,* with the sense that the many had compiled connected narratives out of reports of individual incidents, as these had been available in the tradition; in which case the precise *kathōs* was not the word to use.

were delivered: This verb, *paradidonai,* belonged to the technical vocabulary of tradition, whether written, or, more commonly in the NT, oral; cf. I Cor. 15³; 11²³, and for the corresponding noun *paradosis,* I Cor. 11²; II Thess. 2¹⁵; 3⁶. Thus the Christian writings Luke refers to rested upon oral tradition, which by its nature of separate units required compilation into a sequence. Appeal to tradition, generally to ground the writer's own authority, was a stock theme in prefaces. It is found in historians (for examples see van Unnik, *Neotestamentica* 7, p. 14), but even more in writers on a science of some kind, where knowledge was often handed down through a succession of teachers; cf. the proverb quoted by Galen (in the preface to *De compositione medicamentorum secundum locos* VI, and very similar to the remark of Papias quoted by Eus. *HE* 3.29.6) that 'to collect information from a book is not the same as, or similar to, learning from a living voice'.

to us: That is, Christians, as they came to be called by the outside world (A. 11²⁶ first at Antioch, Tacitus, *Annals* XV, 44 for Rome in the sixties), but considered as a single whole, whatever the separate areas where, and the different manners in which, the delivery of the tradition had originally taken place. As we do not know the date at which Luke is writing, nor at which the narratives of the many had been compiled, we cannot know how long he saw the process of oral tradition as continuing, nor whether he regarded himself as still, like the many, a recipient of oral tradition. His only certain source, Mark's Gospel, was already a written compilation from it. It is also not clear here, or in v. 1, whether Theophilus is addressed as belonging, or as not belonging, to *us.*

those who from the beginning were eyewitnesses and ministers of the word: In the Greek this is a single phrase. *those who were* renders the participial *hoi genomenoi*

= 'the ones having been', where a single article *hoi* stands at the beginning and governs both nouns, *eyewitnesses* and *ministers*, and *genomenoi* stands between *ministers* and *of the word*. It states the source and character of the tradition behind the written compilations. Its meaning depends not only on the interpretation of its individual constituents, but on their relation to one another.

from the beginning: When and how what was to be written about could be said to have begun was a theological question for Luke as for others (see p. 137). Here, however, the question is limited to the origin of the oral tradition. This is characterized as stretching back to, and emanating directly from (*just as*), those called *eyewitnesses* and *ministers of the word*. Claims of this kind are found in ancient writers, and in their prefaces, and had a twofold basis, (i) a general reverence for antiquity as such and as authoritative in itself (cf. Josephus, *Against Apion* 1), and (ii) a concern to validate a tradition by virtue of its origin in the past. Luke's use of the adjective *archaios* = 'ancient' could reflect (i) in 9$^{8, 19}$; A. 15^{21}, and (ii) in A. 15^7; 21^{16}. In A. 26^4 *from the beginning* refers to what Paul's life had been continuously from his youth to the time of speaking. Here it qualifies two classes of people, *eyewitnesses* and *ministers of the word*, who possibly followed one after the other, and whose beginning would have belonged to different times. Even if a single class of people is referred to, their activities of eyewitness and ministry of the word were not identical in time. The phrase may then be an emotive one, claiming the tradition as venerable rather than furnishing precise information about it.

eyewitnesses and ministers of the word: There are two initial difficulties about this compressed combination. (i) Does it refer to two distinct classes of persons or to a single class acting in dual if related capacities? The parallel pair of nouns in A. 26^{16}, 'minister and witness (*martus*)', both applied to Paul, suggest the latter as more probable. (ii) The combination is strange. If the emphasis is on eyewitness, then a more natural duplication would be with some such word as *martus* = 'witness' (cf. Jos. *BJ* 6. 134, 'spectator and witness'), since *ministers* (*of the word*) does not carry on the thought. If the emphasis is on *ministers* as belonging naturally with *of the word*, then *eyewitnesses* does not prepare for this, and 'eyewitnesses of the word' hardly makes sense. In view of A. 26^{16} 'witnesses (*martures*) and ministers of the word' could have been more natural, since *martus* can mean not only one who was an eyewitness of an event, but one who bore witness to its truth.

eyewitnesses: autoptēs + +. The word, which is absent from the LXX, is comparatively rare in Greek writers, and tends to occur in a limited number of specialist contexts. The principal meaning of *autopsia* is not that generally conveyed by the word in English, i.e. happening to be present so as to see an event when it takes place (the word hardly occurs at all in legal writers with respect to evidence), but is 'seeing something for oneself'. It was thus used by geographers of the knowledge of foreign lands acquired by personally visiting them, or from those who had done so (e.g. Pausanias, *Description of Greece* IV, 'Messenia', 31.5); as also by historians in the not infrequent geographical contexts in their narratives (e.g. Herodotus, *History* II, 29. 1; Diodorus Siculus, *Library of History* I, 4. 1; so in the greater number of the cases in Polybius, who uses it more often than others). In its rare occurrence in the papyri an *autoptēs* is someone commissioned to investigate or inspect – an observer or overseer. In scientific, esp. medical works it belongs closely with the author's claim to experience, and with the necessity of basing the science on the observation of empirical data rather than on dogma, and hence of adhering to a living tradition of empirical teaching (so Galen). The idea was given a special slant by Thucydides (though not the word, which he never uses), when in his account of his sources and method in his preface (I, 22) he refers to his presence at some of the events he records, and to his ability to examine witnesses, which meant that his history had to be for the most part of contemporary events. This established a convention, and is repeated with or without the word *autoptēs*, sometimes in prefaces and sometimes in the narrative itself, in a succession of historians; cf. Polybius, *Histories* III, 4.13 (preface), 'not only an *autoptēs* of most of the events, but a participator in some and an actor in others', and Josephus, *Against Apion* 1. 55, 'My qualification as a historian of the war was that I had been an actor in many, and an eyewitness of most, of the events.' In which tradition Luke stands here is difficult to say, since *autoptai* has no object. If this is to be supplied from *the things which have been accomplished among us* from the previous verse, then the claim could be for eyewitnesses as the basis of the accounts both of the Gospel and of Acts. Or were the eyewitnesses responsible for the events recorded in gospels and the ministers of the word for those recorded in A.? Possibly Luke uses the word conventionally for its prestige value in such contexts, and to assert the general reliability of the living tradition, rather than to establish a precise basis of eyewitness for each and every event in it. Hence perhaps the strange combination of eyewitness and minister.

ministers of the word: A unique expression, of Christian, possibly Lukan, creation. It is not easily intelligible. *minister, hupēretēs,* a common word (though very rare in the LXX) is from one of the classical and Hellenistic Greek verbs for 'to serve', having as its particular nuance the service rendered not by a slave but by a competent subordinate voluntarily executing the will of a superior. Thus Hermes was the minister of the gods as their messenger. Those in authority such as generals, judges, doctors, etc., had their ministers, i.e. executive assistants, and the word was used of government officials in this sense. So in the other NT instances: in 4²⁰ of a subordinate synagogue official, A. 5²⁶ of the Sanhedrin's assistants. In A. 13⁵ John Mark is taken as minister (assistant) by Paul and Barnabas, though the duties involved in this are not specified. What is peculiar here is that the persons referred to are ministers or assistants not of a person or persons but of the impersonal word. The ministry of the word in A. 6⁴ is not a complete parallel, as there the different word for service, *diakonia*, means the serving office, which consists in word or teaching (or, in the context, the dispensation or distribution of the word in preaching).

the word: *ho logos* is used in A. absolutely in a pregnant sense for the Christian message about Jesus; cf. A. 8⁴ (with 'gospelling'), 11¹⁹; 14²⁵; 16⁶ (with 'speaking'); 17¹¹. More often it is used with a genitive – of God (A. 4³¹; 8¹⁴; 11¹ etc.), of the Lord (A. 8²⁵; 19¹⁰, etc.). In 5¹; 8¹¹; 11²⁸ 'the word of God' is used of Jesus' own preaching or its contents. In A. 19²⁰ 'the word' is semi-personified, as it increases and grows strong; it means essentially Christianity, a word which did not yet exist (see Haenchen, *Acts*, p. 567, n. 4). As such it might be said to have attendants or assistants. If that is its meaning here the ministers of the word are those who have participated in the Christian mission. In this context, however, it should not be ignored that Luke can use *ho logos* in a more general sense of the report or account of a matter (5¹⁵; 7¹⁷; cf. A. 1¹), and even of the matter itself (A. 15⁶; cf. its use in the plural in 1⁴ for 'the things'). One may compare also the double use of *rhēma* = 'word' or 'event' in 2¹⁵, ¹⁷. In A. 10³⁷ *to genomenon rhēma* = 'what has happened' is applied to the whole ministry of Jesus and its consequences. It cannot be ruled out that by *ho logos* here Luke means the Christian movement, 'the matter', an equivalent to *the things which have been accomplished among us* (v. 1). If so, *eyewitnesses* could go with it, and the whole phrase denote not eyewitnesses of the gospel events and ministers of Christian preaching, but eyewitnesses and assistants of the Christian movement.

it seemed good to me also: This is the past tense of *dokei moi* = 'it seems to me' ('I think'), or, more explicitly, 'it seems good to me' ('I decide'). This is one of the most familiar idioms in the Greek language, and is found in other prefaces of the author's decision to write. It is very rare in the NT, doubtless because it voiced the Greek humanist confidence in human reason and judgment. While it is (apparently) reproduced in the Muratorian Canon's statement that Luke 'wrote in his own name and from his own thinking (*ex opinione*)', it plainly shocked others, and led to the addition in some Old Latin mss of 'and to the Holy Spirit'. In the only other instance of this formal use, which tended to be that in official decrees and inscriptions, human decision and that of the Holy Spirit are conjoined (A. 15²²⁻²⁸). Cf. also Origen, *Homily on Luke* 1, 'As the attempt on the part of a man to record the teaching and discourse of God may be presumptuous, he (Luke) with good reason justifies himself in the preface.' As the main verb in the sentence it ought to carry weight, but, as it follows after the introductory clause, its force, and that of *also*, is curiously weak. For the natural consequence of many predecessors in the field, unless *undertaken* implies criticism of their inadequacy, would be to make Luke's endeavours unnecessary.

having followed: The perfect participle of the verb *parakolouthein* = 'to follow alongside with' + I Tim. 4⁶; II Tim. 3¹⁰. The meaning of this compound verb, by which Luke states the basis of his own writing, is uncertain. (i) Some of the Fathers took *pāsin* = 'all things' as personal ('all of them'), and Luke as claiming to have been a follower or disciple of all the previously mentioned eye-witnesses and ministers of the word. Though the verb can have this sense – Papias (in Eus. *HE* 3.39.4) has it of disciples of the presbyters and of the Lord – it does so rarely. When used with a personal object it generally refers to things as accompanying them (Mark 16¹⁷) or overtaking them (II Macc. 8¹¹); and the adverb *akribōs* = 'accurately' hardly fits this sense. (ii) With *pāsin* as either personal or impersonal a possible meaning is 'to follow' in the sense of 'to rely on' as authorities or models, as in the other NT instances; and cf. Josephus, *Against Apion* 1.130, 'Berosus . . . following most ancient records has, like Moses, described the flood.' Generally, however, some other compound of *akolouthein* is used for this, and the participle is in the present ('relying on') rather than, as here, in the perfect. The following adverb *anōthen* hardly fits this sense. (iii) 'To follow' in the sense of 'to investigate'. Luke will then be indicating the length and accuracy of the personal research he had undertaken for his writing. This is apparently presupposed by the rendering of NEB 'as one who has gone over the whole course of events' and of the Jerusalem Bible, 'after having informed myself of all things . . .' It is supported by Kümmel (*Introduction*, p. 127) and by Bauer (s.v. *parakolouthein*), who quotes two passages from Demosthenes and Josephus (*Against Apion* 2.18), which may not, however, bear it out. Cadbury (*Beginnings* II, p. 502) dismisses this as a typically modern interpretation, noting that the force of the perfect participle is that Luke's information came to him as the events took place and not as the result of subsequent reading and study. (iv) 'To follow' in one or other of a range of figurative meanings – more precisely, 'to understand' what is heard or read (but Luke hardly means that he has understood the narratives he had read or the traditions he had heard); 'to keep up with' an argument; 'to follow' a course of events; or, more generally, 'to be in touch with', 'conversant with'. This last was originally espoused by Cadbury (op. cit. p. 501), who quotes Demosthenes, *On the Crown* 53, 'having followed the matters from the beginning'. It is found with this meaning in Greek authors, including their prefaces, sometimes in conjunction with *pragmata* = 'affairs' and *akribōs* = 'accurately' or its cognates, though this is generally with reference to the activity of the books' readers rather than their authors. So Artemidorus, *On the Interpretation of Dreams*, preface, 'In this book I shall give the necessary division of the subject; I ask from you that you follow the sequence of events (*pragmatōn*) and the accuracy of the judgments', and Archimedes, *Arenarius*, preface, 'I shall attempt to demonstrate by geometrical proofs, so that you may be able to follow . . .' L. C. A. Alexander ('Luke–Acts', p. 110) also adopts this interpretation, suggesting 'being thoroughly familiar with the whole affair', and quotes as a close parallel (though lacking this verb) Galen's preface to his *De Theriaca ad Pisonem*, 'I have written this book on antidotes for you, most excellent Piso, after examining all things accurately', where a participial clause refers to the activity of the author in general terms. She concludes 'Luke leaves us completely in the dark as to the manner and scope of his knowledge: whether he knew the same tradition as that on which the accounts of his predecessors were based, or whether he was already familiar with the story on his own account, he does not say. Possibly he would not have distinguished clearly between the two possibilities (as the use of *us* in verses 1 and 2 suggests), but certainly his *having followed* conveys no additional information on this point.' (v) Cadbury also argued[i] for a more precise meaning of presence at, or participation in, the events referred to, with the corollary that *anōthen* was not a synonym for 'from the beginning', but must mean 'from some time back'. On this view the emphasis of the preface would be tilted, and, at least at this point, would be directed primarily to the contents of Acts, and especially towards the 'we' passages. This interpretation, though supported by J. H. Ropes,[j] has not been generally accepted. Its weakness is that the passages adduced in support fall short of demonstrating this meaning for the verb; the Loeb translator of Josephus, *Life* 357, renders it by 'acquainted yourself with', of *Against Apion* 1.53, by 'have been in close touch with the events (rather than 'present at'), and of Philo, *On the Decalogue* 88, by 'all you have seen and heard and been in touch with'. The adverb *akribōs* = 'accurately' does not support this sense, so that Cadbury was forced to suggest that it was to be taken with the following adverb – 'accurately in an orderly way' – which is very harsh.

all things: Such a general and all-embracing claim was conventional in passages dealing with an author's subject matter and his information. Luke is in any case particularly fond of an exaggerated use of 'all'; cf. in this respect A. 1^1, 'all that Jesus did and taught'. It cannot be taken literally, whatever meaning is given to *followed*.

closely: akribōs. In the Greek this follows *all things*, but it is certainly to be taken with *followed* and not with *to write*. The root meaning of the word is 'exact', 'accurate' or 'strict'; cf. A. 22^3 for the cognate noun *akribeia* + + of Paul's education in the strict observance of the law, and the adjective *akribēs* + + in A. 26^5 of the Pharisees as the strictest party in Judaism, A. 18$^{25f.}$ of Apollos being instructed more accurately, and A. 23$^{15, 20}$ of knowing something more exactly. Thus *accurately* (RSV margin) is preferable to *closely* (RSV text), which is

i Briefly in *Beginnings* II, p. 502, at greater length in *The Expositor* 8, 1922, pp. 401ff.

j 'St Luke's Preface', *JTS* 25, 1924, pp. 67–71; see also the sympathetic discussion by Dupont, *The Sources of Acts*, pp. 104ff.

otiose, since this is already conveyed by the preposition *para* in *parakolouthein*, or to 'carefully', the meaning in Eph. 5^{15}. The claim to accuracy was almost a cliché in prefaces and passages where an author is referring to his sources or methods of presentation, and not only in historians (Thucydides I, 22.2), but also, as was to be expected, in scientific works. It is found with 'to follow' in Josephus (*Against Apion* 1.53), Demosthenes and other writers. It would fit best with the sense 'investigate' for *parakolouthein*, if that were allowed, but would also fit with 'being familiar, conversant with'.

for some time past: anōthen, characterizing Luke's activity of following, not that which he had followed. The word occurs again in L–A only at A. 26^5, also in proximity to *ap'archēs* = 'from the beginning'. The two could be synonyms (see Cadbury, *Beginnings* II, pp. 502f.), and both could be used effusively and without precise reference to express completeness or thoroughness. In that case Luke would be stressing that his personal activity and familiarity with the events went as far back, and was as original, as that of the eyewitnesses and ministers of the word. But they could be distinguished, as, in the view of some, in A. 26$^{4f.}$; cf. Josephus, *Ant.* 15.250, 'friends of Herod from of old'. Luke's claim would then be to accurate personal knowledge of the Christian movement from a long time back. This was Cadbury's later view – '*anōthen* carries back not from the ministry of John to Luke's birth stories, but from the time of writing back over a considerable period of the author's own association with the movement he is describing' (*Luke–Acts*, p. 347), and 'Luke does not claim knowledge of this kind (sc. first hand) for all of his two books, but only for a late though substantial period. *anōthen*, "from a good while back", is quite different from *ap'archēs* in the preceding clause about the informants on whom gospel writers including Luke rely.'^{k}

to write an orderly account for you: This renders *kathexēs soi grapsai* = lit. 'in an orderly fashion to you to write', and may be an over-translation. The main verb *to write* is the simplest word possible. It has no direct object describing what Luke has written – contrast A. 1^1, 'The first volume (*logos* = 'account') I wrote concerning all that . . .' It is followed by the intention of writing in the purpose clause in v. 4, as often in letters and prefaces of a letter type. The manner of writing is expressed by the adverb *kathexēs*. This word appears to have achieved literary status; no instance has so far turned up in the more ordinary Greek of the papyri. In the NT it is confined to L–A (five times), as is also *hexēs* (five times), of which it is an intensification by the addition of the preposition *kata*. It is not clear what kind of order is denoted. It is unlikely to be chronological order. Apart from spasmodic attempts at dating (2$^{1ff.}$, 3$^{1f.}$) L–A is notably lacking in chronology, especially for a historical work, and to judge from his redaction of Mark he was not inclined, or more probably was not in

---

k ' "We" and "I" Passages in Luke-Acts', *NTS* 3, 1956–57, p. 130.

a position, to supply it for the originally undated materials of his sources. Nor is Luke's use of the adverb, or of *hexēs*, much guide. In 8^1 he uses it temporally – *en tō kathexēs* = 'in the next (time)', i.e. 'soon after', as *hexēs* in 7^{11}. In 9^{37} *tē hexēs* (*hēmerā*) = 'the following day' is more precise, as in A. 21^1; 25^{17}; 27^{18}. In A. 18^{23} it is used spatially, in A. 3^{24} apparently of the succession of prophets one after another, and in A. 11^4 of Peter's speech (as consisting of the narration of a sequence of events?). What may be meant here is the treatment of one thing at a time and in a smooth sequence, as this could be said to be a feature of his redaction of the material (cf. his organization of the traditions about the Baptist in 3$^{1-20}$); but it is unlikely that he is consciously criticizing a lack of order in previous attempts (e.g. Mark's), of which Theophilus would probably be ignorant. The word is possibly unemphatic and a somewhat conventional addition to the simple verb *to write* so as to give it the force of a compound verb such as *compile* (i.e. order) *a narrative* in v. 1. He will write in a manner to be expected of any decent author, i.e. in an organized fashion.

for you: This rendering of the dative *soi* would be more natural if the verb *to write* had a direct object; without such *to you* is better, as frequently in letters. It is not clear whether *you* distinguishes Theophilus from, or includes him in, the previously mentioned *us*.

most excellent Theophilus: Nowhere more than here does the preface make Luke's Gospel stand in contrast to the others, or indeed to all other NT writings. The convention of dedication was familiar in the Greco-Roman world. It was rare in historians, that in A above (pp. 116f.) being something of an exception, but was standard in prose works of a non-literary and technical kind. It could take two forms, either that of a separate letter complete in itself and attached to the work, or that of a rhetorical address constituting the first paragraph(s) of the work itself, generally in an opening subordinate clause (Luke delays it, cf. A. 24^3). These two forms to some extent corresponded to the two different motives for dedications, the need of scholars who were separated by distance to communicate their work to others in the same tradition, and the need to secure for the work the patronage of a person of rank, royal or otherwise. 'To write a letter authorizing the recipient to communicate it and addressing a work to a dedicatee, were in antiquity two actions barely separable.'[1] Both could be related to what was meant at the time by 'publication'. Dibelius held that L–A was 'published' through the book trade, though with the modification that the Gospel, but not Acts, had from the first a dual existence, in the world and in the church (*Studies in Acts*, pp. 88ff.). For Luke to have done this himself would have meant that he was able to finance the making of copies of his work, and the dedication would have been more formal. In criticizing Dibelius' sug-

---

l H. I. Marrou, *A Diognète*, Sources Chrétiennes 33, Paris 1951, p. 92 n. 4.

gestion A. D. Nock[m] describes the process of publication as follows: 'An author wrote or dictated his ms. and, when it had reached a finished state, he had a fair copy or copies made . . . like what in journalism was called a "release". He often dedicated it to some person, out of friendship, or compliment, or a desire to lend dignity to his work . . . He might ask the friend, if so disposed, to make the book available to kindred spirits . . . We cannot suppose royal or imperial persons being under any supposed obligation to distribute copies of the numerous works dedicated to them. At the most, if it found favour, he might cause copies to be made and put in public libraries . . . What dedication did mean was that the author had put his work in final shape, and was addressing it to a wider circle.' Thus dedication was not a private affair but intended public consumption.[n] It differentiates L–A from all other NT writings both as to its conception and its dissemination. Its particular purpose here would depend on who Theophilus was, and what Luke's relation to him was or had been.

most excellent: kratistos + A. 23^{26}; 24^3; 26^{25} in addressing the prefects Felix and Festus. Strangely it is not repeated in A. 1^1. The particular nuance of the word here, and its possible implications, continue to be debated. On the one hand, as a Greek rendering of the Latin *vir egregius* it is regularly found in documents and inscriptions of the empire of officials of various kinds, generally of those holding a higher rank than the speaker (cf. Jos. *Ant.* 20.12 of the emperor in a letter). In the papyri, which supply evidence for practice in Egypt up to the second century AD, it is used earlier only of the prefect, but later of certain other officials also. The three instances in A. are of this kind, and could suggest that Theophilus is addressed in his capacity as a (Roman?) official of some kind; so NEB 'Your Excellency'. On the other hand, it was widely used in a non-official sense as a term of esteem, affection (cf. 'my dear . . .'), or flattery, and could be a variant

---

m In a review of Dibelius, *Aufsätse zur Apostelgeschichte*, in *Gnomon* 25, 1953, pp. 497–506.

n On this surprisingly obscure subject see *The Cambridge History of Classical Literature, I Greek Literature*, Cambridge 1985, pp. 16ff., and esp. p. 20: the terms used for publication 'imply the activity not of a publisher or a bookseller, but of the author himself, who "abandons" his work to the public; he gives them the opportunity to read it, to recopy it, to pass it on to others. From that moment the text goes off at random'; and *II Latin Literature*, 1982, pp. 15ff., esp. p. 19, 'It was often possible for an author to confine the circulation of his work in the first instance to a limited number of friends; but sooner or later the decision would have to be taken . . . to authorize or at least acquiesce in general circulation. Publication in this sense was less a matter of formal release than a recognition by the author that his work was now, so to speak, on its own in the world . . . A work once relinquished by its author was public property, and in that sense published, whether or not a bookseller was employed to copy and put it into circulation. What mattered was the author's intention.'

for such standing epithets in prefaces as *philtatos* = 'most beloved' or *beltistos* = 'best', 'most worthy'. Thus Galen in his *Method of Physic* addresses Hiero as *philtatos* in Book I and as *kratistos* in Book II. In A above the Epaphroditus who is addressed as *kratiste andrōn* = 'most excellent of men' was both a man of affairs and a scholar, and was Josephus' literary patron (*Ant.* 1.8–9). Luke could then be addressing Theophilus as a friend of some kind, or at least an acquaintance, whose attention he wishes to attract – for whatever reasons (see notes on v. 4). There is no known instance of its use by a Christian of a fellow Christian. Its next appearance in Christian literature is in the *Epistle to Diognetus* 1¹, where it is applied to an official, possibly the emperor.

Theophilus: This Greek name is attested from the third century BC onwards, particularly for Jews in the diaspora (see MM, p. 288). The suggestion that it does not refer to a specific individual, but addresses the reader as 'lover of God' (*theou philos*) is to be rejected as being both unique in, and contrary to the ethos of, prefaces.

4

In accordance with a general pattern the preface reaches its conclusion and climax in a clause that states the purpose of writing, though with a brevity resembling a common formula in letters – 'I have written to you so that you may know ...' It has a certain flourish, with a renewed assonance with the letter *pi* in *epignōs peri* = *you may know concerning*, an attraction of the relative in *hōn logōn* = 'which things', and the sonorous *tēn asphaleian* = 'the certainty' as the concluding words. Unfortunately its precise force remains uncertain because its principal words permit of more than one translation.

you may know: The compound verb here, *epiginōskein*, can have several nuances, as in the other instances in L–A. With the preposition retaining its force it could mean, generally with a personal object, 'to recognize' (24^{16, 31}; A. 3¹⁰; 4¹³; 12¹⁴ Peter's voice; 27³⁹ a land); and with an impersonal object could indicate a process of attaining knowledge, 'to get to know', 'to learn', 'to ascertain', 'to realize' (1²²; 23⁷; A. 9³⁰; 22²⁴; 23²⁸; 24⁸). With the preposition losing its force it could be simply a lengthened form and synonym of *ginōskein* = 'to know' (5²²; 7³⁷; A. 24¹¹; 25¹⁰; in 8⁴⁶ = Mark 5³⁰ Luke substitutes the simple verb for the compound). Its sense here could be determined by that of its object, *tēn asphaleian* = 'the certainty' (?), see next note. Hence 'to recognize (learn/ realize) the certainty of the things ...' This is urged by van Unnik (*Sparsa Collecta*, pp. 13f.). The 'truth' had already been expounded by his predecessors (vv. 1–2), but Luke was concerned with 'the infallibility of the facts ... he wants to remove doubt about the exactitude of Christ's work of salvation, and bring to Theophilus and his other readers the *complete certainty*'. But such a distinction between truth and certainty, and the circumstances in which it needed to be made, are not easy to envisage. Moreover, in papyrus letters (quoted by Cadbury, *Beginnings* II, p. 509) the verb is found closely connected with *to asphales*, the neuter of the adjective with an article used adverbially as an equivalent for the noun *hē asphaleia*, as in A. 22³⁰ (and cf. A. 2³⁶ with the adverb *asphalōs*, and A. 25²⁶ 'nothing definite to write'). In such cases the meaning is not to know that something is certain, but to know for certain about something, as probably here.

the truth: This renders *tēn asphaleian* + A. 5²³; I Thess. 5³, which stands last in the sentence for rhythmical effect and emphasis. The rendering is correct only if by *the truth* is not meant 'the true meaning' or 'the inner (full) significance', for which the proper word would be *alētheia*, but the true as opposed to a false or inadequate account. The original meaning of the word was 'safety', 'security', as in A. 5²³ (securely locked up; it could be used technically for a security in law). For the cognate adjective in this sense, see Phil. 3¹; Heb. 6¹⁹, and for the adverb Mark 14⁴⁴; A. 16²³. But there had been a shift of meaning to 'certainty', as in the adjectival noun *to asphales* in A. 22³⁰. So possibly here 'to have a reliable account'.

concerning the things: *peri hōn ... logōn* = lit. 'concerning which words'. This has been taken of the Christian instruction Theophilus had received, with the accompanying verb *katēcheisthai* given the meaning 'to be instructed' (see next note). But in L–A it is the singular *ho logos* which is used, frequently, for Christian preaching or teaching, sometimes with a genitive 'of God' or 'of the Lord' (A. 6², ⁴; 8⁴, ¹⁴). The plural always refers to specific words spoken, as in 4²²; A. 2²²; in 6⁴⁷; 9²⁶ it refers to Jesus' speech as a whole; in I Tim. 4⁶ it occurs with a genitive 'of the faith', and in II Tim. 1¹³ of 'sound words you have heard from me'. A possible meaning of the singular *ho logos* for Luke is 'report' or 'account', as in 5¹⁵; 7¹⁷ (cf. A. 1¹, though there it is a written account, and hence 'volume'). This can pass over into the contents of the report or account and denote events or matters, as in A. 15⁶, 'about this matter' (cf. the similar ambivalence of *rhēma* = 'word' or 'thing' in 1³⁷ᶠ·; 2¹⁵). So here the plural could be a synonym for *the things which have been accomplished among us* of v. 1, and refer, not to the words of Christian instruction, but to the Christian events.

you have been informed: The verb here *katēchein* (not LXX), is not attested in Greek literature until late in the second century AD, though this may be chance, as it is found once each in Josephus, Philo and the papyri, and the corresponding noun *katēchēsis* is found from the second century BC onwards. Elsewhere in the NT it occurs three times each in Acts and Paul, in the latter always of religious instruction (Rom. 2¹⁸; I Cor. 14¹⁹; Gal. 6⁶, as probably A. 18²⁵). From this the later semi-technical uses for catechetical instruction, catechism, and cate-chumenate were derived. With that sense here Theophilus' instruction before or after becoming a Christian will be meant. But the word could also mean 'to inform' – so in Josephus, *Life*, 336, 'I myself will give you much information', and Philo, *Embassy to Gaius*, 295-7, Gaius was informed of the beauty of the temple. This is the sense in A. 21$^{21, 24}$, where the information about Paul is in fact false report. With that sense here it could refer to what Theophilus had heard tell (falsely?) about the Christian movement.

Thus, according to the alternatives available, two quite different renderings of the clause are possible. (i) 'that thou mightest know the certainty of those things wherein thou hast been instructed' (AV); 'concerning those things (marg. 'words') wherein thou hast been instructed' (marg. 'which thou wast taught by word of mouth') (RV); 'so that your excellency may learn how well founded the teaching is that you have received' (JB); 'that thou mayest understand the instruction that thou hast already received, in all its certainty' (Knox). The picture drawn from this is of Theophilus as a Christian convert (neophyte?), and of the Gospel, or Luke–Acts, as conceived and written to further (establish?, deepen?, expand?) his knowledge of the Christian faith (and that of others like him?). This interpretation is strained in more than one respect. Firstly, it would seem to imply that Theophilus (and others like him?) had become a Christian on the basis of an instruction which Luke regarded as in some way defective, the defect being in 'certainty', whatever that is to be taken to mean. If this defect attached to the predecessors referred to in v. 1, then he is indeed criticizing them and intended to replace them; but is it to be presumed that Theophilus had read them, or that his instruction had been based on them? Secondly – and here the question whether the preface is to the Gospel only or to both volumes is once again important – Luke–Acts would seem a strange work to conceive for the purpose of correcting or supplementing, and that in the case of a single individual, instruction in the Christian faith, at least as that came to be given catechetical form later. Was the Christian convert expected to be conversant with, for example, the missionary career of Paul?

(ii) 'your Excellency . . . so as to give you authentic knowledge about the matters of which you have been informed' (NEB). Similar, though less explicit, is RSV in its rendering of *tēn asphaleian* by *the truth* and of the verb by *have been informed*. Here Theophilus might be a Christian, but is more likely a (sympathetic and influential?) outsider; and Luke–Acts is conceived and written with the apologetic intent of giving him a reliable account, for whatever reason, of the Christian movement. This might be held to accord better with the shape and character of Luke–Acts itself, and with some of its language.

1^5–2^{52} *The Birth Narratives*

The decision how to begin his work will have been particularly acute for an evangelist, since how, when and where Jesus and what he effected 'began' were theological questions that permitted more than one answer – cf. 1^2; 3^{23}; Mark 1$^{1ff.}$, Matt. 1$^{1ff.}$, John 1$^{1ff.}$, A. 1^{22}; 10$^{36ff.}$. Luke's infancy stories supply a highly distinctive and remarkable beginning. They were to exercise considerable influence on the doctrine of Jesus as Son of God, Lord and Saviour, on the liturgy through the canticles, and on the observance of Christmas; and, as the galleries of Europe testify, they were to capture the Christian imagination as few others. They nevertheless stand apart from the gospel narrative they introduce, which is not continuous with them, and nowhere refers back to their contents. Nor does A., or any other NT writing apart from Matt. 1–2, refer to the circumstances of Jesus' birth. Since the gospels of Mark and John show that it was not only possible, but in accordance with the character of the story of Jesus as the agent of God's salvation, to begin with his appearance as an adult on the public scene (cf. also A. 2$^{22ff.}$; 3$^{13ff.}$; 10$^{36ff.}$; 13$^{23ff.}$), Luke's Gospel is conceivable without them.^{o} They are, however, along with Matt. 1–2, evidence that in some (limited?) circles at some (later?) stage of tradition attention came to be given to the birth of Jesus and to his origin (his *genesis*, Matt. 1^1). This will not have been from biographical motives; the statements in 1^{80}; 2$^{40, \, 51–52}$ are very general, and 2$^{41–50}$ is the solitary account between birth and public ministry. And while there may have been an element of hagiography, which was often attached to the birth and origins of outstanding personages, that is unlikely to have been the dominant motive. Rather it will have been to trace back to the beginning the belief, which appears to have emerged first through the resurrection, that humanly speaking Jesus was 'son of David', but was also 'Son of God' through 'spirit' (Rom. 1$^{3–4}$), and to give concrete narrative

---

o For the hypothesis that they were a later addition to a first draft of the Gospel, see V. Taylor, *Behind the Third Gospel*, pp. 164ff., or to L–A as a whole, see R. E. Brown, *The Birth of the Messiah*, pp. 239ff. (for their absence from Marcion's version of the Gospel, see J. Knox, *Marcion and the New Testament*, Chicago 1942, pp. 77ff.).

expression to what had been a confessional statement of faith, as, in the later creed, 'conceived by the Holy Spirit, born of the virgin Mary'.

The Lukan and Matthaean versions of such traditions have the following in common – in the reign of Herod an angelic annunciation of the conception of a child through the agency of the Holy Spirit by a virgin named Mary while betrothed to, but not yet cohabiting with, a Davidite named Joseph; the child, whose name prescribed by the angel is Jesus, as a future saviour, is born at Bethlehem but brought up at Nazareth. The form and manner of the presentation of these common elements differ very widely. In Matt. 1–2 the narrative of the infancy of Jesus (his birth is not described) falls into six sections – a genealogy, an appearance to Joseph in a dream of an angel advising him of the true nature of Mary's pregnancy, a journey of magi to worship the child at Bethlehem by way of Jerusalem and a visit to Herod, an appearance to Joseph in a dream of an angel commanding him to take mother and child into Egypt in face of Herod's hostility, Herod's slaughter of children, an appearance to Joseph in a dream of an angel bidding him to return to Israel and subsequently to go to Nazareth. All these, with the exception of the first are written in good narrative style, and are organized in relation to an OT text. Joseph is at the centre and Mary is a purely passive figure. Comparison with Luke shows differences which 'are more drastic than anywhere in the canonical gospels – the synoptics *versus* the Fourth Gospel included.'[p] It is thus hardly possible that one evangelist knew and used the work of the other. Luke shows no knowledge of the events in Matthew's account – his angelic annunciation is entirely different in kind and purpose, and his genealogy lies outside the birth stories – and his own account consists of a series of events of which Matthew betrays no knowledge. Further – and this is a major difference – Luke does not narrate the birth of Jesus on its own, but in parallel and interconnection with the birth of John. Nor does he anywhere cite an OT text; the scriptural flavour is imparted by the LXX style, and by statements of fulfilment in the canticles.

Luke's presentation falls into seven sections (the number is probably not significant here), each with the character of a tableau. These are: (i) annunciation of the birth of John made by Gabriel to Zechariah in the temple (1^{5-25}); (ii) annunciation of the conception and birth of Jesus made by Gabriel to Mary in Nazareth (1^{26-38}); (iii) visit of Mary to

p K. Stendahl in *The Interpretation of Matthew*, ed. Graham Stanton, London and Philadelphia 1983, p. 57.

Elizabeth and a psalm of praise (1^{39-56}); (iv) birth, circumcision and naming of John and a psalm of praise (1^{57-80}); (v) birth of Jesus with angelic annunciation to shepherds, a hymn of praise, his circumcision and naming (2^{1-21}); (vi) presentation of Jesus in the temple with a psalm of praise and return to Nazareth (2^{22-40}); (vii) Jesus in the temple at the age of twelve (2^{41-52}).

These tableaux can be seen as separate units; (vii) is obviously so. And while (i)–(iv) now form a single story, this is not taken up in (v)–(vi), where there is no further mention of John nor reference to a virginal conception – Joseph and Mary are called Jesus' parents. They are, however, arranged in two diptychs with a pendant. Thus there are (*a*) two annunciations linked by the physical conjunction of the two unborn children, and a statement of the superiority of the second to the first, and (*b*) two narratives of birth, circumcision, naming and designation of destiny, each followed by a celebration of the future salvation of Israel, for which John is to prepare and which Jesus is to achieve. The parallelism, while considerable, cannot be exact, since more attention has to be given to the birth of Jesus as the superior, and this is underlined by the pendant (2^{41-52}), where Jesus is already engrossed with his divine Father in anticipation of his future destiny. Some have argued for a greater measure of schematization and more complex parallelism. q

Luke has used these units so as to tell an almost continuous story with a considerable amount of movement and characterization. Thus in a period described as 'the days of King Herod' (1^5), and after the completion of Zechariah's temple ministry ($1^{23f.}$), it is after five months of Elizabeth's pregnancy that Gabriel visits Mary, and he expressly refers to the fact as confirmation of his message ($1^{36f.}$). As a result Mary leaves Nazareth 'in those days' to visit Elizabeth as a kinswoman, and stays three months, i.e. until near the time of John's birth ($1^{39, 56}$). At the time of the imperial census 'in those days' (2^1) Joseph and Mary leave Nazareth for Bethlehem, where Jesus is born, and is laid in a manger as a sign for shepherds to find him ($2^{7, 12}$). Eight days later, as prescribed by law, he is circumcised, and at the end of his mother's purification is taken by her to the temple; and since his parents observe Passover annually he is taken to the temple at the age of twelve ($2^{21, 22, 41}$).

There are also parallel expressions which impart a certain symmetry.

q See R. Laurentin, *Structure et Théologie de Luc I–II*, ch. 1; Fitzmyer, pp. 313ff., Brown, *Birth*, pp. 248f.

Thus, the two annunciations are similar in form and wording, and the second is connected to the visitation by the word *greeting*. The same angel Gabriel is sent from God to announce the *good tidings* of the birth of John and the conception of Jesus, whose birth is then announced as *good tidings* by an angel of the Lord ($1^{19, 26}$; 2^{10}). The verb *to fill* of a period of time is used of Zechariah's ministry, Elizabeth's pregnancy, John's birth, Jesus' circumcision and Mary's purification ($1^{23, 57}$; $2^{6, 21, 22}$). The stories of John and Jesus are rounded off by similar but significantly varied notices of development (1^{80}; $2^{40, 52}$), while the remarkable character of the events is observed by those who keep them in mind ($1^{65f.}$; $2^{18f., 51}$).

The most distinctive feature, especially in comparison with Matt. 1–2, is the presentation of the births of John and Jesus in parallel. This is certainly the creation of Luke, and is probably to be accounted for by reference to the composition of L–A. Whereas Matthew's Gospel, like Mark's and John's, is a narrative of the life, teaching, death and resurrection of Jesus as the eschatological event which permits no sequel, but to which an account of his birth as the divine fulfilment of prophecy could be a fitting introduction, L–A is concerned rather with the divine origins and character of the Christian movement as a whole. Here the ministry, death and resurrection of Jesus, crucial as they had been, were intended by God to have a sequel in history, and their origins in Judaism, including the prophetic and preparatory ministry of John, continued to play a part (A. $1^{5, 22}$; 10^{37}; 11^{16}; $13^{24ff.}$). Three further threads serve both to bind the birth stories together and also to connect them with the rest of L–A. Firstly, the Holy Spirit is the agent of the destiny of John and of the conception of Jesus, and is the author of prophetic comment on both ($1^{15, 35, 41, 67, 80}$; 2^{25-36}). This prepares for the Spirit as the agent of Jesus' ministry (4^{1-21}) and of the Christian movement and message (A. 1^{4-8}; 2^{33-38} and passim). Secondly, the meaning of the events is conveyed by the term *salvation* and its cognates ($1^{69, 71, 77}$; $2^{11, 30}$), and this prepares for Jesus and the Christian message (3^6; 19^9; A. 4^{12}; 5^{31}; 13^{23-26}; 16^{17}). Thirdly, this salvation is represented as the fulfilment of God's promises to Israel ($1^{16-17, 32-33, 46-55, 68-79}$; 2^{29-32}), which is to be a major characteristic of the ministry, death and resurrection of Jesus (4^{16-27}; $24^{25-27, 44-46}$) and of the Christian movement and message ($24^{47f.}$, A. 2^{17-39}; 3^{13-26}; 10^{43}; 13^{16-41}; 26^{2-23}).

Critical analysis of these narratives has proved particularly difficult, and there is no consensus on whether Luke used sources here, and, if so, in what form, written or oral, they reached him, and what purpose they had previously served; or on the extent of his editing or authorship. This is partly due to the lack of literary parallels, apart from the very different, and differently structured, accounts in Matt. 1–2, but also to the form of the individual episodes. With the exception of 2^{41-50}, which has some of the characteristics of a pronouncement story, these have the protracted manner of 'legend', with an emphasis on supernatural agency, and on the piety of the actors. The combination of John's story with that of Jesus raises the question whether the former had originated as a tradition in the community of the Baptist's disciples about the birth of their master, or was a product of a specifically Christian interest in John as Jesus' precursor. Closely connected is the disputed linguistic question whether the predominantly Semitic style requires that sources originally in Hebrew or Aramaic had been at some stage translated into Greek, or can be adequately accounted for by a consistent use on Luke's part of the translation Greek of the LXX, departing from it only at $2^{1-5, 41-51}$. A special problem of origin and source is provided by the canticles, the Magnificat, the Benedictus and the Nunc Dimittis. In form there is nothing like these elsewhere in L–A or in the NT. In their content and function of interpreting the events the nearest parallel is the speeches in A. Apart possibly from the Nunc Dimittis they cannot have been transcriptions on the spot of what had been spoken spontaneously by the persons concerned. They are relatively independent of their context, and their removal would not affect the narrative, to which they are minimally related in content. In his study of them S. Farris[r] reaches the conclusions (i) that they fall under C. Westermann's classification of a certain type of Jewish psalm as a 'psalm of praise', with the basic structure of a statement of praise followed by the reason for it in an action of God; (ii) that the linguistic evidence points to dependence on Semitic, probably Hebrew originals; and (iii) that they originated in a Jewish-Christian (Palestinian?) community as celebrations of its belief that in fulfilment of God's promises salvation had come to Israel in the appearance of the Davidic messiah.

Hence in the wide spectrum of scholarly opinion[*] there is at the one end H. Sahlin (*Der Messias und das Gottesvolk*), who sees these chapters as the opening of a continuous Hebrew and Aramaic source underlying

[r] *The Hymns of Luke's Infancy Narratives, JSNT(S)* 9, Sheffield 1985.
[*] Summarized by H. H. Oliver, 'The Lucan Birth Stories and the Purpose of Luke–Acts', *NTS* 10, 1963–64, pp. 202ff.

1^5–A. 15, translated and edited by Luke, but lacking 2^{41-52}, and with the Magnificat assigned to Zechariah and the Benedictus to Anna. P. Winter, in a number of studies,* postulates the use by Luke of a Greek version of a Hebrew source, which had been compiled by the combination of a Baptist document containing an annunciation to Elizabeth as well as to Zechariah and incorporating two Maccabaean hymns, with a temple source made up of the stories of the presentation and of Jesus at twelve, to which the compiler had added the birth of Jesus. M. Dibelius[s] finds an Aramaic document about John, to which Luke has added a number of independent and even contradictory traditions about Jesus' birth, incorporating the Magnificat and Benedictus as ancient songs, and himself creating the story of the visitation. Laurentin (*Structure*, p. 13) postulates a redaction of material in Hebrew, but without further specification. At the other end are those who assign the whole composition to Luke. This is either on linguistic grounds – the language is his, and he is working on oral tradition with the LXX in mind;[t] he is writing 'with a rather more Biblical flourish than was his usual wont', possibly on the basis of Hebrew sources;[u] he is the composer with the aid of oral traditions and on OT models, though the Benedictus may be pre-Lukan.[v] Or it is on theological grounds – the whole is a typological construction by Luke on the basis of Genesis.[w] P. S. Minear[x] argues on stylistic, structural and linguistic grounds that the birth narratives are homogeneous with the rest of L–A, and that Luke has made them, whencesoever he derived them, integral to his whole work.

---

* Listed by Fitzmyer in his bibliography, pp. 332f.

s *Botschaft und Geschichte*, Gesammelte Aufsätze I, Tübingen 1953, pp. 1ff.

t So A. Harnack, *Luke the Physician*, ET London and New York 1907, pp. 96ff. and Appendix II.

u Nigel Turner, 'The Relation of Luke I–II to Hebrew Sources and to the Rest of Luke–Acts', *NTS* 2, 1955–56, pp. 100–9.

v P. Benoit, 'L'enfance de Jean Baptiste selon Luc I', *NTS* 3, 1956–57, pp. 169–94.

w M. D. Goulder and M. L. Sanderson, 'St Luke's Genesis', *JTS* ns 8, 1957, pp. 12–30.

x 'Luke's Use of the Birth Stories' in *Studies in Luke–Acts*, ed. Keck and Martyn, pp. 111–30.

This is basically an account of the divinely planned birth, during Herod's reign, of John, who is to be the future prophetic Elijah figure in Israel, and who is recognized as such by his father through prophetic inspiration ($1^{5-25, \ 57-80}$). Intercalated in it is a parallel annunciation, and advance prophetic recognition, of Jesus' birth ($1^{26-38, \ 45-56}$), which will take place in the same period ($2^{1f.}$). These two constituents are locked together by means of an angelic reference to the kinship of the two mothers concerned, by the visit of one to the other, and by her acclamation by the other ($1^{36-45, \ 56}$). The account of John could have existed independently, with its origin in the community of his disciples as a story about their founder, who was depicted as the forerunner not of Jesus but of God. Luke has used it to establish in a more explicit and detailed manner the mutual relationship of John and Jesus, and of the movements to which they gave rise, which was a matter of Christian concern (cf. 7^{18-35}; A. 10^{36-38}; 13^{23-26}; $18^{24}-19^7$; Mark 1^{1-8}; Matt. 3^{13-15}; John 1^{6-42}; 3^{22-30}).

1^{5-25} THE WONDROUS BIRTH OF JOHN ANNOUNCED

[5]*In the days of Herod, king of Judea, there was a priest named Zechariah, of the division of Abijah; and he had a wife of the daughters of Aaron, and her name was Elizabeth.* [6]*And they were both righteous before God, walking in all the commandments and ordinances of the Lord blameless.* [7]*But they had no child, because Elizabeth was barren, and both were advanced in years.*

[8]*Now while he was serving as priest before God when his division was on duty,* [9]*according to the custom of the priesthood, it fell to him by lot to enter the temple of the Lord and burn incense.* [10]*And the whole multitude of the people were praying outside at the hour of incense.* [11]*And there appeared to him an angel of the Lord standing on the right side of the altar of incense.* [16]*And Zechariah was troubled when he saw him, and fear fell upon him.* [13]*But the angel said to him, 'Do not be afraid, Zechariah, for your prayer is heard, and your wife Elizabeth will bear you a son, and you shall call his name John.*

¹⁴*And you will have joy and gladness,*
and many will rejoice at his birth;
¹⁵*for he will be great before the Lord,*
and he shall drink no wine nor strong drink,
and he will be filled with the Holy Spirit,
even from his mother's womb.
¹⁶*And he will turn many of the sons of Israel to the Lord their God,*
¹⁷*and he will go before him in the spirit and power of Elijah,*
to turn the hearts of the fathers to the children,
and the disobedient to the wisdom of the just,
to make ready for the Lord a people prepared.'

¹⁸*And Zechariah said to the angel, 'How shall I know this? For I am an old man, and my wife is advanced in years.'* ¹⁹*And the angel answered him, 'I am Gabriel, who stand in the presence of God; and I was sent to speak to you, and to bring you this good news.* ²⁰*And behold, you will be silent and unable to speak until the day that these things come to pass, because you did not believe my words, which will be fulfilled in their time.'* ²¹*And the people were waiting for Zechariah, and they wondered at his delay in the temple.* ²²*And when he came out, he could not speak to them, and they perceived that he had seen a vision in the temple; and he made signs to them and remained dumb.* ²³*And when his time of service was ended, he went to his home.*

²⁴*After these days his wife Elizabeth conceived, and for five months she hid herself, saying,* ²⁵*'Thus the Lord has done to me in the days when he looked on me, to take away my reproach among men.'*

This is not a traditional pericope in the ordinary sense. In form it is a comparatively protracted and consequential narrative, and in content it combines factual and biographical detail with vivid dialogue between a statutory angel and a human being. In marked contrast to 1¹⁻⁴ it is Semitic in style, being a series of paratactic sentences almost throughout. Not only is the language predominantly that of the LXX in general, but the structure is stereotyped, being modelled on certain OT stories, in which divine intervention is responsible for the births of notable figures in the divinely governed history of Israel. Thus there are (i) an appearance of the angel of the Lord (v. 11; cf. Gen. 16⁷; Judg. 13³); (ii) the human reaction of fear (v. 12; cf. Gen. 17³; 18¹⁵; Judg. 13⁶); (iii) a personal address by the angel announcing the conception and birth, contrary to human possibilities, of a child, whose name, character and destiny are prescribed (vv. 13–17; cf. Gen. 16⁸, ¹⁰⁻¹²;

17$^{15-16, 19-21}$; 18$^{10-11}$; Judg. 13$^{2-5}$); and (iv) human unbelief in the face of this (v. 18; cf. Gen. 16^{13}; 17$^{17-18}$; 18^{12}). Peculiar here are the setting in temple piety (but cf. I Sam. 1$^{3-28}$), and the priestly origins of John, the future eschatological prophet.

∞∞

5

in the days of: A vague expression for a king's reign characteristic of the opening of pious narrative with a historical setting (cf. Judith 1^1; Tobit 1^1; Matt. 2^1). It is possibly from a source, as it does not recur in L-A, and contrasts with Luke's attempts at exact dating in 2$^{1-3}$; 3$^{1-2}$.

Herod, king of Judea: The complex story of Herod, called the Great, of his rise to power, his political aims, intrigues and successes, his wars, alliances and marriages, is told by Josephus in *Ant.* 14.1–17.199 – 'one of the most glittering figures in one of the most glowing periods of human history'.^{y} An Edomite, and hence hated by the Jews however hard he tried to win their favour he rose from obscure origins under the tutelage of Rome to be the native ruler (this is the meaning of *king* in Roman political terminology) of *Judea*. If used correctly here this denotes, not the Roman province created in AD 6 out of the southern part of Palestine (as in 2^4; 3^1; A. 9^{31}), but the Roman satellite kingdom ruled by Herod, which included Galilee, Samaria and parts of Peraea and Coele Syria. It is not always clear what Luke means by Judaea; in 6^{17}; 7^{17}; A. 10^{37} it appears to include Galilee. Herod's rule was from 27–4 BC, and Luke places this event at some unspecified time within it; Matt. 2$^{15-20}$ places Jesus' birth some (little?) time before Herod's death.

a priest named Zechariah: John comes from exalted stock, the priesthood being something of an *élite* in Israel limited to certain families, 'the sons of Aaron'. *named* is here onomati = 'by name', as usually in L-A. Though importance can be attached to a name, it is doubtful whether the name Zechariah (which is fairly common in the OT and Jewish tradition) or Elizabeth, has any particular significance here.

of the division of Abijah: This refers to the organization of the priesthood. The word rendered *division, ephēmeria*, means 'daily (sc. duty)', and was used by transference of the groups into which the priests were divided for duty at the temple. These had been twenty-four in number in David's time (I Chron. 23^6; 24$^{7-18}$), and apparently that number had been restored, with their antique names attached, from the four that had returned from Babylon (Ezra 2$^{36-39}$),

---

y S. Perowne, *The Life and Times of Herod the Great*, London 1956, New York 1959, p. 15.

though Josephus can still refer to four (*Against Apion* 2. 108) and seven (*Ant.* 7.365f.). If J. Jeremias is correct in his estimate of the number of priests (just over 7000, *Jerusalem in the Time of Jesus*, pp. 202ff.), each division, consisting of a number of priestly families (from four to nine), would comprise some 300 priests. Each did two separate weeks' duty in the year. In I Chron. 24^{10} the division of Abijah comes eighth.

a wife of the daughters of Aaron: That is, a priest's daughter; cf. II Chron. 2^{14}, 'the daughters of Dan' expressing membership of a tribe. Though intermarriage among priestly families was no doubt common, it was not compulsory. John was doubly of priestly stock.

her name was Elizabeth: Literally 'the name of her Elizabeth', a less elegant construction, which recurs only at v. 27.

6

John comes not only from the priestly but also from the ideal pious in Israel, here described as *righteous (dikaios) before God,* that is, perfectly observant of his declared will, which is then explicated by *walking in all the commandments and ordinances (dikaiōmata) of the Lord blameless.* For such expressions of Jewish piety, see Deut. 6$^{20-25}$ and passim, I Kings 8^{61}, Ps. 119$^{1-2}$ and passim, 1QS 1 (Vermes, *Scrolls*, p. 72).

7

The supernatural character of John's birth is underlined. It meant the removal by God's power of barrenness, regarded in Israel as a supreme misfortune, and possibly as a punishment for sin. Here the scriptural model is Hannah, the mother of Samuel (I Sam. 1$^{2ff.}$; but cf. also Rebekah, the mother of Jacob, Gen. 25^{21}, Rachel, the mother of Joseph, Gen. 30$^{22ff.}$, and Manoah's wife, the mother of Samson, Judg. 13$^{2ff.}$). But it meant further the gift from God of a child to those beyond the time of begetting and childbearing; *advanced in years,* literally 'advanced in their days', a LXX expression, cf. Gen. 18^{11} – of which Abraham and Sarah were the models (Gen. 16^1–18^{15}; Rom. 4$^{18-21}$).

8

while he was serving: The first occurrence of *egeneto* = 'it happened' (with a description of attendant circumstances) followed by a verb in the indicative (here *it fell to him by lot*). This is not a Greek but a LXX construction reproducing Hebrew idiom. There are many instances of it in the gospels, some of which are undoubtedly from Luke's hand (e.g. 9$^{18, 33, 37}$; 20^1, where Luke revises Mark), and all may be. It is absent from A. A second construction is *egeneto* joined to a following verb in the indicative by 'and' ('he' or 'they'). This is also LXX and Hebrew idiom, and is also frequent in the Gospel (in 5^{17}; 6$^{6, 12}$; 8^{22}; 9^{28} Luke is revising Mark). The only occurrence in A (5^7) is doubtful. A third construction is the Greek idiom of *egeneto* followed by an accusative and infinitive. This occurs in 3²¹; 6¹˙ ¹²; 16²², and is common in A. Here the construction introduces an overloaded sentence (vv. 8–10). giving the attendant circumstances of the angelophany, and concentrating, somewhat artificially, on Zechariah performing his duties alone, and the crowd outside waiting for him to come out alone.

when his division was on duty: On one of the two weeks in the year when it was the turn of the division of Abijah to be at the temple. But the Greek, literally 'in the order of his course', could mean 'in the succession of priestly actions which fell to it on duty'.

9–10

The *mise en scène* may be somewhat idealized, constructed from OT texts rather than taken from life, and approximating Zechariah to the figure of the high priest. (i) The ritual of burning incense morning and afternoon goes back to the prescriptions of Exod. 30¹⁻¹⁰, where the picture is muddled, since *the altar of incense*, regarded as *the* altar (elsewhere that is the altar of burnt sacrifice), is before the mercy seat in the holy of holies, and beyond the veil through which the high priest went once a year to cleanse it (Exod. 30⁶˙ ¹⁰ᶠ˙; so also Heb. 9⁴). Here it must be in the temple, *naos* = 'sanctuary', i.e. the rest of the temple outside the holy of holies. (ii) For details of the scene reference is made to the Mishnah tractate Tamid = 'The Daily Offering'. This has the various priestly duties, including the burning of incense, distributed by lot, and describes the offering of incense as a corporate action of a priest with assistants. This tractate may be in part an ideal reconstruction of rituals which had long since ceased to be performed. (iii) *the whole multitude of the people* (a somewhat fulsome phrase) *praying outside at the hour of incense* (probably here in the afternoon), will be in the courts beyond the porch at the end of the sanctuary. But there is no evidence that such a congregation waited for the priest who had offered the incense to emerge alone to pronounce the Aaronic blessing (Num. 6²⁴⁻²⁶). In Tamid 7² this is done by all the priests on duty. Tractate Yoma 5¹, 'He came out by the way he went in, and in the outer space (of the sanctuary) he prayed a short prayer' refers to the high priest on the Day of Atonement.

11

an angel of the Lord: Not, as generally in the OT, *the* angel of the Lord. He reappears in the birth stories (vv. 26, 28), but, apart from 23⁴³ (where the text is doubtful), not in the rest of the Gospel, though he is found frequently in A. (5¹⁹; 8²⁶; 10³; 12⁷⁻¹¹˙ ²³; 27²³). *angelos* means messenger, and in the case of individual angels retains this functionary sense. It denotes an intermediary delivering God's message, and can be a synonym for God himself (cf. Gen. 16⁷⁻¹³; 22¹¹⁻¹⁴; Judg. 6¹¹⁻¹⁴).

appeared: *ōphthē*, the passive of *horān* = 'to see', is an apocalyptic word for the manifestation of heavenly beings. It is used elsewhere in the synoptists of Moses and Elijah at the Transfiguration (9^{31}), but in the tradition of appearances of the risen Lord (I Cor. 15$^{5-7}$; 24^{34}; A. 9^{17}; 13^{31}; 26^{16}), and in A. of tongues of flame (A. 2^{3}) and the God of glory (A. 7$^{2, 35}$; cf. 16^{9}). The corresponding noun *optasia* = 'vision' (v. 22) is, apart from II Cor. 12^{1}, confined to L–A (24^{23}; A. 26^{19}). No description is given of the angel by means of which he was recognized. The nearest parallel is Josephus' account (*Ant.* 13.282) of the heavenly voice heard by John Hyrcanus in the temple when he was offering incense as high priest.

on the right side: In the ancient world the propitious side, here fitting for the delivery of good news (v. 19).

12

In such scenes, biblical and non-biblical, the human reaction to heavenly vision is bewilderment – *tarassein* = 'to trouble', elsewhere in the NT in this sense 24^{38} – and *fear (fear fell upon* + A. 19^{17}).

13–17

The purpose of the angel's appearance is to deliver the divine message, which is not simply for Zechariah personally, but primarily through him for many in Israel (cf. v. 16). This is given in exalted language in rhythmical couplets with a concluding line (as printed in RSV; v. 13 could be printed in the same way). It is a miniature canticle, declaring from angelic lips (cf. vv. 32–33, 34–35; 2^{14}) the divine significance of coming events, as is done by human lips in vv. 46–55; 68–79; 2$^{29-32, 34-35}$.

13

The message begins with the customary divine response to human fear, which is to forbid it and to give the reasons (cf. Gen. 15^{1}; Dan. 10^{12}; the sequence will be repeated in vv. 29–30; 2$^{9-10}$).

your prayer: deēsis = petitionary prayer, common in the epistles, but elsewhere in the gospels 2^{37}; 5^{33}. It is assumed in this that Zechariah had been petitioning for the removal of childlessness, though this is artificial from those past the age of begetting and bearing.

you shall call his name: An expression combining 'call him' and 'name him' (cf. 2^{21}; Matt. 1^{21}; Gen. 3^{20}; Isa. 9).

John: Here, as dictated by God, the name must be significant, but nothing is made of it (contrast vv. 59–66), and the Greek reader is unlikely to have known that *Yôhānān* meant 'Yahweh has shown favour'.

14

Not only the rhythmic tone but the content begin to impart the special atmosphere of rejoicing over salvation, both by individuals and a wider circle, that characterizes Luke's infancy narratives (it is absent from Matt. 1–2).

joy and gladness: the first (*chara*) is repeated in vv. 28, 46, 58; 2¹⁰. The second (*agalliasis* + v. 44; A. 2⁴⁶; Heb. 1⁹ LXX; Jude 24) is a forceful word denoting spiritual exaltation, as does the corresponding verb in v. 47; 10²¹; A. 16³⁴. For the two in combination, Matt. 5¹²; I Peter 1⁸; 4¹³; Rev. 19⁷. The joy and gladness are for both Zechariah and for the rest of Israel in the future when John fulfils his divine destiny – *for he will be.*

15

great: megas, repeated of Jesus in v. 32, is surprising. It is infrequent in this sense in the NT, which is not concerned with human greatness (cf. Mark 10⁴²f.). In the OT it is used absolutely of God, and is here qualified by *before the Lord,* i.e. in God's eyes and through his place in God's purposes. It is presumably in this sense that he is the greatest of men in 7²⁸.

he shall drink no wine nor strong drink: The latter, *sikera,* is a transliteration of the Aramaic *sikra,* and refers to alcoholic drink other than wine. The precise force of the prohibition as an explication of John's greatness is not clear. In Lev. 10⁹ it applies temporarily to priests to secure their holiness on entering the sanctuary, and, along with other injunctions, to anyone undertaking a special Nazirite vow of separation to the Lord (called 'great' in Num. 6²), but only for the period of the vow. Hence it could denote asceticism in general (7³³). But it is laid on Samson's mother because he is to be a Nazirite for life (Judg. 13⁷), and this may be the force of its addition in the LXX text of I Sam. 1¹¹. It could then prescribe a lifelong Nazirite state for John *from his mother's womb.*

filled: pimplanai, almost confined to L-A in the NT. Followed by *with the Spirit* it recurs in vv. 41, 67; (4¹); A. 2⁴; 4⁸, ³¹; 9¹⁷; 13⁹). Here perhaps in contrast to intoxication with wine, as in Eph. 5¹⁸.

the Holy Spirit: Or 'holy spirit', neither word having the article, though the two forms are interchangeable – cf. 2²⁵ without and 2²⁶ with, A. 2⁴ without and 2³³ with, the article. The term is comparatively rare in the OT (Isa. 63¹⁰; Ps. 51¹¹), though always to hand in the frequent reference to the spirit, i.e. breath or effective (moral) power of the God who is holy. It is rare also in the inter-testamental literature and in the synoptic teaching of Jesus (see Barrett, *Holy Spirit*). It is common in the later rabbinic writings, and in A. and the epistles, where it is a hallmark of Christian life. In the OT, as later with the rabbis, 'the (holy) spirit of God' is closely associated with prophecy (Isa. 61¹; Ezek. 11⁵; Joel 2²⁸ff.; Zech. 7¹²), and here Luke introduces another special feature of his infancy narratives, viz. that the events of the births of John and Jesus were the occasion of, and accompanied by, a renewed outburst of prophecy in Israel (cf. vv. 44–45, 67; 2$^{27-35, 36-38}$; contrast Matt. 1–2, where they occur in fulfilment of past prophecy). This is underlined with respect to John by *from his mother's womb*, meaning 'while still in the womb' rather than simply 'from birth'. It prepares for Luke's presentation of Jesus as at least a spirit-endowed prophet throughout his ministry (4$^{1ff.,\ 18ff.}$, 10^{21}; 24^{19}), and as the inaugurator of the era of the Spirit at his exaltation (A. 2$^{17-33}$).^{z}

16–17

This explication of v. 15 could be variant statements of the same thing, based largely on the text of Malachi.

he will turn many of the sons of Israel to the Lord their God: This may echo Mal. 2^6, where the priests are told about their father Levi, the originator of the covenant, that he 'turned many' (from iniquity).

he will go before him in the spirit and power of Elijah: The spirit with which John is to be filled is further defined as *the spirit and power* (a familiar combination, cf. v. 35; 4^{14}; A. 1^8, and almost a hendiadys, since spirit is effective power) of Elijah. This rests on Mal 3^1, 'I send my messenger to prepare the way before me', regarded as being taken up in Mal. 4$^{5-6}$, 'I will send you Elijah the prophet before the great and terrible day of the Lord comes.' On the score of his career and his assumption into heaven (I Kings 17–21; II Kings 2) Elijah became an eschatological figure who was expected to return to reform Israel before the end. While *in the spirit and power of* is more general than the full-blown doctrine of Elijah *redivivus*, with whom John is identified in Mark 9$^{9-13}$ (omitted by Luke), it is still an obstacle to the thesis of Conzelmann (*Theology*, pp. 18ff.) that Luke had a consistent view of John as the last of the old prophets and not the eschatological precursor, and he has to set it aside, along with A. 10^{37}; 13^{24}, as an inconsistency.

to turn the hearts of the fathers to the children: That is, to achieve harmony in Israel. This also echoes in a general way (the plural *hearts, fathers, children*) the standard role of the messenger-Elijah (Mal. 4^6; Ecclus 48^{10}).

to the wisdom of the just: This renders *en phronēsei dikaiōn* = 'in (by) the way of thinking of the righteous'. This has no direct parallel in Malachi, though Mal. 4^4 bids Israel remember the law of Moses, the statutes and (righteous) ordinances (*dikaiōmata*), and it is to obedience to these and not to wisdom that those who are *disobedient* need to be turned.

to make ready for the Lord a people prepared: This somewhat tautologous statement concludes and summarizes the role of the eschatological prophet. *make*

z See G. W. H. Lampe, 'The Holy Spirit in the Writings of St Luke', in *Studies in the Gospels*, ed. Nineham, pp. 159–200.

ready, hetoimazein, is OT language (Isa. 40³ with a 'way', II Sam. 7²⁴ LXX with a *people*). *prepared, kataskeuazein* = 'equip' is used of the messenger in Mal. 3¹, quoted of John in 7²⁷.

18

As in other such scenes the human being, instead of accepting the announcement of the seemingly impossible, questions it (cf. Gen. 17¹⁷⁻¹⁸; 18¹¹⁻¹⁵), though here in the mild form of requesting a verifying sign (cf. Gen. 15⁸; Judg. 6³⁶⁻⁴⁰; II Kings 20⁸⁻¹¹), such as is given without request in 2¹².

19–20

Despite the mildness of Zechariah's request, but because of the importance of the moment for Israel's redemption, the angel now brings his full weight to bear by giving his name and his credentials as the spokesman of God, and so further underlines what he has said about John in vv. 13–17.

19

Gabriel, who stands in the presence of God: This reflects the speculative theology of angels that developed in Judaism from the second century, in apocalyptic circles but also in popular piety (though according to A. 23⁸ rejected by the biblically conservative Sadducees). Here individual messenger angels have become a plurality of denizens of heaven forming a divine entourage, who partake in the divine glory and judgment, and are engaged in heavenly worship (Rev. 5¹¹), though some can still be spoken of with reference to their function (9²⁶; Mark 13²⁷). Two features of the development were (i) the differentiation of angels into orders, one of which was 'the angels of the presence', i.e. those nearest to God (four or seven in number, cf. Tobit 12¹⁵; I Enoch 20; Rev. 8²), and (ii) the naming (by a combination with *-el* = 'God') of principal (guardian) angels, such as Michael, the protector of Israel (Dan. 12¹; I Enoch 9¹; Rev. 12⁷), and Gabriel, who appears as a man (Dan. 8¹⁵⁻¹⁶), at the time of the evening sacrifice (Dan. 9²¹), and prophesies the messianic reign (9²⁵; cf. I Enoch 9¹; 20⁷; 40⁹; 54⁶; 71¹³).

I was sent: A reverential passive = 'God sent me'.

to bring you this good news: The first occurrence of the verb *euangelizesthai* = 'to announce good news'. This became a standard term in the church for Christian proclamation (so in the Pauline epistles, Heb. 4²; I Peter 1¹²). Apart from Matt. 11⁵ (Q) it is confined in the gospels to Luke (ten times, fifteen in A.), while, except for A. 15⁷; 20²⁴, he studiously avoids the corresponding noun *euangelion* = 'gospel'. It had a significant background in Isa. 40⁹; 52⁷; 60⁶; 61¹, being used of the announcement of the good news of God's coming salvation, but Luke can also use it in a reduced sense of 'preach', 'teach' (3¹⁸; 8¹; 9⁶; 20¹; A. 8¹²; 14⁷).

20

For Zechariah's failure to hear God's speech and to utter the appropriate response the angel gives him the corroborative sign he has asked for in striking him dumb (and deaf?, cf. v. 22, where the word rendered *dumb* is *kōphos*, which generally means 'deaf', and v. 62). This is dramatic, and is introduced by the first instance of *and behold*, *kai idou*, a LXX phrase absent from Mark, John and Paul, and rare in Matthew, but frequent in Luke's Gospel, sometimes clearly from his own hand (eight times in A.). It is also strange. Its purpose is to go beyond punitive judgment, and to secure that the revelation and power shall be recognized as God's by the fact that they are effective in human conditions of hiddenness and silence and despite human incapacity (this is spelt out in vv. 59–66).

fulfilled in their time: Literally 'filled into their time'. The expression is a mixed one. The verb here *plēroun* = 'fill', can be used of the completion of a specified or divinely predestined time, which is *kairos* (cf. 12^{56}; 19^{44}; 21^8; A. 7$^{23, 30}$; not *chronos*, which is undifferentiated time; cf. Mark 1^{14}). Generally Luke uses for this *pimplanai* (see on v. 23), and *plēroun* for the fulfilment of the words of God in scripture (4^{21}; 24^{44}; A. 1^{16}; 3^{18}; 13^{27}).

21–22

The congregation's expectation for Zechariah to emerge alone as the priest for the day, the supposed delay caused by the (lengthy?) vision, and their miraculous divination that his dumbness (in failing to give the priestly blessing?, and deafness in failing to hear their enquiries?) was the result not of a stroke but of heavenly vision, all belong to the dramatic technique and legendary character of the story.

23

his time of service was ended: Literally 'the days of his service were filled'. The verb here, *pimplanai* = 'fill' is, apart from two instances in Matthew, confined to L–A in the NT. Its use with a period of time is confined to the birth stories: v. 57; 2$^{6, 21, 22}$.

he went to his home: According to v. 39 a town in the Judaean hill country. This hardly supplies sufficient evidence for commentators to refer to him as a simple country priest.

24

After these days: A vague expression introducing the fulfilment of God's promise in Elizabeth's conception but giving no date for it.

hid herself: Both the action and the reason for it are surprising because artificial (a literary device, Klostermann, p. 11). The opposite action was to be expected, viz. to advertise openly God's grace and power in the removal of barrenness and its reproach even from one beyond childbearing, and to give utterance to the joy promised in v. 14 (cf. Gen. 21$^{6f.}$; 30^{23}). Total concealment of pregnancy during the first *five months* – this note of time is solely for the purpose of Gabriel's reference to the sixth month in v. 36 – would be scarcely possible.

25

This reason is not to be interpreted naturalistically – e.g. to avoid further reproach (Plummer, p. 19), to retire for prayer (Easton, p. 7). It is theological. *Thus* is emphatic. Her concealment, like Zechariah's dumbness, is to match the fact that it is God himself who has *looked on* (*epeiden* + A. 4^{29} = 'be concerned with') her, in a way that goes beyond human capacity and is therefore to be hidden from human eyes. Hence only Gabriel, God's messenger, is in a position to know about it (v. 36).

I$^{26-38}$ THE WONDROUS BIRTH OF JESUS FORETOLD

^{26}*In the sixth month the angel Gabriel was sent from God to a city of Galilee named Nazareth,* ^{27}*to a virgin betrothed to a man whose name was Joseph, of the house of David; and the virgin's name was Mary.* ^{28}*And he came to her and said, 'Hail, O favoured one, the Lord is with you!'* ★ ^{29}*But she was greatly troubled at the saying, and considered in her mind what sort of greeting this might be.* ^{30}*And the angel said to her, 'Do not be afraid, Mary, for you have found favour with God.* ^{31}*And behold, you will conceive in your womb and bear a son, and you shall call his name Jesus.*

^{32}*He will be great, and will be called the Son of the Most High;*
    and the Lord God will give to him the throne of his father David,
^{33}*and he will reign over the house of Jacob for ever;*
    and of his kingdom there will be no end.'
^{34}*And Mary said to the angel, 'How can this be, since I have no husband?'*
And the angel said to her,

    'The Holy Spirit will come upon you,
    and the power of the Most High will overshadow you;
    therefore the child to be born† *will be called holy,*
    the Son of God.
^{36}*And behold, your kinswoman Elizabeth in her old age has also conceived a son; and this is the sixth month with her who was called barren.* ^{37}*For with*

153

God nothing will be impossible.' ³⁸*And Mary said, 'Behold, I am the hand-maid of the Lord; let it be to me according to your word.' And the angel departed from her.*

★ Other ancient authorities add *'Blessed are you among women!'*
† Other ancient authorities add *of you*

This is the crucial pericope in chs. 1–2, not so much in announcing the virginal conception as in making known from a divine source, and in advance of his conception, who and what Jesus is predestined to be. It has the same mythological pattern of angelic appearance and dialogue as the previous story in vv. 5–20 (for a detailed comparison Brown, *Birth*, pp. 249ff.), and could have been modelled on it. The differences are that the setting is now minimal – in Nazareth at the home of an unmarried girl named Mary betrothed to a Davidite named Joseph; it is not referred to as vision, and Mary's question (v. 34) is not evidence of unbelief, but is the occasion of further christological statements going beyond what has been predicted of John. It is less diffuse, and the Greek rather more idiomatic – *named* (v. 26) is in the Greek 'to which the name', as also in v. 27, *greatly troubled* is *diatarassesthai* ++, and *what sort . . . might be* is the more stylistic *potapos* followed by the rare optative. Luke could have been the first to write it down, and could have been responsible for the awkwardness of *betrothed* and the mention of Joseph in v. 27, and of Mary's question in v. 34; he was almost certainly responsible for the connecting links with what precedes and follows (vv. 26, 36). The Davidic christology in vv. 32f. does not necessarily argue use of an early Judaeo-Christian source, since it appears alongside 'Son of God' in the preaching in A. 13²²⁻³⁶.

In what form Luke knew the tradition of a virginal conception, and what historical facts may have lain behind it, are very difficult to detect. For, despite its place here it plays no part in the rest of the gospel, except in the editorial parenthesis *as was supposed* (3²³) adjusting the genealogy to it. Nor is it referred to in A., including the christological speeches, nor elsewhere in the NT (Gal. 4⁴ simply states a Jewish human birth), including the gospels ('son of Mary' in Mark 6³ need not imply it, but could simply indicate that Joseph was now dead). The only exception is Matt. 1¹⁸⁻²⁵, but that in some ways heightens the problem. For while it also reflects a tradition of a virginal conception before Mary and Joseph cohabit, it does so in the entirely different form of first an *ex post facto* statement of Mary's pregnancy through the agency of holy spirit (Matt. 1^{18}), and then of an annunciation, presumably in Bethlehem and through the OT medium of a dream, with the apologetic purpose of securing that Joseph accepts the fact as divinely intended in view of a possible slander of adultery and illegitimacy (Matt. 1^{19-25}). Simply to join together these two forms of the tradition as an explanation of its historical origin would require that the Mary of Luke 1^{26-38} had said nothing at all on the matter in the meantime to the Joseph of Matt. 1^{19-25}.

These factors also militate against the common view that its source is to be traced in the memories and family traditions of Mary (and/or Joseph), pondered perhaps over many years (2^{19}), and eventually publicized, though in these widely different versions, and so as to reach only a limited circle of Christian communities; it was apparently unknown to the Markan, Pauline and Johannine churches, and did not belong to the early Christian message. It may be noted also that the earliest Christian writers to refer to it, Ignatius and Aristides, appear to know it from sources other than the gospels, and only in Irenaeus is there the first clear reference to Luke 1–2. Some have, therefore, accounted for it theologically rather than historically as arising from Christian meditation on Isa. 7^{14} LXX, but this is unlikely apart from some report directing attention to this text, as it does not appear to have been taken currently as a prophecy of the birth of the messiah (in the Hebrew the word translated 'virgin' meant 'a young woman'). Even in Matt. 1^{22-23} it gives the impression of being appended to the story rather than creative of it. That it lay behind Luke's version is asserted by some (e.g. Ellis, Leaney, Marshall, Schürmann) but is denied by others (e.g. Brown, *Birth*, Fitzmyer). Apart from 'virgin' the parallels adduced – 'will conceive', 'bear a son', 'call his name' – have a wider provenance in the OT, while central ideas here – 'Son of the Most High', 'Son of God', 'the throne of David' and eternal rule over the house of Jacob – are absent from Isa. 7^{14} (though some of them are present in Isa. 9).

Others have argued for influence here of the traditions of the divine paternity of 'sons of God', divine men or heroes which are to be found in the increasingly syncretistic religious thought, mythology and folk lore in the world outside Judaism. Later Christian writers were not unaware of these, sometimes dismissing them as fables and sometimes using them as analogies of Christian truth – cf. Justin, *Apology*, I, 22f.,

33, 54; *Dialogue*, 67, 70; Origen, *Against Celsus*, 1.37, 6.8. They are of various kinds, and their quality as evidence is difficult to assess – e.g. the claim to divinity which the fourth-century romancer, in his polemic against the first century heretic Simon Magus, puts into his mouth, 'I am not the magician ... nor the son of Antonius. For before my mother Rachel and he came together she, still a virgin, conceived me, while it was in my power to be small or great ... and to appear as a man among men' (*Clementine Recognitions* II, 14). To be ruled out are stories of the procreation of gods, or of immortals who were purely mythical figures, through sexual union of a god, generally in the form of an animal, with a woman (not necessarily a virgin), as in the case of Apollo, Dionysus, Asclepius, Perseus, Heracles, etc.; as also the birth of Mithras from a generative rock. Nor are Egyptian traditions likely to be relevant, either of the parthenogenesis by which the goddess Net conceived the sun god Ra, or of the birth of the sun god Horus from the goddess Isis, or of the legend which secured the divinity of the Pharaoh, however actually born, by making him the offspring of the god Re, the generative principle, and a woman (queen or priestess), which Alexander had to adopt for himself before he could be considered the legitimate ruler of Egypt.

More significant could be the traditions of divine paternity (not virgin conception) of great men and saviour figures. These also were at various levels. The divine parentage conjectured along with human parents for Romulus belonged still to the sphere of antique legend (Plutarch, *Life of Romulus* II, 2–6 calls it fable). The oft repeated story of the birth of Plato (Plutarch, *Moralia*, 717E; Diogenes Laertius III, 2; Apuleius, *Plato* 1.1; Olympiodorus, *Life of Plato* 1) did not, as may be seen from Origen's introduction of it in connection with the birth of Jesus (*Against Celsus* 1.37): 'For some have thought fit (not in respect of any ancient stories and heroic tales but of people recently born) to record as though it were possible that when Plato was born of Amphictione Ariston was prevented from having sexual intercourse with her until she had brought forth the child which she had by Apollo. But these stories are really myths, which have led people to invent such a tale about a man because they regarded him as having superior wisdom and power to the multitude, and as having received the original composition of his body from better and more divine seed, thinking that this was appropriate for men with superhuman powers.' The religiously minded Plutarch records (*Life of Numa*, 4) an

Egyptian belief that it was possible for the spirit of a god to approach a woman and to beget the beginnings of birth. In commenting on the story of Plato's birth as a 'child of God', and not by 'seed' but by some other power, he seems to make this belief his own (*Moralia* 717D–718A): 'I do not find it strange if it is not by physical approach like a man's, but by some other kind of contact or touch, by other agencies, that a god alters mortal nature and makes it pregnant with a more divine offspring.' The 'saviour' in the NT period was pre-eminently Augustus; cf. the Priene inscription (AD 6) referring to him as 'most divine' and to his birthday as that of a god and as the beginning of glad tidings for the world. Virgil's *Fourth Eclogue*, often cited in this connection, does not refer to a miraculous birth, but develops the motif of the wonderful child who inaugurates a new age, which might be reflected in Luke 2$^{8-14, \ 28-35, \ 41-50}$ (but cf. Isa. 9$^{6ff.}$). A miraculous conception for Augustus, taken from a treatise on the gods of a certain Asclepias, is recorded by Suetonius (*Augustus*, 94.1–4) in the form that his mother Atia spent the night in the temple of Apollo, and was approached in sleep by a snake which left its marks permanently on her (the snake was a regular symbol of the 'genius' or tutelary deity of a person; cf. Plutarch, *Life of Alexander* II, 4, where it appears in connection with a miraculous birth of Alexander). It is doubtful, however, whether these essentially polytheistic stories do anything more precise than to illustrate a universal religious tendency to presuppose something mysterious and miraculous about the births of god-like persons. Knox (*Hellenistic Elements*, pp. 22ff.) notes this as the motive in the legendary embellishments in Jewish apocalyptic and rabbinic writings of the births of notable OT figures – Noah, Abraham, Isaac, Moses – where, however, they take the form of marvellous accompaniments of the birth and not of its divine causation.

In view of the form the tradition takes in Matt. 1^{18} and Luke 1^{35} a more likely origin of it would be a Christian preoccupation with, and explication of, the person and work of Jesus as uniquely 'the Son of God'. This already appears in the probably pre-Pauline formulation in Rom. 1$^{3-4}$. There Jesus is said to be God's Son, and this is then further defined as having been first humanly speaking (according to the flesh) of Davidic lineage, and after that designated or appointed 'Son of God in power', i.e. effective for what being Son of God entails; and this is by virtue of the eschatological act of resurrection to the new age, and is brought about 'according to a spirit of holiness', i.e. by the agency of holy spirit. In A. 13^{33} the text of the divine begetting of a son (Ps. 2^7) is also applied to the resurrection of Jesus; cf. in a different mode Heb. 5^5, and I John 5^{18} for Jesus as the one who had been begotten by God, and John 3^6 for begetting from flesh (man) and from spirit (God). In the synoptic tradition this divine begetting of Jesus through the holy spirit for his eschatological work has been retrojected into his baptism as the divine appointment to, and empowering for, his ministry (3$^{21-22}$; 4$^{1-21}$; Mark 1$^{9-15}$; Matt. 3$^{13-17}$; cf. John 1$^{33-34}$). The tradition of a miraculous conception could reflect a further retrojection, so that the divine begetting of Jesus through the spirit, now of necessity expressed in 'realistic' and quasi-physical terms (see note on the verbs in 1^{35}), shall govern his entire existence from birth. Illustrative here could be Gal. 4^{29}, where Isaac, though born of two human parents, is said to be 'born according to the spirit', i.e. by a special operation of God so as to be at the heart of his purposes. Illustrative also, though in a quite different mode and not as a direct background, might be Philo's use of the idea of divine impregnation of a virgin as an allegorical device for underlining the wholly divine source of the immortal qualities the patriarchs possessed as 'sons of God' (*On the Change of Names* 130–4; *On the Cherubim* 43–7, 49–52; *Allegories of the Laws* III, 219). In 1$^{26-35}$ Mary's virginity serves primarily to point to the existence of Jesus and his future function as entirely the product of the action of God. In Matthew it is not particularly stressed, being referred to in retrospect by the citation of Isa. 7^{14}, while it is conception through the Spirit that is communicated to Joseph in explanation of her pregnancy. In Luke, where it is more stressed by the repetition of 'virgin' in 1^{27} (though not as in later apocryphal and theological traditions, where it becomes the main point), her conception through the Spirit is treated to some extent as parallel to, even if exceeding, Elizabeth's conception by divine agency as an old but barren wife. Though later combined with the Pauline doctrine of the pre-existence of the Son of God, and with the Johannine doctrine of the incarnation of the eternal Word, as explanatory of them, it was different from them in origin and intention, as it was also from the genealogies. See further Brown, *Birth*, Appendix IV; Barrett, *Holy Spirit*, Part One, ch. 2.

∞

26

In the sixth month: This cannot have been the opening of an originally independent pericope as it dates the event by reference to Elizabeth's already mentioned
pregnancy (v. 24). It effects a continuation of narrative with vv. 5–25, and along
with v. 36 prepares for the further continuation in vv. 39–56. Thus the event is
part of an overall divine plan.

the angel Gabriel was sent from God: This also effects continuity with vv. 5–25,
though here Gabriel does not announce himself by name, and there is no
indication that Mary knows who he is.

a city of Galilee named Nazareth: Galilee, which is to figure, though less prominently than in Mark, as the scene of Jesus' ministry (cf. A.10³⁷; 13³¹), was a
region of Palestine stretching from Samaria and the Jordan in the south and
east to the borders of Syrian Phoenicia in the north and west. It still retained the
mixture of races that had earned it the epithet 'of the Gentiles' (Isa. 9¹; I Macc.
5¹⁵). The present Nazareth is a hillside town north of the plain of Esdraelon, but
it was so insignificant that it is not mentioned in the OT, in any Jewish talmudic
or midrashic writing, or by Josephus (cf. John 1⁴⁶). Its existence is now confirmed
by an inscription of the fourth century AD listing it among the residences of the
priestly courses (1⁵). It is here the village residence of Mary, and presumably of
Joseph (cf. 4¹⁶; Mark 1⁹, ²⁴), though this is not so in Matt. 1¹⁸ᶠᶠ·, where the
impression is that their home was at Bethlehem (Matt. 2¹¹), and their residence
at Nazareth a new departure long after the birth as the result of prophecy
(Matt. 2²²⁻²³).

27

a virgin betrothed: For the expression cf. Deut. 22²³. The Greek word *parthenos*
primarily denoted the bloom of youth, and was used of a young (generally
unmarried) girl with or without reference to virginity in the technical sense.
In view of v. 34 it is rightly rendered here by *virgin*. The dispute about it, dating
from at least the time of Justin (*Dial.* 43), arose with respect to Matt. 1¹⁸⁻²³ as to
whether the LXX translator was justified in so rendering the Hebrew word
'almâ = 'young girl' in Isa. 7¹⁴, and thus creating the possibility of a prophecy
of the virgin birth of the messiah. The precise significance of *betrothed* (*mnēs-
teuein*) is also not easily determined. According to Jewish sources (see Jeremias,
Jerusalem, pp. 367ff.) betrothal or consent, generally for girls at the age of twelve
and a half, was the beginning of the marriage procedure, i.e. the acquisition of
the woman by the man. It took the form of agreement before witnesses based
on the marriage contract and payment of the bride price; but it was more than
simply the first stage, since the betrothed was already called 'wife' (cf. Matt.
1²⁰, ²⁴), and as such could be divorced or punished for adultery. The marriage
was concluded, generally a year later, by cohabitation with the transfer of the

woman to the man's house, though there is some evidence for cohabitation before this (cf. Tobit 6–8, and the statement quoted by Jeremias, op. cit., p. 367, that a wife is acquired by money or by writ or by intercourse). Hence in Matt. 1¹⁸ 'betrothed to Joseph' is expressly glossed by 'before they came together'.

Joseph, of the house of David: So Matt. 1²⁰ in the angel's announcement to him of the virginal conception, as also the genealogy in Matt. 1⁶⁻¹⁶ and the subsequent events in Matt. 2. Here he plays no part. His Davidic lineage (for *of the house of David* = David's family, cf. I Kings 12¹⁹, etc.) which is referred to again in 2⁴; 3²³⁻³⁸, in both cases somewhat artificially, is mentioned here as somehow conferring Davidic descent on Jesus (cf. vv. 32–33; Rom. 1³; II Tim. 2⁸).

Mary: Here, as elsewhere in L–A and Matt. 13⁵⁵ *Mariam*, the LXX form of Miriam, Moses' sister (Exod. 15²⁰), but in 1⁴¹; 2¹⁹; Matt. 1¹⁶–2¹¹ the form is *Maria*.

28

came to: Greek 'entered', sc. into her house.

Hail, O favoured one: The Greek *chaire kecharitōmenē* has a certain assonance. The first word, the imperative of *chairein*, could mean (i) 'rejoice', the reason for the command being given in what follows (some would connect it closely with Zeph. 3¹⁴⁻¹⁷, and deduce that Mary is addressed as the equivalent of Sion; but this is unlikely), or (ii) *Hail*, a form of greeting in Greek literature (not LXX; cf. Mark 15¹⁸; Matt. 26⁴⁹; John 19³; A. 15²³). This is how it is regarded in v. 29, *what sort of greeting*. The second word is the perfect participle passive of *charitoun*, a rare and choice word (+ Eph. 1⁶; only Ecclus. 18¹⁷ in the LXX) connected with *charis* = 'grace', 'favour'. The apostrophe is thus of one who is already the object of divine choice. This is repeated in the causal clause in v. 30a. It raises the question 'favour for what?', and this is answered in vv. 32–35. ('Blessed are you among women' is a secondary addition to the text introduced from v. 42.)

the Lord is with you: This follows on from *favoured one*. For God 'to be with' someone is a common OT expression for divine assistance (cf. Gen. 21²⁰; 26³, etc., John 3²; A. 7⁹; 10³⁸; as a greeting in the OT only Judg. 6¹²; Ruth 2⁴). Since there is no verb the Greek could be rendered 'May the Lord be with you', but this is less likely in the context.

29–30

Though only a girl Mary is depicted as more intellectual than Zechariah (cf. 2¹⁹). Her reaction is not one of fear at the vision but of extreme perplexity (*greatly troubled* is an augmented form of the verb in v. 12) at the angel's statement (*logos*), and of pondering its implications. Hence *do not be afraid* is a somewhat formal and conventional element due to the pattern of such visions – for parallels in Greek poetry to this and to v. 28 in the approach of a god to a woman with whom he is to beget a child, cf. Aeschylus, *Prometheus Bound*, 647ff., 'O greatly happy maiden . . .' and Moschus, *Europa*, 154, 'Have courage, O virgin one, do not be afraid.' Here it simply enables the angel to explain.

31

And behold, you will conceive in your womb and bear a son: This is based on OT accounts: cf. Gen. 16¹¹, the angel of the Lord to Hagar, 'Behold, you have in the womb (are pregnant), and shall bear a son'; Judg. 13³⁻⁵, the angel of the Lord to Manoah's wife, 'Lo, you shall conceive and bear a son.' The verb *sullambanein* = 'to grasp' was used, either absolutely or with 'in the womb', in the technical sense of 'to conceive' in biblical and non-biblical literature. It is not indicated when Mary will conceive.

you shall call his name Jesus: For the command and its expression see v. 13. *Iēsous* is the Greek form of the common Jewish name Joshua = 'Yahweh saves', but it is not in the ethos of Luke's birth stories to draw out the significance of names for his Greek readers, not even the name of Jesus – contrast Matt. 1²¹, ²³.

32–33

A proclamation by the angel of the divine destiny of Jesus parallel to that of John (vv. 15–17). It is in four lines, v. 32a and v. 33 being chiastic, and is concerned with the future divine sonship of Jesus (repeated in v. 35), but even more with his 'messiahship' in the form of Davidic kingship.

32

He will be great: For *great* see on v. 15. It is repeated here without any qualification (cf. II Sam. 7⁹ of David).

will be called: Generally taken as 'called by men', but it could be a reverential passive meaning 'God will call him'; cf. the voice from heaven in 3²², 9³⁵.

the Son of the Most High: Or 'son of'; there is no article in the Greek. It need not mean, even in this context, 'begotten by' in a physical or metaphysical sense, but could retain the Semitic connotation of 'specially close to', 'obedient to', 'reproducing the character of', as with the disciple in 6³⁵, though here uniquely so, as in 3²²; 9³⁵. *the Most High (ho hupsistos)* as a title for God is, apart from Mark 5⁷, Heb. 7¹, confined to L–A in the NT (cf. v. 35, v. 76; 6³⁵, all without the article, and A. 7⁴⁸). Used absolutely and without the article, or in combination with Zeus or God, it is found in pagan literature (cf. A. 16¹⁷), but it was a standard epithet in the LXX for Yahweh as exalted, and belonged to Jewish religious speech; cf. Jubilees 16¹⁸; I Enoch 10¹; Josephus (*Ant.* 16.163), Philo (*Flaccus* 46).

will give him the throne of his father David: This could be an extension of 'Son of the Most High' expressed in terms of the Davidic king, who was called God's Son' (Ps. 2⁷). This was one form of the hope of Israel; cf. Ps. Sol. 17²³, 'Lord, raise up for them their king, the Son of David' – which was based on the promise in II Sam. 7¹²⁻¹⁴ of a son of God from David's line on the throne of his kingdom. For literal fulfilment Jesus as the Son of David (18³⁸; 20⁴¹) must have David as well as God for *his father*, and in the birth narratives this is established somewhat artificially through the line of Joseph.

33

This verse continues and explicates v. 32 with the permanence of the line of David and his rule (*kingdom* = kingship), promised in II Sam. 7¹³ and reiterated in e.g. Ps. 89³⁶ᶠ·; Isa. 9⁶ᶠ·. It is now interpreted as a perpetual rule of Jesus over *the house of Jacob*, an expression for Israel (Exod. 19³; Isa. 2⁵ᶠ·). Whether responsible for such statements himself, or reproducing a Jewish-Christian tradition which thought of Jesus in terms of a national and this-worldly eschatology, Luke will presumably have understood them in the sense they have in A. 13²²⁻³⁷. There Jesus, as the saviour provided by God for Israel, is of David's line, and is made God's Son by resurrection, through which he is also given, as now freed from mortality, 'the holy and sure blessings of David', so as to exercise a rule *for ever* and without *end*.

34

How can this be, since I have no husband?: This euphemistic translation is incorrect, and obscures the difficulties. The Greek is *epei*, the ordinary word for *since* (though strangely rare in the NT and only here in L–A); *ou ginōskō* = 'I do not know', where 'know' refers to sexual intercourse, as often in the LXX, but also in Greek authors, e.g. Plutarch, though generally used of the man (cf. Gen. 4¹; Matt. 1²⁵); *andra* = 'a man' or 'a husband'. Whether taken in a present or a future sense – 'since I do not have (shall not have had) sexual relations' – the verb denotes a condition that is the result of previous behaviour. It is remarkable that the question, though standing at the kernel of the story (for its omission by the Old Latin ms b see Creed, pp. 13f.), should be barely intelligible, and have led to such tortuous exegesis (on which see Fitzmyer, pp. 348ff., Brown, *Birth*, pp. 298ff.). For it would make sense only in a form of the story in which there was no mention of betrothal; since if Mary was betrothed to Joseph she would expect to have sexual relations with him in due course. Leaney (p. 21) supposes such a form, to which Luke added *betrothed* to bring it into line with 2¹ᶠᶠ·, where 'Joseph and Mary have no knowledge *before* Jesus' birth of His special origin and character'. It will hardly do to suggest that the question shows Mary to have understood the angel's words as referring to an immediate conception, whereas the end of the betrothal period, when she would have sexual relations with Joseph, might be some months ahead. Even more forced, and increasingly abandoned, is the patristic interpretation of the question as a vow of perpetual virginity – 'since I shall never know a man' – undertaken either on ascetic grounds, or through meditation on Isa. 7^{14}, and as an indication that her marriage was to be one in name only. Hence some scholars take the question as primarily a literary device, albeit a clumsy one, dictated by the pattern of such scenes, where angelic annunciation is always met by human incomprehension, which serves to continue the dialogue by providing an opportunity for the original announcement to be explicated (see Fitzmyer, pp. 348ff.).

35
The angel's reply is in four rhythmic lines, especially if 'of you' is read. What Mary is to understand by it, and how precisely it answers her question, are disputable.

The Holy Spirit will come upon you, and the power of the Most High will over-shadow you: Literally 'holy spirit . . . power of Most High' (see on v. 15, v. 32). These are equivalent expressions (for the conjunction of *spirit* and *power*, cf. v. 17), since 'the (holy) spirit of God' is a term for God himself as operating with effect in the world. The general force of the statement is that the conception and birth of Jesus for the fulfilment of his divine destiny will be entirely the work of God. What is implied as to this work by the verbs used is difficult to say, and perhaps cannot be said. In Matt. 1^{18} Mary is also said to be pregnant 'of' the Holy Spirit, where the preposition *ek* = 'from', 'out of' denotes cause or instrumentality, which could be understood as of a more concrete and direct, or a more indirect and figurative, kind. Similarly here the language is open to a more or a less metaphorical interpretation.

(i) *come upon (eperchesthai)* is, except for Eph. 2^7, James 5^1, confined to L–A in the NT. Apart from the neutral use in A. 14^{19} it has the hostile sense of persons or events invading or supervening, as in 11^{22}; 21^{26}; A. 8^{24}; 13^{40}. A close parallel, however, is A. 1^8 of the Spirit's 'coming upon' the apostles with physical accompaniments to produce in them ecstatic speech and prophecy. In the OT the Spirit, which is nowhere connected with begetting or conception, is said to 'come upon' Saul and David for prophecy or leadership (I Sam. 10^6; 16^{13}, though the verb there is the more violent, 'leap upon' as in A. 19^{16}). It is also said to 'come upon' Israel to produce fruitfulness in the desert (Isa. 32^{15} LXX, the Hebrew has 'poured upon'), and in Ezek. 37^{14} Yahweh 'puts' his spirit within Israel to bring new life from the dead. This is hardly sufficient basis for seeing (with Ellis, pp. 71f., Brown, *Birth*, p. 314) Mary's conception as inaugurating the 'new creation' (II Cor. 5^{17}) on the analogy of the Spirit's part in the first creation (Gen. 1^2; Ps. 104^{30}).
(ii) *overshadow (episkiazein)* occurs in the NT (apart from A. 5^{15}) only in accounts of the Transfiguration (9^{34}; Mark 9^7; Matt. 17^5) with reference to the

divine glory or 'being' (Shekinah) physically present in the cloud. This comes from the OT, where the divine glory as a cloud casts its shadow over Israel (Deut. 33^{12} LXX; Num. 10^{34}), over the tabernacle in the desert (Exod. 40$^{34f.}$; Num. 9^{18}), or Mount Sion (Isa. 4^5). There would seem to be in it a double symbolism of a protective covering against enemies and of proximity to the otherwise unapproachable divine presence with its sanctifying power (cf. 9^{34}: the disciples are afraid to go into the cloud, and it produces temporarily on the face of Moses and on the garments of Jesus the conditions of heavenly existence). Here, since Mary does not need protection, it is the latter. But of what kind is the proximity that it should produce the results stated? In Ezek. 16^8 'cover' is used with a more explicit sexual connotation of God's action towards Israel as a girl. Daube (*NTRJ*, pp. 27ff.) sees in the book of Ruth the background not only of the whole of this story, but specifically of the verb *overshadow* in Ruth's request to Boaz (3^9) 'spread your skirt over (i.e. have sexual relations with) your handmaid, for you are a redeemer', a request that rabbis later interpreted as having been made to God.

therefore: This is emphatic – *dio kai* = 'therefore indeed'. Its force depends on the interpretation of the preceding verbs. (i) If directed primarily to 'since I do not know a man', the meaning could be that in some way the Holy Spirit and the power of God 'beget' Jesus, with the result that, on the principle that like begets like (cf. John 3^6), he will be holy because begotten by holy spirit, and Son of God because God-begotten. (ii) If directed primarily to 'How can this be?', the meaning could be that the Holy Spirit and power of God will somehow attend Mary in her conception (whatever its circumstances) and in the birth of Jesus, and in doing so will enable him to fulfil the role of holy and Son of God that the angel has predicated of him. Only in the former does the operation of the Spirit in the birth of Jesus exceed that in the birth of John, who 'will be filled with the Holy Spirit, even from his mother's womb'; and only in this case is Jesus Son of God because virgin-born.

the child to be born: This renders *to gennōmenon* = 'that begotten', 'beget' being the usual meaning of the verb *gennān*. The emphasis would then be on the divine paternity. But used of the woman the verb can mean 'to bear' (so vv. 13, 57; 23^{29}), and so in the passive *to be born*, where the emphasis is on Mary's maternity (underlined further by the reading 'of (*ek*)you', cf. Matt. 1^{16}).

will be called holy, the Son of God: Gabriel reiterates his statement about Jesus in vv. 32–33, reinforcing it in the light of what he has just said in v. 35a. *holy* now replaces 'great' in view of the Holy Spirit's part in the conception, and *Son of God*, as a variant of *Son of the Most High*, reflects the divine paternity implied in it. But the juxtaposition, with *Son of God* in apposition to *holy*, is strange, since *holy* = 'separate', 'apart', applied to anyone or anything in a close relation to the holy God (cf. 2^{23}), and was not specially distinctive. Perhaps, despite the absence of the definite article, 'the Holy (One) of God' is intended; cf. the alternation of this with 'the Son of God' in the confession of the demons in 4³⁴, ⁴¹. Some would translate 'the holy thing to be born will be called . . .', though the word order does not favour this.

the Son of God: Or 'Son of God'; there is no definite article. This is the first mention in the Gospel of what was to become a distinctive term in Christian confession for the uniqueness of the person and work of Jesus (A. 9²⁰; John 1³⁴; 20³¹; II Cor. 1¹⁹; Gal. 4⁴; Heb. 4¹⁴; I John 4¹⁵; Rev. 2¹⁸). Its origins, usages and meanings continue to be debated.[a] Basic to the term on a Jewish background would be the force of the Hebrew idiom 'son of'. This could convey both God's choice for a specially close relationship with himself of one who was to do his will and reproduce his intentions, and also the response of obedience on the part of the one so chosen. In this sense it could be variously applied to angels (Gen. 6²; Job 1⁶), to the collectivity of Israel by virtue of its covenant relationship with Yahweh (Exod. 4²²⁻²³; Deut. 8⁵⁻⁶; Hos. 11¹), and, in accordance with the royal mythology adopted by Israel from outside, to the Davidic king as an embodiment of that relationship and its permanence (II Sam. 7¹¹⁻¹⁶; Ps. 2⁷, where appointment by adoption is expressed by 'beget', Ps. 89, esp. vv. 26–37; I Chron. 22¹⁰). In the Wisdom literature it came to be applied to individual righteous Israelites (Ecclus 4¹⁰; Wisd. 2¹²⁻¹⁸; 5⁵; cf. Luke 6³⁵). One text at Qumran (see Vermes, *Scrolls*, p. 244) shows that 'he shall be my son' of II Sam. 7¹⁴ was a subject of speculation, the person referred to being identified with 'the Branch of David' who will arise at the end of time with the Interpreter of the Law; while another (mutilated) fragment speaks of someone, not clearly identified, who is to be called the Son of God and Son of the Most High.[b] Vermes (*Jesus the Jew*, pp. 206ff.) cites later rabbinic texts in which holy and charismatic (miracle-working) figures such as Hanina ben Dosa are called God's son, and are accredited by God as such. There would seem so far to be no unequivocal evidence in Jewish sources for 'the Son of God' as a designation of an, or the, eschatological figure. It is this which appears in what may be the earliest form of Christian confession, Rom. 1³⁻⁴. There Jesus, who is of the line of David in his earthly existence, is, through his resurrection and with a view to his parousia (cf. I Thess. 1¹⁰), appointed the Son of God in power; and this involves the agency of holy spirit. There is a similar perspective, though without reference to the parousia, in A. 13¹⁶⁻⁴¹, where Jesus is physically descended from David, but is 'begotten' as the Son of God (Ps. 2⁷) by his resurrection (cf.

a See e.g. R. H. Fuller, *The Foundations of New Testament Christology* for an analysis of different strata, H. Conzelmann, *An Outline of the Theology of the New Testament*, London and New York 1969, pp. 76ff., and, with reference to previous discussions, M. Hengel, *The Son of God*, ET London and Philadelphia 1976.

b See J. A. Fitzmyer, 'The Contribution of Qumran Aramaic to the Study of the NT', *NTS* 20, 1973–74, pp. 391ff.

Heb. 5$^{5-10}$). In the gospel tradition a unique sonship is affirmed to be already operative within, and to be governing, Jesus' earthly ministry. The affirmation is made by the voice of God at two crucial points, his Baptism, when divine sonship is connected with a special endowment of the Holy Spirit (for healing?), and is taken in this sense by Satan (4$^{1ff.}$), and his Transfiguration, when (in anticipation of his parousia?) Jesus is temporarily invested with divine 'glory'. In Luke's account of the trial Jesus' divine sonship, which in Mark is combined with his messiahship (cf. also Matt. 16^{16}) becomes a separate issue (22$^{66-71}$). In Luke's birth narratives it is brought back further still. Here it embraces, and is defined in terms of, his conception by the agency of the Holy Spirit and the power of God (in Matt. 2^{15} this is barely glanced at). For all the reserve with which this is expressed it was bound then to approximate to the more physical idea of divine sonship characteristic of pagan religions.

36

The story takes an unexpected turn, passing abruptly from the exalted announcement of divine salvation to an individual domestic concern, though of such a kind as to bear on one aspect of that salvation. Uninvited the angel gives Mary a sign of the truth of his statement, and a supplementary answer to her question, by communicating to her as proof of the limitless power of God the miraculous conception of Elizabeth, to which he alone, apart from Elizabeth and Zechariah, is privy.

And behold: Cf. 1^{20} as introducing a corroborative sign.

kinswoman: *sungenis*, a feminine form of *sungenēs* = 'relative' without specifying the degree of kinship. Thus there emerges here alone, and almost casually, that along with the co-existence in Israel of two such religious figures as John and Jesus there was a physical relationship between them on the mothers' side.

37

A common religious dictum (cf. Mark 10^{27}; Job. 42^2), here possibly echoing Gen. 18^{14} – 'Can any thing (*rhēma*, as here) be impossible (*adunatein*, as here) with God (*para theō*, here *para tou theou*)?' In the context it relates to Elizabeth's barrenness, but originally it may have been a continuation and conclusion of the answer to Mary's question in vv. 30–35.

38

Behold, I am the handmaid of the Lord: Literally, 'Behold, the slave of the Lord'. There is no verb, and *handmaid* is *doulē* = female slave, the correlative of *kurios*, the master and owner of slaves (cf. Ruth 3^9).

let it be to me: *genoito*, one of the rare instances of the optative in the NT. The sense is: 'Let it happen to me as you have said.' This is not a statement of co-operation with divine action, which will take place anyway, but of acceptance of the angel's assertions as fact and a willing submission. This can be called faith (v. 45).

THE VISITATION

39*In those days Mary arose and went with haste into the hill country, to a city of Judah,* 40*and she entered the house of Zechariah and greeted Elizabeth.* 41*And when Elizabeth heard the greeting of Mary, the babe leaped in her womb; and Elizabeth was filled with the Holy Spirit* 42*and she exclaimed with a loud cry, 'Blessed are you among women, and blessed is the fruit of your womb!* 43*And why is this granted me, that the mother of my Lord should come to me?* 44*For behold, when the voice of your greeting came to my ears, the babe in my womb leaped for joy.* 45*And blessed is she who believed that there would be★ a fulfilment of what was spoken to her from the Lord.'*
    46*And Mary said,*
        'My soul magnifies the Lord,
    47*and my spirit rejoices in God my Saviour,*
    48*for he has regarded the low estate of his handmaiden.*
        For behold, henceforth all generations will call me blessed;
    49*for he who is mighty has done great things for me,*
        and holy is his name.
    50*And his mercy is on those who fear him*
        from generation to generation.
    51*He has shown strength with his arm,*
        he has scattered the proud in the imagination of their hearts,
    52*he has put down the mighty from their thrones,*
        and exalted those of low degree;
    53*he has filled the hungry with good things,*
        and the rich he has sent empty away.
    54*He has helped his servant Israel,*
        in remembrance of his mercy,
    55*as he spoke to our fathers,*
        to Abraham and to his posterity for ever.'
56*And Mary remained with her about three months, and returned to her home.*

    ★ Or *believed, for there will be*

This story is not an additional pieces of biographical anecdote of an intimate and personal kind. It is the linchpin from both a literary and theological point of view of the narrative of the conceptions and births of John and Jesus in parallel. For in consequence of the angel's communication to Mary in v. 36 these are now locked together by the encounter of the mothers of the two children concerned in the two previous separate annunciations; and this in such a way that the pre-eminence of the future Jesus is asserted in advance. The scene is not naturalistic, but is governed throughout by the supernatural and miraculous. In response to a normal greeting Elizabeth is inspired to discern, and to confirm from human lips, the divine revelation of the angel to Mary, and a normal movement of the child in her womb she interprets as its inspired recognition of the coming salvation years ahead. She joins Mary, the first Christian believer (v. 45), by acknowledging Jesus in advance of his birth (his conception?) with what was to become the distinctive Christian confession of him as 'my Lord'; and Mary in the Magnificat sets her personal destiny in the context of the ultimate purposes of God for Israel. This accords with the infancy narratives as a whole, where the future gospel is already contained in a nutshell, and is accepted in advance by the protagonists concerned.

The story is very Semitic in style, consisting largely of a series of paratactic sentences joined by 'and', and with the verbs at the beginning. Its phraseology is biblical and antique, but also elevated, as befits its subject matter. Since it cannot stand on its own but effects a transition, it was either written by Luke for the purpose, perhaps on the basis of an oral tradition but in a pronounced biblical style, or was taken from a written source with such a style, which had already combined the traditions of the births of John and Jesus.

ಚಿ

39
In those days . . . with haste: A rather strange combination; for the vague term *in those days,* cf. 6¹² etc., and for *meta spoudēs* = 'with haste', cf. Mark 6²⁵; Exod. 12¹¹. It seems to mean 'immediately'.

arose and went: A LXX expression, frequent in L–A. No motive is given for the journey (e.g. womanly concern), and while it is prepared for by the angel's words in v. 36 it was not commanded by them explicitly or implicitly. Indeed a journey to confirm them by establishing that Elizabeth was pregnant could be a sign of unbelief. The motive is literary and theological, viz. to bring the two women together as being both involved in a single plan of God, which will later take effect with the relationship between John and Jesus. The feasibility of such a journey of some eighty miles, taking perhaps four days, by a woman alone is not germane to this type of story.

the hill country: hē oreinē, an adjective presupposing *chōra* = 'region' used with an article as a noun. This is fairly frequent in the LXX, where, however, when not used of the central mountainous ridge running right down Palestine (Num. 13^{29}; Josh. 11^{16}), it refers to the uplands of a particular region (of Jericho, Josh. 2^{16}; of Judah, Josh. 20^7; cf. Josephus *BJ* 4.451, 'the hill country over against Jerusalem'). Probably 'of Judah' is to be supplied here, called 'the hill country of Judaea' in v. 65.

a city of Judah: This identifies the region of Zechariah's home (v. 23).

of Judah: Iouda seems to be the genitive of *Ioudas* (as in Matt. 2^6 = Micah 5^2; Heb. 8^8 = Jer. 31^{31}; Rev. 5^5). It is an old fashioned biblical name for Judaea as the land once belonging to the tribe of the patriarch Judah (II Sam. 2^1). This, together with the fact that the city remains unnamed, possibly points to the use of a source.

41
filled with the Holy Spirit: A further reference in the birth narratives to a special operation of the Holy Spirit (for the expression see v. 15). Here it is to endow the human agent with prophetic divination of events and their significance. It is to be repeated in v. 67; 2^{25ff}.

42
exclaimed with a loud cry: Emphatic language: *exclaimed, anaphōnein* + +, five times in the LXX, all of (loud) liturgical music; *cry, kraugē*, frequent in the LXX, generally of a loud lament to God; to introduce an extended utterance under plenary inspiration. This, in a variety of forms of expression – a beatitude in the second person, an interrogative self-reference, a causal explanation and a beatitude in the third person – extols Jesus as Lord and the author of salvation, and Mary as the mother of such and as the instrument of the divine purpose (vv. 42–45). The double beatitude in v. 42 is rhythmic. Plummer's arrangement (p. 27) of the rest metrically is not convincing.

Blessed are you among women: Blessed is *eulogemenē*, the passive participle of *eulogein* = 'to bless', generally of blessing, i.e. praising God, but also of blessing men, i.e. invoking the favour of God on them. Here it is not a wish but a statement of fact, and corresponds to *makarios*, the word of beatitude used in v. 45 (see on 6^{20}). It is thus from human lips the equivalent of the angel's 'O favoured one' (v. 28). *among women* gives the sense 'superlatively blessed' (so Judg. 5²⁴ of Jael; Judith 13¹⁸ of Judith; Song of Sol. 1⁸), here as the mother of *my Lord*.

the fruit of your womb: An OT expression (Gen. 30²; Lam. 2²⁰; Ps. 132¹¹), here for the offspring that 'blessed' Mary is certain to bear because by divine promise, whether already conceived or not.

43

why is this granted me . . .?: The superlative character of the double blessing is further conveyed by this deprecatory question (its form is Semitic, cf. II Sam. 24²¹), and by both parts of *the mother of my Lord*.

my Lord: The least that this could mean would be 'my master' (*kurios*) as from slaves to their owner or from pupils to a teacher, but neither applies here. It possibly denotes the royal messiah, as perhaps in Ps. 110¹ (in II Sam. 24²¹ it is used of the actual king). More likely it reflects the later Christian application of *my* (our, the) *Lord* to Jesus as a result of his resurrection (John 20²⁸; see on 2¹¹), which Elizabeth is here made to use prophetically.

44

What was narrated in v. 41 as event is now prophetically interpreted by Elizabeth – *for behold* and *the voice of . . . came to my ears* are in LXX style – as the grounds of her salutation. Verse 45 implies that Elizabeth knows the angel's words to Mary, but this is not necessarily because they had been part of Mary's *greeting*. Her recognition of Mary and Jesus are wholly inspired and miraculous. For she interprets a natural phenomenon of pregnancy, a movement of the child in the womb, as a leaping (*skirtan* + 6²³, with 'rejoice'; there is no connection with Gen. 25²²); and this as a supernatural witness conveyed to her by the unborn John, himself already inspired in her womb (v. 15), to the unborn Jesus as the author of the eschatological *joy* of salvation (*agalliāsis*, see on v. 14). The Christianizing of the Baptist as witness and subordinate to Jesus (cf. John 3²⁵⁻³⁰) is here read back to his conception and birth.

45

A third beatitude, not now addressed to Mary but formulated about her as the first Christian believer. The variant translations reflect the two possible meanings of *hoti*. (i) 'because' (so RSV margin 'for'), where *believed* is used absolutely in the sense of 'accepted as certain, however incredible' to sum up Mary's whole attitude (contrast Zechariah's unbelief in asking 'how?', v. 18). Such belief is blessed because it pre-empts the future and goes along with what will certainly happen by divine determination. (ii) *that* (RSV text) states this in a more pedestrian manner as the content of what she believed.

The first of the 'canticles', exhibiting both common and individual features. (i) Its character. It may be classified as a 'declarative psalm of praise', i.e. a declaration of the praise of God followed by a statement of the reason for this praise in an action of God (see p. 41); but it is a diffuse form of this. An initial utterance of praise in poetic parallelism (vv. 46–47) is here followed by three successive causal statements, two in the past tense and one in the future (*for, hoti* = 'because' v. 48a, *For behold*, v. 48b, *for, hoti* = 'because' v. 49a). These issue in two generic statements about God in the present tense loosely connected by *and* (v. 49b, v. 50), which are followed by three rhythmic couplets referring to particular divine actions in the past, the first with synthetic, the second and third, which are closely connected and chiastic, with antithetical parallelism (v. 51, v. 52, v. 53). A summarizing conclusion (vv. 54–55) is without rhythm or parallelism. Analyses into a more compact structure with a more connected sequence of thought, such as two equal strophes with introduction and conclusion (Brown, *Birth*, pp. 355ff.), or four strophes (Plummer, p. 31), are not compelling.

(ii) Its position. It is only loosely attached to the narrative, which would not be disturbed by its removal. The change of speaker with *And Mary said* (v. 46) is abrupt, and provides no basis for an utterance of Mary at this point, e.g. divine inspiration, as at v. 67; 2$^{26ff.}$, while the concluding *And Mary remained with her* (v. 56) is awkward, since *her* refers back to Elizabeth as the speaker in vv. 42–45. This loose attachment is underlined by a textual variant. *Mary said* is given by almost the entire ms tradition and that of the Fathers, but *Elizabeth said* is the reading of representatives of the Western tradition – the Old Latin mss a b l, mss of the Latin text of Irenaeus, *Against Heresies* IV, 7.1, and of Origen's *Homily on Luke*, 7, and the text of a sermon of Niceta of Remesiana (A. von Harnack suggested an original 'she said', which was taken correctly of Elizabeth and incorrectly of Mary). Since reasons can be suggested for an alteration of Elizabeth to Mary, but none except scribal blunder for the reverse, this reading has been, and still is, espoused by some scholars.[c] Further, the contents could fit

c For a review of the debate see S. Benko, 'The Magnificat: A History of the Controversy', *JBL* 86, 1967, pp. 263–75.

Elizabeth better if *the low estate* (*tapeinōsis*, v. 48a) refers to barrenness, as it does in the statement of Hannah (I Sam. 1¹¹), upon whose song (I Sam. 2¹⁻¹⁰) the Magnificat is to some extent modelled. Against this reading, apart from the overwhelming weight of the textual evidence, is that for Elizabeth to pass straight from ecastatic praise addressed to Mary as blessed among women to speech about herself as the one who will be called blessed would be forced. The canticle can be understood in its context (attempts to place it elsewhere are not convincing) as Mary's hymn of praise for her destiny, located, not as might have been expected at the annunciation itself, but, as with the Benedictus, at a specific occasion arising from that, viz. the salutation of Elizabeth (a comparison has been made with Judith, who is saluted as blessed among women in Judith 13¹⁸ᶠᶠ·, and responds with a canticle in Judith 16¹⁻¹⁷). Nevertheless the fact that there can be such a debate is 'eloquent proof of the non-specific character of the canticle' (Brown, *Birth*, p. 348), while the awkwardness of v. 56 is taken by S. Farris (*The Hymns of Luke's Infancy Narratives*, p. 111) as 'a sign that the Magnificat was secondarily inserted into its present context'.

(iii) Its origin. That it is a transcript of what was spontaneously uttered by Mary (in Aramaic or Hebrew?) on a particular occasion and repeated verbatim (in Greek translation?) in tradition as part of a narrative so as to reach Luke in that form is a scarcely tenable hypothesis (see Fitzmyer, p. 359). If so, how is its composition as a separate and independent unit to be accounted for? If Luke himself composed it in Greek – there is no compelling evidence for its being a translation – and on OT models (for the scholars who have proposed this, see S. Farris, op. cit., p. 162, nn. 7 and 9), it might have been expected to match more closely the context for which he composed it, and to show clearer marks of his hand. The latter consideration is complicated by the difficulty of establishing what would be Lukan vocabulary here over and above the LXX phraseology which he can adopt, and of which the canticle is largely composed (see the critique in S. Farris, op. cit., pp. 21ff., of A. von Harnack's analysis in favour of Lukan composition). If Luke did not compose it, but incorporated it into his narrative (at a later stage, so Brown, *Birth*, p. 349), how and where did it originate as a hymn which combines the praise of God by the speaker for her own personal benefits with a wider praise of him for his acts of redemption towards Israel in the past? And all this in what is largely a cento of OT commonplaces – for the parallels see the Notes, and in tabular form Creed, pp. 303f., and Brown, *Birth*, pp. 358ff. A closely related question is how the past tenses of the verbs are to be understood. These have been taken as 'gnomic' aorists with a present sense conveying what is permanently characteristic of God (as do the present tenses in vv. 49b–50); or, but only if it is a translation, they have been taken to render in Greek the Hebrew prophetic perfect, by which future (eschatological) events were spoken of as if they had already happened. In either case the psalm could be simply Jewish. But *has regarded* and *has done* (vv. 49–50) appear to be genuine aorists referring to specific events in the past, as may the others also. In pursuance of this question Brown (op. cit., pp. 349ff.) is led to postulate an origin in a Jewish Christian community of the Anawim or Poor Ones. It was a Jewish Christian community, since only they would be in a position to celebrate a recent past event, the whole event of Christ and not simply his birth, as constituting their salvation, which is given in hymnic form an interpretation somewhat similar to that given in kerygmatic form in the speeches in A. (A. 3[17–26]; 10[34–43]; 13[26–41]). It is a community of the Poor Ones since it breathes a Hasidean piety of the pious poor such as is found notably in psalms of the OT and of the intertestamental period, as also at Qumran, where the speaker can praise God for what has happened to the whole community as the 'poor ones' (cf. Ps. 37, 1QM 11[9], 1QH 3, 5 – Vermes, *Scrolls*, pp. 241f., 138, 156, 159). Such a psalm on the lips of Mary makes her a representative of this piety and an interpreter of the birth of Jesus as anticipatory of the whole gospel, which has been revealed to her in advance (vv. 31–35). This does not, however, get rid of the artificiality that the personal benefit for which Mary praises God is not parallel to, or a participation in, the salvation of Israel, but the cause of it; nor is her elevation to be the mother of the messiah parallel to, or a particular instance of, the elevation of the poor through the overthrow of the mighty or the supply of the hungry through the rejection of the rich. It may be that the model here, in general scope as well as in detail, is the Song of Hannah, a royal psalm in which 'although attributed to her, there is only one line that is even remotely relevant to Hannah's situation . . . The opening verse celebrates a triumph over enemies with the help of Yahweh, and there follows a hymn of praise to Yahweh who controls human lives and fortunes.'[d]

d L. H. Brockington, *Peake's Commentary*, rev. ed. by M. Black and H. H. Rowley, London and New York 1962, p. 319.

৩৩

46–47

An individual statement of exultation and praise in synthetic parallelism (cf. I Sam. 2¹). *soul* (*psuchē*) and *spirit* (*pneuma*) are synonymous expressions for the self (cf. Isa. 26⁹; Ps. 77²ᶠ·). *magnifies* (*megalunein* = 'to make great' in the sense of 'extol' + A. 5¹³; 10⁴⁶; 19¹⁷; Phil. 1²⁰; frequent in the OT, and esp. the Psalms, cf. Ps. 34³) is taken up by *rejoices* (*agalliān*; see on 1¹⁴; so in Pss. 35⁹; 40¹⁶; 70⁴), though strangely this verb is in the aorist. *the Lord* = Yahweh is taken up by *God*, characterized, as often in the OT, as *saviour*, i.e. the author of salvation or deliverance from enemies, oppression or afflictions (cf. I Sam. 2¹; Ps. 25⁵; Hab. 3¹⁸). This is a note of the Lukan birth narratives (1⁶⁹, ⁷¹, ⁷⁷, 2³⁰), though neither here nor in what follows is it said in what sense God has been Mary's saviour.

48

The praise in vv. 46–47 could be followed naturally by the reason for it in v. 49. Here two causal statements are first made which are individual to Mary as the speaker, both with reference to a model mother in Israel. They are somewhat forced, and could be an insertion by Luke (*For behold, henceforth – apo tou nun –* and *generations* could betray his hand) to make a connection with the surrounding context (*handmaiden*, cf. 1³⁸, *call me blessed*, cf. 1⁴²⁻⁴⁵), and by implication to identify the salvation being extolled with that to be brought about by Mary's son (1³²⁻³⁵).

he has regarded the low estate of his handmaiden : This corresponds almost verbatim with Hannah's address to God (I Sam. 1¹¹). But there *low estate* (*tapeinōsis*) = '(state of) humiliation' refers to her 'affliction' of barrenness (as also in Gen. 16¹¹; 29³²; 31⁴²). This cannot apply here, nor can the wider meaning that the word can bear of the oppression from which God delivers (Deut. 26⁷; Judith 6¹⁹; Ps. 31¹⁷ etc.). In being chosen as the mother of the messiah Mary is hardly the prototype of those of *low degree* (*tapeinous*) who are advanced through the divine act of reversal in overthrowing rulers (v. 52).

all generations will call me blessed : This echoes the words of Leah 'for all (the) women will call me blessed' (Gen. 30¹³ LXX). In the context it expresses the uniqueness and the universality of the salvation, which – though this is only implied and not stated – will be brought through the birth of her son.

49a

As it stands this is an additional ground for praise in the *great things* (*megala*, cf. *magnifies* in v. 46) which *he who is mighty* (*ho dunatos*, not elsewhere in the NT of God as a warrior, and in the OT only Zeph. 3¹⁷) has done (cf. Deut. 10²¹). But while this leads naturally to the amplifications in vv. 51–55, it is not evident what it can refer to in Mary's case (securing her pregnancy? or that her child will be what is said of him in vv. 32–33?).

49b–50
Two loosely appended conclusions of a general kind about the character of God as seen in his actions (cf. the sequence in I Sam. 2¹⁻²). That God's *name* is *holy*, i.e. that he is himself distinct from any other, is a core of Jewish piety (cf. Ps. 111⁹, holy because doing great things). That his *mercy*, i.e. his covenant love, operates continually (*from generation to generation*, lit. 'to generations and generations', is without exact parallel) towards *those who fear him* is a commonplace of the psalms both inside and outside the OT (cf. Pss. 103¹⁷; 111⁴⁻⁹; Pss. Sol. 2³³; 13¹²; 15¹³). *those who fear him* comes last in the sentence in the Greek, and it has been suggested that it should begin the next sentence, thus improving the rhythm of both v. 50 and v. 51.

51–53
Mary's praise is now for God's actions in the past. These are described in OT language, but are not further specified.

51
he has shown strength with his arm: God is depicted as a warrior. *shown strength* (lit. 'has done strength') is not Greek, but there is a parallel in Ps. 118¹⁵. God's *arm* is a common OT symbol for his effective power; cf. Ps. Sol. 17³, a psalm of the future kingdom of the Son of David: 'We hope in God our saviour, for the might of our God is for ever with mercy.'

has scattered the proud: For the sequence of thought, cf. I Sam. 2³⁻⁴. *scattered* (*diaskorpizein*) is common in the LXX, and esp. in the Psalms, for Yahweh's action towards his enemies. *the proud* (*huperēphanoi*), with its cognates, is particularly frequent in the Psalms and the Wisdom literature for the enemies of God as being arrogant, self-sufficient and unwilling to acknowledge his sovereignty (cf. Isa. 2¹²; 13¹¹; Ps. Sol. 17⁸, the proud have laid waste the throne of David). While rare in the NT (+ Rom. 1³⁰; II Tim. 3²; James 4⁶ and I Peter 5⁵, quoting Prov. 3³⁴), it could here refer to the opponents deemed proud in this sense (e.g. Pharisees) with whom the gospel is presented as being in victorious conflict.

in the imagination of their hearts: Rather 'in the thought (*dianoia* = 'way of thinking') of their minds', a Semitic expression; cf. Ps. Sol. 17¹⁵, 'the (foreign) enemy acted proudly, and his heart was alien from our God.'

52
The divine reversal of status and fortunes in the abasement of the lofty and the corresponding exaltation of the lowly is a common OT theme, and is variously

stated (cf. Ps. 18²⁷; Ecclus 10¹⁴). The same language could later state a principle of the gospel (e.g. 14¹¹; 18¹⁴; Phil. 2⁸⁻⁹; James 1⁹ᶠ·). It is not evident what is being referred to here.

has put down the mighty from their thrones: There is no exact parallel to this in the OT, but cf. Ecclus 10¹⁴, where the lowly take the place of the rulers (*dunastēs*, the word used here). In I Sam. 2²⁻⁸ they are exalted to join them. This can hardly apply to either Mary or the Christian gospel.

those of low degree: tapeinos (see on v. 48). This word is found in the OT in conjunction with, and as a synonym for, the needy, those of low social status, who are the opposite of the wealthy in Israel, and are oppressed by them (cf. Pss. 82³; 10¹⁸; Isa. 11⁴, etc.). Exaltation of such would be to a position of power, independence and self-sufficiency. Condemnation of wealth and the blessing of the poor is marked in Luke. But the word could be used for those who, as the antithesis of the proud, were humbly dependent on God and looked to him for succour. Exaltation of such would be to some favoured relationship with God, but this is not specified here.

53
The reversal is continued in terms of God's replenishment of the hungry (Ps. 107⁹, fills with good things, Ps. 146⁷) and his deprivation of the rich. For this sequence of thought, but in reverse order, cf. I Sam. 2⁵⁻⁸, and the Lukan beatitudes and woes (6²⁰⁻²¹, ²⁴⁻²⁵), where the language appears to be literal. There the reversal is part of the eschatological promise of the kingdom; here it is represented as having taken place.

54–55
The previous divine action (actions) is now summarized in LXX language as the scripturally promised deliverance of Israel (cf. vv. 68–70; 2³⁰ᶠ·; A. 3¹⁵⁻²⁶; 5²⁹⁻³²; 10³⁴⁻⁴³; 13¹⁶⁻⁴¹).

54
helped: antilambanesthai = 'take hold of' (+ A. 20³⁵ in the sense of 'help') is a regular word in the OT, and esp. the Psalms, for Yahweh's succour both of the individual Israelite and of the nation.

his servant Israel: for this expression see Isa. 41⁸; 44¹, etc. Here it is unreflective, since the proud and rich who have been rejected were themselves members of Israel. Nevertheless their removal has served to purify Israel as the people of God.

in remembrance of his mercy: In the Greek 'to remember', an explanatory infinitive (cf. v. 72). In acting so God calls to mind his covenant relationship with Israel (cf. Ps. 98³).

55

This could be a revised version of the concluding words of Micah (7^{20}), where God's steadfast love will be shown to Jacob (= Israel), further defined as to Abraham (here *to Abraham and to his posterity*), and as in accordance with a past oath to *our fathers* from of old (here ecstatically as being *for ever*).

56

This editorial notice – Luke favours *about* with numbers (cf. 3^{23}; 9$^{14, 28}$; A. 1^{15}), *returned* (*hupostrephein*) is his word – removes Mary from the scene (cf. vv. 23, 38) at the latest possible time in Elizabeth's pregnancy to allow the birth of John to be narrated as a separate incident.

I$^{57-80}$ THE BIRTH, NAMING AND PRAISE OF JOHN

^{57}*Now the time came for Elizabeth to be delivered, and she gave birth to a son.* ^{58}*And her neighbours and kinsfolk heard that the Lord had shown great mercy to her, and they rejoiced with her.* ^{59}*And on the eighth day they came to circumcise the child; and they would have named him Zechariah after his father,* ^{60}*but his mother said, 'Not so; he shall be called John.'* ^{61}*And they said to her, 'None of your kindred is called by this name.'* ^{62}*And they made signs to his father, inquiring what he would have him called.* ^{63}*And he asked for a writing tablet, and wrote, 'His name is John.' And they all marvelled.* ^{64}*And immediately his mouth was opened and his tongue loosed, and he spoke, blessing God.* ^{65}*And fear came on all their neighbours. And all these things were talked about through all the hill country of Judea;* ^{66}*and all who heard them laid them up in their hearts, saying, 'What then will this child be?' For the hand of the Lord was with him.*

^{67}*And his father Zechariah was filled with the Holy Spirit, and prophesied, saying,*

^{68}*'Blessed be the Lord God of Israel,*
    for he has visited and redeemed his people,
^{69}*and has raised up a horn of salvation for us*
    in the house of his servant David,
^{70}*as he spoke by the mouth of his holy prophets from of old,*
^{71}*that we should be saved from our enemies,*
    and from the hand of all who hate us;

^{72}to perform the mercy promised to our fathers,
   and to remember his holy covenant,
   ^{73}the oath which he swore to our father Abraham, ^{74}to grant us
   that we, being delivered from the hand of our enemies,
   might serve him without fear,
   ^{75}in holiness and righteousness before him all the days of our life.
   ^{76}And you, child, will be called the prophet of the Most High;
   for you will go before the Lord to prepare his ways,
   ^{77}to give knowledge of salvation to his people
   in the forgiveness of their sins,
   ^{78}through the tender mercy of our God,
   when the day shall dawn upon* us from on high
   ^{79}to give light to those who sit in darkness and in the shadow of
      death,
   to guide our feet into the way of peace.'
^{80}And the child grew and became strong in spirit, and he was in the wilderness
till the day of his manifestation to Israel.

* Or *whereby the dayspring will visit* Other ancient authorities read
since the dayspring has visited

This section returns to the perspective of vv. 5–25, following more
naturally after vv. 24–25 than after v. 56, and could originally have belonged with it. In an artistic and dramatic narrative it continues the
combination of the human with the supernatural and miraculous that
had marked the annunciation of John's conception into the circumstances of his birth, or rather of his naming – contrast the matching
narrative in 2$^{8-21}$, where the miraculous events attend the birth and the
naming is simply mentioned. The Benedictus, which sets John in the
context of divine purpose and promise (cf. the Magnificat), is linked
with the narrative as the prophetic utterance of Zechariah on his divine
release from his divinely caused dumbness in view of his faithful
adherence to the name already prescribed by God.

ଚଉ

57
the time came for: Lit. 'the time was filled for' – see on v. 23 for Luke's use of 'fill'
with time. It is hardly, as Brown alleges (*Birth*, p. 368), an echo of Gen. 25^{24},
where wording and construction differ.

58

Apparently Elizabeth has been able to maintain the concealment of her pregnancy (v. 24) to the end, so that neighbours and relatives discover her to be a mother only at the birth. This is wholly improbable, but it serves to impart a certain quality of the marvellous to the story at the outset.

has shown mercy: Lit. 'has magnified (*megalunein* = 'make great', but in a different sense from v. 46) his mercy with her' (*eleos,* cf. 10^{37}, the only other instance in L–A of the word in connection with an individual).

rejoiced with her: At the deliverance from barrenness; not in fulfilment of v. 14, which is a rejoicing at John's having been born in view of what he becomes.

59

This further sets the scene, though not without artificiality.

on the eighth day they came to circumcise: The construction is *egeneto* with a verb in the indicative; see on v. 8. This refers to the law's injunction of circumcision on the eighth day after birth (Lev. 12^3). It was a token of membership of the covenant people with its benefits and obligations, and was based on God's command to Abraham (Gen. 17$^{10-14}$). It took precedence over any other commandment (cf. John 7$^{22-23}$).

the child: to paidion as in vv. 66, 76, 80, rather than *to brephos* = 'the babe' as in vv. 41, 44; 2$^{12, 16}$. Fitzmyer (p. 380) sees it as probable evidence of a source.

they would have named him Zechariah after his father: There are three difficulties here. (i) Naming appears to have taken place at birth (cf. Gen. 4^{25}; 21^3, etc.); naming at circumcision is not attested in Judaism until the eighth century AD (SB II, p. 107). Some have suggested that Luke here assimilates to a Hellenistic practice of naming seven or ten days after birth. (ii) *they* refers to the previous neighbours and kinsfolk, but there is no evidence, nor is it at all likely, that they had any standing in the matter of naming another's child. Here they are introduced with their human suggestions to provide a foil to the parents who are obedient to divine revelation. (iii) Naming after the father was in fact rare.

60–64

A dramatic and circumstantial scene. There is no indication that it centres on any mention of the name John (see on v. 13), or that the reader is supposed to know that it meant 'Yahweh has shown favour'. The focus of the story is the conflict between natural and human suggestion and miraculous and divine revelation.

61

Elizabeth, as the parent able to speak, is the first spokesman. She makes a blunt reply *Not so* (*ouchi alla* = 'not at all but') *he shall be called John*. It is perhaps to be understood that Zechariah had already communicated this somehow to Elizabeth, but the narrative may intend to convey that Elizabeth has been divinely inspired at this moment to know the name.

62

In response to the objection that the name is one unknown in the family the father is appealed to as the ultimate source of authority. The language here is Luke's – *made signs, enneuein* + + (because *kōphos* in v. 22 means 'deaf and dumb'?); *what he would have* is an articular interrogative (*to ti*, as in 19^{48}; 22$^{2, 4, 24}$; A. 4^{21}; 22^{30}) with the rare optative (as in 9^{46}; 22^{23}).

63

writing tablet: The diminutive *pinakidion*, only here in the Greek Bible. It was of wood covered with wax (parchment, Lagrange).

they all marvelled: At the concurrence of the parents over such a name. This imparts the quality of miracle; cf. 8^{25}; 9^{43}; 11^{14}.

64

For his faithfulness in these circumstances to the angelic message Zechariah is miraculously released from the punishment for his previous disbelief, as the angel had predicted – *until the day that these things come to pass* (v. 20). This is stressed by *immediately* (the first occurrence of the Lukan *parachrēma*), and by the emphatic zeugma – lit. 'his mouth was opened and his tongue' (*was loosed* is not in the Greek).

65–66

The Benedictus could have followed here as the content of what Zechariah *spoke, blessing God* (v. 64), but Luke first gives in his own language (note the typical repetition of *all*) a series of reactions to the whole event, stretching from annunciation to naming, which characterize it as miracle, and give it wide publicity leading to continuing speculation about John.

65

fear came on all their neighbours: As at a miracle; cf. 5^{26}; 7^{16}; A. 19^{17}.

these things: ta rhēmata tauta, cf. 2$^{19, 51}$; A. 5^{32}; 13^{42}. *were talked about, dialalein* + 6^{11}.

66

laid them up in their hearts: tithenai = 'place', 'retain', with 'in their hearts =

minds', a LXX expression, + 21^{14}; A. 5^4 (with 'ears' 9^{44}). It was not passing gossip.

What will this child be? : Because of the circumstances of his birth; but the following *For* suggests that marks of divine favour were already evident in him.

the hand of the Lord was with him: A LXX expression for success under divine direction (cf. II Sam. 3^{12}; A. 11^{21}). This is a statement of Luke, not of those who ask the previous question. It looks forward to v. 80 which itself looks forward to 3$^{1ff.}$.

67

And his father Zechariah: An awkward resumption after vv. 65–66, so that the canticle appears as an addition, and it is not clear when Zechariah uttered it.

was filled with the Holy Spirit, and prophesied: In this introduction Luke underlines his theme of a renewal of the spirit and prophecy as attending the births of John and Jesus; cf. v. 41; 2$^{25ff.}$; for 'filled with holy spirit', as here, see on v. 15. By prophecy must be meant here recognition of divine action and truth as well as discernment of the future (cf. vv. 41–45).

68–79

The second canticle, the Benedictus, resembles the first, the Magnificat (vv. 46–55), in being basically a psalm of praise with accompanying grounds (see p. 141); in combining, though in reverse order, a general praise of God for past actions with statement of a more individual kind; and in being largely a cento of OT expressions (see notes, and in tabular form Creed, pp. 305f.; Brown, *Birth*, pp. 386ff.). And while there is here no doubt as to its speaker, it is oddly placed after v. 67 rather than after v. 64, and is relatively independent of its context (v. 80 could follow after v. 66). It is, however, distinctive in certain respects.

(i) The general section, vv. 68–75, is less structured than the Magnificat with a paucity of rhythmical couplets or balanced parallel statement. It is, in effect, a single sentence made up of a succession of loosely connected assertions in the past tense celebrating for Israel (*we, us, our*) God's redemption of his people (v. 68). Hence it 'gives the impression of a rather ramshackle construction. There is no great distinction, in reality, between the saving act itself and the result of the act. Rather, one amplifying description of the act is piled on another' (S. Farris, op. cit., p. 133). Attempts to establish a more compact structure – e.g. of two equal strophes with balanced ideas (Brown, *Birth*, p. 382) – are not compelling.

(ii) In the individual section, vv. 76–79, which alone links the canticle to its setting, there is an abrupt change of style with an address to the infant John, and with verbs in the future tense referring to his role. This is without biblical parallel, and has been compared to the Hellenistic *genethliakon*, or birthday ode in honour of a child; though in vv. 78–79 a return is made to the manner of vv. 68–75.

Despite the differences of these two parts the canticle is judged by many a unitary composition,[e] though for some the child addressed was originally Jesus,[f] and in the view of Sahlin, *Messias*, p. 287, Leaney, pp. 24f. was originally spoken about him by Anna (2²⁸). Another widely held view is that an original (Jewish or Jewish-Christian) composition, vv. 68–75, ending with *all the days of our life*, has been supplemented by vv. 76–77 to adapt it to the context of John's birth. Another is that an original canticle comprising vv. 68–75, 78 (77)–79 has been edited by Luke with the addition of v. 76 (so Bultmann, *History*, p. 296) or of vv. 76–77 (so Brown, *Birth*, p. 381), where the language could reflect a Christian estimation of John in Lukan form; cf. 3²⁻⁶ = Mark 1³⁻⁴; A. 13²⁴.

A further distinction is that the actions of God that are praised include, or even consist in, the appearance of the Davidic messianic saviour (v. 69, and possibly v. 78), and are described in martial language as deliverance of Israel from her enemies. If the past tenses are genuine aorists and not, as has been suggested, instances of the prophetic future, then the canticle, if not composed by Luke, can only have emanated from a community that believed the Davidic messiah to have come. Unless this was a Baptist community which believed John to have been that messiah (so P. Winter and others; cf. 3¹⁵; John 1⁶⁻⁸, ¹⁹ff.), it can only have been a Christian, or more precisely a Jewish-Christian, community. Zechariah is then made the mouthpiece of this belief, and in the context speaks in the light of the angel's words about Jesus as the Davidic messiah (vv. 32–33), and sets John from birth in relation to him as such. It nevertheless remains awkward that Zechariah passes so abruptly from a past deliverance to John's future part in it; that no distinction is made between the believing community which celebrates this salvation and Israel as a whole; and that the salvation should be described in martial terms, which in the context cannot refer to actual happenings but can only be stereotyped OT expressions.

68

Blessed be the Lord God of Israel: Lit. 'Blessed Lord the God of Israel', as at the conclusion, not the opening, of Ps. 41 (v. 13); Ps. 72 (v. 18); Ps. 106 (v. 48). Cf. also I Kings 1⁴⁸, David's blessing. *blessed, eulogētos*, only here in L–A, is the familiar form of the Jewish *berakah* or blessing of God (v. 64) through praise

e See D. R. Jones, 'The Background and Character of the Lucan Psalms', *JTS* ns 19, 1968, p. 34.

f So L. Gaston, *No Stone on Another*, *NovTest* Suppl. 23, 1970; J. A. T. Robinson, 'Elijah, John and Jesus: an Essay in Detection', *NTS* 4, 1957–58, pp. 280f. (reprinted in *Twelve New Testament Studies*, SBT 34, 1962, pp. 28–52).

and thanksgiving. The verb has to be supplied, either the hortatory subjunctive *be*, or, as perhaps here in view of the confident declaration of God's acts, the indicative 'is'. 1QM 14⁴ (Vermes, *Scrolls*, p. 142) shows this form with a similar combination of 'salvation', 'covenant' and 'redemption' as possibly a living liturgical tradition.

visited: episkeptesthai, the ordinary word for 'visit', as in A. 7²³; 15³⁶, or 'inspect', 'examine', as in A. 6³, but often in the LXX for God's action in examining his people, either for judgment or, generally, for their good (cf. 7¹⁶).

redeemed: Lit. 'made a redemption for', which is without exact parallel (cf. Ps. 111⁹ 'sent redemption'). *redemption, lutrōsis*, + 2³⁸; Heb. 9¹², with its cognates (e.g. the verb, 24²¹; Titus 2¹⁴; I Peter 1¹⁸) had a technical meaning of the ransom by payment of captives and slaves, but also a wider meaning of deliverance from various kinds of captivity.

his people: Israel as a whole, with whom the speaker identifies himself, though if the redemption being celebrated is brought through Jesus, that was largely rejected by Israel.

69

And has raised up: And may be explanatory = 'in that'. *raised up, egeirein*, is frequent in the OT of God's providential action, and means 'bring into effective existence' (cf. Judg. 2¹⁶; A. 13²²).

a horn of salvation: A Semitic expression in which the noun *horn*, a symbol of power derived from horned animals (cf. Ps. 89¹⁷), acts adjectivally, and *of salvation* = 'effecting salvation' acts as a noun. The meaning is 'powerful saviour'.

salvation: Repeated in vv. 71, 77. Though only once in the gospel on the lips of Jesus (see on 19¹⁻⁹ for its meaning and biblical background) it is an important word for Luke as a designation of the results of the Christian message (A. 4¹²; 13²⁶; 16¹⁷), as is also the equivalent *to sōterion* = 'the saving thing' in 2³⁰; 3⁶; A. 28²⁸. In Luke alone of the synoptists is Jesus called 'saviour' (see on 2¹¹).

in the house of his servant David: horn appears to have had a semi-technical and personalized sense in association with David and his line; cf. I Sam. 2¹⁰ LXX, 'the horn of his anointed'; Ps. 132¹⁷ in connection with salvation; Ezek. 29²¹. Cf. also the fifteenth benediction, 'Cause the shoot of David to spring up speedily, and raise his horn in your salvation . . . Blessed art thou, Lord, who causest the horn of salvation to shoot forth.'

his servant: For David as the servant of the Lord cf. Isa. 37³⁵; Ps. 18 (heading); A. 4²⁵; *Didache* 9²; the last three are liturgical.

70

The only qualifying clause in the canticle, which either runs on from the previous verse or is a parenthesis. It is unrhythmical and somewhat prosaic. Fitzmyer (p. 384) sees it as a Lukan addition establishing a favourite Lukan theme of the Christian salvation as the fulfilment of prophecy. In favour of this could be the language – *by the mouth of* is a Lukan expression (cf. A. 1¹⁶; 3¹⁸, ²¹; 4²⁵; 15⁷) and the stylistic word order – lit. 'the holy from of old prophets of him' occurs again at A. 3²¹. *the holy prophets*, + A. 3²¹; II Peter 3², is a pious expression of later Judaism (Wisd. 11¹; II Baruch 85¹).

71

that we should be saved: Lit. 'a salvation'. This begins a series of statements in apposition amplifying the redemption. It is introduced here by 'salvation', either as picking up the word in v. 69 with v. 70 as a parenthesis, or as giving the content of what God spoke to the prophets. *our enemies* and *all who hate us* are in parallel (cf. Ps. 106¹⁰), and could be religious stereotypes which go with salvation, and not refer to anyone in particular.

72

A further amplification, made by verbs in the infinitive and having a measure of parallelism, which moves backwards from David to the patriarchs.

mercy: eleos (without the article, as in v. 54) is, as often in the LXX, God's *hesed* or covenant love. *to perform mercy* followed by 'with' (as here; + 10³⁷) is a LXX expression (Gen. 24¹²; Judg. 1²⁴), a synonym for redemption or salvation as the operation of that love (cf. Titus 3⁵). But that it has been with *our fathers* = the patriarchs, i.e. that they have been the recipients of it (*promised to* is not in the text), is very obscure. It can hardly mean that the patriarchs have lived after death in expectation of the redemption brought by Christ.

to remember his holy covenant: A Semitic expression for 'in accordance with', 'in fidelity to' (cf. v. 54 with 'mercy', Pss 105⁸; 106⁴⁵ with 'covenant'). *his holy covenant* is, like *the holy prophets* in v. 70, a pious term of later Judaism (I Macc. 1¹⁵, ⁶³). This is taken by some to refer to the Mosaic covenant, but in A. 3²⁴⁻²⁵, where there is a similar sequence of thought, the covenant is that with Abraham. This would lead on to v. 73.

73

the oath: horkon, 'an oath', accusative in apposition to *covenant* in v. 72, though that is in the genitive (cf. Ps. 89³). The thought moves backwards again from the patriarchal ancestors to *our father Abraham* (Gen. 26³), the originator of Israel, who are sons of Abraham. But how imprecise such thought can be is illustrated by Micah 7²⁰, 'Thou wilt show faithfulness to Jacob and stedfast love to Abraham, as thou hast sworn to our fathers from the days of old.'

74
Here the articular infinitive (Lukan) *to grant us* (*didonai* = 'to give' with acc. and infin. = 'to make it possible for us') follows on from, and explicates, the *oath* in v. 73. This refers to Gen. 22$^{15-18}$, which to some extent recapitulates the promise in Gen. 17$^{1-8}$, where it is called a covenant. There the promise is of the multiplication of the nation, victory over enemies and the possession of Canaan to the blessing of all nations (from which A. 3^{25} selects the last). Here the benefit is specified as a permanent deliverance from enemies so as *without fear* to *serve* God – *latreuein*, a cultic word of temple worship, but with a wider meaning of the performance of religious duties (A. 24^{14}).

75
in holiness and righteousness before him: For a similar combination as the ideal for Israel living under the covenant in the promised land, see Josh. 24^{14}, 'serve him in sincerity and in faithfulness'. It could have been an elaboration of the command in Gen. 17^1, 'Walk before me and be blameless'.

all the days of our life: This has been taken to mark the end of the original hymn, but apart from Isa. 38^{20} it, or its equivalent, does not function as a concluding formula (cf. Pss 90^{14}; 128^5; 27^4; 90^9). In Ps. 27^4; Isa. 38^{20} it characterizes the cultic service of God as continual. Here it reflects a this-worldly form of messianic existence in which men still die.

76
An abrupt and emphatic change to the second person singular – *kai su de* = 'And as for you' – and the future tense brings the canticle back from the celebration of an already realized salvation to the occasion of its utterance, and makes it prophetic in the literal sense, thus answering the question in v. 67.

will be called: i.e. will be acknowledged as (vv. 32, 35).

the prophet of the Most High: This designation 'prophet' (there is no article) 'of the Most High' (on which see v. 32), since it is explained by the following clause (*for*), probably depends on, and perhaps reflects, a Christian application of the messenger figure of Mal. 3^1, who is said by God 'to prepare the way before me', and in Mal. 4^5 is Elijah the prophet (cf. v. 17; 7^{27} = Matt. 11^{10}). *go before the Lord to prepare his ways* is not an exact reproduction of Mal. 3^1, or of the similar passage Isa. 40^3 applied to John in 3^4 = Mark 1$^{2-3}$. Leaney (p. 20) and others have cited Test. Levi 8^{15} as evidence for the designation as a messianic title (see AP II, p. 309), and Leaney argues that this makes the Benedictus messianic throughout, and that the child addressed must originally have been Jesus. But the passage adduced is somewhat obscure and may have Christian elements in it; and 'a prophet of the Most High' appears to be used there adjectivally to state that the king-messiah, who will exercise a threefold office that is Mosaic, Aaronic and Maccabaean (in being 'a priest of the Most High God'), will also be a prophet. In Luke's narrative Jesus is Davidic messiah because Son of the Most High (v. 32).

before the Lord: Some take this as referring to Jesus, to whom John is forerunner, as in the Christian adaptation of such texts as Mal. 3¹; Isa. 40³ to make them apply to him (cf. 3⁴⁻⁶; Mark 1²⁻³; 7¹⁷). But in vv. 16–17 the Lord before whom John goes is Yahweh, and the parallelism suggests that here it corresponds to *the Most High*, even if in between Jesus has already been called *the Lord*, at least by implication (v. 43).

77

to give knowledge of salvation: This unparalleled expression appears to be Christian and Lukan; cf. II Cor. 4⁶; 10⁵; Phil. 3⁸; II Peter 3¹⁸ for the only other instances in the NT of *knowledge* followed by a genitive (of God, of Christ). It appears to mean 'experience', and the *salvation*, which has previously consisted of deliverance from external enemies (vv. 69, 71, 74) is now interpreted more internally as *the forgiveness of sins*. This term is absent from the OT, and is comparatively rare in the NT (in Matthew only at 26²⁸, not at all in John, in the epistles Eph. 1⁷; Col. 1¹⁴; cf. Heb. 9²²; 10¹⁸) apart from L–A, where it can summarize God's gift through Christ (24⁴⁷; A. 2³⁸; 10⁴³; 13³⁸; 26¹⁸). Surprisingly it was attached in one form of the tradition to John's baptism (3³ = Mark 1⁴, the only occurrence in Mark except for 3²⁹), though this is corrected in Matt. 3¹¹ (a baptism of repentance only, as in A. 13²⁴; 19⁴).

As they stand this and the following verse provide the wider eschatological context in which John's baptism takes place; but if vv. 76–77 are a Lukan addition they will originally have continued, through a number of subordinate clauses, the explication of the redemption in v. 68.

the tender mercy: In the Greek *splankna eleous* = 'bowels of mercy', an unparalleled expression in the Greek Bible (cf. Test. Zeb. 7³; 8²). In the ancient world the entrails were considered the seat of the emotions (+ seven times in Paul, I John 3¹⁷), though this is strangely rare in the OT (only Prov. 12¹⁰; Wisd. 10⁵; Ecclus 33⁵). Here it characterizes the *mercy* of v. 72 as stemming from a deep compassion in God.

when the day shall dawn upon us from on high: A further explication closely linked by *en hois* = 'in which' (sc. bowels), with the sense perhaps of 'whereby' rather than *when*. The statement is exceedingly obscure on account of both the noun and the verb. (i) The Greek word rendered in the RSV text by *the day* is *anatolē*, here without any definite article. When derived from the verb *anatellein* in its intransitive sense of 'to rise' (generally of the sun, cf. Mal. 4² LXX) it meant the act of rising of the sun, or possibly of a star (Matt. 2², ⁹). By extension it could mean the area of the sun's rising, the east (as in Rev. 7², and, in the plural more usual in this sense, 13²⁹; Matt. 2¹; 24²⁷). It is by a further extension that RSV renders it by *a day* (which dawns). This could accord with the temporal *when*, and with the shining light in v. 79; a day *from on high* (i.e. from heaven, from God, cf. 24⁴⁹; Eph. 4⁸ LXX) might be an eschatological expression (cf. Mal. 4¹⁻³). But it would not accord with the verb *episkeptesthai*, which means 'to visit' (v. 68) and cannot mean 'to dawn'. One suggestion is that the rising, which could be associated with stars, is by metonymy a star itself, denoting an eschatological figure (cf. Num. 24¹⁷, a star from Jacob . . . a sceptre from Israel; Rev. 22¹⁶, Jesus the offspring of David, the bright morning star; II Peter 1¹⁹, the day dawns and the morning star rises in your hearts). A further complication is that the noun *anatolē*, when derived from the verb in its transitive sense of 'to cause to sprout', had already been used in the LXX to translate the Hebrew *semah* = 'sprout', 'shoot', 'scion' as a term for the Davidic heir (Jer. 23⁵; Zech. 3⁸; 6¹², rendered in English by 'the Branch'). This personalized sense would accord with the verb 'visited', and perhaps with *from on high* (sc. God's messiah), but not with the function in v. 79 of shining as light in the darkness.

(ii) There is an insoluble textual problem with regard to the verb.

(*a*) 'will visit' (RSV margin) is read by B, the original hand of ℵ, a few other mss and the Syriac version.

(*b*) 'has visited' (RSV margin) is read by a corrector of ℵ, by A C D and a large number of mss, and by the Latin version.

Some judge (*a*) to be original and (*b*) to be an assimilation to the past tenses of an already realized salvation found in the rest of the canticle. Others judge (*b*) the harder reading, which has been altered to the future so as to make the whole of vv. 76–79 prophetic, and to place John's mission in the context of a future messianic coming. If vv. 76–77 are a Lukan insertion (*b*) is likely to have been what he wrote.

79

The canticle is rounded off by a twofold statement of the purpose (or result) of the visit of (the) *anatolē* to Israel.

to give light to those who sit in darkness and in the shadow of death: If this reproduces the context as well as the language of such passages as Ps. 107¹⁰⁻¹⁸; Isa. 42⁷; 49⁹⁻¹⁰; Micah 7⁸, it could refer to captives in the darkness of prison and in expectation of death there. To these (the) *anatolē* appears. This is the meaning of *epiphainein* (cf. A. 27²⁰ of sun and stars), but here probably it has the more positive sense of 'shine upon' in such a way as to deliver from darkness (cf. Isa. 42⁷; 49⁹; Deut. 33²⁻³).

to guide our feet into the way of peace: This may be an additional purpose, but there is no 'and', and it may denote the positive consequence of deliverance from captivity in the directing of Israel (*our feet*) in *the way of peace* (cf. Isa. 59⁸), i.e. an existence marked by wholeness and fullness of life (see on 2¹⁴).

80

Luke supplies a hagiographical conclusion to the narrative of the birth of John, which also prepares for that of his adult ministry. The first part is somewhat conventional, since of course *the child grew* (cf. Judg. 13²⁴). *became strong* (*krataiousthai* + 2⁴⁰; I Cor. 16¹³; Eph. 3¹⁶, not LXX) is often said of heroes, though generally with reference to physical stature and prowess. That John's strength was in (divine) spirit takes up the promise in v. 15.

he was in the wilderness: Lit. 'in the desert places'. This was a LXX expression of a more general kind, but here it must denote the same as the singular in 3², i.e. the desert of Judaea situated on the eastern hills of Judaea stretching to the Jordan. This is not necessarily based on any knowledge. Thus it is not said at what age John began to live on his own in the desert (that he was made a member of the Qumran community by his parents is pure hypothesis), nor why he chose to do so – to live an ascetic life? or because prophets were often associated with the desert? The statement simply prepares for the desert provenance of John's mission and baptism, which was already established in the tradition (3²⁻⁴ = Mark 1³⁻⁴; 7²⁴; Matt. 11⁷; John 1²³).

his manifestation: anadeixis + +. This Hellenistic word (in the LXX only Ecclus 43⁶, and then in a different sense) denoted a solemn and formal public appointment and presentation to an office, e.g. the investiture of a king (cf. 10¹ for Luke's use of the corresponding verb). In 3² the inauguration of John's ministry will be described in more biblical terms of the call of a prophet – 'the word of God came to . . .'

THE WONDROUS BIRTH OF JESUS

As the annunciation to Mary has followed that to Zechariah, so now the birth of Jesus follows that of John, though ch. 1 is complete in itself, and ch. 2, which hardly presupposes it, makes a fresh beginning. The account falls into two parts of different length, style and character, which are linked by reference to Bethlehem as David's city and to the new-born child in a manger. The first, vv. 1–7, is brief, factual and notably lacking in any detail of a wondrous birth. The second, vv.

8–16, is extended, and itself falls into two parts, vv. 8–14 and vv. 15–16, which form a single whole through the promise of the discovery of a sign (v. 12). It has the character of supernatural wonder throughout, and contains a third angelic annunciation, which, together with a doxology, interprets the birth in relation to salvation. In vv. 17–18, 19 and 20 the whole is given a threefold conclusion, the first extending the knowledge and wonder of the event, the second relating it to Mary, and the third, perhaps the original one, closing the story of the shepherds.

2^{1-7}   THE BIRTH AT BETHLEHEM

2 *In those days a decree went out from Caesar Augustus that all the world should be enrolled.* *²This was the first enrolment, when Quirinius was governor of Syria.* *³And all went to be enrolled, each to his own city.* *⁴And Joseph also went up from Galilee, from the city of Nazareth, to Judea, to the city of David, which is called Bethlehem, because he was of the house and lineage of David,* *⁵to be enrolled with Mary, his betrothed, who was with child.* *⁶And while they were there, the time came for her to be delivered.* *⁷And she gave birth to her first-born son and wrapped him in swaddling cloths, and laid him in a manger, because there was no place for them in the inn.*

The statements in vv. 1–5 serve a double purpose. (i) They bring together in their own way the two traditions that Jesus was a Galilean, whose home was in Nazareth, and that as 'the Son of David' he was, or ought to be, of Bethlehemite origin. Hence the detailed precision of v. 4. The first tradition is widely attested, but only in the gospels and A., by the appellation *Nazarēnos* (so Mark and Luke) and *Nazōraios* (so Matthew, L–A and John), which Luke regards as synonyms (18^{37} = Mark 10^{47}), and by statements that he came from Nazareth (Mark 1^9; Matt. 21^{11}; Luke 1^{26}; 4^{16}; John 1^{45}, though John 1^{46} represents this as the last place to look for a messiah). The second, that he was born at Bethlehem, is in Matt. 2^{1-6} first stated as a fact, though probably not without reference to Joseph as a Davidite and to the genealogy of Jesus as Davidic (Matt. 1^{20, 1-17}), and is then urged as a dogma by the appeal of Jewish authorities to Micah 5^{1-3} to establish Bethlehem as the necessary birthplace of the messiah (hence it is the subsequent residence at Nazareth that has to be specially justified by prophecy, Matt. 2^{23}). It may be reflected, and used with Johannine irony, in the dispute over Jesus' messiahship in John $7^{42f.}$. It is possible that Luke knew of the Bethlehem tradition only from the story of the shepherds (v. 15), and wished to give it a basis not in doctrine – there is no trace of the use of Micah here – but in historical causes. To be 'the Son of David' in a messianic sense ($18^{38f.}$; Ps. Sol. 17^{23}), and to be given the kingdom of his father David (1^{32}; A. 13^{22-37}), would require for some, though not necessarily for Jesus himself (cf. $20^{41ff.}$), the qualification that, like many others, he should be physically descended from David (cf. Rom. 1^3, possibly a pre-Pauline statement). It did not require, however, that he should be born at Bethlehem, and this may represent a final stage of the extension of Davidic sonship back into his earthly life (see Fuller, *Foundations*, pp. 188ff.).

(ii) The statements also provide the otherwise non-chronological traditions of the birth with a fixed point. The origin of Christianity in the birth of the messiah is marked by an event in secular history which was well known to the Jews, even notorious (cf. A. 5^{37}, 'in the days of *the* census'). It is here a decision of the highest temporal authority in the exercise of its universal power, and not scripture, which dictates the circumstances of the birth (contrast Matthew). If this synchronism had already been made in the tradition Luke will have reproduced it as significant; but as the other stories in chs. 1–2 lack this kind of precision it is more likely to have been the creation of Luke, and so is indicative of his mind. As a factual statement in semi-technical language it does not give the impression of oral tradition, and it does not require a Semitic original, being largely in idiomatic Greek.

These two purposes are, however, only achieved by the conjunction of three factors – a universal census of the empire, a local census at that time in Judaea as its consequence, and the registration of inhabitants in their tribal town. In all three Luke appears to be in error.[g]

---

[g] For some of the vast literature on the historical problems of these verses, see Bauer under *apographē*. In the notes here the following are specially referred to: A. N. Sherwin-White, *Roman Society and Roman Law in the New Testament*, pp. 162ff., H. Braunert in *Historia* 6, 1957, pp. 192ff., L. R. Taylor, *American Journal of Philology* 54, 1933, pp. 120ff., and T. Corbishley, *Klio* 29, 1936, pp. 81ff.

1

This historical notice is, like others in L–A, a mixture of the precise and the imprecise.

In those days: This vague introductory phrase (cf. 6^{12}; A. 6^1; 9^{37}; 11^{27}) gives the impression in the context that it refers to Herod's reign (cf. 1^5). Assuming the latest date in that reign for the annunciation to Zechariah and on the presumption (1$^{5ff.}$) that 1^{24} does not indicate a long elapse of time, and that Mary is supposed to be pregnant in 1$^{39-56}$, the period indicated here for the birth of Jesus could not be more than a year or two after Herod's death in 4 BC. In Matt. 2$^{1ff.}$ it falls within Herod's reign. Either date is impossible for what follows with regard to the census. If Mary is not supposed to be pregnant in 1$^{39-56}$ and the census is to be identified with that in AD 6/7, then some ten years could have passed between the annunciation to Mary and her conception; but this can hardly be what was intended.

a decree: dogma, which in general conveyed the idea of a 'positive ordinance, emanating from a distant and unquestionable authority' (MM) was the regular word in Greek for a decree, first of the Roman Senate, and later of the emperor (cf. Jos. *BJ* 1. 392; Octavian confirms Herod in his kingdom by a decree – *dogmati*).

went out: In the Greek *egeneto* followed by a verb in the indicative (see on 1^8), by which in some cases, as perhaps here, a more dramatic effect is produced. The normal word with *decree* would be *poiein* = 'make' or *egeneto* = 'there was'. *went out* is less technical and more dramatic and 'biblical' in style (cf. Dan. 2^{13}).

from Caesar Augustus: from (para) signifies that the decree reached Palestine from the imperial source; cf. the conclusion of the edict in Pap. Fayum 20.22 commanding that copies 'of this my decree' should be set up by rulers of the several cities so as to be read. *Caesar Augustus* is Gaius Julius Caesar Octavianus, who in 30 BC emerged from the civil war as the sole ruler (imperator) of the Roman world. *Augustus,* here transliterated into Greek, but generally translated by *Sebastos* = 'to be revered', 'his majesty' (as in A. 25$^{21, 25}$), was a title conferred on him by the Roman Senate in 27 BC, but could become, as here, a proper name.

the world: hē oikoumenē = 'the inhabited world', as perhaps here, with the idea of giving the birth of the universal saviour a universal setting, even though such an enrolment was not remotely feasible. But the word is found, especially in inscriptions, of the empire as the equivalent of the civilized world – the Latin *orbis terrarum.* This is probably the meaning here, and points at the outset to a certain connection in Luke's mind between Christianity and the empire.

should be enrolled: apographesthai, probably middle rather than passive with the sense 'to register oneself'. This could be for various purposes, e.g. military service. In the LXX the word occurs in this sense only in II Macc. of Jews registered under Ptolemy with a view to their extermination. It is specially common of censuses in the papyri, which contain a considerable number of census returns. While much is known from ancient sources, including inscriptions and papyri, concerning matters of census and taxation in the empire, the documentation is not complete, so that there can be debate over the dates at which they were carried out, and over the procedures adopted, in the areas involved.

No single census for the whole empire, the natural interpretation of Luke here, is known from the sources, which in fact suggest the contrary. Various arguments have been deployed to save Luke's veracity. Thus a universal census has been seen in, or has been postulated by inference from, the registration which Augustus, revising what had taken place spasmodically under the republic, prescribed in 28 BC, 8 BC and AD 14 (Suetonius, *Augustus,* 27.5: 'he thrice carried out a census of the people'). This, however, is irrelevant, since it was concerned only with Roman citizens, first those in Rome and Italy, and then by extension those throughout the empire. Irrelevant also, and for similar reasons, are Vespasian's census in AD 74/5, and Augustus's statistical survey of the whole provincial area – *breviarium totius imperii* – both of which have been appealed to as instances of a universal enrolment (e.g. by Taylor and Corbishley; contradicted by Braunert; see n. *g* above). The census and taxation of the provinces and of their non-Roman inhabitants were a distinct matter, and took a different form.[h] The emperor claimed the taxation as his by right, and no doubt planned it in systematic fashion, but it appears to have been undertaken piecemeal. Of the existing provinces the senatorial were already provided with a municipal administration which could be used for the purpose, while in the less developed imperial provinces machinery had to be created for it. A census was one of the first results of the Lex Provincialis which was drawn up on the occasion of the annexation of a region as a province. It could be repeated at intervals, though not necessarily at regular intervals. Thus a census is recorded for Gaul in 27 BC and 12 BC in connection with its formal annexation by Augustus, and again in AD 14–16 (Livy, *Summaries,* 134, 138f.; Tacitus, *Annals* I, 31, 33), the first perhaps being a preliminary survey, since the second was regarded as a novelty and gave rise to unrest. In Egypt, generally a special case, the Romans took over and reorganized some of the financial arrangements already in existence under the Ptolemies, and there a fourteen-year cycle for the census is attested from AD 33/34, and is possibly traceable as far back as 10/9 BC. The concurrence of the second census in Gaul in 12 BC with (supposed)

h For the differences in form, see B. P. Grenfell and A. S. Hunt, *Oxyrhyncus Papyri* II, London 1899, pp. 207ff.

censuses in Spain and Egypt does not justify the conclusion of T. Corbishley (op. cit.) that it reflects a period of general registration stretching from 12–7 BC. Only in exceptional cases were the inhabitants of a client kingdom brought under Roman taxation by the initiative of the native ruler, and there are no adequate grounds for supposing (with Rengstorf, Grundmann and others) that the political difficulties and financial embarrassments of the latter years of Herod's reign, which even led him to require an oath of allegiance to himself and to Caesar (Jos. *Ant.* 17.42; 15.368), make it probable that he brought Judaea under the Roman census. It is highly unlikely that he would have risked the offence, so obnoxious to the Jews, of 'numbering the people', or that if he had it would have gone unrecorded. For Judaea the situation is, therefore, precisely that described by Josephus for AD 6: 'the territory subject to Archelaus was added to (the province of) Syria, and Quirinius, a man of consular rank, was sent by Caesar to take a census of property in Syria and to sell the estate of Archelaus' (*Ant.* 17.355; cf. also the similar statements in *BJ* 2.117; 7.253). The order for the census would be issued in the name of Quirinius as imperial legate, but it is likely that in it he referred his action to the will and authority of the emperor (cf. Jos. *Ant.* 18. 1, and the census form in Grenfell and Hunt, op. cit., p. 208). Thus in a very general sense the Judaean census of AD 6 could be said to be the outcome of imperial policy, and Sherwin-White (*Roman Law*, pp. 168f.) takes Luke in this sense, presupposing some sort of preamble relating the decree to the principles of Augustus' financial and provincial policy. Luke's statement, however, clearly intends a much more precise connection than that between the Judaean census and his putative general enrolment of the empire, and in this he was mistaken.

2

This verse is a historical notice passing from the general to the particular. It specifies the time at which – the governorship of Quirinius (*hēgemoneuein*, see on 3¹, used of the imperial power and local prefects, and here of the imperial legate in a province) – and the area through which – the province of Syria – the imperial edict affected Judaea. The absence of a connecting particle makes it a parenthesis separating the statement in v. 1 from the consequences in v. 3, and the reason for its insertion is uncertain owing to textual variants and doubt as to its meaning. The text varies according to the position of the verb *egeneto*.

(i) *hautē apographē prōtē egeneto* – so B and a few other mss (the majority have this word order with an article before *apographē*).

(ii) *hautē egeneto apographē prōtē* D.

(iii) *hautē apographē egeneto prōtē* ℵ.

(i) has been translated 'This (the neuter *touto* assimilated to the feminine *hautē*) was a first census (and it took place) when Quirinius . . .' (so Loisy, Klostermann and others); but the Greek is awkward, as is the ellipse before the genitive absolute, and *hautē* goes more naturally with *apographē*. 'This census was the first (and it took place) when Quirinius . . .'* would fit better the secondary reading with the article before *apographē*. Another suggestion, more pertinent to (ii) and (iii), has been to take *prōtē* in the sense of *proteron* = 'before' – 'this census took place before Quirinius was governor' (so Lagrange and others). But while *prōtos* can have this force, it only does so when followed by a noun and not by a genitive absolute, and there is no other instance of this in L–A. Plummer's rendering (p. 49), which he regards as not really doubtful, 'This took place as a first enrolment' (*apographē prōtē* in apposition) seeks to remove a historical error in Luke by making a distinction between a preliminary enrolment under Quirinius' authority and the later one in AD 6/7. But was there such a previous enrolment, and was Quirinius in office in Syria to order it? (see next note).

when Quirinius was governor: The lengthy career under Augustus of Publius Sulpicius Quirinius (called by Luke *Kurēnios*, in some mss *Kurinios*) is summarized in an obituary by Tacitus (*Annals* III, 48), and is documented, though incompletely, elsewhere.[i] A *novus homo*, he was consul in 12 BC, conducted a successful campaign against the Marmaridae of the African desert (*c.* 15 BC, perhaps as proconsul), and some time between 12 BC and AD 1 subjugated the Homonadenses, Cilician brigands to the south of Galatia, probably operating from a command in Galatia rather than from Syria (Tacitus, *Annals* III, 48). Between AD 1–4 he acted as guide to Gaius Caesar in Armenia and Syria (Dio Cassius lv 10a, 4–5), and was rewarded with the legateship of Syria. Evidence of his having held a census there is contained in an inscription (ILS 2683), where Q. Aemilius Secundus refers to conducting a census of Apamaea under Quirinius as legate of Syria; but no date is given (Sherwin-White, *Roman Law*, p. 169, n. 1, suggests it was the second, and had been preceded by a census under Sentius Saturninus *c.* 9 BC), and in any case it refers to a census of Roman citizens and not to an enrolment of provincials. The sequence of legates in Syria is not fully known, but is fairly complete for the period covering Herod's rule – M. Titius *c.* 10 BC, C. Sentius Saturninus 9–6 BC, P. Quintilius Varus 6–4 BC. Place, however, has been found for a legateship of Quirinius in Syria previous to that he held in AD 6 on the basis of a funerary inscription from Tivoli (ILS 918) to be dated sometime after AD 14. It is mutilated in several places, including the name of the person concerned. It refers to the conferring on him by the Senate of triumphal decorations, a proconsulship in Asia, a legateship (if the words for this are supplied) of Syria a second time (if these words are to be

* So F. Hauck, *Das Evangelium nach Lukas*, Leipzig 1934, ad loc.

i See E. Gloag's article on Sulpicius in Pauly-Wissowa, *Real-Encyclopädie der classischen Altertums*, 2nd series, 7, Stuttgart 1931, cols. 822–43; R. Syme, *The Roman Revolution (60 BC to AD14)*, Oxford and Toronto 1939, passim; Taylor, op. cit. (n. g above).

taken together). T. Mommsen was so sure that all this fitted Quirinius and no one else that he filled in the gaps in the inscription on this assumption. This identification has been widely espoused, in English notably by W. M. Ramsay[j] though with a modification of Mommsen's date from 3/2 BC to 11–7 BC, and the improbable supposition that Quirinius was military governor of Syria while M. Titius and C. Sentius Saturninus were its civil governors. Also improbable is the suggestion of E. Stauffer[k] that he held an extraordinary *maius imperium* in the East from 12 BC to AD 17. The identification remains doubtful. Syme (*Roman Revolution*, pp. 398f.) thinks it possible but unlikely; Sherwin-White (op. cit., p. 165 n.) thinks it improbable, in that the reference does not fit the Homonadensian war, and that nothing is known of Quirinius as proconsul in Asia. Solutions of the problem based on the view that it is Josephus who is in error in misplacing events and misdating legates (T. Corbishley, op. cit., pp. 81ff.), or in misunderstanding his source in putting the census after Herod's death, may be disregarded. Mistaken also is the appeal to Tertullian's reference (*Against Marcion* IV, 19) to census activity in Judaea of C. Sentius Saturninus (Easton, pp. 20f., regarded this as settling the question), since Tertullian is referring to a census subsequent to that at which Jesus was born.[l] H. Braunert (op. cit., pp. 212ff.) attributes Luke's error in 2^2 to a source emanating from a Christian Zealot group, which wished to synchronize the birth of the messiah with the origin of the Zealot movement, associated by them confusedly with the disturbances both at the death of Herod (4 BC) and at the census (AD 6). But apart from doubt about the existence of such a group, and about the propriety of the word 'Zealot', which Josephus reserves for the later followers of John of Gischala, the verse does not read like a source, and in view of the similar error in A. $5^{37f.}$ confusion on such matters could as well be ascribed to Luke. Possibly he intended to contrast by juxtaposition *the* census with its sinister connections and the birth of the true Davidic saviour, but this would be very cryptic for his readers. More likely the statement in v. 2 is simply a historical notice by Luke arising out of his previous putative universal enrolment in v. 1, and bringing that into relation with Judaea. If so, it illustrates Luke's quality as a dramatic historian and also the limitations of his historical knowledge.

3–5

These statements require for their cogency certain circumstances of enrolment of which we are imperfectly informed.

j *Was Christ Born at Bethlehem?*, London and New York 1898, pp. 227ff.

k *Jesus and His Story*, London 1960, pp. 33f.

l C. F. Evans, 'Tertullian's References to Sentius Saturninus and the Lukan Census', *JTS* ns 24, 1973, pp. 24–39.

3
all: If taken closely with v. 1 this means the whole empire (excluding Roman citizens?), which would of course be fanciful.

each to his own city: The procedure here resembles that laid down in Egypt for the *apographē kat'oikian* – the enrolment by household – in which were returned a person's age, address, household, property, slaves etc., for the purpose of poll-tax, to be distinguished from the *apographē* of house and land property which was sent in from time to time (see Grenfell and Hunt, *Oxyrhyncus Papyri* II, pp. 207ff.; ibid. p. 203 for a papyrus recording a change of residence, and p. 208 for a census return). There is evidence of edicts issued in Egypt ordering the return of those who for various reasons were absent from home, though this was not necessarily linked with taxation. There is a decree of the Prefect of Egypt for AD 103/4 ordering this with reference to a census (Grenfell and Hunt, op. cit., pp. 177ff.). The complex administrative system of Egypt was in some respects peculiar in the empire, and may not be automatically taken as applicable to other provinces, but 'nothing would be more natural than that when a census was instituted every one without distinction of race should be ordered to go to his own city' (Grenfell and Hunt, op. cit., p. 211). Two difficulties arise in applying this to Luke's text. (i) It is not known for certain whether the census in Judaea affected Galilee at all. Josephus (*Ant.* 18.26ff.) gives the impression that Herod Antipas in Galilee continued in his previous status as native ruler with the good will of Rome. If the census in Judaea was not simply a registration (i.e. for poll-tax, which was never universal in the empire), but was (also?) a valuation of property (Josephus uses for it the Greek word *apotimēsis* = 'valuation'), then it has to be supposed that Nazareth in Galilee was not, as the gospel tradition on the whole suggests, the permanent residence of Joseph (*his own city,* v. 3), and that he was there away from home (Leaney, p. 45, suggests as a journeyman-carpenter), and had property in Bethlehem which he must declare. But the reason given in v. 4 for his journey is not of this kind, but is theological.

(ii) It is not known from other sources what lay to hand in Judaea by way of administrative machinery for carrying out the census. Luke suggests that the method was for registration to take place by attendance at ancestral centres, and this has been held likely in deference to local patriotism (so Braunert, op. cit., Lagrange, Easton). Originally each of the twelve tribes had been made up of clans (*patriai*) and the clans of families or 'fathers' houses' (*oikoi patriōn:* so frequently in the LXX, e.g. Num. 1ff., I Chron. 1ff.). Apart from 'tribe' these terms had come to be used more loosely. Hence *oikou kai patrias* = *of the house and lineage* (v. 4) could be a hendiadys, picking up *of the house of David* (1^{27}), with an official sound and a biblical flavour. But to achieve its object a system of registration must apply to all concerned, whereas one based on *patria* would be defective in two respects. It could not cover non-Jewish inhabitants, and it would effectively cover Jews only if they could without exception trace a family and tribal lineage, and if there was a still living tradition of an area or town serving in each case as the tribal or family centre, as perhaps Bethlehem for Davidites. This is scarcely conceivable. Jeremias (*Jerusalem*, ch. xiii) assembles the evidence for the remarkable ability not only of Jewish priests but also laymen to trace their ancestry for at least a few generations, the genealogies probably being kept in public archives. But he admits that the majority of references are to members of the tribes of Judah and Benjamin, and that it is never a matter of a census of the whole population (as in I Chron. 9^1, 'All Israel were reckoned by genealogies'). It is thus more likely that the system used, because it was already in use, was that of 'toparchies'.^{m} There are two lists of them for Judaea, one in Josephus (*BJ* 3.54ff.) for the time of Nero, and the other in Pliny (*Hist. Nat.* 17.70), possibly for AD 6 and perhaps from an official source. There were eleven districts (so Josephus; Pliny has ten), all with the exception of Jerusalem made up of villages with a larger village for the administrative centre under a government representative. The slight variations between the two lists indicate that the partition was subject to revision. But the word 'toparchy', like 'nome', was a technical term of the Ptolemaic system of administration; it is used in I Macc. 11^{28} of three Samaritan areas transferred to Judaea. This system appears to have continued throughout the Seleucid period and to have been adopted by Herod (cf. Jos. *BJ* 2.167, Salome at her death bequeathed her toparchy to Julia, wife of Augustus). These would then be the natural registration districts covering the whole of Judaea at the time of the census in AD 6. Such a system would not bring Joseph to Bethlehem unless it could be shown that Bethlehem was the administrative centre of a toparchy, and in any case would not bring him there for the reason given by Luke that he was of the house and lineage of David.

4

This statement is made with some solemnity and detail.

went up: anabainein is often used of 'going up' to Jerusalem or to the temple. Though Bethlehem was somewhat higher than Nazareth the eighty or so miles between them could hardly be described as ascent all the way.

the city of David: This epithet, repeated in v. 11, is emphatic. It belonged expressly to Jerusalem (Sion), which David captured from the Jebusites and made his capital (II Sam. 5$^{7, 9}$). Its application, only here, to Bethlehem of Judah, a small town (called in John 7^{42} a village) five miles south-west of Jerusalem, depends on the description of David as originally the son of a Bethlehemite (I Sam. 17^{12}). In the context it gives theological import to the

m On these, of which not a great deal is known, see A. H. M. Jones, *Cities of the Eastern Roman Provinces*, Oxford 1937, pp. 274ff.

place and the journey thither; 'the Son of David' is to be born in 'the city of David'; cf. John 7⁴² and the use of Micah 5² in Matt. 2⁵ᶠ·. Some, e.g. Creed (pp. 31f.) and Brown (*Birth*, pp. 421ff.) postulate dependence on Micah 4–5 as background here and also to account for the shepherds in Luke's story. They suggest that 'the Tower of the Flock' (Migdal Eder), which in Micah 4⁸ is a designation of Jerusalem as about to be delivered by a shepherd ruler from Bethlehem (Micah 5²⁻⁴), has been transferred to Bethlehem itself, and they refer to Gen. 35¹⁹⁻²¹, where Bethlehem and Migdal Eder are also mentioned together though as being at some distance from each other, and to the statement in the (late) Targum Pseudo-Jonathan that the king messiah will be revealed at the end of the days from the Tower of the Flock. But this is highly speculative.

to be enrolled with Mary: So RSV and other translations, taking *with Mary* with *to be enrolled* in view of its distance from *went up*, which in the Greek is the opening word of the sentence. Others render 'went up with Mary'. Again there is uncertainty over attendant circumstances. Such evidence as we have (cited in Schürer, *Jewish People* I, p. 403), suggests that in the case of the poll tax in Syria females from the ages of twelve to sixty-five were subject to it, but not that they had to appear. Information about them, as about anything else, was presumably supplied by the head of the family. Two mss transpose to here 'because of the house of David', and read 'they' for 'he', so as to make Mary a Davidite and the reason for the journey cover her as well. This is later editing.

his betrothed: See on 1²⁷. Some Old Latin mss and syrˢⁱⁿ read 'wife', which appears also in the conflate reading in some mss 'betrothed wife'. In favour of this is that it could have shocked a Christian scribe as a designation of Mary before she had given birth to the virginally conceived child and so been altered to *betrothed*. On the other hand the journey together of a betrothed couple could have been shocking to a Gentile Christian scribe ignorant of Jewish marriage procedure and have been made respectable by 'wife'. The evidence referred to in the previous note does not help to determine the choice of reading by settling such questions as whether only as Joseph's wife would Mary attend registration, and hence whether they are supposed to have been married in the meantime and Joseph was now ready to acknowledge the future child as his son.

6–7

Like vv. 1–5 these verses have a long history of debate, but for the different reason that they are very brief and imprecise. If the story of the shepherds came to Luke in tradition it may have had an introduction stating more precisely where Joseph and Mary lodged and the birth took place. The new historical framework provided by Luke in vv. 1–7 lacks precision at these points and is detailed only where it prepares for the message to the shepherds – *wrapped in swaddling clothes . . . laid in a manger.*

6

while they were there, the time came: In the Greek Luke's construction of *egeneto* = 'it came to pass' followed by a verb in the indicative 'the days were fulfilled' (for 'fill' as an expression of time see on 1^{57}) together with the articular infinite *en tō einai* = 'in their being'. No length of time is given for the stay. It is sufficient that the birth coincides in general with the census. Its exact time is given to the shepherds (v. 11 *this day*). Any emphasis here is on place – *there*, i.e. Bethlehem, the city of David.

7

her first-born son: In the context Mary's previous virginity is expressed but also Jesus' pre-eminence in the family, as the *first-born* opened the womb, and, if a *son*, was dedicated to God (Exod. $13^{11ff.}$). For Luke this prepares for $2^{22ff.}$. The word *first-born* (*prōtotokos*), rather than *monogenēs* = 'only born' (cf. 7^{12}), while suggesting the birth of later children, does not absolutely require it.

wrapped . . . in swaddling clothes: In Greek the single word *esparganōsen* = 'swaddled'. The verb derived from the noun *sparganon* = 'cloth', found in Greek literature mostly in the plural of the cloths or bands with which new-born infants were wrapped so as to prevent their limbs moving. Hence 'she treated him as a baby at birth', cf. Ezek. 16^4, where lack of such bands means not to have been treated properly as a new-born babe. But the detail is here dictated by what is to come when it will serve as part of a supernatural sign (v. 12). What the shepherds will find is *brephos esparganōmenon*, a child recognizable from its clothes as recently born.

laid: anaklinein + + in this sense. She 'put him to bed'.

manger: This could mean (i) a feeding trough for horses or cattle; so generally in Greek literature and in Job 6^5; Prov. 14^4. This could take various forms,[n] the most likely being a flat tray on the floor; (ii) a stall for horses or cattle, as in II Chron. 32^{28}; Job. 39^9; Isa. 1^3; probably in a courtyard, and no more than an enclosure in the open air. (i) might be indicated by *laid*, but (ii) by *no place in the inn*. In either case what is to constitute the sign, guaranteeing the truth of the angel's message of a saviour, is the strange sight of such a babe (new-born) in such a place. Incongruity is suggested, and not necessarily either poverty, or obscurity, or humiliation.

no place for them in the inn: As with *manger* the picture is unclear, and has given rise to much discussion (see Brown, *Birth*, pp. 399ff.). The word rendered *inn* here, *kataluma*, is said by MM to be a Hellenistic equivalent for *katagōgeion* = 'resting place', but is probably over-translated by *inn* = 'public hostelry' (for

n See G. Dalman, *Sacred Sites and Ways*, ET London and New York 1935, pp. 40ff.

Luke this is *pandocheion*, cf. 10³⁴). In that case *in a manger* (stable) will not mean in the manger (stable) belonging to an inn, and *there was no place for them* will not mean that they were refused accommodation at the local inn because it was full or for any other reason. A sufficient rendering of *kataluma* in most cases is 'lodging'. In the plural it meant 'lodgings', and the corresponding verb meant 'to lodge for a night' (cf. 9¹²; 19⁷). In the only other NT instance (22¹¹ = Mark 15¹⁴), as also in the LXX, it refers to an *anageion*, a guest room or one for meals (cf. I Sam. 1¹⁸ LXX; 9²²), but this hardly applies here. What is indicated by the definitive article *to kataluma* = 'the lodging' is not clear – perhaps a caravanserai, with separate caravans under a common roof or shelter. Nor is it clear whether the birth took place there. The suggestion is unlikely that with the birth of the child there was no longer sufficient space (so *topos* = 'room' in the sense of 'space') for Joseph and Mary in the lodging where they were already staying, so that the babe had to be slept outside (or in the manger (stall) inside if it was a farmhouse consisting of a single room occupied also by the cattle). That would require 'no place for him'. The reason for so placing the child is that the whole family (*them*) were unable to find room in the lodging, whatever and wherever that was. Whether Luke thought the journeying to the town for the census to be the cause of overcrowded conditions is not clear, as also whether *in a manger* is intended to stand in contrast to 'in the lodging' in the sense of 'out in the open' as opposed to indoors.ᵒ The suggestion of Laurentin (*Structure*, pp. 57f.) that Luke was influenced here by Micah 4⁸⁻¹⁰ is improbable, for the single verbal parallel adduced, 'he shall go forth from the city' refers to something quite different, and Luke's text cannot be said to have in common with Micah's 'a childbirth outside the city in the field'. Some have seen the *kataluma* as a (the?) caravan shelter with a place for animals attached. This could be a cave dwelling; though Justin's reference (*Dialogue* 78) to the birth as taking place in a cave is unlikely to rest on a reliable tradition, as it is prompted by his argument that heathen myths, including the begetting of Mithras from a rock and the initiation of his followers in a cave, were parodies of the truth invented by demons. Some give the details here a more recognizable theological content by reference to OT passages – Wisd. 7⁴ᶠ·; Solomon has no other beginning of existence than in swaddling clothes; Isa. 1³ LXX, 'The ox knows its owner, and the ass its master's (lord's) manger'; and Jer. 14⁸: Israel is not like an alien who goes to a lodging for the night. The biblically expert shepherds, or readers, are to understand that the babe is to be found, not in a lodging like a stranger in Israel, but swaddled as the future Davidic king in the Lord's manger (see Fitzmyer, pp. 394f.). This is surely far-fetched.

ᵒ So H. J. Cadbury, 'Luke's Interest in Lodging', *JBL* 45, 1926, p. 318.

⁸*And in that region there were shepherds out in the field, keeping watch over their flock by night.* ⁹*And an angel of the Lord appeared to them, and the glory of the Lord shone around them, and they were filled with fear.* ¹⁰*And the angel said to them, 'Be not afraid; for behold, I bring you good news of a great joy which will come to all the people;* ¹¹*for to you is born this day in the city of David a Saviour, who is Christ the Lord.* ¹²*And this will be a sign for you: you will find a babe wrapped in swaddling cloths and lying in a manger.'* ¹³*And suddenly there was with the angel a multitude of the heavenly host praising God and saying,*

¹⁴*'Glory to God in the highest,*
and on earth peace among men with whom he is pleased!' ★

¹⁵*When the angels went away from them into heaven, the shepherds said to one another, 'Let us go over to Bethlehem and see this thing that has happened, which the Lord has made known to us.'* ¹⁶*And they went with haste, and found Mary and Joseph, and the babe lying in a manger.* ¹⁷*And when they saw it they made known the saying which had been told them concerning this child;* ¹⁸*and all who heard it wondered at what the shepherds told them.* ¹⁹*But Mary kept all these things, pondering them in her heart.* ²⁰*And the shepherds returned, glorifying and praising God for all they had heard and seen, as it had been told them.*

²¹*And at the end of eight days, when he was circumcised, he was called Jesus, the name given by the angel before he was conceived in the womb.*

★ Other ancient authorities read *peace, good will among men*

This story is markedly different from that in vv. 1–7. In form it is not part of a continuous narrative, but an independent unit inserted here; vv. 6–7 could be naturally followed by vv. 21ff. In content it is no longer simply factual, giving information about events in the affairs of men. It is revelatory, communicating to men through the heavenly media of angelic appearance, speech and praise the divine significance of the events. It is the only story in the birth narratives to do so consistently (in vv. 26–32, 36–38 this is done by the insertion of divinely inspired prophecy). It is very vividly told with a contrast and conjunction between heaven and earth – night/heavenly light, vv. 8–9,

heavenly praise/earthly praise, vv. 14, 20, heavenly communication/
earthly communication, vv. 15, 17 – and with the heavenly message
underlined by the repetition of *rhema* = 'word' (thing) in singular and
plural (vv. 15, 17, 19) and *lalein* = 'speak', 'tell' (vv. 15, 17, 18, 20).
The style is correspondingly 'biblical'. Unless Luke has specially
affected it for the purpose it will be evidence of a Semitic original; so
the parataxis throughout, and the expressions *keeping watch* (*phulassein*
phulakas = 'to watch watches', cf. Num. 3⁷; 8²⁶), *angel of the Lord*
(but cf. A. 5¹⁹; 8²⁶; 12⁷, ²³), *glory of the Lord, filled with fear* (*phobeisthai*
phobon megan = 'to fear a great fear'), *I bring you good news of a joy*
(*euangelizesthai . . . charan* = 'to announce as good tidings a joy', cf.
A. 10³⁶), *all the people* = Israel (cf. A. 10⁴¹?), *this* (will be) *a sign* (cf.
I Sam. 10¹). To Luke could be ascribed *region* (*chōra* = 'land', 'territory'), *out in the field* (the verb *agraulein* + +, not LXX, = 'to live out
of doors'), *appeared* (*ephistanai*, frequent in L–A and rare elsewhere in
the NT), *shone around* (*perilampein* + A. 26¹³ of heavenly light; not
LXX), *suddenly* (*exaiphnēs*, apart from Mark 13³⁶ only L–A in the NT),
praise (*ainein* v. 13, and with *glorifying* v. 20), *when* (*hōs* = 'as' used
in a temporal sense), *go over* (the Lukan *dierchesthai*, here followed by
the rare particle *dē* = 'indeed' expressing urgency), *that has happened*
(*to gegonos*, the perfect participle used adjectivally), *made known* (*gnōriz-
ein*, only here in the synoptists), *found* (*anheuriskein* + A. 21⁴), *returned*
(the Lukan *hupostrephein*). Verse 19 is supplied by Luke to connect the
story with the whole infancy narrative.

ന്ദ

8

Literally 'And there were shepherds in that region living out of doors and
watching night watches over their flock.' In this scene, which has the character
of 'legend', it is not clear (i) how many shepherds were involved, and whether
in that region means that they are all Bethlehemites; (ii) why they are specified as
living out of doors, and whether this indicates a time of the year, the summer
months, or simply expressed 'outdoors' in contrast to the 'indoors' of vv. 6–7;
(iii) whether they are all guarding a single large flock, or each his own flock
(which he owned?), but in sufficient proximity to one another to be addressed
as a single audience; and (iv) whether night watches refer to an overnight
refuge with different conditions from a daytime watch, or simply provide a
setting for the shining light of divine glory. Why shepherds should be the first
recipients and disseminators of the heavenly news and interpretation of the
birth has often been discussed. The use of 'shepherd' inside and outside the Bible

for the wise and beneficent ruler of a people is hardly relevant, as that usage is purely metaphorical. Their presence in Greek bucolic poetry, e.g. Virgil's *Fourth Eclogue*, as idealized figures has been suggested, as also their mention in legend in connection with the births of (divine) heroes including Mithras (Creed, p. 31), but there is little sign of this in Jewish tradition. There, at least in some (later) rabbinic statements, shepherds are disreputable characters; though this is hardly strong enough evidence for the conclusion that the gospel is made known to them as such, as later to tax collectors and prostitutes. Any ideal element here is likely to be derived from the place, and the association of Bethlehem with David, who was called there as shepherd to be king (I Sam. 16¹¹⁻¹³; Ps. 78⁷⁰ᶠ·).

9–11
See on 1¹¹⁻¹⁴, where the same language and sequence are present: *angel, fear, be not afraid, because, I bring good news, joy*.

9
an angel of the Lord: Here he remains anonymous (contrast 1¹⁹, ²⁶ – from a different source?), but is reinforced by an angelic host (v. 13), and his utterance is that of God (v. 15).

appeared: The verb *ephistanai* = 'to stand by' is used here, as elsewhere in L–A and Greek literature, for the appearance on the scene, generally sudden, of human or heavenly beings (cf. A. 12⁷; 23¹¹).

the glory of the Lord: The first appearance in L–A of the important word *doxa*. In Greek this meant 'appearance', 'opinion', 'reputation'. In the LXX it underwent a transformation, and was given a special force as the translation of the Hebrew word *kabhodh* = 'weight', 'splendour' with reference to Yahweh's self-manifestation and presence in the form of luminous cloud (Exod. 16¹⁰; Num. 14¹⁰; so here *shone around*). It was then constantly associated with Yahweh, and with heavenly beings around him. It was the nearest Hebrew thought came to speaking ontologically of God's 'being' (cf. A. 7⁵⁵; Titus 2¹³; Rev. 15⁸), and could be a synonym for God, especially in the form 'the glory' (so some mss here).ᵖ

bring good news: For this Lukan celebratory verb from the OT see on 1¹⁹. One element in Luke's thought here could be that suggested by the inscription from Priene dated AD 6, which celebrates the birth of the emperor Augustus as 'the beginning of good news (the noun) for the whole world'.

ᵖ See *TDNT* II, pp. 232ff., L. Brockington, 'The Septuagintal Background to the New Testament use of *doxa*', *Studies in the Gospels*, ed. Nineham, pp. 1–8.

11

This verse supplies the interpretative core of the story, of the birth narratives as a whole, and to some extent of the whole Gospel. the *great joy* (1^{14}), which will be that of Israel (*all the people*, v. 10), is over the arrival for the shepherds, as here the representatives of Israel, of the time of salvation. *this day* is the first occurrence in the gospel of *sēmeron* = 'today', which is here a precise note of time, but in the context carries something of the emphasis of the advance into the present of the eschatological future, as in 3^{22} (v. l.); 4^{21}; 5^{26}; 19^9; 23^{43}; A. 13^{33}. Here that is attached to the moment of Jesus' birth, and so prepares for Christmas Day.

a Saviour: sōtēr = 'deliverer'. The noun here is semi-adjectival, 'one who is a saviour'. This can have a background in the OT, where it is used of God (Ps. 25^5 etc.; so in 1^{47}, the only other instance in the Gospel) in his activity towards Israel of salvation (*sōteria*, 1^{69}); as also of those God empowers to deliver his people from oppression (e.g. the Judges, cf. A. 13^{17-23}). But it was also a familiar term in Hellenistic piety for (divine) heroes (e.g. Heracles), or great men, to mark their special position as conferring benefits on mankind, whether political (e.g. the emperor Augustus), philosophical (e.g. Epicurus), or medical (e.g. Aesculapius). It was also applied to cult divinities such as Mithras or Isis. It is this latter background which may be responsible for its application to Jesus, which takes place in the later strata of christology. Thus in the gospels it occurs again only in John 4^{42} in the Hellenistic expression 'the saviour of the world' (cf. I John 4^{14}). In the other instance in A. (5^{31}) it is combined with the Hellenistic image of the *archēgos*, the pioneer. In its only occurrence in Paul (Phil. 3^{20}) it refers to the future transforming power of the risen and exalted Lord at his parousia, and it is frequent only in the Pastorals as one of the Hellenistic elements there (of God I Tim. 1^1; 4^{10}; Titus 1^3; 2^{10}; 3^4; of Christ II Tim. 1^{10}; Titus 1^4; 2^{13}; 3^6). See Bauer (s.v. *sōtēr* and the literature cited there) and Cullmann (*Christology*, pp. 238ff.).

Christ the Lord: One of the most important statements in the Gospel, since it defines (*who is*) Jesus, saviour even from his birth, in terms which only came to be used of him later. It is, however, unique in the NT, and is very obscure. The Greek is *Christos Kurios*, which, if taken as the conjunction of two anarthrous nouns, is literally 'Christ, Lord' – cf. A. 2^{36} for a similar conjunction, though in reverse order, and with the nouns joined by 'and'. Apart from Lam. 4^{20} LXX, where it is an error for the normal *Christos Kuriou* = 'anointed of the Lord', the only parallel is in Ps. Sol. 17^{36}, where some hold it to be a similar error in view of three occurrences of 'anointed of the Lord' in the following Ps. Sol. 18 (title, 6, 8).

Christ: The first component of the expression, *Christos*, originates as a verbal adjective from *chriein* = 'to smear with oil'. In the LXX, where it renders the

Hebrew *mašiah* (messiah), it gains a special force from the Israelite practice of anointing as the sign and means of divine appointment and investiture of the king (I Sam. 24[6], 'the Lord's anointed'; II Chron. 6[42], 'thy anointed one'; cf. Isa. 45[1], 'his anointed, Cyrus'). It is still found with this kind of genitive in I Enoch 48[10], 52[4]; II Baruch 39[7]; 70[9]; 72[2]; IV Ezra 7[28]). With a different kind of genitive cf. 'the messiah of Israel and (the messiah of) Aaron' at Qumran (Vermes, *Scrolls*, pp. 47ff.). In Lev. 4[3, 5, 16] it is used without a genitive in 'the anointed priest' = 'the priest duly (divinely) appointed' (cf. Lev. 6[19, 22] 'when he is anointed . . . the priest who is anointed'). Here, therefore, *Christos* could be adjectival, 'an anointed Lord'; cf. Luke's own expression in 23[2], *Christos Basileus* = 'an anointed king'(?), though this would be tautologous if 'anointed' still retained any connotation of kingship. Used absolutely and with the definite article – 'the anointed one', 'the messiah' – it became a term for the future (Davidic) king in the coming age, but this is not clearly attested in Judaism before AD 70 (e.g. II Bar. 29[3]; IV Ezra 12[32]), and it is regular only in the later Talmud and Targums, which preserve rabbinic statements from AD 70 onwards. The only widespread evidence for an earlier use of this is in the NT itself (e.g. Rom. 9[5]; Mark 8[29]; cf. Luke 3[15]; 4[41]; 24[26, 46], but in 9[20] altered to the earlier form 'the Christ of God', cf. 23[35]). If such passages as 20[41] = Mark 12[35]; 22[67] = Mark 14[61] represent what was actually said and are not later Christian formulations they point to an already established usage of 'the messiah' in Judaism. A further complicating factor is the surprising development by which among Christians *Christos*, with or without the article, became an alternative personal name for Jesus (e.g. Rom. 5[6], I Peter 2[21] etc.), or could stand on either side of 'Jesus' as an additional personal name (Mark 1[1]; Matt. 1[1]; Rom. 1[1] etc.). In such instances it is difficult to determine whether the word retains anything of its adjectival or titular sense of 'an (the) anointed'. So here the translation could be 'who is Christ (personal name) the Lord'.

Lord: The second component, *Kurios*, is also originally a verbal adjective meaning 'owner of', 'ruler of (over)'. With or without an article it is ubiquitous in the LXX as an equivalent of the tetragrammaton, the divine name YHWH (so already 1[6, 9, 11, 16] etc.). Its application to Jesus is difficult to trace. It would appear to have arisen out of his resurrection and exaltation (A. 2[36]; Rom. 10[9]; Phil. 2[11]), and would express for Greek-speaking Christians something of what 'the Christ' no longer did. The application probably originated with 'our Lord' (Aramaic *maran*, cf. I Cor. 16[22]) as a Christian community's title for Jesus as their present and future owner, of whom they were the slaves, and as the object of their worship (cf. Col. 1[3]; Eph. 4[5]). There were no parallels to this in Judaism with reference to any other than the one God YHWH, who is the Lord. It resembled, and possibly reflected the influence of, the use of the word by devotees for a cult divinity (Lord Mithras, Lady Isis, etc.), and even for the emperor. With the omission of 'our' '(the) Lord' became a designation for the exalted Jesus in his delegated divine authority and power, first over Israel and the church and then over the universe (A. 10³⁶; Phil. 2¹¹). This allowed statements in the OT about YHWH as Lord to be taken as referring to Jesus (e.g. Mark 1³). Only Luke uses 'the Lord' of Jesus in the narrative of his earthly life, and he may be here bringing it back to his birth. A possible translation is 'Christ (a personal name) the Lord'. If, however, *Christos Kurios* is allowed to stand as the true reading in Ps. Sol. 17³⁶ it could be evidence in Judaism of the conjunction of 'Lord' in an honorific sense with 'anointed' as a title, on the analogy of such Hellenistic phrases as *kurios basileus* = 'Lord king', and the translation here could be 'Lord anointed one'. (See *TDNT* III, 1039ff., Cullmann, *Christology*, pp. 195ff.)

a sign to you: Generally in the OT 'the sign to you', as in some mss here. *sign* (*sēmeion*) has several meanings in the Bible. Here it is something that will corroborate the divine or angelic statement (= 'I told you so'). This could be either something still in the future, as Zechariah's dumbness (1¹⁸⁻²⁰; cf. Exod. 3¹²; II Kings 19²⁹), or something already present, as Elizabeth's pregnancy (1³⁶⁻³⁷) and here. Often the sign bears some relation to the thing signified – e.g. Isa. 8¹⁻⁴; II Kings 19²⁹, where future prosperity will show that God has triumphed over Israel's enemies. Here it simply serves to establish the angel as someone to be believed because he is able to direct the shepherds to an unexpected and incongruous sight which he already knows about, a new-born babe in a manger. This does not say anything about the character of the messiahship and lordship, e.g. that it is manifested in humility.

13–14

Strictly this interrupts the story, which continues in v. 15 with the shepherds verifying the statements of the single angel in vv. 10–12. It is a very miniature canticle, now on the lips of angelic and not human beings, in the form of two parallel and chiastic lines, though of unequal length. It provides a further divine setting for, and interpretation of, the angel's announcement, with doxological praise of God followed by a declaration of salvation for men. There are no verbs, which are generally supplied in the jussive. But while this would fit the first line – 'let there be glory given to God' – it would not fit the second, where the sense appears to be 'there is (will be) peace . . .'; and this would require 'there is glory being given to God.' Both the praise and the peace are already actual in view of the birth of a saviour.

13

the heavenly host: An expression from the vocabulary of angelology, literally 'the army of heaven', with angels as the divine soldiery; for the phrase, cf. I Kings 22¹⁹; Neh. 9⁶; and for the idea, Rev. 12⁷.

praising God: That is, extolling him for what he brings about; particularly the function of angels as denizens of heaven (Ps. 148^{1-2}).

14

Glory to God: A different use of *glory* from that in v. 9 and more akin to the Greek meanings of the word, 'renown', 'honour'. To give glory (17^{18}; Rom. 4^{20}) is the equivalent of praise and thanksgiving (Phil. 1^{11}). It was a formula in the vocabulary of Jewish worship.

in the highest: The neuter plural of *hupsistos* (1^{32}) = 'the highest places', the abode or presence of God, here contrasted with *on earth*.

peace: This word, *eirēnē*, has an altogether richer content than absence of conflict, which it means in ordinary Greek. As the LXX rendering of *shalom*, its basic meaning is 'totality', 'wholeness', and it expresses the ideal state of life in Israel. This was prosperity, happiness and untrammelled growth in a harmonious community, and its source was God.q In the prophets, who announced it as the life of the restored community beyond judgment and deliverance, it is brought into relation with salvation, along with truth and righteousness (Isa. 49^{22-26}; 52^7; 55^{12}; 60^{12-17}; Zech. 8^{16-19}). It can thus be an eschatological term for the conditions under the rule of the future ideal king (Isa. 9^{2-7}; Zech. 9^9; Micah 5^5), or a paradisal existence in which all forms of strife have been removed (Isa. 2^{2-4}; $11^{1ff.}$; Ezek. 34^{25-28}).

among men in whom he is pleased: This translates *en anthropois eudokias*, where the noun *eudokia* is in the genitive qualifying *men*, and v. 14 is then a twofold statement. In the variant, *peace, good will among men*, *eudokia* is in the nominative, which gives a threefold statement: Glory to God in the highest, and on earth peace, good will towards men. There is no doubt that the former, which is the reading of the better textual authorities, is to be preferred, but there still remains dispute over the meaning of *eudokia*. This word, confined to Jewish and Christian writers, can refer to men as being 'of good will' (Phil. 1^{15}), and would denote in that case those minded to look for, and receive, peace. But it is frequent in the LXX for the good will and favour of God shown in his gracious and saving action – so in the only other instance in L-A, 10^{21} = Matt. 11^{26} (Q), and cf. Eph. $1^{5, 9}$. 'men of his good pleasure', to which there are similar expressions at Qumran (Fitzmyer, p. 411) would then be somewhat tautologous – God's peace (salvation) to those who are the objects of his salvation'.

15

thing: *rhēma* = 'word', but with *what has happened* must have the meaning *thing* (see on 1^{37}).

q See J. Pedersen, *Israel* I–II, London and Copenhagen 1926, pp. 263–335.

16

the babe lying in a manger: Both nouns now have the article, i.e. they found *the* babe lying in *the* manger which they had been told they would find. This, and not any awareness of a virginal conception, is what authenticates the angel's message of a saviour who is Lord Christ, and provides the incentive for communicating it to others.

17

they made known the saying: All the angel has said is here a single *rhēma* = 'saying', 'statement'. Whether they are supposed to understand what they tell is not evident.

18

wondered at: As at the end of a miracle story (8^{25}; 9^{43}; and cf. 1^{63}; 2^{33}). Again it is not clear whether this is wonder at a marvel that is comprehended or not comprehended.

19

This verse, repeated without 'pondering them' in v. 51b, is clearly from Luke's hand. It singles out the response of Mary, who is here called *Maria* (elsewhere in L–A only at 1^{41}), from that of the rest (no mention is made of Joseph). The grounds for this are given in the following words, the meaning of which is disputed.

kept all these things, pondering them in her heart: Or 'kept all these things in her heart, pondering them'. There are three difficulties here. (i) *all these things* (or 'words', *rhēmata*, see on v. 15; 1^{37}), if it is not a typical Lukan exaggeration, could refer not only to the report of the shepherds, who, apart from 'saviour' would not be communicating anything she had not heard already (cf. $1^{32-35, 43}$), but to all that had happened, or been spoken to her, since 1^{26}.

(ii) The verb rendered *kept, suntērein* (+ Mark 6^{20} = 'imprison', Matt. 9^{17} = 'preserve'), if taken with *in her heart*, could mean 'kept to herself' (and continued to do so; the tense is imperfect). This would have no point except on the improbable hypothesis that the purpose of Luke's notice here is to indicate Mary as his source of information for the birth stories. The verb is found in Dan. 4^{25} LXX, 'he kept the words (*logous*) in his heart', of Nebuchadnezzar's response to Daniel's interpretation of his dream, where it means at least 'kept them in mind', and perhaps more positively 'paid attention to them' as due to be fulfilled. For the same expression, perhaps taken from Daniel, cf. Test. Levi 6^2, of a vision whose 'message is to be guarded until the time appropriate for its disclosure'.[r] The variant used in v. 51b, *diatērein*, occurs in Gen. 37^{11} of Jacob's

r *The Old Testament Pseudepigrapha*, ed. J. H. Charlesworth, London and New York 1983, p. 790.

response to Joseph's 'saying' (*rhēma* = the narrative of his dream), either in reflecting on it in puzzlement, or in paying attention to it with an inkling of its future fulfilment.

(iii) *pondering* is the participle of *sumballein*. As such it is subordinate to the main verb *kept*, and either extends or qualifies its meaning. Elsewhere in L–A, to which the verb is confined in the NT, it is used with a dative of the person with the sense 'to engage with' (in battle, 14³¹; in dispute, A. 17¹⁸), or with *pros* + accus. = 'to confer with' (A. 4¹⁵). Here it is used with a direct object. Its basic meaning is 'to throw together', and here this has been taken in the sense of 'puzzled over' in extension of *kept* = 'reflected upon'. In that case the purpose of the notice is to say that though Mary was the most personally and intimately connected with the events of salvation she remained baffled by them. Van Unnik (*Sparsa Collecta*, pp. 72ff.) points to its use in Greek literature in the context of oracles, dreams and visions, where it has the meaning 'to arrive at the interpretation of', 'to establish the right meaning of'. In that case the purpose of the notice would be to present Mary as the first Christian believer, who, in distinction from the mere marvelling of others, came to understand the mystery of the gospel from the beginning. Against this view could be the subordinate position of the participle to *kept* if that is to be rendered 'kept in mind', and that the similar comment, though without *sumballein*, in v. 51b follows on from 'they did not understand the saying which he spoke to them'. A special status of Mary as privy to the truth from the first is not found elsewhere in L–A.

21
This verse should probably be taken with vv. 1–20 as supplying a typically Jewish conclusion to a birth, though the repetition of the same form of words ('And when the days were filled for . . .') in both v. 21 and v. 22 is clumsy, and the introduction of *he* ('the child') is abrupt. Circumcision and naming (for which see on 1⁵⁹) match those of 1⁵⁹⁻⁶⁶, though they can now be stated concisely in a single sentence, since through Mary's obedient response in contrast to the questioning and dumbness of Zechariah there is no hiatus in giving the name which has been prescribed by God before conception.

2^{22-40} JESUS AS A BABE IN THE TEMPLE

²²*And when the time came for their purification according to the law of Moses, they brought him up to Jerusalem to present him to the Lord* ²³(*as it is written in the law of the Lord, 'Every male that opens the womb shall be called holy to the Lord'*) ²⁴*and to offer a sacrifice according to what is said in the law of the*

Lord, 'a pair of turtledoves, or two young pigeons.' ²⁵Now there was a man in Jerusalem, whose name was Simeon, and this man was righteous and devout, looking for the consolation of Israel, and the Holy Spirit was upon him. ²⁶And it had been revealed to him by the Holy Spirit that he should not see death before he had seen the Lord's Christ. ²⁷And inspired by the Spirit* he came into the temple; and when the parents brought in the child Jesus, to do for him according to the custom of the law, ²⁸he took him up in his arms and blessed God and said,

²⁹'Lord, now lettest thou thy servant depart in peace,
 according to thy word;
³⁰for mine eyes have seen thy salvation
³¹which thou hast prepared in the presence of all peoples,
³²a light for revelation to the Gentiles,
 and for glory to thy people Israel.'

³³And his father and his mother marvelled at what was said about him; ³⁴and Simeon blessed them and said to Mary his mother,

'Behold, this child is set for the fall and rising of many in Israel,
 and for a sign that is spoken against
³⁵(and a sword will pierce through your own soul also),
 that thoughts out of many hearts may be revealed.'

³⁶And there was a prophetess Anna, the daughter of Phanuel, of the tribe of Asher; she was of a great age, having lived with her husband seven years from her virginity, ³⁷and as a widow till she was eighty-four. She did not depart from the temple, worshipping with fasting and prayer night and day. ³⁸And coming up at that very hour she gave thanks to God, and spoke of him to all who were looking for the redemption of Jerusalem.

³⁹And when they had performed everything according to the law of the Lord, they returned into Galilee, to their own city, Nazareth. ⁴⁰And the child grew and became strong, filled with wisdom; and the favour of God was upon him.

★ Or *in the Spirit*

This story is striking both in itself and in providing a closer link between the birth of Jesus and the rest of the Gospel. It is of the 'legend' type in stressing the piety of, and the divine favour towards, those concerned, but is difficult to analyse and assess. Like what precedes and follows, it is basically a story of the mother and child, here with special reference to the mother (vv. 34f.); but the double reason for their joint

appearance in the temple – purification and presentation – lacks verisimilitude. Further, it contains two other named persons, of whom
Simeon, who is not connected with either purification or presentation,
occupies the centre of the picture. It is his entrance into the temple at
the right time and his prevision of the babe as the future messiah that
provide the miraculous divine element, which in vv. 9–14 has been
supplied by angels, and it is for the sake of what, through divine
inspiration, he prophesies about mother and child that the story is told.

Its place in the composition of chs. 1–2 is unclear. It could stand in
parallel either with the Benedictus (1^{67-79}), which is the only statement
about John between his birth and naming and the summary of his life
(1^{80}), or with the Visitation (1^{39-45}), which also contains a recognition
of the babe (as yet unborn) through inspiration by the Spirit. It is in
some tension with 2^{1-21}, since the parents are astonished at Simeon's
statements about the child as though they had not heard anything of
the kind before, either from the shepherds' report of the angelic
announcement (2^{17-19}), or, in Mary's case, from Gabriel (1^{32-33}). Thus
the story could have had an independent existence in some form, and
have been incorporated by Luke into his consecutive narrative. Certain
features suggest this. (i) It is not an entirely coherent unity. Verses 25–
32 constitute a story with a beginning of its own (*Now there was a
man . . .*), and a single theme of Simeon's acknowledgment of the babe,
including a canticle which is briefer and more personal. Verse 40, which
corresponds to 1^{80}, concludes both the incident itself and the whole
account of Jesus' birth, and could well follow v. 35. Verses 36–38 have
the appearance of an addition to make a pair of prophetic witnesses, and
Anna, in contrast to the elaborate details about her, has nothing to say
after Simeon. (ii) The framework in vv. 22–24 is artificial and confused, and is likely to have been supplied by Luke in making the story
part of the birth of Jesus. (iii) While the possibility that Luke wrote the
story cannot be ruled out, the strong Semitic flavour suggests that he
is reproducing and editing a written source: note the parataxis of
sentences beginning with 'and' in vv. 25–26, the repetition of 'man' in
v. 25, and the clumsiness of the Greek in vv. 27–29 and in vv. 36–37a,
where it is barely translatable.

६०६

22–24

The confusion here may be due to the need to bring mother and child to the temple together through pious observance of the law as that was deduced (erroneously) from the OT text. The transition from v. 21 might have been suggested by the text of Lev. 12, where in the laws for a woman's purification there is a passing reference (12^3) to the child's circumcision.

22

And when the time came: Literally 'When the days were fulfilled', *pimplanai*, a Lukan word with time (see 1^{23}).

for their purification: For *purification* Luke uses the more common *katharismos* in place of the *katharsis* of Lev. $12^{4, 6}$ LXX. This comprised after a male birth seven days of uncleanness and a further thirty-three days of house confinement, concluded by sacrifice offered in the temple at the Court of the Women. This concerned the woman only. The strange but best attested reading *their* extends it to another. (The variants *autou* = 'his' (sc. Jesus') in D and a few others, *eius* = 'his' or 'hers' in the Vulgate, are probably corrections, though some see *their* as a conflation of 'his' with an original 'hers'). Some commentators take the other person to be Joseph in view of *they brought*, but the rest of the story would suggest Jesus. Either would be nonsensical and betray ignorance of Jewish custom, where neither father nor child were involved in purification. *their* has been held to reflect an influence on Luke of Greek purification rites, which did involve the child, but it is more likely a clumsy device of Luke to bring the child into the proceedings. These are to be about him and not the mother's purification, which plays no further part in the story.

according to the law of Moses: There is a fourfold stress in the story on the observance of the law, here called *the law of Moses* (only Luke and John in the NT), and in vv. 23, 24 *the law of the Lord* (only Luke in the NT). The future messiah of Israel is from birth a member of a family of the strictest religious observance. The law is, however, incorrectly explicated in what follows.

they brought: This refers to Mary and Joseph (v. 16), later to be called *the parents* (v. 27).

Jerusalem: Here the Greek form *Hierosoluma*, the usage in the other gospels and frequent in A., though only four times in this Gospel. In v. 25 it is *Hierousalēm*, a transliteration of the Hebrew form, frequent in this Gospel and A., and eleven times in the rest of the NT. This latter often, though not always, has the religious nuance of 'the holy city', as in Matt. 23^{37}, the only gospel instance outside Luke. It is doubtful whether any conclusions can be drawn from this variation as to Luke's sources. He seems to use the two forms indifferently; in 6^{17}; 18^{31} he changes Mark's *Hierosoluma* to *Hierousalēm*, but in 13^{22}; 19^{28} writes with his own hand *Hierosoluma*.

to present him to the Lord: This secondary, but in the story primary, purpose of the visit to the temple compounds the confusion. For it has nothing to do with any purification of the child, which was not prescribed by the law, and to which the citation in v. 23 is not referring; nor is it naturally followed by the further purpose clause in v. 24, *to offer a sacrifice.*

23

The law cited here, though not exactly, is that of the sanctification of the first-born to God's possession (Exod. 13$^{2, 12, 15}$; cf. 22^{29}; 34^{19}; Num. 3^{13}). This was no longer taken literally, the tribe of Levi having been set aside for Yahweh's permanent possession instead (Num. 8$^{17f.}$). It was put into effect by the father's redeeming the child with a payment of five shekels (Exod. 13$^{13f.}$; Num. 18^{16}). This however did not have to be paid at the temple, but could be paid to a priest in any appropriate place. In itself the payment, which is not mentioned here, would simply mean that Jesus was a first-born son. It is nowhere described in the texts as a 'presenting to the Lord', nor did the law anywhere prescribe a 'presentation' of the first-born to Yahweh. *to present him to the Lord* might be a relic of an original purpose of the story to depict a permanent dedication of the child to God as a Nazirite in the temple after the model of Samuel (I Sam. 1$^{21-28}$). More probably Luke has himself coloured the story with reference to the Samuel model. None of the OT texts referred to above has of the first-born that he *shall be called holy to the Lord*, and Luke appears to have manipulated the text so as to produce a 'presentation' scene that shall contain the fulfilment of what the angel had announced in addition to the child's name (1^{35}). The view of R. Laurentin (op. cit., pp. 58ff.) that the story is motivated by fulfilment of the prophecy in Mal. 3 that the Lord will visit his temple is based on tenuous parallels of thought and language.

24

This indicates the comparative poverty of the parents, as Lev. 12^8 allows the birds for sacrifice in the case of those too poor to afford a lamb.

according to what is said: This formula elsewhere in Rom. 4^{18}; cf. A. 2^{16}; 13^{40}.

25

Simeon: His name is preserved, as in some gospel pericopes, and is necessary in stories of the legend type. It is unlikely to be symbolic, as the patriarch Simeon offers little to the typologist.

righteous and devout: The double characteristic is stylistic (cf. 1^6; A. 10^2; 11^{24}; 22^{12}). The conjunction of the two adjectives *dikaios* and *eulabēs* in Plato illustrates only by contrast, as there the first has the Greek political sense of 'just' and the second means 'circumspect', whereas here the first has the Jewish religious sense of 'righteous', and the latter (+ A. 2^5; 8^2; 22^{12}) had increasingly in Hellenistic authors, including Josephus and Philo, the meaning of 'reverent towards God', and hence pious in religious observance. Thus Simeon makes his appearance not in any official position (later tradition turned him into a priest offering the sacrifice), nor is the reputed custom of having a child blessed by a venerable rabbi (SB II, p. 31) relevant. He is a godly and inspired layman.

looking for the consolation of Israel: Significantly in the context Simeon's piety includes an eschatological element. For 'to look for' in this sense, cf. 2^{38}; A. 24^{15}; Mark 15^{43}; Titus 2^{13}; Jude 21. *consolation* is *paraklēsis*, which could have various senses (e.g. instruction or exhortation, A. 13^{15}). *the consolation of Israel*, which may be from Luke's source, was a semi-technical term for the last days based on the 'Comfort ye' of Isa. 40; cf. II Bar. 44^7, and SB II, pp. 124ff. for rabbinic usage, which included the idiom 'May I not see the consolation if I do not . . .'). In v. 26 it is identified with the appearance of the messiah.

the Holy Spirit was upon him: There is no exact parallel to the use of 'to be upon' (cf. v. 40) with the Holy Spirit (here without the article, see on 1^{15}). It may recall Isa. 61^1, and be intended to show Simeon as a prophet, an exceptional figure in Judaism. If so this is probably due to Luke, who from his Christian experience of the Spirit and prophecy sees them as characteristic of the Christian movement from its beginnings. But the phrase may mean that Simeon's piety included an inspired element, which put him in touch with God and made him look for Israel's hope, the result being the gift to him of revelation rather than prophecy.

26

it had been revealed to him by the Holy Spirit: The verb here, *chrēmatizein*, possibly from *chrēsmos* = 'oracle', is found in pagan authors for a divine oracle, admonition or instruction (cf. A. 10^{22} from an angel, Matt. $2^{12, 22}$ through a dream, Heb. 11^7 with 'devout'). It is unlikely to have been derived from the LXX, where in the few instances it means little more than 'speak'. That the oracle was of divine origin is contained in the word itself (v. 29), and *by the Holy Spirit* (here with the article), like *inspired by the Spirit* (v. 27), may be additions by Luke to enclose the whole incident within the operation of the Spirit.

that he should not see death before he had seen: Though the revelation is private and personal to him, with a play on the word *see* – 'to see death' is a Semitic expression for 'to die' (Ps. 89^{48}; John 8^{51}; Heb. 11^5) – it is connected with the divine purpose for Israel as a whole.

the Lord's Christ: See on 2^{11}. The anointed of the Lord was a regular expression for the actual king (Ps. 2^2 = A. 4^{26}; Ps. 18^{50}; II Sam. 1^{14}), and then for the expected king (Pss. Sol. 17^{36}; 17^{44}; $18^{6f.}$, which also contains the sentiment that those are blessed who live in the days when they will see the works of God through his Anointed).

27–28

This, somewhat clumsily expressed, provides a dramatic framework for the canticle, though the picture is blurred. Simeon is divinely guided to meet the parents and child by coming at a certain moment into the temple. This is *to hieron*, the temple courts, and, since Mary was allowed there, either the Court of the Women or the Court of the Gentiles. It is to be distinguished from *ho naos*, the sanctuary (see on 1⁹). Simeon is not a priest, and the scene has nothing to do with purification or presentation.

the parents: This, repeated in v. 43, and the references in vv. 38 and 48 to Joseph as the father, have been taken by some (e.g. Creed, Easton) as evidence that this and the following story emanated from circles ignorant of the virginal conception (as of the previous prophecies about the child); but they are hardly conclusive either way. The Greek *hoi goneis* has no Hebrew equivalent, the few instances in the LXX being either in books written in Greek or a translation of an original 'father and mother'. If Luke, who did know of the virginal conception, found the phrase satisfactory – and it is difficult to see what other could have been used – the same might have been the case with a source.

the child Jesus: In the context he is now named.

to do for him according to the custom of the law: A further grounding of the event in pious observance of the law of God. It is certainly framed by Luke – *the custom* translates the article with the perfect participle passive of *ethizein* + + = 'accustom' – but it is not intelligible, as neither purification of the child nor his presentation in the temple were prescribed in the law.

28

took up in his arms: As the result of miraculously inspired recognition, and without any sign such as was given to the shepherds. If the basic meaning of the verb here, *dechesthai* = 'to receive', is to be pressed, it might imply that the parents were also miraculously inspired to recognize Simeon as someone special, and to 'present' the child to the Lord by offering it to him.

blessed God: The following canticle is, like the Benedictus, a blessing (*eulogia*), though not beginning with 'Blessed be . . .' It is probably also meant to be prophetic (cf. 2²⁵⁻²⁶ with 1⁶⁷).

29–32

The third canticle, the Nunc Dimittis, has some of the same language as the Magnificat and Benedictus – *servant* (cf. 1⁴⁸), *according to thy word* (cf. 1⁵⁵, ⁷⁰), *peace* (cf. 1⁷⁹), *salvation* (cf. 1⁴⁷, ⁶⁹, ⁷⁷), *people Israel* (cf. 1⁵⁴, ⁶⁸). If v. 29 is to be taken as a statement of praise in extension of *blessed God*, then it is, like them, a psalm of praise with the motive of praise for an action of God. It differs from them in being not diffuse but compact in form and content. It is a poetical construction of three closely knit couplets, each with lines of the same length, the last with synonymous parallelism. While its removal would not disrupt the narrative, and Simeon's blessing of God might have been unspecified like Anna's in v. 38, it is less detachable than the other canticles from the story, whose meaning depends on it, and which may have been suggested by it. Thus *now lettest thou . . .* corresponds with *should not see death before, according to thy word* with *it had been revealed*, and *thy salvation* with *the Lord's Christ*. In an intensely personal manner the celebration of Israel's and the world's salvation is intimately bound up with the fate of the speaker.

29

Lord, now lettest thou thy servant depart: now stands first in the sentence, and together with the present tense of the verb expresses forcefully an eschatology that is being already realized merely in the existence of the child, and long in advance of anything he may do (contrast 10^{23f.}). The language here of *depart* (*apoluein* = 'release') and *Lord* (*despotēs* = 'master') has been taken to be derived from the manumission of a slave by his owner, 'You are discharging your slave from your service.' But this may overstress *doulos* = 'slave', which was conventional for the pious man in his relation to God, and *despotēs*, which was a Hellenistic synonym for *kurios* = 'lord', almost entirely confined to later books of the LXX and to the context of prayer (as in Josephus; cf. A. 4²⁴), and in which the accent is not on God as the master of slaves but as the lord of all things. *apoluein* = 'release, despatch' presupposes 'from the earth', and is an idiom for 'to die' that is not entirely Semitic (cf. Sophocles, *Antigone* 1268, 1314). It is more common in the passive (as in Gen. 15², with the only instance of *despotēs* in the Pentateuch), but is also found in the active (Tobit 3¹³; II Macc. 7⁹). RSV and others take it as modal, 'mayest thou despatch', but it would be more emphatic as a statement of fact, 'thou art despatching', which would then go beyond v. 26, where it is not said he would die once he had seen the Christ. For the sentiment 'Now may I die since . . .' cf. Gen. 46³⁰; Tobit 11⁹.

in peace: Not, as in 2¹⁴ in the full sense of salvation, which at this stage in the Gospel is still to be thought of as confined to those on earth, but in the formal sense in greetings and farewells of 'well-being' (cf. Gen. 15¹⁵). Simeon is prepared himself to go into oblivion once satisfied that God's salvation has appeared for those on earth.

thy salvation: Not 'the Saviour', as though Simeon was looking at the infant, but *to sōterion*, the article with the adjective, a more concrete form of the noun *sōteria*, a LXX word for 'the saving work'. That this for Luke was to be universal is evident from his use of the term, in the only other NT instances of it except Eph. 6¹⁷ = Isa. 59¹⁷, to bracket almost his whole work by extending the

Isaiah quotation at 3^6 and by the closing words of Paul in A. 28^{28}. That this universality is expressed somewhat ambiguously in vv. 31–32 may indicate that he did not compose them himself.

31

prepared: For this word in the sense of planned by God, cf. Mark 10^{40}; Matt. 25^{34}; I Cor. 2^9; I Enoch 25^7. Here it covers, not an item in salvation, but the whole salvation itself as the goal of divine activity in and through Israel.

in the presence of all peoples: This, with the following expression, is somewhat obscure. It need not mean that the Gentiles will participate in the salvation, but only that they will behold it, as in Isa. 52^{10}; Ps. 98^2; Isa. 40^5. But these passages refer to *ethnē* = 'Gentiles', whereas here the word is *laoi*, the singular of which denotes Israel (as does the plural in A. 4^{27}). *all peoples* may therefore here refer to Israel with the Gentiles.

32

This further specification of the salvation is compressed and obscure both in syntax and meaning. *light* and *glory* could be in apposition to *salvation* or be governed by *prepared*; and *glory* could be parallel to *light*, or governed by it and parallel to *revelation*. Gentiles – Israel is the opposite of the expected order.

a light for revelation to the Gentiles: phōs eis apokalupsin ethnōn. The difficulty of this expression can be seen from the variant renderings. 'a light to lighten the Gentiles' (AV) requires *apokalupsis* to have the meaning of *phōtismos* = 'enlightening'. 'for a revelation to the Gentiles' (RV), and 'that will be a revelation to the heathen' (NEB) require *Gentiles* to be in the dative. 'for the unveiling of the Gentiles' (RV margin) is ambiguous, but is true to the sense of *apokalupsis* followed by a genitive in the four other NT instances. In the OT *salvation, light* and *glory* can be associated terms, especially in II Isaiah, which provides the eschatological picture here. For God's glory is his splendour, often described as visible radiance, and his nature seen as his effective power for salvation. For *salvation* and *light*, cf. Isa. $51^{4f.}$; Ps. 43; for *salvation* and *glory*, cf. Isa. 40^5; for *light* and *glory*, cf. Isa. $60^{1,\ 19}$; 58^8; for all three together, cf. Isa. 60^{1-6}. Some of these passages concern the Gentiles, perhaps the most significant being Isa. $42^{6,\ 16}$; 60^{1-3}, where darkness is said to cover the earth for the Gentiles, but is removed by the light shining on Israel. The meaning here may therefore be 'a light for the unveiling of (the darkness upon) the Gentiles'.

glory to thy people Israel: This is not immediately intelligible, since *glory* is generally that which belongs to God. It may rest on Isa. 60^{1-3}, where Jerusalem's light is synonymous with the Lord's glory over her, which becomes her own light and brightness. This will be the form of Israel's destined salvation.

33–35

These verses are difficult both grammatically and in their sequence of thought. In view of v. 26 and the tone of the canticle the story might have been expected to end at this point with a reference to Simeon's departure from the temple, but in contrast to the Magnificat and Benedictus the canticle has a supplement.

33

The 'parents' are here referred to as *his father and his mother*, which is Semitic in style, but also, probably, in thought, Joseph being reckoned the father for legal and genealogical purposes. They interpret the general statements of the canticle directly of the child – *about him*. They repeat the wonder of $2^{17f.}$. This is a conventional trait belonging to miracle stories, and, when repeated in the individual pericopes, imparts a strong sense of the miraculous to the birth narratives as a whole.

34

Both parents are blessed, but since the story is basically of mother and child she alone is addressed with words of prophecy. These presumably are not intended to be the content of the blessing, though the wording *blessed them and said to Mary* suggests this.

Behold, this child . . . many in Israel: Simeon also passes from the general to the particular (cf. 1^{76}), but not in continuation of the canticle, as the form is no longer poetical and the tone changes abruptly from that of blessing. In terms which, even if put into his mouth *ex eventu*, are very allusive, he speaks of the divine appointment of *this child* to be the instrument of the twin activity of judgment and salvation. It is striking that this is uttered by way of an address to Mary.

is set for: keitai eis, a classical usage (cf. Phil. 1^{16}; I Thess. 3^3), used here in two somewhat different senses of the consequences for men and of the destiny of the child.

for the fall and rising: Some take this to refer to a double experience of the same people, who will be brought low and then exalted by the gospel, but that is unlikely. *fall, ptōsis*, with its verb *piptein*, is so common in the LXX for the effect of the judgment on the wicked that it need not be tied down to the specific prophecy of the stone of stumbling in Isa. 8^{14}, a proof text in the early church (Rom. 9^{33}; I Peter 2^8). *rising, anastasis*, refers to rising up out of humiliation or oppression, not to standing upright in the judgment. It is rare as an antithesis to *fall* (cf. Ps. 20^8, but not Isa. 24^{20}, where it is getting up after falling). The thought is similar to 1^{52-53}.

of many in Israel: Not the same as 'the many' as a term for all Israel. Its effect is to be widespread in Israel; no mention is made of the Gentiles.

for a sign that is spoken against: This continues and develops the thought. The instrument is not to be successful in effecting the divine purposes without itself being subject to the judgment of men. *sign, sēmeion*, is capable of a variety of meanings, the most likely here being 'banner' or 'ensign', which in Isaiah God commands to be raised as a summons and warning to the nations that he is about to demonstrate his power for the judgment and rescue of Israel and the Gentiles (rendered *sēmeion* or *sussēma* in Isa. 5^{26}; 13^2; 18^3; 49^{22}; 62^{10}, and in 11^{10-12} connected with the scion of David). *spoken against, antilegein* = 'contradict', is a classical word, rare in the LXX but occurring at Isa. 22^{12}; 50^5; 65^2 in the sense of 'disobey'.

35

(and a sword shall pierce through your own soul also): A very obscure statement. The Greek *kai sou de autēs tēn psuchēn* is literally 'and moreover (or 'but') of thee further thyself the soul (shall a sword pass through).' With the utmost emphasis it directs attention to Mary and to her personal experience as a result of what is being prophesied. Yet syntactically it is to be taken as a parenthesis, as by most commentators and in some Greek texts, even though parenthesis is foreign to Semitic speech, and is here very violent. Plummer (pp. 70f.) rejects this on the ground that 'a statement of such moment to the person addressed would hardly be introduced parenthetically', but in effect treats it as such in taking the words that follow, 'that thoughts . . .', as dependent on the whole of 'Behold . . . soul also', and on *is set for* and not on *will pierce*. Other attempts to avoid the parenthesis involve treating Mary as identical with, representative or symbolical of Israel: so Sahlin (*Messias*, pp. 272ff.), who takes *your own soul* as an apostrophe of Zion; Black (*Aramaic Approach*, pp. 153ff.) who amends the text to 'Through thee thyself (O Israel) will the sword pass'; Leaney (p. 100), 'if Mary "is" Israel the sword passing through her soul passes through the land' (cf. Laurentin, *Structure*, pp. 89f.). But this is intolerably forced. If it is a parenthesis, justifying the address of the whole prophecy in vv. 34-35 to Mary, it is likely to have been added by Luke – *kai . . . de* and *dierchesthai* = 'pass through' are in his style. It would be uniquely 'Mariological' in the birth narratives in the extent to which the course of the divine purpose was linked with her personal experience (for *psuchē*, soul, in the sense of 'self', see on 1^{46}). To what does Luke intend this to refer? See Fitzmyer (pp. 429f.) for a proper insistence that it is to be interpreted in relation to Luke's Gospel alone, and for the rejection on this account of some traditional interpretations. The parallel in wording with *Sybilline Oracles* 3.316, 'For a sword shall go through the midst of thee' has often been noted, and has been taken by some as evidence of literary dependence, but the line, which is unmetrical and possibly corrupt, seems to refer to the destruc-

tion, confusion and famine resulting in Egypt from the struggle between rival Ptolemies. The expression could have been proverbial for distress (cf. Ps. 37^{15}; Judith 6^6). If related to what precedes and follows, it could refer here to the distress for Mary personally of the future mission and message of her son in bringing about such divisions, and the unveiling of secret antagonisms, in Israel; or, more specifically, in spelling a repudiation of natural family ties that could apply even to her (cf. v. 48; 8^{21}; 11$^{27f.}$).

thoughts: dialogismoi could be neutral; the effect will be to bring to light what people are really thinking. But generally in the NT it has the sense of hostile thoughts.

36–38

The provision of a second witness to the child's destiny in respect of the coming salvation is probably made, either with a view to the pairing of a man and a woman, of which there is some evidence elsewhere in the gospel, or with reference to the law in Deut. 19^{15}. For Anna has nothing specific to say in her own right about the child either to God or man, and she only generalizes Simeon's testimony. Like Simeon she is a model; the descriptive biographical detail precludes her from being a 'type'.[s] The model is that of a woman of advanced years who persists in widowhood and in devoted religious practice – for this model in Judaism, see Judith 8$^{1-2, 4-8}$; 11^{17}; 16$^{22f.}$, and in the church I Tim. 5^5. Anna is a phenomenal representative of the model if the clumsy Greek here means that after marriage (at what age?) she lived for seven years as a married woman and eighty-four years as a widow. The devotional practice here of *worshipping* is appropriate to a story of the temple, to which she may have been in some way permanently attached; *epistāsa*, rendered *coming up*, could mean 'being there'. That she is called *a prophetess* may be due to Luke in his desire to represent the rebirth of prophecy in the emergence of Christianity. Prophetesses were rare in Judaism, the rabbis reckoning seven in Israel's history, but they could have been more common in the church.

38

Anna, like the parents and Simeon, combines the general and the particular. She *gave thanks to God* – the verb *anthomologeisthai* + + is a Hellenistic word found very occasionally in the later LXX books – and *spoke of him*, sc. the babe. In broadcasting, presumably what had been revealed to Simeon, she performs the same function in the story as the shepherds in vv. 17–18.

[s] The interpretations of *Phanuel, Asher* and the *seven years* and *eighty-four* suggested by M. D. Goulder and M. C. Sanderson, 'St Luke's Genesis', *JTS* ns 8, 1957, p. 24, to bring her within an overall typological pattern for the birth stories are very strained.

all who were looking for the redemption of Jerusalem: Like Simeon she belongs to the eschatologists, who in Luke's typical exaggeration *all who* are regarded as a class. *looking for*, see on v. 25. *the redemption of Jerusalem* is synonymous with *the consolation of Israel* (v. 25), with Jerusalem, as often in the OT, standing for the nation, and *redemption*, *lutrōsis*, having the general sense of 'release' or 'deliverance' without reference to ransom or any particular means (cf. 1^{68}; 24^{21}; Pss. 111^9; 130^7).

39

Like vv. 22–24 this shows how Luke envisaged the setting and importance of the events. The future Lord of Israel is from the beginning completely a member of Israel. When they have *performed* (*etelesan* = 'completed', cf. A. 13^{29}) *everything according to the law*, i.e. everything required by the law, the family returns home from Bethlehem – this, differently from in Matthew, will have been by way of Jerusalem.

40

The child Jesus' development is described in idealized and conventionally biblical terms (cf. I Sam. $2^{21,\,26}$), as was John's in 1^{80}, the first part of which is repeated here. Conventional too for the future great man is *filled with wisdom* (e.g. A. 7^{22} of Moses). It is not clear whether Luke makes a deliberate distinction between John's desert discipline in the prophetic spirit till the time of his mission and Jesus' domestic growth in wisdom, i.e. the knowledge of God and divine things, to be demonstrated in the next episode; and between God's *favour* (*charis* = 'grace') upon Jesus (deduced from his subsequent life?) and his guiding hand on John.

2^{41-52} JESUS AS A YOUTH IN THE TEMPLE

[41]*Now his parents went to Jerusalem every year at the feast of the Passover.* [42]*And when he was twelve years old, they went up according to custom;* [43]*and when the feast was ended, as they were returning, the boy Jesus stayed behind in Jerusalem. His parents did not know it,* [44]*but supposing him to be in the company they went a day's journey, and they sought him among their kinsfolk and acquaintances;* [45]*and when they did not find him, they returned to Jerusalem, seeking him.* [46]*After three days they found him in the temple, sitting among the teachers, listening to them and asking them questions;* [47]*and all who heard him were amazed at his understanding and his answers.* [48]*And*

when they saw him they were astonished; and his mother said to him, 'Son, why have you treated us so? Behold, your father and I have been looking for you anxiously.' [49]*And he said to them, 'How is it that you sought me? Did you not know that I must be in my Father's house?'* [50]*And they did not understand the saying which he spoke to them.* [51]*And he went down with them and came to Nazareth, and was obedient to them; and his mother kept all these things in her heart.*

[52]*And Jesus increased in wisdom and in stature,* * *and in favour with God and man.*

* Or *years*

The same characteristics of the Christian message as ensured that only later was interest to be shown in the circumstances of the messiah's birth are likely also to have limited any early growth of traditions about the interim period between birth and adult public ministry. There are none in Matthew, and those found in later apocryphal gospels are fanciful and bear little if any relation to the gospel. This is the only instance in the canonical gospels, and may have been all that was available to Luke for bridging the gap, and providing a modicum of continuity and transition from infancy to ministry. This it does with some theological effect in depicting Jesus as already showing in youth such preoccupation with the Father as will underlie his ministry. Since the story is clearly a pendant, attached by a special introduction in vv. 41f. and provided with a triple ending at vv. 51f., it does not throw light on the question how far Luke was himself responsible for the composition of 1^5-2^{40}.

The story is not easy to classify. It is correctly called a 'legend' in being designed to exhibit a person's sanctity, though it is of a peculiar type, since the sanctity is conveyed by the statement in v. 49, which is implicitly if not explicitly doctrinal and christological. Vincent Taylor's category of 'Stories about Jesus' fits well here, for while it may belong to a cycle of stories about Jesus and his mother, who is the spokesman in v. 48, it is concentrated on Jesus (note the repetition of *him* and *his*). It is a pericope with a single motif, though of a more biographical kind than usual, and in content it conforms to a type – 'the law of biographical analogy' (Dibelius, *Tradition*, p. 108). The precocity of the child who shows advance evidence of his future destiny was not uncommon in ancient literature. Thus Cyrus reveals his identity with a noble remark (Herodotus I, 114f.); Alexander, when very young, and in the absence of his father, asks far from childish questions of Persian ambassadors (Plutarch, *Life of Alexander*, 5); Apollonius, on reaching the age of learning his letters, copes with the best teachers (Philostratus, *Life of Apollonius*, 1.7). In the Jewish tradition it can be seen in the romanticising description of Moses in Josephus (*Ant.* 2.230) as having an understanding far beyond his years that gave promise of the greater deeds to be wrought in manhood, and by Philo (*Life of Moses*, 1.21) as advancing in a short time beyond the capacities of his teachers and forestalling their instruction. The context here is again that of pious Jewish observance, and what is presaged is not, as generally in apocryphal gospels, the future wonder-worker ('mighty in deed', 24^{19}; 5^{17}), but the future teacher ('mighty in word', 24^{19}), who will later exercise a teaching ministry in the temple (19^{47}; 20^{1}), and behind whose authoritative words is a knowledge of the whole purpose of God in scripture by one who as the Son is privy to the Father's secrets (4^{22}; 24^{27}; 10^{22}). Peculiar to the story is that these features, and especially the boy's theological self-consciousness, are brought out through an antagonism between child and parents.

The story is distinguished from the rest of the infancy narratives not only in form and content but in language, and Luke was probably the first to commit it to writing. The syntax is more polished – the double genitive absolute in *they went up* and *when the feast was ended*, the double participle in *supposing* and *did not find*, and the classical *nomizein* with accusative and infinitive in *supposing to be*. So also is the phraseology – *every year, kat' etos* + +, *company, sunodia* + + = 'caravan' (so Strabo), *a day's journey, hēmerās hodon*, rare in the LXX and never in that order, *sought, anazētein* + A. 11^{25}, a classical word found in the papyri but very rare in the LXX, *understanding, sunesis*, classical and LXX but rare in the NT and only here in L–A, *anxiously, odunasthai* + 16$^{24f.}$; A. 20^{38} = 'to be in pain', a classical poetic word, rare in the LXX.

∞

41

his parents: See on v. 27. The variant 'Joseph and Mary' here and in v. 43 is clearly a correction.

went: The imperfect of the Lukan verb *poreuesthai* has the sense 'used to go', i.e. as pious Jews. The law was not binding on women and they were exempt from pilgrimages, but some would seem to have attended the feasts, and the law was debated accordingly (see SB II, pp. 141f.). For a story of Jesus and his mother Mary is necessary, and her action may be modelled on that of Hannah (I Sam. 1³⁻⁷).

the feast of the Passover: hē heortē tou pascha + John 13¹, a Christian formulation, not found in the LXX or Judaism, which spoke of 'the Passover' or 'the feast of unleavened bread'. For this feast see on 22⁷.

42

twelve years old: This age appears frequently in the ancient world as that of adolescence, and may be too conventional to argue (as in SB II, p. 147) that since thirteen years and one month was the time when a Jewish boy undertook the obligations of the law this journey was a preliminary visit to accustom the boy Jesus to the future.

according to custom: In the Greek 'according to the custom of the feast'. What this means is not clear – perhaps 'in pilgrimage caravan' to prepare for the search in v. 44.

43

when the feast was ended: In the Greek 'having completed (*teleioun*, cf. A. 20²⁴) the days'.

as they were returning: In the Greek the articular infinitive of the Lukan verb *hupostrephein* = 'in the returning'.

the boy: ho pais and no longer the babe (*brephos*, vv. 12, 16) or the child (*paidion*, vv. 17, 27, 40). He now emerges as the subject of the action and in distinction from the parents; the text in v. 42, except in a few Old Latin mss, does not say expressly that they took him with them. He now acts independently in that he *stayed behind* (*hupomenein* + A. 17¹⁴ in this sense). How he did this at the conclusion of the seven days of the feast, or maintained himself in the meantime, are irrelevant to this kind of story. His parents act naturally, he does not.

44–46

It is not clear whether they missed him before starting out but supposed him to be somewhere in the caravan, or discovered him to be missing only at the end of a day's journey. *three days* is too conventional an expression to permit calculation of how much time was spent in journeying or searching.

44

sought: The verb *anazētein* is found in papyri for the search for human beings under difficult circumstances, especially for escaped prisoners.

46

Our knowledge of the circumstances is too limited to say how far the scene is idealized. Parts of the temple area were apparently used for theological instruction and discussion (19^{47}; 20^1), though some have speculated whether there was a synagogue in the area for the purpose (SB II, p. 150). Ellis (p. 85) refers to tractate Sanhedrin (88b) for the Sanhedrin's informally receiving questions and giving instruction on feast days and sabbaths; but here the feast is over.

sitting: The posture of pupils, though generally at the feet of individual rabbis (A. 22^3).

among the teachers: among, en mesō = 'in the midst of' (Lukan) means that he is the cynosure of a concourse of rabbis. Only here in the gospel is *didaskalos* = 'teacher' applied to them.

asking them questions: The boy listens but also interrogates, and is himself interrogated (*his answers*, v. 47). But the verb *eperōtān* is often used in the gospels to introduce a point of debate (as in 6^9; 17^{20}; 20^{21}; Mark 12^{18}), and may here denote, not requests for information, but success in disputation, which was to be a mark of his ministry. Josephus (*Life* 9) can say of himself, 'When I was a mere boy about fourteen years old I was universally applauded for my love of letters, insomuch that the chief priests and the leading men of the city used constantly to come to me for precise information on some particular in our ordinances.'

47

Luke underlines the marvel of such religious knowledge beyond his years by a typical *all who heard*, and by the verb *existasthai* = 'to be astonished', used seven times in A. of astonishment at miracle. The scene nevertheless exhibits a certain reserve compared with later apocryphal stories about the relations between the young Jesus and his teachers, e.g. in the Infancy Gospel of Thomas 19^2, where they are reduced to silence by him. And the wonder does not, as generally, form the climax of the story, but is only the prelude to its main point.

his understanding and his answers: A Lukan double expression forming a hendiadys, 'his penetrating answers' (Fitzmyer, p. 442).

48

The language is vigorous. The parents are also astonished (a different verb, *ekplēssesthai*, cf. 9^{43}; A. 13^{12}), but for the different reason that he has shown such independence of them. This leads to complaint, which, characteristically in a Lukan birth story, is voiced not by Joseph but by Mary. It is so phrased as to produce a reply which subjects natural ties to supernatural, which possibly for Luke is the beginning of Mary's experience of the sword (v. 35). For the reproach *Son, why have you treated us so?* is met by a counter reproach *How is it that* (ti hoti = 'what that', classical and LXX) *you sought me?*, and *your father and I* (predictably altered in some mss to 'we') is taken up by *my Father's house*.

49

Did you not know . . .?: Their actions belied all that they were in a position to know.

I must be: The first use in the gospel of *dei* = 'it is necessary' of the divine compulsion which will mark his ministry, here retrojected into his youth.

in my Father's house: en tois tou patros mou = 'in the (things) of my Father'. 'It is unfortunate that the very first words which can be certainly known to have been uttered by our blessed Lord are of doubtful interpretation' (Field, *Notes*, p. 50). RSV's rendering takes the neuter plural *ta* = 'the things' followed by a genitive to mean 'the house of', as in classical and Hellenistic usage (for instances see Field, *Notes*, pp. 53ff.), and occasionally in the LXX (Esther 7⁹; Job. 18¹⁹), and *einai en* = 'to be in' of location. The temple context then determines the meaning, which is 'There was no need to search; you should have known where to find me – where God my Father lives'. But for this one would have expected *oikos* = 'house' in view of its frequent use for the temple (cf. 19⁴⁶), and what he is engaged in, discussion of the law, is not so naturally associated with the temple as were sacrifice and prayer. AV's rendering 'about my Father's business' follows the regular classical and Hellenistic usage of *ta* = 'the concerns' (cf. Mark 8³³; I Cor. 7³²) and *einai en* = 'to be occupied with' (cf. I Tim. 4¹⁵). The saying would then be of a more widely applicable and permanent kind, for which the temple context is only a frame – 'Why be upset when you found me missing? You should have known what I would be about – occupied with the truth of God.' It takes, as frequently in the Gospel, the form of a rhetorical question, which does not in either rendering really answer the complaint. It is also christological. Jesus speaks as one conscious of being the Son of God (1³⁵) in relation to God whom he calls *my Father*.

50

they did not understand the saying: The ignorance already referred to in v. 48 is not removed. This is not evidence that the story is unaware of the virginal conception; 'your father and I' (v. 48) suggests the opposite. What was to be expected of a child so born still lay open. It is idle to speculate what it was that, despite their previous knowledge, they failed to understand. Luke here assimilates the event to the later gospel story. As with his disciples, so here, Jesus speaks on a different plane, and is met with human incomprehension even from his intimates (cf. 9⁴⁵; 18³⁴).

51-52

The saying in v. 49 brings the incident to a close. With a triple ending (cf. vv. 17-20 and the double ending in vv. 39-40) Luke now ties it into the infancy narratives as their conclusion.

51

Jesus continues to be the subject, the parents now accompanying him rather than he them, but it is emphasized that the divine filial consciousness expressed in v. 49 did not spell rebellion, and was not incompatible with a continuing state of parental obedience. *was obedient* renders *hupotassesthai*, a verb found only here in the gospels, though regularly in the household codes in Eph. 5²⁴; Col. 3¹⁸; Titus 2⁵; I Peter 3¹, where, however, it is used of the obedience of wives to husbands, that of children to parents being expressed by *hupakouein*.

kept all these things in her heart: The mother is again cited (see on v. 19) as a witness to the remarkable character of events – here all the events of the infancy – in their bearing on the future. In the context this mitigates somewhat the incomprehension in v. 50.

52

The verse returns to Jesus with a repetition of v. 40, which approximates more in thought, though not in phraseology, to I Sam. 2²⁶ LXX.

increased in wisdom: The verb here, *prokoptein*, is a regular classical word for making outstanding progress; but it is the possession of the fullness of wisdom rather than growth in it that is suggested by the scene in the temple and by *filled with wisdom* (v. 40).

in stature: The Greek word *hēlikia* makes little sense here in either of its two meanings. That of 'age' (RSV margin 'years'), which is the regular meaning in the papyri, is strangely dismissed by Creed (p. 46) on the ground that 'it goes without saying that Jesus grew older'; for it presumably goes without saying that from the age of twelve he grew taller. Perhaps what is meant is the outstanding stature and appearance to be predicated of the great, as in the idealized portrait of Moses in Josephus (*Ant.* 2.231), 'When he was three years old, God gave wondrous increase to his stature (*hēlikia*); and none was so indifferent to beauty as not, on seeing Moses, to be amazed at his comeliness', and in Philo (*Life of Moses* 1.19), 'He was noble and goodly to look upon; and the princess, seeing him so advanced beyond his age (*hēlikia*) . . .'

in favour with God and man: A formula in which *charis, favour*, is used in a different sense from v. 40 for approbation. That it increased among men could only be presumed.

3^1-4^{13} *The Prophetic Mission of John as the Forerunner and the Installation of Jesus as the Son of God*

In these chapters John prepares a people for the Lord (3^{1-20}); the focus then shifts to Jesus, as we see him designated, legitimated and tested as the Son of God ($3^{21}-4^{13}$).

The parallelism of John and Jesus with respect to their births (chs. 1–2) is continued with respect to their adult ministries, but in such a way as to remove John from the scene and to focus on Jesus alone. John, who was destined to be called 'the prophet of the Most High', to go before the Lord (God) to prepare a people for him by turning men to the way of peace (salvation), by reconciling them to one another, and by the remission of sins ($1^{16-17, \, 76-79}$), and who in the meantime has had his abode in the desert until his appointment by God to Israel (1^{80}), now receives in the desert God's call to be a prophet (3^2). He appears publicly to announce a baptism for remission of sins (3^3), exhorts those who would be God's true Israel to repent in face of an imminent judgment (3^{7-9}), bids men be reconciled to one another and to follow the paths of justice (3^{10-14}), and declares his baptism in water preparatory to a baptism in spirit by a mightier one to come (3^{15-17}). Jesus, destined to be called 'the Son of the Most High' ($1^{32, \, 35}$), is the anointed one ($2^{11, \, 26}$), and, though subject to human parents, calls God his Father (2^{49-51}). Now through the medium of John's baptism he is publicly anointed with the holy spirit, and is declared by God to be his Son (3^{21-22}). He is legitimated as such by his descent (3^{23-38}), and is proved such by a victorious conflict with the devil (4^{1-13}).

Luke is here still concerned with beginnings (3^{23}). Although, like Matthew, he has carried the gospel story further back than Mark, and has given it a pre-history in the birth of Jesus (and of John), he is compelled to start again from the perspective already established in the tradition, where the gospel had in effect 'begun' with, and from, the preaching and baptism of John (so Mark $1^{1ff.}$, John $1^{6ff.}$, $^{19ff.}$, reproduced by Luke in A. 1^{22}; 10^{36-38}; 13^{24}). The events of 1–2, though full of promise for the future, and to some extent bruited abroad (1^{66}; 2^{38}), had been confined to a small circle of the pious in Israel. But the events of the gospel were 'not done in a corner' (A. 26^{26}), and the moment when they begin to pass from the private to the public domain is heavily underlined by Luke. The story, which in his version is to reach its end with Paul at the centre of the civilized world preaching a salvation of God that is universal in scope and import (3^6; A. 28^{28}), is brought at its beginning into relation with the history and government of that world. It is unnecessary to account for $3^{1ff.}$ by postulating (with Taylor, *Third Gospel*, pp. 164ff., and others) a first draft of the gospel, which had lacked 1–2, and had begun at this point.

3^{1-20} THE PROPHETIC MINISTRY OF JOHN

3 *In the fifteenth year of the reign of Tiberius Caesar, Pontius Pilate being governor of Judea, and Herod being tetrarch of Galilee, and his brother Philip tetrarch of the region of Ituraea and Trachonitis, and Lysanias tetrarch of Abilene, ²in the high-priesthood of Annas and Caiaphas, the word of God came to John the son of Zechariah in the wilderness; ³and he went into all the region about the Jordan, preaching a baptism of repentance for the forgiveness of sins. ⁴As it is written in the book of the words of Isaiah the prophet,*

'The voice of one crying in the wilderness:
Prepare the way of the Lord,
make his paths straight.
⁵Every valley shall be filled,
and every mountain and hill shall be brought low,
and the crooked shall be made straight,
and the rough ways shall be made smooth;
⁶and all flesh shall see the salvation of God.'

⁷He said therefore to the multitudes that came out to be baptized by him, 'You brood of vipers! Who warned you to flee from the wrath to come? ⁸Bear fruits that befit repentance, and do not begin to say to yourselves, "We have Abraham as our father"; for I tell you, God is able from these stones to raise up children to Abraham. ⁹Even now the axe is laid to the root of the trees; every tree therefore that does not bear good fruit is cut down and thrown into the fire.'

¹⁰And the multitudes asked him, 'What then shall we do?' ¹¹And he answered them, 'He who has two coats, let him share with him who has none;

and he who has food, let him do likewise.' ^{12}Tax collectors also came to be baptized, and said to him, 'Teacher, what shall we do?' ^{13}And he said to them, 'Collect no more than is appointed you.' ^{14}Soldiers also asked him, 'And we, what shall we do?' and he said to them, 'Rob no one by violence or by false accusation, and be content with your wages.'

^{15}As the people were in expectation, and all men questioned in their hearts concerning John, whether perhaps he were the Christ, ^{16}John answered them all, 'I baptize you with water; but he who is mightier than I is coming, the thong of whose sandals I am not worthy to untie; he will baptize you with the Holy Spirit and with fire. ^{17}His winnowing fork is in his hand, to clear his threshing floor, and to gather the wheat into his granary, but the chaff he will burn with unquenchable fire.'

^{18}So, with many other exhortations, he preached good news to the people. ^{19}But Herod the tetrarch, who had been reproved by him for Herodias, his brother's wife, and for all the evil things that Herod had done, ^{20}added this to them all, that he shut up John in prison.

In pursuit of an orderly account (1^3) Luke here gathers into a single section almost all the information about John available to him (7^{18} is vague, and says nothing about John's whereabouts, and 9^{7-9} presumes his death, which is not described). This information was evidently fragmentary, brief and highly compressed in the tradition, being largely such as served to indicate John's role in Christian eyes. Hence it is difficult to get him into focus, or to arrive at a coherent account of his teaching (see on vv. 7–9, 15–17).[t] Luke has, however, made out of the traditions a more connected narrative than that in the other gospels. John is depicted in miniature as a prophet with a call (v. 2b), a sphere of operations (v. 3), a diversified message (vv. 7–9, 10–14, 15–18), and a span of activity which is rounded off by an advance notice of his imprisonment (vv. 19–20), even though this removes him from the story before he has baptized Jesus. The representative character of all this for Israel is stressed by all (vv. 3–6, 15–16), the multitudes (vv. 7, 10) and the people (vv. 15, 18; cf. $7^{29f.}$; $20^{3ff.}$).

The question of sources is complicated by two factors. (i) Even if Luke (and Matthew) were primarily dependent on Mark here, they

[t] For the problems involved in reconstructing from the gospels and any other sources, e.g. Josephus, the person, message and movement of John, see W. Wink, *John the Baptist in the Gospel Tradition*, NTS monograph 7, 1968, and the literature there cited.

would not have shown it by reproducing Mark's beginning, which is very compressed and awkward. (ii) If vv. 7–9, 16–17 are to be ascribed to Q (the very close verbal agreement between Matthew and Luke here has been a starting point for the Q hypothesis) it is still uncertain what kind of a writing Q was, and how it would have introduced John and his teaching. A possible analysis of this section is that its major content, John's preaching (vv. 7–9, 16–17) was taken from Q (with vv. 10–14 a piece of oral tradition added by Luke to this Q material), but that its framework in *preaching a baptism of repentance for the forgiveness of sins* (v. 3b) and in the citation from Isa. 40³ (vv. 4–6) was supplied by Mark. The introductions and transitions binding material from different sources into a smooth narrative suggest Luke's hand.

❧❧

1–2
This synchronism must have involved research on the part of Luke, who was writing at a later, perhaps much later date. Strictly speaking it introduces the prophetic activity of John, but it is clearly intended to place the events of the Gospel as a whole (and possibly those of A. also) on the background of world history (cf. 2¹ff.) – the only attempt in the NT to do so. The sixfold reference to contemporary rulers, civil and ecclesiastical, is far more elaborate than anything of the kind in the OT, e.g. the dating in prophetic books or in Judith 1¹, and is after the manner of the secular historians (cf. Thucydides II, 2, perhaps a model in being sixfold, Polybius I, 3, Diodorus Siculus XVI, 2, Dionysius of Halicarnassus, *Roman Antiquities* 9.61, etc.) and of Greek inscriptions. It may be something of a literary flourish, as the last two civil rulers are otiose, playing no part in L–A. Further the fifteenth year of Tiberius' reign would function as a fixed chronological datum only if accompanied in the Gospel itself by precise dates for the births of John and Jesus, and for, at least, the passion. These Luke does not provide, and perhaps was not in a position to provide, even if he had wished to do so. The incidental historical references in L–A can be made to yield a chronology only by reference to statements outside it, and Luke is no more concerned with exact chronology than the other evangelists, but is for the most part content with vague and general notes of time.

1
In the fifteenth year of the reign of Tiberius Caesar: The synchronism begins at the centre of the world, Rome, and with a date, the regnal year of the Roman emperor. *reign (hēgemonia)* is a general word for governorship (Dio Cassius 60.17 for the prefecture of Egypt). Josephus uses it both of the office of Caesar

(*Ant.* 18.33, of Tiberius), and of a particular Caesar's period of rule (*BJ* 6.269). If the regnal years are reckoned, as generally, from the death of Augustus (19 Aug. AD 14), *the fifteenth year of Tiberius* is from 19 Aug. AD 28 to 18 Aug. AD 29; if reckoned by the Jewish civil year it is from 1 Oct. 27 to 30 Sept. 28, counting the first year as from 19 Aug. to 1 Oct. AD 14; if by the Jewish ecclesiastical year it is from Nisan 28 to Nisan 29. Some have argued for a reckoning from the association of Tiberius as co-regent with Augustus in AD 11–12 (mentioned by Suetonius, *Tiberius* 26; Velleius Paterculus 2.21; Tacitus, *Annals* I, 3), as this could reconcile the date with the birth of Jesus in 4 BC and his age in 3[23]; but the evidence of these Roman writers themselves, and that of papyri and coinage, are against this.[u]

Pontius Pilate being governor of Judea: The remaining statements in v. 1 are not chronological, but refer to the rulers contemporary with the previous date. They begin with the emperor's representative in the Roman province of Judaea. *being governor* is the participle of the verb *hēgemoneuein*, corresponding to the previous noun. D and Eusebius have *epitropountos* = 'being procurator' (the Old Latin and the Vulgate have *procurante*), but this was the correct terminology only at a later date. Smaller areas requiring special treatment as being either new or difficult provinces – such as was Judaea – were governed by men of second (equestrian) rank. These were called *praefecti* = 'prefects', as is Pilate in an inscription discovered at Caesarea, the Roman headquarters. Only from AD 53, as the result of a decree of the emperor Claudius, were they called 'procurators'. While the usual Greek word for *praefectus* was *eparchos* (Jos. *Ant.* 18.33), a possible word was the more military term *hēgemōn* (Jos. *Ant.* 18.55, of Pilate). While the prefect was directly responsible to the emperor, who appointed and dismissed him, he enjoyed full authority (*imperium*) in his province. Pilate was prefect from AD 26 to AD 36 (37?). *Judaea* was one of the three administrative districts into which Palestine was divided under Roman rule, stretching from the northern border of Samaria to include Idumaea in the south, and from the sea to beyond the Jordan (so 1[65]; 2[4]; 5[17]; 21[21]). But elsewhere Luke is less precise. In A. 1[8]; 8[1]; 9[31] it excludes Samaria; in A. 12[19] it excludes Caesarea; in 23[5]; A. 10[37] it includes Galilee; and in 1[5]; 4[44]; 6[17]; 7[17]; A. 26[20]; 28[21] it seems to be used as a general term for Palestine as the land of the Jews, which it had been under Herod the Great, and had again become from AD 41, when Claudius restored to Herod Agrippa I 'all the country over which Herod his grandfather had reigned' (Jos. *Ant.* 19.274).

Herod being tetrarch of Galilee: This and the following notices reflect the partition of Palestine made by Augustus in 4 BC (Jos. *BJ* 2.93–95), which was substantially that made by Herod the Great in his will (Jos. *BJ* 1.664). It lasted until AD 6, when

u See G. Ogg, *The Chronology of the Public Ministry of Jesus*, Cambridge 1940, pp. 170ff.

Archelaus was deposed and Judaea became a province. A tetrarchy, originally one of the four regions into which a kingdom was divided, had become a general term for a division of a Roman protectorate (Tacitus, *Annals* XV, 25). A tetrarch ranked below a king (see Luke's correction in 9⁷ of Mark 6¹⁴). Herod Antipas, the son of Herod the Great and Malthace, was tetrarch of Galilee (Luke does not mention his territory of Peraea) until banished to Lyons by Caligula in AD 39. He is the Herod who figures prominently in this Gospel (3¹⁹; 8³; 9⁷ff.; 13³¹; 23⁷⁻¹⁵; also A. 4²⁷; 13¹).

his brother Philip tetrarch of the region of Ituraea and Trachonitis: Philip, Herod's half-brother, the son of Herod the Great and Cleopatra of Jerusalem, ruled peacefully until his death in AD 34 over what Luke calls *the region of Ituraea and Trachonitis*. *Ituraea* could be an adjective = 'the Ituraean and Trachonitid region', but is more probably a noun = 'Ituraea and the Trachonitid region'. Precise specification of the territories included in this tetrarchy, to which Philo (*The Embassy to Gaius* 326) gives the name 'Trachonitis', would be difficult without giving a long list of names (cf. Jos. *BJ* 2.93–95), even supposing the names and boundaries were fixed, and that Luke knew them. Until the first century BC the principality of Ituraea, under its ruler Ptolemy and his son Lysanias, covered a large area stretching from Laodicea in the north to Galilee in the south, and from Mediterranean outposts in the west to the environs of Damascus in the east. The transference to Herod in 24 BC of Batanea, Trachonitis and Auranitis, and four years later of Ulatha and Paneas (rebuilt by Philip as Caesarea Philippi), was part of the gradual disintegration and dismemberment of the Ituraean principality. Thus *Ituraea* would have been the most convenient term to designate Philip's territory other than Trachonitis, and though imprecise was not altogether incorrect.

Lysanias tetrarch of Abilene: The tetrarchy of Abilene, with its capital at Abila, and including parts of Lebanon (Jos. *Ant.* 19.275), was also the result of the dismemberment of the Ituraean kingdom. Josephus refers to it as both the tetrarchy (*Ant.* 18.237) and the kingdom (*BJ* 2.215) of Lysanias. Two inscriptions from near Abilene, one certainly from the time of Tiberius, attest the existence of a tetrarch Lysanias. It is surprising that Luke should mention such a small territory that plays no part in the gospel story. This is perhaps for the sake of completeness, since Abilene was part of the territory of Herod Agrippa I, or for the sake of a rhythmical sentence as fully as possible in the historical style.

2a

in the high-priesthood of Annas and Caiaphas: The genitive absolutes give place here to the preposition *epi* with the genitive, a regular construction in dating. When the noun is, as here, without an article it denotes a period of time during the person's actual office = 'at the time when Annas and Caiaphas were high priests'. What does this mean? The plural 'high priests' could refer, as frequently in the gospels, to those who had been high priest, and those who belonged to high priestly families, but there was only one high priest in office at any one time, as Luke was aware (A. 4⁶). Some have supposed that *Caiaphas* was added by a scribe as a correction of *Annas* in the text, and was then, and at A. 4⁶, incorporated into the text. If so Luke would be in error, since Annas, who was appointed high priest in AD 6, was deposed by the prefect Gratus in AD 15, his son-in-law Caiaphas holding the office from AD 18 (17?) to 36. Josephus (*Ant.* 20.198) says that men counted Annas most happy in that after he himself had enjoyed the office all his five sons became high priests, which was unprecedented. Hence it might be supposed that he continued to exercise great influence, and could still be called in a sense high priest. There is a similar combination, or confusion, of names in John (cf. 18¹³, ²⁴ with 18¹⁹). Possibly Luke is making a general deduction from such data, oral or written, as his sources provided. If he had been more precisely informed he would probably have given a name to the high priest who presided at Jesus' trial (22⁵⁴).

2b–3

the word of God came to John the son of Zechariah: Luke shows his versatility by passing within a single sentence from the manner of secular history to the hallowed language of the OT. For *the word of God came*, only here in the NT, and *the son of* in the call of a prophet, cf. Jer. 1¹⁻²; Hos. 1¹; II Baruch 1¹, where it prepares, as here, for some action or announcement to follow. While in the other gospels John simply makes his appearance in fulfilment of scripture, Luke traces this appearance back to a divine call. This could be significant in itself if, as is often said, scribal exegesis of scripture had by this time replaced prophecy, which was held to have disappeared from Israel until some significant time in the future. Some statements – e.g. 7¹⁶, ²⁶; Matt. 7¹⁵ – suggest, however, that prophecy was a live possibility.

in the wilderness: *hē erēmos* = 'the desert'. The place of a prophet's call is not generally recorded in the OT. The tradition had, however, firmly associated John with the desert (7²⁴ = Matt. 11⁷; Mark 1⁴). This may have come about through the application to him of Isa. 40³ in the LXX version, which has 'the voice of one crying in the desert', whereas the Hebrew connects 'in the desert' with 'prepare'. By *hē erēmos* was not meant a sandy waste, but a desolate, un-cultivated region, generally uninhabited. Without specification it was vague. It could denote the wilderness of Judah west of the Dead Sea (so Matt. 3¹, and possibly here in view of 1³⁹, ⁶⁵, ⁸⁰). If so, v. 3a marks a change of scene between the call and the preaching in an inhabited area. Or it could denote land east of Jordan (cf. John 1²⁸; 10⁴⁰). It could, however, be less a geographical than a religious term. The forty years' sojourn in the wilderness came to be regarded as an ideal time when Israel saw the saving acts of God and was made his people

(Hos. 9¹⁰; 13⁵; Amos 2¹⁰; Jer. 2²; A. 7³⁶), and as such it supplied features of the coming age (Hos. 2¹⁴ᶠᶠ·; 12⁹; Micah 7¹⁵; II Baruch 29⁸). There was an expectation that the salvation of God would be immediately preceded by a journey into the desert in the belief that there God would give tokens of deliverance (cf. Matt. 24²⁶; A. 21³⁸). In the theology of Qumran retreat to, and residence in, the desert were not unconnected with the community's conception of itself as a community of penitents, the remnant or true Israel of God. It is doubtful whether Luke had any more precise geographical knowledge. He has probably taken the two places with which John had been associated in the tradition, the desert and the Jordan, perhaps under the influence of the stories of Elijah and Elisha in I Kings 17³ᶠᶠ·; II Kings 2⁶ᶠᶠ·), and has brought them together by a call in the desert and a subsequent preaching mission in *the region about* (Greek *perichōros* = 'neighbourhood') Jordan, which draws the crowds to John.

preaching a baptism of repentance for the forgiveness of sins: This highly compressed and possibly Christian formulation is probably taken from Mark 1⁴, where it is the sole description of John's ministry. It presents difficulties in its parts and in their relation to one another.

(i) *preaching:* The Greek verb *kērussein* means to perform the function of a *kērux* or herald, to announce. Very occasionally it is used in the LXX for a prophet's announcement of a coming action of God (e.g. Isa. 61¹), but it became the standard term in the Christian tradition, first for Jesus' announcement of the imminent coming of God's kingdom (4⁴⁴; 8¹; Mark 1¹⁴ etc.), and then for the Christian proclamation of Jesus himself as messiah and saviour (A. 8⁵; I Cor. 1²³ etc.). Its use here of John may indicate that he is being seen through Christian eyes as part of the gospel (cf. A. 10³⁷; 13²⁴).

(ii) *a baptism:* The Greek word here *baptisma* is a passive verbal noun meaning 'the act of being baptized'. It is only found in Christian writings. To 'preach a baptism' is a highly uncommon expression. If the verb is to be given the pregnant sense in (i) above, then the baptism announced is itself a work of God or produced by God. In connecting repentance with baptism John differs from his prophetic predecessors, as is indicated both in Jewish and Christian tradition by his title 'the Baptist' (so Jos. *Ant.* 18.116, the synoptic gospels and Acts; Mark 1⁴ has 'the one baptizing'). His practice has been variously accounted for by reference to the religious lustrations that were increasingly common in the ancient world. including Judaism;ᵛ or in particular to the baptizing of Gentile proselytes for membership of Israel, if, as is not established beyond dispute, this was already practised in Judaism in the first century AD.ʷ But the NT evidence

ᵛ Cf. Josephus, *Life* 11; *BJ* 2, 129; J. Thomas, *Le Mouvement Baptiste en Palestine et Syrie*, Paris 1935, for the theory of a widespread baptist movement at the time; for lustrations at Qumran, see G. Vermes, *Scrolls*, p. 45.

ʷ See W. F. Flemington, *The New Testament Doctrine of Baptism*, London 1948, New York 1949, Part I.

is too scanty for certainty, and possibly it is not necessary to look further than the OT. In the prophets repentance and the new life had already been associated with washing (cf. Isa. $1^{16ff.}$; 4^4; Ezek. $36^{25ff.}$; Zech. 13^1; Jubilees 1^{23}). Interpreted realistically under the influence of a fervent eschatological expectation such passages could have given rise to a practice such as John's baptism. It is also possible that the priestly origin ascribed to him by Luke ($1^{5ff.}$) could have influenced John in his choice of a practice that was levitical in character (cf. John $1^{19ff.}$, where priests and Levites interrogate him about his baptizing), and that he may have shared the expectation of a deliverer from the house of Levi (Test. Levi $8^{12ff.}$).

(iii) *of repentance*: Greek *metanoia* = 'change of mind'. This is nowhere defined in the NT, and the OT had no technical term for it. What it referred to, however, was very familiar to the OT and Jewish piety (though not to Gentiles), i.e. a turning from idols and sin and to God with complete devotion once and for all. This is the characteristic demand of God through the prophets (Amos $4^{6ff.}$; Hos. $6^{1ff.}$; Isa. $55^{6ff.}$; Jer. $25^{4ff.}$; Ezek. $18^{30ff.}$; Deut. 29–30). Later Jewish literature, in which *metanoia* and the corresponding verb are increasingly the terms used, show that it became the background of Jewish piety, corporate and individual, and of the teaching of the synagogue (Ecclus $17^{24ff.}$; Wisd. 11^{23}–12^{19}, the prayers of penitence in Dan. 9; Tobit $3^{2ff.}$; Prayer of Manasses 4ff.). In connection with eschatological hopes the urgent note of the prophets reappears in the expectation of a single act of repentance which God will give to Israel as the prelude to the coming of the kingdom (Assumption of Moses 1^{18}; Ps. Sol. $18^{4ff.}$; Jubilees 23^{26}). This note could have become the more urgent in the preaching and practice of John in proportion as he believed his hearers to be faced with an imminent final judgment. The connection between baptism and repentance remains, however, obscure. The genitive *of repentance* is generally taken to mean that the baptism accompanied repentance as an outward sign or symbol of it, though it is not clear why it was necessary. But pure symbolism was foreign to ancient religion, including Judaism, and in the view of some scholars the meaning is that the act of submission and submersion was efficacious, and itself produced the required repentance. This would make it an eschatological sacrament, and so unique in Jewish piety.[x] The question in v. 7 implies that the baptism is efficacious in respect of the coming judgment, though the demand in v. 8 for the fruits of repentance shows that it was not automatically so.

(iv) *for the forgiveness of sins*: In the Greek *for* is *eis*, with the meaning 'resulting in' rather than 'with a view to', and *forgiveness of sins* is *aphesis hamartiōn*, with the meaning either 'cancellation of' or 'release from' sins, according to the two meanings of the verb *aphienai*. This is surprising here, since elsewhere in the NT forgiveness (remission) of sins is a gift granted by the exalted Christ (A. 5^{31}),

---

x See the discussion and references in U. W. Mauser, *Christ in the Wilderness*, SBT 39, 1963, pp. 84ff.

or is 'in Christ' (Eph. 1^7; Col. 1^{14} – the only Pauline instances), or is given through his name (24^{47}; A. 10^{43}; I John 2^{12}), or in Christian baptism (A. 2^{38}). Hence Matthew removes it from here to Matt. 26^{28}, and characterizes John's baptism as one of repentance only (Matt. $3^{2,\ 11}$). The fact that it is nowhere else in L–A attached to John's baptism, which is said to be one of repentance (A. 13^{24}; 19^4), indicates the influence of Mark's text on Luke here (Josephus, *Ant.* 18.117, perhaps in anti-Christian polemic, expressly denies that John's baptism was for the remission of sins). The statement is more intelligible to the extent that (i) John's mission was thought of as so intimately connected with the gospel as to form part of it (3^{4-6}; 16^{16}?; Mark 1^{1-4}), and (ii) it had not necessarily acquired everywhere in the Christian tradition the meaning of a forgiveness always available through the atoning death of Jesus, and could still have the more Jewish sense of the removal by God in response to repentance of the sins of the past and of a single unrepeatable act preceding the judgment (as perhaps in 1^{77}). Cf. I Enoch 5^6; 12^5 for release from sins as belonging with the peace and salvation of the saints.

4–6

This, the first OT citation in the Gospel after that in the birth narratives, 2^{23-24}, could have been taken, as in Matt. 3^3, from Mark 1^{2-3}, though Mark's abrupt use of it in parenthesis and attached to a citation from Malachi wrongly ascribed to Isaiah, cried out for revision. This Luke makes by removing it to the end of his description of John and as a comment on it, and by a more formal mode of citation: *in the book* (cf. 20^{42}; A. 1^{20}; 7^{42}) *of the words* (this is unique) *of the prophet Isaiah* (he will use the Malachi quotation of John in the Q passage 7^{27} = Matt. 11^{10}). The citation may be seen as an example of that use of *testimonia* or proof texts to establish the gospel events as being 'according to the scriptures', i.e. according to the divine plan, which constituted the earliest exercise in Christian theology (see Dodd, *According to the Scriptures*). The use here, as often elsewhere, is probably an 'atomic' one, i.e. the text is taken in isolation without regard for its original context. Here the connecting links are *in the wilderness* and *the Lord*, which in Isa. 40^3 refers to God, but is now made to refer to Jesus as the Lord of Christians, and consequently the LXX text itself has been altered from 'of our God' to *his* (ways). In this way John, his preaching and movement, do not stand in their own right, as references to 'John's disciples' (5^{33}; 7^{18}; 11^1; A. $19^{3f.}$) suggest that they could, but are essentially the necessary divine prelude to Jesus. Luke further makes the citation serve as an introduction to the whole story of the Gospel and Acts in its universal appeal by having it run on until it reaches *all flesh shall see the salvation of God*, which is echoed in the final words of Paul in A. 28^{28}.

7–9

John's eschatological preaching. Somewhat surprisingly in view of 1^{17}, Luke does not reproduce Mark's further description of John as Elijah *redivivus* (Mark 1^6; cf. Mal. 4^5), but there is a similar omission of Mark 9$^{11-13}$ (and of the saying in Matt. 11^{14}?), which may indicate that Luke rejected the doctrine. He passes straight to a specimen of John's preaching – *he said* is in the Greek the imperfect, which could mean 'he used to say' – which is taken from Q, the agreement with Matthew being verbatim apart from two words. Apparently no audience was supplied in Q, and each evangelist provides his own, Matthew's 'Pharisees and Sadducees' perhaps suggested by *brood of vipers* (cf. Matt. 12^{34}; 23^{33}), and Luke's perhaps a condensed form of Mark 1^5, 'there went out to him . . . and they were baptized by him'. The preaching reads like a summary, the separate sentences being only partially made into a logical unity by the connecting links – *oun* (untranslated in RSV), *and* (v. 8), and *even now, therefore* (v. 9); but the sequence of condemnation of the hearers as in an almost hopeless case, appeal for repentance, and demand for specific actions from particular classes (as in vv. 10–14), is one frequently found in the messages of the prophets to the nation (cf. Isa. 1^5; Hos. 4–5; Amos 5–6). The language is that of eschatological preaching, but it is not conventional, and has a character and force of its own. By means of the connecting particle *therefore* (v. 7a) Luke makes it an explication of the previous prophecy, the *fruits of repentance* (v. 8a) corresponding to the removal of all obstacles and the straightening of what is crooked (vv. 4–5), and the power of God to raise up children to Abraham (v. 8b) corresponding to the sight of God's salvation by all flesh (v. 6).

the multitudes: A favourite term with Luke, as with Matthew, whereas (apart possibly from Mark 10^1) Mark always uses the word *ochlos* = 'multitude' in the singular. It is more likely that as a prophet John spoke in these terms to all who came to him (i.e. to the Jordan for baptism, not to the desert) than to a specific group, as in Matt. 3^7. Generally, however, Luke is not so pessimistic about them (cf. 7^{29}). In v. 15 he calls them *the people*, an LXX term very common in L–A. It could denote God's people (cf. A 13^{24}), and this would correspond with the tenor of the passage here as an address to Israel with the purpose of creating the true people of God.

brood of vipers: Found again only in Matt. 12^{34}; 23^{33}, where it is glossed by 'serpents' and a similar question asked. For evil nature denoted by reference to origin, cf. Isa. 57^4; John 8^{44}; hence Matt. 12^{34} interprets by 'being evil'. The viper was the most poisonous and malignant type of snake (Job 20^{16}; Ps. 140^3; cf. Isa. 59$^{4f.}$).

Who warned you?: Or, in accordance with the general meaning of the verb, 'Who showed you how?' Either appears to be a rhetorical question implying that in their case the advice was well nigh useless.

the wrath to come: This phrase is, perhaps by chance, little attested (cf. Ignatius,

Letter to the Ephesians 2[1]). *the wrath* (Dan. 8[19]; 11[36]), meaning God's final judgment and condemnation, generally on the heathen but also on all sinners, including Israelites (Jubilees 15[34]; 36[10]; Ps. Sol. 15[6]; I Enoch 84[4ff.]), dominates the thought of later, esp. apocalyptic Judaism. *to come* (*mellein*) is part of the vocabulary of apocalyptic (Matt. 11[14]; 12[32]; Baruch 4[9]; I Thess. 1[10]).

Bear fruits that befit repentance: The hearers are already, as in v. 9, being treated as trees. The injunction does not follow logically from the preceding question, as it implies that their case is not hopeless, as also that the moral consequences of baptism are to be a qualification for it. *fruits* (Matthew 'fruit') perhaps prepares for the separate injunctions in vv. 10–14.

begin: This is thought by some to be less elegant that Matthew's 'presume' and therefore from Q, but others take the opposite view. The auxiliary *begin* with 'to say' is fairly common in Luke. *to yourselves* (*en heautois* = 'in yourselves') fits 'presume' better, and may be an intrusion from Matthew's text (it is omitted by the Old Latin and some other mss).

We have Abraham for our father: This also does not follow on logically, and would seem to be addressed to those who believed that as Israelites they did not need baptism. 'A lot in the world to come . . . is ultimately assured to every Israelite on the ground of the original election of the people by the free grace of God.'[y] Despite some voices to the contrary (e.g. IV Ezra), this is the general view of Israel's election, based on such passages as Deut. 7[6-11]; cf. Ps. Sol. 9[17] and the Mishnah, tractate Sanhedrin 10[1], 'All Israel has part in the world to come', Justin, *Dialogue* 140. Thus John's baptism is radical in placing Israelites on the same footing as proselytes, who were generally denied a share in the world to come. His conception of the miraculous power of God as able to make a true Israel for himself from the offspring of stones is not the same as, but in a way prepares for, the conception of Christians as the true children of Abraham (Rom. 4; Gal. 3). Some have supposed a word play here on the Aramaic for 'stones' and 'sons'.

9
Even now: Greek *ēdē de kai* = 'What is more'. The judgment is immediately impending.

the axe is laid to the root of the trees: The axe is not found elsewhere as a symbol of judgment. Lagrange (p. 108) thinks that a wedge is meant, placed by the feller against the root and ready to be driven home at any moment with a hammer. But the figure of the axe placed at the root of many trees, of which all that are bad are to be felled, nothing being said of those that are good, is

---

y G. F. Moore, *Judaism*, Cambridge, Mass. and Oxford 1927–30, II, p. 94.

obscure. Perhaps the original had a single tree representing Israel; in which case v. 9b would not be a threat of what is to happen to some trees, but, as in Matt. 7^{19}, a gnomic statement, using the present tense *is cut down, thrown*, about the fate of bad trees.

10–14

John's practical teaching. Peculiar to Luke. This passage on the fruits of repentance in detail (*What then shall we do?*, v. 10) is unusual both in structure and thought, and differs markedly from vv. 7–9. Luke may have composed it himself on the basis of oral tradition. The form of a thrice repeated question, variously introduced, with answers appropriate to each group of enquirers, is elegant. The question asked by each group *What shall we do?*, differentiated in v. 10 by *then* (i.e. in the face of vv. 7–9), in v. 12 by *Teacher*, and in v. 14 by *and we*, recalls the same question in A. 2^{37} in a similar context of a call to repentance and baptism, and may reflect the influence of Christian baptismal catechetical practice. Nowhere else do tax collectors and soldiers provide the audience for a particular teaching. Either oral tradition has retained a precise setting here, or more probably, it is Luke's creation; cf. 7^{29}, where he abruptly inserts into a Q passage the people and the tax collectors as those receptive to John's baptism. In John's replies, which show evidence of Luke's hand, the apocalyptic preacher of imminent judgment appears as a teacher of the law and of practical wisdom, which corresponds more closely with Josephus's account of him as 'a good man who commanded the Jews to exercise virtue, both as to righteousness towards one another and piety towards God' (*Ant.* 18.117).

11

A rhythmical, largely participial sentence; *share* (*metadidonai*) five times in the NT, only here in the gospels. It calls, like the prophets, for greater equality in Israel through the voluntary exercise of the two 'works of love', which were commanded and highly prized in Jewish religion, the clothing of the poor (the *coat*, *chitōn*, was an undergarment worn next to the skin), and the feeding of the hungry (cf. Job 31^{17-20}; Tobit 1^{16-17}; Matt. $25^{35f.}$; SB IV. I, pp. 565ff.). This resembles some teaching of Jesus (e.g. $6^{29ff.}$), but falls short of its radical demand.

12

Tax collectors: telōnai = 'those who have bought a toll', Latin *publicani* from *publicum* = 'public property', hence 'publicans' (AV). They are mentioned only in the synoptic gospels in the NT. They belonged to the financial system in the form it took once Judaea became a Roman imperial province (the Seleucid rulers and Herod had previously collected taxes in their own way). The Roman method in general, because of the lack of a permanent civil service, was to farm out the right to collect the taxes of a province to the highest bidder (those of senatorial rank were not allowed to bid). He then set the taxes at a rate which enabled him to recoup his price and also to make a profit from their collection. This he did through agents, who were generally recruited from the native population. These are the tax collectors of the gospels. They in their turn set out to make a profit. Taxes were of two kinds; direct taxes, i.e. those on produce and the poll tax, and indirect taxes, i.e. tolls and customs duties. They were collected on the coast and at Jerusalem, Jericho and other places, e.g. Capernaum. In Judaea direct taxes were under the control of the prefect, and were collected by agents of the Sanhedrin; indirect taxes were farmed out (in Galilee the taxes, also farmed out, went to Herod Antipas). The tax collector was thus doubly despised and detested as both the instrument of a hated alien power – particularly in Israel with its horror that God's people should be under foreign domination – and as one who was automatically an extortioner. He was classed with thieves, and was regarded as specially unclean through his necessary contact with Gentiles (cf. 18^{11}), and as excommunicate from Israel (cf. Matt. 18^{17}).

13

Collect no more than is appointed you: Idiomatic in the Greek. *than is appointed* is *para* = 'compared with', and the perfect participle passive of *diatassein* (mostly L–A in the NT) used as a noun. *collect* is *prassein* = 'to do' used in a technical sense (+ 19^{23}). There is no questioning of the rights of the occupying power; only a demand for social justice in the form of avoidance of the corruption endemic to the profession.

14

soldiers: In the Greek the participle of *strateuesthai* = 'men serving in the army'. It is not clear who these were, nor why they should appear as a special class. That they were Jews employed in the army of Herod Antipas is possible, and in the context likely, as Luke would hardly introduce Gentiles so indirectly. Plummer (p. 92) suggests they were employed as police to support the tax collectors in collecting (extorting) their dues. The reply to them, again expressed in literary fashion, appears to be directed to the observance of the eighth, ninth and tenth commandments.

rob by violence: diaseiein + + = 'to extort by intimidation'. A papyrus contains the word used about a soldier.

by false accusation: sukophantein + 19^8 = 'to accuse falsely'. Hence 'do not accuse anyone falsely'. A papyrus contains the word in connection with tax collectors, and in another it is combined with the previous verb, while the corresponding nouns are also found together.

wages: opsōnia = 'provisions', 'rations', as perhaps here; but it was a regular word for a soldier's pay, which was low. If the injunctions in this verse are to obedience to the commandments, and those in v. 11 are to 'works of love', it may be noted that these are often found together, with Abraham as the exemplar of both (see SB IV, pp. 538ff., 565ff.; III, p. 180). John would then be exhorting his hearers to become genuine sons of Abraham.

15–18
While the previous extracts from John's preaching could have been important for Christians in pointing to imminent divine judgment as the immediate background of Jesus' own mission, this extract would have been most important as testimony by John himself, in terms of his own mission, to that of an immeasurably greater one, who could be identified – though not necessarily by John at the time (cf. 7^{18-20}) – with Jesus. This testimony in the form of a contrast of two baptisms is very compressed, and is made more obscure by the existence of two variant versions, those of Mark and Q. Basically Luke follows the Q version; v. 16 agrees with Matt. 3^{11}, and against Mark $1^{7f.}$, in the word order *I baptize ... he who is mightier ... he will baptize*, and v. 17, absent from Mark, is in verbatim agreement with Matt. 3^{12}. If, however, Matt. 3^{11} in any way reproduces the language of Q, Luke will have assimilated it to the language of Mark 1^7. In contrast to both Mark and Matthew, where the pronouncement follows straight on from what precedes, Luke has pointed it up by framing it with an introduction (v. 15) and a conclusion (v. 18).

15
Style and vocabulary show this verse to be from Luke's hand – so the genitive absolutes in *were in expectation* (*prosdokān*, chiefly L–A in the NT) and in *questioning concerning* (the classical *dialogizesthai peri* + +), and *he were*, one of the rare cases of the optative in the NT. From John's words in v. 16 he deduces, perhaps correctly, a concrete setting, and makes them a reply to a particular theological speculation (typically represented as universal – *all men, all*) aroused by John's person and work. The setting perhaps reflects later Christian polemic against claims made for their leader by the group known as 'John's disciples' (5^{33}; 7^{18}; 11^1; A. 19^3?).

the Christ: For this term see on 2^{11}. Luke takes *he who is mightier* as denoting the messiah, and so interprets John's words as primarily a disavowal of messiahship (cf. the more official scene in John $1^{19ff.}$).

16
This remarkable but difficult verse forms an important transition, since John himself not only relates, but also subordinates, his eschatological mission to that of Jesus, and 'signs off' as his precursor. This is done in terms of an antithesis between two baptisms, the meaning of which is disputed (cf. the similar but more extended testimony of the Baptist to his subordination in John $1^{25-27, 30-33}$).

I baptize with water: The verb *baptizein* meant in ordinary Greek 'to dip, immerse (in water), drown'. It could naturally be adopted for ritual washings, especially for that of John if he immersed the postulant in the Jordan. *with water* (the simple dative, as in Mark; Matthew has 'in water') is placed for emphasis immediately after *I*, and states a limitation. This cannot, however, be that such a water baptism was external only, since it conveyed the interior gift of the forgiveness of sins (v. 3). Perhaps what is meant is that while water baptism, in effecting remission of sins, was immediately preparatory to God's judgment of right and wrong, it fell short of conveying that to which it pointed, viz. the life of righteousness in the coming age. That will depend on the meaning of the contrasted baptism.

he will baptize you with the Holy Spirit and with fire: Better *with holy spirit*; the article is absent, as also in Mark and Matthew. The striking phrase 'baptize with spirit' is not found previously, but it is not unnatural to the extent that spirit could be thought of as a fluid (cf. Joel 2^{28} 'poured out', John 7^{38} 'flow'), and as parallel to water (Isa. 44^3; Ezek. 36^{25-27}; John 3^5). *spirit (pneuma)* was a widespread term in religion, including the Jewish, for effective power, the equivalent of *dunamis* (cf. 1^{17}). *holy spirit* (see on 1^{15}) is the effective (inward) power of God, who alone is holy (Ps. 51^{11}; Isa. $63^{10f.}$; 1QS DR 2, Vermes, *Scrolls*, p. 98). But to what does the promise refer? In its Markan form of baptism with holy spirit only it could refer to Jesus' victorious conflict with, and liberation of men from, 'unclean spirit' in the exorcisms and healings which play such prominent part in that gospel. But in Luke and Matthew the promise is of baptism *with holy spirit and with fire*. How do these belong together, and to what do they refer? Fire is also a widespread religious symbol. In the Jewish tradition it is generally used of destructive judgment (Amos 1^4; 7^4; Isa. 66^{15}; Dan. 7^{10}; IV Ezra 13^{10}), though occasionally of purification (Num. 31^{23}; Isa. 4^4). In Joel 2^{28-30} it occurs along with 'spirit', but as the opposite of it as being destructive (cf. 1QS CR 4, Vermes, *Scrolls*, pp. 76-7). It is generally held that Luke saw the promise as fulfilled at Pentecost. Against this is (i) that in A. $2^{3f.}$ fire has a different sense of inspiration or illumination, and (ii) that in A. 1^5; 11^{16} the Pentecostal gift is expressly interpreted by reference to John's promise in its Markan form of baptism with holy spirit only. There is therefore much to be said for the following conjectural reconstruction – originally the promise in Q was of a baptism with wind (the Greek word *pneuma* can mean 'wind' or 'spirit') and fire, i.e. a baptism of judgment upon *you* (sc. those warned in v. 7); this thought was carried on in the following verse in Q (v. 17) by reference to the winnowing wind of judgment and the fire that destroys the chaff; that Mark's version was a Christianized form of the saying, in which 'fire' was dropped, *pneuma* taken as 'spirit', and 'holy' added; and that the present text of Matthew and Luke is the result of a conflation of Mark's version with that of Q, which was made either at some stage in the tradition of Q itself, or by Matthew and Luke independently in combining Mark's text with Q.

he who is mightier than I is coming: he who is mightier translates the comparative of *ischuros* with an article = 'the mightier one', i.e. mightier in executing the purposes of God. In 11$^{21-22}$ the same word is used (perhaps in dependence on Isa. 49^{24ff}.) in a parable about the conflict between Jesus and Satan. Some take it as a title of a particular expected figure (with *is coming* cf. 7^{20}, 'he who is to come'), but there is no firm evidence for this, and *mightier than I* is descriptive rather than titular. Some think John is referring to Elijah, others, including Luke (v. 15), think the messiah (cf. John 1$^{19-21}$, the messiah, Elijah, the prophet).

the thong of whose sandals I am not worthy to untie: So Mark 1^7; John 1^{27}; Matt. 3^{11} has 'carry'. An extreme expression of inferiority and of the distance between the baptisms. With respect to the mightier one John ranks himself below a slave, being unfit to perform the slave's duty of taking off his master's shoes (said by later rabbis to be below even a slave). The relative positions of John and Jesus were a theological problem. In John 1^{15} it is raised by Jesus' coming after John in time. This is hinted at in Mark 1^7; Matt. 3^{11}, but Luke omits *opisō* = 'after', 'behind'.

17

winnowing fork: This was a shovel for throwing the threshed grain into the wind to separate it from the chaff. The baptism of judgment will be both positive and negative, producing the harvest of the good grain and the destruction of the useless chaff.

19–20

A single summarizing sentence in Lukan language (note the typical *all the things*) which is probably dependent on Mark 6$^{14-29}$ (omitted by Luke). It is a literary device for rounding off the section on John. It does not appear to have the special force, either of marking the end of the old era and the beginning of the new (so Conzelmann, *Theology*, p. 21), or of drawing a parallel with the fate of Jesus on the cross (Luke refers only to John's imprisonment, not to his death).

^{21}*Now when all the people were baptized, and when Jesus also had been baptized and was praying, the heaven was opened,* ^{22}*and the Holy Spirit descended upon him in bodily form, as a dove, and a voice came from heaven, 'Thou art my beloved Son;* with thee I am well pleased'†*

* Or *my Son, my* (or *the*) *Beloved*
† Other ancient authorities read *today I have begotten thee*

The divine empowering rather than the baptism of Jesus expresses the content of this story, especially in its Lukan form. In its present position the baptism of Jesus by John forms the transition from the prophetic, and by the divine will precursory, ministry of John to the filial, messianic ministry of Jesus. It also begins the fulfilment of John's prophecy, inasmuch as he who is to baptize with holy spirit, and is to perform all his ministry, both earthly ($4^{18ff.}$) and heavenly (A. 1^5; $2^{33ff.}$), through it, must first be shown to possess it pre-eminently. Mark may have been the first to make the transition in this way. There is no firm evidence for an account of the baptism in Q, the two minor agreements of Matthew and Luke against Mark – the ordinary word for 'opened' with the heavens rather than Mark's vulgar word meaning 'split asunder', and the preposition *epi* = *upon* rather than Mark's *eis* = 'into' – are readily explained as natural improvements of Mark. Q may thus have passed from John in the desert to Jesus in the desert (4^{1-13} = Matt. 4^{1-11}).

Form-critically the story, especially in its Lukan form, has been termed a 'legend' in the technical sense of a story which aims to depict the religious character of a man, and his status and calling as these are seen by God. Perhaps it would be better classified as a 'myth' in the technical sense of a story which aims to present the divine origin and basis of something that is central in the relationship of God and man, here the earthly mission and activity of Jesus as the unique Son of God. Its source is unlikely to have been Jesus himself, unless it is supposed that he narrated retrospectively his personal religious experience to his disciples, and spoke to them directly of himself as the Son of God. The latter would certainly not be borne out by the evidence. It is entirely lacking in the personal details, characteristic of visions and prophetic calls (see Bultmann, *History*, pp. 247ff.). Rather, theological reflection on the person and work of Jesus when judged 'according to the Spirit' (Rom. 1^4; I Cor. 12^3; II Cor. 5^{16}), i.e. as God revealed them to be, is here attached to the historical fact – it cannot have been invented – that Jesus submitted to John's baptism. Through the symbolism displayed it is declared at the outset that the earthly career of Jesus is to be understood throughout as the work of God through, and in union with, his most intimate possible agent (A. $2^{22ff.}$; $10^{37ff.}$; $13^{33ff.}$). Mark alone, with his christology of the Son of God whose sonship and power are revealed in and through humiliation, betrays no embarrassment at the thought of Jesus submitting to a baptism of repentance for the forgiveness of sins. Contrast the apologetic dialogue introduced in Matt. 3^{14-15}, and the absence of any reference to the baptism itself in John 1^{32-33}. Luke's account also betrays embarrassment. He has rewritten it as a single sentence, in which, astonishingly, the man Jesus is introduced on to the scene for the first time by means of a subordinate participial clause (*and when Jesus also had been baptized*). This is only partly accounted for on grounds of style (in the Greek *egeneto* = 'it came to pass that' followed by verbs in the infinitive and participial clauses with genitive absolutes is in the Greek *chria* style; see on 17^{20} below), or by the necessity of narrating the baptism in impersonal terms once John has been removed from the scene (v. 18). It is also due to a desire to pass over the baptism itself, and to concentrate on the supernatural elements.

ରେ

21

when all the people were baptized, and when Jesus also had been baptized: The situation depicted by these successive subordinate clauses in the genitive absolute is unclear. Mark and Matthew represent Jesus as coming from Galilee to the Jordan to ask for baptism during John's baptizing. His motive for this might have been to show solidarity with Israel, or with that part of Israel which had sought renewal through penitence, or to associate himself with the eschatological mission and message of John, whom, as the divine messenger, he is to hail as the greatest born of women (7^{24-28}). Luke appears to envisage Jesus' baptism as taking place separately, and after John's baptizing activity had ceased, since *all the people* (all Israel? or all of Israel who had responded?) had been baptized.

and was praying: The descent of the Spirit is no longer coincident with Jesus' emergence from the waters of baptism (Mark 1¹⁰; Matt. 3¹⁶), but with his subsequent prayer. The suggestion is unlikely that this addition by Luke reflects a distinction in the early church between baptism and the gift of the Spirit (cf. A. 8⁴⁻¹⁸); in A. Luke has no consistent doctrine of the Spirit in relation to baptism. It is due rather to a desire to make the story religiously more comprehensible, and to his interest in Jesus as a man of prayer, who prays at the critical moments (cf. 6¹²; 9¹⁸, ²⁸⁻²⁹; 22⁴⁰ᶠ·; 23³⁴ – also 5¹⁶; 11¹; for the Spirit given to Christians while praying, cf. A. 1¹⁴; 2¹ᶠᶠ·; 8¹⁵⁻¹⁷; 13¹⁻³).

the heaven was opened: Conventional language in visions and epiphanies for the divine origin of what (who) is then to make its (his) appearance as God's representative (cf. Ezek. 1¹; III Macc. 6¹⁸; John 1⁵¹; A. 7⁵⁶; 10¹¹; Rev. 19¹¹). In Mark/Matthew this, and what follows, are the object of Jesus' own vision ('he saw'). Luke makes them objective for all to see.

22

the Holy Spirit descended: Here *holy spirit* has the definitive article, as in 2²⁶; 10²¹; 12¹²; and frequently in A; but comparison with 4¹ (without article), or of A. 1⁵ (without article) with A. 1⁸ (with article), shows that no essential difference is implied. 'The personal categories used to describe the activity of the Spirit are not designed to present Him as a special heavenly being but rather to bring out the fact that He is an objective divine reality which encounters and claims man ... The decisive thing is that man stands here before a reality which comes from God, which in some sense represents the presence of God, and yet which is not identical with God' (*TDNT* VI, pp. 387f.). *descended* is a more dramatic form of the sending of the Spirit by God.

in bodily form: sōmatikō + + *eidei* + 9²⁹; John 5³⁷; II Cor. 5⁷; I Thess. 5²². This Lukan addition is not meant as a qualification ('so far as outward appearance goes'), but on the contrary to accentuate the concreteness already expressed in 'like' (Mark 1¹⁰; Matt. 3¹⁶; cf. John 1³²). It is characteristic of Luke to objectivize the supernatural (cf. 24³⁹ᶠᶠ·; A. 2²⁻⁴). It is his way of saying that the incidence of the Spirit *upon* Jesus (v. 21; 4¹⁸) brings about a plenary inspiration with the breath of God (cf. John 1³²ᶠ·; 3³⁴), so that he is not from time to time possessed by, but is the permanent possessor of, the Spirit (4¹, ¹⁸ᶠ·).

as a dove: This symbol in the synoptic story (cf. also John 1³²), which is taken for granted as immediately recognizable and is not explained, remains baffling. The association of the dove with divinities was widespread in ancient religions, and there are faint reflections of this in the OT, but this does not justify the assertion that 'in the hour when God acknowledged His Son the dove could be the recognisable and almost exclusively suitable phenomenal form of the Holy Spirit' (*TDNT* VI, p. 69). Abrahams (*Studies*, I, pp. 47–50) assembles statements of varying dates in which (i) the voice of God, in the rabbinic form of the *bath qol* (see below), is compared to the chirping of a bird or is heard moaning as a dove, and (ii) the Spirit of God in Gen. 1^2 is described as moving over the face of the waters like a dove brooding over its young. But (i) is irrelevant, since it is the Spirit and not the voice which is here compared to a dove, and while (ii) is suggestive in its reference to the Spirit's work in creation, it remains a simile only, and hardly accounts for such a confident use of the symbol for the Spirit itself. In rabbinic literature the dove also represents Israel (SB I, p. 123), but for a heavenly Israel to descend on Jesus at his baptism makes no sense. The most striking instance of the dove in the OT is in Gen. 8, and this might conceivably be the origin of its use here in view of the interpretation of baptism as an antitype of the flood (I Peter $3^{18ff.}$), and of certain similarities between Jewish traditions about Noah and Christian traditions about John and his baptism: preaching of repentance (II Peter 2^5; Heb. 11^7; Jubilees $7^{20ff.}$), salvation through the waters of judgment in face of a future judgment of fire (I Enoch $10^{1ff.}$; 106–108; II Peter 3^{4-12}), and the renewal of God's covenant with Noah as a second Adam (Ecclus 44^{16-18}; II Esdras 3^{11}; II Enoch 35^1). The suggestion (cf. Jeremias, *Theology* I, p. 52) that 'like a dove' refers to the manner of the Spirit's descent, i.e. 'gently', leaves unstated what was seen to descend in this way, and certainly does not apply to Luke's *in bodily form*. None of the suggested explanations carries much conviction, and it remains possible that the symbol is a Christian creation for the Spirit which 'rests' upon the king (Isa. 11^2).

a voice came from heaven: A statement of an objective reality, as in Matt. 3^{17} (in Mark 1^{11} it could have been heard only by Jesus, and in John 1^{33} is privately vouchsafed to John). It is often interpreted by reference to the *bath qol*, a rabbinic term for the echo of God's voice (it means literally 'daughter of the voice'), or that measure of revelation still given when, after the disappearance of prophecy, the Holy Spirit had ceased to speak directly to Israel (SB I, pp. 125ff.). But this is improbable, especially for Luke, who saw in the appearance of Jesus the occasion of the rebirth of prophecy in Israel (chs. 1–2). This could bring with it a renewal of the direct address of God (cf. Dan. 4^{31}), the more so when what is involved goes beyond the call of a prophet, and is the installation of Jesus as the beloved Son.

Thou art my beloved Son; with thee I am well pleased: The source and precise implications of these words have been much discussed (see on 1^{35}). They have commonly been taken as a combination of Ps. 2^7 LXX, 'my son art thou', and Isa. 42^1 LXX, 'Jacob, my chosen servant (*pais* = also 'son'), I will uphold him ... Israel my chosen one, whom my soul has received (ms Q, margin, 'delights in'); I have put my spirit upon him' (cf. also Isa. $44^{2ff.}$ LXX, 'Fear not Jacob, my servant, and the beloved one Israel, whom I have chosen ... I will put my spirit upon your seed'). The reference to Ps. 2 may be unnecessary; in the similar utterance in 9³⁵ *Thou art*, which is characteristic of the psalm, disappears; and the alteration of word order from 'my Son art thou' to *Thou art my Son*, which applies the words more directly to Jesus, may reflect the influence the direct address in Isa. 42¹, 'Jacob, my servant . . .' Further, what is distinctive in the address is *with thee I am well pleased*, which is strictly unnecessary after *my beloved Son*, and this is certainly derived from Isa. 42¹. Further, there is an immediate connection between the 'servant' of Isaiah and the gift of the Spirit (Isa. 42¹; 44³; 61¹; cf. 11²), while that between the Son and the anointed one of Ps. 2 and kindred passages and the Spirit is less immediate (but see Barrett, *Holy Spirit*, pp. 41ff.). If *beloved* (*ho agapētos*) is more than an adjective meaning 'only' (so Gen. 22², ¹², ¹⁶ of Isaac), and is a title 'the Beloved' (so RSV margin; cf. Luke's substitution of 'the chosen one' for it in 9³⁵),ᶻ it could also be based on 'the beloved one' of Isa. 44² LXX. There, as in Deut. 32¹⁵; 33⁵, ²⁶, it translates Jeshurun as a title for Israel (cf. also Isa. 5¹, and the version of Isa. 42¹ff. quoted in Matt. 12¹⁸, if that is not influenced by the baptism story). The derivation of *my Son* (*huios*) from 'my servant' (*pais*) would not be possible in circles which kept close to the Hebrew text but would be possible in Hellenistic Judaism – cf. Wisd. 2–5, which is dependent on Isa. 52–53 but interprets the servant of the Lord as the son of God (2¹³⁻¹⁸). Such an identification would be further strengthened by the specifically Christian doctrine of Jesus as the unique Son of God that emerged from belief in his resurrection (A. 9²⁰; Rom. 1³⁻⁴; John passim).

I am well pleased: The verb *eudokein* is a word of election. It combines will and affection, especially in conjunction with (the) *beloved*, and denotes the installation to a particular function and status of one who is a special object of delight. If *Son* is derived from Ps. 2⁷ this will be to the office of Israel's king or anointed one (cf. II Sam. 7¹⁴; connected with the Spirit Isa. 11²; Ps. Sol. 17³⁷). If it is derived from Isa. 42¹ it is to the function of the true and obedient Israel, created such by the Spirit of God.

The variant reading 'Thou art my beloved Son today I have begotten thee' = Ps. 2⁷, is found in the Lukan, though not the Markan or Matthaean, text of D and in all the Old Latin texts except e; is the only version found in Justin; and receives support from other Fathers, including Origen and Augustine. It is surprising and has been variously explained. Some have taken it to be original, and to have been later assimilated to the text of Mark (not, as is more general in such cases, to that of Matthew). If original it need not be from a different account of the baptism, for which there is no other evidence in Luke; nor is it necessarily 'adoptionist' in the later doctrinally heretical sense (Jesus became at the baptism what he previously was not). The same text is applied in A. 13³³

z See J. Armitage Robinson, *St Paul's Epistle to the Ephesians*, London and New York 1903, pp. 299ff.

(cf. Heb. 1⁵) as the divine attestation of Jesus' sonship at and through his resurrection, and Luke would not have thought it inconsistent with a divine sonship at and through birth (1³⁵). Justin (*Dialogue* 88) sees the address in this form as a recognizable sign for men of Jesus' messiahship because it was in words in which the OT had already said that the Father would address the Son. That is, Ps. 2⁷ was a proof text of messianic sonship, and Luke may himself have preferred it here because he, and only he, is to follow the baptism with a genealogy of Jesus' (divine) begetting. If it is not original the alteration was presumably made by scribes for the same reason.

The collocation of language and thought in the baptism story can be illustrated from what is said about the new priest of the coming age in Test. Levi 18⁶, 'The heavens shall be opened, and from the temple of glory shall come upon him sanctification, with the Father's voice as from Abraham to Isaac. And the glory of the Most High shall be uttered over him, and the spirit of understanding and sanctification shall rest upon him (in the water).' But this may be a Christian or Christianized writing itself dependent on the baptism story.

3²³⁻³⁸   THE LEGITIMATION OF JESUS AS
                      SON OF GOD

²³*Jesus, when he began his ministry, was about thirty years of age, being the son (as was supposed) of Joseph, the son of Heli,* ²⁴*the son of Matthat, the son of Levi, the son of Melchi, the son of Jannai, the son of Joseph,* ²⁵*the son of Mattathias, the son of Amos, the son of Nahum, the son of Esli, the son of Naggai,* ²⁶*the son of Maath, the son of Mattathias, the son of Semein, the son of Josech, the son of Joda,* ²⁷*the son of Joanan, the son of Rhesa, the son of Zerubbabel, the son of Shealtiel, the son of Neri,* ²⁸*the son of Melchi, the son of Addi, the son of Cosam, the son of Elmadam, the son of Er,* ²⁹*the son of Joshua, the son of Eliezer, the son of Jorim, the son of Matthat, the son of Levi,* ³⁰*the son of Simeon, the son of Judah, the son of Joseph, the son of Jonam, the son of Eliakim,* ³¹*the son of Melea, the son of Menna, the son of Mattatha, the son of Nathan, the son of David,* ³²*the son of Jesse, the son of Obed, the son of Boaz, the son of Sala, the son of Nahshon,* ³³*the son of Amminadab, the son of Admin, the son of Arni, the son of Hezron, the son of Perez, the son of Judah,* ³⁴*the son of Jacob, the son of Isaac, the son of Abraham, the son of Terah, the son of Nahor,* ³⁵*the son of Serug, the son of Reu, the son of Peleg, the son of Eber, the son of Shelah,* ³⁶*the son of Cainan, the son of*

Arphaxad, the son of Shem, the son of Noah, the son of Lamech, [37]the son of Methuselah, the son of Enoch, the son of Jared, the son of Mahalaleel, the son of Cainan, [38]the son of Enos, the son of Seth, the son of Adam, the son of God.

This section owes its presence here to the significance attached to genealogies in the ancient world. Stemming originally from the close connection of religion with physical consanguinity, especially with the gods, they had become of great importance to Jews as evidence of belonging to the people of God as the 'children of Abraham' (cf. 3^8), and particularly with reference to the preservation of the purity of the priesthood through descent from Aaron and the validation of the authority of rabbis (SB I, pp. 4ff.). I Chron. 1–9 consists largely of genealogies designed to establish the continuity of the later Jewish community with the beginnings of Israel's history and to secure its Davidic character. There were apparently materials available in public records for the reconstruction of genealogies both of individuals and of families (Josephus, *Life* 3–6; *Against Apion* 1.30ff.), though it is doubtful whether this would apply to all, or even to most. Concern with the ancestry of Jesus may thus have arisen in Jewish Christian circles with a view to establishing his Davidic origin (2^4), perhaps against Jews who denied it.[a]

Some genealogies, however, were primarily symbolic and theological rather than strictly historical documents, and were constructed according to a system of sacred numbers designed to reveal a schematized history as evidence of the divine government of the world. Thus Jubilees is written on a heptadic system, and divides the generations of mankind from creation to the giving of the law into forty-nine jubilee periods of weeks of years, Israel entering the promised land at the close of the fiftieth jubilee. The Apocalypse of Weeks in I Enoch 93 has ten weeks of years, the first seven, each marked by some event in Israel's history, stretching from creation to the author's own time, and the last three from the inauguration of the messianic kingdom to the judgment. The genealogy of Matt. 1^{1-17} is of this kind, being expressly divided into three periods, each of which covers two weeks of generations (Matt. 1^{17}). Luke's genealogy also appears to have been artificially

a For a discussion of the matter see M. D. Johnson, *The Purpose of the Biblical Genealogies*, SNTSM 8, 1969.

constructed. It consists of seventy-seven human names. This may represent eleven weeks of generations between creation and the advent of the messiah, who stands at the close of the eleventh week, to be followed, perhaps, by the twelfth and final week in which the times of the Gentiles are fulfilled (21²⁴) and the messiah returns to establish all things (A. 3²¹). Its introduction at this point, compared with Matthew's place for it before the birth of Jesus, is not unsuitable, and does not require the hypothesis of a first draft of the Gospel, which lacked the birth stories and began at 3¹. It follows after the first mention of Jesus as a grown man and his reception of the Spirit. The manner of its introduction emphasizes that the messianic era, which is still a promise for the future at his birth (1³²ᶠ·; 2³⁸), 'begins' with his public ministry. Moses' genealogy is also given after his public appearance before Pharaoh (Exod. 6¹⁴⁻²⁷). It concludes the opening section of the Gospel which is concerned with beginnings, and in its own fashion it provides a transition by carrying over the thought of divine sonship and mission from the baptism to the temptation.

The ascending form of the genealogy with the repeated *son of* (cf. Tobit 1¹; Esther 2⁵; in Greek it is the genitive of the article, *tou* = 'of the', referring to the name that follows) is less common in the LXX, especially at this length, than the descending form in Matthew, with 'was the father of' (Greek *egennēsen* = 'he begat'); but given that it starts from Jesus it is neater here. The lists of names in the two genealogies differ very considerably at certain points, and attempts to harmonize them were early (see Eus. *HE* 1.7; Origen, *Against Celsus*, 2.32); but the task is impossible, and has had to be abandoned.[b] Such harmonizing attempts, together with the difficulty of transcribing accurately Hebrew names in Grecized form, have led to many variants in the text. Between Joseph (of Nazareth) and David (vv. 23–31) there is scarcely any agreement between the two genealogies. Matthew traces a royal descent of actual kings and rulers through Solomon by means of names drawn from scripture. Luke traces descent through Nathan and his descendants, who are not mentioned in scripture, nor otherwise known. They were presumably drawn from a Jewish tradition which held that the royal line through Solomon had become extinct with Jeconiah (cf. Jer. 22¹⁰; Zech. 12¹²). From David to Abraham

---

[b] For details of these attempts and comments on individual names, see Marshall, pp. 158ff.

(vv. 31–34) the two almost coincide (*Sala* and *Admin* in Luke correspond to *Salmon* in Matthew, *Aram* in Matthew is absent from Luke and *Arni* in Luke is absent from Matthew). The extension beyond Abraham, the founding father of the holy community, to Adam and creation is peculiar to Luke. It may be drawn from Gen. 10¹⁻²⁷ and Gen. 5 (or from I Chron. 1²⁻²⁹), and from the LXX text (*Cainan*, v. 36, is absent from the Hebrew text of Gen. 10²⁴ and I Chron. 1¹⁸). It is an expression of Luke's universalism. The conclusion with *son of God* attached to *Adam* is astonishing, and without parallel in any genealogy of the OT or of Jewish tradition. Adam cannot be a son of God in the same physical sense in which the others were sons of their fathers. It is either a literary device to make the end of the genealogy match its beginning with Jesus, the Son of God, or it is a simple unreflective expression of the divine activity in creation and redemption through a man. The peculiar argument of A. 17²⁴⁻³¹ – men are the offspring of God, who has appointed final judgment in a man – offers something of a parallel, whereas it is doubtful whether the Pauline conception of Jesus as the second Adam and Son of man (I Cor. 15²⁵⁻⁴⁹) is present. These considerations, together with the symbolic structure of the genealogy, suggest that Luke was responsible for its final form, if not its compiler.

ကာ

23
A genealogy is not easily introduced into narrative. The awkwardness of the introductory words here has led to variants in text and word order.

Jesus: Greek *kai autos Iēsous*. Ordinarily *kai autos* is emphatic and would yield 'Jesus himself'. Here it seems to be used in a less emphatic manner (cf. 1²²; 9³⁶), and to pick up the name = 'Now Jesus . . .' This is made necessary by Luke's rewriting of the baptism story in such a way that the name *Jesus* is introduced *en passant* (v. 21).

began his ministry: began (*his ministry* gives the right meaning but is not in the Greek) is the present participle *archomenos* = 'beginning', agreeing with *Jesus*, and is loosely attached in an adverbial sense. For a similar, though not identical, use of this participle, cf. 23⁵; 24⁴⁷; A. 1²²; 10³⁷, the last two linking 'beginning' with John's baptism.

about thirty years of age: Luke seems to use about (*hōsei*) with numbers without wishing to make them less specific (9¹⁴, ²⁸). The figure *thirty* may have been governed by David's age when he was anointed king over Israel (II Sam. 5⁴; Luke 1³²; cf. Gen. 41⁴⁶ of Joseph before Pharaoh); but Dionysius of Halicarnassus, *Roman Antiquities* 4.6, mentions it as a recognized fact in the Greco-Roman world that men were called to public service from their thirtieth year onwards.

(*as was supposed*): It is unnecessary to regard this parenthesis as an addition by Luke to a source which considered Jesus to be the natural son of Joseph in order to adapt it to the virgin birth. If Luke was the compiler of the genealogy it cannot be so. Both genealogies are those of Joseph, and could hardly be otherwise where ancestry was almost always traced through the father. Both Matthew and Luke were faced with the difficulty of linking Jesus, who was without human father, with sacred history through a genealogy which could only be that of a father. Each has met the difficulty in his own way. In SB II, p. 155 examples are given of 'common presumption' having the force of proof in cases where it was doubtful whether a man and a woman were married. So Jesus could be 'commonly presumed' to be Joseph's son (2³³, ⁴³).

4^{1-13} THE TESTING OF THE SON OF GOD

4 *And Jesus, full of the Holy Spirit, returned from the Jordan, and was led by the Spirit ²for forty days in the wilderness, tempted by the devil. And he ate nothing in those days; and when they were ended, he was hungry. ³The devil said to him, 'If you are the Son of God, command this stone to become bread.' ⁴And Jesus answered him, 'It is written, "Man shall not live by bread alone." '*
⁵And the devil took him up, and showed him all the kingdoms of the world in a moment of time, ⁶and said to him, 'To you I will give all this authority and their glory; for it has been delivered to me, and I give it to whom I will. ⁷If you, then, will worship me, it shall all be yours.' ⁸And Jesus answered him, 'It is written,

"You shall worship the Lord your God,
and him only shall you serve." '
⁹And he took him to Jerusalem, and set him on the pinnacle of the temple, and said to him, 'If you are the Son of God, throw yourself down from here; ¹⁰for it is written,

"He will give his angels charge of you, to guard you,"
¹¹and

> *"On their hands they will bear you up,*
>> *lest you strike your foot against a stone."'*

[12]*And Jesus answered him, 'It is said, "You shall not tempt the Lord your God."'* [13]*And when the devil had ended every temptation, he departed from him until an opportune time.*

In its present position this story closes the prelude to the Gospel. Whether ultimately derived in some way from the visionary experience of Jesus himself, or the product of Christian midrashic interpretation of his messiahship and lordship, it sets his earthly ministry in the context of a supernatural conflict between the sole representative of God and his kingdom and the representative and ruler of the kingdom of evil. The devil's words in vv. 6–7 show theological reflection on this, and the editorial note in v. 13, taken together with 22^{28}, indicate that Luke saw the whole life of Jesus as one of temptation, which comes to a head in the passion ($22^{3, \ 31, \ 53}$; cf. A. 26^{18}). But the story, which in Mark 1^{12-13} has the form of brief notice without specific content, could have stood on its own. Luke's use of Mark to introduce it (vv. 1–2) and Matthew's use of Mark to conclude it (Matt. 4^{11}) suggest this. The close connection between baptism and temptation through the action of the Spirit in both could have been made first by Mark. Another source could have passed straight from John in the wilderness to Jesus in the wilderness with the Spirit playing no part.

The story, like that of the baptism, is a 'myth' without personal or psychological details. It is, however, of a highly distinctive kind in being a supernatural dialogue in the form of a scriptural debate. Its motive cannot have been simply to demonstrate the humanity of Jesus (Heb. $2^{17f.}$; 4^{15}), since the temptations are not those of common humanity but of the Son of God, albeit the Son of God as man and not as angel or purely supernatural being. 'To tempt' here, as generally in the Bible, is not to entice to sin in the ordinary sense, but to test the godly for his fidelity to God. The agent can be either God himself or Satan. The classic temptation in this sense had been in the forty years' sojourn in the wilderness when Israel as God's son (Exod. $4^{22f.}$) had been put to the test so as to learn to trust him entirely and not to put him to the test. This is summarized in Deut. 6–8, which is probably to be regarded as the immediate background of the story here; see especially the wording of Deut. 8^{2-5}. The choice of these three particular temptations, which governs the choice of the OT texts employed, their character and order, is best explained in the light of the testings of Israel.ᶜ According to Deut. 6¹⁰⁻¹⁶, 8¹⁻9²² these were, (i) Israel is allowed to starve and is then supplied by God so as to learn complete dependence on him (Deut. 8³), but fails to do so (Deut. 9⁷ᶠᶠ·); (ii) Israel is commanded to preserve her special relationship to God and to ensure that she serves him alone by driving out the heathen and refusing to compromise with their idolatry (Deut. 6¹³ᶠᶠ·; 7¹ᶠᶠ·) but fails to do so (Judg. 3⁵⁻⁷); (iii) Israel, doubting God's power, puts him to the test by compelling Moses to force God's hand (Deut. 6¹⁶; Exod. 17¹⁻⁷; Num. 20¹⁻¹³; Ps. 95⁸⁻¹¹), for which Moses is refused entry into the promised land (Deut. 32⁴⁸⁻⁵²). On this background Jesus would be presented as the true Son of God, in whom the destiny of Israel was recapitulated and the divine purpose accomplished in that he renders to God the obedience and trust that Israel had failed to give. (I Cor. 10¹⁻¹³ provides an instance of such midrashic reflection on Israel's temptations to lust for food, to commit idolatry and to test God despite his saving acts and supernatural gifts, now applied to Christians as the true Israel.)

Close parallels both in the selection and wording of the LXX citations and in such phrases as *all the kingdoms of the world, set him on the pinnacle of the temple*, and *throw yourself down from here*, indicate Luke's use either of Matthew or of Q. If Luke were dependent on Matthew he would be unlikely to have produced the inconsistency in v. 2 (temptation throughout, and at the end of, forty days), which is due to his use of Mark, and which Matthew has avoided. Most of the differences between Matthew and Luke can be attributed to the style or interests of each evangelist. Puzzling, however, is the difference of order of the second and third temptations. It is generally held that Luke reproduces the order of Q, Matthew having transposed to make the offer of the kingdoms of the world a climax, which Luke would hardly have altered if it had stood thus in Q. The suggestions that Luke has transposed, either to bring the temptation to throw himself down from the temple into immediate juxtaposition with the following incident when an attempt is made to throw Jesus down from a hill, or to reach a climax in Jerusalem, are not particularly convincing. The order in Q, if that is represented by Luke, could reflect the OT view that the supreme temptation was that of testing God.

ᶜ On this see J. A. T. Robinson, 'The Temptations', *Theology* 50, 1947, pp. 43–8, reprinted in *Twelve New Testament Studies*, SBT 34, 1962, pp. 53ff.; B. Gerhardsson, *The Testing of God's Son*, Lund 1966.

1

This verse is influenced by Mark, especially *in the wilderness*, which in the Greek follows immediately and awkwardly after *by* (Greek 'in') *the Spirit*. The connection between baptism and temptation, broken by the genealogy, is restored by *from the Jordan*, belatedly mentioned as the scene of the baptism (Mark 1⁹). *returned* (*hupostrephein*) is Lukan, but has no precise meaning here (returned to where?). *full of the Holy Spirit* – an expression confined to Luke, A. 6³, ⁵; 7⁵⁵; 11²⁴ – is not necessarily a softening of Mark's violent 'drove into', as that verb had a weakened sense in Hellenistic Greek, but it does replace an external compulsive force by an inward directing influence, and emphasizes that from now on Jesus is the possessor of, and his whole activity directed by, the Spirit (cf. 4¹⁸). *led by* (*agesthai*) is the word used for God's leading Israel in the wilderness (Deut. 8², ¹⁵). Thus while the proximate agent of temptation is the devil, behind it is the action of the Spirit of God, who not only allows it but brings it about.

2

This verse is a mixture of Mark and Q. *tempted* for *forty days* is possible for Mark, who has no specific temptations nor any reference to fasting. It is awkward here when conjoined with the different picture (Matt. 4²) of forty days' fasting with temptations at the end. *in those days* is necessary to unite the two.

forty: A round number, only here in the gospels, with years (for Israel's sojourn in the wilderness, A. 7³⁶), or days (A. 1³).

the devil: *ho diabolos* (so Matt. 4¹), a word used in the LXX to translate Satan (cf. Mark 1¹³) in the sense of the accuser or counsel for the prosecution allowed by God in the heavenly court (Job 1⁶; Zech. 3¹; the corresponding verb means 'to bring charges with hostile intent'). He later develops into the more hostile figure of Israel's tempter (II Chron. 21¹; cf. Matt. 4³), 'the one who tries to disrupt the relation between God and man, and especially between God and Israel' (*TDNT* II, p. 76). By a further development he becomes a semi-independent personal supernatural power and source of evil (see on vv. 6–7). Victory over him here is to be distinguished from that in exorcisms. 'As the tormentor he is overcome by miraculous power, as the tempter by humble faith and obedient surrender to God's will.[d]

he ate nothing: Luke interprets 'fasted' (Matt. 4²) exactly (cf. A. 9⁹). Fasting, along with prayer and almsgiving, was a primary religious duty, and was especially conjoined with prayer (A. 13²). It could be in preparation for receiving divine revelation, as in the forty days' fast of Moses (Exod. 34²⁸; Deut. 9⁹),

d R. Leivestad, *Christ the Conqueror*, London and New York 1954, p. 52.

or of Elijah (I Kings 19^8), but it is not so here, since the revelation has already been received, and is taken as the basis of the temptation (*if you are the Son of God*). It would seem to be determined here by the first temptation as a necessary prelude to it (*he was hungry*, cf. Deut. 8^3, 'he suffered them to hunger').

3

The devil said to him: Apparently from Q. Matt. 4^3, less abruptly, 'And the tempter (participle of the verb 'to tempt') came and said to him'.

If you are the Son of God: This is often taken to express doubt, to be resolved by successful miraculous action, but *ei* = *if* could mean 'since', and the divine sonship be assumed as a starting-point. In the context *the Son of God* has the same meaning as in 3^{22}, i.e. either the true Israel and servant of God, or God's king. By itself it could denote a different kind of figure – a divine man – who was to be recognized as such by his miracles.

command this stone to become bread: The first temptation is to miraculous transformation. This is strange, since the performance of miracles was not associated in Jewish tradition with the messiah or servant of the Lord (but cf. the vulgar request for a sign from heaven, 11^{16}, and the signs of false prophets and false messiahs, Mark 13^{22}). In Matt. 4$^{3-4}$, which has the plural 'stones' and 'loaves' and the full reply from Deut. 8^3, the temptation could be interpreted on the background of Deut. 8 as being to usurp the prerogative of God in supplying heavenly manna by miraculous power, which is repudiated in favour of the proclamation of God's word as the means of feeding men. But this is not possible for Luke's *this stone* and *bread* (i.e. 'loaf'), where the temptation is reduced to a miraculous satisfaction by Jesus of his own present and personal hunger. The reply (*answered, apokrinesthai pros*, is apart from John 8^{33}, confined to Luke in the NT) of *Jesus* (the name would be necessary at the beginning of the Q account, and occurs in both evangelists in the other two temptations) is in Luke also reduced to a general ascetic spiritual principle. *It is written* – in holy scripture; i.e. God has said it.

5–8

The second (in Matthew third) temptation has its basis in Deut. 34$^{1-4}$, where from Mount Pisgah God shows Moses the promised land, which has been secured for Israel by its destruction of the heathen peoples *en route*. This is now expanded to a world-wide view.

5

Luke's description is less naive and more visionary than Matthew's – *took him up* (so Matthew) is not to any place (Matthew's mountain from which the whole world is visible is chimerical), and the highly literary *in a moment of time* (*en stigmē chronou* + +) is imaginary. *the world* is properly in the context *hē oikoumenē*, i.e. the civilized world of the nations and their power.

6–7

This is a temptation which attends one who exercises power and rule, and preeminently the one who exercises the world-wide power of God for God (sc. God's Son, Ps. 2$^{7-11}$, though this is not said here). It is not a temptation to perform spectacular miracle, but to subvert the spiritual order of things at their heart on the false supposition that this order can be effectively established by an accommodation to the forces of evil. In v. 6 the devil himself supplies an extended theological basis for this, which has no parallel in Matthew. *their glory,* which is appropriate in Matt. 4^8 but awkward here, suggests that Luke's interest in Satan and his authority (*exousia*, cf. 22^{53}, here probably 'sphere of rule') has led him to write up the dialogue. *To you, to me, If you, shall be yours,* are all emphatic in the text, and point up the issue at stake. The devil's statement that he is by divine permission lord and disposer of the world goes beyond what is found in Jewish sources, where Satan is not lord of the world; but it is not out of harmony with an increasing dualistic tendency in Judaism (where, nevertheless, he is always subject to God and never an object of worship), and it underlies such passages as John 12^{31}; II Cor. 4^4; Eph. 2^2; Rev. 13^{2ff}.

8

The reply is from Deut. 6^{13}, which forbids the provoking of God's jealousy by following other gods or the gods of the nations. In common with Matt. 4^{10} Luke has *shall worship* for the LXX's 'shall fear', but places it first in the sentence, thereby forming a chiasmus, and emphasizing it in response to the devil's offer in v. 7.

9–12

The third temptation returns to the form of the first (*If you are the Son of God*) and to an even more bizarre suggestion of miracle. Its background, revealed in the reply, is the temptation to put God to the test, which is the most heinous of all. As a warrant for it the devil himself quotes a word of God in scripture.

9

he took him to Jerusalem: In contrast to v. 5 a specific place is mentioned, not the whole world but the centre of God's religion (Matthew 'the holy city'), and the centre of that, the temple. The journey thither is in the imagination (cf. Ezek. 8^3).

the pinnacle: pterugion = 'little wing', hence 'edge'. Various identifications of this have been made, none conclusive. Whether the statement in Eus. *HE* 2.23.11 that the Jews threw James the Just from the wing of the temple is an independent witness to it as a notably precipitous area, or is dependent on this passage, is not clear.

throw yourself down from here: There is no known basis for this, certainly not the late rabbinic tradition that the messiah would reveal himself on the roof of the temple (SB I, p. 151). The demonstrative proof is not to be for the benefit of others – there is no suggestion of any spectators – but for Jesus himself.

10–11

The devil provides a scriptural basis in Ps. 91, in which the psalmist throughout addresses the godly man and assures him of divine protection. The devil takes the one addressed to be the Son of God, though there is no evidence for a messianic interpretation of the psalm in Judaism. Verses 11–12 of the psalm are strangely divided into two separate quotations, perhaps to underline the protection as (i) angelic, and (ii) consisting of 'bearing up', though the latter does not fit the context here, since it refers to angelic support for the feet on a journey ('in all your ways', omitted from (i)).

12

Jesus repudiates the suggestion by applying Deut. 6[16] to himself.

13

There is no final 'Begone, Satan!' as in Matt. 4[10], but a typically Lukan conclusion – *had ended* (the participle of *suntelein* + v. 2; A. 21[27]; Mark 13[4]; Rom. 9[28] LXX; Heb. 8[8] LXX), *every temptation* (*panta peirasmon* = 'the whole gamut of temptation').

until an opportune time: *achri kairou*. The preposition *achri* = 'until' is a favourite with Luke, and he can use *kairos* in a weakened as well as a precise sense (e.g. 8[13]). Conzelmann (*Theology*, passim) makes the phrase, taken in a precise sense, a basis for his theory that Luke consciously presents the earthly ministry of Jesus as a paradisal period in which the devil is banished, to be allowed back only at the appointed time of the passion. But in the only other instance of the phrase in the NT, A. 13[11], it means 'for a while'.

$$4^{14}-9^{50}$$

The Ministry in Galilee

After the extended prelude in 1–2; 3^{1}–4^{13}, which imparts to his narrative something of the character of a 'life' of Jesus, Luke proceeds with a long section descriptive of Jesus' public ministry in Galilee. This comes to an end at 9^{50}, where it is succeeded by the journey to Jerusalem. It is composed largely of pericopes from Mark ($4^{14-15,\ 31-44}$; 5^{12}–6^{19}; 8^{4}–9^{50}) set within the predominantly Galilean framework that Mark had supplied for them ($4^{14-16,\ 31}$; 5^{1}; 6^{17}; 7^{1}; 8^{26}; 9^{10}). To this is added material from Q (6^{20}–$7^{10,\ 18-35}$) and of his own (4^{16-30}; 5^{1-11}; 7^{11-17}; 8^{1-3}).

4^{14-44} Preaching and Healing

4^{14-15} INTRODUCTORY SUMMARY

¹⁴And Jesus returned in the power of the Spirit into Galilee, and a report concerning him went out through all the surrounding country. ¹⁵And he taught in their synagogues, being glorified by all.

Luke rejoins Mark (1^{14-15}) with the notice that *Jesus returned*, a Lukan word which, if used exactly, requires it to be supposed, since it is not stated as in Mark 1^{9}; Matt. 3^{13}, that he had come from Galilee to be baptized ($2^{39,\ 51}$; 4^{16}). The link is not made, as in Mark, by John's imprisonment, since that has already been used to conclude the section on John (3^{19-20}), but by *the power of the Spirit* (a Lukan combination, cf. 1^{17}; A. 1^{8}; 10^{38}) already apparent in baptism and temptation. Luke then substitutes for Mark's highly compressed programmatic summary of Jesus' 'preaching' of the 'gospel' (a word he always avoids) a general statement of his reputation as a preacher throughout the region (taken in advance from Mark 1^{28}; *report, phēmē* + Matt. 9^{26}), and of widespread synagogue teaching which meets with universal acclaim (*doxazesthai* of human approval + Matt. 6^{2}). Of this he is to give a specific and also paradigmatic instance in 4^{16-30}.

Galilee: See on 1^{26}; 3^{1}. According to all the gospels Jesus began his work not at the centre of Judaism, i.e. Judaea and Jerusalem, but on its outskirts in Galilee (in Mark and Matthew it is confined there, though this is less so in Luke, and in John is not so at all). This was presumably because he was a Galilean (23^{6}; 4^{16}). Whether this in any way affected his strategy or message is uncertain. There is little reliable information about first-century Galilee in the later rabbinic sources. Whether there were any significant differences of belief or practice in Galilee compared with Judaea and Jerusalem is debated. Its epithet 'of the nations (Gentiles)' in Isa. 9^{1}; I Macc. 5^{15} indicates that it was looked upon as surrounded by aliens and as racially mixed. This could have led either to a stress on Jewish separateness (Galilean Jews were reported to be devoted to the temple), or to a Jewish way of life that was in closer touch with, and not uninfluenced by, the Hellenistic.[a] It possessed some towns, but was predominantly rural with a peasant population; and it is disputed how far Pharisaism, which was urban and middle-class, had made its presence felt there. Under the indirect rule of Rome, exercised directly by Herod Antipas, it enjoyed by contrast with Judaea relative prosperity and stable conditions, though it was probably heavily taxed, and there was an unequal distribution of wealth. Whether the reputation for Zealotism and insurrection given it later by Josephus (*Ant.* 18.274, 284; cf. Judas the Galilean, A. 5^{37}) was either fair, or fitted the earlier period of the gospel story, is uncertain. Vermes (*Jesus the Jew*, pp. 223ff.) sees the piety of men like the charismatic healer R. Hanina ben Dosa as having been influential in Galilee at that time.[b]

taught in their synagogues: sunagōgē = 'collection', 'assembly' (LXX 'congregation' – of Israel) is not used in the OT for a building or place of assembly. It first appears in this sense in the first century AD in Josephus, Philo and the NT. On the origins of the synagogue as an institution, which rabbinic sources ascribed quite unhistorically to Moses, there are divergent views: (i) It emerged in Palestine in the time of Ezra to give effect to his requirement that the people should be taught the law. (ii) It emerged in the Diaspora in the Hellenistic period to provide worship for those who lived far from the temple, and was transplanted thence to Palestine. (iii) It was copied from secular assemblies in the Greco-Roman world and given a religious character. Eventually there was a large number in the Diaspora and in Palestine, and through them Jewish worship was decentralized. While synagogue worship stood alongside temple worship, by which it was not uninfluenced, it was primarily lay, and was shaped by the central place in Judaism of the law and the prophets, and of their

a The view has been held that in Mark Galilee has less a geographical than a symbolic sense – see Marxsen, *Mark the Evangelist*; R. H. Lightfoot, *Locality and Doctrine in the Gospels*, London and New York 1938.

b On the whole subject see S. Freyne, *Galilee from Alexander the Great to Hadrian, 323 BC to 135 CE*, Wilmington, Del., 1980.

reading and exposition. Synagogues either had schools attached or were themselves used as schools. When the temple was destroyed they survived.

When a competent person was present the readings could be followed by an
exposition of the passages, generally the prophetic passage, which had been
read (cf. A. 13^{15}). This is what is meant in this context by *taught*, the verb
didaskein used absolutely – i.e. taught the will of God through the exposition of
scripture. Jesus was evidently seen as a competent person, and some of his
teaching is placed in this context. That it was felt to be in some way out of the
ordinary, and so cause wonderment, is a generalizing statement here, which is
to receive partial illustration in what follows.

4^{14-44} *Preaching and Healing*

4^{16-30} THE OPENING PROCLAMATION

^{16} *And he came to Nazareth, where he had been brought up; and he went to
the synagogue, as his custom was, on the sabbath day. And he stood up to
read;* ^{17}*and there was given to him the book of the prophet Isaiah. He opened
the book and found the place where it was written,* •

^{18}'*The Spirit of the Lord is upon me,*
    because he has anointed me to preach good news to the poor.
    He has sent me to proclaim release to the captives
    and recovering of sight to the blind,
    to set at liberty those who are oppressed,
    ^{19}*to proclaim the acceptable year of the Lord.*'

^{20}*And he closed the book, and gave it back to the attendant, and sat down; and
the eyes of all in the synagogue were fixed on him.* ^{21}*And he began to say to
them, 'Today this scripture has been fulfilled in your hearing.'* ^{22}*And all
spoke well of him, and wondered at the gracious words which proceeded out of
his mouth; and they said, 'Is not this Joseph's son?'* ^{23}*And he said to them,
'Doubtless you will quote to me this proverb, "Physician, heal yourself; what
we have heard you did at Capernaum, do here also in your own country."'*
^{24}*And he said, 'Truly, I say to you, no prophet is acceptable in his own
country.* ^{25}*But in truth, I tell you, there were many widows in Israel in the
days of Elijah, when the heaven was shut up three years and six months,
when there came a great famine over all the land;* ^{26}*and Elijah was sent to
none of them but only to Zarephath, in the land of Sidon, to a woman who
was a widow.* ^{27}*And there were many lepers in Israel in the time of the
prophet Elisha; and none of them was cleansed, but only Naaman the Syrian.'*

^{28}When they heard this, all in the synagogue were filled with wrath. ^{29}And they rose up and put him out of the city, and led him to the brow of the hill on which their city was built, that they might throw him down headlong. ^{30}But passing through the midst of them he went away.

Each evangelist has his own way of presenting Jesus' first public utterance of his message. Luke's has affinities with Mark's, in that the highly compressed summary in Mark 1$^{14-15}$, 'preaching the gospel (*euangelion*) of God, and saying, "The time is fulfilled" ' could be echoed in vv. 18, 21, 'to preach good news (*euangelizesthai*)' and 'Today this scripture has been fulfilled'. There could be an affinity with the OT citation in Matt. 4$^{12-17}$ showing the shores of the sea of Galilee and not Nazareth to be the appointed scene of salvation. But Luke's opening is far more artistic and impressive, being perhaps the most dramatically elaborated story in his Gospel. Jesus is depicted as reading a particular synagogue lection from the OT, and by this means proclaiming himself the Spirit-empowered servant or prophet of God, and announcing the purpose and content of his mission as the fulfilment of the promises of salvation, with a further hint that it will concern non-Jews.

Luke will have found in his sources more than one reference to synagogue preaching as a regular practice of Jesus, and to the mixture of astonishment and opposition it aroused (cf. Mark 1$^{21f.,\ 27f.,\ 39}$; 3$^{1ff.}$; cf. Matt. 4^{23}; 9^{35}), but nowhere any account of its content. This deficiency cried out to be made good, and where better than at the opening of the ministry? Luke, therefore, departs from Mark's order, picks out an event which comes later in Mark, and so narrates it as to characterize the message and activity of Jesus as a whole, and the response of Jews to him. The story thus has a formal and paradigmatic character unique in the gospels. It contains in very brief form the pattern of the sermons preached in A. to Jews, beginning with an OT passage, proceeding to an announcement of present salvation in fulfilment of it, and leading to the rejection of the preacher by his own people (A. 13$^{17ff.}$; 17$^{2ff.}$). There are parallels in thought and language with A. 10$^{34-39}$, and the scene in the synagogue, the reference to God's messengers as sent outside Israel, and the violent ending, could recall the story of Stephen in A. 6$^{8ff.}$. Luke may then have wished to show at the outset that the missionary experience of the apostles had its basis in that of Jesus, and this could explain why he chose the episode at Nazareth for the purpose, since for Luke Nazareth is where Jesus had belonged (2³⁹, ⁵¹; 4¹⁶; and cf. the frequent appellation 'Jesus of Nazareth'), and where the ministry should be solemnly inaugurated.

His omission of Mark 6¹⁻⁶ from a section where he is following Mark closely indicates that he regarded his own story as an equivalent. The general outline is the same, and *his own country (patris)* occurs only here in Mark and Luke. He may have possessed an alternative version which he preferred (so a number of scholars); but language, composition and content suggest that he was largely responsible for the account, based on Mark's, with the help, perhaps, of additional oral material. There is a high proportion of literary words and phrases. *where he had been brought up* (+A. 7²⁰ᶠ·; 22³), *went . . . as his custom was* (+A. 17²), *on the sabbath day* in the form *tē hēmerā tōn sabbatōn* (+A. 13¹⁴; 16¹³), *was given . . . opened (anaptussein* + + = 'unroll' of a scroll), and *the place where* and *closed*, are all good literary usage. Noteworthy also are *fixed on* (*atenizein*, only L–A in the NT apart from twice in Paul), *in your hearing* (lit. 'in your ears', a LXX expression akin to that inserted by Luke at 9⁴⁴), *spoke well of (marturein*, elsewhere in the synoptists Matt. 23³¹, and in this sense A. 6³; 10²²; 16²; 22¹²), *gracious words* (see note), *doubtless* (*pantōs* only here in the gospels), *proverb (parabolē*, in this sense cf. 5³⁶), the neat construction in v. 23b (for that in vv. 25–27 see notes), *filled with wrath* (apart from two instances in Matthew confined to L–A in the NT; cf. A. 5¹⁷; 13⁴⁵; 19²⁸ of Jewish opposition to the apostles), *put him out of the city* (cf. A. 7⁵⁸ of Stephen, A. 13⁵⁰ of Paul and Barnabas), *brow (ophrus* + +), *throw down headlong* (the literary *katakrēmnizein* + +), and *through the midst* (the literary *dia mesou*). Luke's attempt to make the story programmatic illustrates his strength and weakness as a writer. In a series of paratactic statements, which here serve to create a vivid impression, the successive actions in the scene are described – 'and he went . . . and he stood up to read . . . and there was given him . . . he opened the book and found the place', and then, after the reading, in reverse 'he closed the book . . . gave it back . . . and sat down'. The favourable effect on the audience is highly dramatic, so that their later fury and murderous intent stand in the strongest possible contrast. In the transition from the one to the other, however, the story limps and lacks verisimilitude, since this is made by means of three awkwardly connected sentences, containing two proverbs which are given a forced interpretation by reference to events which have not yet taken place, and OT precedents which hardly apply.

16a

Nazareth: See on 1²⁶. Here it is *Nazara*, which occurs elsewhere only in Matt. 4¹³. This is strange. It can hardly be explained, either by the use of a common source, as Matt. 4¹²⁻¹⁷ is simply his revision of Mark 1¹⁴⁻¹⁵, or by the use of Matthew by Luke, as the occasion is quite different.

where he had been brought up: A link with the birth narratives (2³⁹, ⁵¹), such as was not possible for Mark. *brought up* (*trephein* + + in this sense) probably denotes mental and spiritual nurture rather than simply rearing.

as his custom was: This belongs to the formal style of the narrative. Jewish readers at least would assume that a pious Jew automatically attended the synagogue on the sabbath. The parallel in A. 17² refers to Paul's strategy of seeking out the synagogue on arriving at a town in foreign parts, and that in Mark 10¹ to a (peculiar?) habit of Jesus of teaching crowds in public.

on the sabbath day: The seventh day set aside for abstention from work and for worship. In Greek literally 'on the day of the sabbaths', *sabbath* being a transliteration of the Hebrew *sabbat* = 'rest', with an *a* added to reproduce its sound, which then turned it into a plural in Greek.

16b–20

For this particular occasion of Jesus' attendance and teaching in the synagogue Luke includes some of the ritual involved, and his is the earliest account to survive. According to later rabbinic sources the sequence of the sabbath morning service appears to have been as follows: recitation of the Shema or confession of faith (Deut. 6⁴⁻⁹, with, possibly, 11¹³⁻²¹); prayers, including the Eighteen Benedictions; the reading in Hebrew of a passage from the law (*seder*), probably according to a fixed lectionary compiled for a three-year (one-year?) cycle, the reading, made from a dais, being of one verse at a time by different readers, with a targum or Aramaic paraphrase being provided of each verse as read; a reading from the prophets (*haftarah*), also targumed; an exposition based on the lection(s); the Kaddish prayer and a benediction. The service was ordered by 'the ruler of the synagogue' (cf. 8⁴¹), who appointed the readers and those to lead the prayers, and invited the preacher (cf. A. 13¹⁵). Some of these duties might be performed by his assistant (*hazzan*, Greek *hupēretēs* = 'attendant', v. 20), who took out the scrolls and handed them to the readers. Whether the *haftarah* was from a fixed lectionary is not known for certain. If it was not, v. 17 would indicate a specific request by Jesus for what he wished to read and preach about. If it was, he either happened, or deliberately chose, to attend when the passage was due to be read (and secured that he would be asked to read it and preach?). But Luke is primarily concerned to show Jesus as in command.

18–19

The kernel of the story. The fulfilment of Isaiah's message of salvation, already hinted at in 3^{4-6} ($^{22?}$) is now made explicit through the only passage in Isaiah where the prophet speaks in person of the character and purpose of his mission, and of his appointment to it by an endowment with the spirit of God (cf. Isa. 42^{1-9}; 49^{1-6}). This is a striking use of a particular passage of scripture, and is difficult to classify. Despite the occasion it is not the text of a sermon. The words of this *graphē* = a particular passage of scripture are simply said to be fulfilled (v. 21). It could then be said to belong to the familiar category of prophecy-fulfilment, but this would be in a formal sense only. For Isaiah speaks in the present and not the future tense (contrast A. 2^{25-31}), and about himself and not another (contrast A. 8^{34}); and there is no suggestion that he had failed, and that it remained for someone else in the future to carry out his charge. Rather Jesus himself is the starting-point as the spirit-endowed prophet, and the character of his mission; and the text is appropriated, and as it were re-enacted, in order to give these their divine origin and purpose.

The dramatic scene is again somewhat blurred. What is read here as *written* is from the LXX text (*recovering of sight to the blind* differs from the Hebrew text, which has 'the opening of the prison house to those who are bound'), but differs from that text in the following respects: (i) 'to heal the brokenhearted' (Isa. 61^{1d}) is omitted; (ii) *to set at liberty those who are oppressed* is imported from Isa. 58^{6}; and (iii) *to proclaim (kērussein)* replaces 'to call'. These alterations cannot have been made by the reader in the course of his reading. They are examples of early Christian activity, possibly here of Luke himself, in adapting the scriptural text in order to make particular theological points. What these points were depends on what the various expressions in the text were understood to mean in Luke's time, and by Luke himself in applying them to Jesus, which is not easy to determine.

18a

The Spirit of the Lord is upon me, because he has anointed me: Jesus is the prophet whose appointment to his office, and his execution of it, are governed by God's Spirit. *upon (epi)* implies a compelling force rather than an indwelling (cf. $4^{1, 14}$). *anointed (echrisen)* was used literally of the consecration to their office by oil of kings and high priests, and here is used figuratively to designate the prophet's relation to God, and his function (cf. Isa. 42^{1}). In the context it interprets in these terms Jesus' evident reception of the Spirit at his baptism (3^{21-22}). In A. $10^{38f.}$ 'how God anointed Jesus of Nazareth with (the) holy spirit and power' may also refer to the baptism, but is primarily concerned with its effects in the healing ministry. In A. 4^{26-27} 'whom you anointed' expresses through the verb what is implied by the adjectival noun 'his anointed', i.e. his anointing by God is Jesus' appointment, not as effective prophet, but as God's messiah or anointed one.

18b

to preach good news to the poor: This could either stand as a headline with a full stop after it, the subsequent statements being different ways of saying the same thing, or be the first, if principal statement, to be followed by additional specifications of what was involved in Jesus' mission (in 7^{22}, also influenced by Isa. 61^1, it comes last). The verb *euangelizesthai* corresponds to the noun *euangelion* = 'the good news' (from God) from or about Jesus, which Mark employs for the opening of Jesus' ministry (Mark 1^{14-15}), and which Luke consistently avoids. It meant 'to announce good tidings' (originally of victory), but in L–A, where it occurs fifteen times (it is absent from Mark and John, and occurs in Matthew only in a citation, 11^5), it has a wide spread. It is used of John's teaching (3^{18}), and of the preaching and teaching about Jesus, or of the word (A. 5^{42}; $8^{4, 12}$; 11^{20}; 14^{15}). The noun *ptōchoi* (absent from A.) is also more frequent in Luke than in the other gospels. Its occurrence here raises the question whether it, and the following expressions, are to be taken in a figurative sense, since it has, probably in Isa. 61^1 and certainly often in the psalms, the meaning of 'humble', 'meek'. In all other instances in Luke, however, it denotes literal poverty; see esp. 6^{20} in contrast to Matt. 5^3. It has been maintained that the omission from Isa. 61^1 at this point of 'to heal the broken hearted' was deliberate on Luke's part, and that he wished to confine the Spirit with which Jesus is endowed to the spirit of prophecy in Jesus' words, which is to be fulfilled in the audience's ears (v. 21), without reference to his healing activity (contrast 7^{21-23}, 24^{19}, A. 10^{38}). This raises the question of the interpretation of the expressions to follow.

18c

He has sent me to proclaim release to the captives: Jesus' presence and activity are a mission from God. For *apostellein* = 'to send', cf. 4^{43}; 9^{48}. It is frequent in A., and esp. in John for God as the sender of Jesus and Jesus as the one sent. *proclaim* (*kērussein*) is the action of the herald, whose announcement is effective for what he announces. It became part of the Christian vocabulary for Jesus' announcement of the coming of the kingdom of God, and for the subsequent announcement of the kingdom and of salvation in and through Jesus. In II Isaiah (Isa. 40–55) *release to the captives* would refer to God's coming deliverance of the exiles from Babylon (cf. Isa. $49^{8ff.}$). What such language meant in the situation of III Isaiah (Isa. 56–66), when this deliverance had taken place, is not clear. In Isa. 58^6 it is used by extension for an analogous action towards fellow Israelites in releasing from their confinement those subject to oppression. It could be intended by Luke to refer to Jesus' promise of release for the physically hungry and oppressed, as for the literally poor (cf. 6^{21-23} following 6^{20}, and the antitheses in 6^{24-26}). The problem here is that *release* (*aphesis*) could have, and in Christian language certainly came to have, the double meaning of liberation from captivity of various kinds, and (with or without *hamartiōn* = 'of sins') forgiveness, in the sense of liberation from, or cancellation of, debt. Hence it has been taken here as referring to that aspect of Jesus' prophetic mission, the forgiveness of sins, which is particularly illustrated in 7³⁶⁻⁵⁰.

18d

and recovering of sight to the blind: Here the LXX text, in its translation, alters the meaning of the Hebrew text, which, in continuation of the previous thought of the liberation of captives, has 'and the opening of the prison to those who are bound'. For the sequence of thought cf. Isa. 49⁹, where 'saying to the prisoners, "Come forth"' is followed by 'and to those who are in darkness, "Appear."' The text may then have meant no more than the exchange of the darkness of prison for the light of day. Against a spiritualizing interpretation – e.g. the conversion from sinful blindness to the perception of divine truth – could be the fact that in 7²², where Isa. 61¹ is filled out from Isa. 35⁵⁻⁶ with the restitution of sight as part of the deliverance in the coming time from all human ills, Luke clearly takes this as literal (see his deliberate insertion of 7²¹).

18e

to set at liberty those who are oppressed: Lit. 'to send away in freedom (*aphesis*) those who have been broken in pieces', a strange but forceful mixed metaphor. In Isa. 58⁶, from which it is introduced here, it is one of a number of injunctions on Israelites to behave towards one another as God had behaved towards them in removing all forms of oppression, e.g. feeding the hungry and inviting the homeless. It is doubtful whether *aphesis* should be taken as forgiveness, and the whole applied to a purely spiritual release. Luke may have understood by it deliverance through exorcism from the captivity and oppression of Satan (cf. 13¹⁶). If so this could explain the previous omission of 'to heal the broken-hearted', since Luke can approximate healing to exorcism (cf. 4³⁸ᶠ·; 13¹⁶).

19

to proclaim the acceptable year of the Lord: This means the time in which the Lord shows favour; cf. Isa. 49⁸, where it is further specified as 'a day of salvation'. The language is based on the institutions of the Sabbath Year and the Jubilee Year described in Lev. 25. Their hallmark was liberty (Lev. 25¹⁰; Jer. 34⁸, ¹⁵, ¹⁷), since they involved the emancipation of slaves, the suspension of debts, the restoration of property and the return of the land to fallowness. The Talmud, Sanhedrin 102a, 'This is the time ordained for salvation' shows it being given an eschatological flavour. Thus v. 19 is a summary of the previous statements. It may be that Luke stopped at this point, and did not continue the citation with 'and the day of vengeance of our God', in order to underline the gracious aspect of Jesus' ministry, avoiding here the aspect of divine judgment.

20

sat down: This is generally taken as the posture of the preacher in the synagogue, as it was for the teacher in the schools (cf. Matt. 5^1; Mark 4^1, etc.); but Philo (*Special Laws* II, 62) refers to the preacher as standing, and in A. 13^{16} Paul stands. Here it may be for dramatic effect. Though he has so far done no more than read the prophetic lection, Jesus, seated on the dais, is already the cynosure of all eyes – the addition in the Greek of *eyes* with the verb *atenizein*, which already meant 'to look intently upon', is emphatic. This already presupposes some sort of identification of *me* in the Isaiah quotation with Jesus, which has not yet in fact been made.

21

And he began to say to them: began is purely auxiliary, but it provides a more formal introduction than simply 'he said' to the first public words of Jesus in this Gospel.

Today this scripture has been fulfilled in your hearing: A very brief and pregnant statement in temporal terms (cf. Mark 1^{14-15}; II Cor. 6^2) of the actualization in some way of the lengthy contents of the Isaiah citation. For *today*, the emphatic first word in the sentence, as indicating the presence of the promised eschatological future, see on 2^{11}. *this scripture* means 'what this passage is talking about'. The exact force, however, is not clear. The verb *peplērōtai* continues the temporal accent in *today*, being in the perfect tense = 'is in the state of having been', but is doubtfully rendered by *has been fulfilled*, as this would answer to a prophecy couched in the future. A possible rendering is 'has been (already) accomplished' (with the tacit assumption that in Isaiah's case it had not been?). The verb may be proleptic, speaking as if the whole of Jesus' ministry is over, but this does not fit with *today*. Or it may refer to Jesus' mission from God and his endowment with the Spirit as already accomplished, with the inevitable consequences to follow. *in your hearing* (Greek 'ears') can hardly mean that the prophecy has been accomplished because Jesus has read it and they have heard him read it. The sense may be 'with you for witness', which may then prepare for the objection put into their mouth in v. 23 – how can they be witnesses to the accomplishment of the prophecy if he has not yet done any works amongst them?

22

In Mark 6^{2-3} the reaction to the (unspecified) teaching of Jesus is astonished bewilderment that such wisdom and works of power should come from a compatriot carpenter, whose origins and family they know, and then offence at the incompatibility between such mundane circumstances and what was expected for the glorious origins of the messiah. In Luke there is an awkward transition in the course of a single verse from high approval to some sort of disapproval, which is then assumed in v. 23. The approval is total; *all spoke well of him*. It expressed itself as astonishment at *the gracious words* (lit. 'words of grace') *which proceeded out of his mouth*. Here *grace* (*charis*) could mean 'salvation' (cf. A. 6⁸ of Stephen, A. 14³ of Paul), 'of grace' describe the content of the words, and the whole refer to the words of Isa. 61¹ read by Jesus and appropriated to himself. Or it could mean 'attractiveness' (+ Col. 4⁶), as in the classic phrase from Demosthenes onwards *charis logōn* = 'charm of speech', and refer to further words of Jesus after those in v. 21, which are not recorded. If the latter it would be the only humanistic description of Jesus' mode of speech. The question *Is not this Joseph's son?* could possibly continue the approval and voice local pride. More probably it is intended to mark an abrupt though unexplained change from approval to incredulity and hostility. If so, it could be an abbreviated form of the prolix questions in Mark 6²⁻³, where 'the carpenter, the son of Mary', if the right reading, is difficult, since among Jews a man was not denoted the son of his mother unless illegitimate. This would not do for Luke, for whom Jesus is the son of Mary by miraculous divine conception. Luke may have framed the question in this way for christological purposes, and in the context to pose the alternative – the Son of God by the reception of the Spirit at baptism and therefore equipped for the divine work, or the son of Joseph (cf. 3²³, *the son* (*as was supposed*) *of Joseph*).

23

However v. 22b is to be taken, the sequence of thought here, which is peculiar to Luke's version, is awkward. The rejection to which the story moves is anticipated and manufactured by Jesus himself. He voices the opposition by putting into the mouths of the audience (*doubtless you will quote to me*) the *proverb*, '*Physician, heal yourself*'. This proverb is found in ancient literature,[c] where it is applied in various ways to a person's need of that which he is able to supply for others but not for himself. Its explication here – wrongly printed in RSV as part of the proverb – is to the effect that what Jesus needs, if he is to substantiate his claims made in vv. 18–21 so that they can witness to them, is to make good the deficiency of not having reproduced in Nazareth the kind of things he is reported (though not in Luke) to have done already in Capernaum. This criticism seems to presuppose some such statement as that in Mark 6⁵⁻⁶, where the inability to do mighty works in Nazareth concludes the story, and is the consequence, not the ground, of the opposition. It also seems to imply that the expressions in v. 18 are to be taken literally as denoting mighty works of a physical kind. *here also in your own country* is so formulated as to introduce the word *patris* = 'home town' or 'fatherland', which is the key word in the next statement.

c See J. J. Wetstein, *Novum Testamentum Graecum . . . necnon commentario pleno*, Amsterdam 1751, on Matt. 13⁵⁷.

24

Truly, I say to you: The first instance of this form of introduction, the others being at 18^{17, 29}; 21^{32} (all from Mark), 12^{37}; 23^{43}. *Truly* renders *amēn*, which is the transliteration into Greek of a Hebrew word meaning 'so let it be'. It is found eight times in the LXX, always at the end, either of a sentence (five times as a liturgical response, cf. I Chron. 16^{36}, and in the NT I Cor. 14^{16}; Eph. 3^{21}; Rev. 5^{14}, etc.), or of a book, as in Tobit and III and IV Maccabees. Its use at the beginning of a sentence as an asseverative word in conjunction with the similar *I say to you* is well attested in the synoptic tradition – in John it is always re-duplicated. Jeremias held it to be unique to Jesus, and to reflect a consciousness of divine authority replacing the prophetic 'Thus says the Lord';[d] but while it was, perhaps, popularized by Jesus, it was not unknown before him.[e] Luke appears to be ambivalent in his attitude to it, or perhaps simply careless. It is the only transliteration of a Semitic original he allows in his Gospel (it is absent from A.), but he more often omits it (as in 10^{12}; cf. Matt. 10^{15}), or replaces it by 'truly' (*alethōs*, 9^{27} = Mark 9^1; 12^{44} = Matt. 24^{47}; 21^3 = Mark 12^{43}), or by 'for' (22^{18} = Mark 14^{25}), or by 'yea' (*nai*, 11^{51} = Matt. 23^{36}). J. C. O'Neill has argued[f] that in the six instances where Luke has the word it serves a special purpose of underlining the importance of statements about God's plan of salvation, and the conduct of Christians in relation to that; though the statements in 9^{27}, 12^{44}, where it is altered, could be held to belong to that category. If Luke does reserve it for special emphasis, its occurrence here, reinforced by *in truth* (*ep' alētheias*) in the next verse, could be to mark at the outset a governing theme of L–A, viz. Jesus' rejection by Israel as a whole and his reception outside.

no prophet is acceptable in his own country: This statement, also of a proverbial kind, accentuates the rejection implied in the application of the previous proverb, and perhaps in *Is not this Joseph's son?* In form it is more concise than Mark's affirmation followed by exceptions (Mark 6^4, shortened in Matt. 13^{57}), and is nearer to John 4^{44}, though more exclusive (*no prophet; acceptable, dektos,* may have been carried over by Luke from v. 19). In all versions the force of the saying depends on the meaning given by each evangelist to *patris*, a word found in the gospels only in this statement. In Mark it seems to refer to Nazareth itself as Jesus' 'home town', rather than to Galilee as his 'home country', since up to that point in Mark's story the Galileans have on the whole accepted him. In John it refers to Judaea and Jerusalem, the chief scene of Jesus' ministry and of his rejection in that Gospel, so that he leaves them for Galilee. Here, in view of its further explication in vv. 25–27, it seems to denote Israel as a whole, which is

d The Prayers of Jesus, SBT 2.6, 1967, pp. 112ff.
e See J. Strugnell, ' "Amen, I say unto you" in the Sayings of Jesus in Early Christian Literature', *HTR* 67, 1974, p. 180 n. 6.
f 'The Six Amen Sayings in Luke', *JTS* ns 10, 1959, pp. 1–9.

to reject him – cf. A. $7^{22ff.}$, the midrash on Moses who, mighty in deed and word, undertook to visit his brethren, the children of Israel, and thought that they understood God to be giving them salvation by his hand; but they did not.

25–27

These verses develop the previous statement, and prepare for the violent climax that the story has in Luke (there is no parallel to this in Mark), by provoking the fury of the inhabitants. Nevertheless, they fit here very loosely, if at all. For the OT precedents cited of Elijah and Elisha are not of a prophet's mission being first directed to Israel, and subsequently, after rejection there, to those outside, but of a 'mission' directed to a particular non-Israelite from the outset in the form of miraculous succour from a prophet. Only in a forced and muted fashion do they suggest that Jesus' message is due to go to Samaritans and Gentiles after a previous rejection by Israel (cf. A. 13^{46}; 18^6). Their parallelism in form and their internal rhythms resemble those of other passages commenting on the ministry (cf. 11^{31-32}; 10^{13-15}), and they are possibly a fragment of oral tradition belonging to a different context, which Luke has written up for use here – 'they bear the stamp of Lukan vocabulary' (Leaney, p. 53).

29

put him out of the city . . . that they might throw him down headlong: Cf. A. 7^{58}. Knox (*Hellenistic Elements*, p. 18) argues that the latter verb (*katakrēmnizein*) shows Luke to be using a source which knew that the official Jewish punishment of stoning began with the victim being precipitated from a higher to a lower place, although Luke, who uses a different word for stoning (*lithobolein*) in A. 7^{58}, was himself unaware of this. But there is no other evidence that the word, which is generally found in scenes of violence, was used in such a technical sense. Luke's mention of *the hill* suggests a greater height than that prescribed for precipitation before stoning ('twice the height of a man' according to the Mishnah, tractate Sanhedrin 6^4), from which witnesses were then to roll down stones on the one so precipitated. A lynching is meant.

30

Jesus possesses a mysterious invulnerability, as in John 8^{59} (where these words in Luke have got into some of the mss), and John 10^{39}.

4^{31-44} = Mark 1^{21-39}

THE OPENING TRIUMPHS OF THE MINISTRY

The section in Mark is a single unit sketching the character of the ministry through events gathered into a single day ('A Specimen Day', Nineham, *Saint Mark*, p. 73). Luke incorporates it as such, preserving its sequence and notes of time, underlining its typical nature (vv. 31f., 40f., 43f.), and in v. 41 reinforcing it from similar material in Mark 3^{10-11}. By omitting the conventional Markan trait of Jesus' accompaniment by disciples (who in Luke have not yet been called), he focuses attention on Jesus alone, who is the subject of the action throughout. The section then follows well after 4^{16-30}. The synagogue preaching is continued, and the notes of wonder and approval (vv. 14–15, 20, 22) reappear in vv. 32, 36, 42. *Jesus of Nazareth* (v. 34) is now intelligible after v. 16; with the concluding statement in v. 43, where 'I came out' is altered to *I was sent*, a return is made to *he has sent me* in vv. 18–19; and *preach good tidings* is repeated from v. 18, now with the addition of *the kingdom of God* from Mark 1^{15}. In adding v. 41, and in treating the fever as a demon (v. 33), Luke stresses exorcism, and the whole section becomes an illustration of *the good tidings* and *release* of vv. 18–19, and of the ministry of Jesus through the Spirit. As the Christ (4^{41}) and the Son of God (3^{22}; 4^{1ff.}; 4^{41}) he is the stronger one (3^{16}), who baptizes with the holy Spirit he himself possesses. His work, which is recognized by the demon world, is part of a supernatural conflict between holy and unholy spirit. His successful exorcisms mean the victory of the rule of God over the rule of Satan, achieved by means of his divine power, which is spirit. Thus vv. 18–19 have already provided the setting in which exorcism and healing can be seen as evidence of the liberating action of God through his anointed one. The section is thus an excellent example of how Luke, without possessing any additional information, and by means of additions, omissions and modifications, fits the Markan material into his own design, and makes explicit what is hinted at in Mark's more abrupt and vigorous account.

4³¹⁻³⁷

4³¹⁻³⁷ = Mark 1²¹⁻²⁸

AN EXORCISM IN THE CAPERNAUM SYNAGOGUE

³¹*And he went down to Capernaum, a city of Galilee. And he was teaching them on the sabbath;* ³²*and they were astonished at his teaching, for his word was with authority.* ³³*And in the synagogue there was a man who had the spirit of an unclean demon; and he cried out with a loud voice,* ³⁴'*Ah!** *What have you to do with us, Jesus of Nazareth? Have you come to destroy us? I know who you are, the Holy One of God.'* ³⁵*But Jesus rebuked him, saying, 'Be silent, and come out of him!' And when the demon had thrown him down in the midst, he came out of him, having done him no harm.* ³⁶*And they were all amazed and said to one another, 'What is this word? For with authority and power he commands the unclean spirits, and they come out.'* ³⁷*And reports of him went out into every place in the surrounding region.*

* Or *Let us alone*

ಬಃ

31–32

These become link verses. By omitting from Mark 'immediately' and 'entered the synagogue', and by taking over *was teaching* and *on the sabbath* (*en tois sabbasin*, probably to be understood here as a genuine plural = 'on the sabbath days'), Luke here, as elsewhere, generalizes the specific statements in Mark. He thus conveys the impression of a ministry of some duration, of which the events of vv. 33ff. are a specimen.

31

went down: katerchesthai = 'to arrive'. Apart from James 3¹⁵ the verb is confined in the NT to L–A, where it can be used in missionary contexts (A. 9³²; 19¹).

Capernaum, a city of Galilee: The impression left by Mark and Matthew that Capernaum was the residence of Jesus, and for some time his headquarters, disappears in Luke, where it is just one of the cities of Galilee. It is now identified as such for Gentile readers, which it could not be in v. 23. The site, which is imprecisely located in literature, is identified by archaeologists with Tel Hum on the north-west shore of the Sea of Galilee. As adjoining the east-west trade route it would be prosperous, and is probably correctly called a *city*.

32

his word was with authority: Cf. v. 36, *What is this word? For with authority and power* ... Mark's statements in 1²², ²⁷ are obscure, since *exousia* can mean

277

either 'authority' or 'power', and exorcism and teaching are curiously inter-twined, the one being an example of the other. Healing and teaching are twin activities in the gospel tradition (10^{13}; 7^{22}; Mark 2^{17}; 6^2; Matt. 11^5, etc.), and it is significant that in both Mark and Luke the ministry begins with beneficent acts of power rather than with examples of Jesus' teaching. Luke has not entirely removed this obscurity (*teaching*, v. 31, *his teaching*, v. 32), but the contrast with the teaching of the scribes and the reference to 'A new teaching' in Mark are dropped, and *exousia* is made synonymous with *dunamis* = *power* (v. 36; cf. 9^1; 10^{19}; A. 8^{19}). The *word* (*logos*) of Jesus is thus his healing and exorcistic word (cf. $7^{7, 14}$; Matt. 8^{16}; John 4^{53}) by which demons are made to come out, rather than, as in Mark, his teaching with authority which they have to obey.

33–37

In Mark this is of special importance as the opening event of the ministry, which gives an important clue to the whole. It is so also for Luke, since although the meaning of the mighty works has been indicated in advance in vv. 18–19, none had been done in Nazareth.

33

had the spirit of an unclean demon: Behind this and cognate stories in the synoptists lies the demonology which had developed in Judaism under Persian and other foreign influences, and which may have been more prevalent in Galilee than in Judaea. The evidence for it is found in the pseudepigraphic and rabbinic litera-ture, the latter being dated *c.* AD 150–450 and largely in the Babylonian Talmud, which, however, reflects earlier popular beliefs. In the OT demons are heathen idols. Subsequently demonology developed in two directions. (i) In apocalyptic demons take their origin from the fall of the angels (I Enoch $15^{6ff.}$; 69^{12}; Jubilees 5^7; $10^{1ff.}$), and attain a quasi-metaphysical status. They are united in a kingdom of Satan, are characteristic of this age and its corruption, and are destined to be destroyed in the coming age (Jubilees 10^{8-11}; 23^{29}; I Enoch 55^4; Test. Levi 18^{12}). They seduce men to idolatry, witchcraft and war, and except that they afflict men with every kind of ill, they have no particular connection with sickness. (ii) In rabbinic writings, which are not uniform in their teaching, and in magical writings, which sometimes show a strong Jewish element, they are not said to be a kingdom of evil, but are thought of after the manner of popular animistic belief in spirits as individual. They are intimately connected with the daily life of men, threatening them with uncleanness, and especially with sickness and madness. Various types of illness were called by names of demons. 'The spirit of uncleanness' is a common rabbinic expression, and is opposed to the holy spirit. In the synoptic tradition these two conceptions appear to have been brought together, and to be both simplified and intensified. The demons are never connected with temptation or sin, but exclusively, and very literally, with entry into and taking possession of men's bodies and minds (11²⁴⁻²⁶). Their influence is to be seen, especially in Luke, in various forms of illness (4³⁹; 7²¹; 8²; 13¹¹; A. 10³⁸). Nevertheless they form a supernatural kingdom of evil and are agents of the lord Beelzebul (11¹⁷ff·) or Satan, who, as 'the evil one' or 'the enemy' (10¹⁹), is the source of temptation and sin, and is the adversary of the rule of God. The casting out of demons from individuals can therefore be a sign of the overthrow of Satan, and of the deliverance of men from all evil (9¹ᶠ·; 10¹⁹ᶠ·; 11²⁰). Thus 'the dualism of Jewish apocalyptic is sharpened, and the metaphysical conflict has become central.'ᵍ

Luke here explains demoniac possession on its first occurrence in the gospel; cf. Jos. *BJ* 7.185; 'the so-called demons are the spirits of evil men entering into the living.' A demon is called *daimonion* (Ps. 91⁶; I Enoch 19¹, and frequently in rabbinic and magical writings), or *pneuma* (*spirit*. Jubilees 10⁵), or *akatharton pneuma* (unclean spirit, a cultic term, cf. Test. Benj. 5²; Zech. 13²). Luke's *spirit of an unclean demon* – it is not clear whether the genitive is possessive or appositive – is without parallel (but cf. Rev. 16¹³⁻¹⁶), and is designed for Gentile readers, for whom *daimonios*, from which *daimonion* is the noun, does not necessarily have an evil connotation, but denoted simply the supernatural (cf. A. 17¹⁸). Luke's *had a spirit* (cf. 7³³), as also the verb with the preposition *hupo* (A. 5¹⁶), and the preposition *apo* = 'from' rather than *ek* = 'out of' for the spirit's departure (7²¹), could suggest a less complete possession than Mark's 'with' (Greek *en* = 'in') a spirit', which Luke reserves for the agency of the Holy Spirit.

34-37

Though the story is vivid it has received the form common for such accounts in oral tradition – a statement of the patient's affliction, the technique of healing or formula of exorcism and a chorus of wonder from the audience (for examples, see R. Bultmann, *History*, pp. 218ff.). The language cannot be understood apart from the technical terminology of thaumaturgy. The confession in v. 34 and the question in v. 36, which carry the weight, are distinctive Christian elements.

34

This verse could belong to the thaumaturgical tradition, and be modelled on apotropaic formulae for warding off the attack of a demon by declaring, 'I know who thou art, M'. The demon would then be making a counter-attack in these terms. This would involve a change of roles, since here it is the demon and not the exorcist who feels threatened (but cf. Euripides, *Alcestis*, lines 28ff., for a similar address from a lesser deity who is lord of demons to a major deity). Here

---

g R. Leivestad, *Christ the Conqueror*, New York and London 1954, p. 40; on the whole subject see also J. M. Hull, *Hellenistic Magic and the Synoptic Tradition*, for whom Luke's Gospel is the one most deeply penetrated by thaumaturgy, and Vermes, *Jesus the Jew*.

it serves to introduce a confession of faith, and Luke transfers to it *with a loud voice*, which in Mark refers to the inarticulate cries of the demon.

Ah! Greek *Ea* + +. This is an expression of surprise or disapproval. Since it could be connected with the verb *eān* = 'to let go', 'to leave alone', it could be taken as the imperative of that verb (so RSV margin).

What have you to do with us?: *ti hēmin kai soi* = 'What to us and to thee?' is a Hebraism, though not unknown in colloquial Greek. Here it is 'a protest against hostile measures' (Bauer). In conjunction with *Have you come to destroy us?* it could be based on I Kings 17^{18}.

Jesus of Nazareth: Nazarēnos, as in 24^{19}. Otherwise Luke uses *Nazōraios* (see on 18^{37}). Knowledge of the name was important in magic as it brought with it power over the opponent. But while the demon's address takes the form of a conjuration of the name of Jesus, that may owe its place here to a motive more closely connected with the practice of exorcism in the church, which was through the confession of the 'name' of Jesus as the one whose advent spells the destruction of the demons; cf. the specification of the name *Iēsous ho Nazōraios* in the healing in A. 3^6 (cf. A. 4^{10}; 2^{22}).

Have you come to destroy us?: This could be a statement, not a question. As originally angels or servants of God, demons were able to recognize other supernatural beings (cf. 4^3, where Satan knows that Jesus has been designated from heaven the Son of God). They could also have knowledge of the divine purposes and foretell the future. Here, as previously, the demon speaks for the whole demon world. In his own way he makes a confession of faith in acknowledging Jesus not simply as an individual exorcist, but as one destined to destroy that world.

the Holy One of God: An address rather than a predicate (cf. Ps. 106^{16} of Aaron, II Kings 4^9 of Elisha). It does not seem to have been a messianic title, but it is appropriate here as a cultic term. The 'holy' is found in magical writings as the enemy of the unclean. Holiness makes Jesus' name effective, and 'holy' is applied to Jesus in connection with healing and 'the name' in A. 3^{14-16}; 4^{27-30}. The address is crucial to the story, as it provides it with theological meaning, and interprets what could otherwise be understood as collusion with Satan.[h]

35
This verse is also in the language of thaumaturgy. *rebuked* (*epitimān*, cf. 4^{39}; Mark 9^{25}) is the equivalent of the 'threats which are a constant feature of magic'

---

h For the Jewish tradition that Jesus was a sorcerer, see J. Klausner, *Jesus of Nazareth*, ET London and New York 1925, pp. 18ff.

(S. Eitrem, *Papyri Osloenses*, Oslo 1925, p. 36 and references); *be silent (phimō-thēti* = 'be muzzled') is a technical term for spellbinding or reducing a demon to silence (Eitrem, op. cit., pp. 76f.), which is an equivalent of exorcism; *come out* is the technical term for exorcism itself. It may be noted that, despite close parallels, the healings and exorcisms of Jesus have a relatively greater simplicity and directness than generally in the thaumaturgical tradition. He does not conjure with names, not even with the name of God, nor use repeated formulae or elaborate techniques, but expels with a single authoritative word. The imperative of his healing may be compared with the imperatives of his teaching.

thrown him down in the midst: This, in place of Mark's 'convulsing him', shows the reality of the exorcism – cf. Jos. *Ant.* 8.48; Philostratus, *Life of Apollonius* 4.20, for demons demonstrating by some action that they have come out.

36

As elsewhere in such stories the audience acts as a chorus and supplies the Christian theological comment, here in the form of a question. An exorcism did not ordinarily raise questions about the person and status of the exorcist. It indicates the purpose for which the story was told in the context of preaching about Jesus.

37

An addition, as in Mark, fitting the individual event into the ministry of Jesus as a whole, and showing his reputation as spreading (cf. $6^{17ff.}$).

4^{38-39} = Mark 1^{29-31}

THE HEALING OF PETER'S MOTHER-IN-LAW

³⁸*And he arose and left the synagogue, and entered Simon's house. Now Simon's mother-in-law was ill with a high fever, and they besought him for her.* ³⁹*And he stood over her and rebuked the fever, and it left her; and immediately she rose and served them.*

In taking over Mark's story Luke makes a number of stylistic improvements – *and he arose and left (anastas apo* = 'having arisen from' +22^{45}) *was ill with* (analytical imperfect of *sunechein* = 'suffer from', so A.28^8, also with *fever*). He omits the names of the disciples in Mark 1^{29} since in his narrative they have not yet been called, which makes the necessary retention of *Simon* awkward (cf. v. 23 with Capernaum). He adds certain touches which are characteristic of miracle stories. The difficulty and completeness of the cure are underlined (*high fever, immediately she rose* – cf. 5^{25}; 8^{47}; 13^{13}; A. 3^7). There are parallels in thaumaturgical technique to the healer 'standing over' the patient. But Mark's pairing of this healing with the previous exorcism, which is taken up in the summary in Mark 1^{32-34}, is destroyed by Luke, who, in treating the fever as produced by a demon (*rebuked*), assimilates the technique of healing to that of exorcism (contrast A. 28^8).

4^{40-41} = Mark 1^{32-34}

HEALINGS AND EXORCISMS

⁴⁰Now when the sun was setting, all those who had any that were sick with various diseases brought them to him; and he laid his hands on every one of them and healed them. ⁴¹And demons also came out of many, crying, 'You are the Son of God!' But he rebuked them, and would not allow them to speak, because they knew that he was the Christ.

Luke rewrites Mark more idiomatically, and makes additions from Mark 3^{10-12} which are more appropriate here than in the introduction to the sermon at 6^{17-19} (*all those who had*, cf. Mark 3^{10}; *crying, You are the Son of God*, cf. Mark 3^{11}). By the imperfect tenses of the verbs, and by omitting the local detail in Mark, Luke underlines the typical character of the events. The number of healings is vastly increased, the techniques used are varied, and the success is complete. But this is more than a record of healing success, since it contains two christological statements. The demons now pass in their confession from *the Holy One of God* (v. 34) to echo the voice from heaven at the baptism, which is taken up by the devil in the temptation, and acknowledge Jesus the healer and exorcist as *the Son of God* (v. 41a; see on 3^{22}), which for Luke is evidently a synonym for *the Christ* (v. 41b).

ΩΩΩ

41
would not allow them to speak, because they knew that he was the Christ: Here, as elsewhere, Luke reproduces the injunctions to silence. Since W. Wrede's book

The Messianic Secret[i] these have often been regarded as doctrinal insertions which Mark made when he ordered the individual pericopes into a continuous story, and which had as their object to explain how it was that, although he performed messianic actions, Jesus was not acknowledged as messiah in his lifetime. This theory, however, fails to explain why Mark has not carried through the theme of secrecy consistently (e.g. Mark 5$^{19, 25-34}$; 9$^{14-27}$; 10$^{46-52}$), or why he was at pains to point out that sometimes the injunctions failed of their purpose (Mark 7$^{36-37}$). Nor does it explain why Matthew and Luke apparently saw no incompatibility between such injunctions and other material they include in which messiahship is clearly hinted (7$^{18ff.}$; 10$^{23f.}$; 11$^{20ff.}$). Possibly not all injunctions to secrecy are of the same kind or origin, and some may be more closely related to the earliest form of the tradition than others. Injunctions to demoniacs should perhaps be considered on their own. Their aim appears to be not to suppress knowledge of the exorcisms but the confessions of demons, and this could be accounted for by the ambiguous nature of demonic testimony (cf. the charge of collusion with Beelzebul). The demonic could be taken for the divine and vice versa, since both belonged to the 'supernatural' world, and demons could counterfeit the voice of heaven. They are nevertheless evil, and their testimony must be disavowed. Judgment on the historicity of these injunctions will depend on the difficult question whether demoniacs are likely to have made such precise utterances. Possibly the silencing of demons was originally part of the technique of exorcism, and was only later interpreted in the light of the belief that Jesus the exorcist was messiah.[j]

4$^{42-44}$ = Mark 1$^{35-39}$

THE MISSION ELSEWHERE

^{42}And when it was day he departed and went into a lonely place. And the people sought him and came to him, and would have kept him from leaving them; ^{43}but he said to them, 'I must preach the good news of the kingdom of God to the other cities also; for I was sent for this purpose.' ^{44}And he was preaching in the synagogues of Judea.*

* Other ancient authorities read Galilee

The differences from Mark here are striking. The explanation of V. Taylor (Third Gospel, p. 79) is that Luke has used Mark 1$^{21-38}$ as a single

i Published in Germany in 1901, ET London 1971.
j See C. Tuckett, ed., The Messianic Secret, Philadelphia and London 1983.

section, and his memory of it is fading as he comes to its end, but they are better explained as (i) stylistic improvements of Mark's Greek, which is very rough here, and (ii) deliberate editing to make the section end more impressively. In (i) belong *And when it was day* (gen. abs.), *departed* (*poreuesthai* is Lukan), *sought* (*epizētein*, cf. A. 12^{19}) for Mark's verb *katadiōkein*, which generally has a hostile sense = 'pursued', *to* (*heōs* = 'up to', used spatially with a person + A. 9^{38}), *kept* (*katechein* in the classical sense of 'restrain' + II Thess. 2$^{6f.}$), *from leaving them* (*tou mē* with the infinitive), *the other* (*ho heteros* in the plural + Phil. 2^{4}). (ii) Luke's version, while losing the vividness of Mark's detail, serves to mark a stage in the ministry and to indicate its character. Since Jesus is not yet accompanied by disciples in Luke, it cannot be Peter and his companions who pursue Jesus to inform him of the crowds' enthusiasm but the crowds themselves, whose enthusiasm has been marked since 4^{15}. Jesus' retirement is a deliberate plan of which the crowds are aware; and the climax of the incident, and so of the whole section is, more clearly than in Mark, an explicit statement of the intended scope of the divine constraint, content and origin of his mission. 'I came out' in Mark 1^{38} is obscure (from Capernaum to the desert, from private life into Galilee or from heaven to earth?), whereas *I was sent* (cf. 10^{16}) picks up *He has sent me* in the Isaiah quotation in v. 18, and recalls the frequent use in John of the same verb on Jesus' lips for the divine origination of his person and work. The omission of 'he prayed' in Mark 1^{35} is not surprising, as attached to this incident it might suggest that Jesus was still uncertain of the nature and range of his mission, whereas he has been certain of it since his baptism (vv. 16–30). The omission is repaired in 5^{16} by an addition to a generalizing summary from Mark, where it more aptly suggests that retirement from crowds for solitary prayer was a constant feature of the ministry.

ஐ

43

I must preach the good news of the kingdom of God: Luke introduces here the term *the kingdom of God* which he is to use some thirty-five times, finding it in all his sources as the subject of Jesus' teaching in a wide variety of utterance (beatitude, parable, miracle and pronouncement story, isolated saying), and sometimes adding it himself, as here and at 19^{11}. While very frequent in the synoptic gospels it is comparatively rare in the rest of the NT, as also in Jewish literature. The Greek *hē basileia tou theou* renders the Hebrew *malkuth Yahweh*, which is one of the few abstract theological expressions in Judaism. Its sense, however, is concrete and dynamic, as it refers to the activity of God in governing his people (cf. Ps. 145$^{11f.}$, where 'power' and 'mighty deeds' are synonyms for 'kingdom'). It is properly rendered by 'sovereignty' or 'rule'. It could be said to exist already, or to come or be manifested, i.e. to be exercised completely. Because of this concreteness it could have as a secondary meaning the sphere in which the rule is exercised (I Chron. 17^{14}), which could be entered. The term is not found as such in the OT; it is a later concretion of the concept deeply rooted there of God as the king who creates, sustains and renews Israel and the world (Pss. 93, 96, 97 – 'the Lord reigns' = 'renews his rule'). This is seen particularly in his deliverance of Israel from her captors (Isa. 33^{22}; 52$^{1-10}$; Zeph. 3$^{14-15}$). In times of external oppression or of internal disharmony and disaffection it could be a symbol of what was to be expected of God in the future. The symbol was elastic, and what it denoted could vary according to differing religious emphases in groups or individuals. (i) In the period of the monarchy, when perhaps the concept first became a feature of Israelite religion, the rule of God was embodied in the king, his anointed one or son (Ps. 2$^{7ff.}$). This subsequently gave rise to the hope of the actualization of God's righteous rule over Israel (and over the world through attraction to, or subjugation by, Israel), perhaps through an ideal Davidic king (Ps. 89; Isa. 11, 61; Jer. 23$^{5ff.}$; Ps. Sol. 17$^{23ff.}$). (ii) In the circumstances of the first century AD this hope might be expressed, in a reassertion of the faith of the Maccabees, as resistance to the heathen oppressor and the contamination he had brought. This would involve the expulsion of the Roman occupying power, so that the land would once more be holy to the Lord and the people free to be subject to God as their sole ruler (cf. Ps. Sol. 17; Jos. *Ant.* 18.23). (iii) For those of a Pharisaic cast of mind the sovereignty of God, which was already present in the commandments of God in the law and their observance, could be said to come through a more complete obedience to them, and a greater holiness, individual and corporate; so perhaps the Kaddish prayer, 'May he establish his kingdom in your lifetime and in your days and in the lifetime of all the house of Israel, even speedily and at a near time.' This may be seen in the later rabbinic expression 'to take on the yoke of the kingdom of heaven' – cf. Berakoth 14b: R. Johanan said, 'If one desires to accept upon himself the yoke of the kingdom of heaven in the most complete manner, he should relieve himself, and wash his hands, and put on tephillim, and recite the Shema and say the tephillah; this is the complete acknowledgement of the kingdom of heaven.' (iv) By others, more eschatologically minded, its coming could be thought of in more transcendental and cosmic terms as the irruption of a present heavenly order of righteousness, which would bring about a resolution of the conflict between good and evil through a warfare, in part at least heavenly, a final judgment and destruction of sinners, and a (resurrection to) new life on (a renewed) earth (Dan. 7$^{12ff.}$; I Enoch 46–51; 84–90; II Baruch 72–73, Assumption of Moses 10, the Qumran War Scroll (Vermes, *Scrolls*, pp. 122ff.)). Here the expressions varied greatly, and the heightened and often bizarre imagery make it difficult to know what was contemplated. These conceptions were not entirely self-contained, and elements of one can be found in another. The sources also differ over whether a single representative figure or agent was to be involved, and who he would be.[k]

Here the kingdom of God is the object of the verb *euangelizesthai* = 'to announce good tidings', regarded by Luke as a synonym for *kērussein* = 'to proclaim' (cf. v. 44 = Mark 1³⁸; 16¹⁶; A. 8¹²). This word in Isa. 61¹ (quoted in v. 18) and kindred passages (Isa. 40⁹; 52⁷; Ps. 96²) belongs to the vocabulary of salvation. It announces that Yahweh is returning to Sion and is entering on his reign. If this is the force here it admirably sums up the narrative so far, with special reference to the use of the equivalent noun *euangelion* in the summary in Mark 1¹⁴⁻¹⁵. But for Luke, who, apart from Matt. 11¹⁵, is the only evangelist to use the verb (he has it fifteen times in A.), it can have a weakened sense less closely connected with Jesus' whole activity, and means simply 'to teach', 'to instruct about', with 'the word', 'Jesus', 'Christ' or 'the Lord' as object.

44

Judaea: The reading of p⁷⁵ B and others; it is probably original, *Galilee* being an assimilation to Mark's text. Even so the meaning is not certain, since in addition to its narrower sense Judaea can have for Luke the meaning of the whole of Palestine (A. 26²⁰; 10³⁷; possibly Luke 23⁵; 6¹⁷; 7¹⁷), as it could for some non-Jewish writers (cf. Strabo, *Geogr.* 16.2.21). Luke will not have had any further information here; his alteration will have intended to convey that the ministry was from the outset directed to Israel as a whole. *the other cities* (v. 43; Mark 'the next towns') will then be the cities of Palestine, including the rest of those in Galilee.

5^1-6^{11} *The Making of Disciples and Apostles*

Apart from 5¹⁻¹¹ the material in this section is taken from Mark, except for 6¹²⁻¹⁹ in the Markan order. So far the narrative has been of the activity of Jesus alone. Now – previously in Mark – disciples begin to

k On the whole subject see S. Mowinckel, *He that Cometh*, ET Oxford and New York 1956, John Gray, *The Biblical Doctrine of the Reign of God*, Edinburgh 1979, R. Schnackenburg, *God's Rule and Kingdom*, ET Edinburgh and London 1963. For the discussion of the relation of Jesus' teaching to such conceptions, see N. Perrin, *The Kingdom of God in the Teaching of Jesus*, London and Philadelphia 1963, G. E. Ladd, *The Presence of the Future*, Grand Rapids 1974, London 1980.

figure ($5^{30, 33}$; 6^1). From amongst these some are chosen who are specifically named 'apostles' ($6^{13ff.}$), and who will be responsible for extending Jesus' healing and preaching mission further afield ($9^{1ff.}$), and eventually to all Israel and to the world (A. 1^8). The contents of the section are, therefore, of fundamental importance in the perspective of L–A.

5^{1-11} THE CALL OF PETER (AND OF JAMES AND JOHN)

5 *While the people pressed upon him to hear the word of God, he was standing by the lake of Gennesaret. ²And he saw two boats by the lake; but the fishermen had gone out of them and were washing their nets. ³Getting into one of the boats, which was Simon's, he asked him to put out a little from the land. And he sat down and taught the people from the boat. ⁴And when he had ceased speaking, he said to Simon, 'Put out into the deep and let down your nets for a catch.' ⁵And Simon answered, 'Master, we toiled all night and took nothing! But at your word I will let down the nets.' ⁶And when they had done this, they enclosed a great shoal of fish; and as their nets were breaking, ⁷they beckoned to their partners in the other boat to come and help them. And they came and filled both the boats, so that they began to sink. ⁸But when Simon Peter saw it, he fell down at Jesus' knees, saying, 'Depart from me, for I am a sinful man, O Lord.' ⁹For he was astonished, and all that were with him, at the catch of fish which they had taken; ¹⁰and so also were James and John, sons of Zebedee, who were partners with Simon. And Jesus said to Simon, 'Do not be afraid; henceforth you will be catching men.' ¹¹And when they had brought their boats to land, they left everything and followed him.*

Luke introduces appropriately here, and before the call of non-apostolic persons like Levi (v. 27), an impressive account of the attachment to Jesus of his three principal apostles. In view of their place in the gospel narrative and that of the early church (8^{51}; $9^{28, 54}$; A. 3^1; 4^{13}; $8^{14ff.}$; 12^2), and especially of Peter as the leading apostle and missionary of Jew and Gentile (9^{20}; 22^{31}; A. $2^{14, 37}$; 5^{29}; 10–11; 15^{14}), Luke will hardly have been content to reproduce, either here or earlier, Mark 1^{16-20}, which is so terse, abrupt and without explanatory background as to be barely intelligible, and where Peter appears only as one person in two pairs of brothers. As Paul is to be given a special call (A. $9^{1ff.}$), so must Peter be (cf. Matt. $16^{17f.}$; John 1^{40-42}).

Luke's substitute story presupposes, like Mark's, that Jesus is already well known, and is well known to Simon, who has been mentioned previously without introduction (4^{38}); but it gives a strong impression of having been originally concerned with Peter alone, and of having been written up, probably with Mark 1^{16-20} in mind. As a result, like 4^{16-30}, it is vivid overall but awkward and unconvincing in some of its details. In the kernel, vv. 4b–6, 8–9, the verbs are in the singular and the dialogue confined to Jesus and Peter, culminating in an individual promise = *you* (singular) *will be* – in response to an individual confession (v. 8). There are breaks at vv. 3b–4a, at v. 10a – an awkward addition to make the incident cover the call of James and John (*and so also, homoiōs de kai,* elsewhere in the gospels 10^{32}; cf. v. 33), and at v. 11. These breaks can be explained as due to Luke's use of Mark. If the *partners (metochoi)* in v. 7 are the same as the *partners (koinōnoi)* in v. 10, v. 7 could also be an addition based on the double call in Mark (Andrew is not mentioned in L–A except in apostolic lists), and the reaction of Peter will have followed directly on the filling of the net; though the original could have been a story of two boats, one of them Simon's, with v. 10b making an impressive ending.

Judgment on whether there is any connection here with John $21^{1-13\ (18)}$ is difficult in view of the highly symbolic character of that story, which is written in the Johannine manner. In both there is a miraculous catch of fish after a fruitless night of toil; the unbroken (breaking) net; Peter as the leader with the sons of Zebedee accompanying him; and a reference to his penitence and reassurance. In Luke, however, Jesus is in the boat, while in John he directs operations from the shore; and the story is not, as in John, an allegory of the success of the apostolic mission, but is of a miracle inducing awe, to which is somewhat loosely attached a promise of future apostolic work. A highly plausible suggestion is that both are variant versions of the appearance of the risen Lord to Peter, which, in view of its primacy in the resurrection tradition (I Cor. 15^5; 24^{34}), is so strangely absent from the resurrection narratives. If so, Luke either did not recognize it as such – always a possibility when a resurrection story stood on its own and apart from its context after the passion – or he used it here because his theology required that resurrection appearances took place in, or near, Jerusalem.[1] Peter's

---

[1] See C. H. Dodd, 'The Appearances of the Risen Christ: an Essay in Form-Criticism of the Gospels' in *Studies in the Gospels*, ed. D. E. Nineham, pp. 22f.

reaction in v. 8 would then be explicable as a consequence of his previous denial (see note ad loc.).

Whether Luke knew the story in oral or written form is difficult to say. The style is somewhat refined, with participial and infinitive constructions, and with a high proportion of literary or quasi-technical words: *had gone out of (apobainein)*, *washing (plunein*+Rev. 7¹⁴; 22¹⁴), *put out (epanagein* + +), *the deep (to bathos*, rare in the sense of deep water), *a catch (agra* + +), *enclose (sunkleiein* + + in this sense), *beckoned (kataneuein* + +), *help (sullambanesthai* + Phil. 4³), *to sink (buthizesthai* + I Tim. 6⁹), *to catch (zōgrein* + II Tim. 2²⁶). The following could be ascribed to Luke's hand: *pressed upon* (cf. 23²³), *the word of God* (see note), *standing* (cf. A. 16⁹; 25¹⁰), *lake* (cf. 8²², ³³), *asked*, *a little (oligon* as an adverb of space + Mark 1¹⁹), *when (hōs)*, *had ceased speaking* (LXX), *Master, at your word* (cf. the LXX 'according to your word' in 1³⁸; 2²⁹), *to come and help* (infinitive of purpose with participle), *filled, both, fell down at the knees of* (see note), *was astonished (thambos* = 'astonishment' + 4³⁶; A. 3¹⁰ and *periechein* = 'to take hold' + + in this sense), *henceforth*. Also characteristic of Luke is the use within a short space of the same word in different senses, as in *hestōs para* = 'standing by' in v. 1 and 'moored at' in v. 2, and *agra* = 'a draught' in v. 4 and 'a catch' in v. 9.

 beta

1
While . . . he was standing: Literally 'It came to pass in the crowd's pressing (infinitive) . . . and he' followed by a finite verb. For this construction see on 1⁸.

the people: The first mention of *ho ochlos* (singular = 'the crowd', not *the people*, which in Luke is *ho laos*). This crowd forms a regular undifferentiated audience for Jesus' actions and words. This could also be from Mark, who, with one exception, always has the word in the singular, though for Luke it is interchangeable with the plural – in v. 3 *the people* is *hoi ochloi* = 'the crowds'. They are represented throughout as enthusiastically favourable to Jesus until the last moment in the passion, when they are found amongst his opponents (23¹³⁻²⁴), but then only temporarily (23²⁷, ⁴⁸). The incident is placed on the background of an instruction of this crowd from a boat (possibly taken from Mark 3⁷⁻⁹; 4¹), but from v. 4 this fades from the scene.

the word of God: Apart from the specialized use for an OT statement (Mark 7¹³; Matt. 15⁶; John 10³⁵) this expression is confined to Luke amongst the evangelists.

For him it is a general term for the message of Jesus (8^{11}; 11^{28}), and frequently in A. for the apostles' message about Jesus (A. 4^{31}; 6^{2}; 8^{14}; 11^{1}, etc.).

the lake of Gennēsaret: A name for 'the sea of Galilee', which Luke does not use, and is not found outside the NT. *limnē* = 'lake' is found in the NT only in Luke apart from its use in Rev. for the lake of fire. Gennēsaret was the fertile and populated plain bordering the north-west shore, and in the form Gennēsar is the regular word for the lake in Josephus (*BJ* 3.506, cf. I Macc. 11^{67}).

4

Put out into the deep: Where the large catch required for the story was possible, as it was not for hand nets cast from the shallows.

5

Master: The first of Luke's six instances of *epistatēs* (a word confined to his Gospel in the NT) as an address to Jesus, except for 17^{13} on the lips of disciples. In the Hellenistic world it was a title for various kinds of officials including those in education. For Luke it was an equivalent for rabbi (9^{33} = Mark 9^{5}) in the sense of 'my great man' which it had before it became an official title in Judaism. It emphasized authority over the pupil more than the function of teacher (*didaskalos*), for which it was also a synonym (8^{24} = Mark 4^{38}; 9^{49} = Mark 9^{38}). With this corresponds *at your word*. In contrast to Mark 1$^{16-20}$ it implies that Peter is already a disciple and not about to become one.

8

Simon Peter: Only here in L–A, where he is named either 'Peter', 'Simon called Peter', or, as in the rest of this story, 'Simon', but regularly in John, including John 21$^{1-11}$. In view of 6^{14} it is anachronistic here, and could be due either to a source reflecting the resurrection tradition, or to Luke's marking Peter's call by the use of his later and more official apostolic designation in the church (cf. II Peter 1^{1}).

fell down at Jesus' knees: An expression of profound prostration unique in the Bible but found in classical and Hellenistic writers (Bauer s.v. *prospiptein*).

Depart from me, for I am a sinful man, O Lord: This reaction, which with v. 10 forms the pregnant climax of the story, is puzzling. Conviction of sin is not elsewhere a natural or expected response to miracle, and some explanations are hardly convincing – 'the acted parable of the catch of fish reveals the remedy for Peter's lack of spiritual qualification' (Ellis, p. 103), 'The revelation of Jesus' divine power in this epiphany sufficed to demonstrate that he was in the presence of the Holy One and to make him aware of his own inadequacy' (Marshall, p. 205).

a sinful man: The first occurrence of *hamartōlos*, which Luke in the Gospel uses more often than any other NT writer (it is absent from A.), whether as a noun, or as here an adjective with *man* (cf. 19⁷). Who precisely are classified by the word, by whom and on what basis they are so classified, are matters of dispute.[m] In ordinary Greek it had no religious connotation, but denoted one who opposed or disrupted law, order or custom. In the LXX in general it is rare, but it springs into prominence in the Psalms and Wisdom literature, where it denotes one who is the opposite, and enemy, of the pious or righteous man, who delights in and observes the commandments of God (Pss. 1; 119; a synonym is *asebēs* = 'impious'). The sinners were those who were heedless of the covenant and the requirements of the law, and who persistently and openly flouted the commandments without sign of repentance. How in the circumstances of the first century AD were they identified as such? In some cases it would be by their occupation. Tax collectors, in performing the work of the heathen power, were automatically outside the covenant as traitors to God and his people (cf. Matt. 18¹⁷, 'as a Gentile and a tax collector') These are singled out in the synoptists (5³⁰ = Mark 2¹⁶; 7³⁴ = Matt. 11¹⁹; 15¹; 18¹⁰; 19²); but the conjunction 'tax collectors and sinners' raises the question who '(the) sinners' were that they were so conjoined. Other sinners by profession would be usurers, whose occupation contravened Lev. 25³⁵⁻³⁸ (they may be referred to by 'extortioners' in the list in 18¹¹), and also prostitutes, who are conjoined with tax collectors in Matt. 21³¹ (cf. 7³⁹, if the woman is a prostitute). Beyond these there would be those who were known in the community to be (unrepentant) thieves, adulterers (cf. 18¹¹), and possibly perjurers, sabbath-breakers (John 9¹⁶), and others. Disputable is whether, and how far, the term was extended by those in a position to determine such matters (rabbis? scribes? the Sanhedrin?) to cover such as were recognizably more lax (but more lax than whom?) in religious worship and in the observance of e.g. dietary and purity laws.

What *sinful man* means here is not clear. No mention is made in Mark 1¹⁶⁻²⁰ or elsewhere of the religious status or spiritual condition of the first disciples when called. Their occupation as fishermen did not carry any stigma. A confession of sinfulness here, especially if Peter is already a disciple, would have point if it was not a general one, but an acknowledgement of the guilt of his previous denials of Jesus when the miraculous catch demonstrates his lordship. The vocative *kurie* need mean no more than 'Sir', but on Peter's lips here it is more likely to be the vocative of *ho kurios* = 'the Lord', the peculiarly post-resurrection title of Jesus (cf. John 21⁷). However, the conviction of sin in the one who was to be the chief apostle is appropriate at the opening of a section where the dominant note is that Jesus calls not the righteous but sinners to repentance (5³²), and Luke has used the story for this purpose (cf. 22³²).

[m] See the discussion of E. P. Sanders, *Jesus and Judaism*, ch. 6, who takes issue with the view that the term covered the *'amme ha-arets* or common people.

10

Do not be afraid: Except for 8^{50} = Mark 5^{36} and 12^{32} this belongs to epiphanies of supernatural beings (1^{13}; 2^{10}; Mark 6^{50}; A. 18^{9}; 27^{24}), and conveys divine reassurance or empowering (cf. 12^{32}). This, and neither the declaration of forgiveness to be expected after v. 8, nor the summons to follow in view of v. 11, is the response to Peter's adjuration.

henceforth you will be catching men: A more literary and less proverbial statement than 'I will make you become fishers of men' (Mark 1^{17}).★ The verb here, *zōgrein,* means 'to capture alive' (the noun *zōgreion* could mean a fishpond), and perhaps continues the thought of *a catch* (v. 9). In Jer. 16^{16} the deliverance and judgment of Israel are secured by fishers and hunters from the Lord. In Mark the sense appears to be 'I will change your occupation from fishing for fish to fishing for men', and stresses the power of Jesus to change and enable. In Luke, where the verb with a continuous sense stands at the end, the meaning seems to be 'From now on you will be successful in taking men alive.' This could well be a post-resurrection promise and commission.

11

they left everything and followed him: A conclusion tacked on to, rather than arising from, the story, making it serve the same purpose as Mark 1^{16-20}, even though no demand to leave all or to follow has been made either to Peter or to the others (*they*), who are now somewhat awkwardly included. It is couched in the stereotyped language of the call to discipleship, though following is not the consequence of 'from now on you will be a missionary'.

left everything: A generalization of the cost of discipleship. In Mark 1^{18} they leave their nets, and in 1^{20} their father, servants and boats. Cf. $18^{22, \, 28}$ = Mark $10^{21, \, 28}$, and Luke's addition in 5^{28}. It cannot have applied to all of the large numbers represented as being disciples.

followed him: The first mention of *akolouthein* = 'to follow' (cf. also 'to go behind' 9^{23}; 14^{27}, 'to follow behind' Matt. 10^{38}) with the meaning 'to become a disciple'. It could already have a metaphorical sense in Greek – e.g. to follow an argument, or to follow (imitate) a god. The latter is not found in the OT, where Israel is not said to follow Yahweh. In the NT it is, apart from Rev. 14^{4}, confined in this sense to the gospels, where it is used of following the earthly Jesus. This gives it a pregnant sense, in that it refers to an actual physical accompaniment of Jesus, and thereby a participation in, and commitment to, the destiny of one whose actions and movements constitute a divinely appointed

★ For the metaphor see W. H. Wuellner, *The Meaning of 'Fishers of Men'*, Philadelphia 1967.

journey to be accomplished ($9^{23, \, 49, \, 57f.}$; 13^{33}; 14^{27}; 22^{33}); with which journey are bound up the kingdom of God and eternal life ($9^{61f.}$; $18^{22, \, 26-30}$). This cannot apply to the vast crowds who are said to follow (Mark 3^7), and it partly conflicts with the picture of the disciple (*mathētēs* = 'learner'), who is not a peripatetic but a stationary figure, sitting as a pupil at the master's feet.

$5^{12}-6^{11}$ JESUS' AUTHORITATIVE WORKS AND WORDS

In reproducing Mark $1^{40}-3^6$, which he perhaps regarded as a single section (some scholars see Mark 2^1-3^6 as a collection of controversy stories that came to Mark as a single unit), Luke provides further instances of the work and word of Jesus in fulfilment of $4^{18f.}$ (cf. to *proclaim release*, 4^{18}, with 5^{17-26}), as that is now evidenced in the existence and behaviour of a body of disciples. In this way he leads up to the address to hearers and disciples in $6^{20ff.}$. Each incident embodies a decisive pronouncement on an important element in Jewish belief and practice – so $5^{13f., \, 24, \, 32, \, 34}$; 6^5 (cf. 4^{32}). Together they present the single theme of Jesus wielding the power and authority of the new order, within which his disciples are enclosed, and evoking enthusiasm from the people and hostility from the authorities. Luke underlines this with *so much the more* (5^{15}), *from every village of Galilee and Judaea and from Jerusalem* (5^{17}), *strange things* (*paradoxa* + +, a strong word), *murmured* (*gonguzein*, a sinister word in the LXX, only here in L–A, but cf. 15^2; A. 6^1). Luke follows Mark closely except at the beginnings and ends of the pericopes, where he rewrites with a view to a smoother sequence and for clarification. So *egeneto* = 'it came to pass' in $5^{12, \, 17}$; 6^1 (RSV *while, as, while*); 5^{17} connects with 4^{44}; 5^{15} indicates a further expansion of Jesus' influence and sets the stage for 5^{18-39}, in which four separate Markan incidents are combined into one; an introduction is supplied for $5^{36ff.}$. There is an unusual number of agreements with Matthew against Mark in wording and omission, from which it could be deduced that Luke had Matthew before him as well as Mark; but they are probably to be explained as accidental (see notes on individual passages), and Luke shows no knowledge of the material in this section peculiar to Matthew (Matt. 9^{13}; $12^{5-7, \, 11-12}$).

5^{12-16} = Mark 1^{40-45} THE LEPER

^{12}*While he was in one of the cities, there came a man full of leprosy; and when he saw Jesus, he fell on his face and besought him, 'Lord, if you will, you can make me clean.'* ^{13}*And he stretched out his hand, and touched him, saying, 'I will; be clean.' And immediately the leprosy left him.* ^{14}*And he charged him to tell no one; but 'go and show yourself to the priest, and make an offering for your cleansing, as Moses commanded, for a proof to the people.'*★ ^{15}*But so much the more the report went abroad concerning him; and great multitudes gathered to hear and to be healed of their infirmities.* ^{16}*But he withdrew to the wilderness and prayed.*

★ Greek *to them*

An independent pericope for which Luke does not provide any more precise setting. It presupposes Jesus to be already well known as a powerful and worshipful figure (*fell on his face*, v. 12, is frequent in the LXX for obeisance before God or a king). The importance of the story for Luke is shown by his inclusion of another healing of leprosy (17^{11-19}) and by his own addition of 'lepers are cleansed' to the Isaiah quotation in 7^{22}. Although he omits, with Matthew, the expressions of strong emotion and of violence in Mark ('was angry', 'strictly charged' – lit. 'roared at him' – and 'sent him away' – lit. 'threw him out', Mark $1^{41, 43}$), which may have been as baffling to him as to the modern commentator, the story still has puzzling features (see on v. 14).

12

and behold: Not rendered by RSV = Matt. 8^2, not in Mark. The word is characteristic of both evangelists in miracle stories, as also *Lord* = Matt. 8^2 (which may have stood in Mark).

a man full of leprosy: As often Luke magnifies the disease. The elaborate precautions of Lev. 13–14, such passages as Num. 5^2; 12^{12}; II Chron. $26^{16ff.}$, and statements of the rabbis, show that leprosy (probably not the modern leprosy but skin eruption) was regarded with particular horror as defiling the holiness of the people and as a visitation from God. Although rigid exclusion was not enforced except from Jerusalem and walled towns, so that a leper could have been found *in one of the cities* (a LXX phrase, cf. II Sam. 2^1), the leper's life was a living death (Num. 12^{12}; Jos. *Ant.* 3.264). Israel was held to have been free from leprosy at Sinai (SB I, pp. 594ff.), and its removal could be a mark of the coming age (7^{22}; Matt. 10^8).

13

touched him, saying, 'I will; be clean,': Stress is placed on *clean,* vv. 12, 13, 14. This is no ordinary healing, nor is touching simply part of the healing technique, as in 7^{14}; 13^{13}, etc. Jesus is not only able to heal the man of his leprosy by his authoritative word, but in doing so to touch him without himself becoming thereby unclean.

14

Curiously Luke only half emends the construction of the sentence. *he charged him to tell no one:* The mysterious injunction to silence (see on 4^{41}) is taken over from Mark though it plays no part in the narrative and the fame of Jesus spreads (v. 15). Perhaps Luke took it here as a command to concentrate on the one thing necessary.

go and show yourself to the priest, and make an offering for your cleansing, as Moses commanded, for a proof to the people: This, which indicates the meaning of the cure, is obscure. The law made no provision for the healing of leprosy. The function of the priesthood was limited to pronouncing after examination that the leprosy, for whatever reason, had disappeared, and that the person was cultically pure and could partake in the sacrifices. The eleborate sacrificial ritual he was to undertake is prescribed in Lev. 13–14. The purpose of Jesus' injunctions here is generally taken to be to show his deference to, and compliance with, the law, but this depends on the meaning of *eis marturion autois* = 'for a testimony to them' (RSV margin). To take *them* of the general public (*the people*, RSV text) is forced, and there is no reason to suppose that the man would not have himself have followed the customary procedure. If *to them* means 'to the priests', it is not evident to what his actions would witness, since the sacrifice would be offered as a result of their own pronouncement of him as clean. In the other two instances of the phrase in Mark (Mark 6^{11}; 13^9) it has the sense of 'to witness against them' (cf. 9^5 *ep' autous* = 'against them'). So here perhaps the leper's actions are to spell the end of purificatory sacrifice, since Jesus is able to cleanse from leprosy without himself becoming unclean.

15–16

Luke's paraphrase (note the similar statements, variously expressed, in 4$^{14, 37}$) does not indicate clearly whether he took Mark's ambiguous statement (Mark 1^{45a}) in the sense that 'he', the leper, disobeyed the command and broadcast the matter, or that 'he', Jesus, preached and disseminated the word. The result is a further extension of Jesus' fame and increased crowds for hearing the word and healing. *But he withdrew* is in the periphrastic tense 'he was (in the habit of) withdrawing' (*hupochōrein* + 9^{10}), not to avoid the crowds, but to punctuate the healing and preaching ministry with retreat to the desert (it is not said where this is), and for prayer (omitted from Mark 1^{35} = 4^{42}, where it refers to a specific instance, and reproduced here as habitual).

5^{17-26} = Mark 2^{1-12} THE PARALYTIC

^{17}*On one of those days, as he was teaching, there were Pharisees and teachers of the law sitting by, who had come from every village of Galilee and Judea and from Jerusalem; and the power of the Lord was with him to heal.*★ ^{18}*And behold, men were bringing on a bed a man who was paralyzed, and they sought to bring him in and lay him before Jesus;*† ^{19}*but finding no way to bring him in, because of the crowd, they went up on the roof and let him down with his bed through the tiles into the midst before Jesus.* ^{20}*And when he saw their faith he said, 'Man, your sins are forgiven you.'* ^{21}*And the scribes and the Pharisees began to question, saying, 'Who is this that speaks blasphemies? Who can forgive sins but God only?'* ^{22}*When Jesus perceived their questionings, he answered them, 'Why do you question in your hearts?* ^{23}*Which is easier, to say, "Your sins are forgiven you," or to say, "Rise and walk"?* ^{24}*But that you may know that the Son of man has authority on earth to forgive sins' – he said to the man who was paralyzed – 'I say to you, rise, take up your bed and go home.'* ^{25}*And immediately he rose before them, and took up that on which he lay, and went home, glorifying God.* ^{26}*And amazement seized them all, and they glorified God and were filled with awe, saying, 'We have seen strange things today.'*

★ Other ancient authorities read *was present to heal them*
† Greek *him*

The twin themes of deliverance from paralysis by the power of God exercised by Jesus in response to *faith*, and of deliverance from sin by the divine authority of *the Son of man* in the face of the unbelief of *the Pharisees* (all three introduced here for the first time), make this an outstanding pericope. It supplies both the most direct fulfilment of 4^{18} (*to proclaim release – aphesis – to the captives*, *The Spirit of the Lord is upon me* being picked up by *the power of the Lord was with him to heal*, v. 17), and also, apart from $7^{36ff.}$, the only basis in an incident from the life of Jesus for the proclamation of the forgiveness of sins in his name which, according to Luke, was a principal part of the apostolic message (24^{47}; A. 2^{38}; 5^{31}; 10^{43}; 13^{38}). This will have secured its place in the tradition and perhaps influenced the form of the story. There is no attempt to preserve secrecy. The miracle is explicitly interpreted as evidence of salvation in accordance with the interrelation of the physical and the spiritual which runs through this section ($5^{14, 31-32}$; 6^9). He who effects the cleansing of physical and ritual impurity which the priests could only acknowledge, here effects for an individual the forgiveness which the priests alone could declare for the whole people through sacrifice.

The story is dramatically told from the point of view of the narrator, who deduces the faith which evokes the action of Jesus, and who, especially in Mark, knows the unspoken thoughts of the adversaries and Jesus' supernatural knowledge of them. The combination of themes, however, gives the story an unnatural twist reflected in the awkward *he said to the man who was paralyzed* (v. 24). Those who voice the chorus of approval typical of the ending of a miracle story here include the opponents (v. 26 *them all*), who do not answer the question addressed to them in v. 23, and of whose charge of blasphemy (v. 21) no more is heard. Both Matthew and Luke attempt to relieve the awkwardness, Matthew by shortening the miracle, Luke by introducing the opponents at the beginning. Attempts to recover an original are hardly convincing. Bultmann (*History*, pp. 14f.) suggests that Mark 2^{5b-10} were an insertion at some stage to base the Christian claim to forgive sins on Jesus' authority and were composed for the miracle; but it is not evident why they should be so inserted unless v. 5b already belonged to the story, but it cannot have belonged as a passing remark in a miracle story. Taylor (*Formation*, p. 166) supposes alternative versions, one a miracle story and the other a pronouncement story from which beginning and end have been removed; but the latter must have concerned the healing of a paralytic, and there would have been no reason for removing its beginning and end. The awkwardnesses may perhaps be accounted for by the story's importance, which ensured that it be told in lengthy, dramatic and naive form compared with the shorter and smoother combination of miracle and controversy in e.g. Mark 3^{1-6}, and that a conventional miracle ending be added, the opposition of the Pharisees being reserved for the end of the section in Mark 3^6. There are agreements with Matthew against Mark in *And behold* (v. 18 =

Matt. 9^2; see on v. 12), *bed* (*klinē*, v. 18 = Matt. 9^2, a natural substitution for Mark's vulgar word 'pallet', and varied by Luke with 'little bed' (*klinidion*, vv. 19, 24) and with '*that on which he lay*, v. 25), *and went home* (v. 25 = Matt. 9^7, a natural addition from Mark 2^{11}), *with awe* (v. 26 = Matt. 9^8, a frequent accompaniment of miracle in Luke, but in Matthew only here and 14^{26}).

17

On one of those days: A Lukan expression (8^{22}; 20^1) providing the vaguest possible chronology. Whereas Mark sets the scene with a crowd outside a house and refers incidentally to the opponents (Mark $2^{1, 6}$), Luke rewrites to underline the importance of the incident as a test case by assembling an (impossible) audience of *Pharisees and teachers of the law . . . who had come from every village of Galilee and Judea and from Jerusalem* (for what?), and refers to the crowd incidentally (v. 19).

Pharisees: The first mention of those who are to be, as in the other gospels, standing opponents of Jesus. Despite the references to them in the NT (confined to the gospels, A. and Phil. 3^5), and the fairly detailed statements that Josephus, once a Pharisee, makes about them, albeit in popular philosophical terms intelligible to his Greek readers, the origins of the Pharisees, their history, their character and role in the first century AD, are extremely difficult to reconstruct.[n] The name *Pharisaios* is a Grecized form, though it is disputed whether this is of the Hebrew *parash* – in the sense either of 'one who is separate' (from uncleanness? the community? or someone else?), or of 'one who divides', i.e. interprets the text of scripture – or of 'Persian', with the sense of one who introduces foreign ideas. It is not known at precisely what point in the Persian or Greek periods, or in what circumstances, they emerged as a group within a developing Judaism – in A. 15^5; 26^5 they are called a *hairesis*, to be rendered 'group' or 'party', not 'sect'. In *Ant.* 13.171ff., 288ff., Josephus shows them to be such already in opposition to John Hyrcanus (135–105 BC), and in other references illustrates their fluctuating fortunes in the first century BC in a three-sided struggle with the Sadducees and the Hasmonean rulers. They appear to have been a lay, non-priestly, movement, whose primary intention was to inculcate, and bring about, in Israel a maximum holiness, and that in forms which were possible for all to achieve through a strict obedience to the law in the conditions of daily life, and without recourse to the special circumstances of close associa-

n 'Virtually impossible' according to J. W. Bowker, *Jesus and the Pharisees*, Cambridge and New York 1973, p. 1. This book prints the relevant texts. See also E. Schürer, *The History of the Jewish People in the Age of Jesus Christ*, rev. ed. II, pp. 388ff., J. Neusner, *The Rabbinic Traditions about the Pharisees before* 70, Leiden 1971, I–III, and Sanders, *Jesus and Judaism*, passim.

tion with the temple or retreat into the desert (they are to be distinguished from *haberim* = 'the associates', who were smaller groups binding themselves to observe priestly rules of ritual purity). To this end they undertook an interpretation of the law (and of the rest of scripture as itself interpretation) through oral traditions which would make it intelligible in, and applicable to, the changed conditions of life since Moses – they were said 'to make a fence around the law'. They were thus a flexible, progressive and probably popular movement in comparison with the static, literalist and aristocratic Sadducees. It is debated whether by the first century AD they had ceased to be political and were a purely religious group; whether they had become more middle-class and orientated on Jerusalem, with little or no presence and influence in Galilee; and whether they had lost popular support on account of an excessively detailed and rigorous interpretation of the demands of the law. It is not known for certain how numerous they were – Josephus (*Ant.* 17.43) puts their numbers at 6000 in the time of Herod – nor how authoritative they were in Judaism; they did not control the temple or the Sanhedrin. They are commonly characterized as 'legalists', and the source of their hostility to Jesus is located in his attack upon their harsh and narrow 'legalism'; but these are question-begging terms in respect of a religion in which the Torah was central as the gracious gift of God to establish Israel.[o] Even in denunciations such as that in Matt. 23²³ it is not clearly legalism, however defined, that is under attack, while Jesus' own demands for a righteousness exceeding that of the Pharisees (Matt. 5¹⁷ᶠᶠ·) could be seen as rigorous in the extreme. Particular Pharisaic concerns may underlie some of the disputes in the gospels, e.g. those over purity, fasting, the sabbath (Mark 2¹⁴ᶠᶠ·, ²³ᶠᶠ·; 3¹ᶠᶠ·; 7¹ᶠᶠ·), but there is justice in the view that the Pharisees can serve the evangelists as a 'narrative convention'. 'When the narrator needs someone to ask a question that allows a stunning response on the part of Jesus he calls forth the Pharisees. When a villain is needed to exemplify obviously unsavoury traits he calls forth the Pharisees.'[p] They can then be introduced into the narrative, quite unrealistically, as a single, ubiquitous and inquisitorial body – *the* Pharisees – who dog Jesus' footsteps. In this Luke is more discriminating. In A. Pharisees appear in a favourable light. Some are found among the Christians, whose cause is protected by a Pharisee, Gamaliel, and Paul defends himself by appeal to his membership of the Pharisees, who, like the Christians, believe in resurrection (A. 15⁵; 5³⁴; 23⁶; 26⁵). In the Gospel also it is only 'some Pharisees' who interrogate Jesus (6²), or warn him (possibly with good intentions, 13³¹; cf. 19³⁹),

---

o See the observations of Abrahams (esp. *Studies in Pharisaism and the Gospels* II, pp. 4ff.) that joy was of the essence of Pharisaic religion, and one source of the joy was the multiplicity of laws, which gave so many opportunities of serving God.

p J. Neusner, *From Politics to Piety: the Emergence of Pharisaic Judaism*, Englewood Cliffs, N.J., 1973, p. 74.

and he is a guest at the table of individual Pharisees, even if hostility develops there ($7^{36ff.}$; $11^{37ff.}$; $14^{1ff.}$). This, however, does not prevent Luke from having *the Pharisees* as a single body in attendance with inimical intent (6^7; 11^{53}; 14^3; 15^2; 16^{14}, where they are slandered as lovers of money).q

teachers of the law: A compound word *nomodidaskaloi* + A. 5^{34} of Gamaliel, I Tim. 1^7, found otherwise only in Christian writers, and possibly a Christian (Lukan?) creation to distinguish Jewish from Christian teachers. It is introduced here before the first mention of *grammateis* = 'scribes' (5^{21}), in explanation of the specialized meaning of that word in Judaism (cf. Jos. *Ant.* 17.149, 'exegetes of the ancestral laws'). It should be noted, however, if *village* is to be taken literally here, that the village scribe could be a person of inferior status and limited capacity (Jos. *Ant.* 16.203, where they are referred to slightingly as mere 'village clerks').

the power of the Lord was with him to heal: A powerful comment (the variant *them* weakens it), which is added by Luke to preface the first of the individual healings (*iasthai* = 'to heal' is more common in L–A than elsewhere in the NT), the fever in 4^{39} having been treated as a demon, and the leprosy in vv. 12-13 requiring a special type of cleansing. It is meant to cover all the healings. That Jesus was a healer as well as an exorcist was deeply rooted in the tradition and is particularly stressed by Luke (cf. 24^{19}; A. 2^{23}; 10^{38} for his characterizing Jesus as such). Many stories of his healings were preserved, both as evidence of the nature of his mission, and because Christians healed in his name (A. $3^{1ff.}$; 4^{30}; 5^{12-16}; I Cor. 12^9). As healer Jesus participated in the widespread practice of thaumaturgy in the ancient world (see Hull, *Hellenistic Magic*), which had a place, though not an official one, in Judaism, especially, it is claimed, for the *hasid* or charismatic figure in Galilee, perhaps acting with Elijah and Elisha as models (R. Otto, *The Kingdom of God and the Son of Man*, pp. 333ff., Vermes, *Jesus the Jew*, pp. 58ff.). Such actions were, however, in themselves ambiguous; 'mighty in deed and word' (24^{19}) could redound simply to the reputation of the healer, and in any case raised the question of the relation of the 'deed' to the 'word' (cf. *teaching*, v. 17, and for the combination of teaching and healing cf. $4^{31ff.}$; 5^{15}; 6^{17}; $13^{10ff.}$). Here Luke refers them to *the power of the Lord* (= God; for *power* and *spirit* as closely related in Luke, cf. 4^{15}; 1^{35}; 24^{49}; A. 10^{38}). That the healings are the direct work of God heralding the coming age of salvation, and

q For a detailed examination of this, see J. T. Sanders, *The Jews in Luke–Acts*, ch. 4. His explanation is that the favourable references to Pharisees are to serve Luke's purpose of presenting Christianity as the true Judaism and as in continuity with Judaism, while the unfavourable references are retrojections into the Gospel of the fundamental error of the Christian Pharisees in demanding of Gentile converts circumcision and the keeping of the Mosaic law (A. $15^{5ff.}$).

redound to the glorification not of Jesus but of God, is a special mark of Luke's narration of them (vv. 25–26; 7^{16}; 13^{13}; 17^{15}; 18^{43}).

18–19
The situation in Mark 2^{3-4}, which Matthew simply ignores, is elaborated by Luke, improbably, with a tiled roof rather than one of rushes.

20
their faith: The *faith* (*pistis*) in healing stories, generally of the patient (7^{50}; 8^{48}; 17^{19}; 18^{42}; A. 3^{16}; 14^9), here of those who bring him (vv. 18–19), has the specialized meaning of confidence in the healer and his powers.

Man, your sins are forgiven you: The vocative *anthrōpe* in classical usage expresses rebuke or contempt (cf. 12^{14}; 22^{58-60}), and may be used here to imply that the patient was indeed a sinner. But the sudden transition from healing to forgiveness (cf. John 5^{1-14}) rests on the general connection in Jewish thought between sickness and sin, and therefore between physical and spiritual wholeness (cf. Ps. 103^3). Paralysis could be specially significant since it had been the divine punishment upon tyrants and the destroyers of God's people (I Macc. 9^{55}; II Macc. $3^{22ff.}$; III Macc. 2^{22}), and the strengthening of 'weak hands' and 'feeble knees' (LXX *paralelumena*, the same word as here), was promised in the important prophecy of Isa. $35^{3ff.}$.

are forgiven you: *apheōntai*, from *aphienai* = 'to cancel', 'remit', or 'let go', 'release'. The perfect expresses completed action, and the passive is reverential = 'God has forgiven'. It is not evident how this statement was open to the charge of blasphemy (v. 21), the most heinous of crimes in Judaism since it consisted of acting or speaking in such a way as to infringe a sole prerogative of the only God. The issue here would seem to be, 'Who has the right to declare authoritatively and with privy knowledge that God has forgiven?' (cf. II Sam. 12^{13}). The priests had such a right, but within the sacrificial ritual prescribed by God himself. Jesus, as holy man or prophet, declares it authoritatively to an individual outside the prescribed ritual.

22–23
For Luke Jesus has the power to divine men's unspoken thoughts. The force of the question here is probably not that one is easier than the other, but that both are very difficult (cf. 16^{17}; Mark 10^{25}); and that the achievement of the one implies the achievement of the other.

24
But that you may know . . . .: Dibelius (*Tradition*, p. 67) sees this as a comment of a preacher addressing his Christian audience, which has become incorporated into the text; but the style may be modelled on Exod. $8^{10, 22}$; 10^2.

that the Son of man has authority on earth to forgive sins: 'Judaism never, from Old Testament times to the present day, has ventured to make any such assertion in regard to the Messiah' (G. Dalman, *Words of Jesus*, p. 262). If so, v. 24, whether spoken by Jesus or attributed to him, does not amount to a claim to be messiah, but implies a development in the conception of the Son of man. The *exousia* (either *authority* from God, or 'power') to exercise the judgment and deliverance of God at the end of the days in the heavens is already anticipated in the actions on earth of the human Jesus ('the Son of man . . . I say'), and his actions, being those of the Son of man, have an ultimate character (cf. John 5^{19-29}).

the Son of man: Luke here introduces the term 'the Son of man', which he found in all his sources – here, 6^5; $9^{22,\ 26,\ 44}$; 21^{27}; 22^{69} from Mark, $6^{22?}$; 7^{34}; 9^{58}; 11^{30}; $12^{8?,\ 10?,\ 40}$; $17^{22?,\ 24?,\ 26?}$ from Q, and 18^8; 19^{10}; 21^{36}; 22^{48}; 24^7 from special sources or supplied by himself. The origins, usage, authenticity and meaning of the term remain matters of acute debate.[r]

The term occurs frequently in the gospels (the only instance outside them is in A. 7^{56}) without explanation, and as recognizable by audience or readers, and almost always on the lips of Jesus, who is apparently referring thereby to himself in the third person. At its base is the Semitic idiom 'son of', so that '(a) son of man' (Greek *huios anthrōpou*) means a member of the human genus, 'a man' (cf. Ps. 8^4; Ezek. 12^2, etc.). Whatever else it may express it must retain this basis, which in some cases may be its whole content – e.g. possibly here (cf. Matt. 9^8, 'had given such authority to men'), 6^5 in its Markan form (Mark 2^{27}, 'The sabbath was made for man . . . so the Son of man (= man?) is lord of the sabbath'), possibly 9^{58} = Matt. 8^{20}, and 12^{10} = Matt. 12^{32}, blasphemy against the Son of man being perhaps a variant translation of Mark 3^{28}, 'the blasphemies of men'. It has been held, however, that this does not account for an emphasis to be detected in the definite article, 'the Son of man' (Greek *ho huios tou anthrōpou*). Such an emphasis could be derived from a specific use of the idiom in the vision in Dan. $7^{13f.}$, where 'one like a son of man' = 'one with the appearance of a man' in contrast to the preceding beasts, comes 'with the clouds' before the Ancient of Days (= God) to be given by him an everlasting dominion

[r] From the vast literature on the subject the following may be selected as reviewing both the texts involved and the interpretations: B. Lindars, *Jesus Son of Man*, London 1983; C. F. D. Moule, *The Origin of Christology*, Cambridge and New York 1977; F. Hahn, *The Titles of Jesus in Christology*, ET London and Cleveland, Ohio, 1969; F. H. Borsch, *The Son of Man in Myth and History*, London and Philadelphia 1967; G. Vermes in M. Black, *Aramaic Approach*, Appendix E, and *Jesus and the World of Judaism*, London and Philadelphia 1983, ch. 7; M. Casey, *Son of Man: the Interpretation and Influence of Dan. 7*, London 1979; I. H. Marshall, 'The Synoptic Son of Man Sayings in Recent Discussion', *NTS* 12, 1965–66, pp. 327–51.

(kingdom) over all peoples. This figure is then identified in Dan. 7[18, 22, 27] with 'the saints of the Most High', who are generally taken to be the Israelites who had remained faithful under the persecution by Antiochus Epiphanes (though interpreted by some as angels or an angel). The definite article would then refer to, and specify, this figure in Daniel – *the* or *that* son of man – and could be evidence of a theological development of the Danielic figure in some areas of Judaism. The chief evidence for this has been seen in the Similitudes in I Enoch 37–71, where *the* or *that* Son of man appears, no longer as a corporate entity, but as a heavenly, eschatological intermediary, who is the leader of the saints, and who executes for God the judgment and destruction of the sinners. This could be the recognizable background of such sayings as those in 21[27] = Mark 13[26] ('with the clouds'), 21[36]; 17[24, 30], and also possibly of those which speak of the heavenly witness, the vindication or judgment by the Son of man (9[26]; 12[8]; 18[8], cf. Mark 8[38]). If the term still has this sense in statements of a different kind – that the Son of man is destined to be rejected, to suffer and be killed (9[22, 44]; 18[31]; 22[22]), whether spoken by Jesus or later formulations – it affirms a paradox that it is the heavenly arbiter and judge of men who is judged and rejected by men. Such a precise background could explain why the term ceased to be operative in the church, since in Greek it was a barbarism (= lit. 'the son of the man'), and it may have been replaced by 'the man' in the sense of a (new) Adam (cf. I Cor. 15[45ff.], and the heavenly Son of man in John 3[13]; 6[27, 33, 53, 62], etc.); though it must have been current usage for some time amongst Christians, if, as has been argued, it was placed on the lips of Jesus, or substituted for an original 'I'. Problematic for this view has been uncertainty over the date and character of I Enoch, and its reliability as a source for a pre-Christian Jewish theology, and this has been increased by the absence of the Similitudes from the text of I Enoch at Qumran. Recently Vermes has challenged this reconstruction of a titular, eschatological use of the term, and accounts for it by a rabbinic idiom in which a speaker refers to himself, generally in embarrassing circumstances such as humiliation and death, in circumlocutory fashion as '(the) man' or 'the son of man' = Aramaic *bar enash(a)*. In that case the statements of the suffering, rejection and death of the Son of man in the gospels would be the more original, even if later formulations in the tradition. Statements about his coming 'with the clouds', or his heavenly witness, vindication or judgment, would then be the products of a subsequent theological development, whereby a non-eschatological tradition was 'eschatologized', or its implicit eschatology made explicit, sometimes with assistance from the imagery of Daniel.

26
The importance of the event is signalized by the forceful and duplicated language of the chorus ending. *amazement (ekstasis)* is frequent in the LXX for an *awe* or dread sent by God (cf. also Wisd. 5[2] on those who afflict the righteous).

strange things is *paradoxos* + +, a word found frequently in Greek historians for a surprising turn of events, and used by Josephus of miracles.

$5^{27-28, 29-32}$ = Mark 2^{13-17}

THE CALL OF LEVI AND OF SINNERS

²⁷*After this he went out, and saw a tax collector, named Levi, sitting at the tax office; and he said to him, 'Follow me.'* ²⁸*And he left everything, and rose and followed him.*

²⁹*And Levi made him a great feast in his house; and there was a large company of tax collectors and others sitting at table* with them.* ³⁰*And the Pharisees and their scribes murmured against his disciples, saying, 'Why do you eat and drink with tax collectors and sinners?'* ³¹*And Jesus answered them, 'Those who are well have no need of a physician, but those who are sick;* ³²*I have not come to call the righteous, but sinners to repentance.'*

* Greek *reclining*

This is a particularly pointed conflict story, and one of great importance for the Christians. It is concerned with the authority of Jesus, and concludes with a statement of the character of his mission. The Markan version has a number of obscurities, not all of which are removed by Luke. Thus, it is unclear whether the call of Levi and the subsequent meal are integrally related, or were originally independent, and were brought together at some stage so that the one should provide the framework of the other. Also, what is meant by 'sinners' in the collocation 'tax collectors and sinners', what is the relation between the two parts of Jesus' reply, and what is the precise meaning of 'call'?

27

he went out: from the house implied in vv. 18–19. For Luke the sequence is one of thought from the forgiveness of sins of the paralytic to the call of sinners to repentance, and he omits, as does Matthew, the transition in Mark of teaching before a crowd on the seashore.

a tax collector, named Levi, sitting at the tax office: For tax collector see on 3¹². No location is given. In Mark it is Capernaum, where there would be a customs post for dues on goods coming into Herod's territory of Galilee. *Levi,* changed in Matt. 9⁹ to 'Matthew', appears only in this incident in the NT. Luke drops 'the son of Alphaeus', perhaps to avoid confusion with James, the son of Alphaeus, in the list of the Twelve (6^{15}).

'Follow me': See on 5^{11}.

28

left everything: As in 5^{11}, with a different verb. No demand for this has been made (for renunciation of possessions as a condition of discipleship, see 14^{33}); it marks the 'following' as total.

29

In Mark 2^{15} 'his house' probably means Jesus' Capernaum house (cf. Mark 9^{33}), especially if there 'were sitting with' means 'were fellow guests of' (cf. Mark 6^{22}) and not 'were guests with'. Luke makes it Levi's house, as yet unrenounced; and this is the first of several occasions in Luke when Jesus teaches from the position of a guest at a meal ($7^{36ff.}$; $10^{38ff.}$; $11^{37ff.}$; $14^{1ff.}$; $19^{5ff.}$; cf. $15^{1f.}$). Luke provides an adequate setting – *made* (*poiein* with a feast + $14^{12,\ 16}$) *a great feast* (*dochē* + 14^{13}; cf. Gen. 21^8; Dan. 5^1) – for what he judges a *large company* (*ochlos* with gen. + 6^{17}; A. 6^7), though it is not indicated where such a number of tax collectors would come from.

tax collectors and others sitting at table with them: Text and meanings are uncertain. *them* could refer to the tax collectors or to Jesus and his disciples. Some mss have *him*, sc. Jesus, or perhaps Levi; D reads simply 'others sitting'. Strange, especially in view of vv. 30, 32, is Luke's substitution of the vague *others* for 'sinners' in Mark. In Mark 2^{15a} 'tax collectors and sinners', both nouns without the article, could refer to a single group, i.e. tax collectors, who by definition were sinners in the technical sense of those outside the covenant, though the same words with the article in Mark 2^{16b}, and in the reverse order in Mark 2^{16a}, must refer to two groups. Even so it is not clear whether in this conjunction (cf. 7^{34}; 15^1) 'sinners' is being used in a technical sense, nor to whom precisely it refers (see on 5^8). Possibly for Luke it has a general religious sense, and is inappropriate as a description of those who, like Levi, have repented and are already disciples of Jesus.

30

the Pharisees and their scribes: For Mark's 'the scribes of the Pharisees', which means scribes who were of a Pharisaic persuasion (cf. A. 23^9). For *the Pharisees*, see on 5^{17}. The word *grammateus* = 'scribe' (Hebrew *sopher*), introduced in 5^{17} as 'teacher of the law', meant one concerned with writing, and was in widespread secular use for a secretary or clerk, often concerned with legal documents (A. 19^{35} + +; so also in Israel in pre-exilic times, cf. Jer. 36^{26}). Only in post-exilic times, with the increasing importance of the law, did the word acquire a technical professional sense of one qualified, first in the accurate transmission of the OT text, and then in its interpretation (Ezra 7⁶). This activity included application of the interpretation in cases of law. This interpretation was done under the aegis of the temple, and scribes were drawn from priestly families and Levites; the ideal of such is depicted in Ecclus 38²⁴ᶠᶠ·. With the emergence of the Pharisees, perhaps not unconnected with the *hasidim* of the Maccabaean revolt (I Macc. 7¹¹⁻¹⁷), a different kind of lay, non-priestly interpretation and application grew up, but the Pharisees did not produce their own scribes as such. Scribes could attach themselves to the Pharisaic movement, and associate themselves with its mode of interpretation. The relation between the two appears to have been fluid. Pharisees could themselves be interpreters of the law without being official scribes, while some scribes were confined to writing out the text.

his disciples: The episodic and pre-formed character of the gospel material is illustrated by the presence in the story without explanation of disciples, nor does Luke offer any explanation in incorporating the story into his narrative, where they are mentioned for the first time. This feature, that it is the disciples who are interrogated or their behaviour attacked, which is found elsewhere (e.g. v. 33; 6¹ᶠ·), has been held to indicate that the reason for handing on the story in the oral tradition was that it bore on problems which Christians had to face. The meaning of *disciples*, here and elsewhere, is, however, far from clear. The word *mathetēs*, from the verb *manthanein* = 'to learn', was a correlative of *didaskalos* = 'teacher', one who is learnt from, whether alive or dead, and was widespread in the Hellenistic world for a pupil in one or other of the schools of thought or philosophy, and a student of their traditions; it could further denote membership of a fellowship composed of teacher and pupils. It is absent from the LXX, because the teacher/pupil relationship is not found in OT religion. It emerges in Judaism, not without Hellenistic influence, for one who studies scripture, especially the law, under a qualified teacher (later called a rabbi), under whom alone it could be done. He would be a member of a group or school – e.g. in this period of the school of Shammai or of Hillel – whose traditions he would learn and represent. In the NT the word is confined to the gospels and A. In the latter, where it is found from 6¹ onwards, it is used absolutely to denote believers or Christians. In the former it is used, implicitly or explicitly, of an unspecified group of the followers of Jesus in his earthly ministry – 'the disciples' (10²³; 16¹), 'his disciples' (so generally) or 'my disciple' (14²⁶⁻³³). There are sufficient similarities, some of a more than formal kind, between the gospel picture and the teacher/pupil relationship in Judaism to raise the question whether Jesus stood in the position of 'rabbi' to pupils (cf. 6⁴⁰). Such are (i) his synagogue preaching: see Daube (*NTRJ*, pp. 205ff.), who takes Mark 1²² to indicate that Jesus, though not ordained, spoke with the authority of a rabbi in contrast to an ordinary teacher, who had no power to make decisions; (ii) being addressed as 'Teacher' by followers who are instructed by him ($6^{20ff.}$; Mark 4^{34}), though not 'in school' or through systematic interpretation of the scriptural text, and who are thereby representatives of his particular teaching ($5^{30, 33}$; 6^2; Mark 7^{1-5}); (iii) a similar address by others, who approach him as competent to deliver judgments on, or from, scripture ($20^{21, 28, 39}$). There are, however, considerable dissimilarities. Whereas a young man of the requisite ability would request an accredited teacher of reputation to admit him to his 'school', generally in the hope of himself becoming a teacher, Jesus is represented in more Hellenistic fashion as itinerant (9^{57}; 10^{1-20}; Mark 3^7; 6^1), with itinerant disciples, and as himself taking the initiative in summoning men, and those without previous qualifications, to a discipleship which is permanent. These features are, however, themselves problematic. The itinerant character of Jesus is possibly exaggerated in the gospels;[s] and while individuals, or an inner group, are depicted as being personally called by Jesus, this cannot have applied to the 'great crowd' of his disciples (6^{17}; 19^{37}; Mark 2^{15}), who, if there were such, will have become adherents in some other way.

Why do you eat and drink . . .?: Luke has the question addressed to the disciples about their own behaviour (in Mark about Jesus' behaviour, cf. 15^1), even though it is Jesus who replies (cf. 6^{1-5}). This is perhaps because he was aware that a similar question about eating with the unclean (Gentiles) was a grave issue in the churches; see A. 10^1–11^{18}; 15^{1-29}; cf. Gal. 2^{11-16}; I Cor. 8–10. Luke has the more conventional *eat and drink*, as in v. 33.

31–32
The question has, unusually, a double answer (cf. 4^{23} and 4^{24-27}). The first is proverbial, impersonal and defensive, the second personal, positive and programmatic of Jesus' mission. The form is the same in both ('not . . . but'), though not the force; and the second does not follow naturally from the first, as healing in answer to need and going out to call are different kinds of activity.

31
A proverb with Hellenistic parallels (see J. J. Wetstein, I, p. 358). Its form here – only the sick need a physician, the healthy (*hugiainein* + 7^{10}, 15^{27} in the gospels) do not – is very emphatic. The language may be more than proverbial illustration if the healings of Jesus are indicative of his mission (in the Gospel of Thomas 31 the statement is brought together with the physician proverb in 4^{23}).

---

s See F. Borsch, 'Jesus, the Wandering Preacher', in *What about the New Testament?*, ed. M. Hooker and C. Hickling, London 1975, pp. 45–63.

32

Here the force may be dialectical rather than exclusive – 'I am concerned with sinners rather than with the righteous.'

I have not come: Luke introduces, here from Mark, the first of the sayings beginning with the formula *I have (not) come* followed by an infinitive of purpose (cf. 12$^{49, 51}$ (4^{43}), varied by 'the Son of man came' in 7^{34}; 19^{10}, cf. Mark 10^{45}; Matt. 5^{17}). The verb (*ēlthon*) is in the aorist, except here, where Luke alters to the perfect, perhaps with the added nuance 'I have come and continue to . . .' The formula introduces a reflective summary of the character and purpose of Jesus' mission seen in its totality and as already completed. As such it is likely to be a Christian product – cf. I Tim. 1^{15}, where it is incorporated into a credal statement; it can be seen continuing in 'I came to destroy the works of the female' in the Gospel of the Egyptians, and 'I came to destroy the sacrifices' in the Gospel of the Hebrews. It has no real parallels in Hellenistic religion, nor any basis in the OT, where the 'coming' of God cannot presuppose a 'being sent', as generally in this form of statement (cf. 4^{43}), and the prophets do not speak of their mission in the first person, but of God who sends them (Jer. 1^5; Isa. 6^8; but cf. Dan. 9^{23}; 10^{14} of a heavenly envoy). Nor is it connected with 'he who is to come' (7^{19}), which means 'the future coming one'. It could be a fresh creation, expressing with a certain intensity a prophetic sense of mission with a more than prophetic sense that this involves the destiny of men. The nearest Jewish parallels are in later rabbis, who used the formula to convey divine purpose – e.g. 'scripture comes to . . .', meaning 'the purpose of scripture is . . .'^{t} This is the primary meaning in the synoptists. It does not presuppose pre-existence, though it could be taken to do so, and is so taken in the development it receives in John's Gospel through the addition of 'from the Father' and 'into the world' (John 16^{28}).

to call: The verb *kalein* used absolutely (cf. Rom. 8^{30}; 9^{11}; I Cor. 7^{17}; I Peter 1^{15}) is found of God's summons to Israel to partake of the blessings of redemption and to participate in his purposes (Isa. 41^9; 42^6, etc.). So here in Mark it could express a function which exceeds the prophetic. Jesus is the agent of the divine summons to the blessings of the kingdom, and, if the context is to be pressed, could refer to the summons to follow him as leader, and to share in his activity and fate, of which the summons to Levi is a particular instance. But the verb could also mean 'to invite' (to a meal), and since the kingdom can be depicted under the image of a meal this may be its meaning in Mark. In the context the saying would then link not only with Levi's call, but with the subsequent meal of Jesus with disciples; and in the Markan form it gives as the ground of the

---

t See E. Arens, *The ELTHON-Sayings in the Synoptic Tradition*, Freiburg 1976, pp. 265ff.

offence that Jesus gave that he invited sinners to the kingdom without further ado, and without previous conditions.

to repentance: Luke's addition shows that he took *call* in the sense of 'summon' and not of 'invite', and is characteristic, *repentance* (see on 3³) being for him the core of the Christian message (24⁴⁷; A. 5³¹; 11¹⁸; 17³⁰; 20²¹; 26²⁰). But, if the Markan saying is correctly interpreted above, Luke's addition renders it innocuous, since no right-minded Jew could take offence at a summons of sinners to repentance, which was integral to Judaism, and was to be expected of a spiritual leader.

5³³⁻³⁵, ³⁶⁻³⁹ = Mark 2¹⁸⁻²²

THE NEW ORDER

³³*And they said to him, 'The disciples of John fast often and offer prayers, and so do the disciples of the Pharisees, but yours eat and drink.'* ³⁴*And Jesus said to them, 'Can you make wedding guests fast while the bridegroom is with them?* ³⁵*The days will come, when the bridegroom is taken away from them, and then they will fast in those days.'* ³⁶*He told them a parable also: 'No one tears a piece from a new garment and puts it upon an old garment; if he does, he will tear the new, and the piece from the new will not match the old.* ³⁷*And no one puts new wine into old wineskins; if he does, the new wine will burst the skins and it will be spilled, and the skins will be destroyed.* ³⁸*But new wine must be put into fresh wineskins.* ³⁹*And no one after drinking old wine desires new; for he says, "The old is good." '★*

★ Other ancient authorities read *better*

In Mark this is a separate pericope introduced by a statement about fasting and the impersonal 'they come to him and say'. Its connection with what has preceded is, however, close, since the mission of Jesus as divine summons could lead to the question of the nature of that to which men are summoned. It could be closer still if 'call' has overtones of 'invite'. The newness of that order of life to which men are summoned is established by a contrast between feasting and an important element in Jewish piety, fasting. Luke runs the pericope on from the preceding (*And they said to him* refers to the previous speakers in v. 30), so that vv. 33–39 become conversation at table with Pharisees and scribes (cf. 7³⁶ᶠᶠ·; 11³⁷ᶠᶠ·; 14¹ᶠᶠ·). However, the previous addition of *to repentance* alters the connection, since penitence goes with fasting rather than with feasting (but cf. $15^{7, 10}$; $10^{22ff.}$), and the question could become 'Why do those called to repentance not fast?' Whereas in the previous pericope Luke has the actions of Jesus laid at the disciples' door, here he follows Mark, and the actions of the disciples are laid at Jesus' door.

33

The preliminary statement in Mark 2^{18} of what was going on as the basis of the question asked becomes in Luke part of the question itself.

the disciples of John: These are mentioned elsewhere as a distinct religious group at the time: in 11^1; in A. $18^{24}-19^7$ (here possibly Christians who knew only John's baptism and not Pentecost), and especially in John's Gospel; cf. John 4^1, where they appear to be numerous, 3^{25}, where they engage in dispute over (baptismal?) purification, and $1^{35ff.}$, where their leader directs some of them to become disciples of Jesus. Our scanty knowledge of the Baptist and his movement makes it difficult to envisage what would be meant in his case by *disciples* (see on v. 30). The synoptists depict him as directing to Israel as a whole a call to repentance in face of an imminent final judgment, and this was hardly likely to produce a separate religious group of adherents of a teacher with its own cast of belief and piety. How any such beliefs and practices developed after his death, and in consequence of the non-appearance of the judgment he had announced, is not known. Were John's disciples a 'baptist' or 'adventist' group, and what happened to them? Their relation to the disciples of Jesus and later to Christian churches, and vice versa, could have been a continuing problem, not unconnected with the co-existence of their respective leaders (7^{18-35} = Matt. 11^{2-19}; Luke 1–2), and with ambiguities arising from that (John was Jesus' forerunner, Mark $1^{2ff.}$; 9^{9-13}; A. 13^{25}, but Jesus was baptized by John).

fast often: For fasting in Jewish religion, see Abrahams, *Studies* I, pp. 121ff., *TDNT* IV, pp. 927ff. Originally an apotropaic, public and private, to ward off demons, and then the divine judgment, and to secure relief and blessing, it had become for the individual an act of self-denial that was meritorious and pleasing to God in itself, and was thus characteristic of the most pious in Israel (18^{12}; Tacitus, *Histories* V, 4 shows it to have been for some Gentiles a hallmark of the Jew). Along with prayer and almsgiving it constituted the duties of religion (cf. Matt. 6^{1-18}). While fasting often expressed penitence or remorse, the frequent fasting of John's disciples could have been of a different kind, and a mark of an asceticism stamped on his disciples by John's emphasis on judgment and repentance. The pericope could originally have been concerned only with the disciples of John in contrast with those of Jesus, since in 7^{31-34} = Matt. 11^{16-19} a contrast is drawn in the same terms between their leaders.

and offer prayers: An addition by Luke; cf. 11^1, where he knows that John taught his disciples a particular way of praying. It produces the regular Jewish combination of 'prayer and fasting' (2^{37}; Dan. 2^{18} LXX; A. 13^3; 14^{23}). It may have been made to provide a rhythmical balance with Luke's 'eating and drinking', but it is inept here, as logically it should lead to a question 'Why do not your disciples pray?'; and the contrast is shifted from that between asceticism and non-asceticism to that between pious and not pious.

and so do the disciples of the Pharisees: Lit. 'and likewise also those of the Pharisees' for 'the disciples of the Pharisees' in Mark 2^{18} (Matt. 9^{14} 'the Pharisees', but cf. Matt. 22^{16}). This is even more puzzling than *the disciples of John.* The Pharisees (see on v. 17), in distinction from scribes, were lay Jews bound together by the ideal of ordering their lives according to a strict interpretation of the law. As such they did not have disciples in the sense of those under the instruction of a teacher, even if they themselves could undertake the scribal work of interpretation. The expression was, perhaps, modelled on *the disciples of John,* and was added to a pericope originally limited to a specific contrast between the disciples of John and those of Jesus so as to make it cover at the same time, or even primarily, a contrast with, and a criticism of, an aspect of Pharisaic practice in general.

34

The question is possibly proverbial (cf. v. 31; 4^{23}), though it is not wholly parabolic, since 'fast' is contained in both the saying and in that to which it applies. *the wedding guests* renders *hoi huioi tou numphōnos* = 'the sons of the bridechamber', a designation of a group of guests who played a particular part in the wedding ceremonies as the bridegroom's attendants. It may have here a more precise reference to the custom of dispensing guests during the seven days of wedding festivities from religious duties, which might include fasting (so SB I, p. 505). The sense is that fasting is entirely inappropriate during a wedding (that is the meaning of *while the bridegroom is with them*), since that is throughout an occasion of joy. The implied application is that fasting is impossible for Jesus' disciples (underlined by Luke's *can you make them* for Mark's 'can they'), since what has made them disciples is a proclamation of a present salvation (for wedding language used parabolically of salvation, cf. Isa. 61^{10}; Jer. 33^{11}).

35

This verse is almost certainly a later adaptation and application of v. 34 in a christological sense. The language is no longer parabolic but allegorical. The bridegroom is now a specific bridegroom, Jesus; the sons of the bridechamber are his disciples; *while he is with them* is now taken literally of a particular period of time, his earthly ministry, lasting until *the days will come* (a prophetic-apocalyptic type of utterance, cf. 17^{22}; 21^6) when the bridegroom *is taken away from them* (sc. his death; there is nothing analogous to this in wedding practice). This no longer answers the original question about the present time and mode of Jesus' ministry as exhibited in the conduct of his disciples, but, in conjunction with v. 34, contemplates two times, and justifies some kind of fasting for Christians at a later date – emphasized by Luke with *in those days* for Mark's 'in that day'.

36–38
Luke punctuates by inserting as an introduction to the following sayings *He told them a parable also*, as in 6^{39}. In their present context the sayings in Mark 2$^{21-22}$ bear generally on the contrast and incompatibility between the newness of the order of life Jesus has initiated and the oldness of the Jewish order within which he has done so. For *new* (*kainos*, an eschatological word, cf. 22^{20}; Mark 14^{24}; II Cor. 3^6; Rev. 3^{12}) and *old* in this respect, cf. Rom 7^6; II Cor. 5^{17}; Heb. 8^{13}. They are, however, obscure both in expression and intention. Luke clarifies by rewriting the first saying (v. 36), though by reference to a wholly improbable practice of cutting up a new garment to patch an old, and by assimilating it to the second (a double *kai* = 'both . . . and' in v. 36 as well as in v. 37). They then make the same point that new and old are so incompatible that the attempt to combine them ruins both. What this is meant to convey about the mutual relation of Christianity and Judaism – e.g. whether they are to continue as separate entities alongside each other – is by no means evident.

39
This isolated verse is very strange. Its absence from D, the Old Latin, Marcion, Irenaeus and Eusebius suggests it is a later scribal addition. If genuine it is impossible to say how Luke came across it. In either case it makes a triad of sayings beginning with *no one*, but it fits very ill; the connection is the purely verbal one of *new wine*. It may be a piece of proverbial wisdom (cf. Ecclus 9^{10}), to be understood here, either as reinforcing the view that new and old are to be allowed to exist alongside each other (*The old is good*), or as an ironical comment on the religious perversity of Pharisaic conservatism in refusing Jesus and his message (v.l. *The old is better*).

6$^{1-5}$ = Mark 2$^{23-28}$
THE FIRST SABBATH DISPUTE

6 On a sabbath,* while he was going through the grainfields, his disciples plucked and ate some ears of grain, rubbing them in their hands. ²But some of the Pharisees said, 'Why are you doing what is not lawful to do on the sab-

bath?' ³*And Jesus answered, 'Have you not read what David did when he was hungry, he and those who were with him:* ⁴*how he entered the house of God, and took and ate the bread of the Presence, which it is not lawful for any but the priests to eat, and also gave it to those with him?'* ⁵*And he said to them, 'The Son of man is lord of the sabbath.'*

    * Other ancient authorities read *On the second first sabbath* (on the second sabbath after the first)

This, and the following, will have been of special importance in the tradition, since the divine institution of the sabbath, far more than fasting, was (with circumcision) a principal hallmark of Judaism (cf. Mark 2²⁸ 'even of the sabbath'). Freedom of Christianity from Judaism could involve a break with sabbath observance (Col. 2¹⁶). If Jesus acted authoritatively towards Judaism he cannot have avoided the question of the sabbath, and any actions or words which went beyond the bounds of legitimate discussion of what was implied by the sabbath law would raise acutely the question of his authority (v. 2 *what is not lawful*). This is because God himself had directly established the sabbath (Gen. 2²).ᵘ The tradition represents Jesus as healing on the sabbath, and even as going out of his way to do so (Mark 1²¹ff., ²⁹; 3¹ff.; Matt. 12¹¹; Luke 13¹⁰ff.; 14¹ff.; John 5¹ff.; 9¹⁶ff.). The question thus arises whether more was intended here than a protest against an over-rigid legalism in favour of humanitarian action (cf. 14⁵), and whether the intense opposition aroused (cf. Mark 3⁶) was to something more than the performance of a right action on the wrong day (cf. 13¹⁴). What was meant by the establishment of the sabbath and by God's rest on the seventh day could be matters of debate (SB II, pp. 461f.). Thus Philo (*Allegories of the Laws* I, 3ff., *On the Cherubim* 86ff.) denies that God's rest spelt inactivity, but only that having ceased to create mortal things he began to create divine things; and he interprets the sabbath positively to mean that God alone in a true sense keeps festival and possesses joy, because his working is alone with absolute ease and without toil and suffering. There is some evidence in Jewish thought for the sabbath as a symbol

ᵘ On the sabbath in Judaism, see G. F. Moore, *Judaism in the First Centuries of the Christian Era*, Cambridge, Mass. 1927–30, II, pp. 21ff., E. Schürer, *History*, rev. ed. II, pp. 467ff., *TDNT* VII, pp. 6ff. For the interpretation of the sabbath law, its fluidity, and the humanity of some rabbinic views, see Klausner, *Jesus of Nazareth*, pp. 278f., Abrahams, *Studies*, I, pp. 129ff., Vermes, *Jesus and the World of Judaism*, pp. 46 and 162 n. 22.

of the world to come.^{v} The sabbath could then be the day proper to the performance of those actions which proclaimed the advent of the kingdom of God, and which were signs of a joyful and untrammelled existence with God (cf. the interpretation of Jesus' works as sabbath works of the Father in John 5$^{17ff.}$, and of Christian existence as sabbatical in Heb. 3–4). Some such background may be required here by the fact that the disciples in the cornfields are not represented as acting out of danger of starvation, but naturally out of a freedom they possess as Jesus' disciples, nor is the man in the synagogue in danger of his life.

ಬಃ

1

Many mss have here *deuteróprōtō* = 'a second-first', see RSV margin. This has been taken as a technical term for either 'the first sabbath in the second year (of a jubilee)', or 'the first sabbath after the second day of Passover', or 'the second sabbath after the fifteenth day of Nisan' (see SB II, p. 158), but none of these is likely to have produced such a Greek equivalent. It is better taken, as first by Westcott and Hort, as an ancient corruption (it is absent from p^4 p^{75} B $\aleph$) resulting from a later combination of two separate scribal glosses, 'second' in view of 4^{31} and 'first' in view of *another* in 6^6.

ate: An agreement with Matthew against Mark but required by the sense.

rubbing them in their hands: The verb *psōchein* + + is extant only twice elsewhere. Luke's addition makes the disciples transgress two of the secondary prohibitions derived from the major sabbath prohibitions, viz. threshing as well as reaping (*plucked*).

2–4

As in 5^{30} the question from the ubiquitous Pharisees is directed to the disciples but Jesus covers them in reply. The citation of David's action (I Sam. 21$^{1-6}$) in compelling the priest at Nob (the incorrect name in Mark, Abiathar, is omitted by Matthew and Luke) to give up the holy bread for himself and his hidden companions, is curious. The method of argument is rabbinic, an appeal by rhetorical question to scripture to establish a notable exception to the law (cf. 20$^{41ff.}$), but its force here is weak, since there is no indication in the OT text that it happened on a sabbath or was a case of dire need (though a later midrash says both). Hence the need in Matt. 12$^{5-7}$ for further OT instances, and perhaps in

v Life of Adam and Eve 51.1 (*AP* II, p. 153); SB III, p. 687; E. C. Hoskyns, 'Jesus the Messiah' in *Mysterium Christi*, ed. Bell and Deissmann, pp. 74ff.

the tradition for the addition of Mark 2^{27-28} to make Jesus' judgment on the sabbath less indirect and ambiguous. But the choice of this precedent may have lain in a parallel between the situation of David, the anointed but as yet un-recognized king of Israel, together with his companions (note *he and those who were with him*) and Jesus the anointed but persecuted one with his disciples. If before David the law thus yields, how much more before Jesus at the present time.

5

The above interpretation could be strengthened in Luke's version, which passes straight to the lordship over the sabbath of the Son of man. The omission (as by Matthew) of the intervening 'The sabbath was made for man, not man for the sabbath' (Mark 2^{27}) is notable but natural, as this introduces a new thought which does not arise from the OT precedent, nor lead to ('so', Mark 2^{28}) the function of the Son of man. *And he said to them*, reproduced from Mark, may indicate that originally Mark 2^{27-28} were independent sayings that were added; or that Mark 2^{27}, which could stand on its own, was later glossed by Mark 2^{28}. It is, however, wider in scope than the oft-quoted parallel from R. Simeon b. Menasya (*c.* AD 180) commenting on Exod. 31^{14}, 'To you (Israel) is the sabbath given over, and you are not given over to the sabbath', and the choice of 'man' rather than 'you' or 'Israel' may point to a desire to extend the sabbath, estab-lished by God at creation, to mankind (cf. Mark. 10^{2ff}.). This does not, however, indicate the source and meaning of *the Son of man* here. Some see it as simply a variant for 'man'; and even as once reading 'the sabbath was made for the son of man, not the son of man for the sabbath'. This is unlikely. The establishment of the sabbath by God for (the good of) man does not issue in man's being *lord of* (*kurios* = 'ruler' or 'disposer' of) the sabbath. Any radical modification of it could only come from God himself or his representative. *The Son of man* may here be a name in the church for Jesus acting in such an authoritative role as man (cf. 5^{24}).

6^{6-11} = Mark 3^{1-6}

THE SECOND SABBATH DISPUTE

6*On another sabbath, when he entered the synagogue and taught, a man was there whose right hand was withered. 7And the scribes and the Pharisees watched him, to see whether he would heal on the sabbath, so that they might find an accusation against him. 8But he knew their thoughts, and he said to the man who had the withered hand, 'Come and stand here.' And he rose and* *stood there.* ⁹*And Jesus said to them, 'I ask you, is it lawful on the sabbath to do good or to do harm, to save life or to destroy it?'* ¹⁰*And he looked around on them all, and said to him, 'Stretch out your hand.' And he did so, and his hand was restored.* ¹¹*But they were filled with fury and discussed with one another what they might do to Jesus.*

In the context this is a particular instance of Jesus' lordship of the sabbath. The story, which Luke gives in a less compressed but also less dramatic form than Mark, is somewhat artificial. It is a conflict story in which the healing is entirely subordinate. It presupposes that Jesus is already known to contravene sabbath regulations and to heal on that day, thereby raising a crucial issue; but the presence in the synagogue of a man with a paralysed hand would not of itself lead to the presumption that a healing would take place. As in 5^{17–26} the narrator is privy to the unspoken thoughts of the opponents, specified by Luke as *the scribes and Pharisees* (in Mark they appear at the end as 'the Pharisees'), and to Jesus' discernment of their *thoughts* (*dialogismous* in a bad sense) as malign, i.e. they were ready to oppose a healing which they were sure would take place.

6–8

Two of Luke's additions are conventional – *taught* for a synagogue scene, and *right* as the more important of two limbs. The omission of 'him' after *heal* underlines the incident as a test case. Jesus takes the initiative with the patient, who is almost a cipher, and the offensive with his opponents.

9

The force of the rhetorical question, which Luke frames more formally (*I ask you*) and improves (*to destroy it*, i.e. 'life' for Mark's 'to kill'), is not clear. Some take it to be that to refrain from doing positive good is the equivalent of doing evil, and to decline to heal is to kill; but that would require the case to be an urgent one (hence the addition in Matt. 12^{11–12}). Others take *to do good* and *to save life* of Jesus' healings and *to do harm* and *to destroy it* (life) of the will of his opponents towards Jesus. The question would not then state a general principle, but be directed to the actual situation. Jesus' healings are good and are signs of salvation (the deeper meaning of 'to save life' = salvation, cf. 9^{24, 56} v. l., is probably not absent), but in the hearts of his adversaries are murderous intentions towards him. Which befits the intentions of the sabbath?

10–11

With Matthew Luke omits the silence of the opponents (he has it at 14⁴) and the consequent anger of Jesus, and the combination of the Pharisees and the Herodians (elsewhere Mark 12^{13}/Matt. 22^{16}) and their abortive plot, which comes too early in the narrative. He substitutes a vaguer statement that *they were filled with fury* (a slight variation of 4^{28}), and that they *discussed . . . what they might do to Jesus*. It nevertheless serves to round off the section on a note of hostility, and to prepare for the following address to disciples and adherents.

6^{12-49} *The Establishment of the Israel of God and its Way of Life*

In Mark $3^{7-12,\ 13-19}$ Jesus is thronged by crowds for healing, and ascends 'the mountain' to appoint the Twelve, but with no immediate consequences. In Matt. 4^{23}–7^{29} Jesus on a similar occasion withdraws from large crowds, and ascends 'the mountain', where there is no appointment of the Twelve, but he delivers to disciples 'the Sermon on the Mount'. Luke uses the two Markan sections in reverse order to depict, first an ascent of 'the mountain' for the appointment of the Twelve as apostles, and then a descent to crowds gathered for healing, who, together with disciples, provide the audience for the equivalent 'Sermon on the Plain'.

6^{12-19} = Mark 3^{7-19}

JESUS' APPOINTMENT OF THE TWELVE AND THEIR DESCENT TO THE CROWDS

^{12}*In these days he went out into the hills to pray; and all night he continued in prayer to God.* ^{13}*And when it was day, he called his disciples, and chose from them twelve, whom he named apostles;* ^{14}*Simon, whom he named Peter, and Andrew his brother, and James and John, and Philip, and Bartholomew,* ^{15}*and Matthew, and Thomas, and James the son of Alphaeus, and Simon who was called the Zealot,* ^{16}*and Judas the son of James, and Judas Iscariot, who became a traitor.*

^{17}*And he came down with them and stood on a level place, with a great crowd of his disciples and a great multitude of people from all Judea and Jerusalem and the seacoast of Tyre and Sidon, who came to hear and to be healed of their diseases;* ^{18}*and those who were troubled with unclean spirits were cured.* ¹⁹*And all the crowd sought to touch him, for power came forth from him and healed them all.*

A certain solemnity of diction in vv. 12–13 marks a new stage in which the character of Jesus' mission is further disclosed. Though the Twelve are mentioned as such only once in A. (6²), and nothing is reported of any one of them except Peter, John and James, 'the apostles' as a corporate body dominate the first part of A. There alone in the NT their activity is recounted, and they appear as the original nucleus, the effective leaders and the permanent authority in Jerusalem (A. 1², ¹³ᶠ·, where their names are again rehearsed; 2³⁷⁻⁴³; 4³³⁻³⁷; 5¹², ²⁹; 6², ⁶; 8¹, ¹⁴; 9²⁷; 11¹; 15²⁻²³). Behind them stands the authority and effective work of Jesus, vindicated by his resurrection, to testify to which is one of their prime functions (A. 1⁸, ²²; 3¹⁵; 5³²; 10³⁹, ⁴¹). Very significant, therefore, for Luke is the moment of their selection by Jesus (through the Holy Spirit, A. 1²) in accordance with the will of God (*in prayer to God*, v. 12; cf. A. 1²⁴ᶠᶠ·, where God appoints Matthias as an apostle), and his conferring on them a status beyond that of disciples.

The juxtaposition of two such similar scenes at the same point in the narrative as well as similarities of wording – *into the hills, a great crowd, a great multitude* (twice in Mark 3⁷ᶠ·), *from Judea and Jerusalem, Tyre and Sidon, unclean spirits, were cured, to touch him* – make it unnecessary to postulate any other source here than Mark 3⁷⁻¹⁹. That vv. 13–18, however punctuated, is not a complete sentence (*chose*, v. 13, is in the Greek 'having chosen') could be due to Luke's use of two Markan incidents in reverse order. The differences from Mark, including the reversal of order, are such as are required by his adaptation to his own purposes of two disconnected passages which have no immediate sequel in Mark, and they betray his hand – *in those days* (cf. A. 1⁵; 6¹), *to pray* (cf. Mark 6⁴⁶, a section omitted by Luke) *all night he continued* (*dianuktereuein* ++), *when it was day* (cf. 4⁴²).

☙☙

12–13
The meaning of the scene is conveyed largely by its symbolism. Nothing is said of any reason for, or principle of, the choice of 'the Twelve', nor of what was involved in being an 'apostle'. It has to be supposed that those not selected went

down again immediately for Jesus and the Twelve to make a separate descent together (v. 17).

12

into the hills: This is a possible rendering of *to oros* = 'the mountain', but in this context, and without further specification, it is likely to be theological rather than topographical, and to denote 'the mount of God', a new Sinai, where Israel begins to be reconstituted, and new commandments are uttered (cf. Exod. 19² for Sinai as 'the mountain').

all night . . . in prayer to God: For Luke's emphasis on Jesus at prayer cf. 3²¹; 5¹⁶; 9¹⁸, ²⁸; 11¹. Reference to an all-night vigil of prayer, which is unique, marks the importance of the occasion, and perhaps implies that the decision to appoint twelve at all, as well as their selection, was communicated by God in prayer (in A. 1² the Greek could mean 'whom he had chosen through the Holy Spirit').

13

his disciples: For Mark's 'those whom he desired', which could mean only those to be 'appointed' as the Twelve, Luke substitutes an already existent body called *his disciples*, which has begun to appear since 5³⁰. *chose* (*eklegesthai*, so A. 1²) preserves Mark's phrase and his 'appointed' since the verb is used in the LXX of divine selection (Deut. 4³⁷; Isa. 41⁸, etc.).

twelve: The expression 'the twelve' is moderately attested in the tradition – I Cor. 15⁵; Mark 6⁷, ⁴³; Matt. 10¹; John 6⁶⁷⁻⁷¹; Rev. 21¹⁴. Their constitution as such is likely to have gone back to Jesus if only because most of them are not recorded as playing any part individually in the church in Jerusalem. Their number was significant because the original composition of Israel was held to have been of twelve tribes descended from the sons of Jacob–Israel (Gen. 49²⁸; cf. James 1¹). Hence they expressed symbolically that Jesus' mission was addressed with divine authority to the empirical Israel with the intention of bringing into being the true Israel or God's people (for a similar conviction at Qumran, with its three priests and twelve laymen in authority, see Vermes, *Scrolls*, pp. 16–18, 85). The Twelve are a sign that there is in the process of being prepared (for Luke ultimately as the outcome of the completed work of Jesus, 24⁴⁴; A. 1²⁻³) a community of the last days for the salvation and judgment of the empirical Israel. The only saying relative to them, in whichever version, 22³⁰ = Matt. 19²⁸, presents them as eschatological figures, who are to be co-judges (cf. Dan. 7⁹) of Israel at the judgment (perhaps for this reason the number has to be made up at the outset of the church's mission to Israel, A. 1¹²⁻²⁶). In the changed perspective of A. this is no longer relevant and they do not perform this function. There they appear as a survival from the past without any specific task at the Twelve.

whom he named apostles: This stands for Mark's 'that they might be with him, and that he might send them out to preach and to have authority to cast out demons' (cf. 9^{1-2} reproducing Mark 6^7). Luke expresses by the passive noun *apostolos* = 'one sent' what Mark gives by the verb *apostellein* = 'to send (out)', and he traces the designation of the Twelve as (the) *apostles* back to Jesus himself. The origin of the word and its development in the church are, however, complex. By contrast with its frequent occurrence in the NT – over seventy times, of which nearly half are in the Pauline or deutero-Pauline epistles, and twenty-eight in A. – the word is very rare in secular Greek, where it has such meanings as 'naval expedition' or 'admiral'. It is found only once in the LXX (I Kings 14^6, ms A) of a prophet who is a messenger of bad news, and in the single instance in Josephus (*Ant.* 17.300) it means 'a sending forth'. One view (*TDNT* I, pp. 407ff.) is that it is a Greek rendering of, and is in its meaning wholly governed by, the Hebrew *shaliach*, a rabbinic term for a personal delegate or authorized agent, who was commonly empowered in Jewish legal practice to carry out a commission for another with his authority (cf. Berachoth 5^5, 'He who is sent by a man is as the man who sends him', which could lie behind sayings which have the verb, 10^{16}; Matt. 10^{40}). The word is secular except in so far as the commission was itself a religious one, and it was not used in Judaism for missionaries. The Christian content will then have derived from the finality of Jesus who commissions, and from the fact that what the apostles represent – temporarily in his lifetime (cf. 9^{10}) and then permanently after his resurrection (cf. A. 1^{2-11}) – is the eschatological mission from God of Jesus, first to Israel and then to the world. But it is not certain that the office of *shaliach* existed at the time, and in the majority of NT instances, i.e. in the Pauline epistles, the natural meaning is 'missionary'. It would be simpler to account for the noun as a precipitate of the verb, which is frequent both of Jesus as sent by God (9^{48}, John passim), and of those sent to extend his mission. But as missionaries apostles were not limited to the Twelve (Paul is one; and cf. Rom. 16^7; I Cor. 15^7). That they are so limited in L–A (if in A. $14^{4, 14}$ the word means envoys of the church at Antioch) could be the creation of Luke (but cf. Matt. 10^1; Rev. 21^{14}), as also that the sedentary, non-missionary figures of the Twelve become a kind of governing body of the church in Jerusalem. He may also be responsible for the absolute use of the word, which properly requires 'my' or 'his' (cf. Paul's 'an apostle of Jesus Christ'). Further, the qualification in A. 1^{21} that an apostle must have companied with Jesus – presumably to be a guardian of the tradition about him – may have led Luke here to ascribe the term 'apostles' for the Twelve to Jesus himself.

14–16
There are variations in the four lists of the Twelve in Mark 3^{16-19}; Matt. 10^{2-4}; Luke 6^{14-16}; A. 1^{13}, and variations of order even in the last two. But in view of the lack of information in the tradition about them individually, and their

insignificance as a body, the extent of agreement is striking, as the list is unlikely to have been rehearsed in preaching or teaching.

14

Simon, whom he named Peter: The names are introduced in the accusative, though not wholly grammatically, as there is no main verb; but this is an improvement on Mark's broken sentence here. Peter stands at the head of all lists. He has already been referred to as 'Simon' (4[38]; 5[3–10]), and also by his 'Christian' name 'Simon Peter' (5[8]). Here, as in Mark, he is given that name without explanation (contrast Matt. 16[18]; John 1[42]). *Andrew* is paired with him as his brother (Mark 1[16]), which was not possible in 5[1–11]. *James and John* are already known to the readers as brothers (5[10]); their nickname 'Boanerges' is omitted as unintelligible.

15–16

The order of the last four names is perhaps for the sake of rhythm, the first and third being followed by the father's name, the second and fourth by a description, and the two Judases brought together.

15

Simon who was called the Zealot: *zēlōtēs* could mean 'zealous', 'an ardent enthusiast' (e.g. 'for the law' A. 21[20]), but it was also used by Josephus for one group of revolutionaries in the later Jewish War. It stands for 'Cananaean' in Mark 3[18] = Matt. 10[4], correctly in the view of some scholars, who see that word as a transliteration of an Aramaic word which could mean 'zealot' in the technical revolutionary sense.

16

Judas the son of James: So A. 1[13]. This is the only serious difference from Mark's list, which has 'Thaddaeus' (so Matt. 10[3]); but that there were difficulties in Mark's text here is shown by different spellings in the mss – 'Daddaeus', 'Taddaeus', and by the variant 'Lebbaeus' in D and mss of the Old Latin.

Judas Iscariot: This, not unnaturally, is the last name in all lists. The meaning of *Iscariot* is disputed. It is generally taken geographically, 'a man of Kerioth', located in southern Judaea, perhaps implying that he was the only non-Galilean. Others take it as meaning 'false', which is then further explicated by *who became a traitor*. Others[w] connect it with *sicarius* = 'dagger-man', another term used by Josephus for revolutionary zealots.

w Cf. O. Cullmann, *The State in the New Testament*, New York 1956, London 1957, p. 15.

This scene is perhaps intentionally reminiscent of Exod. 19²⁴, where only Moses (and the elders) go up mount Sinai, while 'the people' wait beneath the mount to be told the words of the Lord, to which they reply 'All the words of the Lord will we do and hear' (Exod. 24³ LXX; cf. Luke 6⁴⁶ᶠᶠ·). *a level place* could correspond with this, as well as providing a more plausible site for a sermon than the top of the mountain in Matt. 5¹, since *pedinos* + + could mean not only level in contrast to uneven but also lowland in contrast to hill country.

17

came down with them: Cf. Mark 3¹⁴ 'to be with him'. This is perhaps intended to suggest that Jesus is now surrounded by the twelve apostles, who are not addressed by him, but stand with him as he addresses the *great crowd of his disciples* in the presence of *a great multitude of people.* Luke perhaps understands by *Judaea* the whole of Palestine, retaining also from Mark the capital city and the coastal districts (*paralios* + +) of Tyre and Sidon (cf. Judith 2²⁸), which may represent the wider world (cf. Deut. 33¹⁹; Isa. 9¹; Josephus, *Against Apion* 1.60).

18

In view of the setting he is providing for 6²⁰⁻⁴⁹ Luke alters 'hearing all that he did' (Mark 3⁸) to *come to hear him and to be healed* (v. 17) and omits the instructions about the boat – his level place at the foot of a mountain cannot be the shores of the sea of Galilee – and the injunctions to silence (Mark 3⁹, ¹²). The gracious and powerful healing work of Jesus is rehearsed again in forceful terms – *all the crowd, power came forth from him, healed them all* – as a prelude to his gracious and authoritative words (for words and deeds of the apostles in the presence of the people, cf. A. 2³⁷⁻⁴³; 4³³; and esp. 5¹²ᶠᶠ·).

6^{20-49} THE LIFE OF THE ISRAEL OF GOD

²⁰*And he lifted up his eyes on his disciples, and said:*
   '*Blessed are you poor, for yours is the kingdom of God.*
   ²¹'*Blessed are you that hunger now, for you shall be satisfied.*
   '*Blessed are you that weep now, for you shall laugh.*
   ²²'*Blessed are you when men hate you, and when they exclude you and revile you, and cast out your name as evil, on account of the Son of man!* ²³*Rejoice in that day, and leap for joy, for behold, your reward is great in heaven; for so their fathers did to the prophets.*
   ²⁴'*But woe to you that are rich, for you have received your consolation.*

25'*Woe to you that are full now, for you shall hunger.*

'*Woe to you that laugh now, for you shall mourn and weep.*

26'*Woe to you, when all men speak well of you, for so their fathers did to the false prophets.*

27'*But I say to you that hear, Love your enemies, do good to those who hate you,* 28*bless those who curse you, pray for those who abuse you.* 29*To him who strikes you on the cheek, offer the other also; and from him who takes away your cloak do not withhold your coat as well.* 30*Give to every one who begs from you; and of him who takes away your goods, do not ask them again.* 31*And as you wish that men would do to you, do so to them.*

32'*If you love those who love you, what credit is that to you? For even sinners love those who love them.* 33*And if you do good to those who do good to you, what credit is that to you? For even sinners do the same.* 34*And if you lend to those from whom you hope to receive, what credit is that to you? Even sinners lend to sinners, to receive as much again.* 35*But love your enemies, and do good, and lend, expecting nothing in return;* ★ *and your reward will be great, and you will be sons of the Most High; for he is kind to the ungrateful and the selfish.* 36*Be merciful, even as your Father is merciful.*

37'*Judge not and you will not be judged; condemn not, and you will not be condemned; forgive, and you will be forgiven;* 38*give, and it will be given to you; good measure, pressed down, shaken together, running over, will be put into your lap. For the measure you give will be the measure you get back.*'

39*He also told them a parable: 'Can a blind man lead a blind man? Will they not both fall into a pit?* 40*A disciple is not above his teacher, but every one when he is fully taught will be like his teacher.* 41*Why do you see the speck that is in your brother's eye, but do not notice the log that is in your own eye?* 42*Or how can you say to your brother, "Brother, let me take out the speck that is in your eye," when you yourself do not see the log that is in your own eye? You hypocrite, first take the log out of your own eye, and then you will see clearly to take out the speck that is in your brother's eye.*

43'*For no good tree bears bad fruit, nor again does a bad tree bear good fruit;* 44*for each tree is known by its own fruit. For figs are not gathered from thorns, nor are grapes picked from a bramble bush.* 45*The good man out of the good treasure of his heart produces good, and the evil man out of his evil treasure produces evil; for out of the abundance of the heart his mouth speaks.*

46'*Why do you call me "Lord, Lord," and not do what I tell you?* 47*Every one who comes to me and hears my words and does them, I will show you what he is like:* 48*he is like a man building a house, who dug deep, and laid the foundation upon rock; and when a flood arose, the stream broke against the* *house, and could not shake it, because it had been well built.† ⁴⁹But he who hears and does not do them is like a man who built a house on ground without a foundation; against which the stream broke, and immediately it fell, and the ruin of that house was great.'*

> * Other ancient authorities read *despairing of no man*
> † Other ancient authorities read *founded upon the rock*

The Composition of 6^{20-49}

INTRODUCTION
And he lifted up his eyes on his disciples and said:

(i)	6^{20-23}	Four blessings in two pairs, the last with four verbs followed by two commands and two reasons	Matt. 5^{3-12} nine blessings
(ii)	6^{24-26}	Four corresponding woes, the end of the last matching the end of the last blessing	Not in Matthew

PART I
But I say to you that hear (the whole audience):

(iii)	6^{27-28}	Four commands to charity, the first two of action, the second two of speech, with verbs at the beginning, in the last three the recipients expressed by participles	Matt. 5^{44}, the first and fourth in relation to command to love the neighbour
(iv)	6^{29-30}	Four commands to generosity, first and third positive, second and fourth negative, with verbs at the end, the recipients expressed by participles	Matt. 5^{39-42} has the first three, and a version of the fourth, in relation to 'an eye for an eye'
(v)	6^{31}	A single command summarizing vv. 27–30 with reference to ideal human behaviour	Matt. 7^{12} has this as a summary of law and prophets in context of giving
(vi)	6^{32-34}	Three exhortations – to love, do good and lend – in the form of conditional clause, question and statement, the last being varied	Matt. 5^{46-47} has the first and a variant of the third in relation to command to love the neighbour
(vii)	6^{35}	A single command to love, do good and lend, with two reasons, the first repeating v. 23, the second with reference to the behaviour of God	Not in Matthew, but cf. Matt. $5^{42b, 45b}$

(viii)	6^{36}	A single command to mercy with reference to the behaviour of God	Matt. 5^{48}, a similar command in relation to commandment to love
(ix)	6^{37-38}	Four commands to mercy in two pairs, one negative, one positive, ending with measure qualified fourfold and saying 'With what measure'	Matt. 7^{1-2} has the first command followed by the saying

PART II

He also told them (the disciples?) *a parable:*

(x)	6^{39-40}	Parable, blind leading blind, double question applied in double statement	Matt. 15^{14} has parable in debate on clean and unclean; Matt. $10^{24f.}$ has application in mission charge
(xi)	6^{41-42}	Second parable, speck and log, double question applied in double statement	Matt. 7^{3-5} has parable and application after 'With what measure'
(xii)	6^{43-44a}	Third parable, good and bad trees known from their fruits	Matt. 12^{33} has a version in Beelzebul discourse, Matt. 7^{16a-17} another version in warning against false prophets
(xiii)	6^{44b-45}	Fourth parable, figs and thorns, brambles and grapes, with threefold application	Matt. 7^{16} has parable in warning against false prophets Matt. 12^{34b-35} has application in Beelzebul discourse

CONCLUSION

(Jesus speaks of himself and his words)

(xiv)	6^{46}	Why call me 'Lord, Lord' and not do what I tell you?	Matt. 7^{21} has a version in warning against false prophets
(xv)	6^{47-49}	Antithetical parable, houses built on rock and earth, with fourfold clauses and final statement	Matt. 7^{24-27} also concludes with this parable, the verbs being in fours

This, though placed in a context supplied by Mark, begins the section 6^{20}–8^3 of non-Markan material that Luke inserts into the Markan narrative framework. Linguistically it is a careful and artistic whole.

Some have distinguished vv. 27–38 in it for their closely knit and
poetic structure, but the balance, rhythm and fourfold arrangement run
throughout. As a series of radical ethical demands, enclosed between
antithetical beatitudes and woes and an antithetical parable about the
speaker's own words, it is unique in form, and is inappropriately
termed a 'sermon', whether judged by ancient or modern conceptions
of a sermon. To call it an 'ordination sermon'[x] ignores that it is precisely not directed to those just appointed apostles, while Farrer's
suggestion (*Studies in the Gospels*, ed. Nineham, p. 80) that in being
spoken 'after' rather than, as in Matthew, 'on' the mount it is an
ordination sermon for the apostles as the new Levites rests on the doubtful hypothesis that the Gospel is composed on a hexateuchal pattern
with this falling in the Leviticus section.

It is not, however, unified in thought ('loose and rambling', Fitzmyer, p. 628).[y] The woes intrude in an address to disciples, and its
redirection to *you that hear* (v. 27) does not illuminate. The rule in (v)
makes a weak connection, and the mercy enjoined in (ix) is not the
same as that in (vi)–(viii). The second articulation *He also told them a
parable* (v. 39) marks a break rather than secures continuity, and any
sequence of thought in what follows is difficult to discern. Some of the
material, e.g. (x), (xi) and (xii), seems originally intended to convey
something different from what it teaches in this setting.

Agreement with the discourse in Matt. 5–7, of which it is a third the
length, both in order (as in (i), (iii)–(iv), (vi)–(viii), (xi)–(xv)), and also
in wording (as in (i), (iv)–(xi), (xii)?, (xiii)?, (xv)), raises the question of
sources. Since Luke's version generally appears the more literary, and
therefore probably, secondary, it may be argued that it is an abbreviated form of Matthew's, deliberately limited to the two themes of love

x K. E. Kirk, *The Vision of God*, London and New York 1931, p. 72.

y Hence analyses vary. Lagrange, pp. 183ff., divides into exordium, love of
enemies, dispositions for this, peroration; J. Dupont, *Les Béatitudes*, 2nd ed.,
Bruges 1958–9, vol. I, pp. 189ff., into exordium, love of enemies, brotherly love,
the necessity of works; Klostermann, pp. 77f., according to form rather than
content, into prophetic, gnomic and parabolic sections; Ellis, p. 111, into setting,
the promises and principles of the kingdom (which is only mentioned in 6^{20}) and
the meaning of discipleship. S. Agourides (in *Mélanges Béda Rigaux*, Gembloux
1970), attempts to establish a single theme throughout by taking vv. 27–38 as
injunctions to those already pronounced blessed for their poverty not to hate their
enemies, the rich, and vv. 39ff. as condemnations of those teachers who encourage
them to do so.

and true discipleship. In favour of this could be that both evangelists set the discourse in the context of 'the mountain', and that Luke immediately, Matthew almost immediately, follows it with the Centurion's Servant, which is not easily accommodated in a sayings source. On this view Luke, in pursuing a predominantly fourfold arrangement, selects the first two and the last two of Matthew's beatitudes and has them addressed to disciples. He takes the two commandments to radical love in Matt. 5^{44}, adds two more of the same kind, gives examples of these taken from the preceding verses Matt. 5$^{39-42}$ (omitting Matt. 5^{41}), and rounds off with the golden rule from Matt. 7^{12}, where it appears out of place. He then takes the rest of the commands to love, reproducing the questions in Matt. 5$^{46-47}$ and adding a third on lending from Matt. 5^{42b}, translates them into equivalent commands (v. 35), and rounds off by transposing the first of Matthew's two references to the character of God (Matt. 5^{45}), using the second (Matt. 5^{48}) to introduce the following injunctions to mercy. Passing over the treatment of Jewish religious duties and teaching on possessions in Matt. 6$^{1-34}$, he takes up the two sayings 'Judge not . . .' and 'With what measure . . .' (Matt. 7$^{1-2}$) and fills them out to four. The remainder, vv. 39–49, could then have been reproduced from Matt. 7$^{3-5, 16-27}$, reworded but in the same order, except that the comparison of men to trees will have been taken from Matt. 12$^{33-35}$.^{z} Against this hypothesis, apart from its failure to account for (ii), (x) and (xii), is that it requires a selective procedure in removing sayings or groups of sayings from their admirable contexts in Matthew which has no parallel either in Luke's use of Mark or in the other non-Markan material he has in common with Matthew. And the resulting sequence is in places very forced. An alternative hypothesis is that some such specimen collection of Jesus' sayings stood in Q; that in sequence though not necessarily in wording it was substantially as in Luke; and that Matthew made it part of a more elaborate discourse governed largely by antithesis between Jewish and Christian belief and practice. If, however, it is judged that not all the differences here can be reasonably put down to the editorial work of one or other evangelist, this hypothesis would have to be modified to their use of variant versions of this Q tradition. Luke places it at the first convenient place in his narrative for the disciples as a body to hear it.

z See further Drury, *Tradition*, pp. 131ff.

An exordium parallel to, but different from, that in Matt. 5^{1-12}. (i) There are four beatitudes in two pairs – poverty and hunger, tears and suffering (= Matt. $5^{3-4, \, 6, \, 11}$). This may be original to a source, as they all concern the future reversal of a present condition, whereas those in Matt. 5^{7-9} affirm the future consequence of a present disposition, to which the others are also conformed. (ii) They are apostrophes in the second person, whereas in Matthew they are gnomic statements in the third person. This could also be original to a source rather than Luke's creation, as the last and extended beatitude in Matt. 5^{11-12} is in the second person – though Daube, *NTRJ*, pp. 196ff., argues that a lengthened form with change to the second person was an established Jewish pattern of expression. (iii) When followed by four converse woes they provide a different kind of exordium from Matthew's pronouncements of blessedness followed by ethical demands, viz. prophetic antithetical blessings and curses on the righteous and unrighteous in Israel (cf. Deut. 28; 30^{15-20}; Isa. 3^{9-12}; Jer. 17^{5-8}; I Enoch 9^{8-9}).

20

lifted up his eyes on: A solemn expression, elsewhere in the NT (16^{23}; 18^{13}; John 17^1) of looking up to heaven. It focuses attention on the disciples as the recipients of a prophetic address. In Matt. 5^1 Jesus sits as a teacher.

Blessed: makarios = 'happy', 'fortunate'; hence 'macarism' for the extolling utterance it introduces (Latin *beatus*, hence 'beatitude'). This type was widespread in Greek literature, generally with the relative pronoun in the gnomic form 'Blessed he who . . .' (so 7^{23}; 14^{15}). In the LXX often 'the man who' (Ps. 34^8; Prov. 3^{13}; literally 'the happiness (or happy things) of the man who . . .'). Generally in the NT *blessed* is followed by a descriptive noun, e.g. the poor. Matthew's form as the commoner has been held to be original, and Luke's due to assimilation to the last beatitude (Matt. 5^{11-12}), but in the OT in intensified address to Israel by God or his prophet the second person is also found (Deut. 33^{29}; Isa. 32^{20}; Mal. 3^{12}; Baruch 4^4). This could fit the context of a personal address to disciples, and Matthew may have adopted the more common form for catechetical purposes. Like *makar*, of which it was a subsidiary, *makarios* was originally in Greek applied to the gods, whose life was untroubled by care and death, and then to men in so far as they could share that life. In popular philosophy it came to be applied to those in possession of what was held there to contribute to the good life, e.g. wealth, wife, children, etc. So occasionally in the OT (Ps. 127⁵; Ecclus 25⁷⁻¹⁰), where it is generally related to an aspect of piety; that man is blessed who trusts in God, is forgiven, possesses wisdom or keeps the law (Ps. 2¹²; 32²; Prov. 3¹³; 29¹⁸). It was appropriate for eschatology with its promise of a future perfect relationship with God (14¹⁵; Rev. 14¹³; 19⁹; 20⁶). Here present and future are integrally related. The future state is the ground of being counted happy in the present. In this form, and spoken by one whose words have the authority claimed in vv. 46–49, the macarism goes beyond ascription or congratulation and approximates to the blessing which secures what it utters.

you poor: Literally 'the poor, because yours . . .' *ptōchos* means a beggar, one who is destitute. In the LXX it is used for the materially poor and needy in Israel, sometimes perhaps as a class, 'the poor ones' (Ps. 149⁴). This poverty is often a scandal, especially when the result of oppression or dispossession by the wealthy, and it is to be removed by God (Pss. 9¹⁸; 10; 72²⁻⁴, ¹²⁻¹³; 82²⁻⁴, etc.). Through this connection with God it can take on the meaning of 'pious', in the sense of one who looks in his need to God for succour. At Qumran 'the community of the poor' is a term used for the sect or for a portion of it, though it is not clear whether, or how, this was related to the voluntary poverty and communal possession practised there. A spiritual sense of some kind is indicated by the obscure expression in Matt. 5³ 'the poor in spirit' (= 'those who are poor, i.e. humble, in inward disposition'?; in the only parallel, 1QM 14⁷ (Vermes, *Scrolls*, p. 142), it means 'faint-hearted'). These considerations are not necessarily determinant for Luke's text or his understanding of it. In this Gospel the word, absent from A., always refers to the materially poor (with the possible exception of the LXX quotations in 4¹⁸; 7²², where it is uncertain how Luke took it). When taken with the corresponding woe in 6²⁴ it is likely to do so here – cf. the parable in 16¹⁹⁻³¹, where v. 25 exactly reproduces the teaching of this beatitude and the woe, and where 'rich' and 'poor' have no moral connotation. If this is the meaning it can only be the sole meaning and not an ancillary one, as in the comment (Marshall, p. 249) that the word means 'pious' but that the saying is 'at the same time addressed to those who are literally poor'. For Luke the disciple is either drawn from the literally poor or is to make himself such (14³³, cf. James 2¹⁻⁶).

for yours is the kingdom of God: The eschatological basis of the blessing, which is that to the disciples (*yours*, the relative pronoun *humeteros*, is Lukan and more stylized than 'of them' in Matt. 5³) will belong (*is* should be taken as a future – cf. the verbs in vv. 21–23) *the kingdom of God* (for which see on 4⁴³). Only here is the kingdom of God said to belong to persons (but cf. 12³²). The sense seems to be that as the dispossessed they will be made rich by their possession of the kingdom, either in participating in the conditions brought about by its coming, or in themselves exercising God's rule (on a renewed earth?, cf. Matt. 5^5).

that hunger now, for you shall be satisfied: Again in the Gospel *peinān* (absent from A.) denotes literal physical hunger (so 1^{53}, and cf. 'are full now', v. 25), and this is here the sole meaning. The metaphorical 'hunger for righteousness' in Matt. 5^6 spiritualizes, and has possibly involved the addition of 'and thirst' as better expressing spiritual desire (cf. Pss. 42^2; 143^6). Luke's *now* underlines the eschatology, pointing to 'then' as the time of divine satisfaction. *shall be satisfied* is probably a reverential passive and means 'God will satisfy you'. For such satisfaction under the figure of eating in the kingdom see 14^{15}; 13^{29}.

that weep now, for you shall laugh: This sounds more vivid, concrete and original, with the actual tears of bitter experiences giving way to the hilarity of eschatological joy, when compared with the more conventionally religious 'those who mourn, for they shall be comforted' in Matt. 5^4, if mourning there is for the sin and judgment of Israel and the comforting her redemption by God (cf. Isa. $61^{2f.}$; $66^{10f.}$, etc.). On the other hand *weep* (*klaiein*) is frequent in Luke (cf. 7^{32} = Matt. 11^{17} 'mourn'), and may be due to him, and *mourn and weep* (v. 25b) and *your consolation* (v. 24) could indicate that Luke read 'mourn' and 'comforted' in his source. Further *laugh* (*gelān* + v. 25) is difficult, (i) because in the LXX, apart from Eccles. 3^4, it always means 'to scoff at', and (ii) because if here it denotes the laughter characteristic of the time of the kingdom (a Hellenistic idea *TDNT* I, pp. 66of.) it has to have in v. 25 the quite different meaning of the careless enjoyment of the worldly (as the noun in James 4^9 ++).

22-23

This, the last macarism as in Matthew, is different in form, in that the description of the circumstances of those blessed (v. 22) is extended, with, in Luke, four matching verbs – *hate, exclude – revile, cast out* –, and the blessing is followed by a command, and only then by its ground, to which a further reason is attached. It also differs in content, which is specific rather than general, and may be coloured by Christian experience. In this position it may be intended to govern the previous three macarisms, and to suggest that the poor, hungry and tearful are blessed in so far as they are disciples of Jesus ready to undergo persecution.

22

when men hate you: This, which can prepare for the continuation in v. 27, refers to a concrete situation (the Greek means 'whenever') of the disciples (cf. 21^{17}). 'Those who hate us' became 'in the literature of the post-apostolic epoch almost a technical term with Christians for their adversaries' (Harnack, *Sayings*, p. 61; cf. I Clement 60^3; Polycarp, *Letter to the Philippians* 12^3; *Diognetus* 2^6, 5^{17}). *men* both widens the range of what are chiefly Jewish hostile actions (cf. v. 26a; 21^{17}), and also provides with *in heaven* the antithesis man-God.

exclude you: aphorizein = 'to separate' is a semi-technical term for expulsion from the people of God (cf. Isa. 52^{11}; 56^3). The only other instance in the NT in this sense, A. 19^9, refers to Paul's removal of his disciples from the synagogue at Ephesus. The equivalent in Matt. 5^{11}, *diōkein* = 'persecute' is used of Paul's actions towards Christians with such expulsion in mind. Later (*c.* AD 85) this became official Jewish policy towards Christians (cf. John 9^{22}; 16^2).

revile: oneidizein, so Matt. 5^{11}; the only other NT instance in this sense is the macarism in I Peter 4^{14} on Christians persecuted for the name of Christ.

cast out your name as evil: This has been accounted a Semitism and compared with Deut. 22^{14}, 'bring an evil name upon' = 'destroy the reputation of', but the parallel is not close, and the classical meaning of 'reject' or 'spurn' would fit here, possibly with the suggestion of excommunication (cf. John 9^{34}). With the more polished *as evil* it could be a revised version of 'utter all kinds of evil against you' (Matt. 5^{11}). *your name* can only be a designation which they have in common as disciples of Jesus or of the Son of man – cf. the remarkable parallel in the context of rich and poor in James 2$^{6-7}$. The name came to be 'Christian', and appears in I Peter 4$^{14-16}$ as the subject of a macarism in the context of persecution.

on account of the Son of man: 'on my account' Matt. 5^{11}. Originality and meaning are difficult to establish. The personal 'I' for the indirect 'the Son of man' (for which see on 5^{24}) is likely to have been a later development both doctrinally and in the context of persecution, though Matthew is unlikely to have changed 'the Son of man' if it was in his text. On the other hand some have detected a tendency in the tradition to substitute 'the Son of man' for an original 'I' (see Jeremias, *Theology*, pp. 262ff.), and in 18^{29} Luke can be seen replacing 'for my sake' in Mark by 'for the sake of the kingdom of God'. On Vermes's view the two expressions would be exactly equivalent, the speaker referring to himself indirectly as the Son of man because of the embarrassing circumstances of persecution. On the 'titular' view the reference could be to persecution for the claim to be disciples either of Jesus who is to come as the Son of man, or of the Son of man who on earth was himself the subject of persecution (9^{22}; 18^{31}).

23

rejoice in that day, and leap for joy: The verbs in the aorist add precision, as does *in that day*, a phrase generally denoting the day of judgment, and perhaps here indicating the ultimate character of the reward to follow. *leap for joy (skirtān +* 1$^{41, 44}$) is, like *laugh* (v. 21), vivid. It is found in the LXX for the leaping of animals; its use for festive dance is more Greek than Jewish.

your reward is great in heaven: The first of two reasons for joy in persecution, expressed generally in terms of the moral concept, Jewish and non-Jewish, of merited *reward* (*misthos* = 'payment due', 'wages earned', as in 10⁷, the only other instance in Luke, Matt. 5¹²; 6¹⁻¹⁸; Rom 4⁴; James 5⁴). This is *in heaven* (*ouranos* singular, as generally in Luke; Matthew's plural 'in the heavens' occurs only five times in L–A); i.e. it is God's valuation conveyed by the reversal of the human situation. It is *great* because the Son of man and his cause stand highest in God's estimation.

for so their fathers did to the prophets: A second reason for joy in persecution. The predecessors of the disciples' persecutors acted in the same way towards God's prophets; *did* covers all the actions described in v. 22. Behind this lies the tradition that developed in Judaism of the prophets as all subject to persecution (see on 13³⁴, and the formulation in A. 7⁵¹⁻⁵²). *their fathers* (Matt. 5¹² 'they') is secondary, as it presupposes disciples who are separated from the Jews. The injunction could be either general, 'rejoice because you are treated like none other than God's prophets of old', or specific, 'as yourselves prophets rejoice that you are treated as such' (so probably Matt. 5¹², 'the prophets who were before you'). In the latter case disciples are not simply those who profess allegiance to Jesus and his cause but are active proponents of them, and for that reason are persecuted.

24–26

The woes are difficult on any hypothesis; 'There is no entirely satisfactory solution to the problem' (T. W. Manson, *Sayings*, p. 49). To suppose that Luke composed them himself as parallel to his version of the beatitudes is to credit him with great clumsiness, as they interrupt his articulation of the discourse as delivered to disciples. They might have belonged to a collection of sayings which was not concerned with audience or sequence of thought, and which conceived beatitudes and woes as contrasted like blessings and curses in the OT.

24

But: The strong adversative *plēn* = 'only', though not in A., is more common in this Gospel than elsewhere in the NT; cf. 6³⁵; 10¹¹; 11⁴¹; 12³¹; 22²¹; with 'woe' 17¹; 22²². It is certainly needed here to make a connection.

woe: ouai, an interjection of distress, 'alas', found occasionally in Hellenistic literature but frequently in the LXX, predominantly in the prophets, and, in the NT, in the synoptists and Revelation. In this context it could also, like the macarism, go beyond an expression of feeling, and amount to an effective proclamation of doom or a curse.

you that are rich: Who could be meant by these in an audience of disciples does not appear. In one strand of the OT the rich are assumed to be arrogant and oppressors of the poor. There is no reason to suppose that here, but only the intense dislike of wealth evident in this Gospel, particularly in its special material.

you have received your consolation: The judgments in the woes are probably intended, like those in the macarisms, to be eschatological, though it is difficult to give this content to them. The ground of the condemnation of the rich is that they *have received* (*apechein* in its commercial sense of receiving a sum in full + Matt. $6^{2, 5, 16}$; Phil. 4^{18}) their *consolation* (*paraklēsis* + 2^{25} in the gospels, four times in A.), often used of God's resolution of conflict or suffering; here perhaps 'satisfaction'. This is the teaching of 16^{25}, where it is more explicitly eschatological, since the poor and rich are in Abraham's bosom and Hades respectively. Here the eschatology is only implicit. The rich are condemned as godless in finding their satisfaction in wealth; cf. I Enoch 94^8, 'Woe to you rich, for you have trusted in your riches, and from your riches you shall depart; because you have not remembered the Most High in the days of your riches.'

25

are full now: empimplanai + 1^{53}; A. 14^{17}; John 6^{12}; Rom. 15^{24}, all except the last of physical satiety.

shall hunger: Required as the antithesis to v. 21a, though nowhere else is perpetual hunger a condition of the condemned.

laugh now: For the difficulty of this see on v. 21b.

mourn and weep: For this as a condition of the condemned 13^{28}; Rev. 18^7.

26

An antithetical parallel to vv. 22–23, though brief and not exact, since *all men* (*pantes hoi anthrōpoi*, a classical expression, not LXX) stresses the universality of the human approval rather than provides the required contrast of man and God, as in v. 22. *speak well of* (*kalōs legein* with accusative + +, also classical) suggests that Luke read 'utter evil' in v. 22, as in Matt. 5^{11}, to which this is the proper antithesis. Again it is not evident who in an audience of disciples was likely to qualify for the role of false prophet (in the church?).

27–38   *The Absolute Demands on Those Who are to Enjoy Ultimate Blessedness*

27–35

A single section on love of enemies, but only so because this theme announced in vv. 27–28 is resumed in vv. 32–35 after the analogous but not identical theme of (self)-giving in vv. 29–31. The six commands with parallels in Matthew –

vv. 27a, 28b, 29, 30 – appear more as independent sayings held together by style and sense. This may reflect an origin in a sayings source. They read more naturally (esp. 'love your enemies') as part of the separate antitheses in which they appear in Matthew.

27a

But I say to you that hear: A fresh introduction required by the abruptness of what is to follow. It is unique in form, and extends the audience to all those assembled in v. 17 – cf. Luke's introduction to the parable in v. 47, 'Every one who comes to me and hears my words.'

27b–28

A statement, without ground or qualification, of the commandment to love 'the neighbour' in its most extreme possible form. In Matt. 5⁴³ it stands in antithesis to a supposed command to hate the enemy which it is impossible to establish in the OT or Judaism. In movements to establish an ideal Israel hatred of the enemy could be obligatory, e.g. for the Zealots, or at Qumran, 1QM, 1QS 10²⁰, where however it stands alongside the opposite sentiment 'I will pay no man the reward of evil, I will pursue him with goodness' (Vermes, *Scrolls*, pp. 124ff., 90f.). This love is not a matter of feeling, as is shown by the three following verbs, making two of action and two of speech. *do good to* (*kalōs poiein* with dative of person + + classical and LXX) refers to beneficent action towards those who *hate* (see on v. 22). *bless* and *curse* are antonyms of speech (cf. James 3⁸⁻⁹; Rom. 12¹⁴), and intend to procure good or harm. *abuse* (*epēreazein*, classical not LXX) refers to insults; in the only other NT instance, I Peter 3¹⁶, it is used of the misrepresentation of Christians by outsiders or opponents, which is to be met with gentleness, here with a corresponding mode of speech in intercession.

29–30

These four commands in two pairs also enjoin extravagant response to the actions of others, but with a rather different point of total self-giving, differently made in v. 30 from v. 29. They are in the second person singular and envisage more specific situations. In Matt. 5³⁹⁻⁴² they are in antithesis to the principle of 'an eye for an eye', and illustrate non-resistance to evil, though the second pair is not well fitted for this. Luke's version, which runs straight on from vv. 27–28, is neater in structure, syntax and vocabulary.

29

who strikes you on the cheek: The occasion, and hence character, of this insult are not indicated.

takes away your cloak do not withhold your coat as well: In Matt. 5⁴⁰ the situation seems to be of a lawsuit for possession of the *coat* (*chitōn*, the more valuable inner garment) in which the *cloak* (*himation*, the outer garment) is thrown in as well. Here the action seems to be that of a robber who snatches the outer garment and is to be offered the inner, which, however, he could have taken for himself.

30

The first command is to unrestrained giving on request. The second (in Matt. 5⁴² to lend) is approximated to v. 29 – not to ask back what has been taken by force.

31

These commands, which on their reiteration in vv. 32–35 are to have as their basis imitation of the character of God, are here grounded in the prudential rule 'Do as you would be done by'. This has many parallels inside and outside Judaism, and in both a positive and negative form, between which there is no essential difference. It is found combined with reference to the character of God in the different though analogous context in Matt. 7⁷⁻¹², where it is said to fulfil the law and the prophets.

32–34

This argumentation in interrogative form for the commands of v. 27 is parallel to Matt. 5⁴⁶⁻⁴⁷, where it follows directly after the commands to love in imitation of God.

what credit is that to you?: So in vv. 32, 33, 34; Matthew has 'what reward?' or 'what more do you do?' *credit* is *charis*, a word confined to Luke in the synoptists, and with a wide range of meaning. In 1³⁰ it means 'favour', 'approval' (cf. A. 2⁴⁷; 7⁴⁶); here the concrete expression of approval, so approximating to 'reward' (*misthos*, the word used in v. 35b; cf. I Peter 2²⁰; in Paul it is the free gift which is the opposite of earned reward, Rom. 4⁴). Only a love, beneficence and giving which altogether exceed the ordinary human bounds of *quid pro quo* earn divine approval (see further on v. 35b).

even sinners: So vv. 32, 33, 34; Matthew varies with 'tax collectors' (combined with 'sinners' in 5³⁰), and 'Gentiles' (*ethnikoi*), which Luke never uses.

33

do good to: *agathopoiein* with an object + +, a LXX and not classical usage, has a wider scope than 'salute' (Matt. 5⁴⁷). For similar language I Peter 2²⁰.

34

Possibly framed by Luke on the model of vv. 32–33 with reference to borrowing, which is absent from v. 30 = Matt. 5⁴². The language appears to be his:

hope (*elpizein*, apart from the quotation in Matt. 12²¹ only Luke in the synoptists), *to receive* (*apolambanein* = 'to receive back', apart from once in Mark confined to Luke in the gospels), *as much again* (*ta isa* + + = lit. 'the equal things', a well-known classical phrase).

35a

The previous questions translated into equivalent commands, introduced by the strong adversative *plēn* = 'but'. This also could be Luke's creation; it is absent from Matthew.

expecting nothing in return: apelpizein + +. The normal meaning of the verb is 'to despair'; hence the variant reading, with masculine instead of neuter object, 'despairing of no man'. The sense required by the context is 'expect in return', which will have been created (by Luke?) by catachresis from *apolambanein* = 'receive in return' and *hope to receive* in v. 34. This sense is not found in Greek literature before Chrysostom in the fourth century.

35b

This provides the climax of the section; its equivalent in Matt. 5⁴⁵ comes earlier. *your reward will be great:* This indicates the meaning of *charis* in vv. 32–34; cf. 6²³ for *reward* (*misthos*). In the light of the section, and e.g. of Matt. 6¹ff., the teaching on reward is marked by two features, (i) reward is promised to those who act without any thought of it as a motive; (ii) it is not an adjunct to the action but is the activity in its perfected form, since it derives from the character of the God who gives it.

you will be sons of the Most High: The commands in v. 35a, and by implication those in vv. 27–34, are now given a basis beyond the prudential counsel in v. 31 in the imitation of God himself. *sons of* is the Semitic idiom for 'like', 'reproducing the character of' (cf. 'chips of the old block'). the *Most High* (the Matthaean 'your Father who is in heaven', Matt. 5⁴⁵) translates the anarthrous *hupsistos* = 'most high', a term widespread in Greek religion with Zeus or 'god', used by Gentiles of the God of the Jews and by Diaspora Jews of Yahweh (frequently in Ecclesiasticus). Apart from Mark 5⁷, uttered in pagan country, and Heb. 7¹, from Gen. 14¹⁸, it is confined to L–A in the NT. For *sons of the Most High* cf. Ecclus 4¹⁰; Ps. 82⁶.

he is kind to the ungrateful and selfish: Different from the appeal in Matt. 5⁴⁵ to God's evident benevolence in nature. It is abbreviated to make the single summarizing point 'gracious to the ungenerous' without any indication where this character of God is to be discerned.

kind: chrēstos, used in Greek literature especially of the gods, and in the LXX of God. In the gospels only in Luke (cf. Rom. 2⁴; I Peter 2³).

ungrateful: acharistos: (+ II Tim. 3²), a refined word, chosen for its assonance with *chrēstos* and its connection with *charis* in one of its meanings of 'generosity'.

selfish: This translates *ponēros*, which occurs in Matt. 5⁴⁵, but there in its ordinary meaning of 'bad'. Here it has a specialized sense of 'mean' (cf. Jos. *Ant.* 6.305 for this sense in combination with *acharistos*).

36

Be merciful even as your Father is merciful: This is very different in wording and use from Matt. 5⁴⁸. There it concludes the section on love of enemies with a statement of consequences – to be perfect (*teleios* = 'whole', 'complete') as the heavenly Father is perfect. Here it introduces the next section with a command to be *merciful* (*oiktirmōn* + James 5¹¹; frequently in the LXX of God) as a quality of God (here *your Father*) to be imitated. This is awkward, since God's mercy cannot consist in his abjuring all judgment (v. 37).

37–38

These four commandments are not prudential but voice again an absolute eschatological ethic. The passives are Semitic idiom for 'God will not judge, condemn, will forgive, give'. So also is the third person plural in *will be put* (Greek *dōsousin* = 'they will give'). The commands are simply to *forgive* (*apoluein* = 'to release', probably here from debt, i.e. to pardon) with the consequence (Matt. 7¹ the purpose) that they themselves will not be judged or condemned (by God), and will be pardoned by him. Of the two comparisons in Matt. 7¹⁻², 'with what judgment' and 'with what measure' Luke has the latter only, and uses it somewhat differently in connection with the further commandment to give (cf. v. 30). The fourfold abundance of the measure with which God will respond to this giving is literary in expression: *pressed down* (*piezein* + +, once in LXX) *running over* (*huperekchunnein* + +, rare), *lap* (*kolpos* = 'bosom', and then the fold in the garment falling from the chest, + + in this sense). So also *the measure you get back* (the very rare *antimetrein* + +).

39–49 *Illustrative Parables*

39

He also told them a parable: For this Lukan use of *parable* in the sense of proverb, cf. 4²³; 5³⁶. *them* presumably refers to the wider audience of v. 27.

Can a blind man . . . into a pit?: A more vividly phrased version, with double question, of the saying in Matt. 15¹⁴, where, in a different context, it is applied to the Pharisees and their disciples. Why it is placed here, and to what it applies, do not appear.

40

Another independent proverbial maxim. It is found variously formulated and applied. In Matt. 10²⁴⁻²⁵, in the duplicated form of pupil/teacher, slave/master, it teaches that both share a common fate (cf. John 15²⁰; in John 13¹⁶ that the slave is to imitate his master). Here it is limited to pupil/teacher, perhaps because it is in a discourse to disciples from Jesus as exclusive and authoritative teacher. This context may also have determined the curious application in Luke that *everyone* (the Lukan *pās*; here 'every disciple') *when he is fully taught* (*katartizein*, only here in L–A, in the specialized sense of 'fully trained') *will be like his teacher.* If the disciple listens to, and puts into practice, the words of Jesus (vv. 46ff.) he will become as Jesus (with respect to teaching in the church?).

41–42

Parabolic teaching in the form of questions and injunction, which is in almost verbatim agreement with Matt. 7³⁻⁵; there is a terser but probably secondary version in Gospel of Thomas 26. *speck* . . . *log* betrays the element of the grotesque found elsewhere in the parabolic teachnig of Jesus. There is a parallel in a saying of R. Tarphon (*c.* AD 100) where it illustrates resistance to criticism. In Matthew, where it immediately follows the command not to judge, it seems to base that prohibition on the incapacity of human beings for judgment because of distorted vision. Here, where it is somewhat removed from the command, there may be an association of ideas between *see clearly* and *blind* (v. 39), and *take the log out of your own eye* may indicate the necessary self-criticism if the pupil is to be *fully taught.*

42

hypocrite: So Matt. 7⁵. The word is puzzling (see note on 'hypocrisy', 12¹). In the NT the word is confined to the synoptists (12⁵⁶; 13¹⁵, Mark once, Matthew thirteen times), and is always on the lips of Jesus. It occurs only twice in the LXX – Job 34³⁰; 36¹³ – where it renders a Hebrew word for 'godless', as also in other Greek translations of the OT. In Greek it meant 'one who replies', 'speaker', and so 'actor'; cf. *Letter of Aristeas*, 219 (*AP* II, p. 114) where the king is told to imitate the actor who studies his part carefully. It seems, however, to have acquired the bad sense of 'play-acting', 'dissembling', as in Jos. *BJ* 2.587, where in the context of the lies and craftiness of John of Gischala he is said to be *hupokritēs philanthrōpias* = 'he affected humanity'. But lack of self-criticism and unawareness of disqualifications for passing judgments on others are hardly forms of deliberate dissembling.

43–46

Further parabolic teaching. As a tree's fruits are evidence of its species and quality, so a man's speech is evidence of the quality of his inner being. Despite *For* (v. 43) this thought is not evidently a continuation or further explication of that in vv. 41–42. Again Luke appears to be reproducing a source which consists of independent sayings of a general character with little connection between them and capable of varying application. Verses 43 and 44 are found together with considerable similarity of form and wording, but in reverse order, in Matt. 7$^{16-21}$, where they are applied to the detection of false prophets (in the church?). Verses 43 and 45a b are found together with considerable similarity of form and wording but with v. 45a b in reverse order in Matt. 12$^{33-35}$, where they are applied in denunciation of those who call Jesus' good works evil. Perhaps for Luke the passage is intended to teach, *en route* from v. 39 to vv. 46ff., that the effectiveness of the disciple will depend upon his having his eye and mind purified and rendered sound by obedience to the Lord's teaching. There is a parallel in Gospel of Thomas 45 which agrees with Matthew's version in the order grapes/figs, but with Luke's in being limited to vv. 44-45 in that sequence.

43-44

For no good tree ... for each tree ...: This is more neatly formulated, with balancing statements in v. 44b, than either Matt. 7$^{17-18}$ or Matt. 12^{33}.

figs are not gathered: sullegein (so Matt. 7^{16} = 'collect together') *suka* = 'figs' (Matthew 'grapes') has assonance.

grapes picked from a bramble bush: picked is *trugein*, the customary word for picking fruit, esp. grapes; *bramble bush* is *batos*, the more customary and generic word than Matthew's.

45

produces: propherein = 'to bring out' is, because of its classical meaning 'to utter', preferable in the context to Matthew's *ekballein* = 'to send out'.

good treasure of his heart: Matt. 12^{35} 'out of his good treasure'. Luke either identifies the *good treasure* with the *heart* (= the mind, see on 1^{51}), or sees the *heart* as the storehouse of it. This prepares for the next saying which concludes the passage, but which in Matt. 12^{34} introduces it.

out of the abundance of the heart: In contrast to Matt. 12^{34} both nouns are anarthrous, thus stressing their qualitative aspect. *abundance* is a rare noun *perisseuma* from the verb *perisseuein* = 'to be in abundance', and the thought seems to be that a man's speech is the result of what predominates in his heart = mind.

46

An isolated saying. In Matt. 7^{21} it also stands between the parable of the trees and that of the two houses, but is differently formulated in Matthaean phraseology with reference to entry into the kingdom and doing the Father's will; and it is further developed in 7$^{22-23}$ by sayings of an eschatological kind which appear in Luke 13$^{26-27}$. Luke's version with *and not do what I tell you* makes it an immediate introduction to the following parable.

call me: Perhaps for an original 'say to me', as in Matt. 7²; Luke 13²⁵⁻²⁶. If it means 'address me as' the reduplication is awkward.

Lord, Lord: If this is the post-resurrection title 'the Lord' in the vocative, it cannot have been spoken by Jesus; but it could be a title of high respect, as e.g. of a rabbi (cf. John 13¹³).

47–49

A parable – for *I will show you*, confined to L–A in the NT, cf. 12⁵; for the double *is like* introducing a parable, cf. 7³¹ᶠ·; 13¹⁸ᶠ·. It is clearly the same parable and occupies the same position as Matt. 7²⁴⁻²⁷. Form and content may be conventional; cf. Pirke Aboth 3²² (*AP* II, p. 702), R. Eleazar b. Azariah (*c.* AD 50–120) 'used to say: Every one whose wisdom is greater than his deeds, to what is he like? To a tree whose branches are many and its roots few; and the wind comes and roots it up and turns it over on its face ... But every one whose deeds are more than his wisdom, to what is he like? To a tree whose branches are few and its roots many, which, if all the winds that are in the world come and blow upon it, they move it not from its place.' It is, however, particularly forceful here as the conclusion of the discourse, and as a comment of the speaker on the character of his own words. It is not, however, to be allegorized. The distinction drawn is not, as in I Cor. 3¹⁰ᶠ·, between having Jesus or some other as the *foundation* (a key word in Luke's version), but between two possible kinds of association with him as teacher (cf. James 1²²ᶠᶠ·). In Matthew the contrast is more between hearing and doing; in Luke it is between confession with the lips and confession in deeds. And this is not between discipleship which is partial or complete, but between discipleship and what turns out to be not discipleship at all. Implied in this is that the teaching of Jesus is never simply descriptive or informative, to which it is enough to be a disciple to give assent; it is always imperative, and assent consists in obedient action.

There are considerable differences between the two versions. (i) In structure Matthew's is, characteristically, fully antithetical, with the second part corresponding exactly with the first, whereas Luke varies the second part. (ii) In expression Luke's is the more literary; *dug deep* renders two verbs, *skaptein* + 13⁸; 16³ = 'to dig' and *bathunein* + + = 'to go deep down'; *laid the foundation, tithenai themelion* + 14²⁹ in the gospels; *flood, plēmmura* + +, a technical term for a flood tide in a river, gives a different picture from the force of the elements in Matt. 7²⁵; *broke against* is the very rare *prosrēssein* + +; *shake* is *saleuein* (cf. A. 4³¹; 16²⁶); *because it had been well built* is the articular infinitive after the preposition *dia* = 'on account of': *he who hears and does not* are aorist participles; *fell* is the compound verb *sunpiptein* + +; *ruin* is *rhēgma* + + = 'fracture' (it was used of a breach of the Nile dam), but here given the sense of 'destruction' by its assonance with *prosrēssein* above.

7^{1-10}

7^1-8^3 *Jesus as the Prophetic Deliverer*

After the 'sermon', and before rejoining Mark at 8^4, Luke places six paragraphs in three pairs, drawn from different sources but forged into a unity by connections within and between them. Together they reinforce the picture already emerging in chs. 3–6 of Jesus as a prophet mighty both in deed and word (cf. 24^{19}). In the first pair a centurion's 'boy', precious to his master, is healed at the point of death by a word from a distance (7^{2-10}, Q), and a young man, the only son of a widowed mother, is raised from death by a word (7^{11-17}, L). In the first case Jesus is astonished at the faith of a Gentile exceeding any in Israel, and in the second God is extolled in a report going beyond the confines of Israel that he has sent a great prophet. In the second pair this report calls forth an enquiry from the Baptist about the person of Jesus, who replies by interpreting his actions as signs of salvation and blesses those not offended by him (7^{18-23}, Q). This leads to Jesus' testimony to the Baptist as more than a prophet and as the immediate herald of salvation, and to the praise of God by the people and tax collectors who had received John's baptism, in contrast to the Pharisees and lawyers who have rejected both John and the Son of man who is the friend of tax collectors and sinners (7^{24-35}, Q). In the third pair a woman who is a sinner lavishes devotion on Jesus and receives forgiveness and salvation for her faith, in contrast to a Pharisee, who takes offence at Jesus and concludes from his actions that he cannot be a prophet (7^{36-50}, L). Then on a preaching tour women who have been delivered from various ills minister out of their possessions to Jesus and his apostles (8^{1-3}, L; this supplies a transition to what then follows). Thus in the face of Jewish leaders (vv. 3, 36ff.), a Gentile (v. 6), the Baptist (vv. 18ff.) and increasing crowds (vv. 12, 24, 29; 8^1) Jesus is set forth as a prophet (vv. 16, 39) and more than a prophet (vv. 7f., 19 ff., 27f., 34, 49) in his power over disease, death and sin.

7^{1-10} THE HEALING OF THE CENTURION'S SLAVE

After he had ended all his sayings in the hearing of the people he entered Capernaum. ²Now a centurion had a slave who was dear* to him, who was sick and at the point of death. ³When he heard of Jesus, he sent to him elders of the Jews, asking him to come and heal his slave. *And when they came to Jesus, they besought him earnestly, saying, 'He is worthy to have you do this for him, *for he loves our nation, and he built us our synagogue.' *And Jesus went with them. When he was not far from the house, the centurion sent friends to him, saying to him, 'Lord, do not trouble yourself, for I am not worthy to have you come under my roof; *therefore I did not presume to come to you. But say the word, and let my servant be healed. *For I am a man set under authority, with soldiers under me: and I say to one, "Go," and he goes; and to another, "Come," and he comes; and to my slave, "Do this," and he does it.' *When Jesus heard this he marvelled at him, and turned and said to the multitude that followed him, 'I tell you, not even in Israel have I found such faith.' *And when those who had been sent returned to the house, they found the slave well.

   * Or *valuable*

This striking story, taken with its parallel in Matt. 8⁵⁻¹³, and with what is almost certainly another version in John 4⁴⁶⁻⁵⁴, raises questions of textual transmission, sources and editorial revision. Common to all three are the reputation of Jesus as a powerful healer, Capernaum as the locale, a Gentile official whose dependent is ill, a dialogue between him and Jesus containing an objection, and the cure performed by word from a distance. Differences are (i) in John the official is a *basilikos*, a royal (Herodian?) functionary, in Matthew and Luke a centurion (but see on v. 2); (ii) the one ill (in Luke and John near to death) is in John the official's son, in Luke his slave, in Matthew his *pais*, which could mean either; (iii) in Matthew and Luke the story is not primarily, as in John, a miracle story, but a pronouncement story, with the healing as a subordinate element, and in them there is almost verbatim agreement in the dialogue but wide difference in the surrounding narrative. T. W. Manson (*Sayings*, p. 63) saw the dialogue as alone belonging to Q, each evangelist supplying his own narrative; but to be intelligible it must have had some such brief setting as in Matthew. That Luke is largely responsible for his narrative is suggested by the excellence of the Greek in vv. 2, 4–7a, and by similarities with the story of Cornelius in A. 10. By contrast v. 3 is in poor Greek – abrupt change of subject, and two instances of the Semitic redundant pronoun, *him, his* – which could indicate that Luke's Q version already differed from Matthew's in having a deputation sent to Jesus.

1

A transition verse. As in Matt. $7^{28f.}$ the 'sermon', at its opening addressed primarily to disciples, is at its conclusion referred to the people by a solemn formula. Each is in the style of the evangelist – *after* (*epeidē* + + in a temporal sense); *ended* (*plēroun* = 'fill', 'complete', cf. 9^{31}; A. 12^{25}; 13^{25}; 14^{26}); *sayings* (*rhēmata*, cf. A. 5^{20}; 10^{44}); *in the hearing* (*eis tas akoas* + A. 17^{20}).

Capernaum: Only here and 4^{31} in L–A as a place to which Jesus goes. It connects what follows with the Galilean ministry. If in Matt. 8^5 'after these things' and not 'As he entered Capernaum' is the right reading this connection could have been made by Luke.

2

The English translation does not bring out the idiomatic Greek: 'Of a certain centurion a slave, dear to him, being ill was about to die.'

centurion: The Greek form *hekatontarchēs* (Matt. 8^5 *hekatontarchos*), as elsewhere in the NT except Mark 15^{39-45}, which has the Latin form *kenturiōn*. It means 'one in command of a hundred', and refers to a rank which formed the principal working officers in the Roman army. He cannot be that here, as Galilee was not occupied by the Romans until AD 44, and it has to be supposed that he was a non-Jew of some kind in the troops of Herod Antipas, and that these were modelled on the Roman army. In Matthew there is slight textual evidence for *chiliarchos* = 'ruler of a thousand', i.e. a cohort, the equivalent of the Roman military tribune (for such at Herod's court see Mark 6^{21}), and *centurion* could represent a downgrading by Luke in the interests of his story which has affected Matthew's text.[a]

who was dear to him: This supplies a reason for the request with respect to a slave which would be unnecessary in John with respect to a son, or in Matthew if *pais* there means 'son'. *dear* (*entimos*) is found in papyri of a soldier who has done honourable service (cf. 14^8; Phil. 2^{29}). Here it probably means 'held precious' (cf. I Peter 2^4), and perhaps corresponds with 'only son' in v. 12.

3

elders of the Jews: Unique in the NT. Elsewhere 'the elders (of the people)' denotes prominent citizens as 'lay' members of the Sanhedrin (cf. 19^{47}; 20^1). Here the reference is to local civic leaders, and underlines the Jew–Gentile aspects of the story.

4–6

That these verses are from Luke is suggested by (i) the idiomatic Greek, notably

---

a G. Zuntz, 'The "Centurion" of Capernaum and his Authority', *JTS* 46, 1945, pp. 183–90.

he is worthy to (*axios estin hō*), a Latinism found 'mostly in connection with
Roman officials' (Blass-Debrunner, p. 7), and (ii) the parallels with A. 10$^{1-33}$.
In Matthew the main point is the faith in Jesus of a Gentile such as had not been
found in Israel, and the tension between his request for healing and his scruples
at inviting Jesus as a Jew to his house is overcome by a healing at his own
request by a word at a distance (cf. Mark 7$^{24ff.}$). For Luke the faith of Gentiles
in Jesus was of prime importance, but in A. this comes about through the
extension of the gospel by way of Jews to pious Gentiles, and the initial distance
is reduced because these are already closely associated with Judaism and its
piety. The archetype of this, on which the question of the admission of Gentiles
is settled in A., is the case of Cornelius (A. 10^1–11^{18}). There are parallels between
that story and this in a pious centurion (A. 10$^{1f., 22}$), who does not approach
directly but sends a deputation to make his request (A. 10$^{5-9}$), who vouch for
him as being in good standing with Judaism (A. 10$^{20-23}$). Thus Luke appears to
have written the extended introduction here to make the story a paradigm in
the earthly ministry of Jesus of the admission of Gentiles into the Israel of God
by faith (A. 11$^{17f.}$; 14^{27}; 26^{18}).

5

he loves our nation, and he built us our synagogue: Piety among soldiers was not
uncommon, and Tacitus (*Histories* III, 24) mentions that Roman soldiers often
adopted the religion of the region in which they were stationed. Judaism was
certainly a live religious option in the empire for those dissatisfied with pagan-
ism. An Egyptian inscription of the second century BC refers to a pagan official
helping to build a Jewish house of prayer (quoted by Creed, p. 101). It is
questionable whether the pay of a centurion, even of a chief centurion, would
allow him to cover the whole cost of building a synagogue.

6–7a

An awkward turn in the story in two respects. (i) As a result of the success of the
deputation of elders in closing the gap between Jesus and the Gentile through
their commendation of his piety, a second deputation has to be sent of *friends*
(*philos*, a Lukan word, cf. A. 10^{24}) to reopen it from the centurion's side, so that
it may then be overcome by his faith which Jesus is to commend. (ii) The
highly personal *I am not worthy* . . . and *say the word* are artificial when uttered
by others on his behalf. Further the demur, which in Matthew appears to arise
from compunction at asking a Jew to defile himself by entering a Gentile house,
could in Luke express a self-deprecating humility. For this seems to be what is
conveyed by the somewhat confused sequence of statements, (i) *do not trouble
yourself* (*skullein* + Mark 5^{35} = 'harass', but often in papyri in the reduced sense
of 'bother'), (ii) *for I am not worthy*, which contradicts the initial request, and
(iii) *therefore* (i.e. because *not worthy to have you come under my roof*) *I did not*

344

presume to come to you (*oude ēxiōsa emauton*, a Greek idiom = 'I did not consider myself worthy', sc. to come myself).

7

But say the word: In Luke's refashioning of the scene this request has less force than in Matthew.

8

For I am a man set under authority: kai gar ego (so Matt. 8⁹) is more correctly 'For I also', and the argument from the soldier's experience to the request for a healing by word only requires 'in authority' 'I also, like you, exercise authority over others, and I know the word of command which effects what it utters.' That the point of comparison is with Jesus as one who acts under the authority of God is forced. A few mss in Matthew have 'in authority', and his text may have been early assimilated to Luke's (so Zuntz, op. cit.). *set* (*tassein*, Lukan) *under authority* may be Luke's alteration to further the picture of a self-effacing junior officer. The argument for the effective word of command then has to proceed entirely out of the next words *with soldiers under me*.

9

This encomium provides the climax. It voices the wonder not, as generally in miracle stories, of the audience at the healing, but of Jesus himself, and is uttered solemnly (*I* (Matt. 8¹⁰ 'Truly' – 'Amen') *tell you*) to a crowd that is now said to be following. Its emphasis in Luke is slightly different from Matthew's 'from no one in Israel'. *not even in Israel* = not even in God's people, where such faith is to be expected.

10

A conventional ending compared with Matt. 8¹³, where the word of command is linked to the soldier's faith. It resembles Mark 7³⁰, also in a healing from a distance (omitted by Luke). The combination of proximity and distance is maintained to the end; it is the intermediaries who discover the efficacy of Jesus' healing word.

7^{11-17} THE RAISING OF THE WIDOW'S SON

¹¹*Soon afterwards* he went to a city called Nain, and his disciples and a great crowd went with him. ¹²As he drew near to the gate of the city, behold, a man who had died was being carried out, the only son of his mother, and she was a widow; and a large crowd from the city was with her. ¹³And when the Lord saw her, he had compassion on her and said to her, 'Do not weep.' ¹⁴And he*

came and touched the bier, and the bearers stood still. And he said, 'Young man, I say to you, arise.' 15 And the dead man sat up, and began to speak. And he gave him to his mother. 16 Fear seized them all; and they glorified God, saying, 'A great prophet has arisen among us!' and 'God has visited his people!' 17 And this report concerning him spread through the whole of Judea and all the surrounding country.

* Other ancient authorities read *Next day*

This story continues the theme of the power of Jesus' word and en-hances it. The raising, unpetitioned and not in response to anyone's faith, of one who is undoubtedly dead (contrast 8⁵³) is supreme evidence of the sheer power of him who is called for the first time in the gospel 'the Lord', and prepares for 'the dead are raised up' as the climax of the mighty works Jesus cites in v. 22. It has the conventional marks of a miracle story, ending with a chorus, which is here duplicated to under-line the outstanding character of the act; which, if *Judaea* means Palestine, receives the widest possible publicity.

While there is evidence of Lukan style and vocabulary (see notes) the story as a whole is strongly Semitic, a 'typical bit of translation Greek worse than the average' (Knox, *Hellenistic Elements*, p. 1). It has eighteen main verbs, mostly in parataxis and joined by 'and', and eight instances of the redundant personal pronoun. Either it is to be ascribed as an isolated story to a written source, or Luke has been content here to reproduce a Semitic style current in oral tradition for narrating miracles.

The frequently quoted account of the resuscitation of a young girl by the philosopher thaumaturge Apollonius (Philostratus, *Life of Apol-lonius* 4.45, printed in English in Taylor, *Formation*, p. 127) illustrates the thaumaturgical background in general and provides particular parallels – the accompanying crowd, the promise to banish weeping, the putting down of the bier – though in its literary flavour and mild scepticism it is very different. (Klostermann, p. 87, gives other pagan parallels.) Luke's story has rather been influenced by that of Elijah in I Kings 17¹⁷⁻²⁴: 'a widow (woman)', 17⁹, 'the gate of the city', 17¹⁰; 'the child revived', 17²²; 'delivered him to his mother', 17²³; 'Now I know that you are a man of God, and that the word of the Lord in your mouth is truth', 17²⁴. This could reflect an intention either of the tradition or of Luke himself to present Jesus in terms of Elijah – cf. also Ecclus 48.4f., 'How wast thou glorified, O Elijah, in thy wondrous deeds! ... who did raise up a dead man from death, and from the place of the dead, by the word of the Most High.'

11

A connecting link supplied largely by Luke – *he went* renders the Lukan 'it came to pass he went'; *called* (*kaloumenos* regularly with place names in L–A); *his disciples*, who play no part, *went with him* (*sunporeuesthai* + 14^{25}; 24^{15}; Mark 10^1).

Soon afterwards: This translates *hexēs* = 'next' (only L–A in the NT) with the masculine article in the sense 'in the following (sc. time, *chronos*; cf. the similar *en tō kathexēs*, 8^1). As this differs from Luke's use elsewhere with the feminine article = 'on the following (sc. day, *hēmera*, as in 9^{37}; A. 21^1; 25^{17}; 27^{18}) it is likely to be the correct reading here, unless it was prompted by a scribe's reflection that Nain would be more than a day's journey from Capernaum.

a city called Nain: The preservation in an individual story of a place name is rare, especially of one not mentioned elsewhere. The *city* is generally identified with the modern village of Nein, some twenty-five miles south of Capernaum. Whether Luke knew of its whereabouts does not appear from his curiously vague geographical reference in v. 17.

12

Lukan language in *As* (*hōs* used temporally), followed by (and) *behold* (cf. A. 1^{10}; 10^{17}) and *drew near* (*engizein* with dative, cf. 15^{25}; 22^{47}; A. 9^3; 10^9).

carried out: ekkomizein, only here in the Greek Bible, was the correct word for carrying a corpse to burial.

the only son: monogenēs, a word inserted at 8^{42}; 9^{38} into a Markan story for greater pathos.

13

the Lord: ho Kurios. Unless this title is to be presupposed in the vocatives in $5^{8, 12}$; 6^{46}; 7^6, where it could be an honorific address 'Lord' = 'Sir' (Aramaic *mar*), this is the first instance in the Gospel of its use for Jesus in narrative. This usage is confined to Luke among the synoptists (if the sole occurrence in Mark 11^3 = Matt. 21^3 has the meaning 'the master'), and in Luke to non-Markan sections 7^{19}; $10^{1, 39, 41}$; 11^{39}; 12^{42}; 13^{15}; $17^{5f.}$; 18^6; 19^8; 22^{61}; 24^{34}. It may have been characteristic of his special source, but in some cases is clearly from his hand (e.g. 10^1; 11^{39}; 12^{42}; $17^{5f.}$), and could be so in all cases. It emerged as a designation of Jesus (the most frequent in A.) in his risen and exalted state, as thereby uniquely related to God, and as exercising ultimate authority and control over the church, and over the world (24^{34}; A. 2^{36}; Rom. 10^9; Phil. 2^{11}, etc.). Its origin has been much debated as having been either in Hellenistic Christianity through the attachment to Jesus of a term denoting a cultic divinity (e.g. the Lord Mithras; cf. I Cor. 8^{4-6}), or in Palestinian Christianity, first in the form 'our Lord' (Aramaic *maran*, I Cor. 16^{22}), the heavenly owner and ruler of the Christians, whose coming to complete his work and manifest his rule is urgently expected (I Cor. 16^{22}; Rev. 22^{20}; I Thess. 4^{16f.}). See Fuller, *Foundations*, the relevant sections and literature cited, and Fitzmyer, pp. 201ff. In either case it could come to suggest 'divinity' for Jesus inasmuch as *Kurios* was in use for the Hebrew *adhon* = 'the Lord' as a designation of Yahweh, and became regular in Christian texts of the LXX. It was evidently natural in e.g. I Cor. 11^{23}; 9^{14}; 7^{10, 12} to use the title in referring to an action, or in introducing a saying, of the earthly Jesus, and it is surprising that it penetrated the gospel tradition so little. In his (limited) use of it Luke invests the life of the earthly Jesus with something of the aura of his later exalted state.

had compassion: Only here and Matt. 20^{34} as the motive for performing a miracle.

Do not weep: As in 8^{52}, Luke's version of Mark 5^{39}. The injunction is in view of the certainty of what is about to happen.

14
touched the bier: soros + + is 'coffin', which was evidently an open one, rather than a bier for carrying it. *touched* is generally taken as a sign for the bearers to stop, but it may reflect thaumaturgical technique (cf. 4^{40}; 8^{47}; 13^{13}; 22^{51}).

Young man, I say to you, arise: As in Mark 5^{41}, where it is modified by Luke at 8^{54}. The word of command now penetrates to the sphere of death, cf. John 11^{43}.

15
sat up: anakathizein + A. 9^{40}.

16
The chorus response begins in Lukan fashion with *fear* = 'awe' and *they glorified God*, as in 5^{26} where Luke rewrites Mark 2^{12}, and it may be Lukan throughout; *has arisen, ēgerthē*, is a LXX expression for God's bringing of someone on the scene (cf. A. 13^{22}), and *visited, episkeptesthai* = 'inspect', has the sense the word acquires in the LXX of divine visitation for judgment or salvation (+ 1^{68}; 7^8; A. 15^4). If so the statements will express Luke's theology, and even if he took them from tradition he will not have regarded them as an inadequate response. That Jesus is a prophet is for him not superseded by, but included in, his being messiah or Lord (cf. 24^{19} with 24^{26-27}; A. 3^{18-23}; 7^{37}). *great, megas*, when applied to gods or their representatives, has the sense of 'powerful', and here refers to prophets who like Moses and Elijah were effective in deed and word (4^{24ff.}; 24^{19}; A. 7^{22}; Ecclus 45^3; 48^{4f.}).

17

This is couched in the same language as 4$^{14, 37}$, and here prepares for vv. 18ff. It is, however, imprecise. If by *Judea* is meant the province it does not follow naturally here, as it was not contiguous with Galilee where the miracle had taken place. Some take it to mean Palestine. In either case it is not clear to what *the surrounding country* refers – round Nain or round Judaea?

7$^{18-35}$ JESUS AND JOHN

This is made up of three sections, vv. 18–23, John's enquiry and Jesus' reply; vv. 24–30, Jesus' testimony to John; vv. 31–35, their common rejection. These do not necessarily belong together except as having a common subject matter. Since, except for the insertions at vv. 21, 29f., they are found in the same sequence and wording in Matt. 11$^{2-19}$ (except for Matt. 11$^{12-15}$, which has equivalents in Luke 16$^{16f.}$), they had presumably been brought together in Q. They were clearly of great importance, and will probably have owed their preservation to a continuing concern amongst Christians with the connections and distinctions between John and Jesus, who had been contemporaries, both of whom had initiated a prophetic, eschatological (and baptizing?) movement in Judaism, and both of whom had gathered a community of disciples. For evidence of theological reflection on these facts, cf. in preaching A. 10^{37}; 13$^{24f.}$; with respect to doctrine John 1$^{7f., 15f., 19-23}$; 3$^{26ff.}$; with respect to baptizing A. 1^{5}; 11^{16}; John 1$^{24-28}$; 3$^{25-30}$; with respect to disciples 5^{33}; 11^{1}; A. 18$^{24-28}$; 19$^{1-7}$. The 'Christian' character of such passages make a precise historical picture difficult to reconstruct. Thus there is no information of how long the two ministries ran parallel, or of what time had elapsed between Jesus' own baptism and John's imprisonment, or of what John expected to follow his baptizing ministry, or of whether he wished his movement and disciples to continue in face of those of Jesus.

7$^{18-23}$ JOHN'S ENQUIRY AND JESUS' REPLY

^{18}*The disciples of John told him of all these things.* ^{19}*And John, calling to him two of his disciples, sent them to the Lord, saying, 'Are you he who is to come,* *or shall we look for another?' * ²⁰*And when the men had come to him, they said,* '*John the Baptist has sent us to you, saying, "Are you he who is to come, or shall we look for another?"* ' ²¹*In that hour he cured many of diseases and plagues and evil spirits, and on many that were blind he bestowed sight.* ²²*And he answered them, 'Go and tell John what you have seen and heard: the blind receive their sight, the lame walk, lepers are cleansed, and the deaf hear, the dead are raised up, the poor have good news preached to them.* ²³*And blessed is he who takes no offence at me.'*

In comparison with Matt. 11²⁻⁶ there is, as in vv. 1–10, close agreement in what is spoken but wide variation in the narrative, which each evangelist could have supplied for himself. Luke's is the more articulated, and affords a good example of how he produces a narrative out of such sayings material. As in vv. 1–10 the centurion, hearing reports of Jesus, sends a deputation to justify granting his request, so here John, having been informed about Jesus, sends a deputation to ask a question; v. 21 is an insertion on which to base the reply.

18

A link verse provided by Luke. The widespread report of v. 17 reached *the disciples of John.* For these see 5³³. Here they seem to be referred to as a single body resident in one place. These *told* (*apangellein*, common in L–A) John of *all these things,* a typically Lukan expression of a general kind, here intended to cover at least the previous two miracles, and perhaps everything from 4¹⁴ onwards.

19–20

It is not said where John was or what his circumstances were. Matt. 11² has him in prison, and presumably for that reason compelled to send disciples. Luke, who has mentioned the imprisonment in advance (3²⁰), may, but does not necessarily, presume the same. From Luke are *calling two of his disciples* (Greek 'a certain two', a conventional expression, cf. A. 23²³); *the Lord,* as in v. 13; *the men* (*hoi andres,* predominantly L–A in the NT), *had come* (*paraginesthai,* almost exclusively L–A in the NT); and the repetition of the question in vv. 19, 20 for the sake of liveliness in narrative.

20

John the Baptist: So in v. 33, 9¹⁹, Matthew, Mark and Jos. *Ant.* 18.116, 'John surnamed Baptist'. It sounds like a later formal designation, though his baptizing could have been unusual enough for him to be called this in his lifetime.

Are you he who is to come, or shall we look for another? This could (i) presuppose a previous acknowledgment by John of Jesus as *he who is to come*, and voice a subsequent doubt whether Jesus' activities matched what was expected of such a one – though why in that case had not John in the interim brought his movement to an end and directed his disciples to Jesus (as in John 1²⁹ff.)? or (ii) express a dawning faith in John that Jesus, by virtue of his activities, was to be identified with the anonymous 'he who is mightier', to whose coming after him he had previously referred (3¹⁶). For Matthew, in view of Matt. 3¹⁴ and 'the deeds of the Christ' (Matt. 11²), it must be the former, and in view of 1⁴¹ff. and *the Lord* (v. 19) Luke probably understood it so. Originally it could have been the latter.

he who is to come: *ho erchomenos* = 'the one coming' has a pregnant sense imparted by the Jewish mode of conceiving salvation in temporal terms – 'the (future) coming one' (cf. 'the (future) coming age'). It will have been interpreted by Christians as the messiah (cf. John 11²⁷, with the Johannine addition 'into the world'); but though there is frequent reference in later Judaism to the fact that the messiah 'comes', there is no evidence there for 'the coming one' as a term for him. It can hardly refer to the Son of man, as in Jewish as opposed to Christian tradition he 'comes' to God on the clouds (Dan. 7¹⁴). In Matt. 11¹⁴ (absent from Luke) Elijah is referred to as 'who is to come', and in Mark 9¹¹ his 'coming first' (before whom or what?) is a scribal tenet. In Mal. 3¹ff. God's messenger of the covenant, identified in Mal. 4⁴ with Elijah, 'comes' to judge and refine Israel with fire – cf. the Baptist's prophecy of one who will baptize with spirit (wind?) and fire (3¹⁶f.). John's question may therefore arise from doubt whether Jesus – *you* is emphatic – is performing Elijah's role. The connection with vv. 11–17 may indicate that Luke took it that way. John would then have seen himself as the herald of the returning Elijah, and the identification of John himself with Elijah could have been a Christian theological creation, perhaps initiated by words of Jesus (Mark 9¹³; Matt. 11¹⁰f.). (For the evidence, somewhat exiguous, in Judaism for the belief presupposed in some NT passages that Elijah was to be the forerunner of the messiah, see *TDNT* II, pp. 929ff.). In John 6¹⁴f. 'he who comes' (into the world) qualifies 'the prophet' (of Deut. 18¹⁵ff.?), but the expectation of the prophet like Moses is attested for Samaritan and Christian rather than Jewish belief – it may have existed at Qumran, see Vermes, *Scrolls*, pp. 48–50. In John 6¹⁵ 'the prophet' is connected with 'king', and in Mark 11⁹ 'he who comes' (in the name of the Lord, Ps. 118²⁶) is glossed by 'the kingdom of our father David', in 19³⁸ by 'king' and in Matt. 21⁹ by 'the Son of David'. If John thought of himself as a prophet of the last days the 'mightier one' is likely to have been the (messianic) king, who exercises saving power. In Mark 10⁴⁷; Matt. 9²⁷; 12²³; 15²²; 21¹⁴f. 'the Son of David' is associated with healing.

another: *allos* could mean another person than Jesus who would fulfil the required role, or a different kind of person (*heteros*, as Matt. 11³). The use of these two words in the NT is too loose to press this.

21

A highly artificial insertion to provide the basis for the reply in v. 22. This then refers not, as in Matt. 11⁴, to the ministry in general ('what you hear and see'), but to what the two disciples have just had demonstrated to them, *what you have seen and heard* – for the order cf. 10²⁴. It is from Luke – *in that hour* cf. A. 16³³; *bestowed, charizesthai,* apart from Paul only L–A in the NT – but illustrates his unpredictability, as it contains his only use of *plagues* (*mastix,* perhaps in compensation for its omission in 6¹⁸ᶠ· = Mark 3¹⁰). Blindness is singled out, the other cures specified in v. 22 being covered by *diseases, plagues* and *evil spirits,* and by the raising in vv. 11–17. Even so no basis is supplied for the preaching to the poor.

22–23

The reply is not direct but oblique, and in terms not of status but of function. It is a free rendering of Isa. 35⁵ᶠᶠ·, 'Then (when Yahweh will come and save, v. 4) the eyes of the blind shall be opened, and the ears of the deaf unstopped; then shall the lame man leap as a hart, and the tongue of the dumb man shall sing for joy . . . the unclean shall not pass over it' (the holy way; this is perhaps taken up in *lepers are cleansed*). Cf. also Isa. 29¹⁸ᶠ·; 32³ᶠ·. Isa. 28–35 form a distinct group of prophecies (they have nothing to do with the 'Servant' of Isaiah) which relate to the divine judgment and redemption of Judah and Jerusalem in reply to the cry for mercy (Isa. 33²), and to the reign of the future king (Isa. 32¹; 33¹⁷). The addition of *the poor have the good news preached to them* from Isa. 61¹ (absent from some mss of Matt. 11⁵) links the healings to the rest of the ministry (cf. 4¹⁸), and further interprets them as signs of the era of salvation. The force of the reply is linked to the meaning of the preceding 'he who is to come' (v. 20) and of the following beatitude (v. 23).

23

takes . . . offence: skandalizesthai is, with its noun skandalon = 'trap', almost entirely confined to the LXX and NT. It should probably be rendered 'snared', and so mean enticed into error, unbelief or sin, sometimes by what is contrary to accepted custom or belief (Matt. 15¹²; 17²⁷; John 6⁶¹; I Cor. 8¹³). The beatitude (see 6²⁰) may then be either (i) an integral part of the reply in v. 22: those are blessed who continue to believe in Jesus even if the beneficent character of his deeds contradicts a different programme predicated of *he who is to come*; or (ii) added to the reply: Jesus may not be recognizably the kind of person whose deeds are to be held to mark the era of salvation.

^{24}*When the messengers of John had gone, he began to speak to the crowds concerning John:* '*What did you go out into the wilderness to behold? A reed shaken by the wind?* ^{25}*What then did you go out to see? A man clothed in soft raiment? Behold, those who are gorgeously apparelled and live in luxury are in kings' courts.* ^{26}*What then did you go out to see? A prophet? Yes, I tell you, and more than a prophet.* ^{27}*This is he of whom it is written.*

"*Behold, I send my messenger before thy face,*
who shall prepare thy way before thee."

^{28}*I tell you, among those born of women none is greater than John; yet he who is least in the kingdom of God is greater than he.*' ^{29}(*When they heard this all the people and the tax collectors justified God, having been baptized with the baptism of John;* ^{30}*but the Pharisees and the lawyers rejected the purpose of God for themselves, not having been baptized by him.*)

This stands out as vigorous, colourful and circumstantial. In counterpoint to John's previous tentative enquiry, Jesus, by a series of rhetorical questions leading to a solemn affirmation, pronounces authoritatively about John and the divine plan for Israel. Verses 24–28 are in almost verbatim agreement with Matt. 11^{7-11}. The differences are mostly to be ascribed to Luke as more literary – *messengers* (*angelos* + 9^{52} of human messengers), *gorgeously apparelled*, *live in luxury* (*truphē* + II Peter 2^{13}), *kings' courts* (*basileion* ,++ the classical word for 'palace'). This and the previous pericope represent the contribution of Q to the question of the relative position and function of John and Jesus, which would seem to have been much debated; cf. Mark 9^{9-13}; Matt. 17^{9-13}; John 1^{19-28}; 3^{25-30}.

24–26

What . . .?: The interrogative *ti* can also mean 'why?'. It must do so in Matt. 11^9, and this probably determines the punctuation of the other questions in Matthew, and also in Luke (so Gospel of Thomas 78). Hence 'Why did you go out . . .? To behold a reed . . .?', and so with the other questions.

into the wilderness: This indirectly confirms the desert as the scene of John's prophetic activity (3^2; Mark 1^4), though not necessarily of his baptizing, and it presupposes that the crowds addressed had taken part in a mass exodus to him there ($3^{7ff.}$).

A reed . . .? : The argument moves by a progression from the ridiculous to the sublime. It starts from what was such an ordinary sight in the desert – *to behold* (*theasasthai* = 'to gaze at') *a reed* – as to be a ludicrous reason for going out there; some take *a reed shaken by the wind* of an unreliable person, but this is very doubtful. It then moves to a human portent, a man of splendour and luxury, perhaps with Herod in mind, who imprisoned John. This would also be ludicrous; for the dress appropriate to the desert cf. Mark 1⁶; Josephus, *Life* 11, of the desert ascetic Bannus, who wore 'only such clothing as trees provided'. It then moves to a divine portent, *a prophet*; for the desert as the rendezvous of the followers of prophets and rebels, cf. Matt. 24²⁶; A. 21³⁸; Josephus *BJ* 2.259–262. This last was indeed the case – *Yes, I tell you* – and, did they but know it, someone (something) *more than a prophet.* This, while very general, can in a Jewish perspective only refer to someone (something) that occupies a place between the prophets and that which they announced. It hardly supports Conzelmann's thesis (*Theology*, p. 25, etc.) that Luke places John firmly within the old order of Israel, the law and the prophets.

27

This, the only explicit OT citation in Q, defines *more than a prophet*. Its form of introduction, *This is he of whom it is written*, is found at Qumran (cf. Vermes, *Scrolls*, pp. 243, 97). Its text is in the first part closer to Exod. 23²⁰, which speaks of Yahweh's messenger who is to lead Israel. Its second part is from Mal. 3¹, which speaks of the messenger who prepares for Yahweh's coming in judgment. With *before thy face* from Exodus, and *thy way* in place of 'my way' in Mal 3¹, it becomes an address by God to his messiah. This is likely to be a Christian creation. If the messenger of Mal. 3¹ is to be identified with Elijah in Mal 4⁵ᶠ·, then, when uttered by Jesus, it pronounces John as Elijah redivivus to be the precursor of the messiah, who is himself. This also appears to be a Christian creation.

28

This remarkable saying may originally have been independent. The first part does not carry on the thought of vv. 26–27 – to be the greatest of men is not a further definition of being more than a prophet – but is simply a foil to the second part. There is here a particularly radical expression of the eschatological conception of salvation. John surpasses all human beings. He does so presumably by virtue of his proximity to the coming eschatological crisis as its immediate herald. Nevertheless, so great is the distinction between the coming of God's kingdom and anything in human life that he is, or could be, surpassed by the most insignificant in that kingdom. From such a compressed and hyperbolic statement it can hardly be decided whether John is here excluded from the kingdom, whether there are grades in it, and whether it is regarded as already present.

he who is least: mikroteros is a comparative = 'smaller', but the comparative was by this time often used as a superlative = 'the smallest', here in counterpoint to 'the greatest' of v. 27a. Some commentators from Tertullian onwards have taken it as a real comparative and as a cryptic reference of Jesus to himself (cf. 17^2 for his use of *mikros* = 'little one' for the disciple). It could then be a statement from Jesus' side resolving the problem that he and John were contemporaries and John temporally prior to himself; cf. John $1^{15f.,\ 24-31}$; 3^{28-30} for its resolution from John's side.

in the kingdom: See on 4^{43}. Here it has its secondary meaning of 'realm'.

29–30

Some take these verses as a continuation of Jesus' words (see NEB margin). But their prose style is in marked contrast with the sayings on either side, and they are rather to be seen as a somewhat awkward editorial comment which Luke has felt it necessary to add in order to articulate the previous section, and to provide the different groups required for the favourable address in vv. 24–28 and the condemnation in vv. 31–34 (*you say*, v. 34; and cf. 20^{1-8}). They resemble the application attached to the parable in Matt. 21^{32}, though the persons contrasted and the basis of the contrast are different. The language is heavily Lukan.

all the people and the tax collectors: An odd combination of a favourite Lukan expression in narrative, *all the people* (with *heard* cf. 19^{48}; 20^{45}) with a specific group, *the tax collectors* (see on 3^{12}), who are added awkwardly to prepare for v. 34.

29

justified God: For 'justify' in the sense of 'prove right' cf. v. 35; Rom. 3^4; Ps. Sol. $8^{7,\ 27}$; IV Ezra 10^{16}, with the comment of *AP* II, p. 604, 'To acknowledge the justice of God's decree is equivalent to pious submission to his will.'

having been baptized with the baptism of John: With some exaggeration the whole nation, apart from its spiritual leaders, is said to have undergone the rite. In doing so they had recognized the divine origin of John's mission as a prophet of a special kind (cf. 20^{1-8}).

30

the Pharisees and the lawyers: A combination peculiar to Luke (+ 11^{53}; 14^3) for the more usual 'the scribes and Pharisees'. For the former see on 5^{17}. *lawyer* (*nomikos*) is, apart from Titus 3^{13}, confined to Luke in the NT, and to non-Markan sections of his gospel. It is widely attested in papyri and inscriptions for 'lawyer' in the ordinary sense, though rarely in Jewish documents, and never there for 'scribe'. Its use here and in 10^{25}; 11^{45-53}; 14^3, probably reflects Luke's hand, and an intention to supply his readers with the nearest equivalent in

Greco-Roman society to the Jewish scribe, i.e. an exegete of the (religious) law; cf. 5¹⁷, where on the first reference to 'scribes' he adds as explanation 'teachers of the law' (*nomodidaskaloi* + A. 5³⁴; I Tim. 1⁷).

the purpose of God: purpose (*boulē*) is largely confined to L–A in the NT, and *the purpose of God* entirely so (+ A. 2²³; 13³⁶; 20²⁷). Here it specifies John's mission and baptism as an indispensable part of the divine plan for Israel's salvation.

for themselves: Absent from some mss. It could be taken either with *rejected,* i.e. on their own responsibility, or with *the purpose of God,* i.e. which had them in mind.

7³¹⁻³⁵ JESUS' COMMENT ON JOHN AND HIMSELF

³¹'*To what then shall I compare the men of this generation, and what are they like?* ³²*They are like children sitting in the market place and calling to one another,*

> "*We piped to you, and you did not dance;*
> *we wailed, and you did not weep.*"

³³*For John the Baptist has come eating no bread and drinking no wine; and you say, "He has a demon."* ³⁴*The Son of man has come eating and drinking; and you say, "Behold, a glutton and a drunkard, a friend of tax collectors and sinners!"* ³⁵*Yet wisdom is justified by all her children.*'

The unit is close in wording to Matt. 11¹⁶⁻¹⁹. To suppose that Luke is following Matthew here would mean that he has omitted Matt. 11¹²⁻¹⁵, only to retain part of it in a revised form in a strange new context at 16¹⁶. This is far less likely than that he is following Q, and that Matthew has supplemented, and has carried further the process in Q of bringing together material about John. The connection here (*then*) is only possible because of Luke's editorial comment in vv. 29–30. Even so it is weak when Jesus' words are resumed after the intervening comment, and when they are addressed to all Israel (*you say*) and not to the limited section of it referred to in v. 30.

31

The interrogative introduction to a parable, here a double question (cf. 13¹⁸ = Mark 4³⁰), is rabbinic. 'Most of the rabbinical parables begin with the words . . . "a parable: like a king . . ." This usage is an abbreviation of "I will relate a parable to you. With what shall the matter be compared? It is the case with it as with . . .''' (Jeremias, *Parables*, p. 100). In these parables the 'it' is generally a statement in scripture which the parable elucidates. Here the referent is the behaviour of contemporary Israel, who is addressed through the parable; *you say*, vv. 33, 34 (Matthew 'they say').

this generation: A rabbinic expression, found in the LXX (Deut. 32$^{5, 20}$; cf. A. 2^{40}) but not in ordinary Greek, with the sense of the sum total of those born at the same time, contemporaries. Luke underlines this by adding *the men of* (cf. 11^{31}).

32

The content of the parable, a children's game, is far from a stock figure, but is drawn from life. The details are, however, unclear; for this and the various interpretations of the parable see Lagrange, pp. 223ff. In Matt. 11$^{16f.}$ groups of children sitting in market places address others (*heteroi*), complaining that whether they have piped or mourned (played at weddings or funerals?) these other have not made the appropriate response; i.e. 'whatever we do is wrong.' In Luke there are two groups who either make this complaint to each other (*allēlois*; but this is very artificial), or, more probably, who make alternate complaints in a kind of tit for tat – i.e. 'everyone is in a contrary mood.' Luke's version can be a genuine similitude, which is applied to the successive treatment of John and Jesus in Israel. Matthew's suggests the more allegorical picture of John and Jesus jointly confronting Israel with a combination of dourness and joviality.

33-34

The application is more directly supplied (*For*) than with most parables. It pre-supposes a close connection between John and Jesus. Its formulation in terms of 'coming' could suggest later reflection on what is already past and complete (see on 5^{32}). This is increased by Luke's more formal *John the Baptist*, though decreased by his use of the perfect tense *has come* (Matt. 11$^{18f.}$ 'came'). Since the point appears to be to accuse Israel of frivolous perversity, it is not clear what precisely the actions had been which had been perversely interpreted.

eating no bread and drinking no wine: Matt. 11^{18} has 'neither eating nor drinking'. Taken literally this is nonsense, and presumably refers to abstention from ordinary life when that is expressed as 'eating and drinking', as in v. 34 = Matt. 11^{19}. Luke is more specific. *no bread* perhaps implies the special desert fare mentioned in Mark 1^6 (though not by Luke in 3$^{2f.}$), and *no wine* the special ascetic vocation as a Nazirite (cf. 1^{15}).

he has a demon: Possibly another way of saying 'he is mad' (cf. John 7^{20}; Mark 3$^{21, 30}$), though actual demonic possession may be meant (cf. John 8^{48}; 10^{20}). In either case John's asceticism must have been regarded as peculiar and extreme to have occasioned such a judgment, however perverse. In 5³³ = Mark 2¹⁸ the abstinence of his disciples is an approved act of piety alongside that of the Pharisees.

34

The Son of man has come: This raises some of the problems connected with the Son of man (see on 5²⁴). Bultmann (*History*, p. 155) regards the statement as a Hellenistic formulation since it applies the eschatological title to the earthly life of Jesus, and conjectures an original 'man'; but man in general cannot be called the friend of tax collectors and sinners. Jeremias (*Theology*, pp. 261f.) thinks it replaces an original 'a son of man' = 'a man' = 'I'; but the context seems to require a reference to a specific figure who is recognizably as closely connected with the objects of John's mission as John himself, and perhaps more so. If 'the Son of man' is original here, and has the titular sense, it invests the earthly life of Jesus with an eschatological character. Such a use could always lie to hand, since even when referring to a heavenly being it did not lose its underlying meaning of 'man', and required the earth as the sphere of his operations.

eating and drinking: Again, if this refers to ordinary life and does not mean 'specially given to eating and drinking', it is difficult to see how it gave rise to the perverse judgment.

a glutton and a drunkard: Of these the first, *phagos* (so Matt. 11¹⁹) appears for the first time in Greek literature, and the second, *oinopotēs* (so Matt. 11¹⁹) occurs only here in the NT, only once in the LXX, and is rare in Greek literature.

a friend of tax collectors and sinners: An additional and specific judgment based on the actual behaviour of Jesus (cf. 5²⁹; 15²). It does not belong with, or proceed out of, the general antithesis of fasting/feasting, since eating and drinking with the outcast is not evidence of gluttony and drunkeness.

35

A semi-proverbial saying which would be capable of different applications. Here it qualifies the otherwise entirely negative judgment on this generation by making exceptions.

Yet: Greek *kai* = 'and' in the adversative sense 'and yet'. But in Luke, who adds *all* to *children*, it could continue the thought of *friend of tax collectors and sinners*, and look back over the whole chapter, and especially to vv. 9, 22, 29, where there is abundant evidence of the success of John and Jesus.

wisdom: The personification which had developed in Jewish theology to express the divine activity in certain of its aspects, especially creation and the instruction of men in God's truth and ways (cf. Prov. 8; Ecclus. 24; Wisd. 7).

Here the missions both of John and Jesus are placed under the aegis of this Wisdom.[b]

is justified: As in v. 29 'to be proved right', here with *apo* = 'from' in the sense 'as the result of'. The existence of those who have responded to John and Jesus shows the effective operation of the divine Wisdom.

her children: This is the language of the Wisdom tradition, where men are addressed as children or sons (so Ecclus passim), including by Wisdom herself (Prov. 8[32]), who communicates to them the divine purpose (Wisd. 9[17]). In Matt. 11[19] 'deeds' (works) is clearly secondary. Some take the *children* as John and Jesus themselves, but this cannot be so for Luke with his addition of *all*.

[36]*One of the Pharisees asked him to eat with him, and he went into the Pharisee's house, and sat at table.* [37]*And behold, a woman of the city, who was a sinner, when she learned that he was sitting at table in the Pharisee's house, brought an alabaster flask of ointment,* [38]*and standing behind him at his feet, weeping, she began to wet his feet with her tears, and wiped them with the hair of her head, and kissed his feet, and anointed them with the ointment.* [39]*Now when the Pharisee who had invited him saw it, he said to himself, 'If this man were a prophet, he would have known who and what sort of woman this is who is touching him, for she is a sinner.'* [40]*And Jesus answering said to him, 'Simon, I have something to say to you.' And he answered, 'What is it, Teacher?'* [41]*'A certain creditor had two debtors; one owed five hundred denarii, and the other fifty.* [42]*When they could not pay, he forgave them both. Now which of them will love him more?'* [43]*Simon answered, 'The one, I suppose, to whom he forgave more.' And he said to him, 'You have judged rightly.'* [44]*Then turning toward the woman he said to Simon, 'Do you see this woman? I entered your house, you gave me no water for my feet, but she has wet my feet with her tears and wiped them with her hair.* [45]*You gave me no kiss, but from the time I came in she has not ceased to kiss my feet.* [46]*You did not anoint my head with oil, but she has anointed my feet with ointment.* [47]*Therefore I tell you, her sins, which are many, are forgiven, for she loved much; but he who is forgiven little, loves little.'* [48]*And he said to her, 'Your sins are for-*

b For Wisdom thought of as a feature of the Q tradition, see M. J. Suggs, *Wisdom, Christology and Law in Matthew's Gospel*, Cambridge, Mass. 1970.

*given.' *⁴⁹*Then those who were at table with him began to say among themselves, 'Who is this, who forgives sins?' *⁵⁰*And he said to the woman, 'Your
faith has saved you; go in peace.'*

This story, peculiar to Luke, illustrates his characteristic excellencies and
deficiencies as a redactor of tradition. It is a highly circumstantial narrative written in lengthy sentences, and includes dialogue and parable
written in short sentences which are particularly animated. As a result
it is more dramatic and moving than the corresponding stories in the
other gospels (Mark 14³⁻⁹ = Matt. 26⁶⁻¹³; John 12¹⁻⁸). The picture is,
however, at times a blurred one, and inconcinnities in the story raise
questions of the form in which Luke received it, and of how far he was
the master of his material.

Style and language suggest that Luke was largely responsible for its
present written form. Thus in the initial setting (vv. 36–38) *sat at table*
is the classical *kataklinein* for reclining at a solemn banquet, and is confined to Luke in the NT; in vv. 37–38 the actions to be picked up in
vv. 44–46 are described idiomatically by participles (*learned, brought,
standing, weeping*) leading to main verbs (*began to wet, wiped, kissed,
anointed*); *brought, komizein,* is in the active sense confined to Luke in
the NT; *wet, brechein,* elsewhere in the Greek Bible Ps. 6⁶ of tears;
wiped, the literary *ekmassein* + v. 44, John 11²; 12³; 13⁵. In the parable
and dialogue, Lukan are the participial *ho kalesas = who had invited*
(v. 39) cf. 14⁹, and the two classical senses of *echein* = 'to have' (v. 40)
and 'to be able to' (v. 42), cf. A. 23¹⁷; 25²⁶. Stylistic are the semi-
technical terms *creditor* (*chreopheiletēs* ++) and *debtor* (*daneistēs* ++)
and (the) *one, the other* (v. 41); *forgave, charizesthai* in the classical sense
'to grant a favour' (v. 42); *I suppose* (*hupolambanein* + A. 2¹⁵); *judged*
(*krinein* in the classical sense 'to decide', cf. 12⁵⁷; A. 4¹⁹; 20¹⁶; 25²⁵)
(v. 43); and the rhythm in vv. 44–45 with the nouns standing first in the
clauses, the repetition of *she,* the alternation of the possessive pronouns
your, my and *her,* and *ceased* (*dialeipein* ++) in the classical construction
of negative with participle. The conclusion in vv. 48–50 appears to be
Luke's compilation. The comment in v. 47, which presumes the
woman's forgiveness, would make an appropriate ending. The pronouncement, despite this, of forgiveness in v. 48 changes the character
of the story from one of dialogue and comment to one of action. The
question in v. 49 relates the story to the rest of the chapter with its
emphasis on Jesus as effective prophet. In v. 50 a formula for the con-

clusion of healings, which does not arise naturally here, turns the story into one of salvation, and aligns it to vv. 9–10, 21ff.

Whether Luke had in mind Mark 14$^{3-9}$, which he deliberately fails to reproduce, is debated (see Fitzmyer, pp. 684ff.). Mark's story is more christological and mysterious, and Luke may have seen the anointing on the head there as giving a handle to the charge that Jesus had made himself an anointed king (23^2). His own version is more straightforward and human. In Mark the anointing is a premeditated honorific act, whereas in Luke the weeping and wiping with the hair would be most natural as the unpremeditated act of a grateful penitent. In that case *brought an alabaster flask of ointment*, which is premeditated, could be an intrusion, probably taken from Mark. These considerations make the original form of the tradition received by Luke difficult to determine – perhaps the substance of vv. 36–39, 44–47. For a review of the various analyses see Marshall, pp. 304ff.

36–38

There is no time reference, nor is the city named. The link with what precedes is provided by what in the story itself is a subordinate and somewhat artificial element, viz. that *one of the Pharisees* (see on 5^{17}), i.e. of those condemned in vv. 30ff. for failure to discern a prophet, is unfavourably contrasted with *a sinner* (see on 5^8), i.e. a friend of the Son of man and one of the children who justify Wisdom.

36

asked him to eat with him: For this setting of a meal see on 5^{29}. No motive is given for the invitation. *Teacher* (v. 40) might imply the intention to honour an outstanding religious figure, but in that case the neglect implied in vv. 44–46 becomes even more inexplicable.

a woman: One of the instances, more frequent in Luke, of Jesus' contacts with women; cf. in this section vv. 11–19; 8$^{1-3}$.

a sinner: One of those coupled with tax collectors in v. 34. In contrast to Pharisee this could denote a transgressor of the Pharisaic code of righteous behaviour, but her *many* sins (v. 47) indicates an evident wrongdoer. Some take it here to mean prostitute, noting the conjunction in Matt. 21$^{31f.}$ of tax collectors and prostitutes. How such a person is present at the meal is not explained.

an alabaster flask of ointment: A common term found in the papyri. It may have been taken from Mark 14^3, where its use on the head of Jesus is vital to the story, whereas here its use on his feet is supplementary and somewhat superfluous.

38

A highly affecting scene. As Jesus reclines at table the woman stands behind him in such a way as to be over against his feet. On these she lets drop tears, and in order to turn this into a footwashing uses her hair, perhaps let down for the purpose, as a towel to wipe them off. She then continues kissing the feet (the verb is in the imperfect), though at one point anointing them (the verb is in the aorist) with oil brought for the purpose. The meaning and motive of these actions are not given until later, and then indirectly, in Jesus' references to them in vv. 44–47. It has to be presumed that she knew herself to be one of the company with whom Jesus, the Son of man, associates, that he had already declared her sins forgiven, and that her actions were expressions of gratitude for this (not of penitence; the title The Penitent Woman for the story is a misnomer). That is, the woman's actions can only be accounted for by reference to something the story does not itself contain.

39

In vv. 39–47 the narrative takes on something of the form of a conflict story, with hostile question and counter-question refuting it, though here the hostile question is unspoken, and the counter-question does not really answer it.

said to himself: The soliloquy of a chief character is a regular and crucial feature in some of the special Lukan parables (cf. 15¹⁷ff.; 16³ff.; 18⁴f., ¹¹f.). Here it is part of an actual incident; and as the reflection that in allowing himself to be treated in this way by a sinner Jesus shows himself to be no prophet it is not crucial to the incident. For this is not concerned with the question of Jesus as prophet in itself, but only in the context of ch. 7. And although Jesus' words in vv. 40ff. must be supposed to follow from his reading of the Pharisee's unspoken objection, they are not directed to that objection.

a prophet: Some mss read 'the prophet', but the sense is that a prophet is one who discerns the heart and keeps himself from sin (cf. John 4¹⁹; 9¹⁷). Prophetic discernment Jesus does indeed have in knowing the Pharisee's inner thoughts (cf. 11¹⁷).

40

Simon: The naming of a character in a story, especially at this late stage, is unusual, and may reflect the influence of Mark 14³. It serves to introduce as lively a dialogue as any in the gospels, as does also *he answered,* Greek *phēsin* = 'he says', one of the few historic presents in Luke, which is used here for dramatic effect.

What is it?: Literally in the Greek 'Say (on)'.

Teacher: didaskalos, which Luke introduces here for the first time as an address to Jesus (in 3¹² it is applied to the Baptist). He can take it over from Mark (so at 8⁴⁹; 9³⁸; 20²¹, ²⁸, ³⁹; 21⁷; 22¹¹ – never apparently from Q), or from, or can insert it into, his special material (10²⁵; 12¹³; 11⁴⁵ into Q). With the partial exception of 22¹¹ = Mark 14¹⁴ he never has it used of Jesus by disciples (contrast Mark 4³⁸; 9³⁸; 10³⁵); for that his word is *epistatēs* (see on 5⁵). As a rendering of rabbi (cf. John 1³⁸; 20¹⁶),ᶜ it would denote in Judaism one regarded as an influential, authoritative, and perhaps accredited teacher of religion.

41-43

The parable, which is not called such, nor is Jesus expressly said to be the speaker, is brief and succinct. It may be compared with the extended parable in Matt. 18²³⁻³⁵ in being about the cancellation for those unable to pay of a larger or smaller debt with emphasis on the expectation of a corresponding gratitude. It may be an example of parabolic material of Q origin which has been used in different ways.

42

love him: For *agapān* = 'to love' in the sense of gratitude, see Jeremias, *Parables*, p. 127.

44-47

The parable is given a more direct application than usual. It takes a dramatic form – Jesus turns towards the woman but addresses Simon – but is somewhat forced. Each of the woman's previously narrated lavish actions is made the foil for a corresponding niggardliness and churlishness, hitherto unmentioned, in the host's hospitality. They are then interpreted as expressions, from one who had been aware of many sins, of gratitude for a forgiveness (presumably at Jesus' hands) which is also hitherto undisclosed, and which was not hinted at in the description of her as a sinner (v. 37). This is contrasted according to the logic of the application with the ingratitude of the host, which is due to his awareness of having had only a few sins forgiven (or of having had none at all to be forgiven?). With such an application the parable has no bearing on the original objection in v. 39.

44

no water for my feet: This is strange. Such a provision would appear to be automatic, especially at a banquet (cf. 11³⁷ᶠ·; John 13¹⁻¹⁰). Would the other guests (v. 49) have made the same complaint?

45

no kiss: The kiss of greeting on the cheek could perhaps mark the difference

ᶜ See R. E. Brown, *The Gospel according to John*, Anchor Bible, New York 1966, p. 74, for its occurrence on a Jewish ossuary dated before AD 70.

between a warm and a purely formal invitation, but there is evidence for it as a custom only in Greek and not in Jewish hospitality. Here it is in counterpart to an act of devotion described hyperbolically in *from the time I came in she has not ceased to kiss my feet*.

46

anoint my head: This action, generally self-administered and as part of a bath, was an expression of well being and enjoyment (cf. Matt. 6¹⁷, where it is the opposite of what is penitential). There is no evidence that provision for it at a meal was *de rigeur*. It may be a foreign element in the story due to Mark 14³. It is taken up, somewhat awkwardly, by the woman's superfluous action of anointing the feet.

47

The syntax of this crucial interpretative verse is uncertain at two points. (i) *Therefore, hou charin* + + = 'on account of which', can be taken closely with *I tell you* and refer backwards – 'On account of this (the woman's actions) I tell you that ...' (so apparently RSV). Or it can refer forwards with *I tell you* in parenthesis (so some Greek texts) – 'It is for this reason (I tell you) that ...' (ii) *For* is *hoti*. This can have its causal sense, i.e. her forgiveness is the consequence of her love; but this contradicts both the parable and the following *he who is forgiven little, loves little*. Or it can be elliptical, i.e. her sins have been forgiven, which is shown by the fact that she loved much (so NEB).

48–50

These verses secure that the story ends as an action of grace, with Jesus addressing the woman and not Simon. They are a curiously lame conclusion, being apparently borrowed from other contexts where they are pertinent.

48

Your sins are forgiven: See on 5²⁰, whence Luke may have taken this. The argument of vv. 41–47 depends on the woman's knowledge that her sins have already been declared forgiven. A declaration of forgiveness here can only be a confirmation of what has already taken place, and hence loses much of its force.

49

The questioning objection raised by the other guests, who are now introduced for the purpose, may also be taken from 5²¹. Here it is an interjection without any consequences.

50

Your faith has saved you: For this concluding formula in healing stories, with its significant double meaning of *faith* and *saved*, see on 8⁴⁸ (and for healing and forgiveness connected with faith, see 5²⁰⁻²⁴). It is hardly appropriate here, where it has been a question of the woman's love, not of her faith.

go in peace: A conventional formula for dismissal and departure under the divine protection; cf. Judg. 18⁶; A. 16³⁶.

8 *Soon afterwards he went on through cities and villages, preaching and bringing the good news of the kingdom of God. And the twelve were with him,* ²*and also some women who had been healed of evil spirits and infirmities: Mary, called Magdalene, from whom seven demons had gone out,* ³*and Joanna, the wife of Chuza, Herod's steward, and Susanna, and many others, who provided for them* out of their means.*

* Other ancient authorities read *him*

This brief notice, with its combination of the general and the particular, could be suggestive. It is not a self-contained unit of oral tradition, and unless the L material constituted a connected narrative it will not have reached Luke in documentary form. It is a single, somewhat over-loaded sentence, with marks of Luke's hand in *Soon afterwards, en tō kathexēs* ++, with *kathexēs* = 'successively' (confined to L–A in the NT) used in a temporal sense, *went through*, the literary *diodeuein* + A. 17¹, *bringing the good news, infirmities (astheneia)* and *means (ta huparchonta)* It could then reflect independent historical research on his part. He uses it as a transition to the remainder of the 'Galilean' ministry, 8⁴–9⁵⁰, which he takes over from Mark 4¹–9⁵⁰, and sets within the context of a constant journeying (cf. 4⁴⁴; 9⁵¹ᶠᶠ·).

1

through towns and villages: It is not said where these, and the towns in v. 4, are. The previous region of Jesus' preaching has been Judaea (4⁴⁴; cf. 7¹); the last mentioned places have been Capernaum, which was in Galilee (7¹), and Nain (7¹¹), which may have been so. While the material Luke is about to incorporate had a predominantly Galilean locale (Mark 4¹; 5²¹; 6¹, ⁵³; 7³¹; 8²²; 9³⁰, ³³), he nowhere makes this clear.

preaching and bringing the good news of the kingdom: A summarizing hendiadys. For the expressions see on 3³; 4⁴³ᶠ·.

And the twelve were with him: These are now added in view of their previous appointment, perhaps with 'to be with him' of Mark 3¹⁴ in mind, which Luke omitted in 6¹³.

2–3

and also some women ... Mary ... and many others who provided for them: To Jesus and his now permanent companions in travel and mission, the Twelve (*them*; *him* is a reverential alteration), Luke adds a large company of ministering women, naming three. Such a group, with three named, is abruptly introduced in similar manner in Mark 15⁴⁰⁻⁴¹ (cf. Matt. 27⁵⁵⁻⁵⁶; in Luke 23⁴⁹ none are named). The same, or similar, named women continue as witnesses of the burial and empty tomb (Mark 15⁴⁷; 16¹; Matt. 27⁶¹; 28¹; Luke 23⁴⁹ unnamed; 24¹⁰ named ones with others; A. 1¹⁴ unnamed). For all this Luke here prepares in advance. For such a large female contingent, including at least one married woman, to accompany a rabbi or itinerant prophet would be unusual. It would be an important feature for Luke, who appears to underline by his choice of material the place of women in the gospel story and in A.

who had been healed: This applies to the three named women.

Mary, called Magdalene: She is the only one common to all specifications of named women (cf. Mark 15⁴⁷; 16¹; Matt. 27⁶¹; 28¹; Luke 24¹⁰; John 19²⁵; 20¹), and was plainly an important figure in the passion and resurrection tradition. *Magdalene* means the woman from Magdala, a place not mentioned elsewhere.

seven devils had gone out: It is not clear whether in the vocabulary of exorcistic diagnosis *seven* is meant literally (cf. Legion in 8³⁰), or metaphorically of an exceptionally severe possession by one demon.

3

Joanna: She appears again only in 24¹⁰, as one of the women visiting the tomb.

Chuza, Herod's steward: This, together with the mention of Manaen in A. 13¹, may indicate that Luke was in touch with traditions about the court of Herod Antipas. It is not certain what *steward* (*epitropos* + Matt. 20⁸; Gal. 4²) denotes here; probably the administrator of an estate, as in Josephus, *Ant.* 18.194. So there was at least one highly placed convert among the disciples, and she from amongst the opposition.

Susanna: She does not reappear later in the gospel, and is otherwise unknown.

provided for them out of their means: Some presumably, and Joanna certainly, were women of substance. This is the only explicit explanation (Mark 14⁵⁰ᶠ· is only implicit) of how Jesus and his immediate companions were able to travel so extensively, especially in Luke's account, without working to support themselves. It also establishes the function of women disciples as material care and not preaching and healing. Luke may also have had in mind conditions in the later Christian mission, cf. A. 16^{15}.

8^4–9^{50} The Remainder of the Mission Before the Journey to Jerusalem

Luke now returns to the Markan narrative at the point where he had left it after the introduction to the 'sermon' (6^{12-19} = Mark 3^{7-19}), and is then dependent on it until Mark 10^1, where Jesus leaves Galilee for Judaea, at which point Luke also begins the journey to Jerusalem via Samaria ($9^{51ff.}$). He thus seems to have regarded Mark 3^{20}–9^{50} as a single section. From it he incorporates four units of parable teaching (8^{4-8}, $9-15$, $16-18$, $19-21$), four acts of power (8^{22-25}, $26-39$, $40-56$), the mission of the Twelve, Herod's consequent enquiry, the feeding of the five thousand and the confession of messiahship (9^{1-6}, $7-9$, $10-17$, $18-27$), the transfiguration, cure of the epileptic, prophecy of the passion and dispute over greatness (9^{28-36}, $37-43a$, $43b-45$, $46-48$), concluding with the strange exorcist (9^{49-50}). Although, as the agreement in wording and order shows, there is nothing in 8^4–9^{50} which is not from Mark, Luke does not take over all that is in Mark 3^{20}–9^{50}. To have done so would, no doubt, have unduly lengthened this 'Galilean' section, which is almost exactly equal in length to the 'Judaean' section (3^1–8^3) and the journey to Jerusalem (9^{51}–19^{27}), but there seem to be other reasons for his variations from Mark here. These may be considered under three heads. (i) Variations at the beginning and end of the whole section; for these see notes on 8^{4-18} and 9^{37-48}; (ii) Omissions of units inside the Markan section; for the omission of the parables in Mark 4^{26-32} see notes on 8^{4-18}, of the Nazareth episode (Mark 6^{1-6}) see notes on 4^{16-30}, of the material about the Baptist (Mark 6^{17-29}; 9^{9-13}) see notes on 3^{20}; (iii) The so-called 'Great Omission' of the seventy-four consecutive verses, Mark 6^{45}–8^{26}. For this see Introduction, p. 18.

8^{4-18} = Mark 4^{1-25}

PARABLE AND THE WORD OF GOD

⁴*And when a great crowd came together and people from town after town came to him, he said in a parable:* ⁵'*A sower went out to sow his seed; and as he sowed, some fell along the path, and was trodden under foot, and the birds of the air devoured it.* ⁶*And some fell on the rock; and as it grew up, it withered away, because it had no moisture.* ⁷*And some fell among thorns; and the thorns grew with it and choked it.* ⁸*And some fell into good soil and grew, and yielded a hundredfold.*' *As he said this, he called out,* '*He who has ears to hear, let him hear.*'

⁹*And when his disciples asked him what this parable meant,* ¹⁰*he said,* '*To you it has been given to know the secrets of the kingdom of God; but for others they are in parables, so that seeing they may not see, and hearing they may not understand.* ¹¹*Now the parable is this: The seed is the word of God.* ¹²*The ones along the path are those who have heard; then the devil comes and takes away the word from their hearts, that they may not believe and be saved.* ¹³*And the ones on the rock are those who, when they hear the word, receive it with joy; but these have no root, they believe for a while and in time of temptation fall away.* ¹⁴*And as for what fell among the thorns, they are those who hear, but as they go on their way they are choked by the cares and riches and pleasures of life, and their fruit does not mature.* ¹⁵*And as for that in the good soil, they are those who, hearing the word, hold it fast in an honest and good heart, and bring forth fruit with patience.*

¹⁶'*No one after lighting a lamp covers it with a vessel, or puts it under a bed, but puts it on a stand, that those who enter may see the light.* ¹⁷*For nothing is hid that shall not be made manifest, nor anything secret that shall not be known and come to light.* ¹⁸*Take heed then how you hear; for to him who has will more be given, and from him who has not, even what he thinks that he has will be taken away.*'

Mark 4¹⁻³⁴ is unique in the synoptic tradition in serving a double purpose of providing a collection of parables, the only one in Mark, and a rationale of parable teaching as a whole. The section is, however, disjointed, and both elements in it are obscure. For (i) it is not evident why the parable of the sower should raise the question of parables in general (Mark 4¹³), or what the relation is between it and the sayings and parables in Mark 4²¹⁻³². And (ii) Mark 4¹¹⁻¹² appears to teach, in contradiction to Mark 4³³⁻³⁴, that the purpose of parables is to conceal the truth.ᵈ Luke, however, is to include more parables, and other collections of parables, from other sources. Here, where he introduces for the first time the extended parable proper (the word in 4²³; 6³⁹ denotes a proverbial saying, and 7⁴¹ᶠ· is not called a parable) he is concerned with the latter aspect of interpretation (Matt. 13 is concerned with extending the collection of parables). This has determined Luke's redaction. His expression *in a parable* (v. 4) shows that, like Mark, he regarded the situation as typical and representative. So he rewrites to produce a single literary and compact unit in four connected and smoothly flowing paragraphs (vv. 5–8, 9–10, 11–15, 16–18), which focuses on the parable of the sower alone (upon which in Mark 4¹³ the understanding of all parables is said to rest). Hence the awkward statement in Mark 4¹⁰, 'asked him concerning the parables' followed by Mark 4¹³, which presumes a request for an interpretation of the sower parable, is replaced by *asked him what this parable meant* (v .9), and by *the parable is this* (v. 11). Hence also the omission (along with Matthew) of the parable of the Seed Growing Secretly (Mark 4²⁶⁻²⁹), and the reservation to later of the parable of the Mustard Seed (Mark 4³⁰⁻³²) in its Q form as a twin with the parable of the Leaven (13¹⁸⁻¹⁹ = Matt. 13³¹⁻³²). Further, having provided as a preface to the section a widespread public preaching of the kingdom of God (v. 1) he concentrates on parabolic teaching as revealing the secrets of the kingdom. The esoteric element is reduced by the omission of the retreat of Jesus and disciples into privacy, the substitution of *secrets* for 'secret', and the revision of the citation in v. 10. The meaning of the sower parable is now the missionary lesson that the preaching of the word of God will with patience produce a harvest of hearers, and the sayings on the lamp (vv. 16–18) exhort disciples to missionary effort. This is further underlined, and the section rounded off, by the transposition of the incident of the visit of Jesus' family (vv. 19–21 = Mark 3³¹⁻³⁵), so that the vast listening crowd becomes evidence of the harvest of hearers and doers of the word, and thereby constitutes Jesus' true family.

d For discussion of the section see D. E. Nineham, *Saint Mark*, pp. 125ff.; G. H. Boobyer, 'The Redaction of Mark 4.1–34', *NTS* 8, 1961–62, pp. 59–70; C. F. D. Moule, 'Mark 4.1–20 Yet Once More', in *Neotestamentica et Semitica*, ed. E. E. Ellis and M. Wilcox, Edinburgh 1969, pp. 95–113.

4–8

Luke has pruned the vivid but verbose Markan original in the interests of style and sense. In vv. 4, 5a, 8b the participles (so in the Greek *came together, came to, a sower, as he said*) allow each sentence to have three clausulae. In vv. 5b–8a are four carefully balanced two-line sentences, with what happens to each kind of seed compressed into a single statement; hence the addition of *and was trodden under foot* (v. 5, though inappropriate for the interpretation) to balance *as it grew up* (v. 6), *grew with it* (v. 7) and *grew* (v. 8), and the single *a hundredfold* for Mark's ascending scale, which plays no part in the interpretation in Mark.

4

The boat as a pulpit for teaching the crowds (Mark 4¹) has already been used by Luke in his construction of 5¹⁻¹¹ and is omitted here. The teaching has no particular setting except somewhere in the course of, or as the result of, the preaching journey supplied in 8¹. *came together* (*suneinai* + +) and *came to* (*epiporeuesthai* + +) are present participles and describe something still taking place.

he said in a parable: dia parabolēs. This unique expression may be intended to have a general character, 'he spoke in a figurative manner, parabolically'; in any case through the single parable of the sower and not, as in Mark 4¹⁰f., in parables.

5

his seed: ton sporon autou added for alliteration with *sower* (the generic participle *ho speirōn* = 'the one sowing') and *to sow* (*speirai*), but it further aids the transformation of a parable of a sower into a parable of seeds.

fell along the path: This, with *on the rock* (v. 6) and *among thorns* (v. 7) depicts seemingly senseless acts. Jeremias (*Parables*, pp. 11f.) argues from rabbinic statements for a Palestinian custom of ploughing after sowing which would make them natural. This has been contested,[e] and they may be an instance of a deliberately bizarre element present in other parables of Jesus, which is necessary to the point. If so, before being turned into a parable of the soils by allegorical interpretation, it could have been a genuine parable of contrast, in which a sowing affords an abundant harvest contrary to all appearances and expectations. This would be the point also of the following parables in Mark of the seed growing mysteriously, the smallest seed producing a large tree, and an obscured lamp giving light. These could then be parables, not of the kingdom of God in general, but of its paradoxical manifestation in the preaching and

[e] J. Drury, 'The Sower, the Vineyard and the Place of Allegory in the Interpretation of Mark's Parables', *JTS* ns 24, 1973, 367–79.

ministry of Jesus, where it is obscure and goes unrecognized before being manifest.

birds of the air: A biblical expression, found in the Q material (9⁵⁸; 13¹⁹; cf. also A. 10¹²); but *of the air*, absent from some mss, should probably be omitted on grounds of rhythm.

6

grew up: Hardly an adequate basis for *receive it with joy* (v. 13).

moisture: ikmas, a refined word, elsewhere in the Greek Bible Jer. 17⁸. In Theophrastus (*Enquiry into Plants* 6.4.8) it is, as here, contrasted with *withered* (*xērainesthai* = 'become dry'). When interpreting (v. 13) Luke returns to Mark's 'had no root', which can be moralized (cf. Col. 2⁷), whereas *withered* cannot.

8

a hundredfold: A single expression of maximum yield replacing Mark's graduated scale, though it is not clear whether it means a hundred seeds harvested for each seed sown,* or a hundred fruits.

He who has ears to hear, let him hear: This injunction underlines the importance of the parable, especially when supplied by Luke with a solemn introduction *he called out* (imperfect tense, 'he repeatedly called out'). It was perhaps a common formula (it reappears in 14³⁵, and is added in some mss at 12²¹; 13⁹; 21⁴), and may ultimately go back to Ezekiel, the only OT prophet to be associated with enigmatic parables. It may then refer to the ability to penetrate the mysterious (cf. Rev. 2⁷; 3⁶). In Ezek. 3²⁷, however, 'hear' means 'obey' what God demands, and this may be the sense in Mark 4⁹, ¹³, where Jesus is surprised that disciples, those who have already obeyed, do not understand the parables.

9–10

Mark 4¹⁰⁻¹², of which this is Luke's revised version, is very obscure both in itself and in conjunction with Mark 4³³⁻³⁴ (omitted by Luke), and is probably misplaced and misapplied. The context requires a contrast between understanding and not understanding parables, not between knowledge conveyed with parables and without parables; and a question about the use of parables in general is hardly answered in terms of insiders who do not need them and outsiders for whom they are effective only in judgment. Jeremias (*Parables*, pp. 16f.) conjectures that 'in parables' (Greek *en parabolais*, Mark 4¹¹) originally rendered an Aramaic adverbial phrase 'enigmatically', 'in riddling fashion', and this led the saying to be taken as applying to the purpose of parables. In favour of this is 'everything is' (Greek *panta ginetai* = 'all things take place', Mark 4¹¹), which

---

* So K. D. White, 'The Parable of the Sower', *JTS* ns 15, 1964, p. 301.

appears to refer to happenings rather than teaching (cf. also 'perceive' and 'hear' in the Isaiah quotation, Mark 4¹²). The saying may thus originally have been a comment on the puzzling hidden character of Jesus' mission as a whole. It would apply only indirectly to parables as enigmatic because comments on this.

9

The transition from parable to interpretation is the most concise in Luke, where *his disciples* (for Mark's 'those who were about him with the twelve'), not in private but in the presence of the crowd, ask not about parables in general but about the parable just spoken. It is, however, over concise, since their question leads directly to the interpretation in vv. 11ff., and leaves the difficult statement about parables in general (v. 10) hanging in the air.

what this parable meant: That a parable should itself require elucidation is completely foreign to Greek usage, where *parabolē* denoted an illustration, or an example having probative force in an inductive proof (Aristotle, *Rhetoric* 2.20), which would fail of its purpose if it were not crystal clear. The association of parable with enigma derives (i) from the wider meaning *parabolē* acquires as a LXX translation of the Hebrew *māsāl*, and (ii) from the loss in the church of the original contexts and intentions of Jesus' parables, and their consequent treatment as allegories with cryptic reference to a later state of affairs. (i) *māsāl* can cover the proverb of traditional wisdom (Ezek. 12²²), the saying of the 'wise' in Israel (Prov. 1⁶; Ecclus 3²⁹), an oracular utterance or taunt (Num. 23⁷ff.; Micah 2⁴), a veiled revelation in symbolical form of a future divine action (Ezek. 17²²ff.; 24³ff.), a figurative representation of eschatological events seen in a vision and requiring a seer or angel to interpret them (I Enoch 37⁵ and passim; IV Ezra 4¹²ff.), and, among the rabbis, a story told to aid exegesis of an OT text. In a surprising number of passages the word carries with it the sense of enigma (cf. Prov. 1⁶; Ecclus 39²ᶠ·; Num. 23–24; Deut. 28³⁷; Ps. 49⁴; 78²; Ezek. 17²; 20⁴⁹). This is not because the parable is itself complicated or an intellectually subtle form of speech, but because it is the vehicle of a revelation of the will of a God whose thoughts are not as men's thoughts, and whose intended actions run counter to human expectations. The parables of Jesus are sometimes rabbinic in form, less so in their content, and he does not seem to have used them for expounding the OT text.[f] They would seem to be primarily oracular utterances in story form urging attention to some aspect of the rule of God or the divine purpose. In so far as this aspect was unexpected or mysterious the parable could be enigmatic. For (ii) see on vv. 11ff.

10

To you it has been given to know the secrets of the kingdom of God: Or, 'The secrets

[f] See Abrahams, *Studies* I, ch. xii; M. D. Goulder, *Midrash and Lection in Matthew*, London 1974, pp. 47ff.

of the kingdom have been given to you to know'. In either case the passive is reverential, and means 'God has given'.

the secrets: The plural of *musterion* = 'mystery', 'secret' (so Mark 4¹¹), a word confined to this passage in the synoptists (the idea is present in 10²¹ = Matt. 11²⁵; it is not in John). In the NT it is predominantly a Pauline word for the divine purpose, hitherto hidden but now published in the death and exaltation of Christ (cf. I Cor. 2¹, ⁷; Col. 1²⁶ᶠ·; 2²; II Thess. 2⁷; Eph. 3³). There it may owe something to the idea of a secret in Hellenistic 'mystery' cults (cf. I Cor. 2⁶ᶠᶠ·) but it had already entered Judaism through the LXX of Dan. 2¹⁸ᶠᶠ·, ⁴⁴ᶠᶠ· for the veiled announcement of the future establishment of the reign of God. In subsequent apocalyptic literature the revelation of the secret (more commonly 'secrets') of the eschatological age was a common idea (I Enoch 63³; 103²; IV Ezra 12³⁶; Damascus Rule 3²³ – Vermes, *Scrolls*, p. 100; cf. Amos 3⁷). What the single all-inclusive secret of the kingdom is which God had given to the inner circle is not stated in Mark. In the context of the parables of Mark 4¹⁻³⁴ it could be the paradoxcial but necessary hiddenness, and the apparent insignificance, of what should by its nature manifest itself in an opposite manner. This is too difficult for Luke, who, with Matthew, substitutes the more normal and comprehensible *to know the secrets* (cf. Wisd. 2²).ᵍ This could envisage a multiplicity of separate truths about the kingdom to be conveyed by different parables. The sequence of thought, however, remains obscure, since it is not said when and how the disciples have shown a capacity to know the secrets, and their request for an interpretation shows that the parable has not had the desired result. Perhaps Luke means that the disciples are right to ask the question because they have the capacity to understand the secrets from a parable when it is interpreted, in contrast to those who have not, and who must be left with uninterpreted parables.

but for others: hoi loipoi = 'the rest' (Lukan) is less exclusive and predestinarian than Mark's 'those outside'.

they are in parables: There is no verb in the Greek, which is literally 'but to the rest in parables', perhaps evidence of Luke's embarrassment with Mark's text. If 'the secrets are given' is to be supplied, the contrast may be between the direct knowledge of the disciples, and the indirect knowledge of the same secrets by others through parables (cf. Num. 12⁸, where to Moses God speaks

ᵍ Unless 'the secret' is read in Matt. 13¹¹ with C k Clement and Irenaeus, *to know the secrets* is a notable agreement of Luke and Matthew against Mark, and has been taken as evidence of Luke's knowledge of Matthew. It is not, however, impossible that both hit on the same emendation of the obscure Markan original, and Luke shows no other signs of having read Matthew's heavily revised version of Mark here.

mouth to mouth, clearly, and not in dark speech). But this does not lead to v. 10b.

so that seeing . . . may not understand: This is a stylistic abbreviation of Mark's version of Isa. 6⁹ᶠ· LXX, and not an alternative form of the LXX text. The passage was a proof text of Israel's obduracy and unbelief (cf. A. 28²⁶ᶠ·, John 12⁴⁰). Luke retains *hina = so that*; the purpose of parables is to conceal the truth (Matt. 13¹³ softens with *hoti* = 'because', and some wish to take *hina* in that sense). He omits the final words from Isaiah in Mark 4¹², and so stops short of saying that their purpose was to prevent conversion and forgiveness.

11–15

In itself the parable of the sower (of which there is a version in the Gospel of Thomas 9 without any interpretation attached) could be a genuine parable with a single point, the details having no significance in themselves. The rule of God, as it is being proclaimed by Jesus, is in the riddle form of an apparently fruitless sowing, which nevertheless will produce its harvest. This would be doubly paradoxical in that (i) harvest rather than sowing was the appropriate metaphor for God's rule (cf. Joel 3¹³; Jer. 51³³; Hos. 6¹¹; II Baruch 70²; IV Ezra 4²⁸ᶠᶠ·; Mark 4²⁹; Matt. 13³⁹; John 4³⁵; Rev. 14¹⁵), and (ii) the kingdom, as God's, should manifest itself for all to see, and should carry all before it. The interpretation in Mark 4¹³⁻²⁰, which is reproduced by Matthew and Luke (it is the only one in Luke), is in various degress an allegorical treatment of details, and shows reflection on them – e.g. that seed sown on rocky ground is somehow more hopeful than that sown on hard ground (this then provided a basis in the gospels for the subsequent allegorical interpretation of all the parables). This is plainly artificial, since the seed has to become both the word sown and those in whom it is sown. Moreover it reflects the concerns of a later time in having a high proportion of words and concepts which are rare, or confined to this passage, in the synoptists, but are characteristic of didactic or exhortatory passages in A. and the epistles.

Luke is wholly dependent on Mark's interpretation, even to the point of reproducing or revising it rather than commenting on his own version of the parable, e.g. in v. 13 the comment is on having no root, as in Mark 4¹⁷ = Mark 4⁶, and not on having no moisture (v. 6, his own version of Mark 4⁶). He has, however, rewritten Mark's version, which is clumsily expressed, so as to produce neat single sentences – *the ones.* (vv. 12, 13), *as for what* (*that*, vv. 14, 15) – with participles for main verbs. In v. 13 *for a while* (*pros kairon*) is taken up by *in time of* (*en kairō*); in v. 14 *mature* (*telesphorein*, only here and IV Macc. 13²⁰ in the Greek Bible) balances *bring forth fruit* (*karpophorein*, v. 15); *honest and good* (v. 15) is the classical *kalos kai agathos* + +. He also carries further the process of ecclesiastical application, turning the parable into an exhortation to steadfastness in face of external and internal obstacles (cf. A. 14²²), and, as addressed to disciples, an instruction in missionary experience.

11

the word of God: This expression, for Mark's 'the word', is nowhere else on the lips of Jesus, but is frequent in A. and epistles for the later Christian message.

12

that they may not believe and be saved: An addition to Mark in later Christian language (cf. A. 14⁹; 16³¹; Eph. 2⁸). Some take it as an equivalent for the words omitted from the Isaiah quotation in v. 10, which makes impenitence and damnation the work of the devil and not of parables.

13

receive it: For 'receive the word', not elsewhere in the gospels, cf. A. 8¹⁴; 11¹; 17¹¹; I Thess. 1⁶; 2¹³ for receiving the Christian message.

in time of temptation: More general than Mark's 'tribulation or persecution on account of the word'; cf. A. 14²²; 20¹⁹; II Tim. 4²ᶠᶠ·; I Cor. 10¹³; James 1²; I Peter 4¹²; Rev. 3¹⁰.

fall away: aphistanai = 'apostasize', not elsewhere in the gospels in this sense; cf. I Tim. 4¹; Heb. 3¹².

14

pleasures: hēdonai, only here in the gospels; cf. Tit. 3³; James 4¹ᶠᶠ·; II Peter 2¹³.

life: bios, in this sense only here in the gospels; cf. I Tim. 2²; I John 2¹⁶; 3¹⁷.

15

hold it fast: Luke's addition; cf. I Cor. 11²; 2¹⁵; Heb. 3⁶; A. 9²³.

patience: hupomonē, elsewhere in the gospels 21¹⁹ (see note); cf. James 1³ᶠ·; Col. 1¹¹.

16–18

In Mark 4²¹⁻²⁵ a series of cryptic and loosely connected sayings is introduced as spoken to an unspecified audience ('them' could be either the inner circle of Mark 4¹⁰ or the crowds of 4³³). Luke makes this a single unit, which runs straight on as an extension of the interpretation of the parable spoken to disciples. For this he omits Mark 4²³ as repetition and the reference to 'the measure' Mark 4²⁴ (already used at 6³⁸), revises with reference to variant versions of the sayings in Q, and articulates the whole ('And' or 'But', v. 16, untranslated in RSV, *For,* v. 17, *then, for,* v. 18). He also modifies the sense. In

Mark the sayings are curiously formulated in terms of purpose, and would appear to present the hiddenness of the kingdom as a temporary necessity with a view to future manifestation ('brought in to be . . . and not . . .?', 'nothing hid, except to be . . .'). In Luke eventuality replaces purpose. The sayings now disavow secrecy, and become assurances that all will be made plain.

16

This is recast as in 11³³ = Matt. 5¹⁵, Q, with *No one after lighting* (*haptein* = 'kindle' + A. 28²), and *those who enter may see. covers it with a vessel* in place of Mark's 'under a bushel-measure' makes the two halves of the sentence evenly balanced, and the word order *may see the light* makes it an exact chiasmus. In Mark 4²¹ 'the lamp' (a definite article in the Greek) could be precise; for 'lamp' as a figure for the kingdom given by God to David, cf. Ps. 132¹⁷; II Kings 8¹⁹; I Kings 11³⁶; 15⁴; 'brought to be put under a bushel' could comment on the present contradictory state of the kingdom by means of an action as senseless in illumination as is random sowing in farming. Here it is a piece of general wisdom. No one in his right mind behaves in this way with lamps, which is guaranteed by the following statement (*for*) that nothing remains concealed. There is a parallel in Gospel of Thomas 33b, which corresponds more closely. though not exactly, with Luke's form here and at 11³³, and is connected with proclaiming from housetops.

17

The first half is a chiasmus, and in the second the verb is at the end. Again the idea of purpose in Mark is replaced by consequence. Truth will out. Some take vv. 16–17 of the need of the disciples to be missionaries, but the following injunction (*then*, v. 18) is concerned with their understanding, as is Luke's addition here of *shall not be known* (so 11³³ = Matt. 10²⁶, Q), which makes a connection with knowing the secrets of the kingdom (v. 10).

18

how you hear: In place of Mark's curious 'what you hear'.

for to him who has will more be given . . .: A proverbial statement capable of varied application – in 19²⁶ to stewardship in the kingdom. Here it may refer to the special kind of hearing required, i.e. in an honest and good heart (v. 15), which produces fruit (further knowledge of the secrets?).

thinks he has: This rationalizes the extreme paradox in Mark (contrast 19²⁶).

8¹⁹⁻²¹ = Mark 3³¹⁻³⁵

HEARERS AND DOERS OF THE WORD

¹⁹ *Then his mother and his brothers came to him, but they could not reach him for the crowd.* ²⁰ *And he was told, 'Your mother and your brothers are standing outside, desiring to see you.'* ²¹ *But he said to them, 'My mother and my brothers are those who hear the word of God and do it.'*

The Markan section on parables could be said to begin, not at Mark 4¹ but at Mark 3²²⁻³⁰, where Jesus instructs the crowds 'in parables' (Mark 3²³) in reply to the accusation about Beelzebul. This is sandwiched between an obscure reference to 'his friends' (Mark 3²¹; so RSV for *hoi par autou*, but Bauer suggests 'family' or 'relations'), who wish to apprehend him as being mad, and a visit of his family (possibly the same persons) for reasons unstated, in the context of which Jesus pronounces his true family to be those sitting around him, who do the will of God (Mark 3³¹⁻³⁵). In revising this whole Markan section Luke has preferred the longer version of the Beelzebul controversy in a different setting (11¹⁴⁻²³ = Matt. 12²⁴⁻³⁰), and has concentrated on the single parable of the sower and its attendant interpretation and sayings, omitting the other parables in Mark and the summary in Mark 4³³ᶠ·. He has transposed the visit of the family to serve as a conclusion to his parable section. To do this he has both remodelled it and modified its sense.

19

his mother and his brothers: A curious designation of the family, perhaps because Joseph is dead, taken from Mark 3³¹⁻³³ (cf. John 2¹²). It is not found again in the Gospel. Luke omits Mark 3²¹, and there is no suggestion here that they were those who thought Jesus mad. They are absent from 4¹⁶⁻³⁰, contrast Mark 6¹⁻⁶. They reappear in A. 1¹⁴ along with the apostles and 'the women' as believers. *his mother* was last mentioned at 2⁵¹ in terms which suggest that she would be a believer, and does not appear again in the Gospel. *his brothers* (*adelphoi*) are mentioned only here in the Gospel. In the light of 2⁷ they would most naturally be blood brothers born to Mary after Jesus (for the possibility that, at any rate in Mark, *adelphoi* could have a wider meaning of 'relations', see Fitzmyer, pp. 723f.). There is no reference to hostility or unbelief on their part, as in John 7³, ⁵.

came: *paraginesthai,* Lukan. No object of their coming is indicated.

reach: suntunchanein, elsewhere in the Greek Bible only II Macc. 8^{14}.

for the crowd: Since the previous parable has not been interpreted in private (Mark 4^{10}) the crowd of 8^4 is still present as a setting, and it is they who provide the only obstacle to access to Jesus.

20

was told: apangellein, Lukan; with *paraginesthai* A. 5^{25}; 28^{21}.

standing outside: An awkward relic of Mark 3^{31}, where it refers to outside the house.

desiring to see you: For 'seeking you' in Mark 3^{32}, which, if taken with Mark 3^{21}, could have a hostile intent. Again no purpose is stated.

21

In Mark 3^{33-35} the response of Jesus is in three stages: (i) a rhetorical question, 'Who are my mother and my brothers?', which could be dismissive of the physical family; (ii) an indicative statement, 'Here are . . .', pointing to his hearers as his family (in the view of some this is where the pericope originally ended); (iii) a generalizing statement defining his family as whoever does the will of God. Luke omits (i) and (ii), and concludes with a revised version of (iii). The Greek, however, is unusual – literally 'mother of me and brethren of me (the nouns without the article), these are those hearing and doing (participles)'. This can be given the generalizing sense of RSV, *My mother and my brothers are those who hear the word of God and do it*, which establishes the basis of Jesus' kindred without necessarily excluding his physical family. Or it could be rendered 'are these, those who are hearing and doing . . .', in which 'these' indicates the audience, as in (ii) above. Fitzmyer (p. 725) interprets very differently, taking *mother* and *brothers* as pendant nominatives ('as to my mother and my brothers') and 'these' as resumptive ('it is they who are hearing and doing . . .'), so that it is his kindred who are held up as model disciples.

hear the word of God and do it: An awkward revision of Mark 3^{35} – *do* goes with 'will' not with *word*, which is heard – which results from Luke's fresh setting at the end of a parable section on hearing the word of God.

$8^{22}-9^{50}$ THE MYSTERY OF THE PERSON OF JESUS

This constitutes a single section made from material selected from Mark but reproduced in Mark's sequence. It begins with four mighty works in two pairs (8^{22-56}), which are followed by an extension through the Twelve of the twin activities of preaching and healing, and by Herod's consequent enquiry (9¹⁻⁹). Then comes the supreme miracle of the feeding, which is brought into immediate proximity to two moments of revelation. The first is when Peter, in response to the prayer of Jesus, confesses him the Christ, and the first announcement is made of the suffering of the Son of man, and a promise given of the vision of the kingdom. The second is the direct revelation by God himself, in response to the prayer of Jesus, of him as the elect Son (9¹⁰⁻³⁶). The section closes with four units – the exorcism of an epileptic, the second prediction of the passion, teaching on true greatness and the anonymous exorcist. The last rounds off admirably with *he that is not against you is for you* (9⁵⁰), while Luke's alteration of 'was not following us' (Mark 9³⁸) to *does not follow with us* (9⁴⁹) prepares for the journey of Jesus and his disciples to Jerusalem in 9⁵¹ff..

The section thus constructed has as a dominant motif 'Who is Jesus?' Hence the question at the beginning (8²⁵). The whole region of the Gerasenes (so Luke, 8³⁷) in fear beg Jesus to leave, while the demoniac proclaims what Jesus has done for him (8³⁸⁻³⁹). Jesus himself declares (so Luke, 8⁴⁶) that power has gone out from him. The resuscitation of Jairus' daughter takes place in secrecy, and to the amazement of the parents (8⁵¹⁻⁵⁶), and the extension of Jesus' powers to the Twelve makes Herod ask 'who is this?' (9⁹). The crucial question 'who do you say that I am?' is asked by Jesus himself (9²⁰), and the divine voice itself declares to an inner circle the answer to the question, and urges them to listen to him (9³⁵). Jesus affirms the incompatibility between himself and this generation (9⁴¹), and urgently (so Luke, 9⁴⁴) repeats the prophecy of the passion, which (so Luke stresses) the disciples completely fail to understand (9⁴⁴⁻⁴⁵). Jesus then declares that to receive him is to receive him who has sent him (9⁴⁸), and that others who use his name effectively in exorcism belong with his disciples (9⁵⁰).

8²²⁻²⁵ = Mark 4³⁵⁻⁴¹

THE STILLING OF THE STORM

²²*One day he got into a boat with his disciples, and he said to them, 'Let us go across to the other side of the lake.' So they set out,* ²³*and as they sailed he fell asleep. And a storm of wind came down on the lake, and they were filling with*

water, and were in danger. ²⁴And they went and woke him, saying, 'Master, Master, we are perishing!' And he awoke and rebuked the wind and the raging waves; and they ceased, and there was a calm. ²⁵He said to them, 'Where is your faith?' And they were afraid, and they marvelled, saying to one another, 'Who then is this, that he commands even wind and water, and they obey him?'

The great significance of this event in the tradition is indicated, as often in miracle stories, by the concluding chorus (v. 25), where the implied answer to the disciples' question is that Jesus, like God, is lord of the forces of nature, and as such is the saviour of his church and the creator of its faith. It is, however, incorrectly termed a 'nature miracle', since this particular disorder in nature is treated as the work of the demon world and is quelled by exorcism. Thus Jesus' lordship over nature and his salvation of men are by way of his domination of the evil cosmic powers.

Luke tells the story in a less vigorous but more polished manner than Mark (there is possible influence from Jonah 1). In v. 22 *he* renders 'it came to pass and he' (for which see on 5¹); *got into, embainein,* the technical term for 'embark'; *set out, anagein,* only L–A in the NT in the technical nautical sense of 'to put to sea'. In v. 23 *sailed, plein,* + four times in A., Rev. 18¹⁷; the mention of Jesus' sleep before the storm is more elegant narrative; *fell asleep, aphupnoun,* ++, rare in this sense, its meaning being generally 'to wake from sleep'; *were filling with, sumplērousthai* + Jer. 25¹² in the Greek Bible, its meaning with ships being generally 'to be manned'; *were in danger, kinduneuein,* + I Cor. 15³⁰, rare in LXX; cf. Jonah 1⁴. In v. 24 *raging, kludōn* = 'swell', cf. Jonah 1⁴, ¹¹ᶠ·; *ceased, pauesthai* used absolutely + 11¹; A. 20¹; I Cor. 13⁸.

22

One day he got into a boat: Having abandoned the setting in Mark 4¹ of a boat used for teaching in parables, and having transposed the visit of the family to conclude the parable section, Luke also abandons Mark 4³⁵⁻³⁶, with the departure from the crowd, the obscure 'they took him with them, just as he was', and the 'other boats', which play no further part in Mark's story. He is content with the briefest and vaguest of connections – *one day* (see on 5¹⁷), and *a boat,* not 'the boat' of Mark 4³⁶.

to the other side: From Mark, where probably, though not clearly, it means the other side from Capernaum. It is even more vague in Luke.

the lake: See on 5¹.

fell asleep: From Mark. but briefer. It is not clear whether this detail simply looks back to Jonah 1⁵ᶠ·, or is intended to provide a foil for the disciples' panic, or to suggest that Jesus lives permanently in the calm which he is to produce.

a storm of wind: lailaps = a hurricane, such as is common on the sea of Galilee, since the wind is funnelled between the surrounding hills. But in Mark certainly, and here probably, something more than a natural phenomenon is intended. For the Hebrews the sea was a symbol of turbulence (Ps. 107²³ᶠᶠ·), and in the form of 'the abyss', which Luke introduces at 8³¹, was the primeval sea or chaos, controlled by God (Gen. 1²; Job. 38⁸ᶠᶠ·; Isa. 51⁹ᶠ·; II Enoch 28¹ᶠᶠ·), but still a sphere of the domain of evil, and the abode of disobedient spirits to be overcome in the last days (II Enoch 29⁵; Assumption of Moses 10⁶; Rev. 9¹; 21¹). In Dan. 7² the winds are associated with the sea and stir it up (cf. IV Ezra 13²).

24

Master, Master, we are perishing: For *Master* as Luke's equivalent for Mark's 'Teacher', see on 5⁵, and for the duplication for emphasis, cf. 10⁴¹. This is the kernel of the story, but it can hardly be given a naturalistic basis. It is not said who the disciples were, but their reaction of terror is not that of men who were likely to be thoroughly familiar with local storms, especially if they included any of the fishermen who were amongst the first disciples (5¹⁻¹¹). Nor is it evident why they should appeal to Jesus; to be their Master would not mean that he was specially qualified to handle boats in storms (in 'do you not care if we perish?', Mark 4³⁸, they speak like strangers rather than disciples). Thus the language is already symbolic, and such as to make the story from the first a paradigm of the religious truth that Jesus is the saviour of those who are perishing (cf. Matt. 8²⁵, 'Save, Lord; we are perishing').

rebuked the wind and the raging waves: For Mark's 'rebuked the wind, and said to the sea, "Peace" (lit. 'be silent'), "Be still" ' (lit. 'be muzzled', see on 4³⁵), where the storm is addressed as a demon and exorcized with a binding spell. Luke may have omitted these injunctions as inappropriate for inanimate objects, but his reduced form *rebuked* could still refer to an adjuration to a demon (see on 4³⁵, ³⁹).

25

Where is your faith?: Luke omits the charge of cowardice in Mark, and his form of the question suggests a temporary loss of the faith which, according to 8⁴⁻²¹, the disciples already possess rather than a total absence of it in 'Have you no faith? (or 'Do you not yet have faith?') in Mark. Again the language seems to be dictated by the religious message and not by any actual situation. Generally faith in such stories means confidence in Jesus' powers as a thaumaturge, and is mentioned either before the performance of the miracle (5²⁰, and here

Matt. 8²⁶) or as a comment on it (7⁵⁰, etc.). Here it seems to mean confidence that no harm of the kind represented by 'perishing' could possibly come while Jesus is present as saviour.

and marvelled: Luke may have taken this from Mark 5²⁰, where he removes it (8³⁹) to procure a better ending. Here he adds it to qualify the fear, which is customary in such stories, and to lead to the question that follows.

Who then is this . . . obey him?: This supplies interrogatively the theological point. In the light of such passages as Ps. 69¹ᶠᶠ·, ¹⁵ᶠᶠ·; 89⁹ᶠ·; 93³ᶠ·; 29³; 46², the answer to the question is God, or one who wields directly the divine power. But Luke has assimilated the question to Mark 1²⁷, which deduces from a single exorcism the lordship of Jesus over the whole demonic world, and this may be the sense here.

8²⁶⁻³⁹ = Mark 5¹⁻²⁰
THE EXORCISM OF LEGION

²⁶*Then they arrived at the country of the Gerasenes,*★ *which is opposite Galilee.* ²⁷*And as he stepped out on land, there met him a man from the city who had demons; for a long time he had worn no clothes, and he lived not in a house but among the tombs.* ²⁸*When he saw Jesus, he cried out and fell down before him, and said with a loud voice, 'What have you to do with me, Jesus, Son of the Most High God? I beseech you, do not torment me.'* ²⁹*For he had commanded the unclean spirit to come out of the man. (For many a time it had seized him; he was kept under guard, and bound with chains and fetters, but he broke the bonds and was driven by the demon into the desert.)* ³⁰*Jesus then asked him, 'What is your name?' And he said, 'Legion'; for many demons had entered him.* ³¹*And they begged him not to command them to depart into the abyss.* ³²*Now a large herd of swine was feeding there on the hillside; and they begged him to let them enter these. So he gave them leave.* ³³*Then the demons came out of the man and entered the swine, and the herd rushed down the steep bank into the lake and were drowned.*

³⁴*When the herdsmen saw what had happened, they fled, and told it in the city and in the country.* ³⁵*Then people went out to see what had happened, and they came to Jesus, and found the man from whom the demons had gone, sitting at the feet of Jesus, clothed and in his right mind; and they were afraid.* ³⁶*And those who had seen it told them how he who had been possessed with demons was healed.* ³⁷*Then all the people of the surrounding country of the Gerasenes*★

asked him to depart from them; for they were seized with fear; so he got into the boat and returned. ³⁸ *The man from whom the demons had gone begged that he might be with him; but he sent him away. saying,* ³⁹*'Return to your home, and declare how much God has done for you.' And he went away, proclaiming throughout the whole city how much Jesus had done for him.*

* Other ancient authorities read *Gadarenes*, others *Gergesenes*

The close connection in Hebrew thought between hostile powers in nature and the tormenting spirits (SB II, p. 9), and the use of the storm figure for disorder and madness in mankind (Ps. 65^{5ff.}; 46²⁻⁶; Isa. 17^{12ff.}), make the juxtaposition of this and the preceding pericope significant. While the storm at sea is represented as a demon, whose exorcism brings calm, the description of the demoniac here, which is unique in Mark for its elaborateness and is only slightly attenuated in Luke, is designed to depict a tempestuous and storm-ridden creature, whose exorcism involves the return of demons to the deep. The weight lies not on the actual exorcism, which in Luke (v. 29a) is referred to retrospectively and in parenthesis, but upon the magnitude and drama of the conflict between Jesus and the demon world and the effect on the spectators. To this the protracted form of the narrative, and its detailed thaumaturgical features ('fantastic and grotesque', Fitzmyer, p. 734), contribute. Thus the demand for the surrender of the demon's name is primarily to bring to light the extent of Jesus' power over a veritable army of demons. While the previous miracle concerns the lordship of Jesus in relation to disciples and their faith, here disciples play no part and there is no mention of faith. The locale is heathen, and the conflict a violent one between 'the Most High God' incorporate in his 'Son' and heathen abomination and uncleanness typified in the swine. The conclusion is neither a chorus of wonder nor an injunction to silence, but – a unique feature in exorcisms – the enlisting of the erstwhile demoniac, now 'saved' by Jesus and become his disciple (both Lukan additions), as a missionary to his own terrified and hostile city. Many have followed Wellhausen in supposing this a folk tale of a Jewish exorcist later transferred to Jesus; but since Jesus was a Jewish exorcist operating in Galilee and its environs this hardly seems necessary.

26–29

Luke begins more stylishly – vv. 26–27a, *arrived, kataplein* + + = 'sail down (to the shore)', *opposite, antipera* + +, *met, hupantān* – but is then content to reproduce, comparatively unaltered, the diffuse and lively Markan original. The over-loaded sentence in Mark 5³⁻⁵, where the illness has to be deduced from the demoniac's behaviour, is divided into two. In v. 27b, when the man is first introduced, there is a description of his general manner of life – *a long time, chronos hikanos*, only L–A in the NT, *had worn no clothes* supplies the basis, lack-ing in Mark, for *clothed* in v. 35. In v. 29b, in parenthesis and as an explanation of Jesus' repeated attempts at exorcism, there is a more particular account of the activity of the possessing demon and its severity – *many a time, pollois chronois* (this could mean for 'many years', Bauer, s.v. *chronos*), *seized, sunharpazein* + + of paroxysm, *into the desert*, the special abode of demons.

26

the country of the Gerasenes: This name is found as a variant with 'Gadarenes' and 'Gergesenes' in the manuscript tradition of all three synoptic accounts. The general critical judgment is that *Gerasenes* was the original reading in Mark 5¹ and was taken over by Luke here – it is strongly attested by p⁷⁵ B D the old Latin – and that 'Gadarenes' was the original reading in Matt. 8²⁸, being a deliberate alteration of Mark to bring the region nearer to the lake. But 'Gergesenes' is comparatively well attested in Luke – ℵ L Θ fam 1, 33, Bohairic and Armenian versions – and is printed in the text in the United Bible Societies edition, *Gerasenes* being judged an assimilation to Mark. The problem was known to Origen. In his *Commentary on John* (6.24), where he says that he had visited places to enquire about the footsteps of the Lord but is also con-cerned with the prophetic character of place names, he dismisses 'Gerasenes' because Gerasa is a town in Arabia 'and has near it neither sea nor lake', and for the same reason 'Gadarenes' from Gadara in Judaea. He then continues, 'But Gergesa, from which "Gergesenes" is taken, is an old town in the region of the lake, on the edge of which is a steep place, from which it is pointed out that the swine were cast down by the demons. Now the meaning of Gergesa is "dwell-ing of the casters out", a prophetic reference to the conduct towards the Saviour of the citizens of those places who "besought him to depart from their coasts".' It is not clear whether 'Gergesenes' is here a textual variant on which Origen is commenting, or is his own conjecture based on his supposedly local knowledge, which was inaccurate in any case, since Gerasa = Jerash was not in Arabia nor Gadara in Judaea, but both in the Decapolis, the first some forty miles south-east and the latter some twelve miles south of the sea of Galilee. Excavations have been made at a town on the shore with the Arabic name Kursi, but this does not have overhanging cliffs. It is unlikely that either evange-lists or subsequent scribes had any reliable topographical knowledge to decide between what would have seemed outlandish sounding names. In the view of Dibelius (*Tradition*, p. 73n.) the variants arose from attempts to identify the un-named city (vv. 27, 34ff. = Mark 5¹⁴) by reference to its region (*country*) and the inhabitants.

opposite Galilee: Luke refers indirectly to the Galilean character of the previous events, and indicates a pagan region for what is to follow, even if he omits the reference to the Decapolis in Mark 5²⁰.

had demons: This indicates already the plurality of the possession in a way that Mark's more usual 'with an unclean spirit' could not.

no clothes . . . among the tombs: Nakedness is mentioned as a feature of demoniacs; for graves as a resort of demons, SB I, p. 491. For God as the deliverer of such, Ps. 67⁷ (LXX); Isa. 65⁴.

28

This verse is moulded by the ideas and language of Hellenistic magic. Mark 5⁷ depicts a battle of spiritual powers in which the demoniac acknowledges Jesus by kneeling to him, but nevertheless counter-attacks through the knowledge of Jesus' name and status. He attempts to ward off exorcism by an invocatory formula summoning superior power, 'I adjure you by God' = 'I invoke God against you'. This is somewhat softened by Luke with *fell down before him* (unless the verb *prospiptein* is given a violent meaning, as by Fitzmyer, p. 738, 'lunged at him'), and *I beseech you*, which makes the demoniac an already vanquished suppliant for mercy.

cried out: For *krazein*, applied to demonic cries, see *TDNT* III, pp. 898f.

What have you to do with me?: For this apotropaic formula, see on 4³⁴.

Jesus, Son of the Most High God: Possession of the name and status, with the power that conferred, was a crucial weapon for both participants in a combat of this kind (cf. v. 30). Sometimes it is introduced by 'I know who you are' (cf. 4³⁴); here it takes the form of a direct naming.

the Most High God: This is to be distinguished from 'the most High', which is a pious Jewish periphrasis for God (as in 6³⁵; 1³², ⁷⁶). It is basically a pagan title, adopted in the LXX, where it is predominantly on the lips of non-Israelites for Yahweh (Gen. 14¹⁸ff.; Num. 24¹⁶; Isa. 14¹⁴; Dan. 3²⁶), and it is found in Hellenistic magical formulae (Hull, *Hellenistic Magic*, p. 67). *Son of the Most High God*, only here and Mark 5⁷ in the NT (cf. A. 16¹⁷), is thus a christological confession in heathen form.

do not torment me: As For (29) shows, the torment was to be exorcised.[h]

[h] For *torment* (*basanos*) as a technical term for the punishment of a demon by superior magic, see S. Eitrem, *Some Notes on the Demonology of the New Testament*, 2nd ed., Symbolae Osloenses 20, 1966, p. 71.

29

he had commanded: The verb is in the imperfect = 'he was commanding' or 'he repeatedly commanded', indicating the difficulty of the case, which the parenthesis in v. 29b accounts for.

30

What is your name?: The severity of the case is shown by the fact that Jesus here, though not elsewhere, employs the common exorcistic technique of making the patient expose his name and so his condition (Hull, op. cit. p. 69). In doing this he begins to acknowledge defeat, and can only attempt to negotiate terms.

'Legion'; for many demons had entered him: From Mark 5⁹, with 'for we are many' turned into an explanatory comment. There has now to be an awkward alternation between the singular 'he' of the man and the plural 'they' of the possessing demons. *Legion* (*legiōn*, feminine) was a Latin loan word in Greek for a body of front line soldiers in the Roman army, generally 6000 strong, and often with the same number of auxiliaries attached. It is used here, but as masculine, to express plural possession in the sense, not of multiple personality (the demons speak together and with one voice), but of irresistible force (v. 29b). It possibly represents a final resistance; their strength is in their numbers, which Jesus will find too much for him. A legion is unlikely, however, to have sunk as low as the 2000 required by the number of the swine (Mark 5¹³), and in popular speech the word may have meant simply a large number. In Matt. 26⁵³, its only other occurrence in the NT, it reflects speculation on the hierarchy of the heavenly host, and the demonic host of the rival kingdom of Satan may have been thought of as organized in troops (Rev. 12⁷ᶠ·; Matt. 25⁴¹; II Enoch 29⁴ᶠ·; Test. Asher 6; SB I, pp. 983f.), the demoniac considering himself possessed by one such troop.

31–33

A strange denouement conceived in terms of thaumaturgical technique. There is no specific word or moment of exorcism, which has been going on continuously (v. 29a), but a bargaining between the demons, who are now willing to depart, and the exorcist, who is in a position to direct their departure. What follows is an instance of a feature common in thaumaturgy, the demonstration of spiritual success by external phenomena (Dibelius, *Tradition*, p. 89). But Bultmann (*History*, p. 210), following Wellhausen, thinks that there is a more particular point of 'the devil deceived'. In return for leaving the man the demons extract a concession to be allowed to take up another habitation in the same region (for domicile as a problem for demons, cf. 11²⁴ᶠᶠ·). But their appropriate choice of unclean swine proves their undoing, as they perish through the panic of the swine their possession produces. Luke's deliberate alteration of 'not out of the country' (Mark 5¹⁰) to *not into the abyss* (v. 31) may be intended to underline this. For *the abyss* was a term both for the deep (sea) and for the underworld prison in which the evil spirits were to be locked up until the end (I Enoch 18–21; Rev. 9¹ᶠ·, ¹¹; 20¹). So by way of the drowning swine the demons actually go to their destined and dreaded place of punishment.

34–39

In contrast to other such stories the sequel is almost as long as the account of the exorcism. If this is not the garrulousness of a secular tale later transferred to Jesus (so Dibelius, *Tradition*, pp. 87ff., 101f.), it may be due to the Gentile provenance of the incident, and reflect the importance attached in the evangelism of the early church to mastery over the spirits and magic of the pagan world; see Harnack, *The Mission and Expansion of Christianity* I, pp. 125ff. ('It was as exorcists that the Christians went out into the world', p. 131), and the evidence from the Fathers assembled there; cf. also A. 16¹⁶ᶠᶠ·; 19¹¹⁻⁴¹; Matt. 21¹⁻¹²; Mark 16¹⁷.

Four elements are interwoven.

(i) In v. 34, through the flight of the swineherds, knowledge of the event is extended to the city and region, and eventually to the whole population (v. 37).

(ii) In vv. 35–36 the demoniac is seen as completely recovered from his dire condition and restored to sanity (cf. the repeated designations of the man as *from whom the demons had gone*, v. 35, *who had been possessed with demons*, v. 36, and *from whom the demons had gone*, v. 38). He speaks in his own name (*begged*, v. 38) and no longer in the mixed singular and plural of possession, and (so Luke adds) has been 'saved' (*healed*, v. 36, renders *sōzein*, with its double meaning, see on 7⁵⁰), and sits at Jesus feet as a disciple (v. 35; cf. 10³⁹).

(iii) In vv. 37–38 the unanimous reaction of the inhabitants is not so much to reject Jesus as to secure his departure, because they were *seized with great fear*, a Lukan addition, probably denoting pagan terror at such a manifestation of supernatural powers (contrast the godly fear of 5²⁶; 7¹⁶).

(iv) In vv. 38–39 the exorcized man asks to accompany Jesus back to Jewish soil as a permanent companion disciple. This he is refused, and is instead commissioned to return to the home he had previously abandoned (v. 27), and there to *declare* (*diēgeisthai* = 'report', as in 9¹⁰; A. 9²⁷; 12¹⁷) what God had done for him. Further, he becomes a lone and advance Gentile evangelist in *proclaiming* (*kērussein*, see on 3³) the mighty work of God himself in the work of Jesus (*how much God has done for you, how much Jesus had done for him*). On this Christian missionary note Luke concludes, omitting Mark's conventional ending 'and all men marvelled'.

8⁴⁰⁻⁵⁶ = Mark 5²¹⁻⁴³

THE HEALING OF THE WOMAN WITH AN ISSUE AND THE RAISING OF JAIRUS' DAUGHTER

⁴⁰*Now when Jesus returned, the crowd welcomed him, for they were all waiting for him.* ⁴¹*And there came a man named Jairus, who was a ruler of the synagogue; and falling at Jesus' feet he besought him to come to his house,* ⁴²*for he had an only daughter, about twelve years of age, and she was dying.*

As he went, the people pressed round him. ⁴³*And a woman who had had a flow of blood for twelve years* and could not be healed by any one,* ⁴⁴*came up behind him, and touched the fringe of his garment; and immediately her flow of blood ceased.* ⁴⁵*And Jesus said, 'Who was it that touched me?' When all denied it, Peter† said, 'Master, the multitudes surround you and press upon you!'* ⁴⁶*But Jesus said, 'Some one touched me; for I perceive that power has gone forth from me.'* ⁴⁷*And when the woman saw that she was not hidden, she came trembling, and falling down before him declared in the presence of all the people why she had touched him, and how she had been immediately healed.* ⁴⁸*And he said to her, 'Daughter, your faith has made you well; go in peace.'*

⁴⁹*While he was still speaking, a man from the ruler's house came and said, 'Your daughter is dead; do not trouble the Teacher any more.'* ⁵⁰*But Jesus on hearing this answered him, 'Do not fear; only believe, and she shall be well.'* ⁵¹*And when he came to the house, he permitted no one to enter with him, except Peter and John and James, and the father and mother of the child.* ⁵²*And all were weeping and bewailing her; but he said, 'Do not weep; for she is not dead but sleeping.'* ⁵³*And they laughed at him, knowing that she was dead.* ⁵⁴*But taking her by the hand he called, saying, 'Child, arise.'* ⁵⁵*And her spirit returned, and she got up at once; and he directed that something should be given her to eat.* ⁵⁶*And her parents were amazed; but he charged them to tell no one what had happened.*

* Other ancient authorities add *and had spent all her living with physicians*

† Other ancient authorities add *and those who were with him*

These two incidents Luke leaves interwoven, as in Mark, but revises by slightly condensing and by refining, sometimes with language of a LXX flavour. They furnish notable instances of the wide reputation of Jesus as a healer and of his exercise of power, which Luke makes a self-confessed power (v. 46). Both are so described as to proclaim salvation through faith, especially by Luke (v. 50). Disciples are present (vv. 45, 51), but play a subordinate part. The stories are about Jesus and the two individuals concerned (*Daughter*, v. 48, *do not fear*, v. 50), with, in the first case, the previous enthusiastic crowd (vv. 4, 19f.) still in attendance (v. 40, *welcomed, apodechesthai*, only L–A in the NT; *waiting for, prosdokān*, is Lukan, but no reason for their expectation is given), and, in the second case, a group of mourners (v. 52).

ᴔᴔ

40

Here only four words agree with Mark. Presumably Jesus is still on the move (8¹ff.). *returned*, the Lukan *hupostrephein*, is very general; perhaps returned from foreign soil, but it is not said to where.

41

And there came a man . . . who was: Literally, 'And behold (LXX) there came a man . . . and this one . . .'. For this form of sentence cf. 19²; *houtos* = 'this (man)' for 'he' cf. 7¹².

named: Generally Luke writes *onomati* = 'by name' (as in Mark 5²²). Here he has 'to whom the name', as in 1²⁶ᶠ·; 2²⁵; A. 13⁶.

was: huparchein, of a continuing state or status, only Luke in the gospels.

a ruler of the synagogue: Mark has the compound *archisunagōgos* = 'synagogue-head', as does Luke in 13¹⁴; A. 13¹⁵; 18⁸, ¹⁷. Here he alters to *archōn* (= 'one ruling', participle used as a noun) *tēs sunagōgēs* = 'of the synagogue', perhaps in order to explain the term at its first occurrence (Matt. 9¹⁸ has here simply 'a ruler'). The office is attested for both Jewish and Gentile assemblies, but in Judaism *archisunagōgos* denoted specifically one who had general supervision of the order and arrangements of synagogue worship in a place. It could also be an honorary title borne by more than one person in a place (cf. Mark 5²²; A. 13¹⁵). Thus a local religious official knows of Jesus' reputation as a healer and solicits his aid.

to his house: Advanced in the story from its position in Mark 5³⁸. The reason for his petition, on the man's own lips in Mark, here becomes a statement (contrast the opposite in v. 46).

42

only: Luke, whose only source here is Mark, cannot have known this. It is added to heighten the pathos (cf. 9³⁸), thus making a pair with 7¹².

about twelve years of age: Advanced in the story from its belated mention in Mark 5⁴². Luke is fond of 'about' with numbers.

pressed round: An odd word, *sunpnigein*, meaning 'to choke', as in the only other NT instances, Mark 4.⁷, ¹⁹; Matt. 13²²; Luke 8¹⁴; the last of which may still be in Luke's mind. The pressing crowd provides the setting for what is to follow.

43

a woman with an issue of blood: issue is *rhusis* = 'flow'; hence *ceased* ('stopped') in v. 44. The reference here is to Lev. 15²⁵⁻³⁰, where, in the context of the preservation of Israel from ritual uncleanness, discharges of blood other than, or beyond, menstruation are treated very seriously as defiling everyone or everything coming into contact with them. On their cessation a seven-day quarantine is prescribed, ending with sacrifice which restores the woman to the life of the community. *for twelve years,* i.e. without cessation, thus indicates the severity of the woman's condition. 'and had spent all her living with physicians' is a more concise and elegant version of Mark 5²⁶, and could have come from Luke's hand, but its omission in B (D), the Sinaitic Syriac and Sahidic and Armenian versions suggests it is a scribal addition.

44

fringe: kraspedon, if genuine (it is omitted in D the Old Latin and Marcion) is an agreement with Matt. 9²⁰, and may be a reminiscence of Mark 6⁵⁶, its only occurrence in Mark (omitted by Luke). It could refer either to the extremity of the outer garment or to one of the four tassels that could be worn on it. In either case the power resident in Jesus is regarded as effective even at the furthest point.

45-46

In this revision of Mark may be seen two of Luke's editorial habits, (i) that of generalizing the scene with *all,* though it is not plausible that each member of such a crowd should be interrogated and deny, and (ii) that of particularizing in dialogue, here with *Peter* in place of 'his disciples' in Mark 5³¹ (the variant 'and those who were with him' should probably be omitted with p⁷⁵B and others). But most important is Luke's concern to explicate further the *power* (*dunamis*) of Jesus. This he has already introduced in 4¹⁴ as the driving power of the spirit, in 4³⁶ along with authority over demons, at 5¹⁷ as the power of God made present at the time for healing, and at 6¹⁹ to explain why the sick touched Jesus (it will recur at 24⁴⁹; A. 1⁸; 3¹²; 4⁷; 10³⁸). Here Luke omits all references to the woman's own consciousness in Mark 5²⁸⁻²⁹ – her previous knowledge of Jesus' deeds, her expression of her intentions and her interior knowledge of her cure. He replaces this by the consciousness of Jesus. The question in Mark 5³⁰, 'Who touched my garments?', regarded there as nonsensical, is not adequately answered by reference to the contact of pressing crowds, since it implies that the *power* is a *mana* resident in Jesus, which is beyond his control and is automatically released by the special touch of someone who, deliberately and with faith in his powers, seeks it for healing. In v. 46 this is expressly put into the mouth of Jesus himself, who thus gives the reason for his question, which in Luke's form (*Who was it that touched me?*) emphasizes the touching. He knows that he must have been touched in this special way because it had been registered in his consciousness by a discharge of power. (For this magical conception of power in the ancient world and in the NT, especially L–A, see J. M. Hull, *Hellenistic Magic*, pp. 105–14.)

47

A heavily revised version of Mark 5³³. The woman takes Jesus' public statement about the emission of power as evidence that he has discovered her secret (*hidden* is the idiomatic *lanthanein* + A. 26²⁶; Mark 7²⁴; Heb. 13²; II Peter 3^{5, 8}). With the *trembling* and prostration appropriate in the presence of the numinous she makes public profession – *in the presence of all the people* is Luke's addition – of the reason for her action, i.e. as v. 47 makes clear, her confidence in the extent of the power of Jesus, and the immediacy of its result. Thus the unclean has made contact with the holy, and so far from either defiling it or being destroyed by it has released it.

48

For this formula in healing stories, see 7⁵⁰; 17¹⁹; 18⁴². In Mark 5³⁴ it relates the impersonal act of healing with the personal quality of saving faith, and is therefore followed, though illogically after the previous statement that the woman knew she had been healed, by a personal word effecting the cure. Luke omits this, so that *your faith* can here only mean confidence in Jesus as the source of power.

49–50
Almost verbatim from Mark.

49

While he was still speaking: This binds the two miracles together. Luke has an individual messenger for Mark's impersonal 'there came', and his message has greater finality – the verb *is dead*, in the perfect tense, stands at the beginning – and peremptoriness, *do not trouble . . . any more.* The opportunity for a cure is over, and Jesus' power stops short at death. This sets the scene for what follows.

50

Do not fear: This is generally uttered in the context of the appearance of the supernatural (cf. 1^{13, 30}; A. 18⁹; Mark 6⁵⁰). Here it is awkward as a transition.

Has Jairus at the news begun to show fear of death, or is he being reassured that his original request for recovery from sickness is still possible?

and she shall be well: sōthēsetai = also 'she shall be saved'. This addition by Luke to the command *only believe* makes the miracle conform in its own way to the interpretative formula in v. 48 *your faith has made you well* (saved you).

51–53

Luke's rewriting here is loose and confusing. In Mark 5³⁸⁻⁴⁰ Jesus is met on arrival by a throng of weeping mourners who mock him, and whom he ejects from the house, taking the three disciples and the parents into the part of the house where the child was. In Luke Jesus on arrival enters the house with the three disciples and the parents (the mother appears belatedly here); but *all who were weeping and bewailing her*, who are rebuked and who answer by mockery (vv. 52–53), must refer not to the five who have gone in, but to a crowd, which thus appears to be inside the house, and witnesses of the miracle.

51

Peter and John and James: The first appearance in Luke of an inner circle of three, which, for reasons not apparent, was established in the Twelve, and was allowed to share certain experiences of Jesus (cf. 9²⁸). The order John before James (cf. A. 1¹³) is probably due to the close association of John with Peter in A. (cf. A. 3¹; 8¹⁴), which is already there in Luke's identification of 'the two disciples' of Mark 11¹ with them. In Mark it is only they of the disciples, followers or crowd who are allowed to accompany Jesus to the house; in Luke only they who are allowed into it (is this for them to learn how to raise the dead? cf. A. 9³⁶⁻⁴¹).

52

she is not dead but sleeping: This statement, as a rebuke to mockery, is crucial in the context, but is nevertheless obscure. This is because of the ambivalence of the language used. Thus 'to sleep', generally *koimāsthai*, is common in Greek literature, the LXX and the NT as a synonym for death (e.g. I Cor. 15⁵¹), and occasionally the verb here *katheudein* is so used (Ps. 87⁶ LXX; Dan. 12²; I Thess. 5¹⁰). Further, the words used in the NT for resurrection – *egeirein* = 'to raise erect', in the middle 'to arise' (so v. 54), and *anistanai* = 'to get up' (so v. 55) – can also both mean 'to awake out of sleep'. For examples of this ambivalence, cf. the hymn in Eph. 5¹⁴, and the deliberate *double entendre* in John 11¹¹⁻¹³. Here, however, death is not spoken of as sleep but is contrasted with it – 'she is not dead but is dead' would be nonsense. The words can hardly represent an alternative diagnosis of the child's condition as not death but a coma – Luke's addition *knowing that she was dead*, v. 53, is substantiated by the return of her spirit, v. 55. Nor can they be a tautologous statement that all death is a sleep. Perhaps they are a way of saying that this particular death is not an instance of death proper with all its power and finality, since it is to be reversed and overcome by an 'awakening' at the hands of Jesus.

54

But taking her by the hand he called: Ignoring the mockery of the bystanders Jesus (*autos de* = 'but he') employs a gesture fitted for 'raising up', grasping by the hand (only here in Luke; with 'raise up', cf. Mark 9^{27}; 13^{1}; Matt. 12^{11}; A. 9^{41} of Peter raising Tabitha). He then summons the girl back from death with a shout; *called* is *phōnein*, which in L–A, when it does not mean 'to summon', is 'to shout' (cf. 16^{24}; for the idea John 11^{43}; A. 9^{40}).

Child, arise: As elsewhere Luke omits the Aramaic supplied here in Mark, and uses the nominative 'the child' as a vocative. *arise* is the word for resurrection, which could equally mean 'wake up' (cf. Eph. 5^{14}).

55

her spirit returned: An addition by Luke accounting for the result in terms of current belief that the *spirit* (*pneuma* here in the sense of the principle of life), though it may leave the body, remains for a time in the vicinity, and can be summoned back.

got up at once: This translation preserves the possible double meaning of *anestē* as 'arose' and 'woke up' (cf. A. 9^{40} 'opened her eyes'). The result was immediate as in vv. 44, 47; 4^{39}; 5^{25}; 13^{13}; A. 3^{7}. Luke omits 'and walked', and improves Mark's order by closing the scene with the command to give the girl food, the motive of which is to demonstrate the reality of her resuscitation to earthly existence (cf. $24^{41ff.}$).

56

The injunction to silence imposed by the Markan dogma of secrecy is reproduced. It is more than usually artificial in Mark, for how could the parents possibly conceal what had happened? It is even more so in the more public scene which Luke depicts, when all knew that she was dead.

9^{1-6} = Mark 6^{6-13}

THE MISSION OF THE TWELVE

9 And he called the twelve together and gave them power and authority over all demons and to cure diseases, ²and he sent them out to preach the kingdom of

God and to heal. ³*And he said to them, 'Take nothing for your journey, no staff, nor bag, nor bread, nor money; and do not have two tunics.* ⁴*And whatever house you enter, stay there, and from there depart.* ⁵*And wherever they do not receive you, when you leave that town shake off the dust from your feet as a testimony against them.'* ⁶*And they departed and went through the villages, preaching the gospel and healing everywhere.*

Luke passes over the rejection of Jesus in his home town, which stands on its own in Mark 6¹⁻⁵, as it disturbs the connection between Jesus' miracles and the extension of his powers through the Twelve, and he has already included the gist of it in 4¹⁶⁻³⁰.

The choice of the Twelve (6¹³ff.) and their existence as a group (8¹ff.) already betoken that the activity of Jesus, rabbi and healer, is directed to the whole nation, and that his intention is to constitute the true people of God, the Israel of the last days (22³⁰; cf. the Qumran Community Rule, 8¹, where so long as the twelve men and three priests are in the Council of the Community it will be established in truth, and be an Everlasting Plantation, a House of Holiness for Israel (Vermes, *Scrolls*, p. 85). Their sending out gives further expression to this, as the accent on 'to send out' (*apostellein*, frequent in the LXX for the divine mission of the prophets) is on the will and purpose of the sender and the commission he gives. It is, however, difficult to bring this mission into focus, as it is described only in the vaguest terms, and the instructions, which alone are preserved in detail, doubtless as models for later Christian missionaries, are obscure. In the perspective of the synoptic gospels (there is no such mission in John, but cf. John 4³⁸) its purpose is a temporary extension through the Twelve of Jesus' activity, and a rehearsal for their mission to the world (24⁴⁶ff.; A. 1⁸; Matt. 28¹⁶ff.). No motive, however, is given for such a mission, and there are statements in connection with it which could suggest that it was originally conceived as a single decisive mission to Israel to herald the end and to gather in the final harvest (10² = Matt. 9³⁷f.; 10¹⁴ = Matt. 10¹⁵; Matt. 10²³).

Luke differs in distributing the material available from Mark and Q in two such missions, that of the Twelve here and that of the Seventy (10¹⁻¹⁶). Here he reproduces Mark, but with reminiscences of Q represented in Matt. 10⁵ff. (see on 10¹ff.). Agreements with Matthew are: *gave, cure diseases* (v. 1), *preach the kingdom of God* (v. 2; cf. Matt. 10⁷), direct speech, *no staff, money* (v. 3) *whatever* (v. 4), *town, dust* (v. 5). By omission and alteration Luke produces a smoother version. The conferring of power and its purpose (v. 1), a sentence in four parts with two duplications, precedes the mission, which (v. 2) has a double object corresponding to what Luke omits from Mark 3¹⁴⁻¹⁵ in 6¹³. With the omission of 'belt' and 'sandals' and with *no staff* v. 3 is a sentence in four parts, the two middle parts making two pairs, with *bread (artos)* and *money (argurion)* placed together for alliteration. Verse 6 is balanced – Lukan are *went through, the villages, preaching the gospel* – and ends in typical Lukan fashion with *everywhere*.

∞

1

The conjunction of preaching and healing characterized the mission of Jesus, and is here perhaps a model for the similar conjunction in A. The relation between them is not obvious, and is variously expressed. In Mark the Twelve are sent to exorcize, though they preach repentance and heal the sick as well (Mark 6⁷, ¹³). Luke also emphasizes exorcism (*all* with *demons* is typically Lukan), but adds *to cure diseases*, which is then repeated (*to heal, iasthai*, Lukan) along with preaching as the object of the mission.

gave them power and authority: The transference of Jesus' power (here *power and authority*, a Lukan hendiadys, cf. 4³⁶) to his apostles was of vital importance to the church (A. 2⁴³; 3⁶; 4⁷; 5¹²; 9³⁴), but no account is given of how this was envisaged as taking place.

2

Luke omits Mark's 'two by two' (though he has it at 10¹), perhaps because, while apostolic practice sometimes followed this (A. 8¹⁴; 13²), it did not invariably do so (A. 9³²).

to preach the kingdom of God: Only in Luke is *the kingdom* the direct object of *to preach (kērussein)* both in the mission of Jesus and of the church (A. 20²⁵; 28³¹), for which preaching the gospel of the kingdom is a synonym (*euangelizesthai*, v. 6; cf. 4⁴³; 8¹). Whether this always means proclaiming the kingdom to be near, as in the parallel mission of the Seventy (10⁹, ¹¹), is not clear.

3

The missionary manner. Such injunctions are likely to have been preserved as guides to missionary practice, but there is difficulty, increased by variations between the evangelists, in determining their intention and the situations they reflect.

Take nothing for your journey . . . nor bag, nor bread, nor money: These prohibitions

– *bag*, probably the mendicant's rather than the provisions bag (Bauer s.v. *pēra*); *bread* is absent from Matt. 10⁹; *money, argurion* = 'silver', is the Roman rather than the Greek copper coinage of Mark 6⁸ – may express that in the special circumstances all needs will be supplied (cf. 22³⁵, verbally referring to the mission of the Seventy but actually addressed to the Twelve), by others (I Cor. 9¹⁴), or by God.

no staff . . . do not have two tunics: These prohibitions – *no staff* = Matt. 10⁸, but contradicts Mark 6⁸ – are different from those above. Along with 'to wear sandals' (Mark 6⁹) and 'to salute no one' (10⁴) they could imply that the mission was of great urgency, or would be short, but that would not apply to the command to stay in a house (v. 4) nor to the prohibition of bag and money (unless that meant they were not to look like beggars). Manson (*Sayings*, p. 181), referring to the injunctions in the Mishnah, tractate Berakoth, 9.5, that no man was to enter the mount of the temple with staff, shoes or purse so as not to defile it, suggests here that the mission is a specially sacred undertaking; but this is somewhat forced, and does not account for the other prohibitions. Perhaps what is meant by all of them together is that the missionaries are to embody in themselves the extreme simplicity and detachment from the world that their eschatological message of the kingdom is to bring about (cf. 12²⁰; I Cor. 7²⁵⁻³¹).

4

whatever house you enter, stay there, and from there depart: The missionary method. They are to evangelize a town from a single residence in it (cf. A. 9⁴³; 10⁴⁸; 16¹⁵; 17⁵). This is very compressed, and is stated more fully in 10⁵⁻⁷. Is it to enjoin concentration of effort or to forbid search for better accomodation? *from there depart* could mean 'go out only from there to preach in the town', or 'when you leave the town (v. 5) let it be from this single residence'.

5

If they are not received (*dechesthai* of receiving apostolic messengers, 9⁴⁸; Gal. 4¹⁴; Col. 4¹⁰; II John 10; or their message A. 8¹⁴; 11¹; 17¹¹; I Thess. 1⁶; 2¹³), they are to *shake off the dust* from their *feet*. For this gesture see on 10¹¹. *as a testimony against them* here (from Mark) suggests that it is a prophetic sign by which the missionaries disclaim further responsibility, and pronounce upon the town which rejects the eschatological rule of God the now inevitable judgment of God in the last days (cf. 9²⁶; A. 18⁶; Matt. 27²⁴ᶠ·).

6

through the villages: Neither Luke, nor the other evangelists, have any idea of the location or territorial scope of the mission.

7Now Herod the tetrarch heard of all that was done, and he was perplexed, because it was said by some that John had been raised from the dead, 8by some that Elijah had appeared, and by others that one of the old prophets had risen. 9Herod said, 'John I beheaded; but who is this about whom I hear such things?' And he sought to see him.

The curious fragment, Mark 6^{14-16}, placed between the mission of the Twelve and their return from it, is primarily (in Matt. 14^{1-2} entirely) concerned with Herod's fear of John (as a possible leader of an uprising as in Jos. *Ant.* 18.117f.?), and with his echoing the superstitious deduction from Jesus' fame that he is John redivivus. It becomes in Mark the platform for a lengthy retrospective account of John's death, but into it are artificially inserted other popular speculations about Jesus, which are to reappear as the prelude to the confession of his messiahship (9^{19} = Mark 8^{28}). Luke omits the intercalated story of John's death, perhaps for stylistic reasons, and because it suggested a parallel between John and Elijah, which he tends to avoid. He rewrites in a more polished manner, and so as to make it a testimony by Herod, who dismisses the idea of Jesus as John redivivus, to the mystery of Jesus.

🙢🙠

7a
the tetrarch: So Matthew, and correctly for Mark's 'king'; see on 3^1.

heard of all that was done: Luke rewrites Mark's awkward sentence, and supplies a typical object to *heard of*, which could refer to the whole activity of Jesus, perhaps now coming into the open through the apostolic mission in Herod's territory.

perplexed: diaporein, perhaps suggested by *aporein* in Mark 6^{20}, omitted by Luke. In the other NT instances, A. 2^{12}; 5^{24}; 10^{17}, it expresses reaction to the miraculous or supernatural, but Luke omits the reference in Mark 6^{14} to Jesus' 'powers', and makes Herod's perplexity a reaction to popular opinion.

7b–8
These suppositions – because *it was said by some . . . by some . . . and by others* is an elegant articular infinitive = 'on account of its being said' – are probably to

9⁷⁻⁹

be taken as three variant expressions, of decreasing definiteness, of current expectation that the eschatological time would be marked by the renewal of prophecy (Joel 2²⁸; I Macc. 4⁴⁶).

7b

John had been raised from the dead: This is the most concrete affirmation, being dependent on events more or less recent. It is a testimony to the impression created by John as a, or the, prophet that prophetic activity subsequent to his death should be taken as evidence of his continued existence, and therefore in popular belief of his corporal resurrection. But it is very curious as well as superstitious, since it could only be held by those who had never seen John and Jesus together or as contemporaries (see Cullmann, *Christology*, pp. 31ff.). It possibly belongs to a later period when the distinction between John and Jesus and their respective roles was a problem (cf. 3¹⁵; 7¹⁸ff.; A. 18²⁴ff.; 19¹ff.; John 1–3).

8

Elijah had appeared: The most specific and traditional form of prophetic expectation, based on Mal. 3¹; 4⁵ (cf. Ecclus 48¹⁰f.; Mark 9¹¹; Matt. 11¹⁴). Thus *had appeared* means 'had made his expected appearance'. This took two forms, an earlier, that Elijah would appear, as one who had been taken up into heaven, to prepare directly for God (cf. 1¹⁷), and a later, almost certainly of Christian origin, that he would be the precursor of the messiah. If John were believed to be Elijah, confusion between Jesus and John could lead to the belief that Jesus was Elijah; and if 'he who is to come' refers to Elijah, John may have been partly responsible for this. On one interpretation of A. 3²⁰f. Elijah's task of restoring all things (cf. Mark 9¹²) was still to be accomplished by Jesus as messiah.

one of the old prophets: More precise than Mark 6¹⁵, 'a prophet, like one of the prophets of old' (but D has 'one of the prophets'; cf. Mark 8²⁸), but less precise than 'the prophet' (John 1²¹; 6¹⁴; 7⁴⁰). Belief in the return of a notable prophet, either unspecified or variously identified (Jeremiah, Matt. 16¹⁴) was in some cases based on Deut. 18¹⁵, as in the Samaritan expectation of Ta'eb, or the restorer, as Moses redivivus, and, possibly, at Qumran (see Vermes, *Scrolls*, pp. 49f.). Enoch has been suggested as belonging to the patriarchal period, but *old* (*archaios*, as in v. 19) is not as precise as that in the other Lukan instances (A. 15⁷, ²¹; 21¹⁶), and in apocalyptic expectation Enoch appears as a companion of, not an alternative to, Elijah.

had risen: anestē, not from the dead; it means 'had appeared on the scene'.

9

Luke has rephrased. *John I beheaded* does service for the whole of the account of the Baptist's fate in Mark 6¹⁷⁻²⁹, and also dismisses the popular view that Jesus

398

is John redivivus as out of the question. This leaves Herod bearing witness in his own way to the mystery of the person of Jesus with his question, *'who is this about whom I hear such things?'* (cf. 4^{36}; 8^{25}). With his addition of *And he sought to see him* Luke prepares for the special incident he will insert in 23^{6-12}.

9^{10-17} = Mark 6^{30-44}

THE FEEDING OF THE MULTITUDE

[10]*On their return the apostles told him what they had done. And he took them and withdrew apart to a city called Bethsaida.* [11]*When the crowds learned it, they followed him; and he welcomed them and spoke to them of the kingdom of God, and cured those who had need of healing.* [12]*Now the day began to wear away; and the twelve came and said to him, 'Send the crowd away, to go into the villages and country round about, to lodge and get provisions; for we are here in a lonely place.'* [13]*But he said to them, 'You give them something to eat.' They said, 'We have no more than five loaves and two fish – unless we are to go and buy food for all these people.'* [14]*For there were about five thousand men. And he said to his disciples, 'Make them sit down in companies, about fifty each.'* [15]*And they did so, and made them all sit down.* [16]*And taking the five loaves and the two fish he looked up to heaven, and blessed and broke them, and gave them to the disciples to set before the crowd.* [17]*And all ate and were satisfied. And they took up what was left over, twelve baskets of broken pieces.*

Mark underlines the two feedings of a multitude as together constituting a profound mystery, which provides a clue to the ministry and person of Jesus, but which the disciples fail to grasp (Mark 6^{52}; 8^{11-21}; cf. John $6^{26ff.}$). By his omission of Mark 6^{45}–8^{26} Luke allows this to disappear, and also avoids the feeding of the four thousand as a doublet. He nevertheless brings the feeding of the five thousand thereby into immediate proximity to the confession of Jesus' messiahship, his first announcement of the passion, and the Transfiguration. These together (cf. also $9^{41, 43ff.}$) form a section concerned with the mystery of Jesus' person, death and glorification as the climax of the Galilean ministry before the departure to Jerusalem.

What took place to give this particular meal of Jesus with his followers its unique place in the tradition is now irrecoverable. The context in Mark, partly reproduced by Luke, suggests a special occasion created by the massing of crowds as a result of the apostolic preaching of the imminent kingdom, and that the meal was connected with that kingdom. Even so, was the original intention to withdraw with the Twelve as the nucleus of the true Israel into the desert as a retreat, or as a place of God's revelation and redeeming mercy in the past? And was Jesus subsequently moved by the presence of crowds to include them with their leaders, and to enact a symbol of the coming kingdom? Apart from any such context the story has distinctive features. It is not a miracle in the sense of an act called out by clamant need. For it does not take place because the request of the apostles to dismiss the crowds is impossible, or would involve intolerable hardship (contrast Mark 8^2), but simply because of the peremptory command of Jesus, who has decided otherwise, to feed them out of their own resources. The miraculous is not conveyed by any descriptive action (it is not said that Jesus multiplied the food); nor by a chorus of wonder from the crowds; indeed it is not evident from the narrative that the crowds were aware of anything extraordinary; nor even by the conversation between Jesus and the Twelve, who are alone privy to what happens, but who nevertheless do not ask, 'Who is this?' If at all it is conveyed by the mention of the twelve basketfuls of remains. This is clearly symbolical of the feeding of Israel by God, and suggests that the whole story may have been a theological construction to express this from the first. For while Mark's story of the five thousand, in comparison with the more stylized account of the four thousand (Mark 8$^{1-9}$), has vivid factual details, both are deeply coloured by OT stories of the feeding of Israel by God.[i] Thus the incident appears to have been told from the standpoint of the expectation, attested in apocalyptic (II Baruch 29.8), in rabbinic literature (see SB IV, p. 954) and in the NT (I Cor. 10$^{1ff.}$; Rev. 2^{17}), that the conditions of the ideal wilderness period would be

---

[i] So the hosts of the twelve tribes (cf. Num. 10–11) with thousands on foot (Mark 6^{33}; cf. Exod. 12^{37}; Num. 11^{21}) in the desert (Mark 6^{32}; 8^4; cf. Exod. 15^{22}; Num. 10^{12}), for three days (an artificial element in Mark 8^2; cf. Exod. 15^{22}; Num. 10^{33}), where they are fasting and faint (Mark 8^3; cf. Exod. 16^3; Ps. 107$^{4f.}$), and are sheep to be given rest and refreshment by the divine Shepherd of Israel (Mark 6$^{31, 34}$; cf. Pss. 77^{20}; 78$^{52f.}$; 107$^{1-9}$). For 'You give them something to eat' and 'Shall we go . . . give them to eat?' (Mark 6^{37}; 8^4) cf.II Kings 4$^{42ff.}$; Num. 11$^{13, 22}$; fish, cf. Num. 11$^{4f., 22}$; they are satisfied to the full (Mark 6^{42}; 8^8) cf. Pss. 107^9; 78^{29}; and food is left over (Mark 6^{43}; 8^8) cf. II Kings 4^{44}; Exod. 16$^{23ff.}$.

repeated in the new age, and the Christian belief that the new age had dawned. Jesus, the divine shepherd, feeds the true Israel of his followers by the hands of their leaders, his ministers. That this does not take the form of a portent of supernatural bread raining from heaven (cf. the demand for a sign from heaven in Mark 8^{11-12}; John 6^{30}), but of a meal in natural circumstances with Jesus as host, preserves the necessity of faith and the possibility of misunderstanding, and so throws the main weight on the interpretative element.

That the story has been influenced by liturgical practice related to the Last Supper can hardly be demonstrated, since the words for the ritual acts – *taking, blessed, broke, gave* – are the customary words for the host at any Jewish meal; but it is unlikely that a Christian would have thought of the former without the latter. If so, then the Feeding, Eucharist and Eschatological (Messianic) Banquet will be connected. The first two are distinct in that the Feeding does not refer the gift of the person of Jesus, and the Supper concerns only Jesus and the Twelve. Both could be united in being in some sense anticipations of the third.

Luke has smoothed Mark's vivid but somewhat ungainly version into a consecutive narrative in three parts, each of four sentences: introduction (vv. 10–11), dialogue (vv. 12–14a) and meal (vv. 14b–17). There is agreement with Matthew in *withdrew* (v. 10), *the crowds followed him* (v. 11a), the healing in v. 11b, *food, we have no more than* (v. 13), *about* (v. 14) and *what was left over* (v. 17). This Easton (p. 137) judges 'rather more than can easily be accidental', though his suggestion of the use of a pre-Markan source is hardly feasible.

გე

10–11

In Mark the pericope could originally have begun with 6^{34}, to which 6^{30-33} were added to provide a vivid, if rather confused, introduction to connect what follows with the apostolic mission, and to explain how Jesus' intention of retirement was frustrated. Luke's abbreviated version is in his own words: *return* (*hupostrephein*, of the return of missionaries to base, A. 8^{25}; 12^{25}; 13^{13}); *withdrew* (*hupochōrein* + 5^{16} to the desert; no reason is given for this); *welcomed* (*apodeches-thai*, of receiving missionaries, A. 18^{27}; 21^{17}; 28^{30}). There is no interruption of a previous plan, and the presence of crowds is natural and welcome.

10

what they had done: So Mark, but Luke makes it cover preaching and healing, which Jesus now continues.

a city called Bethsaida: Probably the right reading (so B 33 and others), unless 'a village' (so D) was altered to *city* in the light of Matt. 11²⁰, 'a desert place' (so Θ) being an assimilation to Matthew/Mark. It is, however, clumsy as contradicting both *for we are here in a lonely* (desert) *place* (v. 12) and Mark 6⁴⁵, where they go across the lake to Bethsaida after the feeding. The omission of Caesarea Philippi from Mark at 9¹⁸ and of Capernaum at 9⁴⁶ suggests that Luke is content with general indications of place in this section. The last to be named in Mark is Nazareth (Mark 6¹, ⁶), and as Luke is dispensing with the section Mark 6⁴⁵–8²⁶ with its detailed but bewildering itinerary, he seems to have fixed on Bethsaida as occurring at both its beginning and its end (Mark 6⁴⁵; 8²²). It was a village converted into a town by the tetrarch Philip, and situated at the north-east end of the Lake Gennesaret. But Luke may not have known where it was, and there is no mention of going there by boat, as in Mark 6⁴⁵.

11

Luke supplies an object for the teaching in Mark – for *spoke of* (concerning) *the kingdom,* cf. A. 1³; 8¹²; 19⁸ – and, like Matthew, interprets the compassion of the shepherd (Mark 6³⁴) as healing. Jesus thus returns to his twofold work to which he had just commissioned the Twelve.

12

Does this imply a temporary break, the crowds to return the next day? The suggestion that five thousand should find *provisions* (*episitismos* + +, the word used in Ps. 77²⁵ LXX, a passage which may lie behind the whole story) in the neighbourhood is scarcely feasible, and Luke's rationalizing addition *to lodge* (*kataluein* + 19⁷) is even less so. Here it serves to magnify the divine provision over against human lack of resources.

13

food for all these people: For *food* (*brōmata*) cf. Ps. 77¹⁸ LXX, and *all these people,* cf. Num. 11¹³.

14

about five thousand: For the mention of the numbers at this point in the story, cf. Num. 11²¹. *about* is common in Luke with numbers.

companies: klisia + +, of a group of people eating together in place of Mark's *sumposia* = drinking party.

fifty each: For this as one natural division of a company, cf. Exod. 18²¹.

16

Jesus, having determined what he proposed to do (cf. John 6⁶), and having ordered the crowds to be disposed according to his wishes, now acts as their host, with the Twelve as assistant ministers (*gave* is the imperfect tense of re-peated action). Dibelius (*Tradition*, p. 90) refers to the ceremonial acts as 'miraculous media'. But apart from *he looked up to heaven*, which is attested, though not widely, as an attitude of prayer (cf. Job 22²⁶; Susanna 35; Jos. *Ant.* 11.64), and which may be intended to stress Jesus' confident access to God, they are all the characteristic ritual of a Jewish meal (cf. A. 27³⁵). The wording, verbatim from Mark, may have been moulded by the liturgical tradition of the Last Supper in the formal participle *taking* (*labōn*, cf. 22¹⁹); and *blessed* with *them*, which is foreign to the Jewish conception, whereby it is God, not things, that are blessed, may reflect a Christian conception of the holiness of the eucharistic bread.

17

they took up what was left over: Since it would suffice that the multitude was satisfied (cf. Exod. 16¹⁸), the provision of more than enough, and the deliberate collection of what was left over (repeated in Mark 8⁸), must have a special point, which is in view in Mark 8¹⁴ᶠᶠ·. Nothing is said of the purpose of such a collec-tion or of what was to be done with the remains. It is just the fact of twelve basketfuls of them that is significant. They presumably symbolized in some way the completeness of the divine sustenance of Israel (cf. the legend in the Talmud, Yoma 75a, that the number of omers of manna gathered by each family miraculously corresponded with the number of its members). This may rest upon Exod. 16²²ᶠᶠ·, where the day before the sabbath a double quantity of manna is collected, 'two omers apiece', which the leaders of the congregation report to Moses, who then orders that 'all that is left over' shall be laid up for the sabbath. In that case the feeding, as involving both divine sustenance with bread and the sabbath, could be in a double sense a foretaste of the age to come.

9¹⁸⁻²⁷ = Mark 8²⁷⁻9¹

JESUS THE SUFFERING MESSIAH AND HIS DISCIPLES

¹⁸*Now it happened that as he was praying alone the disciples were with him; and he asked them, 'Who do the people say that I am?'* ¹⁹*And they answered, 'John the Baptist; but others say, Elijah; and others, that one of the old pro-phets has risen.'* ²⁰*And he said to them, 'But who do you say that I am?' And Peter answered, 'The Christ of God.'* ²¹*But he charged and commanded them to tell this to no one,* ²²*saying, 'The Son of man must suffer many things, and be rejected by the elders and chief priests and scribes, and be killed, and on the third day be raised.'*

²³*And he said to all, 'If any man would come after me, let him deny himself and take up his cross daily and follow me. ²⁴For whoever would save his life will lose it; and whoever loses his life for my sake, he will save it. ²⁵For what does it profit a man if he gains the whole world and loses or forfeits himself? ²⁶For whoever is ashamed of me and of my words, of him will the Son of man be ashamed when he comes in his glory and the glory of the Father and of the holy angels. ²⁷But I tell you truly, there are some standing here who will not taste of death before they see the kingdom of God.'*

This composite section, taken over from Mark 8²⁷–9¹, raises acute problems. Its form in Mark is considerably due to the redactional work of the evangelist.ʲ Its content raises the question of the relation of the Christian message about Jesus to his ministry and teaching. It has often been taken as a watershed in the gospel story in recording the historical moment when the disciples recognized for the first time who Jesus was, and were consequently initiated into the necessity of his passion. Matthew may have understood it so (Matt. 16¹⁷ – but cf. Matt. 14³³ – and Matt. 16²¹ 'from that time . . .'), but not necessarily Mark ('he began', Mark 8³¹, may be an example of the auxiliary use of the verb). In Luke it is almost entirely without setting, geographical or temporal. In all its three parts it is too compressed for any precise historical context in the ministry of Jesus or psychological background in the disciples to be determined, and its function in the tradition would seem to have been doctrinal. The statements of messiahship and rejection are simply juxtaposed, and no explanation is given of what messiahship means or of why it is elicited only to be banned, or of who the Son of man is and why the prophecy of rejection should be made in terms of him. The shape of the first part, vv. 18–20 = Mark 8²⁷⁻²⁹, with its parallel questions, indicates that the main point lay in the contrast between the inadequate belief of the populace and the confession of disciples that Jesus is the Christ. Taken together with the second part, vv. 21–22 = Mark 8³⁰⁻³¹, it provides a succinct paradigm of the basic, perhaps original confession by which a Christian was constituted and was separated from the world, viz. that the crucified but risen Jesus was the Jewish messiah (A. 9²²; 17³). That the primary purpose was not historical but didactic is suggested by the third part, vv. 23–27 = Mark

j See E. Dinkler, 'Peter's Confession and the Satan Saying: the Problem of Jesus' Messiahship', in *The Future of our Religious Past*, ed. J. M. Robinson, London and New York 1971, pp. 169ff.

8^{34}–9^1, which consists of instruction on the way of the cross as the universal law of discipleship. In his editing Luke underlines this element.

૮૦૨

18

Despite his large omission of the intervening material in Mark 6^{45}–8^{26}, Luke's context is essentially the same as Mark's, viz. the popularity of Jesus with the crowds. This gives point to the question in v. 18b, where Luke substitutes *the people* (*hoi ochloi* = 'the crowds') for 'men' in Mark. In place of the circumstantial detail in Mark 8^{27} Luke carries on from the Feeding and the previous opinions of people about Jesus (vv. 7–17), and provides a very general setting (*Now it happened that*).

praying: Luke has Jesus praying at crucial moments (3^{21}; 6^{12}, etc.), here perhaps how to meet the reply he knows he will provoke by his question to the disciples. In this case the prayer may be derived from the sequel to the Feeding in Mark 6^{46}.

alone: *kata monas*, a curious construction, found in classical and Hellenistic Greek, which requires a feminine plural noun to be understood. It is perhaps dependent on the only other instance in the NT, Mark 4^{10}. Jesus is alone after the Feeding in Mark 6^{45-47}; John 6^{15}.

were with him: suneinai + A. 22^{11}, the reading of p^{75} D and others. This is awkward after *praying alone* (Mark 4^{10} is not a parallel, as 'alone' there means away from the crowds). Hence the variant in B 'came to meet him'. It is not clear whether *the disciples* still refers to the Twelve as in vv. 10–17.

19

For the threefold reply see on vv. 7b–8, which is almost exactly repeated here, with the difference that it is now in answer to an enquiry which for some reason Jesus deliberately initiates about himself, and is a foil to a further question and reply.

20

you: In the Greek the word stands first in the sentence for emphasis. It suggests the Twelve, of whom Peter here as elsewhere is the spokesman, rather than a larger and undifferentiated body of disciples. The presupposition of this further question is that the previous categories – Baptist? Elijah? prophet? – are not adequate for the nature of Jesus and his mission.

The Christ of God: A deliberate alteration of Mark's 'the Christ' (for which see on 2^{11}). The expression is unique in the NT. While probably incorrect on the lips of first-century Jews, who would avoid the divine name (hence more correctly 'the Lord's Christ', 2^{26}), it nevertheless recovers, and preserves for Gentile readers, what was entirely correct and essential. 'the anointed one' was not an absolute term, even though it became such when used of Jesus after his resurrection or in later Judaism, but needed to be followed by a descriptive genitive. The one so designated did not exist in his own right with a function that was self-explanatory. He belonged to Yahweh and was the agent of his redemptive purpose however that purpose was conceived – so 'his (or my) anointed' of the reigning monarch in I Sam. 2^{10}; Ps. 2^2, etc., of the future king of the new age, Ps. Sol. 18^6; II Bar. 39^7; A. 2^{36}; 3^{18}; 4^{26}, and the messiahs of Aaron and Israel of the priestly and royal figures expected at Qumran (Vermes, *Scrolls*, p. 87). However varied the conceptions of 'the anointed one' (of Yahweh) at the time, it would express a unique category, beyond which there were no further questions to be asked except of the ultimate relation of his messiah to God (I Cor. 15^{24}). Peter's reply probably means that he expects Jesus to inaugurate or establish God's kingdom; hence the section ends appropriately with the statement in v. 27.

21

In Mark the injunction under censure (*epitimān*, an important word repeated in Mark 8$^{30-33}$, means 'to lay under penalty') is not to speak about Jesus at all, and belongs with his doctrine of secrecy over the person of Jesus. Both Matthew explicitly (Matt. 16^{20}) and Luke implicitly with *this*, restrict the command to silence about messiahship, and here *epitimān* (*charged*) means at the most 'rebuke', as in Mark 8^{32}. No reason is given for the command. It could imply that messiahship is repudiated under any form, or, more likely here, that it is accepted as true, but to be preserved as a secret between Jesus and the disciples (the Twelve?), which will be made public later by God in resurrection when it has gone the way of suffering and death (A. 2^{36}).

22

The first of the four (in Mark three) announcements of the divine necessity of the suffering of the Son of man, the others being 9^{44} = Mark 9^{31}; 17^{25}, cf. Mark 9^{12}; 18$^{31-34}$ = Mark 10$^{33-34}$. They have the ring of a formula, and vary in explicitness and in the extent to which they are framed in the light of later events. They can hardly have been preserved in oral tradition as three recognizably separate statements of the same thing, and their repetition and disposition are likely to have been Mark's work in articulating his narrative. Creed observes (p. 130) that the 'great central section of the Gospel divides the first two Marcan prophecies of the Passion from the third, and the many other themes which intervene divert the steady movement towards the end which controls the arrangement of Mark.' For Luke 'the Christ' has been Christianized as an appellation of Jesus, and the doctrine of a suffering messiah is no longer scandalous but natural and intelligible (cf. 24²⁵ᶠ·, ⁴⁶ᶠ·, and 'that the Christ must suffer' as a proposition demanded by the OT in A. 26²³). So here the announcement of the passion, which in Mark is given a separate introduction and stands over against the confession of messiahship, is made to run on (*saying*) as an explication of it. And by the omission of Mark 8³²⁻³³ Luke boldly suppresses the hostile reaction of Peter to the announcement and his consequent rebuke as Satanic.

the Son of man: These predictions of the passion are framed in terms of the Son of man (for which see on 5²⁴). In Mark this appears to be juxtaposed to 'the Christ'; here it is a synonym for it and a name for Jesus (cf. 24⁷; in Matt. 16²¹ it is dropped and 'he' substituted). If by the Son of man the eschatological figure was originally meant, the force of the statement would have lain in its paradox and irony; the supreme agent of the divine purpose would become totally passive and ineffective. If it was a circumlocution for the speaker in embarrassing circumstances the saying could be more easily ascribed in some form to Jesus. Even then he will have spoken from some (unstated) conception of himself and his destiny which would be contradicted by suffering and rejection.

must: This refers not to fate but to the will of God, which elsewhere can be expressed by an appeal to scripture (cf. 18³¹).

suffer many things: pathein polla, a remarkable phrase without Jewish parallels except Assumption of Moses 3¹¹ *multa passus*. The verb *paschein* acted in Greek as the passive of the verb *poiein* = 'to do'. Its basic meaning was not, as in the modern use of 'suffer', the endurance of physical or mental pain, but 'to be done to', to be the 'patient' or object and recipient of the actions of others, almost always in a bad sense. Since Hebrew lacks a word for this, *paschein* is an insignificant word in the LXX, and is not found in passages dealing with the sufferings of Israel (e.g. in Job or the Psalms), nor is any OT reference suggested when it is used in the NT. In some, generally kerygmatic passages it is a synonym for death (22¹⁵; 24²⁶, ⁴⁶; A. 1³; 3¹⁸; 17³), but not here, where it is distinguished from *be killed. many things* is probably used adverbially in the sense of 'much'.

be rejected: apodokimazein = 'to prove and find wanting', applied to metals and stones (Ps. 118²²), animals (14¹⁹) and then to persons for office and to God's judgment (Jer. 6³⁰). The paradox continues. The Son of man, whose role includes the testing of men in the execution of God's judgment, the vindication of the righteous and destruction of sinners (John 5²⁷; I Enoch 69²⁷ᶠᶠ·) – or Jesus whose words voice the judgment of God – is himself to be put to the test by men and found wanting.

by the elders and chief priests and scribes: The rejection which in 17²⁵ is general is here made specific. The three groups could denote the classes that mattered in Israel – prominent laymen, the priesthood and the theologians – or the components of the Sanhedrin (in Luke they are governed by a single article). The composition of the Sanhedrin is not known for certain and the terminology for it varies considerably in the gospels: in Mark generally, and sometimes in Matthew and Luke, these three groups, though in varying order (and Mark 15¹ adds the Sanhedrin to them); in Matthew generally the chief priests and elders (of the people), as also in A. (with rulers for chief priests in A. 4⁵); in Luke chief priests and scribes (19⁴⁷; 20¹⁹; 22²; 23¹⁰) constitute the council (22⁶⁶; A. 22⁵), but in 22⁵² it is chief priests, captains and elders and in 24²⁰ chief priests and rulers. If the Sanhedrin is referred to here the rejection is official excommunication from Israel.

be killed: The excommunication will be for a capital offence, and would result in stoning. In 18³² the killing would be at the hands of Gentiles.

on the third day be raised: For 'after three days rise again' in Mark 8³¹ and in agreement with Matt. 16²¹. The phrases mean the same, *on the third day* (so 18³³; 24⁷, ²¹, ⁴⁶; A. 10⁴⁰) being probably the form taken in the tradition (cf. I Cor. 15⁴; cf. Hos. 6²). *be raised*, the passive of *egeirein*, preserves more clearly than the other word for resurrection, *anistanai* = 'to rise', that God is the author of the resurrection of Jesus. These concluding words are more evidently in the light of events, and Peter's remonstrance in Mark 8³² would be more natural without them. They transform the prophecy into one of ultimate divine triumph, as the suffering, rejection and death are to be reversed by God through the eschatological act of the resurrection of the righteous, which, in being applied to a single individual in advance, betokens the approach of the end of the ages. Any interpretation of the death and resurrection here will depend on the meaning to be given to the Son of man. In Jewish eschatology resurrection preceded, and brought men to, judgment. In the person of the Son of man, if he is the eschatological leader of Israel, the final things are rehearsed of necessity in reverse order, since in his case resurrection is his vindication at the hands of God in face of the false judgment of Israel, and reveals his death as itself righteous.

23–27

Luke follows Mark closely in reproducing a complex of sayings which apply, on the principle of like master like pupil, the previously stated doctrine about the Son of man to disciples (cf. 6⁴⁰ = Matt. 10²⁴ᶠ·; John 12²³⁻²⁶). For them also the possession of (eternal) life is to be by way of a certain death. Originally these very compressed sayings, reduced by Luke to four and rounded off by a fifth, could have been separate. Variants of them are found in isolation in other settings (e.g. 14²⁷; 17³³; Matt. 10³⁸ᶠ·; John 12²⁵ᶠ·). Here they are linked in a progression (*for* in vv. 24, 25, 26) by reference to the person of Jesus. The first (v. 23) is more concrete and closely related to v. 22; the second (v. 24) states a more general principle (cf. 17³³), though it is still *for my sake*; the third (v. 25) continues the second by the omission of Mark 8³⁷, but introduces the thought of final loss, which leads to the fourth (v. 26) on the ultimate sanction of discipleship in the judgment of the Son of man on those who are ashamed of Jesus; while the fifth (v. 27) pronounces on the authority of Jesus the certainty and imminence of the consummation.

23

The general homiletic character of the sayings as statements of the nature of Christian discipleship is indicated by the audience provided – in Mark a crowd specially summoned from nowhere, in Luke his favourite *all*.

would: thelei = 'wishes', here in the sense of 'intends'.

to come after: opisō erchesthai, a synonym for *akolouthein,* 'to follow' (for which see on 5¹¹). It means 'to fall in behind', and hence 'to share the destiny of'. Here, with the addition of *daily,* it takes on more of the meaning 'to imitate'.

deny himself: arneisthai means to renounce or disown by a judicial act (cf. A. 3¹⁴f.), and in 12⁹ brings with it rejection by God in the judgment. But 'to renounce oneself' has no parallel in Greek or Jewish literature. The sense may be that to be a companion of the Son of man the would-be disciple must pass on himself in his natural existence the same rejection and excommunication as is passed by others on Jesus.

take up his cross: See on 23²⁶. This may be a Christian formulation in the light of the fact that the messiah rejected by Israel was executed in Roman, not Jewish, fashion (cf. Heb. 12²; 13¹³, where the cross is interpreted as excommunication from the 'camp' of Israel). Simon of Cyrene will then have been a symbol of the true disciple (23²⁶). Alternatively Jesus, without any prevision of his own crucifixion, could have used a violent metaphor based on the familiar sight in Palestine of columns of outcast criminals (Varus is said to have crucified two thousand after the death of Herod). Crucifixion was reserved for the worst offences – murder, sedition, robbery and sacrilege; and although under the Empire it was extended to others, it remained in public estimation what it had always been under the Republic, the most shameful death because the punishment of slaves. Hence it would be a figure proper to those who throw in their lot with the utterly despised Son of man.

daily: One of Luke's most momentous editorial additions. It softens the stern realism of the metaphor in Mark of a once for all accompaniment of Jesus to the gallows, and originates the more conventional spiritualizing conception of continual cross-bearing and self-denial in Christian piety.

24

The paradox is found in varying forms; cf. 17³³; Matt. 10³⁹; John 12²⁵f.. Here it is connected with Jesus – *for my sake*, either on account of being my disciple, or in my service.

life: psuchē = 'soul', but should not be translated so except in the Hebrew sense of 'living being', 'self' (so *himself*, v. 25). *save his life, psuchēn sōzein* means 'to escape death', 'to preserve one's life in the face of imminent death' (Gen. 19^{17}; I Sam. 19^{11}; Amos 2^{14}, etc., as also 'seeks to gain'. 17^{33}). *lose life, psuchēn apollunai* occurs in the LXX only at Ecclus 20^{22}, where it appeasr to mean 'to destroy oneself' (cf. Matt. 10^{28}; in Matt. 10^{39} 'lose' is the opposite of 'find'). The meaning is perhaps, 'He who is set on preserving his natural existence (preserving himself alive in the world) will destroy himself (in the judgment), and whoever destroys himself (in the world) for my sake, he it is (*houtos* = 'this man') who will preserve himself (will receive eternal life – 17^{33} 'will make [preserve] alive').

25

The issue in v. 24 is supreme since possession of the self is the supreme possession, for which there is no adequate exchange. For this hyperbole *the world* is used, without exact parallel in the NT, for the sum of possessions. The contrast *gains/loses* suggests 'gain as a possession' and 'lose as a forfeit'; but this gives a strained sense. Enjoyment of the world and loss of the self cannot be compared, since the latter would exclude the possibility of the former. *forfeits, zēmioun,* which Luke takes from Mark, adding *loses* to connect with v. 24, could bear its other meaning of 'be punished'. There is a remarkable parallel in II Baruch 51$^{15f.}$, 'For what then have men lost their life, and for what have those who were on the earth exchanged their soul? For then they chose not for themselves this time, which, beyond the reach of anguish, could not pass away; but they chose for themselves that time, whose issues are full of lamentations and evils, and they denied the world which ages not those who come to it, and they rejected the time of glory'. A. Schlatter[k] takes *gain* and *lose* as missionary terms (cf. I Cor. 9$^{19ff.}$; I Peter 3^{1}) with the sense, 'What if an apostle converts the world but is himself lost?' For *what does it profit?* as a rabbinic expression, see SB I, p. 749.

26

The previous truths are now given an expressly eschatological basis, first of a negative and then of a positive kind (v. 27).

whoever is ashamed: The verb *epaischunesthai,* only in this saying in the gospels, like its opposite *homologein* = 'confess' (cf. 12^{8}) belongs in the vocabulary of Christian confession, sometimes in a situation of persecution (cf. II Tim. 1$^{8, 12}$; Rom. 1^{16}).

k *Der Evangelist Matthäus*, Stuttgart 1929, pp. 521f.

me and my words: Who Jesus is and what he says are inseparable. They are of such a kind that to fail to be identified with them has ultimate consequences. This does not fit well with the injunction to silence in v. 21. Some mss do not have *words*, leaving *my*, *emous*, to mean 'those who are mine'. In that case acknowledgment of Jesus involves acceptance of his disciples, and the saying would be addressed to a wider circle excluding disciples.

him: touton stands first for emphasis, as *he* in v. 24, and makes a chiasmus.

will the Son of man be ashamed: Here the Son of man is clearly an eschatological figure, whether another than Jesus who establishes in heaven what relates to Jesus on earth, or Jesus himself in his future role. In the variant 12^9 = Matt. 10^{33} the scene is more clearly forensic, with the Son of man giving testimony in favour of the confessing disciple before God's angels. Here he appears to deliver the judgment himself. (For disavowal by the Son of man, cf. I Enoch $46^{4ff.}$, by Jesus as the Son of man/king-messiah, Matt. $25^{31ff.}$, and as Lord Matt. 7^{23}.)

when he comes: Originally this may have referred to a 'coming' before God on the clouds, like that of the one like a son of man in Dan. 7^{13}, in order to give testimony, and have been transformed in later Christian thought to a 'coming' or parousia from heaven to execute the judgment itself. A difficulty in such passages is the often inconsistent character of eschatological imagery. Thus some hold that the figure in Daniel already has divine attributes, and in I Enoch the two conceptions of the Son of man (or Elect One) as standing before God in a subordinate position and as seated on the throne of glory as God's associate in the judgment lie side by side (cf. I Enoch 49^2; $48^{2ff.}$; $61^{8f.}$; $62^{2ff.}$; $69^{26ff.}$, and cf. Rev. 3^5; 14^{14}).

in his glory and the glory of the Father and of the holy angels: The eschatology can still be seen in the process of development in Luke's revision of Mark here. *glory* denotes heavenly effective majesty, divine radiance and power. It belongs to God and can be almost a synonym for him – so Mark 8^{38}, 'in the glory of his Father'. The composite triadic glory here is Luke's creation. Firstly, the Son of man now has a glory of his own – for the Son of man's own glory, cf. I Enoch 49^2; 69^{27}, and for the Christ as possessing a glory of his own 24^{26}; Mark 10^{37}; II Cor. 3^{18}; II Thess. $1^{9f.}$. In the context this is mentioned before, but as accompanied by and representative of, *the glory of the Father*, a more developed conception than 'his Father' (Mark 8^{38}; Matt. 16^{27}). Mowinckel (*He That Cometh*, pp. 368ff.) argues that for the Son of man to have a father he must have been known also as the Son of God, but the only evidence is this passage, where it could reflect either (i) the extension to the Son of man of a sonship already attributed to the angels and the righteous in heaven (I Enoch 71^1), or (ii) a Christian identification of both the Son of man and the Son of God with Jesus (John $5^{26f.}$), or (iii) a combination made by Jesus himself of the Son of man concept with his own conviction of God as his Father (cf. Matt. 10^{33}). Thirdly, there is the glory *of the holy angels*. These accompany God and share his judgment in Deut. 33²; Dan. 7¹⁰; II Baruch 51¹¹; I Enoch 1⁹ and passim, and in the NT can accompany the Son of man or Jesus (Matt. 25³¹; Mark 8³⁸; II Thess. 1⁷; in Luke 12⁸ᶠ·; 15¹⁰, they are almost synonymous with God).

27

The most explicit statement in temporal terms of the certainty of the kingdom, solemnly introduced (*truly* for Mark's 'Amen', cf. 12⁴⁴; 21³), and couched in periphrastic oracular language that is not to be pressed too hard.

some standing here: Not *some* in contrast to 'others', nor *standing here* of bystanders, whether disciples or not, but a formal expression for 'those alive', 'the present generation'.

taste death: Attested only once in Greek literature, but found in John 8⁵²; Heb. 2⁹; IV Ezra 6²⁶, and in rabbinic texts, where, however, it marks the bitterness and enigma of death as not belonging to God's purpose for the righteous.

before: Hardly that having seen the kingdom they will then die, but rather that their death will be anticipated by the vision of the kingdom. In IV Ezra 6²⁶ 'those who have not tasted death from their birth' are those assumed to heaven before death to appear as companions of the messiah in his advent. In Mark the reference may be to the gathering of disciples on earth into the company of the elect (Mark 13²⁶ᶠ·).

they see the kingdom of God: For Mark 9¹ 'they see the kingdom of God come with power', which, with Mark 8³⁸, provides an eschatological climax to the whole section on discipleship of Jesus, messiah and Son of man (see Kümmel, *Promise and Fulfilment*, pp. 25ff.). Matthew's revision 'see the Son of man coming in his kingdom' shows that he took Mark 9¹ of the parousia. Luke's revision, with *kingdom* as the direct object of *see* (only here in L–A, the nearest to it is 19¹¹) shows that he took it of a future vision of the kingdom, and not, as proposed by Dodd and others, of an awareness that it had already come. In face of the non-fulfilment of such a precise prophecy Luke substitutes a more general expression open to wide interpretation. It cannot be taken, as by some, of the Transfiguration, which was only a few days away. Perhaps Luke intended the events of the successful mission in A. as evidence of the rule of God in operation (A. 1³).

9^{28-36} = Mark 9^{2-8}

THE TRANSFIGURATION

²⁸*Now about eight days after these sayings he took with him Peter and John and James, and went up on the mountain to pray.* ²⁹*And as he was praying, the appearance of his countenance was altered, and his raiment became dazzling white.* ³⁰*And behold, two men talked with him, Moses and Elijah,* ³¹*who appeared in glory and spoke of his departure, which he was to accomplish at Jerusalem.* ³²*Now Peter and those who were with him were heavy with sleep but kept awake, and they saw his glory and the two men who stood with him.* ³³*And as the men were parting from him, Peter said to Jesus, 'Master, it is well that we are here; let us make three booths, one for you and one for Moses and one for Elijah' – not knowing what he said.* ³⁴*As he said this, a cloud came and overshadowed them; and they were afraid as they entered the cloud.* ³⁵*And a voice came out of the cloud, saying, 'This is my son, my Chosen;* listen to him!'* ³⁶*And when the voice had spoken, Jesus was found alone. And they kept silence and told no one in those days anything of what they had seen.*

* Other ancient authorities read *my Beloved.*

This pericope is unique in form, character and position. Like the bapt-ism story it is a 'myth' in depicting the activity of the supernatural in physical terms. Factual detail is lacking, such as the location of the mountain, how the heavenly figures are identified, and the return of Jesus to a natural state. Unlike the baptism story it is no longer possible to determine what, if any, historical occasion lay behind it. And whereas at the baptism theophany Jesus hears the voice but remains unchanged, and in the post-resurrection Christophanies is in some sense changed but there is no accompanying heavenly voice, here theophany and Christophany are combined, and divine attestation is matched by heavenly condition. Further, only here are disciples also recipients of the theophany (but cf. Matt. 3¹⁷; II Peter 1¹⁶ff·). Hence there is a certain ambivalence, especially in Mark's version, where it is not clear whether metamorphosis has significance in itself and for Jesus himself (he is pas-sive throughout), or takes place for the sake of the disciples, to prepare them for the words from heaven spoken only to them. Some have judged it a story of a resurrection appearance that has been misplaced, but neither the form nor the symbolism are those characteristic of resurrection appearances (see J. E. Alsup, *The Post-Resurrection Appearances in the Gospel Tradition*, pp. 141ff.). Similarly the symbolism of 'cloud' not 'clouds' and the address 'This is my Son . . . listen to him' tell against its categorization as a vision of the parousia in advance. Taken by itself it could be a theological construction of Christian creation proclaiming the glory of God in the face and words of Jesus (cf. II Cor. $1^{19f.}$; 3^7–4^6; I Cor. $2^{7ff.}$; Col. 1^{27}; John 1^{14}; 3^{13}; $7^{17f.}$; Heb. $1^{1ff.}$). 'Before the earliest gospel had assumed its present shape, the Church had fixed upon the Transfiguration as the central moment of the Lord's earthly life. It had surrounded that moment with a glamour of allusion and allegorism so complex that it cannot now with any certainty be analysed into its constituent elements. And it has done this as though to remind itself that the *whole* gospel, from beginning to end, must be read and regarded as one great vision of God in Christ.'[1] In its present position, which may be due entirely to Mark, it dominates the gospel narrative theologically, providing both a climax to the Galilean ministry with divine confirmation of the revelation in vv. 18–27, and also the proper standpoint for understanding the coming rejection of the Son of man. Historically it is difficult to account for the continuing failure of disciples to see who Jesus is, and in particular for the denial of Peter, after participating in such an experience, and the dialogue in Mark 9^{9-13}, almost entirely omitted by Luke, appears to be a somewhat artificial attempt to deal with this.

Luke's version shows both close parallels with Mark, and that in distinctive expressions, in vv. 28, 29, 30, 33, 34–35, 36, and also considerable differences. As Luke has been following Mark hitherto, and will continue to do so (v. 36b presupposes Mark 9^{9-13}), and any special source was not sufficiently continuous to include a story beginning with a note of time, it is unlikely that Luke is dependent on any other source than Mark here. The differences can be explained as curtailments to improve stylistically a somewhat disjointed original, and expansions designed to make what is compressed in Mark psychologically more comprehensible, and to integrate the story into his own theology. In particular Luke has tried to get rid of the ambivalence in Mark by dividing the story into two. In the first part, vv. 29–31, the transfigura-

---

1 Kirk, *The Vision of God*, p. 101. See also the studies of G. H. Boobyer, *St Mark and the Transfiguration Story*, Edinburgh 1942, and A. M. Ramsey, *The Glory of God and the Transfiguration of Christ*, London and New York 1949.

tion takes place as an objective event, which concerns Jesus and his heavenly companions, and of which the disciples are not, as in Mark, the spectators. The second part, vv. 32–35, concerns the disciples only, who become aware of what is happening on waking, and who are addressed from the cloud. The two parts are drawn together in the two sentences in v. 36, though the connection between them remains unclear.

ಜಿ

28

This introductory sentence contains a number of Lukan characteristics.

Now . . . he took with him . . . and went up: This renders the Lukan construction 'It came to pass . . . having taken . . . and he went up' (see on 5¹).

about eight days: A hanging nominative with a period of time (cf. A. 5⁷) for Mark's 'after six days'. Such precise chronology is unique in Mark outside the passion narrative, and is probably symbolic. It might mean 'on the sixth day' (see on v. 22), or 'on the seventh day' ('after two days' in Mark 14¹ appears to mean 'on the third day'). For 'six days' as days of preparation for a sacred occasion, cf. Gen. 1¹⁻²⁴; Exod. 24¹⁶. Luke's expression (*about* with numbers is characteristic of him) is too imprecise to be symbolic. He appears to have taken Mark's 'six days' as a rough equivalent for a week, which was not observed by Greeks or Romans, and to have translated them into the required number of days by inclusive reckoning (cf. the Roman *nundinum* for an eight-day period).

after these sayings: A substitute for Mark's 'after six days'. The expression is unique in the NT. It could mean 'after these things' (*logoi* = 'things' as in the LXX of II Chron. 32¹; I Macc. 9³⁷), but more likely it emphasizes the connection between the express words of vv. 21–27 and the Transfiguration as a visible sign of their fulfilment.

Peter and John and James: For these names, and in this order, see on 8⁵¹.

the mountain: This is conventional for Mark's 'a high mountain' (cf. II Peter 1¹⁸, 'the holy mountain'). It is less an actual mountain than the locale proper for prayer (cf. 6¹²), and here for theophany and revelation (cf. Exod. 24¹⁶).

to pray: A typical Lukan motif (see on 3²¹). Here it weakens the impression in Mark that Jesus knows what will take place and deliberately conducts the three apart to be witnesses of it. In Luke prayer is the object of the retirement and transfiguration supervenes upon it (*as he was praying,* v. 29).

29

the appearance of his countenance was altered: For Mark's single word 'was trans-figured', *metamorphousthai.* This word, absent from the LXX, meant 'to be changed into something else', and could be suspect on account of its associations with crude mythology (cf. the literary versions of the motif in Ovid's *Metamorphoses* and Apuleius' *The Golden Ass*), with magic and the divinization claimed in mystery cults. Metamorphosis was, however, found in Jewish apocalyptic as an extension to individual saints at the resurrection of the eschatological renewal of the world (cf. Dan. 12[2f.]; II Baruch 49–51; Assumption of Moses 10[9], transformation into the likeness of angels or stars: I Enoch 38[4]; 104[2]; I Cor. 15[39ff.]). The emphasis there is less on change of form than on the light and the splendour of the face and appearance (cf. Rev. 1[16] of the Son of man). This feature, curiously lacking in Mark, is supplied here. *altered* is *heteros* = 'different', the verb from which could be a synonym for *metamorphousthai*. This is not the same as the reflected light of Moses' face in Exod. 34[29ff.] (cf. Dan. 10[8]), which did not betoken a change of state and could fade (cf. II Cor. 3[12ff.], where the true metamorphosis from Christ's glory is contrasted with the light on Moses' face).

his raiment became dazzling white: This is not embellishment; the state of the garments shows the completeness of the metamorphosis (they are referred to in mystery cults as outward signs of transformation). *white* became in apocalyptic, though not in the OT, the eschatological colour, corresponding to light as a heavenly substance; cf. I Enoch 71[1], angels with white garments and faces shining like stars; 62[15f.], the elect clothed in garments of glory composed of light, Rev. 3[4f.] and passim. Hence Luke's intensive *dazzling*, the rare *exastraptein* = 'white as light' in place of the homely simile of the fuller in Mark 9[3]. Momentarily on earth Jesus becomes what he is to be permanently, the denizen of heaven.

30

And behold: Luke rewrites dramatically. *behold* introduces divine revelation (cf. 1[31]; 2[10]; A. 1[10]; 7[56]), and here further revelation. The mystery is not simply the transfiguration of Jesus but its heavenly purport.

two men: From Luke; not however the same as the two unidentified men in 24[4]; A. 1[10], who are in the dress of angels, but two special human beings in Israel's history, now located in the heavenly sphere, who are identified – the Greek, not translated in RSV, has *hoitines ēsan* = 'who in fact were', 'none other than'.

Moses and Elijah: In their historical order (so Matt. 17[3]; cf. Mark 9[5]) in place of Mark's remarkable 'Elijah with (accompanied by) Moses' (and cf. Mark 9[9-13], where only Elijah occurs). Their joint appearance is a highly distinctive feature in the story, and must contribute to its interpretation, though that is not easy to establish. Traditional exegesis has taken them as representing 'the law and the prophets', a rare expression outside the NT, which witness to Jesus; but this is not possible for Mark, and is unlikely for Matthew and Luke. While Moses could stand for the law (cf. 16^{29}; $24^{27, 44}$; II Cor. 3^{15}), there is no firm evidence that Elijah, a much elaborated figure in Jewish tradition, stood for prophecy (if *listen to him* in v. 35 echoes Deut. 18^{15}, Moses could stand for prophecy). The priority of Elijah in Mark suggests the heralding of the coming kingdom (see on 7^{20}, and Mark 9^{11}), and the two together may be representatives of the heavenly elect. In the context Enoch and Elijah would be more natural as the two OT figures who had been translated to heaven (cf. I Enoch 89^{52}–90^{31}; IV Ezra 6^{26}). There is some evidence for a belief that Moses also belonged with 'those who had been taken up, who had tasted death from their birth' (IV Ezra 6^{26}), e.g. in the Assumption of Moses (see *AP* II, pp. 407f.) and the tradition mentioned by Josephus (*Ant.* 4.326; see the Loeb edition, pp. 632f., with the note comparing similar accounts of the translation of Aeneas and Romulus). For evidence of the transference to Moses of functions belonging to Enoch as recipient of the secrets of the last things, cf. II Baruch $59^{5ff.}$; IV Ezra 14^5. In Rev. $11^{3ff.}$ God's two prophetic witnesses in heaven are described in terms of Elijah and Moses in that order. Such a conjunction could have been read out of Mal 3^1; 4^6, with the reference to a messenger twice in 3^1 and to Elijah in connection with the law of Moses in $4^{4f.}$. If Moses here derives his role from Elijah, their appearance together may portend the imminence of the final age of judgment and renewal.

31

appeared: That is, made the transition from heaven to earth; the word is that used for appearances of the risen Lord (24^{34}). In Mark the 'appearance' is to the disciples.

in glory: Strangely it is left to Luke to introduce the one word, *glory*, that is demanded by the whole narrative, since it stood for the manifested being and presence of God, and for the nature of those belonging to the heavenly eschatological realm. The three central figures are now in the same state of being.

spoke of his departure . . .: Mark's 'were talking with Jesus' (reproduced in v. 30) was perhaps intended simply to indicate that Jesus had been transported to the same plane as the two heavenly figures; cf. 'the angel who talked with me', Zech. 1^9 etc.; II Enoch $1^{2ff.}$; Rev. 4^1, for examples of heavenly conversation as a feature of apocalyptic vision. But it invited elaboration. For Luke, who may not have understood the significance of Moses and Elijah in the context, their importance lies in the subject of their conversation. This he supplies in a form which brings the transfiguration into harmony with the remainder of his Gospel as focused on Jerusalem, and with its message of 'through suffering to glory' (24^{26}).

spoke of: legein with a noun as direct object is rare in the NT, and comparison with the same usage in Mark 10³²; A. 1³; I Cor. 15⁵¹ suggests 'declare to', 'narrate' rather than 'speak with about'. If so the christology is more human than in Mark. Jesus is given instruction by the heavenly witnesses in the divine secrets which concern him.

his departure, which he was to accomplish at Jerusalem: The word rendered departure, *exodos* + Heb. 11²²; II Peter 1¹⁵) can mean simply 'end' (Exod. 23¹⁶ of the end of the year), and, possibly derived from this, can be a synonym for 'death' (Wisd. 3²). The continuation in Wisd. 3³ with 'their journeying away from us . . .' suggests 'departure'. Josephus (*Ant.* 4.189) has the full phrase *exodus tou zēn* = 'exit from life', and Philo (*On the Virtues* 77) equates it with *apoikia* = 'departure' in an account of the death of Moses. The verb *accomplish*, *plēroun* in the sense of 'execute' (cf. A. 14²⁶; Rom. 15¹⁹; Col. 1²⁵), favours 'departure'. Thus the word is a solemn, in the LXX semi-poetical, word for death (its counterpart *eisodos* = 'entrance' is used in A. 13²⁴ of Jesus' appearance on the human scene), and it fits the context in suggesting departure through death to glory (24²⁶). *was to*, *mellein*, has the sense of fulfilment of divine purpose, and *at Jerusalem* covers the rest of the gospel from 9⁵¹. As the subject of the instruction by the two heavenly witnesses the death of Jesus is ratified as divine event. There are no good grounds for giving *exodos* the further theological meaning of 'deliverance (from Egypt)' and so 'redemption'.

32
Peter and those who were with him: Lukan, cf. 5¹⁰; A. 5¹⁷; 19³⁸.

kept awake: The theme of sleeping and waking, introduced here by Luke, is conventional in visionary scenes (cf. A. 12⁶ff.; II Enoch 14ff.), and is different from that in Gethsemane (22⁴⁵f.). The verb *diagrēgorein* + +, is found here for the first time in Greek literature. It should mean 'to keep awake', but its use here in the aorist participle suggests 'when they were fully awake'. The disciples do not witness the transfiguration of Jesus nor the appearance of Moses and Elijah, but only the consequences on waking.

33
And as the men were parting from him: A connecting link in the narrative by which Luke supplies a reason for Peter's otherwise unexplained suggestion to make booths. The vision is beginning to fade and Moses and Elijah to leave (*diachōrizesthai* + +) Jesus, and they must be made to stay. It is Lukan editing which produces the impression that Peter's intention was to prolong the event.

it is well that we are here: This is the correct translation of the Greek, where *it is well* is followed by an accusative and infinitive, rather than 'it is good for us to be here' (so RV), which would require *us* to be in the dative, and logically that the disciples should have booths as well. The meaning is therefore, 'It is fortunate that we are here, so that as your servants (*Master* for Mark's 'rabbi' is Lukan) we can build booths for the three of you', and not 'It would be good for us (all) to stay here, so let us make places of abode.'

let us make three booths: The point of this abrupt proposal, why it was retained in the story if it was judged to be made out of bewilderment and fear (Mark 9^6) or incomprehension (v. 33), and whether it is simply a foil for what then takes place, are all obscure. Some interpret by reference to a quite specific background, that of the Feast of Tabernacles (Booths).[m] But there were two lines of thought in Judaism connected with *skēnē* = 'tent', 'booth', which, while sometimes employing the same language, are to be distinguished. *Skēnopēgia*, the Feast of Tabernacles, commemorated the dwelling of the Israelites in booths under divine protection in the desert, and the promise it looked forward to was that of divine protection from wrath in the judgment. On the other hand there was a close connection between 'the tent' and God's dwelling with Israel, his glory and revelation. God talked with Moses from heaven (Exod. 20^{22}) not only in the cloud of glory (Exod. $24^{15ff.}$), but within the tent, at the doors of which the pillar of cloud stood, and which had been constructed on a heavenly model (Exod. $33^{7ff.}$; $25^{8f.}$, a passage on which there was much rabbinic speculation). Apocalyptic knew of heavenly abodes for the elect along with the angels (cf. 16^9; I Enoch 41^2; $39^{4, 7f.}$, etc.). In Rev. 13^6 the tabernacle of God is identified with 'those who dwell in heaven'. It is on this background that the building of tabernacles for heavenly beings would make sense, and the specification *one for you and one for Moses and one for Elijah* singles the three out as supernatural figures.

34

There is a hiatus in the story here, as Peter's proposal, judged to have been made in ignorance of what he was talking about, receives no response, unless Luke's addition *As he said this* indicates that the arrival of the cloud is God's response to it.

a cloud came and overshadowed them: This cloud is to be distinguished from the apocalyptic 'clouds', which are the vehicles of locomotion for God or the Son man (Mark 13^{26}). This is the cloud of theophany, which in Jewish belief descends, rises, or remains stationary over the tabernacle, as the localized manifestation of the presence of God (Exod. 19^9; 33^9; $34^{5ff.}$; $40^{34ff.}$; II Macc. 2^8). When the tabernacle is finished the cloud, which is the divine glory, envelops it outside (Exod. 40^{35}, *episkiazein*, the verb used here), and fills it inside in fulfil-

---

[m] See especially H. Baltensweiler, *Die Verklärung Jesu: historisches Ereignis und synoptische Berichte*, Zurich 1959, who cites a rabbinic ordinance that travellers during the feast should at least spend the night in tents, and who dates the event within the feast.

ment of the divine promise to dwell with Israel. Its arrival at this point may imply that for the disciples to build tabernacles to house the three heavenly figures is unnecessary and inadequate, since the divine presence envelops them personally. Since the disciples are addressed *out of the cloud* it could be that they remain outside it, and that *them* refers to Jesus, Moses and Elijah. This may be already implicit in Peter's proposal, and Luke's addition *and they were afraid as they entered the cloud* could mean fear that Jesus was about to be taken from them (cf. A. 1⁹ᶠᶠ·). But *out of the cloud* need not be taken so literally (cf. Exod. 24¹⁶ᶠᶠ·), and Luke's moving of the disciples' fear to this point (contrast Mark 9⁶) is better explained if he understood them to be enveloped in the cloud. If so the scene is unique. Though distinguished from Jesus, and told to listen to and obey him, they are nevertheless united to him as the elect by the divine presence.

35

It has been argued that originally the story ended with the appearance of the cloud and the discovery of Jesus alone, the voice being introduced later to place the disciples at the centre, and to make it a christological statement for the edification of Christians. But it is doubtful whether the story was ever told for any other purpose, and the connection between the presence of God in the cloud and his speaking out of it was close (cf. Exod. 24¹⁶; 34⁵; Deut. 5²²).

And a voice came out of the cloud: More proximate and intense than 'from heaven' (3²²; II Peter 1¹⁸).

This is my Son, my Chosen: The address at the baptism is repeated (see on 3²²), but now in declaratory form to the disciples. So far Jesus has been depicted as a companion of Moses and Elijah, who have instructed him. He is now divinely declared unique as God's own Son and as the eschatological Elect One, whose words are to be received as the words of God by the nucleus of the elect.

my Chosen: Or 'the Chosen (One)'. *ho eklelegmenos*, the perfect participle passive, is to be preferred as the best attested (p⁴⁵ p⁷⁵ ℵ B) and most unusual reading to 'Beloved', widely attested but probably an assimilation to Mark, or *ho eklektos* (cf. 23³⁵) = 'the Elect One', which is weakly attested. Like this last it is a title in apposition – 'the Chosen One' rather than 'my Chosen' – and may be based on Isa. 42¹, 'my servant . . . my chosen'. In the Similitudes of Enoch 'the Chosen One' is a regular designation, alternative to the Son of man, for the lord of the elect ones, and the source for them of wisdom and righteousness. Having a specially close relationship with the Lord of Spirits he is the object of his special favour, is appointed by him to a glorious heritage, and will carry out his final purposes (I Enoch 39⁶ᶠᶠ·; 45³ᶠᶠ·; 49²²ᶠᶠ·; 51³ᶠᶠ·; 61⁵ᶠᶠ·). As in 23³⁵ 'the Elect One, along with 'the Christ' and 'the king of the Jews' appears to the crowd the title most clearly contradicted by Jesus' actual situation on the cross, so here, in face of his divinely certified suffering and rejection, he is declared to be nevertheless (for Christians, thereby) the supreme heavenly agent and the lord of the elect. Luke may have something of this in mind in making the alteration.

listen to him: Not rather than to anyone else, e.g. Moses or Elijah, but because he is who he is. The words echo Deut. 18¹⁵, in Luke in the same word order – 'to him listen'. There they refer not to a single individual, but to a provision of prophets whenever the need arises, who shall be like Moses the representatives of Yahweh, so that Israel may fulfil its promise of obedience at Horeb (Deut. 18⁹ff.; 5²⁷f.; cf. Exod. 24³). In rabbinic literature the text, which is rarely referred to, is interpreted either of prophecy in general or of Jeremiah. At Qumran it appears in a 'messianic' anthology, and may have been behind the expectation there of the Prophet (see Vermes, *Scrolls*, pp. 245, 49ff.). It is applied to Jesus as messiah in A. 3²³; 7³⁷. Only with these closing words, additional to the address at the baptism, is the intention of the theophany disclosed and is it a medium of revelation. The transfiguration is not simply a manifestation of the heavenly status of Jesus. Since that status is inseparable from a teaching and prophetic activity it also establishes the ultimate authority of his words on earth for his church. When the story was told on its own that would cover the whole of Jesus' ministry of the word. In its present context it applies particularly to his teaching on the rejection of the Son of man, which the disciples fail to comprehend.

36
And when the voice had spoken: en tō followed by the infinitive *genesthai*, a predominantly Lukan construction in the NT = 'after the vision', perhaps as a result of it.

Jesus was found alone: Or, 'there was found Jesus alone'. A dramatic conclusion, implying either that the voice effects what it says and leaves Jesus the Son as the sole person for the disciples to heed, or that the supernatural cloud has departed, taking Moses and Elijah with it, and leaving Jesus once more in his earthly state.

And they kept silence: As a conclusion to the vision, and to account for its lack of effect among the disciples, Mark appends one of the injunctions to silence that belong to his doctrine of the messianic secret. In this case it is imposed until the resurrection of the Son of man, and itself gives rise to a discussion of what was meant by resurrection (Mark 9⁹⁻¹⁰). Luke changes this into a statement of fact that the disciples remained silent and refrained from telling anyone anything about it *in those days*, though no reason is given for their behaviour. The subsequent dialogue during the descent of the mountain (Mark 9¹¹⁻¹³) Luke omits, perhaps because of the strangeness of its context (it concerns Elijah alone) and the obscurity of its contents.

9^{37-43a} = Mark 9^{14-29}

THE CURE OF THE EPILEPTIC BOY

^{37}*On the next day, when they had come down from the mountain, a great crowd met him.* ^{38}*And behold, a man from the crowd cried, 'Teacher, I beg you to look upon my son, for he is my only child;* ^{39}*and behold, a spirit seizes him, and he suddenly cries out; it convulses him till he foams, and shatters him, and will hardly leave him.* ^{40}*And I begged your disciples to cast it out, but they could not.'* ^{41}*Jesus answered, 'O faithless and perverse generation, how long am I to be with you and bear with you? Bring your son here.'* ^{42}*While he was coming, the demon tore him and convulsed him. But Jesus rebuked the unclean spirit, and healed the boy, and gave him back to his father.* ^{43a}*And all were astonished at the majesty of God.*

Luke follows Mark's sequence of descent from the glory and certainty of transfiguration in the heavenly sphere into the intolerable world of evil and impotence, and by the omission of Mark 9^{11-13} brings them into more immediate proximity. Mark's story of the cure of the epileptic boy is striking in several respects. It is long and diffuse, and contains along with the healing a number of different motifs – (i) the excitement of the crowd, (ii) the failure of the disciples, (iii) the dialogue with the parent on faith, (iv) the necessity in face of the gravity of the case of a double technique of healing, exorcism and the raising of the apparently dead, and (v) private instruction of the disciples on what was required for exorcisms of this type. Matthew and Luke agree in condensing this to the normal pattern and proportions of a healing story, and in the portions of Mark they omit (viz. Mark $9^{14-16,\ 21-24,\ 25b-27,\ 29}$). Of the above motifs they agree in retaining only (ii), though Matthew has his own version of (iii) and (v).

๛

37
A combination of Mark 9^9 and 9^{14}. *come down*, *katerchesthai*, and *met*, *sunantān*, are almost confined to Luke in the NT. The latter summarizes the situation in Mark 9^{14-15}. *next day*, *tē hexēs*, is Lukan. It is too general to indicate whether Luke thought the Transfiguration took place at night, as is also the reading in some mss 'during the day'.

9^{37-43}

38

Luke increases the drama and pathos with *And behold*, *cried* (*boasthai*, only L–A in the NT apart from OT quotations and the cry on the cross), *I beg* (*deomai*, only L–A in the NT), *look upon* (*epiblepein* + 1^{48}; James 2^3 in another sense, frequent in the LXX, but not elsewhere, in appeals for divine succour), and *only* (cf. the addition to Mark in 8^{42}, and 7^{12}), with the father's request based on it (*for*).

39

In this overloaded sentence Luke brings together in a fourfold statement the details of the case (less medical than Mark, so Lagrange) which are scattered in Mark: *a spirit* (without adjective) = Mark 9^{20}, *seizes* = Mark 9^{18}, *suddenly* = Mark 9^{20}, *cries out*, *convulses* = Mark 9^{20}, *foams* (literally 'with foam', more usual than the corresponding verb in Mark $9^{18, 20}$). *hardly* (*molis*, only here in the gospels, four times in A.) *leaves* (*apochōrein* + A. 13^{13}; Matt. 7^{23}) summarizes the severity of the possession corresponding to 'from a child' and 'never enter him again' in Mark $9^{21, 25}$. The forceful *shatters* (*suntribein* = 'crushes') = Mark $9^{22a, 18}$. 'dumb' (Mark 9^{17}) is dropped because the demon cries out.

40

In the story taken on its own this would provide in the context of a healing a contrast between the power of Jesus the teacher and the impotence of the disciples. In the context, if the disciples included any of the Twelve, it stands in strange disaccord with 9^{1-6}, particularly when Luke omits any reference to this type of possession as a special case (Mark 9^{28-29}).

41

This expostulation has particular force in Luke, being all that is left of Mark's version to distinguish this exorcism from any other exorcism. Its language is influenced by the Song of Moses (Deut. 32^{1-43}; there is another version in the Odes at the end of the LXX), which 'shows great originality of form, being a presentation of prophetical thoughts in poetical dress on a scale without parallel in the Old Testament'.[n] Only there in the OT is *generation* used of contemporary Israel – *faithless* for 'crooked' (Deut. 32^5) may be a Christian creation based on this context, cf. Deut. 32^{20} – and Matthew and Luke recognize the allusion by adding *perverse*. The Song celebrates the faithfulness of Yahweh in face of the faithlessness of his people in turning to idolatry, especially the idolatry of the Golden Calf which Moses encounters on his descent from the holy mount. In the context the expostulation is evoked by the impotence of the disciples, who are thus ranged with the rest of Israel (mankind?) as faithless and perverted.

n S. R. Driver, *Deuteronomy*, ICC, 1895, p. 345.

It falls short of being an utterance of 'the God who appeared only temporarily in human form, quickly to return to heaven' (Dibelius, *Tradition*, p. 278), but is more than an expression of weariness in the face of ingratitude.[o] *with you* seems to betray the consciousness of one who knows he has an earthly ministry that is limited in time and scope, its fulfilment to be looked for elsewhere (cf. 12^{50}; $13^{32ff.}$). Readers of the Gospel know that Jesus' departure is already determined.

42–43
Luke passes over the dialogue on faith and the subsequent discussion of the disciples' impotence (Mark 9^{28-29}), and the difficulties of the case, and brings the story quickly to a conventional end, Jesus performing the cure with ease to the astonishment of all.

42
As the demon (*daimonion*) *tore* (*rhēssein* = 'dash to the ground,' cf. Mark 9^{18}) *and convulsed* (= Mark 9^{20}) the boy, Jesus *rebuked* (*epitimān*, see on 4^{34}) *the unclean spirit* (= Mark 9^{25}). *and healed the boy*, coming after the exorcism, preserves a trace of the double cure in Mark. *and gave him back to his father* (as in 7^{15}) balances *Bring your son here* (v. 41).

43
As elsewhere in Luke the work of Jesus issues in the magnification of God (cf. 5^{26}; 7^{17}; 8^{39}).

majesty: *megaleiotēs* appears for the first time in Greek literature in the LXX (four times, for the majesty of Solomon, of God's truth and kingdom), is used by Josephus of divine majesty, and elsewhere in the NT of Artemis (A. 19^{27}) and of Christ at the Transfiguration (II Peter 1^{16}) – cf. the similar *megalōsunē* in the Song of Moses (Deut. 32^3). This grandiose word fits the scene following the Transfiguration.

9^{43b-45} = Mark 9^{30-32}
THE SECOND PREDICTION OF THE PASSION

[43b]*But while they were all marvelling at everything he did, he said to his disciples,* [44]*'Let these words sink into your ears; for the Son of man is to be delivered into the hands of men.'* [45]*But they did not understand this saying, and*

o M.-J. Lagrange, *Évangile selon Saint Marc*, Paris 1911, ad loc.

it was concealed from them, that they should not perceive it; and they were afraid to ask him about this saying.

That Mark is Luke's source here is indicated both by the occurrence of a second prediction of the passion at this not very obvious place, and by the common sequence of its constituent elements – *to be delivered into the hands of men* (only here in the passion predictions), *they did not understand this saying* (agnoein = 'to be ignorant of', only here in Mark and Luke), and *they were afraid to ask him* (only here in Mark and Luke). Luke's forceful rephrasing shows its importance and meaning for him in the context.

ᴥ

43b

Luke does not reproduce the journey through Galilee, which in Mark 9^{30a} leads to, but is hardly required as a setting for, this single passage. His geography remains vague; there has been no place reference since the unspecified journey of $8^{1ff.}$ except a visit to the Gerasene country, Bethsaida and the mountain. Further, Luke substitutes for the desire of Jesus to remain incognito in Mark 9^{30b} the very opposite setting of a universal acclamation of his mighty deeds – *marvelling at*, confined to Luke in the NT, *all, everything, he did* is imperfect = 'he was doing'. So for Luke a principal aspect of the passion, which made it difficult for men, including disciples, to accept Jesus as messiah, was that it contradicted their natural expectation of a hero and saviour; cf. $4^{22ff.}$; $24^{19ff.}$; Heb. 2^{10}.

44

Let these words sink into your ears: This, in place of Mark's 'he was teaching', is most emphatic, and is unique in the Bible. *into your ears*, often with 'to speak' = 'to announce to the people', is of LXX origin (cf. Deut. 31^{30}; 32^{44}), and is found in the NT (except for James 5^4) only in L–A (1^{44}; cf. 4^{21}; A. 11^{22}). *tithesthai* = 'put' with such a phrase, as here, is both classical and LXX (cf. I Sam. 21^{12}), and is also confined to L–A in the NT (1^{66}; 21^{14}; A. 5^4; 19^{21}). The sense is 'Do you (emphatic, as opposed to men in general) receive into your ears, sc. take completely to heart'.

these words: Some take *logous* to mean 'things' (see on 9^{28}, and cf. $1^{4, 65}$; I Macc. 7^{33}), since what Jesus says is described in v. 45 as a single *rhēma* = 'saying', and *for* could have its ordinary force. The meaning would then be, 'Lay up the memory of these mighty works, for you will need to recall them when the opposite happens.' But the close connection of *words* with *ears* favours *these words* (cf. Jer. 9^{20}); in which case *for* will have the sense, not found elsewhere in

L–A, of 'namely' (cf. 24⁴⁴). The meaning will then be, 'Take to heart the hand-ing over of the Son of man as the only clue to what is to happen '(cf. 24⁶⁻⁸, ⁴⁴ᶠᶠ.).

the Son of man: See on 5²⁴.

is to be: mellei (so Matt. 17²²). Luke is fond of this verb, and generally it denotes a simple future of human intention; but in this kind of context it probably includes divine predestination (cf. 3⁷; 9³¹; A. 17³¹; 26²³).

delivered into the hands of men: It is unnecessary to refer, as do some, to Isa. 53⁶, ¹² as a background, since 'to be delivered into the hands of', which is not found there, is a common LXX expression for the delivery of men, generally by God, into the power of their enemies to wreak their will (see on 22⁴). Limiting the prediction to this single, compressed and general statement – there is no reference, as in Mark 9³¹, to death and resurrection – underlines the basic contradiction of the passion, that Jesus, as the Son of man and Chosen One, belongs with God and his purposes, and not to men, who, for all their acclaim, remain enemies of evil will.

45

The emphatic injunction to comprehend in v. 43 is now matched by an equally emphatic statement of incomprehension (cf. 18³⁴). Luke makes the double com-ment in Mark 9³² fourfold, including in *perceive* the standard Greek word for intellectual perception, *aisthanesthai* + + (cf. 24²⁵).

was concealed from them: A Hebraism, which, when followed by *that,* suggests the concealment is by divine purpose (cf. 24¹⁶), and is only temporary (8¹⁷; 12²). It is to be removed by God in due time through the risen Christ's exposition of divine purpose in the scriptures (24²⁵⁻²⁷, ³², ⁴⁴ᶠᶠ.).

were afraid to ask him: From Mark, with *this saying* repeated; it suggests a deep-seated abhorrence accompanying, and perhaps the cause of, the intellectual incomprehension.

9⁴⁶⁻⁵⁰ = Mark 9³³⁻⁴¹   DISCIPLESHIP

⁴⁶*And an argument arose among them as to which of them was the greatest.* ⁴⁷*But when Jesus perceived the thought of their hearts, he took a child and put him by his side,* ⁴⁸*and said to them, 'Whoever receives this child in my name receives me, and whoever receives me receives him who sent me; for he who is least among you all is the one who is great.'*

⁴⁹John answered, 'Master, we saw a man casting out demons in your name, and we forbade him, because he does not follow with us.' ⁵⁰But Jesus said to him, 'Do not forbid him; for he that is not against you is for you.'

Luke refashions, and brings together, two units in Mark loosely connected in thought by a contrast between Jesus and his disciples in their conception of discipleship, and verbally by *in my (your) name*. They thus serve as a preparation for the long non-Markan section 9^{51}–18^{14}, in which Jesus both acts through his disciples (9^{51}–10^{24}) and himself instructs them ($11^{1ff.}$; $12^{22ff.}$; $16^{1ff.}$; $17^{1ff.}$, $^{22ff.}$). He concludes with the inclusive missionary principle *he that is not against you is for you*, and ignores the heterogeneous collection of sayings that follow in Mark 9^{41-50}. Further, by omitting Mark 10^{1-12} he is able to rejoin Mark with a similar incident of Jesus with the children ($18^{15ff.}$ = Mark $10^{13ff.}$).

The first unit, vv. 46–48 = Mark 9^{33-37}, is itself composite, containing two themes – the least to be the greatest and the receiving of Jesus in the person of a child; but the connection between them, and the relation of the second to the original question about greatness, are obscure. It is the first rather than the second which would follow naturally from the introduction of a child. So Luke, like Matthew, has rewritten to produce a single unit in which both themes are related to the figure of the child (*for*, v. 48b).

༄༅

46
Luke omits the details of place and movement and the question of Jesus in Mark 9^{33}.

an argument arose among them: Either (i) 'there arose a dispute (*dialogismos*, see on 2^{35}) amongst them'; but there is no parallel in L–A to *eiserchesthai* = 'to enter' in the sense of 'arise', and v. 47a implies that the disputation was internal to each disciple, or (ii) 'there entered a deliberation into their hearts', which would be the only instance in the NT of the classical use of the verb with thoughts, and no reason is given why they should all have the same thoughts. The imprecise expression may be due to Luke's combining a summary of Mark 9^{33-34} with a favourite idea, implicit also in Mark, of Jesus as the reader of men's thoughts (v. 47, cf. 5^{22}; 6^8; 24^{38}).

as to which of them was the greatest: Luke formulates the issue clearly by a construction almost confined to him in the NT, the indirect question introduced by the article *to* and the verb in the optative. *greatest*, *meizōn* is the comparative used as a superlative. The question about precedence, and the definition of greatness it drew from Jesus, clearly made a deep impression in the tradition (cf. $22^{24ff.}$; 14^{11}; 18^{14}; Mark $10^{13-16, \, 42-45}$; Matt. 18^{1-6}; John $13^{12ff.}$). It may have had a precise origin in the sudden elevation of simple men from their ordinary occupations to be leading figures in the eschatological mission to Israel, and to be successful preachers and exorcists.

47

took a child and put it by his side: paidion could mean (i) an infant, as apparently in Mark 9^{36}, unless 'taking in his arms' should be 'putting his arm around', or (ii) a (young) child, as here, where he is placed alongside so as to be associated with Jesus. The choice of *a child* as an analogue of the disciple appears to be a departure from Judaism, where children are those who owe obedience, and need discipline and instruction. Among the rabbis 'the little one' was the immature one, whether as pupil or teacher – see SB I, p. 592, and cf. Rom. 2^{20}; I Cor. 3^1; 14^{20}; Eph. 4^{14}; Heb. $5^{13f.}$. Its force is debated – it is certainly not innocence or sinlessness, which are nowhere suggested. In Mark 10^{14} the kingdom is said to belong to such, and is to be accepted 'as a child' (accepts?). In Matt. $18^{3f.}$ disciples are to turn and become as children to enter it, which means to make themselves *tapeinos* = 'lowly' or 'insignificant' rather than 'humble'. The point of comparison may be smallness as such – cf. the reading of syr^{sin} at 9^{48b}, 'he that is small and is as a child to you' – and there may be more than analogue here, since Jesus would appear to have called his disciples 'the little ones'. In $17^{2f.}$; Matt. $18^{10ff.}$; 25^{45} the term probably, and in Mark 9^{42}; Matt. 10^{42}; 18^6 certainly, refers to disciples. It is not a term of affection, as 'children' or 'little children' in Mark 10^{24}; John 21^5, but a characterization of his mission by reference to the paradoxical status of those who receive it (cf. 10^{21}). It may have had its origin in Zech. 13^7, where 'the little ones' are the sheep who suffer when the shepherd is smitten but are the remnant that becomes the people of God (cf. 12^{32}). Here the matter is complicated rather than elucidated when the child is primarily introduced not to teach true greatness (in Mark 9^{35} this has already been done, and in Luke is a secondary object), but as a figure of the one to be received in Jesus' name (see next note).

48a

In its present form and context this states two things at once. (i) On the Jewish principle of the *shaliach*, viz. that the one commissioning is received in the person of the one commissioned, the mission of Jesus, and that of the disciples dependent on it, are authoritative, having their origin in the divine will and conveying the divine presence; for this principle, stated also in 10^{16}; Matt. 10^{40}; John $12^{44f.}$; 13^{20}, see *TDNT* I, pp. 414ff. (ii) Smallness is the characteristic by which the mission is recognized at each of its stages – the disciple, Jesus and God. But (i) combines awkwardly with the figure of the child, as may be seen from the strained interpretation given to *receives* in relation to *this child* – 'cares for' (Easton), 'the service of children' (Schlatter, Rengstorf, W. Manson), 'the service of love' (Klostermann, Creed); see the discussion in Lagrange, p. 282. In the NT 'to receive', *dechesthai*, when not used of receiving the word of God, generally has the semi-technical sense of accepting a divine messenger. *in my name* in such a context would most naturally mean 'as my representative' (cf. 21⁸; A. 4¹⁷ᶠ·; 9²⁷ᶠ·; Matt. 7²²). But a child cannot be received in this way, not having been sent like an apostle, prophet or righteous man (Matt. 10⁴⁰⁻⁴²). The statement may originally have been made not to disciples but about them as 'little ones' (cf. Mark 9³⁷), which, when no longer understood as meaning 'disciples', suggested the introduction of a child to explain it, perhaps on the analogy of Mark 10¹³ᶠᶠ·, where Jesus 'receives children', and the kingdom is to be 'received as a child'. In this form it may have been understood to have reference to infant baptism in the church; see on 18¹⁵⁻¹⁷.

48b

This arises more naturally from the figure of the child, and relates more closely than v. 48a to the question about greatness. Luke has changed its position, sentence structure and wording so as to conclude with the most emphatic possible statement of the paradox. *for*, i.e. the child is the symbol of the fact that *he who is* (*huparchein* suggests a state of being) *the least* (*mikroteros*, comparative as superlative, 'the littlest'?) *among you all* ('the little ones'?), *is the one who is great* (*houtos megas* is emphatic = 'he is the one who is (already) great').

49-50

The preservation in the tradition of this strange little pericope, including a personal name, could be explained by the important part played by exorcism in the Christian mission (see on 4³³), and by the problems to which it gave rise in competition with Jewish exorcism, itself deeply affected by Hellenistic thaumaturgy and magic (cf. 11¹⁹, Justin, *Dialogue* 85, Jos. *Ant.* 8.45ff., SB IV, Excursus 21). Illuminating as background is A. 19¹³ᶠᶠ·, where the exclusive attitude, in contrast to Jesus' reply here, may reflect increased hostility between Christians and Jews. By the second century the use of the name of Jesus in exorcism was forbidden to Jews.

49

John answered: It is impossible to say why it is John (so Mark 9³⁸) rather than Peter or an anonymous disciple who is made to raise the question. *answered*, the participle *apokritheis*, is often used simply as a copula and does not have to be translated, but Luke may have added it here with its full force to link the pericope to what precedes. John's observation is now a rejoinder to Jesus' statement about receiving someone in his name.

in your name: There is no substantial difference between *en* = 'in' and *epi* = 'upon' (as in v. 48) with 'the name', though the former, which is probably the correct reading here, is more usual in exorcism (cf. 10^{17}; A. 3^6; 4$^{7-12}$; 16^{18}; Mark 16^{17}). Since in ancient, and especially Semitic thought 'the name' denoted the nature and person of, and could stand as an equivalent for, a divinity, it was always capable of development in accordance with further revelation of the divinity whose name it was. Thus in the NT 'the name of Jesus' comes to stand for all that Jesus is (cf. Phil. 2^{10}), and for the means, particularly in baptism, by which the believer is associated with him. In the synoptic gospels this has its roots in the widespread conception of the name of the divinity as an instrument of power (cf. A. 19^{13}; 4^{30}; 9^{34}). A. 4$^{7-12}$ shows a close connection between 'name' and healing power, and also a more spiritual conception of the latter arising from the former. That the disciples themselves made use of the name of Jesus in his lifetime, and that this constituted the power and authority given to them when sent out on a mission (9^1), cannot be concluded with certainty from this passage, but it is possible, and Luke appears to have thought so (cf. 10^{17}). Here the name is effective apart from any personal relation with, or commission from, Jesus. The disciples do not deny its effectiveness, and nor does Jesus. Their objection is to its unauthorized use by one who is not an accredited disciple. The pericope could owe something to Num. 11$^{26-29}$, Joshua's protest at the irregularity of Eldad and Medad's prophesying outside the number of the seventy elders, and Moses' reply, and if so would be appropriately placed in Luke near the appointment of the Seventy.

with us: This, with *you* in v. 50, distinguishes between Jesus and the disciples, whereas *us* in Mark 9$^{38, 40}$ unites them.

50
forbid: kōleuein, from Mark, is the opposite of 'receive', and seems to have had a semi-technical sense of refusing to receive into the Christian community (cf. 18^{16}; A. 8^{36}; 10^{47}; III John 10).

he that is not against you is for you: Luke omits the more specific part of Jesus' reply in Mark 9^{39}, that the use of the name is evidence of a minimal relation and of a general support of Jesus which is unlikely to change. By omitting also the string of sayings in Mark 9$^{41-50}$ he is also able to conclude the Galilean ministry with a variant version of Mark 9^{40} which makes it a maxim for the missionary church. It is only formally in contradiction with 11^{23}, also in a discussion on exorcism, since there by the use of the name the exorcist is engaged in the same work 'with' Jesus and 'harvests' with him. Matt. 7$^{22f.}$ does represent a contrary position.

$$9^{51}-18^{14}$$

The Central Section

The chapter division here is misleading. The sentence in 9[51], the solemn character of which is hardly reproduced in the English rendering, marks a turning point in the Gospel. All that remains to be narrated about Jesus is now placed under the sign manual of his impending assumption. It begins here to be set within the framework of a journey from a place unspecified to Jerusalem via Samaria and Jericho. In this way the division between the Galilean ministry and what followed is more definitely marked in this Gospel, which thus acquires a different structure from that of the other synoptic gospels. Much of its individual character comes from this expansion of the approach to the passion in Jerusalem to a length greater than that of the Galilean ministry, and to constitute almost a third of the Gospel ('the centre and core of the Third Gospel', Streeter, *Four Gospels*, p. 203).

Luke's plan and procedure here have been much discussed.[a] This is particularly because this section, stretching from 9[51], where Luke leaves Mark, to 18[14], where he rejoins him, has the appearance of a largely amorphous aggregate of material . To judge from 8[1ff.]; A. 8[4ff.]; 9[32ff.]; 13[14ff.]; 15[36ff.], Luke would not have been averse to casting his narrative into what was a popular literary form at the time, viz. the travel story of an itinerant teacher. To call this section The Travel Narrative (as in Huck's *Synopsis*, p. 112) would, however, be to describe it by its most formal aspect, and to leave its distinctive character unexplained. Only the vaguest indications of time and place are provided as connecting links (9[52, 56f.]; 10[1, 21, 38]; 11[14, 27]; 13[10, 31]; 14[1, 25]); cf. the comment of Lagrange (p. xxxviii), 'In this section we search in vain to know where we are.'

At two points (13[22]; 17[11]) the reader has to be reminded, somewhat awkwardly, that a journey is in progress. It is therefore unlikely that Luke derived the concept of such a journey from the material he has selected to include in it, for this does not by its content demand, or for the most part even hint at, a journey as its necessary context. It is more

---

a See H. Conzelmann, *Theology*, pp. 60ff., L. Girard, *L'Évangile des voyages de Jésus*, Paris 1951, and the bibliography in Marshall, p. 402.

likely that he derived it from Mark, who in 10^{1-12}, a passage omitted by Luke, refers in obscure terms to a journey 'to the region of Judaea and beyond the Jordan', while later (10^{32}) referring solemnly to a journey to Jerusalem for death. Luke does not appear to have any more accurate information, and his journey, though greatly extended, is equally obscure – a missionary(?) tour in Samaria ($9^{52ff.}$), a further mission or teaching tour somewhere *en route* to Jerusalem (13^{22}), a sojourn(?) in Herod's territory (Galilee or Peraea $13^{31ff.}$), a journey through, or along the borders of, Samaria and Galilee (17^{11}), and a sudden arrival at Jericho (18^{35}). This is hardly capable of being traced on a map. The frequent reference to Jerusalem as the goal ($9^{51, \, 53}$; 13^{22}, 13^{33-35}; 17^{11}; $19^{11, \, 28}$) is governed less by geographical than by theological considerations of the necessity of the passion, which has already been divinely determined and supernaturally announced (9^{31}; cf. $13^{33ff.}$; 22^{22}; A. 2^{23}). Though it begins from the firm determination of Jesus to go to Jerusalem the journey itself becomes desultory until the final stage from Jericho.

Judged by its form the section thus appears to be a construction of Luke. Judged by its content it is almost entirely a depository of the teaching of Jesus, such as was available to Luke, and which he judged appropriate for inclusion. This is delivered either to disciples specifically, or to the spiritual leaders of Israel as opponents, or to both together, and occasionally to crowds in general. None of this is derived from Mark, but either (i) has parallels with Matthew and is taken from a common source, Q, or sources, or (ii) is peculiar to Luke (L). With respect to (i) it is possible that Q provided Luke not only with the picture of Jesus as a teacher, but with a sequence of teaching, which in its order (though not in its wording) he has reproduced more faithfully than Matthew, who has conflated it with other material in the composition of discourses.[b] With respect to (ii) it is debated whether it came to Luke as a teaching section in a single document (cf. Easton, pp. 23ff.), which was jointed to the Q material, or represents individual units of tradition which Luke found available and selected for inclusion. There would seem to be evidence for editorial work by Luke in the construction of larger complexes of teaching out of smaller units, in which generally the L material is attached to the Q material (see the introductions to the several chapters in the commentary). While occasionally

b See V. Taylor, 'The Order of Q', *JTS* ns 4, 1953, 27–31.

this teaching may be linked to the picture in 9^{51} of Jesus as the rejected and suffering messiah on his way to death, this is not the case with most of it, which does not exhibit any dominant theme or themes. Luke's main motive may have been to preserve from available traditions, written or oral, what he thought most significant in the teaching of Jesus either for the direction of Christians or over against current Judaism. For the suggestion that he was governed in his selection and arrangement here by a desire to present Jesus as the prophet like Moses and his teaching in Deuteronomic terms, see Introduction, pp. 34ff.

9^{51-62} *A Mixed Reception*

⁵¹*When the days drew near for him to be received up, he set his face to go to Jerusalem.* ⁵²ᵃ*And he sent messengers ahead of him,*

This is a sonorous sentence by reason of its strongly 'biblical' style and phraseology. It was undoubtedly framed by Luke, as it is intended as a heading for material drawn from more than one source, and in some sense for the rest of the Gospel. It reveals his understanding of what he has still to relate.

৩৩

51
When: In the Greek literally 'It came to pass . . . and he'. For this LXX construction see on 5^1.

the days (of): Another LXX expression; cf. 1^{23}; 17^{22}; 21^{22}; A. 12^3; 21^{26}.

drew near: A lame rendering of the compound verb *sumplērousthai* = 'to be fulfilled', here used in a rare temporal sense (cf. A. 2^1; Jer. 25^{12}, and the corresponding noun in II Chron. 36^{21}; Dan. 9^2, of the divinely appointed years of the captivity). In this construction a period of time is characterized by the event to which it is leading, and which governs it. Hence, 'When the days of his assumption were reaching their (divinely appointed) term'. The course of the story is entirely determined by Jesus' foreknowledge and his consciousness of his destiny (cf. 9^{31}).

to be received up: In the Greek 'of his assumption'. The noun here (*analēmpsis*) is not found in the LXX. In Pss. Sol. 4²⁰, its earliest occurrence in extant Greek literature, it means 'death', retaining from the Hebrew original the double meaning of 'uplift' and 'remove'; but eventually it followed the verb (used in II Kings 2¹¹; I Macc. 2⁵⁸; Ecclus 48⁹; IV Ezra 6²⁶; A. 1²; I Tim. 3¹⁶) to become a semi-technical term for the translation by God to heaven of certain OT saints – notably Enoch, Elijah and Moses – to remain there until the consummation of the ages, in which they were to play a role (cf. A. 3²¹; II Baruch 76², the pseudepigraphical book The Assumption of Moses, *AP* II, pp. 407ff.). The plural *the days* shows that 'assumption' is not limited here to the ascension, but is extended, like 'to be lifted up' in John's Gospel, to embrace passion and the approach to it, resurrection and ascension as a single divine operation.

he set his face: This expression is confined to the LXX, though there followed by the preposition *epi* with the sense 'to oppose', 'to threaten'. Luke has used it with an infinitive of purpose in the sense 'firmly determine' (for the phrase in this sense, though with a different verb, II Kings 12¹⁷; Isa. 50⁷).

52a
he sent messengers ahead of him: cf. Gen. 24⁷; Exod. 23²⁰; Mal. 3¹. It is not clear what this means; see on v. 52b.

9^{52 b-56}　　　　REJECTION BY SAMARITANS

⁵²ᵇ*who went and entered a village of the Samaritans, to make ready for him;* ⁵³*but the people would not receive him, because his face was set toward Jerusalem.* ⁵⁴*And when his disciples James and John saw it, they said, 'Lord, do you want us to bid fire come down from heaven and consume them?'* ★ ⁵⁵*But he turned and rebuked them*† ⁵⁶*And they went on to another village.*

★ Other ancient authorities add *as Elijah did*
† Other ancient authorities add *and he said, 'You do not know what manner of spirit you are of; for the Son of man came not to destroy men's lives but to save them'*

As the Galilean ministry had opened with a scene of rejection, and with appeal to precedents in the careers of Elijah and Elisha (4¹⁶⁻³⁰), so does the journey. *when his disciples saw it they said* is awkward if they have been sent on ahead of Jesus, and may indicate that Luke is here utilizing an original story in which Jesus and disciples entered a village (for preaching) and were rejected, and adapting it to the different setting of a journey with disciples sent on in advance.

 басы

52-53

a village of the Samaritans: The story may belong to the L tradition, which alone of the synoptic traditions mentions Samaritans (10^{33}; 17^{16}), though there the reference is favourable, and here they are singled out as the first to rebuff Jesus on his journey.[c] They were sectarian Jews who were not alone in their hostility to the Jerusalem temple and priesthood (cf. Qumran), but whose distinctive tenet was that Mount Gerizim was the holy mountain on which God should be worshipped.

to make ready: Only here in the NT is the verb *hetoimazein* = 'to prepare' used without an object. The preparation is not specified, and could mean in the context something more or other than securing hospitality. There is a fresh situation here and in $10^{1ff.}$, which is neither that of Jesus travelling in company with disciples ($8^{1ff.}$), nor that of sending out envoys who return to him ($9^{1ff.}$), but half-way between. It would seem that Luke intends the journey to be a royal progress. This could be analogous to the situation of Moses, who, in leading Israel to the promised land, sends out messengers 'to search the land for us, and bring us word again of the way we must go up, and the cities into which we shall come' (Deut. 1^{22}).

because his face was set towards Jerusalem: In the Greek 'his face was going' (to go), a unique expression. There is an apparent parallel in II Sam. 17^{11}, but there 'face' stands for the person, whereas here it is determined by *he set his face* in 9^{51}. Dalman (*Words of Jesus*, p. 31) sees it as an instance of Luke's habit of using an expression 'that slips from his pen a second time after a short interval, and then perhaps never again'. The hostility of the Samaritans is generally explained with reference to Jos. *Ant.* 20.118 and *Life* 269 as that customary with Samaritans towards Galileans, who took this, the shorter route, to the festivals at Jerusalem. But in the first passage Josephus describes only the taking of this route as customary and the disturbance on it as a special occurrence, and in the second seeks safe conduct for his envoys through Samaria because it had fallen to the Romans. Since the main ground of dispute between Samaritans and Jews was the place of the Jerusalem temple and cultus, hostility would be likely towards pilgrims thither, but it is unlikely that this is what Luke intends by *because his face was set towards Jerusalem*. This rather links the incident with 9^{51} and the

[c] On the vexed questions of the origins and character of the Samaritans see R. J. Coggins, *Samaritans and Jews*, Oxford and Richmond, Va., 1975.

passion of the rejected Jesus. After the assumption the rejection will be reversed (A. 1⁸; 84ff.).

54

James and John: Cf. Luke's identification of the two disciples in 22⁸. Only here and in 12⁴¹ are individual disciples named in this central section. Elsewhere James and John are represented as acting together only in Mark 10³⁵ff. (omitted by Luke).

Lord, do you want us . . . and consume them?: The question echoes the words of Elijah in his protest in Samaria against the king's consultation of a foreign god, and his proof that he is a man of God by the destroying fire (II Kings 1¹⁰ff.; the variant 'as Elijah did' simply makes this plain). This is wrongly called typological, since Elijah's action is here repudiated. That the two disciples should believe that, permission being granted by Jesus, they could effect this destruction, if it is anything more than a foil to Jesus' rebuke, could betoken an intense messianic (Zealot?) fervour amongst the disciples.

55

The rebuke is emphatic. *he turned* (Greek the participle *strapheis*) occurs seven times in Luke (not in A.), always in non-Markan contexts, and gives a special point to what follows. *rebuked (epitimān)* is a strong word, used in exorcisms of rebuking demons, and only here and Mark 8³³ pars. of rebuking disciples. This terseness gave rise to additions to the text with the object of closing the incident with a pronouncement of Jesus, who otherwise does not speak, and of making its lesson explicit. 'You do not know what manner of spirit you are of' is a striking saying, though *pneuma* = 'spirit' in the sense of 'disposition' has no parallel in the gospels, but only in the epistles (I Cor. 4²¹; Gal. 6¹; I Peter 3⁴). It should be omitted with p⁴⁵ p⁷⁵ and the major uncial mss. The Son of man saying should also be omitted with the same textual authorities. The double sense, physical and spiritual, of 'destroy' and 'save' is more forced than in 6⁹. These additions illustrate the continuing vigour and inventiveness of the tradition, particularly with respect to Son of man sayings.

56

This is vague, and serves simply to continue the thought of a journey. It is not said whether it was a Samaritan village, or whether they were accepted there.

[57] *As they were going along the road, a man said to him, 'I will follow you wherever you go.'* [58] *And Jesus said to him, 'Foxes have holes, and birds of the air have nests; but the Son of man has nowhere to lay his head.'* [59] *To another he said, 'Follow me.' But he said, 'Lord, let me first go and bury my father.'* [60] *But he said to him, 'Leave the dead to bury their own dead; but as for you, go and proclaim the kingdom of God.'* [61] *Another said, 'I will follow you, Lord; but let me first say farewell to those at my home.'* [62] *Jesus said to him, 'No one who puts his hand to the plough and looks back is fit for the kingdom of God.'*

Luke now follows with a triplet of sayings on requirements of discipleship. All have a proverbial ring, though the last is too specific to be a proverb. They could have stood on their own, a suitable setting to be deduced from their content. Though the form is that of dialogue the weight falls on the saying of Jesus on the demands for discipleship, and for this they were preserved. It is not said what effect the sayings had.

The first two are in almost verbatim agreement with Matt. 8^{19-22}, where they are inserted into a collection of miracle stories and immediately previous to a crossing of the lake of Galilee, and they are addressed, somewhat implausibly, to a scribe and a disciple. In placing them here Luke may indicate that he saw the journey as a progress which gathers followers *en route* until on arrival they form a multitude (19^{37}). The third, peculiar to Luke, is modelled on the second, and shows evidence of his hand – *say farewell* (*apotassesthai* + 14^{33}; A. $18^{18, 21}$; Mark 6^{46}; II Cor. 2^{13}), *plough* (*arotron* + +), *fit for* (the literary word *euthetos* + 14^{35}; Heb. 6^{7}). Luke may also have refashioned the second to make it a fourfold statement by the addition of v. 60b, which 'word by word, forms a contrast to the man's request' (Plummer, p. 267). He has woven all three together by having the affirmation of the first, *I will follow you* (v. 57b) and the petition in the second *let me* (v. 59) combined in the third, *I will follow you . . . let me* (v. 61).

❧

57
As they were going along the road, a man said: Generally *said* is taken with *along the road*, but this phrase (*en tē hodō* = 'in the way') could be a Christian expression for discipleship (cf. Mark $10^{32, 52}$), here intensifying *were going*.

wherever you go: This voices a total readiness for discipleship. For 'to follow' in the sense of 'to be a disciple', see on 5^{11}. In this context there is a certain irony, since Jesus can now go only to one place, Jerusalem.

58

What this haunting saying means precisely, and what it implies for the disciple, is not clear. It is a saying about the Son of man, and the would-be disciple is expected to recognize the term, and to know that Jesus is speaking of himself. In the context it appears to mean that Jesus is homeless on earth because on his way to Jerusalem, which, though it is the city of God, will reject him. It could then be another way of saying that to be a disciple is to take up the cross and follow (9^{23}). Bultmann (*History*, pp. 27f.) thinks that a proverb on the homelessness of man on earth (the Son of man = man) has been attributed to Jesus. Manson (*Sayings*, p. 72) objects to this that as a statement about man it would be simply untrue, but the striking parallel in Plutarch, *Life of Tiberius Gracchus* (quoted in Creed, p. 142), contrasting the beasts of Italy, which have holes and somewhere to sleep, with those fighting for Italy, who wander homeless, shows a similar sentiment applied to a particular situation, and this could have been generalized in the manner of e.g. Ecclesiastes. Manson further insists that the choice of *foxes* and *birds of the air* has to be explained. On the basis of I Enoch 89, where 'foxes' stand for the Ammonite enemies of Israel, and of such passages as Ezek. 17^{23}; Dan. 4^{12}, where 'the birds of heaven' may stand for Gentiles, he interprets the saying to mean that everyone is at home in Israel except the true Israel (the Son of man). The Roman overlords and the Edomite interlopers (cf. 'that fox' of Herod in 13^{32}) have made their position secure, while the true Israel is disinherited by them. But Edomites are represented in I Enoch by boars, and it is not certain that 'the birds of heaven' was, without more specific reference (as in Mark 4^{32}), an equivalent for Gentiles. And it was not only the true Israel but all Israel that was politically disinherited. Foxes may be chosen as solitary and vagabond animals (cf. Lam. 5^{18}; Ezek. 13^4 – hence 'even foxes'), and birds as the most restless (*nests, kataskēnoseis*, should rather be 'dwelling places'). As an individual person Jesus seems in the gospels to have had a home, and to be given hospitality when on the move. Perhaps the meaning is that as the Son of man, the eschatological redeemer, the world should belong to him (cf. Ps. 84^{4-6}, as expounded in Heb. $2^{5ff.}$), but paradoxically it is denied to him (cf. I Enoch 42^1; 94^5 for the homelessness on earth of Wisdom). But no parallel is cited for 'to have somewhere to lay the head' (= 'to sleep') as a synonym for 'to have a home'.

59

In the parallel, Matt. 8^{21}, the request is strange from one who is already a disciple; there is nothing for 'first' to refer to, and the command to follow precedes *Leave the dead to bury their own dead*. Luke has the incident initiated by the command to follow, which gives better sense to *first*, and *Leave the dead* . . . *own dead* is succeeded by a fresh thought, probably introduced by Luke himself, that to be a disciple is to be engaged in proclaiming the kingdom of God (*diangellein* + A. 21²⁶; Rom. 9¹⁷ LXX).

Let me go and bury my father: This request was imperative, as the burial of parents was a supreme obligation of Jewish religion and family piety, the neglect of which was a gross impiety. The refusal of such a request serves to express in the most ruthless possible terms the breach with natural life required by discipleship and its engagement with the kingdom of God (cf. 14²⁶).

leave the dead to bury their dead: This seems to require the literal and the figurative use of *dead* in a single sentence. The latter (cf. 15²⁴; I Tim. 5⁶) is not found in the OT, but is common in Hellenistic, especially Stoic literature, and was known to the rabbis (SB I, p. 489). Again the implication is very rigorous. Only those preoccupied with God's kingdom are alive – *but as for you*, Greek *su de* = 'but you (who are alive)'. The rest of the world is in the sphere of death.

61–62

This third instance is the most general. Its injunction to carry through what has once been undertaken would be more appropriate for one who is already a disciple. It is plainly modelled on Elijah's summons of Elisha. With v. 61 cf. I Kings 19²⁰, 'Let me kiss my father and mother, and then I will follow you.' *puts his hand to the plough* (v. 62) is not paralleled as an expression for undertaking a task, and probably arises here from Elisha's ploughing when Elijah called him.

10^{1-24} *The Successful Mission of the Seventy and its Import*

This is one of the most crucial sections of the Gospel, by reason both of its sustained elevated tone, which is continued from 9⁵¹ᶠᶠ·, and of the character of the materials Luke has assembled for it. The journey to Jerusalem now takes on for a time the character of a mission foreshadowing the harvest of the end through the Lord's appointment of Seventy in addition to the Twelve. He commissions them at greater length than the Twelve as heralds of the kingdom and of himself. To reject them is to incur, like the Galilean cities that have rejected him, the supreme judgment. Their success in exorcism, which they report with jubilation, is interpreted – in advance of his own (11¹⁴⁻²³) – by a visionary experience of the Lord himself, unique in the gospels, as evidence of the end of Satan's dominion, and of the existence in their persons of the heavenly elect. In an ecstatic prayer of thanksgiving to God they are declared the recipients of an open revelation of the Father, itself grounded in the mutual and exclusive knowledge of the Father and the Son; and they are pronounced blessed as being witnesses of nothing less than the fulfilment of Israel's hope.

All this is of the greatest importance, since the powers, status and insight of the Lord are now depicted, even more explicitly than in the case of the Twelve, as being passed on from him to his church. But the section also provides a signal illustration of Luke's aptitude for painting a picture which combines impressiveness in general with lack of veri-similitude in particulars. Thus, *the Lord appointed seventy others* (v. 1) suggests something momentous, and *sent them two by two* that it is a mission over a wide area. And this is resumed in the return of the missionaries as to a centre of operations (v. 17; cf. 9^{10}). But the addition of *on ahead of him* and of *into every town and place where he himself was about to come*, if pressed, yields the preposterous situation of thirty-five (six) pairs of missionaries either spread out at intervals along the direct route to Jerusalem, to be caught up by Jesus as he follows the same route, or operating radially in all directions from some centre along the route, each pair to be followed up in turn by Jesus. There is no trace elsewhere in the NT of a body of seventy disciples or apostles, and the question in 22^{35}, which refers back to 10^4 and not to 9^3, is addressed not to them but to the Twelve. The woes on the (Galilean) towns (vv. 13–16) continue the mood of vv. 10ff., but they are out of place in a mission charge; and while vv. 23–24 follow well after vv. 21–22 there is no hint that the previous sayings had been addressed to any other audience than the disciples.

THE APPOINTMENT
AND CHARGE OF THE SEVENTY

After this the Lord appointed seventy* others, and sent them on ahead of him, two by two, into every town and place where he himself was about to come. ²And he said to them, 'The harvest is plentiful, but the labourers are few;

pray therefore the Lord of the harvest to send out labourers into his harvest. ³Go your way; behold, I send you out as lambs in the midst of wolves. ⁴Carry no purse, no bag, no sandals; and salute no one on the road. ⁵Whatever house you enter, first say, 'Peace be to this house!' ⁶And if a son of peace is there, your peace shall rest upon him; but if not, it shall return to you. ⁷And remain in the same house, eating and drinking what they provide, for the labourer deserves his wages; do not go from house to house. ⁸Whenever you enter a town and they receive you, eat what is set before you; ⁹heal the sick in it and say to them, "The Kingdom of God has come near to you." ¹⁰But whenever you enter a town and they do not receive you, go into its streets and say, ¹¹"Even the dust of your town that clings to our feet, we wipe off against you; nevertheless know this, that the kingdom of God has come near." ¹²I tell you, it shall be more tolerable on that day for Sodom than for that town.'

* Other ancient authorities read *seventy-two*

The question of Luke's sources here is complex. It is likely that something as important to the church as a mission charge (cf. *Didache* 11³ᶠᶠ·; I Cor. 9¹⁴, one of the very few references by Paul to a word of the Lord) should have existed in more than one version in the tradition, and should have attracted other relevant material to itself. A comparison of Matt. 9³⁵–11¹ and Mark 6⁷⁻¹³ shows that each evangelist will have had his own conception of it. Luke has already used Mark 6⁷⁻¹³ for his commissioning of the Twelve (9¹⁻⁶), and 10²⁻¹² is unlikely to have been simply a rewriting of that for a fresh occasion, since, both in the material here which overlaps Mark and that which does not, there are agreements with the conflate charge in Matt. 9³⁵–11¹. This could indicate a mission charge in Q, though if so the extent of the Q material, its order (vv. 3–4, 5–7a, 7b, 9⁹⁻¹⁶ = Matt. 10¹⁶, ⁹⁻¹⁰ᵃ, ¹¹⁻¹³, ¹⁰ᵇ, 7, ¹⁴⁻¹⁵, 40), and the wording (e.g. vv. 5–6 ‖ Matt. 10¹¹⁻¹³), remain uncertain (see Harnack, *Sayings*, pp. 8of.). When the Markan material is subtracted from the composite charge in Matt. 9³⁷–10¹⁶, what is left is not the same as Luke 10¹⁻¹², ¹⁶, even when allowance has been made for editing by each evangelist. In some places Luke would appear to be secondary (see Knox, *Sources* II, pp. 48ff.). It is unlikely that Luke derived the Seventy from Q, as there is no sign of them, or of a mission other than that of the Twelve, in Matthew. Manson (*Sayings*, pp. 73f., 18of.) assigns the material peculiar to Matthew and Luke respectively to their special sources M and L, so that a mission charge would then be attested in four sources; but this is probably too mechanical, and produces units that are too short and disconnected to be recognizably from a source. Thus he assigns vv. 2–3 and probably vv. 8–12 to Q and vv. 4–7 to L, but the latter, even with the addition of v. 1 and vv. 17–20, is too brief to stand on its own as a mission charge. Whatever his sources Luke would appear not simply to have transcribed and joined them. He has produced out of them a distinctive and polished construction of ten balanced sentences with introduction and conclusion, which, as in 6$^{20-49}$, show predominantly a fourfold structure.

ಐಐ

1

after this: Both time and place are very vague.

the Lord appointed: The post-resurrection title is used for this official action. The verb here (Greek *anadeiknunai*), besides its ordinary meaning of 'to show forth', had acquired in Hellenistic historians (e.g. Polybius, Josephus) the technical sense of 'to authorize', 'to appoint to an office'. In the LXX it is generally used of the appointment of a king, successor or governor, but this is not entirely secular, as in I Esdr. 2³ it is used of God's appointment of Cyrus as king of the world, and in 8²³ of judges who would know the law of God. Its use here could indicate that Luke saw the Seventy (and by implication the Twelve) as office bearers and rulers in the church.

seventy: As with the Twelve the intention will depend on the significance of the number. This had two symbolic references in Judaism. (i) Seventy elders (Greek *presbuteroi*) attend Moses at Sinai (Exod. 24$^{1ff.}$), and in Num. 11$^{1ff.}$ Moses, on complaining that the number of the people is too great for him, is told by God to take 'seventy men of the elders of Israel, whom you know to be the elders of the people and officers over them', and upon them God will place some of the spirit that is on Moses, so that they may share Moses' burden, in addition to his twelve attendants from the tribes (Num. 1$^{5ff.}$). This became the statutory number for ruling bodies in Israel, e.g. the Great Sanhedrin and the Sanhedrin in Alexandria (Mishnah, Sanhedrin 1^6; SB III, p. 166). Josephus appointed seventy of the older men to act under him (*BJ* 2.570; see *Life* 56 for a combination of a body of twelve and of seventy), and the Zealots appointed a body of seventy judges (Jos. *BJ* 4.336).

(ii) It came to be held that the Gentile nations numbered seventy (Jubilees 44^{34}) on the basis of the list in Gen. 10 and the statement in Deut. 32^8 that the nations were fixed by God 'according to the number of the children of Israel' (i.e. the seventy persons who went into Egypt, Gen. 46^{27}). The LXX reads 'according to the number of the angels of God', which reflects, or gave rise to, the doctrine that the angel guardians of the nations (Dan. 10¹³, ²⁰ᶠ·) were seventy in number (Testament of Naphthali, 8⁴ᶠᶠ·; *AP* II, p. 363).

The Seventy in Luke have generally been interpreted with reference to (ii), and their mission as a 'prefiguration' in the ministry of Jesus of the church's future mission to the Gentiles. Against this is that content (except perhaps v. 8b) does not suggest it, nor does the context (if a Samaritan locale is still to be supposed; Samaritans were not counted as Gentiles). Luke appears to be describing not a symbolic prefiguration but a mission as actual as that of the Twelve to Israel, and in the plan of L–A the Gentile mission must wait until after the Lord's resurrection, and even then is connected primarily with the Twelve (see Wilson, *The Gentiles and the Gentile Mission in Luke–Acts*, passim). It may then be (i) that Luke has in mind, especially if the figure of Moses is in the background of much of the material in this central section, and that he is concerned with the order of elders in the church, which is to figure prominently in the story in A. (cf. A. 11³⁰ where they are suddenly introduced as officers of the church in Jerusalem, 14²³, where they are appointed by Paul and Barnabas in 'every church', 20¹⁷; 21¹⁸; I Tim. 5¹⁷; Tit. 1⁵; James 5¹⁴; II John 1; Rev. 4⁴). It may be noted that while the Jewish rulers in the gospel – chief priests (scribes), and elders (9²², 20¹) – continue in A. (A. 4⁵ᶠᶠ·; 23¹⁴; 24¹), so far as the church itself is concerned they are replaced by the Christian combination of 'apostles and elders' (A. 15², ⁴, ⁶; 16⁴). Luke may have thought of the latter as a kind of Christian Sanhedrin in Jerusalem under James, and he may here be ascribing, unhistorically, to Jesus the institution of the presbyterate alongside the apostolate.ᵈ While they do not receive the Spirit, as in Num. 11¹⁷, they share the task of Jesus, exorcize in his name and are rejoiced over in the spirit. Against this is that the elders both in Numbers and in Acts are not missionaries, but local bearers of office; but, as with the Twelve, these two functions may be fused in Luke's mind, his chief concern being with the latter.

It is not possible to decide with any certainty between the readings *seventy* and 'seventy-two'.ᵉ The mss and patristic support are fairly evenly divided. The choice of symbolism does not decide the matter, since in the case of (i) the obscurity of the text in Num. 11²⁴⁻³⁰ allowed Eldad and Medad to be counted as two extra elders (cf. *Clementine Recognitions* 1⁴⁰, 'He chose other seventy-two, that recognizing the pattern of Moses the multitudes might believe'), while in the case of (ii) the LXX text of Gen. 10 has seventy-two names. It is perhaps more likely that seventy-two was altered to the more hallowed number seventy. Manson (*Sayings*, p. 257), who considers the mission to be a doublet of the mission of the Twelve to Israel, opts for seventy-two as being, like the number

---

ᵈ See A. M. Farrer, 'The Ministry in the New Testament' in *The Apostolic Ministry*, ed. K. E. Kirk, London and Toronto 1946, pp. 135ff.

ᵉ For a detailed discussion, see B. M. Metzger, 'Seventy or Seventy-two Disciples?', *NTS* 5, 1958–59, pp. 299ff.

of the apostles, determined by the thought of the twelve tribes; but a similar consideration, or simply a preoccupation with the LXX text, could have led a scribe to alter seventy to seventy-two.

others: With *appointed,* and in the context of a mission charge, this is likely to refer back to the appointment of the Twelve ($9^{1ff.}$) rather than to 9^{52}.

two by two: This, which is strangely not reproduced from Mark 6^7 in 9^2, corresponded with apostolic practice (A. 13^2; $15^{27, \ 39}$; 17^{14}; 19^{22}). According to J. Jeremias[f] this was to increase the force of their testimony on the principle in Deut. 19^{15}. But this would not apply to all pairings (e.g. 22^8), and it may be here simply conventional.

into every town and place where he himself was about to come: No attempt is made, or could be made, to show this actually happening. The mission is as artificial in conception as is the whole journey to Jerusalem. The Seventy do not prepare for the coming of Jesus, but like the Twelve in $9^{11, \ 16}$, preach and heal on his behalf, and vv. 2–12, 17 reflect the same pattern as $9^{2, \ 6}$. The picture here is out of focus because Luke has superimposed it on the situation in 9^{51}, perhaps having in mind the sending of messengers by Moses to inspect the land and its harvest (Deut. 1).

2

This is identical in wording with Matt. 9^{37}, where it is placed before the appointment of the Twelve. Though readily associated with mission it hardly belongs in a mission charge, and the command to the missionaries to pray for an increase in their numbers is not particularly appropriate on the occasion of the commissioning of a further seventy. Verse 2a could be a proverb, though no parallel is cited, as could indeed be the whole verse if *the Lord* is rendered 'the master' – cf. Pirke Aboth 2^{19}, 'The day is short, the task is great, the workmen are sluggish, the reward is much, and the master of the house is urgent.' But *harvest* could be more than proverbial, and stand for the ingathering of the elect and the destruction of the wicked, which it does occasionally in Judaism (Joel 3^{13}; Isa. 27^{12}; II Baruch $70^{2f.}$), and more definitely in the NT (Matt. $13^{30ff.}$; John $4^{35ff.}$; Rev. $14^{15f.}$). There is no parallel to *the Lord of the harvest* as a description of God. In this context the saying characterizes the mission as a time of fulfilment, and of grace and judgment, though there is no indication of when the sowing had been done of which they are to reap the harvest. The labourers are human agents engaged on an extended task, and not the angels executing the sudden and catastrophic reaping of the end, of whom there would always be the required number.

f Abba: *Studien zur neutestamentlichen Theologie und Zeitgeschichte,* Göttingen 1966, pp. 132ff.

3

Go your way: Again very brief and general, without any specific directions such as are given in Matt. 10$^{5f.}$. Luke is perhaps more concerned with providing a model for the church's mission than with a particular situation.

I send you out as lambs in the midst of wolves: 'The contrast is as old as Homer' (Bauer, s.v. *arēn*). The saying could readily attach itself to a mission charge. In Matt. 10^{16} it introduces warnings of persecution, and a certain kind of behaviour is deduced from it. Here it is isolated, neither following from v. 2, nor leading to v. 4. Language and context are too general to identify the *wolves* – but cf. the constant Jewish opposition in A. to Christian missionaries (in A. 20^{29} wolves probably refers to Christian false teachers).

4

A balanced statement with two nouns between two prohibitions (cf. 9^3), but so compressed that the meaning of *carry* (*bastazein*) with *sandals* is unclear (= 'wear'?, 'carry in addition to sandals worn'?). The prohibition of sandals (so Matt. 10^{10}, but not Luke 9^3), in contrast to their express permission in Mark 6^9, could be taken as an ascetic element introduced out of competition with Cynic travelling preachers (so Knox, *Sources* ,II, p. 48).

purse: This (*ballantion* + 12^{33}; 22^{35}), which could itself be carried in the belt, seems to be Luke's equivalent for the money in the belt of Matt. 10^9; Mark 6^8. They are to be without means of purchase, but will not be mendicants and will not lack (22^{35}).

5–7

These verses deal with the strategy of setting up headquarters for the mission in a town. For apostolic practice on this, cf. A. 9^{43}; 16^{15}; 17$^{15ff.}$; 18$^{3, 7}$. In Matthew the strategy is different – to enquire in a town or village for a worthy household, to stay there, and if it proves worthy to let peace abide on it. Luke treats houses and towns separately, dealing with houses first, and leading through the treatment of towns to the woes on impenitent towns. Hence the discrimination is not, as in Matt. 10$^{11-13}$, between households in a town, but between persons in a household. This may be due to 'later reflexion' (Harnack, *Sayings*, p. 80), as Luke also has the greeting first to the whole house (v. 5). As in vv. 9, 11, what the missionaries are to say is given more vividly than in Matthew in direct speech. Here also Luke may be secondary, since *peace* was the customary word of greeting and farewell in eastern countries, and would be what any Jew would take for granted. It can, however, have a more concentrated theological meaning of 'salvation' (see on 2^{14}), and this is probably so here in view of (i) the realistic conception of blessing, which is regarded, like its opposite 'woe', as having an objective force able to be recalled (v. 6b), (ii) the context, in which the disciples are announcing the arrival or proximity of the kingdom (v. 9), and

(iii) the Hebraism *a son of peace* (v. 6a), which is a unique expression, meaning either a peaceful type of man, or one destined for peace, i.e. salvation (cf. Pirke Aboth 1^{12}, SB II, p. 166, I, pp. 476f.). The Hebraism could be due to Luke, who introduces two such in 20^{34-36}.

6

rest upon: anapauesthai, used of the spirit of Moses upon the seventy (Num. $11^{25f.}$) and of Elijah upon Elisha (II Kings 2^{15}).

return: anakampein + A. 18^{21}; Matt. 2^{12}; Heb. 11^{15}.

7

Once in a house they are to stay there, and not *go* (metabainein, elsewhere in L–A A. 18^{7} of Paul moving headquarters) *from house to house*. The reason for this is not clear – to achieve concentration, to avoid suspicion of mendicancy, to banish any sense of being burdensome? – and formally it contradicts *Whatever house you enter* (v. 5). While in the house they are to have no scruples about accepting hospitality; *what they provide* is in the Greek ta par'autōn + Phil. 4^{18}; Mark 5^{26} = 'the things from them'. In I Cor. $9^{4ff.}$ Paul defends this for himself. It is this, rather than travelling without provisions (Matt. 10^{10b}), that is justified by the proverb *the labourer deserves his wages*. Matthew's 'his food' would fit Luke's context better, but *wages* is the more natural correlative of *labourer* (cf. Matt. 20^{8}; Rom. 4^{4}, etc.). In its Lukan form the proverb is quoted as scripture in I Tim. 5^{18}, alongside Deut. 25^{4}, as a basis for the payment of outstanding 'elders', while Paul, who also quotes Deut. 25^{4}, refers to some form of it as a word of the Lord in justification of the payment of apostles (I Cor. 9^{14}). That the question could be a burning one in missionary practice is evident from Paul's avowals (I Cor. $9^{5ff.}$; II Cor. $11^{7ff.}$; 12^{13}; I Thess. $2^{6ff.}$; II Thess. 3^{8}). Rabbis were not paid for their teaching.

8–9

Luke now deals with towns that accept. That they are called towns (Mark 6^{11} 'place', Matt. 10^{11} 'town or village') is not necessarily 'a reflexion of the later conditions of Christian missions' (Knox, *Sources* II, p. 52), as the word could belong to the vocabulary of Jesus (Matt. $10^{5, 15, 23}$), and in the OT many small places were so called (but note Luke's introduction of the word in 9^{5}). In Mark 6^{11}, Matt. $10^{14f.}$ only those places that do not receive are mentioned, and v. 8 may be a Lukan construction to match vv. 10f., since *eat what is set before you*, clearly a parallel to *eating and drinking what they provide* (v. 7), does not fit here. They would not be entertained by whole towns, and towns which *receive* are those which receive the message, not those which provide hospitality.

eat what is set before you: This reflects in its wording the later problem of eating unclean meats which faced Christian missionaries when they moved out of

Israel into the Gentile world (cf. A. 10⁹ᶠᶠ·; 15²⁹; I Cor. 10²⁷, 'eat (not eat and drink) what is set before you').

9

The statement of what the missionaries are to do and say, which in Mark 6⁷; Matt. 10⁷ᶠ· stands more naturally at the beginning of the charge, is delayed to this point to give positive content to the instructions about towns that receive. For the combination of healing and preaching, cf. 9⁶; A. 8⁵ᶠᶠ·.

heal the sick: Compared with Matt. 10⁸ this is compressed. *sick* (*asthenēs*, only here in the Gospel; in A. at 4⁹; 5¹⁵ᶠ·) is the most general word. No mention is made of exorcism, which is the only healing reported in v. 17 (Luke can use *heal* in connection with exorcism, 6¹⁸; 8²).

The kingdom of God has drawn near to you: Again direct speech as in v. 5 (cf. Matt. 10⁷, and contrast 4⁴³; 8¹). For *the kingdom of God* see on 4⁴³. *draw near* (*engizein*) is used more often by Luke than by any other NT writer. It imparts a certain tenseness to the narrative of the journey to Jerusalem as the goal is approached (18³⁵; 19¹¹, ²⁹, ³⁷, ⁴¹). It is used here for the first time in connection with the kingdom of God (contrast Mark 1¹⁵; Matt. 4¹⁷). For the debate whether the verb has a spatial or temporal sense, and means 'draw near' or 'arrive', see Kümmel, *Promise and Fulfilment*, pp. 19ff. Lukan usage elsewhere favours *has come near*, though the addition of *to you* (*eph'humas* = 'upon you', cf. 11²⁰) intensifies this, possibly to the point of 'arrival'. In the persons and message of the missionaries the rule of God has come so close that they should be able to recognize it, and to accept or reject them is to accept or reject the kingdom.

10–12

The rejection of the towns that reject. Verses 10–11 are parallel to vv. 8–9, also ending with a statement about the kingdom. In view of v. 8 it is uncertain what is involved in *do not receive you* – do not accept their message, or do not give them hospitality to preach it? In Matt. 10¹⁴ it is both, and the condemnation is of individuals in a household or a town. Here it is more elaborately stated in direct speech and in a somewhat overloaded sentence, and is more indiscriminate, being judgment of whole towns as wholes once they are considered to have rejected. In A. 13⁵¹ this condemnation is carried out over Antioch as a whole, even though there are believers within it, and the missionaries return later to it.

10

go into its streets and say: The condemnation is public and formal. It is not clear whether *go* (Greek 'go out') means to go outside a house or outside the town, which would perhaps fit the act of repudiation better.

11

Even the dust of your town that clings to our feet, we wipe off against you: In comparison with Mark 6^{11}; Matt. 10^{14}, Luke's version is both more dramatic in being spoken to the inhabitants in interpretation of the symbolic gesture, and more literary – *clings* (*kollāsthai*, used only here in the NT of the adhering of material substance), *wipe off* (*apomassesthai* + +, used for 'shake off' in the absence of sandals). The meaning of the gesture is debated (see *Beginnings*, V, pp. 269ff.). One interpretation, based on the Jewish belief that dust from heathen lands destroyed Levitical purity, is that the gesture was one of self-purification and possibly, that the towns, though belonging to Israel and the recipients of the message of Israel's hope, are to be regarded as heathen. Another is that the departing missionaries dissociate themselves completely from the towns and disclaim any further responsibility for them (Luke's *even* perhaps support this). Also implied may be that they are handed over to judgment (v. 12).

nevertheless know this: It is not clear to what *nevertheless* (Greek *plēn*, cf. v. 20) is exceptive – 'though you may think this a purely personal gesture on our part, know this (cf. 12^{39}) that it is nothing less than God's kingdom that has come (to you)'?

12

I tell you: This rounds off the charge proper, and assures the missionaries of the ultimate character of their mission.

it shall be more tolerable on that day for Sodom: The rejection of the pairs of messengers, being the rejection of the eschatological rule of God, involves final consequences greater than the physical destruction of Sodom for rejecting the two angels (Greek *angeloi* = 'messengers', Gen. 19$^{1\mathrm{ff}}$). For the sin and punishment of Sodom as less than those of God's people, cf. Lam. 4^6; Ezek. 16$^{45-58}$. What fate can be worse for a city than Sodom's physical destruction, or in what sense whole towns can be judged as such, are not indicated. The sense is that the rejection of what is ultimate involves ultimate rejection. *tolerable* is the classical *anektos*, found only vv. 12–14 and Matt. 10^{15}; 11^{22} in the Greek Bible. *that day*, is not the day on which the missionaries are rejected, but, as often in the prophets, the day of judgment.

10$^{13-16}$ WOES ON THE IMPENITENT TOWNS

^{13}'*Woe to you, Chorazin! woe to you, Bethsaida! for if the mighty works done in you had been done in Tyre and Sidon, they would have repented long ago, sitting in sackcloth and ashes.* ¹⁴*But it shall be more tolerable in the judg-ment for Tyre and Sidon than for you.* ¹⁵*And you, Capernaum, will you be exalted to heaven? You shall be brought down to Hades.*

¹⁶*'He who hears you hears me, and he who rejects you rejects me, and he who rejects me rejects him who sent me.'*

Verses 13–15 are puzzling here. They fit ill with a mission charge since they look backwards rather than forwards. They fit particularly ill here since they look back on a Galilean mission that is already over, and they break the connection between vv. 1–12 and v. 16. Knox (*Sources* II, pp. 53ff.) thinks they belonged here in a source common to Matthew and Luke, but in a mission charge to the Twelve when they were being sent to Galilean cities other than Chorazin, Bethsaida and Capernaum, which had already rejected; and that in Matt. 11^{21–23} they have been moved to a different context of rejection of Jesus. But they could have stood as a separate unit in Q and been brought here by Luke because of similarity in thought and style (cf. also, possibly, the influence of Num. 20–21, esp. 21²⁹, the woe on Moab for not allowing Israel to pass through). In contradiction to the general impression of the Galilean ministry conveyed by the synoptic narratives they represent the Gali-lean ministry as a failure. It is unlikely that Luke intended them to indicate that the mission of the Seventy was also a failure. So far as they go vv. 17–20 represent it as a success.

တလ

13–14
These verses combine remarkably the historical and the eschatological. These two towns in Israel were quite insignificant – Chorazin is not mentioned any-where else, and its site is unknown – but because of what had happened there, and its rejection, they are now more notorious, and are destined for a worse fate, than Tyre and Sidon. The combination of these latter as symbols of heathen prosperity and pride (Isa. 23^{1–12}; Jer. 25²²; 47⁴; Joel 3⁴; Ezek. 27–28) was perhaps responsible for a single woe on Chorazin and Bethsaida instead of separate woes on each.

the mighty works done in you: Nothing is said of any preaching by Jesus or the disciples in these places (cf. v. 17 and contrast Mark 6^{12f.}). They have been the scene of *mighty works* (*dunameis*, used here for the first time in Luke), which are the product of the power (*dunamis*, singular) for healing and exorcism which resides in Jesus and is transferred by him to the missionaries (5¹⁷; 6¹⁹; 8⁴⁶; 9¹). They are not simply wonder-working, but are integral to the presence of the rule and power of God. As such they are intended to evoke repentance (see on 3³).

long ago: Not if Jesus' works, but if works similar to them, had been done here in ancient times.

sitting in sackcloth and ashes: A mark of humiliation (cf. Dan. 9³). Luke's *sitting*, if taken by itself, could be another such mark (cf. Job. 2¹³). If not it is awkward, since the penitent sat in the ashes (Jonah 3⁶) clad in sackcloth; but cf. Isa. 58⁵.

14
This repeats with respect to Tyre and Sidon the lesson of v. 12. It shows how woes that are retrospective could be attached to a mission charge with woes that are prospective.

15
And you, Capernaum: Capernaum is singled out as having been, at least in Mark and Matthew though less so in Luke, a headquarters of the Galilean ministry. Its condemnation, in a remarkable distinction from the previous woe form, is in the form of an apostrophe. It is modelled on the late passage in Isa. 14¹²⁻¹⁵, where Babylon is characterized by apostrophe as the acme of blasphemous arrogance, who is made by God to exchange her lofty pretensions to heavenly pre-eminence for life in the underworld, the sphere of death and shades. It is not clear how far the words may be pressed – e.g. that *will you be exalted to heaven?* refers to a claim by Capernaum to be of unique importance because so closely associated with Jesus and his mission even though unreceptive to them.

16
This verse returns abruptly to, and concludes, the mission charge with a statement of the principle of the *shaliach* (see on 9⁴⁸). This, which is attached to mission and is variously formulated in the gospels, is here constructed chiastically throughout in the Greek, and in comparison with Matt. 10⁴⁰ is primarily negative, perhaps because it follows woes. Matthew's 'receive' is a more natural continuation of *receive* in vv. 8, 10, and belongs to the vocabulary of this type of saying (cf. Mark 9³⁷ pars., John 13²⁰). Luke's *hears* picks up the message of the kingdom in v. 9. *rejects* is here the Hellenistic word *athetein*, which was not generally used with persons, but which in the LXX had acquired a menacing sense of rebellion and treacherous dealing.

17 The seventy* returned with joy, saying, 'Lord, even the demons are subject to us in your name!' 18 And he said to them, 'I saw Satan fall like lightning from heaven. 19 Behold, I have given you authority to tread upon serpents and scorpions, and over all the power of the enemy; and nothing shall hurt you. 20 Nevertheless do not rejoice in this, that the spirits are subject to you; but rejoice that your names are written in heaven.'

* Other ancient authorities read *seventy-two*

This ecstatic passage, peculiar to Luke, would be more compact without v. 19, which somewhat breaks the sequence between vv. 17–18 and v. 20 without adding to the thought. *I have given you*, which in the context is retrospective – 'you have been successful because I have given you . . .' – would be more natural if prospective – 'I have given you . . . therefore go' (cf. Mark 16^{17f.}). An original pericope on exorcism and its implications (vv. 17b–18, 20) may have been edited by Luke to serve as a conclusion to the mission of the Seventy. That it is not entirely appropriate, since they had not been commissioned to exorcize, underlines how important to Luke, more than to any other NT writer, was the tradition of healing and exorcism, doubtless because of its exercise in the church which he will show in A. (see Hull, *Hellenistic Magic*, ch. vi).

∞

17
returned with joy: The Greek verb *hupostrephein* is almost exclusively Lukan in the NT; cf. 9^{10} = Mark 6^{30}. Matthew does not record any return of the missionaries. The section of woe and condemnation gives place to one of joy and congratulation, which continues to v. 24. This is no ordinary joy, but the triumphant exultation that belongs to life under the shadow of the victorious kingdom (see on v. 21, and A. 2^{46}).

Lord: In this triumphant moment Jesus is addressed by his title as ruler of the church.

even the demons are subject to us: Though not expressly bidden to exorcize this is the sole evidence they report of the success of the mission. The demons, as members of the kingdom of evil organized under Satan, were the most powerful opponents of the kingdom of God they were to proclaim (cf. 11^{14-23}). This may be the force of *even*, though it may also express the disciples' surprise at their powers exercised for the first time. *subject* (Greek *hupotassesthai*; v. 20; 2^{51}, not otherwise in the gospels or A.) is the word, taken from Ps. 8^6, which was used in the church for the subordination of the hostile heavenly powers to the risen and exalted Christ (I Peter 3^{22}; I Cor. 15$^{24ff.}$; Eph. 1$^{21f.}$; Phil. 3^{21}; Heb. 2^8). Here it is applied to the lower earthly sphere of the demons, and belongs in the vocabulary of exorcism along with such words as 'command' and 'obey' (cf. 4^{36}; 8^{25}; Mark 1^{27}).

in your name: See on 9^{49}. This is the only explicit statement in the gospels of the use by the disciples of the name of Jesus in exorcism during his lifetime. It provides a firm basis for the use of the name of the exalted Lord in similar circumstances in the church (cf. A. 3^1–4^{12}; 19^{13}).

18

I saw Satan fall like lightning from heaven: This is unique in the gospels as an indication by Jesus of visionary experience. Here it sets the exorcisms of individual demons by Jesus or disciples in his name within the apocalyptic drama of the fall of Satan.

I saw: The Greek verb *theōrein* was used in all the ordinary senses of 'to see', but also had in Greek literature and in the LXX the particularly religious sense of visionary sight, and the imperfect tense was customary in introducing visions (cf. Dan. 4^{10}; 7$^{2f.}$). The language is pictorial and should not be pressed in detail – e.g. at which of the exorcisms did Satan fall? *fall* is in Greek the aorist participle, and probably denotes what is contemporaneous with the seeing (cf. Dan. 7^2; Rev. 9^1; I Enoch 86^1; A. 7^{56}; 10^{11}). The meaning will then be 'I saw Satan fall when you were being successful', rather than with Otto (*The Kingdom of God and the Son of Man*, p. 103) 'I was beholding (at some time previously, or in a pre-existent state) Satan fallen', the exorcisms then being the outcome of a previous expulsion of Satan.

Satan fall like lightning from heaven: This could mean 'I saw Satan fall (from power) like lightning falls from heaven', i.e. headlong. There may be a further reference (cf. v. 15) to the fall of Babylon as the day star from heaven (Isa. 14^{12}). But the passage in Isaiah may itself have been drawn from a wider tradition of the fall of individual stars = celestial beings (cf. I Enoch 86^1; 88^1; Rev. 8^{10}; SB II, p. 167), which could become a way of expressing the expulsion of Satan from heaven. The position of Satan in Jewish thought was ambiguous. One tradition held that on his attempt to claim equality with God he had already been hurled from heaven to inhabit the bottomless air or the earth (II Enoch 29$^{4f.}$; see *AP* II, p. 447). In that case *from heaven* could be 'from the sky', which was his sphere, his fall being into the abyss (8^{31}). A more widespread view was that he still had a place in the heavenly sphere, and was due for expulsion in the mythical war to come between the heavenly and the evil powers (cf. I Enoch

454

$16^{1\text{ff.}}$; $54^{4\text{f.}}$; $90^{21\text{ff.}}$; Test. Jud. 25^3; Test. Levi 18^{12}; Rev. $12^{7\text{ff.}}$). In the Assumption of Moses 10^{1-10} the appearance of the kingdom of God is the destruction of Satan and the abolition of sorrow. In Rev. $12^{7\text{ff.}}$ the expulsion of Satan from heaven to earth by the establishment of the kingdom of God and the authority of the heavenly Christ means woe to the inhabitants of the earth to which he comes. This is not the view here. The exorcisms of Jesus, and now of the disciples, are evidence that Satan's rule on earth is already over (cf. 11^{14-22}; John 12^{31}; 16^{11}).

19

This is also unique in the synoptists as a personal statement by Jesus of the nature of that charismatic power (this rather than *authority* for *exousia*, here with the definite article 'almost peculiar to this passage', Plummer, p. 279), which, as Elijah and Elisha, he has transmitted to his disciples (see Otto, op. cit., pp. 346ff.).

to tread upon: patein epanō. This could mean 'to tread on top of', as in 11^{44}. The promise would then be of invulnerability (cf. A. $28^{3\text{ff.}}$; Mark 16^{18}), and this could be continued in *and nothing shall hurt you*, with *ouden* = *nothing* as the subject of the verb. But this is hardly relevant here, and *epanō* may derive some of its force from *exousia* = 'power' (cf. 19^{17}), and intensify *patein* to give it the sense of the compound verb *katapatein* = 'to trample upon', 'to destroy' (cf. Ps. 91^{13}; Test. Levi 18^{12}, where the new priest is to bind Beliar (= Satan), and to give his children power to trample upon the evil spirits (cf. also Test. Simeon 6^6; the spirits of deceit are to be trodden underfoot).

serpents and scorpions: Behind this is probably Ps. 90^{13} LXX, 'You will tread on the asp and basilisk (a fabulous monster)'. SB II, pp. 168f. cite a midrash on this psalm which has 'serpents and scorpions'. For this combination threatening the Israelites in the wilderness, cf. Deut. 8^{15}; in a commentary on Deuteronomy they are combined with evil spirits. They could thus be meant as particular manifestations or symbols of *the power of the enemy* (cf. II Thess. 2^9), and so not dangers to be escaped but evils to be destroyed. The Greek would allow 'to tread upon serpents and scorpions and upon the power of the enemy' (cf. Test. Levi 18^{12}), but the rendering of RSV is probably correct with '*power (authority) to tread upon serpents and scorpions, and over all the power of the enemy. the enemy* appears as a title of Satan only in later apocalyptic writings (Test. Dan 6^3; Life of Adam and Eve 17, *AP* II, p. 137), and in the NT only here (but cf. Matt. 13^{39}). It could be the subject of the verb *shall hurt*, with *ouden* meaning 'not at all' (cf. A. 15^9; 18^{17}). For *adikein* = 'to injure' in an eschatological sense, cf. Rev. 7^3; 11^5.

20

The colloquial exceptive adverb *plēn* = 'nevertheless', 'rather', qualifies the preceding statement and refers back to vv. 17–18, indicating that v. 19 is an addition. Its force seems to be that the jubilation should not be over the fact (*in this, en toutō*, + A. 24^{16}) that *the spirits* (a variant for 'demons', emphasizing their supernatural status in the cosmic drama) are subject to them (because that could go to their heads and induce a concern with their performance and reputation as wonder-workers?). It is not the power and its sensational achievements of destruction as such which are to be the subject of eschatological joy (cf. 6^{23}; 15^7), but the salvation they portend, and the fact that they are the instruments of such.

your names are written in heaven: written (Greek *engraphesthai* + II Cor. $3^{2f.}$) was the regular word for enrolment on the public register of a city. That meaning could suffice here, *in heaven* (Greek 'in the heavens') being the equivalent of the heavenly city (cf. Phil. 3^{20}). But in the background, though not explicit, is probably the conception of God's book. The idea of divine books is as old as human writing.[g] It is found in the OT in the form of a register of Israelites who are to share in the blessings of the chosen people (cf. Exod. 32^{32}; Ps. 87^6; 69^{28}; Isa. 4^3; Ezek. 13^9; Mal. 3^{16} – to be distinguished from the books recording good and evil, and those containing the heavenly secrets). This was developed in apocalyptic as 'the book of life', containing the names of those destined for eternal life (cf. Dan. 12; I Enoch 47^3; 104^1; Jubilees 19^9; Phil. 4^3; Heb. 12^{23}; Rev. 3^5; 13^8, etc.). Thus the Seventy belong to the elect. Schlatter (p. 279) maintains that Satan here is the accuser of men before God, and that his expulsion means that the elect can now be acknowledged for what they truly are; cf. Rev. 3^5, where the promise not to blot out of the book of life the name of him who overcomes is followed by Christ's confession of his name before the Father and his angels. But the context suggests by the expulsion of Satan the destruction of evil power rather than the removal of the heavenly accuser.

10^{21-24} JESUS' JUBILATION

[21]*In that same hour he rejoiced in the Holy Spirit and said, 'I thank thee, Father, Lord of heaven and earth, that thou hast hidden these things from the wise and understanding and revealed them to babes; yea, Father, for such was thy gracious will.** [22]All things have been delivered to me by my Father; and no one knows who the Son is except the Father, or who the Father is except the Son and any one to whom the Son chooses to reveal him.'*

g See J. A. Montgomery, *Daniel*, ICC 1927, p. 299.

²³ *Then turning to the disciples he said privately, 'Blessed are the eyes which see what you see! ²⁴For I tell you that many prophets and kings desired to see what you see, and did not see it, and to hear what you hear, and did not hear it.'*

* Or *so it was well-pleasing before thee*

The sense of spiritual triumph in 10¹⁷⁻²⁰ is continued and intensified by Luke in placing here two jubilant utterances of Jesus (= Matt. 11²⁵⁻²⁷) which are unique in the synoptic tradition, and by introducing them by an expression of spiritual exaltation which is also unique. Taken together they are dubiously called 'Johannine'; for while the thought and language of v. 22 have parallels in John – for *All things have been delivered*, cf. John 5²⁰; 13³; 15¹⁵; 16¹⁵; 17², and for the mutual knowledge of Father and Son, cf. John 10¹⁵; 14⁷; 16³; 17²⁵ – the vocabulary of v. 21 is entirely foreign to John, as indeed largely to the synoptists.

Source, form and origin of these isolated and highly concentrated sayings have been much debated, as also the original text.ʰ As to source, the close agreement with Matt. 11²⁵⁻²⁷ can only mean the use of one evangelist by another (and in view of the secondary *who is* after *know* the use of Matthew by Luke), or, since in Matthew also these verses follow the condemnation of the impenitent towns (Matt. 11²¹⁻²³), the use of a common source Q, Luke having disturbed the sequence by the return of the Seventy. In the latter case it is not clear whether the note of time was in the source (*In that same hour*, i.e. after the return of the Seventy, is a Lukan expression, while 'At that time', i.e. of the condemnation of the towns, is a Matthaean one); or to what *these things* referred to in the source; or whether it included Matt. 11²⁸⁻³⁰. As to form, E. Nordenⁱ argued that Matt. 11²⁵⁻³⁰ was original on the grounds

h On the text see Harnack, *Sayings*, pp. 272ff.; Dom John Chapman, 'Dr Harnack on Luke X 22: "No man knoweth the Son" ', *JTS* 10, 1909, pp. 552–66; P. Winter, 'Matt. 11.27 and Luke 10.22 from the First to the Fifth Century', *NovTest* 1, 1956, pp. 112–48; J. N. Birdsall, in *The Cambridge History of the Bible* I, ed. Ackroyd and Evans, pp. 337ff. On origin see A. E. J. Rawlinson, *The New Testament Doctrine of the Christ*, London and New York 1926, pp. 251ff.; T. W. Manson, *The Teaching of Jesus*, Cambridge 1931, New York 1932, pp. 109ff.; W. Manson, *Jesus the Messiah*, London 1943, Philadelphia 1946, pp. 71ff.; Jeremias, *Theology*, pp. 56ff.; I. H. Marshall, 'The Divine Sonship of Jesus', *Interpretation* 21, 1967, pp. 87–103.

i Agnōstos Theos, Leipzig and Berlin 1923, pp. 277ff.

that it was an organic whole reproducing a common pattern of
Hellenistic-Semitic religious utterance, which consisted of (i) a Prayer
of Thanksgiving, (ii) an Avowal of the Reception of Knowledge, and
(iii) an Appeal to Men to Learn. Examples of such a pattern are Ecclus
51.1–12, 13–22, 23–30, and the close of the Hermetic tractate Poimandres (where, however, the thanksgiving comes at the end). Perhaps in
favour of such a schema is that apart from it the connection between
the first two sayings is not close ('reveal' is the only connecting link),
and each could stand on its own, the first being addressed to God and
more apocalyptic in tone, and the second a declaration to no one in
particular and having more the character of a wisdom saying. The
second is so complete in itself that a third would not be expected to
follow it, as is the case in both Matthew and Luke. Luke could then
have suppressed the third saying (Matt. 11^{28-30}) as being a general
invitation to mankind, and have replaced it by one better fitted to his
context in being addressed to disciples as a blessing. On the other hand
the parallel with Ecclus is not very close. The thanksgiving there is not
for revelation but for deliverance from evil, and v. 22 = Matt. 11^{27}
does not refer to the reception of wisdom. The unit in the source may
then have been vv. 21–22 = Matt. 11^{25-27}, to which each evangelist has
made his own addition. As to origin, the mutual esoteric knowledge in
v. 22 has been held to betray a source in a Hellenistic (gnostic) form of
Christianity; cf. the statement in the Magical Papyrus (London), 122.50,
'I know thee, Hermes, and thou knowest me.' But the parallels with
Ecclus could indicate that it is unnecessary to go outside the Jewish,
especially Wisdom, tradition for such thought and language (see further on v. 22). With reference to the conjunction of vv. 21 and 22 it
should be noted that Jewish apocalyptic not infrequently incorporated
themes from the Wisdom tradition.

נצב

21

Thanksgiving for revelation. This is couched in the language of psalm (*I thank
thee*) apocalypse (*hidden, revealed*) and wisdom (*wise and understanding, babes*).

he rejoiced: The verb here (*agalliāsthai*) is often found in conjunction with 'joy'
and 'rejoice' (*chairein*) as in Matt. 5^{12}; John 8^{56}; I Peter 1^8, and with 'thank', as in
Ps. $9^{1f.}$; 32^{11}; 67^5; 70^4, and it may have been suggested by these words in
vv. 17, 20, 21. In this form it is confined to biblical and ecclesiastical writers,
being in the LXX especially frequent in the psalms and poetical passages of the

prophets. It denotes a specifically religious joy before God, and a praise which makes known his works, particularly those that exalt his people. It became an eschatological word for the joy of the coming age (Ps. 96[11]; Isa. 12[6]; 25[9]; Rev. 19[7]; Assumption of Moses, 10[1], 'Then Satan shall be no more and sorrow shall depart'). In A. 2[46] the corresponding noun describes an aspect of the life of the first Christians.

in the Holy Spirit: holy is absent in some mss, including p[45]; it could have been added to make the passage trinitarian. If 'in the spirit' means 'in the holy spirit' (cf. 2[27], and possibly A. 18[25]; 19[21]; 20[22]), the expression 'to rejoice in the spirit' is unique, and may indicate ecstasy rather than simply prophetic inspiration. Nowhere else is Jesus said to make a particular utterance in the spirit. This creation of Luke conveys the exceptional importance he attached to the sayings. The mutual knowledge of the Father and the Son now embraces the disciples.

I thank thee: exhomologeisthai = 'to praise' is a liturgical word of thanksgiving in the LXX, especially frequent in the psalms (Pss. 75 and 138 begin with it), and also found in Chronicles, Daniel and Tobit (cf. Ecclus 51[1ff.]). In this sense it is found, apart from the LXX citations in Rom. 14[11]; Phil. 2[11], only here in the NT.

Father, Lord of heaven and earth: The text is uncertain. p[45] and Marcion have 'Father, Lord of heaven', and some Old Latin mss 'Lord, Father of heaven and earth'. The original may have been 'Father in heaven'. *Father* and *yea Father* are characteristic of the relation of Jesus to God in the gospels, but cf. Ecclus 51[10] (Hebrew), 'I said, O Yahweh, my Father art thou.' *Lord of heaven and earth* may be an embellishment of the text. Though biblical in idiom (cf. Gen. 1[1]; Ps. 115[3]; Isa. 45[18]; Dan. 4[34]) it is found in precisely this form only in Tobit 7[17] LXX (cf. A. 17[24], and in prayer A. 4[24]; Gen. 24[3]; Judith 9[12] LXX). It corresponds to the address 'Lord of the world' customary with the rabbis. Here it emphasizes the right of the Father to dispense as he pleases.

that thou hast hidden these things from the wise and understanding and revealed them to babes: In the source, and even in their present position in Luke, *these things* and *them* hang in the air. They would more naturally follow, and refer back to, *all things* in v. 22. If this is the connection then they will be the secrets of divine wisdom (see further on v. 22). This is further suggested by *hidden* and *revealed* (the verbs are in the aorist but have the force of the perfect). For these had become semi-technical verbs in wisdom, apocalyptic and Hellenistic mysticism (possibly under the influence of Judaism) for the concealment and disclosure to appropriate persons of the heavenly secrets or knowledge (cf. Wisd. 6[22]; Dan. 2[47]; I Enoch 16[3]; 46[3]; 51[3]; I Cor. 2[7-10]; II Cor. 3[14]; Eph. 3[9f.]; Col. 1[25f.]; the thought is already present in Deut. 29[29]). Also may be compared the Qumran hymn, 1 QH 7[1, 26], 'I thank thee, O Lord . . . Thou hast given me knowledge through thy marvellous mysteries . . .' (Vermes, *Scrolls*, pp. 160–3). There is a remarkable parallel to the Lukan context in Test. Levi 18¹²⁻¹⁴ (which may not be pre-Christian), 'And Beliar shall be bound by him, and he shall give power to his children to tread upon the evil spirits. And the Lord shall rejoice in his children, and be well pleased in his beloved ones for ever. Then shall Abraham and Isaac and Jacob exult, and I will be glad, and all the saints shall clothe themselves with joy.' It is distinctive of the Jewish conception of revelation that it is not simply the unveiling of what has hitherto been secret, but that God himself both reveals and conceals at the same time. So here God is praised both for his revelation and concealment, with their obverse in human acceptance and rejection, and for the paradox involved. *wise and understanding* are in the Greek without the article, and so denote a class, (as does also *babes*). Apart from 'wise' in the Wisdom saying in Matt. 23³⁴ neither word occurs in the gospels, but they are often found together in Wisdom literature for the natural recipients of divine wisdom (cf. Ecclus 3²⁹; 8²⁸; IV Ezra 12³⁸; 14²⁶, and the quotation from Isa. 29¹⁴ LXX in I Cor. 1¹⁹). Here they probably refer to such as the scribes and Pharisees. *babes*, in the gospels only here and the OT quotation in Matt. 21¹⁶, means the unlearned, those in need of elementary instruction (Ps. 19⁷; 119¹³⁰), who can be contrasted with 'the spiritual' (I Cor. 3¹), with teachers (Rom. 2²⁰) or with the mature (Heb. 5¹³). Here it refers to the disciples.

yea, Father: This paradox of revelation is here grounded in the divine will by the fervent *yea* (*nai*), and by the, possibly liturgical, repetition of *Father*.

for such was thy gracious will: In the Greek *houtōs eudokia egeneto emprosthen sou* = literally 'so it was well-pleasing before thee' (RSV margin). This is a thoroughly Semitic form of expression, which was common with the rabbis in prayer. *eudokia* = 'good will', 'pleasure' is not found in Koinē Greek, Josephus or Philo, and is almost confined to the LXX, where it first appears, and to Christian literature (Origen and Jerome regarded it as a new creation). In the LXX the greater number of instances are in Ecclesiasticus, where it means the divine pleasure or the divine decree (33¹³; 39¹⁸; 41⁴; cf. I Enoch 49⁴). 'before' (Greek *emprosthen*) is derived from the oriental court style.

22

All things have been delivered to me by my Father; (a):
and no one knows who the Son is except the Father, (b):
or who the Father is except the Son (c):
and any one to whom the Son chooses to reveal him. (d):

There are a number of variants in the text. In some mss *my* is absent. It is more likely to have been added than omitted, though it could have been omitted to assimilate to *the Father* in (b) and (c) and to make the statement doctrinal throughout. More important, (b) is absent from some mss. This would give a logical sequence for (a), (c), (d); all things have been transmitted to the Son by the Father, so that the Son alone is privy to the Father and is able to reveal him to others. (b) interrupts both the thought, since if the Son is unknown to anyone but the Father he cannot be the agent of revelation to anyone, and the sequence, since (d) cannot be construed with (b) but only with (c). In some citations in the Fathers (b) follows (c), and it is suggested that it was an early interpolation to provide a parallel doctrinal statement to (c), the order of the clauses being later reversed in order to lessen the incongruity when (b) follows (c), and to make the subject of (c) and (d) the same. Both as it stands, and in any possible previous form, the text presents problems for interpretation.

All things have been delivered to me by my Father: The Greek could mean (i) absolute power and authority have been delegated (cf. Matt. 28¹⁸ of the risen and exalted Jesus, Dan. 7¹³ᶠ·), *all things* meaning creation (cf. John 1³; 13³; Rom. 9⁵). This would separate v. 22 from v. 21, where it is a matter of truths revealed rather than of divine power exercised; it would fit 'the Son of man' rather than 'the Son' (sc. of God); and it does not lead on to the mutual knowledge of Father and Son as a natural expansion (though it could do so if (b) were absent, and in the Lukan form, where 'to know who the Son is' might mean to know that he is the one who now wields the divine power). (ii) 'All things have been transmitted', i.e. all knowledge and the divine secrets due for revelation (cf. John 21¹⁷; 3³⁵?; I Cor. 2¹⁰, ¹⁵). This would connect v. 22 more closely with v. 21, *all things* corresponding to *these things*. It would give a precise sense to *have been delivered*, the Greek verb *paradidonai* being used sometimes in the NT and Judaism for the 'tradition' or transmission of divine truths. In Judaism this 'tradition' was of the teaching of the elders (Mark 7³), in Paul of his own teachings (I Cor. 11²; 15³), which could come not from a human but a divine source (I Cor. 11²³; I Thess. 2¹³; II Thess. 3⁶). This divine *paradosis* is paradoxically hidden from those who were guardians of a tradition they supposed divine, and is revealed to those ignorant of it (cf. Matt. 11²⁸⁻³⁰). This leads more naturally to (c)–(d). It introduces, however, an important modification, since what is said in v. 21 to be revealed directly by the Father to the disciples, is now said to be revealed to them only mediately through the Son (cf. John 15¹⁸; 16¹³⁻¹⁵; 17⁷⁻⁸). This could indicate that originally v. 21 and v. 22 were separate unconnected sayings.

and no one knows who the Son is except the Father, or who the Father is except the Son: It is not clear whether the emphasis in (a) is on (i) *all things have been delivered*, with the consequence that since everything has been resigned by the Father to the Son the latter is the sole agent of revelation (this leaves no room for (b)), or on (ii) *by my (the) Father*, when the whole passage in its Matthaean, though not in its Lukan, form could be taken as two parallel statements, (a)(b)–(c)(d), with the sense that anything the Son has is derived from the Father, and this has its basis in the Father's certain knowledge of the Son (cf. John 5¹⁹⁻²⁷), while the revelation of the Father to men has as its basis the Son's exclusive knowledge of him.

knows who is: Luke's use of *know* (*ginōskein*) with an indirect question is secondary in comparison with Matthew's *know* (*epiginōskein*) with a direct object. It shows that Luke understood the knowledge involved as concerned with identity. This would be possible for the Father's knowledge of the Son (cf. I Enoch 46³; 48³, ⁶; 62⁷, where the identity of the Son of man is known only to God), but no Jew could say that knowledge of who the Father is was entirely veiled from men. The mutual knowledge (in the Matthaean form) has been explained on the basis of the OT conception of the communion of knowledge between God and Israel. God's knowledge of Israel means his choice of them (Amos 3²; Hos. 13⁵; Deut. 34¹⁰; Jer. 1⁵), and Israel's knowledge of God means her obedience to him (Hos. 6³, ⁶; Isa. 1³; Jer. 2⁸). This is possible, and there is evidence at Qumran of a Jewish type of gnosis, including esoteric, i.e. apocalyptic gnosis.ʲ But this would involve two different, if connected, meanings of 'to know' in a single sentence that suggests rather a mutual (possibly pre-existent) knowledge of Father and Son which is identical in kind. And since Israel had already participated in this knowledge, it would not account for the exclusiveness of *no one knows the Father.*

the Son: This absolute use, which is perhaps already implicit in *All things have been delivered to me by my* (the) *Father*, is frequent in John, but occurs elsewhere in the synoptists only at Mark 13³² = Matt. 24³⁶ (omitted by Luke). This could be accidental in view of the frequent references by Jesus to 'Father' or 'my Father'.ᵏ Its rarity can hardly be explained (as by Cullmann, *Christology*, p. 286) as due to a deliberate reserve on Jesus' part, since the way it is used here presumes that it is familiar and immediately recognizable. There is in the saying as a whole an absence of any messianic secret about the person of Jesus on the one hand, and an extreme doctrine of the concealment of the Father on the other hand. This is likely to reflect a later and more developed theology in some area of the church (see Hahn, *The Titles of Jesus in Christology*, pp. 307ff.). Jeremias (*Theology*, I, pp. 56ff.) takes (*b*) and (*c*) together as not specific and theological but as generic and illustrative statements. He takes them as a kind of parenthesis and renders 'Only a father knows his son, and only a son knows his father' as a general truth of life. But this is artificial when following on from the specific statement in (*a*), where the Father is God, and when issuing in (*d*), which must also refer specifically to the Son's revelation of the Father, since it is not part of human life that sons seek to 'reveal' their fathers to others.

j See W. D. Davies, 'Knowledge in the Dead Sea Scrolls and Matt. 11.25–30', *HTR* 46, 1953, pp. 113–39.

k For a discussion of the evidence, see H. F. D. Sparks, 'The Doctrine of the Divine Fatherhood in the Gospels' in *Studies in the Gospels*, ed. Nineham, pp. 241–62.

chooses to reveal him: Early patristic authorities have simply 'reveals' or 'will reveal'. *chooses* may have been added for euphony, or to match the last clause of v. 21.

23–24

The same sayings as in Matt. 13$^{16-17}$, but with different context and meaning. In Matthew they follow the explanations of teaching in parables. The disciples' eyes and ears are blessed as seeing eyes and hearing ears in contrast to others, and strictly 'eyes' are not relevant, and are suggested by Isa. 6^9 quoted in Matt. 13^{15}. In Luke those are pronounced blessed (destined to participate in the age to come, see on 6^{20}) who see what the disciples are seeing, i.e. the events presaging the age to come (cf. 10$^{17ff.}$). There is no mention of 'ears'. F. Blass★ wished, though on slender textual evidence, to omit *and to hear what you hear, and did not hear it*; but Luke may have only partially adapted the saying to his context.

Then turning to the disciples he said privately: The specification of an audience of disciples here rather than at v. 22 is awkward (*turning* is Lukan; *privately* is absent from some mss, and may have been a conventional addition; cf. Mark 4^{34}; 6^{32}; Matt. 17^1; 20^{17}). It may indicate that Luke realized a third member was necessary after vv. 21–22, which needed to be supplied with an introduction.

24

prophets and kings: and kings (omitted in some Old Latin mss and Marcion) is generally held to be more original than 'and righteous men' (Matt. 13^{17}), but see Knox (*Sources* II, p. 56), who thinks that Luke has accomodated to a Hellenistic convention in which kings were regarded to a far greater extent than in the OT as the proper recipients of revelation.

IO$^{25-42}$ *The Commandment of Love*

The teaching of Jesus on the journey now becomes more public. A dialogue with a representative of Judaism asks for his authoritative judgment as *Teacher*, and this produces a statement of the two commandments as together the basis of the future possession of eternal life. Compared with Mark 12$^{28-34}$ = Matt. 22$^{34-40}$, which Luke omits in that context, the statement is practical rather than theological, and is made primarily, if somewhat artificially, for the sake of the second commandment and its exposition in the following parable of the Compassionate Samaritan. Luke could here be reproducing an independent

★ *Evangelium secundum Lucam*, Leipzig 1897, ad loc.

tradition describing a separate occasion; but it is not impossible that vv. 25–28 represent his removal of Mark 12^{28-34} from the position of one among a series of controversial dialogues to occupy this more prominent position, and his reformulation of it with the parable in mind.

10^{25-28} THE COMMANDMENT OF LOVE

^{25}*And behold, a lawyer stood up to put him to the test, saying, 'Teacher, what shall I do to inherit eternal life?' ^{26}He said to him, 'What is written in the law? How do you read?' ^{27}And he answered, 'You shall love the Lord your God with all your heart, and with all your soul, and with all your strength, and with all your mind; and your neighbour as yourself.' ^{28}And he said to him, 'You have answered right; do this, and you will live.'*

This is in the form of a controversial dialogue, with question, counter-question, reply and comment.

ಬಬ

25

And behold: As the beginning of a fresh narrative this is Septuagintal and Lukan (cf. 2^{25}; 23^{50}; 24^{13}; A. 16^1).

a lawyer stood up to put him to the test: The scene changes from the address to disciples, but without any specification of place or time. For *a lawyer* (in the Greek 'a certain lawyer', a construction frequent in L–A and almost confined to Luke in the synoptists), see on 7^{30}. There is an agreement with Matt. 22^{35} (Mark has 'scribe'), though there is some textual evidence for the omission of 'lawyer' there.

to put to the test: In Greek the reduplicated verb *ekpeirazein* + 4^{12} = Matt. 4^7 LXX; I Cor. 10^9, a word confined to the Greek Bible. There is also an agreement with Matt. 22^{35} (*peirazein*), but the idea is somewhat conventional in encounters between Jesus and authorities assumed to be hostile (cf. Mark 10^2; 12^{15}).

what shall I do to inherit eternal life?: In Mark $12^{28ff.}$ the occasion for the rehearsal of the commandments is the question of a principal or foundation commandment, from which the others are to be deduced, and the form in which it is asked implies that it was a matter of debate (see Abrahams, *Studies* I, pp. 18ff.). Here the question is not the same, but exactly reproduces Luke's version of that asked by the rich ruler (18^{18} = Mark 10^{17}), upon which it may be modelled. This is perhaps because that story also is in two parts, with obedience to the commandments tested by a further demand. *to inherit* (*klēronomein*) is especially Deuteronomic, generally with 'the land', and introduces the recital of the prime commandment in Deut. 6^4, to which is also attached the promise of life ('that we might live', Deut. 6^{24} LXX; cf. also the promise of life attached to the commandments in Lev. 18^5). There 'life' means the permanent existence of Israel in the promised land. Here it is *eternal life*. The term (*zōē aiōnios*) is the product of the late Jewish doctrine of the two ages (*aiōnes*), the present and the future (eschatological) age. The adjective *aiōnios* = literally 'of the age' means 'eternal' not in the sense of 'timeless', but of what is characteristic of the coming (final) age (cf. Dan. 12^2; IV Macc. 15^3; I Enoch 40^9). It is found elsewhere in L–A only at $18^{18, 30}$ (from Mark) and A. $13^{46, 48}$ as the consequence of the fulfilment of the Jewish law freed from its nationalist restrictions.

26

A double question to be taken up by the double comment in v. 28.

in the law: This stands first in the sentence and is emphatic. It is assumed that the answer lies in the commandments and their observance (cf. 18^{20}, 'you know the commandments').

How do you read?: pōs is used here in the more Hellenistic sense of 'in what way?', and *anaginōskein* in the sense of 'understand'. Hence 'What is your reading of it?' (NEB), rather than the rendering of Jeremias (*Theology* I, p. 187) 'How do you recite (i.e. your creed, the *Shema*)?', as this could only produce the first commandment in reply.

27

Whether the combination of the two commandments as a summary of the law was the work of Jesus or had already been made in Judaism before him is still debated in the absence of literary evidence other than Test. Dan 5^3, Test. Issachar 5^2; 7^6 and a possible Jewish sourceu nderlying *Didache* 1, since these texts may not be pre-Christian. In Mark 12^{28ff}. Jesus makes the combination of 'first' and 'second' commandments, and the scribe approves. Luke shows that he thought it had been already made by putting it in the mouth of the lawyer, and Jesus approves (the suggestion of Manson, *Sayings*, p. 260, that the lawyer simply repeats what he had heard from Jesus on a previous occasion, is forced). With the omission of 'you shall love' before *your neighbour* Luke runs the two commandments together to become in effect one commandment. (i) The first commandment, from the *Shema* or creed (Deut. 6^5), was the core of Jewish, especially Deuteronomic religion, yet its text seems not to have been precisely fixed even in quotation (cf. the variation between Mark 12^{30} and 12^{33}). The text in Matt. 22^{37} and the Western text of Mark 12^{30} and of Luke here agree with the Hebrew and LXX text of Deut. 6^5, with II Kings 23^{25} LXX and with Jewish exegesis in having three nouns: *kardia* ('heart' in the sense of 'mind'), *psuchē* ('soul', or 'heart' in the sense of 'feelings'), but with *dianoia = mind* in place of *dunamis* = 'power' (some mss of Deut. 6^5 have *dianoia* for *kardia*, and II Kings 23^{25} has *ischus* = 'strength' for *dunamis*). And in Matthew the nouns are preceded by the instrumental *en* = 'by', a literal rendering of the Hebrew, as against the *ex* = 'out of' of the LXX. Luke and Mark agree in alone having four nouns, *ischus* being added (Luke has the last two in reverse order from Mark, perhaps for the sake of chiasmus); and while Mark has *ex* throughout, Luke begins with *ex* (perhaps in view of the regular phrase *ek kardias* = 'from the heart'), but continues with *en*. It is thus possible that Luke derived his text here from Mark. (ii) In the second commandment (Lev. 19^{18}) *plēsion*, an adverb meaning 'near', has the article as always in the LXX, except in Ps. 35^{14}; Song of Sol. 5^{16}, where it means 'friend'. It is the equivalent of 'brother' in the OT, denoting a fellow Israelite who is within the covenant (Lev. 19^{18a}). It was extended to include the foreigner permanently resident in Israel (Lev. 19^{34}; Deut. 10^{19}), and, in rabbinic Judaism, the proselyte (SB I, pp. 354ff.). There is evidence for a wider interpretation based upon the common origin of mankind (see note on v. 29).

28
A double comment. (i) The answer on the essence of the law is correct (cf. Mark $12^{28, \, 32}$). *right* (*orthōs* + 7^{43}; 20^{21}; Mark 7^{35} in a different sense) is Lukan. (ii) An exhortation to action proceeding from the correct judgment, to be partly repeated in v. 37 (cf. Gen. 42^{18}). The Greek would allow a double imperative – 'do this and live'.

10^{29-37} THE PARABLE OF
           THE COMPASSIONATE SAMARITAN

29But he, desiring to justify himself, said to Jesus, 'And who is my neighbour?' 30Jesus replied, 'A man was going down from Jerusalem to Jericho, and he fell among robbers, who stripped him and beat him, and departed, leaving him half-dead. 31Now by chance a priest was going down that road; and when he saw him he passed by on the other side. 32So likewise a Levite, when he came to the place and saw him, passed by on the other side. 33But a Samaritan, as he journeyed, came to where he was; and when he saw him, he had compassion, 34and went to him and bound up his wounds, pouring on oil and wine; then he set him on his own beast and brought him to an inn, and took care of him. 35And the next day he took out two denarii* and gave them to the innkeeper, saying, "Take care of him; and whatever more you spend I will repay you when I come back." ³⁶Which of these three, do you think, proved neighbour to the man who fell among the robbers?' ³⁷He said, 'The one who showed mercy on him.' And Jesus said to him, 'Go and do likewise.'

* The denarius was worth about a shilling

Although the previous dialogue is brought to a conclusion by the command in v. 28, it is made to continue as a controversy (*And*, v. 29, is resumptive) by a further question from the lawyer arising out of it, which provides a somewhat artificial transition to the parable.

This is the first of the special Lukan parables of the lengthy 'tale' type, which teach by narration of a particular incident rather than by analogy. In style and vocabulary it is exceptional even in Luke. Field's judgment (*Notes*, p. 61) that 'throughout this beautiful narrative all is as classical as the most determined Anti-Hellenistic would require' may be exaggerated, but so is that of Knox (*Sources* II, p. 59) that the sixteen participles look like 'a superficial attempt to get rid of the parataxis of a Semitic original'. There is an unusually high concentration of choice words and phrases (see notes). It would seem that Luke used here a more literary source than usual, or was himself the first to put the parable in writing. In favour of the former is that if he had written it himself he is likely to have made it fit the context better.

While the parable is clear in its general lesson – love of the neighbour is to know no bounds or boundaries – it has proved difficult to interpret with precision in relation to its context and to other elements in the Gospel. (i) Strictly the question in v. 36, when taken in relation to that in v. 29 (v. 27b), asks which of the three passers-by was neighbour to, i.e. was the object of the love of, the wounded man, to which the only possible answer would be 'he who came to his rescue'. This hiatus could be avoided if *proved neighbour to* could have the subjective force of 'acted in a neighbourly manner towards', but there is no evidence that the Greek can bear this meaning. The proposal of Jeremias (*Parables*, pp. 205ff.) to render *plēsion* as 'friend' ignores its semi-technical meaning in the commandment (v. 27, v. 29), and leads to the tautology that a friend is one who is a friend. Nor are those interpretations convincing which see the change in the form of the question in v. 36 as deliberate and as holding the key to the parable – 'a subtle shift . . . "Neighbour" is not an object that one defines but a relationship into which one enters' (Ellis, p. 158), 'the original question is unanswerable and shouldn't even have been asked . . . his concern should not be for who the neighbour is, but for who he himself is in relation to the neighbour (any neighbour).[1] The allegorical exegesis of the Fathers[m] avoided the difficulty by identifying the Samaritan with Jesus, who is to be loved by fallen man as the neighbour who saves him. Attempts have been made to revive this, e.g. by K. Barth[n], 'The good Samaritan, the neighbour who is a helper and will make him a helper, is not far from the lawyer. The primitive exegesis of the text was fundamentally right. He stands before him incarnate . . .' B. Gerhardsson[o] on the basis of an etymological relation between the Hebrew words for 'neighbour' and 'shepherd', interprets the parable of Jesus the good shepherd, who binds up wounded Israel as her leaders do not. But apart from the general question of the legitimacy of treating the parables as allegories, such interpretations cannot lead naturally to the concluding exhortation *Go and do likewise*. The hiatus has to be admitted (with Wellhausen, Klostermann, Loisy, Creed and others). It is probably to be put down to Luke's capacity for combining fine writing with confusion in presentation. (ii) As often with parables of this kind it is uncertain how far details are to be pressed as pointing to the meaning. The choice of priest, Levite and Samaritan (the familiar three persons in a parable) is clearly significant. But of what? It has been supposed that originally it was 'priest, Levite and Israelite (i.e. layman)', and the parable was anti-clerical (see SB II, pp. 182f., Montefiore, *Synoptic Gospels* II, p. 467); but *Samaritan* would not convey this. A special line of interpretation (suggested cautiously by Jeremias, *Parables*, pp. 203ff., and worked out in detail by Derrett, *Law in the NT*, pp. 208ff.) sees the main point in the behaviour of the priest and Levite as determined by the laws against ritual defilement of priests through touching a corpse (Lev. 21[1] – or of approaching to see whether it was a corpse), which prevail over the command to succour the wounded. But this gives the affective description of the man, *half dead*, a technical sense of that which tests ritual purity, and it weakens the force of the Samaritan's actions, since he was

l V. P. Furnish, *The Love Commandment in the New Testament*, London and New York 1974, p. 40; see also Marshall, p. 450.

m For references see C. Wordsworth, *The New Testament in the Original Greek*, 1859 (often reprinted), ad loc.

n *Church Dogmatics* I.2, ET Edinburgh and New York 1956, p. 419.

o *The Good Samaritan – The Good Shepherd?*, ConjNeot 16, 1958.

not governed by such levitical regulations. Derrett himself draws attention to the defect of this interpretation when he calls the parable 'a highly scientific piece of instruction clothed in a deceptively popular style', and comments 'The specific dilemma of persons belonging to specific castes does not by itself afford any rule of life for the ordinary man' (p. 227). One of the lessons he draws – love 'has nothing to do with community or sect, but is a spontaneous natural thing' (p. 223) – does not arise from such an interpretation. *Samaritan* is probably chosen as the traditional enemy, one who as a schismatic is excluded from the covenant fellowship of neighbours (i.e. Israelites), but who, in contrast to the embodiments and representatives of the covenant people, carries out the requirements of the covenant. This need not be an attack on law as self-defeating, when one commandment prevents another, or on the callous effects of 'legalism', as the Samaritan was also subject to the Pentateuchal law. (iii) Certain OT passages lie in the background and suggest thoughts and language, though not necessarily to the extent that the parable is 'a kind of midrash on Hos. vi.6' (Derrett, p. 227), or that the incident in II Chron. 28$^{8-15}$ 'supplies Luke with plot, location, characters, and detail for his story' (Drury, *Tradition*, p. 78).

კოე

29

to justify himself: This provides the basis for the (awkward) transition from a satisfactory summary of the commandments to a parable concerned with the second command only; but it is not clear what it means. Luke alone has the expression (cf. 16^{15}, there 'before men', of the Pharisees), which is not found in classical Greek, the papyri, or the LXX. It is unlikely to have the technical sense of justification in Paul. Perhaps in the context the lawyer is justifying his original question in v. 25 by referring to an area of uncertainty in the commandments.

who is my neighbour?: There is no evidence that this was a matter of debate like the question of which was the great commandment (Mark 12^{28}), but there are rabbinic statements concerning the fundamental principle of the law which relate it to the second commandment. Thus (Sifre on Lev. 19^{18}) 'Thou shalt love thy neighbour as thyself'; Rabbi Aqiba said, 'This is the greatest general principle in the law'. Ben Azzai said, ' "This is the book of the generations of man" (Gen. 5^{1}) is a greater principle than that' (i.e. every man must be loved as a fellow creature). Also Hillel's famous reply to the proselyte who wished to be taught the whole law while standing on one leg, 'What thou hatest for thyself do not to thy neighbour; this is the whole law, the rest is commentary; go, learn' (cf. Rom. 13$^{8ff.}$; Gal. 5^{14}, and possibly James 2^{8}).

30

replied: Greek *hupolambanein* + +, a classical usage.

was going down: To be taken literally. The road drops 3,300 feet in 17 miles.

fell among robbers: Greek *peripiptein* + A. 27⁴¹; James 1². robbers is *lēstai* = 'brigands'. Strabo (XVI, 2.41) records Pompey as destroying a stronghold of such near Jericho. *beat* (*plēgas epitithenai* + A. 16²³, possibly a Latinism). *half dead* (*hēmithanēs* + +).

31–32

a priest . . . a Levite: These are often conjoined in the OT as together responsible for the temple worship in Jerusalem. According to rabbinic tradition Jericho was the chief priestly city, half the total of the twenty-four courses of priests, or of those serving at any one time, being resident there, and responsible for providing their fellows with provisions. This rather reduces the force of *by chance* (*kata sunkurian* + +, a rare form). The Levites, who numbered about 10,000, and were also divided into twenty-four courses, were a kind of inferior clergy with subordinate tasks in the temple service (Jeremias, *Jerusalem*, pp. 207ff.). *passed by on the other side* (*antiparerchesthai* + +, only one other instance is known of the verb in this sense); *to the place* (*kata ton topon* + +).

33

a Samaritan: The word stands first in the sentence for emphasis. Just what it would have conveyed to the audience is not clear. The origins and character of the Samaritans are still matters of debate (see Coggins, *Samaritans and Jews*). They were schismatics, and as such could be the object of greater hatred than Gentiles. They claimed descent from the patriarchs, but this was denied by the Jews, who slanderously ascribed to them a heathen origin (cf. 17¹⁸, *allogenēs* = 'foreigner'). They held to the Pentateuch as alone scripture, but the chief point of difference was their insistence that Mount Gerizim was the only proper place of worship. In this respect the Samaritan stood at the opposite pole to the priest and Levite. Relations between them and the Jews fluctuated, but are said to have deteriorated seriously in the first century AD (Jeremias, *Jerusalem*, pp. 352ff.).

as he journeyed: participle of *hodeuein* + +; *where he was: kat' auton* + +.

had compassion: The verb *splankgnizesthai* is very rare outside the synoptists (elsewhere in Luke at 7¹³; 15²⁰; not in A.). It is derived from the noun *splanknon* = 'the bowels' or seat of emotion. It here defines the source and character of the Samaritan's love of his neighbour.

34–35

The actions arising from the Samaritan's compassion are described in some detail – *bound up* (*katadein* + + in this sense), *wounds* (*trauma* + +), *pouring on* (*epichein* + +, *oil and wine* were medicaments, cf. Theophrastus, *Enquiry into Plants* 9.11, 1); *set on* (*epibibazein* + 19³⁵, A. 23²⁴), *inn* (*pandocheion* + +, a word from the comic writers, not in LXX, Philo or Josephus), *take care of* (*epimeleisthai* + I Tim. 3⁵, a classical usage); *the next day* (*epi tēn aurion* + A. 4³, ⁵, an unusual phrase); *repay* (*prosdapanān* + +); *come back* (*epanerchesthai* + 19¹⁵). For some of the language cf. II Chron. 28¹⁵. The details are not important in themselves, but emphasize the extent of the Samaritan's compassion and his generosity in crossing the religious (and racial?) gulf in the face of human need.

36
The one who showed mercy on him: This is the one thoroughly Semitic expression in the parable, literally 'the one who did mercy with him'. *mercy* (*eleos*) is first God's grace and mercy in succouring men in their need, especially his gracious act, and then acts of succour to be expected of those who have claims on one another.

37
Go and do likewise: kai su = 'and thou' are to be taken together – either 'Do you also go, do likewise', or, with *go* as an auxiliary, 'Go, and you also do likewise.'

³⁸*Now as they went on their way, he entered a village; and a woman named Martha received him into her house.* ³⁹*And she had a sister called Mary, who set at the Lord's feet and listened to his teaching.* ⁴⁰*But Martha was distracted with much serving; and she went to him and said, 'Lord, do you not care that my sister has left me to serve alone? Tell her then to help me.'* ⁴¹*But the Lord answered her, 'Martha, Martha, you are anxious and troubled about many things;* ⁴²*one thing is needful.* Mary has chosen the good portion, which shall not be taken away from her.'*

* Other ancient authorities read *few things are needful, or only one*

Observance of the two commandments, and especially the first, as the way to the inheritance of eternal life is now followed by exclusive devotion to Jesus the Lord as the pre-eminent and inalienable inheritance of the true disciple. The story, peculiar to Luke, is striking for the close connection of its spiritual truth with individual features of the scene through which it is brought to light. An excerpt from private table talk is given a form which makes the concluding words of Jesus a governing principle of the Christian life (cf. I Cor. $7^{34f.}$, 'the unmarried woman or girl is anxious about the affairs of the Lord . . . to secure your undistracted (*aperispastos*) devotion to the Lord'). Bultmann (*History*, p. 56) classifies it as a biographical apophthegm presenting an ideal scene. The two sisters certainly became types of contrasting spiritual attitudes, the contemplative and the active; and the naming of characters in a story can argue against rather than for its authenticity. Nevertheless, the point of the saying of Jesus, for which the pericope was framed and preserved, cannot here be isolated from the attendant circumstances, including the naming of the women ('Mary has chosen . . .'). How far John 11–12 can be taken as an independent witness to the place and the characters of the women in the tradition (John 11^1, 'the village of Mary and her sister Martha', 12^2, 'Martha served') is bound up with questions of the historical reliability of John 11, and of a possible use by John of Luke's story.

Vocabulary suggests Luke may have been the first to put the story in writing – *as they went on their way* (*en tō* with the infinitive of the Lukan verb *poreuesthai*, a frequent construction in Luke); *a village* (Greek 'a certain village', cf. 9^{56}; 17^{12}); *a woman named* (Greek 'a certain woman by name', cf. 16^{20}; A. $5^{1, 34}$ etc.); *received* (*hupodechesthai* + 19^6; A. 17^7; James 2^{25}); *she had* (*tēde ēn* = 'to this one there was', + James 4^{13} for this use of the demonstrative); *sat at* (*parakathizesthai* ++, classical not LXX), *at the feet* (*para tas podas*, i.e. as a learner, + A. 22^3); *was distracted* (*perispasthai* ++); *serving* (*diakonia* ++ in this sense); *went to* (*ephistanai*, apart from Paul only L–A in the NT); *to help* (*sunantilambanesthai* + Rom. 8^{26}, a rare word); *troubled* (*thorubazesthai* ++, very rare); *is needful* (*chreia* = 'need' with the verb 'to be' + Heb. 7^{11}); *portion* (*meris*, only here in the gospels, cf. A. 8^{21}).

☙❦❧

38

The resumption of the journey is formal. It is not to be supposed that Jesus is here following up the work of disciples (10^1), who play no part in this story. The identification of the village as Bethany is the work of the fourth evangelist (John 11^1; 12^1). It is out of the question here, as Jesus does not arrive there until 19^{29}.

39

The person and word of Jesus are brought into great prominence here. The setting for his utterance is the highly unusual one in Judaism of a woman as a pupil of a rabbi, who is here given his post-resurrection title 'the Lord' expressive of his relation to the church.

41–42

While the general sense is clear, the reply of Jesus, which is likely to have attracted particular attention in the church, is textually uncertain. The following are the main variants, each of which has found support from scholars.

(i) Martha, Martha, (you are troubled D) Mary has chosen the good portion is read by most Old Latin mss, syr^{sin} and Ambrose.

(ii) Martha, Martha, you are anxious and troubled about many things, but one thing is needful. And Mary . . . is read by p^{45} p^{75} A C some Caesarean texts some Old Latin mss syr^{cur} Basil.

(iii) As (ii), but with 'few things' for 'one thing', is read by some mss and by the Bohairic and Armenian versions.

(iv) As (ii), but with 'few things are needful, or one. For Mary . . .' is read by p^{3}B $\aleph$ 33 some Caesarean texts thet Ehiopic version Origen.

(i) is clear, and is taken as original by some; but the conjunction 'Martha, Martha, Mary' is very harsh, and even with 'you are troubled' is tame as having nothing in answer to Martha's busyness or her complaint. It could be an abbreviation through the omission of words, perhaps as they stood in (iv), which were no longer understood. (iv) is printed as the text by Nestle and Kilpatrick (cf. Easton, p. 174), but despite the strength of its attestation it reads like a conflation of (ii) and (iii). Either 'few' or 'one' is a proper contrast to 'many', but hardly both together. 'few things' (iii) is less likely to have been a creation of the church than 'one thing', but it is very weakly attested to be the basis of such a conflation, and it could be, with (ii), a precipitate of (iv). (ii) corresponds not only with later Christian asceticism but also with the radical tone found elsewhere in the gospels (cf. 'one thing you lack', 18^{22}), and may be original.

Martha, Martha: For the reduplicated name in an apostrophe of concern, cf. 22^{31}; A. 9^4.

you are anxious and troubled about many things: Klostermann (p. 123) quotes Pirke Aboth, 4¹⁰,' Do little with business and be busy with the Torah.'

the good portion: The Greek word *meris* is found in connection with meals (for examples, Field, *Notes*, pp. 63f.), and Moffatt, following (i) above, translates 'Mary has chosen the best dish'. Others have taken 'few' or 'one' to refer to dishes; so Easton (p. 173), 'a few dishes, or only one would have been enough for necessary food'. But such interpretations may be misguided. In connection with meals *meris* does not denote a 'dish' which could be chosen from other dishes on a menu, but a portion, helping, mess or rations (cf. Gen. 43³⁴; Deut. 18⁸; I Sam. 9²³; Lucian, *On Salaried Posts in Great Houses* 26). It can hardly have that meaning here with *has chosen. much serving* and *many things* should probably be given a wider meaning than preparation of dishes for a meal – i.e. busyness about many things, leading to anxiety and distraction. In the LXX *meris* is most frequently found, as with its synonyms *klēros* = 'lot' and *klēronomia* = 'inheritance', for the inheritance of the promised land (Josh. 14⁴), or in Israel (Num. 18²⁰; Deut. 10⁹), or for Israel's inheritance in the Lord (Pss. 16⁵; 73²⁶), or for Israel as the Lord's inheritance or portion (Deut. 32⁹; Ecclus 17¹⁷). In this sense it could be used eschatologically (IV Ezra 7⁹; I Enoch 39⁸). Attention to Jesus and his word is the blessed lot that Mary has chosen. This meaning could explain the use of *good* (*agathos*) with *meris*, since this is the standing adjective for the promised land in Deuteronomy.

which shall not be taken away from her: either 'which she shall not be deprived of by being told to help with the housework', or, more probably, 'which is of such a kind (i.e. a certain and lasting possession) that she will never be deprived of it'.

Chapter 11

This chapter, though it is rounded off by a forceful conclusion (vv. 53–54), is not a closely knit unity. It consists of three blocks of material, largely but not entirely drawn from Q. These are: (i) vv. 1–13, teaching on prayer, (ii) vv. 14–36, controversy over exorcism combined with condemnation of the search for signs, and (iii) vv. 37–52, denunciation of Pharisees and lawyers. While each section has a certain coherence in itself, the connection between them is limited to a contrast between good and evil.

I I$^{1-13}$ *Prayer, its Pattern, Necessity and Efficacy*

I I *He was praying in a certain place, and when he ceased, one of his disciples said to him, 'Lord, teach us to pray, as John taught his disciples.'* ²*And he said to them, 'When you pray, say:*

'Father, hallowed be thy name. Thy kingdom come. ³*Give us each day our daily bread;** ⁴*and forgive us our sins, for we ourselves forgive every one who is indebted to us; and lead us not into temptation.'*

⁵*And he said to them, 'Which of you who has a friend will go to him at midnight and say to him, 'Friend, lend me three loaves;* ⁶*for a friend of mine has arrived on a journey, and I have nothing to set before him';* ⁷*and he will answer from within, "Do not bother me; the door is now shut, and my children are with me in bed; I cannot get up and give you anything"?* ⁸*I tell you, though he will not get up and give him anything because he is his friend, yet because of his importunity he will rise and give him whatever he needs.* ⁹*And I tell you, Ask, and it will be given you; seek, and you will find; knock, and it will be opened to you.* ¹⁰*For every one who asks receives, and he who seeks finds, and to him who knocks it will be opened.* ¹¹*What father among you, if his son asks for† a fish, will instead of a fish give him a serpent;* ¹²*or if he asks for an egg, will give him a scorpion?* ¹³*If you then, who are evil, know how to give good gifts to your children, how much more will the heavenly Father give the Holy Spirit to those who ask him?'*

* *our bread for the morrow*

† Other ancient authorities insert *bread, will give him a stone; or if he asks for*

Luke here constructs a single section on prayer out of more than one type of material. He supplies a context of Jesus at prayer (vv. 1–2) for introducing the Lord's Prayer. As that Prayer is petitionary throughout, or because it contains a petition for bread, a parable (peculiar to Luke) is added of a man who asks loaves of a friend (vv. 5–7). This requires to be interpreted by Jesus (v. 8, *I tell you*) as teaching the efficacy of urgent prayer. This theme is developed in vv. 9–13 by commands of Jesus (v. 9, *And I tell you*) to bold prayer based on confidence in the goodness of God. These commands are in almost verbatim agreement with Matt. 7⁷⁻¹¹ (Q). They also have similarities with the parable both in form (*What father among you?*, v. 11; *Which of you?*, v. 5), and in content (the friend, who is a reluctant friend, v. 8a, opens the door, v. 7, and gives when asked, v. 8b; men who are evil give good things, v. 13, and must ask and knock at the door, vv. 9–10).

With respect to the Lord's Prayer there are problems of text, origin and form, as well as of interpretation.[p]

(i) Text. This was very widely assimilated in the textual tradition to the longer, more Jewish and possibly more liturgical version in Matt. 6$^{9-13}$ (as in AV). The true text, given only in B and a few other mss, is that translated in RV and RSV.

(ii) Origin. The Prayer is not attested elsewhere in the NT, though echoes of it have been detected in Rom. 8^{15}; Gal. 4^6; I Peter 1^{17} and John 17. The existence in Matthew and Luke of closely similar but also variant versions could argue, however, that it was in use in different churches.[q] The evangelists might have derived it from Q, Matthew's version being an expanded form of the shorter form in Luke. But this is not necessary. Each could be giving the version with which he was familiar in his church. The wording was evidently not sacrosanct from the first. Hence an exact original may not be recoverable, especially if both versions had had behind them a history of liturgical usage. C. F. Burney[r] pronounced Luke's version a mutilated torso in comparison with Matthew's. E. Lohmeyer (op. cit., p. 29) claims, however, that when turned back into Aramaic it exhibits a regular Aramaic verse form of seven lines of seven syllables each. This may be fortuitous, since at certain points where it appears secondary it seems to reflect the influence of Greek style, e.g. *Father* (cf. 23, 46), *each day* (*to kath hēmeran*, cf. 19^{47}; A. 17^{11}), *for* (*kai gar*, cf. 6^{32}), *ourselves* (*autoi*, cf. A. 24^{15}; 27^{36}), *everyone who is indebted* (*pas* with the participle, cf. 6^{30}). It is impossible to determine whether such differences from Matthew's version already belonged to Luke's, or were further modifications by his hand.

(iii) Form. The Prayer is not at all distinctive in its language (see

[p] Origen was aware of some of these. See his treatise *Concerning Prayer*, 18.2–3, 26.1, 29.1. On the whole subject see E. Lohmeyer, *The Lord's Prayer*, ET London 1965 = *Our Father: an Introduction to the Lord's Prayer*, New York 1966; C. Taylor, *Sayings of the Jewish Fathers*, 2 vols., 2nd ed., Cambridge 1897–1900, Excursus V; J. Jeremias, 'The Lord's Prayer in Modern Research', *ExpT* 71, 1959–60, pp. 141–6; J. Carmignac, *Recherches sur le Notre Père*', Paris 1969.

[q] Cf. also *Didache 8*; for discussion of the Rotas-Sator square, see H. Last, *JTS* ns 3, 1952, pp. 92–7.

[r] *The Poetry of our Lord*, Oxford 1925, p. 113.

notes), though it might be in its sequence. What is characteristic of it is its brevity and compression. This was already noted by Tertullian (*Tract on the Prayer*, 1) and Cyprian (*On the Lord's Prayer*, 28). It falls into two parts. (i) An address, followed by two (Matthew three) petitions, without link except that it is God who is addressed and his action sought. Jewish parallels show that such petitions 'originally expressed one idea only, the petition that the messianic kingdom might appear speedily, yet always subject to God's will' (K. Kohler, *JE* VIII, p. 183). (ii) Three (Matthew four) petitions linked by 'and' and by a common reference to disciples' needs. There may be some correspondence between the two parts, *Give* answering to *Father* (cf. v. 13), the sanctification of the name involving the removal of sins, and the coming of the kingdom bringing with it the deliverance from temptation. This brevity and compression may be the effect of the heightening of eschatological tension in the teaching of Jesus. The verbs are in the aorist. This is not simply because that is 'the truest tense of "instant" prayer' (J. H. Moulton, Grammar I, p. 173). It is also, as the single exception in Luke (*Give*, the present tense in Greek) indicates, because the petitions are not for recurrent everyday needs, but for a single unrepeatable act of divine deliverance (cf. 18^7). Some elements in the Prayer reappear in the passion narrative – *Father*, *the kingdom* with its coming (in Matthew the doing of the Father's will), *temptation* (Matthew's 'the evil one'), as in 22$^{3, 18, 29-32, 40-46}$; cf. Matt. 26^{42}. This, together with the somewhat Mosaic character of the first part of the Prayer, has led to the suggestion that its origin was not in Jesus himself, but in disciples, who knew his career and interpreted his mind (Abrahams, *Studies* II, p. 101).

∞

1

This introduction is supplied by Luke; *in a certain place, when he ceased, said to him (eipen pros)* are all Lukan. So also is the setting of Jesus at prayer, and as a man of prayer (cf. 3^{21}; 6^{12}). The Lord's Prayer in the church is thus given an origin in the personal communion of Jesus *the Lord* with God, and in specific instruction arising from that communion. Only here in the gospels is *didaskein* = 'to teach' used of Jesus' teaching on a specific subject (*to pray*). The request is somewhat unusual. As pious Jews the disciples would know how to pray. It is, however, as a disciple of Jesus that one of them requests a special way of praying. It was customary for rabbis to use, or compose, a favourite form of prayer (Abrahams, *Studies* II, pp. 103ff.). The precedent cited here is somewhat different, *as John taught his disciples*. This reflects Luke's interest in John and his relation to

Jesus, and in John's disciples as a concurrent religious group (cf. 7^{18}; A. 19$^{3f.}$, and especially his addition to Mark of 'and offer prayers' in 5^{33}). It could serve to mark off John and Jesus from Jewish teachers who prescribed for their pupils out of the Jewish tradition. For both had created radically eschatological communities within Israel, each of which could be expected to have prayers expressing their characteristic beliefs. The prayer that follows is that of the community of Jesus' disciples (*us, our*).

2–4

The traditional character of the Prayer may be seen from the following parallels in contemporary, or near contemporary, Jewish prayers, especially the Eighteen Benedictions.[s]

Father:	Benediction 4:	O favour us our Father . . .
	Benediction 6:	Forgive us, our Father . . .
	New Year:	Our Father, our King, disclose the glory of thy Kingdom speedily.
Hallowed be thy name:	Benediction 3:	Holy art thou, and thy name is to be feared.
	Kaddish:	May his great name be hallowed in the world, and may he establish his kingdom speedily.
	'Al ha-Kol:	Magnified and hallowed be the name of the supreme king of kings.
Thy kingdom come:	Benediction 10:	Blow the horn for our liberation, and lift a banner to gather our exiles.
	Benediction 11:	Restore our judges as at the first . . . and reign over us.
	(Berakoth 40b):	'Any benediction that is without mention of the name is no benediction. Any benediction without *malkuth* (mention of God as king) is no benediction.
Give us:	Benediction 9:	Bless for us, O Lord our God, this year for welfare with every kind of produce thereof.
Forgive us:	Benediction 6:	Forgive us, our Father, for we have sinned . . .
	New Year:	Our Father, our King, forgive and remit all our debts.
Lead us not:	Benediction 7:	Look upon our affliction and plead our cause, and redeem us for the sake of thy cause.
	Evening Prayer:	Bring me not into the power of sin . . . nor into the power of temptation.

2

When you pray, say: In Matt. 6^9 the Prayer is given as illustrating a mode of

---

[s] For the text of these see C. W. Dugmore, *The Influence of the Synagogue upon the Divine Office*, Oxford and Toronto 1944, Appendix.

praying – 'like this', i.e. unostentatiously and briefly in distinction from Jewish hypocrites and the Gentiles. Here it is given as the model and formula for all occasions (*hotan* = 'whenever').

Father: In Greek the vocative *Pater*. This probably translates Abba, an Aramaic vocative form by contraction from Abbai. It survived in the tradition as the address of Jesus himself to God (Mark 14^{36}), and as a bilingual feature in the prayer of Greek speaking Christians (Rom. 8^{15}; Gal. 4^6). There it is immediately glossed by a Greek equivalent, *ho patēr*, the nominative used as a vocative (in Matt. 26$^{39, 42}$ by the vocative *pater mou* = 'my father'). For God as Father see on 2^{49}. While Father is not used of God in the Jewish pseudepigraphic writings, and he is only once addressed as such in the Psalms (Ps 89^6), the concept of God as the Father of Israel and of individual Israelites was well established in Judaism, especially in prayer (Ecclus 23^1; 51^{10}; Tobit 13^4; Wisd. 14^3; III Macc. 5^7; 6^4). The word conveys primarily authority, lordship and the status which calls for obedience rather than love, care or insight. Hence it is frequently combined with 'king', 'lord' and 'master' (Ecclus 23^1; cf. I Peter 1^{17}), and 'Our Father, our King' is a regular formula in Jewish prayer (see SB I, p. 175). In the Lord's Prayer the address is thus naturally followed by petitions about the name and the kingdom of God (cf. Zech. 14^9). What distinguishes Abba is that it was the familiar form of address used by children of their earthly fathers (cf. the Greek *pappa*), and it was not employed in Jewish public prayer. Its use by Jesus has been judged unique and revolutionary, and indicative of his concept of God and of intimacy with him (so Jeremias frequently; see his *Theology*, pp. 61ff.). What kind of familiarity the address conveyed, and how far this can be adequately reproduced (e.g. by the English 'daddy'), are problematic.* That is was unique to Jesus is not certain. K. Kohler (*JE* I, p. 28) claims that it was 'the formula for addressing God most familiar to Jewish saints in the NT period'. He quotes the rebuke of Onias by Simeon ben Shetah (second to first century BC) for too great boldness in prayer, 'I would excommunicate thee for thine irreverent mode of prayer, were it not that before God thou art a privileged son, who sayeth to his father, "Abba, do this and do that for me", and the father granteth him whatever he wisheth'. Also Simeon's grandson, Hanan, when children came during a drought crying, 'Abba, give us rain', prayed: 'O Ruler of the word, for the sake of these little ones who cannot discriminate between the Abba who giveth rain and the Abba who can only pray for, but not give, rain, hear my prayer' (see also Vermes, *Jesus the Jew*, pp. 210ff.). The familiarity of approach reflects the conviction that Jesus as 'the son' is cognizant as none other of the counsels of God (so especially throughout John's Gospel). As extended to his disciples it reflects their position as the true Israel intimately connected with the fulfilment of the divine purposes. It is not as the Father of all

* See J. Barr, 'Abba, Father', *Theology* 91, May 1988, pp. 173–9.

men, but as the Father of Jesus and as their Father, that God is so addressed.

hallowed by thy name: The Jewish background of the prayer is particularly evident here. The *name* of God was one of the dominant conceptions of Judaism, yet it is found only here in the synoptists on the lips of Jesus (contrast John 17⁶, ¹¹ᶠ·, ²⁶; Matt. 28¹⁹ is clearly a later Christian creation). This is also the only reference in the synoptists to the concept of 'hallowing the name' (cf. John 12²⁸) which was so frequent in Judaism as to be almost a synonym for religion (see Moore, *Judaism* II, pp. 101ff.). God's name is the extension of his person. It denotes his divine being as that is disclosed in his personal action. That 'being' is by definition 'holy', i.e. unique and separate from evil.ᵗ It alone is so. For God's name to be hallowed, i.e. to be made holy, is for him to be acknowledged for the God he is. That is 'the most characteristic feature of Jewish ethics, both as principle and motive' (Moore, op. cit. II, p. 101). The passive voice of the verb is probably a reverential passive, avoiding a too direct address to God (contrast John 17¹⁷). As in the OT the sanctification of his name is more often predicated of God than of man, the meaning is probably 'Do thou sanctify thy name', i.e. procure that thou art acknowledged as God. The aorist tense probably means that the petition is not general but specific. God is asked to act decisively in such a way that this acknowledgment may come about. Some, however, take the words not as a petition, but as a preliminary ascription added to Father, as in the familiar 'Blessed be He' after the mention of God (cf. *Didache* 10²).

Thy kingdom come: This stands in marked contrast to the previous petition. For its language is characteristic of the synoptic tradition (cf. 17²⁰; 22¹⁸; Mark 9¹ etc.; for the kingdom of God, see on 4⁴³), but it has no exact parallel in the OT, the pseudepigraphic writings or the rabbis. When these spoke of the kingdom of God they referred to its appearance (cf. Assumption of Moses 10¹), or to its being manifested or brought about, rather than to its coming.ᵘ There is a clear instance here of the kingdom as the object of expectation. This appears to have been enhanced rather than negated by the condition that in some sense it had already come (11²⁰; cf. the prayer of the church in I Cor. 16²²; Rev. 22²⁰; *Didache* 10⁶). The connection with the previous petition is close. God hallows his name by establishing his rule (cf. Ezek. 36²²ff·; for the combination of Father and ruler of the world, cf. 10²¹). The intransitive verb in the aorist imperative, *elthatō*, probably has the sense of 'Do thou cause to come'. In place of this peti-

---

t Cf. N. H. Snaith, *The Distinctive Ideas of the Old Testament*, London 1944, Philadelphia 1946, ch. 2.

u Lohmeyer (*The Lord's Prayer*, p. 108) quotes Bengel: 'The sanctification of the divine name is taken over from the Old Testament into the New, to be continued and increased by us; the advent of the kingdom of God is in a measure peculiar to the New Testament.'

tion there is a remarkable variant reading in Luke, 'Let thy holy Spirit come upon us and cleanse us', found in the mss 162 and 700, in the text of Luke used by Gregory of Nyssa and in Maximus of Turin; Marcion had something similar before 'hallowed be thy name'. They can hardly be authentic words of Jesus, who spoke very rarely of the holy Spirit (see Barrett, *Holy Spirit*), and in the synoptists uses 'cleanse' (*katharizein*) only of ritual washing or healing. They more likely represent a liturgical adaptation of the Prayer, perhaps for use at baptism. As such, however, and despite the weak textual attestation, they might have stood already in Luke's version of the Prayer, or have been inserted by him (cf. his reference to the holy Spirit in v. 13). For a detailed discussion, see Leaney, pp. 59ff.

3

Give us each day our daily bread: In the Greek *ton arton hēmōn ton epiousion didou hēmin to kath' hēmeran.* This begins the second half of the Prayer. The petitions are now direct, the verbs being in the active. They concern the needs of the disciples (*thy* changes to *our*), which arise from what is involved in the previous petitions. Somewhat surprisingly bread is placed first among those needs (contrast 12³¹). The petition is distinctive in being the only one to have the verb, not at the beginning, but in the middle of the sentence, and to contain an epithet (*epiousion*), which determines the sense. The petition is highly problematical, since the meaning of the epithet is uncertain, and is still debated (for the literature see *TDNT* II, pp. 590ff.). Already Origen appears not to have known what the word *epiousios* meant. He comments (*Concerning Prayer*, 27.7) 'it is not employed by any of the Greeks or learned writers, nor is it in common use among the ordinary folk'. He then adds, 'It seems likely to have been coined by the evangelists.' This is very unlikely, especially if the Matthaean and Lukan versions reflect independent oral traditions. Easton (p. 175) speculates that it belonged to the popular Jewish Greek of Jerusalem. The only other instance of it is in a fifth-century AD papyrus account book (since lost). One item in this read 'half an obol of *epiousi*', an abbreviation of *epiousiōn* = 'of epiousian things'. This does not fix the meaning of the word, but it has been equated with the Latin word *diaria* = 'daily rations' (of food or pay) found in a list of household articles in a wall inscription at Pompeii (E. C. E. Owen, *JTS* 35, 1934, p. 377). In default of a reliable parallel recourse has been had to possible derivations. The following suggestions have been made: (i) It is to be derived from the preposition *epi* = 'upon' and the verb *einai* = 'to be', especially the noun from it *ousia* = 'being'. This can give either (*a*) 'answering to our nature', 'spiritual', or (*b*) 'that which belongs to existence'. (*a*) was the interpretation of Origen and of other Fathers following him (Jerome rendered the Matthean petition by *supersubstantialis*). It is to be dismissed as determined by a philosophical understanding of *ousia* foreign both to the gospels and to vernacular usage, where it meant 'property'.

(ii) It is to be derived from the phrase *epi tēn ousan* (sc. *hēmeran*) = 'for the present (day)' – so Blass-Debrunner, §123, p. 66. The petition may then be for a limited supply, the bread necessary for the coming day and no more (so *TDNT* II, p. 599). There is, however, no example of *hē ousa* without the noun *hēmera* to mean 'the present day', and there were more usual words for this – e.g. *ephēmeros* in James 2^{15} of daily food, and *kathēmerinos* in A. 6^1 of daily distribution.

(iii) It is to be derived from *epi* and the verb *ienai* = 'to come' or 'to go', either through the participle *epiousa*, or through the standing expression *hē epiousa* (sc. *hēmera*) = 'the next day (as in A. 16^{11}). So Moulton, *Grammar*, II, pp. 313f., and a considerable number of scholars. This could give either (*a*) 'future', 'next', 'of the morrow', or (*b*) 'that which is coming on', 'for the next day', which, according to the Jewish time reckoning, would mean 'for the next day' if prayed in the morning, or 'for the dawning day' if prayed in the evening. (Jerome, who rendered *epiousion* in Luke by the Latin *cotidianum* = 'daily', mentions with reference to Matthew's text that the Gospel according to the Hebrews read *mahar*, which he interpreted as meaning 'of tomorrow'.)

Of the derivations (iii) is the more probable. Of the interpretations (ii) and (iii) (*b*) would best fit Luke's text – 'our necessary bread give us daily' – to which there are rabbinic parallels (see SB I, pp. 420f.); though if 'our bread' means 'the bread we need', and *epiousios* means 'necessary' the prayer is tautologous. Further, in view of the aorist tenses throughout, and the aorist imperative *dos* in this petition in Matthew, Luke's present imperative *didou* looks secondary, as is *to kath' hēmeran* = 'daily' in comparison with Matthew's *sēmeron* = 'today'. The emphatic position of 'today' at the end of the sentence in Matthew could indicate that *epiousion* at the beginning should have a temporal but contrasted sense, e.g. 'of tomorrow'. The sense would then be – 'our bread of tomorrow give us today'. Behind this could lie the story of the manna, the bread specially given by God (Exod. 16^{15}; Neh. 9^{15}; Ps. 78^{24}; Wisd. 16^{20}; cf. John 6$^{32-34}$). In that story the bread for the sabbath was supplied the day before, and belief that it would be so was a test of trust in God (Exod. 16$^{22-30}$). There is evidence that in rabbinic thought the sabbath was treated as a symbol of the coming age, and manna as a symbol of the food of that age. Thus in its Matthaean form this petition, like the others, could be eschatological, i.e. a prayer for the coming of the kingdom in terms of receiving already in advance the (sabbath) bread of the age to come (cf. 13^{29}; 14^{15}; John 6^{34}). *our bread* would then mean 'the bread which belongs to us as heirs of the kingdom'. Luke has given the petition a more general sense of prayer for daily necessity (cf. his addition of 'daily' in 9^{23}).

4

and forgive us our sins, for we ourselves forgive everyone who is indebted to us: This petition, like the one (in Matthew two) following, concerns the removal by

God of what stands in the way of the fulfilment of the previous petitions. Here again Luke appears secondary. (i) Matthew has *debts* (*opheilēmata*), and the verb (*aphienai* = 'to let go') has one of its possible meanings, 'to cancel', 'to remit'. The metaphor is financial-legal, and is used only here in the Greek Bible of the relation between God and men, who by neglect of the commandments fall into arrears. The religious use of 'debt' for 'sin' is rare in the OT, but is common in later Judaism, and in the teaching of Jesus (7^{41ff.}; Matt. 18^{23ff.}; 6¹⁴ – in Aramaic the same word serves for both). But it was foreign to Greek thought, and alteration to the more conventional 'sins' was natural. That it was an alteration is evident from the second half of the sentence, where the idea of debt is retained. This is awkward, as *who is indebted to us* (in Greek the participle followed by the dative) is not a complete equivalent for 'who sins against us', which is required by the first half of the sentence; and the verb now becomes a hybrid, mixing cancellation of debts with forgiveness of sins. This petition could also be eschatological, the remission of sins belonging to the last days (1⁷⁷; Jer. 31³¹⁻³⁴; Col. 1¹⁴).

(ii) This is the only petition with a qualification attached. Its force is not certain. Abrahams (*Studies* II, p. 95) takes it as a condition, without parallel in Jewish liturgical prayer. Divine forgiveness is conditional upon men's forgiveness of their fellows (cf. Ecclus 28^{2ff.}; SB I, p. 421). But while Matt. 6^{14f.} interprets the clause so, the natural force of the conjunction in Matt. 6¹², *hōs kai* = 'as also', is not conditional or causative, but is to establish exact similarity ('precisely as', cf. A. 10⁴⁷; 22⁵; I Peter 3⁷; II Peter 2¹), or even an appeal for imitation (Matt. 18³³). This could also be the force of Luke's probably secondary *for we ourselves* (*kai gar autoi* = 'for also we'). In that case the sense will be that a direct request for forgiveness can be made by those who, as disciples of Jesus, are already in the position of having forgiven others (Matthew *aphēkamen*, aorist), or of habitually doing so (Luke *aphiomen*, present). They are already living the life of the kingdom and reproducing the character of the Father, and it is for the Father to follow suit.

and lead us not into temptation: In the Greek *mē eisenenkēs* (= 'do not bring us', i.e. in the future, which is the force of the aorist subjunctive here; see Moulton, *Grammar* I, p. 122) *eis peirasmon* ('into trial'). In Luke's version the prayer ends with this, its only negative petition (in Matt. 6^{13b} it is followed by the corresponding positive, 'But deliver us from evil (or, the evil one'), which is also found interpolated into some mss of Luke; see AV. It early caused difficulties. The reflections that God cannot be the author of temptation (cf. James 1¹³), or that temptation is inseparable from the godly life (cf. James 1¹²), led to exegetical modifications, some of which affected the text. Thus Marcion seems to have known the petition in the form 'do not allow us to be led' (Tertullian, *Against Marcion* 4.26). In the East Dionysius of Alexandria glossed it with 'that is, do not allow us to fall into temptation', and in the West Tertullian (*Concerning Prayer* 8) glossed it with 'that is, suffer us not to be led, of course by the one who does tempt'. Cyprian (*On the Lord's Prayer* 25) had 'The Lord admonishes us to say in prayer, "And do not suffer us to be led into temptation",' and he read the petition in this form in his Bible (the Old Latin ms k). Augustine referred (*The Lord's Sermon on the Mount* 9) to many who prayed the petition thus, and (*On the Gift of Perseverance* 6) to its occurrence in this form in very many mss, though not in any Greek mss known to him. Further, a succession of Latin Fathers glossed the petition from I Cor. 10$^{12f.}$ to mean that we were not to be led into temptation 'which we are not able to bear', and this gloss found its way into some Eastern liturgies. The Greek work *peirasmos*, which is found only three times outside the Bible, is used in the LXX, along with the verb, in the sense of 'proving'. This is sometimes of men proving God. More often it is of God putting men to the test to see whether their loyalty to, and trust in, him are well established. So of the godly man, such as Abraham (Gen. 22) or Job, or of Israel as a people on the way to the promised land (Exod. 20^{20}; the gift of manna proves Israel. Exod. 16^4; Deut. 8^2). Behind this lies the conception of the world as the scene of conflict between good and evil in the form of the personal will of God meeting the recalcitrant will of men. In the Wisdom literature this takes the milder form of training by experience (Ecclus 2^1). In apocalyptic, where the conflict between good and evil is sharpened, *temptation* (sometimes with the definite article) could be a synonym for the tribulation (*thlipsis*) which it was believed would immediately precede the end (cf. Dan. 12^1; Rev. 3^{10} with 7^{14}; 2$^{9f.}$), and which not even the elect could survive unless it was shortened (Mark 13$^{19ff.}$; I Cor. 7$^{26ff.}$; cf. SB IV, pp. 977ff. for Jewish pictures of its horror). This is possibly the meaning of *temptation* here, as also in 22$^{40-46}$, where the disciples are commanded to pray this petition, while Jesus, who prays to the Father that his will may be done, also asks for the cup to be removed. The petition will then be for such a speedy and powerful deliverance from God as shall by-pass even the woes which were to precede it. It illustrates the characteristic uncertainty of Jewish thought about the ultimate origin of evil and trial. In apocalyptic Satan is increasingly thought of as the source of evil, and as the instigator of the trials of the righteous. Nevertheless his ultimate subordination to the permissive will of God (cf. Job) is never entirely abandoned. Hence God can be said both to deliver men from him (so Matt. 6^{13b}) but also through him to bring men to trial.

5–8

The parable – a vignette of Palestinian village life (Jeremias, *Parables*, pp. 157ff.) – is intended to provide a transition from the model prayer given in vv. 2–4 to the injunctions to urgent prayer in vv. 9–13. It is, however, both clumsy in its form and confused in its content, and could have had originally a different context. (i) With respect to form, questions beginning with the formula *Which of you?* need to be brief to make their point. They are meant to introduce what is self-evident and so to elicit the immediate response 'Obviously no one' (cf. 12²⁵) or 'Everyone, of course' (cf. 14⁵). Here the question is lengthy, continuing in a series of paratactic sentences throughout vv. 5–7, and loses its way in a protracted description and dialogue. It is not always clear what action is being ascribed to whom – contrast *Which of you who has a friend will go to him* (RSV) with 'Suppose one of you has a friend who comes to him' (NEB). Hence the question can lead to opposite interpretations, e.g. 'The request is outrageous. "Which of you" would ask such a thing? Yet persistence is rewarded' (Ellis, p. 163), and 'Can you imagine . . . that you would call out, "Don't disturb me . . .?" Unthinkable! Under no circumstances would he leave his friend's request unanswered' (Jeremias, *Parables*, p. 158). Since the question eventually ends on a negative note – *I cannot get up and give you anything?* – the point has to be established by an addendum in v. 8. (ii) The point of v. 8 is itself unclear, and wavers between two lessons. The emphasis is on *friend*, not only what he asked for, but everything he needs at whatever inconvenience (with the inference that God treats men likewise, so Jeremias, p. 159). But this is relegated to a negative conditional sentence in a parenthesis – *though he will not get up and give him anything because he is his friend*. The basis of giving is now the friend's *importunity*. The Greek word here (*anaideia* + +) can mean either 'importunity' or 'shamelessness' (Ecclus 25²²). If the former is meant the parable is assimilated to that of the Unjust Judge (18¹⁻⁸), with which some have seen this parable as a pair. But in 18⁵ 'bothers me' (the same Greek phrase as in v. 7 here) refers to the importunity of repeated requests, whereas here only a single request is made. If the latter is meant it does not proceed naturally out of the parable, where it is implied that the request of a friend in such circumstances would not constitute 'shamelessness' or 'impudence'. The same applies if 'because of his shamelessness' is taken to mean 'so as not to lose face in the matter' (see Jeremias, p. 158), whether that refers to the petitioner or the one petitioned.

9–10

Apart from the Lukan introductory formula *And I tell you*, these verses are in exact agreement with Matt. 7⁷⁻⁸ (Q). Their compressed proverbial form, and the absolute use of the verbs, would leave them open to take their meaning from the context in which they are placed. The first two are found variously used in the Mandaean literature (Bultmann, *History*, p. 87); the second was used by rabbis of the study of the Torah (SB I, p. 458). In Luke's context, though not necessarily in Matthew's, they are used to ground petitionary prayer in the certainty that God will answer it. The passives *be given, be opened*, mean 'God will give, will open'. *ask* (*aitein*) has the sense of *demand*. *seek* (*zētein*) could also have the sense of 'require', though it might have the religious connotation of 'seeking the Lord', i.e. 'having recourse to', 'longing for the intervention of' the Lord (cf. Rom. 10²⁰, quoting Isa. 65¹). The door implied in *knock* and *opened* could be, but is not necessarily, a figure of entry into the kingdom and of access to God (cf. 13^{24f.}; Rev. 3^{7f.}; Isa. 26^2). The unequivocal imperatives in v. 9 and affirmations in v. 10 voice the boldness and assurance of life in the kingdom. This does not reckon with the possibilities or otherwise of normal life, e.g. that not all seeking results in finding, or that not all asking is right asking (James 4^{2f.}).

11–13

In this context, though not necessarily in Matt. 7^{9-11}, these sayings also concern prayer – *ask, give*. They are more closely related to the parable in vv. 5–8, if that teaches the generosity of God, than they are to the injunctions to confidence in asking in vv. 9–10.

11

What father among you, if his son asks for a fish, will instead of a fish give him a serpent?: This translation smoothes out a sentence which in the Greek is barely grammatical, and which is difficult to account for in comparison with the clearer statement in Matt. 7^{9-10}. Further, while Luke and Matthew have in common the pair *fish/serpent*, Luke lacks Matthew's bread/stone (the variant reading inserts it from Matthew), and Matthew lacks Luke's *egg/scorpion*. These differences are not easy to account for (see Marshall, pp. 268f.). The question *What father . . .?* could be an appeal to the ridiculous, expecting the answer 'No one, of course'. If so it would not be necessary to the argument, as some suppose, that serpents and scorpions should look like, and possibly be mistaken for, fish and eggs. The argument is *a minore ad maius*, but its precise force depends on the meaning of *who are* (v. 13). In the Greek this is the participle of *huparchein*. If this verb, as commonly in Hellenistic Greek, is simply a synonym for *einai* = 'to be', then the saying could be spoken to opponents. Though they are evil, they still *know how* (*oidate* = 'you know' in the sense of 'you are able'; it is the capacity, not the knowledge, of men and God that is compared) to give the opposite kind of (i.e. 'good') gifts. If the verb retains its original nuance of 'to be by nature' (i.e. 'irretrievably'), the saying will be about mankind in general. If men, who are evil (malevolent) by nature, are still able as fathers by nature to give beneficial gifts, how much more the Father, who is by nature good (beneficent).

13

the heavenly Father: The Greek text generally printed here has *ho patēr ho ex ouranou*, which means literally 'the Father (the one) from heaven'. This is unique, and barely intelligible. Variants in the mss attempt to assimilate it to Matthew's 'your Father (the one) in the heavens'.^v Some mss, including p^{75},

---

^v Blass-Debrunner, § 437, p. 225, take *ex* = 'from' as an equivalent of *en* = 'in'; C. B. Winer, *A Treatise on the Greek of the New Testament*, ET by W. F. Moulton, Edinburgh 1870, p. 784, see here a compound phrase 'he who is in heaven gives from heaven'.

lack the second definite article, which would allow the translation 'how much more will the Father give from heaven'. This would stress the heavenly origin of the gifts of the divine Father compared with earthly gifts of earthly fathers.

the Holy Spirit: This is almost certainly secondary and due to Luke – variants in the mss reflect assimilation to, or conflation with, the 'good things' in Matt. 7¹¹. It is a very significant alteration by Luke. For the section on prayer is concluded, and the objects of the petitions of the Lord's Prayer, and of prayer in general, are summed up, by placing on the lips of Jesus a promise of the gift which in Acts is the characteristic possession of the Christian (A. 2²⁸; 10⁴⁵; 11¹⁷; 19²ᶠᶠ·), and which is given in answer to prayer (A. 2¹ᶠ· with 1¹⁴; 8¹⁵⁻¹⁷; 9¹¹⁻¹⁷; 11⁵⁻¹⁵; 13²ᶠ·).

11 ^{14–36} *True and False Signs*

This section is made up of three units from Q, which are separated in Matthew: vv. 14–23 = Matt. 12²²⁻³⁰, controversy over exorcism; vv. 24–26 = Matt. 12⁴³⁻⁴⁵, the exorcised spirit; and vv. 29–32 = Matt. 12³⁸⁻⁴², seeking for signs. These are linked in vv. 27–28 by a beatitude, which is peculiar to Luke, and are concluded in vv. 33–36 by sayings on interior light. Some of these latter have parallels: v. 33, the lamp = Matt. 5¹⁵, vv. 34–35, the eye as the light of the body, = Matt. 6²²⁻²³. Streeter (*Four Gospels*, p. 278) assigns the whole of vv. 14–36 in its Lukan form to Q. There is too much evidence of Luke's hand in wording and in the ordering of material to make this likely. Knox (*Sources* II, pp. 62ff.) supposes a tract containing vv. 14–32 (but probably not vv. 33–36) compiled by Christian controversialists to meet a double charge that Jesus used evil spirit but never wrought a really convincing miracle. Matthew will then have made two separate stories out of it, and Luke will have gone some way towards this by slovenly editing in v. 29a. The beatitude, which has no place in such a tract, could then only be accounted for as genuine reminiscence of an actual order of events – accusation of possession and a reference to Jesus' family – similar to that in Mark 3²¹⁻²⁵. But the beatitude is surely from Luke's hand (see note), and it is more likely that Luke has composed a single section on the unbelief of Israel, and has done so by bringing together two unbelieving accusations against Jesus, introducing them in vv.

14–16. These are distributed between two different groups in the same crowd – vv. 14–16, *the people* (*hoi ochloi* = 'the crowds') marvelled. *But some of them said . . . while others . . .* The reply to the first is in vv. 17–23, to the second in vv. 29–36. There is no break with the beatitude (v. 27, *As he said this*), and the crowds mentioned in v. 14 are picked up and augmented (v. 29) to provide an audience for an address to 'this generation'. The sayings in vv. 33–36 make the section end with an appeal to repent of spiritual blindness. The sequence of thought may be: exorcisms are not evidence of Jesus' possession by evil but of its disposssession by him; they are not this in themselves or as spectacular actions, but only if the previous evil power is replaced by the power and presence of the good; the demand for the spectacular is itself evidence of evil nature; it betrays blindness to what is apparent in the activity of Jesus for those whose eye, and so their whole self, is not darkened by evil.

11$^{14-23}$ CONTROVERSY OVER EXORCISM

[14]*Now he was casting out a demon that was dumb; when the demon had gone out, the dumb man spoke, and the people marvelled.* [15]*But some of them said, 'He casts out demons by Beelzebul, the prince of demons';* [16]*while others, to test him, sought from him a sign from heaven.* [17]*But he, knowing their thoughts, said to them, 'Every kingdom divided against itself is laid waste, and house falls upon house.* [18]*And if Satan also is divided against himself, how will his kingdom stand? For you say that I cast out demons by Beelzebul.* [19]*And if I cast out demons by Beelzebul, by whom do your sons cast them out? Therefore they shall be your judges.* [20]*But if it is by the finger of God that I cast out demons, then the kingdom of God has come upon you.* [21]*When a strong man, fully armed, guards his own palace, his goods are in peace;* [22]*but when one stronger than he assails him and overcomes him, he takes away his armour in which he trusted, and divides his spoil.* [23]*He who is not with me is against me, and he who does not gather with me scatters.'*

The issue raised here was of crucial importance. Not only is it the unanimous testimony of the synoptic traditions that exorcism played a (considerable?) part in the ministry of Jesus (in 13^{32} it belongs in the definition of that ministry), but it also played a part in the mission of the church (cf. 9$^{49f.}$; 10^{17}; A. 5^{16}; 8^7; 16^{16}; 19$^{12f.}$). It was therefore necessary to establish the connection of exorcism with the major concerns of that ministry and mission. The importance of the issue is reflected in the preservation of two distinct but overlapping versions of the controversy in Mark 3$^{22-27}$ and in Q (Matt. 12$^{22-30}$/Luke 11$^{14-23}$). The literary evidence here is complex, but it would appear that Matthew, who records the controversy in its Markan context, has conflated the Markan and Q versions, while Luke, who passes over it in its Markan context, reproduces the Q version alone.^{w} The accusation of being possessed could stand on its own, as in Mark 3^{22}, where it is voiced by Jerusalem scribes (cf. John 7^{20}; 8^{48}; 10^{20}). In Q it is introduced by way of an actual exorcism of a dumb (Matthew, blind and dumb) demoniac. This leads to astonishment on the part of the crowds (v. 14 = Matt. 12^{22}), but to a charge from opponents (*some*, v. 15; 'the Pharisees', Matt. 12^{24}) of casting out demons by the agency of Beelzebul. Thus the theological issue of exorcism is discussed only in terms of a particularly perverse charge that in Jesus' case the exorcising of evil spirit was an activity of evil spirit itself, and in terms of a rebuttal of this charge. In Q the rebuttal is in four (in Mark, two) stages. (i) vv. 17b–18, the charge could only be true if the realm of evil was at civil war, which, so it is implied, is not the case; (ii) v. 19, an appeal to the contemporary Jewish practice of exorcism, which logically should be subject to the same charge; (iii) v. 20, an assertion interpreting the exorcisms of Jesus as evidence of the direct action of God in relation to his kingdom; and (iv), vv. 21–22, developing (iii) in parabolic form, the exorcisms are the spoil of a victorious conflict with Satan. Each of these arguments is forceful in itself provided it is not pressed too far, but they do not together present a logical progression.^{x}

w See G. F. Downing, 'Towards the Rehabilitation of Q', *NTS* 11, 1964–65, pp. 169–81.

x In the view of Bultmann (*History*, pp. 13f.) the charge originally had a single reply, that in vv. 17f. (as in Mark), and the other verses were added. In the view of E. Schweizer (*The Good News according to Matthew*, ET London 1984, p. 284) the charge about Beelzebul received a single reply in terms of Beelzebul (v. 19), the statements in terms of Satan being later accretions.

ஐ

14

The verse shows the pattern of a miracle story in its briefest possible form – illness, cure, result of cure, effect on audience. *he was casting out* (in the Greek the periphrastic tense = 'he was in the process of casting out') is put first in the sentence to provide the framework for the controversy. *who was* (kai auto ēn = 'and it was') is absent from some mss. *dumb*: a dumb demon is one which makes the patient dumb.

15

He casts out demons by Beelzebul, the prince of demons: For demon possession and exorcism see on 4³³. The popular character of the tradition here is indicated by *Beelzebul*. The name is found in Greek literature only in this passage and parallels, and in Matt. 10²⁵. Spelling, origin, history and meaning are all obscure. Some mss have Beelzebub = 'lord of flies', which is found elsewhere only in II Kings 1²ff. as a derogatory form of the name of the god of Ekron. B has Beezebul in contrast to the mass of textual authorities, which have Beelzebul. The latter is found in the form Baalzebul = 'lord of the high place (or, lofty dwelling)' in the Ras Shamra texts as a description or name of the god of Syria, and hence for Israel a false god or idol. How it entered the bizarre world of demonology is not known, nor what precisely it denoted there. It could have become simply a bogey term. 'He has Beelzebul' (Mark 3²²) looks like a popular form of 'He has an unclean spirit' (Mark 3³⁰). He is called *prince* (archōn = 'ruler') of 'the demons', who are thus thought of as constituting a single realm. In Matt. 12²⁴ he is 'a' ruler, possibly one of a number of subordinate rulers under Satan. In that case the division of Satan against himself (v. 17) could mean that in allowing exorcism Beelzebul was a rebel ranged against the other rulers of the demons. Luke and Mark have *the* ruler. Even this might mean that under Satan he was in sole charge of the demon world, which was only one department of the whole realm of evil. The division of Satan against himself could then mean that in allowing exorcism Beelzebul would be setting the demon world in opposition to the rest of Satan's kingdom. In the rebuttal in vv. 17–18 he appears to be identified with Satan, and this may be underlined by Luke's explanatory addition in v. 18b. In Jewish theology, however, Satan was not thought of as a demon or presented in demonic terms. But precision of thought is hardly to be expected in this sphere, especially at the popular level.

16

This verse is plainly out of place. It is put here to prepare for the subsequent controversy in vv. 29–32, and to make that arise out of the present occasion. For *seeks a sign*, see on v. 29.

17

knowing their thoughts: In Q (cf. Matt. 12²⁵) Jesus' rebuttal of the charge proceeds from his ability to divine men's thoughts to the letter and to reproduce their words. This is a magical trait, but it is unnecessary here, since the charge had already been uttered aloud.

Every kingdom divided against itself is laid waste: In Mark throughout, and in Luke and Matthew after this verse, *kingdom* could have the sense of 'rule', and v. 18 could mean 'how will his rule continue?' (cf. I Sam. 13¹⁴). Here, and in Matt. 12²⁵, it must have the sense of 'realm'. Civil war in a realm devastates it (so the verb here *erēmousthai* + Rev. 17¹⁶; 18¹⁶⁻¹⁹), or, more precisely, 'depopulates it' (cf. Isa. 6¹¹, and generally in the LXX). The statement is possibly more than simply parabolic, and is already to some extent allegorical. Evil spirits actually constitute a single realm of evil, which is in conflict with the kingdom of God (v. 20). Thus individual exorcisms are given a cosmic setting.

and house falls upon house: In Matt. 12²⁵ᵇ/Mark 3²⁵ there is a repetition with respect to a house of what has been said about a kingdom. If 'divided' is supplied that could also be the sense here; but in that case 'against itself' is to be expected. Luke's wording, which is certainly secondary, is better taken as a further description of what happens when a kingdom is laid waste – either, 'house falls on top of house' (for *piptein epi* = 'to fall upon', cf. 13⁴; 20¹⁸), or, 'house after house falls' (for *epi* in this sense cf. Phil. 2²⁷, 'sorrow after sorrow'; *piptein* = 'to fall' is suggested by *stand* in v. 18).

18

The first part of the verse, 18a, is introduced by *de kai* = 'but also', 'so then', and applies the parable in v. 17 emphatically. It is more exactly modelled on v. 17 (*Satan . . . divided against himself*) than is the corresponding verse Matt. 12²⁶ ('Satan casts out Satan'), which is influenced by Mark 3²³. In either case *Satan* seems to stand both for the ruler of the demon world and for that world itself. Verse 18b, which is probably Luke's addition, giving vv. 17–18 a fourfold structure, identifies Beelzebul with Satan, and shows Jesus divining the thoughts of the opponents. The argument here is not watertight. It does not allow for the possibility of the antichrist appearing to perform exorcisms as a sign of Satan's power (cf. II Thess. 2⁸ᶠᶠ·; Matt. 24⁴ᶠ·). Further, it presupposes that the kingdom of Satan is evidently intact and shows no sign of being fatally divided, whereas in vv. 20ff. it is supposed that it is on the point of collapse.

19

This throws the accusation back on the opponents, and asks whether they are prepared to make the same judgment on the exorcizing activities of their fellows. *your sons* means 'those closely connected with you' (cf. 'the sons of the bridegroom', 5³⁴). Bauer (s.v. *huios*) suggests the more precise sense 'your pupils'. This would require that the charge was brought by scribes, as in Mark 3²². Again the argument cannot be pressed in the context, as if to say that when

Jews exorcized, then, as with Jesus' exorcisms, the kingdom of God came upon men (v. 20). But those who dub his exorcisms diabolical in origin must be prepared to suffer condemnation (at the last judgment?, cf. v. 31) from those of their fellows who could point to successful exorcism through the invocation of what was divine in origin.

20

This is not argument, as then it would yield the tautology that what is done by God is divine action. It is unequivocal assertion, based on the speaker's authority, of the origin and significance of his acts. Exorcisms are not in themselves conclusive, nor is their meaning immediately perceptible. They mean what Jesus says they mean. They are part and parcel of his effective proclamation of the kingdom of God. 'Jesus is thinking in distinctly dualistic terms. What is not of God is of the devil; what is not of the devil is of God. *Tertium non datur*' (Leivestad, *Christ the Conqueror*, p. 45).

by the finger of God: This is generally taken as original in Q compared with 'by the Spirit of God' (Matt. 12^{28}), which Luke, with his emphasis on the Spirit, is unlikely to have changed. But this is not absolutely certain. For all its frequency in L–A 'the Spirit' is nowhere there associated with healing or exorcism (except perhaps 4$^{18ff.}$). For the agency in healing Luke tends to use OT terms such as 'the power of the Lord' (5^{17}; 6^{19}) or 'the hand of the Lord' (A. 4$^{28-30}$; 13^{11}). 'the finger of God' was another such, going back to Exod. 8^{19}; Deut. 9^{10}. It stresses that the action of Jesus is nothing less than the personal redeeming action of God, but is also dependent on God.

then: ara, which emphasises the apodosis in a conditional sentence. Hence 'to be sure'; perhaps here 'as I have already told you'.

has come: ephthasen. For the dispute over the meaning of this verb here, see Kümmel, *Promise and Fulfilment*, pp. 105ff. Current usage, including that of the NT, is overwhelmingly in favour of 'has arrived' (perhaps 'has arrived in advance of its time', cf. Matt. 8^{29}), rather than of 'has drawn near', which would make it a synonym of *engizein* (10$^{9-11}$). This would hardly have been questioned but for its contradiction of other statements in the gospels that the kingdom is still to come or has only drawn near. This contradiction, however, lies too deep in the gospel traditions to be eliminated, and must be allowed to stand.

21–22

The parable in Mark 3^{27}/Matt. 12^{29}, introduced by formula or question, depicts a private affair of assault and plunder. In Luke it is more self-contained, being introduced by *When*, is more rounded and didactic in form (Lagrange, p. 332), and is literary in its phrasing: *fully armed* (the participle of *kathoplizesthai* + +), *goods* (the participial *ta huparchonta*), *assails* (*eperchesthai*, apart from Eph. 2⁷; James 5¹ only L–A in the NT), *overcomes* (*nikān*, elsewhere in the gospels John 16³³), *armour* (*panoplia* + Eph. 6¹¹, ¹³), *divides* (*diadidonai* + 18²²; A. 4³⁵; John 6¹¹), *spoil* (*skulon* + +). It is transformed, appropriately in the context, into a battle of giants, in which one contestant *overcomes* (not 'binds' as in Mark/Matthew) the other. All three versions are probably to some extent allegorical. Although 'the strong one' (not as in RSV 'a strong man'; *ho ischuros* has the definite article) is not found as a title for Satan, its use here probably indicates that in the language of popular belief it had become so. Bauer (s.v. *ischuros*) cites from the Paris Magical Papyrus references to a demon called 'strong', to a 'strong one' who is 'armed', and to 'Fear, fully armed' (the same adjective as in v. 21) who fights against a 'stronger'. Behind all three versions, and especially behind Luke's, may lie the promise of God in Isa. 49²⁴f. to deliver Israel by conquering the strong giant and taking his spoil (cf. also Isa. 53¹², and the proverb in Pss. Sol. 5⁴, 'No man takes spoil from a mighty one'). But while the two contestants – Satan and Jesus (or God) – are allegorized, the details may not be pressed. Thus *divides* forbids the *spoil* to be interpreted of the possessed who are healed. Otto (*The Kingdom of God and the Son of Man*, pp. 101ff.) refers *overcomes . . . and takes away his armour* to a previous victory by God over Satan, which enables Jesus as exorcist to collect the spoils subsequently. But this is too precise, and rests on Otto's erroneous belief that Luke's version is the most original. The general sense of all the versions is that the exorcisms of Jesus are themselves the conquest and spoliation of Satan.

23

A double proverbial saying, which could be attached to almost any passage of controversy with opponents. In view of the context an opposite view of neutrality with respect to discipleship is expressed to that in 9⁵⁰, where the issue is also one of exorcism, but where the exorcist could have been one of those here called 'your sons'. The second half of the saying could be more than simply proverbial. *scatters* is in the Greek *skorpizein*. This is found only here in the synoptists. It is a late Greek word which is found in the LXX for the scattering of Israel (Ezek. 5¹²; Tobit 3⁴) as sheep (Zech. 11¹⁶). This could determine the meaning of *gather* here, which is also used in the LXX of the gathering of Israel by God (Isa. 11¹²; 66¹⁸, etc.) as sheep (Isa. 40¹¹; Ezek. 34¹²f.). In Isa. 40¹⁰⁻¹¹ there is also an abrupt transition from the figure of God as the mighty one with his spoil, which is the rescued exiles, to that of the shepherd who gathers the flock of Israel. If this is to be pressed here the exorcisms are interpreted as evidence of the divine restoration of Israel through deliverance from Satan the oppressor. Those who do not accept them but oppose them (the religious leaders?) destroy Israel.

493

²⁴'*When the unclean spirit has gone out of a man, he passes through waterless places seeking rest; and finding none he says, "I will return to my house from which I came." ²⁵ And when he comes he finds it swept and put in order. ²⁶ Then he goes and brings seven other spirits more evil than himself, and they enter and dwell there; and the last state of that man becomes worse than the first.*'

This Q passage (in the Greek wording and word order are almost identical with those in Matt. 12⁴³⁻⁴⁵) is a very strange one. It reads like an extract from a text book on demonology. It is given something of a didactic character by the concluding proverb (with which cf. Matt. 27⁶⁴; II Peter 2²⁰). Its original purpose is not clear. Matthew, who has it after the condemnation of this generation for its failure to appreciate what is present in Jesus' ministry, interprets it of the future condition of the Jews. In Luke it seems to teach that exorcism is in itself negative, and is not conclusively proof against evil. Positive possession of, and by, the good is necessary, and a state of neutrality between good and evil is impossible.

∽

24–26
The passage is deeply rooted in popular belief. The natural habitat of demons is presumed to be the desert, for which *waterless places* here is a synonym (Isa. 34¹⁴f·, where the LXX has 'demons' for 'wild beasts', Baruch 4³⁵; IV Macc. 18⁸; Rev. 18²; see SB IV, p. 516). But they are driven by their nature to look for permanent abode (*my house*, v. 24, *dwell*, v. 26) in the bodies of men. Josephus (*BJ* 7.185) refers to 'the so-called demons, in other words the spirits of wicked men who enter the living and kill them unless aid is forthcoming'. In *Clementine Homilies* 9¹⁰ 'The reason why demons delight in entering men's bodies' is said to be that 'Being spirits, and having desires after meats and drinks and sexual pleasures, but not being able to partake of these by reason of their being spirits, and wanting organs for their enjoyment, they enter the bodies of men.' In *Ant.* 8.45 Josephus attributes to Solomon skill in devising forms of exorcism by which the demons were driven out 'never to return'.

24
rest: The Greek word *anapausis* denotes in classical and Hellenistic Greek a temporary abode. Only in the LXX does it mean, as here, a permanent abode

(Isa. 32¹⁶; 57¹⁵), sometimes in connection with demons (Isa. 13²¹; 34¹⁴ 'to seek rest').

25

swept and put in order: This describes the result of the previous exorcism, the effect of possession being regarded as filth and interior chaos.

11²⁷⁻²⁸   BLESSEDNESS

²⁷*As he said this, a woman in the crowd raised her voice and said to him,* '*Blessed is the womb that bore you, and the breasts that you sucked!*' ²⁸*But he said,* '*Blessed rather are those who bear the word of God and keep it!*'

Both origin and purpose of this little pericope are puzzling. It is one of the few doublets in the Gospel, being similar to Mark 3³¹⁻³⁵ (= Matt. 12⁴⁶⁻⁵⁰) in its context of the Beelzebul controversy, its reference to Jesus' family, and in its pronouncement on hearing and doing the word of God (cf. 8²¹, Luke's version of Mark 3³⁵). Distinctive here is the beatitude form, both of the effusive remark of the woman in the crowd and of the reply to it; ejaculatory beatitude of this kind is confined to Luke or his sources (cf. 1⁴⁵; 14¹⁵). The introduction in v. 27a is entirely from Luke's hand. If there is any connection with what immediately precedes (*As he said this*), it may be that a positive cleaving to the word of God is necessary if the object of exorcism is to be obtained.

೧೪

27

Blessed is the womb . . . that you sucked: A fulsome ejaculation of piety. It recalls the birth stories (cf. 1⁴², ⁴⁵, ⁴⁸); cf. II Baruch 54¹⁰, of Baruch himself; Shemoth Rabba 45, 'Blessed is she who bare him' (of Moses); Pesikta 149a, 'Blessed is the womb from which he came forth' (of the messiah).

rather: menoun + +. The degree of confirmation and inclusion or repudiation and exclusion implied by the word is uncertain. The Latin versions vary between a rendering 'Yes, blessed indeed, but also blessed . . .' and 'Not at all; blessed rather . . .' (cf. 8²¹ = Mark 3³⁵).

the word of God: In the context of the blessing of Jesus' person this probably refers not to the word of God in general, but to that word as proclaimed by Jesus.

keep it: The Greek verb here, *phulassein,* is rare in the NT but frequent in the LXX, especially Deuteronomy, for the continued observance of the divine commandments. For 'hearing and keeping' cf. Exod. 23^{22}; Deut. 7^{12}.

I I$^{29-36}$ SIGNS

^{29}*When the crowds were increasing, he began to say, 'This generation is an evil generation; it seeks a sign, but no sign shall be given to it except the sign of Jonah.* ^{30}*For as Jonah became a sign to the men of Nineveh, so will the Son of man be to this generation.* ^{31}*The queen of the South will arise at the judgment with the men of this generation and condemn them; for she came from the ends of the earth to hear the wisdom of Solomon, and behold, something greater than Solomon is here.* ^{32}*The men of Nineveh will arise at the judgment with this generation and condemn it; for they repented at the preaching of Jonah, and behold, something greater than Jonah is here.*

^{33}*'No one after lighting a lamp puts it in a cellar or under a bushel, but on a stand, that those who enter may see the light.* ^{34}*Your eye is the lamp of your body; when your eye is sound, your whole body is full of light; but when it is not sound, your body is full of darkness.* ^{35}*Therefore be careful lest the light in you be darkness.* ^{36}*If then your whole body is full of light, having no part dark, it will be wholly bright, as when a lamp with its rays gives you light.'*

Luke now picks up the second controversial subject for which he has prepared in v. 16. The request by *others* is treated as an expression of the attitude of Israel as a whole. An augmented crowd (*epathroizein* = 'to collect in addition' is found only here and once in Plutarch) supplies an audience for a wholesale condemnation of the present generation of Israel on this score. Verses 29–32 are a Q passage, agreement with Matt. 12$^{38-42}$ being close, at times verbatim. That in Q it followed the Beelzebul controversy (so in Matthew; Luke combines them) does not of itself establish its meaning – e.g. that the sign requested is something more spectacular or conclusive than exorcism. It is an independent pericope, carrying its meaning in itself. It may already in Q have been composite, since although vv. 29–30 and vv. 31–32 are connected by a

reference to Jonah they are making different points. Jesus already pronounces condemnation of Israel for the request for a sign as such. This
will be borne out by the only sign to be given, which is the Son of man
as the sign of Jonah (in judgment?). Further, at the final judgment the
present Israel will stand condemned on the testimony of Gentiles, the
queen of Sheba and the inhabitants of Nineveh, on the ground that it
has failed to recognize in its midst, and to make the appropriate response to, something greater than the wisdom of Solomon or the
preaching of Jonah. Luke somewhat tempers this wholesale condemnation by a collocation of sayings on light, which stress the need for
possessing the good in the form of interior spiritual perception.

തരു

29

a sign: Greek *sēmeion.* It is not clear what this, called in v. 16 *a sign from heaven,*
meant for Luke, nor whether it was evil in itself (*to test him,* v. 16, meaning 'to
make a diabolical suggestion'), or whether it would not be granted because this
generation was too evil to receive it. One meaning of *sēmeion* in classical Greek
was an omen from the gods, but its use for divine miracle is rare outside the
Greek Bible and writers dependent on it. Throughout the OT (where it is not
found with 'from heaven') it has the favourable sense of (i) divine miracle
accompanying or guaranteeing redemption (so in Exod., Deut., Num., Pss.), or
(ii) a symbolic act of a prophet heralding a future action of God (Ezek. 4³;
24²⁴), or (iii) a catastrophic portent of the end produced by God (Joel 2³⁰ only,
but characteristic of apocalyptic, cf. IV Ezra 4⁵¹ᶠ·). In Mark, and in Matthew
apart from Matt. 16³; 24³⁰, it is used in the bad sense of either (i) a lying portent
of the end produced by false prophets or messiahs (Mark 13²²/Matt. 24²⁴; cf.
II Thess. 2⁹; Rev. 19²⁰), or (ii) probably, a celestial wonder on earth of an overpowering kind (Mark 8¹¹ᶠ·; cf. John 4⁴⁸; I Cor. 1²²; Rev. 13¹³ᶠ· 'from heaven';
16¹⁴, produced by demons). Throughout L–A, however, apart from this passage, it is used in a good sense – signs from heaven produced by God (21¹¹, ²⁵),
miracles as divine attestation of Jesus (A. 2²²), healings attesting the preaching of
the apostles (A. 2⁴³; 4¹⁶⁻³⁰; 5¹²). Here in Q it may have denoted some undeter-
mined but conclusive wonder which would guarantee the status of Jesus, and
which did not require spiritual perception (was Luke thinking of something
like the request in 9⁵⁴; cf. Rev. 13¹³?).

except the sign of Jonah: This is very difficult, both (i) in relation to the tradition,
and (ii) in itself. (i) As a concession it is in flat contradiction to the explicit
refusal of any sign (from heaven) in Mark 8¹², which is in a section not reproduced by Luke, and which in Matt. 16⁴ is modified to agree with this Q passage.

The suggestion is very doubtful that Mark, or the tradition he records, knew of this concession and deliberately suppressed it. The two traditions, whatever their origins, are simply irreconcilable. (ii) *the sign of Jonah* appears to mean the sign that Jonah himself was. But to what does this refer? The continuation in vv. 31–32 suggests that it was Jonah's preaching. But these verses need not originally have belonged here; if they did, a 'sign' of Solomon would seem to be required. Preaching is an unlikely meaning for *sign*, especially when attached to the Son of man, who is not generally thought of as a preacher. Further, if Jesus here refers to himself as the Son of man, and *shall be given* and *will be* are to be taken as real and not simply logical futures, then the reference cannot be to his preaching, which is not future but is already going on. In Matt. 12^{40} Jonah's sign is his residence for three days and nights in the whale's belly as a prophecy of the death, burial (and resurrection?) of the Son of man. This could be what the figure of Jonah would naturally suggest (cf. III Macc. 6^8; SB I, p. 646), and it preserves the future tenses. It is, however, suspiciously allegorical and explicit, and almost certainly represents a later Christian midrash (according to K. Stendahl, *The School of Matthew*, pp. 132f., possibly an addition to Matthew's text, which originally was the same as Luke's here). If it had stood in Q Luke is hardly likely to have omitted it. Perhaps Jonah is here a figure of judgment, and this is what the Son of man will be to this generation in his parousia. It has been suggested that *of Jonah* (Greek *Iōna*) is an early corruption of *of John* (*Iōannou*; cf. Matt. 16^{17} 'bar Jonah' with John 1^{42} 'son of John'), and that the reference was to the Baptist as the only sign, perhaps as the coming Elijah. In that case Matt. 12^{40} and Luke 11^{30} would be Son of man sayings arising subsequently to, and out of, this corruption, and to explain it.

31–32

Two parallel statements which are compressed in form and oblique in reference. In Matt. 12$^{41-42}$ the statement about the Ninevites comes in immediate proximity to the sign of Jonah. Luke has the reverse and historical order, which was probably that of Q. The connection with v. 30 will be closer if the sign of the Son of man means his parousia, since Jonah appeared to announce the imminent destruction of Nineveh. Jesus, as himself privy to the final judgment, pronounces in advance the condemnation then of the present generation of Israel on the testimony of Gentiles. This will be for its failure to recognize the presence now in Israel of something greater than the wisdom of God in Solomon which drew the queen of Sheba, or the preaching of the prophet Jonah, which secured the repentance of Nineveh. It is not clear whether the selection of these two was governed by the desire for two examples of non-Israelites who took note of, and were involved in, what God was bringing about in Israel, or by a model of divine activity as consisting in wisdom and prophecy (cf. Matt. 23^{34}), or a characterization of Jesus' ministry as itself consisting in wisdom and prophecy. If the last, then under wisdom would be included the proverbial and parabolic teaching as well as such explicit wisdom sayings as 10²¹ᶠ. Jonah will have been selected to represent prophecy as the only prophet in the OT who is instructed to 'preach' (cf. Jonah 3², where both verb and noun are found, the latter only there in the LXX of 'preaching'), which preaching is characteristic of Jesus' ministry.

31

The queen of the South: The queen of Sheba is meant (I Kings 10¹ᶠᶠ.). Her kingdom of Sabaea is variously placed in the sources in northern or southern Arabia. Josephus (*Ant.* 8.165) reflects a tradition which made her queen of Egypt and Ethiopia. But there was no region called 'the South', and the genitive probably means 'from the south' ('the southern queen').

will arise at the judgment with the men of this generation and condemn: It is not clear whether *arise* means stand up to give her testimony at the judgment, or be resurrected in order to do so, this being one form of resurrection belief in Judaism (cf. II Baruch 50–51); nor whether this generation will have died and also been resurrected for judgment, or will be still alive on earth and judged there. *condemn* might mean more than that she will testify to the condemnation of this generation. As approved by God she will carry it out (cf. I Cor. 6²; Wisd. 3⁸; Ecclus 4¹⁵; Rev. 3²¹).

something greater: This is notably indirect and reserved. If the *something* (not 'someone') *greater* is of the same kind as wisdom and prophecy, it is presumably that which wisdom and prophecy foreshadow – the presence of the eschatological kingdom? It is here held to be sufficiently evident in the activity of Jesus to render culpable those who fail to recognize it.

33–36

Sayings of various origins are here brought together to provide a conclusion to the discourse, and are spoken without change of audience. The connecting link with what precedes is failure to recognize the truth when present. They are used by Luke in highly individual fashion to locate the condemnation of this generation in its blindness. *your* throughout is in the singular. This fits the context in Matt. 6²²⁻²³ where it is disciples who are being addressed, but not here where it is crowds. The language of light and darkness is parabolic. It hardly needs to be taken in the theological sense of salvation and judgment (as by Ellis, pp. 166f.), or the lamp taken as a figure of God and his law (as by Leaney, pp. 192f.).

33

An isolated parabolic saying capable of different applications (cf. 8¹⁶ = Mark 4²¹; Matt. 5¹⁵). Here it serves simply to introduce the following saying about the eye as the body's lamp, and to connect it with what has preceded. The function of a lamp is not to be obscured, but to emit light to be seen – though what is required here is rather 'light by which to see'.

34

Your eye is the lamp of your body: Reference to parts of the body as expressing functions of the person is frequent in Wisdom sayings. The common view in the ancient world was that of the Empedoclean school of philosophy, according to which sight was due, not to rays entering the eye from the object (as the Stoics thought), but to a searchlight thrown out by the eye upon the object. So here *the light in you* (v. 35).

sound . . . not sound: The Greek words here, *haplous* and *ponēros*, can mean 'healthy' and 'sick'. This is the most natural meaning for the saying in itself and in this context, and it continues the thought of v. 34a. If the eye is able to perform its functions the whole body (person) is illuminated and able to see. But in Matt. 20¹⁵ *ponēros* with 'eye' means 'ungenerous', and one of the meanings of *haplous* = 'single-hearted' was 'generous'. This, however, would not continue the thought, would involve an abrupt change to a purely metaphorical use of 'eye', and would hardly prepare for v. 35, which envisages a total loss of the eye's function.

35-36

Rhythm and sense require the passage to end with v. 35 and the pessimistic conclusion similar to Matt. 6²³. Plato (*Timaeus* 47a) remarks that sight is the greatest blessing because it gives us everything else. Verse 36 is flat and tautologous, and is difficult to explain. There is considerable textual variation here. D and some Old Latin mss substitute Matt. 6²³ᵇ for vv. 35-36; syrᶜ has this after v. 35 and one ms after v. 34; syrˢ and two Old Latin mss have, with variations, 'if your body has no lamp shining it is dark to thee; how much more when the lamp shines does it lighten thee.' If Luke wrote the text printed he presumably wished to end as he had begun with *a lamp*, and on a very positive note – *having no part dark, with its rays* (*astrapē* = 'lightning', i.e. the most brilliant light).

II³⁷⁻⁵⁴ *Denunciation of the Pharisees and Lawyers*

³⁷*While he was speaking, a Pharisee asked him to dine with him; so he went in and sat at table.* ³⁸*The Pharisee was astonished to see that he did not first wash before dinner.* ³⁹*And the Lord said to him, 'Now you Pharisees cleanse the outside of the cup and of the dish, but inside you are full of extortion and wickedness.* ⁴⁰*You fools! Did not he who made the outside make the inside*

also? ⁴¹*But give for alms those things which are within; and behold, every-thing is clean for you.*

⁴²*'But woe to you Pharisees! for you tithe mint and rue and every herb, and neglect justice and the love of God; these you ought to have done, without neglecting the others. ⁴³Woe to you Pharisees! for you love the best seat in the synagogues and salutations in the market places. ⁴⁴Woe to you! for you are like graves which are not seen, and men walk over them without knowing it.'*

⁴⁵*One of the lawyers answered him, 'Teacher, in saying this you reproach us also.' ⁴⁶And he said, 'Woe to you lawyers also! for you load men with burdens hard to bear, and you yourselves do not touch the burdens with one of your fingers. ⁴⁷Woe to you! for you build the tombs of the prophets whom your fathers killed. ⁴⁸So you are witnesses and consent to the deeds of your fathers; for they killed them, and you build their tombs. ⁴⁹Therefore also the Wisdom of God said, "I will send them prophets and apostles, some of whom they will kill and persecute," ⁵⁰that the blood of all the prophets, shed from the foundation of the world, may be required of this generation, ⁵¹from the blood of Abel to the blood of Zechariah, who perished between the altar and the sanctuary. Yes, I tell you, it shall be required of this generation. ⁵²Woe to you lawyers! for you have taken away the key of knowledge; you did not enter yourselves, and you hindered those who were entering.'*

⁵³*As he went away from there, the scribes and the Pharisees began to press him hard, and to provoke him to speak of many things, ⁵⁴lying in wait for him, to catch at something he might say.*

In spite of v. 36 the condemnation of this generation as evil (cf. v. 51 with vv. 29, 32, and v. 39 with vv. 29, 34) is continued, but now with reference to its spiritual leaders, the Pharisees, and those who furnished the basis of Pharisaic piety by their interpretation of scripture, the lawyers. Both are sweepingly denounced as a class, and both are roused to bitter antagonism (vv. 53–54).

Questions of source and composition are especially difficult here. On the one hand there is close agreement in thought and wording with parallel passages in Matthew – cf. v. 39 with Matt. 23^{25}, v. 42 with Matt. 23^{23}, v. 43 with Matt. 23$^{6-7}$, v. 46 with Matt. 23^4, v. 47 with Matt. 23^{29} and vv. 50–51 with Matt. 23$^{35-36}$. On the other hand there are considerable differences of thought and wording in what is plainly the same material, as in vv. 40–41 (cf. Matt. 23^{26}), v. 44 (cf. Matt. 23^{27}), v. 48 (cf. Matt. 23$^{30-31}$), v. 49 (cf. Matt. 23^{34}) and v. 52 (cf. Matt. 23^{13}). These differences appear to be too great to be accounted for in all cases by the editing of one or other of the evangelists or of both together. Hence hypotheses of a common source have generally been modified to allow the possibility that Matthew and Luke have used variant versions or translations of the same tradition (of Q, so Streeter, *Four Gospels*, p. 254; of a common tract, so Knox, *Sources* I, pp. 94–101). Manson (*Sayings*, pp. 94ff.) assigns vv. 42–44, 46–52 to Q and most of Matt. 23 to Matthew's special source M. He explains the agreement in order of the woes on tithing, sepulchres and the tombs of the prophets as a coincidence between Q and M. But in several instances Luke's version seems to be too compressed to be a straight reproduction of Q (see notes on vv. 44, 47f.). Easton (pp. 195f.) assigns vv. 37–41, 44, 47–48 and vv. 53–54 to L; but this seems too short a collection to have vv. 53–54 as a conclusion.

The differences in the order of the woes could be put down largely to the fact that Matt. 23 is an elaborate compilation of seven woes against scribes and Pharisees with anti-Pharisaic material and ending in an apostrophe of Jerusalem, all set in the context provided by Mark 12$^{37bff.}$. There are, however, signs of compilation in Luke also. The normal 'scribes and Pharisees' (cf. 5^{21}, etc.) are separated, and six woes are equally divided between them. Those against the confusion of greater and less, against ostentation and against hypocrisy are directed to the Pharisees. Those against binding legal burdens, building monuments to the prophets and withholding knowledge are directed to the lawyers (a Lukan term for scribes), though these are not notably aimed at what is characteristic of scribes rather than Pharisees, and the woe against ostentation (v. 43) is in 20$^{46f.}$ directed against scribes. This symmetry is disturbed in the first half by vv. 39–41, and in the second half by the utterance of Wisdom in vv. 49–51. The sayings in vv. 39–41, while not unrelated to those in Matt. 23$^{25-26}$, form a separate unit with its own sequence of thought; but this sequence is dependent on a contrast between the outside of the cup and the interior of the Pharisees, which is unlikely to be original, and may be due to Luke's understanding of 'the inside' in terms of the inward light in vv. 34–36. It is difficult to envisage a natural setting for such a double series of woes, and the introduction to both may have been provided by Luke. An invitation from a Pharisee to dine is an artificial scene for the denunciation of 'the Pharisees' as a class, but has parallels in 7^{36}; 14^1. Similarly artificial is the intervention of a lawyer at the meal with the remark that in the attacks on the Pharisees the lawyers are also involved, and the consequent denunciation of the lawyers as a class. The conclusion in vv. 53–54 appears to be from Luke's hand (see note), and the juxtaposition of the hostility of the leaders and the enthusiasm of the crowds (12^{1}) is possibly meant to prepare for the repeated contrast between them which Luke makes, especially in the passion narrative (cf. 14$^{1-3}$ with 14^{25}; 15$^{1-2}$; 19$^{47-48}$; 20$^{1-8, 19, 26}$; 21^{38}–22^{2}).

ಬಜ

37

While he was speaking: The Greek, which has the preposition *en* with the aorist infinitive of the verb, should be translated 'When he had spoken'.

to dine: Greek *aristān* + John 21$^{12, 15}$. There is nothing in what has just been said to prompt such an invitation. The setting is Luke's.

38

was astonished that he did not first wash: This could mean that Jesus neglected a bowl standing ready for the purpose (cf. John 2^{6}), or refused a bowl at table (in 7^{44} a Pharisee neglects to provide the necessary water). There is nothing corresponding to this in Matt. 23^{25}, but there is in Mark 7$^{1-8, 14-23}$, where Pharisees and Jerusalem scribes object to Jesus' disciples eating with unwashed hands, and there is a similar transition from unclean hands to unclean vessels to the distinction between inner and outer cleanliness (cf. A. 10$^{9ff.}$, where the pronouncing of animals clean is a sign of the cleansing of the heart of the Gentiles). The Markan passage is part of a section omitted by Luke, and may have influenced him here. According to Mark 7$^{3ff.}$ such rules of cleanliness did not belong to the law but to 'the tradition of the elders' based on it, and the impression given there is that they were many and varied. On the other hand the evidence of the Mishnah is that ritual washing before eating was not obligatory except when the person's hands were certain to be defiled, and the only case of this was that of biblical students, since, according to the Pharisees but not the Sadducees, touching the scrolls of scripture automatically defiled the hands.

39–41

The reply of Jesus (*the Lord* is Lukan) to this (spoken?) objection opens with the only case in the gospels of the non-temporal use of *nun* (= 'now'), with the sense 'so then'. In Luke it is in three (Matthew, two) parts – the contrast between exterior and interior cleanliness (v. 39), the connection between exterior and interior (v. 40), the cleansing of all things from what is interior (v. 41).

39

Though not in the form of a woe this verse corresponds fairly closely with the fifth woe against the scribes and Pharisees in Matt. 23^{25}. However, if *inside you are full* is the right translation of *esōthen humōn gemei* (= 'your inside is full'; a possible, though not likely, rendering is 'it (sc. the vessel) is full of your extortion'), then the statement is very different in form and meaning from Matthew's 'They (sc. the cup and dish) are full.' J. Neusner[y] sees both versions as deriving from an original which ran, 'You cleanse the outside of the cup and plate but not the inside. Hypocrites. First cleanse the inside and the outside will be clean.' This saying was intended from the first to apply metaphorically to the inside and outside of persons (as in Mark 7$^{1-8}$), but its formulation rested on (i) the separation made in laws of ritual purity between the outside and inside of a vessel, and the debate whether the one affected the other in respect of cleanness and uncleanness, and (ii) the tenet of the school of Shammai, which was dominant until AD 70, that the condition of the outer was not influenced by that of the inner (the subsequent dominant tenet of the school of Hillel was that the state of the inside was the sole determinant of purity, since the outside was always unclean). Matthew's version is the more natural, with its contrast between the outside and inside of the same object. Luke's application of 'the inside' to the Pharisees themselves is forced. It could have been made by Luke himself to continue the thought of interior light in vv. 34–36, or have already been made in his version, which he placed here because of its affinity with vv. 34–36. But already in Matthew's version 'the inside' of the vessel refers no longer to its inside surface, but to what is inside it, i.e. its contents. These are now identified as vices – that of *harpagē* (RSV *extortion*, though the more natural meaning of the word is 'plunder'), and that of *akrasia* = 'intemperance', which does not go with *harpagē* in the latter sense. In Luke 'the inside' also means 'the contents', but now of the Pharisees, and they are also full of *harpagē* = *extortion*, though now in the sense of 'rapacity', and of *wickedness* (though in v. 41 the contents, if that is the right interpretation of *ta enonta* there, consists of valuables, which can be given as alms).

40

The corresponding statement in Matt. 23^{26} appears to begin from the position of the school of Hillel; cleanse the inside of the cup (though here its contents), since the cleanness of the inside is all that matters; though it continues differently with the cleansing of the inside securing that of the outside. In Luke's chiasmus the point is quite different. There is no distinction between inside and outside since both have the same maker. For their inability to see this the Pharisees are called *fools* (*aphrōn*, a strong word characteristic of the Wisdom literature). Knox (*Sources* I, p. 97) conjectures that without *fools* this verse formed the conclusion of a pronouncement story in the form of a polite reply to

---

y 'First Cleanse the Inside', *NTS* 22, 1975–76, pp. 486–95.

Pharisees, and was later combined with v. 39 (originally a woe, as in Matthew) to produce the present violent attack. But 'the outside' and 'the inside' sound suspiciously abstract; contrast 'the outside of the cup' (Matt. 23²⁵), 'whatever goes into a man from outside' (Mark 7¹⁸); and *he who made* as a term for God as creator is not found elsewhere in the synoptists (cf. A. 4²⁴; 14¹⁵; 17²⁴). The verse looks like an attempt to derive a general principle from a particular rule. There is a variation of word order in the Greek which could affect the sense. 'He who made the outside made the inside' appears to mean 'if God requires external purity, how much more does he require internal purity', whereas 'he who made the inside also made the outside' appears to mean, 'Why such anxiety about external things, since God is their maker too?' (cf. A. 10¹⁵).

41

This introduces the wholly new thought that almsgiving cleanses everything. This is difficult to account for, and possibly represents a further attempt to moralize and spiritualize the whole matter. The only parallel with Matthew is *clean* (katharos, the same word as in Matt. 23²⁶), and, possibly, *those things which are within* (ta enonta, cf. Matt. 23²⁶ 'the inside', *to entos*). Many have adopted the conjecture of Wellhausen that the differences between Matthew and Luke go back to a confusion in translation of the Aramaic verbs *dakkau* = 'cleanse' and *zakkau* = 'give alms'. This is criticized by C. F. D. Moule,ᶻ and it would not account for the variation in the second half: *and behold, everything is clean for you* (Luke), 'that the outside also may be clean' (Matt. 23²⁶ᵇ). Further, *those things that are within* (the participle of *eneinai* + +), when not followed by 'them' (i.e. the vessels), would be awkward even if v. 41 were to be taken as an isolated saying. When placed after v. 39, which refers to what is inside the Pharisees, it is barely intelligible. It could be taken in the classical idiomatic sense of 'to the best of one's ability'. So, *give alms* (didonai, as in 12³³; generally in the NT the verb is *poiein* = 'do alms') as much as you can, and that will cleanse everything (cf. Rom. 14²⁰; Titus 1¹⁵).

42

With *But* (cf. 6²⁷) there is an abrupt transition from the unit in vv. 39–41 to a series of woes independent of it. For *Woe* see on 6²⁴. In Matthew it is followed by the vocative, in Luke here by the dative (in 6²⁴⁻²⁷ he varies the two). The parallels with Matt. 23²³ are close, including the Judaistic sentiment *these you ought to have done*. The condemnation is not of concern with trivialities, but of religious behaviour which allowed observance of minor commandments to stand alongside neglect of major, called in Matt. 23²³ 'the weightier matters of the law' (not in Luke, perhaps because *barus* = 'weighty' could mean 'burden-

ᶻ In his *Idiom Book of New Testament Greek*, Cambridge and New York 1953, p. 186.

some', as in Matt. 23⁴). The OT prescribed the tithing of produce, i.e. its dedication in some way to the Lord (Deut. 14²²⁻²⁹; 26¹²⁻¹⁵; Num. 18²¹⁻³²). There is rabbinic evidence for the application of this to dill and cummin (Matt. 23²³) but not *mint* (Matthew and Luke); while if the passage cited in SB II, p. 189 refers to this time *rue* was not tithed, and may be an addition by Luke. His *every herb* (*lachanos* = 'vegetable') is very general and sweeping, and could alter the meaning to a condemnation of oppressiveness and extortion. In Matthew the three objects of tithe are matched by three duties towards man – 'justice' (*krisis*, often in the LXX for justice towards the neighbour), 'mercy' (*eleos*, often in the LXX with *krisis*) and 'faith' (*pistis* = 'keeping faith'). Luke has a different formulation of twin commandments of duty towards man (*justice*) and towards God (*love* of him). This is clearly secondary. The noun *agapē* is very rare outside the NT (elsewhere in the synoptists Matt. 24¹²), and as the love of God, i.e. human love for God, is a Christian creation (cf. John 5⁴²; I John 2¹⁵; 3¹⁷; 5³). The unusual order of duty to man and then duty to God indicates that Luke is editing an original which had *justice* first.

43

This woe against pride and ostentation is one of the few doublets in the gospel. It is parallel to two out of the four accusations (not in woe form) which Luke takes over from Mark at 20⁴⁶, and which forms the beginning of Matthew's discourse against the scribes and Pharisees in Matt. 23. See further on 20⁴⁶. Here *salutations* comes after *best seat* (in the singular), and is more applicable to scribes than to Pharisees (cf. Matt. 23⁷, 'being called rabbi by men').

44

Though there is little agreement in wording this is clearly the same woe as in Matt. 23²⁷⁻²⁸. The meanings are different, and in either case puzzling. In Matthew the scribes and Pharisees are compared to whitened tombs as belying their real state by a fair outward appearance. But tombs were whitened not to conceal what was inside, but in order to make their existence clear, so that men might avoid the defilement of touching them (cf. Num. 19¹⁴ᶠᶠ·; *Beginnings* IV, p. 287, commenting on A. 23³, suggests that the term had become one of general abuse, the meaning of which had been forgotten). In Luke's version defilement is the main point. The Pharisees are condemned as being *like graves which are not seen* (*adēlos*, in this sense only here in the NT), over which men walk unawares, and are thus made unclean. This is so brief as to be barely intelligible, and there is no indication of what aspect of Pharisaic behaviour warrants this description. Knox (*Sources* I, p. 97) thinks Luke may have abbreviated the saying through failure to understand it.

45

One of the lawyers: For *lawyer* see on 7³⁰. Here by an intervention of one of them the woes, which in Matthew are addressed to 'scribes and Pharisees' jointly, are distributed between the Pharisees and the lawyers separately, and the latter are personally addressed, and their characteristics as a class portrayed.

reproach us also: Perhaps generally, because by their exegesis of scripture they provided the bases of Pharisaic piety, or with special reference to the condemnations in vv. 42 and 43. *reproach* (*hubrizein*, only here in the NT in the classical sense of 'to insult with words').

46

The first woe against the lawyers (*Woe to you lawyers also* corresponds to *Now you Pharisees* in v. 39), that on legalistic oppression, is plainly equivalent to what, in the form of a statement, stands at the head of Matthew's whole chapter of denunciation (Matt. 23⁴). Luke's version is more literary – *load* (*phortizein* + Matt. 11²⁸, in a similar context), with the cognate accusative *burdens hard to bear* (*phortia dusbastakta* + +, cf. A. 15¹⁰; Gal. 6²⁻⁵); *you yourselves*; *touch* (*prospsauein* + +, cf. Jos. *BJ*, 7.348, where the word is taken from Sophocles); *one of* is Lukan. The general sense seems to be that the lawyers (in Matthew the scribes and Pharisees) adopt the stricter rather than the milder interpretation of the law, i.e. they bind rather than loose (cf. Matt. 16¹⁹; 18¹⁸; SB I, pp. 913f.). In Matthew, however, they are reproached for not removing again the very traditions they have already bound upon men. Luke's *touch*, perhaps suggested by *finger*, is too general to indicate clearly what is meant.

47–48

Condemnation of the building of tombs for the prophets might be more fittingly directed against the nation, as lawyers (scribes and Pharisees) are unlikely to have had a special responsibility for the erection of memorials. Its expansion in both Matthew and Luke by statements about the blood of the prophets shows that there is some relation here between the evangelists with respect to source, though what that relation is, and the meaning of the woe, are alike obscure. According to Knox (*Sources* I, p. 99) the argument in vv. 47–48 = Matt. 23²⁹⁻³¹ is 'hopelessly weak and disingenuous, and would appear to have grown up in a rather low level of anti-Jewish controversy'. To build memorials for martyr prophets would be prima facie evidence of disagreement, not of agreement, with their murderers (hence the variant 'not consenting to' in some Old Latin mss and Marcion). The thought required here is that they show themselves the genuine offspring of those who killed the prophets. Something of this is supplied in Matt. 23³⁰⁻³¹ in the disclaimer, 'If we had lived in the days of our fathers', in which they confess that they are their fathers' sons (i.e. like them). Luke's version shows signs of his hand – *So* (*ara*, not found first in the sentence in classical Greek, as here; cf. A. 11¹⁸); *witness* (*martus*, cf. 24⁴⁸; frequent in A.); *consent to* (*suneudokein* + A. 8¹; 22²⁰; three times in Paul); *the deeds*, not elsewhere in

Luke, perhaps suggested by Matt. 23³⁻⁵). This version is without logic as it stands. The lack of an adequate antecedent to *So* suggests that there has been excessive abbreviation here. Black (*An Aramaic Approach*, pp. 11f.) proposes a mistranslation of the Aramaic in which 'you are children of' was rendered 'you build'.

49-51

This generation fills up the sum of the rejection of God's messengers. These verses are placed here because they refer to the murder of the prophets. While in Matt. 23³⁴⁻³⁶ they lead into an apostrophe of Jerusalem, in Luke they are added to a woe, which thus becomes distended. While sentence structure and a good deal of the wording are the same in Matthew and Luke the differences alter the import. In Matthew Jesus, continuing to speak in his own person, addresses the present generation as prophet-killers, and avers that he is in the act of sending (or will send) to it prophets, wise men and scribes – a very Jewish (Matthaean?) description of the spiritual leaders of the community, 'scribes' being surprising as the object of 'to send', and in this context where they are denounced. Some will be killed and suffer Roman death, others subjected to Jewish persecution. This can only refer to the sufferings of Christian leaders, largely at the hands of fellow Jews. The purpose is that this generation may incur responsibility for the innocent deaths of all the righteous as the last generation, which rejects the emissaries of the messiah (cf. I Thess. 2¹⁵). In Luke Jesus quotes, in justification of the woe on the lawyers as murderers like their fathers (*Therefore*), a prophecy of the Wisdom of God that (she?) will send, at a date unspecified, *prophets and apostles*. Despite the curious order this appears to be a Christian coinage; for the reverse order of Christian apostles and Christian prophets, cf. Eph. 2²⁰; 3⁵; Rev. 18²⁰ (I Thess. 2¹⁵). Some of these will be persecuted, so that *the blood of all the prophets, shed from the foundation of the world* (*hē katabolē tou kosmou*, from Q, only here in L–A) *may be required of this generation*. Luke's version gives the impression of something missing. (i) *Therefore also* (v. 49), in referring backwards and not forwards, as in Matt. 23³⁴, makes a weak link between the previous woe and this passage, originally independent of it. (ii) There is a hiatus between Wisdom's prophecy, extending apparently as far as *persecute* and the following clause, to which, since it refers back to v. 48, it does not provide an antecedent. (iii) *some* (v. 49) is lame, rhythm and sense requiring a corresponding 'others', as in Matt. 23³⁴. (iv) *all the prophets* (v. 50) ignores the previous *apostles*, and makes Abel a prophet.

49

the Wisdom of God said: This is likely to have been reproduced from Q. Luke will hardly have substituted it for 'I send' (Matt. 23³⁴), whereas Matthew (or his source) could have identified Wisdom with Jesus, and applied the whole saying to the Christian mission. It is, however, curious, and has been variously explained as (i) a periphrasis for 'God in his wisdom' (Creed, p. 167), though without any indication of when God has said it, (ii) an introductory formula for a saying from a lost (Christian?) Wisdom writing (Bultmann, *History*, p. 114), which summarizes OT history (cf. Jer. 7²⁵ff.), or (iii) an introduction to an oracle, possibly on the destruction of Jerusalem, uttered by a Christian prophet, for whom Jesus and the Wisdom of God were identified (Ellis, pp. 170ff.).

51

the blood of Zechariah: This is generally taken to refer to Zechariah the son of the priest Jehoiada (confused by Matt. 23³⁵ with the prophet Zechariah, son of Berechiah, Zech. 1¹), who was stoned 'in the court of the house of the Lord', when, after God had repeatedly sent prophets in vain, the Spirit of God came on him (i.e. he was a prophet; II Chron. 24¹⁷⁻²²; cf. Jos. *Ant.* 9.168f., and SB I, pp. 940ff. for rabbinic traditions about his death). Since II Chronicles may by this time have stood at the end of the OT, 'from Abel to Zechariah' could mean 'from first to last', and be a semi-proverbial expression for all the rebellion against God in the divinely ordered history of God's people. This would, however, be somewhat literary, and would refer to a period long closed, whereas the sense would seem to require that the speaker covers the whole period up to the time of speaking. Some have suggested that the Zechariah referred to is the son of Baris (or Bariscaeus), who, according to Jos. *BJ* 4.335-344, was killed by the Zealots in the temple itself (*between the altar and the sanctuary?*). This would date the saying after AD 70.

52

This concluding woe corresponds to the opening woe in Matt. 23¹³. Both versions are obscure through brevity. Luke's denounces what the lawyers have done in the past, whereas in Matthew it is their continuing and present practice that is condemned. In Matthew the image is tolerably clear. The scribes and Pharisees (as exegetes of scripture?) possess the keys of the kingdom for opening and shutting (cf. Matt. 16¹⁹; Rev. 1¹⁸; 3⁷), but do not use them for admission either of themselves or others (because their judgments are legalistic and burdensome?). This image is still present in Luke's *did not enter yourselves, and you hindered those who were entering*, but it is blurred by the substitution, either by Luke or in his source, of *the key of knowledge* for 'the kingdom'. This is clearly secondary. *knowledge* (*gnōsis*) is foreign to the vocabulary of the gospels (elsewhere 1⁷⁷), though it is found in Paul for the knowledge of God consequent on Christian faith, in Qumran ('They withhold from the thirsty the drink of knowledge', Vermes, *Scrolls*, p. 161), and widely in Hellenistic religion. Black (*An Aramaic Approach*, pp. 193ff.) conjectures an original, fuller than either version, 'You are the holders of the keys (of knowledge), who shut the kingdom of heaven against men, and take away the key. You enter not in yourselves, and them that enter in you hinder.'

the key of knowledge: This could mean either 'the key (of the kingdom?) which consists in knowledge', presumably the knowledge of the scriptures (rabbis could speak of the knowledge of the Law as a key, *TDNT* III, p. 747), or 'the key to knowledge' (of divine things), which is more Hellenistic in tone. If the former is meant it would explain why Luke places this woe as a climax. That which constituted the pride and instrument of the lawyers, their interpretation of scripture for the instruction and guidance of God's people, proves in their actual use to be the supreme impediment to divine knowledge both for themselves and those they instruct.

53-54

Luke rounds off the section by underlining the extent of the breach in thought and teaching between Jesus and the spiritual leaders of Israel, *the scribes and Pharisees* (if this is the right reading he reverts to the language of his source; some mss read, perhaps by way of correction in the light of Luke's text, 'the Pharisees and the lawyers'). He does so by a concentration of literary words expressing intense hostility – *press hard* (*deinōs enechein* + + = 'to be exceedingly hostile'), *provoke to speak* (*apostomatizein* + +, the meaning is uncertain = 'cross-examine'?, 'catch him in speech'?, 'watch his utterances closely'?; see Bauer), *lying in wait* (*enedreuein* + A. 23²¹), *to catch at* (*thēreuein* + + = 'to hunt'). There is a remarkable number of variant readings in this verse designed to provide either a public setting for the woes ('in the sight of all the people'), or a more precise anticipation of the passion ('that they might find wherewith to accuse him', cf. 19⁴⁷; 22²⁻⁴).

12 *The Disciples and the World*

This chapter of teaching follows without break. Its importance for Luke is indicated by his provision of a double audience. An undifferentiated body called *his disciples* is addressed *first*. This is in the presence of milling crowds, which, even allowing for Luke's propensity to exaggerate, now reach fantastic proportions. To this audience are delivered four addresses, two longer to the disciples and two shorter to the crowds. These are – (i) vv. 1b–12; the disciples are warned against hypocrisy and fear of men. They are assured of divine care and of acknowledgment by the Son of man: (ii) vv. 13–21; the crowds are warned against avarice and the belief that life consists in possessions;

(iii) vv. 22–53; the disciples are warned against anxiety about earthly things, are assured of divine care and possession of the kingdom, and are exhorted to sell possessions and to have treasure with God. Blessing is pronounced on those found faithful and ready for the Son of man. The mission of Jesus is critical and divides men; (iv) vv. 54–59; the crowds are condemned for failure to discern the times as critical and to take the appropriate steps.

This is one of Luke's more diffuse compositions. It gives the impression that separate units, which had already undergone some development in the tradition, have been connected together by purely verbal links or through a general similarity of ideas. This is also to say that Luke has attempted to find room for diverse traditions even if he was not sure of their original context and meaning. Streeter (*Four Gospels*, p. 291) considers the material of the chapter, apart from vv. 11–21, to have stood in Q in its Lukan order. There are two reasons against this. (i) The three sections Luke has in common with Matthew – vv. 2–9 = Matt. 10$^{26-33}$, vv. 22–34 = Matt. 6$^{25-33, 19-21}$ and vv. 39–46 = Matt. 24$^{43-51}$ – do not belong together apart from the links Luke has forged for them. (ii) It is not this common material that determines the rest of the material in this chapter, but vice versa. Thus the theme of vv. 2–9 is introduced by a saying (v. 1) which is probably taken from Mark 8^{15}. The theme of vv. 22–31 has already been set by vv. 13–21, which is L material. The theme of vv. 39–46 has already been set by vv. 35–38, which is also L material. It is possible that vv. 36–38, 39–40 and 42–46 were three parables in Q in that order, and that Matthew rearranged them within the Markan framework he uses.

12 *In the meantime, when so many thousands of the multitude had gathered together that they trod upon one another, he began to say to his disciples first, 'Beware of the leaven of the Pharisees, which is hypocrisy. ²Nothing is covered up that will not be revealed, or hidden that will not be known. ³Whatever you have said in the dark shall be heard in the light, and what you have whispered in private rooms shall be proclaimed upon the housetops.*

⁴*'I tell you, my friends, do not fear those who kill the body, and after that*

have no more that they can do. ⁵*But I will warn you whom to fear: fear him who, after he has killed, has power to cast into hell;** *yes, I tell you, fear him!* ⁶*Are not five sparrows sold for two pennies? And not one of them is forgotten before God.* ⁷*Why, even the hairs of your head are all numbered. Fear not; you are of more value than many sparrows.*

⁸'*And I tell you, every one who acknowledges me before men, the Son of man also will acknowledge before the angels of God;* ⁹*but he who denies me before men will be denied before the angels of God.* ¹⁰*And every one who speaks a word against the Son of man will be forgiven; but he who blasphemes against the Holy Spirit will not be forgiven.* ¹¹*And when they bring you before the synagogues and the rulers and the authorities, do not be anxious how or what you are to answer or what you are to say;* ¹²*for the Holy Spirit will teach you in that very hour what your ought to say.*'

* Greek *Gehenna*

The bitter antagonism of, and towards, the Pharisees (11³⁷⁻⁵⁴), and the indiscriminate enthusiasm of enormous crowds, provide a vivid setting for the instruction of disciples. This is a composite section, consisting of three separable units, vv. 2–3, 4–7, 8–12, of which vv. 2–9 are also found in the same sequence in Matt. 10²⁶⁻³³ as part of the mission charge to the Twelve. Their different position here does not necessarily reflect their place in Q. It is more likely due to Luke's understanding of vv. 2–3 as bearing on the theme of hypocrisy, with which in v. 1 he chooses to open the whole discourse. Thus, compared to the specific command to disciples to make public the message they have received in private (Matt. 10²⁶⁻²⁷), v. 2 has become an utterance of general wisdom that truth will out, and v. 3 a warning to disciples that what they speak in private will certainly come to light.

The independent unit vv. 4–5 is connected with vv. 2–3 by a fresh beginning, *I tell you*, and a form of address, *my friends*, which is unique in the synoptists. The teaching shifts to a charge not to fear men, but only God, who alone has the power of life and death. In Matt. 10²⁸ this charge follows naturally from the previous command to proclaim the message openly. In Luke it does not follow naturally from a previous warning against private hypocrisy (v. 3), and no explanation is given of why disciples may be faced with the threat of death.

In vv. 6–7, as in Matt. 10²⁹⁻³⁰, the connecting link with what precedes is 'fear'. Originally these verses could have been independent of

vv. 4–5, and also separate from each other. For there is a shift from
'fear' to 'do not fear' in respect of the relation to God, and from the
constraint of God's omnipotence as judge as the basis of action to confidence in his omniscience as creator. The thought now is that if the
cheapest things do not escape God's notice, how much less those who,
as disciples of Jesus, are the special objects of God's attention. But the
continuation in v. 7a with *alla kai* = 'not only, but also' (RSV *even*)
shows more clearly than in Matt. 10^{30} the hiatus here. For v. 6 would
be followed more naturally by v. 7b, and the numbering of the disciples' hairs by God as additional evidence of their value to him (v. 7a)
is an interposition.

And I tell you (v. 8) marks a development with a transition from a
general truth about disciples to a particular situation, that of their public
confession or denial of Jesus. In Matt. 10^{32} this transition is more cogent
after a previous injunction to preach without fear. In Luke the link is
largely verbal, *before men* and *before the angels of God* picking up *before
God*.

A possible occasion for confession or denial, the disciples on trial, is
treated in vv. 11–12, but this is by way of v. 10 as a transition. Again
the link is verbal; *the Son of man* connects with v. 8 and *the Holy Spirit*
with v. 12. Comparison with the parallels in Matt. 12^{32}, Mark 3^{28}, suggests that this verse is completely out of context, and the use to which
Luke puts it is obscure (see note). In vv. 11–12 a return is made to the
theme *do not fear* (v. 4), but now in the form of *do not be anxious* when
on trial. They are not to be anxious about their defence, because, as
they are assured with complete foreknowledge and certitude, the Holy
Spirit will instantly instruct them in what needs to be said.

৩৩

1

In the meantime: en hois (+ A. 26^{12}), literally 'in which things'; perhaps here 'in
which circumstances'. This is unique in the gospels as a connecting link.

so many thousands of the multitude had gathered together: The crowds, who were
'increasing' in 11^{29}, are now said to have *gathered together* (*episunagein*, used of
crowds in Greek historians) to the number of *many thousands*. The Greek word
here is *murias* = 'ten thousand' (cf. A. 21^{20} of believers; Heb. 12^{22}; Jude 14;
Rev. 5^{11}; 9^{16} of the hosts of angels); hence 'many tens of thousands'. It is pointless to ask how or where such numbers could gather in the course of a journey,
or how Jesus made himself heard. The scene is clearly an ideal one.

Beware of the leaven of the Pharisees, which is hypocrisy: Or, with a different punctuation of an awkwardly worded sentence, 'Beware of the leaven, which is hypocrisy, of the Pharisees'. This is probably taken from Mark 8^{15}. *Beware: prosechete.* Since this is also the word used in Matt. 16^6, but not in Mark 8^{15}, it has been taken as evidence that there was such a saying in Q. This is unlikely, as (i) there is no further indication that Matt. 16$^{5-12}$ is dependent on anything other than Mark 8$^{14-21}$, and (ii) the verb here is followed by *heautois* = 'to yourselves' = 'be on your guard'. This is a LXX expression, and is peculiar to Luke in the NT. It is not clear whether *leaven* had a bad sense in itself ('corruption', as perhaps in the alternative rendering above), or a neutral sense ('influence'), which takes on a bad sense when applied to the Pharisees. The bad sense in I Cor. 5$^{6ff.}$ is imparted by 'old', with reference to the Passover regulations (Exod. 12$^{15-20}$). In 13^{21} leaven is a quickly spreading influence, as in Gal. 5^9. It is found in the rabbis for the effective working of the law (SB I, p. 729). It could, however, be associated with corruption, as in Lev. 2^{11}, in the rabbis and in Plutarch. *the leaven of the Pharisees*, left unidentified in Mark 8^{15}, is identified in Matt. 16^{12} with their teaching. Luke identifies it with their *hypocrisy*. In the NT generally hypocrisy (*Greek hupokrisis*) does not have the meaning of deliberately playing a part, which is ultimately derived from Greek drama, where the verb *hupokrinesthai* meant 'to answer from under', i.e. from under the mask, which all actors wore. *hupokritēs* (= 'hypocrite', see on 6^{42}) was the normal word for an actor, and never for 'one who pretends'. Nevertheless, in its only occurrence in the LXX (II Macc. 6^{25}, repeated in IV Macc. 6^{15}) *hupokrisis* does mean deliberate dissimulation. In view of Luke's use of the verb in 20^{20}, this is probably what he means by the noun here. If so, it shows he understood (or misunderstood) the sayings in vv. 2–3 as concerned with hypocrisy in that sense.

2–3

In Matt. 10^{26} the reference is to a message that is of necessity concealed in the present, but is so only in order to be brought out into the open (cf. Mark 4$^{1-32}$, and especially Mark 4^{22}). In Luke this has become the general statement that hypocrisy in the sense of dissimulation is foredoomed; everything, however secret, will come to light (cf. 8^{17}, Luke's version of Mark 4^{22}). In v. 3 the application of this to the disciples is made by *anth' hōn* (+ 1^{20}; 19^{44}; A. 12^{23}; II Thess. 2^{10}), which means 'because' (it is not translated in rsv). In Matt. 10^{27} Jesus commands the Twelve to speak in open day that which has been communicated to them under cover of obscurity. and to proclaim on the housetops that which he has whispered as a secret in their ears. This is an intelligible use of these vivid images. In Luke this has become the assertion that anything the disciples speak in a concealed manner under cover of darkness cannot be prevented from coming into the light of day; and what they speak to one another in whispers in private rooms will nevertheless become public property. This is a hardly intelligible use of these same images. For it is not apparent why, or what, disciples would be speaking in the dark or whispering to one another; nor is it evident what particular form of hypocrisy this would be. In an attempt to make sense of v. 3 G. Friedrich (*TDNT* III, p. 705) takes v. 2 as referring to the hypocrisy of the Pharisees, which the disciples are assured will be unmasked, and takes v. 3 as a proverb. But *what you have whispered in private rooms shall be proclaimed* is too diffuse in expression for a proverb. It reads more like an adaptation of the Q text as found in Matt. 10²⁷ to the theme of hypocrisy as Luke understood it. *in private rooms* may be an addition by Luke to balance *upon the housetops* (= for all to see, cf. II Sam. 16²²).

4–5

In comparison with the single antithetical sentence in Matt. 10²⁸ Luke has a longer and more polished unit here, with an introduction, *I tell you, my friends*, and a reiterative conclusion, *yes, I tell you, fear him!* The language is partly from Luke's hand – *after that* (*meta tauta*), *have* (*echein* = 'to have' in the sense of 'to be able', a classical usage), *I will warn* (*hupodeiknunai* = 'to show', apart from Matt. 3⁷ confined to L–A in the NT), *has power* (*echein exousian*, cf. A. 9¹⁴), *to cast into* (*emballein* + +). Nevertheless Luke lacks Matthew's sharp antitheses between the capacity to kill the body only and not the soul as well, and God's capacity to annihilate both in Hades. These concepts have been held to be more Greek than Hebrew, and therefore secondary in Matthew; but the separation of soul and body at death, to be reunited for resurrection or eternal punishment, was good apocalyptic and rabbinic doctrine (so Moore, *Judaism* II, pp. 311ff.; cf. IV Ezra 7³²). It may, however, have been a desire to avoid the idea of killing the soul as puzzling to his readers that led Luke to produce the rather flat equivalent here *and after that have no more that they can do*, and to limit God's capacity to casting into Hades at death.

my friends: Cf. Justin, *Dialogue* 8, 'A love of the prophets and of those men who were friends of Christ possessed me.' The nearest NT parallel is John 15¹³ᶠᶠ·, where the eleven are not addressed as friends (though cf. John 15¹³), but are told that they are to be called *philoi mou* (without the article = 'friends of mine') because they know what their lord is doing. Here, with the article (= 'the friends of mine'), and as a designation of a group by their common relation to one person, the term is less personal and more formal. It could reflect the widespread technical usage of 'the friends of' as a court title for the leading officials of a king. This appears among the Persians (cf. Esther 1³; Dan. 3²⁴), and Alexander had his 'Companions', as did his successors (cf. I Macc. 6¹⁰; 10⁶⁰).ᵃ Luke may

---

a For further examples see A. Deissmann, *Bible Studies*, ET London and New York 1901, pp. 167f., and *Light from the Ancient East*, ET, new ed., London and New York 1927, pp. 378f.

have introduced it here to emphasize that it is as 'the companions of Jesus' that the disciples are especially precious to God, particularly when they share his lot and suffer extreme penalties.

do not fear ... whom to fear (v. 5): The distinction between fear of men and fear (awe) of God is made by the use of the same verb *phobeisthai*, followed in the first case by *apo* with the genitive, and in the second case by the direct object. For God's power over life and death, cf. Wisd. 16$^{13-15}$; IV Macc. 13^{14}; James 4^{12}.

5

hell: Greek *geenna* = Gehenna. This originally denoted the valley of Hinnom to the south and west of Jerusalem. It appears in II Kings 23$^{10ff.}$ as a place of idolatrous fire sacrifice to Molech, which Josiah 'desecrated' in his reform. It became in apocalyptic the name of the abyss (hence *cast into*, cf. Matt. 5^{29}; Mark 9^{47}) of eternal punishment, corporeal and spiritual, for apostate Jews after the judgment (I Enoch 90$^{26f.}$; Isa. 66^{24}). It is found in the NT, apart from James 3^{6}, only in the synoptists, and only here in Luke.

6

five sparrows ... for two pennies: The Greek word rendered *sparrows* emphasizes the point, being the diminutive *strouthion* = 'little sparrow', though this was not in fact eaten. That rendered *pennies* is *assarion*, a Latin loan word in Greek for the Roman copper coin, the *as*. This was a coin of very small value, and was worth one sixteenth of a *denarius* (see on 20^{24}). Bauer translates by 'halfpenny', AV and RV by 'farthing'. The variation between Luke and Matthew in the selling price of sparrows (Matt. 10^{29} 'two for a penny') is likely to be due less to an interest in, or knowledge of, market values, than to Luke's interest in rhythm, which has produced the chiasmus – literally 'five sparrows for pennies two, and not one of them ...'

forgotten before God: The Semitic idiom *before* (*enōpion*) is a favourite with Luke. Here it adds a certain vividness to *forgotten* (*epilanthanesthai*, a rare word in the NT, only here in Luke) in what is otherwise a less colourful statement than 'fall to the ground without my Father' (Matt. 10^{29}). *God* may be secondary here, due to the reflection that he is not the Father of birds but their creator.

7

are all numbered: This is emphatic, not only with *all*, but with the verb in the periphrastic tense – the perfect participle with the verb 'to be' = 'are in the state of having been numbered'. The statement is generally found in the form 'not one of your hairs shall fall to the ground' (cf. I Sam. 14^{45}; II Sam. 14^{11}; I Kings 1^{52}; Luke 21^{18}; A. 27^{34}), and as a promise of protection. This could be the sense in Matt. 10$^{29-30}$ – the hairs of the disciples have been numbered by

God, and he will not allow them to perish, any more than the sparrows to fall, without his knowledge and will.

you are of more value than many sparrows: The disciples are assured of the providential care of God, which extends to the cheapest things on the market.

8–9

The language here – *acknowledge* (*homologein*) and *deny* (*arneisthai*) – is that found in the later Christian confession of Jesus' messiahship or lordship (cf. I John 2²²ff.; 4²f.; A. 3¹³f.; II Tim. 2¹²; in the context of persecution John 9²²; I Tim. 6¹²f.). In the case of *acknowledge* here the form is more primitive, the verb being followed by *en* = 'in' ('to confess in' + Matt. 10³²), which is an Aramaism. The primitive form of 'deny' would be 'to be ashamed of' (9²⁶). In what this confession or denial are to consist (confession of Jesus' messiahship?) is not stated, nor in what circumstances they are to be made. They will have ultimate consequences when the heavenly advocate, the Son of man, either acknowledges them as his own or repudiates them. The picture is the Jewish one of the judgment as a juridical process in the heavenly court. Here that picture has two special features. (i) The Son of man (see on 5²⁴). Various views are held on this – that the title stood in Q, and was altered by Matthew to the more christological 'I also' (Matt. 10³²); that in Q the title stood also in v. 9 and was altered there by Luke; that in Q the verb was, as in v. 9, in the passive, and Luke introduced the title on the analogy of 9²⁶, and to prepare for v. 10. If the last were the case he will have created an otherwise unknown function for the Son of man, that of heavenly mediator and advocate of men before God (contrast 21³⁶; but cf. Rev. 3⁵ of the exalted Jesus). This is, along with 9²⁶ and Mark 8³⁸, a form of statement, the most natural interpretation of which would be that Jesus and the Son of man are distinct persons. (ii) *the angels of God.* This is an unfamiliar idiom in Jewish literature, and may be Luke's own (cf. 15¹⁰, but also Rev. 3⁵, confession before God and the angels). Angels are often mentioned in apocalyptic and rabbinic writings as agents of judgment and punishment (e.g. I Enoch passim; cf. Matt. 13³⁹, ⁴⁹), but not as constituting the court itself. Here Luke may have introduced them to make a contrast with the plural *tōn anthrōpōn* = *men. will be denied before*, by the Son of man; but it could be a periphrasis, with the meaning 'the angels (i.e. God) will deny'.

10

This assertion of an unforgivable sin, defined simply as blasphemy against the Holy Spirit, in contrast to speaking against the Son of man, which is forgivable, is very severe (for suggestions made to mitigate its severity, see Nineham's Pelican Commentary, *Saint Mark*, pp. 121ff.). The parallel in Matt. 12³² (cf. also Mark 3²⁸f.) within the controversy over the origin and significance of Jesus' exorcisms is more intelligible. For there the Holy Spirit is referred to as the agent of the conflict with the kingdom of evil, victory in which brings about the coming of the kingdom of God (Matt. 12^{28}, 'If it is by the Spirit (Luke 11^{20} 'the finger') of God that I cast out demons . . .'). To attribute the exorcisms to a source in evil spirit is to confound good and evil, and to introduce a logical contradiction at the heart of God's saving work. It is to be guilty of an 'eternal' sin (Mark 3^{29}) which has no forgiveness either in this world or the world to come (Matt. 12^{32}). If Matt. 12^{32} = v. 10 stood in the Q account of this controversy (which Matthew has conflated with Mark's), it is strange that Luke did not reproduce it in his account (11^{17-23}). If it was an isolated statement in Q which Matthew brought into connection with the controversy, it is still puzzling that Luke should have used it here. For (i) the Son of man is now, in contrast to v. 8, someone on earth against whom the disciples could speak; and if this is equivalent to the denial of Jesus, which results in condemnation at the judgment (v. 8), it is presumably not forgivable; and (ii) there is nothing in Luke's context to account for the abrupt introduction of the Holy Spirit and blasphemy against him.

A distinction is drawn between blasphemy against the Spirit and speaking a word against the Son of man, or, in Mark 3^{28} (by an alternative translation of the Aramaic?) the blasphemies which the sons of men blaspheme. The ground of this distinction is not specified, and the language used is difficult to assess. The verb 'to blaspheme' (*blasphēmein*) with a direct object (which is perhaps presupposed in Mark 3^{28}) meant 'to defame', 'to revile'. When followed by the preposition *eis* = 'to blaspheme against' (as in v. 10b, Mark 3^{29}; cf. Dan. 3^{29}) it is a Semitism, and could denote blasphemy in the technical sense of the violation of the power and majesty of God. The phrase 'to speak a word against' (*legein logon* (*eis*, v. 10a, *kata*, Matt. 12^{32})) is also a Semitism, and could have a general or a specific sense. In Job 2^9 it means to curse God. In A. 6^{13} it is the equivalent of 'blasphemous words' (A. 6^{11}), which are, however, spoken against Moses as well as against God. In Matt. 12^{32} the phrase is used with reference both to the Son of man and the Holy Spirit. For this language at Qumran, cf. The Damascus Rule, 5^{11} (Vermes, *Scrolls*, p. 102), where certain who disregard marriage laws are said to 'defile their holy spirit, and open their mouth with a blaspheming tongue against the laws of the Covenant of God'. Conzelmann (*Theology*, pp. 179f.) attempts to make sense of v. 10 in this context by taking it as a gloss on v. 8. That is, speaking against the Son of man (denial of the earthly Jesus) is forgivable, even if he is already in his ministry the bearer of the Holy Spirit, because it is not until Pentecost that it is plainly revealed who he is. To deny him after that is to blaspheme the Spirit. But if a change from one period of time to another is to be presupposed in the course of a single sentence, the tenses of the verbs would suggest that it is in the opposite direction. For *speaks* is in the Greek *erei* = 'shall speak', and refers to the future, while *blasphemes* is in the Greek the present participle, and refers to the present. Barrett (*Holy Spirit*, pp. 105ff.) favours the patristic interpretation, according to which those who speak against the Son of man are the heathen. Their sin could be forgiven, as are all sins in baptism. Those who blaspheme against the Holy Spirit are Christians, who already possess the Spirit but apostasize. Again, a change of persons in the course of a single sentence would be awkward, and blasphemy against the Spirit would be a curious expression for apostasy.

11–12

The source of this saying is uncertain. There is a doublet of it in 21$^{12, 14-15}$, which occupies the same position in the apocalyptic discourse as Mark 13^{11}, though its form is strikingly different from Mark 13^{11} and from the saying here (which in form is close to Mark 13^{11}). There is a fourth version in Matt. 10^{19}, but that is taken from Mark 13^{11}, and put in a fresh context. All versions are concerned with a situation in which disciples are 'handed over' to courts for trial (*bring, eispherein* = 'to bring forcibly', only here in the NT in this sense). The courts will be Jewish (*synagogues*, so also 21^{12}; Mark 13^{9}; Matt. 10^{17}; cf. John 9^{22}; 12^{42}; A. 9^{2}; 22^{19}; 26^{11}), and – reflecting the later universal mission – Gentile (cf. 21^{12}; Mark 13^{9}; Matt. 10^{18}). Luke's *the rulers and the authorities* is a more literary expression. The words are often found separately in Hellenistic Greek in this sense, and are combined in Plato (cf. Titus 3^{1}). The disciples are not to *be anxious* (*merimnān*; see on v. 22) *how* (or *what*, omitted by some mss, is probably an assimilation to Matt. 10^{19}) *to answer*. This verb is, as in 21^{14}, *apologeisthai* (only L–A in the NT). It is the technical term for 'to conduct a defence at law', and reflects Luke's strong apologetic interest. The reason for such freedom from anxiety in these circumstances is that the Holy Spirit will be the speaker (so Mark and Matthew); here, more emphatically, that the Spirit will instruct them *in that very hour* (a Lukan expression) *what* they *ought to say* (*ha dei eipein*, also Lukan). Barrett (*Holy Spirit*, pp. 131ff.) argues that this is a secondary formulation reflecting later Christian experience of the Spirit, and that the promise by Jesus of his own assistance in 21$^{14-15}$ is more primitive in wording and thought. See on 21$^{14-15}$ for the contrary suggestion that Luke, having referred here to the promise of the Spirit (which may indeed be a Christian formulation), has refashioned Mark 13^{11} for his own purposes. The fact that Luke has a doublet of this saying shows that it will have been of special importance to him. It is relevant to much of the story in Acts, and he will give accounts of such situations in the cases of Peter and John (A. 4$^{6-13}$), Stephen (A. 6$^{5, 10-15}$; 7$^{55ff.}$) and Paul (A. 20$^{22f.}$; 22–26).

12^{13-21}

WARNING TO THE CROWDS ABOUT POSSESSIONS

¹³One of the multitude said to him, 'Teacher, bid my brother divide the inheritance with me.' ¹⁴But he said to him, 'Man, who made me a judge or divider over you?' ¹⁵And he said to them, 'Take heed, and beware of all covetousness; for a man's life does not consist in the abundance of his possessions.' ¹⁶And he told them a parable, saying, 'The land of a rich man brought forth plentifully; ¹⁷and he thought to himself, "What shall I do, for I have nowhere to store my crops?" ¹⁸And he said, "I will do this: I will pull down my barns, and build larger ones; and there I will store all my grain and my goods. ¹⁹And I will say to my soul, Soul, you have ample goods laid up for many years; take your ease, eat, drink, be merry." ²⁰But God said to him, "Fool! This night your soul is required of you; and the things you have prepared, whose will they be?" ²¹So is he who lays up treasure for himself, and is not rich toward God.'

The teaching now passes to the subject of possessions. It is directed to the crowds following an intervention from one of their number (for this cf. 10²⁵ff.; 11²⁷ff.; 14¹⁵ff.). The section shows signs of composition. The dialogue in vv. 13–14 is another instance of a 'biographical apophthegm' (Bultmann, *History*, pp. 55ff.) preserved by Luke, i.e. a saying of Jesus which is inseparable from a specific historical situation. In itself it probably shows Jesus refusing a position of arbitrator over mundane affairs, though no reason is given for the refusal. In its present context it has become a foil for a warning about avarice (v. 15). It has then to be supposed that avarice lay behind the request for the inheritance to be divided (v. 13).

The parable Luke then appends (*And he told them a parable* is his form of introduction) is intended to reinforce the teaching of v. 15. It is not well fitted for this, since the story is not naturally one of avarice. It begins with a man who is already prosperous, and his plans for the future are not motivated by acquisitiveness, but by desire for the security to enjoy to the full what he already has. The lesson drawn in v. 21 is that death deprives a man of his possessions unless he is *rich toward God*; but it does this in any case. Apart from its context, and without v. 21, the parable depicts one who thinks himself abundantly secure. He is unmindful of the ultimate crisis of death, which will supervene to render that security nugatory. He is called a fool for his pains by God, who is the author of the crisis. If the parable is not teaching the truism, either that life is always threatened by death, or that in death a man cannot take his possessions with him, its point could be, as in other parables, the crisis which comes upon men through the approach of the kingdom of God (so Jeremias, *Parables*, pp. 164f.). That the crisis is portrayed in terms of a rich man does not mean that the parable is about riches.

בּאּ

13

Teacher: It is not clear whether this form of address here means that Jesus is approached as a layman whose reputation is so high that he is treated virtually as a rabbi, or as an outstanding rabbi well qualified to adjudicate in legal matters.

divide the inheritance with me: The situation is generally taken to be that of two sons who have been left an inheritance in the form of joint ownership of an undivided property. The petitioner wishes to enjoy his portion separately (cf. 15^{12}). If so, it is not evident why this should be accounted avarice, or be the occasion for the statement in v. 15. In the Gospel of Thomas (72) there is a version of the dialogue which is followed not by v. 15, but by 'He turned to his disciples and said to them, "I am not a divider, am I?".'

14

Man: This vocative (*anthrōpe*) is confined to Luke in the gospels. It is generally brusque or contemptuous (cf. 22$^{58, 60}$), but not always so (cf. 5^{20}).

who made me a judge or divider over you?: Bultmann (*History*, p. 55) warns that the biographical character of the incident does not guarantee its historicity, as sayings of this gnomic type were put into the mouths of great men. This is unlikely to have happened here, as (i) Jesus is approached as a rabbi, and the early church no longer thought of him as such, but as the Lord, and (ii) the rhetorical question in response to the request is not at all obvious, but is enigmatic. It could amount to replying, or perhaps refusing to reply, by means of a scriptural tag suitably adapted for the purpose (*made me ... over you* in place of 'made you ... over us', and *divider* for 'prince'). In Exod. 2^{14} the question is addressed by an opponent to Moses in repudiation of his authority. As cited by Stephen in A. 7$^{27, 35}$ the answer to the question is 'God', who has indeed appointed Jesus as judge and ruler over the Israel, who has rejected him. Here it is used out of context and in a modified form (and in a mocking way?) by Jesus to repudiate his own authority so far as matters of this kind are concerned. Too much may be read out of it when it is taken, either as an explicit rejection of the position of a second Moses (Leaney, p. 176), or at a definition of Jesus' mission as being other than that of a social reformer or an arbiter in personal disputes (Ellis, p. 176). Some textual witnesses lack *or divider*. It was perhaps omitted because in v. 51 Jesus says he comes for 'division'.

15

Take heed, and beware: This emphatic double warning – *take heed (horāte* = 'see'), *beware (phulassesthai apo* + +, cf. A. 21²⁵; I John 5²¹, not LXX = 'guard yourselves from') – could be a further reminiscence of Mark 8¹⁵ (cf. v. 1), where there is a similar double warning.

all covetousness: This is an inadequate rendering. *pāsēs* = 'every kind of', and *pleonexiās* = not 'covetousness', which in Greek is *epithumia* (cf. Exod. 20¹⁷), but 'avarice'. The corresponding verb means 'to get the better of', 'to defraud', and the basic meaning of the noun is 'insatiableness'. It does not belong to the vocabulary of the gospels (elsewhere only Mark 7²² in a formal list of sins), but does belong to that of the early church (in Col. 3⁵ it is identified with the prime sin of idolatry).

for a man's life does not consist in the abundance of his possessions: Literally, 'In the superabounding to anyone his life is not from his possessions.' The sentence is overloaded, perhaps through an attempt to combine two separate thoughts suggested by the following parable – (i) a man's life does not consist in superabundance, and (ii) a man's life does not consist in his possessions. *life* here is *zōē*. Generally in the NT this refers to spiritual or eternal life, and not man's physical existence, which is *psuchē*, as in v. 22 (but cf. A. 17²⁵).

16-21

This parable of the 'tale' type is only loosely attached to the dialogue in vv. 13–15 (in the Gospel of Thomas 63 there is a version of it which is separate from the dialogue in 72). It is vividly and stylishly written, which could suggest that Luke was the first to put it into writing; and it has some unusual features (see on vv. 19, 20). The opening sentence in the Greek word order is, *of a rich man* (cf. 7²) *brought forth plentifully (euphorein* + +, not LXX) *the land (chōra* = 'estate' + +, not LXX). For the soliloquy in vv. 17–19 cf. 16³ᶠ· and Luke's addition in 20¹³. *I have nowhere* (v. 17) is the classical idiom *ouk echo pou* + + = 'I have not where'. There is chiasmus in vv. 18, 19 and 20. In v. 18 *pull down* is *kathairein* + 1⁵²; A. 13¹⁹; 19²⁷, *barns* is *apothēkai* in the sense of storehouses for grain, and *goods* is the neuter plural of *agathos* = 'good', a Hellenistic usage only here in the NT. The imperatives in v. 19 have two longer enclosing two shorter verbs.

19

I will say to my soul: This address to the soul is found in Egyptian wisdom literature, and in the OT (Ps. 42⁵; Ps. Sol. 3¹). It is unique here in the NT. *soul* (*psuchē*) is used here of the animate life of the individual in the body. It is regarded as a loan from God in Wisd. 15^8, and in some Hellenistic philosophers (e.g. Cicero, *Republic* III, 3.4; Epictetus IV. 1.172); hence v. 20, *your soul is required of* ('back from') *you*. There is a striking parallel to the words of this address, and to the thought of the parable, in Ecclus 11$^{17-19}$ (cf. also Ps. 49$^{16-20}$; 39^6; Eccles. 2$^{24f.}$; Job 27$^{16ff.}$).

take your ease, eat, drink, be merry: This is taken by some as voicing the attitude of the godless man, and therefore as evidence that the rich man is already presented in the story as one who has not been rich toward God, i.e. has neglected God. But the last three verbs are often found together as terms of well-being, which is approved of (Eccles. 8^{15}; Tobit 7^{10}). They do not in themselves express selfishness or neglect of God, but satisfaction and security. Only in the form 'Let us eat and drink, for tomorrow we die' (Isa. 22^{13}; quoted in I Cor. 15^{32}) are they the words of the godless, and plainly they could not have been quoted here in that form without wrecking the parable. The Old Latin has a much abbreviated text here – 'ample goods; be merry'.

But God said to him: Only here in the parables is God represented as taking part in the action and as addressing an individual. There is no need to enquire whether he is supposed to do this by a dream. The writing is naive and unreflective. Only God can deliver this message, as it was held that he alone made the decision over the time of a person's death.

Fool: In Greek *aphrōn*; elsewhere in the gospels 11^{40}, of those who cannot see the logic of the situation. This has also been taken as an indication that the man is godless, since in Ps. 14^1 it is the fool who says 'There is no God'. That is unnecessary in the context.

this night: In contrast to *many years* (v. 19), and marking the suddenness of the crisis. This is not the night in which the man attains his security and addresses his soul, but the night on which he confidently affirms that he will one day do so.

is required: Greek *apaitousi* = 'they will ask back' is taken by some as a reverential rabbinic periphrasis for God. This is unlikely on the lips of God himself. It may be a conventional expression for death – 'they (the angels?) will come and ask for your life back' (cf. 16^{22}).

21

A terse participial sentence – literally, 'So the one storing up treasure for himself but toward God not being rich' – which draws a moralizing conclusion, and both connects the 'abundance' in the story with the avarice in v. 15, and also leads into the subject of earthly cares in vv. 22ff. 'to be rich toward God' (*ploutein eis theon* + +) is a unique expression, and may be Luke's coinage (the parallel in Rom. 10¹² of God's generosity to all men is a different idiom). It is not clear what it means, nor how it is the opposite of *lays up treasure for himself.* Some take it as an equivalent of laying up treasure in heaven (cf. v. 33). Jeremias (*Parables*, p. 106) interprets it of entrusting earthly wealth to God, whatever that may mean. The whole verse is absent from Codex Bezae and three Old Latin mss.

12^{22-53} A SECOND ADDRESS TO DISCIPLES

This diffuse address falls into three sections, vv. 22-34, vv. 35-48 and vv. 49-53, which are distinct from one another both in form and subject matter.

12^{22-34} (i) CARE ABOUT EARTHLY THINGS

²²*And he said to his disciples, 'Therefore I tell you, do not be anxious about your life, what you shall eat, nor about your body, what you shall put on.* ²³*For life is more than food, and the body more than clothing.* ²⁴*Consider the ravens: they neither sow nor reap, they have neither storehouse nor barn, and yet God feeds them. Of how much more value are you than the birds!* ²⁵*And which of you by being anxious can add a cubit to his span of life?* ²⁶*If then you are not able to do as small a thing as that, why are you anxious about the rest?* ²⁷*Consider the lilies, how they grow; they neither toil nor spin;† yet I tell you, even Solomon in all his glory was not arrayed like one of these.* ²⁸*But if God so clothes the grass which is alive in the field today and tomorrow is thrown into the oven, how much more will he clothe you, O men of little faith?* ²⁹*And do not seek what you are to eat and what you are to drink, nor be of anxious mind.* ³⁰*For all the nations of the world seek these things; and your Father knows that you need them.* ³¹*Instead, seek his‡ kingdom, and these things shall be yours as well.*

³²*'Fear not, little flock, for it is your Father's good pleasure to give you the kingdom.* ³³*Sell your possessions, and give alms; provide yourselves with purses that do not grow old, with a treasure in the heavens that does not fail,*

where no thief approaches and no moth destroys. ³⁴*For where your treasure is, there will your heart be also.'*

  ★ Or *to his stature*

  † Other ancient authorities read *Consider the lilies; they neither spin nor weave*

  ‡ Other ancient authorities read *God's*

Of this section vv. 22–31 form a closely knit and rhythmical unit (which corresponds closely with Matt. 6²⁵⁻³³). This is especially so if *hēlikia* (v. 25) means 'age', as then two similar strophes, vv. 23–26 and vv. 27–28, expand respectively *your life, what you shall eat* and *your body, what you shall put on* (v. 22). This theme is then repeated and rounded off in vv. 29–31. To this unit Luke had added v. 32, an independent saying without parallel, but with a verbal link with v. 31 in *the kingdom.* He has then continued with sayings on true wealth, vv. 33–34, in a form that combines close agreement with, and wide divergence from, Matt. 6¹⁹⁻²¹. In this way a rhythmical conclusion is provided of two sentences, each with two parts (vv. 32, 34), enclosing one with four parts (v. 33). The completed unit, vv. 22–34, then consists of eight statements, each with a fourfold structure.

    The thought in vv. 22–31 is not, however, unified. The logic, both of the unit as a whole, and of individual statements within it, is not easy to establish. Anxious preoccupation with the means of existence is condemned on four distinct grounds – (i) that life is more than the means of life, vv. 22–23; (ii) that it is attempting the impossible, vv. 25–26; (iii) that the God who provides for birds and flowers will much more provide for disciples, vv. 24, 27–30; and (iv) that such things will accrue anyway to those who seek the kingdom. These are all commonplaces of Jewish wisdom, except the last, which is eschatological, and which may be intended to provide the context in which the others are now to be understood. The sequence of thought may be as follows – do not be anxious about the means of existence; behind these is that about which to be anxious, viz. God and his kingdom; birds and flowers show by their lack of anxiety that God is completely reliable; so there is a sustaining and clothing by God which is certain, and which banishes anxiety; do not seek for things in themselves, but seek the kingdom, which brings all else with it.

22–31

With *And he said to his disciples* Luke shows that he judges what follows to be concerned with the way of life proper to disciples. It might originally have been spoken more generally about men, who as such are of greater value than the things of nature. The very close verbal agreement with Matt. 6^{25-33} (which as part of the Sermon on the Mount is also spoken to disciples) requires dependence either of one evangelist on another, or, more probably, on a common source. *Therefore* (*dia touto*, elsewhere in Luke $11^{19, 49}$, where it appears due to Q) also opens this section in Matt. 6^{25}. There the connection with what precedes (Matt. 6^{24}, 'You cannot serve God and mammon'), while less artificial than here, is also not a particularly strong one. It could have stood in Q as a link with whatever preceded there. Some of the differences of wording may be due to Luke – e.g. *ravens* (*korax* = 'crow' + +), in place of the more conventional 'birds' (Matt. 6^{26}, *peteina*), which reappears at the end of v. 24; *neither storehouse* (*tameion*, as in v. 3, but with a different meaning) *nor barn*, compared with Matt. 6^{26}, 'nor gather into barns', a fourfold in place of a threefold statement; perhaps the whole of v. 26, again a fourfold statement; and *seek* (v. 29) to prepare for the same word in v. 31. On the other hand 'your heavenly Father' (Matt. 6^{26}) and 'his righteousness' (Matt. 6^{33}) are due to Matthew. It is not clear whether Matthew or Luke was responsible for the different form of sentence – question or statement – in v. 23 = Matt. 6^{25b}, v. 24b = Matt. 6^{26c} and v. 28b = Matt. 6^{30b}.

22

do not be anxious: The Greek verb is *merimnān*, and the force of the argument throughout depends on the meanings to be given to it (cf. Bultmann, *TDNT* IV, p. 592, 'Only in this passage is there an explicit discussion of care, and this passage must be expounded separately'). Jeremias (*Parables*, pp. 214f.) renders by 'to put forth effort', and sees it as an equivalent of *zētein* = 'to seek' (v. 29). In that case the injunction to imitate the birds and flowers, who do not sow, reap or labour, may be commanding an attitude to normal affairs which is eschatological (cf. I Cor. 7^{29-31}, because of the shortness of the time, 'let those who buy be as though they had no goods, and those who deal with the world as though they had no dealings with it', and I Thess. 2^9; 4^{11}; II Thess. 3^6, where some took the imminence of the parousia as a ground for not working). On the other hand, the basic meaning of the verb is 'to care', 'to be concerned about' (e.g. someone's welfare, Phil. 2^{20}), and then 'to be unduly concerned', 'to be anxious'. The question then at issue is when a proper concern has become an improper anxiety. Here the anxiety is the general one about the means of existence, which is caused by the future (*what you shall eat*, cf. Matt. 6^{34}) and its insecurity (vv. 28, 33). This is referred to in pagan literature as characteristic of human life, and as a cause of its troubles (cf. also Ecclus 30^{24}; $31^{1ff.}$). It is not condemned here as such, but by reference to its object, which is life itself.

Your life ... your body: These two words are taken by Bultmann (*TDNT* IV, p. 592) as a synthetic parallelism for 'life'; but they appear too distinct here for that. Rather is *life* the more embracing term ('physical existence', cf. Prov. 6^{30}), and *body* one aspect of it.

23

life is more than food: The force of *more than* is not clear. That life is more than eating is obvious. It nevertheless depends on food to be life. Concern with food and clothing could be evidence of the value put on existence; cf. 'For the soul's sake we must take care of the body' (Plato, cited by Clement of Aexandria, *Stromateis* IV, 4.18). What may be implied is that anxious concern about means leads to a preoccupation with them as ends (cf. v. 30); but in the gospels there is no analysis of human life in itself, and apart from its relation to God. By *life* here may already be meant the goal of human existence, i.e. life in the kingdom of God.

24

consider the ravens: Cf. Job 38^{41}; Ps. 147^9, making the same point of God's provision for them. The Stoics also condemned anxiety about earthly require-ments by an appeal to animals as showing that providence supplies all creation with what is necessary. The argument here can hardly be that God provides for men in the same manner as he nurtures birds and produces flowers, i.e. without any necessary toil or contriving on their part. It could be that the harmony of birds and flowers with nature, itself considered as governed in all its details by God, is evidence of a creator who can be trusted to make all necessary provi-sions for disciples. *Of how much more value are you* (cf. *how much more*, v. 28) incorporates the argument of vv. 6–7. Disciples are not simply included in the creation for which God cares. They are distinguished from it (and from the rest of mankind?) by their status as specially valuable objects of the divine care in view of their relation to the kingdom (cf. v. 32).

25–26

add a cubit to his span of life?: This question is an interruption, and separates the treatment of food and clothing, which were introduced together in v. 22. It makes a different point. The word translated *span of life, hēlikia,* 'is ambiguous, signifying either "age" or "stature"; in classical Greek more frequently "age", in biblical "stature" ' (Field, *Notes,* p. 6). He decides for the latter on the ground that *cubit* (Greek *pēchus*) 'is not only *a* measure of length, but that by which a man's *stature* was properly measured'. On the other hand, MM report (p. 279) that in the papyri 'we are unable to quote any example ... in which "stature" is the natural meaning, and hardly any in which it is possible; while for "age" we can produce a long list.' In v. 26, which is a more prosaic statement possibly

from Luke's hand, *as small a thing as that* (*to elachiston* + 16¹⁰; 19¹⁷) suggests a
temporal sense, 'a brief span' (though Bauer can only quote one instance in
Greek literature of *pēchus* in this sense). As a measure of height a cubit, i.e.
eighteen inches, would not be a very small, but a very considerable addition to
make. *the rest* (*ta loipa*) seems to mean 'any other things of the same kind' (cf.
Mark 4¹⁹; I Cor. 15³⁷).

27

Consider the lilies: krinon is used in the LXX for flowers in general, and has been
identified with several: the lily, the anemone, etc. (see Bauer).

how they grow; they neither toil nor spin: This is the reading of the majority of
mss, but it could be an assimilation to Matt. 6²⁸. A few textual authorities have
'how they neither spin nor weave' (*huphainein* + +, a refined word, but more
usual than 'toil' in conjunction with 'spin'). This would make the slightly different point that they do not have to employ high skills to outmatch Solomon's
glory (*doxa* in the sense of 'splendour', proverbial in Solomon's case, and
somewhat vulgarly described in II Chron. 9).

28

The lessons of vv. 24, 27 are summarized in a third example, *the grass*. Despite
its being so short-lived and dispensable (cf. the cheapness of sparrows in v. 6), it
nevertheless has a vesture from God. For 'the grass of the field' (Matt. 6³⁰) Luke
has 'If in (the) field . . .', which almost amount to 'in nature'. This is a pointer
to God's capacity to clothe disciples, who are of much greater value. If they fail
to live by this truth they are men *of little faith*; cf. the Talmud, Sota 48b (quoted
in SB I, p. 439), 'He who has bread in his basket and says, "What am I to eat
this morning?", he belongs to those of little faith.' The word here, *oligopistos*,
is not found in Greek literature before this and the four occurrences in Matthew;
and subsequently, apart from a single instance in Sextus (second century AD) it
appears only in Christian writers. Generally in the synoptists 'faith' has a
specific reference, e.g. to have confidence in Jesus as a healer. Here it is a more
general confidence in the providence of God, but only as that applies to
disciples.

29

There are two significant differences here from Matt. 6³¹. (i) The verb *seek* is
introduced as a synonym for 'be anxious'. This prepares for v. 31. With *kai
humeis* at the beginning of the sentence (= 'and do you'), the statement is
emphatic. (ii) *nor be of anxious mind* is added by Luke. This makes a double command, to be followed by a double statement in v. 30, and underlines that anxious

seeking of the wrong kind is meant. The Greek verb here, *meteōrizein* + +, is called by Lagrange (p. 364) 'un mot recherché'. It meant 'to be lifted up', either physically or metaphorically, and so, in the LXX, 'to be presumptuous'. In this context, however, it must have one of the meanings belonging to the cognate adjective *meteōros* = 'in mid-air', 'in suspense'. Hence 'to be anxiously uncertain', as in Polybius and the papyri.

30

For all the nations of the world seek these things: This translation is probably incorrect. In the Greek *tauta gar panta ta ethnē*, the word *panta* = 'all' goes not with *nations* but with *these things*, and in that word order has the sense 'these things taken together'. In the reverse order the same words mean in Matt. 6³¹ 'all these actual things'. Hence 'all' does not have to be repeated at the end of the verse and in v. 31 (contrast Matt. 6³²⁻³³). *the nations of the world* (Matt. 6³² 'the Gentiles' = 'the nations') occurs only here in the Greek Bible, but corresponds to a frequent rabbinic expression for mankind apart from Israel (SB II, p. 191, I, p. 204). Only here in the synoptists is there a characterization of the Gentiles. Their life is determined by a concern for (the compound verb *epizētein* = 'to seek after') earthly necessities. It is for that reason godless. The life of the disciples, as the true Israelites, is godly, being determined by God's knowledge of them as their Father. The word order in the Greek – 'but of you the Father knows' . . . – is very effective.

31

This saying (= Matt. 6³³) appears to have rounded off the section of teaching in Q. It does so, however, by introducing a new factor, that of *the kingdom* – so in v. 32; here, to connect with v. 30, it is *his*, i.e. the Father's *kingdom*, though some mss have 'the kingdom of God'. Hence it is attached somewhat forcibly by the adversative conjunction *plēn* = 'only' (in Matt. 6³³ the connection is made by 'first'). Nowhere else in the synoptists is the kingdom said to be the object of search. If for Luke *seek* is equivalent to *be anxious* (v. 29), the command will be to be preoccupied with the kingdom. Even so it is very general, and what it meant in practice would depend on how the kingdom was envisaged. If the command has any connection with what has preceded, to seek the kingdom might be to cultivate the attitude of total confidence in God as the provider of men's highest good. *these things shall be yours as well* makes clear that the detachment demanded in vv. 22ff. is not ascetic but theocentric. Here the eudaimonistic ethic of Deuteronomy – 'if you keep the commandments you will be happy' – is brought to a sharp point in an eschatological concern with the kingdom. Sufficiency of worldly things is not even, as in Deuteronomy, the reward of devotion to God and his commandments. It is now simply an addendum thrown in with it.

32

In view of the finality of v. 31 it is unlikely that, as Streeter contends (*Four Gospels*, pp. 284, 291), v. 32 followed in Q, and was dropped by Matthew. The verse is complete in itself, and appears too isolated to have belonged to a document. Luke may have derived it from oral tradition, and placed it here because of the catchword *Fear not* (cf. v. 4), and in order to continue from vv. 30–31 the connection between the kingdom and the Father (cf. 11²; 22²⁹; Matt. 13⁴³; 26²⁹). It will then have to be taken with what precedes as reinforcing the command to be preoccupied with the kingdom, which is by divine decree to be theirs, rather than, as by Easton (p. 203), with what follows. It is, however, so brief and compressed that the original context, and consequently the meaning, can only be guessed. (i) With regard to its context, the language is 'biblical', but points to the early church rather than to Jesus. *flock* has in Greek the definite article (*to poimnion* = 'the little flock'). It refers to the flock of God, not to the flock of Jesus (reference to such passages as Mark 6³⁴ is irrelevant). This is common in the OT either as descriptive of Israel (Ps. 78⁵²; Isa. 40¹¹; Ezek. 34¹⁰ff.) or as a designation of her (Micah. 5³f. as the remnant; Jer. 13¹⁷; Zech. 10³; cf. Ps. Sol. 17⁴⁵; I Enoch 89¹⁰–90³⁶). In the NT it is found in later books – A. 20²⁸f., where it is perhaps descriptive, I Peter 5²f., probably as a designation (cf. also I Clement 16¹; 44³, etc.). *it is the good pleasure* (*eudokēse* = 'he is pleased') is an OT term for the divine favour, and is generally followed by *en* = 'in' (Ps. 147¹¹; Jer. 14¹²; Luke 3²²). With an accusative and infinitive, expressing divine decision (= 'he has decided that') it is found only here in the gospels, but is a natural expression for Paul (I Cor. 1²¹; Gal. 1¹⁵; Col. 1¹⁹). Also only here in the gospels is the kingdom said to be 'given'. In Paul, the only other NT writer to mention the kingdom of God, it is given and received as an inheritance (I Cor. 6⁹; 15⁵⁰; Gal. 5²¹; cf. James 2⁵). (ii) With regard to its meaning, this is only hinted at in *fear not*, *little*, and *to give you the kingdom*. The first could refer to some particular situation in which disciples would have cause to fear (cf. vv. 4, 11). Or it could be general, and be linked with *little*. If this is more than a term of endearment, it could indicate that it is because the disciples (the Christians? the Twelve?) are so few in number, and are so insignificant compared with Israel as a whole, that they have to be reassured that they are indeed God's flock, the remnant of Jewish expectation. *the kingdom*, as that which is given by God, probably has the active sense of the exercise of God's rule either among men (as in Dan. 7²²⁻²⁷, where it is given by God to the saints to be exercised over the nations), or in the coming age (cf. 22²⁹f., where it applies only to the Twelve). The saying has been taken by some as originating in the church as a reassurance to those discouraged in their Christian vocation by the delay of the parousia.^b

b See H. F. D. Sparks, 'The Doctrine of the Divine Fatherhood in the Gospels' in *Studies in the Gospels*, ed. Nineham, Oxford 1955, p. 250.

It is taken by others as a genuine word of Jesus preparing disciples in advance for the shock of his coming death.

33–34

These verses, whatever their origin, but particularly if they owe something of their form to Luke's editing, illustrate his concern with the question of wealth and poverty in the church. Verse 34 (= Matt. 6²¹, but sharpened into a chiasmus) provides a forceful ending for an instruction of disciples on true possessions. Hence *your* is plural. In Matthew, where it introduces the theme, 'your' is in the singular of the individual disciple. The disciples' treasure is the measure of where their *heart* (i.e. their mind, preoccupation) has been. But *For* shows that the verse originally stood as a conclusion drawn from the antithetical statement of the two ways of amassing treasure, as those are set out in Matt. 6¹⁹⁻²¹. Of this antithesis only v. 33b now remains as a tail end. For the negative statements *where no thief approaches* (*engizein*, Lukan) and *no moth destroys* (*diaphtheirein* + II Cor. 4¹⁶; I Tim. 6⁵; Rev. 8⁹; 11¹⁸) presuppose a preceding positive form of the same statement, such as in Matt. 6¹⁹. Further, v. 33b does not follow naturally from v. 33a. As an extension of (heavenly) *purses* (*ballantion* + 10⁴; 22³⁵f.) it is awkward, since moths eat clothes, not purses; and there is some discordance in style and thought between the literary phraseology of *do not grow old* (the participle of the verb *palaioun* + Heb. 1¹¹ LXX; 8¹³ = 'eternal') and *does not fail* (*anekleiptos* + + = 'inexhaustible'; cf. Wisd. 7¹¹⁻¹⁴; 8¹⁸, where wisdom brings inexhaustible riches and treasure), and the concrete language of the parable in the *thief* and *moth* which rob and consume. In v. 33a Luke appears to be offering an interpretation of *treasure in the heavens* (cf. Matt. 6²⁰). This was a rabbinic expression for the reward for good deeds, especially almsgiving, which God confers in the world to come.ᶜ Here Luke gives it content by taking the demand made on the rich ruler as a would-be disciple (18²²) and generalizing it as a radical requirement from all Christians (or all ministers?, cf. v. 41) of complete poverty and of almsgiving. It is not clear from the gospel narrative whether those who had become disciples of Jesus were still supposed to have possessions (cf. 5¹¹; 8³; 9⁵⁷f.; 10⁴), but Luke is probably concerned to provide a basis in the teaching of Jesus for the practice of the first Christians of selling possessions and distributing the proceeds, which he is to describe in A. 2⁴⁵; 4³²⁻³⁷. For *provide yourselves* (Greek = 'make for yourselves') together with eternal habitations and riches, cf. 16⁹⁻¹¹. For *give alms* see on 11⁴¹.

---

c Cf. Tobit 4.8ff., SB I, pp. 430f., and E. P. Sanders, *Paul and Palestinian Judaism*, London and Philadelphia 1977, p. 197, who quotes T. Peah 4.18, where a king who gives his earthly treasure to the poor is said to be storing up treasure in heaven or for the world to come.

35'*Let your loins be girded and your lamps burning,* 36*and be like men who are waiting for their master to come home from the marriage feast, so that they may open to him at once when he comes and knocks.* 37*Blessed are those servants whom the master finds awake when he comes; truly, I say to you, he will gird himself and have them sit at table, and he will come and serve them.* 38*If he comes in the second watch, or in the third, and finds them so, blessed are those servants!* 39*But know this, that if the householder had known at what hour the thief was coming, he would have been awake and★ would not have left his house to be broken into.* 40*You also must be ready; for the Son of man is coming at an hour you do not expect.'*

41*Peter said, 'Lord, are you telling this parable for us or for all?'* 42*And the Lord said, 'Who then is the faithful and wise steward, whom his master will set over his household, to give them their portion of food at the proper time?* 43*Blessed is that servant whom his master when he comes will find so doing.* 44*Truly I tell you, he will set him over all his possessions.* 45*But if that servant says to himself, "My master is delayed in coming," and begins to beat the menservants and the maidservants, and to eat and drink and get drunk,* 46*the master of that servant will come on a day when he does not expect him and at an hour he does not know, and will punish★ him, and put him with the unfaithful.* 47*And that servant who knew his master's will, but did not make ready or act according to his will, shall receive a severe beating.* 48*But he who did not know, and did what deserved a beating, shall receive a light beating. Every one to whom much is given, of him will much be required; and of him to whom men commit much they will demand the more.'*

★ Other ancient authorities omit *would have been awake and*
† Or *cut him in pieces*

The command to disciples to be preoccupied with the kingdom and heavenly treasure (vv. 31–34) is directly succeeded by commands to be ready for the Son of man, and to be his true slaves. These are conveyed by means of three parables, each of which is puzzling in form and content.

(i) In vv. 35–38 (peculiar to Luke) an abbreviated parable about slaves in readiness is introduced by a relative clause (*like men who,* v.

36a), which leads out of an injunction to disciples in the second person (v. 35). It continues with a double beatitude in the third person (vv. 37a, 38), but this is divided by a statement with a solemn introduction, which is an intrusion into the parable (v. 37b).

(ii) In vv. 39–40 (in close agreement with Matt. 24$^{43-44}$, Q) there is a parable of householder and burglar, which is supplied with a special introduction, but is reduced to a bare minimum. It leads to a command to be ready for the Son of man.

(iii) In vv. 41–48 (of which vv. 42–46 are in almost verbatim agreement with Matt. 24$^{45-51}$, Q) a question from Peter about the application of *this parable* – i.e. the immediately preceding parable about wakefulness, or possibly the first parable about readiness, or possibly both together taken as a single parable – is answered by a third parable. This is about the different subject of faithfulness. It concerns a steward, who is set over his master's slaves, and who, if faithful in his duties, will be set over his master's possessions. If on account of his master's delay in returning he abuses his position he will be destroyed. This parable also includes a beatitude (v. 43) followed by a solemnly introduced statement (v. 44). It is rounded off by vv. 47–48 (peculiar to Luke, and possibly written by him), which treat of different punishments for different degrees of unfaithfulness in slaves.

The original setting, recipients and purport of parables of this shape are hardly now recoverable. Jeremias (*Parables*, pp. 48ff., 55ff.) sees them as originally directed to the Jewish religious leaders in warning of the impending crisis and judgment. If so, they will have been considerably modified in tradition through application to subsequent and specifically Christian situations. They now give either instruction of a general kind on the eschatological nature of Christian life (cf. I Cor. 7$^{29-35}$ for Christian behaviour as governed by 'anxiety' about the Lord in view of the shortness of the time), or specific instruction for Christian conduct in the face of the delay of the return of Jesus = the Son of man.

ॐ

35–38

As Knox (*Sources* II, p. 70) observes, this unit has a complicated background. The language suggests that Luke took these verses from a source, especially *truly* (*amēn*), which he generally alters or avoids, and *awake* (*grēgorein*), only here in Luke. The thought is essentially that of Mark 13$^{33-37}$ (which Luke omits there), but form and wording are very different. In Mark the parable begins with instructions to slaves, including an order to the doorkeeper to keep watch, and then passes into a command to disciples, in which the fourfold division of the night implies that he is away for an evening. Luke's version begins from a command to disciples to be ready for the return of a master from a wedding (is there an echo here of Matt. 25¹⁰?). No instructions are given, but all are to be ready as doorkeepers however late at night.

35

let your loins be girded and your lamps burning: Both expressions are purely metaphorical. *loins girded* = 'in a state of constant readiness for a journey' (but here not in order to go anywhere); *lamps burning* = 'prepared for action at night' (but not, as in Matt. 25¹ff., so as to go in with the bridegroom). Wellhausen (p. 67) notes the intensity of the language here compared with the serenity of vv. 22ff. This reflects eschatological urgency in the church. *your* as the second word in the Greek following the verb is emphatic, as is also *kai humeis* = 'and do you' at the beginning of v. 36.

36

they may open: That all slaves act together as doorkeepers is an allegorical element, destroying the parable. It is required by the application of the parable to Christians, all of whom are to wait for their Lord and to open the door to him.

37

Blessed: A further allegorical element, since *blessed* (*makarios*, see on 6²⁰) is not a general word of congratulation or thanks, but a specific word for the state of those on whom God confers the kingdom.

awake: grēgorein. This word in a spiritual sense has no background in the LXX. Apart from this passage it is confined in the gospels to the eschatological passages, Mark 13³⁴⁻³⁷; Matt. 24⁴²⁻25¹³. It is, however, a regular word in the ethical vocabulary of the early church (A. 20³¹; I Cor. 16¹³; I Thess. 5⁶, ¹⁰; I Peter 5⁸; Rev. 3²f.; 16¹⁵).

he will gird himself . . . serve them: This breaks the sequence of v. 37a to v. 37b, and has passed over completely into allegory. It does not describe normal behaviour of a master to slaves (cf. 17⁸), nor even a special reward for duty, but only the exceptional behaviour of Jesus the Lord. Elsewhere this behaviour is so paradoxical as to call for explanation (Mark 10⁴²⁻⁴⁵; John 13¹⁻¹⁷; in 22²⁴⁻²⁷ it precedes a promise to the Twelve that they will sit at his table in the kingdom). In this case the reward for disciples who are found waiting for him will be participation in the messianic feast along with a master who is also their servant. The prophetic word put into the mouth of the exalted Jesus in Rev. 3²⁰ illustrates how such an allegorization of the parable could come about in Christian teaching.

38

If he comes in the second watch, or in the third: This reiteration of v. 37 is a further application of the parable to the Christian problem of the delay of the Lord's return. For watches of the night, see on 2⁸. If *second* and *third* reflect the Hebrew and Greek division of the night into three watches, and not the Roman division into four, the meaning will be 'up to the end of the night'. The delay may be long.

39–40

These verses are apt for continuing the discourse. For although they were already connected in tradition with what is to follow in vv. 42ff. (cf. Matt. 24⁴³ff. = Q), they are more closely related in thought to vv. 35–38, since they concern watchfulness for what comes unexpectedly rather than readiness over a long period (v. 45). They are introduced by *know this*, a formula for the disclosure of truth, especially eschatological truth (21²⁰; 10¹¹; A. 2³⁶; II Tim. 3¹; II Peter 3³). Here that truth is conveyed in terms of the thief in the night (cf. Jer. 49⁹; in Luke, at any time, *at what hour*, v. 39) breaking into houses (cf. Job 24¹³⁻¹⁷). This became a figure in the early church for the day of the Lord and the manner of its coming, from which was deduced the necessity of constant wakefulness (I Thess. 5²; II Peter 3¹⁰, where it has become conventional, Rev. 3³; 16¹⁵, where it is used allegorically of Jesus and his coming). Jeremias (*Parables*, p. 50) believes that this Christian usage, which 'is foreign to the eschatological imagery of late Jewish literature', derives from this parable. Against this is (i) that v. 39 = Matt. 24⁴³ is exceedingly compressed in form; it is a parabolic illustration rather than a parable. (ii) It is reduced in content to the conditional statement that the householder would have been awake and ready for the burglar if he had had advance knowledge of the time of his arrival. (This is the sense even if *would have been awake, and* are absent from the text, as in some textual witnesses; they are probably an assimilation to Matt. 24⁴³). The lesson appears to be that one is bound to be unprepared for that for which one cannot be prepared. This figure is then made, not altogether appropriately, a reminder to disciples, who will be waiting for the Lord, that he will come at an unexpected hour. This is unlikely on the lips of Jesus. Other references to the future coming of the Son of man are either to its manner (21²⁷), or to its suddenness for those not expecting it (17²⁶⁻³⁰). It is more likely as a formulation in the early church urging preparedness for the return of Jesus, as in I Thess. 5² for 'the day of the Lord', which Jeremias (*Parables*, p. 50) thinks may have stood here originally when the parable was spoken to the Jewish leaders. There are two variant versions of the parable in the Gospel of Thomas (21b, 103), both of which have a reference to 'loins girded', which is peculiar to Luke. In neither is the parable applied to the coming of the Son of man.

41–46

There are two differences in this passage from Matt. 24^{45-51}, with which it is otherwise in the closest agreement. (i) It is introduced by a question from Peter (v. 41), to which the teaching in vv. 42ff. is introduced by *And the Lord said* as a reply. It has been argued★ that this question stood in Q, and was omitted by Matthew. The language, however, suggests Luke's hand – *Peter said* (*eipen de ho Petros*), *the Lord*, 'to speak a parable for (with respect to)'. If so, a passage beginning in Q with *Who then is . . .?* would pose problems for the evangelists of how to use it and where to place it. *then* translates the Greek particle *ara*. This could be used without any meaning of its own, and simply to enliven a question. Matthew seems to have taken it in this way, and to have used the passage as part of his expansion of the discourse in Mark 13. But *ara* could have an inferential or resumptive sense = 'so then'. Luke seems to have taken it in this sense, and to have framed the question in v. 41, to which the passage is then a response. If so, the question itself could be an indication of how Luke understood the passage as a whole. If by *us* in distinction from *all* Peter refers to the twelve apostles as their spokesman, his question is whether the previous parable applies only to apostles or to all disciples (Christians). (ii) It could correspond with this that in Luke, compared with Matthew, the slave is a *steward* (*oikonomos*). While not ceasing to be a slave (v. 43 *that servant*), he is set over *the manservants and maidservants*, and not simply over 'his fellow servants' (Matt. 24^{49}), and he does not just 'give them their food' (Matt. 24^{45}), but distributes *their portion of food* (*sitometrion* + +, a technical term in the papyri for food ration or allowance). While this could be 'another instance where Luke improves the social status on account of the circles for which the Gospel was intended' (Knox, *Sources* II, p. 70), it more likely reflects the early church's use of *steward* for apostles and church leaders, who are to be *faithful*, and who will be judged only by the Lord at his coming (cf. I Cor. 4^{1-5}; Tit. 1^7; I Peter $4^{10f.}$). They are not to browbeat their fellow Christians or to run riot (v. 45; cf. I Tim. 3^{1-3}; 5^1; Tit. 1^7; II Tim. 2^{21}; I Peter 5^3; A. 20^{28-31}; I Thess. $2^{9ff.}$). Otherwise they will suffer the extreme penalty at the parousia (v. 46).

42

Who then is the faithful and wise steward?: Behind this language may lie the figure of Joseph, the Jewish model of the wise one (*phronimos* = 'prudent'), who was set by Pharaoh over his *household* (*therapeia*, v. 42; cf. Gen. 45^{16}; $41^{33, 39f.}$; Ps. 105^{21}), and who dispenses supplies (Gen. 47^{12-14}, *sitometrein*, only here in the LXX).

★ E.g. by C. F. D. Moule, *The Birth of the New Testament*, London and New York 1962, 147ff.

will set over: In contrast to 'has set over' (Matt. 24⁴⁵) this historicizes the parable as well as applies it to later conditions in the church. The appointment of the apostles over the church at the Lord's departure is still future at the time of speaking (cf. A. 1²ᶠ·). *will set over* in v. 44 will then refer to the eschatological appointment of the apostles over the heavenly church of the saints (cf. 22²⁸⁻³²).

45

My master is delayed in coming: The verb here, *chronizein*, expresses in a single word the delay of the parousia which is referred to in more detail in II Peter 3³ᶠᶠ·.

46

will punish him: This is a conjectural translation. The Greek verb here, *dichoto-mein*, is a strange word to have maintained itself in the tradition (cf. Matt. 24⁵¹). The literal meaning is 'to cut in half' (cf. Jos. *Ant.* 8.31 of Solomon's order in I Kings 3²⁵), and could refer to a method of execution (cf. the similar expression in Susanna 55, 59; in Exod. 29¹⁷ it means 'to cut in pieces' a sacrificial animal). In the context such a punishment sounds excessively savage, and it is not fol-lowed naturally by *and put him with the unfaithful*, unless it is supposed that all the unfaithful met this fate. MM quote an inscription with a milder meta-phorical sense, which would allow 'he will cut him off', i.e. from the faithful. So also O. Betz,ᵈ who sees it as an exaggerated rendering of the Hebrew verb used in the Qumran Community Rule (2.17), 'He shall be cut off from the midst of the sons of light' (Vermes, *Scrolls*, p. 74). C. C. Torreyᵉ conjectures an Aramaic original with the meaning 'he will divide his portion', which would make it a synonym for *put him with*. This latter (*to meros tithenai* = 'to place his portion') is said to be a Semitism for 'to assign him his place' (SB I, p. 969), or for 'to treat as' according to Jeremias (*Parables*, p. 57), who con-jectures an original with the meaning 'he will assign him blows, and treat him as impious'. *unfaithful (apistos)* is very rare in the LXX, and is found again in the gospels only at Mark 9¹⁹ and pars. It is not the opposite of *faithful* (v. 42), but is the word for 'unbeliever', and appears to be a Christian creation (cf. I Cor. 6⁶; 7¹², etc.).

47-48

These verses have no parallel in Matthew, where the parable ends with the plainly Matthaean addition, 'there men will weep and gnash their teeth'. The question therefore arises of their origin and purpose here. Apart from the gnomic statement in v. 48b they cannot stand on their own, but belong in the parable. Linguistic evidence could suggest that Luke has himself supplied them

---

d 'Donnersöhne, Menschenfischer, und der Davidische Messias', *Revue de Qumran* 5, 1961, pp. 43ff.

e *Our Translated Gospels*, London n.d. [1937], pp. 157f.

– *knew, did not make ready, did not know* and *did* are all participles in the Greek; 'to know the will' occurs only here in the synoptists (cf. A. 22¹⁴); *act according to* represents a use of the verb *poiein* = 'to do' followed by the preposition *pros* which is unique in the NT; *deserved a beating* translates two words which may be said to be Lukan, *axios* = 'worthy of', and *plēgē* = 'a blow'. Their purpose appears to be to extend the parable to two further categories in the church. (i) There are those who are not apostles, but are privileged in being privy to the Lord's will (teachers? pastors?, cf. A. 20²⁸). If they do not act according to this knowledge and will, they will receive severe, but not extreme, punishment. (ii) The ordinary Christian, who is in constant danger of error, and needs to be taught, cannot be expected to maintain the same degree of watchfulness, and in the case of failure will receive milder punishment. Finally, v. 48b, with a double chiasmus, enunciates the general principle that responsibility varies according to gift and commission. Again the language suggests the context of the early church. *commit, paratithenai,* in the sense of 'to entrust for safe keeping', is found elsewhere in the NT only in connection with Christian ministers (I Tim. 1¹⁸; II Tim. 2², 'entrust these things to faithful men'; for the corresponding noun, *parathēkē* = 'the deposit of teaching', cf. I Tim. 6²⁰; II Tim. 1¹²⁻¹⁴).

12^{49–53} (iii) THE MISSION OF JESUS

⁴⁹*'I came to cast fire upon the earth; and would that it were already kindled!* ⁵⁰*I have a baptism to be baptized with; and how I am constrained until it is accomplished!* ⁵¹*Do you think that I have come to give peace on earth? No, I tell you, but rather division;* ⁵²*for henceforth in one house there will be five divided, three against two and two against three;* ⁵³*they will be divided, father against son and son against father, mother against daughter and daughter against her mother, mother-in-law against her daughter-in-law and daughter-in-law against her mother-in-law.'*

The thought of the future coming of the Son of man for the reward or punishment of faithful or unfaithful disciples is followed directly by that of the present mission of Jesus among men. This is conveyed by three highly distinctive sayings, which are difficult to assign together to a written source, or to account for individually in an oral tradition. All three are in the 'I' form. The first two (vv. 49, 50) are peculiar to Luke, and are here a pair. Both are very concentrated and cryptic in their use of metaphor, and in combining oracular statement about the present with aspiration for the future. They do not, however, necessarily belong together, and may have been juxtaposed, either by Luke or in the tradition, because of an association of thought between 'fire' and 'baptism' (cf. 3¹⁶; A. 2³ᶠ·; Justin, *Dialogue* 88). In form v. 49 is closer to v. 51 then to v. 50 (*I came*); and there it is the goal of Jesus' mission that is the subject of his wish, whereas in v. 50 it is his present state. Verses 51–53 are parallel in content to Matt. 10³⁴⁻³⁶, but very different in construction.

ཀྶཀྶ

49

I came: See on 5³². It expresses a consciousness of prophetic mission. Only if taken closely with v. 50, and only if that verse voices a constraint of Jesus because he is on earth, need the coming be from heaven to earth, as frequently in John's gospel.

to cast fire upon the earth: An enigmatic statement, as the commentaries show. *Fire* is a widespread religious symbol with varied meanings (see *TDNT* VI, pp. 928ff.). One of them is 'purification' (cf. Mark 9⁴⁹), and could account for the conjunction with baptism in v. 50. More probably, as the object of *cast upon the earth*, the fire of divine judgment is meant, as frequently in prophetic and apocalyptic writings (cf. Isa. 66¹⁵ᶠ·, fire and sword; Jer. 11¹⁶; Ezek. 15⁶ᶠ·; Zeph. 1¹⁸; Joel 2³; I Enoch 102.1; Ps. Sol. 15.4; Jubilees 9.15, sword and fire). The Baptist's prophecy of the one who would baptize with spirit (perhaps originally with the 'wind' of winnowing) and fire (for destruction of the chaff) might be relevant to this saying (cf. 3¹⁶⁻¹⁷). The force of *cast upon* (*ballein epi*) is not easy to determine. The saying may have been modelled on that in Matt. 10³⁴, where 'to cast peace upon the earth' appears to mean 'to establish' it (SB I, p. 586). Something of the apocalyptic expression 'to cast to (*eis*) the earth' may be intended (cf. Rev. 8⁵, fire from the heavenly altar causing earthly disasters; 8⁷, fire mixed with blood; 11⁵; 13¹³). Such fire, however, does not need to be *kindled*, (but cf. Amos 1.14, where 'I will kindle a fire' is an equivalent of 'I will send (a fire)' in 1⁴·⁷·¹¹·¹²). Some take it of the holy Spirit, whose coming still lies in the future (cf. A. 2³, the tongues of fire at Pentecost), though they also wish to associate the Spirit with judgment (cf. Ellis, p. 182).

would that it were already kindled!: This second part of the saying is equally enigmatic. The Greek is *ti thelō* (= 'what do I wish?') *ei ēdē anēphthē* (= 'if it has already been kindled'). This is capable of diametrically opposite translations. (i) 'What will I if it be already kindled?' – so AV and RV. This expresses satisfaction that the mission is in the process of fulfilment. It gives a normal meaning to *ei* = 'if', but not to *ti thelō* = 'what do I want (lack)?', with the expected answer 'Nothing'. (ii) The juxtaposition with v. 50 might indicate that both sayings were understood to contain an unfulfilled wish. Hence the translation of RSV above, which states that the fulfilment of the purpose of the mission has not even begun. This involves two rare Hebraisms in a single sentence – *ti* as the exclamatory 'how!' (cf. II Sam. 6²⁰; Song of Sol. 7⁶), and *thelein ei* = 'to wish that' (twice in the LXX, Isa. 9⁵; Ecclus 23¹⁴). (iii) Some have proposed a separation into question and answer – 'What do I wish?'; 'Oh that it were already kindled!', with *ei* in the sense of *eithe* = 'would that'. This is very abrupt.

50

In this remarkable but mysterious saying Jesus' ministry is orientated towards a crisis which is preordained (*I have*), and through which he will be released from a present constraint (cf. 13³²ᶠ·).

a baptism to be baptized with: *baptisma baptisthēnai* – for wording and construction, cf. 7²⁹, Mark 10³⁸ᶠ·. What this alludes to is obscure. *baptisma* is a passive verbal noun which is not found in Greek literature before the NT. The verb *baptizein* occurs only three times in the LXX, where it is a synonym for the ordinary Greek word for 'to wash' (*baptein*), and does not have its classical and Hellenistic Greek meaning of 'to sink', 'to drown'. Those OT passages which refer to calamity in terms of being overwhelmed by water (Ps. 42⁷; 69²· ¹⁵; 124⁴ᶠ·; Isa. 43²; Song of Sol. 8⁷) do not use this verb. Josephus uses it (*BJ* 4.137) of brigands 'sinking' Jerusalem by consuming its supplies. In its metaphorical use by Plato, Philo, etc., the verb is not absolute; men are 'sunk' in sleep, or 'drowned' by passion. MM cite from a papyrus of the second century BC an instance of the verb used absolutely in the sense of being overwhelmed with troubles, but this is hardly sufficient to attest a popular usage which would make the noun immediately recognizable as referring to this. It is possible that the activity of John the Baptist, and of baptist groups operating at this time, brought about an expansion in the thought and language of baptism (e.g. baptism with spirit, wind, fire), but there is no evidence to connect baptism with the suffering of calamity or death. There is a notable parallel in Mark 10³⁸ᶠ·, which is omitted by Luke, perhaps because he saw the saying here as its equivalent. There the 'baptism to be baptized with' has as a synonym a 'cup' to be drunk, and both apply to the Twelve as well as to Jesus (Matt. 20²² retains from Mark only the cup). But the significance of the 'cup' is also obscure. It could be a symbol, like 'fire' of the divine judgment. This Jesus has to undergo (as possibly here, if v. 49 and v. 50 are to be taken closely together, and the 'fire' he casts on the earth is the same as the baptism with which he is baptized). A connection between baptism and calamity could have been forged by Jesus himself on the basis of a metaphorical usage, for which the documentation is now lacking. Or the connection could have arisen in the early church from an understanding of Christian baptism as baptism into the death of Christ (cf. Rom. 6³).

how I am constrained until it is accomplished!: As in v. 49 the second part of the sentence is as enigmatic as the first. *constrained* is *sunechesthai*, which, when used absolutely, means either 'to be hemmed in' (cf. 8⁴⁵; 19⁴³; Phil. 1²³, 'from both sides'), or 'to be held in captivity' (cf. 22⁶³). The nature of the constraint, and whether it affects only Jesus' person or also his work, are not indicated. Perhaps the restriction consists in the very existence in a world of unfaithfulness and disobedience of the one whose destiny is to be the Son of man, and to effect God's judgment and the consummation of his purposes (cf. 9⁴¹). What would then be looked forward to is the unconstrained life in the age to come, where God's will is freely obeyed. The verb rendered *accomplished* – *telein* – may be characteristic of Luke or of his special material (cf. 18³¹; 22³⁷; A. 13²⁹). In Greek literature it was predominantly a poetic word of elevated tone. Hence it was used of the 'performance' of religious rites. Here it may indicate that the *baptism*, whatever that might be, was not merely to be undergone and passively endured, but was something of great positive significance, which was to be carried through. As a result not only would Jesus himself be released from constraint; his mission would become fully effectual.

51–53
These sayings will have spoken to Christians for whom belief in the gospel had involved separation and opposition from the family (cf. I Cor. 7¹²ᶠᶠ·), and will have provided assurance that they were living in the last days.

51
Compared with Matt. 10³⁴ this looks like a revision. For the question form *Do you think?* (*dokeite*) followed by *No ... but rather ...* (*all'ē*, + II Cor. 1¹³, a classical usage), cf. 13²⁻⁴. *I have come* (*paraginesthai*, a colourless word, almost confined to L–A in the NT). *to give peace on earth* (Matthew's 'to bring', *ballein epi* = 'to cast upon', is awkward with 'sword'). *division* (*diamerismos* + +) is less vivid than Matthew's 'sword'. The reason why Jesus' vocation is of this kind is given in the allusive language of vv. 52–53.

52–53
Peace and harmony, upon which the OT placed such emphasis, especially harmony in the family, were to be characteristic of the age of salvation (cf. 1⁷⁹; 2¹⁴, etc.). But in Micah 7⁶, which is reflected in v. 53, quoted in the parallel passage, Matt. 10³⁵ᶠ·, and may lie behind Mark 13¹², salvation is preceded by a lament of Sion over such corruption in her society that a man may no longer trust even his most intimate fellows. This passage seems to have provided a dogmatic proof text of an internecine conflict that would necessarily precede salvation (cf. Isa.

66^5; Ezek. 38$^{18f.}$; Zech. 14^{13}; I Enoch 56^7; 100^2; Sanh. 97a; see SB I, pp. 585f.; cf. also the vocation of the returning Elijah to reconcile families in preparation for the age to come, Mal. 4^6, quoted 1^{17}). Thus the divisions produced by Jesus' summons to discipleship (cf. 9$^{59f.}$, 14^{26}) are themselves signs of the preliminaries of salvation.

52

henceforth: In the Greek *apo tou nun*, which is Lukan. By contrast with the repetition of 'I have come' in Matt. 10^{35} this places the divisions in the future (perhaps because of the future tenses in vv. 49–50), and in the context lessens their force as a present sign of the approach of the coming age.

in one house there will be five divided: Neither in vv. 52–53 nor in Matt. 10$^{35-36}$ is the LXX text of Micah 7^6 exactly quoted. Luke's version looks like a neat rephrasing of it based on Micah's 'a man's enemies are the men of his own house', and on the reflection that there are five persons involved in the division of the family – father, son, mother (who is also mother-in-law), daughter and daughter-in-law.

12$^{54-59}$ TO THE CROWDS. FAILURE IN
                    JUDGMENT

^{54}*He also said to the multitudes, 'When you see a cloud rising in the west, you say at once, "A shower is coming"; and so it happens.* ^{55}*And when you see the south wind blowing, you say, "There will be scorching heat"; and it happens.* ^{56}*You hypocrites! You know how to interpret the appearance of earth and sky; but why do you not know how to interpret the present time?*

^{57}'*And why do you not judge for yourselves what is right?* ^{58}*As you go with your accuser before the magistrate, make an effort to settle with him on the way, lest he drag you to the judge, and the judge hand you over to the officer, and the officer put you in prison.* ^{59}*I tell you, you will never get out till you have paid the very last copper.'*

The discourse in the chapter ends somewhat lamely with two reprimands to the crowds for their inability to exercise the required discernment. They are both additional – *He also said* (v. 54, *de kai* = 'also'); *And why* (v. 57, *ti de kai*) – and have the appearance of addenda, for which Luke has found a place here.

(i) Verses 54–56 are peculiar to Luke (the parallel in Matt. 16$^{2-3}$ is a later addition to the text there). They have no connection with what has preceded, which has not been concerned with signs of the time (the divisions in vv. 51–53 lie still in the future).

(ii) Verses 57–59 have a close equivalent in Matt. 5$^{25-26}$, but Luke and Matthew differ in their use and interpretation of this parabolic injunction. Originally it may have been eschatological, urging speedy reconciliation in face of the imminence of the final judgment. Something of this may still remain in Matthew, where it is placed in the Sermon on the Mount, and commands speedy reconciliation in place of the anger that incurs condemnation at the judgment. Luke has made of it a further condemnation of the crowds, apparently for their incapacity to arrive at a just settlement of disputes on their own initiative, and without recourse to law (cf. I Cor. 6$^{1-11}$). For this he supplies an introduction which attempts to align it with the lesson of vv. 54–56. So *for yourselves* (Greek *aph' heautōn*, elsewhere in the synoptists 21^{30}) is emphatic. *judge what is right* (*krinein to dikaion* + A. 4^{19}) appears to mean here 'reach a just settlement'. That this application is forced is also shown by the abrupt change from the second person plural of the crowds in vv. 54–57 to the second person singular of the individual in vv. 58–59, which was in Q (cf. Matt. 5$^{25-26}$).

∞

54
a shower: ombros + +. In Palestine rain clouds come in from the sea, i.e. from the west.

55
scorching heat: So in the rare non-biblical instances of the Greek word here, *kausōn*. In the more numerous instances in the LXX the meaning varies between this and 'the east wind', where it renders the same Hebrew word as is also translated by *notos = the south wind*. The first meaning is more likely here as avoiding a possible tautology with *the south wind*, and as providing a parallel to *A shower is coming* (v. 54).

56
hypocrites: See on 6^{42}. Culpable inconsistency seems intended rather than the hypocrisy in v. 1. This implies that events are taking place that should be immediately recognizable by those with spiritual integrity as evidence of the crucial nature of the present time. What these events are, why they should be

so, and whether they are associated with Jesus (e.g. his mighty works, proclamation of the kingdom, etc.), are not indicated.

the ... time: ho kairos: This can be a synonym for the more usual word for 'time', *ho chronos*, as generally in L-A. It had already, however, acquired in Greek the sense of a moment of destiny or decision. This was accentuated in Jewish eschatology, where it was a technical term for the critical period of the end (cf. 21⁸). Here the meaning appears to lie somewhere in between – 'Why do you not discern this period of time in its critical character?'

58–59
Some of the differences from Matt. 5²⁵⁻²⁶ are literary and due to Luke – the *magistrate* (*archōn*, i.e. the heathen magistrate, cf. A. 16¹⁹), *make an effort* (*didonai ergasian*, + + a Latinism = *dare operam*), *to settle* (*apallassesthai* + A. 19¹² = 'to leave', 'to be rid of'), *drag* (*katasurein* + +), *the officer* (*praktōr* + +, a law officer who deals with debts). On the other hand *go, hupagein,* is not characteristic of Luke, and is the language of his source. In Luke the saying seems to have become a piece of practical wisdom that personal settlement of disputes is preferable to imprisonment until the debt is paid. It has to be assumed that the one accused was in fact guilty.

59
copper: In Greek *leptos* = 'small'. Matthew has here *kodrantēs*, a Greek form of the Latin *quadrans*, which Plutarch describes as *to leptotaton* = 'the smallest' of the Roman copper coinage. It was one quarter of an *as* (see on v. 6). But the *leptos* was even smaller, as two went to a *quadrans* (Mark 12⁴²).

13 *Judgment and Salvation: Israel and the Gentiles*

Knox (*Sources* II, pp. 74–83) takes 12⁵⁴–13⁹ as a separate tract on the nationalist peril, and 13¹⁰⁻³⁵ as 'a collection of fragments which Luke has inserted here for no particular reason; they were in his tradition, and had to be put in somewhere'. Although, however, 13¹⁻⁹ could be a further instance of failure to discern the crucial time (12⁵⁶), the note of finality in 12⁵⁹, and the fresh audience in 13¹, justify a chapter division here, and ch. 13 could be said to have a unity of its own. It consists of four sections: (i) vv. 1–9, introduced by new arrivals – doom lies over the nation unless it repents forthwith; (ii) vv. 10–21, introduced by teaching in a synagogue – the salvation of the true Israelite, and, over against the unrepentant hypocrisy of leaders, the acclamation of the works of salvation as evidence of the present operation of the kingdom and of its ultimate expansion; (iii) vv. 22–30, introduced by a notice of the journey which has Jerusalem as its goal – salvation involves the exclusion of many Jews and the inclusion of many Gentiles; (iv) vv. 31–35, introduced by a threat from Herod – the saving ministry will go on, and the triumph of Jesus is certain, though it involves the destruction of Israel. The basis is laid here for a major theme in A., that of the rejection of Israel as a nation for its unbelief, and the inclusion of Gentiles along with believing Jews in the church and in the kingdom of God. The materials Luke has edited here are diverse, but they are bound together by emphasis on the authority of Jesus as teacher, saviour and judge (vv. 2–5, 13–16, 25–27, 32, 34–35), and there is a sense of urgency in the constant address in the second person plural.

13 *There were some present at that very time who told him of the Galileans whose blood Pilate had mingled with their sacrifices. ²And he answered them, 'Do you think that these Galileans were worse sinners than all the other Galileans, because they suffered thus? ³I tell you, No; but unless you repent you will all likewise perish. ⁴Or those eighteen upon whom the tower in Siloam fell and killed them, do you think that they were worse offenders than all the others who dwelt in Jerusalem? ⁵I tell you, No; but unless you repent you will all likewise perish.'*

⁶And he told this parable: 'A man had a fig tree planted in his vineyard; and he came seeking fruit on it and found none. ⁷And he said to the vinedresser, "Lo, these three years I have come seeking fruit on this fig tree, and I find none. Cut it down; why should it use up the ground?" ⁸And he answered him, "Let it alone, sir, this year also, till I dig about it and put on manure. ⁹And if it bears fruit next year, well and good; but if not, you can cut it down."'

Peculiar to Luke. The thought of impending judgment is continued from ch. 12, but is now made the basis of a universal summons to repentance by comment upon a pair of incidents, both occurring in Jerusalem, the one concerned with Galileans and the other with Jerusalemites, and by a parable. Verses 2–5 may have reached Luke as a single unit composed of two closely parallel sayings in question form, and without introduction. For v. 1 is an introduction to the first question only, and it is difficult to conceive an introduction which would cover both. If *whose blood Pilate mingled with their sacrifices* were placed after *these Galileans* it would balance *upon whom the tower of Siloam fell* in v. 4, and it could have been removed from there by Luke to supply an introduction to the whole unit, and replaced by the somewhat colourless *because they suffered thus*. The unit is notable for its topical and circumstantial character; *those eighteen* can only refer to something well known, and probably recent. There is no other record of either incident, but the second would have been too trivial for Josephus to mention, and the scantiness of his sources for this period hardly justifies the assumption (of Wellhausen, p. 71) that Josephus would not have failed to mention the first had he known about it. The numbers involved may have been small.

ಞ

1

Evidence of Luke's hand here could be *there were present* (*parēsan*, the verb only here in Luke, but four times in A.), *at that very time* (*en autō tō kairō* + +) and *told* (*apangellein* = 'to report', frequent in L–A).

whose blood Pilate mingled with their sacrifices: It is not clear to what precise action this referred. 'To mingle the blood with' means 'to slay together' – for Jewish examples see Schlatter, p. 323. Philo (*On the Special Laws* III, 91) sees the command in Exod. 21¹⁴ to remove the murderer from the altar when he takes asylum there as designed to prevent vengeance being taken on him there, which would be 'a profanation of the gravest sort. For the blood of the murderer will mix with the blood of the sacrifices.' If the words are to be taken literally, and the men were killed while in the act of slaughtering their sacrificial victims (which they did at Passover), then the act would have been not only tyrannical, and bloodthirsty, but also a violation of the temple and its precincts. But while Philo (*Embassy to Gaius*, 302) refers to bribery, insult, robbery, outrage, wanton injustices, constant executions without trial and ceaseless and supremely grievous cruelty as characteristic of Pilate's governorship, the only act of sacrilege he mentions is the introduction into Jerusalem of military standards bearing the bust of the emperor. It was his conviction that such a sacrilegious act as slaughtering men in the act of sacrificing in Jerusalem could not have failed to be mentioned by Josephus that led Wellhausen (p. 71) to propose that what stood here originally was a reference to Pilate's massacre of Samaritans at Mount Gerizim c. AD 35, which led to his dismissal (Jos. *Ant.* 18.85).

2

Do you think that?: This construction, followed by 'but unless' (vv. 2, 4) may indicate the same source (L?) as 12⁵¹, but in both places it may be due to Luke.

Galileans: Only here on the lips of Jesus. Some have suggested that it had the nuance of 'revolutionaries'. Judas, a leader in the Jewish revolt, called a Gaulanite in Jos. *Ant.* 18.4ff., is called a Galilean in Jos. *BJ* 2, 118. 'Galileans' are listed amongst Jewish sects by Justin (*Dialogue* 80) and by Hegesippus (in Eus. *HE* 4. 22.7). They could have had a reputation not only 'as heretics but also as rebels. Manson (*Sayings*, p. 273) suggests that Jesus' informants in v. 1 were either patriots attempting to embroil him in revolt, or enemies trying to get him to incriminate himself by making some statement about Pilate. S. G. F. Brandon^f suggests that the passage is residual evidence that Jesus was the kind of person whom some thought it necessary to keep informed on political matters, his reply being intended to discourage the precipitation of events by resort to violence. But this puts undue weight on the introductory statement in v. 1, and the parallel in *those who dwelt in Jerusalem* (Greek 'Jerusalemites', v. 4) suggests that the reference is purely geographical; and the additional instance adduced by Jesus himself in vv. 4-5 could indicate that the first incident was no more political than the second.

4

The pool (reservoir) of Siloam was part of the Jerusalem water supply (cf. John 9⁷), and the incident of the tower could have been connected with Pilate's attempt to improve that supply by an aqueduct, which led to rioting and bloodshed because he paid for the project with misappropriated temple funds (Jos. *Ant.* 18.60ff.; *BJ* 2.175f.). H. G. Wood^g takes the fall of the tower as due to military operations, and Jesus' words as a specific warning to Israel that persistence in present attitudes to Rome would end in messianic war and ruin.

3, 5

Whether or not the incidents had any political background, Jesus treats them from a religious point of view. He sees them as raising questions about a prevalent doctrine that disaster is indicative of, and proportionate to, sin (cf. the

f *The Fall of Jerusalem and the Christian Church*, London 1951, pp. 106f.
g 'Interpreting this Time', *NTS* 2, 1955–56, pp. 262–6.

book of Job). In answering his own questions it is this doctrine that he repudiates and not any judgment on Pilate's action. They were not sinful (*hamartōloi* = 'sinners') *above all others* (sc. Galileans), nor *offenders* (*opheiletai* = 'debtors', a synonym for sinners) beyond all other Jerusalemites. This repudiation is then made, not without some inconsistency, the basis for a call to repentance in the shape of a universal warning that the audience, here representative of the nation, will, if they do not repent (it is not said of what), *all likewise perish*. If *likewise* (*homoiōs* = 'similarly') and *hōsautōs* = 'in the same way' (v. 5) are to be pressed, it must mean that they will meet with comparable disaster. This probably refers to the destruction of Israel (cf. vv. 34–35). The more usual interpretation – if you do not repent (of sin in general) you will be condemned by God – reduces the lesson drawn from these very specific incidents to a religious platitude.

6–10

The parable continues the thought that destruction is certain apart from repentance, adding that the time for repentance is already determined and short. There is nothing to indicate its source, nor whether it came to Luke already attached to vv. 1–5 (*And he told this parable* is a Lukan form of introduction). It is stylishly written, and this comes over in the English rendering, esp. *Lo, these three years have I come*, and in the conditional sentence with an ellipse of the first apodosis (*well and good* is not in the Greek). In content there is a parallel in *The Story of Ahikar* 8^{35} (*AP* II, p. 775): 'My son, thou hast been to me like that palm tree that stood by a river, and cast all its fruit into the river; and when its lord came to cut it down it said, "Let me alone this year and I will bring thee forth carobs." ' Knox (*Hellenistic Elements*, p. 19 n. 4) draws attention to a more striking parallel in popular magic, in which 'the owner of a barren tree should gird up his loins and go up to the tree in anger as if to cut it down. Someone else must come up and ask him to spare the tree, guaranteeing that it will do better in the future; if spared the tree will bear.' The parable here lends itself to allegorization but is nowhere clearly allegorical. None of the OT passages generally quoted (Hos. 9^{10}; Micah 7^1; Jer. 8^{13}; 24$^{1ff.}$) serves to establish the fig tree as a symbol of Israel; to interpret it of the individual within Israel (so Wellhausen, p. 72), or, with others, of Jerusalem within Israel, is unconvincing. It is tempting to take *three years* as indicating the length of Jesus' ministry, but this is improbable, as is also the suggestion of Schlatter (p. 322) that Jesus is here represented as the intercessor with God on Israel's behalf. Placed here the parable expresses a consciousness on Jesus' part that his ministry is the time which calls for repentance of an ultimate kind.

6

fruit: For Luke here and in v. 9 probably the fruit of repentance, but originally it may have meant the fruit of righteousness.

9
next year: The Greek is *eis to mellon* = 'for the coming' (+ I Tim. 6¹⁹) with 'year' understood.

SABBATH HEALING AND
THE KINGDOM

¹⁰*Now he was teaching in one of the synagogues on the sabbath.* ¹¹*And there was a woman who had had a spirit of infirmity for eighteen years; she was bent over and could not fully straighten herself.* ¹²*And when Jesus saw her, he called her and said to her, 'Woman, you are freed from your infirmity.'* ¹³*And he laid his hands upon her, and immediately she was made straight, and she praised God.* ¹⁴*But the ruler of the synagogue, indignant because Jesus had healed on the sabbath, said to the people, 'There are six days on which work ought to be done; come on those days and be healed, and not on the sabbath day.'* ¹⁵*Then the Lord answered him, 'You hypocrites! Does not each of you on the sabbath untie his ox or his ass from the manger, and lead it away to water it?* ¹⁶*And ought not this woman, a daughter of Abraham whom Satan bound for eighteen years, be loosed from this bond on the sabbath day?'* ¹⁷*As he said this, all his adversaries were put to shame; and all the people rejoiced at all the glorious things that were done by him.*

¹⁸*He said therefore, 'What is the kingdom of God like? And to what shall I compare it?* ¹⁹*It is like a grain of mustard seed which a man took and sowed in his garden; and it grew and became a tree, and the birds of the air made nests in its branches.'*

²⁰*And again he said, 'To what shall I compare the kingdom of God?* ²¹*It is like leaven which a woman took and hid in three measures of meal, till it was all leavened.'*

Peculiar to Luke. In the context of sabbath synagogue teaching a healing takes place, which brings to light the obduracy that prevents Israel from recognizing the signs of the times (*hypocrites* v. 5; cf. 12⁵⁴ᶠᶠ.), in this case the signs of salvation. By contrast the crowd acclaims them.

The story has no connection with what precedes, and is perhaps placed here to initiate the alternation between judgment and salvation which runs through the rest of the chapter. It is a blend of miracle story, conflict story and pronouncement story, and resembles 6^{6-11}, on which it may be modelled. At certain points it shows more art than verisimilitude. Thus the controversy follows the cure, and there is in consequence a double chiastic ending. Verse 17a is a literary reminiscence of Isa. 41^{11} (cf. 45^{16}), and concludes the controversy with a conventional worsting of opponents, though only one opponent, the ruler of the synagogue, has been mentioned. Verse 17b, the customary chorus in a miracle story, brings the narrative back with difficulty to the positive note of salvation and acclaim, and so prepares for vv. 18–21 to follow. The cure takes place in a synagogue, but the word translated *the people* (v. 14) is *ho ochlos* = 'the crowd', which is normally used for one of Jesus' audiences, but is found nowhere else in the gospels for a synagogue congregation.

There is considerable evidence of Luke's hand in the more frequent use of participles throughout, and in the following words and phrases: *there was a woman* (Greek 'behold a woman', cf. 5^{12}; $18^{7, 37}$), *a spirit of* (cf. 4^{33}), *infirmity* (*astheneia*, apart from Matt. 8^{17} only Luke in the synoptists; cf. A. 28^9), *bent over* (*sunkuptein* + +), *could not* (participle in the Greek = 'being unable to', as in 1^{20}; A. 21^{34}; 27^{15}), *straighten* (*anakuptein* + 21^{28}), *called* (*prosphōnein*, apart from Matt. 11^{16} only L–A in the NT), *immediately* (*parachrēma*, apart from Matt. $21^{19f.}$ only L–A in the NT), *made straight* (*anorthoun* + A. 15^{16} LXX; Heb. 12^{12}), *praised God, the Lord, ought* (*dei*, cf. 12^{12}; A. 20^{35}), *bond* (*desmos*, only here in the NT for sickness), *glorious things* (elsewhere in the gospels 7^{25}).

ॐ

10

This is the last instance of synagogue teaching in the Gospel, and the only one on the journey to Jerusalem. It may be reproducing, somewhat artificially, the circumstances of the Galilean ministry.

11–13

Description of illness and cure is elaborate and forceful, giving the basis for the exuberant praise in v. 17. It is not clear whether *a spirit of infirmity* prepares for a healing simply or an exorcism, as in 4^{33}. In 8^2 evil spirit and infirmity are distinguished, though the same verb *heal* (*therapeuein*, the word in v. 14) is used of both. In A. 16^{16} 'spirit of divination' refers to possession, and *whom Satan bound* (v. 16) makes it possible that an exorcism is in mind here, though that is not certain, as 'healing all who were oppressed by the devil' (A. 10^{38}) could refer to healing in general. The double action of authoritative word and the laying on of hands (vv. 12–13) may be intended to suggest the difficulty and greatness of the cure (*you are freed*, v. 12, which looks forward to *bound* and *loosed* (v. 16) is addressed to the woman, and not as an exorcistic formula to a demon). This also applies to the length of the illness, *eighteen years* (cf. 8⁴³; John 5⁵, here referred to later by Jesus himself, v. 16), and to *fully* (v. 11). The latter (*eis to panteles*) is a Hellenistic literary expression which, as Josephus uses it, should go with the verb (= 'to straighten herself completely', as RSV), but here may go with *could not* (= 'could not at all'); in either case it is superfluous after *bent over* (i.e. bent double), and is an accentuation of the gravity of the infirmity characteristic of miracle stories.

praised God: edoxasen = 'glorified', a common theme in Luke, especially in cures (5²⁵; 7¹⁶; 17¹⁵; 18⁴³; A. 4²¹). She does so as a believing Israelite (*daughter of Abraham*, v. 16).

14

The controversy within the miracle story is introduced somewhat artificially, since the objection of the ruler of the synagogue is not directed against Jesus and his action, but against the crowd for demanding healing on the sabbath, though there has been no indication of any such demand, nor of any expectation of the woman to be healed. The objection is so stated as to raise a general principle in terms of the fourth commandment (Exod. 20⁹; Deut. 5¹³). There are six days in the week for working, and that includes healing; on the sabbath it is forbidden.

15

Then the Lord answered him: For his authoritative reply Jesus is introduced by his post-resurrection title *the Lord*. The reply is not a direct answer to the objection as stated, and is not addressed to the ruler, but to the Jews in general. This may reflect controversy over the sabbath between the church and Judaism. What constituted work, what was permitted on the sabbath and in what circumstances, were naturally the subject of debate, and judgments varied. The Mishnaic treatise Yoma (8⁶) permits life that is in danger to be saved on the sabbath. So a child falling into the sea may be saved by the use of a net, or into a pit by the use of a ladder. The Qumran community appears to have been more rigorous in ordering that 'no man shall assist a beast to give birth on the sabbath day. And if it shall fall into a cistern or pit, he shall not lift it out on the sabbath.' There were varied judgments on the precedent appealed to here connected with what knots may be tied or untied on the sabbath, and whether, and how far, cattle should be allowed out for pasturing or watering (see SB I, pp. 622ff., Vermes, *Scrolls*, pp. 112f.). In view of *bound* and *loosed from this bond* (v. 16) it is strange that the appeal here is not to any exceptional circumstances of danger, as in 14^5 = Matt. 12^{11}, but to the comparatively trivial act of untying a beast from its manger so as to lead it away for watering because it cannot wait for a day.

16

These interpretative words of Jesus do pick up the ruler's words in v. 15b. With *on the sabbath day* placed last for emphasis they suggest that his healings were not prompted by the need to advocate a more liberal attitude to sabbath observance. They were, rather, part and parcel of the warfare between the kingdom of God and the kingdom of Satan, and their success was evidence of the victory of the kingdom of God. In that case they were not merely to be permitted on the sabbath. The sabbath, as the symbol of the refreshment and restoration of life and of participation in the 'rest' of God (Heb. $4^{9f.}$), was the proper day for doing them.

17

The chorus of acclamation typical of miracle stories is now given by Luke with characteristic exaggeration as the rejoicing of *all the people* at *all the glorious things* (*ta endoxa*, used in Exod. 34^{10}; Deut. 10^{21}, etc., for the divine works of deliverance), and is delayed to this point so that it may be set over against the worsting by Jesus of *all his adversaries*.

18–21

The particle *oun* (v. 18, *therefore*) is rare in Luke at the beginning of a paragraph. It connects the following twin parables closely with what has gone before, and Jesus is made to continue teaching in the synagogue by means of them.

In the Gospel of Thomas these two parables are found separately (20, 96). In Mark 4^{30-32} the first is found on its own, where Luke omits it. They are found as a pair in Matt. 13^{31-33}. Since the second, vv. 20–21, is in almost ver-batim agreement with Matt. 13^{33}, and the first, vv. 18–19, shows considerable agreement with Matt. 13^{31-32} when phrases that Matthew owes to Mark 4^{30-32} have been abstracted, it is likely that Luke is using a common source with Matthew (Q). In Luke, however, they are closely assimilated to each other in form. The opening double question in v. 18 may have stood in Q (cf. 7^{31} = Matt. 11^{16}; Isa. 40^{18}), but it may have been suggested to Luke by Mark 4^{30}. *sowed* (*ebalen* = 'threw') may also be due to Mark 4^{26}, the only other passage where 'throw' is used with 'seed'. Luke may then have deliberately passed over the parable in its Markan context so as to use it as a twin to the parable of the Leaven in this context.

Although the kingdom of God has already been the subject of a variety of statements in the Gospel, this is the first, and with the possible exception of $19^{11f.}$ the only place where it is expressly treated in its nature and presence by means of parable. This, together with the double introductory question provided to two such brief parables, suggest that Luke had a special reason for placing them here. In its Markan form, with emphasis on the smallness of the seed, and along with other parables in Mark 4, the parable of the Mustard Seed appears to be a comment on the paradox that the kingdom of God should ever be small and hidden, and an assurance that it will not always be in its present state of obscurity. In Luke 'smallness' is still indicated by *a grain of mustard seed*, which was itself a figure of this ('small as mustard seed' was a Jewish proverb), and 'hiddenness' is contained in the parable of the Leaven; but the emphasis now is on the certain expansion and the universal scope of the kingdom – *till all was leavened* (v. 21). As the subject of expansion the kingdom here must mean the rule of God as effectively established among men. Originally this may have referred to the consummation at the end of time, but here it points forward to the story in A. Placed here the parables extend and comment upon the jubilant acclamation of the sabbath healing of a true Israelite (v. 17).

19

his garden: Probably a Lukan refinement, as planting mustard in gardens was not Palestinian practice (Matthew has 'his field'). *his* with *garden* is *heautou* = 'his own'. Some have seen an allegorical touch here – Jesus sows seed in his own garden, Israel, and a huge result follows of Gentiles and believing Jews.

the birds of the air . . . its branches: This, which is in all three versions, could echo, though not exactly, the description in Dan. 9^{9-10} LXX of the kingdom of Nebuchadnezzar, with its claim to be universal, though the figure is also found of the restored Israel (Ezek. 17^{23}; cf. 31^9).

20

three measures: The Greek word here, *saton*, renders a Hebrew measure (cf. Haggai 2^{16}) which Josephus (*Ant.* 9.85) says was equivalent to a *modius* and a half in Roman terms, i.e. approximately three gallons. Though in Gen. 18^6 this is what is used to provide cakes for only three visitors, it is a very large amount, and may reflect the element of exaggeration which is a common feature of Jesus' parables, as may also the designation of the mustard bush as a *tree* (v. 19), even if it could grow to six feet.

^{22}*He went on his way through towns and villages, teaching, and journeying toward Jerusalem. ^{23}And some one said to him, 'Lord, will those who are saved be few?' And he said to them, ^{24}'Strive to enter by the narrow door; for many, I tell you, will seek to enter and will not be able. ^{25}When once the householder has risen up and shut the door, you will begin to stand outside and to knock at the door, saying, "Lord, open to us." He will answer you, "I do not know where you come from." ^{26}Then you will begin to say, "We ate and drank in your presence, and you taught in our streets." ^{27}But he will say, "I tell you, I do not know where you come from; depart from me, all you workers of iniquity!" ^{28}There you will weep and gnash your teeth, when you see Abraham and Isaac and Jacob and all the prophets in the kingdom of God and you yourselves thrust out. ^{29}And men will come from east and west, and from north and south, and sit at table in the kingdom of God. ^{30}And behold, some are last who will be first, and some are first who will be last.'*

The fact that vv. 23ff. could well have followed directly after v. 21 suggests that v. 22 is more than a casual and literary reminder to the reader that a journey is in progress. The remainder of Jesus' itinerant ministry is here characterized (i) as consisting of teaching (cf. v. 26), which will not be expressly mentioned again until 19^{47}, and (ii) as directed to a predetermined goal at Jerusalem, which now has a sinister sound (vv. 33–35).

The discourse in vv. 23–30 is regarded by Lagrange (p. 387) as homogeneous in bringing to the fore what has been an underlying theme since 9^{51}, and especially since 11^{14}, that of the blindness of the Jews, who are confounded by Gentiles, and of the fruitlessness of Jesus' appeals to their leaders. It is, however, a composite discourse, and its analysis proves difficult. It consists of three separable units – v. 24, vv. 25–27, vv. 28–29 (30) – and has a double introduction. The first, v. 22, is plainly editorial. The second, v. 23, may also be so in supplying a question to which the materials in vv. 24–30 are assembled as a reply. In these materials there is sufficient similarity in thought and wording with three passages in Matthew occurring, not indeed together, but in the same sequence, to suggest that they come from a common source (Q). The dissimilarities are, however, such as to make it difficult to account for them in every case by the editorial work of one or the other evangelist.

ཉྫ

23

The teaching is introduced by a question from an individual, though the reply is to an unspecified *them*. *those who are saved* is hoi sōzomenoi = 'the ones being saved' or 'the ones who will be saved'; elsewhere in the NT at I Cor. 1¹⁸; II Cor. 2¹⁵, and A. 2⁴⁷ in a general statement of the growth of the Jerusalem church. It seems to have been a semi-technical term belonging to eschatology. How urgent the question was for some Jews in the first century AD as a result of threatening or actual disaster, and of increased apocalyptic foreboding, may be seen especially in IV Ezra, where it constitutes one of the major themes, and where the answer is profoundly pessimistic (see 7⁴⁷ᶠᶠ·, and esp. 7⁶⁰, 'the few that shall be saved', 8³, 'many have been created but few will be saved', 9¹⁴, 'more will perish than shall be saved'). II Baruch 21¹¹ is more optimistic, 'In time past many have sinned, yet others, not a few, have been righteous.' For Luke this is no longer such a problem, for in A., while entry into the kingdom is difficult (14²²), and Israel as a nation is excluded, a great number will belong to the true Israel of the patriarchs (cf. the discussion of the same issue in Rom. 9–11).

24–25

This is obscure, however punctuated. With a comma after *will not be able* and a stop at the end of v. 25 (so Lagrange), there is an abrupt transition from the third person in *many will seek* to the second person in *you will begin*, and an exhortation to strive is immediately followed by a statement that they will be permanently outside. Loisy and others suggest a stop after *will not be able* and a comma at the end of v. 25, with *When once* introducing an extended protasis of a conditional sentence, and *Then* (v. 26) introducing the apodosis. But the beginning with *When once* is abrupt, the construction breaks down with *he will answer*, which is in the indicative, and not, as the other verbs in a conditional sentence, in the subjunctive, and the first *I do not know where you come from* is greatly weakened in force when it is merely a preparation for the second. Klostermann (p. 146) takes v. 25 as a separate sentence with the main clause beginning at *He will answer you*, but only by adopting the reading of syrˢⁱⁿ 'For when once . . .'.

24

This first part of the reply to the question in v. 23 is clearly equivalent to Matt. 7¹³⁻¹⁴, though the form is different. Probably due to Luke are *strive (agōnizesthai*, only here in the synoptists, but belonging to the ethical vocabulary of Paul and the Pastorals; see I Cor. 9²⁵; Col. 1²⁹; 4¹²; I Tim. 4¹⁰; 6¹²; II Tim. 4⁷, its other occurrences in the NT), *seek* (*zētein*, cf. 17³³ with Matt. 10³⁹), the parenthetical position of *I tell you* emphasizing *many*, the only parallel in the gospels being at 15¹⁰, and *be able* (*ischuein* = 'have the strength').

The exhortation to spiritual effort (*strive*) in view of the failure of *many* seems to imply that of those addressed few will be saved. But the picture is blurred. In Matthew the choice between salvation and damnation is presented by a contrast between the narrow lane and the broad highway leading respectively to narrow and wide gates (*pulē*) of a city, and between the few or many who take them. In Luke there is no contrast; and the way to salvation is through the door of a house (*thura*), the narrowness of which prevents many from entry despite their efforts. This is plainly secondary, and is barely intelligible. For it is not the width or narrowness of a door which makes it a symbol of entry or not into salvation, but whether the door is closed or not (as in v. 25). Hence it is not evident how the narrowness of the door is related to the object of striving, nor whether the effort required is from the individual, who may find himself too fat to get through, or from the elect because they will find a scrimmage round the door. Thus Luke's version gives the appearance of being somehow truncated, a remnant of a larger unit, which has been isolated so as to lead to what follows.

25–27

These verses appear to be composite. On the one hand vv. 26–27 describe the same scene as Matt. 7²²⁻²³, though in the second person, with different grounds of association with Jesus, and with a different wording of Ps. 6⁹. On the other hand, following after v. 25 they become the second of two symmetrically constructed examples of a different scene of people knocking on a door and being refused entry; v. 25, which is awkwardly connected with v. 24, is close to wording embedded in Matthew's parable of the Virgins (Matt. 25¹⁰⁻¹²).

25

The narrow door as a symbol of the difficulty of entrance into salvation (v. 24) changes abruptly to the closed door as a symbol of exclusion from it, and those who have been told to strive to enter are now told that they will be permanently excluded. This transition is very awkward whatever punctuation of vv. 25–26 is adopted; and despite the symmetry of what is another of Luke's double examples, these verses are difficult to construe. *when once* could be a connecting link with v. 24; the failure of the many becomes a fact from the moment the door is shut by the owner of the house, and they remain disavowed despite their knocking. In that case v. 25 could be parabolic, and *has risen up*, which is otiose, could suggest that it is an extract from a parable (cf. the similarity of wording with Matt. 25¹⁰⁻¹², though the situation is different). Against this is the change from indirect statement in v. 24b to direct address in *you will begin*. More probably v. 25 is to be taken as an overloaded adverbial clause describing the conditions at the judgment, and leading to the appeal in v. 26. In that case the whole is allegorical. The door is the door of the banqueting hall of the kingdom (already suggested by the definite article in v. 24, *the* narrow door); the householder is both the doorkeeper of the kingdom and the judge. He is here identified with the Jesus they have known – *Lord, open to us* and v. 26; though *he will say to you* (Matt. 7²³, 'I will declare to them') suggests that it originally referred to God. *has risen up and shut the door* denote actions of judgment.

26

With *then* and *you will begin to say* (Matt. 7²², 'On that day – i.e. the day of judgment – many will say'), the situation in v. 25 is continued, and is applied to the audience. The appeal against final exclusion in Matthew is precise. It is made by (Christian?) prophets, exorcists and healers. This may be secondary (but cf. Mark 9³⁸f.). The reply is a judgment of Christ upon the falsity of his earthly representatives. The corresponding appeal in Luke is weak, being based solely on having been Jesus' contemporaries and having provided facilities for his teaching. This reduces the force of their repudiation as workers of iniquity.

We ate and drank in your presence: This is a LXX expression for friendship (cf. II Sam. 11¹³), and *I do not know where you come from* means 'You are no friend of mine' (cf. I Sam. 25¹⁰f.; John 9²⁹). It is possible, but unlikely, that Luke had in mind the apostles, who as chosen witnesses ate and drank before the Lord and proclaimed him as judge (A. 10⁴¹f.).

27

Both Matthew and Luke differ from the LXX text of Ps. 6⁹, which has 'Depart (*apostēte*, so Luke but not Matthew) from me, you workers (the participle *hoi ergazomenoi*, so Matthew but not Luke, who has the noun) of evil (*anomia* = 'lawlessness', only Matthew in the gospels; Luke has *adikia* = 'unrighteousness' only Luke and John in the gospels).

28–29

These verses are closely parallel to Matt. 8¹¹⁻¹², though there they form a single prophecy in two parts in the third person, but in Luke two separate prophecies, one in the second and one in the third person. The three thoughts in Matthew – (*a*) coming from east and west, (*b*) casting out, and (*c*) weeping and gnashing of teeth – appear in Luke in the order *c, b, a,* and Luke has made the section fourfold by adding v. 30, perhaps from Mark 10³¹, a passage also concerned with the question of who will be saved, which Luke omits in that context. The verses have a superficial connection with vv. 25–26 in the ideas of eating with the Lord and of being inside or outside the kingdom; but Luke makes them continuous by advancing to the beginning of the unit what belongs more naturally, as in Matt. 8¹², to its end, *There you will weep and gnash your teeth. There* now refers backwards to the place to which those bidden to depart (v. 27) will have been consigned. But it also looks forward to *when*, and, by a continuation of the second person plural from vv. 25–26, the twofold result of the judgment, blessedness and condemnation, is presented as what those being addressed will themselves behold, *when you see* (contrast Matt. 8¹¹⁻¹²). The unitary description of blessedness in Matt. 8¹¹⁻¹² as the coming to join the patriarchs in the heavenly banquet is in Luke divided into two distinct statements. The first (v. 28b), in the second person plural, is that the audience will see the patriarchs and the prophets as occupants of the kingdom, and will see themselves thrust out. Taken literally *thrust out* means that they had once been in the kingdom and had been expelled (the same word in Matt. 8¹² means that 'the sons of the kingdom', i.e. Israelites who ought to inherit it, will be 'thrust' into the outer darkness). Perhaps a less literal sense is intended: 'you will find yourselves excluded.' There is then added (v. 29) in supplementation of v. 28a, and as a counterpoint to v. 28b, a statement in the third person which now hangs in the air. This is a prophecy of a future coming into the kingdom of a company from the four points of the compass, i.e. the Gentiles. This coming is expressed as participation at table (in company with the three patriarchs, Matt. 8¹¹, though that is not said here). This reversal of places between Jew and Gentile is underlined in v. 30a, a generalized form of a truth that lies at the heart of the gospel, and that is pressed on the disciples in various ways (Mark 9³⁵; 10⁴⁴ᶠ·; Luke 14⁸ᶠᶠ·). Here, and in this form (contrast Matt. 20¹⁶, where all first are last and vice versa) it serves to round off (*And behold*) the answer to the question in v. 23. There can be many saved because there will be Gentiles who will move into the position of Jews.

28

you will weep and gnash your teeth: This translates by verbs what in the Greek are nouns, *ho klauthmos* = 'the weeping' and *ho brugmos tōn odontōn* = 'the gnashing of teeth'. The expression, which occurs seven times in Matthew and nowhere else, appears to be stereotyped. The articles with the nouns indicate an extremity of grief of those who had most reason to expect to be included in the kingdom. *brugmos* in combination with 'weeping' could denote the chattering of the teeth in fright rather than the grinding of them in rage.

when you see Abraham, Isaac and Jacob and all the prophets: With *when you see* Luke introduces, perhaps unconsciously, a feature found in some eschatologies of the saved and the lost being in sight of one another (cf. 16²³; IV Ezra 7³⁸). The named patriarchs are a conventional triad based on Exod. 3⁶ (cf. A. 3¹³; 7³²; Heb. 11⁹), which is representative of the true Israel. *and all the prophets*, absent from Matt. 8¹¹, is probably a Lukan addition, and reflects his emphasis on the prophets as witnesses to the Christian message (cf. A. 3¹⁸, ²¹, ²⁴; 10⁴³; 13²⁶ᶠ·) and to the word of salvation (A. 24¹⁴ᶠ·). A basis is provided here for a recurrent theme in Acts that the God of Abraham, Isaac and Jacob and of the prophets establishes his people despite, and as a result of, the rejection of the Jews as a people (A. $3^{13ff., 24f.}$; $10^{42f.}$; $13^{17ff., 27ff.}$; $15^{14ff.}$; $24^{14ff.}$; $26^{22f.}$; $28^{23f.}$). The salvation and condemnation which will be evident in the last days are already mirrored in the history of the church. Luke would have found 'sons of the kingdom' (Matt. 8^{12}) too positive a term for the Jews, who for him are rather 'sons of Israel' or 'sons of the race of Abraham' (A. 5^{21}; 13^{26}), and only in favourable cases 'sons of Abraham' (19^9; 13^{16}).

29

men will come from east and west and north and south: The last two points are probably Luke's addition to *east and west* (Matt. 8^{11}) to emphasize the universality of the kingdom. In this form the language echoes Ps. 107^3, which speaks of the coming of redeemed Jews from the diaspora to Jerusalem, and it is suggested that this is the meaning here (Leaney, p. 209). But the 'many' in Matt. 8^{11} certainly denotes Gentiles, and it is likely that *men will come* does so here. That God would bring them in miraculously at the end of the days seems to have been Jesus' own expectation of salvation for the Gentiles, which is based on OT pictures of an eschatological pilgrimage of Gentiles to Sion.[h] Nothing is said in this Gospel of how this is related to the historical mission of the church to the Gentiles, which the risen Lord commands in 24^{47}.

sit at table in the kingdom of God: This reflects a Jewish apocalyptic conception of fellowship with God as a heavenly banquet (cf. I Enoch 62^{14}; 25^5; II Baruch 29^{4-8}; Luke 14^5). For rabbinic passages see SB IV, pp. 1145f., 1163ff.

13^{31-33} HEROD AND THE MINISTRY OF JESUS

[31]*At that very hour some Pharisees came, and said to him, 'Get away from here, for Herod wants to kill you.'* [32]*And he said to them, 'Go and tell that fox, "Behold, I cast out demons and perform cures today and tomorrow, and the third day I finish my course.* [33]*Nevertheless I must go on my way today and tomorrow and the day following; for it cannot be that a prophet should perish away from Jerusalem."'*

Peculiar to Luke. This is a second piece of tradition in this chapter of a biographical and highly circumstantial kind (cf. Bultmann, *History,*

h See J. Jeremias, *Jesus' Promise to the Nations,* SBT 24, 1958.

p. 35, 'I have no explanation to offer of this singular item'). If it came to Luke in oral or written tradition it presumably did so as presenting in miniature and from the lips of Jesus a proclamation of his ministry, death and consummation such as is found in extended form on the lips of others in e.g. A. 2$^{22-36}$; 10$^{38-42}$. This, together with some of the vocabulary, might suggest a Lukan origin, but formulation and wording are probably too striking to have been entirely his creation. The incident implies that Jesus is still within the jurisdiction of Herod, which was Galilee and Peraea (3^1 mentions Galilee only), although 9^{52} and 13^{22} might indicate that he had already moved out of it. Luke is hardly concerned with exact geography here, but with the character and purpose of the journey as such – cf. the repetition of his favourite *poreuesthai* = 'to go, travel' in *Get away* (v. 31), *Go* (v. 32) and *go my way* (v. 33). Placed here the pericope reinforced by words of Jesus the impression of a divinely destined itinerary, which has been the context since 9^{51} of much of the non-Markan material Luke has included. It also carries forward the thought of salvation and judgment from vv. 25–30, and leads straight into the prophecy and lament over Jerusalem in vv. 34–35.

ಞಞ

31
At that very hour: An exaggerated connecting link typical of Luke.

some Pharisees: It is not clear whether, in assigning the message that Herod *wants* (*thelei* = 'wishes' in the sense of 'intends') to kill Jesus to 'certain' Pharisees, Luke intends it to be understood as a friendly warning to Jesus to make himself scarce, or as a hostile attempt to frighten him (cf. Amos 7$^{10-12}$). The unfavourable light in which Pharisees are presented in this gospel makes the latter more likely.

32
Jesus' reply is imperious. For all his authority, vaunted power and swagger Herod is from Jesus' point of view to be dismissed as an ephemeral nobody. He is to be informed of this by reference to Jesus' own sovereign activity, which is continuing and inexorable, and to his death, which, so far from being brought about fortuitously and by secular tyranny, lies within the mysterious divine purpose, and will be the way to his personal goal. Most of the phrases here are cryptic and require elucidation.

that fox: tē alopeki tautē; the demonstrative comes after the noun, and expresses contempt (cf. A. 17^{18} 'this babbler'). In literature generally, ancient and modern, the fox has been a symbol of craftiness, but there is no case of this in the OT, and while there are a few instances in rabbinic literature, the fox is more common there for the mean and paltry man as opposed to the lion, the weighty and important man. So perhaps here.

I cast out demons and perform cures: A chiasmus in the Greek. *perform* is *apotelein* = 'to complete', and is used without emphasis on completion only at II Macc. 15^{39}; James 1^{15} in the Greek Bible. The combination of exorcism and more general healing (cf. 4$^{40f.}$; 8^2; 9^1) is meant to characterize the whole ministry (cf. A. 2^{22}; 10^{38}). There is no reference to teaching. This could be because Herod's chief or sole interest is represented as being in miracle (cf. 9^7; 23^8). G. Bornkamm[i] suggests that the intention of the words was to deny any misrepresentation to Herod of the ministry as politically motivated.

today and tomorrow, and the third day I finish my course: If the expression *today and tomorrow, and the third day,* along with *today and tomorrow and the day following* in v. 33, 'refers to a short period of time, the exact duration of which the speaker either cannot or does not wish to disclose' (so Bauer, *Lexicon,* s.v. *sēmeron*), the meaning will be that the healing ministry will, despite Herod's threats, continue for a time yet. The nearest parallel would not be Hos. 6^2, where 'on the third day' is equivalent to the preceding 'after two days', and is not distinguished from it, but could be Exod. 19$^{10f.}$, 'Go to the people and consecrate them today and tomorrow . . . and be ready by the third day; for on the third day the Lord will come down.' There the emphasis is on the third day as that of the divine epiphany, and 'today and tomorrow' simply lead up to it with the meaning 'continuously from now until that moment'. So here the sense may be that the ministry will continue until its divine consummation. But the equivalent in v. 33, *the day following* (*tē echomenē,* an idiomatic use of the participle of *echein* = 'to have' with the sense of 'following on', elsewhere in the Greek Bible I Chron. 10^8; II Macc. 12^{39}; A. 20^{15}) is included along with *today and tomorrow.* This has led to various suggestions. (i) Some authorities, ancient (syr^{pesh}) and modern, have proposed a verb such as 'work' after *today and tomorrow* in v. 33, continuing with *I must go my way;* but then v. 33a simply repeats v. 32a, and *nevertheless* becomes unnecessary. (ii) Wellhausen (p. 76) sees *the third day I finish my course* as an interpolation to make v. 32 complete; and since the verse could not now be followed by what had originally stood next (*and the day following*), a further interpolation into v. 33 of *today and tomorrow* was necessary. If, however, *the third day I finish my course* is suspect as a prophecy of the resurrection (a primitive Easter confession added by Luke, who then appended a separate saying in v. 33 as a prophecy of the passion,[j] it is a very clumsy interpolation, since in this context the previous *today and tomorrow* cannot refer to the passion. (iii) J.

i *Jesus of Nazareth,* London 1960, New York 1961, p. 154.
j So K. L. Schmidt, *Das Rahmen der Geschichte,* Berlin 1919, pp. 265f.

Blinzler[k] takes *the third day I finish my course* as original, and *today and tomorrow* in v. 33 as an interpolation to remove the contradiction between 'I must start my journey the next day' (v. 33) and $9^{51ff.}$; 13^{22}, where the journey is already in progress. If in the text as it stands *I go my way* (v. 33) is given the same meaning as *I finish my course* = 'I go to my end' (cf. 22^{22}), or 'I go to glory through death', it loses the force of a necessary journey to Jerusalem to perish as a prophet. Originally, therefore, v. 32 and v. 33 may have been separate sayings. The view of Conzelmann (*Theology*, pp. 65, 197) that *today and tomorrow and the third day* points to the three stages into which he sees Luke's gospel as divided – Galilee, the journey, Jerusalem – is not convincing.

I finish my course: The Greek is *teleioumai*. Possible meanings are: (i) As a middle, 'I bring (it) to an end.' This usage is rare, and requires an object to be supplied. (ii) As a passive, 'I am perfected (through death)' cf. the perfection of the righteous by death in Wisd. 4^{13}; IV Macc. 7^{15}; Philo, *Allegories of the Laws* 3.45; Heb. 2^{10}; 12^{23}. This is a Hellenistic idea, and is close in meaning to being 'sanctified' or 'glorified' (cf. John $17^{10ff.}$; Heb. $2^{10f.}$; 10^{14}), i.e. established in divine glory or the heavenly sphere. This would be a fresh thought abruptly introduced, unless an underlying conception of the whole is that of Jesus as the *archēgos* or pioneer (A. 3^{15}; 5^{31}; Heb. 2^{10}; 12^2), who blazes the trail to the heavenly places, the healings then being the beneficent labours which, like Heracles, he performs, and for which his reward is apotheosis (cf. Heb. $5^{2ff.}$; A. 10^{38} for the healings as the works of a *euergetēs* = 'benefactor', a word applied to Heracles and the like.[l] (iii) As a middle, 'I come to my end (goal)'. The other two instances of the verb in L–A – 2^{43} (cf. 22^{37}) and A. 20^{24} – suggest this as the most likely meaning, as does *the third day*, if this is continuous with *today and tomorrow*, and not a cryptic reference to the resurrection. Despite Herod's threats the ministry will go on, and nothing will stop it short of its (appointed) end.

33
Nevertheless . . . away from Jerusalem: The strong adversative *plēn* (*nevertheless*) introduces a modification of the thought in v. 32 by means of a statement with similar wording but different content and orientation. Jesus is here a self-confessed prophet, and the scope of his ministry is by implication extended beyond healing. The journey is now that of an itinerant prophet; but prophets are inevitably put to death by God's people to whom they are sent (A. $7^{51f.}$); and where else than in Jerusalem, God's city? Hence the journey of the prophet must be to Jerusalem. *It cannot be* (*endechetai* + +, a literary word found in the

k *Synoptische Studien*, ed. J. Schmid and A. Vogtle, Munich 1953, pp. 42ff.
l See W. L. Knox, 'The Divine Hero Christology in the New Testament', *HTR* 41, 1948, pp. 229–49.

papyri, but in the LXX only at II Macc. 11[18]) *that a prophet should perish away from Jerusalem* expresses in semi-proverbial form the same pessimistic and ironical standpoint as v. 34. If there is any journeying to be done (v. 31, *Get away from here*), it is simply in the course of travelling *en route* to Jerusalem (10[38]; 22[22]; A. 9[3]). And if there is any dying to be done, it is not at the hands of the secular ruler, but a prophetic death within the paradoxical divine purpose. And it is because he is on his destined way, and not for Herod's threats, that he leaves Herod's territory.

13[34-35]   APOSTROPHE OF JERUSALEM

[34]'*O Jerusalem, Jerusalem, killing the prophets and stoning those who are sent to you! How often would I have gathered your children together as a hen gathers her brood under her wings, and you would not!* [35]*Behold, your house is forsaken. And I tell you, you will not see me until you say, "Blessed be he who comes in the name of the Lord." '*

Apart from minor differences this is in exact agreement with Matt. 23[37-39], including such oddities in the Greek as *autēn* (v. 34a) = 'her' (RSV *you*), and *ouk ēthelēsate* = 'you would not', a second person plural with a singular subject (Jerusalem). Such agreement requires derivation from a common written source (Q), its place in which is not easily envisaged (see Knox, *Sources* II, p. 83n). The promise that Jerusalem will not see the speaker again (*ap' arti* = 'from now on', Matt. 23[39], not in Luke) fits the Matthaean context, where Jesus bids farewell to the city before his death, and looks to the parousia as the time when it will see him again. In Luke the apostrophe follows on well, with *killing the prophets* picking up v. 33, and it provides an impressive ending to the discourse. The context is, however, artificial in the extreme. For the apostrophe loses much of its force when not spoken in or near the city, and when *you will not see me until* refers simply to the end of the present journey; and in following without break after vv. 32-33 it is with difficulty prevented from appearing to be part of the message to Herod.

The apostrophe is in three parts – a historical retrospect (v. 34), a prophecy of desolation (v. 35a) and a promise of visitation (v. 35b); but they are not a tightly knit unity.

34

Jerusalem, Jerusalem: The name is duplicated, as often in apostrophes.

killing the prophets and stoning those who are sent to you: This characterization, while less sweeping than v. 33, is very bitter. This bitterness can be seen emerging in Christian polemic as a consequence of the crucifixion of Jesus and the persecution of Christians by the Jerusalem authorities (A. 7^{52}; I Thess. 2^{15}; Rom. 11^3; Rev. 11^8; 16^6; 18^{24}). But it could predate this if the legends of the martyrdoms of the prophets, which are now preserved in Christian texts, go back to Jewish originals emanating from pessimistic Jewish circles (see *Beginnings* IV, p. 82, and Heb. 11^{37}). Stoning does not refer to lynching, but to the official manner of execution in Israel for heinous offences against God and his law. Thus the perversity of Jerusalem, God's city, consists in excommunicating God's prophets (for the prophets as those *sent*, cf. Jer. 7^{25}) from God's community as idolaters or blasphemers.

How often would I have gathered your children together . . . and you would not!: The speaker refers to his repeated intention to gather together (to bring to salvation in blessed community) Jerusalem's *children*, an unusual expression, denoting perhaps not simply the actual inhabitants, but all Jews as belonging to the mother-city. What is meant by this? Taken in conjunction with v. 35b it has been understood to refer to visits to Jerusalem of Jesus himself which have gone unrecorded in the synoptists (there are three such in John). This is very unlikely. A widespread view is that v. 34 is cast in the mould of a wisdom saying, and is either an utterance of Wisdom put into the mouth of Jesus, or a genuine utterance of Jesus speaking as Wisdom or as one of her messengers. Comparison has been made with other sayings (e.g. 11^{49} = Matt. 23^{34}) as evidence of a Wisdom christology in Q (see Bultmann, *History*, pp. 114f., *TDNT* VII, p. 515; Suggs, *Wisdom Christology and Law in Matthew's Gospel*, pp. 63ff.). But it is unlikely that a wisdom saying would be introduced by reference to the sending and rejection of the prophets, or that Wisdom's visitations would be represented as a repeated mission. The saying is not couched in terms of what Wisdom was expected to do, i.e. to seek, but in vain, a dwelling place among men (Ecclus 24$^{7-12}$; Wisd. 7$^{27f.}$; I Enoch 42), but in terms of God's gathering of the dispersed Jews to salvation, peace and blessed life in Sion. The key word is *gathered (episunagein)*. This is never used of the functions of Wisdom, but is the regular word for the hope of God's restoration: Ps. 106^{47}; 147^2 ('The Lord builds up Jerusalem, he gathers the outcasts of Israel'); Isa. 27^{12}; 52^{12} LXX ('the God of Israel, he who gathers you'); Jer. 31$^{8ff.}$; Zech. 2$^{6ff.}$ (LXX), II Macc. 1^{27} (in a prayer); 2^{18} ('he will gather us into the holy place'). The verb is used with 'your children' and 'house' in Isa. 60$^{4-9}$, with 'house' alone in Isa. 56^7, and with 'children' in John 11^{52}. Here this gathering together is illustrated by the familiar figure of a bird gathering her brood under her wings for safety and protection. Thus the statement is most intelligible if God is the speaker, and the reference is to the successive missions of the prophets for judgment and salvation (cf. Jer. 25⁴ff· where the rejection of the prophets has the result of God's scattering of Israel). In that case the utterance may originally have been that of a Christian prophet speaking in God's name.

35

Behold, your house is forsaken: The apostrophe now passes into prophecy (*is forsaken, aphietai,* is a present with a future sense), introduced by *Behold.* The consequence of repeated refusal is now the desolation of Jerusalem's house. This is similar to OT statements (e.g. Jer. 12⁷; 22⁵), but does not appear to be a direct quotation. The association of *house* = 'temple' with prophecies of the destruction and restoration of Jerusalem (Jer. 7¹¹; 26⁶; Ezek. 9⁶f·) might suggest that here also the destruction of the temple is being prophesied (cf. Jos. *BJ* 6.301ff., of the peasant who proclaimed doom in the form of 'woe to the city, and to the people and to the temple'). But *your house* would be unprecedented for the temple, which is God's house (19⁴⁶), and no clear sense would then be given to *is forsaken* (the Greek means 'is left'; hence the addition in some mss of *erēmos* = 'empty' from Jer. 22⁵). Here *house* may be a synonym for *your children* in v. 34, i.e. household. Since it refuses to be gathered (by God), it will be abandoned to its own devices.

And I tell you, you will not see me . . . : The apostrophe concludes with a prophecy connecting Jerusalem and the speaker. Its connection with v. 35a is not close, and it may have been an independent saying, which is placed here by verbal connection, in that Ps. 118²⁶, the blessing of the one *who comes in the name of the Lord,* is uttered in the psalm 'from the house of the Lord'. Its original sense will have depended on its context, which is hardly now recoverable. For the Gospel's readers it can only refer prophetically to the events of 19³⁷ff·, even if there it is disciples only who make this acclamation, though for Luke they do so as representatives of 'the people' of Jerusalem, whom he presents throughout as Jesus' supporters.

until you say: This adds to the obscurity in Luke. *until: heōs hēxei hote* = literally 'until it (he?) shall come when'. This is awkward, and has led to variants, including the simpler *heōs an* = 'until', as in Matt. 23³⁹.

Blessed is he who comes in the name of the Lord: The psalm quoted is one of the Hallel psalms which figure at Passover, Pentecost, Dedication and, especially, Tabernacles, and attempts have been made to locate the context by reference to one or other of these feasts. A suggestion of Goguel that the words were spoken after an unsuccessful sojourn in Jerusalem at Tabernacles, and referred to a promised return to the city at Passover, is dismissed by Manson (*Sayings*, p. 128) on the ground that this would be a 'high-falutin' way of conveying a very prosaic piece of information'. He himself, on the basis of the connection of the psalm with Tabernacles, and of the tenor of the prophetic lections from Zechariah concerning the universal kingdom associated with this feast, took it to refer to the final consummation, with the implication, as in the Matthaean context, that it would then be too late. Manson's criticism could be made of his own later suggestion[m] that the saying in the Lukan context was intended to indicate to the Galilean audience that the Galilean ministry was over, and that they would not meet again until the next festival (with the added difficulty of an abrupt change from *your house* = Jerusalem to *you* = Galileans). Kümmel (*Promise and Fulfilment*, pp. 81f.) sees it as a solemn statement that 'the temple is to be deprived of Jesus' presence, and with this is connected the prophecy that Jesus will remain invisible to the Jews until they can greet him as messiah'. *see me* would then refer to apocalyptic vision and not literal sight (21^{27}); but the festival acclamation would be a peculiar way of expressing what is to happen at the parousia, and this is hardly what the words can mean in Luke's context, where Jesus is on a literal journey to Jerusalem.

14 *Healing and Teaching at a Meal; Discipleship*

Chapter 14 is a unity, with a fresh setting (v. 1) and an emphatic conclusion (vv. 34–35). It is evidently a composition made out of disparate, though superficially similar, materials. Artificiality at certain points indicates that these materials had not always belonged together in a single source, and if Luke is the compiler he will have arranged them according to his conception of the ministry of Jesus. Another meal in the house of a Pharisee (cf. 7^{36}; 11^{37}), perhaps here deduced from *places of honour* (v. 8, cf. 20^{46}; Mark 12^{39}), provides an audience of *lawyers and Pharisees*, i.e. theologians and the pious (cf. 7^{30}; 11^{53}; only Luke has this combination), for a sabbath healing performed in the face of hostility, and for teaching which has 'dining' as its common theme. Verbal links are supplied, chiefly in various parts of the verb *kalein* = 'to invite' (vv. 7, 8, 10, 12, 16, 17, 24), in *when you* (vv. 8, 12), *sit at table* (vv. 10, 15), *the poor . . . blind* (vv. 13, 21), *blessed* (v. 14, v. 15), and in the compound verbs *reply* (*antapokrinesthai* = 'to reply in return' +

m 'The Cleansing of the Temple', *BJRL* 33, 1950–51, p. 279n.

Rom. 9²⁰) *invite in return* (*antikalein* ++) and *repaid* (*antapodidonai* = 'to give in return', only Luke in the gospels). At v. 25 the audience changes to crowds (cf. 12¹) for teaching on discipleship in a closely knit unit (*for*, v. 28, *so therefore*, *oun*, v. 33, repeated, though not rendered by RSV, in v. 34). This is composed of twin parables (vv. 28–32), enclosed between two longer and two shorter sayings arranged chiastically (vv. 26, 27 and vv. 33, 34f.). A connecting link with what has preceded is provided by the kinsfolk in v. 26, who have been introduced in v. 12 along with friends and neighbours to provide an antithesis to the poor. This composition has similarities with ch. 13 in having a sabbath healing, twin parables, a change of audience, and a section on true discipleship following teaching on the inclusiveness of the kingdom (cf. the relation of 14²⁵ᶠᶠ· to 14¹⁵⁻²⁴ with that of 13²²⁻³⁰ to 13¹⁸⁻²¹).

14¹⁻²⁴   HEALING AND TEACHING AT A MEAL

14 *One sabbath when he went to dine at the house of a ruler who belonged to the Pharisees, they were watching him. ²And behold, there was a man before him who had dropsy. ³And Jesus spoke to the lawyers and Pharisees, saying, 'Is it lawful to heal on the sabbath, or not?' ⁴But they were silent. Then he took him and healed him, and let him go. ⁵And he said to them, 'Which of you, having an ass* or an ox that has fallen into a well, will not immediately pull him out on a sabbath day?' ⁶And they could not reply to this.*

⁷Now he told a parable to those who were invited, when he marked how they chose the places of honour, saying to them, ⁸'When you are invited by any one to a marriage feast, do not sit down in a place of honour, lest a more eminent man than you be invited by him; ⁹and he who invited you both will come, and say to you, "Give place to this man," and then you will begin with shame to take the lowest place. ¹⁰But when you are invited, go and sit in the lowest place, so that when your host comes he may say to you, "Friend, go up higher"; then you will be honoured in the presence of all who sit at table with you. ¹¹For every one who exalts himself will be humbled, and he who humbles himself will be exalted.'

¹²He said also to the man who had invited him, 'When you give a dinner or a banquet, do not invite your friends or your brothers or your kinsmen or rich neighbours, lest they also invited you in return, and you be repaid. ¹³*But when you give a feast, invite the poor, the maimed, the lame, the blind,* ¹⁴*and you will be blessed, because they cannot repay you. You will be repaid at the resurrection of the just.'*

¹⁵*When one of those who sat at table with him heard this, he said to him, 'Blessed is he who shall eat bread in the kingdom of God!'* ¹⁶*But he said to him, 'A man once gave a great banquet, and invited many;* ¹⁷*and at the time for the banquet he sent his servant to say to those who had been invited, "Come; for all is now ready."* ¹⁸*But they all alike began to make excuses. The first said to him, "I have bought a field, and I must go out and see it; I pray you, have me excused."* ¹⁹*And another said, "I have bought five yoke of oxen, and I go to examine them; I pray you, have me excused."* ²⁰*And another said, "I have married a wife, and therefore I cannot come."* ²¹*So the servant came and reported this to his master. Then the householder in anger said to his servant, "Go out quickly to the streets and lanes of the city, and bring in the poor and maimed and blind and lame."* ²²*And the servant said, "Sir, what you commanded has been done, and still there is room."* ²³*And the master said to the servant, "Go out to the highways and hedges, and compel people to come in, that my house may be filled.* ²⁴*For I tell you, none of those men who were invited shall taste my banquet."* '

* Other ancient authorities read *a son*

The fact that this account of a sabbath healing (vv. 1–6) is the third (cf. 6^{6-11}; 13^{10-17}) shows the importance Luke attached to the subject. A sabbath meal in a private house is not, however, a very convincing setting for a healing, and Luke could have provided it both for the saying in v. 5 and for the table-talk in vv. 7–24.

ৰুৰ

1

went to dine: As already apparent from 5^{29}; 7^{36}; 9^{16}; 10^{39}; 11^{37}, the setting of a meal for actions and sayings of Jesus, while not necessarily in all cases historically reliable, was for Luke theologically significant. It could be so in the Jewish world, where religious conversation was engaged in at table – for the place of meals in Jewish piety, and for rabbinic parallels to the idea of 'invitation' to the blessings of salvation, see SB I, pp. 878f., IV, pp. 1154ff., and more generally *TDNT* II, pp. 34f. It could also be so in the Hellenistic world, where symposia offered opportunity for philosophical discussion, and meals could be held in temples.

a ruler who belonged to the Pharisees: The Greek could mean 'a member of the Sanhedrin who was a Pharisee'; but in L–A 'ruler' can have a less precise sense than a member of the Sanhedrin, and Luke may have thought that what in A. 15^5; 26^5 he calls 'the party' of the Pharisees had rulers (cf. Jos., *Life* 21, 'the chief men of the Pharisees'). This would give a representative character to the opposition in this final case of sabbath healing, and for Luke the necessary polemical setting for the sayings in vv. 7–24 as he understood them.

2–6

Apart from the detail *who had dropsy* the story is conventionally told, and could have been modelled on 6$^{6ff.}$. Formal elements are the hostile expectancy of the audience that a healing would take place (here at the beginning, *they were watching him*, cf. 6^7), the unexplained presence of the man, presumably an intruder (*let him go*, v. 4), and Jesus' knowledge of their unspoken thoughts (cf. 6^8). Evidence of Luke's hand may be seen in v. 1 – literally 'It came to pass in his going to dine ... and they were watching' – in *a certain man, before him (emprosthen* as in 5^{19} correcting Mark), *lawyers and Pharisees, they were silent (hēsuchazein* + 23^{56}; A. 11^{18}; 21^{14}; I Thess. 4^{11}), *took him (epilambanesthai)*, which is Lukan, as are *healed (iāsthai)*, *let go (apoluein)*, *could not (ischuein* = 'to have the strength') and *antapokrinesthai* for *reply*. This suggests that Luke was the first to commit the story to writing. If so the decision to begin with it here will have been his choice, and this increases the probability that the whole chapter is his composition.

3

Is it lawful to heal on the sabbath, or not: This question before the healing (some mss omit *or not*), together with that after the healing (v. 5), bring together in a single incident the separate issues in the two previous sabbath healings (cf. Matt. 12$^{9-14}$, rewriting Mark 3$^{1-6}$). Here the question may be not simply whether the law forbade it, but whether the sabbath was not the proper day for healing (cf. 6^9 = Mark 3^4).

5

This second question is more decisive (*And he said to them*). It appeals to human behaviour as a precedent. It could be an isolated question, as in Matt. 12^{11}, and 13^{15} could be a third version of it. In having *ox* it resembles 13^{15} (Matthew has 'sheep'), but in all other respects it is nearer to Matt. 12^{11}, both in the interrogative form, which in Luke is more compactly phrased, as is also the conditional sentence, and in the picture of the rescue of an animal fallen into a *well* (in Matthew 'a pit' – contrast watering the animal in 13^{15}). It may have been taken from a source common to Luke and Matthew. But the text is uncertain. (i) *an ass or an ox* (so RSV) is read by ℵ fi f13 and others, some mss of the Latin and Coptic versions: (ii) *a son or an ox* (so RSV margin) is read by p^{45} ^{75}B W 28 and some mss of the Latin and Coptic versions. There are other readings dependent on (i) and (ii), or due to conflation with Matt. 12¹¹. If the background of the question is the law of Deut. 22¹⁻⁴ (cf. Exod. 21³³ᶠ·) that a man should recover his brother's sheep, ox or ass, then, in the case of more than one animal being specified, 'ox or ass' is to be expected as the usual combination (cf. 13¹⁵), or 'ass or ox' as in Deut. 22⁴. This may have produced (i) above. On the other hand 'son' is out of place, either by reference to any OT text, or as an alternative to an animal. It is not so much a harder reading as an incongruous one, the origin of which is difficult to explain. It might perhaps have been introduced because the question is not followed, as in 13¹⁶; Matt. 12¹², by an a fortiori argument that men are more important than animals (see on 13¹⁵ᶠ·). Black (*Aramaic Approach*, p. 126) proposes an original 'Which of you shall have a beast (Aramaic *beʾira*) fallen into a pit (Aramaic *bēra*) . . .?', with the beast being variously explicated as 'sheep', 'ox' or 'ass' in translation, and 'son' arising from a misreading of *beʾira* as *bᵉra* = 'son'. This could account for variations between the Matthaean and Lukan versions, but hardly for variations in the Greek mss of Luke.

6

This conclusion (cf. Luke's addition at 20²⁶) shows the unit to be really a conflict story and the healing for the sake of the pronouncement. The theological issue is decisively settled, and the opponents are reduced to complete silence.

7–11   *To the Guests a Parable about Guests*

This is somewhat artificial, as from now on Jesus behaves not as a guest but as the one in control. The meal is simply a setting for what he has to say to all and sundry, which, if it was spoken in this setting, can hardly have been heard by disciples.

The origins and intention of vv. 8–10 are puzzling. They have the character of the wisdom literature. The teaching is a piece of worldly wisdom of general application – *when you are invited to a marriage feast* (cf. Matt. 22²) – and does not refer specifically to the meal at which Jesus is speaking. It could be based on Prov. 25⁶⁻⁷, 'Do not put yourself forward in the king's presence or stand in the place of the great; for it is better to be told, "Come up here," than to be put lower in the presence of the prince.' *go up higher* would then mean 'Come up here to me' (i.e. to the chief seat, Field, *Notes*, pp. 66f.). The appeal is to dread of social embarrassment and desire for social esteem as motives of conduct. The rabbis used the Proverbs passage to teach that self-abasement is exaltation, and vice versa. Luke calls the teaching a parable, i.e. it conveys gospel truth, but he can only turn it into such by adding in conclusion a form of the gospel paradox of lofty and lowly (cf. 18¹⁴), which draws a general religious lesson (*for* in v. 11 is *hoti* = 'because'). The guest does not have to be promoted from, or demoted to, *the lowest place* (v. 10), and these words may reflect the gospel paradox in its extreme form, 'the last shall become first and the first last' (13³⁰). Here this truth

14$^{1-24}$

is made a rebuke of certain Pharisees or of certain Pharisaic behaviour – *when he marked* (*epechein* + A. 3⁵; 19²²; Phil. 2¹⁶; I Tim. 4¹⁶, generally means 'to hold toward', 'to aim at', and only here has the reduced sense of 'to notice').

12–14   *To the Host an Instruction on the True Host*
This is probably not intended as a continuation of the parable in vv. 7–11 and should be a new paragraph. The context is artificial as the teaching is general (*when you give*, v. 12), and has no connection with what precedes except a certain contrast between lofty and lowly. It is essentially that of 6³²ᶠᶠ· expressed concretely and emphatically in terms of hospitality. This is done in two carefully balanced sentences, each with four clauses and four kinds of guests. But the second tetrad (*poor . . . blind*, v. 13) is more in place in the following parable as an antithesis – the riff-raff in contrast to honoured guests (v. 21) – and it may have been imported from there. If taken along with v. 21 the injunction in v. 13 could mean 'Invite in the same way as God does.' The first tetrad (v. 12) may then have been expanded to match the second; for *your brothers or your kinsmen* prepare for v. 26, and are not a natural antithesis to *the poor . . . blind*. In v. 12 *rich* before *neighbours* stands out as the only adjective in the injunctions (D has 'neighbours nor rich'), and originally the contrast may have been the more simple one between inviting the rich, who can make return, and the poor, who cannot.

12
a dinner: ariston, which, apart from 11³⁸, is found in the NT only at Matt. 22⁴, in his version of the parable which follows here in vv. 16–24.

invite: In the Greek *phōnein* = 'to summon'. This is not found elsewhere in the sense of 'invite', and may have been suggested by the summoning of already invited guests in the following parable (v. 17).

14
This verse lifts the wisdom sayings on human behaviour in vv. 8–14a to a more spiritual plane. Those actions will secure ultimate divine approval (*you will be repaid* is the 'divine' passive, and means 'God will repay you'), and the blessed life of the kingdom (*you will be blessed*, cf. 6²⁰), which are such as completely to exclude calculation on the human level (*lest they also invite you in return*, v. 12; *they cannot repay you*, v. 14), and are thereby total in their commitment (cf. Matt. 5⁴³–6¹⁸).

the resurrection of the just: This term appears here for the first time in Greek, though it corresponds to a Jewish expression. There was no fixed orthodoxy in Jewish thought at this time on resurrection. Opinions wavered between the positive conception that resurrection was to the enjoyment of eternal life, and so was only for those (Israelites) judged to be righteous, and the more neutral

14^{1-24}

conception that resurrection was for the purposes of judgment, and so for all (see SB IV, pp. 1166ff.). It is not clear whether here it is the former (cf. 20^{36}, Luke's addition to Mark), or the positive half of what is said in A. 24^{15} to be the hope of Israel, viz. the resurrection of the righteous and the unrighteous (cf. Rev. $20^{12ff.}$; John $5^{28f.}$).

15–24 To Fellow Diners a Parable on the Feast of the Kingdom
15

The link with what precedes is provided by a pious, perhaps conventional, ejaculation from one of the company. In the context it arises from what has just been heard (*Blessed is he . . . in the kingdom of God*, cf. *blessed . . . at the resurrection of the just*, v. 14). This is unlikely to have been preserved in oral tradition, and could have been provided by Luke (cf. 9^{57}; $11^{27, 45}$; 12^{13}; 13^{23}). The following parable is only to a limited extent a reply to the remark. For the kingdom of God under the figure of a banquet, see on 13^{29}; 'the bread of the age to come' was a rabbinic expression belonging to it.

16–24

The parable, not expressly so called, is evidently the same as that in Matt. 22^{1-10}. There is the same general contrast between two classes of people, those who exclude themselves from the feast, and those who are included as substitutes. There are also details in common in the invitation followed by a message to those *invited* that the feast is *ready*, the refusal of the summons by all, the *anger* of the host, and the gathering in from the streets so that the feast shall be full. The differences are, however, so substantial that considerable interpretative developments of an original story must be presupposed in each case, whether before it reached the evangelist or at his hands. The question frequently arises whether details in each version are allegorical, and are to be taken as indications of what had given rise to these developments. There is a third version in the Gospel of Thomas (64), which in form and content is close to Luke's, though not certainly derived from it.[n] It has a man send a single servant to summon guests to a banquet he has prepared, and they ask to be excused. The excuses, which are four, overlap, though are not identical with, those in Luke, and are more elaborated; and the inclusion of those from the streets is said to be because 'the buyers and the merchants shall not come into the places of my Father'.

16

A man once gave a great banquest: In Matt. 22^2 the parable is expressly of the kingdom in the more rabbinic mode of a king making a marriage feast for his son.

---

[n] For the text see K. Aland, *Synopsis Quattuor Evangeliorum*, Stuttgart 1964, p. 525, and for a discussion H. E. W. Turner and H. Montefiore, *Thomas and the Evangelists*, SBT 35, 1962, pp. 61f.

♦ In Luke context and conclusion show that he understood it as a parable of the future kingdom (*Blessed is he who shall eat . . .* v. 15, picked up in *shall taste of my banquet*, v. 24), to which there is an invitation in the present.

17

He sent his servant to say to those who had been invited: The etiquette of issuing invitations which are then taken up by a subsequent summons was widespread. For the oriental world, see Esther 6^{14}; for the Hellenistic world, Philo, *Creation of the World*, 78, 'Just as givers of a banquet do not send out a summons to supper until they have put everything in readiness for the feast'; for the Roman world, which had a technical term for the servant sent out, *vocator*, Pliny, *Natural History* 35.89, 'He showed his summoners, so as to say by whom he was invited.' If the point is to be pressed in the parable, it could refer to an invitation to God's kingdom already present in his election of Israel, which is now further implemented by the summons of Jesus to Israel with the message, *Come, because things are now ready* ('all' is absent from some mss, and is probably an assimilation to Matt. 22^4). *now* is in the Greek *ēdē* = 'already', which, if pressed, could refer to the mission of Jesus as the beginning of the eschatological age before it was expected. In Matthew the summons is delivered, more naturally in view of the large numbers contemplated, by many servants; in Luke, less naturally, by a single servant, which might also be an allegorical reference to Jesus himself.

18a

all alike: In Greek *apo mias* = 'from one' (feminine), not attested elsewhere. To judge from parallels the feminine noun to be supplied is either *phōnē* = 'voice' or *gnōmē* = 'mind'. Jeremias (*Parables*, pp. 178ff.) regards such a refusal by all as absurd, and explains it as based on a story in the Talmud of a rich tax-collector, whose splendid funeral is justified by his having performed one good deed just before his death, in that having given a banquet for the city aldermen, when all refused to come, he summoned the poor to eat it, so that food should not be wasted. But the element of the absurd is not infrequent in Jesus' parables, and could have been necessary here in order to present refusal and acceptance, exclusion and inclusion, in black and white terms.

18b–20

Here Luke and Matthew diverge considerably. In Matt. 22^{3-6} the rejection of the summons is given in extended form as, first, a point blank refusal; and then, on its renewal through other servants with a more detailed announcement, as disregard of it by some who have better things to do in farm and business, and as abuse and murder of the servants by the remainder. Here Matthew's version ceases to be a parable, is assimilated to the parable of the Wicked Husbandmen (Matt. 21^{33-46}), and becomes an allegory of the treatment of the prophets. In

Luke the summons is met by excuses, of which three are specified, according to the rule of three in parables. The first two – the necessity to inspect a field or five yoke of oxen recently bought – are expressed in polished form with a co-ordination of direct address, *I pray you, have me excused* (cf. 8²⁸; 9³⁸; A. 21³⁹), in which *have* (*echein* = 'to have' in the sense of 'to count as') is followed by the passive participle of *paraiteisthai*, only here in the NT in the sense of 'to excuse'. The third, *I have married a wife, and therefore I cannot come*, is more peremptory.

Jeremias (*Parables*, pp. 176f.) deduces, but improbably, from the *five yoke of oxen* that all the guests are wealthy (so making a connection with v. 12), and that the motive of the refusal was the desire to snub an upstart. E. Linnemann⁰ holds the third excuse to be an addition on account of its difference in form, and takes the first two as requests to be allowed to come late; but this would hardly explain the wrath of the host. More plausible, in view of the strong echoes of Deuteronomy in this section of the Gospel, is the parallel drawn with passages containing regulations for the holy war to be waged by Israel (Deut. 20⁵⁻⁷; 24⁵). In these there are exemptions from army service for (i) one who has built a house but not dedicated it, (ii) one who has planted a vineyard but not enjoyed its fruit, and (iii) a man betrothed to a wife who has not taken her (cf. Deut. 24⁵, 'When a man is newly married, he shall not go out with the army or be charged with any business'). All these are to prevent another man supplanting him. Of these (iii) appears in Luke, and (ii) could do so if *field* (v. 18) were allowed to stand for 'vineyard'.ᵖ The weakness of this parallel is that the excuses would then be valid, being contained in the law (*I cannot come* could mean 'I am forbidden by the law to come'). They could then only be made grounds for the host's wrath if it is to be supposed that there are now conditions of such absolute urgency that even the regulations of the law are no longer valid. (In his elaborate use of the holy war regulations and rabbinic literature as explanatory of the parable, Derrett (*Law in the NT*, ch. 6) is concerned primarily with Matthew's version, which alone refers to any military action, but from which these Deuteronomic excuses are absent). While couched in scriptural language of permissible exemptions from duty, the excuses are probably intended, when taken together, to show the power of economic and social attachments to stand in the way of answering the summons to the kingdom.

21

Then the householder in anger said: In Matthew the host's anger at the refusal takes the form of military action to destroy the now murderous guests and their city,

---

o *Parables of Jesus*, ET London (= *The Jesus of the Parables*, New York) 1967, pp. 88ff., 158ff.

p There is rabbinic evidence for the extension of the exemption beyond a vine-yard – see P. H. Ballard, 'Reasons for Refusing the Great Supper', *JTS*, ns 23, 1972, pp. 341ff.

after which, the delayed feast being still ready, an invitation is issued to others. This violent mixture of metaphor wrecks the parable still further, and turns it into a Christian allegory of the judgment of God upon Israel. In Luke the host's angry response takes the form of a double invitation of substitute guests. This is also likely to reflect development of an original story of two invitations, one leading to exclusion and the other to inclusion, as in Matthew.

the poor and maimed and blind and lame: The despised in Israel, to be found in the streets and lanes of the city. They are the objects of the invitation of Jesus, who, on his rejection of the pious in Israel, preaches to the outcast.

23
Go out to the highways and hedges: This invitation is that of the church which preaches to the Gentiles, represented by the vagrants to be found in the roads leading to the city (Matt. 22⁹ has an expression which could mean 'the exits of the roads'), and in the hedges around the vineyards. The extreme urgency of this is expressed by *compel* (*anankazein* = 'to force', or, in a weakened sense, 'to urge strongly'). It is not said that this order is carried into effect, perhaps because the Gentile mission is still in train.

that my house may be filled: Possibly an allegorical touch indicating the pre-destined number of the elect, as it is not incumbent on an earthly host to fill his house.

24
The parable ends on the negative note that those who refused the original invitation shall not partake of the feast. There will be no second chance for the pious in Israel. This is plainly allegorical, as the householder speaking to his single servant (vv. 21–23) merges without break into Jesus speaking to the audience – *For I tell you* (*humin* in the Greek is plural) – and the feast and the house are now called his (*my house*, v. 23, *my banquet*, v. 24; cf. Rev. 19⁹). Moreover, those excluded are no longer asking to come in, as in 13²⁵ᶠᶠ·. It remains unclear what precise situation the parable, even if reduced to two invitations, reflects, and whether Jesus is telling it at the end of his ministry in the light of his rejection by Israel, and with a mission to the despised already accomplished, or at some point in the ministry in anticipation of the way things will go.

²⁵*Now great multitudes accompanied him; and he turned and said to them,* ²⁶'*If any one comes to me and does not hate his own father and mother and wife and children and brothers and sisters, yes, and even his own life, he cannot be my disciple.* ²⁷*Whoever does not bear his own cross and come after me, cannot be my disciple.* ²⁸*For which of you, desiring to build a tower, does not first sit down and count the cost, whether he has enough to complete it?* ²⁹*Otherwise, when he has laid a foundation, and is not able to finish, all who see it begin to mock him,* ³⁰*saying, "This man began to build, and was not able to finish."* ³¹*Or what king, going to encounter another king in war, will not sit down first and take counsel whether he is able with ten thousand to meet him who comes against him with twenty thousand?* ³²*And if not, while the other is yet a great way off, he sends an embassy and asks terms of peace.* ³³*So therefore, whoever of you does not renounce all that he has cannot be my disciple.*

³⁴'*Salt is good; but if salt has lost its taste, how shall its saltness be restored?* ³⁵*It is fit neither for the land nor for the dunghill; men throw it away. He who has ears to hear, let him hear.*'

The application of the previous parable to Jesus himself (v. 24) prepares for this section on the requirements for discipleship of Jesus, which is now integral to entering the kingdom. Since the lawyers and Pharisees of v. 3 are by implication excluded as possible disciples a fresh audience is needed. This Luke supplies with *great multitudes*, whom he represents as Jesus' fellow travellers to Jerusalem. The immediate connection of the section is with vv. 18–20, the requirements for discipleship being stated in terms of the social and economic attachments which prevent response to the invitation to the kingdom. But there is also a necessary corrective to a possible misunderstanding of the previous parable as teaching that those who enter the kingdom do so simply because they are destitute, and not as those who have made, or are able to make, the response that others have not been able to make (cf. Matthew's addition to the parable of the Wedding Garment, Matt. 22¹¹⁻¹⁴, to deal with the same issue).

The contents here are of different kinds and origins, and may have been woven into a single unit by Luke. The two sayings in vv. 26–27 are also found in combination in Matt. 10³⁷⁻³⁸, and could come from Q. Luke's version is more rhythmical, consisting of two sentences (Matthew has three) bound together by *cannot be my disciple* (Matthew 'is not worthy of me'). But while the single sentence in v. 26 may be more original in form (*if anyone . . . does not*) than Matthew's two sentences with participial construction ('he who . . .'), it is overloaded by having three separate pairs (Matthew, two reciprocal pairs), and by the inclusion of *wife* along with children, and of *his own life* to form a tetrad. Verse 27 is in the negative form, *Whoever does not . . .* (contrast Mark 8³⁴, 'If any man would . . . let him'). The twin parables in vv. 28–32 (cf. 13¹⁸⁻²¹; 15⁴⁻¹⁰) are peculiar to Luke. They are closely parallel, though not identical, in form. The second is shorter than the first, and is brought to the length of the first by the addition of v. 33 to round off both parables (*So therefore*). Both syntax and vocabulary suggest that Luke was the first to commit them to writing. Thus, the following are expressed idiomatically by participles in the Greek – *desiring, sit down, when he has laid* (*thentos themelion*, gen. abs. with assonance), *who see, saying, going, sit down, who comes, is, sends, that he has*. Notable in the vocabulary are: *count* (*psēphizein* = 'to calculate', + Rev. 13¹⁸, not LXX), *cost* (*dapanē* ++), *has enough to* (*echein eis* ++), *complete it* (the very rare verbal noun *apartismos* ++ = 'for the completion'), *is not able* (*ischuein* = 'to have the strength'), *to finish* (*ektelein* ++), *this man* (cf. A. 6¹³; 22²⁶), *going to war* (*poreuomenos* = 'on his way to', the verb is Lukan), *to encounter . . . in war* (*sumballein eis polemon*, a literary expression), *take counsel* (*bouleuesthai* + twice in John and A., and II Cor. 1¹⁷), *embassy* (*presbeia* + 19¹⁴). The section is rounded off (v. 34 has in the Greek *oun* = 'then') by a variant version of the sayings on salt which Luke omitted in their Markan context (Mark 9⁴⁹⁻⁵⁰), and by the solemn *He who has ears to hear, let him hear*, which he omitted from his version of Mark 4²³.

ॐ

26

If anyone . . . does not hate . . .: This may be an example of the Semitic expression of preference by means of antithesis – 'I love A and hate B' meaning 'I prefer A to B' (cf. Gen. 29³⁰ᶠᶠ·; Deut. 21¹⁵; Rom. 9¹³) – which has been altered, but correctly interpreted, in the Matthaean form (Matt. 10³⁷). But in view of the sweeping nature of v. 33, and the addition here of *wife* (cf. a similar addition to Mark in 18²⁹), it may express Luke's rigorous outlook.

yes, and even his own life: This also may be Luke's addition (*yes, and even, eti de kai* + A. 21²⁸ is literary). It is all-embracing rather than a fourth worldly tie, and may have been suggested by analogous, but different, sayings, also connected with discipleship, about losing one's life to find it (cf. Matt. 10³⁹; Mark 8³⁴ᶠ· and pars).

27

does not bear his own cross: The Greek verb rendered *bear* (*bastazein*) can mean either 'to take up' (so John 10³¹, the equivalent of *lambanein* in Matt. 10³⁸), or, more commonly, 'to carry' (of the cross, John 19¹⁷). This makes a different point. It does not belong with the renunciation of particular worldly ties, but with the command to hate one's own life, with which it seems to have been linked in the tradition (cf. Matt. 10³⁸⁻³⁹; John 12²⁵⁻²⁶). Here the Christian doctrine of the cross is stated by means of an extension of the obedience and imitation involved in the relation of pupil (*mathētēs* = disciple) to rabbi (see on 9²³).

28–32

The two parables may be based on the combination of the figures of wise building and wise conduct of war in a biblical text, Prov. 24³⁻⁶, 'By wisdom a house is built, and by understanding it is established ... by wise guidance you can wage your war, and in abundance of counsellors there is victory.' They teach that it is the height of folly, or is courting disaster, to embark upon a (great) enterprise without being as sure as possible in advance of having the resources and the ability to carry it through. They are adjudged by Luke to refer to discipleship; but despite *For* (v. 28) and *So therefore* (v. 33), they do not follow directly from vv. 26–27, where it is a matter of what has to be renounced rather than whether discipleship can in prospect be maintained to the end. They would be in better context at 9⁵⁷⁻⁶², where there are similarities of wording ('let me first ...', 9⁵⁹, ⁶¹), and where would-be disciples are discouraged in advance if divided loyalty makes their entry into discipleship useless. W. Manson (p. 175) interprets them of Jesus himself, who is engaged in a great enterprise, and who must therefore be certain of his disciples if he is to accomplish it; but *which of you* refers the parables directly to the audience, and *So therefore, whoever of you* (v. 33) shows that Luke takes them so.

28

a tower: If the parables are exactly parallel this will be a large construction, as in 13⁴, rather than the watch-tower in a vineyard or farm building, which the Greek word could also denote; though if *which of you* deliberately refers to something within the compass of the audience either of these latter two could be meant.

32

asks terms of peace: The text varies, and with it the precise sense. (i) The majority of mss have *erōtā ta pros eirēnēn* = literally 'asks (requests) the things with respect to peace'. This seems to be a recognized expression; cf. Test. Judah 9⁷, 'They asked from us terms of peace', the same wording with a different verb. (ii) B has *erōtā* (+ *ta* K and others) *eis eirēnēn*; it would be difficult to account for an alteration of *pros* to *eis*, whereas the opposite was possible in view of the established phrase *ta pros eirēnēn* = 'the things pertaining to peace' (19⁴²). (iii) p⁷⁵ has *erōtā eirēnēn* = 'requests peace'. This is the simplest reading (cf. A. 12²⁰, with a different verb), but if original can hardly account for the insertion of either *pros* or *eis*. (ii) has parallels in the LXX, where it renders a Semitic expression meaning 'to ask after the health of', 'to salute' (*eirēnē* = *shalom* in the sense of 'health', 'well-being'), as in II Sam. 8¹⁰; I Chron. 18¹⁰; Ps. 122⁶ (all with the article), and II Sam. 11⁷ (without the article). H. St J. Thackeray argued⁹ on the basis of a reconstructed text in II Sam. 8¹⁰ and of general Semitic and Egyptian usage that the phrase, when used of dealings between kings, took on the meaning 'to surrender', 'to submit to the authority of'. This is doubtful; it is not the meaning in I Chron. 18¹⁰, which is a retelling of II Sam. 8¹⁰, nor in any of the other biblical passages. If the action in v. 32 is to match that in vv. 29–30 in being the object of ridicule, it is because the king, after setting out with such warlike intentions, is compelled, either speedily to ask for peace terms, or lamely to send to offer his respects. In either case *while the other was a great way off* is probably to be stressed. So great is his miscalculation that he comes nowhere near an engagement with the enemy before he realizes it.

33

An isolated saying which could have been first framed by Luke. It has his love of 'all' (*whoever of you* is in the Greek *pās ex humōn* = 'everyone of you'), and *renounce* is the comparatively rare word *apotassesthai* = 'to say good-bye to' + 9⁶¹; A. 18¹⁸; Mark 6⁴⁶; II Cor. 2¹³). Here it serves to enclose the parables within a triad of sayings which have *cannot be my disciple* as their theme, and attempts to interpret them as also teaching complete renunciation. In explicitly demanding absolute poverty as a necessary condition of discipleship it accords with other special Lukan passages (12³³; 6²⁰, ²⁴).

34–35a

These obscure verses have parallels in Matt. 5¹³ and Mark 9⁴⁹⁻⁵⁰, the first certainly, the second possibly, in the context of discipleship. Luke's is the most structured version, with two short sentences enclosing two longer, and with *fit* (*euthetos*, a literary word) *neither for the land nor for the dunghill* as a rhetorical flourish. Basically it is nearer to Matthew's in having an additional sentence

---

q 'A Study of the Parable of the Two Kings', *JTS* 14, 1913, pp. 389ff.

about what happens to savourless salt, which contains 'throw away' and the curious verb for *lost its taste* (*mōrainein* = 'to make foolish', as in the other NT instances (Rom. 1²²; I Cor. 1²⁰). It is slightly assimilated to Mark's in *Salt is good* and in *restored* (*artuein*; Matthew has 'salted', as in the strange 'everyone is salted with fire', Mark 9⁴⁹).

In Mark salt is what men (disciples?) are to have, in Matthew what disciples are. Luke, who has no direct application, appears to waver between the two. The conjunction *oun* in v. 34 (not translated in RSV) may link the salt which is good provided it does not become savourless with the character of the true disciple, who renounces all and is able to maintain discipleship to the end.

But of what is salt the symbol? (i) In Ecclus 39²⁶ it is listed among the necessities of life, which are 'good things for the godly'. Its necessity lay perhaps – though this is nowhere expressly stated – in its capacity to preserve other things from going bad. This could be why *Salt is good*, and why it is especially useless if it loses this capacity, which cannot be renewed from any other source. (ii) Salt came to be associated with sacrifice, and was prescribed in various offerings (Lev. 2¹³; Ezek. 43²⁴; cf. Ezra 6⁹). No reason is given for this other than that it represented the covenant of salt between Israel and God, i.e. a covenant of permanent loyalty such as was made by men eating salt together. Philo (*Special Laws* I, 289), commenting on Lev. 2¹³, takes it as indicating complete permanence, but in the sense of a preservative. 'Salt acts as a preservative to bodies, ranking in this as second in honour to the life principle. For just as the life principle causes bodies to escape corruption, so does salt, which more than anything else keeps them together, and makes them in a sense immortal.' This is probably the sense in the rabbinic saying (SB I, p. 235), 'The Torah is like salt . . . the world cannot endure without salt', i.e. the Torah preserves the world, and perhaps in Matt. 5¹³. The cultic significance, whatever it may have been, is probably not present in the gospel sayings except in the (probably) variant reading in Mark 9⁴⁹ 'For every sacrifice is salted with salt'. (iii) In Job 6⁶ salt is not a preservative but seasoning, without which the tasteless cannot be eaten. In this sense it could be associated with wisdom. In Cornelius Nepos, *Life of Atticus* 13.2, it is a symbol of what is witty and clever, and in Col. 4⁶, 'Let your speech be always seasoned with salt' is equivalent to 'Conduct yourselves wisely towards outsiders' and so that 'you may know how you ought to answer everyone.' This could be the background of Matt. 5¹³, 'You are the salt (wisdom) of the earth' being synonymous with 'You are the light of the world', and it could explain 'become foolish' (Matthew and Luke) as an equivalent of 'become saltless' (Mark). In explanation of salt's losing its savour in Mark's version some have noted that the salt of the Dead Sea, the principal source of supply in Palestine, contains a considerable admixture of gypsum, which can remain when the salt has evaporated, and which, while still looking like salt, has an insipid taste(see Marshall, p. 596). There is, however, no reference to this in Jewish tradition, nor to salt as an unreliable commodity capable of losing its capacity.

A story of R. Joshua b. Hananiah (quoted in SB I, p. 236) runs, 'There was once a mule who had a foal . . . He was asked, "Can, then, a mule have offspring?" He said, "There are fables." He was then asked, "When salt loses its savour, wherewithal shall it be salted?" He answered, "With the young of a mule." He was then asked, "Does the unfruitful mule have young?" He answered, "Can salt lose its savour?" ' This story (c. AD 90), regarded by some as a direct polemic against the gospel sayings, can only make its point if it can be assumed that salt cannot possibly lose its savour. Such explanations may not in any case be required for Luke's and Matthew's versions if salt is there a symbol of wisdom, which becomes not saltless, but foolish.

fit neither for the land nor for the dunghill: This is unclear. If *for the dunghill* means 'for the purpose of manuring', this is also what is meant by *for the land*. If it means 'for the rubbish heap', then 'not fit for' has no meaning. There is no evidence for the use in Palestine of salt for manuring, but rather the opposite. The sites of cities after destruction were 'sown' with salt to render the land barren (Judg. 9⁴⁵; Deut. 29²³).

throw it away: The verb *ekballein* is used for excommunication (cf. Matt. 8¹²; Mark 12⁸; John 9³⁴ᶠ·), and here could be a warning to the disciple of the possibility of apostasy.

He who has ears to hear, let him hear: This solemn adjuration underlines what was of supreme importance for Luke's time, the radical nature of discipleship and the requirement of constancy in it. *ear* has the sense of 'response', and *to hear* means 'to obey', so that the injunction amounts to 'He who has the will to obey, let him obey.'

Chapters 15–16   *Parables*

Chapters 15–16, consisting of five parables, with sayings between the fourth and fifth, could be said to form something of a unit. There is the same audience throughout, for even 16¹⁻¹³, though spoken to disciples, is heard by, and no doubt really directed to, the Pharisees (16¹⁴ᶠ·). The material of these chapters contains some of the most vivid writing in this Gospel, but may not all have been derived from the same source. If so, the fact that Luke has assembled it here, and the editorial notes he has supplied, reveal something of his outlook and purpose. There is not much connection with what has preceded, except that a general contrast between the worldly, wealthy and impenitent, especially Pharisees, and the poor, unworldly disciples, is continued, and is made sharper in respect of penitence and wealth. The main theme would seem to be the opposition of the Pharisees, in their self-justification and hardness based on their observance of the law, to the message of repentance unto life (cf. A. 11¹⁸), which is everywhere winning the penitent sinner. Hence the scene which Luke sets for the two chapters (15¹ᶠ·) is an ideal one of the totality of tax collectors and sinners in Israel listening as penitents to the teaching of Jesus, which is resisted by the Pharisees and scribes as a body. In 16¹⁶ this contrast is formulated as one between the religion of the OT, which has served its purpose, and the message of the kingdom, which has overtaken it, and which meets with universal response. The theme of repentance, introduced in 15⁷, ¹⁰, is taken up in 16³⁰, and the warning there, that those who do not heed the law and the prophets will also reject resurrection, provides an impressive conclusion in the light of the story of Luke–Acts as a whole (cf. A. 26²⁻²⁷, which recapitulates the emphasis in A. on the resurrection of Jesus, and on its fulfilment of the law and prophets). As, however, the editorial note in 16¹⁴ shows, impenitence and resistance to the gospel message are, for Luke, closely allied with wealth; and it is to the proper use of wealth that the parable in 16¹⁻⁸, when interpreted by the sayings attached to it in 16⁹⁻¹³ (as also, in some measure, the parable in 16¹⁹⁻³¹) is addressed. The gospel is not, however, antinomian, but goes hand in hand with the law (16¹⁶ᶠ·, ²⁹⁻³¹), and it secures for the penitent the righteousness that exceeds the righteousness of the scribes and Pharisees (cf. Matt. 5²⁰).

15 Parables of Lost and Found

This chapter consists of twin short parables followed by a longer one; for a somewhat similar arrangement of material cf. 13¹⁻⁹; 13¹⁸⁻³⁰; 14⁷⁻²⁴. Behind them may lie a biblical text, Deut. 21¹⁸⁻²²³, where the cases of a rebellious son and of finding sheep, or anything else, belonging to a fellow Israelite are found together. They are united by a common theme of joy over the recovery of what is lost. This, however, may be the result of Luke's editing, for the third parable does not concern a lost son or searching father, and *was lost and is found* in vv. 24, 32 look like additions to *was dead and is alive* in order to assimilate its message to that of the other two. Conversely, joy over the return of the prodigal, which is integral to the story in vv. 11–32, may have influenced Luke's interpretation of the two short parables as teaching the joy of God over penitents rather than the diligent search for the lost.

EATING WITH SINNERS

15 *Now the tax collectors and sinners were all drawing near to hear him.* ^{2}*And the Pharisees and the scribes murmured, saying, 'This man receives sinners and eats with them.'*

The scene is set by an introduction which vocabulary and style show to be from Luke's hand. He may have reproduced it from 5^{30}, where, in taking over Mark 2^{16}, he also produces the unusual order *Pharisees and scribes* and adds *murmured;* but whereas there the situation is the specific one of an actual meal, which gives rise to objections, here it is impossibly generalized. It would be out of the question for *all the tax collectors* and *all the sinners* (who would they be?) to be gathered as an audience in one place, and once again Luke's fondness for the word 'all' has led him to produce a blurred picture. Nor is it clear whether they were *drawing near* to hear the call to repentance, or, as those who have already repented, to hear further teaching. If the parables which follow are intended to argue the success of Jesus' mission, it will presumably be the latter. Jeremias (*Parables*, p. 39) suggests that *receives* (*prosdechesthai* is found only here in the gospels and A.) means 'receives to a meal in his house', as is perhaps the situation in Mark 2^{15}, though not in Luke's parallel 5^{29}; but applied to such large numbers that would be equally unrealistic. Luke may have in mind here subsequent conditions in the church; for in the only instances in the NT of this word used with persons as the object it means to treat as a fellow Christian (Rom. 16^2; Phil. 2^{29}). It may denote here reception into the fellowship of the true Israel. This was a basic issue in the mission of Jesus, as it was to be later in the church. Also, apart from A. 10^{41}, *sunesthiein*, rendered here by *eats with*, occurs otherwise in the NT with reference to full acceptance of Gentiles in the church (A. 11³; Gal. 2¹²), or the excommunication of gross sinners from the church (I Cor. 5¹¹).

³*So he told them this parable:* ⁴'*What man of you, having a hundred sheep, if he has lost one of them, does not leave the ninety-nine in the wilderness, and go after the one which is lost, until he finds it?* ⁵*And when he has found it, he lays it on his shoulders, rejoicing.* ⁶*And when he comes home, he calls together his friends and his neighbours, saying to them, "Rejoice with me, for I have found my sheep which was lost."* ⁷*Just so, I tell you, there will be more joy in heaven over one sinner who repents than over ninety-nine righteous persons who need no repentance.*

⁸'*Or what woman, having ten silver coins,* ★ *if she loses one coin, does not light a lamp and sweep the house and seek diligently until she finds it?* ⁹*And when she has found it, she calls together her friends and neighbours, saying, "Rejoice with me, for I have found the coin which I had lost."* ¹⁰*Just so, I tell you, there is joy before the angels of God over one sinner who repents.*'

★ The drachma, rendered here by *silver coin*, was about fourteen pence

These twin parables, introduced by a Lukan formula *so he told them*, and as a single parable (cf. 5³⁶), are well written, with a careful parallelism of wording so far as subject-matter permits, but also with stylistic variations. That they need not always have circulated together in the tradition is suggested by Matt. 18¹²⁻¹⁴, which stands on its own, and is evidently a variant version of the same parable as 15⁴⁻⁷. Structure and wording, context and interpretation, are all, however, so different in the two versions as to preclude direct borrowing by one evangelist from another, or probably the use of a common source here. Comparison of the two gives some indication of the extent to which a story could be modified and re-applied in the course of its use in oral tradition. Matthew's version appears to be further from any original, probably in its brevity of form and certainly in its application to internal conditions in the church, but perhaps not in all respects (see below); and it does not follow that because Matthew's version is clearly secondary Luke's is entirely original.

Both the twin parables tell substantially the same story. As the man tends his own sheep he is not wealthy, and when he spares no effort to go after the one that is lost (we are not intended to enquire what happens to the others while he is away), it is not out of feelings of care or pity, but solely because it is a valuable commodity, the loss of which cannot be afforded. This is plainly the motive of the woman's assiduous search (v. 8), where the proportion of loss, one drachma out of ten, is greater, though not perhaps so closely connected with the household's livelihood. The recovery of what was lost is in each case followed by a scene, absent from Matthew's version, of rejoicing with friends and neighbours, though this is more natural in the second case, since the shepherd was not at home when he lost his sheep. This scene is important as supplying the motif of shared joy which is seen as the point of the parable. The language here is Lukan, and the action corresponds with the setting Luke has supplied for the parables, and with his understanding of them as invitations to Jewish religious leaders to rejoice with Jesus at the conversion of sinners (cf. 15^{32}).

The two parables are given an almost identical interpretation (vv. 7, 10). On this Easton comments 'There is something homiletic about the care with which the moral is drawn in Luke; such a didactic repetition is not in Christ's manner' (p. 235). Is it, however, the moral originally intended? Luke and Matthew have in common that there is more joy over the one recovered than over the ninety-nine which had not strayed; but Matthew has this within the parable itself as the shepherd's own statement of joy at the success of his search. Unremitting search and joy at recovery are what is suggested by the parables themselves. In Luke, however, the emphasis is shifted towards the repentance on the part of the one found as the occasion of the divine joy. *Repentance* and *repents* are predominantly Lukan words in the NT, and the subject is a Lukan interest (cf. 5^{32}, where he glosses the invitation to the kingdom of Mark 2^{17} as a summons to repentance); but the theme is somewhat artificial here, since the sheep and coins being found are hardly appropriate symbols for sinners in the act of repenting. It also involves the allegorization of one detail in the first parable, the ninety-nine that are not lost, which produces the questionable idea of *righteous persons who need no repentance* (perhaps modelled on 'those who are well have no need of a physician', 5^{31} = Mark 2^{17}). This is just plausible in the case of the ninety-nine sheep, since straying sheep were already in the OT a figure for sinners (Ps. 119^{176}; Isa. 53^{6}), but it is significant that no such interpretation is offered of the nine drachmae. These parables may, then, have had as their original point that God sets so high a value on the lost that he spares no effort to recover it (cf. Ezek. 34), perhaps with reference to the mission of Jesus as the present, concrete evidence for this. If so, they may have been not so much, as Jeremias maintains (*Parables*, p. 136), a defence of Jesus' message under attack, as part of its original proclamation of divine grace.

ﭏﭏﭏ

4

lost one: It is difficult to decide which is more original as between Luke's *lost*, which would better express his concern with the outcast (cf. 19^{10}, and 'lost sheep' for the despised in Israel, Matt. 10^{6}; 15^{24}), and Matthew's 'went astray' (Matt. 18^{12}), which is used in the NT for 'erring' Christians, and would therefore fit his context. Ezek. 34^{16} has both expressions. *one* is, as in v. 8, placed as the last word in the clause for emphasis, as is also *rejoicing* in v. 5 (cf. 19^{6}; A. 8^{39}).

5

lays it on his shoulders: The sheep has lost all spirit, refuses to move, and has to be carried (so Jeremias, *Parables*, p. 134); but one may suspect an element of pathos entering here, which tends to deflect emphasis away from the recovery of what is valuable towards care and pity for it.

7

in heaven: This, like *before the angels of God* in v. 10, is a reverential periphrasis for God, the latter being peculiar to Luke in the NT (cf. 12$^{8f.}$). 'Joy before God' was a rabbinic expression, though 'joy over' was a classical Greek expression not found in the LXX.

will be: This is probably not to be taken (as by Jeremias, *Parables*, p. 135) as an eschatological future (i.e. at the judgment), since it is varied in v. 10 by *is*; and even if this originally rendered an Aramaic imperfect with a future sense (so Jeremias), it will have been intended by Luke as a present tense for his Greek readers. In the Lukan writings repentance is a present possibility with present consequences.

8

silver coins: This renders the Greek *drachma*. The drachma was a unit of the Greek silver coinage which came to prevail in Palestine from the time of Alexander. A Greek writer of the third century BC could refer to it as the price of a sheep, but, like the rest of the coinage, it suffered depreciation, and is generally given a value in NT times of between eighteen and twenty pence.

^{11}*And he said, 'There was a man who had two sons; ^{12}and the younger of them said to his father, "Father, give me the share of property that falls to me." And he divided his living between them. ^{13}Not many days later, the younger son gathered all he had and took his journey into a far country, and there he squandered his property in loose living. ^{14}And when he had spent everything, a great famine arose in that country, and he began to be in want. ^{15}So he went and joined himself to one of the citizens of that country, who sent him into his fields to feed swine. ^{16}And he would gladly have fed on* the pods that the swine ate; and no one gave him anything. ^{17}But when he came to himself he said, "How many of my father's hired servants have bread enough and to spare, but I perish here with hunger! ^{18}I will arise and go to my father, and I will say to him, 'Father, I have sinned against heaven and before you; ^{19}I am no longer worthy to be called your son; treat me as one of your hired servants.' " ^{20}And he arose and came to his father. But while he was yet at a distance, his father saw him and had compassion, and ran and embraced him and kissed him. ^{21}And the son said to him, "Father, I have sinned against heaven and before you; I am no longer worthy to be called your son."† ^{22}But the father said to his servants, 'Bring quickly the best robe, and put it on him; and put a ring on his hand, and shoes on his feet; ^{23}and bring the fatted calf and kill it, and let us eat and make merry; ^{24}for this my son was dead, and is alive again; he was lost, and is found." And they began to make merry.*

^{25}*'Now his elder son was in the field; and as he came and drew near to the house, he heard music and dancing. ^{26}And he called one of the servants and asked what this meant. ^{27}And he said to him, "Your brother has come, and your father has killed the fatted calf, because he has received him safe and sound." ^{28}But he was angry and refused to go in. His father came out and entreated him, ^{29}but he answered his father, "Lo, these many years I have served you, and I never disobeyed your command; yet you never gave me a kid, that I might make merry with my friends. ^{30}But when this son of yours came, who has devoured your living with harlots, you killed for him the fatted calf!" ^{31}And he said to him, "Son, you are always with me, and all that is* *mine is yours.* [32]*It was fitting to make merry and be glad, for this your brother was dead, and is alive; he was lost, and is found."* '

    * Other ancient authorities read *filled his belly with*
    † Other ancient authorities add *treat me as one of your hired servants*

The interpretation placed by Luke on the two previous parables prepares naturally for a third (*and he said* as an introduction is found, apart from John 12[6], only in Luke in the NT), in which repentance (vv. 17–19, repeated v. 21), joy over the penitent (vv. 22–24, reapeated v. 32), and the righteous who need no repentance (vv. 29–31), could all be considered integral elements. The very title, however, by which the parable has come to be known, the Parable of the Prodigal Son, indicates a problem about it. In fact it concerns two sons (vv. 11, 25); but the elaboration of the first part, which makes it the longest of all the parables, has so thrown the story out of proportion that vv. 11–24 are with difficulty prevented from appearing as a story in its own right, with vv. 25–32 as a somewhat lame appendix. This is so even if, with Jeremias (*Parables*, p. 131), it is taken as an instance of a two-part parable, with the first part setting the stage for the second part, where the chief point is to be found; for then what was intended as a preliminary narrative has through its length and artistry well-nigh captured the whole scene. Possibly something nearer in shape to the story of two sons in Matt. 21[28-32] has been extended into a story of the 'tale' type in a milieu more given to story-telling for its own sake than that of most of the parables, or where literary influences were stronger.

    As in other 'tale' type parables there is a relatively high concentration of words and phrases which have a more literary flavour, and are not characteristic of the vocabulary of the gospels. Such are: *the younger, the share that falls to me* (a common legal formula in the papyri, where also it is used of paternal inheritance), *property, divided* (between parties, cf. I Cor. 12[11]), *living* in the sense of 'property', *gathered* in the sense of 'realized in cash', *squandered, loose living, spent everything* (i.e. wastefully), *famine* with its standing Greek literary epithet *great, joined himself to* (the Greek verb *kollasthai* is almost confined to Luke in the NT), *citizen* (elsewhere in the NT 19[14]; A. 21[39]; Heb. 8[11] LXX), *hired servants* (the Greek word *misthios*, meaning 'day labourer' is rare in the LXX, but common in the papyri and literary authors), *am worthy to* (this classical Greek expression, *axios eimi*, is found elsewhere in the NT only at A.

13^{25} and in Rev.), *embraced him* (lit. 'fell on his neck') *and kissed him* (so A. 20^{37}, a biblical expression; cf. Tobit 11.9ff., of a father and mother greeting a returning son), *is alive again* (elsewhere in the NT Rom. 7^9), *to make merry* (elsewhere in the gospels 12^{19}; 16^{19}), *music* (the Greek word *sumphōnia*, only here in the NT, denotes the music of a band, or, less likely, of a particular instrument), *dancing.* There is also evidence of Luke's own vocabulary and style. On the other hand, Jeremias notes a strong Semitic flavour in the first, though not in the second part (*Parables*, p. 128 n. 64), and this might suggest that Luke is revising a source here, and has done so more carefully in the second part, or that that part is a later addition.

What is the parable intended to teach? Surprisingly for a story that has often been hailed as a literary masterpiece, or as containing 'the gospel within the gospel', this is by no means easy to establish. Elaboration of detail in a parable, as here, can have the result that the main point is insufficiently focused. Easton comments here (p. 236) that 'the student cannot be warned too stringently against the danger of over-interpretation'. Two main interpretations have been offered, sometimes with modifications in respect of each other. (i) Despite the parable's customary title, and the fact that it begins and ends with two sons, it is primarily about the father. Thus, it 'might more correctly be called the *parable of the Father's love* . . . The father, and not the returning son, is the central figure . . . The parable describes with touching simplicity what God is like, his goodness, his grace, his boundless mercy, his abounding love' (Jeremias, *Parables*, pp. 128–31). It has been called the parable of 'The Waiting Father', and 'teaches God's eagerness to welcome any returning sinner immediately' (Easton, p. 241), or 'the love of God for his wayward children' (Marshall, p. 604, who quotes the judgment of G. Quell in *TDNT* V, p. 973, that in the use of 'Father' for the God to whom erring Israelites are called to return in such passages as Jer. 31^{18-20} 'one may clearly perceive the original of the parable of the prodigal'). The weakness of this interpretation is that while the father may be referred to in terms indicating that he is an image of God (*before you*, vv. 18, 21, *had compassion*, v. 20, *your command*, v. 29 – so Jeremias), the picture is inevitably blurred when God is referred to in the parable alongside but in distinction from the father, in *Father, I have sinned against heaven* (unique in this form as a periphrasis for God) *and before you* (vv. 18, 21; cf. Exod. 10^{16}). Nor is the love of the father or his 'waiting' expressed in the story except in so far as it is to be read out of his joy. Easton (p. 239), thinks the parable purposely represents the father as 'somewhat niggardly', and roundly declares that understanding of the parable has been hampered by supposing that the father is a figure of God, except in the form 'If a faulty human father, none too generous towards his sons, is so moved by the return of the prodigal, who can measure God's welcome to an erring child?'

(ii) The central figure is the younger son, and his experience teaches about disobedience, the necessity of repentance, and the joy of the forgiveness with which it is met (so, e.g., Klostermann, p. 157, Rengstorf, p. 181). Hence Marshall's title for the parable is The Lost Son, and he admits this theme, though only as an additional one, in his comment (p. 604), 'But at the same time (sc. as the father is the central figure) the figure of the son is developed; we see his sin and his need, his repentance and his return, and so the parable is also concerned with the "joy of repentance" (J. Schniewind's phrase)'. That this was, at least in part, Luke's own view (the story 'provides the frame for a grand instance of his great doctrine of repentance', Drury, *Tradition*, p. 77), is indicated (*a*) by his placing of the parable in direct continuation of the previous two, which he has understood in this sense, and (*b*) by the insertion (probably by him) of *he was lost and is found* alongside *was dead and is alive* (vv. 24, 32) to make this parable approximate in meaning to that of the other two, despite its manifest artificiality when the son is not lost (*I perish* in v. 17 means 'I am dying'), and when the father does not search. The weakness of this interpretation is that the parable is not particularly well designed to give teaching on sin, repentance and forgiveness. For it is not clear at the beginning which, if any, of the younger son's actions constitutes rebellion against the father's will in contrast to the dutiful obedience of the elder son (v. 29). It could hardly be his claiming the inheritance in advance, since this was his right, nor his leaving home; while his loose living was an offence against the commandments of God rather than against his father. Further, repentance is expressed in the curiously neutral phrase *he came to himself* (v. 17); and even the confession of sin is less evidence of repentance than the basis for the statement *I am no longer worthy to be called your son*, which in turn is the basis for the request to be taken back as a hired labourer. Nor is there a close connection between the penitence of the son and the love of the father, as though the one were elicited by the other; for the father begins to act only on seeing the son already returning, and because he is returning.

Basically the story would seem to be depicting an instance of what the Greeks termed *peripeteia*; that is, a sudden change from an extremity of misfortune and misery to its opposite. The son is so reduced as to be about to perish (so vv. 14–17), so that even hard service with bare necessities is preferable. So he takes the necessary steps. The father's transports of joy and his lavish treatment are due simply to the unexpected return of the son (*this my son*, v. 24, *this your brother*, v. 32) alive and *safe and sound* (v. 27; the Greek word, *hugiainein*, is common in letters for 'I am well'). This element of *peripateia* is restated by the elder son in his own terms in *But when this son of yours came, who has devoured your living with harlots, you killed for him the fatted calf* (v. 30). The point of the parable would then seem to be, not the penitence and conversion of the sinner as such (generally in the gospels these are presumed rather than described), but the miraculous fact that these occur, and that they are equivalent to life from the dead. The only defect of the dutiful son, who is the permanent sharer of his father's company and possessions, is to fail to appreciate the miracle, and the unfairness which, by ordinary standards, it entails.

To make this last point, however, the parable has to be given a twist, as the picture is no longer that of two sons, each of whom has received his inheritance (contrast vv. 29–31 with v. 12). Indeed, the interpretation of the parable as a whole is further complicated by uncertainty over the status and purpose of this second part, vv. 25–32. It has been judged to be an appendix added in the course of tradition, or by Luke, in order to make a further point[r]; or, if not, as 'undoubtedly an anti-climax', with the meaning difficult to find (Easton, p. 238). Marshall attempts to accommodate it by the supposition, surely improbable, that 'in the end it is not so much the repentance of the son as the communal joy of the restored and reunited family which is the culminating note in the parable' (p. 604). Jeremias (*Parables*, p. 131), while recognizing that the first part of the parable appears to be complete in itself and the second part at first sight superfluous, insists that the parable has been constructed from the first as a two-part parable, and that, like all such, it has its main point in the second part. That point here is an appeal to opponents, the Pharisees, through a reiteration of the message of the first part, 'Behold the greatness of God's love for his lost children, and

r So Welhausen, and J. T. Sanders, 'Tradition and Redaction in Luke 15.11–32', *NTS* 15, 1968–69, pp. 433–8.

contrast it with your own joyless, loveless, thankless and self-righteous lives. Cease from your loveless ways and be merciful.' This, however, does not fit either the text or the context. For the objections voiced by the elder son in vv. 29–30 are not dismissed in v. 31, but are acknowledged as justified, or at most are gently put in a different light (so Wellhausen). It is impossible to see the sympathetic words of the father in v. 31 as referring to those who are hostile, loveless and self-righteous, or to the Pharisees as Luke depicts them. Ellis (p. 199) sees this as an indication that the parable came fairly early in Jesus' ministry before he had encountered the opposition of the Pharisees; but we have no sure means of plotting the course of the ministry in this way. What it could indicate is that Luke is not the author of this second part, since it does not accord with the context of Pharisaic hostility which he has supplied, and that it came to him as already part of the parable. In reproducing it he may have been thinking of the necessity for good Jews and converted Gentiles to live side by side in the church.

ಣ

11–12

See Deut. 21^{15–21}, where there are combined the law of inheritance of the sons of two wives and the treatment of a rebellious son who is profligate.

divided his living between them: For a man to make an irrevocable disposition of property during his lifetime appears to have been possible, since it is warned against in Ecclus 33^{19–23} as likely to lead to his dependence on the family. The share of the elder was two-thirds and of the younger one third.

13

gathered: The verb, *sunagein*, is found in papyri with the meaning 'totalled' of sums of money. Perhaps here 'he realized all his property in cash'.

took his journey: The background is the Jewish patriarchal conception of fatherhood, whereby it was the permanent duty of sons to serve the father in the family community. If the obedience of the elder son consisted in his having remained at home to serve him (v. 29), then the sin of the younger against his father (v. 18) may have been in his having left home before the father's death. There is, however, no suggestion of disapproval in v. 12, and in v. 30 it is the dissipation of the father's wealth that constitutes the wrong against him.

a far country: Greek *chōrān makrān*. This is listed by Jeremias as a Semitism; but it is a classical Greek usage, and recurs at 19¹², where it could be due to Luke himself. It helps to depict a situation in which the father's house will seem all the more desirable, and the son's return all the more unexpected.

14

he began: Possibly a case of the purely auxiliary use of the Greek verb *archesthai*, and hence not to be translated. It is not necessarily a Semitism, and Luke can be seen introducing it himself (in 5²¹ = Mark 2⁶). Here it may have the full force of 'he began'.

15

to feed swine: The extreme of degradation for a Jew.

16

fed on: Although not supported by the weightier manuscripts, the variant *filled his belly with* is probably to be accepted as the more unusual and vulgar reading, which will have been refined to *fed on*, itself perhaps suggested by 16²¹.

the pods: Carob pods, the food of extreme poverty. There is a saying of Rabbi Acha (*c.* AD 320) that 'When the Israelites have to eat carob, then they repent.'

no one gave him anything: 'anything' is not in the Greek, but this is the sense required. It prepares for the contrast in vv. 22f.

17

came to himself: Listed by Jeremias as a Semitism with the meaning 'repented'; but the expression is found in Greek and Latin authors, generally with the meaning of coming to one's senses as the result of reflection. This would seem to be what is required here by the young man's reflection (hence the soliloquy form in vv. 17–19) that he is now worse off than his father's labourers.

18–19

There is an ancient prototype of the wicked son and the faithful father called *The Story of Ahikar* (see *AP* II, pp. 715ff.) which has at 8²⁴ᵇ, Armenian version: 'Nathan began to speak and said: My father Khikar, men sin unto God, and He forgives them, when they say: I have sinned. Father, I have sinned unto thee. Forgive me, and I will be to thee a slave henceforth for ever.' Since the story is now known to have been early (there is a version in Aramaic of the fifth century BC) and also widespread, its language could have influenced the parable here.

22–23

best: Greek *prōtos*, meaning 'first', a rare usage found in the LXX (Ezek. 27²²; Amos 6⁶), but not unknown elsewhere. It is not clear whether the father's gifts are intended to denote anything more precise than a lavish generosity transforming the bedraggled young man into the opposite. Since slaves went bare-foot, *shoes on his feet* may indicate that, so far from being accepted as a day labourer, he is being restored to the condition of a free man. Jeremias (*Parables*, p. 130) suggests that the language here is modelled on Pharaoh's treatment of Joseph (Gen. 41^{42}, ring, finger, garment); but the ring would then be the signet-ring of delegated authority, which would not apply here, while his interpretation of the garment as a symbol of the New Age is surely a case of over-interpretation.

29–30

my friends: Perhaps suggested by 15$^{6, 9}$. We are not to enquire how the elder brother knows the details of the younger's life ('poetic licence', Creed).

a kid: i.e. 'so much as a kid' (some mss 'a young kid'), of far less value than the calf.

16$^{\text{I–I3}}$ *The Parable of the Dishonest Steward*

16 He also said to the disciples, '*There was a rich man who had a steward, and charges were brought to him that this man was wasting his goods.* ²*And he called him and said to him, "What is this that I hear about you? Turn in the account of your stewardship, for you can no longer be steward." ³And the steward said to himself, "What shall I do, since my master is taking the stewardship away from me? I am not strong enough to dig, and I am ashamed to beg. ⁴I have decided what to do, so that people may receive me into their houses when I am put out of the stewardship." ⁵So, summoning his master's debtors one by one, he said to the first, "How much do you owe my master?" ⁶He said, "A hundred measures of oil." And he said to him, "Take your bill, and sit down quickly and write fifty." ⁷Then he said to another, "And how much do you owe?" He said, "A hundred measures of wheat." He said to him, "Take your bill, and write eighty." ⁸The master commended the dishonest steward for his prudence; for the sons of this world* are wiser in their own generation than the sons of light. ⁹And I tell you, make friends for yourselves by means of unrighteous mammon, so that when it fails they may receive you into the eternal habitations.*

¹⁰'*He who is faithful in a very little is faithful also in much; and he who is dishonest in a very little is dishonest also in much.* ¹¹*If then you have not been faithful in the unrighteous mammon, who will entrust to you the true riches?*

^{12}And if you have not been faithful in that which is another's, who will give you that which is your own? ^{13}No servant can serve two masters; for either he will hate the one and love the other, or he will be devoted to the one and despise the other. You cannot serve God and mammon.'

* Greek *age*

Another parable of the 'tale' type, beginning with *There was a man* (cf. 10^{30}; 14^{16}; 15^{11}; 16^{19}), and concerned with *a rich man* (cf. 12^{16}; 16^{19}; 18^{23}; 19^{2}). There is a slight verbal link with what precedes in *wasting his goods* (v. 1), where the Greek word *diaskorpizein* is the same as that rendered by 'squandered' in 15^{13}. *The disciples*, an unspecified body, are now added (*also*) to the audience as the immediate hearers of this parable, although the Pharisees remain in the background to overhear and object (v. 14). This double audience provided by Luke may betray a certain ambivalence in his mind as to the intention of the parable. Was its lesson for the wealthy unbeliever or for Christians?

A steward (Greek *oikonomos*) – not, as in 12^{42}, the chief of the servants, but either the factor of an estate or a financial agent – is successfully accused (the verb and construction with it, *diaballein* followed by *hōs* = 'as' and a participle, belong to classical Greek) before his master of mismanagement; whether through dishonesty or inefficiency does not appear, and is immaterial. He is summoned to make a financial rendering of accounts (the Greek phrase *apodidonai ton logon* is common in classical writers and the papyri; elsewhere in the NT A. 19^{40}; Matt. 12^{36}; Heb. 13^{17}; I Peter 4^{5}, the last three in the eschatological sense of giving an account of oneself at the last judgment). This is prior to his dismissal from the stewardship (the noun only here in the gospels). He soliloquizes that he is not strong enough to dig and is ashamed to beg for a living (*to dig* is found elsewhere in the NT at 6^{48}; 13^{8}; *to beg* at 18^{35}; *ashamed* only here in the gospels). In his predicament he reaches a decision on how to guarantee his future by securing that when he is put out of office (Greek *methistanai*, elsewhere in the NT in this sense A. 13^{22}), *they* – the debtors, the sequel being presumed – may receive him into their houses in gratitude to support him. He summons his master's debtors, and is shown interrogating two of them as to their debts (this is for the sake of the reader; the steward himself knows the answers), and telling them to reduce the amounts by writing out another bill in their own hand.

Here the action of the parable ends. Its interpretation has long proved very difficult; for literature on this, which Plummer, writing in 1910, already called 'voluminous and unrepaying', see Derrett, *Law in the NT*, p. 48 n. 1. A primary question is where the parable is to be thought to end and the interpretation to begin. In the text there is no break at the end of v. 7, and v. 8 is part of the parable, the steward then being approved by the master (*ho kurios*, which is also the Greek for 'the lord') for a shrewdness that is appreciated by men of the world. The interpretation in vv. 9–13, introduced by *And I tell you*, (v. 9; cf. 11^9) is partly eschatological and partly moral: (i) evil as it is, wealth is to be handled with a similar shrewdness, so as to win the favour of those certain to gain entry into heaven, who will in return secure the entry of their benefactors (v. 9); (ii) more generally, upon faithfulness or otherwise in the least matters, or in money matters, depends possession of the true riches (vv. 10–12); (iii) the proper use of money entails not being its slave but the slave of God (v. 13).

A notable recent interpretation of the parable in vv. 1–8 and of the whole unit vv. 1–13 is that of Derrett (*Law*, pp. 48ff.), which is carried through by reference to certain precise details of Jewish commercial practice at the time. Thus, the steward is a financial agent. He is also, in contravention of the law of God (Deut. 23^{20}), a usurer. This, which is not stated, is to be deduced from the largeness of the amounts of the debts (over eight hundred gallons of oil and over a thousand bushels of wheat). What these large figures really represent is sums of money lent on interest, but to conceal this, and to evade the scandal of usury, they are fictitiously stated as loans of commodities. The reason for this is that, by a rabbinic legal device, such loans were judged to be non-usurious, provided that the borrower already possessed some, however little, of the commodity concerned. What the steward does, therefore, in having the figures altered is to remit the interest (a hundred per cent and twenty-five per cent) on money loans; and what the parable thus aims to depict is not the steward's dishonesty (even if he is still called 'dishonest' in v. 8), but rather the opposite, his conversion from the law of man, which had come by degrees to countenance usury, to the law of God, which absolutely forbade it. In this way he commends himself to the public as an honest man, and his master, in ratifying his action, shares in the good reputation earned. The steward is then held up to the pious as a model of one who wins the rewards of righteousness by his use of worldly goods.

The weakness of this interpretation is that it depends entirely on what is not apparent but only covert in the parable – that the contracts are usurious – and on the capacity of the audience to recognize this in the brief reference to them. It also gives a diminished sense to the words in v. 4, *so that people may receive me into their houses* ('to obtain the support of public opinion until he finds alternative employment', p. 72), which would hardly have led to the words in v. 8, *they may receive you into the eternal habitations*. Further, the meaning 'ratified', which Derrett proposes for the Greek verb *epainein* (v. 8) is hardly possible when it is followed by a person as object; while his exposition of vv. 10–13 as 'presenting another aspect of the parable, not inconsistent with the first' (p. 81), hardly succeeds in establishing a closer connection between them and the parable.

Analysis of the parable is inseparable from analysis of vv. 1–13 as a whole, since these verses appear to form a single unit, and to be a composition on the subject of wealth (whether made by Luke himself, in whole or in part, or before him). This would seem to follow from the fact that they reach a conclusion in v. 13, which is an independent saying, identical in wording (except for *servant*) with Matt. 6^{24}. And Luke's context is plainly more artificial than Matthew's, since here the saying intends to leave no doubt that it is not the steward's worldliness that is approved (v. 8), and that any faithfulness in the use of wealth (vv. 10f.) depends on a prior devotion to God. This, however, blunts the evident intention of the saying itself to state a radical opposition between the service of God and of mammon. It will have been placed here because of a general similarity of subject matter (wealth and heavenly things) and of wording (*master* and the catchword *mammon*), and to sharpen the controversy with the Pharisees (v. 14).

Working backwards from v. 13, the three preceding sayings in vv. 10–12 belong closely together, being grouped round the words *faithful* and *dishonest* (unrighteous); and the connection would be closer if the Greek words rendered by *faithful*, *true* and *mammon* (*pistos, alēthinos, mamōnas*), all go back to the same Hebrew root meaning 'trust'. The sayings are gnomic in character, the first (v. 10) consisting of two antithetical statements in the form 'He who . . .', and the second two (vv. 11–12) of conditional sentences. They are arranged in step parallelism, i.e. the successive statements are parallel in form, but the argument takes a step forward each time. Taken together, and especially if v. 11 follows closely from v. 10 (*then*), they teach that faithfulness in the use of wealth is a qualification for greater things. This teaching is, however, unclear, since it is not evident what such faithfulness involves (unless it is to be deduced from v. 9 as giving wealth away), nor what the greater things are. In itself v. 10a is no more than a general proverb, but in this context it characterizes wealth as what is *very little* in contrast to what is *much*, and it reproduces in a single sentence the lesson of the Parable of the Pounds (19^{17}, 'Because you have been faithful in very little . . .', though there the *much* is more of the same kind, the rule over ten cities). In v. 11 wealth is expressly introduced, and as *unrighteous* (Greek *adikos*), though here in the sense of lying and untrustworthy (for this meaning of *adikos* cf. John 7^{18}; II Thess. 2^{12}; Rom. 2^{8}), and hence in contrast to *the true riches*. These may be the equivalent of heavenly treasure (cf. 12^{33}; 18^{22}), though *entrust to you* (in Greek *pisteuein*, the verb from the adjective *pistos* = 'faithful') could imply that they were something given to be spiritually administered (by those who were stewards in the church?). In v. 12 wealth is characterized as *that which is another's*, perhaps as that which is alien to the elect through their break with this present age, in contrast to *that which is your own*, the possessions proper to the sons of light. If the word *mammon* were removed from v. 11, where it disturbs the contrast between what is untrustworthy and what is true, all these sayings could be statements of general proverbial wisdom, and not necessarily about wealth at all; but in this context, and with the word *mammon* in v. 11, they are united around the subject of wealth. Nevertheless, they can hardly be said to arise directly out of the parable, where it is an act of untrustworthiness that is commended, and without any hint that this is an earnest of untrustworthiness in greater things. They would seem to have been placed here to give a moral and exhortatory turn to the parable, and advice for Christian disciples. And again the connection with the parable is to some extent verbal (*dishonest*, v. 10 and v. 8; *unrighteous mammon*, v. 11 and v. 9).

It is just possible that v. 9 was once an independent saying on the ultimate value of alms, having affinity with such sayings as 6$^{32-38}$; 12^{33}; Matt. 25^{40}. The general sentiment that on the right use of money may depend an eternal destiny goes more naturally with what follows in vv. 10–13 than with what precedes in vv. 1–8. It fits the parable closely only if certain elements in the parable are given an allegorical interpretation – the debtors stand for friends and their houses for eternal dwellings – and this may indicate that it was composed at some stage as an application of the parable.

That v. 8 stood as the final sentence in the parable, as Luke received it, would appear from the change from the third person of narration in *the master commended* to the first person of Jesus' direct address in *And I tell you* (v. 9). *ho kurios* can then only refer to the steward's master. Except, however, on some such interpretation as Derrett's, it involves an awkward twist in the story that the master should applaud his own loss; and one might have expected 'his' with *ho kurios* (cf. *my master*, v. 3; *his master's*, v. 5). It has, therefore, been suggested that *ho kurios* should here be translated 'the Lord', referring to Jesus, and the whole verse be taken, not as part of the parable, but as a comment made upon it in view of the embarrassment it had caused, which became attached to the parable in the course of tradition. Its purpose will have been to assure the hearer (reader) that the Lord (Jesus) had indeed chosen such a disreputable character as an example to be commended, and to explain why. The explanation is a double one, and is somewhat clumsy in the Greek by reason of the repetition of *hoti* = because – *for his prudence* in v. 8a is literally translated 'because he had acted prudently', and *for the sons of this world* in v. 8b is literally translated 'because the sons of this world'. The first explanation (v. 8a) restricts the Lord's approval of the steward to his shrewdness. The second explanation (v. 8b) adds, almost in parenthesis, that this shrewdness is second nature to such men, who are thus the natural models for it. If v. 8 is taken in this way, it may be noted that there is then a remarkably similar sequence of thought in 18¹⁻⁵ – a parable about a disreputable character who acts from selfish motives; an assurance from the Lord (who here cannot be any one other than Jesus) that, disreputable as he may be, he is still to be taken notice of; and an eschatological interpretation introduced by 'I tell you', and followed by an independent saying.

If, then, the parable is to be taken as having once ended at v. 7 without interpretation (cf. the abrupt ending at 18⁵), it need not have been concerned with wealth as such, any more than 18¹⁻⁵ is concerned with the law, or the parable in 12¹⁶⁻²¹ with agriculture. It would be essentially a parable of crisis. Faced with an immediate threat of disaster to his whole existence, the steward acted quickly and decisively for the future. Let men, therefore, discern the critical situation in which they are placed with the approach of the kingdom of God, and act accordingly. The attached comment in v. 8, however, not only attempts to mitigate the embarrassment of the parable, but in doing so alters the perspective in a more Christian direction. For it presumes that the kingdom has come, and that there are already in existence those who can be referred to as *the sons of light* (i.e. sons of the kingdom, cf. Matt. 13³⁸), who now need to learn shrewdness in their use of the world. Luke, or someone before him, may then have added v. 9 to provide the parable with an application for Christians. It is in part eschatological in looking to eternal life beyond the judgment, but it is primarily directed to instructing disciples in the wisdom of disposing of wealth to the poor in order to secure life. Since 'steward' became a word used of Christians in the church or their leaders (I Cor. 4¹; Tit. 1⁷; I Peter 4¹⁰), and both 'faithful' and 'wise' were naturally associated with it (12⁴²; Matt. 24⁴⁵; I Cor. 4²), the way would be prepared for the addition here (i) of v. 10, which has a remote connection with the parable (*dishonest*), but is basically a wisdom saying stating a general truth of character; and (ii) of vv. 11–12 (also with a remote connection with the parable in *the unrighteous mammon*, v. 11, and *that which is another's*, v. 12), which in part return to the eschatological perspective (*the true riches*, v. 11, *that which is your own*, v. 12), but which may be intended to teach that a proper use of wealth is a qualification for being entrusted with spiritual gifts and responsibilities in the church. Finally, the addition of v. 13 removes all doubt that the steward is not to be followed as a devotee of mammon.

It is likely that the possession and use of money presented a problem for Christians, who preserved the tradition that the first to become disciples had renounced all possessions (5¹¹; 14²⁶, ³³); and it is part of Luke's idyllic picture of the beginnings of the church that all things were had in common, and possessions and goods were sold for the proceeds to be distributed (A. 2⁴⁴ᶠ·; 4³²ᶠᶠ·). Glimpses of the problem may be seen in I Cor. 7²⁹ᶠᶠ·, where Paul delivers an eschatological judgment that in view of the shortness of the time left those who buy should be as those who had no goods and those who deal with the world as those who did not, and in I Cor. 9 where his acceptance of money for preaching the gospel has to be defended against attack. In Tit. 1⁷ the bishop as God's steward has to be free of dishonest gain, and some form of the problem of wealth in the church was plainly present to the author of the Epistle of James (1⁹ᶠᶠ·; 2¹ᶠᶠ·; 5¹ᶠᶠ·).

❧

3
said to himself: Soliloquy is a common feature in the parables peculiar to Luke

(cf. 12¹⁷ff.; 15¹⁷ff.; 18⁴f.; 18¹¹f.; elsewhere in parables, Matt. 24⁴⁸). It is specially appropriate in parables of the 'tale' type, which are more plentiful in this Gospel, imparting vigour to the action of the story when it is seen as the result of the reflection of one of the characters. It could be a sign of Luke's hand, as in 20¹³ he can be seen introducing it into a parable taken over from Mark.

4

people may receive: The verb *dexōntai* is unspecific – 'they may receive'; but coming after '*I have decided what to do*' in the soliloquy, 'they' must refer to those who are to be the objects of his plan.

5

debtors one by one: Debtors, *chreopheiletēs* + 7⁴¹; one by one, *heis hekastos* = 'each one', elsewhere in the gospels 4⁴⁰; Matt. 26²², and six times in A. They are in debt through borrowing goods, or money expressed in goods, though the circumstances of the contracts are not stated. The large amounts involved (a measure of oil – *batos*, a Greek transliteration of the Hebrew *bath* – was between eight and nine gallons, and a measure of wheat – *koros*, a Greek transliteration of the Hebrew *kor* – was about eleven bushels), and the size of the reductions, are to secure that the gratitude and favour of the beneficiaries will be procured.

6

bill: Greek *gramma*, lit. 'letter' or 'writing', and here used in the plural, is found in the papyri for 'bond'.

8

commended: Or 'applauded', the sense required by the Greek verb *epainein* = 'praise' when used with a personal object.

dishonest steward: A literal translation of the Greek would be 'steward of injustice (unrighteousness)'. This type of expression is found in the LXX (e.g. II Sam. 3³⁴; I Kings 2³²) as the Greek rendering of a Semitic idiom, in which a noun in the genitive is the equivalent of an adjective, and was increasingly common in Hellenistic Greek, probably under Semitic influence. It describes the character of the man in general, and not simply his action (cf. v. 1; 18², ⁶).

for his prudence: phronimōs = 'prudently'. This can have the sense of sharp cunning; he knew where his advantage lay. Thus characterized, the steward's action can lead on to spiritual exhortation concerning the right use of wealth.

the sons of this world . . . the sons of light: 'Son(s) of' is a Semitic idiom denoting quality or character in terms of a common participation in something – e.g. 'a son of peace' (10⁶) is a peaceful man. Behind the expressions here is the apocalyptic and rabbinic doctrine of the two ages (cf. Mark 10³⁰; Matt. 12³²). The concept is temporal rather than spatial, and the primary meaning of the Greek word *aiōn*, which is here translated *world*, is 'age'. The present age (I Cor. 1^{20}; Eph. 1^{21}) is generally held, as here, to be under the domination of evil (Gal. 1^4; I Cor. 2$^{6ff.}$), and those belonging to it as perishing (II Cor. 4$^{3f.}$); and the coming age was to be the age of salvation (Heb. 6^5; I Enoch 71^{15}). While 'son(s) of the age to come' was a frequent rabbinic term, 'son(s) of this age' is attested again only in the addition which Luke makes to Mark at 20$^{34f.}$. Light is common to most religions as a figure of the sphere or nature of the divine, and hence in Jewish thought of the coming age. Those destined for, or already possessing, salvation are 'the sons of light'. This expression is not rabbinic, but it played a great part in the Qumran community as a designation of God's elect; one of its documents, which is concerned with the final apocalyptic conflict or Armageddon, is entitled *The War of the Sons of Light and the Sons of Darkness*. It could be used here satirically of the Pharisees as those who, for all their piety, fail to discern the critical time of the kingdom and act accordingly; but if the whole verse is a secondary interpretation, it more probably refers to Christians (cf. I Thess. 5^5; Eph. 5^8).

in their own generation: This is obscure in two respects. Firstly, in the gospels *generation* usually denotes one's own contemporaries (e.g. 21^{32}), but here it seems to have the sense of 'race', 'kind', those who share a common ancestry and so a common nature. They belong to the world. Secondly, it is not clear whether the meaning is (i) the sons of this age are more adept at dealing with their own fellows (i.e. in worldly affairs) than are the sons of light in dealing with their own fellows (i.e. in spiritual matters), or (ii) the sons of this age are more adept at dealing with their own fellows than are the sons of light in dealing with them (the sons of this age; i.e. in the spiritual use of worldly things). This ambiguity may indicate that the verse is a not altogether successful attempt to get over the embarrassment inherent in the parable, and to make it applicable to the sons of light, who, for Luke, are Christians. Shrewdness in general has now become the lesson of the parable, and not shrewdness in a particular critical situation; and as far as shrewdness is concerned, the worldly exhibit it to a greater degree, at least towards one another.

9

unrighteous mammon: In the Greek 'mammon of injustice (unrighteousness)' – for the form of expression see on *dishonest steward* above. *mammon* is in the Greek *mamōnas*, which is a transliteration of an Aramaic word *mamon* or *mamona*, common in the Jewish Targums and the Talmud for wealth, possessions or gain. It is possibly derived from a root with the meaning 'that in which one trusts', or 'that which is entrusted', and it can be translated by the ordinary Greek word for wealth, *ploutos*. The transliterated form is found in the NT only in this section of Luke and Matt. 6^{24}. With the addition 'of injustice' it could mean ill-gotten gain, and a saying of this kind could have been addressed to those, e.g. tax collectors, whose occupations involved them in such; but the word by itself had already acquired in Jewish speech the bad sense that is marked by the addition (cf. I Enoch 63¹⁰, in a section, chs. 62–105, where the rich are condemned simply as being rich). It was perhaps this which caused the word to be transliterated rather than translated. Money as such as evil, and the only thing to do with it is to give it away and buy eternal life. This was certainly Luke's view (cf. 12³³; 14³³; A. 2⁴³ᶠᶠ·; 4³²ᶠᶠ·).

it fails: This is obscure, since it is not evident how the time of the failure of money would necessarily coincide with the time of the reception into heaven. The obscurity may have been produced by an attempt to give an allegorical application to one of the details of the parable, the approaching end of the steward's employment (v. 3). There is a variant reading with the same Greek verb (*ekleipein*) in the second person plural with the meaning 'when you die' (cf. 12²⁰). This Greek verb is used in the LXX for the failing of men and of natural powers in the day of judgment (Hos. 4³; Amos 8¹³; Hab. 2¹³; Zech. 13⁸, etc.), and this thought may be present here – when mammon is brought to nothing along with this evil age (cf. 12³³, 'treasure in the heavens that does not fail').

they may receive you: Here, corresponding to the parable, the friends, perhaps the poor to whom the kingdom belongs (6²⁰); but if the saying was ever independent 'they' could have been a periphrasis for God, as probably in 12⁴⁸; 12²⁰ (Greek 'they require your soul of you'), 6³⁸ (Greek, 'they will give you').

eternal habitations: For the dwelling places of the righteous see I Enoch 39⁴ᶠ·; 41²; 61²ᶠ·. They are here, though not elsewhere, given the solemn description of 'tabernacles', 'tents' (the meaning of the Greek noun here, *skēnē*); for the wilderness dwelling in tents was in Jewish thought the ideal period when Israel and God lived together (Lev. 23⁴²ᶠ·), and was celebrated as such by the Feast of Tabernacles.

10

II Clement 8.5 gives as a statement of the Lord 'in the gospel' an exact parallel to v. 10a, but preceded by 'If you have not kept that which is small, who will give you that which is great?', which is reproduced in that form by later Fathers. This may be an indication that such sayings existed for a considerable time in a fluid state in oral tradition, and without any precise context (the author of II Clement applies these sayings to the necessity of keeping the flesh pure in order to gain eternal life).

13

If this verse is taken from a common written source with Matt. 6²⁴, there is no indication of where it would have stood in such a source. Manson (*Sayings*, p. 133) cites non-biblical parallels to both sentiments separately – the mutual exclusiveness of wealth and its rivals, and the attempt to satisfy both as serving two masters. Here they are combined, and the one is deduced from the other. For this deduction to be made *serve* has to be given the sense of 'to be wholly devoted to', for it was in fact possible for a man to be owned as a slave by two masters at once, and Jewish law knew of such.

16$^{14-15}$ *The Pharisees Rebuked*

[14] *The Pharisees, who were lovers of money, heard all this, and they scoffed at him.* [15] *But he said to them, 'You are those who justify yourselves before men, but God knows your hearts; for what is exalted among men is an abomination in the sight of God.'*

A conclusion supplied by Luke to draw what has just been said and what is to follow (for there is no change of audience until 17^1) within his anti-Pharisaic polemic. Both verses are somewhat awkwardly constructed. In v. 14 *all this* should refer to what has been spoken from 15^1 onwards, but *lovers of money* really refers to what had been said in 16$^{1ff.}$; and it is their ridicule and not, as is suggested by the Greek here, their listening which was caused by their love of money. Verse 15 is in two parts, with a chiasmus in the second part ('what among men is exalted . . .' is the word order in the Greek), but *for* (*hoti* = 'because') does not establish a causal connection between them. They are also written in a curious mixture of biblical and non-biblical language. Thus, *who were* renders the participle of the Greek verb *huparchein* used with a predicative noun or adjective, which is a typically Hellenistic Greek construction, while *lovers of money* (*philarguroi*) is a literary word, found elsewhere in the NT at II Tim. 3^2 and in the LXX only once in the polished work IV Maccabees (2.8). On the other hand, *scoffed at* (*exemuktērizon*, lit. 'turned up the nose at', + 23^{25}), is found in Greek only in the LXX and Testament of Joseph 2^3, and *abomination* (*bdelugma*) is frequent in the LXX and rare elsewhere.

ॐ

14

The charge of 'love of money' is an indiscriminate one, which is often found levelled against opponents (cf. II Tim. 3²; I Tim. 6¹⁰ff.). From our evidence it would be difficult to establish against Pharisees as a class. In agreement with most of the OT they regarded poverty as an evil and wealth as a blessing, but were insistent on the importance of almsgiving (see Abrahams, *Studies* I, pp. 113f.). Here the charge may be the result of a combination of Luke's hostility towards them and his hatred of wealth, for he links love of money with what are his primary charges against them (*You are those who*; for the form of expression cf. 22²⁸) of exalting themselves before men by a false reputation ('justifying themselves', cf. 10²⁹; 18⁹, ¹⁴) and of hypocrisy (12¹; 11⁴³f.). But God is not taken in, for he *knows your hearts*. The heart here denotes the deepest point in man as a spiritual being. God as 'the knower of the heart' can be expressed by a single word in Greek (*kardiognōstēs*), which, although it expresses a common biblical thought (I Sam. 16⁷; I Chron. 28⁹; Jos. *Ant.* 6.263), emerges for the first time in A. 1²⁴; 15⁸, and is then only found in Christian literature. Verse 15b expresses a typically prophetic judgment that what is lofty in human terms is abhorrent to God and is destined to be overthrown (cf. Isa. 2¹¹ff.). For the association of wealth with such loftiness, cf. I Tim. 6¹⁰, ¹⁷; Ecclus 13²⁰, Damascus Rule, 8 (Vermes, *Scrolls*, p. 105).

16^{16–18} *Sayings*

¹⁶'*The law and the prophets were until John; since then the good news of the kingdom of God is preached, and every one enters it violently.* ¹⁷*But it is easier for heaven and earth to pass away, than for one dot of the law to become void.*

¹⁸'*Every one who divorces his wife and marries another commits adultery, and he who marries a woman divorced from her husband commits adultery.*'

Three isolated sayings, of which there are equivalents in Matthew in quite different contexts; with v. 16 cf. Matt. 11¹²⁻¹³; with v. 17 cf. Matt. 5¹⁸; with v. 18 cf. Matt. 5³² and also Mark 10¹¹⁻¹² at the conclusion of the Markan pericope, 10¹⁻¹², which Matthew reproduces (Matt. 19¹⁻⁹) but Luke omits. Each of the sayings gives the impression of being an extract from a larger complex which would throw some light on its meaning. Their presence here individually and together and in this order is puzzling. For even if they had stood thus in a written source which was little more than a collection of unconnected sayings (the only connecting link is the word *law* in vv. 16 and 17), the question would remain why Luke should have incorporated all three together to stand between the context he has already created in vv. 14–15 and the parable of a rich man and a poor man in 16^{19–31}, so that the parable now follows without break as a continuation of them, and not, as might seem more natural, of 16^{1–15}. And they can hardly have been taken over automatically in order to include them somewhere, since all three, and especially the first two, enunciate truths of far-reaching importance. The same objection could be made to the suggestion of Knox (*Sources* II, p. 98) that they had been jotted down in the margin of a tract that Luke was using, or into the margin of his gospel by Luke himself, and in this way got into the text. Possibly Luke himself assembled them together, and placed them here in the important teaching section which he has been constructing from the beginning of ch. 14, so as to provide a concentrated statement of Christianity as the true Judaism, which takes the OT along with it while going beyond it in scope and severity, and which therefore spells the end of Pharisaism with its restricted righteousness (cf. Acts 13^{38ff.}; 15^{19ff.}; 20^{20ff.}; 24^{14ff.}; 26^{4ff.}). Daube (*NTRJ*, pp. 285f.) explains the sequence from evidence that the themes of violence, the permanence of the law and divorce were sometimes related in Jewish thought.

☙❧

16

Basically the same saying as Matt. 11^{12f.}, having in common with it that time is divided into two by the advent of John and that the kingdom of God is in some sense present. There are, however, considerable differences of wording, emphasis and meaning. Matthew's version is primarily a statement about the Baptist as being more than a prophet, and is placed in his Gospel accordingly. Luke's version is primarily a statement about the relation between the OT and the preaching of the kingdom (for *the law and the prophets* as a standing expression for the written OT, see Matt. 5^{17f.}; 22^{40}; Luke 24^{27}; John 1^{45}; A. 13^{15}; Rom. 3^{21}). Matthew's version may be secondary in some respects (e.g. 'John the Baptist', 'kingdom of heaven', 'the prophets and the law', 'until now'), but the verb he uses of the kingdom (Greek *biazetai*, either as a middle = 'makes its violent way', or as a passive = 'suffers violence') is to be preferred to Luke's more conventional *is preached* (Greek *euangelizetai* = 'is proclaimed as good news', found only here in the passive, which is a possible form of the verb in Greek but not of its Aramaic equivalent). Likewise Matthew's parallelism 'has suffered violence/men of violence take it by force' is to be preferred to Luke's *every one* (a typical Lukan hyperbole) *enters it violently,* where the verb is now *biazetai eis,* a classical and Hellenistic Greek usage with the meaning 'forces a way into', 'crowds into'. In Matthew the sense is very obscure – perhaps, that beginning with John as the turning point of the ages the kingdom forces its way, and men who stop at nothing take possession of it in their zeal (or their zealotry?); or, that the kingdom is violently treated, and robbers (Zealots? Pharisees?) snatch it away from men. If anything like Matthew's version had lain before Luke he will have removed its obscurity (and possibly any sinister association of the kingdom with the Zealot movement which it might have suggested), and will have transformed it into an assertion of the present successful proclamation of the kingdom by the church and its continued acceptance by the Gentiles. In Matthew there is a hint of an eschatological future when the case with the kingdom might be different ('until now'), whereas Luke's *since then* stretches up to the time of writing and onwards into an indefinite historical future. In Matthew the prophets, placed first, and the law in its prophetic capacity, perform the functions of prophecy up to (including or not including?) John and are followed by the violence of the kingdom. Luke's version appears to be saying that the OT is valid scripture until John, and is then superseded by the preached word.

Conzelmann (*Theology,* pp. 22ff.) has taken this verse as a principal clue to the structure and theological outlook of Luke–Acts as a whole. In his view it presents the divine dispensation not, as do other NT writers, in eschatological terms with John as the new Elijah ushering in the last days, but as consisting of three historical epochs – that of the OT with John as its last prophet, that of the earthly Jesus which is now in the past, and that of the church in which Luke and his readers are living. This cannot, however, be concluded with certainty from v. 16, since the preposition *until* (*mechri*) can mean either 'up to and including' or 'up to but not including' (for the latter cf. Heb. 9¹⁰; I Tim. 6¹⁴; and possibly Rom. 5¹⁴). Moreover Luke's picture of John would seem to be less precise than this. He has already introduced the statement (7^{26f.}) that John is more than a prophet and is the special messenger of Mal. 3¹. While he distinguishes the ministries of John and Jesus by having the latter begin only after the former has finished (3¹⁸⁻²³), this may have been simply in order to *write an orderly account* (1³) and not to separate them for any theological reason; indeed, he can elsewhere associate them closely (3¹⁻⁶; 7²⁴⁻³⁵; A. 1^{21f.}; 10^{37f.}; 13²³⁻²⁵), as he does also the persons of John and Jesus in the parallel birth narratives of chs. 1–2, which Conzelmann is compelled to ignore. Luke's form of the saying, and his location of it here, may indicate that he saw it as a statement less about John and his place in the history of salvation than about the OT in relation to the Christian message. It may then look back to 15^{1f.}; 16^{14f.} and forwards to 16¹⁹⁻³¹, and may require the following v. 17 as a complementary statement.

17

Evidently the same saying as Matt. 5^{18} in its wording: *heaven and earth, pass away, the law* in the sense of something written down, *one dot* (Greek *keraia* = 'horn') referring probably to a small hook or projection attached to a letter in the Hebrew alphabet to distinguish it from a similar letter, and hence what is very insignificant. The sayings are possibly derived from the same source, Luke's version being the more original; for Matthew's version seems secondary in the introductory 'For truly, I say to you', in the reduplication 'not an iota, not a dot' (Luke would hardly have omitted 'iota', the smallest letter in the Greek alphabet), and in the qualification 'until all is accomplished'. The two formulations are significantly different. Matthew's is a precise statement that the law is permanently binding in its entirety (cf. Baruch 4^1, IV Ezra 9^{37}, and sayings of the rabbis such as that of R. Jochanan (*c.* AD 250) that 'Prophets and writings will have an end, but not the law' – see SB I, pp. 244ff.). This is the case, however, only until the world passes away with the consummation of the age (if that is the right interpretation of Matt. 5^{18d}). Luke's formulation is more general and rhetorical, with the meaning 'It is very difficult, well-nigh impossible, for the law to pass away (for *it is easier* in this sense, cf. 18^{25} = Mark 10^{25}). Further Matthew's statement is part of a wider complex of material, Matt. 5^{17-48}, on the relation of Jesus' teaching to the law, from which it is evident, as from elsewhere in Matthew, that this had been, and perhaps still was, a burning issue for him and for his church. Together with the preceding statement of Jesus that he had come not to destroy but to fulfil the law it prefaces a series of antithetical pronouncements in which he goes beyond, or even abrogates, specific OT commandments; and it is not easy to judge what in this goes back to him and what stems from later Jewish-Christian controversy. By contrast Luke's statement stands quite isolated. For, firstly, he does not include in his Gospel anything further on the subject. The law and its relation to Jesus is not one of his interests, and the Christianity he represents would seem to be no longer involved in disputes over its validity. Acts shows in various ways that the matter had been settled in practice, and that modifications of the law required by the Gentile mission had not constituted any fundamental breach of it (cf. the weakened version of the Pauline teaching on justification in A. 13^{39}, and the procedure of the Apostolic Council in A. 15). In Acts it is Jews rather than Christians who are said to break the law: 2^{23}; 6^{13} with $7^{38f., 53}$; 15^5 with 15^{19-21}; 21^{20} with 21^{24}; 22^3 with 22^{12}; 25^8. Secondly, the verse is isolated in its context. If the Greek connecting particle *de* is to be rendered by *but*, then what may be intended is an emphatic assertion of one side of a paradox over against v. 16: the repentance and radical obedience made possible by the successful preaching of the kingdom after law and prophets have come to an end is nevertheless none other than what had already been demanded by the law; but such a connection would be somewhat forced. If it is to be rendered by 'and', then the purpose of the verse in this setting could have been to assert in general terms a continuing relationship between the gospel and Judaism. Daube (*NTRJ*, p. 293) points to a similar but reverse sequence of thought to vv. 16–17 to be found in Jewish writers – the law is permanent and attracts all men (cf. Philo, *Moses* II, 14ff.). Here the thought may be that the gospel attracts all men, but still carries with it the law as a moral substratum for Gentile converts (cf. 16³¹).

18

For divorce and remarriage as urgent questions for Christians, cf. I Cor. 7¹⁰ff., where Paul makes one of his rare appeals to teaching of Jesus on a matter. This teaching has multiple attestation in Matt. 5³¹f., in the Markan pericope with its attached precepts, Mark 10¹⁻¹² (reproduced in Matt. 19³⁻⁹), and here. In this attestation there are variations of form, wording, context and meaning. So far as form and wording are concerned Luke's version (i) could have had a common original with Matt. 5³², to which it is nearest in some of its wording – *everyone who divorces his wife, marries a divorced woman* – and in its form of two parallel sentences (the latter similarity could, however, be deceptive, as Matt. 5³² can be construed as a single continuous statement primarily concerned with the consequences of divorce for the woman: i.e. everyone who divorces his wife except for unchastity makes her an adulteress [by forcing her to marry again], so that anyone then marrying a woman thus divorced commits adultery [by marrying an adulteress]). In that case *and marries another* in Luke, which makes the judgment one about remarriage after divorce, would presumably have been absent from Matthew's source, unless he replaced it by his own addition 'except for unchastity'. (ii) Luke could, perhaps, have derived his version from Mark 10¹⁰⁻¹², since both have *and marries another* and *her husband*, and Mark's version consists of two genuinely parallel statements, though the second – divorce by the woman – reflects non-Jewish custom (and for that reason is not reproduced in Matt. 19⁹). A third possibility is that Luke's version is the result of a conflation of the Markan and Matthaean versions, which produces parallel statements, as in Mark; though they are not really such, since they refer to the actions of different men, the one marrying after divorce and the other marrying a divorced woman. On any explanation the puzzle remains why Luke should have been content with such a brief formulation of the matter here, and why, on rejoining Mark at 18¹⁵, he should have chosen to do so immediately after the lengthier discussion of it in the Markan pericope, Mark 10¹⁻¹². As regards context, this in Mark and Matthew is the relation of the teaching of Jesus to the law, either as fulfilling it (Matt. 5³¹f.), or as going behind it to the original purpose of God in creation (Mark 10¹⁻¹² = Matt. 19¹⁻⁹). There could be an element of this here when v. 18 is placed immediately after vv. 16 and 17, though it would be in the curious form that the teaching on divorce is an instance of the permanence of the law.

None of these versions can be adequately interpreted on the background of

Jewish law and practice alone, according to which adultery (theoretically punishable by death) was defined as 'the intercourse of a married woman with *any* man other than her husband . . . A man was not regarded as guilty of adultery unless he had intercourse with a *married* woman other than his wife' (Abrahams, *Studies* I, p. 73). The (divine) law, which required divorce in the case of adultery, declared both the divorcing man and the woman divorced (divorce was always the man's act, at most the woman could ask for it) to be free agents to marry again legally, so that intercourse would then not be adulterous, since it would be with the man's new wife or the woman's new husband. Adultery must therefore have here some other meaning than the legal. (*a*) If *divorces* is taken closely with *marries another* the intention may be to pronounce as adulterous divorce undertaken on trivial grounds (glossed by Matthew as 'except on the ground of unchastity'), and simply for the purpose of marrying again. This would fit v. 18a here, a woman so divorced being considered to be still married, but not v. 18b. And remarriage regularly followed divorce. (*b*) Adultery may be employed, as in the prophets, as a 'forceful and challenging synonym for unfaithfulness',★ so that divorce itself and remarriage are outward signs of an infidelity as adulterous as legal infidelity (Matt. 5^{28}). (*c*) A new conception of adultery emerges from the theological basis brought forward in Mark 10^{1-12}, of which Luke 16^{18} and Matt. 5^{32} are shorn. Here the Mosaic law of divorce is overruled by appeal to the prior purpose of God in creation in making male and female so that they become one flesh. Daube (*NTRJ*, pp. 71ff., and on Luke 16^{18} pp. 297ff.) argues that all these gospel texts on divorce only have force on the basis of a rabbinic conception, derived from Gen. 1^{27}, of the original man as a single androgynous being, and of marriage as therefore the reunion of man and woman into the one indissoluble being intended by God. This view condemned not only divorce but polygamy, which, even if rare amongst Jews in the first century AD, was officially countenanced by the law; and only if polygamy is forbidden is remarriage of a man while his first wife lives adulterous.

The Lukan version resembles Matt. 5^{32}; 19^9 in being concerned only with the man, but differs from all other versions in being primarily not a verdict on divorce as such, but a condemnation of second marriage (cf. I Tim. $3^{2, 12}$; Tit. 1^6 – if these are not condemnations of polygamy), and of any marriage to a divorced woman. This may reflect Luke's ascetic interests (cf. his addition in 18^{29} of the wife, without mention of the husband, to those who are to be renounced for the kingdom's sake), and may account for his placing of this saying in the wider context of the condemnation of worldliness in chs. 15–16. In the immediate context of $16^{16f.}$ he is perhaps presenting Christian marriage as a notable example of the strict observance of the law's demands which is made possible by the preaching of the kingdom.

★ D. S. Bailey, *The Mystery of Love and Marriage*, London and New York 1952, p. 91.

16^{19-31} The Parable of the Rich Man and Lazarus

¹⁹'*There was a rich man, who was clothed in purple and fine linen and who feasted sumptuously every day.* ²⁰*And at his gate lay a poor man named Lazarus, full of sores,* ²¹*who desired to be fed with what fell from the rich man's table; moreover the dogs came and licked his sores.* ²²*The poor man died and was carried by the angels to Abraham's bosom. The rich man also died and was buried;* ²³*and in Hades, being in torment, he lifted up his eyes, and saw Abraham far off and Lazarus in his bosom.* ²⁴*And he called out, "Father Abraham, have mercy upon me, and send Lazarus to dip the end of his finger in water and cool my tongue; for I am in anguish in this flame."* ²⁵*But Abraham said, "Son, remember that you in your lifetime received your good things, and Lazarus in like manner evil things; but now he is comforted here, and you are in anguish.* ²⁶*And besides all this, between us and you a great chasm has been fixed, in order that those who would pass from here to you may not be able, and none may cross from there to us."* ²⁷*And he said, "Then I beg you, father, to send him to my father's house,* ²⁸*for I have five brothers, so that he may warn them, lest they also come into this place of torment."* ²⁹*But Abraham said, "They have Moses and the prophets; let them hear them."* ³⁰*And he said, "No, father Abraham; but if some one goes to them from the dead, they will repent."* ³¹*He said to him, "If they do not hear Moses and the prophets, neither will they be convinced if some one should rise from the dead."'*

Another parable of the 'tale' type, with the same kind of beginning, 'There was a certain man . . .', but without any introduction (some mss omit the Greek connecting particle *de* = 'and'). It is not evident why Luke should have placed it here. There is a purely verbal connection with v. 16 in the mention of Moses and the prophets in v. 29, and perhaps a connection that is more than verbal with v. 17 in the thought that the law is permanently there to move men to repentance (v. 29); there may be also a link with v. 9 in that here the rich man fails to gain entry into the eternal habitations of the blessed.

The parable has certain notable features. (i) It is well told in good

Greek style, and with a richer and more varied vocabulary than is customary in the synoptic gospels. E.g., the following expressions are not found elsewhere in the NT or within it only in Luke–Acts – *fine linen* (a Semitic loan word widely used by Greek writers), *sumptuously* (found in Hellenistic authors but not in the LXX), *full of sores* (found in tragic, and of course medical, writers but not in the LXX), *licked* (the verb *epileichein* is not evidenced elsewhere in Greek), *the end of his finger* (cf. IV Macc. 10⁷ found in Philo and Josephus), *cool* (found in Hellenistic writers but not in the LXX), *am in anguish* (used of mental pain in poetical writers; elsewhere in the NT 2⁴⁸; Acts 20³⁸), *chasm* (classical and Hellenistic but not LXX). For further instances of literary vocabulary, see the notes.

(ii) Parallels in Egyptian and Jewish sources suggest that a story of a rich man and a poor man whose fortunes are reversed in the other world was a widespread and well-known folk tale, which had been variously adapted. The Lukan version is more Jewish in the part played by Abraham and in the references to the angels and to Moses and the prophets; but a popular non-Jewish origin is suggested by several features, some perhaps unique in Scripture. Such are, the absence in the first part of the story of any moral grounds for the reversals of fortune (these are commonly read in by commentators), a representation of the other world not recognizably that of Judaism, a dialogue in the other world as a means of conveying the story's message, and the naming of a character in the parable. These features make it difficult to discern how far Jesus, early Christian tradition, or Luke himself is responsible for the story in its present form. Some of them also combine to make the story somewhat discursive, so that it is not clear where the main point lies.

In the popular Egyptian (Demotic) version of the story an Egyptian, Satme Khamuas, is sent from Amnte, the sphere of the dead, by Osiris its ruler to be born in this world as the miraculous offspring of a childless couple in order to confute a powerful Ethiopian magician. He bears the name of Si-Osiris. His father, seeing a rich man carried out for burial with splendour and a poor man carried out in wretchedness, wishes for himself to have the fate of the rich man in the hereafter and not that of the poor man. The son contradicts his father, wishing for him the opposite, and to prove him wrong conducts him through the halls of Amnte, showing him in one hall the rich man now in torment and in another Osiris, and near him the poor man now clad in the rich man's finery. The explanation given for the reversal of fortunes is that in the case of the poor man his good deeds on earth had outweighed his bad deeds, whereas with the rich man it was the opposite. The father is thus persuaded to change his mind.[s]

In Luke's version there is a rich man unnamed ('Dives' in the traditional title of the parable is simply derived from the Latin version in which it is the word for 'a rich man'), who dresses and feeds splendidly. At his gate is a poor man (*ptōchos*, the regular word in classical Greek for 'a beggar'), who is *named Lazarus*. The name, which serves the purpose of the dialogue in vv. 24f. is probably not an addition here, but is retained from an earlier Jewish version. The name itself probably derives from the prominence of Abraham in this version as a kind of lord of the hereafter, since Lazarus is a variant of Eliezer, Abraham's servant and messenger (Gen. 15^{2-4}; $24^{2ff.}$?), and may denote the humble and faithful Israelite. His wretched condition is described, somewhat loosely, as desiring *to be fed* (the Greek word *chortasthēnai* should properly mean 'to be fed to the full', 'to be satisfied') from *what fell from the table* (this must be a conventional term for 'scraps', since Lazarus lay at the gate and not near the table). He is so helpless that he is unable to drive off the dogs from licking his sores; this is the force of *lay* (v. 20) and of *moreover* (v. 21).

The story then passes to the deaths of both men. In some versions of it the rich man's funeral is described in contrast to the poor man's so that later it can be revealed that their positions have been reversed, but here the reversal is stated at the outset, and provides the *mise-en-scène* for the rest of the story. This is depicted in terms that appear to reflect a popular, unsystematic and partly un-Jewish eschatology. At death Lazarus (not his soul only, as later he can be asked to dip his finger) is carried away by *the angels*. These are probably the so-called 'angels of service', who were believed to perform certain divine tasks, including the collection of the souls of the righteous at death. He is conducted *to Abraham's bosom*. This is a very rare expression in Jewish writings. It could denote either a place of honour at table (cf. John 13^{23}) next to Abraham at the heavenly banquet (cf. Matt. 8^{11}), or, more probably, the loving embrace or communion of Abraham. The first, however, would presuppose the final judgment to have taken place, and in either case the settlement of an individual's fate immediately after death and

s For more detail on this story and for derived Jewish versions see K. Grobel, 'Whose Names was Neves', *NTS* 10, 1963–64, pp. 373–82.

before the end of all things is non-Jewish (cf. 23^{43}). The rich man's fate is stated in what is in Greek a single word *buried*. After death the rich man is, also with a body, *in Hades*, which is represented as a place of torment. Between it and Abraham's bosom there is reciprocal visibility but no access either way by reason of *a great chasm*. This picture is neither that of the Jewish Sheol (rendered in the LXX by the Greek word *hadēs*), the underworld to which all departed souls went without bodies until the final judgment, nor that of Gehenna, the permanent abode of the wicked after the final judgment. The nearest parallel would seem to be an earlier conception found in I Enoch 22ff. (Josephus, *Ant.* 18.14, calls it Pharisaic) of Hades as the intermediate abode of all departed souls until the day of judgment. It is separated into three divisions, the first being for the righteous, the second for sinners 'when they die and are buried in the earth and judgment has not been executed on them in their lifetime' and they are 'set apart in great pain' (I Enoch 22^{10-11}, cf. Luke $16^{25, 23}$), and a third for the unrighteous who have already suffered on earth. According to this picture Abraham's bosom would be one department of Hades. On the other hand, v. 31 implies that a return thence to earth would not be from an intermediate state but after resurrection, and *comforted* (v. 25) suggests a permanent rather than a temporary consolation. In that case the picture would approximate to that of IV Ezra 7^{36}: 'And the pit of torment shall appear, and over against it shall be the place of rest: and the furnace of hell (Gehenna) shall be shewed, and over against it the paradise of delight.'

The story proceeds with the rich man from his place in Hades seeing Abraham and Lazarus (*lifted up his eyes* is a conventional expression, and need not imply that Abraham's bosom is aloft), and making request for Lazarus to be sent with water for his temporary relief. This request is refused on the ground that the present condition of both persons is what it should be. Jeremias, who takes the whole story as a designedly two-part parable (*Parables*, p. 186), sees the first part, which ends here (v. 25), as simply preparatory to the second part, where the parable's lesson is to be found. That lesson he understands to have been addressed to Sadducees in repudiation of their request for an authenticating sign. This cannot have been how Luke understood the parable, since he has it addressed to Pharisees as lovers of money, whose loftiness is an abomination with God ($16^{14f.}$). Moreover the verdict delivered in v. 25 so exactly reproduces the first of the beatitudes and of the woes in $6^{20, 24}$ that it stands in its own right with considerable force, and makes a point that is too emphatic to be merely a prelude to something else. Abraham's judgment there is not that the rich man has not helped the poor (the weak variant reading in v. 21 'and no one gave to him', which is borrowed from 15^{16}, may be an attempt to supply this), but, as in 6^{24}, that he has already had his good things. Nor is it said that Lazarus had done good deeds on earth, but only that he had suffered evil things. (For Luke, however, the words 'rich' and 'poor' could of themselves have had something of the added meaning they had already acquired in the LXX of the sinner as such, because self-reliant, neglectful of God and oppressor of the poor, and of the blessed as such because humble and looking to God.)

In its second part, vv. 27–31, the parable takes a new turn. It has in common with the Demotic version the twin themes of a journey between the two worlds and the conversion of members of the family, though these are very differently conceived. The transition to them is, however, awkwardly made with *And besides all this* (v. 26), as though something was here being added on (the Greek here *en pasi toutois* probably means 'in spite of all this', cf. Ecclus 48^{15}; Job. 2^{10}). And the passage now requested from the other world to this world (v. 27) is hardly a natural alternative to, or extension of, the previous request for a passage between two parts of Hades (v. 24). Since nothing can be altered in Hades the rich man asks that his five brothers be warned from Hades of their possible fate. If it is to be presumed that the brothers are also rich it is now clearly implied for the first time in the parable that to be rich is to be a sinner in need of repentance. When this request is also refused on the ground that the law and prophets are sufficient for repentance, the parable comes to an end in v. 31 with what can only be a Christian reflection: '*If they do not hear Moses and the prophets, neither will they be convinced if someone should rise from the dead.*' For only on the Christian background of the resurrection of Jesus is the resurrection of a single individual before and apart from the general resurrection conceivable. That this is a somewhat forced application of the parable is indicated by the expression *goes to them from the dead* (v. 30). This means 'makes a journey from among the denizens of the underworld', and while it arises naturally from the structure and scenery of the story itself, it is inappropriate as an expression for the Christian conception of resurrection (the Greek preposition here *apo* = 'from among' is used with 'the dead' elsewhere in the NT in superstitious statements, Matt. 14^2; 27^{64}, though once of the resurrection of Jesus, Matt. 28^7).

Hence in the concluding words of the parable it has to be altered to the normal Christian wording *rise from* (Greek preposition *ek*) *the dead*. Whether or not Luke was responsible for this application of the parable in its second part, it certainly accorded with his view. For the characteristic message in Acts of which the Jews are not *convinced* (v. 31; for this word cf. A. 17⁴; 18⁴, and, in conjunction with the word rendered *warn* in v. 28; A. 28²³ᶠ·) is a message of exhortation to repentance through the preaching of the resurrection of Jesus (A. 2³⁸; 3¹⁵ᶠ·; 4², ³³; 13³²ᶠᶠ·; 17¹⁸, ³⁰ᶠ·). And this itself is represented as being no more than what the law (Moses) and the prophets had been saying (A. 13²⁷⁻³⁸; 23⁶; 24¹⁴ᶠ·; 26²²ᶠ·, ²⁷; 28²³).

༒

19

There was a rich man: p⁷⁵ adds 'by name Neues', which is probably an abbreviated Grecized form of the name 'Nineue' found in mss of the Coptic (Sahidic) version. Its absence from the rest of the Greek textual tradition and from the Coptic (Bohairic) version makes it unlikely to have been original.

clothed in purple and fine linen: clothed is found again in the NT only at Mark 15¹⁷. For *purple* cf. Dan. 5⁷; I Macc. 10⁶², and for the combination *purple and fine linen* Prov. 31²²; Esther 8¹⁵; Rev. 18¹².

20

named Lazarus: This, the only instance of the naming of a character in a gospel parable, is strange, since Lazarus is the least significant of the three characters in it and does not speak.

21

licked his sores: As well as denoting his helplessness this may be intended to prepare for the request (v. 24) that Lazarus should assuage the rich man's thirst in Hades with water on the tip of his finger.

22

by the angels to Abraham's bosom: For rabbinic statements about the angels of service, see SB II, pp. 223ff., and for Abraham's bosom see *TDNT* III, pp. 825f. In the following verse it appears in the strange form *en tois kolpois autou* (lit. 'in his bosoms'), which is probably a plural of majesty or of supra-terrestrial things. For 'bosom' = 'communion' cf. the apocryphal saying of Jesus in II Clement 4.5: 'If you are gathered with me in my bosom, and do not keep my commandments . . .'

buried: The harsh brevity here may have led to the variant reading in some Old Latin mss and in Marcion 'he was buried in Hades'. In a Jewish milieu, however, the single word could denote distinction. Only notable figures were supplied with graves; cf. the action of Joseph of Arimathea in supplying a grave for Jesus.

24

in water: I Enoch 22⁹ speaks of 'the bright spring of water' in the division of Hades reserved for the righteous as if it were a standing feature there. Grobel (*NTS* 10, p. 380) notes a similar usage in sepulchral inscriptions with reference to Osiris, the lord of death, who is constantly associated with water.

25

good things ... evil things: A classical Greek expression for good and evil fortune. The use of the Greek word *zōē* = 'life' in the sense of *lifetime* is also classical, and is rare in the NT.

26

a great chasm: In I Enoch 18¹¹ a great chasm is said to separate different places of torment.

17¹⁻¹⁰ *Teaching for Disciples*

17 *And he said to his disciples, 'Temptations to sin* are sure to come; but woe to him by whom they come! ²It would be better for him if a millstone were hung round his neck and he were cast into the sea, than that he should cause one of these little ones to sin.† ³Take heed to yourselves; if your brother sins, rebuke him, and if he repents, forgive him; ⁴and if he sins against you seven times in the day, and turns to you seven times, and says, "I repent," you must forgive him.'*

⁵The apostles said to the Lord, 'Increase our faith!' ⁶And the Lord said, 'If you had faith as a grain of mustard seed, you could say to this sycamine tree, "Be rooted up, and be planted in the sea", and it would obey you.

⁷'Will any one of you, who has a servant ploughing or keeping sheep, say to him when he has come in from the field, "Come at once and sit down at table"? ⁸Will he not rather say to him, "Prepare supper for me, and gird yourself and serve me, till I eat and drink; and afterward you shall eat and drink"?

⁹Does he thank the servant because he did what was commanded? ¹⁰So you also, when you have done all that is commanded you, say, "We are unworthy servants; we have only done what was our duty." '

 ★ Greek *stumbling blocks*
 † Greek *stumble*

As there is something of a break at 17^{11} Luke may here be rounding off what has gone before with a brief section of teaching to disciples, who have been introduced as audience at 16^1. The section is made up of four units – vv. 1–2, 3–4, 6, 7–10 – which are sufficiently disparate to require as connecting links *And he said to his disciples* (v. 1), *Take heed to yourselves* (v. 3), and *The apostles said to the Lord* (v. 5). Since equivalents of the first two of these units are found in the same order, though separated from each other, in the composite discourse in Matt. 18, they could be assigned to Q.

 The first, vv. 1–2, is found in Matt. 18$^{6-7}$, though with the two statements in reverse order. That is because Matthew, in following Mark here, has taken over Mark's version of the sayings about 'little ones' (Mark 9^{42}), and has then used the general statement about stumbling blocks to introduce the subsequent Markan sayings about what in particular causes men to stumble (Mark 9$^{43-47}$). Luke's order from the general statement to the particular is more natural, and could reproduce that of a common source. Form and wording are, however, more polished than would be likely in a source – *are sure to come* (*anendekton* = 'impossible', a rare word found only here in the Greek Bible), *tou mē elthein* ('for them not to come', the genitive of the article with the infinitive, an extension of classical usage with verbs of hindering), *it would be better* (*lusitelei*, a literary word, only here in the NT), *one* (*hena*, placed last in the sentence for emphasis).

 The second, vv. 3–4, has parallels in Matt. 18$^{15,\ 21-22}$, where the two sayings are separated, and are concerned with two different themes, the rebuke of a brother and the limits of forgiveness. While Matthew's version of the two sayings may not have been unaffected by the context in which he has placed them, Luke seems to have modified them by approximating them to each other.

 Verse 6 has a parallel in Mark 11^{23} (in a passage omitted by Luke) and in Matt. 17^{20}. Luke's formulation is the most rhythmical, and agrees first with Matthew's (*if you had faith as a grain of mustard seed you could say*), and then with Mark's (both verbs in the aorist imperative, and *in* (Mark 'into') *the sea*; but the curious reference to transplanting a tree rather than removing a mountain points to an independent version of the saying.

Verses 7–10 are peculiar to Luke. They form a parable of the type consisting of a single continuous sentence, which asks a rhetorical question beginning with 'Which of you'. This type tends to collapse under the weight of its subordinate clauses (cf. 11$^{5ff.}$), which is the case here, despite Luke's attempt to control it by the use of participles (*ploughing, keeping sheep*; in the Greek *come in, come* and *gird* are also participles). It is not clear whether syntactically the parable is meant to be a single sentence with *Does he thank* as the main verb, or two sentences, vv. 7–8 and v. 9. In translation it has had to be broken up into two (RV), three (RSV) or four (NEB) sentences. There is some similarity of language with 12$^{37ff.}$, which might indicate a common source for both, but here the style is more literary – *plough, keep sheep* (in the literal sense only here in the NT), *supper, thank* (*charin echein*), *command* (for *all that is commanded*, the participial *ta diatachthenta*, cf. 3^{13}; A. 23^{31}), *our duty* (the verb *opheilein* only here in the synoptists). The concluding *we have . . . our duty* is neatly expressed with the use of a choice Greek metre.

ᛦᚱᚢ

1

Temptations to sin: This translates *skandala* (margin, *stumbling blocks*). The word meant 'a trap'. Its use in a religious sense for what occasions a falling away from the true God, or seduces men from faith in him (as also the corresponding verb *skandalizein* in v. 2), is peculiar to the Bible. It could be used eschatologically, as perhaps originally in this saying, for what occasions an ultimate defection from God in the coming final tribulation (Dan. 11^{41}; Matt. 13^{41}; 24^{10}; Mark 14$^{27ff.}$), or the forfeit of eternal life (Mark 9$^{43ff.}$).

are sure to come: No solution is being offered here and in v. 2 to the problem of evil; both sides are simply stated. That faith should be radically tested in this way is necessary – for the divine purpose? In Matt. 18^7 this necessity is expressed by *anankē*, which is very rare in the Bible, being the word for 'fate', by which Greeks believed all things to be governed in the last restort. Luke puts it negatively – it is impossible for stumbling blocks not to come.

2

Necessary as they may be, the stumbling blocks are so heinous as occasioning the ultimate sin that a man had better avoid responsibility for them, and the eternal damnation involved (this is the force of *woe to him*), by being physically exterminated first (Mark 14^{21} by not being born at all). If *these little ones* is a semi-technical word for disciples (see on $9^{46f.}$), these sayings would originally have been spoken about them and not to them. In having them spoken to disciples, and in applying them in the following sayings in vv. 3–4, Luke would seem to be thinking of the stumbling blocks somewhat less radically, not as coming from outside to tempt to apostasy from God, but as hindrances to faith put in the way of fellow believers (cf. A. 15^{10-29}; I Cor. 8^{13}; Rom. 14^{13}).

3

Take heed to yourselves: This introductory expression, meaning 'be on your guard', is Lukan, occurring elsewhere in the NT at 12^1; 21^{34}; A. 5^{35}; 20^{28}. It is awkward when, as here, it is followed by instructions given in the singular. Its aim is to establish a connection with the statements in vv. 1–2, and to apply them to interior relations between Christians.

if your brother sins . . . forgive him: brother denotes, as often in the OT, Judaism and other religions, a member of the same religious community. This verse belongs with v. 4 only in Luke's formulation of it, which would appear to be secondary. For *if your brother sins, rebuke him* would seem to require what stands in Matt. 18^{15}, 'if he listens to you (i.e. acknowledges that he is sinning and turns from it) you have gained your brother' (i.e. won him back to righteousness or the kingdom – for 'gain' in this sense, cf. I Cor. $9^{19f.}$; I Peter 3^1). Luke has modified this by introducing his favourite theme of repentance/forgiveness. The sin is now specifically that against a brother; the rebuke is made by the one sinned against; and the object of the rebuke is to secure repentance in the form of acknowledgment of this, so that the one sinned against may then exercise forgiveness. This can then lead on to v. 4, which is Luke's version of the limits of forgiveness when sinned against.

4

In Matt. 18^{21-22} this is strikingly expressed in reply to a question from Peter by the hyperbole 'not seven times but seventy times seven' (or, 'seventy-seven times'); that is, there are no limits, and no mention is made of repentance as a prior requirement. Luke's *seven times a day* (Ps. 119^{164}) is less striking, and by again importing repentance he produces the somewhat pedestrian *and turns to you seven times, and says 'I repent'*.

5

The apostles said to the Lord: The only passage in which Luke uses together the post-resurrection title *the Lord* for the earthly Jesus and the formal title *the apostles* which he believed Jesus himself to have given the Twelve (6^{13}). This invests the request and the reply with a solemn, perhaps official character.

Increase our faith: Or, by a rare usage of the verb here *prostithenai*, 'Grant us faith'. This may echo a prayer men addressed to the ascended Lord as the origin and sustainer of their faith as Christians, which is here transferred to the earlier circumstances of the earthly Jesus and the church's future leaders. What is meant by *faith* here is not clear.

6

A version of this saying is found connected with one on forgiveness, though in reverse order, in Mark 11^{22-25}. It is likely to have been highly valued by Christians as bearing on what the NT shows to have been a central concern for them, and also as the only statement about faith in general from Jesus to have been preserved in the synoptic tradition, where, apart from 18^8; 22^{32}, it denotes confidence in the presence or availability of miraculous power. This conception, which is also found in the rabbis, is uppermost in Matt. 17^{20}, where the saying is a pendant to a miracle story, and it is perhaps not absent from Mark 11^{22-33}, where the saying is introduced after the cursing of the fig tree with a unique expression, 'Have faith in God.' The original form and force of the saying are uncertain. 'Moving mountains' (Matt. 17^{20}; by faith I Cor. 13^2) is likely to have been a proverbial expression for achieving the impossible (J. J. Wetstein, *Novum Testamentum Graecum*, on Matt. 17^{20}, and cf. Mark 9^{23}), rather than the more technical rabbinic term for surmounting difficulties in the interpretation of the law (SB I, p. 759). Moving a mountain into the sea (Mark 11^{23}) is a further elaboration of this, perhaps with the idea that the mountain is thereby destroyed; R. Eliezer (*c.* AD 90) is reported to have done this to show God's approval of something he had affirmed (SB I, p. 759). Luke's version combines the impossible – removing a *sukaminos*, either a mulberry tree, or, as in the LXX, a syncamore, a specially deep-rooted tree – with what is fantastic even by the standards of oriental hyperbole – making it grow in the sea. *this sycamine tree* is perhaps influenced by 'this mountain' in Mark 11^{23}, which could refer to the Mount of Olives as due for destruction in the judgment on Jerusalem.

7–10

This has no obvious connection with what precedes or follows. Luke may have placed it here because he understood it to teach a true doctrine of works to stand alongside teaching on forgiveness and faith; cf. A. $13^{38f.}$ for the sequence of forgiveness, law, faith and justification. As apostles are unlikely to be addressed as those who owned fields and possessed slaves, the parable may have been spoken originally to Pharisees in repudiation of the belief that good works established a claim on God, and in support of the contrary view, as expressed in Pirke Aboth 1^3, 'Be not like slaves who serve the master with a view to receiving a present, but be like slaves who serve the master not with a view to receiving a present,' and 2^9, 'If thou hast practised much Torah, take no credit for thyself, for thereunto wast thou created.' The point, however, is not made with clarity. For (i) a lesson which begins to be drawn with *So you also* (v. 10) should follow directly from actions in the parable, but here does not do so, since the parable is concerned with the attitude and behaviour of the master and the lesson is concerned with the attitude of the slave. And (ii) the sequence of thought in vv. 7–9 is obscure. *Come at once and sit down at table* (v. 7) could refer to a treatment of a slave so exceptional that it could only be construed as a special reward equivalent to thanking him (v. 9), and therefore destructive of the proper relationship between master and slave. If so, the purpose served by v. 8 is not evident. Or it could refer to something which would be in order provided it was deferred until certain further necessary duties had been performed, and the purpose of v. 8 is to stress that a master in relation to a slave is one who continues to exact obedience until all duties are done. There is further obscurity in the use in v. 10 of the adjective *achreioi*, either in its normal sense of 'useless', or in its rarer sense of 'wretched', 'unworthy'; for it is neither the uselessness nor the unworthiness of the slave which preclude any claim on his master, but the fact that he is a slave, and his obedience to commands is simply the performance of what is involved in his being such. (*achreioi* may have been a conventional deprecatory adjective with 'slave' – cf. Matt. 25^{30} – which Luke, or a scribe, slipped in unthinkingly.) In view of the special setting he has provided in v. 5 Luke may have taken the parable as applying, not to men in general in their relationship to God, but to apostles, who might be tempted to think that their position and labours in the church carried with them a status which somehow dispensed with, or modified, the relationship of slave to lord.

17$^{11-19}$ *Healing of Ten Lepers*

[11]*On the way to Jerusalem he was passing along between Samaria and Galilee.* [12]*And as he entered a village, he was met by ten lepers, who stood at a distance* [13]*and lifted up their voices and said, 'Jesus, Master, have mercy on us.'* [14]*When he saw them he said to them, 'Go and show yourselves to the priests.' And as they went they were cleansed.* [15]*Then one of them, when he saw that he was healed, turned back, praising God with a loud voice;* [16]*and he fell on his face at Jesus' feet, giving him thanks. Now he was a Samaritan.* [17]*Then said Jesus, 'Were not ten cleansed? Where are the nine?* [18]*Was no one found to return and give praise to God except this foreigner?'* [19]*And he said to him, 'Rise and go your way; your faith has made you well.'*

The story is peculiar to Luke and contains a high proportion of wording which could be assigned to his hand. Thus, *as he entered* (gen. abs. construction in the Greek), *a* (*tina* = 'a certain') *village* (cf. 9⁵²; 10³⁸), *met* (*apantān*, only here and Mark 14¹³ in the NT), *at a distance* (+ Heb. 11¹³), *lifted up their voices* (a LXX expression, only L–A in the NT), *master* (*epistatēs*, confined to Luke as an address to Jesus, otherwise on the lips of disciples), *go* (*poreuesthai*, Lukan), *as they went* (an articular infinitive, as in 8⁴², where Luke rewrites Mark), *healed* (*iāsthai*, the Lukan word for healing), *turned back*, *praising God* (a Lukan feature in miracle stories, cf. 7¹⁶; 13¹³; 5²⁵; 18⁴³; A. 4²¹), *fell on his face* (a LXX expression, cf. 5¹² of a leper), the idiomatic *was found to*, the LXX expression *give praise* (lit. glory) *to* (cf. A. 12²³, not elsewhere in the gospels), *foreigner* (*allogenēs* ++), *rise and go your way* (so 5¹⁸; A. 8²⁷; 9¹¹; 22¹⁰). Luke may thus have been the first to put the story in writing, perhaps modelling it on 5¹²⁻¹⁶. It has mixed features. Technically it is a story of a miracle, and of one unprecedented in the synoptic tradition in being the simultaneous healing of ten persons of the same disease – and that the dire disease of leprosy – by the process of showing obedience to a command to report for inspection by the priests. As such it could stand here as a signal instance of the faith spoken of in v. 6, especially if that referred to confidence in miraculous power. This is not, however, where the accent of the story lies. The cure is a subordinate element, and is hardly reinforced by the concluding formula *your faith has made you well*. Elsewhere this either effects the healing or accompanies it (cf. 8⁴⁸; 18⁴² and the parallels in Mark), but here it comes belatedly as a comment on it, and as a somewhat conventional rounding off of the story as a miracle story. For Luke cannot have meant that only the Samaritan was healed by faith, the rest being healed without faith. The sharp point for which the story is told, and which cannot be made without it, is Jesus' commendation, not of faith as such, nor of thanksgiving in general, but of the genuine piety of a non-Israelite manifesting itself in gratitude. This reflects the same outlook as 4²⁴ᶠᶠ·; 7⁹; 10²⁵ᶠᶠ·, and as the incidents of the Ethiopian eunuch (A. 8²⁶ᶠᶠ·) and Cornelius (A. 10). The story also powerfully glorifies Jesus, who knows at a distance that all ten lepers have been cleansed, and who, in commenting on the fact (vv. 17–18), plays the part generally assigned in miracle stories to a chorus of bystanders. Moreover, he is so intimately related to God that *giving thanks to him* in an attitude of prostration (v. 16) is identified with giving *praise to God* (v. 18).

17^{11-19}

11

On the way to Jerusalem he was passing along: The story is provided with a prelude in the first mention of the journey since 13^{22}. Even so it is designed to introduce Jesus alone, and not to furnish information about the band of travellers and their route.

between Samaria and Galilee: The preposition here is *dia meson*, which is a classical poetic usage found also in Hellenistic prose, and means 'through the midst of'. But that would require here that Samaria comes before Galilee on the route to Jerusalem, which is not the case. This has given rise to a number of variant readings – *dia mesou, ana meson, meson* – all aimed at establishing a geographical region lying between Galilee and Samaria, and this is adopted by rsv here with *between*, and by some commentators. This raises the question of Luke's knowledge of the geography of Palestine, and of his conception of the constituent parts of the country and of their geographical relation to one another. Conzelmann (*Theology*, pp. 68ff.) concludes from a review of the geographical notices in the gospel that Luke was not familiar with Palestine, at least beyond the coastal region, that he thought Galilee and Judaea were directly adjacent, and that Samaria was inland from them with a border running alongside both (this would appear to have been the view of Pliny in his *Natural History* 5.68ff.; and cf. the same order in reverse – Judaea – Galilee – Samaria – in A. 9^{31}). According to Conzelmann the course of the journey as Luke conceived it was from Galilee to the border of Galilee with Samaria, where Jesus is rejected (9^{51-56}), a return into Galilee, and then directly from Galilee into Judaea along the border with Samaria to Jerusalem via Jericho. Even this, however, does not remove the difficulty of 'through the midst of' or 'between'. Possibly Luke has simply juxtaposed the two regional names Samaria and Galilee so as to provide an appropriate setting somewhere short of Jerusalem for a Samaritan to make his appearance along with Jews.

14

Go and show yourselves to the priests: In 5^{12-16} (= Mark 1^{40-45}) this command is an integral part of the cure and a consequence of its having taken place. Here it is to provide a lapse of time for the cure to take place – *And as they went they were cleansed* – and for a return to be made which is to evoke commendation. It is probably to be deduced from vv. 16–18 that *the nine* were Israelites, and that they were sent to representatives of the Jewish priesthood, presumably at Jerusalem; for the elaborate documentation of the rules for establishing purification from leprosy, see SB IV, pp. 757ff. Whether Luke thought that the Samaritan was sent to representatives of his own priesthood does not appear, nor is it known whether the Samaritan priesthood had similar regulations.

16

Klostermann (p. 173) quotes from a Greek inscription concerned with healing: 'He went and gave thanks publicly to God.'

17–18

The point is somewhat strained, since the others had been commanded to go to the priests (at Jerusalem?), and a return thence, or on the way there, to give thanks was not necessarily incumbent on them. It is, however, made with great force by skilful expression – in the Greek 'Were not the ten cleansed? The nine where?', and *except this foreigner* has an emphatic position at the end of the sentence. *foreigner* does not catch sufficiently the religious significance of the Greek word *allogenēs* in this context. This word is common in the LXX and rare outside it (cf. Jos. *BJ* 2.417, and in the inscription on the barrier in the temple warning non-Israelites from proceeding further). It meant a religious alien.

17²⁰⁻³⁷ *The Kingdom of God and the Son of Man*

²⁰*Being asked by the Pharisees when the kingdom of God was coming, he answered them, 'The kingdom of God is not coming with signs to be observed;* ²¹*nor will they say, "Lo, here it is!" or "There!" for behold, the kingdom of God is in the midst of you.'*

²²*And he said to the disciples, 'The days are coming when you will desire to see one of the days of the Son of man, and you will not see it.* ²³*And they will say to you, "Lo, there!" or "Lo, here!" Do not go, do not follow them.* ²⁴*For as the lightning flashes and lights up the sky from one side to the other, so will the Son of man be in his day.*† ²⁵*But first he must suffer many things and be rejected by this generation.* ²⁶*As it was in the days of Noah, so will it be in the days of the Son of man.* ²⁷*They ate, they drank, they married, they were given in marriage, until the day when Noah entered the ark, and the flood came and destroyed them all.* ²⁸*Likewise as it was in the days of Lot – they ate, they drank, they bought, they sold, they planted, they built,* ²⁹*but on the day when Lot went out from Sodom fire and brimstone rained from heaven and destroyed them all –* ³⁰*so will it be on the day when the Son of man is revealed.* ³¹*On that day, let him who is on the housetop, with his goods in the house, not come down to take them away; and likewise let him who is in the field not turn back.* ³²*Remember Lot's wife.* ³³*Whoever seeks to gain his life will lose it, but*

whoever loses his life will preserve it. ³⁴*I tell you, in that night there will be two men in one bed; one will be taken and the other left.* ³⁵*There will be two women grinding together; one will be taken and the other left.'* ‡ ³⁷*And they said to him, 'Where, Lord?' He said to them, 'Where the body is, there the eagles* § *will be gathered together.'*

* Or *within you*

† Other ancient authorities omit *in his day*

‡ Other ancient authorities add v. 36, '*Two men will be in the field; one will be taken and the other left*'

§ Or *vultures*

Questions of source and interpretation are closely connected here. Verses 23–24, 26–27, 34–35, 37 have parallels in Matt. 24²⁶⁻²⁸, ³⁷⁻³⁹, ⁴⁰⁻⁴¹, 24²⁸, which are those passages that Matthew has inserted into his revised version of Mark 13. A possible deduction, therefore, is that a short discourse of an eschatological kind stood in Q, perhaps as its conclusion, from which Matthew made excerpts, and which, perhaps, Luke has incorporated entire, and in something more like its original wording. On the other hand, there are indications that Luke has not simply taken over a single block of material here, but has attempted to make a composition on a particular theme, and that this has involved editorial work with more than one source, and in some instances a modification of an original meaning.

Thus (i) vv. 20–21 are a self-contained unit, peculiar to Luke, which is addressed to Pharisees, and which does not lead on to the following address to disciples. (ii) The address to disciples, vv. 22–37, takes its start from an independent saying, perhaps modelled in part on vv. 20–21 (and resembling Mark 13²¹, omitted by Luke in that context), and from the phrase *the days* (plural) *of the Son of man* (vv. 22–23). Whatever this phrase denotes, it does not lead naturally to what follows, where what is compared to lightning is the final and sudden *day* (singular) of the Son of man (Matt. 24²⁷ has the technical term 'parousia'). (iii) Verse 25, a prediction of the coming rejection of the Son of man, is modelled on 9²² = Mark 8³¹ (for *but first . . . must* in eschatological discourse, cf. Mark 13¹⁰, omitted there by Luke). It does not come naturally here, and is perhaps introduced by Luke to make the discourse cover all aspects of the Son of man when identified with Jesus – his earthly life (days), his death (rejection) and his final manifestation (day). Then the coming destruction of *this generation* can be seen as the consequence of that act of rejection. (iv) Verses 26–27 on Noah and the flood are close in wording to Matthew but different in sense. In Matthew the point of comparison with Noah's generation (the days of Noah) is that the Son of man's parousia will supervene suddenly on those pursuing their daily occupations in ignorance of it. In Luke the comparison is between a sinful heedless behaviour in Noah's time similar to that in the present days of the Son of man (and the time of his rejection, if *and* at the beginning of v. 26 – untranslated in RSV – is meant to bind it closely with v. 25), bringing upon itself total destruction. (v) Verses 28–30 on Lot and Sodom resemble vv. 26–27 in form and wording, and could have stood in Q, being omitted by Matthew. Or, they could have been written by Luke as a duplication of the Noah comparison to reiterate the total destruction brought by the day of the Son of man. (vi) Verse 31 is similar to, though more polished than, Mark 13^{15}, which Luke omits in that context and Matthew reproduces; but while in Mark/Matthew the saying explicates a warning to instant flight in face of the Antichrist horror, here it appears to forbid self-seeking action aimed at securing earthly possessions in the time of judgment. The injunction ends abruptly, and not very intelligibly, with the words *not turn back* (to do what?), and so can lead on to v. 32 (and connect back with vv. 29–30) with a reference to Lot's wife, who perished because she looked *back* (Gen. 19^{26} LXX *eis ta opisō*, as here). (vii) Verse 33 is an independent saying, and a doublet of 9^{24} = Mark 8^{35} (the context from which Luke has taken v. 25), though formulated in a more Lukan style. There it enunciates a law of life for the disciple as a follower of the Son of man who suffers; here it only follows on because in v. 31 Luke has interpreted an injunction to flight in the last days as moral instruction not to hang on to life at all costs. (viii) Verses 34–35, with a fresh introduction, *I tell you*, conclude the theme with a pair of examples, one concerning males and the other females, of discrimination at the judgment (so Matt. 24$^{40-41}$, though Luke's version is better phrased). Since, however, Luke's first example is of two in the same bed, *that day* (v. 31) becomes *that night* (perhaps through reflection on Mark 13$^{33-37}$, omitted by Luke in that context), and strictly the two women in the second example are made to work at the mill at night. Finally, the homeless proverb of the body and the eagles (v. 37), which in Matthew illustrates the instantaneous character of the Son of man's parousia, is here given in answer to disciples' enquiry about the place (*where*) of the Son of man's appearance. This matches the Pharisees' enquiry about the time (*when*) of the kingdom's appearance, and so provides an impressive conclusion to a discourse, which now both opens and closes with an eschatological question, to which Jesus gives a cryptic but decisive answer.

ಞಞ

20–21   *The time of the kingdom*
These verses are the purest example in the synoptists of that form of oral tradition known in Greek literary criticism as a *chria* (or *chreia*), i.e. a pregnant utterance in a single sentence introduced by a participle in the nominative – *Being asked by . . . he answered them . . .* The question is assigned to the Pharisees, either because the reply is intended as condemnatory, or to secure the Lukan convention of address to Pharisees followed by address to disciples.

20

when the kingdom of God was coming: Evidence of a preoccupation, at least in some circles, with the time of the end can be seen in surviving apocalyptic literature (e.g. Dan. $12^{8\text{ff.}}$; IV Ezra $4^{51\text{ff.}}$; $7^{26\text{ff.}}$; II Baruch 24ff.; see further SB IV, pp. 997ff.).

is not coming with signs to be observed: The first of the two negative parts of the reply. *is not coming* has a future sense of 'will not come'; cf. *nor will they say*. *with* is a preposition of attendant circumstances, 'to the accompaniment of'. *signs to be observed* translates a single Greek word *paratērēsis*, found only here in the Greek Bible. It means 'observation' or 'observance', and could be a technical term for the deduction of the future from signs (cf. Matt. $2^{2,\ 7}$ for the detection of events by astrological observation). The meaning is 'so as to be calculable'.

21

'Lo, here it is!' or 'There!': This second negative part of the reply implies a scrutiny not of time, but of space for what may make its appearance in hidden form; cf. Mark 13^{21} of the messiah.

for behold, the kingdom of God is in the midst of you: The positive ground for repudiating both kinds of search (*for*) is now given in answer to the question. It depends on the meaning to be given to the Greek preposition *entos* – thus NEB has 'amongst you' in the text, and in the margin 'within you', 'within your grasp' and 'will be among you'. For some of the literature in the debate over this, s.v. *entos* in Bauer.

(i) The meaning to be expected from general Greek usage is 'within', 'inside' (so in the only other instance in the NT, Matt. 23^{26}), including inside a person.

The Latin versions have *intra vos* = 'within you'. This is also the almost universal view of the Fathers, as is to be expected of their spiritualizing exegesis, as also of Gnostics (e.g. the Naassenes, for whom it was a favourite text as speaking of a kingdom within man). Its difficulties are (*a*) that as Luke has framed the saying *you* refers to Pharisees, whom he generally represents in an unfavourable light; (*b*) that the idea of the kingdom as an inward possession of mind and heart would be without parallel in the NT (Rom. 14^{17} should not be cited here, as what Paul means is that the kingdom is not eating and drinking in such a fashion that just dealing, harmony and joy are not secured thereby); (*c*) that it does not accord with the conception of the kingdom implied by the verbs that are generally used in connection with it: 'come', 'draw near', 'enter'; and (*d*) that what is required as an antithesis to vv. 20b–21a is not inward possession but a different kind of coming.

(ii) C. H. Roberts[t] has proposed, on the basis of two instances in papyri, a modified form of 'within' – 'within your power', 'in your possession'. 'The misconception to be removed is that it is something external to men, independent of their volition.' He cites Tertullian (*Against Marcion*, 4.35), 'that is, in your power, if you are bold, if you perform God's commandments,' and Cyril of Alexandria in his commentary on Luke, 'that is, it lies in your wills and power to take it'. The difficulties of this are (*a*) that the meaning in the papyri concerned is itself disputed, some translating there by 'in the house of', or 'within the domain of'; (*b*) that the moralistic tendency of much exegesis of the Fathers would incline them towards it, especially Tertullian, who is here anxious to show that the gospel is in harmony with Deut. 30$^{11-14}$, where God says of his word that 'it is in your mouth and in your heart to do it'; and (*c*) that *for behold* introduces an antithetical climax rather than an added explanation, and 'outside your power' would not seem to be the force of *coming with signs to be observed*.

(iii) *in the midst of you* (RSV). So one of the Syriac versions, and one of the Syrian Fathers, Ephrem. This meaning is rare (it is found in Lam. 1^3, and in Symmachus's translation of Ps. 88^5), and Luke's regular word for 'among' is in Greek *en mesō*. While linguistically less well founded, it is probably to be preferred in this context as providing the best antithesis. There will be no future coming such as can be calculated; for behold (unrecognized by you) the kingdom is already in your midst – perhaps in the midst of the community of Israel, which may be the force of *entos* as distinct from *en mesō* = among you as individuals. This interpretation may lie behind the version in the Gospel of Thomas 113, 'But the kingdom of the Father is spread out upon the earth, and men do not see it.'

(iv) Others (e.g. Bultmann, *History*, pp. 121f.) hold that *is* here should itself be taken as a future, and that the original meaning was that calculation is ruled out because the kingdom, when it comes, will be suddenly there in their midst.

---

t 'The Kingdom of Heaven (Luke 17.21)', *HTR* 41, 1948, pp. 1–8.

This secures a sharp antithesis (cf. v. 24), but it makes the saying exceedingly compressed, and requires the main point ('suddenly') to be read out of *for behold*.

That the question asks about the time of the kingdom but the answer is in terms of its mode may indicate that Luke was himself responsible for the question. He was clearly anxious to play down the future aspect of the kingdom, and may have seen this saying as a powerful means of doing so. In A. 1⁷, in reply to a question whether the time has come for the risen Lord to restore the kingdom to Israel, the apostles are forbidden to speculate about divine times and seasons, and are bidden to be his witnesses; and there is little if any reference in A. to the future kingdom to come with power. Rather is it there one of the terms for the Christian message, which the risen Lord speaks about for forty days (A. 1³), which Philip preaches as good news (A. 8¹²), which Paul urges, proclaims to believers and unbelievers alike, and testifies to with warnings that entry into it involves affliction (A. 19⁸; 20²⁵; 28²³, ³¹; 14²²); in all of which passages 'it may mean the Church, but in none is the earlier eschatological meaning decisively excluded by the context' (*Beginnings* IV, p. 4). Similarly, in the Gospel so far, Jesus has preached the kingdom as good news, and has sent others to do the same (4⁴³; 8¹; 9², ⁶⁰). It has come upon men, is growing rapidly from small beginnings, and disciples have been given knowledge of its secrets, indeed the kingdom itself (11²⁰; 13¹⁸ff.; 8¹⁰; 12³²). This means that it is closely related to the present activity of Jesus. There is a future form of the kingdom, which is envisaged in two ways, as that which is to come (11²), and as a heavenly banquet with the patriarchs, anticipated in the universal mission of the church (13²⁸f.; 14¹⁵ff.). From this point on Luke seems anxious to divest this future coming of any idea of the power which might ordinarily be associated with the word 'kingdom', having in mind, perhaps, suspicion aroused by the word for Romans rather than any preoccupation of Christians with the delay of the parousia. In 9²⁷ he has edited Mark's potentially dangerous statement that within the lifetime of disciples the kingdom will come with force, and in 19¹¹ he will mark the dangerous approach to Jerusalem, which is to lead to the acclamation of Jesus as king, by a parable which he underlines as told to deny any immediate open manifestation of the kingdom. It is in this context that the question in v. 20a may belong.

22–30   *The day(s) of the Son of man*

The Pharisees having been rebuked for their preoccupation with the future, and with their failure to discern the presence of the kingdom in the activity (and the existence of the disciples?) of Jesus, the disciples are now warned against an analogous temptation (cf. '*Lo there!* or '*Lo here!*' in v. 23 with v. 21) which is likely to afflict them as disciples. This is expressed in more personal terms with reference to the Son of man, a title which, if its origin is ultimately in Dan. 7, is closely connected with the kingdom of God; though it so happens that nowhere in the synoptic tradition are the two found together in the same saying.

22

The days are coming when: The possibility of the disciples' temptation arises from this. The expression generally forebodes a reversal of conditions at present obtaining (cf. 5^{35}; 19^{43}; 21^6; 23^{29}; A. 3^{19}; Isa. 39^6). Taken closely with v. 21 it could mean that the kingdom will no longer be present in the form to which they have become accustomed, and that, as disciples, they will hanker, not after the future, but after a return to the past.

one of the days of the Son of man: The expression *the days of the Son of man* is unique and puzzling – for a discussion of the meanings that have been proposed for it, see Marshall, pp. 658f. It would seem to be modelled on the biblical phrase 'the days' meaning 'lifetime', 'period on earth' (cf. vv. 26, 28; A. 7^{45}; Gen. 5 passim). The nearest parallel might be 'the days of the messiah', which is found in the rabbis, though not before the first century AD, for the fixed and limited period of the rule of the messiah on earth. But this is not applicable to the Son of man, in so far as he is (as frequently in the gospels) the heavenly advocate or judge of men, who gathers God's elect, and whose dominion is everlasting (cf. I Enoch 48^6; 49$^{2-4}$). Such a figure does not have *days* on earth, but only a single *day* (v. 30), which is the end of the world and the final judgment. The expression is thus only intelligible if the Son of man is here being used in a Christian sense, and is identified with Jesus, who before his enthronement as God's vicegerent, and his appearance for judgment and salvation, has a life span on earth. It is for one of such days (D has 'these days of the Son of man'; cf. Heb. 5^7 'the days of his flesh') that the disciples will be tempted to yearn after his departure.

you will not see it: There is no return of this kind to earthly existence, and the disciples are not to be seduced by any suggestion of it.

24

In contrast to the present days of the Son of man, his future manifestation will be, like lightning, instantaneous and all-encompassing.

lights up the sky from one side to another: Literally translated the Greek here is 'lights from the (place) under heaven to the (place) under heaven', and should mean 'from one place on earth to another'; but this hardly fits here, and the expression may denote the two horizons (cf. Matt. 24^{27}, 'from the east as far as the west').

in his day: This should probably be omitted with p^{75} B D Latt. Sah. It presupposes 'the day of the Son of man' as a specific term modelled on the OT expression for the judgment, 'the day of the Lord'.

25

The thought passes to the necessary rejection of this Son of man (= Jesus) between his days on earth and his appearance in judgment. This is clearly out of place if vv. 22–37 are to be taken as a unitary discourse which is eschatological throughout. It is, however, in place if Luke is here constructing a section on the kingdom of God and the Son of man in their relation to Jesus. What is then produced is a miniature Christian proclamation – the Son of man on earth in his days (vv. 21f.), rejected on earth in his death (v. 25), to be manifested as judge and saviour (vv. 26ff.).

26–30

The sequence of thought here is not clear. Matt. 24³⁷⁻³⁹ has a single comparison with the days of Noah. Luke has two comparisons, with Noah and Lot. These two are found in conjunction in Hellenistic Judaism, generally to confirm the belief, based on Plato's *Timaeus*, that the world was invaded first by water and then by fire. Luke, however, may be responsible for the conjunction here, where both are types of a total destruction in which they and their families were the sole survivors (Gen. 7²³; 19²⁹). But despite *likewise* (v. 28) the comparisons are not identical. The first is between the days (the time) of Noah and the days (the time) of the Son of man, and *until that day when* (v. 27) is simply part of the narrative, and is not taken up by any reference to a 'day' of the Son of man. The second is between the actual day when Lot left Sodom and the day of the Son of man's manifestation. The first is connected with v. 25 (or with vv. 22–25) by *as it was* (in the Greek 'and as it was'), and is more general. It appears to teach that the time of Noah and the (remaining?) lifetime of the Son of man are both times when disaster comes upon the world as it goes about its natural pursuits. The second is more specific, and appears to teach that, as destruction came upon Sodom for its continued selfish life on the day that Lot left it, so the day when the Son of man is revealed (*apokaluptetai*, only here in the gospels in this technical sense, cf. II Thess. 2³ᶠᶠ·), will be in the same way one of destruction. Luke thus distinguishes between the kingdom of God and the Son of man, removing any idea of catastrophe from the former and attaching it to the latter.

31–37 *The nature of the judgment*

These verses divide into two, and deal with two aspects of the crisis brought about by the Son of man's manifestation; to which is added a conclusion.

31–33

The similar sayings in Mark 13¹⁵ᶠ· = Matt. 24¹⁷ᶠ· are eschatological warnings that the final crisis will be so acute that, if a man is to escape it, there will be no time for him, on descending from the housetop, to go inside before leaving, nor, if he is in the field, even to pick up a discarded garment. In linking them with the Son of man's appearance (*on that day*), Luke has rephrased both sayings (*likewise*, v. 31) to give them moral content, and they become ethical instructions to disciples on how to behave in the crisis. They are now warnings against any attempt to preserve possessions at that time, either by going down from the roof to fetch them from inside, or by looking back from the field with longing eyes towards the house. The latter can then lead to the citation of Lot's wife (v. 32) as an example of one who perished because unwilling to forfeit everything at the judgment. This thought is then generalized by a forced application of the saying about losing life to find it (cf. $9^{24f.}$), here formulated in a more polished style (*seeks, to gain* – *peripoieisthai* + A. 20^{28} in the sense of 'preserve for oneself'; *preserve* – *zōogonein* + A. 7^{19} in this sense). In the context that is now made to mean that whoever seeks to preserve his life as his own at the judgment will meet destruction, and whoever is willing to give up his earthly life then will find life. This adaptation perhaps reflects Luke's hostility to earthly possessions. It teaches almost the opposite of Mark's 'Save yourselves at all costs' (Mark 13^{14-16}).

34–35

The division into two at the judgment is continued by a double saying. Previously this has been stated from the human side by reference to possible attitudes of the persons concerned, and the final consequences they will suffer. Now it is stated from the divine side as the operation of a judgment that lies totally outside human control and under the sovereign decision of the Son of man. According to this some will be *taken* – i.e. to salvation, probably by the angels (cf. 16^{22}), possibly by the angels of the Son of man (cf. Mark 13^{27}). Others will be *left* – i.e. to destruction (cf. 9^{60}; 13^{35}).

36

This verse is correctly placed in the margin in RSV as being an assimilation of Luke's text to Matt. 24^{40}.

37

The discourse is brought to a close with what sounds like a proverbial saying – *Where the body* (*ptōma* = 'corpse') *is, there the eagles will be gathered together* (cf. Job 39^{30}). The Greek word *aetos* must mean 'vulture' (so RSV margin) rather than eagle, with which it was classed in the ancient world, since the eagle is not a carrion-eating bird. The interpretation of the eagles as the standards of the Roman army (so Leaney, p. 232) is improbable, especially if the proverbial character of the saying is to be retained. The force of it is that two things belong inevitably together, or that to find the one you must look for the other; but, as often with such sayings, its application is enigmatic. In Matt. 24^{28} it is applied to what stands earlier in Luke (v. 24), apparently to state that the parousia will be, like lightning, open and unmistakable. Its placing here is probably Luke's work to secure that the concluding question '*Where, Lord?*' in the mouths of the

disciples as a body matches the opening question of the Pharisees as a body
(v. 20). The question about the location of the day of the Son of man and of its
effects on human beings (vv. 30–35) is barely intelligible; where else could they
be than somewhere on earth? And it is difficult to see what the answer is intended to say; for the variety of interpretations, some of which are answers to
the question 'when?', see Marshall, p. 669. The interpretations 'wherever judgment is called for' (Creed, p. 221) and 'where judgment is required, i.e. universally' (Ellis, p. 212) are platitudinous. Perhaps it is intended to be both a
refusal to reply directly (cf. the similar refusal in vv. 20–21), and also an assertion
that the judgment will certainly take place, and will be seen to take place, as
surely as the presence of vultures proves the existence of corpses.

18^{1–8} *The Parable of the Unjust Judge (Importunate Widow)*

18 *And he told them a parable, to the effect that they ought always to pray
and not lose heart. ²He said, 'In a certain city there was a judge who neither
feared God nor regarded man; ³and there was a widow in that city who kept
coming to him and saying, "Vindicate me against my adversary." ⁴For a
while he refused; but afterward he said to himself, "Though I neither fear God
nor regard man, ⁵yet because this widow bothers me, I will vindicate her, or
she will wear me out by her continual coming." ' ⁶And the Lord said, 'Hear
what the unrighteous judge says. ⁷And will not God vindicate his elect, who
cry to him day and night? Will he delay long over them? ⁸I tell you, he will
vindicate them speedily. Nevertheless, when the Son of man comes, will he
find faith on earth?'*

The theme introducing the previous discourse at 17²⁰ would appear to
have been worked through to a climax and conclusion at 17³⁴⁻³⁷. It is,
however, continued here without break or change of audience by the
addition, probably from a different source, of a parable (vv. 1–8a) and
an attached saying (v. 8b). Both are peculiar to Luke, and taken together
they could be said to bear on one of the questions raised, at least implicitly, by that discourse, viz. what is the proper attitude of disciples
towards the kingdom of God in so far as it was still to come, and towards the Son of man (Jesus) in the interim between his departure and

his return (17^{20-25, 30-37}). The answer given is that they are to petition unceasingly that what God had initiated through the presence of the kingdom on earth in the persons of his elect (the disciples of Jesus) he will speedily bring to its consummation; and they are to maintain themselves in a state of expectation of this. There are, however, difficulties both with the parable itself, and with Luke's use of it here.

The parable is another of the 'tale' type. Its kernel, and perhaps its original extent, are in vv. 2–5. A judge, described paradoxically, and perhaps proverbially, as being without respect for any judgment, divine or human, is besieged by a widow, a biblical type of the needy and oppressed, with the demand for justice to be done in her case; the verb in v. 3, *ekdikein*, has the meaning, found often in papyri but only here in the NT, of 'to obtain justice for', 'to secure a favourable verdict at law for'. For a time the judge remains obdurate; but since (as he reflects) the widow is such a nuisance, and her constant coming could be the end of him, he undertakes to give her satisfaction. Here the parable as such ends, and so far its interpretation remains open. It could be teaching perseverance (in prayer?), or boldness in relation to God, or, as in 11¹¹⁻¹⁵, the compulsion to right action felt even by evil men as illustrating something about God. In v. 6 the parable is supplied with an addendum from Jesus, introduced by his post-resurrection title (*And the Lord said*), in the form of an admonition to pay attention to the words spoken in the parable by the judge, bad character though he may have been (hence the title The Parable of the Unjust Judge). These words are then given an interpretation, apparently also from 'the Lord', in the form of question and answer (vv. 7–8a), though this is very loosely connected with the previous admonition by *and* ('for' would have been stronger). This interpretation is allegorical and eschatological. The widow in her constant coming is a figure of God's elect in their ceaseless cry for their cause to be vindicated (hence the title The Importunate Widow). The judge's words point to God's certain vindication of those elect; here the noun *ekdikēsis*, from the verb in v. 3, has the different sense of 'vengeance', the only sense in the LXX, to which the word is largely confined. The parable then becomes an expression of the familiar eschatological theme of God's avenging his elect by his deliverance of them from oppression (cf. I Enoch 62¹¹; Rev. 6⁹⁻¹¹). This vengeance is then said, on the authority of 'the Lord' himself (*I tell you*, v. 8), to be imminent, despite any appearance to the contrary (if that is the meaning of v. 7b). This is strange, because speediness is not what is suggested by the judge's behaviour in the parable, but rather the opposite; and at 19^{11} Luke goes out of his way to introduce the Parable of the Pounds as told expressly to combat the idea of an immediate appearance of the kingdom. Further, he introduces this parable in somewhat indeterminate fashion as teaching about prayer in general – that it should be constant and unfailing – without explicit reference to a particular kind of prayer for the coming of the end. This somewhat confused picture has given rise to considerable discussion and to various analyses of the material here – see Marshall, pp. 670f.

The parable shares with 16$^{1-8}$ a certain racy humour, and the choice of a knavish character as the central figure, about whom the audience has to be reassured. It also shares (as with 12$^{16-20}$; 11$^{5-8}$) certain stylistic features – the soliloquy form in vv. 4f. (cf. 16$^{3f.}$; 12$^{17ff.}$), the double antithetical negative in *neither feared God nor regarded man* (vv. 2, 4, cf. 16$^{3, 4}$), a comment from *the Lord* (v. 6, cf. 16^8), *the unrighteous judge*, lit. 'the judge of unrighteousness' (v. 6, cf. 16^8); and with *because . . . bothers me* in v. 5 cf. 11$^{7-8}$. Behind the parable, as possibly with other Lukan parables, may lie a biblical text, in this case Ecclus 35$^{12-19}$ (LXX 32$^{15-25}$), 'For the Lord is the judge, and with him is no partiality. He will not ignore the supplication of the fatherless, nor the widow when she pours out her story. Do not the tears of the widow run down her cheek as she cries out against him who has caused them to fall? . . . The prayer of the humble pierces the clouds, and he will not be consoled until it reaches the Lord; he will not desist until the Most High visits him, and does justice for the righteous, and executes judgment. And the Lord will not delay, neither will he be patient with them, till he crushes the loins of the unmerciful and repays vengeance on nations . . . till he judges the case of his people.' These features have led to the suggestion that Luke composed the parable himself (so Drury, *Tradition*, p. 164, 'his most sophisticated parable'), perhaps on the basis of the reading of Ecclesiasticus in his church (Goulder, *The Evangelists' Calendar*, p. 210). In that case, however, it is likely to have been composed more smoothly as a unit, and to have fitted more closely into the context Luke has supplied for it. The awkwardness of vv. 6–8a, which show no clear evidence of Luke's style, suggests rather that he was incorporating, perhaps not wholly successfully, a unit of tradition which already bore marks of use and adaptation in the church. As in 16$^{1-7}$ a story is told involving great urgency. Its point, which is not explained, hangs on the behaviour and decision of a thoroughly

disreputable character. This element of the 'grotesque' is found sufficiently often in synoptic parables to be ascribed with some confidence to
the mind and parabolic method of Jesus; but for a later generation, for
whom a parable ought to be in every respect improving, this element
had to be overcome. This is done by reference to Jesus himself as the
(risen) Lord, and by supplying an assurance, as from him, that the
parable did indeed apply to the situation of his disciples. On the evidence of the NT that situation could often have been one of impatiently
waiting for, and questioning about, the kingdom of God to come, and
the parousia or return of Jesus as the Son of man (cf. II Peter as a later,
and Revelation as an earlier, example of this). That this would take
place *speedily* (v. 8) must already have belonged to the parable, as it
hardly accords with Luke's own view (cf. 19¹¹; 21²⁰⁻²⁴, and the absence
of this thought in A.). Luke may then have incorporated the parable
here, partly because he saw it as a fitting appendix to 17²⁰⁻³⁷, and also
because he was interested in the subject of prayer (see on 3²¹).

∞∞

1

And he told them a parable: For this formula as continuing a theme, cf. 5³⁶; 6³⁹;
12¹⁶.

to the effect that they ought always to pray and not lose heart: This renders a literary
construction with the preposition *pros* governing a verb in the infinitive. It is
found only here in this gospel, and then not in its usual sense of purpose, but in
that of direction. Mention of constant prayer by Christians (*pantote = always*
means in this context 'constantly' rather than 'continuously') is found in Rom.
1¹⁰; Eph. 6¹⁸; Phil. 1⁴; Col. 1³; 4¹²; I Thess. 5¹⁷; II Thess. 1¹¹ (the last two refer,
as here, to prayer of an eschatological kind, though not explicitly). The verb
rendered *lose heart* (*enkakein*) is a late Greek word, not found in the LXX, and
occurring in the NT only here and five times in Paul. It could mean either 'to
grow weary' or 'to despair' – in prayer at the failure to obtain what is prayed
for.

2

who neither feared God nor regarded man: That is, the very contradiction of the
idea of a judge. There is a more literary version in Dionysius of Halicarnassus,
X, 10.7, 'neither fearing divine wrath nor respecting human fate'.

5

will wear me out by her continual coming: The system of justice envisaged by such private encounters between plaintiff and judge is not clear, and is irrelevant to the parable, which is concerned simply to juxtapose the two characters. The Greek *eis telos*, rendered here by *continual*, could have three meanings. (i) 'finally' – 'lest in the end she wears me out'; but this would require participle and verb, 'coming' and 'wear out', to be in the aorist tense, and not, as here, in the present. (ii) 'completely' – 'lest by her coming she has me done for'. This is not unrelated to the translation of the verb *hupōpiazein*, rendered here 'wear out'. This word, absent from the LXX, and only here and at I Cor. 9^{27} in the NT, is taken from boxing, and means literally 'to give a black eye to'; the Vulgate translates by *sugillet* = 'beats black and blue'. In this strong sense it would not need to be amplified by an adverb 'completely', but only if given the weakened sense 'wear out'. (iii) 'continually'. Its position in front of the present participle 'coming' favours this. It is the woman's protracted persistence, threatening to demolish him, which causes the judge to throw in the towel.

7

This verse applies the parable to *his* (the) *elect*, a semi-technical term in eschatological vocabulary for those predestined by God for salvation – so frequently in I Enoch, and in the NT Mark 13$^{20,\ 22,\ 27}$. Christians are described as such in II Tim. 2^{10}, and without the article in Rom 8^{33}; Col. 3^{12}; Tit. 1^{1}; I Peter 1^{1}; Rev. 17^{14}. For their cry for vindication in God's cause for which they suffer, cf. I Enoch 9$^{2,\ 10}$; Rev. 6$^{9-11}$ (of Christian martyrs in face of its delay). The verse, however, is awkwardly constructed throughout, and is unlikely to have been supplied by Luke. (i) As noted above 'for' would make a better connection with v. 6 than *And*. (ii) *who cry* translates a participle in the genitive agreeing with *his elect*, which is a possible way of expressing a relative clause in Greek; but the meaning intended could be 'if they cry'. (iii) *Will he delay long over them?* is an attempt to render what is obscure in the Greek, where it is not a separate question, but follows on with 'and' from the preceding question, and where the verb translated by *delay long* (*makrothumei*) is in the present indicative, whereas the interrogative construction with the Greek *ou mē* = 'surely' requires that, like the previous verb *vindicate*, it should be in the future subjunctive. Hence RV takes it as a statement, 'And shall not God avenge his elect, which cry to him day and night, and he is longsuffering over them?' (NEB 'while he listens patiently to them?'); but such an abrupt transition from question to statement in a single sentence is very harsh, and a new thought is introduced, since in the parable the judge is not longsuffering. When the Greek verb is followed, as here, by the preposition *epi* it means in the LXX 'to defer execution of wrath upon'. This would not apply to the elect but to their enemies, who are not in view here. They are in view in Ecclus 35^{18} (LXX 32^{22}), 'And the Lord will not delay, neither will he be patient with them, till he ... repays vengeance on the nations.' If this passage underlies the parable, it is possible that a clumsy quota-

18^{1–8}

tion of words from it has caused the confusion here. One suggestion[u] is to take the Greek *kai* (= 'and') in an adversative sense ('but') and the verb in the sense of 'hold out against' – even if an unrighteous judge cannot remain unmoved by a widow, *a fortiori* will not God vindicate his elect, but does he hold out against them? This transition from one type of question to another is awkward. Perhaps the best suggestion is to give *kai* a concessive sense ('although') and the verb the rare, non-biblical, sense of 'delay' – 'even though he delays over them'.

8a

I tell you: For this as introducing an affirmation of Jesus interpreting a parable, cf. 16⁹; 11⁹; 15⁷, ¹⁰; 18¹⁴.

speedily: Jeremias (*Parables*, p. 155) appeals to OT passages as providing grounds for translating the Greek here, *en tachei*, by 'suddenly', which accords with what is often said about 'the end' in the NT; but the passages do not really support this, and the translation should be, as elsewhere in the NT (A. 12⁷; 25⁴; I Tim. 3¹⁴) 'quickly' or 'soon'. The sequence of thought then is, as generally when this subject is discussed, an assertion of God's intended vindication of his own, an acknowledgment of its delay, and a reassertion of its imminence.

8b

As it stands this verse is clearly to be taken with what precedes. It provides a conclusion to it as a unit, connecting with what has been said about the Son of man in the previous discourse (17²²⁻³⁷), and giving the parable a further Christian application, with the Son of man (= Jesus) as the agent of God's vindication of his elect. Equally clearly it is an independent saying, which did not arise from the parable or belong to it, but which has been attached to it, somewhat forcibly, by the adversative particle *plēn* = *Nevertheless* – of the instances of this particle used in this way in the NT over half are in this Gospel. Whether this attachment had already been made, or was made by Luke himself, is not certain. The latter is more likely if parable and preceding discourse came to him from different sources, as also if some of the references to the Son of man in 17²²⁻³⁷ are due to him, as he will have wished the parable also to refer to the Son of man. The possibility of isolated sayings about the Son of man circulating in the tradition may be seen from 19¹⁰; 12⁴⁰; 9⁵⁶ (v. l.). The context in which this one could arise can be seen from I Enoch 46–47, where the Son of man appears as the vindicator of the elect when their prayers have not ascended to heaven in vain. It is, however, remarkable in reflecting apocalyptic thought of a pessimistic kind, such as is found in IV Ezra 7⁴⁵ᶠᶠ·, where the seer is perplexed that so few will be saved (cf. 5¹, 'The days are coming when . . . the land will be barren of faith'). Here

u Proposed by H. Ljunvik, 'Zur Erklärung einer Lukas-stelle (Luk. 18.7)', *NTS* 10, 1963–64, pp. 289–94.

the verb *will he find* is preceded by an untranslatable particle (*āra*), which generally (as in the other NT instances, A. 8³⁰; Gal. 2¹⁷) expresses considerable anxiety and doubt – 'he will probably not find'. This presents a contrast with the previous optimism expressed in v. 8a *he will vindicate them speedily*, and also abruptly alters the focus of attention from the divine aspect of God's vindication of the elect in response to their prayers to the human aspect of the spiritual condition of the elect when this happens – for a similar but reverse alternation, cf. 17³¹⁻³³ and 17³⁴⁻³⁷. Luke may thus have added the question here in order to temper the force of *speedily*, with which he may not have wholly concurred (cf. his editing of the eschatological discourse in the same direction in 21²⁴, ³⁴⁻³⁶). The question presumes that the Son of man is a recognized title for a personage, one of whose functions is 'to come', and the original meaning could have been, 'Will the Son of man at his coming (i.e. at his single appearance on the clouds to gather the elect from the earth, cf. Mark 13²⁶⁻²⁷) find *faith* (i.e. confidence in the ultimate triumph of God and his righteousness) among men?' The idea of the Son of man's coming even once to earth was a Christian creation – a creation of Jesus himself if he is responsible for those statements which refer to his own activity in terms of the Son of man (5²⁴; 6⁵, etc.). For Luke and his readers, for whom the Son of man is identical with Jesus, any reference to his coming must now be to a second coming or return of Jesus, and because it is that which delays it is that which is to be prayed for earnestly. Further, *faith* here has the definite article, and could mean 'the (Christian) faith'. In that case the question becomes a Christian formulation – will there be enough faithful Christians to form an elect when Jesus returns? With this may be compared Paul's exhortation to disciples (A. 14²²) 'to continue in the faith, and saying that through many tribulations we must enter into the kingdom of God', which probably represented Luke's view of the matter.

18⁹⁻¹⁴ *The Parable of the Pharisee and the Tax-collector*

⁹*He also told this parable to some who trusted in themselves that they were righteous and despised others:* ¹⁰'*Two men went up into the temple to pray, one a Pharisee and the other a tax collector.* ¹¹*The Pharisee stood and prayed thus with himself, "God, I thank thee that I am not like other men, extortioners, unjust, adulterers, or even like this tax collector.* ¹²*I fast twice a week, I give tithes of all that I get."* ¹³*But the tax collector, standing far off, would*

not even lift up his eyes to heaven, but beat his breast, saying, "God, be merci-ful to me a sinner!" ¹⁴*I tell you, this man went down to his house justified rather than the other; for every one who exalts himself will be humbled, but he who humbles himself will be exalted.'*

Luke here adds a further parable before rejoining Mark at 18¹⁵ (= Mark 10¹³). (On the Proto-Luke hypothesis he will already have placed here a parable involving a tax collector, and followed it immediately with a story of the conversion of a tax collector in 19¹⁻¹⁰.) It might have been the last in a collection of parables which Luke has put here before re-joining Mark; but the conjunction also (*de kai* = 'further'), which is common in Luke, generally aims to make a connection with what pre-cedes (cf. 5³⁶; 12⁵⁴; 14¹²). In that case the connection would seem to be no more than the theme of prayer in general, to which Luke has made the previous parable approximate by his generalizing introduction in v. 1. Any more specific connection – e.g. that the confidence which is to inspire prayer of the elect must not be allowed to pass into self-satisfaction and superiority – would be forced. The parable, which is peculiar to Luke, is another of the 'tale' type. It also may have as a background a scriptural passage, viz. Deut. 26¹⁻¹⁵, the prayer of the true Israelite. It is, however, unique in the synoptic tradition in being entirely a contrast between two individual characters treated as types. Indeed, it might be said to fall outside the category of parable, if that is defined as a story, in whatever form, in which some aspect of nature or of human behaviour is used to point to some aspect of the relationship between God and men, since here the subject matter of the parable is itself that relationship, expressed in the religious activity of prayer. The picture is drawn with the few bold strokes of a cartoon – not even the most Pharisaic of Pharisees is likely to have prayed as though he were the only righteous person in the world (v. 11). It may be this quality, rather than, as Jeremias suggests (*Parables*, p. 140) the Semitic character of the original, which accounts for the abruptness conveyed by the lack of any conjunctions to connect the sentences in vv. 11, 12, 14. As with some other Lukan parables the picture is somewhat blurred by the introduction and conclusion, which may represent Luke's own deduc-tions from the story.

9

He also told this parable to: A customary Lukan introduction (cf. 5³⁶; 12¹⁶; 14⁷; 15³). In the Greek *this parable* is deferred to the end of the sentence for emphasis, so as to underline the appropriateness of such a parable for the persons to whom it is addressed. This would also be the case if *pros* = *to* were given the meaning 'with reference to' – cf. 18¹; 20¹⁹; 12⁴¹ – or even the meaning 'against'.

some who trusted in themselves that they were righteous and despised others: A combination of the unspecific – *some who (tinas tous)* as if to secure a wide application of the parable, perhaps with conditions in Luke's own church in mind – and the specific. But the specification is obscure. The Greek verb rendered by *trusted in themselves (pepoitha* with the preposition *epi)* means in the LXX, to which it is almost confined, 'put one's trust in' (i.e. God, or some rival to him, cf. 11²²; with 'in ourselves', cf. II Cor. 1⁹); and it is never followed by the Greek *hoti* in the sense of *that.* Hence Manson (*Sayings,* p. 309) takes *hoti* here in the sense of 'because' – they trusted in themselves because they belonged to the class of 'the righteous', i.e. the pious who kept the law strictly, in contrast to 'the sinners' who did not. But in the parable itself the Pharisee's prayer of thanksgiving to God does not depict self-trust as opposed to trust in God, but self-advertisement or self-exaltation. The further characteristic *and despised others (tous loipous* = 'the rest') is taken from v. 11 *I am not like other men* = 'the rest of mankind', but this is only one feature in the parable, and that a subordinate one.

10

Both are 'churchmen', members of the religious community of Israel. They go naturally to the temple for private prayer, possibly at one of the two daily set times for public worship there. They are, however, at opposite ends of the religious spectrum. The Pharisee (see on 5¹⁷) is a member of a lay movement which aimed at actualizing the ideal of holiness by maximum observance of the law. Josephus, writing for non-Jews, describes the Pharisees (*BJ* 1.110) as 'a body of Jews with the reputation of excelling the rest of their nation in the observance of religion and as exact exponents of the laws'. The tax collector (see on 3¹²), as a native agent of the unclean and oppressive foreigner, was classed with 'the sinner' as one exceedingly lax in observance of the law, and lived on the verge of excommunication (Matt. 18¹⁷).

went up: See on 2⁴. In connection with the temple, which was on a hill in Jerusalem, Mount Zion, this will have the literal meaning of 'ascend' (cf. Ps. 24³).

11

stood and prayed with himself: Standing was the regular posture for prayer. Some mss take *with himself (pros heauton)* with *stood,* as matching the tax collector's *standing far off*; but it is doubtful whether the phrase can mean 'by himself', 'aloof', or (as suggested by Jeremias, *Parables*, p. 140) 'so as to be visible'. Taken with *prayed* it cannot mean 'silently', as custom required him to pray aloud. It perhaps reproduces in the setting of this story the element of soliloquy which is a stylistic feature in other Lukan parables (see on 16³). His prayer has the character of an internal monologue.

God, I thank thee that I am not like other men . . . or even like this tax collector: The prayer consists of thanksgiving to God in the form of a rehearsal of his piety. This is not to be regarded as hypocritical, even if exaggerated in its exclusiveness. It is an extension of the thanksgiving of Israel for its election by God from among the nations (Deut. 26¹⁸ᶠ·) to cover the distinction within Israel between those who cared supremely for the divine law in its greatest possible application, and those who cared little or not at all. For its spirit, cf. Ps. 26, and the prayer quoted in SB II, p. 240, 'I thank thee, my God, and the God of my fathers, that thou hast given me my portion to sit in the house of learning and in the synagogue, and that thou hast not given me my portion to sit in the theatre and circuses.' This is first stated negatively as thanksgiving for not being like the generality of mankind – *extortioners, unjust, adulterers*, perhaps from a conventional list, as they appear in Paul's enumeration (I Cor. 6⁹ᶠ·) of those who will not inherit the kingdom of God. *or even like this* (*houtos* is contemptuous) *tax collector*. As tax collectors are referred to in rabbinic writings as thieves, it may correspond here to 'thieves' and 'the greedy' in Paul's list. These last words presume that the tax collector, though described as *standing far off*, is within the Pharisee's vision, and is known by him to be a tax collector; but it is part of the parable's artistry to bring the contrasted figures together by having one refer to the other (cf. 16²³ᶠ·).

12

I fast twice a week: The prayer passes to a positive rehearsal of devotional and practical piety. Ps. Sol. 3⁹ describes the righteous Jew as one who 'makes atonement for (sins of) ignorance by fasting and afflicting his soul'. To the outsider the Jews appear to have been known for such; cf. the reference to their frequent fasts by Tacitus (*Histories* V, 4), and the statement of Augustus in a letter (Suetonius, *Augustus Caesar* 76.3), 'Not even a Jew fasts so scrupulously on his sabbaths as I have today.' The fasting here is not just the observance of the obligatory public fasts, which were few in Judaism, but the bi-weekly private and voluntary fasts of pious practice. The commentary on the Jewish work Megillath Ta'anith (first century AD) testifies to the voluntary practice of bi-weekly fast, and it appears in the Christian manual, the *Didache*, 8, 'Let not your fasting be with the hypocrites, for they fast on the second and fifth day, but do you keep fast on the fourth and on the preparation (sixth) day'. Such fasts represent the penitential element in pious practice, even if the penitence were for the sin of Israel as a whole rather than for his own personal sins.

I give tithes of all that I get: His tithing, i.e. his offering to God of a tenth of his income (*all I get*), goes beyond the requirements of the law for the tithing of grain, wine, oil and cattle (Deut. 14$^{22f.}$), and its extension in Pharisaic practice to herbs (11^{42}), and covers anything he acquires, perhaps in case it has not, through neglect of the law, been tithed already. It might extend to an annual tithing of income for charity, in which case it may provide the element of almsgiving, which, together with prayer and fasting, constituted the three staple duties of Jewish religion (cf. Matt. 6$^{1-18}$).

13

The conduct of the tax collector is in complete contrast. He takes a place remote from the sanctuary, not presuming to approach where the pious are. He declines to assume an attitude of prayer at all, not lifting up even his eyes to heaven, let alone the hands of confident prayer. Rather, as an indication of extreme sorrow he beats his breast – a forceful expression not found again in the Greek Bible except at 23^{48}, nor in Greek literature up to this time, which generally used the verb in the middle, *tuptesthai* = 'to beat oneself', and if any part of the body was mentioned it was the head. In this attitude he confines his prayer to a single petition for mercy in a form underlining his distance from God – *hilasthēti moi* = 'be propitiated to me'; the verb (+ Heb. 2^{17}) is rare in this form in the LXX, with a dative of the person only in II Kings 5^{18}. He characterizes himself with the single word *sinner*, one who is very lax in religion and a flagrant contravenor of the law.

14a

I tell you: Jesus pronounces on this scene as one who is privy to the judgments of God upon men.

this man went down to his house justified rather than the other: The judgment is in terms of justification, but is far from clear. The word rendered *justified (dedikaiōmenos)* is the perfect participle passive (with the force 'in a state of') of the verb *dikaioun* = 'to make (or, pronounce) righteous', which is itself derived from the adjective *dikaios* = 'righteous' (the word used in v. 9). This is the vocabulary which figures so prominently in Paul's discussion of man's standing with God (Rom. 1–4; Gal. 2–3), and his contention that the law and the performance of its righteous demands ('works') do not provide the basis for, but can actually debar from, a right relationship with God (righteousness, justification). That is the gift of God himself in his acquital of the unrighteous sinner, and is to be received by faith. It can hardly be supposed that Luke was not acquainted with Paul's teaching in some form, which the parable, with its implied radical criticism of Pharisaic piety, would support. But in what form?

The only reference to it in A. is at 13$^{38f.}$, where Paul is made to say (the Greek is at the vital point obscure), 'through this man (Jesus) forgiveness of sins is proclaimed to you, and by him everyone that believes is freed (Greek justified) from everything from which you could not be freed (Greek justified) by the law of Moses.' This could mean that while the law and its performance brought justification in respect of some things, faith in Jesus and forgiveness proclaimed through him brought justification in respect of those things in which the law could not. This was certainly not Paul's view, but it may have been Luke's, and it could be the view here. The tax collector obtains his petition, is forgiven, and has a greater degree of justification than the Pharisee in receiving what the law could not give. Further, the Greek phrase *par'ekeinon*, rendered here by *rather than the other*, is also obscure. The preposition *para* could have (i) a comparative sense, 'compared with', as in one of the variants (Greek *ē* = 'rather than'; the reading in D appears to mean 'more (justified) in comparison with that Pharisee'); but the idea of degrees of justification is strange, and for Paul impossible; (ii) an exclusive sense, 'and not (the other)'. Even this still makes a comparison between the two in respect of justification, though the Pharisee had not asked for forgiveness or justification. It may be, therefore, that the key word in the judgment, *dedikaiōmenos*, should not be given its theological meaning here, but should be taken in the sense of 'acknowledge', 'approve', which it has to some extent in the other four instances in the Gospel (7$^{29, 35}$; 10^{29}; 16^{15}, as also in the two instances in Matthew, 11^{19}; 12^{37}; Mark and John do not have the word). In that case the two prayers are regarded as being in competition and God gives the verdict over them, approving that of the tax collector but not that of the Pharisee. The implication of such approval is that an acknowledgment of his sinful condition is the one necessary requirement for a man's approach to God and relationship with him.

14b

From the very special circumstances of the parable there is now drawn (*for*) the general moral and spiritual lesson (repeated almost verbatim from 14^{11}) that self-exaltation will result in abasement and self-abasement in exaltation. It is not clear how far in this semi-proverbial form of the sentiment the eschatological force of *will be* is preserved – i.e. will be abased by God, or exalted by him, in the final judgment.

18^{15-17} = Mark 10^{13-16} *Children and the Kingdom*

15*Now they were bringing even infants to him that he might touch them; and when the disciples saw it, they rebuked them.* 16*But Jesus called them to him, saying, 'Let the children come to me, and do not hinder them; for to such belongs the kingdom of God.* 17*Truly, I say to you, whoever does not receive the kingdom of God like a child shall not enter it.'*

Luke rejoins the Markan framework until 18^{43}. By doing so at this point he avoids Mark 10^1, which is where in Mark Jesus begins his departure from Galilee en route for Judaea and Jerusalem. While, with the omission of Mark 10^{1-12} in favour of 16^{18}, he weakens the Markan complex of stories concerned with marriage, children, wealth and relations, he secures for this and the following incident a connection with 18^{14}, the exaltation of the lowly and the overthrow of the exalted – cf. the insertion in Matt. 18^4 of a saying about humbling oneself as a child into a similar pericope about children in Mark 9^{33-37} = Luke 9^{46-48}. This may be the point of *kai* placed before *brephē* here – *even infants*, the smallest. The story is taken over from Mark almost verbatim with a few, mostly stylistic, alterations. The children are now clearly babies. This is the regular meaning of Luke's word *brephos* here (Mark's *paidion* could be a child of up to twelve years old), as in the other instances of its use in the NT $1^{41, 44}$; 2^{16}; A. 7^{19}; II Tim. 3^{15}; I Peter 2^2. Hence *called them to him* must be a loose expression for 'summoned those carrying the children to bring them to him'. With the omission of Jesus' indignation at the disciples (Mark 10^{14}) the statement in v. 16 takes a more universal form, and is addressed to parents in general.

For all its apparent simplicity the story is obscure. Judaism paid little attention to children in relation to the major issues of life and religion, and its attitude is probably represented by the disciples' rebuke of those who brought them to be touched, presumably for blessing. Rabbis are the teachers of adult pupils (disciples), and have something better to do than to concern themselves with babes in arms. Some have seen the background to the story, and the reason for its preservation in the tradition and its inclusion here, in the practice of, and possibly scruples over,

infant baptism in the church.[v] But in such a context 'as a child' (*hōs
paidion*, v. 17) could hardly be taken metaphorically, but only literally
('in childhood'), and then the statement in v. 17 would be an impossible
one to have been made in the church. It is even arguable that, in omitting Mark 10[16], including 'laying his hands upon them', which in
A. 8[17-19]; 19[5-6] can be associated with baptism, Luke has dissociated the
incident from baptism.

 তঃ

16

The basis of Jesus' attitude here is said to be twofold. (i) The necessity of
children being allowed to come to him; but elsewhere 'to come to' (*erchesthai
pros*) means 'to become a disciple' (6[47]; 14[26]), and this is not possible for
infants. (ii) Connected with this (*for*) the kingdom of God belongs to such,
implying a close relation between coming to Jesus and possessing the kingdom.
In the view of W. Manson (p. 203) by *to such* (*tōn toioutōn*) 'some quality not possessed by children alone, but capable of indefinite extension, is indicated', and
he suggests simple and absolute trust. Others suggest humility, receptivity, etc.,
according to their estimates of the nature or principal characteristics of children.
But this hardly applies here, especially to Luke's version, since babes in arms
cannot take the initiative involved in humility, or adopt attitudes of trust; they
are wholly passive, being here brought passively for the touch of blessing on the
initiative of parents. The same objection holds if *such* is given the reduced meaning of *toutōn* = 'these', and the kingdom is said to be the future inheritance
(*belongs* has a future sense, cf. *is* in 6[20]) of the children 'in virtue of their coming
to Jesus and receiving the word of the kingdom';[w] for infants cannot be said in
any realistic sense to do these things. Perhaps originally the saying had a playful
irony about it, and its meaning was that the disciples should recognize it as
altogether appropriate that Jesus should be intimately associated with little
children, inasmuch as by their smallness and insignificance they are pre-
eminently a parable of the disciples of Jesus, who, as those who possess the
kingdom, are known as 'the tiny ones' (see on 9[48]).

17

With its solemn introduction, *Truly I say to you*, this could be an independent

v Cf. J. Jeremias, *Infant Baptism in the First Four Centuries*, London 1960, Philadelphia 1961, pp. 48ff., and O. Cullmann, *Baptism in the New Testament*, SBT 1
1950, pp. 72ff.; the latter sees the Greek verb *kōleuein*, translated here by *hinder*,
as betraying the liturgical language of baptismal practice in the church; cf. A.
8[36]; 10[47], where the word occurs in baptismal contexts.

w So G. R. Beasley-Murray, *Baptism in the New Testament*, London and Toronto
1962, pp. 327ff.

saying, which became attached to the Markan pericope at some stage through similarity of thought and wording (cf. Matt. 18³ in a different context). What is to be understood by a receiving of the kingdom in the present by virtue of which entry into it in the future becomes possible is not clear. *receive (dechesthai)* is generally found with 'the word' or with persons as objects, and nowhere else in the NT with the kingdom. *like a child* translates *hōs paidion* = 'as a child'. This can hardly mean 'from childhood', or 'in the person of a child' (Mark 9³⁷); and 'as a child receives' (i.e. not the kingdom, which is a matter for adults, but anything that is given it) isolates the verb *receive* in the sentence, and places undue weight upon it. Possibly the meaning is 'by becoming a little one'. The renunciation of pretensions to greatness and achievement is the only possible disposition for receiving the kingdom in the present form given it by the message and activity of Jesus. This is how the saying is glossed in Matt. 18³ in the context of a question about greatness in the kingdom.

18^{18–30} = Mark 10^{17–31} *Riches and the Kingdom*

¹⁸*And a ruler asked him, 'Good Teacher, what shall I do to inherit eternal life?' ¹⁹And Jesus said to him, 'Why do you call me good? No one is good but God alone. ²⁰You know the commandments: "Do not commit adultery, Do not kill, Do not steal, Do not bear false witness, Honour your father and mother." ' ²¹And he said, 'All these I have observed from my youth.' ²²And when Jesus heard it, he said to him, 'One thing you still lack. Sell all that you have and distribute to the poor, and you will have treasure in heaven; and come, follow me.' ²³But when he heard this he became sad, for he was very rich. ²⁴Jesus looking at him said, 'How hard it is for those who have riches to enter the kingdom of God! ²⁵For it is easier for a camel to go through the eye of a needle than for a rich man to enter the kingdom of God.' ²⁶Those who heard it said, 'Then who can be saved?' ²⁷But he said, 'What is impossible with men is possible with God.' ²⁸And Peter said, 'Lo, we have left our homes and followed you.' ²⁹And he said to them, 'Truly, I say to you, there is no man who has left house or wife or brothers or parents or children, for the sake of the kingdom of God, ³⁰who will not receive manifold more in this time, and in the age to come eternal life.'*

Luke continues to reproduce Mark. The only link between this and the previous episode is a reference to the kingdom of God. The Markan

pericope is striking in more than one respect. It is comparatively lengthy, being made up of three units (vv. 17–22, 23–27, 28–31), and while these are connected with one another and subserve a common theme of riches, they are also sufficiently distinct to stand on their own; and it is not always clear where the main emphasis is meant to lie, nor what is the sequence of thought. Even the first unit makes three important points – none good save God, the commandments and eternal life, and the renunciation of riches. There are also vivid touches in the writing. Some of Luke's alterations are purely stylistic, producing occasional agreements of wording with Matthew, but others are more substantial, and reflect his intense interest in the subject. Thus, the unspecified 'man' in Mark becomes a *ruler*, one of the group of 'the rulers' who appear in Luke, as also in John, as particular opponents of Jesus, and in A. as opponents of the church (14¹; 23¹³, ³⁵; 24²⁰; A. 3¹⁷; 4⁵, ⁸; 13²⁷). For Luke wealth and exalted position tend to be synonymous (cf. 16¹⁴f.). Luke also removes the vivid touches in Mark that might tell in the rich man's favour ('ran up', knelt before him',' 'looking upon him loved him', Mark 10¹⁷, ²¹), as also his departure from the scene (Mark 10²²), so that he is left confronting Jesus as the representative of the rich, and as the one to whom the severe words of vv. 24–25 are addressed. By omitting Mark 10²⁴ altogether, and by dropping 'he said to his disciples' (Mark 10²³) and 'And they were exceedingly astonished' (Mark 10²⁶), he removes any association of disciples with the worldly attitude expressed in v. 26. In these ways he fuses the first two of the Markan units more completely into a single story, and by omission of Mark's lively details makes it, as Lagrange observes (p. 479), more abstract, and so more serviceable for teaching its main point. Verses 28–30 then become a pendant, in which the disciples are introduced for the first time by way of contrast as those who, in answering the call to discipleship, have already obeyed the command to sell all and give alms (12³³).

৫৫

18–22

The dialogue here is not without awkwardness. It opens as the familiar scene of the rabbi being asked for his authoritative judgment on a crucial matter of religion (as in 10²⁵, which Luke may have borrowed from here, and Mark 12²⁸⁻³⁴). As such it could close with the decisive answer given in v. 20 in terms of keeping the commandments, and (possibly) with the comment of the ruler that he had done this from his youth. With v. 22, however, all this becomes a preamble to a further point, which is then the main point; and simply furnishes the occasion for Jesus to present his demand for personal discipleship, and for the renunciation of wealth it involves, as the single necessary requirement over and above the performance of the commandments – if it is to be assumed that the demand in v. 22 is intended as an answer to the question in v. 18, and that having *treasure in heaven* is equivalent to inheriting *eternal life*, and not simply the opposite of having treasure on earth. For this transition in thought to be made, the ruler's remark in v. 21 has to be taken either (i) as a complacent statement of achievement which needed to be punctured by a further radical demand from Jesus – but in that case what is then the status and value of the previous reply that keeping the commandments is the prerequisite of inheriting eternal life? or (ii) as an expression of uncertainty whether, since he has kept the commandments from youth, something additional might be required, perhaps the works of piety such as are listed in the Pharisee's prayer in 18¹² – but the one thing lacking, discipleship and total poverty, can hardly be regarded as something additional, as they are so radical and all-embracing. Matthew appears to have felt this difficulty, and to have solved it by distinguishing between eternal life, which is secured by keeping the commandments, and being perfect, which is through renunciation of wealth.

18

Good Teacher: This form of address is very rare in Jewish literature. It is by no means certain that it is to be regarded, as by most commentators, as fulsome flattery (accompanied in Mark's 'he knelt before him' by obsequiousness), which then called for stern rebuke. Rabbis were without impropriety highly revered – cf. the title 'lord' applied to them (in John 13¹³ᶠ· along with 'teacher').

what shall I do to inherit eternal life?: For the form and content of the question, see on 10²⁵.

19

Why do you call me good? No one is good but God alone: An unparalleled rejoinder, which remains enigmatic to commentators from Matthew onwards, both in what it says, and in its almost casual occurrence as a preliminary to the story. It appears too weighty to have as its purpose simply a rebuke of flattery and insincerity (in Mark the man is shown marks of love and esteem). One explanation puts the emphasis on *me*, and sees it as a form of the question about the person of Jesus similar to 'Who do you say that I am?' in 9²⁰. 'If only God is good, and you address me as good, do you mean that you regard me as in some sense God?' This is probably to be ruled out as introducing later doctrinal considerations. Another explanation puts the emphasis on *good*, and sees it as challenging the questioner's sincerity in using it, especially as later he does not accept what the 'good teacher' says; but this does not account for the reference to God as the only one who is good. The Greek word *agathos*, which in the

Greek tradition of philosophy and ethics is central, is not common in the NT, and is seldom used there of persons. It is not denied that there could be a person who was morally good (cf. Rom. 5⁷; I Peter 2¹⁸; John 7¹²; Matt. 5⁴⁵), so that in this sense goodness could not be ascribed solely to God. Nor would Luke and Mark have recorded these words of Jesus if they had understood them to cast doubt on his moral goodness (Matthew may have done so when he rewrote them in terms of the Greek moral concept of 'the good' (Matt. 19¹⁷). In the LXX, where the word is more frequent, the predominant meaning, especially when applied to God, is 'gracious', and God is confessed as such in being the source of Israel's blessings, past, present and future (Ps. 118¹ff.; I Chron. 16³⁴ff.; Isa. 52⁷; Prov. 28¹⁰). Dalman (*Words of Jesus*, p. 337) quotes a saying 'Good greeting to the good Rabbi from the good Lord, who in his goodness does good to his people', and a thanksgiving formula provided for the receipt of good news, 'Praised be he who is kind and sends kindness'; and he observes that what is signified is not an ethical quality of moral goodness, but beneficence. The thought here may then be that Jesus, in being asked what is requisite for the ultimate blessing of eternal life, is addressed as though he were the dispenser of it (cf. 12³²; Mark 10⁴⁰), and the ruler is for that reason referred for answer to the commandments which are God's.

20

The form of commandments rehearsed here is unusual in two ways. (i) It is limited to the fifth to tenth commandments, those concerned with relations to other people – contrast 10²⁷, where in answer to the same question the commands to love God and the neighbour are combined (cf. Mark 12²⁹⁻³¹). This is presumably because the commandment of Jesus (v. 22), which is either meant to supplement these (*one thing you lack*), or to be the means of carrying them out completely, is also concerned with relations to others in being a commandment to distribute to the poor the proceeds of the sale of all possessions. (ii) The order in which the commandments are listed is peculiar. In Mark the list begins with the sixth, runs through to the tenth (though in the unprecedented form 'Do not defraud'), and concludes with the fifth. This is followed by Matthew and Luke, except that both omit Mark's tenth, Luke begins with the sixth and seventh in reverse order, and Matthew makes up the number by adding at the end 'You shall love your neighbour as yourself.' The order of the last six of the ten commandments might still have been variable at the time. In one tradition of the LXX text of Exod. 20 and Deut. 5 the order is 'You shall not commit adultery', 'You shall not kill', and this is the order in some mss of Mark here (cf. evidence for this order in Rom. 13⁹; James 2¹¹).

22

The climax, which Luke somewhat sharpens with *One thing you still lack* and *all that you have* for Mark's 'You lack one thing' and 'what you have'. But Jesus utters not one commandment but two, and it is not clear how they are related to each other, and to the original question and answer. If to *have treasure in heaven* is another way of saying *to inherit eternal life*, then selling all in order to distribute to the poor is the primary demand, and this is what the ruler has to do to attain eternal life; and the demand for discipleship is secondary and additional. If, as is more likely, it is the command to become a disciple of Jesus that is primary, with the abandonment of possessions (and the possession of heavenly treasure that goes with it) as an indispensable preliminary to that, then the one further thing needed to obtain eternal life by keeping the commandments is to become a disciple of Jesus. It is not poverty and charity as such that are required, but the surrender of the whole man to God in response to the demands of his kingdom, and the removal of the obstacle to that surrender, which is wealth. In that case, however, one would expect the OT commandments quoted to include, alongside those concerned with relations to others, those concerned with total devotion to God. For *treasure in heaven*, see on 12^{33}.

23

Again Luke somewhat sharpens the issue with *became sad* (*perilupos* = 'deeply grieved') and *for he was very rich*. The man's upset was the greater in proportion to the greatness of his wealth.

24-25

The individual case of the wealthy ruler is now made the basis of a general pronouncement on wealth. *looking at him* comes awkwardly at this point, but it is Luke's version of Mark's 'looking around him', so that the hard sayings about riches are spoken *vis-à-vis* the ruler, and not, as in Mark, in his absence. The pronouncement is of the great difficulty for those possessing wealth of entering the kingdom of God (v. 24). This is reinforced (v. 25) with a proverbial expression of impossibility, the camel being the largest animal in the region of Palestine and a needle's eye the smallest conceivable aperture (Luke's words for *eye* and *needle* are more refined). It is not clear whether the kingdom of God here is a synonym for eternal life in v. 18 (and for being saved in v. 26), and the entry into it, like the inheritance of eternal life, something that belongs to the future, or is a present possibility in anticipation of that future. It will be the latter if the present tense in v. 24 – lit. 'How hardly do those who have riches enter into the kingdom of God' – which Luke substitutes for Mark's future tense ('they will go into') is a genuine present, perhaps commenting on the ruler's failure to enter there and then, or is a generalizing present (such men do not enter). The extreme rigorism of these statements is mitigated in some mss of Mark 10^{24} by the gloss 'trust in' (riches) for 'have' (riches), which makes reliance on wealth, and not simply its possession, the ground for exclusion. Matthew mitigates it by making a distinction between inheriting eternal life, for which obedience to the commandments while still in possession of riches is sufficient, and perfection and having treasure in heaven, for which renunciation of possessions is a necessary qualification. Luke shows no sign of finding such rigorism problematical.

26

Then who can be saved?: If the rich cannot. The question is evoked by the rigorism of the previous statements – in some mss of Mark, in which 10²⁴ (omitted by Matthew and Luke) comes after the saying about the camel and the needle's eye, the question is evoked by an even more sweeping statement, 'How hard is it to enter into the kingdom of God!' If the question is to have any weight, and to be more than an expression of social snobbery or vulgar worldliness, it must rest on the theological conviction that wealth, so far from being a ground for disapproval by God, is itself an outward sign in this world of his approval and blessing. There are passages in the OT, and especially in the Wisdom literature, which voice such an attitude (cf. Prov. 3¹⁶; 22⁴; Ecclus 11²¹ᶠ·), but it cannot be said to be that of the OT, or even of the Wisdom literature, as a whole, which are well aware of a distinction between wealth and righteousness. In some apocalyptic literature (e.g. I Enoch, II Baruch), with its sharp contrast between this world and its goods and the coming age, the opposite is the case, and the rich and powerful tend to be, as in the prophets and some psalms, the godless *par excellence*. This may lie behind the utterances of Jesus here. Wealth is as good as synonymous with godlessness, and possession of it, and the extreme difficulty of relinquishing it, are permanent barriers to surrender to the demands of God and his kingdom.

27

This reply to the question – that what humanly speaking is impossible becomes possible by the operation of divine power – is stated by Luke in more gnomic form, and by his omission of Mark's 'for all things are possible with God' is confined to the subject of wealth.

28

The story now takes a step forward with the appearance, for the first time in Luke's version, of the disciples as evidence of God's effectual power, and as those who have already done what the ruler has refused to do. Through their spokesman, Peter, they state their position as those who have abandoned their possessions to throw in their lot with Jesus. In this context this is not just a statement of fact, but is meant to imply a tacit question (Matt. 19²⁷ makes it explicit) about where they stand in consequence with respect to eternal life and treasure in heaven.

our homes: Luke here as *ta idia* (*idios* = 'one's own') for Mark's *panta* = 'everything'. This could mean *homes* (so RSV), and could then be taken up in v. 29 in house (in the sense of 'household') *or wife or brothers or parents or children.* Apart from the context the reference could then be to the necessary severance of family relationships in becoming a disciple (cf. 14²⁶). This is not possible in Mark 10²⁹ᶠ·, where 'fields' are included, and it is more likely that *ta idia* here is intended to summarize *house* (in the sense of property), *wife ... children* considered as possessions. Luke may have chosen the word (which is found only here in the synoptists), in view of what he will write in A. 4³² of the company of believers, that 'no one said that any of the things he possessed was his own (*idion*)'.

29–30

Jesus' promise in reply to the disciples' question is twofold. In Mark it is that those who have renounced possessions and relations on account of Jesus and the gospel will receive first on earth a hundredfold equivalent possessions and relations in the fellowship of the persecuted church, and then their ultimate reward of eternal life in the coming age. In Luke's revision of this may be noted the extent of his rigorism in adding *wife* to those who are to be abandoned, and his avoidance of Mark's expression 'for my sake and for the gospel' (cf. 9²⁴ = Mark 8³⁵), and its replacement by *for the sake of the kingdom of God,* which is thus closely associated with the present activity of Jesus, but distinguished from eternal life (A. 11¹⁸; 13⁴⁶⁻⁴⁸). *manifold more* (*pollaplasiona,* only here in the Greek Bible; some mss have *heptaplasiona* = 'sevenfold', cf. 17⁴; Ecclus 35¹¹) leaves the compensations of discipleship unspecified. 'wives manifold' would be impossible, and so would Mark's 'fields', for in A. 4³⁴⁻³⁷ Christians do not possess fields, but sell them for distribution of the proceeds. Luke omits Mark's 'with persecutions', for although the church undergoes persecution in Acts, this does not arise over its life of poverty and communal possession, which is represented as an ideal and untroubled state. With the omission of Mark 10³¹, which is rightly judged to be an intrusion here, and for which an equivalent has been given in 13³⁰, the story comes to an end, as it had begun, with eternal life.

18³¹⁻³⁴ = Mark 10³²⁻³⁴ *The Passion Predicted*

³¹*And taking the twelve, he said to them, 'Behold, we are going up to Jerusalem, and everything that is written of the Son of man by the prophets will be accomplished. ³²For he will be delivered to the Gentiles, and will be mocked and shamefully treated and spit upon; ³³they will scourge him and kill him,*

and on the third day he will rise.' ³⁴But they understood none of these things; this saying was hid from them, and they did not grasp what was said.

The evidence that this section has been taken from Mark, and not, as Easton suggests (p. 275) from another source, is conclusive. Firstly, its position here as the third in a series of explicit predictions of the passion corresponds with the position in Mark. So also does *And taking the twelve*, identical in wording with Mark 10³², for the Twelve have not been mentioned since ch. 9, where Luke was last following Mark, and *Behold, we are going up to Jerusalem*, identical in wording with Mark 10³³, which fits the Markan perspective of a journey to Jerusalem about to begin, but not the Lukan perspective of a journey already in train since 9⁵¹ (cf. 13²²; 17¹¹). As the last thing said to them before arrival in the city the Twelve are now told (belatedly in Luke) of the purpose of the journey to *Jerusalem*, which place-name then dominates the subsequent narrative to the end (19¹¹, ²⁸, ⁴¹; 21²⁰,; 23⁷, ²⁸; 24¹³, ¹⁸, ³³, ⁴⁷, ⁵²). Secondly, the close agreement in wording between vv. 32–33 and Mark 10³³ᵇ⁻³⁴ must be due to the influence of Mark's text here, since there is in fact no mention in Luke's passion narrative of spitting and flogging at the hands of the Gentiles. In the previous two predictions Luke has reproduced from Mark what was to happen to the Son of man at the hands of the Jewish authorities (9²²), and then what was to happen described in general terms (9⁴⁴). Here he takes from Mark's double prediction only what pertains to the Son of man's treatment at the hands of the Gentiles. He adds *shamefully treated* (*hubrizein* + 11⁴⁵; A. 14⁵; Matt. 22⁶; I Thess. 2²) probably to cover the treatment of Jesus by Herod, an incident peculiar to his passion narrative (23¹¹; cf. A. 4²⁷, where Herod is linked with Pilate, the Gentile, in his behaviour towards Jesus).

When taken with such close agreement, the striking differences from Mark will be evidence of Luke's editing, and will betray his particular understanding of the passion. Thus, firstly, 'what was to happen to him' (Mark 10³²), which later in Mark (14⁴⁹) is said in general terms to be the fulfilment of scripture, is specifically defined by Luke as *everything* that *will be accomplished* (*telein*) in fulfilment of prophecy. This was later to become the message and language of the church's preaching as Luke presents it – cf. esp. A. 13²⁷⁻²⁹, 'because they did not understand the utterances of the prophets . . . they fulfilled these by condemning him . . . When they had fulfilled (*telein*) all that was written of him . . .'

Here Luke gives that message as basis in the words of the earthly Jesus, as he will also in the words of the risen Lord (24²⁵⁻²⁷), and of both of these together (24⁴⁴⁻⁴⁶). This Lukan theme, which is almost absent from Mark, reflects the early Christians' search of the OT for scriptural proof to verify the passion, and it has produced the striking *gegrammena dia tōn prophētōn* = 'written through (RSV *by*) the prophets', which is a combination of the more normal expressions 'written in the prophets' and 'spoken through the prophets'. Secondly, the numinous awe of Mark 10³² is omitted, to be replaced by a threefold statement of the inability of the innermost band of the Twelve to comprehend the doctrine of the rejected Son of man; cf. 9⁴⁵, a similar threefold statement in somewhat similar language, where it is clearly an elaboration of the single statement in Mark 9³². This total inability of even the inner group to understand what Jesus is saying is, in Luke, to be removed by Jesus after his resurrection, when he expounds the doctrine as obvious and necessary by reference to scripture (24²⁵⁻²⁷, ⁴⁵ᶠ·), so as to become the message of the church. Placed here the section shows Jesus to be in complete control of his destiny, to know that destiny to be governed by God's age-long purpose for man, and to be the only one to know it.

∞

31
written of the Son of man: the Son of man is in the dative case, and if taken with *written* and not with *accomplished* gives the sense of 'written with respect to the Son man', i.e. as bearing witness to him. For the rejection of the Son of man, see on 9²².

18³⁵⁻⁴³ = Mark 10⁴⁶⁻⁵² *The Cure of a Blind Man*

³⁵*As he drew near to Jericho, a blind man was sitting by the roadside begging;* ³⁶*and hearing a multitude going by, he inquired what this meant.* ³⁷*They told him, 'Jesus of Nazareth is passing by.'* ³⁸*And he cried, 'Jesus, Son of David, have mercy on me!'* ³⁹*And those who were in front rebuked him, telling him to be silent; but he cried out all the more, 'Son of David, have mercy on me!'* ⁴⁰*And Jesus stopped, and commanded him to be brought to him; and when he came near, he asked him,* ⁴¹'*What do you want me to do for you?' He said,*

'Lord, let me receive my sight.' ^{42}*And Jesus said to him, 'Receive your sight; your faith has made you well.'* ^{43}*And immediately he received his sight and followed him, glorifying God; and all the people, when they saw it, gave praise to God.*

Luke continues with the Markan paradigmatic story of the blind man at Jericho, whose faith in Jesus as Son of David brings him healing (salvation), and makes him a disciple. The artificiality of Luke's travel narrative is evident here from the fact that Jericho is the first town to be mentioned since its beginning at 9^{51}, and this is only supplied as the result of his rejoining Mark. Moreover, Jericho does not lie on any natural route from Galilee to Judaea via Samaria, nor even on a route along a supposed border between Samaria and Judaea (see on 17^{11}), but only if the Jordan is crossed into Peraea, as happens in Mark 10^1. Luke revises Mark 10^{46} so as to set the scene on the approach to, instead of on the departure from, Jericho. This is to make room for the following (non-Markan) incident, which may have come to Luke already attached to Jericho, to take place inside the town. This could indicate that the Markan framework is dominant for Luke here; for if he were adding extracts from Mark to a previous draft of his gospel which already contained the story of Zacchaeus, he could have placed this story of the blind man after it, i.e. on the departure from Jericho, as Mark has it. Luke's other alterations aim to produce a smoother and more intelligible story, and they both take away from, and add to, the vividness of Mark's account. The disciples are omitted until the entry into Jerusalem (19$^{29, 37}$). The beggar's name is omitted, if it stood in Luke's text of Mark and was not a later addition there (see the commentaries on Mark ad loc.). The crowd, absent since 15^5, is reintroduced from Mark, but not, as there, simply as a background, but as active in causing the beggar, through the trampling of its feet, to ask what is going on (Luke creates this out of Mark's single word 'hearing'). To his question the affecting words *Jesus of Nazareth is passing by* now become the answer; but *those who were in front* (*hoi proagontes*, perhaps from Mark 11^9; the verb only here in Luke) is clumsy, as they would have already passed by the beggar by the time he asked the question. Luke omits Mark's lively, but somewhat improbable, details of the beggar's approach to Jesus; but *stopped* after *is passing by* is dramatic; *commanded* (*keleuein*, common in A. but only here in the Gospel) *him to be brought* takes account of the necessity for a blind man to be led; *Lord* (*kyrie*, so also

Matthew, perhaps 'Sir') is a more fitting as an address to the Son of David than Mark's 'rabbouni' (Jesus is never called 'rabbi' in Luke); and *receive your sight*, emphasizing the cure by a word (Matthew by a touch), is more striking than Mark's 'Go you way'. Mark's ending, with its possible double nuance of following on the road and in the way of discipleship, is reduced to *followed him*, and the episode closes with a typical Lukan ending to a miracle story, with the beggar *glorifying God* (cf. $5^{25f.}$; 7^{16}; $17^{15f.}$; 13^{13}), *and all the people, when they saw it, gave praise to God* (*ainos* = 'praise' + Matt. 21^{16} LXX; for 'give praise to' cf. 17^{18} 'give glory to'). This ending is particularly significant here, since it supplies the language for Luke's version of the entry into Jerusalem, when the words of acclamation are introduced as those of the whole multitude of the disciples who 'began to rejoice and praise God with a loud voice for all the mighty works that they had seen' (19^{37}).

ॐ

35
Jericho: A major city at the southern end of the Jordan valley, a mile south of the ancient Israelite town. It had been richly and expansively built by Herod as his winter capital, with a fortress to guard the road from Jericho to Jerusalem.

37
of Nazareth: Here *Nazōraios*, which is generally agreed to be an adjective from the place-name (see *TDNT* IV, pp. 874ff.), though it remains a puzzle how the 'a' of Nazaret becomes a long ō in *Nazōraios*. For Luke it is an alternative to *Nazaēnos*, which is the only form in Mark (cf. 4^{34} from Mark 1^{24}; 24^{19}), as also to 'the one from Nazareth' (A. 10^{38}). Its single occurrence here is the only preparation in the Gospel for its surprisingly frequent occurrence in A. (where it is the only form, as also in Matthew and John) as an identification of Jesus in speeches (A. 2^{22}; 3^6; 4^{10}; 6^{14}; 26^9), and as Jesus' self-identification (A. 22^8; cf. A. 9^5). In the gospels neither form is used internally by disciples with reference to Jesus, but only by outsiders or in addressing such.

is passing by: This may be intended to have a solemn tone, as of the procession in which Hellenistic kings and rulers (and even gods) manifested themselves to the people.

38
'Son of David, have mercy on me!': By contrast to the crowd's external description of Jesus as 'of Nazareth', the beggar addresses him urgently and repeatedly as *Son of David*. This could mean simply one who is physically descended from

David (Matt. 1^{20}; cf. Luke 2^4), but it clearly means more than that here, where it is made the basis of an appeal for mercy, which goes beyond a beggar's request for alms. Its earliest appearance as a title (or quasi-title) is in the Markan parallel to this verse, unless it is already such in Ps. Sol. 17^{23}, 'Behold, O Lord, and raise up unto them their king, the Son of David.' The rabbinic writings in which it becomes frequent, especially in the form 'The Son of David comes', are later than the NT. This single instance of its use in Mark and L–A with respect to Jesus (it is only implied in 1^{32}) is emphatic, for it prepares for Jesus' entry into Jerusalem, the city of David, and (especially for Luke) into the temple, to the accompaniment of words once used to greet the king on his entry into the temple (Ps. 118$^{25-26}$), 'Hosanna (to the Son of David, so Matthew). Blessed is he (the king, so Luke) who comes in the name of the Lord' – in Mark only, 'Blessed is the kingdom of our father David that is coming.' Despite its sound 'the Son of David' is not necessarily to be taken as expressing a purely political messiahship. In Matthew, where it is more frequent, it is found, as here, in appeals to Jesus for healing, and these are couched in language which is used in the Psalms in appeals to God for health, succour and salvation. *have mercy, eleēson,* means more than pity, and can include loving-kindness, and the help which God gives in faithfulness to the covenant with his people (cf. Ps. 6^2; 9^{13}; 25^6, etc.). Further, the hope of salvation through God's covenant of promise with the Davidic king (Jer. 30^9; Ezek. 34$^{23ff.}$) was a hope for righteousness and peace under the ideal shepherd-king, sometimes to be accompanied by the healing of blind, lame and deaf (Isa. 29$^{1, 17ff.}$; 35$^{3ff.}$). It is not clear whether such associations were already attached to the Son of David in the first century AD, or became attached as the result of a Christian identification of the Son of David with Jesus the healer. The part that could be played by the title in Christian preaching can be seen in the speech attributed to Paul in A. 13$^{17-41}$ – the appearance of Jesus, of Davidic descent, to be a saviour for Israel and to bring the holy blessings of David. See further Fuller, *Foundations,* the relevant sections.

39
rebuked him: epetimōn, as in 18^{15}; they do to the blind man what the disciples had done to those bringing children to Jesus.

19$^{1-10}$ *The Salvation of Zacchaeus*

19 *He entered Jericho and was passing through.* ^{2}*And there was a man named Zacchaeus; he was a chief tax collector, and rich.* ^{3}*And he sought to see who Jesus was, but could not, on account of the crowd, because he was small of*

stature. ⁴*So he ran on ahead and climbed up into a sycamore tree to see him, for he was to pass that way.* ⁵*And when Jesus came to the place, he looked up and said to him, 'Zacchaeus, make haste and come down; for I must stay at your house today.'* ⁶*So he made haste and came down, and received him joyfully.* ⁷*And when they saw it they all murmured, 'He has gone in to be the guest of a man who is a sinner.'* ⁸*And Zacchaeus stood and said to the Lord, 'Behold, Lord, the half of my goods I give to the poor; and if I have defrauded any one of anything, I restore it fourfold.'* ⁹*And Jesus said to him, 'Today salvation has come to this house, since he also is a son of Abraham.* ¹⁰*For the Son of man came to seek and to save the lost.'*

The story is peculiar to Luke. He may have placed it in the context supplied by Mark 10⁴⁶ff·, either because it came to him already associated with Jericho (which, however, is treated here less as the locality of a story than as a place on an itinerary – *was passing through*), or in order to have a pair of Jericho stories, both of which speak of salvation through Jesus, and thereby prepare for his arrival in Jerusalem as saviour (23³⁵⁻³⁹). It combines by way both of similarity and contrast features of the two previous stories. Thus, (i) in comparison with the story of the rich man (18¹⁸⁻²⁷), *ruler / chief tax collector; All these have I observed from my youth / a man who is a sinner; Sell all that you have and distribute to the poor / the half of my goods I give to the poor; Then who can be saved? / Today salvation has come*; and (ii) in comparison with the story of the blind man (18³⁵⁻⁴³), *hearing a multitude / on account of the crowd; inquired what this meant / sought to see who Jesus was; is passing by / was to pass that way; commanded him to be brought to him / make haste and come down.* It is distinguished as the narrative of an event by the extent to which its effect depends on lively human touches – the man's name, his position as chief tax collector, his energetic action motivated by curiosity, his running to climb the tree because of his smallness of stature, his being told to descend with equal speed to act as host to a guest who invites himself, and the precise but limited profession of intent in place of the more conventional statement that he left all and followed. Such circumstantial and humorous details are not characteristic of the oral tradition when it is primarily controlled by interest in the single religious message to be conveyed, and they are likely to be due to the story-teller's art.

In contrast to these lively features there is, as elsewhere in Luke, a certain lack of logical unity in the story as a whole, and of precision in relation to its main point. That point is clearly *Today salvation has come to this house* (v. 9), which matches artistically *I must stay at your house today* (v. 5). But since Luke is here combining two themes – the conversion of the tax collector and the rebuttal of objections to Jesus' consorting with a notorious sinner – this is addressed to Zacchaeus (*to him*, v. 9), but very oddly in the third person, as if it were being spoken to the objectors about him (*since he also is . . .* v. 9). Hence v. 7 strikes as an intrusion, perhaps modelled on the similar scene in 5$^{29ff.}$; but if it is removed the difficulty of the dialogue in vv. 5–9 ending in a statement in the third person is aggravated. There is no mention of any call to repentance. The conversion would seem to be secured simply by Jesus' invitation of himself to the house, which could be understood as a revised version in changed circumstances of his own invitation of sinners (cf. 5^{32}; and contrast 5$^{27-30}$, where Levi invites Jesus after conversion). As an enunciation of conversion, or as a sign of its having taken place – but in the sequence of the narrative as a reply to the objectors – Zacchaeus solemnly, before *the Lord* as witness, makes a double profession of intent, the first part of which (*the half of my goods I give to the poor*) goes far beyond what was expected for charity, and the second part of which (fourfold restoration of what had been fraudulently gained) goes beyond the requirement of the law, which was the amount plus a fifth (Lev. 6^5). Coming immediately after this profession the statement in v. 9a suggests that salvation is the reward for the promise of renunciation and restoration, though no reference is made to that, whereas v. 9b suggests that it comes about entirely through the initiative of Jesus in treating the tax collector as a member of the people of God; which initiative is then stated, also in the third person, to proceed from the mission of the Son of man to seek and save the lost.

ﳥ

2

This verse is in poor Greek – lit. 'And behold, a man called by name Zacchaeus, and he was a chief tax collector, and he (was) rich.' Knox (*Sources* II, p. 112) concludes that Luke obtained the story from 'an intensely Aramaizing source'; but after the clumsy opening sentence the style is idiomatic, and some of the vocabulary and constructions could be ascribed to Luke (see notes below). Luke can write in this clumsy fashion (cf. 23$^{50-52}$).

Zacchaeus: The name, meaning 'the righteous one', is perhaps stressed as one which could denote a true son of Abraham. It is found in II Macc. 10^{19} as the name of one of Judas Maccabaeus's generals, and the famous Rabbi Jochanan (*c.* AD 80) was known as ben Zachai.

chief tax collector: Strangely the Greek word here, *architelonēs,* appears nowhere else in Greek literature, and it is uncertain to what it refers – perhaps to one who was in charge of the farming of taxes in a given area, or to one of the senior agents in the taxation system. As a wealthy place, Herodian Jericho was likely to have been an important tax centre, and although it was not situated on the border, imports would have to pass through it on the route from Peraea to Jerusalem and the north.

3
to see who Jesus was: Cf. 4³⁴, and for the construction A. 21³³.

on account of: The Hellenistic causal use of the preposition *apo* = 'from', as in A. 11¹⁹; 12¹⁴; 20⁹; 22¹¹.

4
In this verse *ahead* is the regular classical Greek phrase for 'forward', *eis to emprosthen, climbed up* is the classical verb *anabainein epi, was to pass* has the idiomatic use of the verb *mellein* = 'to be about to' (9³¹; 10¹; frequent in A.), and *that way (ekeinēs* = 'that'; 'way' is understood) is a local genitive rare in the NT. *sycamore tree (sukomorea* + +) is a mulberry, a very climbable tree.

5
I must stay: In Greek, idiomatically, *dei me menein* (cf. 2⁴⁹; A. 19²¹; 25¹⁰). *stay* here is *menein* = 'abide', but in v. 7 *to be a guest* is *kataluein* = 'to lodge', implying a longer stay; but this is ignored in the story. Cadbury (*Luke–Acts,* pp. 249ff.) draws attention to the interest in lodgings in L–A.

6
In this verse *made haste* (as also in v. 5) is the intransitive use of the verb *speudein,* which is confined to L–A in the NT, *received* is *hupodechesthai* + 10³⁸; A. 17⁷; James 2²⁵, and *joyfully* is the participle *chairōn* = 'rejoicing', placed for emphasis at the end of the sentence, as at 15⁵; A. 8³⁹.

8
A vital step in the story. So far Luke has given examples of two responses of tax collectors to the demands of religion, penitence (by implication), renunciation of wealth and discipleship of Jesus (5²⁷⁻³²), and penitence simply (18¹³). Here it is penitence (by implication), almsgiving and restitution. This brings the case more within the confines of Judaism, for which restitution by the sinner in the appropriate cases was part and parcel of repentance. It also underwrites

Luke's modification of Jesus' invitation to sinners as a call to them to repent (5^{32} = Mark 2^{17}).

the half of my goods I give to the poor: Twenty per cent was reckoned a satisfactory proportion of income to be given as alms.

and if I have defrauded: The Greek does not express doubt, and should be rendered, 'From whomsoever I have extorted . . .' (*sukophantein* + 3^{14}, which see).

I restore it fourfold: For confessed fraud Roman law required in cases of theft *fourfold* (*tetraplous* + +) restitution, and in Exod. 22^1 this is demanded in cases of the theft of sheep.

9

Today salvation has come to this house: Salvation (*sōteria*) is a common word in the OT, generally in the negative sense of deliverance from enemies or afflictions, though not entirely so, the positive sense being that of restoration to a proper wholeness. In the gospels the idea of salvation is not prominent, and the noun is found on the lips of Jesus only here (and John 4^{22}, where it could be a gloss), and otherwise in Luke only at 1$^{69, 71, 77}$, the first two in the OT sense of deliverance from enemies and the third connected with the forgiveness of sins. In Paul, and the NT generally, it is used eschatologically of a final deliverance into a permanent condition of blessedness, and so belongs to the future; but in the only two instances of its use of Christian salvation in A. (4^{12}; 13^{26}) it could denote what is already present. In A. 13$^{23ff.}$ it is said to be sent in the form of the forgiveness of sins to those who are sons of Abraham through the appearance as saviour of Jesus, Son of David. Here in v. 9 it is emphatically present, though it is not said in what it consists. Negatively it is presumably deliverance from the controlling power of wealth, but there is no reference to discipleship of Jesus or entry into the kingdom as its positive side. *this house* has the sense of 'household', on the principle that what happens to the head of the household happens to it; cf. I Cor. 7^{14} for the holiness of parents involving that of the children.

since he also is a son of Abraham: This appears to reflect the view of A. and Paul that the message of salvation goes first to the Jews (Rom. 2^{10}), because it is primarily destined for them and they for it. In face of the adverse judgment of pious objectors the tax collector is to be considered no longer as an outsider, but as now, once more, a member of the people of God; and the action of Jesus towards him establishes authoritatively that this is so. Marshall (p. 698) considers the language and themes of the verse Lukan; but concern with men and women as children of Abraham could be regarded as a feature of Luke's special material (cf. 13^{16}; 16^{23}).

10

A final ground of the presence of salvation is now produced by the loose attachment (*for* does not make a strong connection with v. 9) of an independent Son of man saying of a generalizing kind. For such sayings see 18^8; 9^{56} (v.l.), and Matt. 18^{11} (v.l., probably taken from here, but now in the form 'The Son of man came to save what is lost'). This places the whole episode in a christo-logical setting as being the outcome of the mission of the Son of man (= Jesus) to seek for and save the lost. Jeremias (*TDNT* VI, p. 492) concludes on the basis of the language – seek, save, lost (cf. Ezek. 34) – that the saying was formu-lated to present the Son of man as Shepherd; but as 15$^{8-10}$ shows, seeking what is lost was not confined to shepherds and sheep, and *lost* is a synonym for 'sinner' or 'wicked' as being outside the sphere of the covenant of God. Since *seek* is the natural correlative of *lost*, *save* may be an addition to make the saying more directly applicable here.

19$^{11-27}$ *The Parable of the Pounds*

^{11}*As they heard these things, he proceeded to tell a parable, because he was near to Jerusalem, and because they supposed that the kingdom of God was to appear immediately.* ^{12}*He said therefore, 'A nobleman went into a far country to receive kingly power★ and then return.* ^{13}*Calling ten of his servants, he gave them ten pounds,† and said to them, "Trade with these till I come."* ^{14}*But his citizens hated him and sent an embassy after him, saying, "We do not want this man to reign over us."* ^{15}*When he returned, having received the kingly power,★ he commanded these servants, to whom he had given the money, to be called to him, that he might know what they had gained by trad-ing.* ^{16}*The first came before him, saying, "Lord, your pound has made ten pounds more."* ^{17}*And he said to him, "Well done, good servant! Because you have been faithful in a very little, you shall have authority over ten cities."* ^{18}*And the second came, saying, "Lord, your pound has made five pounds."* ^{19}*And he said to him, "And you are to be over five cities."* ^{20}*Then another came, saying, "Lord, here is your pound, which I kept laid away in a napkin;* ^{21}*for I was afraid of you, because you are a severe man; you take up what you did not lay down, and reap what you did not sow."* ^{22}*He said to him, "I will condemn you out of your own mouth, you wicked servant! You knew that I was a severe man, taking up what I did not lay down and reaping what I did not sow?* ^{23}*Why then did you not put my money into the bank, and at my coming I should have collected it with interest?"* ²⁴*And he said to those who stood by, "Take the pound from him, and give it to him who has the ten pounds."* ²⁵(*And they said to him, "Lord, he has ten pounds!"*) ²⁶*"I tell you, that to every one who has will more be given; but from him who has not, even what he has will be taken away.* ²⁷*But as for these enemies of mine, who did not want me to reign over them, bring them here and slay them before me."* '

* Greek *a kingdom*
† The mina, rendered here by *pound*, was equal to about £7

This parable, which Luke has Jesus tell immediately after the previous episode (*he proceeded to tell*, Greek *prostheis* = 'adding', a LXX use of this verb confined to Luke in the NT), and to the company who were present at it (*as they heard these things*), is as problematic as any passage in the Gospel. The difficulty of finding a satisfactory title for it (The Pounds, so traditionally; Money in Trust, so Dodd, *Parables*, pp. 24, 146ff.; The Rejected King, so Ellis, etc.) draws attention to it as a striking instance of a parable's undergoing development in the course of oral tradition, and acquiring thereby successive layers of application.

(i) There can be little doubt that it is the same parable as the Parable of the Talents, which Matthew has in a different context (Matt. 25¹⁴⁻³⁰), though certainly not taken directly from a common source. The situation is basically the same – a man before going away gives money to three slaves, who on his return render account, the first two being commended and rewarded for making a profit, and the third condemned for his failure to do so. Despite very wide differences there is also considerable verbal agreement, especially in the section about the third slave, and in phrases that are far from conventional, some being peculiar to this parable in the synoptic tradition. Such are: *well done* (*eu*, only here in Matthew and Luke), *good servant, faithful in* (over) *a* (very) *little, I was afraid of you* (I knew you to be) because *you are a severe* (hard) *man, reaping what you did not sow, wicked servant, why did you not put my money into the bank* (ought to have invested my money with the bankers – the sole reference to banking in the NT), *at my coming . . . with interest* (*tokos*, only here in the NT), *take from him . . . give it to him who has . . . to everyone who has will more be given, but from him who has not, even what he has will be taken away.*

(ii) It is difficult to detect at what stage, and for what reasons, some of the variations would have arisen. Thus, Luke's *ten of his servants* (v.

13) is very odd, and points to slovenliness at some stage, for it is disregarded in what follows, which, like Matthew's version, is constructed on the customary rule of three in parables. In no version would all ten have given account of their actions. The 'talents' in Matthew are some sixty times the value of the *pounds* in Luke, but there the situation is different, as the man distributes his property. The express command to *trade* (v. 13 *prāgmateuesthai* ++, classical, twice in the LXX, taken up in v. 15 by *diaprāgmateuesthai* ++, not LXX) is missing in Matthew, where the scene is set very briefly. The distribution in Matthew of five, two and one talents (representing different degrees of responsibility?) is in Luke a loaning of one pound to each of ten, which earns in addition (v. 16 *prosergazesthai* ++, not LXX) ten, five and none (representing different degrees of effort?). In Matthew the actions of the slaves are first described, and are then rehearsed by the slaves themselves when they render account (Matt. 26$^{16-18, 20, 22, 25}$). In Luke they are disclosed for the first time by the slaves themselves. In Matthew the third slave buries his money for fear of burglars; in Luke he lays it up in a handkerchief (*soudarion*, a Latin loan word + A. 19^{12}; John 11^{44}; 20^{7}). The great reward given for faithfulness in what is little is in Matthew described in exactly matching verses (Matt. 25$^{20f., 22f.}$), and in identical terms as appointment (as steward?) over much. In Luke it is described variously, and in descending order, as a rule over cities, which is incongruous. In Matthew the man is hard (*sklēros*), in Luke severe (*austēros* = 'exacting'), because he reaps what he does not sow, and because (in Matthew) he gathers into barns what he has not scattered, (in Luke) he acts contrary to the law 'you only take up what you put down' (see on v. 21). The third slave is condemned (in Luke out of his own mouth) for not having made interest at the bank, and the command is given (in Luke to certain bystanders) to take his money and give it to the first slave, on the principle (uttered in Luke in reply to an objection of these bystanders that the first slave already has ten pounds) that to him who has shall be given. Thus, characteristically, Matthew's version is the more schematized, Luke's the more literary.

(iii) The precise reference of such a parable is not easy to detect. Dibelius (*Tradition*, p. 255) sees it as directed against the Jewish people as a whole, which has failed to use what God has entrusted to it. Dodd (*Parables*, p. 151) and Jeremias (*Parables*, p. 62) see it as spoken against the religious leaders, who, at the present time of reckoning, are accused of defrauding God by negative concern for personal security in hedging the law. This type of interpretation places the whole emphasis on the behaviour of the third slave, but the manner in which the other two are depicted suggests that they are not simply foils to the third. The idea that the slaves are being put to the test is possibly read into the text. A further difficulty, which would also attach to any application to the disciples, is that what is entrusted is said to be little. The crux of the parable may lie in the description of the character of the master (v. 21, repeated by the master himself in v. 22), since it is this which is the basis of the third slave's inaction (and by implication of the actions of the other two), and of his condemnation. This is taken to mean (as by Manson, *Sayings*, p. 247, 'the argument appears to be'), 'If I make a profit the master gets it; if I make a loss he will come upon me to make it good. Therefore the best course is to do nothing.' This, however, is an unlikely argument for a slave, who has no money of his own, with respect to his master's money, and the second part of it has to be read into the text. The argument of v. 21 could rather be, 'I feared you as one who does not live honestly by his own labours, but by fraud and misappropriation (this is the probable force of *you take up what you did not lay down* – see note), and is prepared to make profit at all costs and by all means. I was unwilling to behave like you; I return your pound to you.' The logic of the conclusion which the master then draws from the slave's statement (*I will condemn you out of your own mouth*, v. 22) depends on the maxim that it is the duty of the slave to be exactly like his master (cf. 6^{40}; Matt. $10^{24f.}$; John 13^{16}): 'since you knew me to be such a person, it was your duty to behave as I do, and at all costs to have got interest.' If this is the correct emphasis, then the parable is another of the risqué parables, like those of the Unrighteous Steward and the Unrighteous Judge, in which the central figure is a reprehensible character, and the lesson conveyed, even by a dangerous example, is 'be profitable at all costs and by all means'. This, perhaps the first form of the parable, could have been spoken with either religious leaders or disciples in mind.

(iv) The first(?) adaptation of the parable in both versions would seem to have been the removal of any punishment of the third slave (to be replaced later in Matthew), and the substitution for it of vv. 24–26 (Matt. 25^{28-29}) with its theme 'To him who has shall be given', which, as the parable's conclusion, becomes now the main point, and is addressed to disciples (cf. 8^{18} = Mark 4^{25}, referring to the possibility of further understanding by disciples in virtue of the knowledge they

already possess). This ending is, however, artificial; for in the movement of the story there is no reason for the extra money to be given to
the first slave and not divided between the first two; and neither is said
to have retained possession of the original money given by the master.
This artificiality is evident in Luke in the abrupt insertion of *those who
stood by* (v. 24) as objects of the command *Take the pound from him* (v.
25), which RSV rightly regards as a parenthesis; and in *I tell you* (v. 26),
which is hardly the master speaking to these bystanders in a continuation of the parable, but is Jesus pointing its moral. These additions
resemble those by which other parables involving reprehensible characters are made edifying (cf. 16$^{8ff.}$; 18$^{6f.}$).

(v) The second(?) adaptation has fastened on the subordinate detail
that the master goes away (Matt. 25^{14} *apodēmōn*, the same word as in
Mark 13^{34}; and cf. 12$^{35ff.}$ = Matt. 24$^{42ff.}$), and has made it the chief
point. This turns the parable into an allegory addressed to Christians
about the parousia or return of Jesus after his going away. This has
produced in Matthew's version, 'Now after a long time the master of
those servants came' (Matt. 25^{19}), and the injunctions pertaining to the
last judgment, 'enter into the joy of your master' (Matt. 25$^{21, 23}$), and
'Cast out the worthless servant into the outer darkness . . .' (Matt. 25^{30}).
In Luke it has gone to such lengths as well-nigh to wreck the parable.
The master is now a nobleman, whose departure is for the purpose of
procuring confirmation of a royal authority which is already his (v. 12),
and during whose absence rebellious subjects send an embassy to protest
their unwillingness to have him as king (vv. 14–15a), and are slaughtered on his return (v. 27). It has long been observed that all this corresponds with events in 4 BC in the narrative of Josephus (*BJ* 2.1–111,
Ant. 17.228–339). This tells of Archelaus, who had already assumed the
kingship of Judaea after Herod's death; of his leaving his castles and
treasury in the hands of faithful officers; of a Jewish embassy to Rome
to plead for autonomy because of the tyranny of Herod and Archelaus;
of the award of the tetrarchy to Archelaus with the promise of kingship
if he ruled well; and of his savage treatment of Jews on his return in
view of his previous disputes with them. This political setting would
seem to have produced in Luke's version *nobleman* (*eugenēs*, a word
used by Josephus for a member of the aristocracy), the incongruity of
rule over ten or five cities as a reward for trading with a pound (vv. 17,
19), and a fresh ending to the parable with the slaughter of rebels in the
presence of the victor after the ancient manner (v. 27). To speak here

simply of the fusion of two stories (Jeremias, *Parables*, p. 59) is to pay insufficient attention to the fact that the additional material (vv. 12, 14, 15a, 27) does not constitute a parable or allegory with a point of its own. Rather it glosses the parable so as to give it a new framework and a fresh point, without, however, being integrated into it, since the rebels who send an embassy have no relation to the slaves who have been bidden to trade. Although the Archelaus incident was no doubt notorious, it would have been thirty years old by the time of Jesus' speaking, and considerably older by the time of Luke's writing, and the choice of it might argue a glossator of a literary and historical cast of mind. Was the glossator Luke himself? This could not be ruled out on linguistic grounds, as much of the vocabulary of the additional material is characteristic of him, or is confined to L–A in the NT: *nobleman, far country, return* (*hupostrephein*), *citizen, send an embassy, reign over, return* (*epanerchesthai*); in v. 27, which is a well constructed sentence, *slay* (*katasphazein* ++, a classical and Hellenistic word). An answer to the question will depend to some extent on how far this final form of the parable is judged to have been given it by the same hand as wrote v. 11, which states the parable's purpose.

(vi) The introduction to the parable in v. 11, which is undoubtedly from Luke's hand, gives a twofold reason why it was spoken to those who had been listening to *these things*, i.e. to talk about a present salvation available through the earthly mission of the Son of man (18^{35}–19^{10}). Firstly, it was because *he was near Jerusalem*, and such proximity in those circumstances could generate a messianic fanaticism. This can be illustrated by Josephus's story (*BJ* 2.261f.) of an Egyptian false prophet, who led his followers 'by a circuitous route from the desert to the mount called the Mount of Olives. From there he proposed to force an entrance into Jerusalem, and, after overpowering the Roman garrison, to set himself up as a tyrant of the people, employing those who poured in with him as his bodyguard.' Secondly, and in elaboration of the first reason, it was because *they* (the attendant company in distinction from *he*) *supposed that the kingdom of God was to appear immediately*. This may reflect less an actual situation in the company, known to Luke, than anxieties in Luke's own mind to which he gives expression here, especially anxieties about the possible misinterpretation of the Christian movement in the Empire. If so, the emphasis may be on *appear* rather than on *immediately*. For it was obvious when Luke wrote that the kingdom had not appeared immediately, and his version of the parable, as distinct from Matthew's ('after a long time', Matt. 25¹⁹), makes no reference to any delay, and it is not designed to reflect on the necessity of a delay in the kingdom's coming. On the other hand, the Greek verb translated *appear* (*anaphainesthai*) had been used by Greek writers with 'king' or 'kingdom' in the sense of 'to proclaim publicly', 'to declare'. What still needed to be disavowed was any political conception of the kingdom; perhaps for this reason Luke omitted Mark 10³⁵⁻⁴⁵ with its request of the sons of Zebedee for places in such a kingdom. What will be openly manifested on the plane of history is the judgment on Israel and the destruction of Jerusalem. Luke could then have been the glossator of the parable which now ends with the slaughter in v. 27, and could have chosen the historical precedent of Archelaus because of its connection of rebellious Jews with Rome. The message Luke then intends the parable to convey at this juncture may be that Jesus who is *de jure* king (19³⁸) is going away to receive his *de facto* (spiritual) rule from the Father. In the interim profitable service of the Lord is to be commended as against either the unprofitableness of Jewish unbelief or their political rebellion, which will be punished, and for the punishment of which the Romans are the Lord's historical agents (cf. 21²⁰⁻²⁴ followed by 21²⁵⁻²⁷, and 19⁴¹⁻⁴⁴). As Creed observes (p. 235), v. 27 reproduces the spirit of 18¹⁻⁸, though his further observation that it differs from the spirit of the lament over Jerusalem in 19⁴¹⁻⁴⁴ applies only to 19⁴¹⁻⁴² and not to 19⁴³⁻⁴⁴.

ಐಐ

11

Both structure and wording of this sentence point to its having been framed by Luke himself. *prostheis* = 'going on to' is introduced by Luke at 20¹¹ into a Markan passage (cf. A. 12³), and *tell a parable* (*eipen parabolēn*) is a Lukan expression. *because he was near to Jerusalem* is the infinitive with the article after the preposition *dia* = 'on account of', a construction rare in the NT, but found seven times in the Gospel and eight times in A. *Jerusalem* is here the form *Hierousalēm*, which Luke prefers – contrast the form *Hierosoluma* in 19²⁸, which is taken from Mark. *immediately* (*parachrēma*) is, apart from two instances in Matthew, confined to L–A in the NT. *appear* is *anaphainesthai* + A. 21³ in the active. The sentence is, therefore, a conscious statement by Luke of what he thought the parable meant, or of what he had shaped it to mean, and of why he thought it appropriate, indeed necessary, to place it at this point in the narrative.

13

ten of his servants: Manson (*Sayings*, p. 315) points to the use of 'ten' and 'five' in Palestine as round numbers, like our 'dozen' and 'half-dozen', but, as he admits, this does not explain their occurrence here. This may be due to reflection back from the reward of ten cities and five cities in vv. 17, 19. The Decapolis in Palestine (cf. Mark 5²⁰; 7³¹) was a loose confederacy of ten cities (the list of which varies in the sources) of a more Hellenistic character mostly east of the Lake of Galilee. Pentapolis = 'five cities' was a grouping found in more than one region of the Roman Empire (cf. Wisd. 10⁶, where it is used of Sodom and its environs). Derrett (*Law in the NT*, pp. 17ff.) takes the servants (Greek *douloi*) not as slaves, who could not trade for their masters, but as those in a position of dependance through being taken into temporary business partnership, the arrangements for which he sees as governing the details of the parable. The parallel he adduces of the use of *douloi* for royal officials is not, however, a strong one, as that was a reflection of the absolutist view of monarchy which made the king's officials his slaves; nor does the reward of the servants with their being set over much (Matthew) or cities (Luke) fit easily into such a business arrangement.

pounds: The word here *mnā*, not found in the NT outside this parable, is a Semitic loan word for a Greek coin worth a hundred drachmae (see on 15⁸).

21

severe: *austēros*, a literary word with a favourable sense (the English 'austere') and an unfavourable one, 'harsh', 'exacting'. MM, who give an example of its use in a papyrus of a government official, translate by 'taskmaster', 'one who would get blood out of a stone'.

you take up what you did not lay down: This is often referred to as a proverb or maxim (so Derrett, *Law*, p. 25 n. 1), but it would seem to be more than that. To take up only what you lay down was a legal principle rather than proverbial wisdom, and it did not originate in banking as Jeremias supposes (*Parables*, p. 59 n. 40), though it could be applied there. Aelian (*Varia Historia* 3.46) refers to it as the universal law of the Greeks, and Diogenes Laertius includes it among the excellent provisions made by Solon that a deposit of treasure should not be removed except by the depositor on pain of death. Plato (*Laws* 11.913C) refers to it as 'that most comprehensive ordinance of the noble man (Solon) who said "Take not up what you have not laid down",' and in *Laws* 8.844E applies it to the fining of one who picks another man's grapes, and in *Laws* 12.941C to the theft of public property. In the Jewish milieu Josephus (*Against Apion* 2.216, cf. 208) commends the clarity and simplicity of the Jewish polity in requiring death for sexual crimes and violence to the person, and the severest penalties for 'taking up what has not been laid down', i.e. misappropriation. And Philo (cited by Eusebius, *Preparation of the Gospel* 8.7) states as a principle of Jewish law, written or unwritten, 'not to take up what has not been laid down, whether from a garden, a winepress or threshing floor'. Thus contravention of this law was to be guilty of some kind of fraud or expropriation, and this is what the slave accuses his master of, and what the master admits to be the case.

23

the bank: Greek *trapeza* = 'table', in the sense of the bench used by money dealers, as in Mark 11^{15} = Matt. 21^{12}. There, however, they are those who change one currency into another; here those who lend money on interest. But this was expressly forbidden between Israelites by the law (Deut. 23^{19-20}; Exod. 22^{25}; Lev. 25^{36-37}); it was permitted an Israelite only in dealing with a foreigner (Deut. 23^{20}). Hence Fitzmyer (p. 1237), the only commentator to note the point, concludes 'the master thought that the servant could at least have lent the money to non-Jews'. But the injunction may be continuing the thought of vv. 20–22: since you knew that I was an extortioner, you should, as my slave, have been like me, and have engaged in the unlawful and extortionate practice of usury.

19^{28}–24^{53}

Jerusalem

From this point in the Gospel the narrative, which has already begun to be articulated by the words 'to approach' (18^{35}; 19^{11}), and which continues to be so ($19^{37, 41}$), becomes more of a single story. Told through a connected series of events it is the story of the coming of Jesus to Jerusalem, the centre of the Jewish religion, of his teaching there, his crucifixion and resurrection there, issuing in the promise of a universal mission of the apostles thence. It is to be expected that the character of the narrative, and also of Luke's method of handling his materials, should change. For any account of the passion and resurrection of Jesus with their attendant circumstances, even if still made up largely of separate units of tradition, will have had as its aim to tell *in extenso* what was involved in the statement 'that Christ died for our sins in accordance with the scriptures, that he was buried, that he was raised on the third day in accordance with the scriptures' (I Cor. 15^{3-4}). In Luke's case there is the added reason that for him the mission of the world was to begin from Jerusalem (24^{47}; A. 1^{4-8}), which was also to be a headquarters for the church throughout Acts. So from being a somewhat loose compilation of episodes and teaching units the narrative now begins to be more unified and precise. This is not due to additional chronological or topographical information. Mark has a rudimentary though not strongly marked chronology which was to lead to the conception of Holy Week: entry into Jerusalem and retirement at evening to Bethany (Mark $11^{1, 11}$, one day), return to Jerusalem, cleansing of the temple and retirement at evening to an unspecified place (Mark 11^{15-19}, one day), return to Jerusalem, teaching in the temple and on the Mount of Olives (Mark $11^{20, 27}$; $12^{35, 38}$; 13^{1-37}, one day), Passover after one or two days (Mark 14^{1-12}). Luke, however, omits all these Markan notes of time, and is content with the vague *drew near* of the Passover and its arrival ($22^{1, 7}$). His non-Markan material does not supply him with any chronological information. The period in Jerusalem is of unspecified duration – *daily* (19^{47}), *one day* (20^1), *every day*

(21³⁷), *at that time* (Greek 'in those days', 23⁷) – and some of the incidents could have taken place at any time within it. As elsewhere, but especially here where the events are concentrated in a single period in a single place, Luke's aim is to present as orderly and intelligible a narrative as the traditions allow. He begins from a descent of the Mount of Olives, which brings Jerusalem into view, as providing the setting for the disciples' acclamation of Jesus. His concern is not, however, with Jerusalem as the holy city of Judaism, for he places next Jesus' lament over it and his prophecy of its destruction (to be repeated in 21^{20–24}, 23^{28–31}). His concern is rather with the temple, and even then with the temple not as containing the sanctuary (Greek *nāos*), the scene of sacrifice, but as sacred place (Greek *hieron*), where teaching takes place in its courts. Once inside Jerusalem Jesus' movements are simplified (somewhat belatedly, 21³⁷) to a teaching ministry by day in the temple, which he has taken over by cleansing it, and a nightly retirement to the Mount of Olives. This teaching ministry, which could have been deduced from Jesus' own words at his arrest (22⁵³, par. Mark 14⁴⁹), is stressed repeatedly, and provides the setting for all that takes place in Jerusalem until Jesus' arrest. In 19^{47f.} the main protagonists of the story are described in relation to it as the chief priests, scribes and chief men of the city, who in listening to it become intent on Jesus' destruction, and 'the whole people', who hang on his words.

19^{28–40} = Mark 11^{1–10}

THE ACCLAMATION OF JESUS BY DISCIPLES

²⁸*And when he had said this, he went on ahead, going up to Jerusalem.* ²⁹*When he drew near to Bethphage and Bethany, at the mount that is called Olivet, he sent two of the disciples,* ³⁰*saying, 'Go into the village opposite, where on entering you will find a colt tied, on which no one has ever yet sat; untie it and bring it here.* ³¹*If any one asks you, "Why are you untying it?" you shall say this, "The Lord has need of it." '* ³²*So those who were sent went away and found it as he had told them.* ³³*And as they were untying the colt, its owners said to them, 'Why are you untying the colt?'* ³⁴*And they said, 'The Lord has need of it.'* ³⁵*And they brought it to Jesus, and throwing their garments on the colt they set Jesus upon it.* ³⁶*And as he rode along, they spread*

their garments on the road. ³⁷*As he was now drawing near, at the descent of the Mount of Olives, the whole multitude of the disciples began to rejoice and praise God with a loud voice for all the mighty works that they had seen,* ³⁸*saying, 'Blessed be the King who comes in the name of the Lord! Peace in heaven and glory in the highest!'* ³⁹*And some of the Pharisees in the multitude said to him, 'Teacher, rebuke your disciples.'* ⁴⁰*He answered, 'I tell you, if these were silent, the very stones would cry out.'*

The acclamation of Jesus – miscalled the Triumphal Entry, since the city is entered only after it has taken place – provides a most impressive opening to the story which is to reach its climax in his crucifixion as 'the king of the Jews'. It is not, however, without difficulties. The narratives in all four gospels present the event as a messianic act, i.e. an act of one who is God's destined king of Israel, with its attendant homage. It is remarkable, therefore, that it plays no further part in the story, and no reference is made to it subsequently, unless it is to be included in *these things* (20²), or underlies the statement of the Sanhedrin at the trial (22⁶⁷). Its messianic character is conveyed by the use of Zech. 9⁹: 'Rejoice greatly, O daughter of Zion! Shout aloud, O daughter of Jerusalem! Lo, your king comes to you; triumphant and victorious is he, humble and riding on an ass, on a colt the foal of an ass' (LXX on a new, i.e. untried, colt). This use is explicit in Matthew and John by quotation, implicit in Mark and Luke by Jesus' deliberate instructions for procuring a new, previously unridden, beast. But this makes the connection between the event and its interpretation a literary one.[a] Pilgrims generally went on foot into Jerusalem for a feast, but it is a moot point whether the sight of a rabbi riding to it, even accompanied by disciples, was so exceptional as to guarantee of itself that Zech. 9⁹ would be evoked in the minds of the bystanders; and they would not be in a position to know that the beast was an untried one. That Jesus staged such an act as is depicted here might be said hardly to accord with evidence elsewhere in the gospels of his reticence towards, if not repudiation of, popular messianism, and his insistence on a necessary rejection of the Son of man. It remains a question whether the enactment of the picture of the king in terms of Zech. 9⁹ would itself be

[a] For an assessment of the historical and the literary and symbolic elements in the story, see A. E. Harvey, *Jesus and the Constraints of History*, London and Philadelphia 1982, pp. 122ff.

sufficient to establish a different kind of messiahship. John could have thought so, since in his account (12¹²⁻¹⁶) the procuring of the beast can be seen as a protest on Jesus' part against the crowd's acclamation as showing a misunderstanding of his kingship, the true nature of which is a main constituent of John's passion narrative. In Luke's account vv. 28–36 are clearly taken over from Mark. Verbal agreement is very close, and any variations are readily accounted for as stylistic improvements by Luke. There is, then, no adequate ground for postulating any other source than Mark for vv. 37–38, where there are considerable differences. For these verses are too fragmentary to stand on their own, and there is no other trace of a non-Markan source used by Luke for this story to which they could have belonged. The differences will have to be put down to Luke's editing, and they will show his mind at this crucial point in the narrative – the appearance of Jesus as king.

ಐ

28

Having stated the nature of the kingdom in the parable of the Pounds (*And when he had said this*), Jesus resumes his journey to Jerusalem. In *he went on ahead, going up to Jerusalem* Luke utilizes that part of Mark 10³² which he had not taken over in 18³¹. Attention is concentrated on Jesus. It is his story and his journey, and he is in control of it.

29

In the course of the journey, some fifteen miles out of Jericho, he *drew near to* Bethphage and Bethany, and to (the area of, Greek *pros*) the Mount of Olives. The text of Mark may have had 'to Jerusalem, and to Bethphage and Bethany and the Mount of Olives', and Luke relieves this overloading of place-names by removing Jerusalem into the previous sentence. Even so the geographical reference is overcrowded. The exact locality of Bethphage is unknown. A place named Beth Page is mentioned in rabbinic literature as closely connected with Jerusalem. Bethany, identified with the modern El Azariyeh, was on the east side of the Mount of Olives, two miles south-east of Jerusalem. The Mount of Olives is a ridge two and a half miles long, over one shoulder of which the Jericho–Jerusalem road swings. It commanded a view across the Kidron valley of the holy city, and especially of the temple. The mention of it in the synoptic narratives might be more than geographical, and owe something to its eschatological associations, based on Zech. 14⁴ᶠᶠ·, as the place where the Lord would stand in the day of the Lord to rescue Jerusalem from the nations. Luke seems to have regarded Bethany as virtually identical with the mount (cf. 24⁵⁰ with A. 1¹², and 21³⁷ with Mark 11¹¹ᶠ·). From here Jesus dispatches two disciples as his representatives (as on the mission, 10¹) to procure for him a riding animal.

30–34

The story in Mark is highly and intentionally mysterious. Jesus, who for the only time in Mark is called 'the Lord', acting with supernatural prevision and imperious authority, predicts that in a village opposite – no name or direction are given – they will find tethered a *pōlos* (horse? ass's colt?) hitherto unridden. They are to requisition it in his name and promise its return. Derrett★ argues that it was accepted practice for one in authority – a king, or general, or teacher – to arrange in advance for the requisitioning of transport in this way. In taking over Mark Luke makes four changes. In v. 31 he omits the promise of the return of the animal on loan (but his text may have read 'and he (the owner) will send it'; cf. Matt. 21³. In v. 32 he replaces Mark's repeated description of the animal by *as he had told them*, underlining Jesus' authority. In v. 33 he refers to the by-standers as the animal's owners (*hoi kurioi*) to match the singular *ho kurios* = *the Lord*. In v. 34 he has the authoritative *The Lord has need of it*, thus focusing attention on the word of Jesus as predictive and effective.

on which no one has ever yet sat: Practically speaking an unsuitable animal for the purpose in hand; but this is a symbolic feature found in stories of heroes or divine beings – cf. the unused tomb in 23⁵³, and I Sam. 6⁷. It was added in the LXX version of Zech. 9⁹, and has here entered the story sufficiently to be on the lips of Jesus as part of his instructions. If, as has been suggested, *tied* was intended to recall the oracle in Gen. 49¹¹, that would be a further symbolic element.

35–36

On their return *they* (not only the two disciples, but at some stage others in the company) place their garments on the animal and mount Jesus upon it (the verb Luke uses, *embibazein*, is the correct word for this, and is already in Zech. 9⁹ LXX). They then place garments under the animal as it proceeds. This is probably to be interpreted as a symbolic act of enthronement, acting out Zech. 9⁹ – cf. II Kings 9¹³, 'Then in haste every man took his garment, and put it under him (i.e. Jehu) on the bare steps, and they blew the trumpet, and pro-claimed, "Jehu is king" ', where the garments represent the men themselves, and the piling of them to form a throne indicates submission to Jehu's authority. This is further indicated here by having the animal walk over garments. The setting is thus provided for the acclamation to follow.

37

Mark does not specify where the acclamation takes place; 'And he entered' (Mark 11¹¹) could be taken to separate it from the city itself. Luke follows him, but is more specific. He links it with Jerusalem by a repetition of *drawing near*

★ *Studies in the New Testament* II, Leiden 1978, pp. 165–83.

(cf. v. 29), and makes use of hints in Mark to suppose a route over the Mount of Olives which brings Jesus (the attention is still focused on him, not on any pilgrim crowds) to the beginning of a descent of the mount at which Jerusalem comes into view (v. 41). At this moment of drawing near to Jerusalem, which in 19^{11} was said to be the reason for telling the parable of the Pounds, the act of acclamation of kingship takes place. In comparison with Mark this act is carefully described, so as to divest it of any suggestion of popular messianism. (i) It is not the action of a mob, or even of a pilgrim crowd, but is confined to *the whole multitude of the disciples*. The word rendered multitude, *plēthos*, occurs, apart from two instances in Mark and John, only in Luke's of the gospels, and plays a considerable part in A. With a defining genitive *of the disciples* (cf. A. 6^2) to denote a corporate entity it is confined to L–A in the NT, and in A. is almost a designation of the church (cf. A. 4^{32}; 6^5; $15^{12, \, 30}$). This could be artificial here if it is intended to denote a very large number which has come as a single body on a protracted journey all the way from Galilee. (ii) The reason for the acclamation is one which pertains to disciples only, viz. praise *for all the mighty works that they had seen*, presumably from the beginning of the ministry in Galilee (cf. A. $10^{37ff.}$, 'beginning from Galilee . . . how he went about doing good and healing all that were oppressed by the devil . . . and we are witnesses to all that he did'; also 7^{19-23}; 10^{13}; A. 2^{22}). This makes the entry into the city a climax and continuation of that ministry, and defines the nature of Jesus' kingship. (iii) The act of acclamation is described, in language characteristic of Luke in miracle stories, as rejoicing and praising God (cf. 5^{26}; 7^{16}; 13^{13}; 17^{15}; 18^{43}, and esp. 13^{17}; A. $3^{8f.}$), and is thus the praise of God for Jesus, and not simply the glorification of Jesus himself (cf. A. 2^{22}; $10^{38f.}$).

38
The words of the acclamation vary in the manuscripts, but should probably read, with Codex Vaticanus, as the double chiasmus:

> Blessed is he who comes,
> the king in the name of the Lord.
> In heaven peace,
> and glory in the highest.

In comparison with Mark this involves:
(i) the omission at beginning and end of 'Hosanna' and 'Hosanna in the highest'. No further reason is needed for this than Luke's dislike of Hebrew and Aramaic words as unintelligible to his readers; here perhaps unintelligible to himself (the meaning of 'Hosanna' is still a matter of discussion), and, as unintelligible, capable of giving the impression of a popular messianic cry. The omission, however, removes the most recognizable link with the festival, as the only occurrence of 'Hosanna' in the OT is at Ps. 118.25, one of the psalms recited at the festival, and the cry was closely associated with the waving of branches then,

which feature in the story (Mark 11⁸?; Matt. 21⁸; John 12¹³) Luke also drops:

(ii) the omission of the dangerous statement, unparalleled in any liturgical utterance, 'Blessed is the kingdom of our father David that is coming!', which could be taken as an identification of the coming of Jesus to the city with the fulfilment of popular messianic hopes ('our father David', not 'his father'). This is compensated for by the insertion of 'the king' into the verse of the festival psalm 'Blessed is he who comes in the name of the Lord' (Ps. 118.26 = 117.26 LXX), the separation of 'in the name of the Lord' from 'he who comes' and its attachment to 'the king', thus enabling *he who comes* to refer to an unspecified future ('he who shall come', cf. 7¹⁹), and declaring *the king* to be God-commissioned and God-approved:

(iii) the glossing of both the omitted elements by a form of the acclamation made by the multitude (*plēthos*) of the heavenly host at the announcement of the birth of Jesus as saviour and Lord Christ in the city of David (2¹¹⁻¹⁴), with the difference that there peace is said to be on earth and glory in the heavens, whereas here both peace and glory are in heaven. Both expressions – peace in heaven and glory in heaven – are unprecedented, and no parallels are cited from Jewish sources. The scene of *peace*, a comprehensive word for wholeness of life, and at times almost a synonym for God's salvation, should be on earth (as in 2¹⁴; 12⁵¹, etc.). The nearest parallel to peace in heaven could be Rev. 12¹⁰; 19¹, but that depends upon the apocalyptic conception of a war in heaven and its ensuing peace, and Luke is unlikely to have had that in mind. *glory (doxa*, here in the sense of 'praise') is generally ascribed to God from earth, and while *glory in the highest* is appropriate on the lips of heavenly beings in 2¹⁴ (cf. Ps. 148¹ᶠ.), it is hardly so here. These expressions are best explained as the product of Luke's grappling with what stood in Mark, whose single 'in the highest' has influenced the form of them. In thus reformulating the acclamation Luke has done two things. Firstly, by inserting 'the king' he has deliberately at the outset of the passion narrative brought to the forefront what was its unavoidable issue (23²ᶠ., ³⁷ᶠ. – and was to continue to be a crucial issue in the church's preaching, A. 17⁷). Secondly, by continuing with *in the name of the Lord . . . in the highest* he has made the disciples bear witness that this kingship, so far from being a matter of revolution, of which Pilate will declare Jesus innocent (23², ¹⁴), is a heavenly affair (23⁴²ᶠ.); and, as in v. 37, attention is fixed upon God as much as on Jesus.

39–40

Only in Mark does the acclamation pass without comment. In each of the other gospels a reaction to it is appended by means of an independent saying, which is to some extent characteristic of that Gospel. In Matthew the whole city is agitated by the appearance of the prophet of Nazareth, and when children in the temple repeat the acclamation in its Matthaean form, and an objection is raised, Jesus replies in terms of the fulfilment of scripture (Matt. 21¹⁰⁻¹⁶). In

John the Pharisees observe of the enthusiasm of the crowds that the whole world
has become Jesus' disciple, and Greeks are then introduced as seeking him (John
12¹⁸⁻²⁰). In Luke Pharisees appear for the last time in the Gospel as the customary
objectors and the opponent of the disciples. They speak from the crowd
(*multitude*), which appears here for the first time in Luke's passion narrative
(contrast Mark 11⁸ᶠ·; Matt. 21⁸); and their objection *rebuke your disciples*
depends on the Lukan account, where only disciples have acclaimed. Jesus is
thus asked to do with respect to the devotion of his disciples what they themselves had done with respect to those who brought children to Jesus (18¹⁵), and
what the crowd had done with respect to the blind man (18³⁹). The authoritative reply of Jesus – *I tell you* – is cryptic, and its meaning uncertain.

if these were silent, the very stones would cry out: This is generally taken to mean
that, if necessary, the stones will utter what must be confessed, and what cannot and must not be suppressed, the kingship of Jesus; so there is no question of
silencing the disciples. Reference is made to Hab. 2⁶⁻¹¹, a passage which the
Qumran Commentary on Habakkuk interprets of the conquest of Jerusalem by
the Romans, though it does not refer to v. 11, 'For the stone will cry out from
the wall, and the beam from the woodwork respond.' There the stone cries out
against the corruption of the city's inhabitants, and Jewish exegesis of various
kinds took it to mean that the stones would voice a cry of accusation – for
rabbinic references to the accusing stone based on Hab. 2¹¹, see SB II, p. 253.
There is evidence in apocalyptic writing of the crying stone as a sign of the end
in e.g. IV Ezra 5⁵, 'Blood will drip from the woodwork and stone will give
forth its voice,' and The Lives of the Prophets (a Jewish work, probably of the
late first century AD) 31¹³ᶠᶠ·, 'He gave a sign against Jerusalem and the whole
land; when they see a stone crying bitterly the end draws near.' Schlatter (pp.
409ff.) insists that the Greek requires to be translated by 'shall be silent . . . shall
cry out', and takes it as a factual and not hypothetical statement: 'When the
confession of the disciples comes to be silenced by the opposition of Judaism,
the stones of the already ruined Jerusalem will cry out that Jesus was king, and
was rejected.' With this specific sense the statement would have a more than
purely verbal connection with the following oracle on the destruction of
Jerusalem (*stones . . . one stone upon another*), and could have belonged with it
rather than with the preceding acclamation.

19⁴¹⁻⁴⁴ *Lament Over Jerusalem*

⁴¹*And when he drew near and saw the city he wept over it,* ⁴²*saying, 'Would
that even today you knew the things that make for peace! But now they are*

*hid from your eyes. ⁴³For the days shall come upon you, when your enemies
will cast up a bank about you and surround you, and hem you in on every side,
⁴⁴and dash you to the ground, you and your children within you, and they will
not leave one stone upon another in you; because you did not know the time
of your visitation.'*

The tension mounts with a further mention of the approach to Jerusalem. At the sight of the city Jesus *wept over it* – the Greek expression,
klaiein with the preposition *epi* and the accusative, not classical or LXX,
is a forceful one. This is the only reference in the gospels to Jesus' weeping except John 11³⁵, where the verb used is different and the weeping
is of a different kind. The reason for it here is not private and personal,
but public and theological, viz. Jesus' foreknowledge of the final destruction of the city of God for failure to recognize and acknowledge
God's dealings with her. This is expressed (vv. 42–44) in a rhythmical
prophetic oracle, which is a mixture of doom and lament. It is self-
contained, and could have been uttered at any time. It is not easily
assigned to a source, nor attached to anything else in a source. It is
different in structure, language and tone from the apostrophe of Jerusalem reproduced from Q in 13³⁴⁻³⁵. In a manner not uncharacteristic of
prophecy it moves from the present tense in the wish that Jerusalem
might know (v. 42), to the future tense of her certain fate (vv. 43–44b),
to the past tense of reflection upon what is now over (v. 44c). The
oracle can be divided into twelve lines of unequal length, but it is not
possible to convey in English translation the powerful effect produced
by the succession of verbs at the beginning, and some form of the Greek
word *su* = 'thou' at the end, of each of the statements.

৩৩

42
Without being named the city is apostrophized, possibly as the mother of
children (v. 44, cf. Gal. 4²⁵; though 'children' could be used simply of a city's
inhabitants). The apostrophe can have the force either of an aposiopesis ('If only
you knew . . .'), or of an unfulfilled wish (*would that you knew*). While its
general purport is plain, there is uncertainty over its precise reference in the two
expressions noted below.

even today: The manuscripts vary here between 'in this day, even you', 'even in
this day' and 'even you at least (even) in this your day'. Behind these variations
may lie two different conceptions. 'in this day' refers in the context to the com-

ing of Jesus to Jerusalem, or his whole mission to Israel, as the crucial moment in her history, perhaps as the fulfilment of what prophets had said would happen 'in that day', i.e. in the eschatological time. The failure to recognize this, shown by the rejection of Jesus – which is here seen in advance, and before Jerusalem has been given a chance to show her mind (cf. 9²²; 18³¹ᶠ·, and possibly 13³⁵) – will be the evidence that Jerusalem's eyes have been blinded. 'in your day' means the day of divine visitation (cf. Jer. 50³¹; Ezek. 22⁴); but this generally denotes the day of destruction already determined, when the time for recognition and repentance has passed. If *kai* in the sense of 'even' is to be taken with *today* the meaning could be 'even at this late hour'. If taken with *you* in the sense of 'also', the meaning could be 'you, like my disciples'. But with *you* it should probably be taken in the sense of 'even', with the pessimistic conclusion that the city of God should be the first to recognize God's will and judgment, but has long since won the reputation of being the last to do so.

the things that make for peace: peace here is generally taken in the sense of 'salvation', that true wholeness of life which God wills to give his people in delivering them from all types of oppression in life. But there is no evidence that the Greek phrase here – *ta pros eirēnēn* = 'the things with a view to peace' – could mean that, whereas it is found as a semi-technical term for peace conditions proposed by combatants in war (14³², Testament of Judah 9⁷). This sense would seem to be required by the following description (vv. 43–44) of the physical destruction of Jerusalem at the hands of enemies in war. In that case what is referred to is not the peace (salvation) of God or peace as reconciliation with God, but peace with Rome; for Rome was the only power in the first century AD to be in a position to be Jerusalem's enemy with the capacity for her destruction. The more precisely the phrase is taken the more it fits conditions subsequent to the ministry of Jesus. Some, however, have seen here evidence for a political element in his proclamation of the kingdom of God, for a concern with the growing hostility between the Jews and Rome and a desire to reconcile them.ᵇ This has been disappointed. *But now* (*nun de* = 'as it is', a classical, not LXX, construction) these terms for peace have been hidden (the meaning is probably 'God has hidden') from Jerusalem's (spiritual) sight; and this will be made evident by her destruction (*for*, v. 43, is *hoti* = 'because'). In a typical biblical combination of thought the Jews are held responsible for the city's fall (they could have known), while at the same time it is the result of divine decree.

43–44
The language here is largely that of prophecy, as in *the days shall come upon you* (cf. 21⁶; Amos 4²; Hos. 9⁷), *dash to the ground* (*edaphizein* in this sense confined to the LXX, cf. Isa. 3²⁶ of Jerusalem), *the time of your visitation* (Jer. 6¹⁵; 10¹⁵, not

ᵇ See C. J. Cadoux, *The Historic Mission of Jesus*, London and New York 1941, pp. 266ff.

found outside the LXX). But it also contains more factual and semi-technical language less suited for a prophetic lament – *cast up a bank* (*paremballein charaka* = to invest with a palisade), *surround* (*perikukloun* + +, cf. *kukloun* in this sense in Luke's prose statement 21²⁰), *hem in* (*sunechein*, so II Macc. 9² of investing a city.) These could betray knowledge of the actual course of events in the Roman assault on Jerusalem in AD 70, including the circumvallation of the city to block all exits, which was not an inevitable part of the attack, but was only decided on by Titus at a special council when the usual methods of attack from earthworks had failed (Jos. *BJ* 5.491ff.). It could be that an original poetic lament of Jesus was edited in the light of events, or a Christian prophetic oracle after the event was put in his mouth. Others besides Christians saw Jerusalem's fall as the judgment of God, e.g. Josephus, who records the daily lament of Jesus, son of Ananias, over the city (*BJ* 6.300ff.), and his own lament in warning its defenders (*BJ* 6.96ff.).

one stone upon another: Cf. Josephus, *BJ* 6.413, 7.1ff. for the wall of Jerusalem so levelled to the ground 'as to leave future visitors to the spot no ground for believing that it had ever been inhabited'.

because you did not know the time of your visitation: This is the reason for Jerusalem's destruction (*anth' hōn* = 'in view of the fact that' is emphatic), and its force depends on the meaning to be given to the Greek word *episcopē*, rendered here by *visitation*. The absence of this noun from secular literature must be fortuitous, as the corresponding verbs are frequently found in the sense of guardianship (including that of the gods), and of visiting, examining or inspecting. Verbs and noun are common in the LXX for Yahweh's guardianship of Israel, and for that guardianship taking effect in his action towards her in what is called, as here, *the time* (*kairos*, the decisive moment), or 'the hour' or 'day' of visitation. In the prophets this is primarily a time of destruction (Jer. 6¹⁵; 10¹⁵; 11²³; Isa. 10³; 24²²; 29⁶); but it could also be a day of deliverance and salvation (Isa. 23¹⁶; Wisd. 3⁷); while Ecclus 18²⁰ stands in between, in that visitation is for judgment but allows opportunity for repentance. If *visitation* is to be given here the first sense – destruction – the statement need say no more than that Jerusalem was destroyed by a surprise attack, being taken unawares. If it is to be given either the second or third senses, then Jerusalem is said to be destroyed, either because of her failure to recognize in the mission of Jesus God's offer of salvation and of reconciliation with him, or because of her refusal to repent in response to the utterance of God's final judgment in the words of Jesus. In any case, although Jesus has not yet entered the city, it is spoken of as already a city of the past. By placing the lament here, and by editing Mark at 21²⁰ᶠ· to make a further reference to the city's fall, Luke shows that he regarded that fall, even though brought about by human agency, as occupying a decisive place in the divine plan of history as that was being put into effect in the mission and death of Jesus.

19^{45-48} = *Mark* $11^{11,\ 15-19}$ *Jesus and the Temple*

⁴⁵*And he entered the temple and began to drive out those who sold,* ⁴⁶*saying to them, 'It is written, "My house shall be a house of prayer"; but you have made it a den of robbers.'*

⁴⁷*And he was teaching daily in the temple. The chief priests and the scribes and the principal men of the people sought to destroy him;* ⁴⁸*but they did not find anything they could do, for all the people hung upon his words.*

Mark makes entry into city and temple a single act (Mark $11^{11,\ 15}$). For the Jewish mind the one was involved in the other (cf. Zech. 14^{21}, and Josephus passim, esp. *BJ* 6.99 in his appeal to his fellow citizens, 'You have kept (God's city) pure for God; the Holy Place too remains undefiled'. But it was the temple as God's dwelling, or rather as the dwelling place of his Name, and as the only place of sacrifice, which conferred glory on the city rather than vice versa. The temple was the nerve centre of the Jewish religion, and the priesthood its effective controllers. Luke separates city and temple. He does not refer to any entry of the city as such. By omission of Jesus' preliminary inspection (Mark 11^{11}), and of the enigmatic, and he might have thought unedifying, cursing of the fig tree (Mark 11^{12-14} – for which he has already supplied an equivalent in 13^{6-9} free of any suggestion that fruit was lacking because it was the wrong time, or that the destruction of Jerusalem was imminent), he proceeds at once to a very abbreviated version of the so-called cleansing of the temple.

This is one of the most enigmatic episodes in the gospels. The theme of the temple, absent from the rest of Mark's story, may be said to move into the centre in his passion narrative, though in a series of exceedingly obscure actions and statements, which might be open to interpretation as follows. After an act of cursing, which portends the end of Judaism (the temple?), Jesus, after a preliminary inspection, returns to the temple, and there in symbolic gesture (symbolic because it cannot have effected any permanent results) overthrows and expels the necessary apparatus of sacrifice, and forbids the carrying of sacrificial implements. This could suggest a (messianic?) intention of bringing sacrifice and temple to an end, rather than cleansing or reform of what was corrupt in it. The divine intention of the temple is declared to be, by a quotation of Isa. 56⁷, a house of prayer to which the Gentiles were to flock (in the eschatological time?), but practically speaking it had become, in a phrase used in Jer. 7¹¹ in certifying its destruction, a zealot stronghold. It is possibly these actions which in Mark 11²⁷ᶠ· raise the question of Jesus' authority. In the course of his replies he refers to himself, in the context of a parable concerning the end of Judaism and the passing of its privileges to others, as the rejected stone which is God's choice as the corner-stone (of the temple? Mark 12¹⁻¹²). In Mark 12³²⁻³⁴ a scribe who asserts that the keeping of the commandments is more important than sacrifice is pronounced not far from the kingdom of God. Seated on the Mount of Olives (cf. Zech. 14⁴ᶠᶠ·) Jesus prophesies the total ruin of the temple in the coming troubles (Mark 13¹ᶠᶠ·), and later establishes a sacrificial rite in his own person (Mark 14¹²⁻²⁵). The first charge at his trial, which is dropped, is that he was reputed – though by false and contradictory witness – to have made the revolutionary claim, 'I will destroy this temple that is made with hands (physical? idolatrous?), and in three days I will build another, not made with hands (spiritual? divine?)' (Mark 14⁵⁸), which is thrown at him on the cross (Mark 15²⁹). At the moment of his death the sanctuary veil is split from top to bottom, and a Gentile acknowledges his divinity (Mark 15³⁸ᶠ·). From all this taken together some scholars have concluded that, for Mark at least, Jesus proclaimed in word and act the destruction of the temple and its sacrificial worship, and its replacement by an eschatological counterpart in his own person and death; with the possible corollary that this was the original ground of his arrest, condemnation, excommunication and death, though the gospel narratives no longer make this clear.ᶜ In Luke most of this disappears. The charge of claiming to destroy the temple and to substitute another disappears from his account of the trial and of the scene of crucifixion, to reappear in a modified form in the charge brought – again by false witnesses – against Stephen, that he had said that Jesus would (at some future date) destroy the holy place (A. 6¹³⁻¹⁴; 'one of several cases where a motif in the gospel of Mark is omitted by the parallel in the gospel of Luke only to reappear in Acts', *Beginnings* IV, p. 134). And the only reference by Stephen to the charge is in the sentiment of spiritual and rationalistic religion that the

---

c See, e.g. E. C. Hoskyns, *The Fourth Gospel*, ed. F. N. Davey, 2nd ed. London 1947, pp. 207ff., R. J. McKelvey, *The New Temple, The Church in the New Testament*, Oxford and New York 1969, pp. 61ff., and E. P. Sanders, *Jesus and Judaism*, pp. 61ff.

Most High does not dwell in places made with hands (A. 7^{48}, repeated by Paul, A. 17^{24}). This leaves the ultimate disappearance of the temple as an act of God (or the exalted Christ) performed through historical agents along with the destruction of Jerusalem, without any suggestion either in the Gospel or in Acts that it is to be replaced by a sacrificial worship in the body of Christ (as is suggested by John 2$^{13-22}$). In Luke the rending of the veil precedes the death of Jesus and does not coincide with it; Mark 12$^{28-34}$ is omitted; the citation about the rejected stone is treated differently, being linked with the stone of judgment (20$^{17-18}$), and after 19$^{47f.}$, 'these things' in 20^{2} no longer refers directly to Jesus' action in the temple but to his teaching there. In fact the sanctuary (*naos*) as the place of sacrifice appears in Luke's Gospel only as the scene of Zechariah's vision (1^{9}) and in the statement, taken from Mark, of the rending of the veil (23^{45}). Luke is concerned with the temple courts (*hieron*) as the place of prayer (18^{10}) and prophecy (2$^{27, 37}$), but especially of teaching (2^{46}, Jesus among the teachers), now of the teaching of Jesus until his arrest (19^{47}; 20$^{1, 21}$; 21^{37}), and later of the apostles' preaching of the Christian message in Jerusalem (A. 3$^{1ff.}$; 3^{11}; 4$^{1-4}$; 5$^{12, 20-25, 42}$).

Thus Luke's abbreviated version of the Markan account (vv. 45–46) is the only one to which the title The Cleansing of the Temple properly belongs. The expulsion is limited to *those who sold*, without any hint of what it was that they were there to sell, leaving the impression, typical of Luke, that it was avarice which was being condemned. 'for all the nations' is dropped from the Isaiah quotation, for the coming of the nations to Zion, which it implies, is no longer to occur; the Christian preaching is to go out from Jerusalem to them. Thus the temple mount or courts are 'cleansed' by Jesus so that he may take them over for his own purposes of teaching at the centre of Judaism for the remainder of his ministry to Israel and under the shadow of his coming rejection. In accordance with this Luke proceeds to set the scene of this ministry in terms of Israel (vv. 47–48). On the one hand are Israel's official representatives, *the chief priests and the scribes and the principal men of the people*. The first, as distinct from the single high priest in office, were a group of the prominent members of the priesthood, drawn from priestly families, who had charge of the temple worship and discipline and of its treasury, and had seats in the Sanhedrin. The second were the authorized and authoritative trained exegetes of scripture, who by the first century AD had emerged into prominence as the theologians in Judaism, and whose representatives had seats in the Sanhedrin. The third, the equivalent of 'the elders', were members of the non-priestly aristocracy, which consisted of influential families surviving from an earlier form of society in the Persian and Greek periods of Jewish history, also with seats in the Sanhedrin. Together these three represented official Judaism. They are described as implacably hostile to Jesus, though the grounds for this are not given. Over against them Luke sets *the people* (*laos*). This is Luke's favourite term for Jesus' audiences, and he is by far the chief user of it in the NT – it occurs thirty-seven times in the Gospel and forty-eight times in A., but in Mark three times, in Matthew fourteen (four in OT citations), in John twice and in Paul ten times (all from the OT). Luke has used it already, generally for favourable audiences (3^{21}; 6^{17}; $7^{1, 29}$; 18^{43}); but from now on, sometimes with the addition of 'all' (19^{47}; $20^{6, 45}$; 21^{38}) it becomes a designation of the inhabitants of Jerusalem, a permanent audience, whose enthusiasm for Jesus is very forcefully expressed by they *hung on his words* (*ekkremanunai* + +, rare in this figurative sense). By this enthusiasm they constantly frustrate the murderous intentions of the official representatives (19^{48}; $20^{9, 19, 26, 45}$; 21^{38}; 22^{2}), until induced by Pilate to join in the condemnation of Jesus ($23^{13, 18}$); though even then they accompany Jesus in great numbers to the cross to lament and behold, in contrast to the rulers who scoff ($23^{27, 35, 48}$). They continue on into A. as enthusiastic supporters of the disciples, and for that reason are feared by the authorities (A. 2^{47}; 3^{1-12}; $4^{1f.,\ 17-21}$; $5^{13-16, 20-26}$). The term is elastic. It can be a general word for 'people', but is also a regular OT designation of Israel as the people of God (cf. A. 10^{2}; 21^{28} of the empirical Israel). Luke also uses it of the Christian community (A. 15^{14}; 18^{10}) perhaps suggesting, though not in any systematic manner, that the Christians have become the true Israel or people of God. Thus Luke pictures Jesus in Jerusalem and in its heart the temple as the great divider, whose teaching creates a schism in Judaism between the people, who in their response show themselves to be, at least potentially, disciples, and so members of the true Israel, and its official representatives, who by their rejection of it and of him excommunicate themselves.

20^1-21^4 *The Temple Teaching of Jesus*

The generalizing statement in 19^{47-48} of teaching in the temple as the daily occupation of Jesus over an unspecified period in the presence of a double audience is explicated by seven instances of such teaching.

(i) In 20^{1-8}, while he is teaching and preaching the gospel to the people in the temple the question is raised by the authorities of Jesus' own authority.

(ii) In 20^{9-19}, without change of scene, a parable is told to the people and against the authorities, who are only restrained from arresting Jesus by fear of the people.

(iii) In 20^{20-26}, again without change of scene, Jesus as teacher is faced with a question about the tribute by representatives of the authorities, who are unable to carry out their plan of arresting him in order to arraign him before Pilate in face of the people.

(iv) In 20^{27-40} the question of resurrection is raised by Sadducees with Jesus as a teacher, and is answered in such a way as not only to reduce them to silence, but also to gain approbation from scribes.

(v) In 20^{41-44} these (scribes) are questioned about the messiah.

(vi) In 20^{45-47}, in the presence of the people scribes are denounced to the disciples.

(vii) In 21^{1-4} Jesus, looking up in the temple, sees rich men making their offerings, and compares them unfavourably with a poor widow.

Thus, as the first period of Jesus' public life has been described as a teaching ministry in the synagogues of Galilee and Judaea ($4^{14f., \ 44}$), and the second part presented in the form of a teaching journey from Galilee to Jerusalem ($9^{51}-19^{27}$), so the third and final part is made by Luke into a teaching ministry in Jerusalem; but in such a way that both the teaching itself, and the reactions of the audience to it, are related as closely as the material would allow to the coming passion and its issues. In presenting this picture Luke is entirely dependent on what Mark had to offer at this stage. Except for the omission of Mark 12^{28-34} the succession of separate and unconnected units is identical in both, and there is such a measure of agreement in wording, sentence order and word order that any differences are to be accounted the editorial work of Luke in bringing this material within his overall setting, and in underlining certain elements which were of special importance to him. In the view of some scholars Mark 11²⁷–12³⁷ came to Mark as an already formed collection of conflict stories designed to show Jesus in debate with opponents about certain vital issues, and as victorious over them; and possibly as the second half of a collection which had the sequence of conflict stories in Mark 2¹–3⁶ as its first half. Such stories tend to present the fact of conflict in various forms and over various matters, but with little by way of precise context or setting, and in their present position *en bloc* they supply scant evidence for a historical reconstruction of the grounds on which the authorities determined to get rid of Jesus. Luke has no further historical information with which to clarify this question. He simply points up the conflict in the material to hand in Mark. Indeed, three of these stories, those on authority, the tribute and David's son, are very cryptic and curiously inconclusive, while that on resurrection has to make its point by a strange *reductio ad absurdum*. A. M. Farrer[d] sees the juxtaposition of the parable of the Wicked Husbandmen, the question on resurrection and that on Davidic sonship as a prefiguration by means of teaching units of the coming death, resurrection and exaltation of Jesus. If this was the case, and Luke recognized it, then his only omission from this section of Mark, that of the scribe's question in Mark 12²⁸–³⁴, may have been made to underline this pattern of thought.

20¹⁻⁸ = Mark 11²⁷⁻³³

THE QUESTION OF AUTHORITY

20 *One day, as he was teaching the people in the temple and preaching the gospel, the chief priests and the scribes with the elders came up* ²*and said to him, 'Tell us by what authority you do these things, or who it is that gave you this authority.'* ³*He answered them, 'I also will ask you a question; now tell me,* ⁴*Was the baptism of John from heaven or from men?'* ⁵*And they discussed it with one another, saying, 'If we say, "From heaven," he will say, "Why did you not believe him?"* ⁶*But if we say, "From men," all the people will stone us; for they are convinced that John was a prophet.'* ⁷*So they answered*

d *A Study in St Mark*, London and New York 1951, pp. 170ff.

that they did not know whence it was. ⁸*And Jesus said to them, 'Neither will I tell you by what authority I do these things.'*

This abbreviated and concentrated form of debate, with hostile question, counter-question, the reply which that enforces, and the consequent refutation by inference, has parallels in both Greek and Jewish literature (see Daube, *NTRJ*, pp. 151ff., SB I, pp. 861f.). Whether the question asked was ever a genuine request for information can hardly be gathered from this form of tradition, which aims to present Jesus as victor over an opposition which questions with hostile intent.

Luke reproduces the unit from Mark with stylistic variations. These may be seen in *one day*, picking up *daily* in 19⁴⁷; *came up* (*ephistanai*, confined to L–A in the NT apart from four instances in Paul); *who is it that gave* is more elegant and specific; *discussed* (*sullogizesthai* ++ a technical term used in philosophical argument); *will stone us* (*katalithazein* ++ = 'stone to death'); *are convinced* (the perfect participle passive *pepeismenos* ++).

᛫᛭᛫

1

the chief priests and the scribes with the elders: From Mark, and constituting a variation of 19⁴⁷. They have appeared already in 9²² (in a different order due to Mark 8³¹) as those who reject the Son of man, and they appear again (with 'rulers' for 'chief priests') in A. 4⁵ as the opponents of the apostles. Together they constitute the Sanhedrin, the supreme court and guardian of Judaism. Josephus, writing for non-Jews, has various descriptions of what is probably intended to be the Sanhedrin, e.g. *BJ* 2.411, 'the principal citizens assembled with the chief priests and most notable of the Pharisees'; *Ant.* 20.6, 'the chief priests and leaders of the inhabitants of Jerusalem'; and *Life* 64, with reference to Tiberias, and in terms of the Hellenistic city, 'the council (*boulē*) and the principal men of the people (*dēmos*)'. If *elders* here, probably to be identified with 'the principal men of the people' in 19⁴⁷, were largely of the Sadducean persuasion, then the authoritative body would be strongly representative of the interests of the temple, and they raise here the question crucial in Jerusalem, the centre of Judaism, and in the temple the centre of Jerusalem, of the authority of Jesus. It is, however, improbable that the whole Sanhedrin would come in person, or even a deputation from it. Those to be interrogated on a vital matter of religion were brought to it (22⁶⁶; A. 4⁵; 5²¹).

2

The debate opens very formally with a double question about authority, its

20^{1-8}

nature and origin; cf. a similer double question in A. 4⁷, and the double statement in Mark 3²². The noun *exousia* is from the verb *exesti* = 'it is possible',
which is the verb used in 20²², with the meaning 'Is it possible according to the
law of God?' The word can be a synonym for *dunamis* = 'power' (cf. 10¹⁹), or
used in combination with it (e.g. 4³⁶; 9¹). In comparison with *dunamis* it has the
sense of 'authoritative power', 'the right to act' (7⁸; A. 9¹⁴). The question is,
however, imprecise because of the uncertainty of what is meant by *do these
things*. Apart from any context this could refer to such things as exorcisms. In
Mark the question, though separated by the intervening story of the cursing of
the fig tree, would appear to refer to the actions of Jesus with respect to the
temple, which, since they are accompanied by teaching (Mark 11¹⁸), are to be
taken as deliberate and authoritative actions (cf. Mark 1²¹ᶠᶠ· for authoritative
teaching which is primarily action). In Luke, as a result of his omission of the
story of the fig tree, his editorial statement in 19⁴⁷ᶠ·, and his introduction of
Jesus here as *teaching* and *preaching the gospel* (*euangelizeshtai* in the weakened
sense of 'teach', as in 3¹⁸; A. 5⁴²; 15³⁵), the question becomes entirely, though
somewhat awkwardly, a question about his teaching, and about the authority
and authorization of Jesus as the teacher of Israel in the temple, which he has
taken over for the purpose (cf. Matt. 21²³). In such a form, and in a Jewish
milieu, this could be a specific enquiry whether, and by what rabbi, Jesus had
been ordained, taking *authority* as 'power lawfully exercised' (so Daube,
NTRJ, pp. 217ff.).

3–4

Jesus counters with a question. In Mark the verb is *eperōtān*, a regular word in
the synoptists for interrogation, and a favourite with Mark, and the object is
logos = 'word', 'statement', here in the rare sense of 'question'. In Luke the
verb is *erōtān*, which could mean 'request', and the translation could be 'I too
will ask you to make a statement.' The force of the counter-question about
John's baptism is not immediately obvious, because it is not certain what its
underlying assumptions are. If recognition of John and his baptism by both
parties is to be assumed, then the counter-question answers the original question
about Jesus' authority, though indirectly. Since, for those who recognized John,
the answer to a question about the source of his baptism must be 'from heaven',
the implication is that Jesus' mission and actions are at least as divinely authorized as John's. If, on the other hand, it is to be assumed that the religious leaders
as a whole, in distinction from the common people, had refused John recognition (as they are made to state in their cogitations in v. 5), then the answer will
be 'from men'. The implication would then presumably be that there can be no
reply to the original question about Jesus' authority, since by their previous
refusal of John the questioners had disqualified themselves from making a
proper judgment on a matter of spiritual authority in Israel that was at least

prophetic, if not more than prophetic, in character. In view of his own comment in 7²⁹ᶠ· that the Pharisees and lawyers rejected the purpose of God for themselves in not being baptized by John, this is probably how Luke understood it. The only evidence, however, of the attitudes of the authorities to John and his baptism is that of the gospels themselves, where the rejection of John is seen in the light of the rejection of Jesus and of the Christian conception of a close relation between them. In Matt. 3⁷ Pharisees and Sadducees come to John's baptism, whereas in Luke 3²¹ it is the whole people who are baptized by him. Some see a closer logical connection between question and counter-question, either in the fact that John himself testified to Jesus as the coming one, or in Jesus' having come to a knowledge of his mission through receiving baptism from John, so that to reject the one is to reject the other. But these, especially the latter, can hardly have been explicit matters of public knowledge such as could form the basis of an argument, and could well have been products of later Christian reflection. Gaston (*No Stone on Another*, p. 88) sees the connection to lie in John's baptism for the purification of Israel as bypassing the provisions of the sacrificial cultus for purification from sin, and so as parallel to Jesus' attack on the temple cult. But while this could apply to Mark's version, it does not apply to Luke's, which is not concerned with the temple as a place of sacrifice but only as a place of teaching.

5

discussed it with one another: By introducing this verb *sullogizesthai*, with its suggestions of reasoning and careful deliberation, Luke imparts to the dispute, and perhaps to all the disputes in this part of the Gospel, a strong rational element. They are caught in the logic of the situation, and unable to escape from it they fall back on a confession of agnosticism.

6

all the people will stone us: Cf. A. 5²⁶ in the case of the apostles. Luke makes the gulf between leaders and people as wide as could be, since stoning was the official punishment for grave religious error.

7

they did not know: That no further comment is made on this extraordinary inability of the religious leaders to make a judgment on such an issue is due to the form of the story, in which this is not an important element in itself, but is a means of showing Jesus as victorious over his enemies in debate.

8

Like his opponents Jesus now refuses to reply. For the Christian reader this is sufficient. Since for him the answer to the counter-question is 'from heaven', and John is the divinely appointed precursor of Jesus, the conclusion to be drawn is that Jesus' authority as a teacher is of divine and not of human (rabbinic?) origin.

20$^{9-19}$ = Mark 12$^{1-12}$
PARABLE OF VINEYARD AND TENANTS

9*And he began to tell the people this parable: 'A man planted a vineyard, and let it out to tenants, and went into another country for a long while.* 10*When the time came, he sent a servant to the tenants, that they should give him some of the fruit of the vineyard; but the tenants beat him, and sent him away empty-handed.* 11*And he sent another servant; him also they beat and treated shamefully, and sent him away empty-handed.* 12*And he sent yet a third; this one they wounded and cast out.* 13*Then the owner of the vineyard said, "What shall I do? I will send my beloved son; it may be they will respect him."* 14*But when the tenants saw him, they said to themselves, "This is the heir; let us kill him, that the inheritance may be ours."* 15*And they cast him out of the vineyard and killed him. What then will the owner of the vineyard do to them?* 16*He will come and destroy those tenants, and give the vineyard to others.' When they heard this, they said, 'God forbid!'* 17*But he looked at them and said, 'What then is this that is written:*

"The very stone which the builders rejected has become the head of the corner"?

18*Every one who falls on that stone will be broken to pieces; but when it falls on any one it will crush him.'*

19*The scribes and the chief priests tried to lay hands on him at that very hour, but they feared the people; for they perceived that he had told this parable against them.*

Here Jesus is not the object of hostile questioning, but himself takes the initiative in attack. There could be some connection with the previous pericope, if there the rejection of John as a divinely sent prophet is implicitly linked with the rejection of Jesus, and in Luke some connection with the lament over the doomed city of Jerusalem (19$^{41-44}$) and the parable of the Pounds (19$^{11-27}$).

The parable is taken from Mark, though the differences from Mark led Taylor (*Third Gospel*, pp. 98f.) to suggest that Luke knew it in another, probably oral, version, and Jeremias (*Parables*, p. 72) that this version was less allegorical, and nearer to the non-allegorical form in the Gospel of Thomas 65. Against this is that the parable is a unit in a sequence of conflict stories which Luke would seem to be incorporating as a whole, and agreement with Mark in wording and word order is close. This is so in v. 9 with *he began to tell*, and the parataxis *and . . . and . . . and*; in v. 10 with *when the time came*, and *empty-handed* (*kenon*, only here in Mark, and elsewhere in L–A 1⁵³; A. 4²⁵, both from the LXX); in vv. 14–16, esp. *he will come and destroy*; and in v. 19 with *they feared . . . for they perceived*. The differences are more likely to be due to Luke's revisions, some of which give the impression of reducing the allegorical element, others of increasing it. Thus, in v. 9 *to tell this parable to, a man* standing first in a parable, and *for a long while* (*chronous hikanous*, a combination confined to L–A in the NT), are all in Lukan style. Verse 10 is phrased more elegantly, including *when the time came* (the idiomatic *kairō* without article = 'in due time') and *sent away* (*exapostellein*, apart from Gal. 4⁴, ⁶ confined to L–A in the NT). In vv. 11–12 *he sent another* is expressed by the Lukan verb *prosetheto* = 'he proceeded to send', and *wounded* is the more literary word *traumatizein* + A. 19¹⁶. The sending of many others who are beaten and killed in Mark 12⁵ᵇ, which makes explicit that the prophets are being referred to, is awkward and ungrammatically expressed, and quite oversteps the bounds of a reasonable story. Its absence from Luke need mean no more than that he wished to restore the parable to the customary symmetry of three, making possible an ascending scale of harsh treatment (*beat*, v. 10, *beat and treated shamefully*, v. 11, *wounded and cast out*, v. 12), and leading to a climax in the sending of the son, for whom alone, in Luke, death is reserved. This sending is introduced in more lively fashion by a soliloquy, *What shall I do?*, which has parallels in Lukan parables, though here it may have been suggested by the question form in Mark 12⁹ and Isa. 5⁴. *it may be* (*isōs* ++ = 'perhaps', only once in the LXX) may increase the allegorical element if it is intended to safeguard God from having made a mistake in view of what actually happens; and *cast him out of the vineyard and killed him* (so Matthew), in place of Mark's 'killed him and cast him out (unburied?)', may refer to Jesus' excommunication from Israel as the significance of his death (cf. Heb. 13¹²ᶠ·; for casting out with the intention of killing, 4²⁹; 13²⁸; A.

7⁵⁸). Further, whereas in Mark the parable is not only directed against, but also spoken to, the Sanhedrin, Luke, in accordance with the *mise-en-scène* he has provided in 19⁴⁷ᶠ·, makes it a cautionary tale told to *the people* (v. 9) about their leaders, and it is the relation between these two which dictates Luke's conclusion (vv. 16–19). The statement that the tenants will be destroyed and the vineyard given to others is met with a demurrer from the people in a form unique in the gospels – *God forbid* translates the Hellenistic *mē genoito* = 'may it not be so', 'perish the thought', elsewhere in the NT only as a rhetorical device in Paul. This shows the people to be in danger of sharing the attitude of their leaders, and it is in answer to that that the psalm citation, somewhat loosely attached to the parable in Mark, is solemnly introduced by *But he looked at them* (only here in Luke; he omits the expression in Mark 10²¹, ²⁷), and by a Lukan designation for scripture *that which is written*, so as to warn them to dissociate themselves from their leaders, and not to be among those who reject. These leaders are then named again as *the scribes and the chief priests*, whose recognition that the parable was pointed at them is underlined by *this parable* (v. 19), and by *at that very hour* (a Lukan phrase). Some of this serves to increase the allegorical character of the parable.

בבב

9–16

The parable starts from the *vineyard* of Isa. 5¹ as a symbol of Israel. The extended description of the vineyard in Mark 12¹, reproducing the LXX version of Isa. 5² (the Hebrew is different), secures this, but the details of hedge, winepress and tower play no part in the story, and they could be omitted without removing the symbolism, which, on the basis of Isa. 5¹⁻⁷ and other OT passages, could be established by the word 'vineyard' by itself. The parable has also something of the threefold structure of Isa. 5¹⁻⁶ of the establishment of the vineyard, the expectation of fruit from it, and punishment for failure to produce it (Isa. 5¹⁻², ³⁻⁴, ⁵⁻⁶). In distinction from Isa. 5¹, however, the vineyard is let out by the owner in his absence to tenants. The Greek word *geōrgos* means one who tills the soil, and in this context could be a vinedresser, but he would be an employee, who could simply be dismissed. It should be translated by 'tenant (farmer)', though it is not indicated why there should be more than one such. Thus the parable refers not to Israel as a whole, but to those with charge over her, and the responsibility to God for her fruitfulness. The story continues allegorically when, to collect the produce of the harvest, three slaves are sent one after another, and all defenceless, despite repeated rebuff and ill-treatment, to be followed in similar fashion by the son in the hope that he will be respected; and when the tenants are represented as plotting, while the owner is still alive, to secure ownership of the vineyard for themselves by doing away with the son because he is the heir to it. This story is so artificial and implausible as not to be intelligible by reference to actual conditions of life, or any likely course of events, but only as an allegory of God's dealings with Israel's leaders, first through a succession of rejected prophets, and then through Jesus, the only Son, who is the heir of God's people (Rom. 8^{17}; Heb. 1^2). The final outcome in the story, which is that intended by the owner and not by the tenants, is presented dramatically in the form of question and answer (possibly modelled on Isa. 5$^{4-5}$; it is without parallel in the parables, except, perhaps, 18$^{7-8}$). The answer, which is limited to the vineyard and tenants (the son is not referred to) is a double one. (i) *He* (the owner = God) *will come and destroy those tenants*. This could have precise reference to the destruction of Jerusalem as the manifestation of divine judgment on Israel; but it need be no more than a general statement of the end of Israel's privileged position as God's people as a result of the rejection of the prophets and Jesus (cf. I Thess. 2$^{14-16}$, written before the destruction of Jerusalem). (ii) *and give the vineyard to others*. This also could be a general statement of the transfer of privilege from the Jews to Christians, Jews or Gentiles, as the true Israel of God (so probably Mark; cf. Gal. 6$^{15f.}$; Eph. 2$^{11-22}$). If, however, *tenants* is stressed, and the *others* are other tenants, then Christian leaders in the church as the true Israel will be meant (so probably Luke; Matt. 21$^{41, 43}$ has a double comment which seems to combine both). Against this it has been objected that it contradicts early Christian belief, which made no distinction between the Jewish people and their leaders in their responsibility for the rejection of the prophets, and that the parable, being based on Isa. 5$^{1ff.}$, depicts the whole people as incurring the divine wrath and forfeiting their election to others, who are not identified. This, however, ignores both that the vineyard as a symbol of Israel is not simply taken over from Isa. 5, but undergoes a certain development in being let out to tenants, and also that the evangelists all record the parable as spoken against the leaders. It is, indeed, unlikely that there was a single uniform view among Christians on the very vexed question of Israel's past and her continuing place in the divine purpose (cf. the differing emphases in I Thess. 2$^{14-16}$; Rom. 9–11; Eph. 2$^{11-22}$). Luke in particular goes out of his way in the Gospel and in A. to distinguish between 'the people' as those who support Jesus and the apostles, and the leaders who oppose them, and by his occasional use of 'the people' for the Christian body suggests that Christian believers are the true Israel of God. In A. 4$^{1-12}$ many of 'the people' become believers in contrast to the leaders, who are expressly identified as the builders responsible for having rejected the stone which was to become the cornerstone.

Two notable attempts have been made to penetrate behind the allegory to an original parable (of Jesus), which told a recognizably coherent story in terms of actual conditions of life. The first is that of Dodd (*Parables*, pp. 124ff.). He takes *went into another country (apedēmēsen* in the sense of 'went abroad') as indicating those conditions. 'If we recall that large estates were often held by foreigners, we may suppose that agrarian discontent went hand in hand with nationalist feeling . . . We can see that all the conditions were present under which refusal of rent might be the prelude to murder and the forcible seizure of land by the peasantry. The parable, in fact, so far from being an artificially constructed allegory, may be taken as evidence of the kind of thing that went on in Galilee during the half century preceding the general revolt in AD 66.' The story thus tells of an absentee landlord, who, on failing in several attempts to recover his rent from a distance from tenants inspired by nationalist feeling, sends his son as a personal agent; and the tenants, in hope of forcible possession of the absentee's property, kill the agent, only themselves to be destroyed in a display of force by the returning owner, perhaps with government help. The principal weakness of this reconstruction is that the parable is not concerned with a large estate, but with a comparatively small affair, a single vineyard, which in Mark's version, following Isa. 5², the owner has dug and made himself. The word *apedēmēsen*, which need mean no more than 'went away', is hardly sufficient of itself to establish absentee landlordism as the prerequisite for understanding the story. It simply sets up a distance between the landlord and tenants (though it is curious if applied literally to God), and Luke's *for a long while* attempts to give verisimilitude to the repeated demands through slaves, even though they are maltreated. The owner could not come himself. Moreover, Dodd admits that the story, even when so reconstructed, not only lent itself to later allegorization, but also already contained allegorical features in the word *vineyard*, and in the fact that 'the climax of iniquity in the story suggests a similar climax in the situation to which it is to be applied', that situation being the death of Jesus as 'the impending climax of the rebellion of Israel in a murderous assault upon the Successor of the prophets' (*Parables*, pp. 130f.). The second is that of Derrett (*Law in the NT*, pp. 286ff.), who explains differently by reference to current law and practice, as follows. The vineyard, made by the man himself, is a new one, and would not begin to show profit until the fourth harvest. The owner, who does not necessarily go abroad, employs tenants, who were entitled by the terms of the tenancy to a fixed proportion of the produce. It must be supposed that the owner asserted his ownership from the start, and that by *when the time came* the end of the first year is meant. The demand for rent at that time is repudiated by the tenants as unwarranted in view of the small yield (if anything he owes them money for costs, and this is unmistakably conveyed to him by beating up his slave and sending him back, not only without rent, but stripped of any valuables he had (the meaning of *kenon* = 'empty-handed'). The owner repeats the process in the second and third years, sending slaves (of course not unaccompanied) in the hope that some rent may now be forthcoming through improvement of harvest and decrease of expenditure; but the tenants, having been successful on the first occasion, continue to repudiate the demands with violence. At the last moment (the further sending of slaves in Mark 12^{5b} is to be disregarded as a later allegorizing addition), since if he does not assert his ownership after the third harvest he stands to lose it by default, he sends his (only) son (of course not unattended), who, in distinction from a slave, can act as his personal representative, and establish his legal position. The tenants, being in actual possession, look to translate it into permanent possession by securing that the rent of the fourth harvest is not collected. Supposing the son to be now the owner (*klēronomos* = 'heir' has to be given this sense), though they do not find out first if this is the case, they hit on the idea of doing away with him, and so with any evidence he may have of the true legal position. But they miscalculate; the owner himself arrives to prove his rights, and ruins them financially (*apolesei* = 'he will destroy' has to be given this sense), substituting other tenants. The weakness of this reconstruction, apart from the dubious rendering of certain words ('heir', 'destroy'), is the extent of precise background information which the hearer must be supposed to possess if he is to recognize the purport of the several actions in the parable. Further, the lesson which Derrett supposes it to teach – that God continues to show patience with men (the vineyard is the world) when they question whether they owe him anything, and refuse to pay what they owe – is so general that it is difficult to see how it ever came to be given the allegorical character in the tradition which the evangelists found it to have. Neither Dodd nor Derrett would seem to give sufficient weight to the fact that the parable has, as its concluding point, that as a result of these violent proceedings the vineyard is given to others.

If the parable was an allegory from the first, the question arises whether, both as to its form and its content, it originated with Jesus. It cannot be ruled out in advance that Jesus employed allegory in his teaching, since rabbis used it in theirs, though generally in the exposition of scripture. Nevertheless, the synoptic parables are not generally allegories, but at the most contain allegorical elements in them; and there are good grounds for attributing allegorizing to the church. That Jesus saw his ministry in relation to, and as the climax of, the missions of the prophets is attested elsewhere in the synoptic tradition (e.g. 11$^{45ff.}$); but that in this he spoke explicitly and publicly of himself as 'the Son (of God)' is open to question. The designation could have been available in Judaism, to judge by its occurrence in the messianic scroll at Qumran, where it is derived from II Sam. 7$^{11ff.}$ and Ps. 2^{7} (Vermes, *Scrolls*, p. 244). Nevertheless Luke's expression *my beloved son* (v. 13, perhaps suggested by Isa. 5^{1}, 'Let me sing for my beloved . . . my beloved had a vineyard'), in the only other instances in the Gospel (3^{22}; 9^{35} v.l.), is not uttered by Jesus about himself, but by the voice of God about him. The title 'the Son (of God)' may have originated in the theology of the church, where it is more frequent. If so, the whole parable, of which the mission of the son is the necessary climax, could have originated there. The objection that the parable would have contained in that case a reference to the resurrection of this 'Son', who is cast out and killed, is not a strong one. For it was possible for Christians to make a point about the significance of Jesus by reference to his death alone without mention of his resurrection (e.g. A. 20^{28}; Rom. 5$^{8-10}$). The purpose of the addition of Ps. 118.22–23 is precisely to supplement the parable by a scriptural statement of what in the nature of the case could not appear as an item in the narrative of an earthly story, viz. the exaltation (resurrection) of the Son by God.

17–18

Whether the parable came from Jesus or not, and whether it originally ended with a question (Mark 12^{9a}; so Dodd, *Parables*, pp. 126f.), or with the answer to the question (Mark 12^{9b}; so Jeremias, *Parables*, p. 76, who identifies, improbably, the *others* with the poor to whom the kingdom belongs), the citation of Ps. 118. 22–23 on the lips of Jesus is certainly an addition to the parable made at some stage in its tradition. As such it furnishes an example of what has been deemed the earliest form of Christian theological thinking, viz. the selection of certain OT passages or sentences as being particularly significant of some aspect of Christian truth, and their application to that truth so as to show it to be grounded in the purpose of God. This can be traced in several NT books and the evidence points to the growth of a common stock of such texts, the use of which can be detected in different NT writers.[e] It is likely that Ps. 118 would have been a source of Christian reflection in this way. It was the longest of the Hallel psalms (Pss. 113–118), which were recited in the house at the Passover meal, and in the temple and synagogue at the great festivals. Christians would have found it speaking to them of Jesus, not only in its general picture of one who is beset by his enemies but triumphs through God's help so as to enter the temple, but also in some of its individual statements (e.g. v. 17, 'I shall not die but live'). What the statement in v. 22 here – *The very stone which the builders rejected has become the head of the corner* – was referring to in the psalm itself is uncertain; but in this Christian use of texts original context and meaning were of little or no importance. What was striking was the picture of complete reversal in the use of a stone judged unfit by the builders to provide the chief stone of the building. This could speak of Jesus, of his death – *rejected* (*apodokimazein*) appears in his predictions of it (9^{22} = Mark 8^{31}; 17^{25}), and may have been taken from the psalm – and of his subsequent exaltation; and, when v. 23 is also quoted, of that exaltation as God's act. What the passage is made to say depends on the manner of its citation. In Mark, where it is loosely attached by 'Have you not read this scripture?', the emphasis lies on its positive proclamation of God's exaltation of his rejected Son. Luke uses only v. 22, which by itself could voice a threat to those who have been responsible for the rejection of the one who was destined to be thus exalted – as in A. 4^{11}, where it is directly applied to the Jerusalem

e On this subject see Dodd, *According to the Scriptures* and Lindars, *New Testament Apologetic.*

authorities in condemnation, and in I Peter 2⁷, where it refers to unbelievers. This is how Luke applies it here, linking it more closely with the parable to continue the thought of judgment there. The statement that the original tenants will be destroyed is met by a horrified disclaimer by the people, who in this way show themselves sympathetic towards those who incur judgment. In warning against this the citation is solemnly introduced by *But he looked at them* (fixed on them a look of rebuke?) as a proof from God (*What then is this that is written?*) of the guilt of, and judgment upon, those who are ready to share in the rejection of the one approved by God.

In distinction from Mark and Matthew Luke does not end here. He omits v. 23 of the psalm, which does not assist his application of v. 22, so as to follow with a further passage about a stone which can procure downfall and destruction. In doing this, and in the way he does it, Luke illustrates two further features of this method of exposition by means of OT texts. The first feature is the collection together from different contexts of sayings which have a significant word in common – here the word 'stone'. 'The tendency to group these texts together is one of the clearest examples of the catchword technique in the New Testament' (Lindars, op. cit., p. 169). This can be seen in I Peter 2⁶⁻⁸, where three separate sayings about a stone from three different contexts are brought together. In juxtaposing the stone saying in v. 18 with Ps. 118²² in v. 17 Luke was thus following a model in the church. The second feature is the readiness to adapt the OT text to serve the particular purpose for which the quotation is being made (cf. Rom. 9³³, where two separate passages from Isaiah are welded to form a single statement). In v. 18 this would seem to have gone even further, so that the verse cannot be set in black type in the Greek text as a recognizable quotation from the OT, and RSV does not print it as such. It has the form of a rhythmical couplet. The first line, *Everyone who falls on that stone will be broken into pieces*, links with v. 17 by defining the stone which the builders rejected (*that stone*) as now a stone over which men may trip. It reproduces the sense, but not the wording, of Isa. 8¹⁴, where it is said of God that 'he will become . . . a stone of offence, and a rock of stumbling to both houses of Israel, a trap and a snare to the inhabitants of Jerusalem. And many shall stumble thereon; they shall fall and be broken' (LXX *suntribēsontai*, a synonym for which in the LXX is the verb Luke uses here, *sunthlān* + +). The second line, *but when it falls on anyone it will crush him*, reproduces the sense, but not the wording, of Dan. 2³⁴⁻³⁵, ⁴⁴, where a stone cut by God is his kingdom, and it destroys any part of the idolatrous image it strikes (Dan. 2³⁴), and crushes the kingdoms of the earth, and winnows them (like chaff, Dan. 2⁴⁴; in his Greek translation of the OT Theodotion has here the same Greek verb *likmān*, in the sense of 'winnow', which Luke has here in the sense of 'crush'). Thus the threatening note of judgment in vv. 16–17 is continued and carried further. As God's rejected but exalted stone Jesus will break those who stumble because they do not believe in him, and as the bearer of God's kingdom he will destroy whatever shows itself alien to God in its rejection of him. This couplet may have come to Luke in oral tradition, but he could have created it himself as a further exposition of the parable. *every one who* and *anyone*, which make the judgment on the leaders in v. 16 a universal possibility, are characteristic of Luke's style.

17

the head of the corner: Jeremias (*TDNT* I, pp. 792f.) takes this expression (Greek *kephalē gōnias*), as also the stone in Isa. 28¹⁶ (Greek *akrogōniaios*, cf. Eph. 2²⁰), as a cope-stone of the arch. This is probably incorrect. It was rather a foundation stone on the ground at the corner from which the builder aligned the whole building.[f]

18

This verse is found, with only one word different, at Matt. 21⁴⁴ in most mss. If genuine there it would require that Luke knew the text of Matthew, or vice versa. But it is absent from D, the Old Latin and syrˢⁱⁿ, and should probably be omitted as an assimilation of Matthew's text to Luke's.

19

Mark's concluding statement (Mark 12¹²) is awkwardly expressed. It could mean, either that the knowledge of the authorities that the parable was spoken against them was the reason why they feared the people (because they knew the people were opposed to them), or, with 'they feared the people' in parenthesis, that it was the reason why they sought to arrest Jesus. Luke appears to take it in the first sense, which he underlines by once more specifying who the authorities were, and by the emphatic position of *this* with *parable*; while by adding *in that very hour* he also underlines the extreme provocation of the parable.

20²⁰⁻²⁶ = Mark 12¹³⁻¹⁷

QUESTION ABOUT THE TRIBUTE

²⁰*So they watched him, and sent spies, who pretended to be sincere, that they might take hold of what he said, so as to deliver him up to the authority and jurisdiction of the governor.* ²¹*They asked him, 'Teacher, we know that you speak and teach rightly, and show no partiality, but truly teach the way of God.* ²²*Is it lawful for us to give tribute to Caesar, or not?'* ²³*But he perceived*

f See R. J. McKelvey, 'Christ the Cornerstone', *NTS* 8, 1961–62, pp. 352–9.

their craftiness, and said to them, ²⁴'*Show me a coin.** *Whose likeness and inscription has it?' They said, 'Caesar's.'* ²⁵*He said to them, 'Then render to Caesar the things that are Caesar's, and to God the things that are God's.'* ²⁶*And they were not able in the presence of the people to catch him by what he said; but marvelling at his answer they were silent.*

* Greek *denarius*

This pronouncement story has two peculiar features. It combines, especially in Luke, extreme compression and brevity with an unusually protracted introduction; and it is not purely verbal, but has at its heart a visual element. Except in the introduction and conclusion Luke follows Mark closely, with some abbreviation and stylistic changes. Thus, *show partiality* (*lambanein prosōpon* = 'receive the face' in place of Mark's otherwise unknown expression 'look on the face'); *is it lawful for us* (*exesti* with acc. and infin. ++); for Mark's Latinism *kēnsos* = 'census' (tax) the more literary *phoros* = 'tribute', the regular word for this in Josephus (cf. Rom. 13⁷); *perceived* (*katanoein*, only here in the gospels except Matt. 7³); *craftiness* (*panourgia*, elsewhere in the NT only Paul); *then* (*toinun* first in the sentence, as in later Greek writers to stress logical inference).

Luke's careful rewording of the beginning and the end reflect the importance the story had for him. For what becomes a dominant theme in A., that Christianity is politically innocent, and that it is the Jews who invent political charges against it, makes overt appearance here for the first time; and this is the only unit in the synoptic tradition which directly raises the matter of the relation of the Jews and of Jesus to the imperial system. Hence, in the introduction (v. 20), in place of Mark's impersonal 'they sent', it is the official Sanhedrin who, out of the animosity created by the previous parable (*So*), and with malicious intent (*watched, paratērein* + 6⁷ = Mark 3²; 14¹; A. 9²⁴, here in the sense of 'watched their opportunity'), *sent spies* (*enkathetoi* ++, a literary word). These *pretended* (*hupokrinesthai* ++) *to be sincere* (*dikaios*, either 'righteous', possibly 'pious', i.e. concerned with the law, or 'honest', i.e. having a genuine question of conscience). The interlocutors are not, as in Mark and generally in Luke in religious matters, the Pharisees, whose question is to be followed by that of another religious group, the Sadducees (20²⁷ᶠᶠ·); for this is not primarily a religious matter for Luke. They are representatives of those who in their official capacity will

bring wholly political charges against Jesus in the presence of Pilate
(23²). Their object is to get hold of some public statement such as would
require the cognisance of Pilate as *governor* in the exercise of his *jurisdiction* (*archē kai exousia* = 'rule and authority', a typical Lukan reduplication, elsewhere in the gospels 12¹¹). Thus Luke makes the
occasion less casual and more of a test case. In the conclusion (v. 26)
Jesus' reply foils the attempt to get hold of a public statement – *catch
him* renders the same Greek word as does *take hold* in v. 20; *what he
said* is the Lukan *rhēma* = 'word'; and *in the presence of* is the LXX
word *enantion*, found only in L–A in the NT. The completeness of
Jesus' victory is shown by the reduction of his interlocutors to silence
by his *answer* (*apokrisis* + 2⁴⁷; John 1²²; 19⁹). Luke thus establishes in
advance that the political charges brought against Jesus (23²), and by
implication accusations of this kind brought against Christians before
the Roman authorities (A. 16²¹; 17⁶; 18¹³), are a plain lie.

ఌఌ

21

The original occasion and circumstances, and the motives of the questioners,
can hardly be established in a report of this kind. The unusually fulsome address
of the questioners consists in Mark of interconnected statements, and is largely
concerned with the character of Jesus – 'You are true (honest), for you do not
regard the position of men, but truly teach the way of God.' Luke turns this
into a continuous statement (*and* in place of 'for'), in which the emphasis falls on
the teaching of Jesus. The Sanhedrin's representatives approach Jesus as *Teacher*,
one who speaks and teaches (a Lukan reduplication) *rightly* (*orthōs* + 7⁴³; 10²⁸ in
this sense), that is, whose judgments are correct and therefore authoritative;
who is impartial, and who *truly* (i.e. without being deflected by other considerations) *teaches the way of God*. This last expression occurs again in the NT only at
A. 18²⁶, and is not found in the OT or Jewish writings, though it is clearly based
on the frequent OT expression 'the way (more often "the ways") of the Lord',
meaning the way of life prescribed by God for his people, religion in the form
of commandments (cf. Isa. 2³; Ps. 51¹³). Luke will have valued it, for in A.
18²⁵⁻²⁶ it is identified with 'the way of the Lord (Jesus?)' and with 'the things
concerning Jesus', and it may lie behind the absolute use of 'the way' as a
designation of the Christian movement (A. 9²; 19⁹, etc.), which will here be
given its basis in the life and teaching of Jesus. Taken by itself this opening
address could be intended to establish that Jesus is supremely a person to be
asked for his interpretation and judgment on a genuinely controversial topic,
upon which the law was thought to be either silent or inconclusive. Coming
after v. 20, however, it can only appear as the deceptive flattery of opponents.

This makes it difficult for the rest of the story to be in focus, a hypocritical question providing an inauspicious basis for the utterance of truth.

22

Is it lawful for us to give tribute to Caesar or not?: This is not, as it came to be treated subsequently, a general question about the relations of church and state, but is specific throughout. (i) *Is it lawful for us?* asks whether the law of God in the OT, either in so many words or as interpreted by the scribes, enjoins or permits the Jews, as the people of God subject to that law, to do something. The answer given to such questions was either 'It is permitted' or 'It is forbidden'. The question about tribute could thus be an exegetical question about the basis in the OT for what the questioners had already been doing for some years, and had been content to do – paying tribute. For the prevailing attitude in first-century Judaism, especially of Pharisees, would seem to have been one of acceptance, even if reluctant acceptance, of the Roman empire as a fact, or even of active loyalty towards it, which included the payment of taxes in return for its benefits.[g] This attitude was based on what was said about the Jewish king in Deut. 17^{14-20}, which had been extended in time to native kings exercising rule under Rome (e.g. the Herods). and then to Rome itself. It was manifested in the daily sacrifices and prayers offered in the temple on behalf of the emperor (cf. Jos. *BJ* 2.409, where the abrogation of these was considered to have been the origin of the Jewish revolt in AD 66). On the other hand, that attitude would have been put under considerable strain at various times and in various places. (ii) *to give tribute to Caesar* does not ask about the payment of taxes in general, nor about internal and local imposts and duties, but about the payment of the tribute tax to the emperor. Both Mark's word *kēnsos*, a Greek form of the Latin word *census*, meaning first the registration for tax assessment and then the tax itself, and Luke's *phoros* = 'tribute', were technical terms for the tax on persons (poll tax) which was automatically levied by the emperor himself on any region once it had become one of the imperial provinces of the empire (see on 2^1). This was never a purely fiscal arrangement, but always a consequence of imperial supremacy and a reminder of subject status. The first census in AD 6, when Judaea was made part of the province of Syria for taxation purposes, caused a revolt, both because 'numbering the people' was held by some to be a sinful infringement of God's prerogative (cf. II Sam. 24^{10}), and also because for a theocratic society it could be seen as submission to an idolatrous power (cf. Jos. *BJ* 2. 118, 'Judas incited his countrymen to revolt, upbraiding them as cowards for consenting to pay tribute to the Romans, and for tolerating

---

g For discussions of the Pharisaic attitude towards relations with Rome, see Abrahams, *Studies* I, ch. VIII, C. G. Montefiore, *Synoptic Gospels* I, pp. 276ff., and H. Loewe, *'Render unto Caesar': Religious and Political Loyalty in Palestine*, Cambridge 1940, pp. 65ff.

mortal masters after having God for their lord'). Although this revolt was mercilessly crushed, it was the same spirit of disaffection and independence which was to lead to the revolt of AD 66 and the destruction of the Jewish state. Opinions vary as to how far this spirit had become widespread and dominant in the interim, and had split Judaism into two camps on the issue of loyalty to Rome; on whether this was the immediate background of the question which Jesus is asked; and on whether he was asked it because in the eyes of some his actions and words seemed to identify him with the spirit of revolt. Most commentators take the question to be, not a genuine enquiry on a debated issue, but a trap to exploit a situation, whereby, if he answers 'Yes' he forfeits the support of the nationalist opposition to Rome, and if he answers 'No' he loses the support of the Pharisees, and will be crushed by Rome.

24

'*Show me a coin. Whose likeness and inscription has it?*:' Trick question though this may be (*he perceived their craftiness,* v. 23) Jesus takes it seriously, and replies to it. The reply is not direct, nor made by reference to scripture, as might have been expected by those who have addressed him as teacher. Possibly he judged scripture not to provide an answer. The reply is indirect, and is made by reference to the tribute money as itself containing the logic of the answer to the question. Jesus asks to be shown a denarius, not having one about him; Mark's 'Fetch me a denarius' implies that they did not have one either. The denarius (Greek *dēnarios* from the Latin *denarius*) was the most widely current of the Roman silver coins. It was minted mostly at Rome under the emperor's supervision, but also in the East at Antioch and Caesarea in Cappadocia.[h] It was the coin prescribed throughout the empire for paying the tribute. If it was the standard denarius issued by the reigning emperor, Tiberius, it would have had on its obverse side a bust of the emperor with laurel wreath and an inscription reading Ti Caesar Divi Aug F Augustus (= Emperor Tiberius Augustus Son of the Divine Augustus), and on the reverse side the completion of the inscription with Pontifex Maximus (= Chief Priest), and a figure of the emperor's mother represented as a divinity sitting on the throne of the gods, with an Olympian sceptre in her right hand and an olive branch in her left. The coin was a symbol both of Roman power and of the divinity of the emperor. Having been shown the coin Jesus asks whose image (*eikōn* = 'picture', 'likeness') it is on the obverse side of the coin, and to whom the inscription there refers. Clearly he does not ask this in order to be informed of what every child would know. The question is a didactic device to elicit from the interlocutors' mouths the word 'Caesar's' from which the necessary inference can then be drawn.

[h] For an illustration, see E. Stauffer, *Christ and the Caesars,* ET London and Philadelphia 1955, facing pp. 112–13.

25

Then render to Caesar the things that are Caesar's, and to God the things that are God's: This necessary inference (*Then*) is so terse and epigrammatic as to be valid and meaningful only if certain concealed assumptions are brought out; and it is not immediately evident what those assumptions are. Thus, the force of the question and answer is that the image and inscription establish ownership. This was literally so with the imperial coinage. It was regarded as the emperor's personal property, issued from the royal mint, and in circulation in the imperial provinces for the payment in the first instance of those dependent on him, his soldiers, agents, etc.; and he could withdraw it at any time. If this is the force of the reply 'Caesar's', then the argument could be, 'Since on your own admission the denarius is Caesar's personal property, but is *de facto* in circulation so as to come into your possession for use in your daily life, you should give it back to whom it belongs; and the only way to do that is to pay the tribute, for which it is the prescribed coin.' This, however, would be a forced and superficial argument on which to base a religious obligation (*is it lawful?*) to pay tribute. Or, the assumption may be that, in addition to establishing ownership, the coinage established the authority of the ruler, which was co-extensive with the circulation of his currency; and the force of the reply would be better conveyed by translating 'the emperor's'. The argument could then run, 'Since the coinage is the personal property of the one who represents and governs the empire, and by its circulation among you and your use of it you acknowledge yourselves inhabitants of the empire, and are prepared to take advantage of its benefits, you should render to the emperor the obedience which imperial authority requires.' Stauffer (op. cit., pp. 128ff.) extends this argument further on the basis of the compound verb here, *apodidonai*. This could be a synonym for the simple verb *didonai* = 'to give', which is used in the original question in v. 22, but its literal meaning is 'to give back', and hence 'to repay'; and it was regularly used of the repayment of debt (as possibly in Paul's statement on this subject, Rom. 13⁷). The argument could then be that the Jews, in their acceptance and use of the imperial coinage, had not merely accepted the political obligations of a subject people, but had been willing to partake of its benefits, legal, economic and political. They were thus in debt to the empire, and the payment of tribute was a moral obligation (this could be implied not only by the verb 'repay', but by 'the things that are Caesar's', i.e. what belongs to him as a moral right).

Whatever its further implications, the minimum that the judgment 'Render to Caesar what is Caesar's' asserts is that there is a legitimate sphere of the earthly ruler in which he has rights. This could be asserted against those in Israel who adopted an extreme theocratic position that only God ruled in Israel. The judgment, however, does not end there, but continues with *and* (give, pay back) *to God the things that are God's*. This could be (i) because the two

spheres were already implicit in the original question, *Is it lawful?*, meaning
'Does God in his rule over Israel command or permit the payment of tribute?',
and because in the past payment had been refused on the ground that it was
incompatible with the rights of God. The juxtaposition of the two spheres, each
with its own rights, was to answer 'Yes' to the original question. Or, it may be
(ii) because the argument, having taken its beginning from the imperial coinage,
and having affirmed the rights of the earthly empire, even though heathen,
idolatrous and potentially tyrannical, required that the claims of God and his
rule should be asserted at the same time and over against it. The empire has its
legitimate demands provided these do not conflict with the claims of God. The
two spheres, however, can hardly be regarded as running parallel; though nothing is said on what were to become such vexed questions in applying this text,
viz. where is the line to be drawn between them, and whether Caesar's is a
sphere where God and his things can be served. Nor is there any hint of what
some introduce here, that the judgment was only a temporary expedient, because Jesus believed that the empire, along with the rest of the world, was
doomed to imminent destruction. Nor is anything said of what 'the things of
God' are, that they should be paid to him, or repaid to him as debt. G. Bornkamm (*Jesus of Nazareth*, p. 123) interprets of men themselves, who in biblical
thought bore the image of God (Gen. 1^{26–27}), and who therefore belong to God,
and owe themselves to him; but it is probably pressing 'image' too hard to make
it supply, both an overt logical basis of 'the things that are Caesar's', and a
covert theological basis of 'the things that are God's'.

Two interpretations may be mentioned which derive directly from the
'image'. In his abbreviated version Luke omits from the demand for a coin in
Mark the words 'and let me look at it'. It is these words which lead H. Loewe
(*Render Unto Caesar*, pp. 102ff.) to conclude that originally the incident was not
concerned with the payment of tribute, but with the question which vexed the
conscience of pious Jews, whether it was possible 'to gaze on' coins, which frequently carried symbols of the divinity of the emperor, in the course of commercial practice without thereby committing the sin of idolatry. In Loewe's
view Jesus looked on the coin in order to pronounce that to do so was not to
compromise with idolatry, nor to give to Caesar wɪat belonged to God.
Derrett (*Law in the NT*, pp. 313ff.) also stresses the act of looking, but in a different way. In his view Jesus is being appealed to genuinely as a teacher, and
would be expected to refer to scripture in reply. The text to be assumed here is
Eccles. 8², 'I . . . mark (= 'look intently on') the mouth (= 'face') of the king,
and on account of the oath of the Lord.' One interpretation of this text could be
that it set royal authority and the obligation to God side by side as compatible;
and Jesus, instead of citing it verbally, mimes it by looking on the coin, so
affirming this interpretation. The original meaning is therefore not an evasion,
nor an equivocation, but simply 'Obey the commandment of the king and obey
(thereby) the commandment of God.' Even if such nuances drawn from the

interpretation of an obscure text underlay Mark's version of the incident, they have completely disappeared in the versions of Matthew and Luke.

26

What it was about Jesus' reply to the question, whether its content or its manner, that reduced his questioners to wondering silence is not indicated. If the reply was simply a restatement of a Pharisaic position on the matter it need not have occasioned wonder, though the manner of argumentation from the coin may have struck them as skilful. Since Luke had introduced them as attempting to get hold of a statement which could involve the governor, and now records their failure to do so, he may have meant their reaction to be one of admiration for the epigrammatic skill in saying what needed to be said while evading the dangers.

20^{27-40} = Mark 12^{18-27}

QUESTION ABOUT RESURRECTION

27 *There came to him some Sadducees, those who say that there is no resurrection,* 28*and they asked him a question, saying, 'Teacher, Moses wrote for us that if a man's brother dies, having a wife but no children, the man★ must take the wife and raise up children for his brother.* 29*Now there were seven brothers; the first took a wife, and died without children;* 30*and the second* 31*and the third took her, and likewise all seven left no children and died.* 32*Afterward the woman also died.* 33*In the resurrection, therefore, whose wife will the woman be? For the seven had her as wife.'*

34*And Jesus said to them, 'The sons of this age marry and are given in marriage;* 35*but those who are accounted worthy to attain to that age and to the resurrection from the dead neither marry nor are given in marriage,* 36*for they cannot die any more, because they are equal to angels and are sons of God, being sons of the resurrection.* 37*But that the dead are raised, even Moses showed, in the passage about the bush, where he calls the Lord the God of Abraham and the God of Isaac and the God of Jacob.* 38*Now he is not God of the dead, but of the living; for all live to him.'* 39*And some of the scribes answered, 'Teacher, you have spoken well.'* 40*For they no longer dared to ask him any question.*

★ Greek *his brother*

20²⁷⁻⁴⁰

William Manson (p. 225) suggests as a connection between this and the previous pericope that Jesus, by rejecting the political dreams of the nation, has thrown his hearers upon an other-worldly conception of the kingdom of God; but such a collection of debates was too artificial to have a sequence of thought of its own. The story was probably included in the collection as an encounter of Jesus with another prominent religious group in Judaism, the Sadducees, over an important matter with which they tended to be associated.

Agreement with Mark is close here – in v. 28, which reproduces Mark's free rendering of Deut. 25⁵⁻⁶ (contrast Matthew); in v. 31, including *likewise* (*hōsautōs*, only once elsewhere in the Gospel and not in A.) and *all seven*; in vv. 32–33, where the agreement is almost verbatim; in v. 37, with the curious *in the passage about the bush*; and in v. 39, a conclusion supplied by Luke from Mark 12²⁸⁻³⁴, which he is to omit. It is gratuitous to account for the considerable differences in vv. 34–36 by postulating another source 'roughly parallel with Mark, which Luke has blended with Mark' (Easton, p. 302). They are rather to be taken as evidence of Luke's editing when a subject is of special importance to him, as is the case here. For not only is the emphasis on the resurrection of Jesus greater in A. than anywhere else in the NT – see A. 1³ᶠᶠ·; 2²⁴, ³²; 3¹⁵; 4¹ᶠ·, ¹⁰ᶠ·, ³³; 5³⁰; 10⁴⁰ᶠᶠ·; 13³⁰⁻³⁷; 17³, ³¹ – but also the truth of the Christian message is argued there, as nowhere else, by reference to the concept of a general resurrection (A. 4²ᶠ·; 17¹⁸), of which Jesus is the first instance (A. 3¹⁵; 26²³); and this is particularly the argument of Paul as he is presented there (A. 23⁶; 24¹⁴ᶠ·; 26⁵ᶠᶠ·). It would thus be important for Luke to establish in the Gospel the truth of resurrection, not only over the person of Jesus (as in ch. 24), but also through Jesus' teaching about it; and this would seem to be the only incident available in the synoptic tradition for doing so. Further, the manner in which this vital matter was raised in this pericope inevitably restricted it to the largely negative point that there is no marriage in the resurrection, and this called for some expansion of a more positive kind.

∞

27

some Sadducees: There is not much precise information about these, so that their origins, including that of their name, are obscure. That is because they did not survive the destruction of the Jewish state in AD 70, and there is little, if any, literature that can confidently be called Sadducean. Knowledge of them comes from later and hostile sources, the NT, Josephus and the Talmud. Rabbinic literature, while sometimes preserving sentiments from the period prior to AD 70, reflects for the most part the outlook and standards which came to prevail after that date. Judged by these standards the Sadducees, now extinct, appeared as heretics, agnostics, almost as atheists. The name is probably to be connected with Zadok, who became a chief priest under Solomon (I Kings 1), and from whom the later priesthood was held to be descended (cf. Ezek. 44[15]). From the time of the Maccabean revolt (175 BC) the tenure of the high-priesthood played an important part in Jewish political and religious history, and there were frequent disputes over the legitimacy, and purity of descent from Zadok, of those who held it. In the course of these conflicts the Sadducees appear to have emerged, though it is not clear how they were related to groups called 'Zadokites', who are also mentioned for this period. They appear to have been a closely knit group, predominantly made up of the lay aristocracy, but including members of the priestly classes. They were always connected with the temple, and were in control of it, even if at times they had to submit to rulings coming from their opponents, the Pharisees. The chief point of conflict between the two was that the Sadducees insisted on the plain and literal interpretation of the OT text as the only guide to practice, and so opposed the claim of the Pharisees to justify established customs, and to establish others, by their own methods of interpretation, and the oral tradition to which it gave rise. (See further *TDNT* VII, pp. 35ff., and Jeremias, *Jerusalem*, pp. 228ff.)

those who say there is no resurrection: Luke here uses the verb *antilegein* = 'to speak against', but with a construction not otherwise found with it in the NT of accusative and infinitive and the negative to mean 'to deny that there is'. The Sadducees appear only here in the Gospel, as also in Mark, though they are mentioned in A. 23[6-8], again in connection with the denial of the resurrection, which also probably lies behind their treatment of the apostles in A. 4[1] and 5[17ff.]. As they were wealthy, and combined an openness to Hellenistic cultural influences with a conservatism that was both political in being nationalist and religious in being traditionalist, there was probably a certain practical common sense and worldly wisdom behind this denial as well as a doctrinal position. Josephus (*BJ* 2.166, *Ant.* 18.16f.) expresses it in Hellenistic terms that would be familiar to his non-Jewish readers as a denial of the persistence of the soul after death, of penalties in the underworld and of rewards. In Wisd. 2[1ff.] it is the ungodly who utter this denial (cf. I Enoch. 103[5]); but it could be represented as the only position consonant with scripture, since, with the exception of Daniel (a book possibly still of indeterminate status in scripture), the OT nowhere explicitly teaches resurrection as the hope of Israel, and was throughout content with Sheol (Hades) as the permanent abode of the shades of the departed. Thus the Sadducees regarded emerging doctrines such as that of resurrection as new-fangled dreams of the pious, and they resisted the elevation to the level of scripture of the interpretative tradition by which the Pharisees purported to find such doctrines in scripture. The conflict can be seen in the Mishnah, tractate Sanhedrin (first or second century AD) 10^1: 'All Israel have a portion in the world to come . . . But the following have no portion therein; He who maintains that resurrection is not a biblical doctrine . . .'

Luke's statement here could give the impression that Jews at the time were divided into the majority who held a precise doctrine of resurrection, and a minority who had no such belief; and this is how some take it. 'The opinion must be rejected that the idea of the resurrection was unknown to the majority of Jews at the time of Jesus. I believe, on the contrary, that the great mass of the Jewish population already adhered strongly to it, and that only the somewhat sceptical aristocrats of the Temple staff, who professed to hold strictly to the teaching of the Torah, openly denied it. The fact that the later Apocryphal books are well aware of the resurrection idea while the earlier ones are silent on the subject proves that it was about the time of the birth of Jesus that the new teaching came into its own.'[i] Even this statement, however, allows considerable latitude as to the time at which, and the form in which, the belief became established, and it is possible to see the situation as more complex and fluid, so that the present pericope is only with difficulty brought into sharp focus. The concept of Sheol began to prove inadequate for some at the time of the Maccabean struggle, when faith required that those who had given their lives for God's kingdom should live again to participate in it. The double resurrection to life or condemnation in Dan. 12^2 was probably a product of that faith, but it represented a considerable innovation, and did not become a dogma in Judaism until later. The literature of the first and second centuries BC and AD belongs to a period 'so alive, so progressive, so agitated by controversies, that . . . the most contrasting views could be held – until a greater uniformity was reached after AD 200.'[j] The evidence of such literature is not easy to assess, since the books cannot always be precisely dated, and it is uncertain whether they are voicing majority opinions or those of minority groups. It clearly testifies to a variety of speculative thought in the sphere of eschatology, sometimes even in the same document. The variety can be with respect of the persons concerned (resurrection of righteous Israelites, of all Israelites, of all men for judgment), of form (in a reconstituted body, a transformed body, without body), and of place (to earth, to a renewed earth, to Paradise). There were also various types of mixture of resurrection belief with belief in the immortality of the soul. The latest addition to this literature, the Qumran scrolls, proves curiously non-committal, so that

i C. Guignebert, *The Jewish World in the Time of Jesus*, ET London and New York 1939, p. 120.

j R. H. Pfeiffer, *History of New Testament Times with an Introduction to the Apocrypha*, New York 1949, p. 53.

it has been possible for scholars to hold that there is no unambiguous evidence in them of belief in resurrection, or of what the community's conception of an after-life was (see Evans, *Resurrection*, pp. 14–33 and the authorities cited there). Meanwhile the post-exilic hope of a this-wordly salvation persisted, and was that of the Sadducees, as perhaps of a great many others.

28–33

The Sadducees pose their question – perhaps a stock question with them in defence of their conservative biblical position – by appeal to the incontrovertible authority of the written law, and of Moses himself (*Teacher, Moses wrote for us*). Here it is to Moses' enunciation of the levirate law of marriage, whereby, to prevent the extinction of the family (always one of the worst possibilities), and the alienation of its property, a man was to marry his brother's widow if he died childless, in order to raise up children to his brother. In Deut. 25$^{5ff.}$ this is not laid down in the form of a legal enactment, but somewhat diffusely in narrative; and each evangelist feels free to summarize it in his own way – Luke's *having a wife but no children* (*ateknos* = 'childless') is an improvement on Mark. In Deuteronomy the law is limited to cases where the deceased has left no male heir (but tradition seems to have modified this; the LXX has 'no seed', and Jos. *Ant.* 4.254 has 'childless'), and to cases where the two brothers were living together on the family property. No mention is made of such a duty as incumbent on any after the second brother. How far the law was still operative in the very different society of first-century Palestine is not known; but that would not affect an appeal to it as the text of scripture, and as showing the mind of Moses. Here the enactment is blown up into an imaginary tale of seven brothers who had married the same woman in succession (this is perhaps characteristic of a folk tale, cf. Tobit 3^8), but without issue. If the conundrum to which the tale then leads – *In the resurrection, therefore, whose wife will the woman be?* – is to have force, it must be presumed that current resurrection beliefs, Pharisaic or otherwise, held that resurrection involved a restoration of earthly conditions. This was no doubt true in many cases. The concrete language used, 'to raise up from the dead', lent itself to such a view. In what may be the earliest form of the belief in Israel (II Macc. 7$^{10f.}$), those who had suffered martyrdom for God's cause were to have their bodies restored so as to participate in God's kingdom on earth for which they had given their lives. It is unlikely to have been true of all forms of resurrection belief that were emerging in Judaism.

34–38

The question posed in such an unsatisfactory manner is given a double answer. The first (vv. 34–36) is negative, and rejects the deductions drawn from Moses' levirate law as erroneous. The second (vv. 37–38) is positive, and argues for resurrection from a different passage of scripture connected with Moses. Some maintain that the second is an addition to a story which originally ended with Jesus' pronouncement that in the resurrection there is no marriage. That may be so, for it is very awkwardly introduced (see below); but it is not absolutely necessary, since the original question is really two questions – (i) Does not the levirate law make nonsense of resurrection?, and (ii) Does not this show that Moses (the Law) cannot have entertained the idea of resurrection? In Mark the answer is both vehement, and in its first part very compressed. The Sadducees are said to be in error, in great error (a unique expression in the synoptists). The basis of the error is twofold – ignorance of scripture and ignorance of the power of God. These are then developed in reverse order. The second, ignorance of the power of God, is treated first, though briefly and impersonally, in two related parts – (i) 'when they rise from the dead, they neither marry nor are given in marriage', (ii) 'but are like angels in heaven'. The argument is that the question ignores God's capacity through resurrection to transform earthly existence into a heavenly existence akin to that of the angels, where procreation, and therefore marriage, no longer obtain. Luke omits the negative reference to error, and treats these two related parts of the reply separately and more positively, developing each by a rhythmical passage with a balanced structure, vv. 34–35 and v. 36.

34–35

This is made up of four clauses. Mark's statement that 'they' do not marry nor are given in marriage is now made to stand in antithesis to a previous statement that to marry and to be given in marriage is what human beings do and must do. The antithesis is expressed in the language of the Jewish doctrine of the two ages, though in a reduced and neutral form. Human beings are *the sons of this age*. The term *this age* (*ho aiōn houtos*) is, apart from 16⁸ and Matt. 12³², confined to Paul in the NT, and, as generally in the apocalyptic thought from which it comes, has the sense of 'evil age' (cf. Gal. 1⁴; II Cor. 4⁴; in Luke 16⁸ it stands over against 'the children of light'). Here, however, the contrast intended is not that between evil and good, but that between temporal and non-temporal (cf. Eph. 1²¹, and the parallel expression 'the age now' in I Tim. 6⁷; II Tim. 4¹⁰; Tit. 2¹²). The meaning is that men, as those who are bounded by time and death, can only continue existence by marrying to beget children. Similarly *that age* (*ho aiōn ekeinos*) is not a technical term for the eschatological age, which would be either *ho mellōn* = 'the future (age)' or *ho erchomenos* = 'the coming (age)', but is formed from the conventional antithesis of 'this' and 'that'. This is then given content by being defined as *the resurrection of the dead*. Those to be resurrected, referred to impersonally by Mark as 'they', are then specified as *those who are accounted* (sc. by God) *worthy to attain to the resurrection from the dead*. Here resurrection is given moral content by being connected with God's judgment and approval. Both language and thought are Lukan. 'to be deemed worthy' (*kataxiousthai*) is found elsewhere in the NT at A. 5⁴¹ and II Thess. 1⁵; *to attain to (tunchanein)* occurs only here in the gospels. To be accounted worthy in respect of eternal life or God's kingdom appears again in the NT only at 9^{62}, A. 13^{46} and II Thess. 1^5, though there are parallels in the rabbis (for which see Dalman, *Words of Jesus*, pp. 119f.), in Greek authors (cf. Vettius Valens, IX. 1, 'He was considered worthy by the gods to attain to a safe harbour'), and in the formula used in Greek inscriptions (see Deissmann, *Bible Studies*, pp. 248f.). It is one way of stating what in 14^{14} (and only there in the NT) is referred to as 'the resurrection of the just'. In the emerging forms of belief in the after-life Judaism wavered between, on the one hand, a single resurrection, that of the righteous (Israelites) to a part in the world to come (this is 'the resurrection from the dead', cf. A. 4^2; Phil. 3^{11}, etc. – according to Josephus, *BJ* 2.163, *Ant.* 18.14 this was the belief of the Pharisees), and, on the other hand, a double resurrection of righteous and unrighteous for judgment (this is 'the resurrection of the dead', cf. A. 24^{15}; John 5^{29}). Here, as the context demands, resurrection is limited to those who are to have a positive existence of life with God, i.e. the righteous.

34

marry and are given in marriage: There is considerable variation in the mss here, mostly of Greek words for 'marry' and 'give in marriage'; but some old Latin mss read *generant et generantur* (or in reverse order), which presupposes a Greek original *gennōsi kai gennōtai* = 'beget and are begotten'. This reading is found in some Fathers, and in some mss in combination with 'marry and are given in marriage'. It could be original, and have been altered to conform with the wording in v. 35. It certainly makes the main point, which is not to do with marriage as such, but with procreation.

35

neither marry nor are given in marriage: Again the evidence is not sufficient to establish whether Jesus is here simply reiterating what was the almost universal, especially Pharisaic, view of the matter against the minority opinion of the Sadducees, or was contradicting it. Jewish commentators on the whole affirm the former – e.g. Montefiore, *Synoptic Gospels* I, p. 285, who quotes as probably valid for the first century AD the saying of Rab (third century AD) in the Talmud (Berakah 17a), 'In the world to come there is not eating and drinking or marrying or envy or hate; but the pious rest with crowns upon their heads, and are satisfied with the glory of God.' This is likely to have been the view of those who incorporated some measure of immortality into their belief, as also in Jubilees 23^{31}, 'Their bones shall rest in the earth, and their spirits shall have much joy.' On the other hand, SB I, pp. 889f., refer Rab's saying, and similar sayings, not to the resurrection, but to the intermediate state of souls before it, and roundly declare that the continuation of married life in the resurrection would have been assumed in popular belief.

36

Here the reason for the absence of marriage in the resurrection is made more explicit than in Mark by a further, typically Lukan, double statement.

(i) According to v. 36a, they will not marry because (*for*) they will be immortal (*ou dunantai* = 'they are not able (to die)', or, as in some mss, *ou mellousin* = 'they will not (die).' This is not a statement of the consistent Greek doctrine of immortality, according to which man cannot die because the soul he possesses is by nature imperishable, and so survives death, which is apparent only; for that doctrine is incompatible with resurrection as the act of God recovering men from death. Nor would it be, as such, a ground for the absence of marriage, since men already have immortal souls when they marry on earth. It is, rather, an example of the hybrid to be found in some forms of Jewish belief, according to which, after death, the righteous have conferred on them by God, or are said 'to put on', immortality or deathless existence (cf. Wisd. 3^{1-5} with or without resurrection?, IV Macc. 14–18 without resurrection?, I Cor. $15^{53f.}$ with resurrection). Hence the translation of RSV here, *they cannot die any more.* And that is why they do not need to marry for the temporal purpose of procreation. This immortality is then further defined as being *equal to angels* (in Greek a single word *isangeloi*, which is not found again in Greek literature, and which Luke may have coined himself on the model of the common Hellenistic formation of adjectives with the prefix *iso-* = 'like', 'equal to'). It was doubtless assumed that angels, as denizens of heaven, were immortal, but this is not stressed in Jewish teaching, nor are they cited as types of immortality (in I Enoch 10^5 the fallen angels are destroyed). Indeed, Luke may not have correctly interpreted Mark's text, which may have intended to say that the resurrected ones do not marry because, like angels, they possess an incorporeal nature, and do not have sexual intercourse. In II Baruch 56^{10} the fall of the angels referred to in Gen. $6^{1ff.}$ is said to have resulted from a mingling of angelic, spiritual nature with human corporeal nature; and in an address to the fallen angels in I Enoch $15^{4ff.}$ the immortal and incorporeal appear together, 'Though you were holy, spiritual, living the eternal life, you have defiled yourselves with the blood of women, and have begotten children . . . you were immortal for all generations of the world.' For Luke also 'angel' and 'spirit' were closely connected, and could even be identified (cf. A. $8^{26, 29, 39}$; 23^8); but here he confines the comparison with angels to immortality, and perhaps even intended to avoid any suggestion in Mark that equality to angels meant that the resurrected ones had an angelic, i.e. incorporeal nature.

(ii) According to v. 36b, this immortal existence, equivalent to that of the angels, is further explicated as that of those who are *sons of God* by virtue of being *sons of the resurrection*. Both connection and meaning are unclear. For v. 36b could be simply an extension of v. 36a, making the same point in a different way. Since angels were regularly termed 'sons of God' or 'children of heaven' (cf. Gen. 6^2; Job 1^6; I Enoch 6^2; 13^8, etc.), the meaning could be that through resurrection to an immortal existence men join the angels as denizens of heaven (and for this reason do not marry). On the other hand, *and are* could be introducing a further point which is not applicable to angels, and *sons of God* could have its customary sense in Judaism of those who are obedient to God's will, and reproduce his character (cf. Wisd. 2¹⁸; Matt. 5⁹, ⁴⁵; Rom. 8¹⁴ᶠᶠ·). They will be such in being *sons of the resurrection*. This striking and unparalleled expression is based on the linguistic usage, predominantly though not exclusively Semitic, in which 'son of' denotes character by reference to a common origin or a common participation in something. They are the products of resurrection. This is another way of saying that they are those accounted by God worthy of resurrection (v. 35), and thereby are shown to be his obedient sons. Thus, vv. 34–36 are more than an expanded version of Mark's charge of ignorance of God's power; for they go beyond providing reasons for the absence of marriage in the resurrection, and introduce moral and spiritual elements into what is otherwise a very limited and formal treatment of resurrection.

for they cannot die any more . . . equal to angels: Philo, for whom immortality has displaced resurrection, can say of Abraham (*Sacrifices Offered by Abel and Cain,* 5) that 'when he left this mortal life "he is added to the people of God", in that he inherited incorruption and became equal to angels, for angels – those incorporeal and blessed souls – are the host and people of God.'

37–38
The somewhat lengthy rebuttal of the objection to resurrection in the form the Sadducees had raised it is now followed by a brief, pregnant but also obscure argument for resurrection as being implicit in scripture. Mark's version is forceful, but awkwardly expressed. It begins with a formula, 'Now concerning . . . (*peri de*)' which is generally used to introduce a fresh subject (cf. its use by Paul in I Cor. 7¹, ²⁵; 8¹; 12¹). This gives the impression of something self-contained being added here as a gloss or appendix, and the impression is increased by a a change in both subject matter and manner of argumentation. For while vv. 28–36 have been about resurrection in general, here, despite the introductory words *But that the dead are raised*, it is argued with respect to certain special persons, the patriarchs, that they are alive before, and apart from, the resurrection. The argument is specific, and employs a rabbinic type of exegesis, which might have been that of the Pharisees in expounding and defending their position in the matter. Jesus quotes the text of Exod. 3⁶, where God says to Moses, 'I am the God of Abraham, and the God of Isaac, and the God of Jacob.' In its context this meant that, before proceeding to instruct Moses, God first identifies himself to Moses as being the same one who had been the God of the patriarchs when they were alive. Here the present tense of identification is pressed to yield the conclusion that he is still their God, and that therefore they are still alive.

The relation he sets up with them endures because he, as the living God, endures (cf. John 14¹⁹). *He is not God of the dead but of the living* is probably for Mark not a general statement, but the conclusion of the foregoing argument. God is 'the God of' only those who are alive; and since he 'is' the God of Abraham, Isaac and Jacob, this shows that they must be alive. (It may be noted that in the OT the opposite conclusion can be drawn, that since God is only God of the living he cannot be God of the dead, and the dead do not have him for God – cf. Ps. 6⁵.)

Here Luke rewrites Mark as follows. (i) He throws the whole weight on Moses as someone the Sadducees must acknowledge. In reply to their origianl words *Moses wrote for us* (v. 28) it is now observed that *even Moses* (*kai Mōusēs* = 'Moses himself') bears prophetic witness to resurrection (*showed, mēnuein* + A. 23³⁰; John 11⁵⁷; I Cor. 10²⁸, a classical word, in the LXX only in the Maccabean books, with the meaning 'to indicate', 'to signify'). He does this *in the passage about the bush, epi tēs batou*, where Luke makes the noun feminine, as it was in good Greek, Mark's masculine being a vulgarism. In Mark the phrase is a mode of referring to a section in the OT which, for lectionary purposes, was headed 'At the bush', but in Luke may be referring to a place – it was at (or 'near' – so *epi* with the genitive) the bush that he does so. *where he calls* (*legei* = 'speaks of as', 'calls'). Ellis (p. 237) takes this as an introductory formula, 'it says', and compares Rom. 9²⁵; but that would require a direct citation to follow, with ' the God of Abraham . . .' in the nominative, and not as here, in the accusative. Since *the Lord* (*Kurion*) is without the definite article the translation should be 'where he calls the God of Abraham and God of Isaac and God of Jacob Lord'.

(ii) For Luke *Now he is not God of the dead, but of the living* is a statement of general truth, for he adds in explanation of it a further generalizing statement *for all live to him*. What the addition means is not clear. Commentators rightly refer to IV Maccabees as illustrating it, and as a possible source of it. The author of this Hellenistic Jewish homily (of the first century BC or AD), in arguing his thesis that the passions can be controlled by enlightened reason, and with reference to the immortality of the righteous, cites the Maccabean martyrs as 'believing that unto God they die not, as our partriarchs Abraham, Isaac and Jacob, died not, but that they live unto God' (7¹⁹), and as 'knowing well that men dying for God live unto God, as live Abraham, Isaac and Jacob, and all the patriarchs' (16²⁵). Here it is assumed that the patriarchs enjoy a present immortality, which can be shared by those who die in God's cause. Luke's imprecise use of his favourite word *all* makes it difficult to discern how far the statement extends. Perhaps the sense is that anyone, whether on earth or elsewhere, who can truly be said to be alive, is so only by virtue of a continuing relation to God, who is the living God and the author of life.

Ellis (pp. 235ff.) objects to such an interpretation of the whole passage that it 'assumes a body/soul dualism that is uncharacteristic of the New Testament view of man', and that 'it would defeat the precise point of Jesus' argument. If

Abraham is now personally 'living', no resurrection would be necessary for God to be "his God" '. This objection is logical, but it probably takes too little account of the varieties of, and the illogicalities within, the Jewish forms of belief concerning life after death in the first century AD. Thus, the separation of body and soul, with immortality for the latter with or without resurrection, is presupposed, not only in Alexandrian works such as the Wisdom of Solomon and IV Maccabees, but elsewhere, e.g. Jubilees 23^{31}; I Enoch 103^3. When Luke penned 16$^{22-31}$ he clearly believed that Abraham was alive in heaven (or thereabouts) apart from resurrection. Ellis's own interpretation that God's words affirm that Abraham will be brought back to life at the resurrection in pursuance of the covenant with him, and so will those who partake of the same covenant relationship, is undoubtedly the more logical, but it is also forced in this context. Similarly he probably approximates Luke's thought too closely to Paul's when he takes *for all live to him* as referring specifically to Christians, whose present existence 'in Christ' is to be fulfilled individually in the resurrection and the parousia. It belongs rather with the more vague and general statements which Luke puts into Paul's mouth in A. 17$^{22ff.}$, where, in response to ridicule of the resurrection, it is said that all men are the offspring of God, that they receive life and whatever they have only from him, that they live and have their being in him, but will yet be subject to judgment by Jesus as the man raised by God from the dead.

39–40

In place of Mark's conclusion 'You are quite wrong', Luke rounds off the incident conventionally with an expression of approval from onlookers, and with the silencing of Jesus' opponents. To do so he borrows from the next pericope in Mark, which he will omit. *And some of the scribes answered, 'Teacher, you have spoken well'* (v. 39) is taken from Mark 12$^{28, 32}$, and *For they no longer dared to ask him any question* (v. 40) is taken from Mark 12^{34}. The result is somewhat clumsy, when scribes are introduced abruptly at the end of the story (as opponents of the Sadducees?), and *For they*, which grammatically should refer to them, cannot do so in view of their approval, but must refer to the Sadducees (and others?).

20$^{41-44}$ = Mark 12$^{35-37}$

QUESTION ABOUT THE MESSIAH

^{41}*But he said to them, 'How can they say that the Christ is David's son?* ^{42}*For David himself says in the Book of Psalms,*

20^{41-44}

> "*The Lord said to my Lord,*
> *Sit at my right hand,*
> [43]*till I make thy enemies a stool for thy feet.*"
> [44]*David thus calls him Lord; so how is he his son?*'

This pericope is taken from Mark, and since Mark's setting for it – teaching in the temple – is for Luke the setting for the whole of chs. 20–21, it is made continuous with the preceding debates. By the omission of Mark 12^{28-34} in favour of his own 10^{25-28} Luke brings it into juxtaposition with the teaching on resurrection; but the suggestion[k] that the question is addressed to the Sadducees, and the implied answer is the same as that in vv. 34ff. – the messiah becomes Lord by the same transforming power of God that makes men sons of God through resurrection – would require the priority of Luke here, and the removal of vv. 37–40 from their present place. The scribes introduced by Luke at v. 39 remain as the audience (*But he said to them*), and the tenet about the messiah is not, as in Mark, specified as scribal, i.e. from professional theologians, but is general (*How can they say?*). *For* in v. 42 strengthens the logic. *David himself*, like *even Moses* in v. 37, is emphatic, two chief OT figures deciding the issues at stake. *in the Book of*, for Mark's 'in the holy spirit', is a mode of citation of scripture peculiar to Luke in the NT (cf. 3^4; A. 1^{20}; 7^{42} – though, as is shown by A. 1^{16}; 2^{30}; 4^{25}, David was for Luke a mouthpiece of the Holy Spirit). Luke is the only NT writer to refer to the Psalms as part of scripture. By this last change Luke underlines the exegetical character of the pericope.

The collection of disputes ends with one initiated by Jesus himself (cf. Mark 3^{1-6} in relation to a similar collection in Mark 2^{1-28}). It would suit the evangelist's purpose of showing Jesus to be in command as a teacher to close the series with a counter-attack by him. It resembles the disputes over authority and the tribute money in being inconclusive, with the question left unanswered or only hinted at, and that over resurrection in posing a conundrum based on scripture. It is distinctive in appearing as a scholastic treatment of a point in theology. It is, moreover, so brief and cryptic as to be barely intelligible, so that for all the discussion of it (for which see Marshall, pp. 743–7), there is no consensus of opinion on what the precise question is that is being raised, on why it was thought necessary to raise it, and on why the tradition

---

k Made by F. Spitta, *Streitfragen der Geschichte Jesu*, Göttingen 1907, pp. 161f.

was handed down in this form. More specifically, is it (i) a purely academic question about current messianic doctrine, or (ii) an actual question raised by Jesus with tacit reference to himself, and to his own messiahship as he knew it to be, or (iii) a question raised subsequently in the church in exposition, or defence, of the messiahship of Jesus as that had come to be understood in the light of events?

נ‍ב‍נ

41

How can they say that the Christ is David's son?: The question supposes that 'the messiah' (*ho Christos* = 'the one who is anointed') was already a technical term in use for the coming one whom God would raise up to deliver Israel and be her leader; though it so happens that the earliest written evidence for this absolute use of the expression as a noun is in the NT itself (see on 2^{11}). Previously it appears as still adjectival, requiring a possessive or descriptive genitive after it, as in 'the anointed of the Lord (Ps. Sol. 17^{36}), or 'his (God's) anointed' (Ps. Sol. 18^6), or 'the messiahs (= the anointed) of Aaron (i.e. the priest) and of Israel (the ruler)' in 1QS $9^{10f.}$ (see Vermes, *Scrolls*, p. 87). It is not certain whether the term was an indefinite one, or, since formerly it had been the king who had been anointed for his office (I Sam. 16^3, etc.), it specified of itself the coming deliverer as a king. To the extent that it did so, and that the king was thought of in the terms of the ideal king David, the statement 'the messiah is son of David' would tend to be tautologous. But the priest had also been anointed for office (cf. Zech. 4^{14}, the two anointed ones, king and priest, and the messiahs of Aaron and Israel mentioned above). 'son of David' without the definite article, as here, is adjectival and descriptive, as probably with the definite article in Ps. Sol. 17^{23}, 'Behold, O Lord, and raise up unto them their king, the son of David.' Its immediate and plain meaning is one who is physically descended from David, a Davidite. The question will then be, 'How is it that they say that the messiah is (i.e. must be) a Davidite?' It is not known whether this was a universally held tenet in Israel at the time. On the basis of scripture – e.g. of the hope of a Davidic ruler in such passages as Isa. 9^{1-7}; $11^{1ff.}$; Jer. $23^{5ff.}$; Ezek. 34^{23}; interpreted in Ps. $89^{20ff.}$ as the establishment of David's throne for ever through one of his line – it may have been sufficiently widespread to appear as a dogma.

42-44

Over against this scripturally based axiom is set a passage from scripture, Ps. 110^1, in such a way that it seems to contradict it. The argument depends for this contradiction on (i) the Davidic authorship of the psalm, since only if David is the speaker can the introductory words of the oracle, 'The Lord (i.e. God) said to my Lord (i.e. the king)' be taken as a reference by David to the king (messiah) as 'his lord'; and (ii) the incompatibility of the status of 'lordship' (i.e.

mastership, ownership) and that of 'sonship' (i.e. a derived existence, sub-servience) in a single person. The argument is verbal. It appeals to the words 'my lord' in the quotation, and makes no reference to the words that follow, 'Sit at my right hand, till I make thy enemies a stool for thy feet.' It takes no account of the fact that if a Davidite were to be the messiah, he would be there-by in a position of divinely delegated authority over all Israel, including in principle David himself. Indeed, it appears to prove too much – not that the messiah does not have to be a Davidite, but that he cannot possibly be one. The answer then expected to the question in v. 44b, *how is he his son? (pōs* = 'how can it be?', as translated by RSV in v. 41), is 'not at all'. The same difficulties apply if the question is taken (as by Montefiore, *Synoptic Gospels* I, pp. 288f., and others), not as a theoretical one about messiahship in general, but as a practical one, by which Jesus intended to dispense with Davidic sonship as a necessary qualification for messiahship, because he both believed himself to be messiah, and also knew that he was not descended from David. To which could then be added the further difficulty that, on the evidence of Rom. 1³ (possibly a pre-Pauline formula), A. 13²³; II Tim. 2⁸ (John 7⁴²?), Jesus was believed, rightly or wrongly, in some areas of the church to have been a descendant of David. This was certainly Luke's view, however artifically he has to establish it through Joseph and not Mary (1²⁷, ³²; 2⁴; 3³²), and he cannot have taken the question in this way.

Possibly 'son of David' has here the wider connotation of 'like David'. The question would then be why messiahship had to be thought of as Davidic in character, meaning by that not necessarily, as it is often taken, 'political' or 'nationalist' (the passages referred to above about the Davidic figure depict him as endowed with God's spirit to rule with his wisdom and justice), but 'exer-cised on earth in an earthly manner'. In that case the appeal to Ps. 110¹ could go beyond the antithesis between 'son' and 'lord', and point towards a different kind of sonship or likeness, which was to displace 'son of David' in thinking about the messiah, one more akin to what is suggested by the words 'Sit at my right hand . . .' If so, which sonship is intended? 'Son of God' is in Mark 14⁶² a synonym for messiah (cf. Luke 22⁶⁷⁻⁷⁰), and, on the same principles of psalm interpretation, 'Son of God' is what in Ps. 2⁷ David claims himself to be. 'Son of man' is also in Mark 14⁶² placed alongside messiah, the heavenly messiahship taking up the earthly but not annulling it; and 'Son of man', since it means 'man' and not 'like a man', would not be a true verbal antithesis to 'son of David'. Farrer (*A Study in St Mark*, p. 283) extends the question further to make it ask under which covenant, that with David or that with Adam, the messiah inherits his kingdom. Or, as a variant of this, the question and argument could be intended, not to replace one sonship by another, but to deprive Davidic son-ship of its priority. The messiah is not simply son of David, nor does the Davidic character of his office say the most important thing about it.

Daube (*NTRJ*, pp. 158ff.) sees the passage as an instance of a type of rabbinic argumentation in which two apparently contradictory texts of scripture are reconciled once each is shown to be true in its own context. The question 'how?' then asks how they can be held together and at the same time. In that case it has to be considered whether the pericope is a product of the early church rather than an utterance of Jesus. For, whatever Jesus' beliefs about messiahship and his own messiahship may have been (and these are not easy to discover), it was certainly part of the church's messianic confession that Jesus was both son of David and Lord at the same time, and that in him both statuses belonged together. It may be noted that, while there is no firm evidence that Ps. 110 was applied to the messiah in Judaism at this time, the NT affords ample evidence of its application in the church to Jesus, especially as proving his lordship from scripture. Dodd (*According to the Scriptures*, p. 35) calls Ps. 110^1 'one of the fundamental texts of the kerygma, underlying all the various developments of it'; and he judges it to be the basis of any statment that Jesus is exalted at the right hand of God. Thus, in A. 2$^{33-36}$ the man Jesus is said, through resurrection and exaltation, and in fulfilment of this psalm, to have been made lord and messiah; and in the christological confession in Rom. 1$^{3-4}$ Jesus is said to be the Son of God, who was a descendant of David according to the flesh (i.e. in the conditions of his earthly life), and was designated Son of God with power by his resurrection (cf. A. 13$^{22-37}$, Jesus, of David's posterity, becomes Son of God by resurrection). Possibly, therefore, in answer to Jewish objections, not that Jesus was not a Davidite, but that being a Davidite he had not exhibited in his life (and still less in his ignominious death) the necessary marks of messiahship, it is here stated by implication that 'son of David' and 'Lord' can, and do, co-exist through the exaltation to lordship of the man Jesus. 'son of David' would then be less a term with messianic overtones than (as in Rom. 1^3) an expression for the earthly existence of the Lord Jesus. This is probably how Luke understood it – cf. passages in A. referred to above, and his alteration here of 'son of David' to 'David's son'. But, as has been observed (see Marshall, p. 745), this is an answer not to the question 'How is David's Lord also his son?', but to the rather different question 'How is David's son also his Lord?' It could be that the use of Ps. 110 in the church originated in its use by Jesus himself, and that he had some intention in the question 'How is David's Lord also his son?' which was already opaque to the evangelists when it came down to them in this exceedingly condensed unit of tradition. Cullmann (*Christology*, pp. 127ff.) would combine all aspects: the statement is an authentic utterance of Jesus, is about messiahship in general but also about his own messiahship, and is not intended to deny his Davidic descent but its christological value, in the same way as he denies any fundamental significance to his physical kinship (Mark 3$^{31ff.}$).

42

David himself says: Ps. 110 is generally designated by modern scholars one of the

Royal Psalms, i.e. those concerned with some aspect of the status and function of the king in relaion to God and Israel. There has been considerable dispute about its date, some ascribing it to the Maccabean, others to the pre-exilic period. Even if it were taken back to the time of David it would be uttered by the priest or prophet about him, and cannot be spoken by David about himself.

20⁴⁵⁻⁴⁷ = Mark 12³⁸⁻⁴⁰

WARNING AGAINST THE SCRIBES

⁴⁵*And in the hearing of all the people he said to his disciples,* ⁴⁶*'Beware of the scribes, who like to go about in long robes, and love salutations in the market places and the best seats in the synagogues and the places of honour at feasts,* ⁴⁷*who devour widows' houses and for a pretence make long prayers. They will receive the greater condemnation.'*

Luke is following Mark so closely here that he even reproduces at v. 46 a doublet of Q's version of the denunciation of the scribes and Pharisees (11⁴³ = Matt. 23^{6f.}). That was directed against the Pharisees; this as in Mark, is directed against the scribes. The transition in Mark 12³⁸ from criticism of scribal theology to their practice is weakened in Luke because in v. 41 he has already made the tenet about the messiah general rather than specifically scribal. The only connection with what precedes is perhaps through the thought of exaltation – being exalted by God ('Sit at my right hand . . .') as opposed to self-exaltation. That would correspond with a dominant strand in Jesus' teaching (cf. 14¹¹; 16^{14f.}; 18¹⁴, etc.); but here it is accompanied by an intense hostility to the Jewish religion as represented by its leading practitioners. The condemnation of the scribes is not spoken directly to them, but about them *in the hearing of all the people* (of Jerusalem?). This is a typical Lukan exaggeration, perhaps suggested here by 'the great throng' in Mark 12^{37b}. It fits the context here since ch. 20 consists of teaching against the religious leaders in the presence of an audience of the people, who are distinguished from them and opposed to them. Further, since the condemnation of the scribes begins from a warning not to imitate them, Luke has it addressed to the disciples (as future religious leaders?), who have been in attendance since 19³⁷.

The unit is rhythmical, with six lines enclosed between an opening warning and a closing judgment. The warning could be translated 'Beware of those scribes who . . .', but *Beware of the scribes who . . .* is probably correct. The censure is of the scribes as a class. Like all such general attacks it runs the risk of being too indiscriminate to carry complete conviction. In the charges there is a curious combination of vanity and vulgar ostentation with extortion and hypocritical piety (cf. 16^{14f.}). U. Wilckens (*TDNT* VII, p. 690) sees these as 'not directed so much against specific excesses of personal vanity or avarice, but rather against the general claim of rabbis that in virtue of their teaching, to which they accord the dignity of divine revelation, they held a most important function in the saved community, and should be given appropriate honour by the people'. They would seem, however, to be less concerned than those in 11³⁷⁻⁵² with abuses attendant on the scribes' functions as exegetes of the law and as theological guides, and more with externals; though what their precise character is in each case is not always clear.

ॐ

46

Here the charges are of ostentation and vanity. The scribes are *those who like to go about in long robes*. But the word for *robe* ('long' is not in the Greek) is *stolē*, an ordinary word for clothing; here apparently the Jewish outer garment, *the tallith*, supposedly of a special kind, 'the resplendent coat of men distinguished for piety and scholarship' (Daube, *NTRJ*, p. 125). The emphasis may then be on *go about* (*peripatein* = 'walk about'), which Luke puts early in the sentence. They did not limit the use of these garments to official or ceremonial occasions (the lengthening of phylacteries and tassels, external signs of piety, Matt. 23⁵, may be giving precision to this charge). They also *love* (Luke alters Mark's 'like' to the stronger word) *salutations in the market places* (so 11⁴³); this is glossed in Matt. 23^{7b} by 'to be addressed as rabbi'. They also love *the best seats in the synagogues* (so 11⁴³) *and the places of honour at feasts.* This conjunction appears to be conventional. Josephus (*Ant.* 15.21) records how Herod received Hyrcanus with all honour, assigning him the chief seats in meetings and the most honoured seats at the banquet table; and in *Ant.* 20.61 the same is said of the king of Parthia's treatment of the son of the king of Adiabene. Here it seems artificial, since the principal seats in the synagogue would presumably be the natural places for scribes to occupy. Chief seats at banquets on the score of being religious personages is a different matter. In 14^{8ff.} this is made the basis of teaching on the necessity of abasement.

47

The character of the charges changes abruptly – Mark is ungrammatical here, and Luke improves by the use of relative clauses. The conjunction of some kind of extortion with religious pretence is found in Assumption of Moses 7$^{1ff.}$, where unnamed persons are denounced as dissemblers and devourers of the goods of the poor, 'saying that they do so on the ground of justice, but in reality to destroy them'; though these are called gluttons, which is hardly what is intended by *feasts* here. It is also found in Jubilees 23^{21} of Hellenizers who 'shall exalt themselves to deceit and wealth . . . and they shall name the great name, but not in truth and righteousness'. What is meant by *devour widows' houses* is disputed. Jeremias (*Jerusalem*, pp. 112ff.) stresses that while some scribes may have followed a trade, and some have been employed by the temple, the majority were poor, with no salary for their scribal work, and were dependant on subsidies; and he takes the reference here to be not to any form of legal malpractice in dealing with widows' property, but to 'the scribes' habit of sponging on the hospitality of people of limited means'. Derrett[1] holds that it refers to scribes acting as lawyers appointed to look after widows' estate. *make long prayers* is referred to in Matt. 6^7, but there it is Gentiles who make them, and the wordiness is evidence of unbelief. Here the length of the prayer is part of the ostentation, and of the desire for a reputation as spiritual persons. In that case the Greek word *prophasis* here bears its usual meaning of an ostensible, as distinct from a real, motive (*for a pretence*). In conformity with his general view of this passage Derrett takes *prophasis* in a possible sense of the actual motive; it was to further their work as widows' lawyers that they made long prayers; but this would probably require a definite article with the noun.

the greater condemnation: Because of their position as custodians of the piety of God's people (cf. James 3^1).

21$^{1-4}$ = Mark 12$^{41-44}$

THE POOR WIDOW

2 I *He looked up and saw the rich putting their gifts into the treasury; ²and he saw a poor widow put in two copper coins. ³And he said, 'Truly I tell you, this poor widow has put in more than all of them; ⁴for they all contributed out of their abundance, but she out of her poverty put in all the living that she had.'*

l ' "Eating up the Houses of Widows": Jesus' Comment on Lawyers', *Nov Test* 14, 1972, pp. 1–9.

21¹⁻⁴

This is taken from Mark, Luke's version being more succinct in expression, and altogether more elegant in wording. In Mark it is a separate story, connected with what precedes by the word 'widow'. In Luke it is continuous with what precedes – in the course of his teaching in the temple Jesus *looked up and saw* – and it leads straight on to what follows about the temple. Bultmann (*History*, pp. 32f.) labels the story a biographical apopthegm of a unitary kind, i.e. the saying arises out of a particular situation, and is not intelligible apart from it. It is however an ideal situation, and we are not meant to ask how Jesus knew what the woman put into the treasury, or that it was all she had.

❦

1

into the treasury: The meaning is curiously difficult to establish with precision. The Greek word *gazophulakeion* is used by Josephus (*BJ* 5.200) in the plural for treasury chambers lining the wall of the inner court of the temple for the storage of temple property, and possibly as strong rooms for the deposit of private wealth; and these were burnt along with the temple by the Romans (*BJ* 6.282). It is possible that they were collectively called 'the treasury', and that this area is referred to in John 8²⁰, 'These words he spoke in the treasury'. It is unlikely, however, that these would be used as places for teaching. The Mishnah, tractate Shekalim (2¹; 6¹), refers to thirteen horn-shaped chests in the forecourt of the temple for free-will offerings, but does not say exactly where they were. If it is one of these that the story refers to, it would have had to be in the Court of the Women for the widow to have access.

saw the rich . . . saw a poor widow: Of those who in Mark are said to offer their gifts Jesus in Luke sees only *the rich* (the word is placed last for emphasis), and, in distinction, *a poor widow* – in place of Mark's normal word for 'poor' Luke has the more literary word *penichros* + +, meaning 'needy', 'poverty-stricken'. Thus the scene becomes a typically Luken contrast between rich and poor.

2

copper coins: See on 12⁵⁹.

out of her poverty: This is a doubtful translation of the Greek word here *husterēma*, which means 'lack', 'deficiency'. The statement could be paradoxical – the widow gave of what she did not possess – and could cut deep; for it implies that the rich, since they give out of abundance, cannot really give at all, but only the poor can give, since their giving involves the expenditure of themselves (Greek *bios*, which can mean both 'life' and 'livelihood'). Josephus (*Ant.* 6.149) places a similar sentiment in the mouth of Samuel, that if the pious, from whom no

728

sacrifice is required, should offer any, however modest, God 'the more gladly welcomes this homage from poverty than that of the wealthiest'. In Leviticus Rabbah 107a is preserved a story of a priest who turns away a woman bringing an offering of a handful of meal, and is told by God not to do so, since 'she is as one who has brought her life (i.e. herself)'.

2 1 $^{5-38}$ *The Coming Tribulation and the Last Things*

GENERAL INTRODUCTION

In the synoptic gospels the narrative of the passion is immediately preceded by a lengthy, uninterrupted discourse of Jesus on the ultimate events of the world's history, and what is to accompany them. It forms the last piece of extended teaching; for apart from Luke 22$^{24-38}$ the utterances of Jesus from then on are brief, and either arise directly from the circumstances, or are spoken in reply to others. In Mark such a lengthy and comparatively articulated discourse is unique in form and content. It has been called 'the Little Apocalypse', and that is correct to the extent that it speaks of a sequence of extraordinary and largely catastrophic events related to the end of all things, which culminate in cosmic dissolution, the appearance of the Son of man and his gathering for God of his elect. In doing so it uses such terms as 'the end', 'the beginning of sufferings', 'the desolating sacrilege', 'the tribulation', 'the shortening of the days' and 'the elect'. These belonged to the vocabulary of a type of thinking and writing which had begun to emerge in Judaism in the middle of the second century BC, and which was still active in the first century AD. A full scale example in the NT is Revelation, and there is a glimpse of it in II Thess. 2$^{1-12}$. The name 'apocalyptic' – from the Greek *apokalupsis* = 'unveiling' – has been given to it because one of its distinctive features is the revelation, as from God, of the secrets (mysteries) of the future and of the consummation of all things.^{m}

m For a review of this literature, most of which is contained in *AP* II, see H. H. Rowley, *The Relevance of Apocalyptic*, London 1944, New York 1946; D. S. Russell, *The Method and Message of Jewish Apocalyptic*, London and Philadelphia 1964; K. Koch, *The Rediscovery of Apocalyptic*, SBT 2.22, 1972; and S. Laws, 'Can Apocalyptic be Relevant?' in *What about the New Testament?*, ed. Hooker and Hickling, pp. 89–102.

Mark 13 and its parallels are, however, peculiar as apocalypse in the extent to which the programme of future eschatological events is directed to a particular group, to whom they provide a warning of what is in store for them personally, and exhortation to an appropriate response based upon it. In this way they approximate to a different genre of literature which had also emerged in Judaism, that of the 'testament' or 'farewell discourse', generally that of a dying father to his son(s), in which he gives warnings and advice on the conduct of life in the future (for a miniature example see Tobit 14$^{13ff.}$, and for a full scale example The Testaments of the Twelve Patriarchs, in its present form a Christian work, but based on Jewish originals).[n] This applies less to Luke, since in his Gospel 22$^{14-38}$ could be said to be the testament or last words of Jesus to his disciples.

Standing as the last piece of teaching before the account of the passion, the discourse resembles from a literary angle the eschatological sections at, or near, the end of OT prophetic books, which prophesy judgment on Israel and the nations. In this position it also serves from a theological angle to set the whole ministry of Jesus and its consequences, and especially his death and resurrection, in the widest, and for the first Christians the only possible, context of the end of history and of God's consummation of his creation. It indicates further that they are an anticipation of, and a means to, the final judgment and salvation of God. In its own terms it makes an absolute an affirmation as could be made about the person and work of Jesus. For the one who is to experience humiliation and rejection at the hands of Israel, but exaltation and acceptance at the hands of God, here speaks as God's vicegerent. He is the one who knows that he is to come in glory to complete God's work. It is his present words which will alone survive the dissolution of the cosmos, and in his hands in the meantime is the fate both of the disciples and of the world. In Luke's version this effect is not so strong, because the predictions are sometimes given a more factual and prosaic form less immediately connected with the final things. Nevertheless a power-

---

[n] For this genre of literature, see Stauffer, *Theology*, Appendix VI. J. Munck (*Aux Sources de la Tradition Chrétienne: Mélanges M. Goguel*, Paris 1950, pp. 155–70) notes as a distinguishing feature of these farewell discourses their apocalyptic tone. For John 13–17 as a farewell discourse in a totally different form from Mark 13 but as containing some of its themes, C. H. Dodd, *The Interpretation of the Fourth Gospel*, Cambridge and New York 1953, pp. 390ff. For Paul's 'testament', A. 20$^{17-38}$.

ful impression is conveyed of the speaker as one who knows in advance the course of future history.

Mark 13 has been variously assessed as:

(i) a Jewish apocalypse which has been revised by a Christian hand (Mark's?);
(ii) a Jewish-Christian apocalypse ending with a statement about the Son of man, but supplemented (by Mark?);
(iii) an assembly or mosaic of more or less independent units of tradition, the reference to 'the reader' (Mark 13^{14}) suggesting that it was primarily a literary construction (made by Mark?).[o]

To the extent that the last was the case the probability is increased that Mark's was the basis of the versions of Matthew and Luke. For while the words of Jesus about the last days would undoubtedly have been treasured and often repeated by the first Christians, who believed themselves to be living in them, it is unlikely that they would always have rehearsed them in a form which covered the same subject matter as in Mark, and in Mark's distinctive and somewhat disjointed sequence. Certainly Matt. 24 shows no evidence for any other basis than Mark 13, which is supplemented, clarified and interpreted. The relation of Luke 21$^{5-36}$ to Mark 13 is more complex. Both Mark and Luke cover the same topics in the same order, except that Luke has nothing corresponding to Mark 13$^{21-23}$, false Christs (of which there is some equivalent in 17$^{23-24}$), or to Mark 13^{32}, the ignorance of any but the Father of the day or hour. It is agreed by all that at the beginning, vv. 5-11, and at the end, vv. 29-33, Luke has simply reproduced Mark. In the remaining sections – vv. 12-19, 20-24, 25-28 and 34-36 – the wording varies in its degree of similarity from close agreement in vv. 12-13, 16-17, 23, and 27, to considerable difference in vv. 14-15, 24-25, and especially vv. 34-36.

Explanations of these phenomena have fallen roughly into two types. (i) On the basis of the disagreements it is postulated that Luke possessed a non-Markan version, generally parallel to Mark's, which he incorporated into his Gospel, or into a first draft of it, before becoming acquainted with Mark; and that he later supplemented it from Mark,

---

o For a discussion of the problems and a review of the hypotheses, see G. R. Beasley-Murray, *Jesus and the Future: an Examination of the Criticism of . . . Mark 13*, London and Toronto 1954, chs. 1-3, Marxsen, *Mark the Evangelist*, pp. 151ff., Gaston, *No Stone on Another*, ch. 6.

especially at the beginning, and perhaps revised some of its wording from Mark, thus bringing about the agreements with Mark. Streeter (*Four Gospels*, pp. 215f.) assigned to Proto-Luke only v. 18 and vv. 34–36, judging Luke's divergences from Mark 'well within the limits of editoral conjecture or inference', and not enough 'to justify the assertion that Proto-Luke contained a parallel version of these sections in Mark'. Taylor (*Third Gospel*, ch. iv) saw vv. 12–15, 18, 19 and vv. 20, 21b, 22, 23b–26a, 28, 34–36 as two separate literary unities, which had not necessarily belonged together, but which Luke had joined, interpolating Markan material into them at a later date. Easton (pp. 310f.) sees the whole of 21$^{5-36}$ as largely independent of Mark, though the L material may not have been consecutive, and Luke may have derived an order for it from Mark.^{p} The chief defect of these analyses is that they must presuppose a somewhat wooden type of revision, in which Luke supplements his original version as a whole by inserting into it units from Mark (vv. 5–7, 8–11, which actually supply the discourse with its beginning, and vv. 29–31, 32–33), and supplementing individual paragraphs by inserting into them sayings from Mark (vv. 16–17, 21, 23a, 26b–27), some of which additions appear gratuitous.

(ii) On the basis of the agreements in order of subject matter and wording Luke is judged to have had no continuous written source here other than Mark, though he may have had one or two independent sayings. In that case he will have edited Mark here with a particularly free hand, and will have had good cause to do so. It is this which has produced the divergences. This is the view taken in this Commentary. Observations relating to it will be made in the comment on individual sections. Here two more general observations may be made. Firstly, some of the differences from Mark are literary. They involve words not found elsewhere in the NT, the use of language drawn from the LXX, and recognizably Lukan expressions. These can all be found in sections that are indisputably taken from Mark, and they may be evidence of Lukan editing in the other sections. Secondly, some of the differences are theological, and here the possibility of extensive revision by Luke cannot be ruled out. For it is not only the modern reader who finds the contents of Mark 13 especially difficult. The later evangelists who used it had to wrestle with the meaning for them and their readers of its mysterious and highly coloured apocalyptic language. They were

^{p} For analyses leading to similar conclusions, see Beasley-Murray, op. cit., pp. 72f., 94ff., Gaston, op. cit., ch. iv, Winter, *Studia Theologica* 8, pp. 138–72.

writing at some point within the time scheme presented by its subject matter, and they would wish to write in such a way as to throw light on the events through which, and in the light of which, they were themselves living. This could press particularly hard on Luke. For in Acts he was to be, as was none of the other evangelists, a historian of the church's mission, and of its divine protection under constant opposition and persecution. This involved some account of the relationship between the Christian movement and Jerusalem as the centre of Judaism, and it would be necessary to give some rationale of the destruction of Jerusalem by the Romans. It may be further noted that, in distinction from Mark and to some extent from Matthew, Luke has already included material of a similar kind: on the dangers to disciples and their need for watchfulness (12$^{4-12, 35-40}$), on the suddenness of the last things (17$^{22-37}$), and on the judgment of Jerusalem (13$^{34f.}$; 19$^{41-44}$). He could then have held himself free to adapt the discourse in Mark 13 in a different direction.

In its Lukan form the discourse has a position, coherence and character of its own. It is not less articulated than Mark, but differently articulated. As the climax of a daily teaching ministry in the temple, which begins at 19^{47} and continues throughout ch. 20 and until 21^4, Jesus speaks in full knowledge of the future of Israel, mankind and the church. Beginning from a question about the temple the sequence of thought is:

(i) Verses 8–9, introduced by *And he said*, the danger of defection from discipleship through deception by false messianic figures, and universal disturbances before the destruction of Jerusalem;

(ii) Verses 10–28, introduced by *Then he said to them*, the persecution of disciples at a time of disorders which lead to the destruction of the city, to the times of the Gentiles, and the chaotic conditions supervening upon the parousia;

(iii) Verses 29–end, introduced by *And he told a parable*, the deliverance of the disciples, the coming of the kingdom of God, and the requirement of constancy to the end.

It was presumably to make these particular points that Luke introduced the discourse at all.

21^{5-6} = Mark 13^{1-2}

THE DESTRUCTION OF THE TEMPLE

⁵And as some spoke of the temple, how it was adorned with noble stones and offerings, he said, ⁶'As for these things which you see, the days will come when there shall not be left here one stone upon another that will not be thrown down.'

Close agreement in wording and sentence construction, including the otiose *that will not be thrown down*, shows this to be taken from Mark. The chief difference is one of setting. In Mark there is a change of scene to the Mount of Olives, which may have had eschatological connotations (cf. Zech. 14⁴ᶠᶠ.), and the whole discourse has an esoteric character as delivered to an inner circle of four disciples. This disappears in Luke. The discourse now follows straight on from 21¹⁻⁴, and is delivered inside the temple in response to remarks from bystanders about its beauty. The literary differences correspond with this. Verse 5 is cast in the *chria* form (see on 17²⁰), so that the temple is raised as a topic of discussion by an undefined audience (*some spoke*). Their elaboration of the temple's magnificence is 'in quite the idiomatic phrase of the secular guide book or travelogue' (Cadbury, *Luke–Acts*, p. 244), with its reference to *noble stones* (*kalos* in the normal Greek sense of 'beautiful', only here in the NT), and its being *adorned with offerings*, an expression found in Greek writers. This fresh setting may have been intended by Luke to invest the discourse with the character of an authoritative public pronouncement on the last things for wide consumption, but if so it is impressionistic and slipshod, since the contents of the discourse apply largely to disciples.

ରୋର

5

the temple: For this see on 1⁹. Its dazzling effect from the outside is described by Josephus (*Ant.* 15.392ff.; *BJ* 5.210f., 222f.). Tacitus (*Histories* V, 5) emphasizes its opulence. In connection with this opulence Josephus (*Ant.* 12.249) mentions its very costly dedicatory offerings (*anathēmata*, Luke's word here). What these may have been is indicated in *Ant.* 15.402, 'Round about the entire temple were fixed the spoils taken from the barbarians (sc. Gentiles), and all these Herod dedicated, adding those which he took from the Arabs.'

6

As for these things which you see: As a pendent nominative this is more dramatic. It could conceivably refer to the buildings of Jerusalem as a whole; but the position of Jesus inside the temple (v. 4), and the emphasis on the temple (v. 5), make this unlikely. The sense is that despite its present solidity and splendour to the eye there will be a time when the temple will have disappeared from view.

the days will come when: A solemn introduction to prophecy (cf. 5^{35}; 17^{22}; 19^{43}; 23^{29}).

there shall not be left here one stone upon another: This, which provides the starting point for the discourse, could have been read out of a cryptic and isolated saying such as 'Not one stone shall rest upon another', which is applied to the city in 19^{44}. No reason is given for it here, and it is not clear whether the prediction is of a single event in the historical order, which could permit, as in earlier times, a subsequent restoration of the temple; or of a permanent destruction for the rest of time; or of an eschatological event preluding a new heavenly temple. None of these accords with the 'cleansing' of the temple (19^{45}), unless that is to be seen, not as its purification to serve for an indefinite period as a house of prayer, but as an act of judgment portending its destruction. How far the third would accord with a promise to destroy the temple and build another in three days (Mark 14^{58}, omitted by Luke) is difficult to say in view of the possibly garbled character of those words as false witness.

21^{7-9} = Mark 13^{3-7}
SIGNS OF WHAT IS TO COME

7*And they asked him, 'Teacher, when will this be, and what will be the sign when this is about to take place?' *8*And he said, 'Take heed that you are not led astray; for many will come in my name, saying, "I am he!" and, "The time is at hand!" Do not go after them. *9*And when you hear of wars and tumults, do not be terrified; for this must first take place, but the end will not be at once.'*

ဘ္ဘ

7

Teacher: didaskalos, here probably taken from Mark 13^1, is used by Luke for an address to Jesus only from those other than disciples. Even so, Luke is not able to remove, either here or in other sections (e.g. vv. 12ff., 28, 34ff.), all traces that the discourse concerns, and is spoken to, disciples.

when will this be, and what will be the sign when this is about to take place?: The problem posed by Mark's text is the connection between the temple and the end-of-the-world events. That there is a close connection is suggested by the double question in Mark 13⁴, 'When will these things (sc. the temple's destruction) happen?', and 'What will be the sign that all these things (the end events) will be accomplished (*suntelesthai* = 'consummated')? The question does not arise from what has been said, but from what is going to be said (Marxsen, *Mark the Evangelist*, p. 169). Such a connection is unforced only if the temple had come to occupy such a place in Jewish religion that, in an apocalyptically minded age, its disappearance would spell the end of all things. As the dwelling place of God and the symbol of his presence with Israel it gave the city its glory and not vice versa; and Zion, the mount on which it was situated, and with which it was sometimes identified, was not entirely synonymous with Jerusalem, the city. Destruction of temple and city were not necessarily identical (cf. Mark 14⁵⁸; John 2¹⁹; A. 6¹⁴); but they could be thought of as being so (cf. Baruch 1²; 2²⁶; Jos. *BJ* 5.195, Slavonic version, 'Jesus was crucified because he prophesied the destruction of the city and the devastation of the temple'). Matt. 24³ strengthens this connection with 'the sign of your coming and of the close (*sunteleias*) of the age'. Luke destroys it. His second question about when *this* (Greek 'these things' as in Mark 13⁴ᵃ, i.e. the destruction of the temple) will *take place* (a more factual word than Mark's eschatological term 'accomplished'), is simply a duplication of the first, and is barely intelligible. In Mark the sign requested is given in the words 'when you see the desolating sacrilege set up where it ought not to be' (Mark 13¹⁴, i.e. the temple profaned). In Luke it is given in the similar words 'when you see Jerusalem surrounded with armies', but this is tautologous; the sign of the destruction of the temple is the destruction of the temple. A possible reason for this confusion is that Luke was not really concerned about the destruction of the temple, but about the destruction of the city, which is to be prophesied in vv. 20–24, to which vv. 8–11 are a preface with vv. 12–19 intercalated. While the temple was important for Luke as a focus of Jewish piety (1–2), as the scene of Jesus' teaching (19–20) and as a proper resort of Christians (A. 1–5), its destruction would not be of special importance. For Christians had long worshipped elsewhere and otherwise, and had taken to themselves what was of value in Jewish worship. Its destruction was part of the destruction of the city, which was of ultimate significance.

8

Take heed that you are not led astray: This is an awkward transition in two respects. (i) It is relevant as a reply to a question about the temple's destruction only if that was thought of as the end, or the beginning of the end, and therefore as accompanied by features associated with the end. For *planān* = 'to lead astray' was a semi-technical and sinister term for deception and enticement to apostasy in the last days. One form of this was false prophecy and promises of deliverance with accompanying signs – cf. Deut. 13$^{1f.}$; Sibylline Oracles 3$^{63ff.}$; II Thess. 2$^{1-12}$, and the frequent reference in the Testaments of the Twelve Patriarchs to 'the spirit of error'. Several NT writers reflect this view, and interpret heresy in the church in the light of it (A. 20^{30}; I John 2^{18}; 4$^{1ff.}$; II Tim. 3$^{1ff.}$; II Peter 3$^{1ff.}$; Rev. 2$^{20ff.}$). Josephus uses similar language with a more political reference. Thus misleading (*planoi*) and deceiving men 'under the pretence of divine inspiration, fostering revolutionary changes, [they] persuaded the multitude to act like madmen, and led them out into the desert under the belief that God would give them tokens of deliverance' (*BJ* 2.258ff.; cf. 2.118; *Ant.* 18.4ff.; 20.97, 168ff.). (ii) With *you* it presupposes as the objects of this deception, not, as in Luke, a general audience of enquirers, but, as in Mark, a specific body of God's elect, here Jesus' disciples. Further, is the warning intended for those who, as disciples of the earthly Jesus, are, or will become, so fanatical in their apocalyptic expectations, that they will be prone to misunderstand any untoward occurrences, and need to learn the preliminary and penultimate character of what they will experience? Or is it now addressed to later Christians, whose experience of the delay of the parousia has so discouraged them that they need to be reassured that it will indeed take place, and to be offered some explanation of the delay?

many will come: That the deceivers will be many was also characteristic of descriptions of the anarchy of the last days.

in my name, saying, 'I am he!': These expressions, both obscure, may voice a double deception, or a single deception in two forms. Both presume that Jesus is no longer on earth, and that disciples will be expecting his return.

in my name: This could be a Christian addition, made in the light of Jesus as the messiah, to a conventional Jewish apocalyptic warning against a multiplicity of deceivers. It makes the special error no longer the seduction of Israel in general from loyalty to God and the Jewish faith, but that of the community of Jesus' disciples, who are now the true Israel of the last days. The preposition translated *in* here is not *en*, as in 9^{49}; 10^{17}, etc., but *epi* = 'upon'. The sense generally given is 'with the naming, requisition, of my name'. But if this means the use of Jesus' name in healing, the thought is not continued in *I am he!* If the name requisitioned is 'Jesus' (i.e. saying 'I am Jesus'), the warning would be unnecessary to personal disciples, who had known him, and could see through the claim. If the name requisitioned is 'Christ' or 'the Christ', it would either presuppose the later Christian use of 'Christ' as a proper name for Jesus, or an established claim to messiahship by Jesus in his earthly ministry, which is hardly borne out by the synoptic tradition, and would be an announcement of a second coming of the messiah, which was a Christian creation.

2 1$^{7-9}$

I am he!: Greek *ego eimi* = 'I am'. This is perhaps deliberately obscure and mysterious.[q] Without compliment it could be simply a means of self-identification – 'It is I', as in Mark 6^{50} – or an affirmative answer – 'I am (such)', as in Mark 14^{62}. But it is also found in the revelatory style of oriental cults, where the cult figure announces himself (or herself, as in the Isis cult) in this way. This may lie behind what is said of Theudas (A. 5^{36}) and Simon (A. 8^9) that they 'gave themselves out to be someone' (by saying 'I am'?). Some derive it from the OT periphrasis for God and his presence (cf. *ego eimi* as a mode of divine speech in the LXX of Exod. 3^{14}; Isa. 41^4; 46^4), and suppose it to have had some connection with the messiah. But if some kind of identification of the messiah with God is meant here, which is improbable, that would require *ego eimi ego eimi* = 'I am the I am'.

the time is at hand: This is perhaps added to explain Mark's cryptic 'I am'; Matthew adds to it 'the Christ'. This is the only place where *the time* (*ho kairos*) is used absolutely in L–A. If, with *at hand* (*ēngiken* = 'has drawn near', as in Mark 1^{15}), it has its technical meaning of the decisive moment of history determined by God (cf. Mark 1^{15}; 13^{33}; I Cor. 7^{29}; Rev. 1^3; 22^{10}), it serves here to brand as false the very expectation of an imminent end. But Luke may have had in mind what revolutionaries such as those in A. 5^{36}; 21^{38} would be likely to say, 'The time has come to strike.' According to the circumstances of time and place this could have a more or a less eschatological connotation.

Do not go after them: This is in place of Mark's impersonal statement, 'they will lead many astray', and matches the opening *Take heed.* It secures that the whole of v. 8 applies to those being addressed – surely disciples, though in view of v. 5 Luke cannot say so. The only two instances in A. of *go after* are in 5^{37} and 20^{30}, where it is a matter of following religious deceivers. By the time Luke was writing it had become clear that in general Christians had not followed such pretenders.

9

And when you hear of wars and tumults, do not be terrified: The exhortation continues with the command not to be terrified at the news of wars. The connecting link is that wars and disturbances belonged traditionally in apocalyptic with false prophets (cf. Rev. 16$^{12ff.}$); but the logic is not clear. If wars are preliminaries to the end, they are to be welcomed by those looking for the end. Perhaps the sequence of thought is, 'When you hear of wars, do not give way to the natural reaction of fear; for it is these which have to happen before the desired end; but even so the end does not follow immediately after them.' Luke's version is more factual and prosaic than Mark's, which is coloured by the language

[q] For the expression, see *TDNT* II, pp. 352, 398f., and R. Schnackenburg, *The Gospel according to St John* II, London 1980, pp. 79ff.

of Dan. 2[28]; 11[44]; Isa. 19[2]. His word *tumults* (*apokatastasia*, only here in the Greek Bible) has in Greek authors a semi-technical sense of 'political disturbances', 'insurrections' (so esp. in Vettius Valens, second century AD, who uses it along with 'deception' and 'revolution'). Luke may be thinking of pretenders whose announcement of themselves and of an appointed hour had led to such (cf. A. 5[37]; 21[38]), or of the battle for Jerusalem, when the people were deluded by false prophets (Jos. *BJ* 6.285ff.). *terrified* (*ptoeisthai* + 24[37]; 12[4]?) is more literary than Mark's 'alarmed'.

for this must first take place: This modifies Mark's quotation from Dan. 2[28], *dei genesthai* = 'it must be'. It is now a statement of fact about an extended period of history, when conflicts of a more local kind, which the audience will be in a position to hear about, will eventually give place to a more universal strife and disaster (vv. 10–11). The events of this period are to happen *first*. Does this mean before the events of vv. 20–24, or before the end? Probably the latter, as v. 9b is a chiasmus – 'for this must take place first, but not at once the end' – and this gives *first* an emphatic position. It is a semi-technical term when applied to what comes before the end (cf. Mark 13[10]; II Thess. 2[3]).

but the end will not be at once: the end (*to telos*, only here in L–A) is also a technical word for the final consummation of all things in the divine plan (cf. Mark 13[7]; Matt. 24[6]; I Cor. 15[24]; I Peter 4[7]). *at once* for Mark's 'not yet' stresses that these events are preliminary, and are not even the immediate preliminaries to the end.

21[10-19] = Mark 13[8-13]
SUFFERINGS AND SECURITY OF DISCIPLES

[10] *Then he said to them, 'Nation will rise against nation, and kingdom against kingdom;* [11] *there will be great earthquakes, and in various places famines and pestilences; and there will be terrors and great signs from heaven.* [12] *But before all this they will lay their hands on you and persecute you, delivering you up to the synagogues and prisons, and you will be brought before kings and governors for my name's sake.* [13] *This will be a time for you to bear testimony.* [14] *Settle it therefore in your minds, not to meditate beforehand how to answer;* [15] *for I will give you a mouth and wisdom, which none of your adversaries will be able to withstand or contradict.* [16] *You will be delivered up even by parents and brothers and kinsmen and friends, and some of you they will put to death;*

¹⁷you will be hated by all for my name's sake. ¹⁸But not a hair of your head will perish. ¹⁹By your endurance you will gain your lives.'

Some such title as the above is required by the contents of this section, which clearly concern, and are addressed to, disciples, though Luke's generalizing of the audience in v. 5 prevents him from saying so. In Mark 'For nation will rise . . . famines' (Mark 13⁸) belongs with 'wars and rumours of wars' (Mark 13⁷); and only with 'But take heed' (Mark 13⁹) does he pass from general statement to particular address. This is not so in Luke's revision. By omitting Mark's 'For', and providing a fresh introduction, *Then he said to them*, he distinguishes the world-wide internecine strife and its attendant horrors (vv. 10–11) from the previous insurrections (v. 9) as following after them; and he makes of these a framework for the trials of the disciples with *But before all this* (v. 12). The intercalating and dating of the disciples' sufferings in this way are awkward, and indicate that Luke is editing Mark here. He does so in such a way as to bring the disorders of vv. 10–11 into closer connection with the fall of Jerusalem in vv. 20–24, and to place the persecutions of the disciples, which is to be one of his concerns in A., before those events. The subject matter of vv. 10–19 is the same as that of Mark 13⁸⁻¹³, with the exception of v. 18 and the lack of any equivalent of Mark 13¹⁰; and it is in the same sequence. Along with considerable similarity of wording there are considerable differences; but these can probably be put down to Luke's editing.

෴

10–11

Luke's revision here is literary. Verse 11 is written with matching parallels. *earthquakes* were a regular part of the apocalyptic scenario, though also a feature of historical records, and *great*, added by Luke, was a conventional adjective with them (cf. A. 16²⁶; Rev. 6¹²). The conjunction *famines and pestilences* (*limoi kai loimoi*, in reverse order in some mss), in place of Mark's 'famines' only, was a well-worn assonance in Greek writers from Hesiod onwards. Luke's addition *terrors* (*phobētra* + +) was a bogey word used by Hellenistic writers for fearful objects which present themselves to the imagination of the sick. Along with his further addition *great signs from heaven* it could also have a historical rather than eschatological reference, as monstrosities and celestial portents were a not uncommon feature in ancient history writing (Dio Cassius 51.17.5 is typical), and they are mentioned at the siege of Jerusalem not only by Josephus (*BJ* 6.288f.) but also by Tacitus (*Histories* V. 13). By omitting the eschatological terminology of Mark 13^{8c}, 'this is but the beginning of the birth pangs', Luke presents these events as part of secular history.

12–19

Taylor (*Third Gospel*, pp. 106f.) notes that, with the exception of vv. 16–17, the tone of vv. 12–19 is very different from the unrelieved gloom of Mark 13^{9-13}, and he accounts for this by Luke's use of a non-Markan source here, the optimism of which he has reduced by inserting vv. 16–17 from Mark. The evidence can be interpreted differently, that Luke has revised Mark freely with reference to the success story he is to tell in A., and that in using the Markan text for his own purposes he has not been able to avoid all contradictions. The warnings in Mark 13^{9-13} presuppose a situation after Jesus' death of a universal mission of the gospel, which has already reached beyond Palestine, since Christians will be handed over to the heathen and not simply to the Sanhedrin, or turned out of synagogues. They are still, however, couched partly in impersonal terms used for the description of the end events (Mark $13^{10, 12, 13b}$), and it is not clear how the mission is related to those events, except that it takes place before them. The whole section will have been of great importance to Luke – hence, perhaps, his willingness to repeat what has already been said in 12^{11-12} – for it must have played some part in prescribing the form and content of A. An explanation of some of his differences from Mark here could be that he has revised Mark with the kind of phraseology he uses in narrating the experiences of Christians in A.

12

Luke does not give any examples in A. of Christians being examined by local synagogues, though he refers to Paul's harassment of them as having been 'throughout their synagogues' (A. 9^2; 22^{19}). In Mark the emphasis is on arraignment and witness before courts, in Luke on oppression and imprisonment, which corresponds to the frequent reference to imprisonment in A. In Luke's revision all this will happen *for my name's sake* (Mark 'for my sake' – for this pregnant use of 'the name', see on 9^{49}). 'In the early chapters (of Acts) . . . the story is told of a great struggle between the Disciples and the Jewish authorities, which centred in the use of the name of Jesus' (*Beginnings*, V, p. 132). This struggle was continued, first through the agency of Paul as persecutor, and then in his own person as a Christian (cf. A. 4^{7-18}; $5^{28, 41}$; 9^{10-29}; 21^{13}, and the frequency of 'the name' in these passages).

13

This will be a time for you to bear witness: This succinct statement of the opportunities for Christians on trial could be Luke's substitute for Mark 13^{10}. For that breaks the sequence of thought in the section, and is obscure. It could mean that the gospel (a word Luke avoids in his first volume and has only twice in A.) is determined temporally ('first') by relation to the end time, and its preaching precedes the suffering of the disciples; whereas in L–A it is determined spatially by relation to the ends of the earth (24$^{47f.}$; A. 1^8), and the sufferings accompany, and are caused by, its preaching. But both punctuation and meaning of Mark 13^{10} are in doubt. 'to all the nations' could go with what precedes ('as a witness to them and to all the nations'), or with what follows ('first must the gospel be preached to all the nations'). If for Luke it was the latter, and he took 'as a witness to them' closely with what precedes, he could have produced his statement in v. 13 as a terse equivalent. But the meaning of v. 13 is also doubtful. *This will be a time* renders a single Greek word *apobēsetai*, a nice classical form (+ Phil. 1^{19} LXX) meaning 'it will turn out as', 'it will have as its result'. *to bear witness* is, as in Mark 13^9, *eis marturion* = 'for witness'. L. Hartman[r] argues that *marturion* does not refer to the act of witnessing, which is *marturia*, but to the witness borne, and that the sentence means either (i) that the persecution undergone by disciples will turn out to be a testimony to them, speaking for their cause before God's throne at the judgment, and against their enemies; or (ii) with the verb used impersonally, that the result will be that God, or the Son of man, will bear witness to them (cf. 12^8, and possibly A. 7^{55}). The reversal indicated by the verb will then be that, whereas they are brought before tribunals on charges proffered against them, this will turn into a favourable judgment on them by God. This interpretation would be more convincing if in the Greek *for you* followed rather than preceded 'for witness'. The alternative is to give *marturion* the sense of the act of bearing witness (as perhaps in A. 4^{33}, the only instance of it in A.). In that case the connection between v. 13 and v. 14 would be closer. The disciples on trial will be given the necessary speech and wisdom for bearing witness, which act, as in Mark 13^{9c-10}, would be related to the preaching of the gospel.

14

This injunction to disciples on trial introduces (*therefore*) the theme of *apologia* or defence, which is a major theme in A. For the progress of the Christian mission is accompanied there by a series of public judicial scenes, in which representative figures – Peter and John (chs. 3–5), Stephen (chs. 6–7), and finally and principally Paul (chs. 13–28) – face charges from the authorities of proclaiming either heresy, which would overturn the tenets of Judaism, or sedition, which threatened the stability of the Pax Romana; and in Paul's case both. What distinguishes this verse from Mark 13^{11} is that it uses the technical language of *apologia*.

Settle it in your minds: In Greek *thete* (= 'place') *en tais kardiais* (= 'in your hearts', i.e. 'minds'). This is very emphatic, and could well be Lukan – cf. the

r *Testimonium Linguae*, ConjNeot 19, 1966, pp. 57ff.

identical expression in A. 5⁴ = 'determine', the same verb with 'in the spirit' (A. 19²¹), and the solemn addition to Mark in 9⁴⁴ (the same Greek verb).

to meditate beforehand: *promeletān* + +, a classical and Hellenistic word (not LXX), found in Aristophanes for practising a speech beforehand. In Greek law a lawyer could be employed to write a speech beforehand, which the client could learn by heart.

to answer: Greek *apologeisthai*, a technical term for defence at law, found only in L–A in the NT.

15

The defence of Christianity on trial consists not simply in the rebuttal of specific charges, but in using the occasion for inspired utterance, commending the message as the hope of Judaism and of mankind. This can be called 'speaking in the name of Jesus' (A. 4¹⁷ᶠ·; 5²⁸, ⁴⁰). Hence the urgent injunction here not to rely on their own intellectual or rhetorical capacities, but on spiritual assistance. The assertion of the earthly Jesus here that he will – presumably in some future undefined state or sphere, and by undefined means – provide this assistance, and be the author of the apostolic speech, is unique in the synoptists. The nearest parallels are Matt. 28²⁰, but spoken by the risen and exalted Lord, and Matt. 11²⁸; 18²⁰, spoken by the earthly Jesus as the present or future Wisdom of God. In view of the emphasis on the Spirit in this Gospel and in A. – including the Spirit as empowering Christians in their defence (A. 4⁸; 5³²) – it is remarkable that Luke, if he is following Mark, has not reproduced from him the promise that the Holy Spirit will be the author of the disciples' speech on such occasions (Mark 13¹¹, one of the very rare references in Mark to the Holy Spirit and its operations). This, together with a supposed Semitic colouring of v. 15 as evidence that it is a more primitive form of the saying than Mark's (see Barrett, *Holy Spirit*, pp. 130ff.), has led to the judgment that Luke is reproducing a non-Markan source here, and perhaps throughout this section. But whatever its origin v. 15 cannot be called more primitive than its equivalent in Mark 13¹¹. It is elegantly constructed, with a relative clause (*which*), and with *mouth* and *wisdom* matched chiastically with *withstand* and *contradict*. *mouth* (*stoma* = 'speech') is a classical poetic usage (cf. 19²²), and could be so here in conjunction with *wisdom*, which is rare in the gospels, but for Luke is the possession of John and Jesus (2⁴⁰, ⁵²), and of the Seven (A. 6³, ¹⁰; cf. 7¹⁰). And whereas in Mark 13¹¹ it is not said that the Spirit-inspired speech will be successful, here this is said most emphatically, and in language which reflects the outlook of A. That the opponents *will not be able to withstand* recalls what Luke writes of Stephen in A. 6¹⁰. *contradict* (*anteipein* + A. 6¹⁴ of the apostles before the authorities) is a regular classical and Hellenistic word for 'gainsay'. *adversaries* (*hoi antikeimenoi*, cf. I Cor. 16⁹; Phil. 1²⁸) is found elsewhere in the gospels only in Luke's own comment in 13¹⁷. The relation between the Spirit and the exalted Jesus is not worked out systematically in A. (as it is in John 14–16), but it is nevertheless close, and is expressed by the fact that they both do the same things. Both stand behind the universal mission of the church (24^{49}; A. 1$^{2, 8}$), the reception of the Gentiles (A. 10^{14}, if 'Lord' means 'Jesus', 10^{19}), the conversion of Paul and the direction of his destiny (A. 9$^{5, 17}$; 18^{9}; 23^{11}; 20$^{23ff.}$), and the mission from Antioch (13$^{2, 47}$). In A. 16$^{6-8}$ the Spirit as the director of the missionary movement is followed by the unique combination 'the spirit of Jesus' (cf. perhaps A. 7^{56}, Jesus the exalted Son of man as the source of Stephen's inspired speech). In view of these considerations it is not impossible that Luke has himself framed this verse, and that having already included from another source (L?) a promise that the holy Spirit will teach the disciples what to say in defence (12$^{11f.}$), he has here deliberately rewritten Mark 13^{11} to make Jesus, the speaker, their promised instructor in his future exalted state.

16–18

The extremity of the opposition to the disciples is now stressed by further instances; v. 16 is connected by *de kai*, to be rendered by 'furthermore' rather than by *even* (RSV). Luke, however, mitigates somewhat the severity of Mark's statements, perhaps because they do not accord completely with the picture to be painted in A., where the Christian message is gladly received by many, and the apostles are opposed by the authorities but find favour with the people.

16

by parents and brothers and kinsmen and friends: A stylized summary of what Mark puts more dramatically, but also more impersonally. For the last three together cf. 14^{12}. *friend* is, apart from Matt. 11^{19}, confined to Luke of the synoptists, and is frequent in A. The hatred will extend from the public to the private sphere. In the OT such hostilities in the family can be seen as a sign of deep-seated corruption, and of judgment (12$^{52f.}$; Mic. 7$^{5f.}$; I Enoch 100^2). In II Tim. 3$^{1ff.}$ they are associated with the last times, as probably here in Mark. In 14^{26} family divisions are contemplated as coming about through the confession of Christ.

some of you they will put to death: Luke qualifies the wholesale slaughter pictured in Mark 13^{12}. *they*, the authorities, will kill some of those delivered to them by kinsmen. In A. only the deaths of Stephen and James are recorded, though Paul is said to have been responsible for others (A. 26^{10}).

17

you will be hated by all for my name's sake: The hatred extends to the widest possible sphere. The presuppositions of this are that the gospel in some measure touches all men, and is such as to arouse the antagonism of all men, so that the disciples and the rest of the world are in opposition (cf. A. 28^{22}; John 15$^{18-24}$; 17^{14}).

18

not a hair of your head will perish: An OT expression for complete immunity, a hair representing what is infinitesimal (I Sam. 14^{45}; II Sam. 14^{11}; I Kings 1^{52}). In A. 27^{34} Luke puts it into the mouth of Paul, and there is a somewhat similar expression in 12^7. Why Luke should have put it into the mouth of Jesus here is difficult to say. It stands in plain contradiction to Mark, and to any version in which the threats to the disciples of harm and death were really meant. It is intelligible here only if spiritualized to mean that even in death they will remain essentially unharmed because protected by God. This is an unlikely meaning (but see v. 19). It is, perhaps, an expression of Lukan optimism, and a somewhat exaggerated preparation for the frequent escapes of Christians from danger through divine overruling (A. 5^{19-26}; 12^{11}; $14^{19f.}$; $16^{25ff.}$; $18^{9f.}$; $19^{23, 30ff.}$; $20^{3, 19, 23}$; $23^{12ff.}$; 26^{17}; $27^{22ff.}$.).

19

By your endurance you will gain your lives: The conclusions of the section in Mark and Luke are plainly on the same note, though they differ typically both in form and content. Mark ends with impersonal statement, Luke continues with direct personal address. Mark ends with a verb *hupomenein* = 'to remain', 'to wait', which is used in the LXX for hope (in God), to convey an eschatological promise that whoever is found waiting (on God? hoping in God?) at the end (time) will secure salvation (deliverance) from God. For Luke this verb means 'to remain behind' (2^{43}; A. 17^{14}), and he has the equivalent noun *hupomonē*. This is a late Greek word, only occasionally with the meaning of 'patience'. It is also related to hope in Paul (Rom. 8^{25}; I Thess. 1^3), and with special reference to the endurance of sufferings (Rom. 5^3; II Cor. 1^6; 6^4). Here the immediate background is probably the usage in IV Maccabees, where it is an important word, coupled in Stoic fashion with *andreia* = 'courage', and denotes the heroic *endurance* of the spiritual athlete in the face of torture, and wins the prize of everlasting life (IV Macc. 9^9; 17^{12}). This probably determines the choice of the verb here, *ktāsthai* = 'to win as a prize'. Schuyler Brown argues for 'perseverance' in the corporate sense of remaning Christians and not apostasizing, but the note is more moral than eschatological – 'it is by your fortitude that you will win the prize of your souls'; cf. Paul's exhortation in A. 14^{22}, which probably expresses Luke's view. Even so *ktēses tas psuchas humōn* = 'you will obtain your lives (souls)' is ambiguous. It could mean either 'you will escape death', or 'you will possess your souls (in the kingdom)', according to the literal or spiritual understanding of the proverb in v. 18.

---

s *Apostasy and Perseverance in the Theology of Luke*, Rome 1969, pp. 48ff., 114ff.

^{20}*But when you see Jerusalem surrounded by armies, then know that its desolation has come near.* ^{21}*Then let those who are in Judea flee to the mountains, and let those who are inside the city depart, and let not those who are out in the country enter it;* ^{22}*for these are days of vengeance, to fulfil all that is written.* ^{23}*Alas for those who are with child and for those who give suck in those days! For great distress shall be upon the earth and wrath upon this people;* ^{24}*they will fall by the edge of the sword, and be led captive among all nations; and Jerusalem will be trodden down by the Gentiles, until the times of the Gentiles are fulfilled.'*

This section is the heart of the discourse in Mark, and probably in Luke also. In Mark it starts from 'the desolating sacrilege' (*to bdelugma tēs erēmōseōs* = 'the detestable thing that causes the desolation (of the holy place)', or 'the abomination which appals'). This phrase appears first in Dan. 9^{27}; 11^{31} (cf. I Macc. 1^{54}) with reference to the installation by Antiochus Epiphanes of the altar and rites of the Olympian Zeus in the temple (168 BC). It became an apocalyptic code word for the extremity of profane evil, the anti-God force, and may have been reapplied to the image of Caesar which P. Petronius was ordered (*c.* AD 40) to erect in the temple (though the order was not carried out). When personalized, as in Mark 13^{14}, it referred to the anti-God figure, who would herald the final conflict between God and evil (cf. II Thess. 2$^{3-10}$; I John 2$^{18,\ 22}$; 4^3, where it takes the Christian form of the Antichrist; Rev. 17ff.). Since the expression originated with the profanation of the temple, it connects in Mark with the initial question about the temple (Mark 13$^{1-4}$), and it establishes Mark's discourse as apocalyptic throughout. The appearance of 'the desolating sacrilege' initiates the final tribulation, hitherto held back, and this involves all the elect, until their sufferings are brought to an end by the appearance of the Son of man. What stands here in Luke is very different – the desolation of Jerusalem, which is divine vengeance in fulfilment of scripture; the death or captivity of its inhabitants, which introduce a period of Gentile rule and anarchy, with Jerusalem remaining a ruin; and the redemption of the disciples at the coming of the Son of man.

How are these two versions related? For, along with these very considerable differences, there is also a similar sequence of sentences, and at some points close agreement in wording.

Mark 13¹⁴⁻²⁰	Luke 21²⁰⁻²⁴
v. 14. *But when you see* the desolating . . .	v. 20. *But when you see* Jerusalem . . . desolation . . .
then let those who are in Judea flee to the mountains . . .	v. 21. *Then let those who are in Judea flee to the mountains* . . .
v. 15. let him who is . . . *not enter* . . .	let those who are . . . *not enter* . . .
v. 17. *alas for those who are with child and for those who give suck in those days*	v. 23. *Alas for those who are with child and for those who give suck in those days*
v. 19. For . . . there will be . . .	For . . . shall be . . .

Taylor (*Third Gospel*, pp. 101ff.) argues for Luke's dependance here on a non-Markan source (L), which he has later supplemented from Mark in vv. 21a, 23a, though he also brackets *But when you see* and *then know* (v. 20) as possible replacements from Mark of what originally stood in the source. Dodd (*More NT Studies*, pp. 69ff.) reaches similar conclusions on the grounds (i) that without vv. 21a, 23a Luke's version would be a homogeneous unit made up of rhythmical couplets in Semitic style and parallelism; (ii) that v. 21a is clearly an insertion, since the proper apodosis to *when you see* is *then know*, and this leaves the apodosis from Mark, *Then let those . . . flee to the mountains* hanging in the air; and *those who are inside the city* and *enter it* should grammatically refer to *Judea*, whereas the sense requires that they refer to *Jerusalem*; (iii) that *surrounded by armies* is so colourless that it does not have to be taken as a prophecy after the event of the fall of Jerusalem in AD 70; and (iv) that the language of vv. 23b–24 is conventional LXX language for the destruction of Jerusalem, and argues a non-Markan source.

These arguments are not conclusive. If Luke was using a non-Markan version of the discourse here he will have preferred its historical to Mark's apocalyptic account. In that case it would be difficult to explain why he should have edited in such wooden fashion a homogeneous unit by the gratuitous insertion of sentences and phrases from Mark which add nothing vital to it. Further, the supposed non-Markan unit is not homogeneous. Like Mark's it begins in the second person and passes awkwardly into the third. Nor is it entirely rhythmical. *Jerusalem surrounded by armies* and v. 22 are prose statements, largely in Lukan language. The grammatical awkwardness in v. 21 could perhaps be better accounted for as a not wholly successful attempt to adapt Mark's text to the conditions of the assault on Jerusalem. It remains open, therefore, to consider Luke's version as a whole as his historicizing revision of Mark's apocalyptic programme.

But when you see is probably taken from Mark, for its somewhat esoteric tone is more appropriate to the dark mystery of the abomination 'set up where it ought not to be' than to the factual identification of the mystery with *Jerusalem surrounded by armies.* So also *its desolation* could have been derived from Mark's 'desolating sacrilege', which literally translated is 'the sacrilege of desolation'. The word *desolation* (*erēmōsis*), could also mean 'desertion', and this sense may be present here, and may be continued in v. 21a, where the language, taken from Mark, echoes the flight to the mountains, and the abandonment of all possessions, required in the crisis brought about by Antiochus Epiphanes (I Macc. 2²⁸; 1⁵⁴). In Luke the first is taken over as applying to the conditions of an attack on Jerusalem. The second is rewritten to fit those conditions and to express the extremity of the city's desertion. Before continuing with Mark's reference to particular hardships involved Luke supplies an interpretation of that extremity in terms of divine purpose (v. 22).

Luke then passes (vv. 23b–24) to a description of the destruction of the city itself. It begins, as Mark's description of the final tribulation, with *For* (there) *shall be*, and what follows is a rhythmical unit of three couplets, partly but not wholly in scriptural language, and more historical and less apocalyptic than Mark's in content. The first couplet, v. 23b, gives the human and the divine aspects of the destruction. It will be *great distress upon the earth* (land?), and also the execution of judgment on Israel. The second couplet, v. 24a, gives the issue (of the siege?) as slaughter and captivity. The third couplet, v. 24b, states the permanent consequences of the destruction, and is built round the word *nations* ([*ta*] *ethnē* = Gentiles), already introduced in v. 24a. Jerusalem will be permanently in subjection to Gentiles throughout a period called *the times of the Gentiles.* This striking expression is clearly of great importance. It comes as the climax of the oracle on Jerusalem, and interprets her destruction by placing it in the context, not of the parousia, but of a certain scheme of history.

20

But when you see ... then know: Marshall (p. 772) suggests for Mark 13¹⁴ the sense 'When you see the desolating sacrilege . . . then let the reader (of Daniel) understand (that it is being fulfilled)'. If that is correct, Mark's statement may have influenced Luke, *then know* being an equivalent to 'let the reader understand'.

surrounded by armies: The language belongs to that of historical statement rather than of prophetic doom. *stratopedon* = 'army' occurs only here in the NT, and in the LXX, apart from Wisd. 12⁸, only in the Maccabean books and the prose account of an attack on Jerusalem in Jer. 34¹; 41². The present participle could mean 'in the process of being surrounded' (i.e. for siege), which would still allow escape (contrast Jos. *BJ* 7.304, where the wall built by the Romans precluded it). Mark's 'the desolating sacrilege' was only intelligible from Daniel, as even Matt. 24¹⁵ has to make clear. Luke would be likely to avoid it as unintelligible to his readers, or, if intelligible, as conveying a wrong identification of historical and apocalyptic events. If the statement here refers to the Roman assault on Jerusalem in AD 70, it will be the only explicit reference in the NT to an event which was so catastrophic for the Judaism of the time that any contemporary historian at all concerned with the Jews must have mentioned it. This would be especially so for Luke, for whom it was no ordinary happening, but one which removed a principal landmark of Judaism. In the perspective of L–A Jerusalem is the holy city of Jewish worship, a home of Christian believers and the centre from which the church spreads, but also the enemy of God (13³⁴), and doomed as guilty of the death of Jesus (9³¹, ⁵¹; 13³³; 19³⁷⁻⁴⁴). For this it is called to repentance by apostles, but refuses to repent, and becomes the persecutor of the Christians, and is responsible for the fate of Paul. Its destruction eventually resolved the mixed situation of the early years of the church, with believers and unbelievers living side by side in her, and distinguished the church as separate from her, and as the inheritor of her privileges.

its desolation: This word in Greek, *erēmōsis*, could also mean 'destruction' (cf. Jos. *BJ* 6.437, of Babylon), but is found in the NT only here and Mark 13¹⁴/ Matt. 24¹⁵, where it is from Daniel, 'the desolating sacrilege' being in Greek 'the sacrilege of desolation'.

21

let those who are inside the city depart,
and let not those who are out in the country enter it: Luke has already included an equivalent of Mark 13¹⁵⁻¹⁶ at 17³¹. Here he may have rephrased Mark's injunctions to instant flight in face of the appearance of the anti-God figure to adapt them to the conditions of ancient warfare. It was customary on the approach of enemy troops for the rural population (*in the country*, in Greek the plural of *chōra* = 'land', + A. 8¹) to take refuge within the city walls. It is, therefore, an

expression of the dire situation that even the city's own inhabitants are to desert her (*depart, ekchōrein* + +, a classical and Hellenistic prose word for strategic withdrawal). Dodd's suggestion (*More NT Studies*, p. 77) that it has here a special sense of 'secede from the community' (Num. 16⁴⁵) fails to provide the necessary antithesis to *enter it*.

22

This is a very important statement at this point in the discourse, and would seem to have been provided by Luke himself – the genitive of the article with the infinitive to express purpose is Lukan; *to fulfil* (*pimplanai* = 'to fill') is, apart from Matt. 22¹⁰; 27⁴⁸, confined to L–A in the NT (though in the sense of 'to complete', as probably here), as is also *all that is written*, cf. 18³¹/Mark 10³³; 24⁴⁴; A. 13²⁹; 24¹⁴. If the fall of Jerusalem is not 'the end', and is to be distinguished from the parousia events, it is nevertheless no ordinary warfare, and it has to be interpreted in relation to the divine scheme of things. Hence the enemy is the instrument of God's judgment and retribution (*vengeance*, Greek *ekdikēsis*, a biblical word for this, see on 18⁷; for *days of vengeance* as the period of the punishment of Israel, Hos. 9⁷, and for similar expressions, Jer. 5²⁹; Deut. 32³⁵; Mic. 7⁴). This is then formally stated to be the completion of the divine purpose in scripture. For prophecies of the destruction, though not permanent, of Jerusalem, cf. Mic. 3¹²; Dan. 9²⁶.

23a

The special hardships of pregnant women and nursing mothers singled out in Mark 13¹⁷ in the context of sudden flight to the mountains (i.e. of eastern Judaea and Transjordan) are perhaps conventional apocalyptic, based on the barbaric treatment of women with young children by Antiochus (I Macc. 1⁶⁰f.). They do not have the same force in the context of the siege of Jerusalem, but Luke retains them, and uses them to introduce (*For*, v. 23b) the description of the destruction of the city itself.

23b–24

At this point in the discourse Mark refers, largely in the language of Daniel, to the final and greatest tribulation (*thlipsis*, a technical term of apocalyptic), which, if God did not shorten it, would not allow even any elect to survive. This would be quite unacceptable to Luke, and the statements here could be his own substitute for it in terms of the fall of Jerusalem. The language is that of the LXX, also primarily from Daniel, though that does not prevent its being from Luke's hand.

23b

great distress shall be upon the earth: distress (*anankē*) is a classical poetic word. It is not in Daniel, but is a frequent and less technical synonym for Daniel's *thlipsis*.

It is found in IV Maccabees for the torture inflicted by the tyrant, and in Josephus (*BJ* 5.571) for the straits of famine in the siege of Jerusalem. *upon the earth* is in Greek *epi tēs gēs*, which could mean 'upon the land', referring to Judaea or Palestine, and this would go better with *upon this people* (v. 24). But this absolute use of *hē gē* to mean the land of Palestine is not found elsewhere in L–A (except possibly 4²⁵), and in v. 25 it clearly means 'on the earth' (as also 18⁸; 2¹⁴). In this sense it is possibly suggested by the universality of the tribulation in Mark 13¹⁹ᶠ·, and sets the destruction of Jerusalem in the setting of world-wide disorder (vv. 10–11, 25–26).

wrath upon this people: This is the only instance of *wrath* (*orgē*) on the lips of Jesus. It is an OT expression for the divine judgment on human sin. It is to be manifested in the last days (Dan. 9²⁶ LXX), but could also be applied to the historical situation of the Maccabean crisis (I Macc. 1⁶⁴, 'And there was great wrath upon Israel'). *this people* (cf. Dan. 9²⁴) was a common term for Israel, generally in condemnation (cf. A. 13¹⁷).

24
The issue of the siege is slaughter and captivity – for this conjunction, cf. Dan. 11³³; Zech. 14²; Jos. *BJ* 6.429, 'When all who showed themselves had been either slain or made captive by the Romans'. *by the edge of the sword* (*stomati* = 'by the mouth') is an OT expression (e.g. Gen. 34²⁶ LXX), but is also found in literary works (e.g. Heb. 11³⁴). The captivity of Israel is a common and bitter theme of OT prophecy. For captivity *among all nations*, cf. Deut. 28⁶⁴; Zech. 7¹⁴. Josephus (*BJ* 6.418) records that the emperor Titus sent the prisoners in Jerusalem to Egypt and to the various provinces.

trodden down by the Gentiles: The Greek verb *pateisthai* is, with its compounds, frequently used in this way of Jerusalem, as in Zech. 12³ LXX, which may be quoted here, Dan. 8²³; Ps. Sol. 17²⁵, 'Cleanse Jerusalem from the Gentiles who tread her down', I Macc. 3⁴⁵, 'the holy place trodden underfoot', II Baruch 67²; Rev. 11²; Jos. *BJ* 4.171, of the holy place trampled underfoot by the Zealots' occupation of the temple. It refers to 'the undisciplined swarming of a victorious army through a conquered city' (Bauer), and means contemptuous treatment. In some cases, e.g. in reference to the holy place, it could refer to defilement by Gentile feet.

the times of the Gentiles are fulfilled: This phrase (*kairoi ethnōn*, both nouns without the definite article, = 'times of Gentiles' is without parallel. It is suggested (*Beginnings* IV, p. 216) that the absence of the articles denotes a technical term, but the opposite is more likely (cf. v. 8, *the time*, as elsewhere). It may be noted that, alone amongst NT writers, Luke uses the plural *kairoi*, and its synonym *chronoi* = 'times', without article in a way that makes the precise meaning difficult to establish. So A. 17²⁶, 'allotted periods', A. 3¹⁹⁻²¹, 'times of refreshing . . .

times for establishing', A. 1^7, 'times and seasons' in contrast to I Thess. 5^1, 'the times and the seasons'. This may reflect Luke's habit of mind, and the phrase here may be his own creation, suitably vague, but suggestive for his purpose. It is Jewish in perspective, with the division of mankind into Jews and Gentiles. A possible background is in Daniel, where there appears for the first time in the OT a theory of history, with divinely appointed periods for nations, the last of which involves the destruction of the city and the temple (Dan. 2^{21}; $7-8$; 9^{24-27}). This theory is, however, specific, and has individual Gentile kingdoms succeeding one another; but the mysterious expression in Dan. 12^7, 'a time, two times and half a time' (LXX 'a time and times and half a time') for the length of the period of 'the shattering of the power of the holy people', at the end of which 'all these things would be accomplished', could have given rise to Luke's more general 'times of Gentiles'. By means of it Luke intercalates into the time scheme of (i) Israel, (ii) the fulfilment in Christ and the church, and (iii) the consummation of all things, which is that of most NT writers (cf. Matt. 28^{20}; I Cor. $15^{23f.}$; Eph. $1^{20ff.}$), the end of historical Israel and divinely appointed Gentile epochs. In this way he makes room in the apocalyptic programme for the period in which he and his readers are living. The Gentiles here are not, as generally in Jewish eschatology, the objects of divine judgment, nor as in Mark 13^{10}, Acts and Rom. $9-11$, the objects of the church's evangelization, but the instruments of divine punishment within the divine plan of history. It is not indicated when these times begin – they could have begun before the fall of Jerusalem, which could be evidence of them – nor how long they will continue before being *fulfilled*, i.e. 'completed'. They are introduced here not for their own sake, but to assert that Jerusalem's ruin will not be such as permitted a future restoration, for which there would be scriptural warrant (Zech. 14^{1-4}; Dan. 8^{13-14}), but permanent, since they themselves will be succeeded by the end (vv. 25–28). In this context there is no room for Mark 13^{21-23} (a curious doublet of Mark 13^{5-6}), since the elect are not involved in the city's destruction, and it is not they who will then be in danger of deception by false prophets, but the city's inhabitants (so Josephus passim).

21^{25-28} = Mark 13^{24-27}

THE CONSUMMATION

^{25}'*And there will be signs in sun and moon and stars, and upon the earth distress of nations in perplexity at the roaring of the sea and the waves, ^{26}men fainting with fear and with foreboding of what is coming on the world; for the powers of the heavens will be shaken. ^{27}And then they will see the Son of man* *coming in a cloud with power and great glory.* ^{28}*Now when these things begin to take place, look up and raise your heads, because your redemption is drawing near.'*

In Luke's version of the discourse there is a break here, because the original question in v. 7 about the destruction of the temple, though not the question in Mark 13^4 about the accomplishment of all things, has been answered, and some transition is necessary for the discourse to proceed. This is effected by *distress of nations* (v. 25), which picks up the threefold mention of *nations* (*Gentiles*) in v. 24, and in this way introduces a characterization of the intervening period of Gentile rule and of the life of the secular world between the fall of Jerusalem and the end. Luke has now reached his own times, and the future tenses of the verbs are no longer speaking prophetically of what is already past or present, but of what is really future. The picture is sombre and ominous because it borrows, adapts and supplements language in Mark designed for the last things and applies it to the historical order.

The section has basically the same sequence as Mark 13$^{24-27}$, cosmic catastrophes followed by the appearance of the Son of man. The chief difference is that Mark's version has poetic rhythm and Luke's is primarily prose. Taylor (*Third Gospel*, pp. 111f.) sees it as taken from a non-Markan source, where it was continuous with vv. 20–24, and as supplemented by Luke by the insertion of Mark 13^{25b-26}. It is, however, unlikely that Luke would have inserted Mark 13^{25b} as well as 13^{26} and so reproduced Mark's double reference to the heavenly bodies, especially as the second then has to come after an intervening statement about the inhabitants of the earth. It is more likely that Luke has summarized in v. 25a Mark's somewhat prolix description of the heavenly bodies (Mark 13^{24-25a}), and then matches it with a corresponding statement of disturbances on earth, which forms a chiasmus with it. Similarly, v. 28, following on the appearance of the Son of man, which is taken from Mark, could be Luke's equivalent for the gathering of the elect, which in Mark is the object of that appearance.

The biblical and poetic language in Mark 13$^{24-25}$ depicts the cosmic dissolution which follows the end of the great tribulation and is the immediate prelude to the Son of man's appearance. The same language is in v. 25 made to depict portents in the heavenly bodies themselves. Contemporary with this on earth is *distress*, which is also a biblical word with the sense of 'straits'. This sense is carried on with another biblical word, *perplexity*, and this perplexity is *at the roaring of the sea and the waves*, a common figure for instability and terror, both in the OT and outside it. This terror is further explicated (v. 26) in more prosaic terms as a despairing human apprehension of the future, and it is caused by heavenly portents. Here Luke seems to be referring to historical events not essentially different from those in vv. 10–11, 23–24, and his mode of expression may reflect a general pessimism in his time over chaotic conditions in parts of the Roman empire, which is one possible meaning of *hē oikoumenē* = 'the inhabited world'.

In Mark 13²⁶ 'And then' is precise, meaning the time of the dissolution of the heavenly bodies. In Luke the shaking of *the powers of the heavens* (v. 26b) is synonymous with the portents in them (v. 25a) and a reason for a period of terror among men (*for*), so that *And then* is imprecise, denoting some time in that period. Whenever that is, *they* (i.e. men) *will see the Son of man coming in a cloud with power and great glory*. In comparison with the detail in the rest of the discourse, this statement of its climax is curiously brief and muted. It sounds like a traditional formula, which required to be filled out from a previous understanding of who the Son of man is, and what his functions are. For *the Son of man*, see on 5²⁴. Some of the problems associated with the term may be seen here. (i) He is referred to as a known figure in the third person, and as if distinct from the speaker, though the evangelist identified them. If Jesus intended this identification, he would be investing his work and person with a future cosmic and ultimate significance and authority. (ii) According to some his *coming* is always to be interpreted as a coming, as in Dan. 7¹³⁻¹⁴, to God to receive at his hands vindication and the kingdom to be exercised. Here his coming is clearly from heaven in the sight of men on earth, and with the kingdom already received to exercise. (iii) Luke's *in a cloud* for Mark's 'in clouds' is a decisive alteration. The latter, derived from Dan. 7¹³, is a standard accompaniment of the Son of man as the vehicle on which he rides either to God or in his manifestation to men (cf. Mark 14⁶²; Rev. 1⁷). The former is the different symbol of the single cloud of divine glory or presence (cf. 9³⁴), and is presumably for Luke the same cloud as receives Jesus at his ascension, and in which, it is emphatically asserted, he will return from heaven to earth (A. 1⁹⁻¹¹). Thus, by this alteration Luke brings the apocalyptic climax of the discourse within the scheme of divine history he is to sketch in Acts.

In Mark the appearance of the Son of man is followed by, and has as its purpose, the assembly of the elect, and the last things are narrated, not for themselves, but for their positive issue as they affect God's chosen. This is missing in Luke. In its place (v. 28) a return is made, though awkwardly, to the personal address of vv. 12–20. The connection with what precedes is not strong, since it is not clear whether *these things* refers to the happenings from v. 20 onwards, or only from v. 25 onwards, nor, if the latter, how the disciples are to recognize when they are beginning. The despondency from which they are to *look up* is presumably not caused by the portents which strike terror to the rest of mankind, nor by the fall of Jerusalem, but by their treatment at the hands of men in the course of the Christian mission (vv. 12–19). *redemption* means the liberation from the oppressive conditions attending faithful witness in the world on the part of those addressed here, who can only be disciples.

∾

25

distress of nations: The Greek word *sunochē* has as its literal meaning 'holding firm' or 'constraint'; hence a better translation might be 'straits'. *nations* without the article may not have here the Jewish meaning of 'the Gentiles' *en masse*, but of the individual nations and peoples of the world, and taken with *upon the earth* may refer to world conditions.

in perplexity at the roaring of the sea and waves: The language here may show the influence of the same, or similar, passages in Isaiah as lie behind Mark 13²⁴⁻²⁵. *perplexity* is in Greek *aporia*, meaning not, as generally, 'the lack of', but 'at their wits' end at'; cf. Isa. 5³⁰, of the advance of the nations on Israel, 'like the roaring of the sea. And if one looks to the land, behold, darkness and distress' (LXX *aporia* = 'straits'), and Isa. 8²², 'they will look to the earth, but behold, distress (LXX *aporia*) and darkness, the gloom of anguish'. *roaring* (*ēchos*) and *waves* (*salos* = 'swell') are also found in the LXX in this connection (Ps. 65⁷).

26a

This is a continuation of the sentence in v. 25, but is in a strikingly different style, which is prose. It begins (*men fainting*) with a gen. abs. of *apopsuchein* + +, a classical and Hellenistic word, only once in the LXX in a different sense, which is followed by *with* (*apo* = 'from'), which governs *fear and foreboding*, a common literary combination, the latter word (*prosdokia* + A. 12¹¹) being followed by an objective genitive, *of what is coming on* (the participle of *eperchesthai*, apart from Eph. 2⁷; James 5¹, only in L–A in the NT) *the world* (*hē oikoumenē*, the secular word for 'the inhabited world', elsewhere in the gospels 2¹; 4⁵;

Matt. 24¹⁴, five times in A.). If this continuation of the sentence is from Luke's hand, so probably is that which it continues, v. 25b. Possibly there is reduced here to a single verse, and applied to the period of history before the end, the remarkable lamentation on the woes of the human race in Ecclus 40¹⁻¹⁰ (note there 'fear', 'foreboding' and 'swell').

27

with power and great glory: The manifestation through the Son of man is of the kingdom of God (cf. v. 31, where what is near is identified by Luke as 'the kingdom of God'), as the heavenly rule of God (*with great glory* = 'manifested in heavenly fashion'). It is exercised with full effect (*with power*). In Mark this full effect is seen in the gathering of the elect, either on the (renewed?) earth, or, as in I Thess. 4¹⁷, in the air. There is no mention of this in Luke, where the dissolution of the universe has no direct consequences for believers, and their relation to the Son of man is not that they will see him, but that they will stand before him (v. 36). The gathering of the elect was unlikely to commend itself to Luke as an image of the mission he is to describe in A., and there is no mention of it there.

28

Construction and vocabulary of this verse suggest that Luke has composed it. *When these things begin to take place* is a gen.abs. of the participle of *archesthai* = 'to begin'. *look up (anakuptein* + 13¹¹, in a literal sense) and *raise your heads (epairein tas kephalas* + +) are both literary figurative expressions for recovery from prostration caused by distress (for both cf. Jos. *BJ* 6.401, 1.629, Philo, *Against Flaccus* 160, *Creation of the World* 158).

your redemption is drawing near: cf. I Enoch 51², 'For in those days the Elect One shall arise, and he shall choose the righteous and the holy from among them. For the day has drawn near that they should be saved.' *redemption: apolutrōsis,* which in the NT need not have its technical sense of ransoming, or liberation through ransom, of prisoners or slaves. Nor does it have here the deeper meaning of deliverance from sin and death found in the Psalms and Paul.

21²⁹⁻³³ = Mark 13²⁸⁻³²
THE TIME OF THE CONSUMMATION

²⁹*And he told them a parable: 'Look at the fig tree, and all the trees; ³⁰as soon as they come out in leaf, you see for yourselves and know that the summer is already near. ³¹So also, when you see these things taking place, you know that*

the kingdom of God is near. ³²*Truly, I say to you, this generation will not pass away till all has taken place.* ³³*Heaven and earth will pass away, but my words will not pass away.'*

This section, consisting of an eschatological parable and two attached eschatological sayings, is clearly taken from Mark, though with editorial changes arising from obscurities in Mark or from Luke's different outlook.

The parable, particularly in Mark, is one of apocalyptic proof. *these things taking place* are as obvious and certain evidence of the proximity of *the kingdom of God* (supplied by Luke; Mark's 'is at the very gates' has no subject) as are the leaves on the trees for the proximity of summer. Precise interpretation depends on identifying *these things*, and here Mark, who has 'all these things', is obscure (see Marxsen, *Mark the Evangelist*, pp. 187f.). For Luke they are synonymous with *these things* which *begin to take place* (v. 28), and the parable is a reinforcement of v. 28 (which thus becomes an introduction to vv. 29-33 as well as a conclusion of vv. 25-27), and a further assurance to the disciples of their liberation. It hints that this will be a consequence of the Son of man's coming to exercise God's rule, or, possibly, a reversal of the position in which they are subject to rulers who are their judges (vv. 12-19) to one in which they themselves rule and judge (cf. 12³²; 22²⁹).

The parable is followed in v. 32 and v. 33 by two emphatic statements of the certainty of the consummation. Both could originally have stood on their own. In their present position they reinforce the lesson of the parable by defining further what is meant by *is near* (v. 31), and by further reassuring the disciples. The first (v. 32), introduced by the solemn *Truly, I say to you*, states that *this generation will not pass away till all has taken place.* Its interpretation depends on the meaning to be given here to *generation* (*genea*), and this is disputed (see below).

The second (v. 33) was perhaps attached to the first because of the common expression *pass away.* It provides an impressive climax to the discourse when the speaker pronounces in this way on his own words. Within the limitations of apocalyptic, with its somewhat impersonal thought and stilted language, it presents a very high christology, since Jesus affirms the ultimacy of his utterances over against the non-ultimacy of anything else (cf. such sayings as 12⁸; Mark 8³⁸; Matt. 5¹⁷; and of the risen Christ, Matt. 28¹⁸⁻²⁰). In this context *Heaven and earth will pass away* probably has a more than figurative sense (cf. Mark 13^{24f.}, contrast 16¹⁷), and this may be responsible for the saying's inclusion here. It is Jesus' utterances on the last things in particular that are immutable, and that survive the dissolution of the universe (cf. Mark 13²², 'I have told you all things beforehand', omitted by Luke). Luke's omission of Mark 13³² would then be understandable, since it appears to qualify Jesus' knowledge of the end and its signs, which have formed the subject matter of the discourse. Jesus' knowledge of the future abides (cf. 23²⁸ᶠᶠ·; 24⁴⁶⁻⁴⁹; A. 1³⁻⁵), nor is it limited by A. 1⁷, which goes no further than saying that the Father's secrets about times and seasons are not for communication to disciples.

בבב

31

the kingdom of God is near: That is, the kingdom or rule of God in its future, glorious and all-powerful form. This may be a correct interpretation of Mark's 'is at the very gates', for which RSV supplies 'he', i.e. the Son of man, as a subject, but which could well be 'the day', or 'the times' or 'the judgment'.

32

this generation shall not pass away: The usual meaning of *genea* = generation is 'those born (living) at a given time', the time being an imprecise and elastic period, generally reckoned to cover about thirty years. This is the sense in the majority of instances in the NT, and, with the possible exception of 16⁸, of all the instances in L–A. *This generation* will then be the generation contemporary with the speaker, and the statement here (cf. the similarly constructed statement in Mark 9¹, also interpreted by Luke with reference to the kingdom of God) will be a temporal one. This period will not have passed (*parerchesthai*, used of time means 'to pass') before *all* (*panta* = 'all things', the total divine plan, including the events mentioned in the discourse; Mark 'all these things') *has taken place.* For Mark, if he was writing *c.* AD 65, this could still be taken literally. For Luke, if he was writing after AD 70, with Gentile epochs to follow after the fall of Jerusalem, and with those addressed by Jesus still awaiting their liberation then, this could only be in error if taken literally. The question is then whether he has stretched the meaning of *genea* in order to preserve an authoritative word of Jesus and to apply it to his own time. Various suggestions have been made to avoid these difficulties – for a detailed discussion of them see Maddox, *The Purpose of Luke–Acts,* pp. 111ff. Marxsen (*Mark the Evangelist,* pp. 195f.) proposes for *genea* the meaning 'race', which it normally had in ordinary Greek, and for 'passed away' the meaning 'disappeared'; but apart from doubt whether the noun could have that meaning in this context, this could hardly make sense in itself – what would the disappearance of the Jews as a race be, apart from the disappearance of all races? Similar criticism would apply to the interpretation of Rengstorf (pp. 229f.), who, surely incorrectly, takes almost all the instances of *genea* in Luke to refer to the (sinful) Jewish people as such, and the statement here as an assurance that, despite their sin, they will not be totally rejected at the judgment. Leaney (p. 263) considers that Luke 'has forced it (*genea*) to bear the meaning "mankind" '; but not only is there no linguistic basis for this, but the sentiment that mankind will not disappear before the things which belong to God's purpose for mankind have had time to take place would hardly be meaningful. Ellis (pp. 246f.) sees Luke as countering expectations of an imminent end, but the context would suggest the opposite, viz. that the hearers need assurance that the end will indeed come (so Marshall, p. 780). He further notes that in the Qumran writings the 'last generation' was a term that could cover several lifetimes, and suggests that *this generation* is a designation for 'the generation of the end-signs'. 'The public revelation of the kingdom *is* just round the corner, but its calendar time is left indeterminate.' This is possible, though the time cannot be left wholly indeterminate if the words are to have force to a particular audience, and the saying is not to be reduced to the tautology that those who belong to the end times will see the end times.

CONCLUSION

34'*But take heed to yourselves lest your hearts be weighed down with dissipation and drunkenness and cares of this life, and that day come upon you suddenly like a snare;* 35*for it will come upon all who dwell upon the face of the whole earth.* 36*But watch at all times, praying that you may have strength to escape all these things that will take place, and to stand before the Son of man.*'

The conclusions in Mark and Luke differ widely in both form and content, and in ways which correspond to the differences between the two discourses throughout. In Mark the discourse constitutes Jesus' final instruction to disciples, and it ends with an artificial collocation of staccato sentences, and, in accordance with its general tenor, on a note of unrelieved eschatological tension. In view of the ignorance on the part of all but the Father of the time of the end, the hearers are given reiterated warnings, largely couched in parabolic language used elsewhere to urge watchfulness in face of the end, to be awake as doorkeepers for the arrival of the day or hour or time. In Luke Jesus instructs his disciples for the last time not here, but at the Last Supper (22^{14-38}), and the discourse is concluded by a rhythmical, sonorous paragraph made up of three carefully constructed sentences in high-flown language. Its teaching is less immediately eschatological and more in the nature of moral exhortation, though it succeeds in bringing the discourse to an end with what, surprisingly, is absent from Mark, viz. the final judgment (cf. Matt. 24^{37}–25^{46}; Rom. 14^{10}; II Cor. 5^{10}; I Peter 4$^{17f.}$). Since, with the omission of Mark 13^{32}, there is no mention of the universal ignorance of the time of the end, 'watching' is now given the moral meaning of constant preparedness for the judgment through godly living, and *that day* (v. 34), which in Mark is simply a synonym for 'the hour' of the master's coming, becomes the day of judgment.

The thought of the passage, despite its lofty diction, or perhaps because of it, is curiously indeterminate. Whether composed by Luke, or derived from current Christian instruction, it reveals his understanding of the whole discourse as primarily moral exhortation and encouragement, and suggests that similar passages in it (vv. 8b, 18–19, 28) are the result of his editing. Even so it does not fit well here, as it picks up neither the theme of *endurance* in the face of persecution (vv. 12–19) nor that of *redemption* (vv. 25–28). It begins from Mark's eschatological watchword *Take heed*, i.e. be on the alert for the unpredictable end (cf. 12$^{38-40}$), but does not continue with this, but with moral exhortation to disciples living in an unspecified period (during the Gentile times before the parousia?) not to be surprised by the day of judgment in a state of gross sinfulness (as can only merit condemnation?); and it reckons with the possibility that they may lapse into insensate drunkenness, literal or metaphorical, and into complete worldliness. This seems to waver between a description of a state of unreadiness for observing the signs of the coming times, and that of a state of sin, of which the day of judgment in its suddenness will allow no time to repent. This exhortation is then given its basis in the assertion that the judgment will be universal in its scope, and therefore inescapable, though why such an obvious assertion has to be made here is not clear.

The assertion of the certainty of universal judgment leads into the final exhortation, though the connection with *but* (possibly 'and') is not a strong one. This again begins from Mark 13^{33} with *watch* (*agrupneite* = 'keep awake'). It refers, however, not, as in Mark, to wakefulness as constant readiness for a parousia that may take place at any time of the day or night, but to wakefulness for constant prayer. The prayer is to have two objects, the relation between which is not clear. The first is the ability *to escape all these things that will take place*, i.e. the events prophesied in vv. 25–28, or, possibly, throughout the discourse. There has been, however, no suggestion in vv. 12–33 that disciples are those who are to avoid the tribulations that come upon men, or that they suffer at men's hands. Rather they are forewarned by Jesus of them, and are to survive them through God's deliverance; and it is doubtful whether the word rendered *escape* (*ekpheugein*) can be given the meaning 'to escape from' in the sense of 'to survive them'.

The second object of the prayer is the ability (through 'escaping' or 'surviving'?) *to stand before the Son of man*. From a stylistic point of view this is a highly fitting conclusion. It is also theologically fitting that the discourse should come to rest with a reference to the Son of man. Since it comes after the mention of the Son of man's cosmic appearance (v. 27) the reference can only be to what belongs with, or lies beyond, that appearance, which is the Son of man's exercise of the judgment; and this accords with the theme of the final judgment which Luke has imported into this last section.

ℬℬ

34–36

Taylor (*Third Gospel*, p. 112) argues from the appositeness of vv. 34–36 as a sequel to vv. 25–28 that they belonged to a non-Markan source, but they are significantly different not only from Mark, but from the rest of the discourse in its Lukan form. Gaston (*No Stone*, pp. 357f.) sees them as 'clearly a Lucan addition based on the eschatological exhortation of the Hellenistic Church, as the numerous parallels to I Thess. 5^{1ff.} show', while Bultmann's verdict (*History*, p. 119) is 'a quite late Hellenistic formulation with a terminology so characteristic and akin to Paul's that one would hazard a guess that Luke was here using a fragment of some lost epistle written by Paul or one of his disciples'. Whatever its origin, the passage has clear affinities with passages in the epistles representative of eschatological admonition (and possibly baptismal instruction) in the church (cf. Rom. 13¹¹⁻¹⁴; Eph. 5⁴⁻⁹; 6¹⁰⁻¹⁸; I Thess. 5⁵⁻⁹; I Peter 4³⁻⁸; Heb. 12²⁵⁻²⁸). The language of Isa. 24, especially vv. 16ff., may also have had some influence, and one may even compare exhortations to renunciation and repentance found in Hellenistic religion, e.g. in the (second-century AD) Hermetic tractate Poimandres, 27–28, 'O peoples, men of earth, who have given yourselves to drunkenness and sleep and to ignorance of God, be sober, and cease from intoxication and brutish sleep.'

That Luke himself has composed this conclusion is suggested by its construction and by the phraseology, which is more literary than any of the NT or OT parallels cited above. The opening sentence (v. 34) is a moral warning, divisible into three clausulae. Of these the first, *Take heed to yourselves*, is a Hellenistic construction confined to L–A in the NT, and could be Luke's version of the first verb in the double warning in Mark 13³³, '*Take heed, watch*'. In the second, *lest your hearts be weighed down with dissipation and drunkenness and cares of this life*, the verb, which stands first, is very rare in the LXX but common in Greek writers, where it is usually followed by 'with wine'. It is followed here by three nouns, *kraipalē* + + = 'hangover', *methē* + Rom. 13¹³; Gal. 5²¹ = 'drunkenness' (these two nouns are found in combination in Greek literature, as also the corresponding verbs in Isa. 24²⁰), and *merimnai biōtikai* = 'earthly cares', the adjective *biōtikos* (+ I Cor. 6³ᶠ·, not LXX) being a Hellenistic word with the meaning, from Aristotle onwards, of 'belonging to life in its earthly aspects'. In the third clause, *and that day come upon you suddenly*, the verb *ephistanai*, apart from I Thess. 5³; II Tim. 4², ⁶, confined to L–A in the NT, also stands first for emphasis, and *suddenly* translates *aiphnidios* (+ I Thess. 5³), and could have been suggested by the corresponding adverb *exaiphnēs* in Mark 13³⁶. The second sentence, v. 35, if it begins with 'For like a snare' (see below), is a statement of eschatological fact giving the basis of the previous warning (*for*). It is made emphatic by a high degree of assonance, with more than half the words beginning with, or containing, the Greek letter *pi* – in the Greek *hōs pagis epeiseleusetai gar epi pantas tous kathemēnous epi prosōpon pāses tēs gēs* – and by the comprehensive *all who dwell upon the face of the whole earth*. For this is a combination of two LXX expressions, viz. 'those who dwell upon the earth' = 'the earth's inhabitants' (cf. Jer. 25²⁹), and 'the entire surface of the earth' (Gen. 8⁹, for mankind A. 17²⁶). The highly structured third sentence, v. 36, is eschatological exhortation. It begins with the second verb in Mark's double warning (Mark 13³³), *agrupneite* = *watch*, and continues with the participle *praying* (*deisthai* in the sense 'to pray' is almost confined to L–A in the NT). This introduces an object clause, *that you may have strength* (*katischuein* + 23²³, Matt. 16¹⁸, but in the common LXX sense 'to prevail over'; in the reduced sense here it is probably chosen as a sonorous word in the context). *to escape* is in Greek *ekpheugein*, only here in the gospels, and elsewhere in the NT with a direct object Rom. 2³; II Cor. 11³³. *these things that will take place* is a Lukan expression (cf. 21⁷; A. 26²²; 27³³).

34

your hearts be weighed down with dissipation and drunkenness and cares of this life: The precise force of this language is not easy to determine. The 'heart' is 'the centre and source of the whole inner life' (Bauer, s.v. *kardia*). In the only LXX instance of its use with *bareisthai* = 'to be weighed down' (Exod. 7¹⁴) the meaning is that Pharaoh was spiritually hardened. The verb when used with 'wine' or 'sleep' (9³²) describes a state of insensibility, but the drunkenness here, especially when combined with *kraipalē* = 'carousing' or 'hangover', seems to be literal, as in Gal. 5^{21}, the list of sins which exclude from the kingdom (cf. also Rom. 13^{13}; I Thess. 5^6; Luke 12^{45}). In I Thess. 5^{3-7}, by a bewildering mixture of images, it is branded as that which prevents readiness for the day of the Lord, on the grounds that the day comes as a thief in the night, whereas Christians are not surprised by it since they are sober in belonging to the day and not the night, which is when men get drunk. In 12^{45} it goes with violence to one's fellows, which brings punishment in the judgment. In 17^{26-29} the judgment comes on those engaged in daily occupations, of which eating and drinking is one. In 8^{14} those who 'go on their way' and 'are choked by the cares and riches and pleasures of life' are those who do not produce the fruit of maturity required at the judgment.

that day: This expression for the day of judgment, or for the day of the Lord, is found again in L–A only at 10^{12} = Matt. 10^{15} 'the day of judgment'. It is probably taken from Christian teaching, where it is common – cf. I Thess. 5^{2-4}; II Thess. 2^2; I Cor. 3^{13}; II Tim. $1^{12, 18}$; 4^8.

34-35

like a snare; for it will come upon: Of the three variant readings here this is the least strongly attested. The weight of the mss evidence is fairly evenly divided between (i) 'like a snare. For it will come in upon . . .', and (ii) 'For like a snare it will come in upon . . .' These variations reflect uncertainty over how v. 35 continues from v. 34. In (i) *like a snare*, if it means 'unexpectedly' (so Bauer, s.v. *pagis*, but with no grounds given except the context here), repeats *suddenly* as characteristic of the day's coming. The element of suddenness could be also imparted to the description of the day as universal (v. 35) by the doubly compounded verb *epeiserchesthai* = 'to break in upon' (sc. mankind), as in its only occurrence in the LXX, I Macc. 16^{16}, where it means to break in suddenly upon an assembly. In (ii) *like a snare* describes how the day comes as that which is universal; but then it can hardly mean 'unexpectedly'. The usual form of that sentiment is that the day comes as a thief in the night (12^{39}; I Thess. 5^2; II Peter 3^{10}). Perhaps the thought is that the day will be universal because it will catch all men like a snare, though a snare is something into which men fall rather than something that comes upon them (but cf. Isa. 24^{18}, where men are caught by it). With either reading v. 35 is curious. It has the appearance of a parenthesis, making a transition from the thought of the suddenness of the day (v. 34) to the thought of surviving it (v. 36). As a statement it is platitudinous except when made (as in II Peter 3^{3-10}, though hardly here) to counter doubt about the coming of the parousia at all in view of its long delay. So Marshall (p. 783) interprets, 'Since the day of the Lord will affect all men, not even disciples can expect to escape from it if they are not ready'; but if, by definition, it affects all men, disciples will not be able to escape it, ready or not ready.

36

to stand before the Son of man: For the Son of man, see on 5²⁴. This is the most express statement in Luke of the Son of man's occupying the position of God in facing men as their judge, rather than that of facing God as men's advocate or as witness against them (9²⁶; 12⁸), or even as 'coming' as God's agent of salvation or destruction, and so as looking for faith or response from men (18⁸). It is thus similar to Matt. 16²⁷; 25³¹f., and could be Luke's statement in terms of the Son of man of the Christian conviction that Jesus had been exalted to the position of judge (A. 10⁴²; 17³¹; Rom. 2¹⁶; II Cor. 5¹⁰; II Tim. 4⁸). Judgment is also what is commonly conveyed by the preposition here *before* (*emprosthen*), as in 12⁸; I Thess. 2¹⁹; 3¹³; II Cor. 5¹⁰; Matt. 25³² (cf. Matt. 27¹¹ for *stand before* of Jesus judged by Pilate). But this cannot be the meaning here, since it is a consequence of the universal character of the coming day of judgment (v. 35) that all men will stand before the judge willy nilly for approval or condemnation; and this cannot be the special object of the disciples' prayer, nor in itself a mark of having obtained salvation. Hence *stand* must have the absolute sense of 'stand fast' i.e. through stedfastness emerge victorious after the conflict, as in Eph. 6¹³, 'having done all to stand' (cf. I Thess. 3⁸; II Thess. 2¹⁵), and *emprosthen* must have the sense of 'in the presence of'. The prayer will then be that they emerge through the judgment as those who have won the Son of man's approval; cf. I Enoch 63⁸⁻¹³, where the elect stand before the Son of man for salvation, while the sinners also stand before him, but are then made to pass away from his presence and given over to destruction; and II Thess. 1⁹, the punishment of eternal destruction and exclusion from the presence of the Lord. All this is Luke's equivalent in terms of the moral and spiritual struggles of the Christians in A. of the apocalyptic concept of the gathering of the elect in Mark 13²⁷, which he has omitted.

21³⁷⁻³⁸

³⁷*And every day he was teaching in the temple, but at night he went out and lodged on the mount called Olivet.* ³⁸*And early in the morning all the people came to him in the temple to hear him.*

Luke rounds off the discourse, as Mark does not, with a return to its setting in v. 5. While the impression created by Mark is of a concentrated time schedule, with the passover falling two days after the utterance of the discourse, Luke provides for Jesus' daily occupation of teaching in the temple (19⁴⁷ᵃ) to continue for an indefinite period, during which the passover is approaching (22¹). The immense popularity of the teaching (19⁴⁸) is reiterated in exaggerated terms, with *all the people* thronging to hear him. Since this teaching ministry is Jesus' way of life at this period, mention is made of how he spends his nights. He repairs to the vicinity of the Mount of Olives and lodges there. It is during this customary night sojourn there that Jesus is arrested (22³⁹).

ကာ

37
lodged on the mount called Olivet: The word translated *lodged – aulizesthai* + Matt. 21¹⁷ of Jesus lodging at Bethany after entering Jerusalem, a chance verbal agreement here – means 'to spend the night'. It need not imply camping out. The location is vague; the preposition *epi* should probably be rendered by 'in the vicinity of' rather than by *on* (RSV).

38
early in the morning . . . came to him: The verb here, *orthrizein* + +, means literally 'to get up at dawn', and this is reproduced by RSV, but with the preposition *pros* = 'to' it could mean 'to throng'.

22–23 *The Passion of Christ*

Character and Origins

The passion narratives – i.e. the accounts of the process by which Jesus came to his death – are noticeably different in character from the rest of the synoptic gospel narratives. While still largely constructed from individual units of tradition, they exhibit a closer connection between these units and a greater, though by no means complete, cohesion and unity. The impression conveyed is that it is a single story that is being told, which, once it has begun, must continue to the end. This greater cohesion has been accounted for on the hypothesis that the passion would have been the earliest part of the gospel tradition to attain a fixed oral, and later written, form. The basis for this hypothesis is evidence in the NT itself that the death (and resurrection) of Jesus as saving event constituted the core of the Christian message from the first (e.g. I Cor. 15³⁻⁴; 1²³; possibly the speeches in A. 2²²⁻³⁶; 3¹³⁻²⁶; 10³⁴⁻⁴³; 13²⁶⁻⁴¹). As such it would have been rehearsed from an early time in a connected sequence of events in a way that was not the case with Jesus' teaching or healing work. This is not to be claimed for the passion narratives in their present form, from which individual pericopes such as those of the Last Supper, or the denial of Peter, can be removed without affecting the main story, but for the basic nucleus of Jesus' arrest, the Jewish trial, the Roman trial and the crucifixion, without which the story could not have been told at all.[t] Of the finished products Luke's exhibits the greatest cohesion. This result, however, has not been achieved by the possession of a superior chronology of the events, for in this he is less precise than Mark; nor through a more exact knowledge of them, at least in those events covered by Mark; nor even by means of additional information, some of which (e.g. Jesus' examination by Herod) can obscure rather than improve the sequence of events; but by skilful arrangement and narration, and by a closer link between diverse materials.

If a passion narrative gave story form to a confession such as 'Christ crucified' (I Cor. 1[23]), it was bound to exhibit in its contents a Jewish side and a Roman side, and in its structure some connection between the two. For 'Christ' was a term only intelligible within Judaism, and crucifixion was a form of capital punishment almost exclusively Roman; and historically the event had taken place at a time when the Jews in Judaea were under Roman rule. Here the passion narratives show extremes of variation. In Mark/Matthew the weight falls heavily on the Jewish side, with an arrest, trial and condemnation by the Jewish Sanhedrin, compared with which the interrogation of Jesus by Pilate is brief, perfunctory and without official verdict and sentence. In John the Jewish side is on the way to disappearing altogether, and from Jesus' arrest onwards the story is of a Roman affair. Luke stands in between, with the Jewish side somewhat curtailed in comparison with Mark, and the Roman side considerably expanded. This is understandable. As a historian of the Christian movement in the empire Luke could not have been insensitive to the embarrassment caused by the fact that its founder figure had been condemned on a charge of sedition as 'king of the Jews', and put to death in a manner reserved by the Romans largely for slaves and revolutionaries. In A. the apologetic theme that Christianity

---

[t] On this see Dibelius, *Tradition*, ch. VII, Bultmann, *History*, pp. 275ff., Taylor, *Formation*, ch. III, and *The Gospel according to St Mark*, London and New York 1952, Additional Note J.

is innocent of political offence, and is shown to be so by the verdicts of Roman officials, any appearance to the contrary being due to the machinations of Jews, becomes dominant in the story of Paul. It is probably already responsible for features which are distinctive of Luke's passion narrative, especially the formal indictment of Jesus by the Jews before Pilate on a threefold charge of sedition, and a threefold pronouncement by Pilate of his innocence.

If the death of Jesus was proclaimed from the first as having been 'according to the scriptures' (I Cor. 15³), i.e. as a fulfilment of the purpose of God to be discerned in the OT, a passion narrative will not have been simple historical narration, as though the events belonged entirely within the categories of historical contingency, human causation or human tragedy. By the use of the OT with respect to the events it will have been indicated that there was in them an indissoluble nexus between human historical action and divine will and intention. It cannot be ruled out that, in the course of tradition, this use was responsible for the way in which the events were narrated, and perhaps in some cases for their invention. The present passion narratives show the end product of this use in three forms. Firstly, the scriptures in general are said to be fulfilled, as in Mark 14⁴⁹ = Matt. 26⁵⁴⁻⁵⁶. This is not found in Luke's passion narrative itself, but is powerfully stated by the risen Lord himself (24²⁶ᶠ·, ⁴⁴⁻⁴⁶). In 22²² the language used is not that of scripture but of divine foreordination, which is a marked feature in A. (A. 2²³; 3²⁰; 4²⁸; 10⁴²; 17³¹). Secondly individual passages from the OT are cited in respect of particular events. This is characteristic of John, but is found in Mark and Luke only once – in Mark 14²⁷ of the disciples' desertion, and in Luke 22³⁷ of the arrest. Thirdly, events are narrated in significant OT language to indicate that they happen by divine direction. Here the evangelists would seem to be drawing partly on a common stock which had established itself in the oral period of tradition. It was composed largely of psalms concerned with a righteous sufferer in God's cause, such as Pss. 22, 27, 38, 69, and language from these is used for the narration of the taunting of Jesus (23³⁵), the actions of the soldiers (23³⁴), the gazing of the people (23³⁵), the presence of friends at the cross (23⁴⁹), the offer of a drink (23³⁶); while for the last words of Jesus Luke replaces Ps. 22¹ in Mark 15³⁴ by Ps. 31⁵ (23⁴⁶).[u]

u For more detailed analysis, see C. F. Evans, 'The Tradition of the Passion', *Explorations in Theology* 2, London 1977, pp. 6ff., and the works referred to in p. 185 n. 12.

The death of Christ was proclaimed not only as a divinely fore-ordained event but as procuring salvation for men (I Cor. 15³, 'Christ died for our sins'). In the passion narratives this saving character is in some measure conveyed by the use of the OT, which sets the events within the context of the 'holy history' of Israel, but also by the selection of the incidents to be narrated, the order and manner in which they are narrated, and by the words spoken by Jesus within them. Here, also, the gospels can exhibit differences. In Mark the element of the pro-clamation of saving event predominates over that of instruction and example. His story begins with a passover meal as the context for the declaration that the disciples share his body and his death as a sacrifice, which inaugurates an eschatological covenant and the kingdom of God (cf. Mark 10⁴⁵, 'a ransom for many'). The sacrifice consists in sub-mission to trial by God to the point of death, and in the surrender of his will in obedience to the Father. This he does entirely alone. In words from Zechariah about God's judgment on Israel total desertion of the disciples is predicted (from which Jesus is to recover them after his resurrection). Before the Sanhedrin he accepts the title of messiah, but sets alongside it the future coming of the Son of man (Daniel) who is to be at God's right hand (Ps. 110¹), his death thus being a spiritual triumph over God's enemies, and the means of the establishment of his reign and his people. Before Pilate he is first non-committal and then silent; indeed after his arrest he speaks only three sentences. From then on the narrative is swift and stark. Jesus is depicted as passive, bereft of human contact and sympathy, and in his dying words as abandoned by God. At the moment of death the veil of the temple is rent as a symbol of the temple's replacement by the body of Christ, and a centurion, speaking for the Gentile world in the midst of darkness and ignorance, confesses Jesus' divine sonship. Luke's narrative, covering the same ground and with the same kind of traditions, paints a significantly different picture. His emphasis is primarily didactic. Jesus teaches by example. There is solidarity between Jesus and his disciples, who are 'the apostles' of the church. They celebrate the passover together as an earnest of the king-dom of God, which is also the kingdom of Christ, where they will feast and rule; and they will serve as he serves. There is no prediction of their communal desertion, nor mention of their flight. Peter's denial is foretold, but in the context of an assurance of his restoration through the prayer of Jesus, and he is recovered by a look. Jesus' replies to the Sanhedrin are non-committal, and his sessions with Pilate and Herod prove his innocence. The theme of the temple disappears, and, if the shorter text of the words at the Last Supper are accepted, there is no reference to an inaugural sacrifice of a covenant. As in A. no salvatory significance is suggested for the death of Jesus except that it moves to repentance. What in its public aspect is the story of a miscarriage of justice in the crucifixion of Jesus as a rebel is in its interior aspect a veritable 'passion' (the Greek word *pathein* = 'to suffer', used absolutely of Jesus' death, is Lukan; cf. 22^{15}; $24^{26, 46}$; A. 1^3; 3^{18}; 17^3). Jesus appears as a martyr, the pattern of humility, who suffers the unjustified hatred of his persecutors (who dies forgiving his enemies), who gathers a penitent with him into paradise, and who commends himself at the last to God, this manner of his dying moving the centurion to declare him innocent (cf. I Peter 2^{21-25}). He is not bereft or alone; others draw near to him. He is not passive but active, not silent but eloquent, in instructing disciples, in commenting on his arrest, in addressing the mourning women. Whereas Mark's story is mysterious, severe and theological, Luke's is more intelligible, human and touched with pathos.

Composition and Sources

The similarities and differences noted above raise the questions of how, and from what, Luke composed his passion narrative. These are not unconnected with the wider questions of how, and from what, he composed the Gospel as a whole (for which, see pp. 15ff.). Literary analysis suggests that the materials of the passion narrative may be divided into three categories.

(i) There is material of substantial length to which there is no parallel elsewhere. This comprises the address at the Last Supper (22^{24-38}), the examination before Herod (23^{6-12}), the address to the women (23^{27-31}) and the incident of the penitent thief (23^{39-43}). This material is comparatively self-contained and detachable from the context.

(ii) There is material of substantial length which is taken from Mark. This comprises the introduction in 22^{1-6}, the preparations for the Passover (22^{7-13}), which provide the initial framework of the story, and perhaps the denial of Peter (22^{54-62}).

(iii) There is material of substantial length in which non-Markan appear to be intermingled with what may be judged Markan elements. This comprises the main body of the narrative, without which the story could not be told – the arrest (22^{47-53}), the session of the Sanhedrin ($22^{54, 63-71}$), the sessions with Pilate ($23^{1-5, 13-25}$), the journey to crucifixion and the crucifixion itself (23[26, 32-38, 44-49]); also the prayer in 22[39-46].

Consideration of the relation of these three categories of material to one another has led to two contrary hypotheses. The first is that the only continuous passion narrative available to Luke was that of Mark. This he supplemented with some additional units of tradition, but also revised more heavily than was his wont with a view to producing a more polished, flowing and coherent narrative, and one which reflected his own viewpoint on certain issues. The second is that Luke had available a continuous non-Markan passion narrative, which at some stage he supplemented from Mark, and which, by the removal of the Markan additions, may be reconstructed, either as part of a larger whole (L, so Streeter, *Four Gospels*, ch. 8; as the passion narrative of L+Q = Proto-Luke, so Taylor, *Third Gospel*, ch. 12), or as an entity on its own (J, a Jerusalem document, A. M. Perry, *The Sources of Luke's Passion-Narrative*).[v]

The issue here is whether the removal from Luke's passion narrative of what is judged to have been derived from Mark leaves behind a recognizably continuous story, or a number of units of tradition, which would require something in addition to make them continuous. This issue is, however, complicated by the difficulty of determining what is rightly to be judged Markan. That is particularly the case with (iii) above, the main constituents of the story. Is this 'mixed' material to be accounted for as Markan material, which Luke has freely revised for his own purposes, but which still retains traces of its Markan origins? Or is it to be explained as material from a non-Markan passion narrative, which Luke has on occasions embellished or filled out by attaching to it phrases or sentences from Mark? A further consideration to be borne in mind is whether the wording in which an event in the passion was rehearsed in the period of oral tradition had become sufficiently stereotyped that it was likely to appear in any written version, Markan or non-Markan. Some attention is given to these questions in introducing the individual sections of the passion narrative.

[v] For a review of the discussion and of the relevant literature, see V. Taylor, *Passion Narrative*.

22^{1-6} = Mark $14^{1-2, \, 10-11}$

THE PLAN OF THE AUTHORITIES

22 *Now the feast of Unleavened Bread drew near, which is called the Passover.* [2]*And the chief priests and the scribes were seeking how to put him to death; for they feared the people.*

[3]*Then Satan entered into Judas called Iscariot, who was of the number of the twelve;* [4]*he went away and conferred with the chief priests and captains how he might betray him to them.* [5]*And they were glad, and engaged to give him money.* [6]*So he agreed, and sought an opportunity to betray him to them in the absence of the multitude.*

This is taken from Mark, as is evident in the agreement in wording in *the chief priests and the scribes* (contrast Luke's different list in 22^{52}), *were seeking*, in the superfluous *went away*, which in Mark is determined by the previous story (omitted by Luke), and means 'went away from Bethany', in *they were glad and* engaged *to give him money*, and in *sought opportunity*. The differences are stylistic – *drew near* in a temporal sense, *called*, *to put him to death* (*anairein* = 'to destroy', common in L–A but rare in the rest of the NT), the participial construction in *who was of the number of the twelve*, *engaged*, *he agreed*, and *in the absence of*. Thus Luke is dependent on Mark for the beginning of the passion narrative (if he did possess a non-Markan passion narrative, it will presumably have been inferior or defective at this point). On what Mark was dependent for his information can only be conjectured. Any passion narrative is likely to have included the arrest, and could well have begun with it; which might then have required an introductory statement to explain why the arrest was made, and who was responsible for it. This itself could have been a later deduction from what had actually happened; for it is unlikely that Christians had access to inside information of what had gone on in official circles.

ॐ

1
Now the feast of Unleavened Bread drew near, which is called the Passover: This is a description for non-Jewish readers (*which is called*), and is a conflation, perhaps suggested by the double reference in Mark 14^1, of what Luke elsewhere calls 'the feast of the Passover' (2^{41}, or 'the Passover', A. 12^4), and 'the days of un-

leavened bread' (A. 12³; 20⁶). These were strictly distinct, but as Passover was immediately followed by a seven days' celebration of unleavened bread, and unleavened bread was prescribed for Passover, they could easily be assimilated, and there was a certain looseness of terminology in referring to them (cf. II Chron. 35¹⁷; I Esdras 1¹⁹, 'the Passover and feasts of unleavened bread seven days' – was Passover included in the seven days?). Josephus can distinguish but also identify them (*Ant.* 14.21, 'the festival of unleavened bread which we call Phaska', *Ant.* 3.249, 'on the fifteenth day the feast of unleavened bread succeeds the Passover'). There is slight rabbinic evidence that the day before Passover (Nisan 14) could be called 'the first day of unleavened bread' (SB II, pp. 813ff.; cf. Jos. *BJ* 5.99). Passover was one of the three chief, i.e. pilgrimage, festivals of the Jewish year, the other two being Tabernacles and Pentecost. It was an annual commemoration of the deliverance from Egypt. It had to be celebrated within the walls of Jerusalem, and in families with a minimum of ten participants at the meal. This had to be eaten after the sunset (when the Jewish day began) which ushered in the fifteenth day of Nisan, the first month of the year (March/April), and before sunrise on that day (cf. Exod. 12¹⁻¹⁴; Num. 9¹⁻¹⁴; Deut. 16¹⁻⁸). On the following day, Nisan 16, the first fruits of the grain harvest were offered in the temple, and the harvest itself commenced.

The passion of Jesus is nowhere dated, either as to the year or to the time of the year, in any kerygmatic statement of it (e.g. I Cor. 15³; A. 13²⁷⁻²⁹, etc.). Nevertheless, both the synoptists and John bring it into connection with Passover time – Mark (and Matthew) more precisely with 'after two days' (which could mean either forty-eight hours after, or, according to an inclusive time reckoning, twenty-four hours after), Luke less precisely with *drew near*, and John (13¹) with 'before'. These chronological data are, however, problematic.ʷ (i) They produce a discrepancy between the synoptists, who describe the supper as a passover meal and the crucifixion as taking place on passover day, and John, who has both on the previous day. Two different resolutions of this difficulty have been proposed. The first takes John's dating to be correct, and the meal 'before the feast of the Passover' (John 13¹) to have been a farewell meal initiated by Jesus himself, and wholly Christian in content. It is then to be supposed that in the traditions of certain (Jewish-Christian?) circles this meal, considered primarily as the framework within which Jesus instituted the Eucharist, was identified with the passover meal, and was set within the context of Jewish paschal practice, even though it lacked some of the principal features of the passover meal, such as the lamb, the bitter herbs and the recital of the passover haggadah or liturgy. Alternatively, the synoptists' dating is taken as correct, and their accounts of the meal, despite a certain brevity and concentration on Jesus' 'eucharistic' actions and words, held to preserve features which were distinctive

w See the discussion in J. Jeremias, *The Eucharistic Words of Jesus*, ch. I, and E. Ruckstuhl, *Chronology of the Last Days of Jesus*, ET New York 1965, pp. 11–55.

of the passover meal. Such are the fact that the meal was held within Jerusalem, in the evening and with an inner group; the act of reclining at table; the breaking of bread after the beginning of the meal; the drinking of wine and the singing of a hymn (though not all these have equal force in marking off the meal from any solemn occasion, and in establishing it as paschal). Further, some of these features may be detected in the meal described in John 13, which may then have been originally a passover meal. John is then to be assumed to have antedated this meal by twenty-four hours. His motive for doing so was to present Jesus as the true paschal lamb, the time of whose death coincides with the time on Nisan 14 when the lambs were being slaughtered in the temple for the passover meal later that night (John 19^{14}, 'It was about the sixth hour' – though this coincidence is not very obvious), and whose death fulfilled the scripture 'Not a bone of him shall be broken' (John 19^{36} – though it is not certain that the reference here is to the passover lamb in Exod. 12^{46}, and not to the words of Ps. 34^{20}).

(ii) These chronological data so condense the narrative as hardly to allow sufficient time for the events to take place. Thus Jesus is arrested after the passover meal (at midnight? later?), and is examined by the Sanhedrin, which is summoned, along with witnesses, during the night (so Mark/Matthew; according to Luke (22^{66}) he is examined for the only time 'when the day came' – at daybreak? later?). After a morning session of the Sanhedrin (so Mark/Matthew) he is taken to Pilate for examination – in Luke is then sent to Herod for examination and returned to Pilate. He is then condemned after a further meeting of Pilate and the Jewish authorities, is mocked by Pilate's soldiers, and is nevertheless crucified by 9 a.m. the same morning (Mark 15^{25}). Not unconnected with this is the further question whether some of these activities contravened the Jewish law. The Mishnah tractate Sanhedrin (4^1) lays it down that 'in capital cases they hold the trial in the daytime and the verdict must also be reached in the daytime' (this would be contravened by Mark's account, but not by Luke's); and further that in such cases 'a verdict of acquittal may be reached on the same day, but a verdict of conviction not until the following day', so that trials for that reason are not to be held on the eve of a sabbath or of a festival day (this would be contravened by both accounts). According to the tractate Betzah, any act that is culpable on the sabbath is also culpable on a festival day, the administration of justice being one such act. It is debated whether these regulations were operative at the time, or represent a later humanitarian revision by Pharisees of a previous harsher Sadducean code, though this is unlikely in the case of the regulation about the culpability of acts on the sabbath and festival days. Speculative also is the suggestion of Jeremias (*Eucharistic Words*, pp. 78f.) that such regulations would have been overruled in the special case of the serious offender, e.g. the false prophet, who, in accordance with Deut. 17^{13}, was to be condemned and executed in the presence of 'all the people', this being possible only when the people were gathered for festivals. The speculative thesis advanced by

A. Jaubert* would have a bearing on all these aspects. From the treatment of Holy Week in the third-century Syriac Didaskalia, and from scattered references in Christian writers to the arrest of Jesus on a Wednesday, she postulates the use at the time by sectarians of a solar calendar, for which there is some evidence in the book of Jubilees and at Qumran. In this festivals fell always on the same day, Passover falling on a Tuesday. Jesus could then have celebrated the Passover on Tuesday night, and have been crucified, as in John, on Friday, the eve of the Passover in the official calendar. The events in between could then have covered a period of two days when the law would not have been contravened. This dating was not recognized by Mark, who therefore telescoped the events to make them fit the official calendar.

2

the chief priests and the scribes: From Mark 14¹. They have already appeared in 20¹⁹, and will appear again at 22⁶⁶; 23¹⁰. They designate the Sanhedrin, the official ruling body in Judaism (for other designations in Luke, see on 19⁴⁷; 20¹). It is their decision that sets the passion in motion.

how to put him to death; for they feared the people: The decision is to take steps to put into effect the intention which, according to Luke, they had had for some time (19⁴⁷; 20¹), viz. 'to do away with Jesus' (this is the meaning of the verb *anairein* which Luke uses here). For this it was necessary, according to Mark, to take him by craft and 'not during the feast' (but before it? or after it?). This is awkwardly expressed and appears contradictory, since, whatever they had planned, they in fact arrest Jesus during the feast. To avoid this contradiction Jeremias (*Eucharistic Words*, pp. 71ff.) proposed for the Greek word *heortē* = 'feast' the possible, but rare, sense of 'the festival crowd'. Luke abbreviates and rewrites Mark, and *in the absence of the multitude* (v. 6) is possibly an equivalent for 'not in the festival crowd'. Here *for they feared the people* may have the sense, different from Mark's, that they deliberated Jesus' destruction for fear of what the people's devotion to him might otherwise lead to (cf. 20¹⁹; 21³⁷ᶠ·).

3–6

Of the two elements in vv. 1–2, the passover and the deliberations of the authorities, the latter is developed first. Luke does not reproduce the story of the anointing at Bethany (Mark 14³⁻⁹), either because he regards it as a doublet of the similar story in 7³⁶⁻⁵⁰, or because Mark's account of the mysterious episode of the advance embalming of Jesus was meant to depict a messianic anointing, which could give handle to the charge of making himself an anointed king (23²). Luke therefore brings together the planning of the authorities and the intervention of Judas.

* *The Date of the Last Supper*, ET New York 1965.

3

Satan entered into Judas called Iscariot: The meaning of Judas's surname *Iskariōtēs* (so always in Matthew and John; in the only other mention in L–A, 6¹⁶ = Mark 3¹⁹, it is *Iskariōth*) is obscure. Some take it as a place name, 'from Kerioth' in southern Judaea, perhaps making Judas the only non-Galilean among the twelve. Others connect it with the Latinism *sikarios* = 'dagger man', Josephus's term for one kind of Zealot. In Mark the action of Judas is simply stated with no reasons given. The NT shows evidence of speculation about it.ˣ In some strands of tradition a sufficient cause was that it was predicted by Jesus and required by scripture (Ps. 41⁹ – so Mark 14¹⁷⁻²¹, developed further in Matt. 26²⁵; Luke 22²²; John 13²¹⁻³⁰). In John 6⁶⁴⁻⁷¹ it is connected with unbelief and the abandonment of discipleship; while John 12⁴⁻⁶ hints at avarice and dishonesty, which fits with, but may have been derived from, his payment by the priests. Luke's interpretation is in terms of the influence of Satan. This affords one of the parallels with the Johannine passion narrative (cf. John 13², ²⁷; cf. 6⁷⁰f.); but it is doubtful whether there is to be seen here the Johannine dualism between God and Satan as the ruler of this world, and the supernatural conflict between them initiated by Judas's action. Luke's picture is probably more individual and psychological (cf. A. 5³; 13¹⁰), and perhaps even exculpatory. That one who belonged to the inmost circle could have handed over his Lord to the enemy (v. 48) was only to be explained if it was not his own act, but the result of satanic possession. For Conzelmann (*Theology*, p. 80) this is the key point in the schema he detects for the whole Gospel, when Satan, who had been banished for the period of Jesus' ministry, is allowed to return for the period of the passion and the church. For Ellis (p. 248) it is intended to indicate a renewal in the passion of the wilderness temptations of Jesus with regard to his messiahship. Neither of these explanations is convincing. It is with Judas and not Jesus that Satan is here concerned, and not in order to tempt him, or through him Jesus (who is already aware of what Judas will do), but to possess him and to prompt his action.

of the number of the twelve: This has been taken to imply that Judas was only counted with the twelve, but did not really belong. But if it is any more than a literary turn of phrase for Mark's awkward '(the) one of the twelve', it might be held to stress the opposite, viz. real membership of an intimate closed circle, cf. Rev. 7⁴, 'the number of the sealed', I Clement 2⁴, 'the number of the elect'.

---

x This has continued down history to the present day. Thus Cullmann, *The State in the New Testament*, pp. 15ff., sees Judas's action as stemming from disillusionment, coming to a head at the Last Supper, at Jesus' refusal to pursue the course of a political messiah; while S. Zeitlin, *Who Crucified Jesus?*, New York and London 1942, p. 162, sees it as stemming from Judas's belief that Jesus was the Son of God, and his fear that the other disciples would make the mistake of proclaiming him a political messiah.

4–6

Luke's account of the interview (which must have been deduced from the events) is more precise – *conferred, engaged* = 'make a decision to', *agreed* (*exhomologein*, nowhere else in Greek literature in the active), and the absence of a crowd in order to be able 'to hand over' Jesus. This is the proper sense of the verb *paradidonai*, used here and often elsewhere in this connection, and not *betray*, for which the Greek is *prodidonai* (in the NT only the noun *prodotēs*, 6^{16}, of Judas as the guide at the arrest, A. 1^{16}). It only acquires the meaning *betray* through its regular association with the action of Judas interpreted in personal terms. This shifts the emphasis from the theological to the subjective. That Jesus is 'handed over' ('into the hands of', i.e. the custody of, cf. Mark 9^{31}) means essentially that he is transferred from the condition in which he is his own master, initiates his actions, and is free to effect the purposes of God, into one where he is under the control of others, is subject to their initiatives and to their actions, which are inimical to him and his purposes. This transfer can be said to be necessary because it is the divine will in scripture (24^7; Mark $14^{41, 49}$). God himself can be said to be the author of it (Rom. 4^{25}; 8^{32}; this is probably the sense of the passive voice in Mark 9^{31} pars, 10^{33} pars, I Cor. 11^{23}). In Gal. 2^{20}; Eph. 5^{25} Jesus is said to hand himself over, and this is the impression conveyed by John's account of the arrest (John 18^{1-9}). In Mark 15^1; A. 3^{13} the Jewish authorities further the process by handing Jesus over to Pilate, and John 19^{11} shows reflection on the responsibility involved. But the word became attached especially to Judas as the initial agent of this transfer, and he is designated 'the one who hands over' (so Mark $14^{42, 44}$; Matt. 26^{25}; John $6^{64, 71}$; 12^4; 13^{11}; $18^{2, 5}$). It is the fact that he accomplished this by means of inside knowledge useful to the authorities that introduces the sense of 'betray'; but this is not stressed, and it is not clear what this inside knowledge was, nor why the kiss (not mentioned here) was necessary. For the more the story, especially Luke's of Jesus' fame and popularity with the whole people, is taken at its face value, the harder it is to suppose that the authorities did not know well enough who Jesus was, and what his movements were, and that they were not able to act on their own, even in crowded conditions, but needed some means of identification.[y]

4

captains: The general sense is clearly that among those who deliberate are members of the temple police, who would be responsible for making the arrest; but the Greek word in the plural (*stratēgoi*) was a popular designation for the chief magistrates in a Hellenistic city (as in A. 16^{20-38}), and in A. 4^1; $5^{24, 26}$ it is used in the singular for 'the captain of the temple', who is designated by Josephus simply as 'the captain' (*BJ* 6.294).

[y] See B. W. Bacon, 'What did Judas betray?', *Hibbert Journal* 19, 1920–21, pp. 476–93.

22^{7-13} = Mark 14^{12-16}

PREPARATION OF THE PASSOVER

[7] *Then came the day of Unleavened Bread, on which the passover lamb had to be sacrificed.* [8] *So Jesus* sent Peter and John, saying, 'Go and prepare the passover for us, that we may eat it.'* [9] *They said to him, 'Where will you have us prepare it?'* [10] *He said to them, 'Behold, when you have entered the city, a man carrying a jar of water will meet you; follow him into the house which he enters,* [11] *and tell the householder, "The Teacher says to you, Where is the guest room, where I am to eat the passover with my disciples?"* [12] *And he will show you a large upper room furnished; there make ready.'* [13] *And they went, and found it as he had told them; and they prepared the passover.*

* Greek *he*

Luke now begins to develop the first element in vv. 1–2, the passover. He provides a framework for his account of the Last Supper as a passover meal, which, if it is to be assigned to a non-Markan source, presumably lacked an introduction. He does this by reproducing with great fidelity Mark 14^{12-16}, which in structure and language is a replica of Mark 11^{1-10}. The factual basis here is difficult to discern. It is profitless to ask how the disciples are to know which of the servants who might be carrying pitchers of water in Jerusalem at festival time was the one with whom they are to have their assignation; or whether the householder who is to be told what *the Teacher* says (v. 11) is a disciple with whom matters have been privately pre-arranged between him and Jesus alone; or whether there would be time for preparations to be made at this stage. The story was not designed to supply such information. An extended account of how a passover meal came to be prepared is unnecessary in itself, as this could be taken for granted. The pericope has been fashioned in the light of the Last Supper as a passover meal, and as an introduction to it. It is designed to show Jesus as endowed with mysterious foreknowledge, and as able to make all things serve his destiny. In his hands the passover meal becomes the Lord's Supper (I Cor. 11^{20}). Luke thus makes modifications to increase the solemnity and vividness of the narrative. The feast which has been approaching (v. 1) now arrives. The initiative of Jesus, and his solidarity with the disciples, are stressed, in that the question in Mark, 'Where will you have us to go and prepare (for you to eat the passover)?' becomes a response to the initial command of Jesus, *Go and prepare the passover for us, that we may eat it* (vv. 8–9). The two disciples sent are named as Peter and John, who are leaders of the apostles in A. 3¹⁻⁴; 4¹⁹; 8¹⁴, and who always stand at the head of the list of the twelve when they are named in pairs (cf. 8⁴⁵ for Luke's provision of a name, and a change in the dialogue, in a Markan pericope). The instructions are introduced by the dramatic *Behold* (v. 10).

፨

7
Then came the day of Unleavened Bread: This is not intelligible, unless Luke's rendering of Mark is (improbably) to be translated 'that day of unleavened bread on which . . .'. There were seven days of unleavened bread beginning on Nisan 15. While there is some evidence that Nisan 14, the day of preparation, could be called 'the first day of unleavened bread' (see on v. 1), there was no such day as 'the day of unleavened bread'. Luke may have coined the expression to invest the preparation of this particular passover meal with special solemnity.

on which the passover lamb had to be sacrificed: the passover lamb is the secondary sense of *to pascha*, of which the primary sense is 'the passover'. *had to be* (edei, an addition by Luke) means that it was obligatory by Jewish law. Jesus acts within the religious observances of Judaism (cf. A. 20¹⁶ of Paul). The sacrifice referred to would have constituted the major element in the preparations, though no reference is made to it in the instructions, unless *eat it* (v. 8) and *eat the passover* (v. 11) mean 'eat the passover lamb'. The sacrifice took place on the afternoon of Nisan 14, when representatives of households went to the temple area with their lambs or goats. There they formed three queues until an area was full. Then the gates were locked and trumpets were blown as a sign that all was ready. To the accompaniment of the Hallel Psalms, 112–118, the animals were slaughtered by their owners, the priests standing in lines to catch the blood in gold or silver vessels. The priests then passed the carcases along the line until they reached the priest next to the altar, where they were offered, i.e. as a sacrifice, and, their entrails having been removed, they were returned to their owners for roasting (see the Mishnah tractate Pesachim 5). The remainder of the preparations would involve the furnishing of the room – here an upper room built on to the roof – with cushions for reclining, which all had to do at Passover (but in this case they would find this already done), and the provision of the required unleavened bread, wine and dishes of herbs.

11
eat the passover: The meaning of this phrase is raised again in v. 15. When *to*

pascha = 'the passover' refers to the feast in general it is said to be kept (Greek *poiein* = 'to perform', so in Exod. 12⁴⁸; Num. 9¹⁰f., ¹³; Deut. 16¹; cf. II Chron. 30²¹; Ezra 6²²). When it is said to be eaten, what is referred to is the passover lamb (so Exod. 12¹¹; Num. 9¹¹). Yet the phrase here appears to be a term for the observance of the feast, involving preparations not confined to the sacrifice of the lamb (cf. I Cor. 11²⁰, where to eat the Lord's Supper probably means more than to consume its contents); and the eschatological fulfilment which is looked to in v. 15 is likely to be that of the passover observance as a whole rather than of the passover lamb.

¹⁴*And when the hour came, he sat at table, and the apostles with him.* ¹⁵*And he said to them, 'I have earnestly desired to eat this passover with you before I suffer;* ¹⁶*for I tell you I shall not eat it* until it is fulfilled in the kingdom of God.'* ¹⁷*And he took a cup, and when he had given thanks he said, 'Take this, and divide it among yourselves;* ¹⁸*for I tell you that from now on I shall not drink of the fruit of the vine until the kingdom of God comes.'* ¹⁹*And he took bread, and when he had given thanks he broke it and gave it to them, saying, 'This is my body.†* ²¹*But behold the hand of him who betrays me is with me on the table.* ²²*For the Son of man goes as it has been determined; but woe to that man by whom he is betrayed!'* ²³*And they began to question one another, which of them it was that would do this.*

²⁴*A dispute also arose among them, which of them was to be regarded as the greatest.* ²⁵*And he said to them, 'The kings of the Gentiles exercise lordship over them; and those in authority over them are called benefactors.* ²⁶*But not so with you; rather let the greatest among you become as the youngest, and the leader as one who serves.* ²⁷*For which is the greater, one who sits at table, or one who serves? Is it not the one who sits at table? But I am among you as one who serves.*

²⁸'*You are those who have continued with me in my trials;* ²⁹*as my Father appointed a kingdom for me, so do I appoint for you* ³⁰*that you may eat and drink at my table in my kingdom, and sit on thrones judging the twelve tribes of Israel.*

³¹'*Simon, Simon, behold, Satan demanded to have you,‡ that he might sift you‡ like wheat,* ³²*but I have prayed for you that your faith may not fail; and when you have turned again, strengthen your brethren.'* ³³*And he said to him,*

'Lord, I am ready to go with you to prison and to death.' ^{34}He said, 'I tell you, Peter, the cock will not crow this day, until you three times deny that you know me.'

^{35}And he said to them, 'When I sent you out with no purse or bag or sandals, did you lack anything?' They said, 'Nothing.' ^{36}He said to them, 'But now, let him who has a purse take it, and likewise a bag. And let him who has no sword sell his mantle and buy one. ^{37}For I tell you that this scripture must be fulfilled in me, "And he was reckoned with transgressors"; for what is written about me has its fulfilment.' ^{38}And they said, 'Look, Lord, here are two swords.' And he said to them, 'It is enough.'

* Other ancient authorities read *never eat it again*

† Other ancient authorities add *which is given for you. Do this in remembrance of me.'^{20} And likewise the cup after supper, saying, 'This cup which is poured out for you is the new covenant in my blood.'*

‡ The Greek word for *you* here is plural; in v. 32 it is singular.

Though evidently a composition out of various materials (note the abrupt transitions in vv. 19, 21, 24, 28, 31, 35), this constitutes a single unit. It is much longer than the corresponding passages in Mark/Matthew, but that is not surprising. For what is extraordinary about Mark's account (followed closely by Matthew) is its extreme brevity and concentration, whereby the passover meal is no more than a framework for the (probably liturgical) text of the actions and words of Jesus in respect of the bread and the wine, preceded by a protracted and vehement prophecy of betrayal (Mark 14$^{17-25}$; cf. a similar brevity and concentration in the oral tradition rehearsed by Paul in I Cor. 11$^{23-25}$). In so far as the meal was thought of in terms of the title which came to be given to it, the Last Supper, this was intolerable, and cried out for expansion in respect both of its passover character, which was indicated by the solemn manner in which it was introduced (Mark 14$^{12-16}$), and of Jesus' last words to the inner circle of the twelve. This is what it is given in Luke's version, which thus stands some way along the road to John's version (John 13–17), where any institution of the Eucharist is absent, and the meal is a framework for a protracted farewell address of Jesus to 'his own' about his and their future.

Luke's version has a distinctive pattern of its own, as follows:

A The Meal

1. Solemn introduction of Jesus with the apostles at the appointed hour (22^{14})
2. Double saying about pass- | Desire to eat it with them before passion (22^{15})
   over: | Its eschatological fulfilment for him | (22^{16})

Either (longer text)

3. Parallel double saying about | Blessing of cup and distribution to them (22^{17})
   passover cup: | Its eschatological fulfilment for him | (22^{18})
4. Parallel double sayings | Blessing of bread – my body for you | (22^{19})
   about bread and cup: | Blessing of cup – covenant in my blood
   for you | (22^{20})

Or (shorter text)

3. Double saying about cup: | Blessing of cup and distribution to them (22^{17})
   | Its eschatological fulfilment for him | (22^{18})
4. Saying about bread: | Blessing of bread – my body | (22^{19a})
5. Transition to Discourse – prophecy of betrayal (fourfold statement) (22^{21-23})

B The Discourse

6. Parting address of Jesus to the apostles:

   (a) Apostles to be great by being servants (eightfold statement) (22^{24-26})
       On the model of Jesus in their midst as waiter (fourfold statement) (22^{27})

   (b) Apostles as past and present participators in Jesus' trials will participate in his messianic banquet and his judgment of Israel (fourfold statement) (22^{28-30})

   (c) Peter's denial prophesied in view of his recovery to strengthen the rest by the prayer of Jesus in conflict with Satan (twelvefold statement) (22^{31-34})

   (d) Reversal of previous lack of possessions as missionary apostles to a present possession of swords,
       So as to share in his condemnation as a criminal by Israel (22^{35-38})

This pattern has considerable coherence. The paschal meal, when all Israel was thought of as gathered in families in joyful thanksgiving for the deliverance from Egypt and in anticipation of God's ultimate deliverance, is celebrated by Jesus with his apostles as the true Israel of God in anticipation of the coming kingdom of God. Bread and wine are blessed and distributed to be consumed by them as symbols of, and the means of union with, his person and his destiny as the inaugurator (through a sacrificial death) of the new covenant of God with Israel. Despite betrayal and denial amongst them, their past and continuing union with him and his destiny will persist into a future kingdom and a period of judgment on Israel, and they will have him as their model and messianic deliverer.

Analysis, however, of the origins and composition of this section proves exceedingly complex, and brings to light a number of inter-related problems.[z] That Luke has simply incorporated entire an alterna-tive account from a non-Markan source is unlikely, as there are indica-tions of his hand in the compilation of the discourse in vv. 21–38. That he incorporated an account of the meal (vv. 14–20) from such a source is possible, though it then has to be supposed, either that it lacked any introduction, or that its introduction was suppressed by Luke, and re-placed with that taken from Mark (vv. 7–13 = Mark 14^{12-16}). This itself raises the question whether Luke's hand is to be seen also in vv. 14–20. The matter is further complicated by (i) the possibility that here, and in the parallel passages in Mark/Matthew (cf. also I Cor. 11^{23-25}), we do not have simply historical traditions of an event, but texts reflect-ing liturgical usage in different areas of the church related to a (repeated) celebration of the Lord's Supper, and (possibly) an (annual?) observance by Christians of the Jewish passover; and (ii) uncertainty whether what Luke wrote was the 'longer' text (i.e. vv. 19–20), or the 'shorter' text (i.e. v. 19a, ending with 'This is my body').

ಐಐ

14

The scene is here set for vv. 15–38, probably by Luke himself with a revised version of Mark 14^{17}, which continues the emphases already apparent in his rephrasing of Mark in vv. 7–13.

when the hour came: This could be purely factual (cf. 14^{17}), and denote any time after the sunset which introduced Nisan 15, and before sunrise, which was the period appointed for the passover meal. But Luke may have intended some-thing more solemn – the appointed hour of the Lord's own passover and supper, for which he had made such deliberate preparation, and of his final words to his disciples.

he sat at table: Attention is fixed on Jesus throughout as host and head. The verb

z On the whole subject see esp. Jeremias, *Eucharistic Words*, A. J. B. Higgins, *The Lord's Supper in the New Testament*, SBT 6, 1952, E. Schweizer, *The Lord's Supper according to the New Testament*, Philadelphia 1967. The most detailed literary analysis of 22^{15-38} is in H. Schürmann's three studies, *Der Paschamahlbericht, Der Einsetzungs bericht*, and *Jesu Abschiedsrede*, Münster 1952–57. See also M. L. Soards, *The Passion according to Luke* (JSNT Suppl. 14) 1987, chs. 2 and 3.

here (*anapiptein* = 'to lie down', 'to recline'), which Luke can use for sitting at table at ordinary meals (cf. 11³⁷; 14¹⁰; 17⁷), could have the sense of the reclining on couches or cushions reserved for banquets, if Luke knew that this was prescribed at passover even for the poorest Israelites as a symbol of Israel's liberation from slavery at the Exodus.

and the apostles: So Luke calls them at 6¹³; 24¹⁰, and frequently in A. (two of them have been named in v. 8). Thus this is not a meal of a private Israelite group, nor even of a rabbi with his pupils (as in v. 11, 'eat the passover with my disciples'), but an official meal of Jesus as the Lord with the future leaders of the church.

15–20

What now follows is not, as in Mark, the prophecy of betrayal, but the meal itself. The form the passover meal would have taken can be reconstructed from available sources with tolerable certainty. The information in the tractate on it, Pesachim, probably goes back to AD 40–70. It had been influenced by the etiquette of the Greek symposium or banquet. It began, possibly outside the room, with the first of four prescribed cups of wine, over which God was blessed as the creator of the grape and of the day itself. This was followed by aperitifs in the form of herbs, generally lettuce, and by a fruit purée. The table was then brought forward, as in Hellenistic banquets, the meal served but not eaten, a second cup of wine prepared and the first of the Hallel Psalms, 113, sung. Then followed the main meal of the lamb, eaten with unleavened bread blessed by the host and bitter herbs. During the meal (in the view of some scholars after it) was the *haggadah* or liturgy of the meal. Originally this was an extempore discussion, but eventually it became formalized as rehearsal of the Exodus story by the head of the household in response to questions put by a younger member of it concerning the distinctive customs of the feast – the lamb, the unleavened bread, the bitter herbs, etc. (cf. Exod. 12²⁶ᶠ·). Grace was then said over a third cup of wine, the cup of blessing, and the whole was concluded by the singing of the remaining Hallel Psalms, 114–118, and by praise over a fourth cup of wine. Interpretation of vv. 15–20 in relation to such a meal is affected by uncertainty over the precise force of some of the expressions there, and by the textual problem in vv. 19–20.

15–16

This opening statement of Jesus at the meal is capable of more than one interpretation.

15

I have earnestly desired: The Greek here, *epithumiā epethumēsa* = 'with desire I have desired', is a construction in which the verb is intensified by its cognate noun in the dative. It is characteristic of the LXX (there is an identical expression in Gen. 31^{30}), though it is not unknown in Hellenistic Greek. It could have come from Luke, who has the construction elsewhere (A. 5^{28}; 16^{28}; 23^{14}; 28^{10}). It expresses the intense longing of Jesus to share the passover meal with the apostles, the reason for this longing being given in v. 16(*for*). But it is possible for the construction to express an unfulfilled wish – 'I would dearly have liked to eat this passover with you (but know that I shall not).' So understood, the words could be taken in two ways. They could be evidence, surviving from an independent account, that the Last Supper was not a passover meal, but, as in John 13–17, took place the day before; and *before I suffer* could express Jesus' conviction that he would not live another twenty-four hours to be able to eat *this* (= 'this coming') passover. Luke can hardly have understood the words in this way, as he has placed them in the context of a passover meal, and the logic of 'I would have liked to eat (but shall not) . . . for I shall not eat until . . .' is not evident. Or, the words could express with respect to the lamb (*this passover* = 'this passover lamb') an avowal of abstinence similar to that which, in the view of some, is made with respect to the wine in vv. 17–18 – 'I would have liked to eat this passover lamb before my death; but I must deny myself that wish; for I do not intend to eat it until God fulfils his promises in his kingdom' (so Jeremias, *Eucharistic Words*, pp. 208–24). Verses 15–16 then voice at the outset a deliberate intention of Jesus to abstain, himself, from the passover meal altogether (so as to enter upon an intercessory fast for the sins of Israel – so Jeremias, pp. 207ff.). This, also, can hardly be how Luke understood the words, as he has underlined the initiative of Jesus in securing preparations for the passover *that we may eat it* (v. 8; cf. *where I may eat the passover with my disciples*, v. 11). Further, in the avowal in v. 16, *ouketi ou mē*, the first word (if it is to be read; it is absent from some mss) would normally mean 'never again', i.e. after eating this meal. The wish is then better taken as one to be fulfilled; and the whole statement could have been framed by Luke with respect to the whole feast on the model of what is said with respect to the wine in v. 18 = Mark 14^{25}.

to eat this passover: Either 'to eat this passover lamb', already before them on the table, or, more likely, 'to eat this passover meal' (cf. Mark 14^{14}).

with you: In the Greek this is placed immediately after the verb for emphasis. The intense desire is to eat the passover with those who are most initimately associated with him in his purpose and destiny (cf. vv. 8–11). This provides the setting for the conversation in vv. 21–38.

before I suffer: This amounts to a further prediction of the passion. It is framed in Lukan fashion, *pro tou me pathein*; the articular infinitive governed by a preposition is more common in Luke than in any other NT writer, and the verb *paschein* = 'to suffer' is his characteristic word for the death of Jesus. The passion is now predicted more exactly as imminent.

16

This gives the reason for the desire expressed in v. 15. It is the certainty (*for I tell you*, in v. 18, which may be taken from Mark 14^{25}) that, in view of his imminent death and what that means, he will not eat another passover on earth (*I shall not eat it again*, so RSV margin, and cf. Mark 14^{25}), but only (with them?) when (*heōs hotou* = 'until') *it is fulfilled in the kingdom of God*, i.e. 'received its completion' (*plērousthai*, as in 7^1; 9^{31}; A. 12^{25}; 13^{25}; 14^{26}). This would correspond with what had become a strong element in passover piety, viz. its eschatological accent, whereby the present celebration of Israel's past deliverance was seen as an earnest of her final deliverance by God. Here Jesus relates that hope to his death and departure as decisive in bringing about the (speedy?) consummation of passover, and what it represented, in the future kingdom which he has proclaimed, and which is already initiated in the existence of his disciples. From this position of eschatological confidence he voices his desire for this last passover meal together.

17–18

There is a measure of parallelism with vv. 15–16, in that an element in the meal, a cup of wine, is related (*for*) with its counterpart in the feast of the kingdom of God. The difference is that the statements here are not, like vv. 15–16, a self-contained couplet, but initiate a 'eucharistic' action, which is then continued in v. 19a.

17

he took a cup: The participle here, *dexamenos* = 'having received', may reflect the ritual of the meal; the cup was handed to him as host. If *passover* in v. 15 means the whole meal, and not the lamb already on the table, this cup could be the first, or preliminary, cup of the passover meal. If v. 18 expresses a vow of abstinence Jesus would be reaffirming by means of this cup his repudiation for himself of participation in the meal to follow.

when he had given thanks: The participle here, *eucharistēsas* = 'having given thanks', appears in Mark 14^{23}/Matt. 26^{27} with respect to the cup which follows the bread, and in v. 19a (cf. I Cor. 11^{24}) with respect to the bread, where Mark/Matthew have *eulogēsas* = 'having blessed'. The two words are virtually synonymous, as in Jewish thought blessing was accomplished by giving thanks to God.

Take this: The injunction occurs also in Mark/Matthew, but in relation to the broken and distributed bread, where it is absent in Luke. It may be part of a liturgical formula in Christian practice. Here it could underline the position of Jesus as the authoritative head of the disciples, and the source for them of all things related to the kingdom of God.

divide it among yourselves: The verb here, *diamerizein*, is unique in the NT eucharistic texts. It is probably due to Luke; the only other NT instance of the verb in the active is in A. 2⁴⁵. It has been held to contradict regulations in the tractate Pesachim, which appear to presuppose individual cups, but Jeremias argues (*Eucharistic Words*, pp. 69f.) that these were a revision of an earlier practice of having a common cup, which would have been operative in Jesus' time. The intention could be different according to the interpretation of v. 18. If that expresses a vow of abstinence, this could be intended to distinguish between Jesus and his disciples; the contents of the cup are for their consumption, as he will not be partaking. If not, it could be intended to unite the disciples as a body with Jesus in his destiny.

18

This verse is closely parallel to what is said in Mark 14²⁵/Matt. 26²⁹ with respect to the eucharistic cup after the bread (though it is absent from the 'longer' text in v. 20), and by that cup is presumably meant the third cup of the passover meal, the cup of blessing (cf. 'after supper' in v. 20, I Cor. 11²⁵). This parallelism has been given two explanations. The first is that Luke is here using an independent liturgical tradition, in which the cup preceded the bread, and was interpreted not by reference to Jesus' blood, but to the eschatological future (cf. *Didache* 8, though there it is the bread that is so interpreted). The second is that it is due to editing by Luke, who, perhaps with knowledge of such a tradition, rejected the sacrificial interpretation of the cup in Mark 14²⁴, and transferred the eschatological reference of Mark 14²⁵ to this earlier cup. *from now on* (the Lukan *apo tou nun*) generally means 'after this present moment'. His destiny is expressed by his drinking of the cup in certain knowledge, and in anticipation, of the coming of the kingdom of God, a more impersonal form of Mark's 'I drink it new in the kingdom of God' (cf. v. 16, 'it is fulfilled in the kingdom of God').

19–20

Interpretation here is bound up with a major textual-critical problem presented by the following:ᵃ

(i) vv. 17, 18, 19, 20 – called 'the longer text' – is read by all mss except D, and by all the versions except mss of the Old Latin and Syriac.

(ii) (*a*) vv. 17, 18, 19a (as far as 'this is my body'), but not vv. 19b, 20 – called 'the shorter text' – is read by D and the Old Latin mss a d ff² i l, and is to be supposed to lie behind c and probably r².

(*b*) a text with the order vv. 19a, 17, 18 is read by the Old Latin mss b and e;

---

a For discussions of it, see R. V. G. Tasker, *The Greek New Testament*, Oxford and Cambridge 1964, pp. 422f., Jeremias, *Eucharistic Words*, pp. 139ff., Leaney, pp. 72ff.

this supports (ii) (*a*), and represents a modification of it to restore the order bread/cup.

(*c*) a text in the order vv. 19 (complete except for 'which is given'), 17, 18, is read by the Curetonian Syriac. This is not derived from (i), which always has 'which is given', but from (ii) (*a*) or (ii) (*b*) – it agrees with D and e in not having 'and' before 'divide it' in v. 17 – and has been supplemented from I Cor. 11²⁴.

(*d*) a text in the order vv. 19 (plus 'and said', and with 'I give' for 'which is given'), 17 (plus 'after supper' and 'this is my blood of the covenant'), 18 (plus 'for', and with 'fruit' for 'product' of the vine), is read by the Sinaitic Syriac. This is derived from (ii) (*c*) ,with additions from I Cor. 11²⁵.

The acuteness of the problem caused by the above evidence at such a crucial point in the narrative as the institution of the Eucharist is indicated by the large number of scholars cited in support of both the 'longer' and the 'shorter' texts by Jeremias in the first (German) edition of his *Eucharistic Words*, and by his own change from support of the 'shorter' to support of the 'longer' text in between the first and second editions of that work (cf. also the change made between the first and second editions of RSV).

So far as abundance, spread and authoritativeness of mss are concerned, the textual evidence is overwhelmingly in favour of the 'longer' text. This in itself, however, makes the appearance of any other text here all the more surprising, and the 'shorter' text becomes the harder reading, especially in face of the texts in Mark, Matthew and I Cor. 11, and therefore the more likely to be original. The 'shorter' text is entirely 'Western' in character. It is thus attested as current early in the second century, in Western Europe (D Old Latin), Africa (*e*) and Syria (syrᶜᵘʳ ˢⁱⁿ). If it is original, it must have been amended early in the chief centres of the church (e.g. p⁷⁵, early third century) to have produced the strong consensus in favour of the 'longer' text in mss from the fourth century onwards. Estimate of it is to some extent bound up with an estimate of the 'Western' text as a whole, which continues to be discussed. For Westcott and Hort, who judged that text to be prone to expansion, the 'shorter' text had originality simply in being shorter. Hence Jeremias (*Eucharistic Words*, pp. 148ff.) conducts a preliminary examination of the 'Western' text throughout Luke's Gospel to show that it was frequently prone to abbreviate, and he judges the 'shorter' text to have been such an abbreviation. The difficulty is then to account for it as such. Dibelius (*Tradition*, p. 211) suggests that it was made simply to reduce the number of actions in vv. 17–20, either by deletion or change of order; but, as Jeremias observes, that would have been achieved more naturally by deleting the first cup (v. 17), thus leaving the order bread/cup; and the absence of words after the bread in v. 19a is not explained in this way. He himself explains by recourse to the *disciplina arcani*, a convention of reserve or secrecy in speaking of central mysteries of the faith to guard against their profanation by the uninitiated – in this case as enjoining cannibalism and the drinking of blood. This is improbable. Our earliest knowledge of such a *disciplina* comes from Cyril of Jerusalem (fourth century), who employed it in the instruction of candidates for baptism; and it would not explain why the other texts of the Last Supper, including those of Mark and Matthew in D, were not similarly affected, nor why the already incriminating words 'This is my body' were not also suppressed. The ascription of the abbreviation to 'some scribal idiosyncrasy' (Marshall, p. 800) is somewhat desperate. Thus, the 'shorter' text could well be original; it is taken as such in the first edition of RSV and in NEB. The 'longer' text could then be the result of scribal supplementation, carried out in somewhat clumsy fashion from I Cor. 11$^{24-25}$ (with assimilation to Mark in the words 'which is poured out for you'), with the object of making it conform to other traditions of the Last Supper, and, perhaps, of inserting the command to repeat the rite into the gospel text.

In the 'longer' text vv. 15–18 appear as two parallel statements concerned with the passover meal (this passover/the (first?) passover cup), which could be self-contained, and which could have been taken by Luke from an independent tradition of the meal. This is followed in vv. 19–20 by two parallel statements made within the meal itself, and concerned with the institution of the Lord's Supper (unleavend bread/(third?) passover cup), which Luke could have received from a liturgical tradition (that of his own church?). The 'shorter' text could be seen either (i) as two parallel statements about the passover (vv. 15–18, as above), to which is added a single statement about bread (v. 19a, perhaps taken from Mark), or (ii) as a single introductory statement about the passover (vv. 15–16), followed in vv. 17–19a by two statements about the institution of the Lord's Supper, but in the order cup/bread, and in a form of words which differs substantially from what stands in Mark, Matthew and I Cor. 11. Either could be Luke's rendering of a liturgical usage. The first could be in a form which prepares for the description of Christian worship simply as 'the breaking of bread' (A. 2^{42}; cf. 24^{35}; A. 20$^{7, 11}$). The second could be in a form which corresponds to the liturgical tradition in *Didache* 9–10, whether that is taken to refer to the Agape (Love Feast) or the Eucharist, in which thanksgiving is made first over the cup and then over the bread, with emphasis on the gathering of the present church into the kingdom (cf. also *Didache* 14, 'On the Lord's day gather yourselves together and break bread and give thanks'). Both would have involved for Luke the suppression of the sacrificial cup after the bread in Mark's text.

19

The conclusion of the 'shorter' text, v. 19a, is identical with Mark 14^{22}, except for Mark's 'as they were eating', which would not follow well after vv. 15–18, *has given thanks* for 'blessed', and *saying* for 'and said'. The action corresponds to the passover ritual, when the host took the unleavened bread for blessing by thanksgiving, and tore it into portions for distribution, his eating of his own portion being the sign for the rest to eat. That the word for ordinary bread (*artos*) is used in all the texts here, and not *azuma*, the word for the unleavened bread prescribed for passover, is probably not significant, since *artos* could mean a 'loaf' of any kind. What is unique is the interpretative statement following the blessing and breaking, and accompanying the distribution, which was generally made in silence.

This is my body: However unusual the statement here, its declarative form – *This (is:* in Aramaic there would be no verb as a copula) *my body* – could also correspond to the passover ritual, *this* (is) being a formula in the passover haggadah for the replies made by the head of the household to the questions asked about the peculiar features of the feast (unleavened bread, bitter herbs, etc.), 'What is this?' The crux of the statement is the sense to be given to the word *sōma* = 'body'. Jeremias (*Eucharistic Words*, pp. 198ff.) sees the principal clue to lie in taking the two statements over bread and cup as in effect a single statement, and hence the words body/blood as a word-pair. This word-pair he takes as equivalent to the LXX 'flesh and blood', the Hebrew word *basar*, generally translated by *sarx* = 'flesh', being occasionally translated in the LXX by *sōma*. This word-pair he locates in sacrifice as descriptive of the two components of a sacrificial animal which are separated in death. On this view the two statements taken together refer to Jesus as a sacrifice, and in particular as the sacrificial paschal lamb. This would by implication supply what has been re-marked as a strange lacuna in the texts, viz. the absence of any reference to what was central in the passover rite, the lamb. This interpretation is vulnerable. It depends on the close conjunction of the two statements to form one statement, and this is threatened by their separation in the 'longer' text and in I Cor. 11$^{24-25}$ by the words 'after supper'. The use of 'body' rather than 'flesh' along with 'blood', and of 'body' in the vocabulary of sacrifice, is said to be 'almost without parallel' (*TDNT* VII, p. 1059). The only NT parallel – 'the bodies of those animals whose blood is brought into the sanctuary as a sacrifice for sin are burned outside the camp' (Heb. 13^{11}) – hardly lends support, as there 'bodies' means 'carcases'. An alternative, and more probable, interpretation is that *sōma* stands on its own, and has the inclusive sense of 'self' or 'person'. This it could have in Greek (what any underlying Aramaic word would have been is a matter of discussion), and is probably to be understood in Paul's term for the church, 'the body of Christ'; cf. esp. I Cor. 10$^{16-17}$, where Christians are renewed as one body through participation in the one loaf, which is the body of Christ. The action with its interpretative statement in the 'shorter' text (as also in Mark/ Matthew here) would then denote the incoporation of the disciples into the 'person' of Jesus, and in Jewish thought that would involve what he does or is about to do (perhaps here with respect to the kingdom of God). Any reference to death or sacrifice would then lie in the action and sayings over the following cup (absent from the shorter text).

which is given for you: This interpretation of the bread in the 'longer' text extends beyond anything in Mark/Matthew. If the 'shorter' text is original, this will have been a scribal addition to fill up what was regarded by the standard of other accounts as a lacuna, and will have been made, either directly from the text of I Cor. 11^{24}, which also has *for you* though not *which is given*, or from the liturgical tradition which is represented by I Cor. 11^{23-25}. Its effect is to make the statement over the bread parallel with that over the cup – given for you/ poured out for you. In the development of the liturgical tradition it may have been created by the statement over the cup, since 'poured out for' with reference to either wine or blood is a natural expression, whereas that bread or body is 'for' them is obscure. Hence in I Cor. 11^{24}, which has 'This is my body, the (body) for you', some mss have 'broken for you', using the ordinary term 'to break bread' in a forced manner as symbolic of the 'breaking' of Jesus' body in death. Here *which is given*, the present participle passive, *didomenon*, with a future sense, represents another interpretation (also forced if it is based on *he gave it to them*), in which the body = person of Jesus is that which God hands over to men (if that is the force of the passive here), or which he himself relinquishes. What is implied by *for you* is uncertain. The preposition used is *huper*, which can mean 'on behalf of', 'for the sake of', or 'in place of'. The sense may be the same as in Mark 10^{45}, 'to give his life as a ransom for many' (though the preposition is not the same), or in I Tim. 2^6, 'gave himself as a ransom for all', and Tit. 2^{14}, 'gave himself for us to redeem us'. In comparison with v. 19a this does not unite Jesus and the disciples, but distinguishes between them as benefactor and beneficiaries. *for you* here, in v. 20 and in I Cor. 11^{24}, is almost certainly secondary to 'for many' (Mark 14^{24}) in applying the benefits internally to the church.

Do this in remembrance of me: This is in verbatim agreement with I Cor. 11^{24}. It provides the only statement in the gospel texts that what Jesus does and says on the particular occasion of the Last Supper is to be repeated as a rite in the church – the verb here, *poiein* = 'to do' has as one of its meanings 'to perform, keep, celebrate' of a feast or sacrifice (cf. Matt. 26^{18}, 'to keep (*poiein*) the passover'). Its insertion here only, and not also at v. 20 (cf. I Cor. 11^{25}), is somewhat slovenly, as it is not clear to what *this* refers – to the action with the bread only, or to the actions in vv. 17–19 (20), or to the whole passover. Jeremias (*Eucharistic Words*, pp. 251ff.) proposed, on the basis of certain OT passages and a passover prayer for God to remember the messiah, that *in remembrance of me* should be understood as 'that God may remember me', and that, as a result of his remembering Jesus, he may bring about the completion of the salvation already initiated by Jesus' death. It is, however, doubtful whether the OT passages are rightly understood in this way,[b] and 'as a memorial of me', 'that you may have me in mind', is the more natural and probable sense.

b See D. R. Jones, '*Anamnesis* in the LXX and the Interpretation of I Cor. 11.25', *JTS* ns 6, 1955, pp. 183–91.

20

That this verse is also a scribal addition is suggested by its slovenly character at two points. (i) Apart from *which is poured out for you* it is identical in wording with I Cor. 11²⁵, except that *likewise* stands after *the cup* for emphasis, and there is no word in the Greek for *is*. That is, the narrative in Mark/Matthew of Jesus taking a cup, giving thanks and giving it to the disciples so that they all drank of it (with the command to drink of it, Matthew), is compressed, as in I Cor. 11²⁵, into the single word *likewise*. But whereas the sequence in I Cor. 11²³⁻²⁵, 'he took bread, and having given thanks he broke it and said . . . likewise (he took) the cup . . . saying . . .' is a natural one, the sequence in vv. 19–20, 'having taken bread and having given thanks he broke and gave it to them saying . . . and the cup likewise . . .' is very awkward. (ii) The only departure from I Cor. 11²⁵, apart from the failure to repeat 'Do this in remembrance of me', is the words *which is poured out for you (to huper humōn ekchunnomenon)*. This is evidently an assimilation to the text of Mark 14²⁴, with *you* in place of 'many', producing a parallel to *which is given for you* in the word over the bread. But it is ungrammatical. *which is poured out* is a present participle passive with the article in the nominative case. This is correct in Mark, where it agrees with 'my blood of the covenant', which is also in the nominative, but it does not agree in v. 20 with 'my blood', which is in the dative after *in*. In Mark/Matthew the accompanying word with the cup, 'This (wine) is my blood of the covenant' is compressed and awkward. The meaning is 'This is my covenant blood.' According to its background this could convey, either that Jesus' death (this is the meaning of 'blood') is to be a sacrifice inaugurating a covenant of God with Israel (as in Exod. 24⁸), or that by his covenant death he is to set free Israel's captives (cf. Zech. 9¹¹). In the corresponding words in v. 20 = I Cor. 11²⁵, the cup itself (its contents?) constitutes this covenant, which is now defined more precisely as the *new* (i.e. eschatological and final) *covenant*, that according to Jer. 31³¹ᶠᶠ· God would make with Israel. It will be set up *in* (Greek *en*, probably used instrumentally = 'by means of') his death.

In Mark/Matthew the narrative of the Last Supper is so concentrated on what pertained to the Christian rite of the Eucharist that the words over the cup bring it to an abrupt end after the singing (presumably) of the remaining Hallel Psalms, 114–118. This brevity is very stark, and it is hardly surprising if, in Luke, the meal continues as the occasion for Jesus to make what is in effect the last address of his earthly life to the apostles, and to instruct them as the future leaders of the church. As such, this will be by definition one of the most important sections in the Gospel as showing a certain perspective, such as Mark and Matthew hardly show at all, on the church and its relation to its Lord. This is particularly so if it was Luke himself who first composed this address by selecting, and bringing together in sequence, sayings which, apparently, had been previously independent of one another, and had been spoken in other contexts. For in doing this he will be revealing something of his own theological perspectives. While the section does not fall completely within the category of the farewell speech of the dying man, since Jesus is to reappear from the dead and instruct the apostles as the risen Lord (24; A. 1¹ᶠᶠ·), it exhibits features commonly found in that literary genre (for which see Stauffer, *Theology*, App. VI). Such are – the leader has a meal with his own; he issues warnings and final commands; he prays for those he leaves behind; and he establishes a successor. So the particular collocation of sayings in vv. 21–38 is designed to give expression to the permanent community of Jesus and his disciples in past, present and eschatological future. Their celebration together of his last earthly passover before his passion is a matter of intense desire for him, since what lies beyond for him, and for them, is life in the kingdom of God, of which eating and drinking was one symbol. Though their unity, and their union with him through receiving his body, are threatened by the betrayal by which the Son of man goes to his appointed destiny, and by their worldly desire for pre-eminence, they have him in their midst for model and authority as the one who serves. Since they have been his constant companions in trial, they will also partake with him at the messianic banquet in a rule which he testates to them as from the Father; and they will fulfil the eschatological role of judges of Israel. Their leader, Peter, despite his coming denial, has already been preserved by Jesus' prevailing intercession from total defection, and with a view to their establishment as brethren; and while in the past they have been maintained without lack under his aegis, they will continue to share his destiny, when, in fulfilment of the divine will in scripture, he is apprehended as a criminal. This complex and sequence of thought are not achieved, as in John 13–17, by a lengthy and closely articulated discourse with uniform vocabulary, but by a collocation of five individual units, some of which are connected by similarity of theme or language, but between which there are also awkward transitions.

21–23 (i) Prophecy of Betrayal

The drama and poignancy of the passion are greatly heightened, both by the fact that, humanly speaking, it was initiated by the agency of one who had been a regular table companion in the inner circle of the Twelve, and also by the fact that Jesus alone knows in advance that this will be the case, and who that agent will be. In Mark, followed by Matthew, Jesus' prediction of it is the only component of the Last Supper other than the eucharistic actions and words, and it is extraordinary there in its location and form. It overshadows a meal already in process as its opening incident, and it takes the protracted form of a rough and agitated sequence of a solemn prediction, partly in biblical language, that he will be handed over by one of those present, a sorrowful question from each one present whether it was he, a repetition that it is one of the twelve who is sharing a common dish, and a solemn reiteration in terms of the Son of man that this handing over is scripturally determined, but that nevertheless the human agent is cursed, and had better not have been born. In contrast to this, and to Matt. 26²⁵ and John 13²¹⁻³⁰, where Judas is progressively unmasked, Luke's equivalent is very different. The incident comes at the end of the meal, and forms the transition from it to the instruction which follows; and it consists of three polished sentences. This could reflect Luke's use of another source for the whole of the Last Supper narrative, but such a hypothesis is unnecessary. It would be understandable if Luke rejected the Markan position for this deeply tragic episode, particularly in view of his emphasis on the solidarity of Jesus and the Twelve at the outset of the meal (vv. 15–17); while the language of vv. 21–23 shows sufficient Lukan traits to be comprehensible as a revision of Mark.

21

But behold: The difficult junction is made with what has preceded, and the thought wrenched abruptly in an opposite direction, by the adversative adverb *plēn*, a colloquial word meaning 'only', 'nevertheless'. It is used in this way more often by Luke than by any other NT writer (cf. 6²⁴, ³⁵; 10¹¹; 11⁴¹; 12³¹; 18⁸; 19²⁷, where it could be due to his sources, as it is not in A.). Here only it is strengthened by the dramatic *idou, behold,* another favourite word with Luke. It cannot be argued that this presupposes the 'longer' text in that the contrast is made with 'poured out for you' as the immediately preceding words; for the contrast would have been as great if what had immediately preceded was the closing words of the 'shorter' text, 'This is my body'.

the hand of him who betrays me is with me on the table: The prediction of betrayal, which is introduced very suddenly, is made more succinctly and stylistically than in Mark 14¹⁸, ²⁰. *the hand of* in the sense of 'the effective action of' can be paralleled in A. 4²⁸; 11²¹; 13¹¹. Here it is the effective action of handing Jesus over into the power of his enemies, and the contradiction is that this murderous intent is now revealed to be present along with the closest companionship with Jesus, which is expressed here by *with me* at *the table* (*epi tēs trapezēs*, as in v. 30; 20³⁷; A. 5²³; not 'on the table' as in RSV), as it had previously been expressed by *eat with you* (v. 15), *divide this among yourselves* (v. 17), and *This is my body* (v. 19) – cf. Mark 14¹⁸, 'one who is eating with me', 20, 'one who is dipping in the same dish with me'.

22

For the Son of man goes as it has been determined: The compressed prediction of betrayal is followed, as in Mark, by a statement of its necessity (*For; hoti* = 'because') in terms of the Son of man and his divinely ordained destiny. In Luke's version *as it has been determined* is certainly from his hand; *horizein* = 'to appoint', 'to determine', occurs only here in the gospels, but is found four times in this sense in A. It replaces Mark's 'it is written'. *goes* is the Lukan verb *poreuesthai* in place of Mark's vulgar *hupagei*.

but woe to that man by whom he is betrayed!: The adversative *but* is, as in v. 21, *plēn. woe to* conveys final condemnation by God (see on 6²⁴), though it lacks the further severity of Mark's 'It would have been better for that man if he had not been born.' It is doubtful whether vv. 21–22 were intended to apply to anyone else than Judas, or that they were ever a general warning that even the closest disciple at the Lord's table could apostasize. The juxtaposition of the divine necessity for something to happen and the human culpability for its happening is simply made without any resolution of the logical problem. Since this culpability is with respect to God's supreme agent, the Son of man, it will meet with ultimate divine opposition and destruction. But Luke, without removing the condemnation, intends somewhat to mitigate it (cf. vv. 3–6, 47–48), and his shorter and smoother version of the whole episode is due to his desire in vv. 21–38 to dwell on the qualifications of the apostles despite their failures.

23

The reaction of the apostles to the two previous statements takes the form of a discussion among them as to the identity of the betrayer – contrast in Mark their individual questioning of Jesus about this, and his reply set between the two statements of betrayal. This verse bears marks of Luke's hand throughout. *which of them it was* is the literary construction of the article followed by the interrogative *tis ara* = 'who then?', and the verb in the rare optative. *that would do this* is the participial 'the one about to' (*ho mellōn*)with the Lukan word for *to do* (*prassein*). This both rounds off the episode in somewhat muted fashion, and also prepares for what follows by reintroducing the Twelve (*And they*) as the audience.

24-27 (ii) *The Character of Apostles*

The allocution moves from the betrayer among the apostles by way of a dispute among them about pre-eminence to instruction on the nature of apostleship. The sequence is not obvious, as there is no suggestion that the betrayer was to act from a desire to be thought great, and the connection is somewhat forced (*de kai* = 'in addition', 'furthermore'). Similarity in thought and language with the pericope in Mark 10^{35-45}, which Luke unaccountably omits from a section where he is otherwise following Mark closely, raises the question whether he has transferred it here in revised form as appropriate to Jesus' parting address to the Twelve, or is reproducing an independent tradition with some of the same wording (and, according to the Proto-Luke hypothesis, omitted Mark 10^{35-45} because he had already done this).

24

In Mark the comparison with Gentile rulers is introduced more specifically in connection with a request from the sons of Zebedee for chief places with Jesus in his coming glory, and the anger that caused among the rest of the Twelve. There greatness means a pre-eminent position in the eschatological kingdom. Luke's introduction is more general. There is *a dispute* (*philoneikia* + +, a highly literary word, with the primary meaning of 'emulation') *which of them was to be regarded as the greatest* (the construction is again, as in v. 23 (cf. 9^{46}), the article with an indirect question, though here the verb is in the indicative). *regarded* – it is not said by whom – is in the Greek *dokei*. This is rare in the NT in this sense of 'to have a reputation', and could well be due to its presence in Mark 10^{42} in the phrase 'those who are supposed to (rule)'. *greatest* is in the Greek *meizōn*, the comparative of *megalos* = 'great (cf. Mark 10^{42}), used in a superlative sense, as in 9^{46} = Mark 9^{34}.

25

the kings of the Gentiles: Mark 10^{42} has 'the supposed rulers of the Gentiles'. *kings* would be a more natural word for Luke in this connection (cf. 10^{24} in comparison with Matt. 13^{17}; 21^{12}; A. 9^{15}), and for him 'rulers' are generally those of the Jews (as in 14^{1}; 23^{13}; A. 4^{5}; 13^{27}).

exercise lordship over them; and those in authority over them: The verbs here, *kurieuein* and *exousiazein*, are in the simple form, whereas in Mark 10^{42} they are in the compound form *katakurieuein* and *katexousiazein*. This is strange in view of Luke's liking for compound verbs, but the explanation could be that Mark and Luke are making different points here. The point in Mark is that those who are supposed to rule the Gentiles actually tyrannize over them, and their great men exercise domination over them (that is the force of the compound verbs); but that is not to be the case among the apostles – in their relation to one another, or in their relation as a body to others (other disciples?)? The point in

Luke is that in the Gentile world it is kings who rule their subjects, and those in authority are hailed by those subjects as benefactors; but you are not to be so (this is a literal translation of the Greek); but the greatest among you is to behave as the most junior, and the leader as the one of lowest rank.

are called benefactors: The word used here, *euergetēs*, is almost certainly due to Luke. It occurs only here in the NT; the verb occurs only at A. 10³⁸; and its cognate noun *euergesia* = 'service' occurs only at A. 4⁹; I Tim. 6². It shows a nice appreciation of the Gentile world, and is perhaps not without a certain irony. For the word is one which is very frequent in classical and Hellenistic literature, being particularly common in inscriptions as a stock epithet for emperors and distinguished men, and found in the papyri as a regular title = 'your beneficence'. It was applied both to gods and to human heroes of various kinds, and it expressed a deeply rooted religio-political concept governing Hellenistic civilization, that of benevolent rule or even despotism. The ruler was hailed by his people as more than simply a ruler, and as their saviour and bene-factor in supplying all their needs. Jesus is thus made to comment on the Hel-lenistic world at one of its central points; and the suggestion in the direct allocution *But not so with you* (v. 26) is that true benefaction proceeds for an apostle from something other than his position as a ruler.

26

In Mark 10⁴³ᶠ· the lesson is that for a member of the Twelve to become 'great' i.e. to have a chief position, he must be the 'deacon' (*diakonos*) of the Twelve, and to enjoy the rights of leadership ('first', *prōtos*, is a word for a chief man) he must play in respect of everyone the part of a slave (*doulos*). Here the lesson is somewhat different, and the language employed indicates adaptation (by Luke?) to conditions as they had developed in the church. It is that the most pre-eminent is to act as if he were *the youngest* (*neōteros*, also a comparative with a superlative sense). This word is found elsewhere in the NT in I Tim. 5¹ᶠ·, ¹¹, ¹⁴; Tit. 2⁶; I Peter 5⁵; A. 5⁶, where it refers to a distinction in the Christian con-gregation between the younger (men and women), the juniors, who as such were at the beck and call of others, and perhaps performed the lowlier tasks, and the *presbuteroi*, the older (men and women), the seniors, who stood at the head; and instructions are given about their respective behaviour and their mutual rela-tions which are based on 'a pattern of popular moral philosophy'.ᶜ Similarly, *the leader* (*ho hēgoumenos*, the participle of the verb which, apart from Matt. 2⁶ LXX, is found only here in the gospels) is used as semi-technical term for those in authority in the congregation in Heb. 13⁷, ¹⁷, ²⁴ (cf. A. 15²²). He is to behave as if he were performing the task of supplying other's needs. The verb here is

ᶜ M. Dibelius, *The Pastoral Epistles*, ET (Hermeneia) Philadelphia 1972, pp. 72, 77f.

diakonein (*he who serves* is the participle matching the leader), and it governs the thought of the next verse.

This verse could have been once an independent unit, which Luke has used as a conclusion to this section in preference to Mark 10⁴⁵, to which it is allied in thought, though it is distinctive in its form of a question answered interrogatively by Jesus himself. The complex of words *diakonein* = 'to serve' (thirty-four times in the NT), *diakonia* = 'service' (thirty-one times) and *diakonos* = 'servant' (twenty-eight times) plays a considerable part in the NT in a wide range of contexts. It would seem to have been a Christian creation, as these words are very rare and unimportant in the OT. It is distinct from the complex *douleuein*, *douleia* and *doulos* (= 'slave'), though this tends to be blurred when both are rendered by the same English word 'serve'. The emphasis in the latter is not on any function performed but on servitude. The slave is the property of his master (Greek *kurios*, which means 'owner'). He has no rights of his own, and he simply does what he is ordered (17¹⁰). The particular emphasis in the former, amongst the various Greek words for 'to serve', is on the personal service done to another in supplying his needs. Its foundation, as this verse shows, is in the ordinary secular activity of waiting at table (cf. John 12²; Mark 1³¹; Luke 10⁴⁰). *one who serves* (*ho diakonōn*, the participle), who could also be a slave (17⁸), is the waiter in distinction from the one upon whom he waits, *one who sits at table* (*ho anakeimenos* = 'one reclining at table', only here in L–A). In A. 6¹⁻⁴ this supplying of needs consists in poor relief called 'serving tables' in distinction from the supply of the word of God in preaching. Paul uses this vocabulary for the collection he makes in the Gentile churches to supply the needs of the poor Christians in Jerusalem (Rom. 15³¹; II Cor. 8⁴, ¹⁹ᶠ·; 9¹, ¹²ᶠ·). From this it can be extended to cover the supply of spiritual needs by spiritual gifts (I Cor. 12⁵; Eph. 4¹²), and the contrast between the law and the gospel as 'serving up' death and life respectively (II Cor. 3⁷; 4¹; 5¹⁸). Here, following upon v. 26, Jesus uses the word to define, not only the true nature of apostles, but also himself as their authoritative model. Since it is also used in a similar way in Mark 10⁴⁵ to complete the pericope there, the question again arises whether Luke is here dependent on Mark, has rejected Mark's saying in terms of the Son of man in the past as too impersonal (as also the sacrificial interpretation of the death of Jesus suggested by 'to give his life as a ransom for many'), and has produced a revised version in the form of a personal statement by Jesus of himself as exemplar. The differences between this verse and Mark 10⁴⁵, however, are probably too great in structure and tone to be accounted for in this way, and it is more likely that Luke has derived it from a tradition, and preferred it to Mark 10⁴⁵. (This could raise the question whether in the tradition personal 'I sayings' of Jesus were transformed into impersonal 'Son of man sayings', or vice versa, see Jeremias, *Theology*, pp. 250ff.).

I am among you as one who serves: In Greek the participle 'the one serving'. This highly personal statement does not refer to a future guiding presence of the exalted Lord (as in Matt. 18^{20}; 28^{20}), nor does it reflect the moment of its utterance, since Jesus is in fact acting as host and not waiting at table – the suggestion that it presupposes the actions in John 13^{4-17} to have taken place is gratuitous, as washing the feet is not the same as waiting at table, and was the mandatory duty of the slave (cf. John 13^{14-16}). It is a formulation of the manner of Jesus' presence with them throughout his ministry, and, if genuine, is likely to have been spoken at some time during it rather than when it is almost over. It could mean either 'I am in your company as the master who serves your needs', or 'as your examplar in serving the needs of men'. There is no indication of what those needs are, nor of how Jesus supplies them; in A. 10^{38} Luke uses *euergetein* + + = 'to be a benefactor to' to characterize the whole ministry of Jesus, perhaps with special reference to his healings.

28–30 (iii) *The Ultimate Destiny of the Apostles*
This is a separate unit, divisible into four long lines. Verbally it is linked simply by 'and' (not in RSV); but the real connection is the continuation from vv. 15f., 17f., 19a of the conjunction of the 'you' of the apostolic company and the person of Jesus, which is stressed here – *You are those who . . . and I* (*kāgō* = 'I also'). In contrast, however, to vv. 21–23, 24–27, it is not now the distinction and separation between Jesus and his disciples that are emphasized, but rather their union in this world, and the unity of their destinies in the age to come.

The origin of the unit – for Bultmann (*History*, p. 158) it is plainly an utterance of the risen Lord – and its development in tradition are puzzling. Thus, v. 30b is evidently the same saying as Matt. 19^{28}, where it stands on its own. The contexts of the two versions are quite different; Matthew's is inserted into a Markan pericope. So also are the introductions – in Luke *You are those who have continued* (*diamenein*, probably due to Luke), in Matthew 'in the new world (*palingennesia*, a technical term probably due to Matthew) you who have followed me'. In what follows – *I assign to you, as my Father assigned to me, a kingdom* (Luke), 'When the Son of man shall sit on his glorious throne' (Matthew) – there may be another instance of the transformation of an 'I saying' into a 'Son of man saying', or vice versa. Verses 29–30a, whether introduced by v. 28 or in some other way, could stand alone. They could have been placed here because they referred to the position of the apostles in the coming kingdom in terms of table fellowship, thus continuing the thought of vv. 15–16, 17–18, 21, 27. Luke could then have attached v. 30b as continuing, albeit by a violent change of symbolism, the thought of the eschatological role of the apostles. Alternatively, vv. 29–30a, eating and drinking in the kingdom by divine appointment, were inserted into an original saying, vv. 28, 30b, about the exercise of eschatological rule and judgment. In either case it is unlikely that Luke and Matthew derived the latter from the same (written) source.

28

You are those who have continued with me: As in v. 27 Jesus is characterized by his relation to the apostles during his earthly ministry as *one who serves*, so now the apostles are characterized by their relation to him in that ministry. The verb here, *diamenein*, means in classical literature 'to endure', but in the LXX, and the other NT instances (1^{22}; Gal. 2^5; II Peter 3^4), it means 'to remain', 'to abide'. The construction here is the definite article with the perfect participle, which implies a long and constant continuance extending to the present moment.

in my trials: The Greek word here, *peirasmos*, means 'testing' (see on 4^2). In the biblical literature, to which it is almost confined, it can refer to a testing by God, or, more frequently, by Satan; but the Twelve can hardly be said in any meaningful sense to have shared with Jesus in such inner spiritual experiences as are described in 4^{1-13}. It can also have a more neutral sense of 'danger', 'trouble', 'oppression', brought about by the opposition of men – cf. A. 20^{19}, where Paul, the model apostle, serves the Lord in humility (cf. vv. 24–27 here), tears and trials which befell him 'through the plots of the Jews' (cf. Mark 10^2; 12^{15} for the verb used of human opposition to the truth). The statement is crucial for the thesis of Conzelmann (*Theology*, pp. 16, 83) that the pattern of this Gospel is determined by Luke's view that Satan had been banished by Jesus for the duration of the ministry and was allowed back to tempt only at the beginning of the passion; but it can only be made to serve that thesis if *trials* here is limited to those which have taken place since the arrival in Jerusalem. This is very forced. The perfect participle suggests a longer period, and a more natural interpretation is that the whole ministry had been one of trials, though there is not much in the gospel narrative to illustrate such a sharing of the apostles in the opposition to, and obloquy of, Jesus. The meaning could be, 'You, the Twelve, are the only ones left who have not deserted from discipleship'; but even so its utterance here, especially along with v. 30b, is awkward in view of the immediately previous prophecy that one of the Twelve will desert and betray. Clearly Luke was bound to omit Mark 14^{27}, which asserts the opposite, a coming total desertion by the Twelve, from which they will be recovered.

29–30

Whatever the precise situation envisaged in v. 28, it is not by virtue of any past merits of their own, nor of any possible future achievements, but by their association in trials up to the present moment with Jesus as God's spokesman and the inaugurator of his kingdom, that their relation to that kingdom is guaranteed. And it is he who is in a position to guarantee it by delegation from God (contrast Mark 10^{40}). The Greek can be rendered either by (i) 'as my Father has appointed for me, so do I appoint for you, a kingdom, that . . .', or by (ii) *as my Father appointed a kingdom for me, so do I appoint for you that . . .* (so RSV). In (i) the sequence of thought is that, inasmuch as God has assigned his rule to Jesus, so Jesus assigns it to the apostles to exercise it (with him) in judging Israel, and the reference to eating and drinking with him in his kingdom is an intrusion. In (ii) the sequence is that since God has determined for Jesus a sphere of rule, Jesus has himself determined for the apostles that they shall be his companions in that sphere by sharing his table, and the reference to judging Israel is an appendix. The verb rendered by *appoint* (*diatithesthai*) can mean 'to covenant', and has as its cognate noun *diathēkē* (they are found together in A. 3²⁵, Heb. 8¹⁰ LXX = Jer. 31³³). It is suggested that this is the meaning here, and that it presupposes the 'longer' text, from which it picks up 'the new covenant'. But this is unnecessary. The saying could well have been uttered originally in a different context from the Last Supper; and with *a kingdom* as the direct object, and *me* and *you* as indirect objects in the dative, the verb is probably to be given its regular meaning of 'assign' (so RSV 2nd ed.), or 'confer upon'. In Jos. *Ant.* 13.407 it is used with 'kingdom' of Alexander Jannaeus conferring the rule on a successor, though there the verb has another of its possible meanings of testamentary disposition in a will. While this could be the sense in *I appoint to you*, if vv. 14–38 are to be regarded as Jesus' last will and testament, it could not apply to *my Father appointed for me*.

that you may eat and drink at my table in my kingdom: This awkward intrusion may be due to the context of the Last Supper, which for Jesus himself foreshadows a future eating and drinking in the kingdom of God (vv. 15–16, 17–18). The background is the heavenly (messianic) banquet as a familiar image in Jewish eschatology for the state of blessedness in the kingdom (cf. 14¹⁵). Its origins can be seen in such passages as Isa. 25⁶; Zeph. 1⁷, and its development in I Enoch 62¹⁴; II Baruch 29⁸; Rev. 19⁹ – for rabbinic parallels, see SB IV, pp. 1154ff. In contrast to the synoptic tradition in general, the table is here said to be Jesus' table and the kingdom his kingdom, a conception which elsewhere in the NT is either found on the lips of others (23⁴²) or, is a christological creation of the church (cf. Matt. 16²⁸/Mark 9¹; Matt. 20²¹/Mark 10³⁷; Col. 1¹³; Eph. 5⁵; II Tim. 4¹; contrast 13²⁹/Matt. 8¹¹).

and sit on thrones judging the twelve tribes of Israel: The origins of this imagery, which is here made to appear as an appendage, is the vision in Dan. 7, where corporate thrones of judgment are set in heaven, and God confers on 'one like a son of man', generally interpreted as a symbol of the faithful Israelites in trial and persecution, a kingdom and dominion over the nations which is everlasting. In subsequent development of this thought 'the Son of man' can become a heavenly figure as the Elect One (= the archetypal Israelite?), who sits on the throne of glory, acts for God as judge, and rules over, and is intimately associated with, the elect and righteous (cf. I Enoch 62⁷ᶠᶠ·; 69²⁷ᶠᶠ·; 51³). This apocalyptic thought and language have influenced the Matthaean form of the saying ('the new world', 'the Son of man shall sit on his glorious throne'); less so the Lukan, which speaks more in the language common in the synoptic tradition – *my*

Father and *kingdom*. That the faithful disciples of Jesus as a body are by divine appointment to share in this kingdom (= rule) is reflected also in 12³² (cf. Matt. 25³⁴). Here the thought is more precise. The apostles, whose selection as twelve in number has been symbolic of Jesus' intention of creating a true Israel (a new, eschatological twelve tribes), will share his eschatological role of exercising final judgment on the empirical Israel (no mention is made of the Gentiles). Or, as has been suggested, *judging* should be given the meaning of 'ruling over' (cf. the book of Judges), and the thought is of the apostles ruling for ever over the true Israel of Jesus' disciples. Comparison can be made with Rev. 3²¹ for a similar promise to the disciple who conquers to sit with Jesus on his throne, as he has sat with God on his throne.

31–34 (iv) *The Apostles and Peter under Trial*
Not only was Jesus' denial by Peter, the chief of the apostles, handed down, for whatever reasons, in the tradition, but also, as with his betrayal by Judas, added poignancy was given it by his foreknowledge and prediction of it. Mark/ Matthew place this in the context of a wider prediction that all the Twelve would apostasize, which is made after the Supper on the way to Gethsemane. The immediately preceding promises based on the constancy of the Twelve (vv. 28–30) make it impossible for Luke to reproduce this, and he brings the prophecy of denial within the Supper discourse itself as contributing to its general theme of the relation of Jesus to the apostles and their relation to one another. As with the prediction of Judas's betrayal, Luke passes more quickly over it than Mark by making it subordinate to a previously expressed confidence that Peter will recover for the benefit of the rest of the Twelve.

The unit is in two parts, (i) vv. 31–32, and (ii) vv. 33–34. Both can be divided into six fairly equal lines. They do not necessarily belong together, as they need not reflect identical situations, and Luke may have been responsible for bringing them together. (i) is without any parallel, and does not have to be spoken at this time. It exhibits considerable dramatic intensity in the use of personal names (*Simon, Simon*; *Satan*), and of personal pronouns – *I have prayed* (in the Greek *ego* is added to the verb) *for you* (*sou* = 'thee'), *that your faith* (*sou* = 'thy') . . . *and when you* (*su* = 'thou' is added to the verb) . . . *your brethren* (*sou* = 'thy'). There is also a high concentration in so short a space of choice vocabulary – *demanded to have* (*exaiteisthai* + +, not LXX), *to sift* (a late Greek word *siniazein* + +, not LXX), *prayed* (*deisthai* = 'to ask', apart from Matt. 9³⁸ only Luke in the gospels; followed by a preposition in the sense 'to pray for' + A. 8²⁴), *fail* (*ekleipein*, + 16⁹; 23⁴⁵; Heb. 1¹² LXX), *when you have* (*su pote* = 'at some time' followed by a participle, an idiomatic construction not found elsewhere in the gospels), *turned* (*epistrephein*, predominantly L–A in the NT), *strengthen* (*stērizein*, only here in the gospels; cf. A. 18²³ in this sense). This could then be a Lukan rendering of an isolated piece of tradition, which nevertheless remains very cryptic.

(ii) is parallel to Mark 14²⁹⁻³¹. In view of its concise form, with the prediction following, and not preceding Peter's expostulation, and its phrasing (*with you* in the Greek placed first for emphasis; *ready, to go* (the Lukan *poreuesthai*), *to prison and to death* (cf. A. 22⁴; 26¹⁰), *that you know me* (accus. and infin., as in 20⁷ revising Mark), it could be a polished revision by Luke of Mark's rougher account.

31

Simon, Simon, behold, Satan demanded to have you: Without any connecting link (some mss have 'And the Lord said'), attention is now focused on one of the apostolic audience, Peter, who is singled out by his personal name Simon (cf. 4³⁸; 5⁵ᶠᶠ·; A. 10⁵ᶠᶠ·; 11¹³). For intensification of feeling by reduplicating the name, cf. 10⁴¹; 13³⁴; 8²⁴; A. 9⁴; 22⁷; 26¹⁴; here there is further intensification with the dramatic *behold*. As their chief – this is nowhere explicitly stated in this Gospel, but is here simply assumed – he is informed of something affecting all the apostles as a company; *you* here is plural, and refers to those addressed throughout vv. 15–30. This is, that in the supernatural conflict attending his ministry (cf. 10¹⁸) Jesus is aware (it is not said how, or for how long, he has been aware of it) that Satan has *demanded to have them*. The verb here means 'to obtain by asking' (Field, *Notes*, p. 76). The situation is that in Job 1¹², where Satan, as the heavenly accuser of men, obtains from God power over Job, and permission to test him.

that he may sift you like wheat: It is not evident to what this refers, when it takes place, or how it differs from the trials referred to in v. 28. The verb means primarily 'to shake'. If the emphasis is on 'sieving', then what may be intended is a separation among the apostles of the true from the false, as of grain from husk. This thought, however, would not be continued in *strengthen your brethren* (v. 32), where the whole apostolic company seems to be envisaged, and not just those separated out as unreliable. The emphasis may be on 'shaking'. In some way Satan is so agitating, or is so to agitate, the Twelve as to undermine their allegiance to Jesus and his cause, and they will need to be re-established by Peter.

32

but I have prayed for you that your faith may not fail: Over against Satan as the accuser and tester of the apostles as a whole is Jesus as paraclete (cf. I John 2¹) and prevailing intercessor for them, but indirectly for them, and directly only for Peter as their chief. The prayer is that his faith may not fail. Generally in the synoptic gospels, where it is not common, *faith* denotes a specific act of response to, or confidence in, Jesus, made at a certain moment. Here something more continuing seems to be meant – the belief in Jesus (as messiah?) that had constituted Peter as disciple and apostle, or, possibly, his loyalty. *fail* is in the

Greek *ekleipein*, a word common in the LXX. It has the sense of 'to give out completely' (in 23⁴⁵ it is used of the sun in eclipse). In this context it is somewhat obscure, for to the extent that vv. 33–34 presume a complete falling away on Peter's part the intercession of Jesus would not have prevailed.

when you have turned again: The verb here, *epistrephein*, belongs to the vocabulary of conversion (as in I Thess. 1⁹; Gal. 4⁹; I Peter 2²⁵), and is used for this by Luke alone among the evangelists (cf. A. 3¹⁹ and 26²⁰, where it is joined with its synonym *metanoein* = 'to repent', and A. 9³⁵; 14¹⁵; 15¹⁹). It implies that Peter is a special case among the Twelve, and that for him something more than a general unsettling is envisaged, viz. actual apostasy, from which he will have to be recovered. And he is not told to convert his brethren, as he will have been converted, but only to strengthen them. The language is so compressed that the picture is somewhat blurred, and Luke may be responsible for this by supplying *when you have turned* in order to link vv. 31–32, the more general threat to the faith of the apostles as a body, to vv. 33–34, the specific and actual apostasy of Peter through his denial.

strengthen your brethren: This would also seem to reflect Christian usage. The verb *stērizein* does not belong to the vocabulary of the gospels; it is found only three times, all in Luke, and only here in this spiritual sense. It does, however, belong to the vocabulary of the early church, where it is used to express various kinds of confirmation or establishment in Christian faith and practice – so in Rom. 1¹¹; 16²⁵; I Thess. 3^{2, 13}; II Thess. 2¹⁷; James 5⁸; I Peter 5¹⁰; II Peter 1¹²; Rev. 3². *brethren* has its origins as an Israelite term for fellow members of the same religious community, and is very frequent in the OT as such. It is comparatively rare in the gospels (in Luke 6^{41f.}; 17³ for a fellow disciple), but it is a standard designation in A. and epistles for Christian believers. Here it is used in a special and restricted sense for the inner company of the Twelve.

33–34

It is in the context of the statements in vv. 31–32 that Luke introduces his more compact and polished account of the prediction of Peter's denial. It is in response to the suggestion of failure under trial implied in Jesus' intercession for him, and to the necessity of conversion, and not, as in Mark 14^{27, 29}, to the prophecy of a wholesale desertion of the Twelve, that Peter professes devotedly (*Lord, with you*) his readiness to accompany Jesus to prison and to death. And it is in reply to this that Jesus, addressing him now solemnly by his apostolic name (*I tell you, Peter*), affirms that on that very day (which has begun already with sunset) he will three times deny him (i.e. cease to be a disciple) by professing that he does not know him.

35–38 (v) *The Apostles and the Immediate Future*

This is perhaps the most puzzling passage in the Gospel, indeed in all the gospels, both in itself, and in its position as the conclusion of the Last Supper discourse.ᵈ It is clearly a separate unit, but is a highly unusual one both in form and content, and it is difficult to envisage it as having been transmitted orally. On the basis of a detailed linguistic study H. Schürmann (*Jesu Abschiedsrede*, pp. 116ff.) proposes an original unit in Luke's special source comprising vv. 35–36, 37b, not linked with Jesus' arrest, which was edited by Luke in vv. 37a, 38 to bring it into connection with the arrest. It begins with a retrospective reference in dialogue to a past event in the ministry, which is then countermanded; it continues with a very explicit citation from scripture, which is said to be on the point of fulfilment in what is to happen to Jesus; and it concludes with a very brief and cryptic dialogue arising from that. This second dialogue (vv. 37–38), while apparently tying the whole passage to the coming arrest of Jesus, is indeed so cryptic – as is the whole unit – that it must have been as baffling to early readers of the Gospel as it has been to commentators ever since.ᵉ

35–36a

As the conclusion of the discourse the section is given an introduction with *And he said to them*. What follows continues the thread running through vv. 14–34 of the union of the apostles in a common destiny with Jesus, which he alone knows in advance, and determines. It begins, however, in unique fashion with Jesus interrogating them with respect to what had made them apostles, viz. their mission (in *When I sent you out* the verb is *apostellein* – cf. 10³; 9² – from which the noun 'apostle' is derived); and with respect to one particular feature of that, viz. that they had gone out without *purse or bag or sandals*. It is perhaps pedantic to observe that these words reproduce, not the conditions which Luke, following Mark, had made Jesus prescribe for the mission of the Twelve (9³), but those he had made Jesus prescribe for the mission of the Seventy (10⁴). This could be simply an editorial slip; but it could be deliberate, in that a purse for money and a bag for possessions or provisions would provide a basis for the contrast to be made in v. 36 in a way that 'staff' and 'tunic' (9³) would not (though the reproduction is still careless, in that *sandals* is unnecessary, and is not taken up in v. 36). The point of the contrast seems to be the following. Their mission as his representatives (10¹⁶) and under his aegis had been so successful, and their message so well accepted, that, on their own admission, they had lacked for nothing, and all their wants had been supplied by those to whom they

---

ᵈ It is a reminder of the singular character of some of the traditions Luke has preserved in his special material; and the classical interpretation of the 'two swords' here as denoting the spiritual and the temporal power is a reminder of the singular vagaries possible in exegesis.

ᵉ For an important recent attempt at its elucidation, see P. S. Minear, 'A Note on Luke 22.36', *Nov Test* 7, 1964–65, pp. 128ff.

went. By contrast (*But now, alla nun*, only here in Luke) the present situation is of an opposite kind, being one of a total rejection of Jesus, and it requires of his apostles an opposite strategy. They must resume the use of purse and bag, if they have them, as an indication that they are now in a position when they will have to fend for themselves.

36b

The argument in vv. 35–36a, if interpreted correctly above, appears tolerably clear. It is thrown into confusion by the strange additional injunction, which does not arise out of v. 35, to buy a sword. As a result the whole sentence in v. 36 is obscure, and can be rendered in a number of different ways, none of which is wholly satisfactory. (i) 'He who (still) possesses a purse, let him take it up again (for use), and likewise his bag; and he who does not have (either), let him sell his mantle and buy a sword (with the proceeds).' Here it is only the less well off among the apostles who is to have a sword, unless it is to be supposed that 'taking up the purse' means finding money to buy a sword (this would not be the case with the bag, unless that was a beggar's bowl for receiving money). The same difficulty attaches to the rendering, 'He who possesses a purse . . . his bag; and he who does not have (anything; the Greek here *ho mē echōn* without an object could mean 'one who has nothing', 'is destitute') let him sell . . .'

(ii) 'Let him who has (a sword) take his purse and bag, and he who does not have (a sword), let him sell his mantle and buy one.' This is grammatically very awkward in requiring the last word in the sentence (*sword*) to be the object of the first words in it ('he who has'), and it destroys the antithesis with v. 35 in making the possession of a sword the primary requirement, already assumed for some, with purse and bag an additional accoutrement. (iii) 'Let him who has a purse take it, and likewise a bag. And let him who has no sword sell his mantle and buy one.' This, the rendering in RSV, treats the verse as two sentences. Its weakness is that it implies that possession of a sword can only come by way of selling the mantle, even for those who already have money in their purse.

Conzelmann (*Theology*, esp. pp. 16, 81f.) finds here an important clue to Luke's construction of his Gospel as a whole, according to which the period of salvation brought about by Jesus' presence and ministry was paradisal in its conditions, but gave away with the approach of the passion to the period of the church (extending now to Luke's own day), when Satan had been allowed back, so that the apostles must be prepared for conflict, even to the point of martyrdom. This, however, involves treating the apostles' mission as representative of the whole ministry, and not as an event, however important, in it; and in characterizing the period of the church as one of conflict it has to give a highly symbolic sense to 'sword' (cf. Matt. 10³⁴). Others interpret in this way. Thus, Schlatter (p. 429): 'Jesus was not speaking of increasing their weapons. But just because he was not thinking of their weapons, the disciples need the courage which regards a sword as more necessary than a cloak, and which will surrender its last possession, but cannot give up the fight.' Taylor says:[f] 'Jesus is speaking metaphorically. He is thinking of the position in which the disciples will find themselves after his death.' The sword is 'symbolic of the seriousness of the situation' (so Grundmann, p. 409), or denotes 'hardship and sacrifice' (so Marshall, p. 825). Easton (p. 328) states, though with reservations, that Luke could not have wished his readers to take the precept literally, and perhaps thought of it in terms on Eph. 6[17]. But, as Minear observes (op. cit.), the other prophecies in this discourse, those of betrayal, and denial, are of what is due for immediate fulfilment, and this could apply to 'a sword', which makes an actual, and not symbolic, appearance in the narrative of the arrest. He suggests that it was the presence of sword-play there (cf. Mark 14[47]; John 18[10]) that produced the dialogue here to prepare for it. The 'sword' here (*machaira*) would not be symbolic of conflict, any more than the 'purse' or 'bag' are symbolic; it would be rather the dagger associated with the bandit and insurrectionary, and this would account better for the solemnly introduced, and extended explanatory statement which follows (v. 37, *For I tell you*). Jeremias (*Theology*, p. 294) takes the sword as literal, but regards the passage as a prophecy of the outbreak of the messianic war, which went unfulfilled – surely a desperate judgment on Luke as as editor. See further on v. 38.

37

The reason why the apostles are to possess swords is a double one. It is because a particular passage of scripture – *this scripture, touto gegrammenon to* = 'this that is written, namely' – has to *be fulfilled* (*telesthēnai* = 'completed' a Lukan word for the fulfilment of scripture, cf. 18[31]; A. 13[29]) in Jesus. And it is because (*kai gar* = 'for also') this fulfilment is imminent, since 'that which concerns me' (*to peri mou* – RSV renders by *what is written about me*) has its fulfilment (*telos echei* = 'is having its fulfilment (now)'). Verse 37b does not simply reiterate v. 37a; it moves from a general necessity of the fulfilment of scripture to the particular situation of that fulfilment. An alternative translation proposed for v. 37b is 'my life (life's work) is coming to an end', but that would be a somewhat forced rendering both of subject and verb.

And he was reckoned with transgressors: This, the only express quotation from Isa. 53 in the synoptic gospels (apart from Matt. 8[17]), is made with great precision. It affords an example of the 'atomic' use of scripture, where only the words quoted, irrespective of any context, are meant to apply. They are not to be taken as a pointer to the whole chapter in Isaiah, or as an indication that Jesus is interpreting his coming death in terms of what is said about the servant in that chapter. The quotation refers to one particular facet, viz. that one who is the

f *Jesus and His Sacrifice: a Study of the Passion-sayings in the Gospels*, London and New York 1937, p. 192.

righteous servant of God is treated by men as a criminal outcast. Its wording differs from the LXX, and is closer to the Hebrew text, in having *with* (*meta*) instead of 'among' (*en*), and in lacking the article with *transgressors*. Luke may be following another version than the LXX, or he may have made the alterations himself to increase the adjectival character of the statement – *he was reckoned with transgressors* = 'he was treated as a criminal'. The quotation explains the reversal and the injunction in vv. 35–36. The Jesus who had inaugurated the mission to proclaim God's kingdom to Israel had been accepted in the persons of the apostles, who for that reason could go out unprepared; but now he is to be decisively repudiated by the authorities in Israel, and treated as a criminal, and the apostles of such a one must adapt themselves to a new role.

38

The response of the apostles to the command to possess swords, now reinforced by an appeal to God's will in scripture, is surprising and terse – *Look, Lord* (*Kurie* with the Lukan *idou* = 'behold') *here are two swords* (lit. 'swords here two'). The reply of Jesus is equally terse – *hikanon esti*. Two renderings have been proposed for this. (i) 'It is enough' in the sense of 'enough of that', breaking off the conversation. No parallel can be produced for this, and it is unlikely that Luke would have brought the passage, and the whole discourse, to an end so inconclusively. (ii) 'It is enough' in the sense that two swords will be sufficient for the purpose in hand. This would correspond with the predominant use of *hikanos* in L–A (where it occurs twice as often as in the rest of the NT) to denote sufficiency of numbers, and is the more likely meaning.

The problem remains why Jesus should here issue the command to possess swords. Minear (op. cit.) sees vv. 35–38 as forming the climax of a discourse which throughout shows the apostles as subject to Satan, and as on the opposite side to Jesus, who, nevertheless, remains in control of events, and is able to set limits to Satan's power. Here his command, if it is any more than a literary device to set the stage for the fulfilment of prophecy, is simply to bring to light the true state of affairs, viz. that in secretly possessing swords the apostles are already in a state of disobedience to their vocation, and are already the 'transgressors' with whom Jesus will be counted. This interpretation may be criticized as unduly minimizing the extent to which, in vv. 14–38, the apostles and Jesus, despite the distance between them, are closely associated, and as ignoring the entirely favourable judgment in vv. 28–30. It may be suggested, alternatively, that vv. 35–38 are governed by a grim but playful irony. In Jesus' mission to Israel through the apostles the conditions were idyllic, and matched the character of the message. Now there is about to supervene a situation which, although divinely decreed, is perverse and nonsensical, in that the representatives of God's people and God's law are to pronounce God's righteous one a member of the criminal classes. In this situation, which has the character of a charade, he and they must look the part. For that a couple of daggers will do. This aspect of things will be touched on again in the Lukan narrative of the passion (vv. 49–51; 23$^{1-25, 32, 39-43}$).

^{39}*And he came out, and went, as was his custom, to the Mount of Olives; and the disciples followed him.* ^{40}*And when he came to the place he said to them, 'Pray that you may not enter into temptation.'* ^{41}*And he withdrew from them about a stone's throw, and knelt down and prayed,* ^{42}'*Father, if thou art willing, remove this cup from me; nevertheless not my will, but thine, be done.'* ^{43}*And there appeared to him an angel from heaven, strengthening him.* ^{44}*And being in an agony he prayed more earnestly; and his sweat became like great drops of blood falling down upon the ground.** ^{45}*And when he rose from prayer, he came to the disciples and found them sleeping for sorrow,* ^{46}*and he said to them, 'Why do you sleep? Rise and pray that you may not enter into temptation.'*

    * Other ancient authorities omit verses 43 and 44

While a narrative of the passion, like the predictions of it in Mark 9^{31}; 10^{33}, could have begun from the arrest of Jesus, perhaps with the place of arrest named, an account of his testing and prayer beforehand would not have been necessary to it. John's account does not have it (though there is some equivalent in John 12$^{27ff.}$), and in Mark the transition from it to the arrest is made only by a passage of great abruptness and obscurity (Mark 14$^{41-42}$). For this was a private and not a public event. Its purpose was to convey the inner theological and spiritual meaning of the external events to follow. This it does by showing the principal actor at prayer, and by specifying the subject of his prayer in terms of 'temptation', 'cup' and 'will'. On its own showing such an account must have been, at least in part, a construct, since the prayer of Jesus, assuming it to have been uttered aloud, could not have been overheard by disciples who are represented as being at a stone's throw distance away, and asleep. The content of the prayer will presumably have been inferred from a particular theology of Jesus as the Son of God in a relationship of obedience to God as Father, and of his death as consequence of that obedience (cf. Rom. 5$^{6-11, 19}$; 8$^{3-17}$; Gal. 4$^{1-6}$; Phil. 2^{8}; Heb. 5$^{5-10}$).

In Mark the story is stylized according to the rule of three, with three selected disciples being addressed three times; though this finally breaks down, as there is nothing to put between Jesus' second and third visits to them, and it is probably all the disciples who are addressed in Mark 14$^{41-42}$. The scene is protracted, dramatic and awesome in its description of the bewildered humanity of Jesus (in Mark 14^{33} the verb *adēmonein* means to be in acute distress, not to know where one is) as he faces an extremity of trial appointed by God (this is indicated by the use of scriptural language in 'My soul is very sorrowful', to which is added 'even to the point of death'). This distress is conveyed to the three intimates, though they show a total lack of comprehension and co-operation, sleep instead of praying, and fail to observe the Christian duty of watching (cf. I Thess. 5^6; I Cor. 16^{13}; Eph. 6^{18}; I Peter 5^8). Luke's story is much shorter, and has a different emphasis. In form it is more consistently a story about Jesus. Apart from *the disciples followed him* (v. 39), the verbs are in the singular with Jesus as the subject of them, and he is concerned with the disciples as a body (vv. 39–40, 45–46). In this way the tenor of vv. 7–38 is continued. In content it is as much about prayer as about temptation, the prayer of Jesus being flanked by exhortations to the disciples to pray to avoid temptation. The isolation of Jesus from them is less marked, and the theme of watching in relation to sleep is absent. There are verbal agreements with Mark in *remove this cup from me* and *Pray that you may not enter into temptation*, but these words, it could be held, would have been contained in any version of the story. If Luke was following a non-Markan source here, clearly much of Mark's more detailed and dramatic account will not have recommended itself to him for inclusion. It is thus possible to explain his briefer version as the result of a revision of Mark's which would depict a more serene Jesus and less faithless disciples. There are literary touches which could be ascribed to Luke – *when he came to* (*ginesthai* (*epi*) as in 24^{22}; A. 13^5; 21^{35}; 27^7, here in the participle), *the place* (cf. 4^{37}; 6^{17}; 11^1; A. 12^{17}), *pray that you may not* (*proseuchesthai* with infin., only here in the NT), *withdrew* (*apospāsthai* = 'to be drawn away', here in a reduced sense + A. 21^1), *about*, the phrase *a stone's throw* for being out of earshot, *knelt down* (of prayer only A. 7^{60}; 9^{40}; 20^{36}; 21^5 in the NT), *if thou art willing* (*boulesthai*, Lukan).

☙❧

39

The transition from the supper to the place of arrest is immediate. If 'when they had sung a hymn' (Mark 14²⁶) refers to the singing of the remainder of the Hallel Psalms at the end of the meal, it is surprising that Luke, with his emphasis on the passover character of the meal, does not reproduce it; but he may not have known the ritual of the meal in detail, or the intervening discourse in vv. 24–38 may have pushed it into the background. In Mark the company ('they') do not return to Bethany (cf. Mark 11¹²; 14³), but go to the Mount of Olives, which, by its eschatological associations (cf. Zech. 14³ᶠᶠ.), would be a fitting place for the prophecy *en route* of the desertion of the disciples by means of the citation of Zech. 13⁷ (Mark 14²⁷), and to a place named Gethsemane. Luke does not reproduce this, not only because Mark 14²⁷⁻³¹ orientates resurrection appearances towards Galilee, whereas his own are to be orientated towards Jerusalem, but also because it supposes a total disruption of the apostolic band by the coming events (Mark 14²⁷, ⁵⁰), and their total failure to comprehend, within which Peter's failure is predicted when he makes a distinction between himself and the rest. Luke has already given a gentler version of this prediction in an opposite context of an assurance of Peter's ultimate steadfastness for the benefit of his brethren (vv. 31–34), and he has already by his editing established somewhere on the mount as a place of regular nightly sojourn (21³⁷). Hence here he has *as was his custom*, and – omitting, as is usual with him, the Aramaic place name – *to the place*, which may be meant, like *the hour* (v. 14), to have a solemn tone.

40

Pray that you may not enter into temptation: Jesus sets the scene as alone aware of what is coming, and of what will be at stake. He sets it not, as in Mark, by an expression of intense agony to an inner circle, but by an injunction to all of them to pray not to enter into temptation. This, like *Father* and *not my will, but thine, be done* (v. 42), recalls the language of the Lord's Prayer. Here, as there, the prayer is not for victory over temptation when it comes, but for the ability to remain outside its sphere; and the implication is that the possibility of entering into it is imminent. It is not clear in what this temptation consists that it can be 'entered into', nor whether Jesus includes himself here, and is praying not to enter into temptation when he asks for the cup to be removed (v. 42; for the hour to pass, Mark 14³⁵), nor whether he enters into temptation on their behalf, so that this is not an occasion when they continue with him in his trials (v. 28). *temptation* (*peirasmos*, see on v. 28, 4²) is a predominantly biblical word with a wide range of meanings according to context. It can denote the afflictions of the righteous, which are in the end educative and purifying in testing their steadfastness to God and his commandments, and as such could even be welcomed (cf. James 1²ᶠᶠ.). That is plainly not the meaning here. It could also designate one aspect of the eschatological conflict with the powers of evil at full stretch, upon which God's cause and kingdom depend (though more clearly so with the definite article – 'the temptation'). Thus, in Dan. 12^{10} LXX the prophecies are sealed until the time of the end when many will be tempted, and Rev. 3^{10} refers to the hour of trial that is coming on the whole world to try its inhabitants. This, which is probably intended in Mark 14$^{33-38}$, is trial of an ultimate kind, when it will be uncertain whether faithfulness to God will hold, or there will be a total defection from him. If that is the sense here it indicates who Jesus is, viz. the eschatological warrior in God's cause. Yet there is an acute and unresolved tension, since Jesus must undergo this trial if the will of God is to be effective for salvation; but it is so dire that even he prays to avoid it, and the disciples must pray not to be involved in it (because of human frailty?, Mark 14^{38}). The word can have a less extreme meaning of trials which can be repeated or are constantly at hand (cf. A. 20^{19}), and in 8^{13} it refers to a testing which undoes a previous faith, though not necessarily to the point of apostasy. This may be the meaning here. If so, it is not its eschatological character as such, but the fact that Jesus is the Son of the Father, that gives this trial its force, and the disciples are to pray to avoid the occasion of defecting from allegiance to him (by resisting with force the necessary humiliation which he accepts?).

41

knelt down and prayed: Jews stood to pray. As the references in A. quoted above show, kneeling is an affective expression of piety for prayer of an urgent kind, though it is not as forcible as 'he fell to the ground' (Mark 14^{35}).

42

Father, if thou are willing, remove this cup from me: Some mss have the verb in the infinitive, giving either a condition followed by an aposeiopesis – 'If it is possible to remove . . . (then may it be so)' – or, with 'if' as interrogative, 'Is it possible to remove . . .?' The Son prays to the Father. The nature of the prayer depends on the meaning to be given to *cup*, and in particular to *this cup*. The figurative use of *cup* is confined to the biblical literature, where it may have developed from ideas expressed in pictures of the gods with a cup of destiny in their hands (see *TDNT* VI, p. 150). It has appeared previously in Mark (10$^{38-39}$, along with 'baptism') as a metaphor for what Jesus and the Twelve both undergo (or, they after him), but in Luke it appears for the first time here. It belongs to God, and is given by him to men (cf. John 18^{11}, an echo of this story transposed into a higher key). It can have the more general sense of 'lot' or 'destiny' (cf. Ps. 11^6; 16^5). If so here, the prayer is to escape the destiny which Jesus has already discerned for himself in scripture, and which he has already delineated as rejection by the authorities of God's people, and as death as the Son of man at the hands of men in accordance with the divine will (9$^{22, 44}$; 18^{31}; 22^{22} – but these may be later formulations). The cup can then hardly be a metaphor for death simply (as Leaney, p. 273), but only for death of a certain kind and in certain conditions, which spell not only failure, but the reversal of the moral order. More frequently in the OT it is specifically God's cup of wrath and judgment, which he gives to the nations and sinners, so that they are stupefied, stagger and fall to destruction (cf. Ps. 75⁸; Isa. 51¹⁷ff.; Jer. 25¹⁵ff.; Lam. 4²¹; Ezek. 23³¹ff.; Hab. 2¹⁶). If so here, Jesus is to be understood as shrinking from the position of being the object of the divine wrath. That is possible in Mark, if the cry from the cross (Mark 15³⁴) is to be interpreted in this way, but it is barely intelligible within the general perspective of the gospels. For in the OT this cup is given to sinners, whereas in the gospels Jesus is known as the obedient Son; and while those who encompass his death may be the instruments of the divine will, they cannot effect the moral reality of divine wrath, since they are themselves sinners and under judgment. The prayer should probably not be interpreted by way of the Pauline paradoxes that God made Christ 'a curse' and 'sin' (Gal. 3¹³; II Cor. 5²¹). The petition in the passive, 'The will of the Lord be done', which resolves the conflict, was a pious Jewish convention. Its setting here in the prayer of the Son of the Father gives it a peculiar intensity – cf. A. 21¹⁴, where Paul uses the same phraseology in face of death.

The character of the scene is affected by whether vv. 43–44 belong to it or not. Without them the conflict in the will of Jesus is reduced to a minimum, and the contrast with Mark's picture is considerable. With them the story reaches a climax with the sole instance in the gospels of an angelic appearance to Jesus, and with highly realistic language about his humanity and piety, as he is moved by heavenly vision to an agony of terror and intense prayer. The textual evidence is evenly divided, as are the estimates of it by textual critics. In the Fathers it is found as early as Justin (quoted from 'the memoirs of the apostles', but with the prayer in the non-Lukan form 'if it be possible'), and in Irenaeus and Hippolytus, but it is lacking as early as Marcion, and is not found in Clement or Origen. It is read by syr^{cur} but not by syr^{sin}; by Θ and fam 1. but not by the somewhat similar grouping W and fam 13; by the original hand of ℵ , but not by its corrector; by D and all the mss of the Old Latin except one, but not by p⁷⁵, B and the Coptic versions and the Armenian version. Hilary, Epiphanius and Jerome knew it, but also knew of mss that did not have it. Evidence in the lectionaries is divided, including evidence in the same lectionary; and there are instances of the transposition of vv. 43–45a to follow Matt. 26³⁹. Those who regard it as genuine generally explain its omission as due to its incompatibility with the Alexandrian doctrine of the divinity of the Son, which would have found such stress on his humanity unpalatable (hence the correction in ℵ), especially as Epiphanius mentions some who objected to it on these grounds. But this was a problem for the theology of the fourth century, and was not necessarily felt in the same way earlier (cf. the absence of the passage from p⁷⁵, early third century, in the same area, Alexandria). It could have been inserted at an earlier date to combat Docetism, the doctrine that Jesus' humanity was apparent only (as in Justin, *Dialogue* 103). The miraculous element, and the elaboration of the piety of the martyr, give it an apocryphal tone; but the line between apocryphal traditions and the passion narratives of Luke and Matthew and certain stories in A. is not easily drawn. The vocabulary shows a high proportion in a brief space of unusual words not found elsewhere in the NT – *agony* (*agōnia* = 'terror', often before the unknown), *sweat, drops* (*thromboi*, with 'blood' generally in the sense of 'blood clots'). Some vocabulary could be ascribed to Luke – *there appeared to him, an angel, strengthening* (*enischuein* + A. 9¹⁹), and *earnestly* of prayer (cf. A. 12⁵); though hardly *katabainein* in the sense of 'to fall down'. If *more earnestly* is a genuine comparative the passage cannot stand on its own, but it could be elative – 'very earnestly'. In the setting the picture is vivid but blurred, since the strengthening by the angel does not come as a mark of divine approval (cf. Heb. 5⁷, 'was heard for his godly fear'), nor to revive one who is weak from conflict, but itself induces a terror not felt hitherto, and a specially fervent prayer. This might imply that the prayer so far had been inadequate because the issues had not been clearly seen (note that in Mark the same prayer has to be repeated). On balance the verses should probably be deleted.

45
When he rose: i.e. from his knees; this could provide a link either with v. 42 or v. 44. He comes to the disciples after having been separated from them, and *found them sleeping for sorrow.* This is a singularly unconvincing explanation of sleep, and Luke may have arrived at it by transferring something of Jesus' words in Mark 14³⁴, 'My soul is very sorrowful' to the disciples, who are thus made sufficiently aware of what is happening to be able to grieve over it. The scene closes as it had begun with the command to pray not to enter into temptation. This could lead directly into the next event, if it is then that the temptation of the disciples, as opposed to that of Jesus himself, is to be seen to take place.

22⁴⁷⁻⁵³   JESUS AND HIS OPPONENTS

⁴⁷*While he was still speaking, there came a crowd, and the man called Judas, one of the twelve, was leading them. He drew near to Jesus to kiss him;* ⁴⁸*but Jesus said to him, 'Judas, would you betray the Son of man with a kiss?'* ⁴⁹*And when those who were about him saw what would follow, they said, 'Lord, shall we strike with the sword?'* ⁵⁰*And one of them struck the slave of the high priest and cut off his right ear.* ⁵¹*But Jesus said, 'No more of this!' And he touched his ear and healed him.* ⁵²*Then Jesus said to the chief priests and captains of the temple and elders, who had come out against him, 'Have*

you come out as against a robber, with swords and clubs? ⁵³*When I was with you day after day in the temple, you did not lay hands on me. But this is your hour, and the power of darkness.'*

This is likely to have been the initial story of any passion narrative, however brief, since it recorded how Jesus was 'handed over', i.e. brought within the control of his enemies, so that the processes might be set in motion, by which, though innocent, he was executed as a criminal. The story will have been shaped by the passion of which it was a part. That would explain its comparative brevity, and the absence of sufficient circumstantial detail for reconstructing actions and their motives. Since the passion is that of Jesus alone, the story is focused on him, and it is not possible to discern from it whether the disciples were, by their presence at the scene, also in danger of arrest. In Mark/Matthew they simply make their escape, and even that is called 'forsaking Jesus' (Mark 14⁵⁰; Matt. 26⁵⁶). In John's highly theological version Jesus procures his own arrest at the price of their immunity (John 18^{8–9}). On this score Luke says nothing at all. The story could have been told in more than one way, since it will have provoked reflection upon the parts played by those concerned – God, Jesus, the authorities, the disciples and Judas. To judge from Matt. 26^{50a}; John 18¹¹, there may have been sayings available in the tradition for elucidating the events.

The main constituents of the story and the sequence of events are identical in Mark and Luke – the arrival of Judas with a 'crowd', the kiss of Judas, the disciples' use of a sword and Jesus' address to his captors. Their accounts are different. Mark's is vivid but disjointed, passing from one participant to another; Jesus is in part the object of the actions of others, who are also unwittingly the agents of the divine purpose. Luke's is briefer, more constructed and more personal. It is hardly at all the story of an arrest, which is only referred to by means of a participle at the beginning of the next pericope (*Then they seized him and led him away,* 22⁵⁴). It is occupied with Jesus, whose personal name is introduced into a story which, in contrast to vv. 39–46, could not be told with him as the subject throughout (vv. 47b, 48a, 51, 52). It falls into three parts – (i) Jesus and Judas (vv. 47–48), (ii) Jesus and the disciples (vv. 49–51), and (iii) Jesus and the arresting authority (vv. 52–53) – each of which has 'Jesus said', the name being (twice) more personal in lacking the article. It depicts Jesus as in command, though not in the same way as John's account. The incident of the kiss is given a different import by a question in terms of the Son of man; the sword stroke is introduced by a request for permission from the disciples as a single body, and is answered by a healing miracle; and the explanation given for the action of the authorities is not the divine will in scripture (that has already been given in v. 37), but darkness and its power. Lagrange observes (p. 563), 'This pericope has a character somewhat unusual in Luke's work. He seems to presume the facts as well known, and his literary revision has as its aim to given them their meaning and to complete them.' These similarities and differences have been explained as due to Luke's use of a non-Markan source which he lightly supplemented from Mark,[g] to his conflation of a non-Markan source with Mark (so Perry, *Passion-Narrative*, pp. 42f.), or to his reflection upon, and improvement of, a somewhat disjointed Markan original, perhaps with the aid of tradition. In favour of the last could be that the agreement in wording with Mark is closest at the beginning and end of the pericope (vv. 47, 52–53); for it is unlikely that a story which is so striking at its centre would have come to Luke with such a deficient beginning and ending that these required to be supplemented, or replaced, by recourse to Mark.

ळ

47–48 (i) Jesus and Judas

This is so brief as to be barely intelligible. Again the question is raised whether this brevity belonged to a non-Markan original, which here Luke chose not to fill out from Mark, or is due to a drastic reduction of Mark by Luke in order to place the emphasis elsewhere, and to transfer the encounter with Judas from the impersonal sphere of public event to the personal sphere of Jesus in the company of his disciples.

47

While he was still speaking: A narrative transition from a scene which conveyed the inner meaning of the passion to a scene which initiated the passion as public event was not easy. That in Mark 14⁴¹⁻⁴² is particularly disjointed and obscure. There the theme of sleeping and waking is brought to an end with the command to sleep on, which is then countermanded by the cryptic 'it is enough', and by an announcement that the hour, the passing of which had previously been prayed for, had arrived, and with it the handing over of the Son of man to

g So F. Rehkopf in his detailed study *Die lukanische Sonderquelle*, Tübingen 1959, pp. 31ff., and others.

sinners (which is not immediately the case if 'sinners' refers to Gentiles). With the vague injunction 'let us be going' the betrayer is said to be at hand, and 'while he was still speaking' (Mark 14⁴³) introduces the betrayer's arrival as proof of the correctness of Jesus' previous statement. It is an indication of Luke's dependence on Mark here that he uses exactly the same words to make the transition, though he intends something different by it. Here the connection seems to be with the repetition of the command to pray not to enter into temptation (v. 46). If that temptation is to active resistance to avoid the rejection, disgrace, suffering and possibly death involved in discipleship of one who is reckoned a criminal in Israel (v. 37), then it can have arrived with the circumstances of the arrest. *While he was still speaking* will then refer to this, and it will indicate that Luke envisaged the story primarily as one of the temptation of the disciples in relation to their Lord, who is no longer touched by that temptation, and that he moulded the story accordingly.

there came a crowd, and the man called Judas, one of the twelve: This is also from Mark, with Mark's 'Judas and a crowd' altered in order, so that the story may proceed immediately with the part played by Judas. He is curiously introduced. Firstly, he is designated *ho legomenos Ioudas*. This is rendered by RSV and others by *the man called Judas*; but when used in this way the participle *legomenos* = 'called' comes after the noun to which it is referring (as in 22¹; A. 3²; 6⁹; cf. Matt. 26¹⁴, 'one of the twelve (who was) called Judas Iscariot'). When used with persons (it is not so used elsewhere in Luke) it generally introduces the person's surname (cf. Col. 4¹¹, 'Jesus, who is called Justus'). Perhaps the expression here was a creation of the Christian tradition with the sinister sound of 'the notorious Judas', 'the Judas they speak of'. Secondly, he is referred to as *one of the twelve*, which is unnecessary after 22³. A proposal to solve both problems is to translate 'the aforementioned one of the twelve, Judas'. But Luke probably reproduces *one of the twelve* from Mark 14⁴³, and uses it to emphasize the personal character of the scene which follows.

He drew near to Jesus to kiss him: For the questions raised by the kiss of Judas – e.g. whether the kiss was routine among the Twelve, or was given by them to Jesus as pupils to a rabbi, etc. – see *TDNT* IX, pp. 140f. The OT passages cited there of the false kiss – Gen. 27²⁷; II Sam. 15⁵; Prov. 7¹³; or II Sam. 20⁹ – do not afford real parallels. The scene in Luke is affecting but indistinct. *drew near to* could mean that Judas approached with the intention of kissing, but was prevented from doing so by Jesus' question, if the verb there has a conative sense, 'Do you intend to hand over . . .?' (so, perhaps, RSV, *would you betray . . .?*) But *drew near* (*engizein*) probably has the sense of 'came up to' (as in 15¹; 24¹⁵; A. 21³³), and an actual kiss is intended. Even so it is no longer integral to the story, since Luke has not reproduced Mark 14⁴⁴ (= Matt. 26⁴⁸), where the kiss is explained in advance as a pre-arranged signal by which Judas was to identify Jesus for his arrest (in John there is no mention of any kiss, and Jesus identifies himself). This may be due to reflection by Luke that Jesus, who had been daily in the temple (v. 53a), and the popularity of whose teaching has been constantly stressed, would not need to be identified. The function of Judas was confined to being a guide to the right place at the right time (v. 47, *was leading them*, cf. A. 1¹⁶). The kiss would then be open to a different construction.

48

would you betray the Son of man with a kiss?: The question makes a connection between *kiss* and 'hand over', though without saying how and why they belong together. *with a kiss (philēmati)* stands first in the sentence for emphasis. A natural interpretation would be 'by means of a kiss', i.e. of identification; but that may be to interpret Luke by Mark. The dative could be one of attendant circumstances, giving the sense, 'Is it along with a kiss (of a friend, cf. Matt. 26⁵⁰, 'Friend . . .', or of a pupil, cf. Mark 14⁴⁵, 'said, "Master!", and kissed him') that you hand over the Son of man?' This introduces a more personal note, and a strong element of the pathos which is found elsewhere in Luke (e.g. 22⁶¹), and it makes 'hand over' approximate to 'betray', i.e. the public action is initiated from within a private circle. Originally the tradition may have done no more than record that Judas kissed Jesus on this occasion, and two different explanations of it were subsequently provided, that in Luke being formulated on the model of Jesus' prediction that he would be handed over as the Son of man (cf. 22²² = Mark 14²¹). If, however, the kiss was in the tradition from the beginning for the purpose given it by Mark, Luke's formulation may have been his own, and was perhaps made in partial exculpation of Judas. Jesus, who already knows that the 'handing over' will take place, and that one of his friends will be the agent of it, here comments on a personal aspect of it with an expression of anguish, that one who is the Son of man should be delivered to his enemies along with a mark of affection, feigned or otherwise, from one of his friends.

49–51 (ii) *Jesus and the Disciples*

The presence in the tradition, at least as represented by Mark (followed by Matthew; cf. also John), of armed resistance on the part of a single disciple (named as Peter in John 18¹⁰) is strange. The incident is difficult to envisage without the arrest of the disciples following as a consequence. It would have been embarrassing as giving colour to the suspicion that Jesus was the leader of an insurrectionary band (cf. v. 52), and apparently it led to the introduction of supposed sayings of Jesus dissociating himself from the act (Matt. 26⁵²⁻⁵³; John 18¹¹). It is also responsible for a certain comic element. Thus, in Mark/Matthew the sword play of this single individual is seen as an attempt at a rescue operation after Jesus' arrest. That it was a ludicrous token resistance, and not at all what was to be expected of the adherents of a bandit leader, is suggested by their abject flight. Luke does not pass over this component of the story. Indeed he develops it by framing the sword stroke itself (v. 50, taken from Mark 14⁴⁷?) with an introduction and conclusion.

49

This verse could well come from Luke's hand. *those who were about him* is in the Greek *hoi peri auton*. This was a regular expression for a group under someone's leadership, varying from a small number (A. 13¹³, 'Paul and his companions'; II Macc. 1³³, 'Nehemiah and his company'), to larger bodies (Jos. *BJ* 5.10, 'Eleazar and his men', *Ant.* 18.354 of an army). Its use for the Twelve (eleven), which is unique in the gospels, may be deliberate here. It invests them with the character of a body of adherents prepared to defend their leader, who is here called *Lord. saw what would follow* is in the Greek 'and seeing', a common Lukan beginning, with the idiomatic future participle of the verb 'to be' used as a noun, *to esomenon* = 'the thing about to happen'. They size up the situation from the armed crowd (not from the kiss of Judas, which interrupts the scene).

shall we strike with the sword? is in the Greek a deliberative question with the future indicative, but referring to the present, a construction without parallel in the NT. It is not a request for information, but a rhetorical question which does not wait for an answer. Thus the sword stroke to follow is made less incidental and individual; it represents the intention of all of them, which they voice in chorus, and it issues from their relationship to Jesus as a body. This may also introduce a comic element of a special kind. For Luke's construction of the scene can hardly be divorced from the previous scene in vv. 35–38. It is presumably one of the two swords there available that is now about to be put to use; and if there was irony there – two swords will be enough to dress for the part of a criminal in fulfilment of scripture – it could be carried over into what Jesus says and does (v. 51) in reply to what the disciples say and do.

50

The linguistic evidence suggests that Luke derived this verse from Mark 14⁴⁷. *one of them* (*heis tis* = 'a certain one') is found only here both in Mark and in L–A, and the word used by both for *cut off* (*aphairein*) means for Luke elsewhere 'to take away'. The differences can be explained as Lukan revision – the more normal word than Mark's for *struck* (*patassein*, as in v. 49; cf. Matt. 26⁵¹); for Mark's 'the slave of the high priest' the different word order 'the high priest's slave' so as to produce, in the manner of classical Greek, the emphasis that it was no less than the high priest's slave who was struck; the ordinary word for *ear* in place of Mark's diminutive here; and *right* as denoting the chief, but conventional with ears (cf. John 18¹⁰, and Luke's addition of it with 'hand' in 6⁶, and Matt. 5²⁹ with 'eye'). It is not known who would be designated by *the slave of the high priest*.

51

The response of Jesus is in word and in action.

No more of this!: This renders *eāte heōs toutou* = lit. 'allow as far as this'. The common Greek verb *eān* = 'to permit', 'to leave go (alone)', is found only eleven times in the NT, nine being in L–A. The words are capable of more than one interpretation. (i) Since they are introduced by 'answered and said' (not reproduced in RSV) they could be a reply to the disciples' question in v. 49, and mean 'Let it come to this point', i.e. of an arrest, which is necessary if the passion is to take place (so Grundmann, p. 414, and others). (ii) Since 'answered and said' does not have to introduce an answer to a question (cf. 9⁴¹), the words could be a double command to the disciples – 'Leave off! Thus far (and no further)!' – (so Klostermann, p. 217, and others). (iii) They could be addressed to the crowd – 'Permit me thus far' – as a request to be allowed, before being arrested, to perform the healing, which he then proceeds to do (less likely, 'Tolerate thus much (of violence from my disciples)', so Plummer, p. 512). If (ii) is preferred, Jesus brings the disciples to a halt, and to that extent dissociates himself from their action, though perhaps with the suggestion that one sword stroke is sufficient to make the point that they are only mock criminals.

he touched his ear and healed him: This is also obscure, as it is not clear whether this healing by touch (cf. 5¹³) meant the replacement of the ear or the staunching of the blood. If Luke is entirely dependent on Mark for this pericope, the healing will be a legendary addition from his own hand, with the purpose of showing Jesus as beneficent to the end, and as overruling, and making good, any destruction inherent in the attitude of his disciples.

52–53 (iii) *Jesus and the Arresting Authority*

In Mark this is the climax and primary point of the story; in Luke it is its third and final component. If the agreement in wording is judged to go beyond what may be expected in variant oral or written traditions of the same event, it will indicate Luke's use of Mark here.

52

Having dealt with Judas, and then with the disciples, Luke now returns to the *crowd*, which was introduced (v. 47) as being led by Judas. This is specified as comprising, or including, *the chief priests and captains of the temple* (in place of 'the scribes', as temple police appropriate for an arrest) *and the elders*. For this collocation see on 19⁴⁷; 22², ⁴. Luke presumably deduces this from the reproach in v. 53, which is directed to those who had been his daily associates in the temple, who were the religious authorities themselves rather than their servants (Mark 14⁴³). But this is awkward since, without any change of subject in what follows, it is they who arrest Jesus, mock him (v. 63), and lead him to their own meeting (v. 66).

who had come out against him: This is Lukan in respect both of the verb used – *paraginesthai* = 'to arrive', very common in L–A, but rare in the rest of the NT – and of the construction – the participle standing between the article and the noun with an attributive sense.

Have you come out as against a robber, with swords and clubs?: Since any arrest anywhere, e.g. in the temple environs, would also have involved the threat of force (*swords and clubs*), the emphasis in the complaint must be on *as against a robber*. This is hardly an adequate translation. The word used here, *lēstēs*, could mean 'robber', but never simply in the sense of 'thief'. The robbery always implied violence of some sort, generally of those compelled to live off the land. In Josephus it is a semi-technical term for those he regarded as irresponsible revolutionaries, or members of 'messianic' groups, who disputed any other rule than the kingdom of God, and were devoted to the overthrow of what the occupying power considered the established order. At their door he placed the disaster of the Jewish war. To government ears the word denoted 'guerilla' or 'bandit'. Barabbas is called such in John 18⁴⁰ (in Mark 15⁷ he is called *stasiatēs* = 'an insurrectionary'). Crucifixion was particularly specified for them in Roman law, and Jesus was crucified along with two of them (Mark 15²⁷); as 'king of the Jews' was crucified as such.

53

When I was with you day after day in the temple: This is the sense of 'daily' here. It was Jesus' constant availability in the temple (despite his previous emphasis on it Luke drops Mark's 'teaching' here) which clearly distinguished him from a guerilla, who would have to be hunted, as they were doing to him now. The fact that they did not arrest him in those conditions shows their hidden motives.

But this is your hour, and the power of darkness: The significance of their present conduct is now stated. In Mark by a strange aposeiopesis, in Matthew more explicitly, it is said to be for the fulfilment of scripture in general. In Luke, where arrest as a criminal has already been interpreted as the divine will by means of a particular passage of scripture (Isa. 53¹² in v. 37), it is said to be evidence of his captors' *hour* and *the power of darkness*. This forceful but cryptic statement cannot stand on its own and unattached, and must have been supplied by Luke if he is following Mark here. Whatever its source – a non-Markan version of the whole story, oral tradition or Luke himself – it is commonly held to have a Johannine ring with the words *hour* and *darkness* (cf. Col. 1¹⁷; A. 26¹³; see the special note on Light and Darkness in Ellis, pp. 166f.). But an interpretation by way of Johannine predestination and metaphysical dualism could be mistaken here. With the emphatic position of *this* at the beginning of the sentence, and with the specification of the hour as *your hour*, the statement could be factual rather than theological. That is, Jesus is not a political or religious deceiver. He has nothing to hide, as is proved by his daily presence in the temple (*day by day, kath' hēmeran*, may carry something of the sense of 'in daylight', cf. 19^{47}; 21^{37}). By contrast it is they who are perfidious, as is shown by the fact that they hunt him as a criminal under cover of night, and the force which can only operate in the dark is typical of them (the reading of D 'But this is your hour and power, the darkness' could be a correct elucidation). These words, and not the actual arrest, close the pericope.

22$^{54-65}$ THE DENIAL OF JESUS BY PETER AND HIS ABUSE BY HIS CAPTORS

54 *Then they seized him and led him away, bringing him into the high priest's house. Peter followed at a distance;* 55*and when they had kindled a fire in the middle of the courtyard and sat down together, Peter sat among them.* 56 *Then a maid, seeing him as he sat in the light and gazing at him, said, 'This man also was with him.'* 57*But he denied it, saying, 'Woman, I do not know him.'* 58*And a little later some one else saw him and said, 'You also are one of them.' But Peter said, 'Man, I am not.'* 59*And after an interval of about an hour still another insisted, saying, 'Certainly this man also was with him; for he is a Galilean.'* 60*But Peter said, 'Man, I do not know what you are saying.' And immediately, while he was still speaking, the cock crowed.* 61*And the Lord turned and looked at Peter. And Peter remembered the word of the Lord, how he had said to him, 'Before the cock crows today, you will deny me three times.'* 62*And he went out and wept bitterly.*

63*Now the men who were holding Jesus mocked him and beat him;* 64*they also blindfolded him and asked him, 'Prophesy! Who is it that struck you?'* 65*And they spoke many other words against him, reviling him.*

The conduct of Jesus after arrest to the high priest's house is linked in all four passion narratives with an account of Peter's denials. This need not have been the case, as the latter could have existed as a unit of tradition on its own, provided it was given a brief introduction connecting it with the passion. It was not integral to a passion narrative, being concerned with Peter rather than with Jesus. Indeed, the purpose for which it was handed on is not obvious. It would hardly have served as a warning to Christians of the possibility of apostasy (an unforgiveable sin, Heb. 6$^{4-6}$; I John 5$^{16f.}$), since Peter was recovered from his desertion. Nor would it explicate a saying like 'He who denies me before men will be denied before the angels of God' (12⁹), since Peter had already confessed Jesus as messiah (9²⁰), and was to do so again (A. 2³⁶), so that his 'denial' here must have been different from that which involved an ultimate rejection by God as its consequence. Perhaps the story always intended a contrast between the weakness of disciples, even the chief of them, and the constancy and fidelity of Jesus himself, and was therefore told in conjunction with his trial. This would explain why in Mark/Matthew and in John (though not in the same way in Luke) Jesus' trial and Peter's denials are narrated as taking place simultaneously, and are interwoven.

ॐ

54a b

The transition from the scene in vv. 47–53 to what is to follow is accurately stated by Luke. Having arrested Jesus (not *seized him*, as in RSV; the verb *sullambanein*, here in the participle, is the technical word for making an arrest, as in A. 1¹⁶; 12³; 23²⁷; 26²¹; John 18¹²), they brought him (i.e. in custody to where he was to appear; the verb *agein*, used absolutely – rendered by RSV by *led away* – can be a technical term for this, as in A. 5²⁶ᶠ·; 26⁶, ¹⁷, ²³). They brought him into (an awkward repetition of the same verb) *the high priest's house*. This is probably an equivalent for 'to the high priest' in Mark 14⁵³, whose house is in Mark the scene of an immediate gathering of the Sanhedrin for a night session, and of Peter's denials (Mark 14⁵⁴⁻⁷²). *the high priest (ho archiereus)* will not have been among *the chief priests* (the same Greek word in the plural), who, in Luke's account, had arrested Jesus (v. 52), but is the single high priest in office, the secular and ecclesiastical head of Israel, and president of the Sanhedrin. That he is not named is characteristic of early tradition, which was not concerned with him as an individual, but as the representative of Israel and its authority, before which Jesus is to be arraigned. There are, however, problems here not unconnected with the question whether Luke is relying on Mark or on independent account. Firstly, the location of an official session of the Sanhedrin at the high priest's house is without parallel (see SB I, p. 1000f.). According to the Mishnah tractate Sanhedrin 11², it was to take place in the assembly hall, probably situated at this time in the temple environs. Secondly, if the regulations in Sanhedrin 4¹ were in force at the time, trials on capital charges were to be held only in the daytime. Both these difficulties disappear in Luke's narrative, where the Sanhedrin does not meet until the morning (v. 66), and does so in the council chamber (if in v. 66 *eis to sunedrion autōn*, rendered in RSV by *to their council*, is to be translated by 'to their council chamber'). Is this because Luke is following a more reliable source for the sequence of events, or because he is correcting what he thought improbable in Mark's? The former might be

22⁵⁴⁻⁶⁵

supported by the parallel scene in John 18¹²⁻¹⁴, though that could be taken as describing an examination at the high priest's house at night, as in Mark. The latter might be suggested by the lack of any reason in Luke's narrative for the night sojourn of Jesus at the high priest's house at all, except for him to be abused by his captors (vv. 63–65), which could have been taken over from the night session in Mark 14⁶⁵.

54c–62

The story of Peter's denial is constructed on the regular rule of three, though here that is dictated by Jesus' own prediction, in which, to emphasize the completeness of the denial in face of Peter's self-confidence, he had promised that it would be threefold (v. 34 = Mark 14³⁰). When included in the gospel narrative as the fulfilment of such a prediction the story acquires the further purpose of demonstrating Jesus' omniscience with respect to his disciples and his control over their destinies (cf. 19²⁸⁻³²; 22^{7-13, 24-32}). There are variations in all four accounts (even in Matthew, who appears to have no other source than Mark) as to persons, places, times, statements (in John questions) and replies. Luke's version is the most polished in (i) preserving a unity of place – Peter does not go outside for the second and third denials; (ii) marking a unity of time with *a little later* and *after an interval of about an hour*, and (iii) varying the interlocutors as a woman and a man followed by another man, whose affirmations are variously introduced (v. 56 *said*, Greek *eipen*, v. 58 *said*, Greek *ephē*, and, as a climax, v. 59 *insisted*, Greek *diischurizesthai* = 'confidently affirm' + A. 12¹⁵, a literary word, not LXX), who are all addressed with a vocative of rebuke (*Woman, Man, Man*), with Peter's denials all in direct speech. Taylor (*Third Gospel*, pp. 48f.) judges this version to be a revision of Mark's, noting that significant verbal agreements make up half of it – *a maid, seeing him, in the light, gazing at him, this man also, but he denied saying, I do not know, one of them, certainly, for he is a Galilean, and immediately, the cock crowed* – that these are evenly distributed throughout the story, and that the differences are explicable as inferences or editorial modifications, especially in the case of the three accusations and the time intervals.^h This is preferable to the view of Perry (*Passion-Narrative*, p. 44) that the time intervals are indications of a non-Markan source (to which Luke has added vv. 54b, 60b, 61c, and possibly 61b, from Mark), for those are Lukan in vocabulary and style; while a defect of the detailed analysis of Catchpole (*The Trial of Jesus*, pp. 160ff.) is that he has to suppose occasional and gratuitous additions of a few words from Mark to an otherwise flowing narrative. If Luke is dependent solely on Mark here, his version affords a signal illustration of his capacity to write in a 'novelistic' manner. For it is less a paradigm of cowardly

h For similar conclusions, see P. Winter, *Studia Theologica* 8, pp. 138ff., J. A. Bailey, *The Traditions common to the Gospels of Luke and John, Nov Test* suppl. 7, 1963, pp. 55ff.

discipleship, and more a dramatic account of a crucial moment in the life of Peter, the chief apostle, as an individual, and of his preservation by the Lord for his future work (cf. vv. 31ff.).

54c

As a solitary exception to the fleeing disciples – so Mark/Matthew, but not Luke, who had not mentioned the flight of the disciples, and provides no information of their whereabouts until the resurrection – Peter is depicted as still 'following Jesus' (Luke and Matthew have the imperfect tense of continuous action). This is *at a distance* (*makrothen*, for Mark's *apo makrothen*, which for Luke means 'from a distance'). No motive is given for this following, such as, for example, that he was still prepared to risk imprisonment or death with Jesus (v. 33; Matt. 26⁵⁸ suggests curiosity 'to see the outcome').

55

Luke here sets the scene more dramatically than Mark. Peter manages to reach the inside of the courtyard of the high priest's house (this is implied here, but stated in Mark 14⁵⁴); though it could be the inside of the house itself. For the Greek word rendered *courtyard* (*aulē*) was used by literary authors for a prince's palace (so Josephus, and cf. I Macc. 11⁴⁶), and in Mark 15¹⁶ it is used of Pilate's official residence. If it has this sense here – the *proaulion* into which Peter goes in Mark 14⁶⁸ (rendered in RSV by 'gateway', but in the margin by 'forecourt') being then the courtyard – the *mise-en-scène* would be somewhere inside the high priest's house, with the two groups, Peter and the servants on the one hand and Jesus and the Sanhedrin (so Mark; his Sanhedrin captors, so Luke) on the other hand, within sight of each other (v. 61). No explanation is given of how Peter succeeded in getting thus far. John 18¹⁵⁻¹⁶ indicates reflection on this; a mysterious 'other disciple', an acquaintance of the high priest, secures Peter's admission from the doorkeeper, who is (improbably in the high priest's ménage) a woman, and becomes Peter's first interlocutor. Luke then elaborates Mark's scene. The centre of the courtyard (or hall) is the locus of Peter's denials in Jesus' presence – *in the middle of, en mesō*, is Lukan (cf. 2⁴⁶; 8⁷; A. 1¹⁵; 2²²; 17²²; 27²¹). There *a fire* (already there in Mark 14⁵⁴) is *kindled* (*periaptein* + +, uncommon for lighting a fire; the simple form *haptein*, read by some mss here, is in this sense confined to L–A in the NT). In the sequence of Luke's narrative those who kindled the fire should be Jesus' captors, members of the Sanhedrin; but the verb is in the genitive absolute construction, and an indefinite 'they' may be meant. It is 'they' who now *sat down together* (*sunkathizein* + +), and Peter *sat among them* (*mesos* with the genitive, a literary construction + John 1²⁶); in Mark 14⁵⁴ it is Peter who 'sits together' with them (the servants). At this point Mark's narrative passes to the trial of Jesus, returning when that is over to Peter's denials (Mark 14⁵⁴ᵇ, ⁵⁵⁻⁶⁵, ⁶⁶⁻⁷²). In John 18¹²⁻²⁷ the two are further dovetailed when Peter's first denial comes before, and the second and third after, the high priest's examination. Luke, who has no account of a night trial, but who nevertheless may intend the abuse of Jesus (vv. 63–65) to be taking place simultaneously, tells the story of Peter straight through.

56–57
Peter is seen first by a servant girl (*tis* = 'a certain' is Lukan) as he sat *in the light*. The Greek here *pros to phōs* is probably taken from Mark 14⁵⁴, where it has the most unusual sense of 'at the fire'. She fixes her gaze on him (*atenizein* in place of Mark's *emblepein* = 'to look upon' is, apart from II Cor. 3⁷, ¹³, confined to L–A in the NT), and announces to the rest, *This man also was with (sun) him*. This is less precise than Mark 14⁶⁷, where one of the high priest's servant girls addresses Peter directly, and accuses him of having been with Jesus of Nazareth. Luke may have preferred that the action should be initiated by a general incriminating statement made to the assembled company. His version is also more literary, as it assumes that the reader will understand who is meant by *him*; it is the same person who has been referred to in v. 54, *they seized him* (sc. Jesus). But this statement, like the two to follow, *You also are one of them* and *this man also was with him* (vv. 58, 59), are, both in Luke and in the other accounts, curiously expressed, as if presupposing a situation which has not been fully described. Apart from their present context *also* in *he also* and *you also* could convey the impression that the disciples of Jesus were known to the servants as a band, that with the exception of Peter they had all been arrested, and that Peter was now in danger of arrest himself if recognized as another of *them*, and as one of those who had been with Jesus. In their present context these expressions have as their purpose to draw attention to Peter. He then denies the truth of the woman's statement by denying any knowledge of Jesus, *I do not know him* (Mark 14⁶⁸, 'I neither know nor understand what you mean'). This is the most emphatic of the three denials in Luke, the two which follow being considerably weaker. It is probably placed first so as to correspond with Jesus' prediction in its Lukan form, 'deny that you know me' (v. 34; 'deny me' Mark 14³⁰).

58
Then, *a little later (meta brachu* = 'after a short (while)'; *brachus* is rare in the NT, and is used of time again only in A. 5³⁴) *someone else (heteros* = 'another' is Lukan; for its use in a series , cf. 9⁶¹; 14¹⁹), this time a man (in Mark the same maid as before, in Matthew another maid; Luke is fond of pairing a man and a woman, cf. 1¹⁸⁻³⁵; 2²⁵⁻³⁸; 7¹⁻¹⁷; 15³⁻¹⁰; 17³⁴⁻³⁶), makes the general accusation personal. He addresses Peter directly with *You also* (in addition to others?) *are one of them*. Peter replies directly with the denial, *I am not* (Mark 14⁷⁰, 'He denied it').

59–60a
The third accusation is made *after an interval of about an hour*. This does not

reflect more precise information but the narrator's art. The language is literary and Lukan – the verb *diïstasthai* = 'to go away' + 24^{51}; A. 27^{28}, used of the passage of time, as is the corresponding noun in A. 5^7 *diastēma* + +, and *hosei* = 'about'. It comes from *another* (*allos*, a variation for *heteros* in v. 58), a man (in Mark/Matthew, somewhat artificially, from all the bystanders together). He reverts to the general accusation of the servant girl, *this man also was with* (*meta*, a variation for *sun* in v. 56). But now he asseverates it (*diïschurizesthai*) and with emphasis (*Certainly*, *ep'alētheias* = 'upon truth', apart from Mark 12^{14} confined to L–A in the NT; cf. A. 4^{27}; 10^{34}). He adds for confirmation, *for* (Greek *kai gar* = 'for also') *he is a Galilean*. This is plainly taken from Mark 14^{70}, but perhaps has a different meaning. In Mark it is added to the statement 'you are one of them', with the implication that all Jesus' disciples as a body were, and were known to be, Galileans; Matthew adds as an explanation of this that Peter's accent gave him away as a Galilean. In Luke the sense may be that Peter is a Galilean because Jesus is a Galilean (cf. 23^6), and for this reason Luke may have altered 'you are one of them' (Mark 14^{70}) to *this man was with him* (sc. Jesus). Peter then, in terms of the milder first denial in Mark 14^{68}, professes ignorance of what is being said.

60b

And immediately, while he was still speaking, the cock crowed: This statement, and the prediction (v. 34) it fulfils, raise questions about the character and formation of the tradition. The essence of the prediction in Mark 14^{30} is contained in the words 'To-day, in this very night (i.e. in Jewish time reckoning sometime during the first half of the day that had already begun at sunset – less emphatically Matt. 26^{34}, 'this night', Luke 22^{34}, 'today') you will deny me thrice.' This stresses both how soon after his profession of loyalty this denial will be, and how complete it will be. This form of prediction hardly lends itself to a dramatic description of its fulfilment, since that could take place any time before daybreak. A further determination by reference to the crowing of the cock, if an actual bird is meant, appears to introduce precision, but in fact does the opposite; for cocks are notoriously unpredictable in this matter, sometimes crowing throughout the night, and so would not provide a sufficiently fixed point of reckoning. It would then be for dramatic purposes that the third denial was predicted as occurring (immediately) before the crowing of the first Jerusalem cock. But, apart from the still debated question whether fowl were forbidden in Jerusalem at the time, this formulation could reflect a tradition which had developed outside Palestine in accordance with the Greco-Roman division of the night into four watches, of which 'cockcrow' (Greek *alektorophōnia* + + Mark 13^{35}, Latin *gallicinium*, originally, but no longer, connected with the crowing of cocks) was the third. Or, it may be supposed that this metaphorical usage was current in Palestine, and was used by Jews alongside the normal Hebrew division of the night into the first, middle and last watches. The meaning of 'cockcrow' would then be 'between 12 and 3 a.m.'. This also would not allow for a dramatic climax of the story by the fulfilment of the prediction. C. H. Mayo[1] suggests that what was being referred to quite precisely was the bugle sounding of the military *gallicinium* to mark the end of the third watch (cf. our reveille) by the Roman garrison in the Antonia fortress in Jerusalem. This would give a determined point of time which could be recognized as such. The prediction would then have been dramatically fulfilled in the nick of time when the third denial was immediately followed by reveille. There is, however, no evidence that *the cock crowed* was a way of saying 'cockcrow sounded', or 'they sounded cockcrow'. A further puzzle is that the climax to Mark's story (Mark 14[72]) is reached with a second cock crow, and this corresponds to the form of the prediction in Mark 14[30], 'before the cock crows twice' (though 'twice' is absent from some mss, and the reading in Mark 14[68], 'and the cock crowed', i.e. for the first time, is also uncertain). In the two passages from classical writers cited by commentators for a double cockcrow (Aristophanes, *Ecclēsiazusae* 389–392, Juvenal IX.106) what is stressed is that the second crowing, either of the same cock or of an answering cock, follows very soon after the first. There would be, however, no point in extending the time limit for the denials by the few minutes between a first and second crowing. Perhaps the original sense of this Markan form of the prediction was that Peter would deny Jesus three times (i.e. outright) in as short a space of time as it takes for one cockcrow to follow another.

61

In Luke the dénouement is not simply, as in John 18[27], that cockcrow followed *immediately* upon the third denial (*parachrēma* is Lukan and stronger than Mark's *euthus*), indeed *while he was still speaking*; nor even that he then recollected Jesus' prophecy, as in Mark 14[72] = Matt. 26[75]. It is that this recollection was brought about when *the Lord* (the post-resurrection title for Jesus), who is now for the first time revealed to have been in proximity all the time, and a spectator of the denials of himself by his leading apostle, *turned and looked at Peter*. If the rest of Luke's story is judged to be a rewriting of Mark's, this immensely affecting statement will have been the product of his imagination, and is further evidence of his propensity for pathos. It brings to a moving conclusion the intimate colloquy between Jesus and the apostles, and especially Peter, which Luke has constructed from 22[1] onwards. The recollection itself, expressed by the more classical verb *hupomnēskein* (= 'to remind'), is phrased in a form that was to become current in oral tradition as a solemn citation formula for the words of Jesus, as in I Clement 13[3]; 46[7], 'Remember the words of the Lord Jesus, how he said . . .', of which A. 11[16]; 20[35] are instances.

i 'St Peter's Token of the Cock Crow', *JTS* 22, 1921, pp. 367–70.

62

The conclusion is curiously problematic. Mark 14⁷² has in Greek *kai epibalōn eklaien*, in which the participle still defies translation (Bauer s.v. *epiballō*; rsv's 'broke down' is only one suggestion). It was probably unintelligible to Matthew and Luke. Their equivalent, *And he went out and wept bitterly* (Matt. 26⁷⁵ᶜ), is in such exact agreement as to require borrowing from Matthew by Luke or vice versa. But the words should probably be omitted from Luke's text with the Old Latin mss a b e ff² i l, and regarded as a scribal assimilation of his text to Matthew's. In that case Luke's story will have ended, not with Peter's bitter tears of remorse, but with Jesus' gaze evoking Peter's recollection; and so with the suggestion that the Lord, by his presence, look and omniscient word, embraced the situation, and preserved Peter from the consequences of his faithlessness (vv. 31–34), as he had preserved the rest from the consequences of their incomprehension and violence (vv. 35–51).

63–65

Meanwhile, or subsequently – it is not clear which – Jesus, in contrast to Peter, patiently and silently endures physical and verbal abuse. The verbs are in the imperfect tense of continuous or repeated action, perhaps to indicate that the abuse was protracted, and took place during Peter's denials and in his sight. The denials would then be juxtaposed with this abuse on a different part of the stage, and not, as in the highly artificial sandwich technique in Mark, with the nocturnal session of the Sanhedrin off stage. In Mark the abuse is an appendage to this session after Jesus' trial and condemnation. That Luke, who moves the session to the morning, is dependent here on Mark is indicated by (i) the awkward connection in v. 63, where *him* (*auton*) after *holding* grammatically refers to the last person mentioned, Peter, but in fact refers to Jesus (rsv supplies *Jesus*, which is not in the Greek text); and (ii) the poor style, with a string of participles (in the Greek holding, beating, blindfolding, saying), and a vocabulary which is either Markan, as in *mocked* (*empaizein*, cf. 18³² = Mark 10³⁴; Mark 15²⁰ omitted by Luke; Mark 15³¹ changed by Luke), *blindfolded, Prophesy!*, or is characteristic of Luke, as in *the men* (*hoi andres*, almost confined to Luke in the NT), *holding* (*sunechein*, predominantly in L–A in the NT, of various kinds of constraint), *beat* (*derein*, used in A. 5⁴⁰; 22¹⁹ of scourging ordered by Jewish synagogues, in A. 16³⁷ by Romans), *many other* (words) (except for Matt. 15³⁰ only L–A in the NT; cf. 3¹⁸; 8³; A. 2⁴⁰; 15³⁵), and *reviling* (*blasphēmein* in a non-technical sense, cf. A. 13⁴⁵; 18⁶). In this way Luke fills in the time between the nightime arrest and the morning trial.

63

Now the men who were holding Jesus mocked him and beat him: In Mark 14⁶⁵ it is (improbably) 'some' of the Sanhedrin who abuse Jesus, being joined by their attendants. Logically this is also the case in Luke, as those holding him in custody are the members of the Sanhedrin who had arrested him and conducted him (vv. 52–54). In Mark the abuse is horse-play; they buffet him (*kolaphizein*, a vulgarism). But it is also theological and religious abuse of one condemned as a religious deceiver, being couched in the scriptural language of the Lord's servant in Isa. 50⁶ LXX, 'I gave my cheeks to blows (*rhapismata*, a very rare word found only there and in Mark 14⁶⁵ in the Greek Bible), and did not turn my face from the shame of spitting.' In Luke this OT colouring is absent – he tends to establish a connection with the OT by general statement, as in 18³¹; 22³⁷; 24²⁷, ⁴⁴, rather than by using its language in description – and the abuse, which precedes the trial, is a more secular buffoonery to be expected of guards whiling away the time. They *mocked him*; the Greek word *empaizein* is found only in the synoptists in the NT, and is used in 18³² of the mocking of the Son of man by the Gentiles, and in 23¹¹ of the mocking (along with insults) of Jesus by Herod. It means that they made fun of him. *beat him* denotes the floggings frequently associated with the treatment of prisoners.

64–65

This, which is certainly taken from Mark, raises problems of text and meaning. If the question *Who is it that struck you?* is to be read after *Prophesy* in Mark 14⁶⁵, it will have been the origin of the identically worded question here and in Matt. 26²⁸, and the situation will be the same in all three accounts. But it is probably to be omitted from Mark with B D L k as an assimilation (some mss – D a f syrˢⁱⁿ – omit the reference to blindfolding in Mark and read 'they began to spit on his face and to strike him'). The situation in Mark would then also be religious. Jesus is derided as a (false) prophet who has just been condemned, and is taunted with the demand 'Prophesy!', i.e. 'Play the prophet!', 'Give us a bit of prophecy!', though there is no reason why for this he should be blindfolded. The question then becomes an agreement of Matthew and Luke against Mark such as would require the knowledge of one by the other. Streeter (*Four Gospels*, pp. 325ff.) considered that it had been inserted from Luke into Matthew in such a way as to affect all the texts of that Gospel, though there is no evidence for this apart from the absence in Matthew of any reference to blindfolding. Thus Luke's is the only intelligible text, since in Mark the blindfolding, if it is in the text, and is anything more than part of the OT colouring, has no consequences; and in Matthew the consequences lack the necessary blindfolding. But even Luke's account may be the result of an attempt to make sense of the Markan constituents of 'buffeting' and 'prophesying', and to create a more normal scene of mockery out of them. In addition to the other mockery (*also*) they play a version of Blind Man's Buff. The attempt is hardly successful, since, even if the Greek verb *prophēteuein*, which in pagan authors means 'to interpret the will of the gods', could have the meaning 'to say in advance', 'to guess', the question required would be 'Who is going to hit you?' W. C. van

Unnik[j] refers to the description by Pollux (*Onomasticon* IX, 113, 129) of two children's games. In the first a child with eyes shut attempts to guess (*manteuesthai* = 'to divine', 'to guess') who touched him, and in the second, called *kollabizein* (= *kolaphizein*, the word in Mark 14^{65}?), one holds his hands over his eyes and tries to guess with which hand the other has struck him. There is, however, no evidence that *prophēteuein* was ever used in this sense of *manteuesthai* = 'to guess'. Derrett (*Law in the NT*, p. 408) proposes a precise background in Jewish official procedure. According to him there was a tradition that 'the true messiah had the power of prophecy, and could prophesy by smell without the use of sight'. The origin of this was a midrash on Isa. 11^3, 'His smell/delight is in the fear of the Lord': and Bar Cochba was put to death as a messianic claimant because he could not 'smell and judge'. Luke, however, is not describing such an official testing of a messianic claimant, but the horse-play of captors engaged in abuse, as appears from the generalizing conclusion by which he rounds off the incident (v. 65), though that is somewhat loosely written, since it implies that the buffoonery in v. 64 could also be described as 'speaking slanderously against him'.

^{66}*When day came, the assembly of the elders of the people gathered together, both chief priests and scribes; and they led him away to their council, and they said,* ^{67}'*If you are the Christ, tell us.*' *But he said to them,* '*If I tell you, you will not believe;* ^{68}*and if I ask you, you will not answer.* ^{69}*But from now on the Son of man shall be seated at the right hand of the power of God.*' ^{70}*And they all said,* '*Are you the Son of God, then?*' *And he said to them,* '*You say that I am.*' ^{71}*And they said,* '*What further testimony do we need? We have heard it ourselves from his own lips.*'

This could be said to be the crucial section of the passion narrative, indeed of the Gospel. For it treats of the final confrontation of Jesus with Israel in the persons of its ruling body, which resulted in his official repudiation and death; which death, along with his resurrection, was to become the kernel of the saving message addressed by God to Israel (cf. I Cor. 15$^{3f.}$; A. 13$^{26-41}$). Yet the synoptic accounts of so vital

j 'Jesu Verhöhnung vor dem Synedrium', *ZNW* 29, 1930, pp. 310f.

a matter – in the Johannine passion narrative it is on the point of disappearing from the story altogether – are so brief and compressed as to be problematic at almost every point, and to require frequent hypothesis and imaginative conjecture to be intelligible.[k] The reason for such brevity could have been that the tradition had been weak here from the first. Since none of the disciples had been an eye-witness of the proceedings, these would have been inferred from their consequences; though it is not out of the question that they derived some knowledge of an event so important for their faith from members of the Sanhedrin (e.g. Joseph of Arimathea as he is depicted in $23^{50f.}$). A more likely reason is that the tradition of the passion had been developed in the context of Christian faith, and as an expression of that faith. Thus, none of the points of conflict which feature in the ministry of Jesus, and which could conceivably had led to his condemnation – accusation of blasphemy in the claim to forgive sins (Mark 2^7), of profaning the sabbath (Mark $2^{23}-3^6$), of exorcizing by Satanic power (Mark 3^{22}) – make any appearance at his trial; nor is what happens there made the basis of the subsequent proceedings before Pilate. The sole issue, apart from, in Mark/Matthew, abortive false witness about a supposed saying over the temple, is that of messiahship and divine sonship. It is not evident why historically this should be so. For if it was intended to bring to a head in this way the conflicts already occasioned by Jesus' authoritative words and actions towards Israel, an affirmative answer to the question 'Are you the Christ?' would not in itself have involved criminal guilt. For it would have been a contradiction in terms if, on the one hand, a 'messiah' was to be expected, but, on the other hand, any one who ever claimed to be such was automatically liable to excommunication, or guilty of a capital offence – unless, indeed, the historical conditions of Roman rule in Judaea were such that no form of the fulfilment of the Jewish religious hope was possible that would not have been promptly regarded as seditious. A negative answer to the question would not have been fatal to Jesus' cause, unless that cause had previously been built around a claim to be messiah, which is not how the synoptic gospels represent it. The tradition may have been less determined by such historical considerations than by the fact that the Christian faith and message had taken the form from the

k On the whole subject, see Catchpole, *Trial*, and the literature cited there, and on aspects of it, *The Trial of Jesus*, ed. E. Bammel, SBT 2.13, 1970, and Harvey, *Jesus and the Constraints of History*, ch. 2.

first of the confession of Jesus as (the crucified and risen) messiah and Son of God, these terms now being understood in a Christian sense (A. 9^{20}; Rom. 1^{3f}; John 20$^{30f.}$; I John 2$^{22–24}$); and that this message had been largely rejected by the Jews. This could have been read back as the substance of the proceedings of the trial, when the preaching of Christ crucified began to be filled out in the form of a narrative of events, and have been responsible for the accounts in their present form. If so, differences in those accounts could be put down to differences in the evangelists' christologies, i.e. their understanding of the nature of Jesus' messiahship and divine sonship, rather than to the preservation in tradition of variant versions of the course of the proceedings.

In Mark's account the Sanhedrin hold (irregularly?) a night-time session, when, after trumped up and inconsistent testimony about a threat to the temple has been heard and discarded, they pass formal sentence of death for blasphemy on the basis of statements which do not warrant it. Then, after insulting Jesus, they hold a morning session, to which no content is given, and take him to Pilate, but without proffering charges. In Luke's account Jesus' captors, after abusing him in the night-time, take him to a single morning meeting of the Sanhedrin, where, in a (preliminary?) examination he is asked about messiahship and divine sonship, and is pronounced self-condemned on the basis of his replies. They then take him to Pilate and proffer charges of sedition. This is certainly smoother and more convincing. 'The Lucan version is free from any suspicion of unreality, and a respectable body of evidence (sc. rabbinic) can be brought in support of it against the opposing Marcan account.'[1] It is, however, a further question whether this greater verisimilitude is achieved through Luke's use of a non-Markan source which was closer to the facts, or through his reflection upon, and rewriting of, Mark.[m] It may be noted that at two points, significantly at the beginning and the end, there is evidence in Luke's text of severe compression, which may have been due to constraint upon him

---

[1] H. Danby, 'The Bearing of the Rabbinical Criminal Code on the Jewish Trial Narratives in the Gospels', *JTS* 21, 1920, p. 61; see also D. R. Catchpole, *Trial*, ch. III, and the writers listed in favour of Luke's account by J. B. Blinzler, *The Trial of Jesus*, ET Westminster, Md., 1959, p. 115.

[m] For the first see Perry, *Passion-Narrative*, pp. 44f., and, with reservations, Taylor, *Passion Narrative*, pp. 81ff.; also writers cited by P. Winter, *On the Trial of Jesus*, Studia Judaica 1, Berlin 1961, pp. 160f. For the second see Bultmann, *History*, p. 271.

of the Markan original. The first is the introduction of the scene by *and they said* (v. 66, *legontes* = 'saying'). With a complete lack of verisimilitude this makes the whole council (in Luke apparently the captors of the previous night) conduct the enquiry in unison. Luke was capable of writing in this way, as is shown by the unison interrogation of the apostles in A. 4^7 and their unison reply in A. 5^{29}; but here it may be due, at least in part, to an omission by Luke of everything between Mark 15^{55}, where the whole council seeks witness against Jesus, to Mark 14^{61}, the particular question from the high priest. The second is the closing of the scene with *What further testimony do we need?* (v. 71 = Mark 14^{63}). This makes sense in the light of previous attempts to obtain testimony against Jesus referred to in Mark 14$^{55–61}$, but these are absent in Luke. Winter (*Studia Theologica* 8, pp. 162ff.) judged the writing in vv. 67–71 to be so slipshod that he proposed a violent solution, that originally there was no examination by the Sanhedrin in Luke, and that it had been inserted by an interpolator, who took Matthew's account as his model. If the beginning and ending were determined by Mark, it might be preferable to explain what lies between – two separate questions rather than a single double question, and two evasive replies enclosing the positive affirmation in v. 69 – as a revision of Mark, which still left behind traces of Mark's saying about the Son of man, rather than as the version of another source, where the replies were evasive, into which Luke has gratuitously inserted the positive affirmation from Mark.

ಉಂ

66

The language is formal. The time and setting for the examination could have been provided by Mark 15^1, though the language is Lukan.

When the day came: hōs (= 'as', used frequently in L–A in a temporal sense) *egeneto hēmera*, a Hellenistic expression + 4^{42}; 6^{13}; A. 12^{18}; 16^{35}; 27$^{29, 39}$. The reader has not been told that the preceding events have been taking place during the night, though he may be expected to conclude this from v. 39 taken with 21^{37}, and from the mention of cockcrow (v. 60). The meeting, in Luke the only one, is thus made to coincide with the second session of Mark 15^1/Matt. 27^1, which also takes place 'as soon as it was morning' (*prōi*, if used technically = the fourth watch, following cockcrow). There are no good grounds for supposing with Ellis (p. 259) that the setting in v. 54 implies a nocturnal session also in Luke, or that in Mark the official condemnation takes place only at the morning session (Mark 15^1).

the assembly of the elders of the people gathered together, both chief priests and scribes:
The authorities in Israel, and the Sanhedrin, are variously described by Luke
(see on 19⁴⁷; 20¹) and by Josephus. The first part of the designation here, *to
presbuterion* = 'the eldership', refers not to a constituent of the Sanhedrin ('the
elders', cf. 9²²; 20¹; A. 4⁵, etc.), but to the Sanhedrin as a whole, as in A. 22⁵, its
only other occurrence in the NT apart from I Tim. 4¹⁴, where it is used of
Christian elders. The fact that the word is found here for the first time in Greek
literature is probably chance, for 'elders' was widely employed for members of
a corporation, and in a sense it corresponds to the word *gerousia* = 'the assembly
of older men', which was a regular term for the governing body of a community (especially in Sparta, but also in Carthage), for the Roman Senate, and
also for the Sanhedrin in Josephus, (cf. A. 5²¹ in the curious form 'the council
and all the senate of Israel'). Here the eldership is *of the people*, i.e. of Israel as
a religious community, not of the populace, with whom Jesus has found such
favour in chs. 20–21. The composition of the Sanhedrin is further specified as
both chief priests and scribes (the stylistic *te . . . kai* = 'both . . . and' is rare in the
NT but common in A.). According to rabbinic sources it was made up of the
quasi-sacred number of seventy members plus the high priest as president.
While the priests, and the elders as influential lay people, were Sadducean in
outlook, the number and influence of the scribes, who were theologians and
exegetes of the law, had increased in the first centuries BC and AD (when reconstituted after AD 70 the Sanhedrin consisted entirely of rabbis). This increasingly
scribal character has led some Jewish scholars to postulate two Sanhedrins at
this time, a larger one concerned with the religious life of Israel, and a smaller
priestly one occupied with political aspects of the nation's life (see Zeitlin, *Who
Crucified Jesus?*, ch. V). *gathered together* is *sunagein* = 'assembled', as in A. 4⁵.

led him away to their council: The sentence is awkward because in Luke Jesus'
captors (v. 63), who have arrested him (54), are themselves members of the
Sanhedrin (v. 52). It could mean that the Sanhedrin assembled consisting of
chief priests and scribes, and *they* (impersonal, or the captors of v. 63) *led him
away* (*apagein* = 'to conduct', cf. A. 23¹⁷) *to their* (sc. the Sanhedrin's) *council*, or,
they (the captors) led him away to their own council. *sunedrion* (only here in
this Gospel) could mean 'council-chamber', and so mark a change of venue
from the high priest's house; but while this is a possible meaning in some
passages, e.g. A. 4¹⁵; 5²⁷, ³⁴; 6¹², ¹⁵, it is not demanded by any of them, and in
others, A. 5²¹, ⁴¹; 22³⁰; 23¹ it can only mean 'council'. For a similar redundant
their in an identical situation of a meeting of the Sanhedrin in the morning after
an arrest the previous night, cf. A. 4⁵.

and they said: The awkwardness continues with this transition (see above). Taken
literally it makes the captors, or the whole Sanhedrin, conduct the interrogation in unison, whereas it can only have been conducted by the high priest, as
in Mark 14⁶⁰/Matt. 26⁶² (cf. John 18¹⁹; A. 5²⁷; 7¹). But Luke can write in this

impressionistic fashion for dramatic effect (cf. A. 2⁷ᶠᶠ·; 4⁷, ¹⁹, ²⁴ᶠᶠ·; 5²⁹), and he may be doing so here to stress the corporate responsibility of Israel for what is to follow.

67–70

In Luke the interrogation proceeds immediately to the question of messiahship. It is not surprising that Luke fails to reproduce the confused preamble in Mark 14⁵⁵⁻⁶¹ᵃ, with its many and abortive false charges, and the discordant testimony about a supposed statement by Jesus that he would destroy the temple, and in three days erect another (regarded by some scholars as echoing the original ground for arresting Jesus). The relation of Jesus to the temple and its cultus will be raised in a more historical and intelligible form in A. 6–7. In what follows in Luke and Mark the sequence of thought is both similar and different. In Mark there is a single question put to Jesus whether he is the Christ and the Son of God, an affirmative reply to which is extended with an assurance to the Sanhedrin that they will see the Son of man exalted and in his parousia. This leads to the dispensing with further witnesses, and to condemnation to death for blasphemy. In Luke there is a question about messiahship, an evasive reply to which is extended by an assertion of the heavenly session of the Son of man. This then becomes the basis for a question about divine sonship, to which the reply is a (qualified?) affirmative. This leads to the dispensing with further witness because Jesus stands self-condemned. If the statements about the Son of man (v. 69) and further witness (v. 71) are subtracted as Markan additions, what remains is not recognizably an independent non-Markan version, but something of a torso, with two unconnected questions without introduction or conclusion. If, however, these two statements are integral to the story, the first in supplying a basis for the question on divine sonship and the second in providing a conclusion, then Luke's account could be better explained as a revision of Mark's.

67a

If you are the Christ, tell us: In Mark 14⁶¹ the direct question of the high priest, opening his interrogation in the face of Jesus' persistent silence, is exasperated, abrupt and peremptory. Plainly Matthew found this too bald, and turned it into an indirect question introduced by a solemn adjuration (Matt. 26⁶³). The words in Luke, voiced by the whole council, are also indirect, though not as a question, but as a demand for an open declaration. The rendering in RSV observes the word order of the Greek better than a proposed alternative, 'Tell us whether you are the Christ.' The sense may be, 'If you are in fact the messiah of Israel, then say so to us, who, as the Sanhedrin of Israel, are the proper persons to hear it.' The question in Mark combines 'the Christ' and 'the Son of God' (in a form 'the Son of the Blessed', which is said, despite its Semitic sound, to be impossible as a Jewish expression; see Klausner, *Jesus of Nazareth*, p. 342). It is not clear whether these were synonyms (if so, why use both?), or terms which always went together, or separate but closely related terms, perhaps with one interpreting the other (the Christ, who is also the Son of God, or that Christ who is the Son of God). Both are regarded here as self-explanatory, though they may have become so only for Christians through the application of both of them to Jesus (Matt. 16^{16}; John 20^{31}). (For the meaning of 'the Christ', and the scarcity of evidence for its absolute use in Judaism at the time for the one who would bring in the coming age, see on 2^{11}.) For Luke the terms were evidently synonymous – see 4^{41}, where he adds to Mark 1^{34} that the demons recognized Jesus as the Son of God, and as the reason for the injunction to silence that they knew he was the Christ, and A. 9^{20–22}, where Paul's preaching is both that Jesus was the Son of God and that he was the Christ (cf. 2^{11, 26} with 1^{35}). Nevertheless, a distinction may be observed between them. In A. 'the Christ' predominates as the term for preaching Jesus and for arguing his status with Jews (A. 2^{31, 36}; 3^{18}; 8^{5}; 17^{3}; 18^{5, 28}; 26^{23}), and it is the necessity and scriptural propriety of a suffering Christ that is frequently so argued (24^{26, 46}; A. 3^{18}; 17^{3}; 26^{23}). This could explain why Luke has two separate questions, one about 'the Christ' and one about 'the Son of God', and why they are answered differently.

67b–68

If I tell you, you will not believe; and if I ask you, you will not answer: The reading in some mss in Mark 14^{62} is, 'You (singular) say that I am', and some have taken this as original on the ground that it would account for 'You (singular) have said so' in Matt. 26^{64}, and for 'You (plural) say that I am' in v. 70 here. However, the deletion from Mark's text of 'You say that' so as to remove any hesitancy on Jesus' part, and to create the first open declaration of messiahship in Mark, is unlikely to have been made by scribes without a corresponding alteration to Matthew's text. If 'I am' is the correct reading in Mark, Luke's account is incompatible with his, and largely contradicts it. What occurs at this point is not a reply, non-committal or otherwise, to a question. It is a refusal to comply with the previous request that, if he is the messiah, he makes an open declaration of it, and ceases to be a hidden messiah; and *tell* in the rejoinder picks up *tell* in the request. This rejoinder is highly stylized, being a couplet in 'four short and well balanced clauses, where the assonance amounts to rhyme' (Knox, *Hellenistic Elements*, p. 11). Though the language is not particularly distinctive of him, Luke may have composed it on the model of 20^{1–8}. There, in the presence of what is equivalent to the Sanhedrin, Jesus, in replying to a leading question about his authority (20^{2}, 'tell us', added by Luke in revising Mark), asks a counter-question (20^{3}, 'I also (added by Luke) will ask you a question'); to this they refuse to reply (20^{5f.}, 'If we say . . .'), and for that reason he refuses to answer their original question. The first half of the couplet justifies refusal of the request on the ground that, even if he told them (whether he was the messiah or not) they will not believe. The verb *pisteuein*, when used absolutely in this way, generally requires an object to be supplied – e.g. 'it' (You will not grant an open declaration to be true any more than you have accepted what has been presented to you already), or 'me' (You will not accept me as telling the truth). The continuation of the couplet with *and if I ask you, you will not answer* ('or release me' in some mss should be rejected as destroying the rhythm) is strange. It does not reflect the situation of a trial, but of a discussion, as in 20¹⁻⁸, and presupposes the necessity of dialogue in any treatment of such matters. What form such a counter-interrogation would take is not indicated. Knox (op. cit., p. 11) suggests that in framing this reply Luke had in mind the position of martyrs before judges who refuse to debate with them. 'Jesus is here the prototype of all martyrs unjustly condemned by courts which would neither accept the Gospel, nor allow its professors to examine them.' It would then be part of Luke's presentation of the trials and death of Jesus as a whole as a veritable 'passion', i.e. as the sufferings of a martyr. It would also imply that the Sanhedrin were incompetent to judge in a central matter of religious belief, viz. messiahship, and were not motivated by the pursuit of truth and justice, but by malice.

69

But from now on the Son of man shall be seated at the right hand of the power of God: This positive affirmation stands in complete contrast to the previous refusal to discuss 'the Christ', and is awkwardly connected by *But.* That it is taken from Mark is suggested by *of the power,* as only here is Ps. 110¹ cited in this form; in Mark it is a periphrasis for God, which Luke has destroyed by adding *of God* (cf. A. 8¹⁰). In Mark there is some sequence of thought, since the affirmation is epexegetic of the previous avowal of messiahship 'I am', and the speaker can readily be understood to be referring to himself as 'the Son of man'. It takes the form of a personal statement that the members of the Sanhedrin will themselves see the speaker, as messiah, both installed as the Son of man at the seat of divinity, and as coming thence to exercise the offices of consummator and judge (for a similar sequence in an address to disciples, cf. Mark 8²⁷⁻9¹). In Luke the affirmation takes the form of a more impersonal and semi-credal statement of the permanent status of the Son of man *from now on* (apo tou nun + 1⁴⁸; 5¹⁰; 12⁵²; 22¹⁸; II Cor. 5¹⁶). Easton (p. 338) argues against Luke's dependence on Mark here on the ground that he would not have weakened Mark's statement by substituting for it a passive *sessio ad dextram*; but this is precisely what he is likely to have done. For this is how he depicts Jesus in A., as the messiah elevated to the right hand of God, to operate from there as the church's Lord and guide, and as the world's judge, but not as coming in the near future; and he is 'seen' there only by believers (A. 7⁵⁶). The awkwardness with which the affirmation follows v. 68, and the necessity of a revised form of it, suggests that Luke did not add it gratuitously from Mark to another version, but that he had only Mark's version, which he edited in accordance with his own christology.

70

And they all said, 'Are you the Son of God, then?': The interrogation, now expressly said to be communal (in *And they all said* vocabulary and word order are Lukan), continues with a question about *the Son of God* (for which see on 1^{35}). This may be a further indication that Luke is writing on the basis of Mark's text, and is here taking up the second component of the double question in Mark 14^{61}. The combination 'the Christ, the Son of God' is not inconceivable in Judaism, if the Son of God referred to the Davidic king, who is in an intimate relationship with God as 'Father'; cf. Pss. 2^7; 89^{27}, and the application at Qumran of II Sam. 7^{14}, 'I will be his father and he will be my son' to the Branch of David who was to come (Vermes, *Scrolls*, p. 244). The treatment of divine sonship as a separate issue on its own, however, betrays a Christian standpoint, as does the deduction of divine sonship (*then*) from the future exalted status of the Son of man. This is only possible for the Christian reader, who knows that Jesus refers to himself as the Son of man (v. 69), that he is both the Son of man and the Son of God, and that *from now on* denotes the period when the crisis inaugurated by Jesus shall have reached its conclusion in his death and subsequent exaltation. The sequence of thought here corresponds with the Christian confession of Jesus as Davidic messiah, who is made, or installed, as the Son of God at his resurrection (A. 13$^{26-41}$; Rom. 1$^{3-4}$).

'You say that I am': This, introduced by a variant Lukan form of introduction *ho de pros autous ephē*, is curiously phrased. You say (*humeis legete*) is the plural, necessary in the context, of the singular *su legeis* = 'thou sayest' (RSV 'You have said so') in the reply to Pilate (23^3); cf. *su eipas* = 'thou hast said' (RSV 'You have said so') in the reply to the high priest in Matt. 26^{64}. The two latter are probably idiomatic, though the meaning is debated. An outright affirmative would presumably have been expressed otherwise, and it can hardly be such in 23^3, where it is the basis of Pilate's declaration of innocence. If an evasive answer is intended, the accent would fall on *you* ('the words are yours'). The form in Luke – *humeis legete oti ego eimi* – could be taken as a strong affirmative, 'it is you yourselves (by using the term "the Son of God") who have said exactly what (taking *hoti* = 'that' as *ho ti* = 'that which') I am'. This throws the responsibility back on to the interrogators, and is taken up by *we ourselves* (v. 71b).

71

'What further testimony do we need?': The question is clearly derived from Mark 14^{63}, where it looks back to the previous attempts to secure witness (Mark 14$^{55-60}$, not in Luke), and is a foil to a ritual pronouncement of guilt for blasphemy and an official sentence of death. Here it looks forward, and is a foil to what is said to be Jesus' own self-condemnation – *apo tou stomatos autou* = 'from his own mouth', as in 4^{22}; 19^{22}; A. 22^{14}, and Luke's editorial note in 11^{54}. This

is a dramatic, but also a vague, conclusion. No less than in Mark's account Jesus is represented as guilty in the eyes of his interrogators, and in a way that makes any further procedures unnecessary; but it is not said what it is that they had heard from his mouth, nor what meaning they attached to the title 'the Son of God' that a claim to it would automatically involve self-condemnation, nor what the extent of the condemnation was (to death?).[n] Thus, Luke does not furnish additional or alternative information for clarifying the issues whether the Sanhedrin did pass a formal sentence of death for blasphemy, or had the power of capital punishment in such a case. Nor is the charge of claiming to be the Son of God proffered before Pilate; contrast John 19^7, where the charge sums up the christology of that Gospel. The absence of any formal condemnation may be an expression of Luke's view that the Sanhedrin were not competent to judge such a vital issue, and were actuated by prejudice and hatred (cf. A. 2$^{22f.}$; 3$^{13ff.}$; 4^{11}; 7^{52}; 13$^{27f.}$). This incompetence left the question of messiahship open to be defined in a Christian sense as a result of the passion and resurrection of Jesus (24$^{26, 46}$; A. 17^3; 26^{23}), as also his status as the Christ, the Son of man and the Son of God (cf. in that order A. 2^{36}; 7^{56}; 9^{20}).

23$^{1-25}$ PILATE, THE JEWS AND JESUS

23 *Then the whole company of them arose, and brought him before Pilate.* *[2]And they began to accuse him, saying, 'We found this man perverting our nation, and forbidding us to give tribute to Caesar, and saying that he himself is Christ a king.' [3]And Pilate asked him, 'Are you the King of the Jews?' And he answered him, 'You have said so.' [4]And Pilate said to the chief priests and the multitudes, 'I find no crime in this man.' [5]But they were urgent, saying, 'He stirs up the people, teaching throughout all Judea, from Galilee even to this place.'*

[6]When Pilate heard this, he asked whether the man was a Galilean. [7]And when he learned that he belonged to Herod's jurisdiction, he sent him over to Herod, who was himself in Jerusalem at that time. [8]When Herod saw Jesus, he was very glad, for he had long desired to see him, because he had heard

n J. C. O'Neill, in *The Trial of Jesus*, ed. Bammel, pp. 72ff., examines the vexed question of what it was in the statements of Jesus under interrogation that constituted blasphemy and produced his condemnation. He concludes, though primarily with reference to John 19^7, that what constituted the blasphemous offence was if anyone laid claim to be messiah or the Son of God before God himself had announced his enthronement as such.

about him, and he was hoping to see some sign done by him. ⁹*So he questioned him at some length; but he made no answer.* ¹⁰*The chief priests and the scribes stood by, vehemently accusing him.* ¹¹*And Herod with his soldiers treated him with contempt and mocked him; then, arraying him in gorgeous apparel, he sent him back to Pilate.* ¹²*And Herod and Pilate became friends with each other that very day, for before this they had been at enmity with each other.*

¹³*Pilate then called together the chief priests and the rulers and the people,* ¹⁴*and said to them, 'You brought me this man as one who was perverting the people; and after examining him before you, behold, I did not find this man guilty of any of your charges against him;* ¹⁵*neither did Herod, for he sent him back to us. Behold, nothing deserving death has been done by him;* ¹⁶*I will therefore chastise him and release him.'* ★

¹⁸*But they all cried out together, 'Away with this man, and release to us Barabbas –* ¹⁹*a man who had been thrown into prison for an insurrection started in the city, and for murder.* ²⁰*Pilate addressed them once more, desiring to release Jesus;* ²¹*but they shouted out, 'Crucify, crucify him!'* ²²*A third time he said to them, 'Why, what evil has he done? I have found in him no crime deserving death; I will therefore chastise him and release him.'* ²³*But they were urgent, demanding with loud cries that he should be crucified. And their voices prevailed.* ²⁴*So Pilate gave sentence that their demand should be granted.* ²⁵*He released the man who had been thrown into prison for insurrection and murder, whom they asked for; but Jesus he delivered up to their will.*

★ Here, or after v. 19, other ancient authorities add v. 17, *Now he was obliged to release one man to them at the festival*

In all the passion narratives there is a hiatus at the crucial point of transition from the Jewish to the Roman side. This adds to the indistinctness of the accounts of the judicial procedures in both, which can only be made coherent by a liberal use of conjecture. The hard core of the tradition was that Jesus was crucified, i.e. put to death by the Romans in Roman fashion; according to the *titulus* on the cross on a political charge of having made a seditious claim to be the king of the Jews. The process by which this was the logical outcome of what had begun as a religious matter within Judaism is, however, nowhere clearly traced. The reason for this may be, in part, that brief and concentrated stories of the Jewish and Roman proceedings, formed perhaps originally for religious purposes, and based on supposition rather than eyewitness testimony, came down as separate units in the tradition, and it remained for the evangelists to try to make a connection between them.

In the background is the general question whether under Roman rule the Jews possessed the power of capital punishment in religious cases. Owing to the paucity and the ambiguous character of the evidence this question 'has been treated with wearying frequency and disappointing inconclusiveness'.[o] The distinctive features of Roman administration of the provinces were 'permanent military occupation, regular taxation and Roman supervision of public order'.[p] The last of these meant jurisdiction in offences, chiefly capital offences, covered by a developing Roman code of statutory law (*ordo*), but also cases not covered by this (*extra ordinem*). They were dealt with by the provincial governor through personal examination (*cognitio*) in virtue of an authority (*imperium*) vested in him alone, which he exercised with considerable initiative and freedom of judgment. Included in it was the power of the death penalty with respect to provincials (but not Roman citizens), and this he jealously preserved. The question at issue is whether in Judaea, when it was brought within the provincial system, these arrangements were in any way modified to accommodate a theocratic people living under the authority of divine law, which prescribed death by stoning for certain offences judged to constitute blasphemy against God, the sentence to be carried out by representatives of the religious community. It has been argued that the Sanhedrin was not only allowed to pass sentence of death for capital offences under the Mosaic law, but to have the sentence carried out by themselves. This would be a natural conclusion from the case of Stephen (A. 7$^{54-58}$), and possibly from other cases also. The express statement to the contrary in John 18^{31} has then to be taken as a statement of Johannine theology rather than historical fact; for John it was imperative that Jesus be crucified and not stoned, so that the meaning of his death as a 'lifting up' should be symbolized by the manner of it (John 18^{32}; 12^{32}). It may then be inferred from the fact that Jesus was crucified that his case was a Roman affair from the first, and the charge one of insurrection. The synoptic accounts could then reflect a tendency, arising from later Christian experience of persecution at the hands of the Jews for the confession of Jesus (e.g. A.

o Catchpole in *The Trial of Jesus*, ed. Bammel, p. 59; see also his own book *The Trial of Jesus*, pp. 221ff. and the literature cited there.

p Sherwin-White, *Roman Law*, p. 12; see Lectures One and Two of this book for the whole subject.

9^{1-2}), to shift responsibility for the crucifixion on to the Jews. If, on the other hand, the historical situation was that the Sanhedrin could pass sentence, but was not allowed to inflict the death penalty on its own authority, cases like that of Stephen have to be explained, either as having occurred during a vacancy in the governor's office, or as instances of lynch law which went unpunished. In the case of Jesus, if he had been found guilty of a capital offence under Jewish law, application would have had to be made to Pilate for confirmation of the sentence and for permission to carry it out, or for the Romans to carry it out. What then has to be explained is why it is not this which took place, but a Roman trial and a Roman execution. It has to be supposed, either that for reasons unstated the Sanhedrin concocted a plot (so Mark 15^1?) to transmute a Jewish capital religious offence (blasphemy, Mark/Matthew, unstated in Luke) into a Roman capital political offence (sedition – did they always have to do this because the governor would not accept a theological charge in his court?), or, that what the Sanhedrin had previously conducted was not a trial issuing in a verdict, but a preliminary (and inconclusive?) hearing (so Luke?, and John?), on the basis of which charges of sedition were formulated *ab initio* for presentation to Pilate. q

This hiatus remains in Luke's account, where the specific charges before Pilate (23^2) do not proceed out of anything recorded of the previous examination by the Sanhedrin, and are not framed in terms of matters which fell within its jurisdiction. It is from a literary point of view that Luke is superior. He provides the only smooth transition from the Jewish to the Roman proceedings, and elaborates the latter in a way that alters the balance between the two. This is done in vv. 1–25, a section which is in marked contrast to what stands here in Mark, and to anything else in this Gospel. The main constituents are, apart from the incident of Herod, the same – Pilate's question, the non-committal reply, the reference to Barabbas, Pilate's wish to release Jesus and his final decision in the face of irresistible demands. Mark's account is, however, compressed, disjointed and lop-sided (four verses given to

q Sherwin-White notes Luke's inferiority to Mark at two vital points. There is 'a somewhat incoherent and allusive account of the session of the Sanhedrin, without a clear statement about a condemnation', and, in comparison with Pilate's conclusion of his *cognitio* with a verdict and condemnation to a stated punishment in Mark, 'Luke is rather less precise at this point' (*Roman Law*, pp. 33, 26).

Pilate's examination, ten verses to Barabbas). Luke's is a single, continuous and articulated narrative of action and dialogue in the interplay between Pilate and the Jews, with the semi-independent story of Herod and the references to Barabbas integrated into it. Its dominant theme is Pilate's repeated declaration of Jesus' innocence, reinforced by that of Herod. In vv. 20–25 it reaches a dramatic climax, marked by assonance and repetition, when Jesus is shown to be condemned to death only because Pilate is overborne by the clamour of the Sanhedrin acting in conjunction with the populace; and it concludes with the remarkable statement (v. 25) that in permitting crucifixion he was handing over Jesus to the Jews to work their own will. Luke's reasons for writing in this way would not be far to seek. With the condemnation of Christianity's saviour figure to the Roman cross his story had reached the point where the shoe pinched hardest for one sensitive to, and perhaps writing for, the outside world of the empire. The apologetic argument in A., that suspicions of Christianity aroused by the disturbances it caused were due to Jewish calumnies, which failed to carry weight with Romans, is here given a basis in the case of Jesus himself. His crucifixion, though a Roman punishment, is represented as essentially a Jewish act (cf. A. 2^{23}; 3^{13-15}; 4^{10}; 5^{30}; 7^{52}; 13^{27-29}). Accordingly the Sanhedrin continues to be depicted less as a responsible religious court than as a malicious mob. It is here ready to proceed out of a hypocritical loyalty to the empire.

ဆ

1

Then the whole company of them arose, and brought him before Pilate: The transition in Mark 15^1 is obscure, as 'and the whole council' is ungrammatical in the sentence and otiose; and according to the sense given to *sumboulion* of either 'counsel' or 'council' the meaning is that they made a plan, though no hint is given of what that was, or that they formed a council (RSV 'held a consultation'). If Luke has used the first half of Mark's sentence to introduce the morning session of the Sanhedrin (v. 66), he could have used the second half here. *the whole company* (*hapan to plēthos*) is confined to L–A in the NT, and can mean a crowd or the whole of a constituted body (cf. 19^{37}; A. 4^{32}; 6^2; $15^{12, 30}$), and could here be the equivalent of Mark's 'the whole council'. The impression in Mark is that Jesus is brought as an already condemned prisoner for Pilate to confirm the sentence and have it implemented. In Luke, where there has been no official condemnation, Jesus is *brought before* (*agein epi*, in this sense also at A. 9^{21}; 17^{19}; 18^{12}) Pilate for trial, and there the whole issue will be decided.

This means before Pilate's tribunal, which was a raised platform on which the seats of the magistrates were placed (in Greek *bēma* = 'judgment seat', as in Matt. 27[19]; John 19[13]). Normally the governor resided on the coast at Caesarea, the capital of Judaea once it became a Roman province, and cases were brought to him there, as in A. 23[23-24, 27]. For the preservation of order at festivals in a city swollen with pilgrims he moved to Jerusalem, reinforcing the garrison there, and he would hear cases there also, as in A. 25[1-9]. This would be at the *praetorium*, originally a praetor's tent in camp, but used of a governor's official residence. According to Josephus (*BJ* 2.301) and Philo (*Embassy to Gaius* 299, 306) this was in the Palace of Herod in the west of the city, described by Josephus as having huge banqueting halls and bedrooms for a hundred guests; but that would not be possible here if it was occupied by Herod when Pilate sent Jesus to him (v. 7). Some have argued that it was in the Antonia Fortress northwest of the temple area, where the troops were garrisoned. The impression left by John 18[28, 33]; 19[9] is that the examination was conducted inside the *praetorium*, with Pilate coming out to communicate with the Jews, whose scruples prevented them from entering. This, however, could be a dramatic *mise-en-scène* provided by that evangelist; in John 19[13] the judgment seat is on a raised place outside. The impression left by the synoptists is that the whole examination was conducted in the open air, and that after it the soldiers took Jesus inside the palace (*aulē*), which is identified as the *praetorium* (Mark 15[16]; Matt. 27[27]). The picture would then be as in Jos. *BJ* 2.301, where Florus 'lodged at the palace (sc. of Herod), and on the following day had a tribunal placed in front of the building, and took his seat. And the chief priests and the nobles and the most eminent citizens presented themselves before the tribunal.' Sherwin-White (*Roman Law*, p. 45) considers Luke's timetable inferior to that of Mark/Matthew, in that an approach to Pilate after a morning session of the Sanhedrin, presumably several hours after dawn, would find him enjoying his leisure with the day's work already done.

Our sources of knowledge of Pilate are too scanty, and probably too biased, to give assistance in assessing the part he plays in the gospel accounts. Apart from a bare statement by Tacitus (*Annals* XV, 44) that he executed Jesus in the reign of Tiberius, they are confined to Philo and Josephus. In referring to an episode when Pilate was forced to revoke his offensive action of introducing the Roman standards into Jerusalem, Philo speaks of his character as naturally inflexible and a blend of self-will and relentlessness, and of his conduct as governor as marked by bribery, insult, robberies, outrages, wanton injuries, constant executions without trial and ceaseless and grievous cruelty. Some allowance would have to be made in this for rhetoric, and for Philo's need, in pursuance of his thesis, to show Tiberius in a good light. Josephus does not offer a character sketch, but describes Pilate as showing considerable ruthlessness and force in quelling opposition to his use of temple monies for building an aqueduct, and in putting down a Samaritan uprising, for which he was ordered to Rome by

Vitellius, the legate of Syria, and deprived of his office (*Ant.* 18.55–62). The fact that he held office for ten years (AD 26–36) could argue that he was highly regarded in Rome as an efficient governor of one of the most difficult of the provinces; though Josephus (*Ant.* 18.176f.) observes that this was because Tiberius deliberately left governors in office for a length of time to prevent provinces being bled by a rapid succession of men intent on getting rich quick.

2

And they began to accuse him: Mark 15$^{2-5}$ is barely intelligible. Without any preliminaries, and not as the result of any stated charges, Pilate asks the crucial question, which is unmotivated by anything that has gone before. The Sanhedrin then belatedly bring charges; but these are many and unspecified, and Pilate refers to them as such, and marvels at Jesus' silence. This would be quite unacceptable to Luke. If Pilate's declarations of Jesus' innocence, which form the main thread of Luke's account, are to have any worth, they must be made with respect to charges that are specific. The Sanhedrin, still speaking as a single body in unison, now act as the official accusers required by Roman law. The verb *katēgorein* can have a general sense of 'to accuse', but it is here used precisely of bringing charges in court, as in A. 22^{30}; 24$^{2-19}$; 25$^{5-16}$.

'We found this man': This could also have a more general sense – 'We have discovered this man to be' – or a more precise and technical sense of findings established by judicial examination – cf. vv. 4, 14, 22, 'I do not find guilt established', and possibly A. 24$^{5, 20}$. With the latter sense the charges are here presented as findings of the Sanhedrin's previous examination; and since in Luke's account there have been no such, the statement may be intended as a further disparagement of the Sanhedrin. So also could be *this man*, if, as is possible, it is contemptuous – 'this fellow'.

The charge, expressed by participles, is a threefold one. There may be a measure of stylization in this – cf. the threefold charge brought against Paul in similar circumstances in A. 17$^{6-7}$, and again in A. 24$^{5-6}$, and Paul's reply to threefold charges in A. 24^{12}; 25^8.

perverting our nation: This is the most general of the charges. The verb *diastrephein* can have a religious meaning of 'to seduce from the true faith' (I Kings 18$^{17f.}$), and has this in A. 13$^{8, 10}$; 20^{30}. It is taken in this sense by the Old Latin mss and Marcion, which continue with 'and destroying the law and the prophets'. This is plainly an addition, as it makes the charge too long and diffuse (for Marcion the charge in this form would be true, not false). The sense is probably political, and the verb a synonym for *anaseiein* (v. 5 = 'to stir up'; Polybius uses it of revolution, 5.41, 1). Or, if 'seduction from' is intended (as in *apostrephein* = 'to pervert', v. 14), then to seduce from loyalty to the empire could be meant (cf. John 19^{15}). Political is also *our nation*, as on Jewish lips *ethnos* is the term for any people other than Jews. When speaking before pagan governors Jews are made to speak of themselves in this way in A. 24$^{3,\ 10,\ 17}$; 26^4 (in A. 28^{19}, Paul speaking to Jews in a political context). Those who have seen the ministry of Jesus as having been more politically orientated than the gospels now allow it to appear would find a measure of truth in this charge.* For Luke the charge is plainly false.

forbidding us to give tribute to Caesar: This is the specific charge of revolution, which would have compelled Pilate to act. It is also the charge which Luke has already ensured shall be manifestly false by his editing of the Markan pericope of the tribute money (20$^{20-26}$). For Luke the false (and malicious) witness lies here rather than in charges about threatening the temple (Mark 14$^{57f.}$).

saying that he himself is Christ a king: This is also a revolutionary charge, but in more personal terms. By means of it Luke, and he alone of the evangelists, provides a basis for Pilate's question, otherwise asked out of the blue, 'Are you the king of the Jews?' Its exact meaning is not clear. The accent is probably on *king*, since this occasions Pilate's question. In the circumstances of the abolition of Herod's kingdom, its replacement by a governor as representative of the emperor (for whom alone the word was becoming appropriated in Roman circles), and the establishment of tetrarchies for kingdoms in the surrounding areas (see on 3^1), the word would carry the sense of 'pretender'. Josephus so uses it (*Ant.* 17.285) to characterize the insurrectionary movements of his time, when he says of Judaea, that it was full of brigandage, and that 'Anyone might make himself king as the head of a band of rebels whom he fell in with, and would then press on to the destruction of the community.' It could even have the sense of counter-emperor; for while the emperors did not use *rex* of themselves, Greeks used *basileus* for both 'king' and 'emperor'; cf. the related charges brought against Paul and his companions of turning the world upside down, of acting contrary to the decrees of Caesar and of saying that there is another king (sc. emperor), Jesus (A. 17$^{6f.}$). If *christos* is here an adjective – 'an anointed king' – it presumes Pilate's acquaintance with the Semitic custom of anointing for kingship. But Luke may be introducing the later Christian usage of *Christos* without the article as a proper name for Jesus, in which form alone it would be intelligible to Romans, and *king* is in apposition, conveying something of its original force – *Christ a king*. Luke could be said to have given a handle to this charge with 'Blessed is the king' in his version of the triumphal entry (19^{38}), though that was an acclamation of disciples only. *saying that he himself is* – the accusative and infinitive construction *legonta heauton einai* is probably contemptuous = 'making himself out to be', as in A. 5^{36} of Theudas, and A. 8^9 of

---

* See S. G. F. Brandon, *Jesus and the Zealots*, Manchester 1967, and per contra M. Hengel, *Was Jesus a Revolutionist?*, ET Philadelphia 1971, with the literature there cited.

Simon – does not correspond with the picture of Jesus in the synoptists. Never-theless, the charge illustrates how, quite apart from any conscious revolutionary intentions, the language of the Jewish religion, and hence of the preaching of Jesus (e.g. 'the kingdom of God'), could not avoid being open to political interpretation.

3

'*Are you the King of the Jews?*': This question, now prompted by the third charge, is the hard core of the passion narratives on their Roman side. Unless there were eyewitnesses from among the disciples at Pilate's tribunal, it was presumably deduced from the *titulus* on the cross. It is political in form; the religious form was 'the king of Israel', as in Mark 15³², Matt. 27⁴², John 1⁴⁹; 12¹³. In the light of the *titulus*, especially in its Lukan form (v. 38), it may be derisory. In Mark 15¹² it is traced, belatedly on the lips of Pilate, to the Jews themselves; John 18–19 is written around it, its origin and meaning (esp. John 18³³⁻³⁷). In Luke its origin lies in the Sanhedrin's misrepresentation of Jesus' whole career (v. 2).

'*You have said so*': In Luke this is the sum total of Jesus' demeanour before Pilate; contrast John 18–19, and Jesus' silence in Mark 15⁵. It is an extraordinary, and possibly significant feature of the passion narratives that the meaning of what was said at such a crucial juncture should be so uncertain. 'It is not clear whether the statement is to be regarded as a denial, or whether Pilate simply refuses to take it seriously; probably the latter is to be understood. But the train of thought is not crystal clear, and it looks as though Luke has omitted something at this point, preferring to use Mark's wording' (Marshall, p. 853). On the one hand *su legeis* is taken as an affirmative, strong or weakʳ though the mockery in v. 11, and the *titulus* on the cross, are not necessarily evidence that Jesus accepted the title, but only that others persisted in applying it to him. Against an affirmative sense is that Pilate would have had to do immediately what he is compelled to do eventually – to order crucifixion for sedition. On the other hand, the expression is taken as a Greek rendering of an Aramaic idiom which intends a non-committal reply (Cullmann, *Christology*, p. 118). The meaning suggested is 'The words are yours' (RSV *You have said so*). Such a nuance could reflect how the matter came to be understood in the tradition, but not necessarily anything said at the trial, which cannot have been conducted in Aramaic. Another suggestion is a qualified affirmative, 'You have rightly understood by your question.' In Luke's context it may have been intended to exculpate Pilate in some measure (John 18³⁴ᶠ·), but neither here, nor when com-bined with the priests' accusations and Jesus' silence in Mark/Matthew, is it able to carry the story forward, or to account for Pilate's reactions ('wondered',

ʳ For a review of the opinions and arguments, D. R. Catchpole, 'The Answer of Jesus to Caiaphas (Matt. xxvi.64)', *NTS* 17, 1970–71, pp. 213–26.

Mark 15^5) or subsequent actions. There is a further hiatus here in all the synoptic narratives, in that there is no interrogation of such a kind as to constitute a real *cognitio*, to justify the words *after examining him* in v. 14, and to lead to Pilate's conviction of Jesus' innocence (contrast John, where, however, the trial takes the form of a theological discussion).

4
Luke ignores Mark's reference to many unspecified charges (Mark 15^3), since it is important for him that the charges be specified so that they may be seen to be refuted. From this point on the story is dominated by the theme of Jesus' innocence, which is already present, but less explicitly, in Mark 15$^{9-10, 14}$. Pilate therefore now makes a formal announcement of it to an audience composed of *the chief priests*, who seem to stand for the Sanhedrin (but may reflect the influence of Mark 15^3), and *the multitudes*. The sudden appearance of the latter (cf. Mark 15$^{8, 11, 15}$) is a literary device for making the action take place on the widest possible stage, and involve in principle the whole Jewish people. While the presence of the seventy-one members of the Sanhedrin at Pilate's tribunal is feasible, that of 'the multitudes' is not, and, like summoning *the people* in v. 13 (the populace of Jerusalem? how could they be summoned?), can only be given a symbolic sense.

'*I find no crime in this man*': *I find* takes up *We found* (v. 2), and means, 'I have established on examination'. *no crime* renders *ouden aition*, which could mean 'nothing culpable', *aition* being a neuter adjective agreeing with 'nothing'; but it is probably a noun, equivalent to the feminine noun *aitia*, which is found in A. 13^{28}; 25^{18}; John 18^{38}; 19$^{4, 6}$ in the technical sense of 'proven charge', 'established guilt of a crime' (v. 22 with *thanatou* of a capital crime). *this man* (cf. v. 14) is common in A., especially in trial scenes – cf. A. 23^9, with 'We find nothing wrong in . . .', and A. 26^{31}, with 'is doing nothing to deserve death'.

5
For the story to proceed, if it is not to be of an interlocution with a mob audience, but of a further examination in which Pilate reiterates the prisoner's innocence, the charges have also to be reiterated. This is done dramatically, but implausibly, by the Sanhedrin and 'the multitudes' together.

they were urgent: In view of Pilate's dismissal of the threefold charge, they press it again (*epischuein* + +) in the form of a single highly political charge.

'*He stirs up the people*': The verb here, *anaseiein*, is uncommon (not LXX). It is found elsewhere in the NT only at Mark 15^{11}, whence Luke may have taken it; though there it is used of the chief priests inciting the mob, and here probably, as by Greek historians, e.g. Diodorus Siculus, of the inciting of mobs by demagogues, or of the fomenting of revolt.

teaching throughout all Judea, from Galilee even to this place: The charge is now
related to Jesus as a teacher, corresponding to Luke's characterization of his
career (4^{15, 31}, teaching in Galilee, 4⁴⁴, teaching in Judaea, 13²², teaching between
Galilee and Jerusalem, 19⁴⁷, teaching in Jerusalem). This is spelt out in language
identical with that in A. 10³⁷ as being *throughout (kath' holēs*, apart from Rom.
16²³ only L–A in the NT) *all Judea from* ('beginning from', not rendered here
by RSV) *Galilee*, with the addition of *even to this place* to bring the danger home
to Pilate. It is uncertain, as elsewhere (see on 1⁵; 3¹; 4⁴⁴), whether Luke means
by Judaea the Roman province, i.e. Palestine shorn of Galilee, Perea and the
maritime cities, or the whole of Jewish territory (Jewry, cf. A. 10³⁹, 'the country
of the Jews'), inclusive of Galilee, which is subsumed under it. In the first case
the statement will be that Jesus' teaching activity, having begun outside the
province, had penetrated into it, and had now reached its centre. In the second
case it will mean that the teaching was throughout Palestine, beginning from
one end of it (Galilee) and arriving at its other end (Jerusalem). This, however,
could hardly be expected to make sense to Pilate, or to prompt his enquiry
whether Jesus was a Galilean. In either case, but more so in the former, where
the mention of Galilee is less necessary, the charge is framed in this geographical
manner so as to provide a peg on which to hang the next episode.

6–12

This story appears only here in the passion narratives. Something like it could
be presupposed in the prayer in A. 4²⁴⁻³⁰, though there with a contrary sense
that Ps. 2² was fulfilled when Herod and Pilate (in that order) were united with
Israel in condemning Jesus, whereas here the point made is that they were
united against Israel in maintaining Jesus' innocence. The story is puzzling from
both a historical and a literary point of view, and has been widely rejected.^s

The episode is introduced when Pilate, picking up the word 'Galilee' from
the geographical statement of the charge in v. 5, ascertains that Jesus is a Galilean, i.e. by domicile, not by origin. This could have a precise legal background.
The question whether the accused was to be tried in the province where he
normally resided (*forum domicilii*), or in the province where the offence was
committed (*forum delicti*), must have been a matter of debate in Roman law,
since a change was made from the second to the first and back again in the
course of the first two centuries AD, though it is not certain when precisely these

s 'A piece of pure hagiography' which does Luke scant credit (C. Guignebert,
Jesus, ET London and New York 1935, p. 467). 'The incident cannot be historical.
The idea that Pilate would recognise that a prince of the family of the Herods
could have the right to exercise a legal function in Jerusalem is highly improbable'
(M. Goguel, *The Life of Jesus*, ET London and New York 1933, p. 515). See also
Creed, p. 280.

changes took place, and the first could have remained as an option.[t] There is a parallel in A. 23[34], where Felix's enquiry about Paul's province makes no sense unless there was an option of sending him back there. The parallel is, however, only partial, as there it is a question of a possible transfer from one province of the empire to another, while here it is a question of a transfer from the jurisdiction of Rome in the province of Judaea to that of a native prince in the tetrarchy of Galilee. Further, Felix does not avail himself of the opportunity, but proceeds to judge the case himself[u], whereas Pilate does avail himself of the opportunity, though in an odd way. He does not remit Jesus to Galilee, but makes use of the fact that Herod was in Jerusalem at the time (by chance? or did he keep Passover?). There is also a parallel in the part played by Herod Agrippa II in the examination of Paul by Festus (A. 25[13]–26[32]), which suggests that the Herods could be appealed to by the prefect to act in the capacity of assessor in cases involving Jewish religious law. But again the parallel is only partial, since it was during a courtesy visit to welcome the new prefect that Agrippa himself offers assistance, whereas Pilate takes the initiative, and remits to another jurisdiction a case he has already tried. This is improbable legally. If the principle of *forum delicti* was in operation, there was no obligation on Pilate to send the prisoner for trial in his place of domicile. It is also improbable politically, as Pilate was unlikely to take the risk that Herod might find Jesus guilty, and in terms of the story itself, if the statement in v. 12 is to be pressed that hitherto Herod and Pilate had been enemies. Those who would maintain the historicity of the event are driven to speculation to account for Pilate's action. Sherwin-White (p. 31) suggests that behind the story may lie remnants of the extraordinary power of extraditing offenders who had fled his realm that had been formerly allowed to Herod the Great. This is rejected by H. W. Hoehner,[v] who advances as hypotheses: (i) that Pilate acted in order to escape his dilemma of showing weakness if he gave in to the Jews, and of making trouble for himself if he did not (but this is plausible only if Pilate could be certain in advance that, as the story requires, Herod would reach the same verdict as himself); (ii) that it was to improve the bad relations caused by his previous massacre of Galileans (13[1]; Sherwin-White rejects this as based on the error that Galileans in Judaea were not subject to Pilate's jurisdiction); and (iii) that Antipas might have been permitted to conduct examinations of offenders from his own territory, perhaps as a preliminary to trying them in Galilee (but Jesus is sent back to Pilate, and the Roman trial proceeds as if nothing had happenned). In default of an adequate historical explanation, the story has been

---

[t] On the whole matter, see Sherwin-White, *Roman Law*, pp. 28ff.

[u] The reason for this is not clear. Sherwin-White (pp. 55f.) suggests that Cilicia was not yet a province.

[v] 'Why did Pilate hand Jesus over to Antipas?', in *The Trial of Jesus*, ed. Bammel, pp. 84ff.

accounted for differently, as based upon a bare tradition that Jesus appeared before Herod, which itself may have been the product of midrash on Ps. 2² with reference to the passion, reflected in A. 4²⁴ff., where more than one ruler is required by 'kings of the earth' in the psalm. In whatever form Luke knew this tradition, he has written it up in order to show the isolation and responsibility of the Jews in Jerusalem in their demand for Jesus' death in the face of the judgments of both the Roman governor and the Jewish ruler.

From a literary point of view the story is strange. It is well written, but it has curiously little content of its own, and appears to have been constructed out of borrowed materials. Thus, it is made up of the desire of Herod to see Jesus and a miracle performed by him (cf. 9⁹; Mark 6¹⁴), a long and unspecified interrogation by Herod, to which Jesus does not reply, together with charges by high priests and scribes who are present (cf. Mark 14⁵⁵⁻⁶³; 15³⁻⁵, omitted by Luke), and a brief reference to mockery by soldiers (cf. Mark 15¹⁶⁻²⁰, omitted by Luke). It was perhaps the occurrence here in general terms of matters dealt with elsewhere in greater detail that led to the omission of vv. 10–12 in syrˢⁱⁿ. The story does not come into sharp focus until vv. 12–15, where it serves Luke's thesis, in that Herod and Pilate not only make common cause over the innocence of Jesus, but are reconciled on the basis of it.

6–7

This transition is a single, relatively polished sentence – *he asked whether* (*eperōtān*, with an indirect question); *when he learned that* (*epiginōskein hoti* = 'to ascertain that', confined to L–A in the NT; cf. A. 19³⁴; 22²⁹); *jurisdiction* (*exousia*, the nearest in the NT to the secular use of this word for 'sphere of rule' is in Luke's addition to Mark at 20²⁰); *sent him* (*anapempein*, a grander form of the verb 'to send', found again in vv. 11, 15, where, as in Philemon 12, it means 'to send back', and A. 25²¹ with the technical meaning of 'to remit to a higher court'); *who was* (a participial construction); *at that time* (lit. 'in those days', common in A.).

he sent him over to Herod: The reader knows from 3¹ that Herod (Antipas) is tetrarch of Galilee, i.e. the other ruler along with Pilate if Jewry is to comprise Galilee. He can thus be included with Pilate as one of 'the kings of the earth' who were gathered against the Lord's anointed (A. 4²⁵⁻²⁷ = Ps. 2²). He is in the background of the gospel story at several points – as having imprisoned the Baptist (3¹⁹⁻²⁰), as desiring to see Jesus because reports of his miracles have suggested that the Baptist he had beheaded had returned (9⁷⁻⁹), and as having murderous intentions towards Jesus (13³¹⁻³³). No reasons are given for his presence in Jerusalem. The tendency to bring him into the foreground has gone much further in the apocryphal Gospel of Peter, where, at the beginning of the first fragment, he displaces Pilate as the chief actor: 'But of the Jews none washed their hands, neither Herod nor any of his judges . . . And then Herod the king commanded that the Lord should be marched off, saying to them. 'What I have commanded to do to him, do ye.'

8

This novelistic notice of Herod's attitude is extraneous to the story's main purpose of confirming Pilate's judgment, and is built around his desire to see Jesus and a miracle (the verb 'to see' is used three times), as a result of having heard about him. This exactly corresponds with the additions Luke makes in taking over the Markan pericope in 9$^{7-9}$ – 'Herod the tetrarch heard of all that was done . . . "Who is this about whom I hear these things?" And he sought to see him.' The language shows Luke's hand – *he was very glad* (*echarē lian*, a common epistolary form in 'I am glad', cf. II John 4, III John 3); *long* (*ex* = 'from', in a temporal sense only Luke in the NT, *hikanōn chronōn* = 'long times', confined to L–A in the NT, and curiously in the plural, as in 20^9); *had desired* (the periphrastic verb 'to be' with participle); *was hoping* (*elpizein* with infinitive, in the gospels and A. only here and A. 26^7); *done by* (*genomenon* = 'happen', as in 9^7; 13^{17}; A. 8^{13}; 12^5).

9–11

This is the heart of the matter if Pilate's judgment is to be confirmed; but clearly Luke had no precise information, and the narrative is general and vague. *He questioned him* (cf. Mark 15^4) *at some length* (*en hikanois logois* = 'some considerable words', a curious phrase, and an example of Luke's tendency to repeat a word – here *hikanos* in the plural – once he has used it, as in v. 8); *he made no answer* (cf. Mark 15^5). In what follows – *The chief priests and the scribes stood by* (*histanai* with participle, as in 23$^{35, 49}$; A. 1^{11}; 9^7; 26^{22}), *vehemently* (*eutonōs*, classical + A. 18^{28}) *accusing him* – the picture is indistinct. Were these, who are introduced abruptly, supposed to be voicing their accusations at the same time as Herod was conducting his interrogation? Verse 11a is also general and colourless. It could be an equivalent for the mockery by Pilate's soldiers in Mark 15$^{16-20}$, which is necessarily excluded there for Luke by his statement (v. 25) that Pilate handed Jesus over to the Jews for crucifixion. Hence, perhaps, the sudden introduction here of Herod's soldiers, who are described in grandiloquent terms as *strateumata*, a word which in the singular meant an armament, and then, as in A. 23$^{10, 27}$, a detachment of soldiers, and in the plural, as here, 'the troops'. Herod's reaction is summed up by *treated with contempt* – *exouthenein*, common in the LXX, where it is sometimes combined with *mocked*. Whether v. 11b is also colourless depends on the significance of *arraying him in gorgeous apparel*. If this is equivalent to the 'purple cloak' of Mark 15^{17} (cf. John 19^5, and the 'royal robes' of Herod Agrippa in A. 12^{21}), then it further specifies the mockery by an abbreviated and faded version of the royal burlesque performed by Pilate's soldiers in Mark 15$^{16-20}$. But the word translated *gorgeous* (*lampros*), when used of clothes, generally, though not always, means, 'shining 'white', and when used with *apparel* can refer to the dress of an angel (cf. A. 10³⁰; Rev. 15⁶; 19⁸). Thus the dress could be intended as a mark of innocence, and so directly related to vv. 12–15. There is, however, no clear evidence that white clothing could have this significance, and the Jews ordinarily wore white.

12

This verse is carefully written, and is plainly from Luke's hand. It is not an addendum to the story, but the point for which it was written and included. *Herod and Pilate* (the stylistic *te . . . kai* = 'both . . . and', which is rare in the NT except in A., makes the connection between the two closer) *became friends* (*philoi*, a Lukan word) *with each other that very day* (*en autē tē hēmerā* + +), *for before this they had been* (*prohuparchein*, a classical and Hellenistic word, once in the LXX = 'to exist before', + A. 8⁹) *at enmity* (*ekthrā*, only here in the NT in a non-theological sense). That Luke is less willing to whitewash Herod than Pilate is suggested by the transference of the mocking to him and his soldiers (cf. also 13³¹). This would serve to strengthen Luke's thesis. Jesus' innocence was so palpable that the two previously irreconcilable rulers in Jewry, one of them a murderous tyrant, came together on this single issue.

13

called together the chief priests and the rulers and the people: The narrative maintains continuity by means of a recapitulation from Pilate of the situation thus far as a result of the remission to Herod. It is made to a concourse summoned (*sunkalein*, apart from Mark 15¹⁶ confined to L–A in the NT, cf. A. 5²¹; 28¹⁷) for the purpose. As well as the chief priests it includes *the rulers*. This designation is absent from the other gospels in this connection, and is used by Luke somewhat loosely – in A. 3¹⁷; 13²⁷ for the whole governing body of Israel (cf. v. 35), in 24²⁰ for such along with the chief priests, in A. 4⁵, ⁸ along with the elders. It stresses the representative and authoritative character of the audience. Even more loose is *the people*. It is not said who these are, nor how they could be summoned, nor, if they are the same as the people whose adulation of Jesus has been so stressed (19⁴⁸; 20⁶, ¹⁹, ²⁶; 21³⁸), why they have so suddenly changed their minds. The language here may have been influenced by that of Ps. 2¹⁻², 'Why do the nations conspire, and the peoples plot in vain? The kings of the earth set themselves, and the rulers take counsel together, against the Lord and his anointed.'

14

Pilate's opening words are very carefully balanced – for vocabulary and construction, cf. A. 24⁸. Translated according to the word order in Greek, they are: '*You* have brought to *me this man* on a charge of perverting the people, and behold, *I*, in *your presence*, have examined him, and have found nothing proven in *this man* of the charges you make against him.' He sums up the previous charges in vv. 2, 5 with the word *apostrephein* = 'to turn (someone) away from', which in this context, and on Pilate's lips, is likely to have the political connotation of seduction from loyalty to the empire. He says that he has examined the prisoner – *anakrinein* is a technical term, corresponding to the Latin *cognitio*, for the examination by magistrates to prepare a suit for trial. The single question in v. 3 cannot possibly pass for this, but none of the synoptists is in a position to fill it out. He reaffirms his previous verdict in a way that combines the dramatic – *behold* – with the formal – *I did not find this man guilty*.

15a

neither did Herod, for he sent him back to us: Pilate reinforces his pronouncement by reference to Herod's judgment, which is now communicated to the public (the priests and scribes of v. 10 are presumably supposed to know it already). The precise force of this is unclear. (i) It is introduced by *all' oude* + A. 19^2 and four times in Paul. If this means 'and neither' it makes Herod's judgment simply supplementary. If it means 'not even', it could imply that that judgment was all the greater confirmation in being a surprise, either because Herod might be expected to support the Jewish authorities as standing nearer to their interests, even if hated by them, or because he was a tyrant quick to detect political and religious opposition, as with the Baptist. But would Pilate have sent Jesus to Herod at all if there was the slightest risk that he would reach a different conclusion from himself? Historical evidence suggests that it was a fixed policy of the Herods to side with the Romans at all costs. (ii) In the basis of the appeal (*for*) the text is remarkably confused. If the correct reading is *he sent him back to us* (with *anapempein*, used in v. 7 for 'send', now having its possible meaning of 'to send back', and *us* as the plural of majesty), Herod's judgment is conveyed in another form. The fact that he had returned Jesus to Pilate, and had not kept him for trial (in Jerusalem? or Galilee?), proved that Herod thought there was no case to answer. But other readings, with varying degrees of attestation, are: 'for he has sent him to you', 'for I have sent you to him', 'for I have sent him (with you) to him', 'for I have sent him to you'.

15b–16

Pilate repeats his verdict once more, again with a combination of the dramatic – *behold* – and the formal: *nothing deserving death has been done by him* (for the vocabulary, *axion thanatou* = 'worthy of death', and the Lukan *prassein* = 'to do' in the perfect, here the periphrastic perfect participle, cf. A. $25^{11,\ 25}$; 26^{31}). He here takes the further step of bringing into the open what has so far been latent, viz. the question of death; and he declares his intention of releasing Jesus after chastisement. The Greek word for this, *paideuein*, meant 'to educate, instruct', as in the only two occurrences in A. (7^{22}; 23^3; cf. I Tim. 1^{20}; Tit. 2^{12}), and then 'to correct, discipline', as in the other NT instances, and possibly in the two LXX examples, I Kings 12^{11-14}; II Chron. 10^{11-14}, which are adduced by

Bauer for the meaning 'to whip'. Only here and in v. 22 is the word used of physical chastisement of an official kind. Pilate may have intended no more than an admonishment for getting into trouble, though he may have meant the lesser flogging (Latin *fustigatio*) prescribed in Roman law as a warning before release – to be distinguished from the greater flogging (Latin *flagellatio*), which accompanied other punishments, including death, as in Mark 15^{15}.

18-19

The narrative in Mark 15$^{6-15}$ is very disjointed. The story is only able to go forward at all after the prisoner's refusal to reply, and Pilate's wonder at that, by an abrupt reference to a custom of Pilate of a festival amnesty for any prisoner of the people's choosing. For then follows the arrival of 'the crowd' (at the tribunal?) to ask Pilate to honour his custom, and the priests' incitement of this crowd to petition for the release of an insurrectionist prisoner named Barabbas in counter to Pilate's own offer to release Jesus (as innocent, or as guilty like Barabbas?), whose delivery to him as a condemned man he knows to have been due to envy. From then on Mark's narrative is dominated by Pilate's repetition of 'the king of the Jews' (Mark 15$^{9, 12}$; cf. 18). By contrast Luke's narrative is relatively smooth. There is no mention of any such custom; v. 17 (see RSV margin) is an interpolation assimilating Luke's text to that of the others, and providing a basis for the otherwise abrupt introduction of Barabbas in v. 18. For Luke Jesus is not an already condemned man, but one whose innocence is a conclusion already drawn by Pilate from his interrogation. There is no further mention of 'the king of the Jews', and Pilate refers to Jesus as *this man* (*houtos*, v. 22 at the end of the sentence, where it is weakly rendered in RSV by *he*). It is *this man* whose death, in reply to Pilate's proposal for his release, is demanded by Israel's representative assembly and its people to a man (*pamplēthei* + +, a rare adverb from the literary word *pamplēthēs* = 'in full abundance', weakly rendered in RSV by *together*). It is in this context that, with curious abruptness, Barabbas is introduced as the one whose release is demanded as an alternative to that of Jesus, which has been offered. He is then further identified in a parenthesis (v. 19).

18

Away with this man!: A common shout of incensed crowds. The Greek *aire* means 'remove', i.e. by force and kill; cf. A. 21^{36}, and, in reduplicated form, John 19^{15}. Its essence can be seen in A. 22^{22}, 'Away with such a fellow from the earth! For he ought not to live.' It is possibly a Latinism – *tolle (e mundo)* = 'remove (from the earth)'.

release to us Barabbas: The episode of the choice between Jesus and Barabbas is the most perplexing, and perhaps the most unpalatable, in the passion narratives. For while it is, at least in the synoptists, the factor which in the end determines that Jesus is put to death as a criminal, it is something quite fortuitous and trivial, and is unconnected with any process of law and justice. The records of the ancient world have been ransacked in vain for any parallel – the passage often appealed to in the Jewish tractate Pesahim 8⁶, 'They may slaughter (the passover lamb) . . . for all whom they have promised to release from prison' refers to the release by the Jewish authorities of prisoners on a few hours' parole to enable them to partake of the passover meal. In itself it appears highly improbable that a Roman governor would commit himself to the release of a condemned revolutionary and murderer by way of an exchange. 'The real problem lies in the absurdity of the very conception of this privilege of the Jews . . . The scene appears more like a stage effect in a childish play than a piece of historical reality' (Guignebert, *Jesus*, p. 469). On the other hand, such a circumstantial story can hardly have been spun out of thin air. One suggestion is that a story of the release of a prisoner in different circumstances somehow became entangled with the gospel tradition of the trial and condemnation of Jesus. There are signs of confusion about it in the way the evangelists have used it. In Mark 15⁶, where it is introduced abruptly as though providing a way round the impasse of Jesus' silence and Pilate's wonder, it is apparently based, not on any regulation, but on a personal favour the governor was in the habit of granting to 'them' of releasing at Passover a prisoner of their own choice ('he used to release'; Matt. 27¹⁵, 'he was accustomed to release'). In Luke, where the Markan story in an abbreviated form is integrated into the flow of his narrative, no basis is given at all. The request, unprepared for, is simply part of the clamour of the people, which overcomes Pilate's resistance – hence the interpolation of v. 17 making it a legal obligation, whether of Jewish or Roman law. In John 18³⁹, where it is loosely attached, it is a Jewish custom which Pilate is prepared to honour. In Mark 15⁸ the choice of Barabbas for release is made by the crowd at the instigation of the priests, but only after it has requested Pilate to repeat his favour of previous years, and had been offered by him the release of Jesus as the king of the Jews, i.e. as a prisoner, perhaps as a condemned criminal. In Matt. 27¹⁶⁻¹⁷ Pilate himself, without any reminder from the crowd and on his own initiative, offers the Sanhedrin the choice between Barabbas and Jesus called Christ. In Luke the request comes late in the proceedings, and without any other basis than the audience's demand for the destruction of Jesus in response to Pilate's declared intention to release Jesus. Perhaps Luke, like some modern scholars, thought any such custom improbable, or was unwilling to lay at Pilate's doorstep a custom which had had such disastrous results, preferring to attribute the demand to the audience's sheer depravity. A further puzzle, not reflected in Luke, is the name. In Mark he is 'the one called Barabbas'. This is not a personal name but a patronymic, which follows a personal name, and means 'the son of Abbas', or 'the son of Abba (= "father")'. In some mss it appears as Barrabbas, meaning 'the son of Rabban', or possibly 'the son of the teacher'. In a significant number of mss of Matthew the name appears as

Jesus Barabbas (or Jesus Barrabbas), and Origen (*Commentary on Matthew*, 121) knew of mss, though not in the majority, which had the name in that form. There can be little doubt that this was original, and that 'Jesus' was suppressed for reasons of piety. Possibly behind Mark's 'the one called Barabbas' there was also an original 'Jesus called Barabbas'.

19

This parenthetical description of Barabbas shows Luke to be following Mark. In Mark 15$^{6-7}$ there is a strange mixture of the precise and the imprecise, as it is not clear whether Barabbas is himself one of those who are called 'the insurrectionists' (or rioters) involved in 'the insurrection' (or riot), or just happened to be in prison along with them. Luke's form of words is probably intended to depict him as a participant in (*on account of*) 'an insurrection' and in murder, and *in the city* (sc. Jerusalem) is his own addition to bring the matter close at hand. These notices are introduced in order to present the death of Jesus in terms of a choice between the good and the evil, and of the triumph of injustice over justice. They are too brief to indicate the character of the revolt, how recently it had taken place and where. In Matt. 27^{16} Barabbas is simply a notable prisoner, and in John 18^{40} a *lēstēs* = 'a revolutionary'. By attaching the parenthesis here Luke makes the Jews side with rebellion, which was the charge they had levelled against Jesus; though the word *stasis* here, which was a technical term for revolt, could have the less precise meaning of 'rioting', as in all its occurrences in A. (15^2; 19^{40}; 23^7; 24^5). In v. 25, where the parenthesis is repeated, it is as much Barabbas as a murderer that provides the foil to the killing of the innocent Jesus.

20–25

This highly dramatic climax is composed by Luke with all the skill that was required by his dilemma of having to present a Roman punishment that is the outcome neither of Rome's real judgment on the matter, nor simply of weakness in Rome's administration of justice. 'If he (Pilate) had been convinced that Jesus was dangerous in the smallest degree he would have condemned him; if he had thought the contrary he would have acquitted him. But the evangelist *cannot* say the one and *will not* say the other. And so he attributes to Pilate a weak leniency which renders him incapable of either condemning or acquitting Jesus' (Guignebert, *Jesus*, p. 467). This weakness is disguised so far as is possible by the forcefulness of the language, with the use of the Greek word *phōne* = 'voice' and of compounds of it in the verbs. Thus in v. 23, where all the language is Lukan, is *loud cries* (*phōnais megalais*) and *their voices* (*phōnai autōn*); in v. 20 *addressed* (*prosphōnein*, apart from Matt. 11^{16} confined to L-A in the NT); in v. 21 *shouted out* (*epiphōnein* + A. 12^{22}; 21^{34}; 22^{24}, the last two of the shouting of a mob). A similar effect is produced by the repetition of the Greek word for

'demand' as in v. 23, *demanding*, v. 24, *their demand* and v. 25, *they asked for* =
'they demanded'.

20–21

Pilate addresses the whole audience a second time, though no details are given
of anything said in support of his now repeated intention to release Jesus. This
leads to an intensification of fury with a reduplicated shout for the Roman
punishment of crucifixion.

22

A third time he said to them: Sherwin-White (*Roman Law*, pp. 26–7) refers to
the usage in Roman law whereby those who refused to defend themselves were
given three opportunities of changing their minds before sentence was given,
as also if they were absentees. Here, however, Pilate addresses the prosecutors
three times, and this is in order to underline by a threefold attestation the
Roman conviction of Jesus' innocence.

'*Why, what evil has he done?*' : This is in response to the demand for crucifixion.
Why is *ti gar* = 'for what?', with the sense 'but this is not possible since . . .'
This is followed by a renewed statement that he had established by examination (*I have found*) Jesus' innocence of any capital crime, and that he proposed
to release him with an admonition.

23

The language here is strongly expressive of the power of mob clamour to pervert justice. *They were urgent* (*epikeisthai* = 'to press upon', elsewhere in the
NT in this sense 5^1, I Cor. 9^{16}). For *loud cries* and *their voices*, see above. *prevailed*
(*katischuein* = 'to be the stronger' + 21^{36}; Matt. 16^{18}).

24

So it comes about that Pilate's judicial sentence (*epikrinein* + +) is not in accordance with his judicial findings, but with the audience's double demand for
Jesus' execution and Barabbas's release.

25

This conclusion is now forcefully expressed in a carefully constructed sentence,
the form and cadence of which are reproduced in the rendering of RSV. The
previous characterization of Barabbas in v. 19 is repeated so as to stand in a
chiasmus with Jesus, but instead of being named he is referred to as the one
whom they asked for. The emphasis is on murder rather than on insurrection, and
this is taken up in the chiastic statement in A. 3^{15}, 'You asked for a murderer to
be granted you, but the author of life you killed.'

he delivered up to their will: Taken literally this amounts to saying that he handed Jesus over to the Jews for them to crucify, as also 24^{20}, 'our chief priests and rulers delivered him up to be condemned to death, and crucified him'. These are preposterous statements, and illustrate the extent to which Luke was prepared to go, for reasons of apologetic, in exculpating the Romans and in stretching the responsibility of the Jews. In view of this, and of the high literary quality of vv. 1–25, there is no necessity to postulate a non-Markan passion narrative as the source of Luke's extended account of Pilate's sessions. It could be explicable as his own development, on the basis of Mark and the story about Herod, of the theme of the innocence of Jesus.

23^{26-49} *The Crucifixion of Jesus*

The conclusion of the passion narrative falls into three sections – the way to crucifixion (vv. 26–31), the crucifixion itself and the reactions to it of others (vv. 32–43) and the death of Jesus and its accompaniments (vv. 44–49). Each of these is a more coherent unit in itself, and the connections between them are closer, than in the corresponding narratives in Mark/Matthew.

23^{26-31} THE WAY TO CRUCIFIXION

^{26}*And as they led him away, they seized one Simon of Cyrene, who was coming in from the country, and laid on him the cross, to carry it behind Jesus. *^{27}*And there followed him a great multitude of the people, and of women who bewailed and lamented him.* ^{28}*But Jesus turning to them said, 'Daughters of Jerusalem, do not weep for me, but weep for yourselves and for your children. *^{29}*For behold, the days are coming when they will say, "Blessed are the barren, and the wombs that never bore, and the breasts that never gave suck!" *^{30}*Then they will begin to say to the mountains, "Fall on us"; and to the hills, "Cover us." *^{31}*For if they do this when the wood is green, what will happen when it is dry?'*

In Luke Pilate, without official sentence, has handed Jesus over to the Jewish authorities to effect their will. There cannot, therefore, follow, as in Mark/Matthew, the mockery and scourging by Roman soldiers inside the *praetorium*, but only the unlikely scene of the Jews proceeding to carry out the Roman punishment of crucifixion. But the writing is rather loose. In v. 26 *they*, which should refer to those to whom Pilate had handed Jesus over, might be impersonal, and the soldiers who appear in v. 36 may be intended (cf. John 19¹⁶⁻¹⁷, ²³). *led away (apagein)* can of itself mean 'led away to execution', as in A. 12¹⁹. In John 19¹⁷ the transition from the praetorium to the place of execution is immediate. In the synoptists there is a walk thither of unspecified distance, with an incident (in Luke two incidents) in the course of it. Mark's account here, and of the crucifixion itself, is somewhat staccato. Luke's shows a greater degree of artistic arrangement, and the participants are more systematically assembled (note *also* in vv. 32, 36) .

ꜩ

26

they seized one Simon of Cyrene, who was coming in from the country: The relative clause, omitted by Matthew, indicates that Luke is reproducing Mark here. Simon, probably a Jew from Cyrene in North Africa, who is either visiting or resident in Jerusalem, is encountered walking in the opposite direction from countryside to city. In Mark 15²¹ this is tied to historical reminiscence by reference to him as the father of Alexander and Rufus. This presumably identified him as someone known to the community in which the tradition circulated, or for which Mark was writing; it is dropped by Matthew and Luke. Despite such precise information no reason is given why he is press-ganged (this is the force of the vulgarism *aggareuein* which Mark uses here, and which Luke replaces by the more polished *epilambanesthai*); nor why an exception was made in Jesus' case to the rule that the condemned man carried his own cross. It could be read out of Mark that this was due to extreme weakness as a result of the previous flagellation, which in Roman law accompanied the execution of the death sentence, and which was sometimes severe enough to inflict mortal wounds. This could not be read out of Luke, where there is no flagellation, and the words spoken in vv. 28–31 are unlikely to have been spoken by one in extreme weakness. Already in Mark, and perhaps in any tradition behind him, the story was paradigmatic. Whatever the actual circumstances, Simon finds himself symbolizing the model disciple, who had already been defined by Jesus, in language drawn from crucifixion, as the one who takes up the cross and follows (Mark 8³⁴). The parallel breaks down in two respects. Simon is compelled, while the disciple acts of his own volition and denies himself; and he does not, like the disciple, carry his own cross, but Jesus' cross for him.

laid on him the cross, to carry it behind Jesus: The cross could take three forms – an upright stake, a stake with a cross-beam at the top, and two intersecting beams. The first would be too heavy for the condemned to carry, and would be already in position. What would be carried would be the cross-beam (Latin *patibulum*, cf. Plautus, *The Braggart Warrior* 359, *The Haunted House* (*Mostellaria*) 55, also called *crux*). It was a yoke placed across the neck, to which the out-stretched arms were affixed, and on which the victim was hoisted up on to the upright beam. It was carried to the place of crucifixion by the condemned him-self – cf. Plutarch, *De Sera Numinis Vindicta* (*On the Delays of the Divine Venge-ance*) 554, 'Every criminal who goes to execution carries his own cross on his back.' The definition of the disciple as one who takes up his own cross (9²³) depends on this. RSV possibly misses the force of the verb Luke uses here, *epiti-thenai*. To mean 'to lay an object on someone' it requires to be followed by *epi* = 'upon' with the genitive or dative of the person. When followed, as here, by the person in the dative, it probably means 'they laid on him the obligation (to carry)'; with the verb *pherein* = 'to bear' in place of Mark's 'take up', and the addition of *behind*, Luke approximates the language further to the description of the disciple in 9²³ and 14²⁷.

27

In Luke, though not in Mark/Matthew, the procession is filled out, and pre-paration is made for the presence at the crucifixion of those whose reactions are to be recorded (vv. 35–41 = Mark 15²⁷⁻⁴¹). There is said to be 'following' Jesus *a great multitude* (*polu plēthos*, a common and conventional expression in L-A), both of *the people* (cf. 1¹⁰; 6¹⁷; A. 21³⁶, Lukan), and of *women*. The attend-ance of the first at executions is attested in Greek and Roman authors, and the presence and attitude of the populace became a regular feature in accounts of martyrdoms. Their presence here is due to Luke's concern with them as ardent supporters of Jesus, and as potential converts of the apostles in Jerusalem (A. 2–6, passim). They are to be mentioned later by him as sympathetic observers of the crucifixion (vv. 35, 48), though no explanation is given of their sudden conversion to, and equally sudden conversion from, their fierce demand for Jesus' destruction (vv. 13–23).

It is not clear why separate mention is made of the large crowd of mourning and wailing women, except as an audience for Jesus' last words before cruci-fixion (vv. 28–31), nor who these are. Jewish parallels refer only to individuals as mourning the condemned. Some commentators refer to Zech. 12¹⁰⁻¹⁴, where a spirit of compassion is to be poured out on the inhabitants of Jerusalem, so that 'when they look on him whom they have pierced, they shall mourn for him as one mourns for an only child (applied to Jesus in John 19³⁷; Rev. 1⁷) . . . On that day the mourning in Jerusalem will be as great as the mourning for Hadad-rimmon in the valley of Megiddo'; and where the women of each family are said to mourn separately. This could point to a particular background for the wailing women here. For 'the mourning for Hadad-rimmon' was a ritual lamentation for the fertility god, elsewhere identified with Tammuz, who was thought to die and descend into the underworld in the dry season, and, bewailed by his sister, to be restored in the spring season for the renewal of nature (cf. Ezek. 8¹⁴, where among the idolatries in the temple the prophet sees women weeping for Tammuz). It is not impossible that relics of this were built into first-century Judaism (see further below).

28–31

The first of Luke's major insertions into the main (Markan?) framework of the story of crucifixion is Jesus' counter to the women's lament by a pronouncement of doom – not, as Grundmann takes it (p. 429), a call to repentance. This is a remarkable unit of tradition. Bultmann (*History*, p. 37) classes it as a biographical apophthegm, i.e. an utterance attached to the life of Jesus, constructed in his view from early apologetic material with an Aramaic background. It is rhythmical (and would be more so without *and your children* and *the barren and*), and is similar in tone to 19⁴²⁻⁴⁴. What makes it distinctive is that, despite its brevity, it is made up of such diverse types of utterance. Thus, v. 28 is a personal apostrophe with chiasmus; v. 29 is a beatitude introduced by an impersonal statement characteristic of prophecy, *For behold, the days are coming* (so 17²²; 19⁴³ where it introduces what is more personal; cf. here the v.l. 'you will say' for 'they will say'); v. 30 is a quotation and application of an OT text (Hos. 10⁸), introduced impersonally by *they will begin to say* (v.l. 'you will begin to say'); and v. 31 is an enigmatic proverbial saying. The last three could belong together, being only loosely connected to the context by *this* (v. 31), if it refers to what is happening to Jesus, and by the apostrophe (v. 28); or vv. 29–30 could belong together, being enclosed within vv. 28, 31, which could also go together.

28

'*Daughters of Jerusalem*': This striking form of address, to be distinguished from 'daughter of Jerusalem' (Zech. 9⁹), which is simply a synonym for Jerusalem, is in the OT confined to the Song of Songs, which it punctuates as the regular address to the chorus (1⁵; 2⁷; 3⁵, ¹¹; 5⁸, ¹⁶; 8⁴). This book was put to liturgical use at the festivals of Mazzoth (Unleavened Bread) in the spring and Sukkoth (Tabernacles) in the autumn, and in the view of a number of scholars it shows both in content and style some connection, however attenuated, with the weeping for Tammuz (see *The Interpreter's Bible* V, pp. 94ff.). It is possible that the mourning women have some relation to this (see on v. 31).

do not weep for me, but weep for yourselves and for your children: This is not without parallel in ancient literature, where also women appear as mourners. Commentators refer especially to Seneca, *Agamemnon* 659ff., where Cassandra says to the chorus bemoaning the tragic events in Troy, 'Restrain your tears, which all time will seek, ye Trojan women, and do you yourselves grieve your own death with groans and lamentations.' Here the apostrophe seems to mean 'Save your tears for the occasion when they will be needed.' This occasion will be when a woeful event (or events) comes to pass soon enough for the women as well as their children to experience it.

29

the days are coming when . . .: Some interpret this as a prediction of the fall of Jerusalem. Easton (p. 346) asserts, 'Of course something far wider than the siege of Jerusalem is contemplated', though he does not specify further. Others refer to Zech. $12^{10ff.}$, but that obscure passage appears to be speaking of the divine protection of Jerusalem.

'Blessed are the barren . . .': In the context the barren are blessed (for the form of expression, cf. 11^{27}; 21^{23}) because they will be spared the additional anguish of seeing their children perish (*yourselves and your children*, v. 28); but originally the meaning may have been that their barrenness will have secured that there were fewer to perish. There is a similar ambiguity about barrenness in II Baruch 10^{13-15}, 'For the barren shall above all rejoice, and those who have no sons be glad . . . For why should they bear in pain only to bury in grief? Or why should mankind have sons? Or why should the seed of their kind again be named, when this mother (Jerusalem) is desolate and her sons led into captivity?'

30

The barren are to be blessed, since those still alive in the catastrophe, whatever it is, will apply to themselves the prayer for obliteration in Hos. 10^8 (cf. Rev. 6^{16}, where it is somewhat differently applied to the desire for somewhere to escape from the divine wrath, cf. Rev. 9^6).

31

The meaning of this verse, and its connection with what precedes (*for*), are obscure, and there is a wide variety of interpretation. Ezek. 20^{47} refers to the green and dry tree, i.e. all trees, as being consumed by the fire of judgment, and there is a similar rabbinic saying, 'When fire consumes the green, what will the dry do?' (quoted in SB II, p. 263). But the metaphor is not necessarily associated with fire. The parallel just quoted stands alongside 'If Leviathan is pulled out with a fish hook, what will the fish in the shallows do? If the rod falls into the flowing stream, what will the water in the cisterns do?' These contrast the more difficult with the less; here the present is contrasted with worse to come.

Grundmann's suggestion (p. 430) that *they do* and *will happen* are periphrases for God is forced. The interpretation of Creed (p. 286), 'If the innocent Jesus meets such a fate, what will be the fate of the guilty Jerusalem?' (so also Easton), may be too precise and allegorical. *when the wood is green* and *when it is dry* (RSV) translate *en tō hugrō xulō* = 'in the green wood' and *en tō xerō* = 'in the dry', and *in* may be taken in the sense of 'in the period of'. The meaning could then be 'If they can do such things (as the condemnation of Jesus) while there is still life, what will happen when death and judgment overtake them?' – less likely that the reference is to the beginning and end of the period of the Gentiles (Leaney, pp. 283f.). But if 'the green (tree = period)' and 'the dry (tree = period)' had originally some connection with the Tammuz rite,[w] then v. 31, which does not continue the thought of vv. 29–30, may be returning to v. 28, thus making the passage a unity; and the meaning could be 'If they do this (i.e. lament) in the green season (of spring, when they should be rejoicing), what shall they do in the dry season (the proper season for lamentation)?'

$$23^{32-43} = \text{Mark } 15^{22-32}$$

THE CRUCIFIXION AND THOSE CONCERNED

[32]*Two others also, who were criminals, were led away to be put to death with him.* [33]*And when they came to the place which is called The Skull, there they crucified him, and the criminals, one on the right and one on the left.* [34]*And Jesus said, 'Father, forgive them; for they know not what they do'.* And they cast lots to divide his garments.* [35]*And the people stood by, watching; but the rulers scoffed at him, saying, 'He saved others; let him save himself, if he is the Christ of God, his Chosen One!'* [36]*The soldiers also mocked him, coming up and offering him vinegar,* [37]*and saying, 'If you are the King of the Jews, save yourself!'* [38]*There was also an inscription over him,†* 'This is the King of the Jews.'*

[39]*One of the criminals who were hanged railed at him, saying, 'Are you not the Christ? Save yourself and us!'* [40]*But the other rebuked him, saying, 'Do you not fear God, since your are under the same sentence of condemnation?* [41]*And we indeed justly; for we are receiving the due reward of our deeds; but this man has done nothing wrong.'* [42]*And he said, 'Jesus. remember me when*

w So A. Jeremias, *Handbuch der altorientalischen Geisterkultur*, Leipzig 1913, pp. 263ff.

you come in your kingly power.' ‡ [43]*And he said to him, 'Truly, I say to you, today you will be with me in Paradise.'*

   * Other ancient authorities omit the sentence *And Jesus . . . what they do*

    † Other ancient authorities add *in letters of Greek and Latin and Hebrew*

    ‡ Greek *kingdom*

Mark's account here is very disjointed. It passes from the crucifixion of Jesus to a note of time, to the inscription, to the crucifixion of the other two, to the mockery of passers-by, to that of the priests. Luke's smoother narrative does not require any other explanation than his editorial hand. All three condemned men are led to crucifixion and are crucified together. This sets the scene for the actions and reactions of those present, which, in contrast to the crucifixion itself, are given a protracted description. A feature of crucifixion as a mode of execution was that, as a warning, it was conducted with great publicity in the street, or at an elevated site. The victim was thus exposed to abuse. After the division of garments Luke introduces *the people* as a constant and not unsympathetic background of spectators (vv. 35a, 48). He then assembles on the scene in succession various types of mockers – *the rulers* (v. 35b; *de kai* = 'but also', not 'but' as in RSV), *the soldiers* (v. 36; 'also'), a mocking *inscription* (v. 38; 'also'), and finally the fellow condemned, one mocking and the other not (vv. 39ff.). The narrative is bound together at more than literary level by the use of Ps. 22 as interpretative of the action.

ဟ

32

Two others also, who were criminals, were led away to be put to death with him: The tradition represented by Mark/Matthew, and that by John, contained mention of the crucifixion of two others along with Jesus, either simply as historical reminiscence, or to mark the fulfilment of prophecy, which Luke has made explicit in 22³⁷. In Mark 15²⁷ this is introduced abruptly; Luke prepares for it artistically by including the two along with Jesus to conclude his description of the procession. Easton (p. 347) insists that, on account of its language and position, this verse is to be ascribed to L, though he admits that *others (heteroi), led away (agein)* and *with (sun)*, are from Luke's hand. To these should be added *put to death (anairein* = 'to destroy', generally by violence, murder or assassination, apart from three instances confined to L–A, where it is used twenty times, in

A. 2^{23}; 10^{39}; 13^{28} of Jesus' crucifixion). In Mark/Matthew the two are called *lēstai* = 'rebels', though it is not clear whether they belonged to the insurrectionists of Mark 15^7. Luke has already underlined the innocence of Jesus on the charge of insurrection, and has emphasized the criminal, as much as the insurrectionary, character of Barabbas in contrast to Jesus (vv. 19, 25); so *criminals* (*kakourgos*, as in vv. 33, 39, + II Tim. 2^9) may be due to him. If so all evidence for a non-Markan source here disappears. The writing is somewhat loose. The Greek *heteroi kakourgoi duo* should mean 'two other criminals', making Jesus a criminal as well, perhaps in continuation of the irony in 22^{35-38}; but most put a comma after *heteroi*, and translate 'there were others led along with him, two criminals'.

33

And when they came to the place which is called The Skull: This concludes the procession. For the form of expression, cf. A. 27^8. *called* (*kaloumenos*) is Lukan. All the evangelists refer here to *the* (Matthew 'a') *place*. Luke, as usual, avoids the Aramaic place name which the others have, Golgotha, replacing it by a Greek equivalent *Kranion* = 'Skull' (not, as in rsv 'the Skull'). John 19^7 has it the other way round, 'to what was called Place of a Skull, which in Hebrew is called Golgotha'. How the place got its name is not known; that it was because executions took place there (so Jerome), or because it was a skull-shaped rock formation, are both guesses. The site, about which there is a vast literature,[x] has not been established for certain. Christians were not interested in holy places associated with the life and passion of Christ until the time of Constantine, who, under the influence of his pious mother, had enquiries made about them to give them official recognition (see Eusebius, *Life of Constantine*, 3.25ff.). One of the matters in dispute is whether the bishop of Jerusalem, in response to Constantine's demand to establish the place of Jesus' tomb, was relying on a living tradition, or only on guesswork, when he located it under the temple of Aphrodite, which was then destroyed, and the Church of the Holy Sepulchre erected in its place. This affects the location of Golgotha, if it was in the vicinity of the tomb (John 19^{41}). In John it is said to be near the city, and thus outside its walls. The Church of the Holy Sepulchre is inside the present walls, though there is evidence that at the time its site lay outside the north wall. If that location is correct (some would place it well outside the present walls), the journey there, if from Herod's palace, would have been approximately a thousand yards, if from the Antonia fortress, rather less.

there they crucified him, and the criminals, one on the right hand and one on the left: The crucifixion of all three is stated by all the evangelists in the barest possible

[x] See esp. Dalman, *Sacred Sites and Ways*, pp. 346ff. and J. Finegan, *Light from the Ancient Past*, Princeton 1946, pp. 434ff.

manner, Luke's being the most polished wording – 'the one, on the one hand, on the right, and the other, on the other hand, on the left'. This would have involved tying them to the cross beam, if not already tied, or to crossed beams, possibly nailing the hands (John 20²⁵), and elevating the whole to an upright stake, and fixing it there with a wooden pin. Crucifixion, of Persian origin, had been adopted by Rome for the punishment of slaves and rebels (not for Roman citizens, except by some tyrannical governors exceeding their powers). It was exercised with great severity in the provinces to maintain law and order, and to suppress any sign of revolt (Josephus mentions mass executions of rebels in Judaea). It was acknowledged to be 'the most cruel and hideous of tortures' (Cicero, *Against Verres* V. 64). The passion narratives, however, show no concern with the physical or mental aspects. For them the cross and its 'suffering' were theological. They expressed the completeness of the rejection of God's chosen one by God's people, and of the humiliation and impotence endured by the one who should have been most honoured and effective (cf. I Cor. 1²²; Heb. 12²). Here the scene is set for the actions and reactions of those present, which, by contrast, are given a protracted description.

34a

And Jesus said, 'Father, forgive them; for they know not what they do' : If this belongs to the original text, the first reaction to the crucifixion is that of Jesus himself, in the form of a prayer to God as Father for the forgiveness of his executioners (or all those responsible) on the ground that they are ignorant of what they are doing. But its status is uncertain, and it should probably be omitted. It is read as early as Marcion, and by Tatian (but after v. 46a), by Hegesippus, Irenaeus, Clement, Gregory Nazianzen, by ℵ (original hand) D (second corrector) A L G f1 f13 565 700 syr^eur and the *Clementine Recognitions* (but spoken on the way to the cross). The evidence for omission is strong – p⁷⁵ B ℵ (a correctng hand) D (original hand) W Θ 38 579 0124 syr^sin a d co^sah boh. Structurally it breaks the sequence, so that *And they cast lots . . .* as the action of the executioners follows awkwardly after it. Marshall (p. 868) argues that 'sayings by Jesus are found in each main section of the Lucan crucifixion narrative (23²⁸⁻³¹, ⁴³, ⁴⁶); the lack of such a saying at this point would disturb the pattern.' But it is not clear what is a main section here; it could extend from v. 33 to v. 43. It could be argued that Luke did not intend to refer to Jesus, or to anything said by him, until those around him had been dealt with in vv. 33–38. As concerns the thought, it is easier to suppose that the sentence was inserted at a later stage from a still fluid oral tradition as an additional characterization of the death of Jesus – perhaps with reference to Isa. 53¹², 'made intercession for the transgressors' – than to suppose that it was suppressed out of anti-Jewish feeling that, as regards the passion, the Jews were past praying for. The parallel in the story of Stephen (A. 7⁵⁹⁻⁶⁰) could point in either direction: (i) that Stephen's prayer for the forgiveness of his executioners and his prayer of self-committal imply that both were present in the gospel text (v. 34a and v. 46), so that Jesus supplied a model for the first martyr; or (ii) that the prayer of Jesus at death was augmented to make it not less than the prayer of Stephen (or than the prayer of James for the forgiveness of his enemies recorded in Eus. *HE* 2.23.16). Ignorance as a ground of forgiveness is fairly widely attested in Hellenistic literature (see Creed, p. 286), and this ignorance does not have to be given the special sense of a sinful moral state (as by Ellis, pp. 267f.). Perhaps the strongest ground for the inclusion of the words in Luke's text (though not necessarily for their authenticity as words of Jesus) could be the ignorance of the Jews and their rulers which Luke puts into the mouth of Peter in A. 3¹⁷ (though not the ignorance at A. 13²⁷; 17²³, which is of a different kind); though there it is not the ground of personal forgiveness for the act of crucifixion, but a basis for the possibility that the Christ could still be a blessing to Israel despite it.

34b

And they cast lots to divide his garments: After the crucifixion itself the first action to be noted, as in Mark, is the division of Jesus' clothes. The condemned were sometimes, though by no means always, stripped of their clothes. These were then the perquisites of those performing the execution. The author of Ps. 22¹⁸, 'They divide my garments among them, and for my raiment they cast lots', had no such custom in mind, but was describing an act of oppression and deprivation. The action here is described in his (scriptural) words in order to state that what was going on was according to God's saving will – 'my' in the psalm now refers to Jesus, and nothing is said about the clothes of the other two condemned. These words will have influenced the account of the incident, clearly so in John 19^{23f.}, where, in defiance of Hebrew parallelism, two different sets of clothing are presupposed or invented. Luke's version – lit. 'and dividing his garments they cast lots' – is more in the narrative style, and is the most compressed form of the LXX text. It is also the least intelligible. It does not mean, as RSV might suggest, that they cast lots as to who should divide the garments, but that having divided the garments they cast lots as to who should have what. The action has lost any connection with soldiers, who are not introduced until v. 36.

35a

And the people stood by, watching: As the silence of Jesus in Mark/Matthew has been modified by the address to the women (vv. 28–31), so also is the Markan picture of total hostility towards him. *the people*, who had previously been so warmly in support of him (19⁴⁷–22²), but who had joined the rulers to demand his death (vv. 13ff.), are the first to be mentioned of the spectators, and are once more distinguished from the rulers. They are represented as standing by (*heistēkei*, the pluperfect tense of continuous action, placed first in the sentence, as in v. 10, v. 49), and as watching (*theorōn* = 'beholding'). While this may have begun as vulgar delight in a spectacle – cf. v. 48, *all the multitudes who assembled to see the sight (theōrian)* – it ends in sensitive lament at what had taken place (*returned home beating their breasts*).

35b

but the rulers scoffed at him: By contrast the next to be introduced simply *scoffed* (*exemuktērizon*, imperfect tense with the sense 'repeatedly mocked'). *the rulers* correspond to 'the chief priests with the scribes' of Mark 15^{31} (cf. A. 3^{17}; 13^{27}), and are amongst those to whom Pilate had delivered Jesus (v. 25), and who had brought him to the place of crucifixion. The verb, and that translated by *watching* in v. 35a, are from Ps. 22^{6-7} (LXX Ps. 21^{7b-8}), which has 'scorned by men and despised by the people. All who see (behold) me mock at me.' Luke may be deliberately rewriting this verse so as to separate 'behold' from 'mock at', and to use it as a neutral word for the attitude of the people in distinction from that of their rulers.

'*He saved others; let him save himself, if he is the Christ of God, his Chosen One*': The scene is too set for Luke to take over from Mark 15^{29-30} the mockery of casual passers by (also based on Ps. 22 in 'wagging their heads'), either the taunt 'Save yourself and come down from the cross', or that about destroying the temple, which refers to a supposed saying of Jesus that Luke has already omitted from his account of the trial before the Sanhedrin. But he does take over the taunts of the rulers in Mark 15^{31-32}. These are also based on Ps. 22; cf. v. 8, 'He committed his cause to the Lord; let him deliver him, let him rescue him'; v. 19, 'But thou, O Lord, be not far off! O thou my help, hasten to my aid!'; v. 21, 'Save me from the mouth of the lion.' They advert to salvation in the sense of deliverance or rescue, and to the messiah as one who delivers. In Mark the taunts are twofold, and make two separate but connected points. The first is in the indicative, and is religious – 'He saved others; he cannot save himself.' Here the reputation of Jesus as one who has delivered others is acknowledged. This presumably refers to his miracles of healing and exorcism (cf. 'Your faith has saved you', 7^{50}; 8^{48}; 17^{19}, etc.), so the taunt is a form of the proverb 'Physician, heal thyself' applied to the present situation; though miracles hardly provide an analogue of deliverance from crucifixion, unless they are to be thought of as acts of rescue from defeat and death. The second is in the imperative, and is politico-religious, 'Let the Christ, the King of Israel, come down now from the cross, that we may see and believe.' The Christ as the King of Israel is by definition a successful and victorious figure; let him show himself such by a miraculous reversal of defeat in descending from the cross, and so provide evidence that he is the messiah. Luke compresses the two into a single concise taunt (he makes the first part a chiamus), which is in the imperative, and is wholly religious – 'Let the one who has rescued others deliver himself if he is (i.e. so as to show himself to be) the Christ of God, the Chosen One.' The term 'the King of Israel' would be for Luke an unacceptable synonym for 'the Christ'; cf. his revision of Mark in 19[38]; and the analogous term 'the king of the Jews' he reserves for the mockery by the Romans in the next section. *of God* could be taken either with *the Christ* or *the Chosen One*. The former is more likely in view of Luke's addition of it in 9[20]. With *the Chosen One* (*ho eklektos* + John 1[34] with 'of God'), common as a 'messianic' title in I Enoch, may be compared Luke's substitution of 'chosen Son' for Mark's 'beloved Son' in 9[35]. It is not the Jewish messiah-king the rulers stand guilty of rejecting, but God's Christ, the object of his special choice and appointment. The taunt 'Let him save himself' continues to dominate in what follows (vv. 36–39), if somewhat artificially.

36

The soldiers also mocked him, coming up and offering him vinegar: The soldiers are now belatedly, and rather awkwardly, brought on to the scene. In Mark they have been the executioners, and are there as bystanders, among them the centurion, who also stands by but opposite Jesus (Mark 15[16, 20, 24, 35, 39]). In Luke they have no necessary part to play, and are auxiliary to the main officiants, Jews. Sanders, *The Jews in Luke–Acts*, pp. 11ff., argues that in his doctoring of the account of the crucifixion to make it an act carried out entirely by the Jews Luke intends these to be Jewish soldiers. But the centurion (v. 47) is certainly a Roman, and Joseph still has to ask Pilate for Jesus' body (v. 52); and it is more likely that the soldiers here are a Roman element which Luke is unable to remove, but which he plays down. They are introduced without explanation as *coming up*; also without explanation is their action of offering vinegar. This is taken from Mark 15[36], where it is a hostile act of the soldiers scripturally motivated by reference to Ps. 69[21], 'They gave me poison for food, and for my thirst they gave me vinegar to drink.' It is there obscurely attached to Jesus' cry from the cross interpreted as a cry to Elijah for help (in John 19[29] it answers Jesus' thirst, which is in fulfilment of scripture). Luke, who omits any cry of Jesus at this point, appears to take the soldiers' action as a form of mockery – the Greek could be translated, 'There also mocked him soldiers by coming up and offering him vinegar and by saying . . .'

37

'If you are the King of the Jews, save yourself!': The verbal mockery of the soldiers is in terms of the Roman ascription *the King of the Jews* (cf. v. 3), which Luke reserves for this section, and which may be intended as a secular equivalent of the religio-political 'The Christ, the King of Israel', as in the royal burlesque in Mark 15[16–20] (omitted by Luke; cf. also John 19[1–7]). It is assimilated to that of the rulers, though in direct speech with *save yourself!*, which is not altogether appropriate for soldiers compared with mock homage.

38

There was also an inscription over him, 'This is the King of the Jews': For this Roman context Luke reserves the reference to the *titulus*, but does so in a curious fashion, which shows him again attempting to play down the part of the Romans in the crucifixion, so far as that was possible. On the way to execution the condemned carried a tablet round his neck indicating his crime (Latin *causa poenae* = 'the reason for the penalty'), and it was then fixed over him, either on the cross beam or the crossed beams. For this cf. Suetonius, *Caligula* 32, where a slave who had stolen silver had his hands cut off, and was made to walk among the guests 'preceded by a placard giving the reason for his punishment', and *Domitian* 10, where one who offended the emperor was thrown to the dogs in the arena 'with a placard tied round his neck reading "A Thracian supporter who spoke evil of his Emperor"'. This is referred to correctly in Mark 15²⁶ as 'the inscription of his charge' (Matt. 27³⁷ 'his charge'), and in John 19¹⁹⁻²⁰ as the *titlos*, a Latinism from *titulus*. Luke, however, introduces it without the definite article as *an inscription*, as though alluding to what was not usual but exceptional, something that just happened to be there to add its mockery. Since he can hardly have been ignorant of the *titulus* as part of official procedure, this may be deliberate. Some mention of the offending title of Roman condemnation, 'the King of the Jews', was unavoidable in the story, but it is here treated, not as representing the official verdict of Rome, but as further piece (*also*) of gratuitous insult. This may be why Luke gives it in a form that can hardly have been the one officially authorized, *ho Basileus tōn Ioudaiōn houtos* = 'The King of the Jews – this one'.

39–43

As in Mark, the description of the various kinds of derision closes with the mention of the two fellow condemned, but in such a way as to contradict the Markan picture of total hostility and isolation. This is done by means of Luke's second substantial insertion into the crucifixion narrative. It is linked to what has preceded by the themes of messiah, kingship and 'he saved others, himself he cannot save', and brings them to a powerful and moving climax. It also resolves the paradox introduced at 22³⁷ (cf. v. 32) of Jesus the criminal. Amidst repeated and almost universal derision, impiety and unbelief, one of the two justly condemned criminals professes the fear of God, attests the innocence of Jesus, and in the form of a request makes a christological confession. As a result the last words of Jesus before his own self-committal to God are not those of judgment (vv. 28ff.), but are a solemn assurance of an immediate salvation transcending death.

Like the previous addition in vv. 28–31 this is a remarkable unit to have been preserved in tradition on its own until such time as Luke came across it. This was presumably in oral form, as vocabulary and style suggest that he was the first to put it down in writing. Thus, Lukan are in v. 39 *one, criminal, hanged, are you not (ouchi)*, in v. 40 *the other, fear God, the same (ho autos* with a noun else-where in the gospels 2⁸; Matt. 26⁴⁴), in v. 41 *justly (dikaiōs* + + in the classical sense of 'deservedly'), *receiving (apolambanein*, only here in the gospels in this sense), *our deeds ... has done* (the Lukan verb *prassein), wrong (atopos =* 'out of place', a Hellenistic word for what is morally evil, + A. 25⁵; 28⁶; II Thess. 3²). But the matter is complex, as may be seen from the comments of Knox (*Hellenistic Elements*, pp. 11–12), 'His first sentence in v. 40 is quite poor; *krima* in the sense of condemnation appears to be peculiar to biblical Greek; but v. 41 breaks out into fine writing, with good rhythm ... a contrast with *men* and *de*, a cretic with the last long syllables resolved to end the second clause, the double assonance ... and a cretic with both long syllables resolved and a trochee to end clause 3. What follows is, however, lamentable. "And he said" ... does not tell us who the speaker is, and we have the unnecessary *sou* (of you) after kingdom to represent the Semitic suffix. The reply of Jesus is equally bad, with its "and he said to him", which does not tell us who is speaking to whom ... The only inference is that Luke had before him a story which puzzled him because of the immense reward promised for so small an act of repentance; he added v. 41 to make the penitence more explicit ... here we have a clear case in which there has been a Lucan addition to, or rewriting of, material that came to him from a very semitic source.'

The story has the flavour of 'legend' in the technical sense of what is told to depict the power and personal piety of a holy man. It is wrongly called The Penitent Thief, as the man is nowhere called a thief, and it is not the moral attitudes of penitence and forgiveness that are prominent, but the religious attitudes of piety and faith. It came to be a standing feature of later accounts of martyrdoms that a bystander (in Jewish martyrdoms a Gentile) was moved by the martyr's example to confess the same faith with him, and so to be united with him in sharing his destiny. Here this takes place in the special circumstances of the con-crucifixion of two criminals with Jesus the martyr.

39

hanged: kremmanunai, a Hellenistic synonym for crucifixion (cf. Plutarch, *Life of Alexander* 59). In A. 5³⁰; 10³⁹ it is used of Jesus' crucifixion in the form 'hanging on a tree', which is due to Deut. 21²³ (quoted in Gal. 3¹³).

railed at him: The verb *blasphēmein* is used here neither in the secular sense of 'slander', nor in the technical theological sense of blaspheming God, but in an intermediate sense required by this type of story of 'speaking impiously' (cf. Mark 15²⁹, whence Luke may have derived it). The man's impious utterance is the same as that of the rulers. It starts from a supposed messiahship of Jesus, which is now put in the rough and ready, and more insulting, form of a question introduced by *Are you not?*; and to the taunt *Save yourself!* is now added *and us*.

40

rebuked him, saying, 'Do you not fear God?' : The addition *and us* is the ground of his companion's rebuke that he does not *fear God* (*phobeisthai theon*). This is a regular Jewish expression for piety. Apart from I Peter 2¹⁷; Rev. 14⁷; 19⁵, it is confined to L–A in the NT (cf. 1⁵⁰; 18²), being a term in A. for pious Gentiles on the periphery of Judaism (A. 10², ²², ³⁵; 13¹⁶, ²⁶). The force of the rebuke is either (i) if vv. 40 and 41 are taken closely together, 'To find yourself in the same condition as one who is innocent ought to lead you to piety', or (ii) if v. 41 is an additional thought, 'To be under (the same) sentence for crime ought to make you remember God, the more so if we are here for crime and he is not'.

42

And he said, 'Jesus, remember me when you come into your kingdom' : On the basis of his previous rebuke, and with an attitude of piety the opposite of that of his companion, the man then makes his request. *Jesus* (*Iēsou*) could be in the dative ('he said to Jesus') or the vocative. If the latter it is both direct and intimate, being one of the few instances in the gospels where Jesus is addressed by his personal name, and the only one where that name is not accompanied by some other designation – e.g. Jesus, Master (17¹³), Jesus of Nazareth (Mark 1²⁴), Lord Jesus (A. 7⁵⁹; Rev. 22²⁰). *remember me* means more than 'call me to remembrance'. As when God is said to remember (1⁵⁴, ⁷²; A. 10³¹; cf. Gen. 40¹⁴) it means 'to pay regard to' with a favourable result (cf. *Didache* 10⁵, 'Remember, Lord, your church to deliver it'). The request for remembrance proceeds from a belief that Jesus is some sort of heavenly royal figure. It is an implicit christological confession, though in a form rare in the NT that Jesus himself has a kingdom – elsewhere in the gospels 22³⁰; Matt. 16²⁸, and outside the gospels, as a result of his resurrection, Eph. 5⁵; Col. 1¹³; II Tim. 4¹; II Peter 1¹¹. Variant readings make the precise content of the request uncertain.

(i) In the form *in your kingdom* – so ℵ A W f1 f13 a b q – it is a request for a favourable judgment when Jesus comes as king in the parousia, *kingdom* meaning the exercise of sovereignty (so RSV 1st ed. *in your kingly rule*; cf. the reading of D 'in the day of your coming').

(ii) In the form *into your kingdom* – so p⁷⁵ B L some Old Latin mss – it is a request to be received as a member of the realm where Jesus is to reign. Easton, p. 350) regards (i) as certainly right, since (ii) can only be a Christianization of an earlier eschatological hope of a coming kingdom of God. But it is not impossible that (i) was a scribal assimilation to that eschatology, and that Luke wrote (ii), since it would correspond to the situation in A., where Jesus at his ascension enters spatially into a heavenly status, and remains there to guide his church and to receive martyrs such as Stephen (A. 7⁵⁹).

43

'Truly, I say to you, today you will be with me in Paradise' : The equally direct and

personal reply of Jesus, which is his final word to men on earth, is prefaced by the solemn formula, *Amen, I say to you*, which is relatively infrequent in Luke. The reply speaks of life beyond death in the form, unique in the gospels, of an eschatology of Paradise. *today* is taken in some mss with *I say to you*; but it should probably stand as the emphatic first word of the reply itself (cf. 4^{21}; 19^9; D has 'Be of good cheer, today . . .'). As a reply to *when you come in your kingly rule* it contradicts the request by granting it there and then and not in a future parousia. As a reply to *into your kingdom* it would declare an immediate entry of both Jesus and his petitioner into a heavenly realm beyond death. The inevitable imprecision and inconsistencies in eschatological language perhaps do not allow either *today you will be* or *with me in Paradise* to be pressed too hard. The concept of *Paradise* (+ II Cor. 12^3; Rev. 2^7) results from the use in Greek of a Persian loan word meaning 'enclosure' or 'park', first for Eden as the garden of God (Gen. 2^8), then for the condition of the redeemed Jerusalem on earth (Isa. 51^3), and finally for an eschatological Eden. The last does not appear in the OT, but is found in apocalyptic writings, alongside other equivalent expressions, for the future state or dwelling place of the righteous after the judgment (II Esdras 8^{52}). In II Enoch 8.1 it is the garden, the Paradise of Eden, in which is the tree of life (cf. Rev. 2^7), against which God rests when he goes there. In I Enoch 61^{12} the Elect One as the head of the heavenly people of God is king of Paradise (cf. also I Enoch 60^8; 70^3). Alongside this, perhaps under Hellenistic influence, there came into being a doctrine of a present hidden Paradise as the abode of (the souls of) the departed after death, which resembles the peculiar eschatology of the parable of the Rich Man and Lazarus (cf. Abraham's bosom, 16^{22}), and possibly here. In II Cor. 12^3 it is a heavenly region, perhaps identical with the third heaven of II Cor. 12^2, into which Paul is caught up in mystical rapture. In second-century Christianity the belief is found that the martyr went straight from death to heaven, and this could already be presupposed in the story of Stephen (A. 7$^{54-60}$; for a similar belief in Judaism, cf. SB II, p. 264). The relation of this (intermediate?) state of Paradise to the normal Jewish doctrine of the general resurrection is inevitably unclear, as is also the relation of Jesus' statement here that he would be in Paradise immediately after death with the prophecy of his resurrection on the third day. Ellis (pp. 268f.) attempts to harmonize by giving *today* a wider meaning of 'in the present time of salvation', and by postulating here something equivalent to the Pauline conception of the believer's inclusion into the body of Christ by corporately dying and rising with him; but this is unconvincing. The statement proclaims the gospel of salvation in that the criminal is treated immediately as righteous, and it is Jesus, the messiah and judge to be, who from the cross determines that it is so (it is not suggested that he will open the gates of Paradise, cf. Test. Levi 18.10). As the innocent martyr Jesus himself belongs with the righteous in Paradise, but as their king; and he takes another with him to be amongst his companions – *with me* (cf. 22^{28}).

23⁴⁴⁻⁴⁹

23⁴⁴⁻⁴⁹ = Mark 15³³⁻⁴¹
THE DEATH OF JESUS AND ITS ACCOMPANIMENTS

⁴⁴*It was now about the sixth hour, and there was darkness over the whole land* until the ninth hour, ⁴⁵while the sun's light failed;† and the curtain of the temple was torn in two. ⁴⁶Then Jesus, crying with a loud voice, said, 'Father, into thy hands I commit my spirit!' And having said this he breathed his last. ⁴⁷Now when the centurion saw what had taken place, he praised God, and said, 'Certainly this man was innocent!' ⁴⁸And all the multitudes who assembled to see the sight, when they saw what had taken place, returned home beating their breasts. ⁴⁹And all his acquaintances and the women who had followed him from Galilee stood at a distance and saw these things.*

* Or *earth*

† Or *the sun was eclipsed.* Other ancient authorities read *the sun was darkened*

It was not uncommon in antiquity for accounts of the death of a famous figure, or of one close to the gods, to mention portents in nature as accompanying it, and to record the dying man's last words. These two elements are already present in the tradition of Jesus' death represented by Mark. In Matt. 27⁵²⁻⁵³ the element of biblical portent is greatly increased; in John's account it is absent. Luke is here wholly dependent on Mark, and any significant modifications he makes show his mind on the matter.

ཪཪ

44
It was now about the sixth hour: Luke marks the occasion by incorporating the only time reference he takes over from Mark's passion narrative. *now* (*ēdē* = 'already') is probably unemphatic, as in 14¹⁷. *about the sixth hour,* i.e. *noon; about* is a typical Lukan addition with numbers. Luke omits the reference to Elijah (Mark 15³⁵ᶠ·), which depends on the cry of dereliction in Mark 15³⁴, which he is to replace. He brings together the two miraculous events which are separated in Mark so that they both precede the death of Jesus, which then becomes the climax. And he underlines the character of these events as portents.

there was darkness over the whole land until the ninth hour: over the whole land (*eph'holēn tēn gēn*) probably refers to Palestine, though it could mean 'over the whole earth' (so RSV margin), and be intended to indicate the cosmic dimensions of the death.

45

while the sun's light failed: In Mark the darkness is primarily scriptural and eschatological; cf. Amos 8^9, 'On that day, says the Lord God, I will make the sun to go down at noon, and darken the earth in broad daylight.' Characteristically Luke makes the supernatural thoroughly factual and physical. The verb *failed* (*ekleipein* + 16^9; 22^{32}; Heb. 1^{12} LXX), when used of the sun, was a technical term for an eclipse (so RSV margin). The variant reading 'was darkened' may have arisen from the knowledge that an eclipse at the time of the paschal full moon was an astronomical *faux pas*. Eclipses were held in the ancient world to be particularly dire portents. This can be seen in the letter from Mark Antony to Hyrcanus (Jos. *Ant.* 14.309), 'Our enemies and those of the empire overran Asia, sparing neither cities nor temples, and committed lawless deeds against men and gods, from which we believe the very sun turned away, as if it were loath to look upon the foul deed against Caesar.' See also the remark of Philo (quoted in Eusebius, *Preparation of the Gospel* 8.14, 395d) that eclipses pertain to the divine bodies of the sun and moon, since they portend either the death of kings or the destruction of cities; and as a particular instance of this Plutarch's statement that when Romulus disappeared in death 'the face of the sun was darkened, and the day turned to night' (*Life of Romulus*, 27.6).

and the curtain of the temple was torn in two: This curtain almost certainly refers to that which hung before the Holy of Holies to conceal it from human eyes and to separate it from the rest of the holy place (Exod. 26$^{1ff.}$), rather than that which hung at the entrance to the holy place itself (Exod. 26^{37}). In Mark the rending of this curtain, placed immediately after the death of Jesus, and followed by the centurion's confession of faith, brings to a climax the theme of the temple, which is a principal thread running through his passion narrative. It could symbolize either the replacement of the temple by the body of Christ as the house of prayer for all nations (Mark 11^{17}; cf. John 2^{21}), or the opening of the way into the presence of God through the death of Jesus (cf. Heb. 10$^{19f.}$). This theme is consistently omitted by Luke, for whom the temple remains a place of prayer for the first Christians (A. 3^1), is not threatened until the appearance of Stephen (A. 6$^{13f.}$), and is to be destroyed in its own time by the Roman armies (21$^{5-20}$). Placed before the death of Jesus, and immediately after the eclipse, the rending of the veil loses any symbolic or theological meaning, and is simply a portent at the central place of Judaism, and appropriate for the death of Jesus, who had made the temple the seat of his teaching ministry in Jerusalem (19$^{47ff.}$).

46

crying with a loud voice, said: There is the same uncertainty here as in Mark 15$^{34, 37}$ = Matt. 27$^{46, 50}$ whether 'the great cry' was itself the last words of Jesus, or preceded (succeeded) them. A. 7^{60} suggests the former.

Father, into thy hands I commit my spirit: The last words of Jesus will have been the subject of Christian reflection. They may also have been the product of it, and of different interpretations of the meaning of his death. Thus, 'It is finished' (John 19^{30}) are fitting last words of the Johannine Jesus, who had previously prayed to his Father 'I glorified thee on the earth, having finished the work thou gavest me to do' (John 17^{4}). The cry of dereliction from Ps. 22^{1} in Mark 15^{34} = Matt. 27^{46} is hardly possible as a final utterance of the innocent martyr, who has just spoken vv. 28–31, v. 43. Luke replaces it by what is more suitable, the trustful self-committal to God 'Into thy hand(s) I commit my spirit' from Ps. 31^{5} (LXX Ps. 30^{6}, 'I will commit'), prefaced by the plain vocative *Father*, characteristic of the speech of Jesus (cf. 22^{42}). This psalm is similar in content and tone to Ps. 22, but lays greater emphasis on the sufferer's confident hope of deliverance by God (cf. vv. 2, 5b, 7, 15–22). Luke's use of this verse with the words *my spirit* (*to pneuma mou*) may have been influenced by the statement that follows, *And having said this he breathed his last*. The verb here, which is used by Mark for the death of Jesus, is *exepneusen*, a classical and Hellenistic expression meaning 'he breathed out', 'he breathed his last'. Since *pneuma* can be both 'breath' and 'spirit' the equivalent to the verb can be 'he yielded up his spirit' (Matt. 27^{50}), or 'he gave up (handed over) his spirit' John 19^{30}). Luke may combine both meanings when the psalm verse *I commit my spirit* is followed by *And having said this he breathed his last*. With Jesus the final expiration is also the handing over of his spirit to the God who gave it. His last words are thus a summary of his relationship to God, and he dies as a martyr should die; cf. A. 7$^{59-60}$, 'And when he had said this he fell asleep'.

47

the centurion: The presence of this person in Mark 15^{39} (*kenturiōn*, a Latin loan word, in Luke the Greek equivalent *hekatontarchēs* = 'commander of a hundred') is more intelligible, where he is presumably the officer of the Roman soldiers in charge of operations, and is described as standing facing Jesus; cf. the expansion in Matt. 27^{54}, 'the centurion and those who were with him, watching over Jesus'. In Luke he is introduced, like the soldiers, abruptly and without explanation.

saw what had taken place, he praised God: In Mark the centurion's confession of faith is evoked by the manner of Jesus' death, i.e. his expiration with the loud cry of dereliction, and this corresponds with Mark's christology. Speaking in the name of the Gentile world he is the first human being to attest in his own way ('a son of God'), the divine sonship of Jesus, which hitherto had been attested only by God himself (Mark 1¹¹; 9⁷) or by supernatural beings (Mark 3¹¹; 5⁷); and he does so at the moment of Jesus' complete depotentiation. In Luke the centurion's reaction is also evoked by *what had taken place* (*to genomenon*, the aorist participle used as a noun, which is Lukan), which will include the eclipse as well as the manner of Jesus' death. This now corresponds with Luke's theology, consisting in the glorification of God, a stereotyped form of words in Luke for a climax, especially of miracle (cf. 5²⁵, ²⁶; 7¹⁶; 13¹³; 17¹⁵; 18⁴³; A. 4²¹, as the result of what had happened A. 11¹⁸; 21²⁰), and an expression of piety.

Certainly this man was innocent!: The centurion thus joins the criminal of vv. 40f. in voicing a godly judgment on Jesus. It is the final and most emphatic attestation (*certainly*, *ontōs*, an adverb from the participle of the verb 'to be', cf. 24³⁴) from the Roman side that *this man* (cf. vv. 4, 14) was *innocent* (so RSV). The word here is *dikaios* = 'righteous', and again Ps. 31 may have had some influence; cf. Ps. 31¹⁸, 'Let the lying lips be dumb who speak insolently (LXX lawlessness) against the righteous.' But the word can mean 'innocent', as in Matt. 23³⁵; 27⁴, ¹⁹; James 5⁶, and with this sense it completes Luke's picture of Jesus the martyr, and finally resolves the paradox of Jesus the criminal.

48

And all the multitudes who assembled to see the sight: In Mark 15⁴⁰ the narrative of the crucifixion is completed by a notice of women watching from a distance, some of whom are named, and provides a link to the subsequent burial and visit to the tomb (Mark 15⁴⁷; 16¹). In incorporating this verse (v. 49) Luke adds *and all his acquaintances* (*hoi gnōstoi*); but before doing so he inserts a description of the effect of *what had taken place* (again, as in v. 47, the aorist participle as a noun) upon the general audience of the people, here called *the multitudes*, whom he alone had introduced as spectators *watching* (*theōrein*, as in vv. 27, 35). This could also reflect the influence of Ps. 31; cf. v. 11 (LXX Ps. 30¹²), 'I am a horror to my neighbours, an object of dread to my acquaintances (*hoi gnōstoi*); those who see (*theōrein*) me . . . flee from me'. Lagrange (p. 593) observes that Luke writes here 'in a style which does not fight shy of rare words'. Such are those translated by *assembled* (the very uncommon Greek word *sunparaginesthai* + +), *sight* (*theōria* + +, with *when they saw*, *theōresantes*, producing a paranomasia), and *beating their breasts*, found elsewhere only at 18¹³). Without exception – the usual Lukan exaggeration – the crowds who had come to view the spectacle return in a state of grief akin to the lamentation of the women they had accompanied.

49

And all his acquaintances and the women who had followed him from Galilee: Luke here turns from the public scene of v. 48 to the more private scene in Mark

15⁴⁰, the link between them being 'looking on' (Mark 15⁴⁰), which is the same word, *theōrein*, as *saw* in v. 48. The disposition of the women in Mark as 'from afar' (*apo makrothen*) reflects the influence of the LXX in certain psalms of a similar character – Ps. 31¹¹ (LXX Ps. 30¹²) quoted above; Ps. 38¹¹ (LXX Ps. 37¹²), 'My friends and companions stand aloof from my plague, and my kinsmen stand afar off (*makrothen*)'; Ps. 88⁸ (LXX Ps. 87⁹), 'Thou hast caused my companions to shun me . . .', v. 18 'Thou hast caused lover and friend to shun me; my companions (*hoi gnōstoi*) are in darkness.' Luke has further approximated Mark's narrative to the language of the LXX by adding *his acquaintances* and *stood* (cf. LXX Ps. 37¹²); and he appears to have taken the parallel expressions in Ps. 37¹² LXX, 'my friends and companions' and 'my kinsmen', as indicating two separate classes of people. Out of the first he has created at this point an undefined group of those in close association with Jesus (*his acquaintances, hoi gnōstoi*), with the typical Lukan exaggeration *all*. These are to play an important part in the rest of the Gospel by providing an element of continuity in it. They are probably meant to include the Eleven, whose flight in Mark 14⁵⁰ Luke has not reproduced, and those referred to as *all the rest* (24⁹), as *them* (24¹³) and as *those who were with them* (24³³), and perhaps Mary and the brethren (A. 1¹⁴ᶠ·). Out of the second he has created, as also standing and watching the events from a distance, a group of women described as those *who had followed him from Galilee*. Here two groups of women mentioned in Mark 15⁴⁰⁻⁴¹ are telescoped, the three named women who had followed Jesus from Galilee, and many other women who had come up with him to Jerusalem. That some women had ministered to Jesus in Galilee has been mentioned in 8³. Their names are omitted here by Luke, being reserved until they become witnesses of the empty tomb (24¹⁰). Here, unnamed, they are witnesses to the death, as also in v. 55 to the burial.

23⁵⁰⁻⁵⁶ = Mark 15⁴²⁻⁴⁷

THE BURIAL OF JESUS

⁵⁰*Now there was a man named Joseph from the Jewish town of Arimathea. He was a member of the council, a good and righteous man,* ⁵¹*who had not consented to their purpose and deed, and he was looking for the kingdom of God.* ⁵²*This man went to Pilate and asked for the body of Jesus.* ⁵³*Then he took it down and wrapped it in a linen shroud, and laid him in a rock-hewn tomb, where no one had ever yet been laid.* ⁵⁴*It was the day of Preparation, and the sabbath was beginning.*★ ⁵⁵*The women who had come with him from*

Galilee followed, and saw the tomb, and how his body was laid; 56*then they
returned, and prepared spices and ointments.*
  On the sabbath they rested according to the commandment.

★ Greek *was dawning*

Whether an account of Jesus' burial always concluded a passion narrative is uncertain, since in its present position it provides a necessary
transition from the crucifixion to the discovery of the empty tomb and
the resurrection appearances. In the early formula in I Cor. 15³⁻⁴ 'that
he was buried' could also be a transitional statement between death and
resurrection, but it could also belong with 'died' to complete the statement 'dead and buried'. K. H. Rengstorfʸ considers that 'he was buried'
intended to indicate that Jesus was a notable figure, as in Jewish tradition only such were represented as having graves; and this could
account for the mention in this pericope of Joseph as a man of substance. The purpose of the pericope, taken on its own and apart from
the tradition of the empty tomb, could be to assert that the corpse of
Jesus was not left on the cross to rot, as could happen, nor thrown into
a common fosse with those of other criminals (see Daube, *NTRJ*,
p. 310).
  The extent of the verbal agreement with Mark, and the character of
the differences, make it unnecessary to postulate any other source than
Mark here. In his general editing Luke concentrates on the main action
of burial, and on the persons involved, first Joseph and then the women.
Mark's somewhat elaborate time reference at the beginning (Mark 15⁴²)
is attached to the death of Jesus, though it serves by implication to
account for Joseph's action in asking for the body for burial while there
was time before the sabbath. Luke removes this to the end (v. 56),
where it governs the actions of the women, and points forward to their
visit to the tomb (Matthew distributes it between 27⁵⁷ and 28¹; John
19⁴² has a form of it, but without any connection with the women).
  In the Greek vv. 50–53 are a single overloaded and ill-constructed
sentence, one of the worst Luke has written in the Gospel. Literally it
reads, 'And behold, a man by name Joseph, being a member of the
council, a man good and righteous, – this man was not consenting to
their purpose and deed – from Arimathea, a city of the Jews, who was
looking for the kingdom of God, this man, going to Pilate, asked for

y Die Auferstehung Jesu, Berlin 1952, pp. 51ff.

the body of Jesus, and taking it down he wrapped it in a linen shroud, and laid him in a rock tomb where no one had ever been laid.' This clumsiness is likely to be the result of a rewriting of Mark: first, of Mark's 'Joseph of Arimathea', which refers to him as someone well known in the tradition (cf. Mark 15²¹), hence the revision in Matt. 27⁵⁷, and Luke's *a man named Joseph*, and *from the Jewish town of Arimathea* (lit. 'Arimathea, a city of the Jews', a vague description, clearly for Gentile readers); second, of Mark's 'a respected member of the council'. The Greek here is *euschēmōn bouleutēs*, and the meaning of both noun and adjective is uncertain – perhaps a man of high rank in Arimathea. Matt. 27⁵⁷ alters to 'a rich man', which was one, though a vulgar, meaning of *euschēmōn* (cf. A. 13⁵⁰ = 'upper class'). Luke takes it in the sense of morally noble, which it generally has in Hellenistic literature and in inscriptions, where it is often found with *kalos* = 'good'. He therefore paraphrases with *good (agathos)* and *righteous (dikaios)*. He takes *bouleutēs* = 'councillor' to mean a member of the Sanhedrin, and so has to make him an exception to its previous unanimous decision to condemn Jesus (22⁷¹; 23¹⁸). Hence the parenthesis in v. 53a, which is clearly from his hand – *consented to (sunkatatithenai* ++, not LXX, but in the papyri for 'to agree with'), *their* (i.e. the Sanhedrin, clumsily introduced), *purpose (boulē*, Lukan) *and deed (praxis* + Matt. 16²⁷; Rom. 12⁴). In vv. 55–56 the style is thoroughly Lukan, and these verses can hardly be taken, as by Taylor (*Passion Narrative*, pp. 99ff.), as the rump of another source having links with the very different story in John 19³⁸⁻⁴², which Luke will then have largely abandoned in favour of Mark.

ဿ

50–51
The tradition in Mark gives no details to explain why Joseph should have a tomb in Jerusalem, or why he should have been anxious to perform the office of burial, except that *he was looking for the kingdom of God* (so also Luke), and was therefore pious. Like Simon of Cyrene and the centurion he is on the Christian side. Matthew makes him a disciple, John a secret disciple. Luke makes him a single exception in the enemy camp, and so perhaps prepares for the curious statement in A. 13²⁹ that the Jews took Jesus down from the cross and placed him in a tomb.

52
went to Pilate: So Matt. 27⁵⁸, an improvement on Mark's 'went in to'. The

action is more natural in the other gospels, where the crucifixion is Pilate's responsibility, than in Luke, where Jesus is handed over by Pilate to the will of the Jews (23^{25}). That the petition is granted is assumed by Matthew and Luke, who pass over Mark $15^{44f.}$.

53

Burial was a duty of the utmost piety. Its method varied. Criminals were thrown into a common pit. The great mass of people were too poor to possess a tomb, and were simply interred in the ground. Tombs cut in rock were the property of the more wealthy. They were of various designs, with a burial chamber approached by either a vertical or a horizontal shaft, and the body laid either on the floor, or in a recess, or on a ledge.ᶻ Here Joseph *wrapped* the body (*entulissein*, so Matthew, probably a more usual word with shrouds than Mark's colloquial word, which could be used of wrapping anything). He then *laid* (*tithenai*, so also Matthew in preference to Mark's 'deposited') *him* (not, as previously, 'it') *in a rock-hewn tomb* (*laxeutos* + +, a curiously rare adjective in Hellenistic literature in view of the frequent mention in the papyri of *laxos* = 'stonemason').

where no one had ever yet been laid: A triple negative in the Greek, expressing reverence for Jesus. This is the language of hagiography, and in the spirit of 19^{30} = Mark 11^2; cf. John 19^{41}, which may be dependent on Luke here, the addition of 'new' in Matt. 27^{60}, and of 'clean' with 'shroud' in Matt. 27^{59}. Strangely Luke omits the placing of the stone at the door of the tomb (Mark 15^{46}), though it is assumed in 24^2. He may have judged the questioning about it in Mark 16^3 to be artificial – why should they set out at all if they knew that they would not be able to move the stone? The connection between the burial and the visit to the tomb is made differently by Luke; see next note.

54–56

There is an element of indefiniteness at this point in the synoptic versions of events. For they do not state that the wrapping of the body had included an embalming with spices, such as John 19^{39-40} depicts Joseph performing in accordance with Jewish burial custom. The hot climate demanded that this be done immediately and before corruption set in. It could hardly be postponed for the twenty-four (thirty-six?) hours required if the visit of the women to the tomb for embalming took place after the intermission of the sabbath, as in Mark 16^1 and here. In that case, however, a sufficient reason for their visit is lacking. John does not have any such visit, and in Matthew no other motive is supplied for it than curiosity. Ellis (p. 271) postulates that it was an act of devo-

---

ᶻ See J. Finegan, *The Archaeology of the New Testament*, Princeton 1969, pp. 181ff.

tion in the form of a supplementary anointing, though there is no evidence for such in Jewish burial custom. This ambiguity may be due to the overlapping of two originally separate stories connected with the tomb, that of the burial and that of the women's visit later. This is perhaps to be seen in vv. 54–56, which serve two purposes, and where the narrative begins to pass from the one to the other, thus making the burial a prelude to the discovery of the empty tomb.

The verses are plainly from Luke's hand. They are carefully constructed as link verses, though this is obscured in all English translations because (i) a full stop is put after *the commandment* (v. 56b), whereas in the Greek the sentence runs on into 24^1, and (ii) the Greek particles *men . . . de* = 'on the one hand . . . on the other hand', 23^{56b}–24^1, which articulate the statements in this single sentence, are not translated. The link can also be seen in the repetition of the reference in v. 49 to *the women who had come with him from Galilee* (v. 55; *sunerchesthai* = 'to accompany' is common in this sense in A.). These are introduced here as those who will later be addressed by the angels at the tomb with the words 'Remember how he told you, while he was still in Galilee' (24^6 Luke's revised version of Mark 16^7). Here their qualifications to be the future witnesses of the empty tomb are stressed, when it said that they *followed* Joseph (the reduplicated verb *katakolouthein* + A. 16^{17} means 'to follow hard on the heels of'), *saw the tomb* (i.e. where it was), and exactly *how* (this use of the conjunction *hōs* is predominantly Lukan in the NT) *his body was laid*. There was no possibility of their going to the wrong tomb. Having done this they returned home (*hupostrephein*, a Lukan word), and prepared in advance *spices and ointments* (*arōmata kai mura*, a frequent combination in the LXX and papyri; cf. Mark 16^1, 'spices that they might anoint him' and Mark 14$^{3-8}$, ointment for embalming). Then on the sabbath they *rested* (*hēsuchazein* = 'to leave off from what one was doing previously', as in A. 11^{18}; 21^{14}), i.e. they desisted from activity, as commanded on the sabbath.

54

It was the day of the Preparation, and the sabbath was beginning: The time references here and in 24^1, as in corresponding verses in the other gospels, are obscure, the precise meaning of the terms used being uncertain.

(i) The burial takes place on *paraskeuē* = 'preparation'; so Mark 15^{42}, in Luke on *the day of* (the) *preparation* (cf. 22^7; A. 2^1; 20^{16}). This could mean either the day before the sabbath, i.e. Friday (so *prosabbaton* in Mark 15^{42}; cf. Jos. *Ant.* 16.163), or the day before passover day (John 19$^{14, 31, 42}$). Here it is clearly the former, being followed by *the sabbath was beginning* (vv. 54, 56b). The time referred to is between 3 p.m. on Friday, the time of Jesus' death (v. 44), and sunset. By the synoptic reckoning, however, though not that of John, it was also passover day, which, as a feast day, was the equivalent of a sabbath, and all work was forbidden except that which pertained to the food for the feast

(Exod. 12¹⁶); though what was necessary for burial was not prohibited on the sabbath (SB II, pp. 52ff.).

(ii) The burial was finished, and the site of the tomb observed by the women, towards the end of Friday as sunset approached and *the sabbath was beginning* ('was dawning' RSV margin). The verb here is *epiphōskein*, a remarkable verbal agreement with Matt. 28¹, its only other occurrence in the NT, where it is translated by 'the dawn of'. The word is very rare, several of the few instances of its use being dependent on these two NT passages. The difficulty of its translation and interpretation arises from the fact that it is derived from the Greek word *phōs* = 'light', and should therefore mean 'to begin to be daylight', 'to dawn with the sunrise'; but that it is used predominantly by Semitic writers, or those using Semitic material, for whom the day began at sunset, and 'daybreak' was the approach of darkness. (It has been suggested that if the verb retained any connection with 'light', it was with the light of the evening star; but it could have lost any such connection, and have meant 'to draw on'). Thus in the apocryphal Gospel of Peter 2 Herod gives as the reason for the burial of Jesus that the sabbath was drawing near (*epiphōskein*), 'for it is written in the law, "Let not the sun go down on a slain man"'. This could be the sense in Matt. 28¹, where time does not have to be found for the preparation, or the buying, of spices, since the women do not go to the tomb to anoint. There they set out 'late on the sabbath', i.e. at the approach of the sunset which began 'the first day of the week' (Sunday), or, since 'late on the sabbath' could be a rabbinic expression for the first day of the week, they set out at the approach of its beginning at sunset. This, however, would make the visit to the tomb and the subsequent events take place in increasing darkness, and would contradict Mark 16², 'very early . . . when the sun had risen', and John 20¹, 'early, while it was still dark'. On the other hand the Gospel of Peter can use the verb to mean the dawn – 8, 'Early (*prōias* = 'early in the morning') when the sabbath was dawning a crowd came from Jerusalem and the countryside to see the tomb sealed', and 9, 'In the night in which the Lord's day (Sunday) dawned . . .' This meaning would accord with 24¹, where the women visit the tomb *orthrou baseōs* = 'at deep (early) dawn' (*orthros* + A. 52¹; John 8² means 'early morning', cf. the adjective used of this visit, *orthrinos* + +, 24²² = 'early in the morning', and the verb *orthrizein* + + 21³⁸ = 'to get up early in the morning'). This follows the end of the sabbath. Luke may then be operating with the non-Semitic calculation of the beginning of the day with sunrise, as possibly in A. 20⁷⁻¹¹ (see *Beginnings* IV, p. 255). In that case he may have thought of Joseph's burial activities as taking place in the night time, and the women's observation of the tomb (v. 55) as made in the dawning light of Saturday. On either interpretation it is not easy to envisage at what time of the day or night the work of preparing the embalming materials took place (v. 56), especially if it had involved buying them.

24 *The Resurrection*

The conclusion of a gospel presented peculiar difficulties. It could not consist of an account of the death and burial of Jesus, with perhaps some kind of epilogue. It involved the narration of an event, or events, of an eschatological character, in which God was directly concerned as effecting through them his final purposes for Israel and mankind. Through them Jesus, and anything he had done, said or suffered, were set in an ultimate and non-historical dimension. Thus a gospel ended where Christian faith had begun, in giving narrative expression to the basic confession that Jesus is Lord (or is God's messiah or the Son of God), or to the second part of such a credal formula as 'Jesus Christ who died, who was raised from the dead' (Rom. 8[34]). This lordship, first over the church (I Cor. 16[22]), and then in principle over mankind and creation (Phil. 2[10-11]), was primarily apprehended through, and expressed in terms of, his resurrection from the dead (Rom. 10[9]), or his exaltation to God or God's right hand (Phil. 2[9-11]). This was so because 'resurrection', in the diverse forms in which it had emerged in Judaism in the first century AD, was itself an eschatological concept.[a] Along with the (last) judgment, it was one term for expressing God's destruction of sin, and of death which was linked with sin, and his establishment of righteousness and eternal life for his elect. The belief that Jesus had been raised by God from the dead was, therefore, belief that these final things were being anticipated in and through him, and that he had now been made the all-powerful agent of God's purposes. This lordship was not apprehended in a vacuum, but through certain effects ascribed to it. Such were the universal mission of the church as the true people of God, its preaching of the message of the cross and resurrection, the faith in God that evoked, and a present experience of what had hitherto been predicated of the age to come – the Spirit, freedom from sin and obedience to righteousness, and a life judged to be of eternal quality.

---

a For the development of various forms of belief in resurrection in Judaism, see Evans, *Resurrection*, pp. 14ff., and the literature cited there.

24

The presentation of such truths of faith and experience in narrative inevitably involved difficulties and limitations. God's act of raising Jesus, often expressed in the passive 'he was raised', could not be narrated, and no evangelist attempts to describe the resurrection itself, though Luke, and he alone, describes the exaltation of Jesus (A. 1⁹⁻¹¹). It had to be presupposed as the basis of any stories about the risen Jesus, if those were to be stories about God and not simply about Jesus. What is narrated as evidence that such a resurrection had taken place is 'appearances' or self-manifestations of Jesus as the risen one; the word commonly used here, ōphthē (v. 34; I Cor. 15⁵⁻⁸) would seem to mean 'he allowed himself to be seen'. These appearances are in a form which both enables Jesus to establish his identity with his former earthly self, and indicates that he appears (from heaven?) as the one who has been raised and exalted as Lord by God. There is considerable variation in this respect. The fact that the gospel accounts do not tally with the list of appearances in I Cor. 15⁵⁻⁸, and the differences between those accounts themselves, show that the traditions about the resurrection were not fixed. Further, the stories are not readily susceptible to form-critical analysis, since they do not fall into generally recognized categories of oral tradition.[b] This could be due to their special character and content, for which there were no precedents or models. There could have been a model for exaltation in the belief that notable figures, such as Elijah, Enoch or Moses, had been assumed by God directly from earth to heaven, and were destined to play a role in God's dealings with Israel in the end-time (cf. II Kings 2¹⁻¹² and Mal. 4⁵; Gen. 5²¹⁻²⁴ and I and II Enoch; Deut. 34⁵⁻⁶ and the Assumption of Moses). There was, however, no previous expectation in Judaism of an appearance on earth immediately after death of any such figure, let alone the messiah. Nor would records in Hellenistic religious traditions of the appearance after death of heroes furnish a model, as these were isolated phenomena, unconnected with anything corresponding to the Jewish faith in the one God and his moral purposes for mankind. Christian faith in the resurrection of Jesus, being unique in character and content, had to create its own forms of narrative expression. In principle a single well-attested story of a resurrection 'appearance' would suffice to affirm that Jesus had been raised from the dead. The fact that there were several available

[b] For an analysis of the resurrection traditions according to their form, and the attendant difficulties, see Dodd, 'The Appearances of the Risen Christ', in *More NT Studies*, pp. 102ff., and Alsup, *Post-Resurrection Appearance Stories*, III and IV.

in tradition, and that they differed considerably in tone and content, suggest that their purpose was not simply to affirm the resurrection of Jesus as a fact, but also to declare its meaning and its consequences. These are conveyed primarily by what the risen Lord says, and it is on his words rather than on the form of his appearance that the emphasis lies. These words are significantly different in the various stories; and as these differences correspond to some extent to differences of theological outlook in the gospels themselves, the stories may be supposed to have developed in tradition as vehicles of different interpretations of the resurrection.

In all this Luke occupies a special position. The other evangelists conclude their works with stories of the appearance of the risen Jesus, which express his universal lordship until the parousia, as each understood that lordship; and they so write as to make it impossible to take up the pen again (Mark 16$^{1-8}$?; Matt. 28$^{16-20}$; John 20$^{19-23, 24-31}$; 21$^{20-25}$?). For Luke, who intended a continuation in a second volume, the perspective is different. The resurrection is now the point of transition from the story of the earthly Jesus to the story of the movement which went by his name, and also the basis of that movement. It was therefore necessary to spell out successive stages from the (temporary?) state of resurrection to that of exaltation, from exaltation to the consequent gift of the Spirit, and to the effects of the Spirit in the historical circumstances, activities and characteristics of the Christian community. This brought with it a special difficulty of how and where to end the first volume of his work, and how and where to begin the second, and of the overlap between them. But the importance for Luke of the final chapter of the first volume can be seen from the place occupied by the resurrection of Jesus in the second. There it is affirmed as the installation by God of Jesus as Israel's messiah, and is argued in detail from scripture (A. 2$^{24-36}$; 3$^{13, 22f.}$; 4^{11}; 13$^{33-37}$), and as that through which salvation is gained (A. 4$^{11f.}$). To bear witness to it is the special function of apostles (A. 1$^{2ff., 22}$; 4^{33}). It is their proclamation of it that evokes the opposition of the authorities, which marks the early years of the Christian movement along with its popularity with 'the people' (A. 4$^{1ff.}$; 5$^{17ff.}$). In a Gentile setting the message can be summarized as preaching Jesus and the resurrection (A. 17$^{18, 31}$); while a special feature of the presentation of Paul in A. is that he is persecuted on account of the resurrection, and defends himself by appealing to the resurrection of Jesus as the fulfilment of the hope of the Jewish race (A. 23$^{6ff.}$; 24$^{15ff.}$; 26$^{8, 23}$; cf. 13$^{32f.}$).

Luke–Acts is thus more responsible than any other NT writing for the presentation of Christianity as a religion of resurrection. This emphasis may reflect Luke's awareness of a widespread concern in the world of his day with death, mortality and fate, and of a yearning there for life and immortality.

In the composition of ch. 24 Luke has used four units. Each of these could stand on its own as a means of proclaiming resurrection faith. They are more diverse than the traditions in the other gospels, and could be of different origins. The story of the empty tomb (vv. 1–11) is similar to Mark's and may be a version of Mark's. The Emmaus story (vv. 13–33) is unique in length, form and content. Verse 34 is a bare kerygmatic statement in a single sentence. The story in vv. 36–44 (49) has some similarity with other traditions (Matt. 28$^{16-20}$, John 20$^{19-23}$). Their collection together places the witness to the resurrection on a wide basis of the testimony of the women, of individual disciples in intimate discourse with the Lord, of Peter as the chief apostle and of the officially commissioned apostles (A. 1$^{3ff.}$, if from Luke's hand, places it on a further apostolic basis of proof extended over a considerable period, though without specific details). Through the combination of these units Luke makes the resurrection faith the result of a series of interlocking events, a kind of 'history' of the risen Lord (especially if A. 1$^{3ff.}$ is included), which does not come to an end until Pentecost (A. 2$^{1ff.}$). He achieves this by various unities of composition.

(i) There is a unity of place. No mention is made of Galilee except as belonging to the past (v. 6, cf. 23$^{49, 55}$). Jerusalem and its environs, towards which the story has been directed from 9^{51} onwards, are stressed as the necessary location of the appearances (vv. 13, 33, 49, 50, 52; cf. A. 1$^{4, 12}$), and as the necessary base from which the Christian movement is to proceed (v. 47, A. 1$^{4-8, 12}$).

(ii) There is a unity of time. The journey to Emmaus takes place on the same day as the visit to the tomb (v. 13), and leads immediately (v. 33) to a return to those for whom, in the interim, the appearance to Peter has become an accomplished fact. This is immediately (v. 36) followed by an appearance of the Lord, his instruction and parting, though this involves a journey at night – contrast A. 1, where a forty-day period of appearances (at Bethany or the Mount of Olives?) is concluded by an ascension.

(iii) There is a unity of persons concerned. It is two of those to whom the women have reported, sc. the eleven and the rest (vv. 9, 13), who go to Emmaus, and only here is a reference to the visit to the tomb brought within the story of an appearance (vv. 22f.). It is the eleven and their companions to whom these two report, and with whom they experience another appearance, and receive instruction and blessing (v. 33).

(iv) There is a unity of theological themes. There is no trace of apologetic in face of Jewish impugning of the resurrection, as in Matt. $27^{62ff.}$ (and perhaps John $20^{11ff.}$). Rather there is in each of the three pericopes an assertion, in the face of unbelief (vv. 4, 11, 41), of the divine necessity, and therefore the propriety, of the passion and resurrection (v. 7, *must be*, v. 26, *Was it not necessary?*, v. 44, *must be fulfilled* – in v. 34 *indeed* may refer back to the unbelief in v. 11). In the first this necessity is traced back by the angels to a prophecy made by Jesus during his earthly ministry, which is thus brought within the story of the empty tomb. In the second it is stated by the risen Lord in credal form as the burden of the entire OT (vv. 26f., 32). In the third these are combined, and the risen Lord shows the passion and resurrection to be the burden of his previous teaching and of the OT together. This doctrine of the divinely ordained suffering and resurrection of the messiah the Christian preachers in A. are to reiterate, and to expound by reference, both general and particular, to the OT (A. 2^{22-35}; $3^{13, 18}$; $4^{11, 25ff.}$; 10^{43}; 13^{33-41}; $17^{3, 11}$; $26^{22f.}$; 28^{23}). Here it is given its origin in the words of the risen Lord himself. Its very repetition as the major theme in both appearances, and its dominance over the other two motifs – those of the knowledge of the Lord in the breaking of bread (vv. 25–27), and of the mission of the church (vv. 44–48) – could indicate Luke's concern with Christianity as the heir of Judaism, especially by virtue of the resurrection (A. 23^6; $24^{14f.}$; $26^{6-8, 22f.}$). Also binding the materials together is that the living one, who is not to be sought among the dead, and who can appear and disappear at will, remains a man, who consorts naturally with other men, who walks and talks and eats as they do, and who is raised and exalted as a man (A. $1^{3f., 10f.}$; $2^{22f.}$; 17^{31}).

A further feature of this chapter is the unusually large number of textual variants, except in vv. 13–35, which is notably free from them. These are in vv. 5, 12, 36, 40, 51, 52. The choice is generally between a longer text attested by most authorities, and a shorter text attested by the Western textual tradition. Each has to be examined on its own, but some scholars opt in all cases for the longer text (e.g. Jeremias, *Euchar-*

istic Words, pp. 149ff.); and this is sometimes linked with the suggestion that in his composition of this chapter Luke was in touch with resurrection traditions also represented in John 20. Other scholars opt in all cases for the shorter Western text (see RSV margin, and Creed, ad loc.), and explain the longer text as due to scribal harmonization with other accounts, especially John's, with a view to filling out, and strengthening, Luke's sequence of events. This could have taken place in the second century, when there is evidence that the resurrection was a subject of considerable controversy in the churches. In the closing verses of the Gospel and the opening verses of A., changes could have been made when, for the purpose of inclusion in the Canon, Luke–Acts was made into two separate volumes, each to be complete in itself.

24 *But on the first day of the week, at early dawn, they went to the tomb, taking the spices which they had prepared. ²And they found the stone rolled away from the tomb, ³but when they went in they did not find the body.* ★
⁴*While they were perplexed about this, behold, two men stood by them in dazzling apparel; ⁵and as they were frightened and bowed their faces to the ground, the men said to them, 'Why do you seek the living among the dead?†
⁶Remember how he told you, while he was still in Galilee, ⁷that the Son of man must be delivered into the hands of sinful men, and be crucified, and on the third day rise.' ⁸And they remembered his words, ⁹and returning from the tomb they told all this to the eleven and to all the rest. ¹⁰Now it was Mary Magdalene and Joanna and Mary the mother of James and the other women with them who told this to the apostles; ¹¹but these words seemed to them an idle tale, and they did not believe them.*‡

★ Other ancient authorities add *of the Lord Jesus*
† Other ancient authorities add *He is not here, but has risen*
‡ Other ancient authorities add v. 12, *But Peter rose and ran to the tomb; stooping and looking in, he saw the linen cloths by themselves; and he went home wondering at what had happened*

This story presents special problems of origin and purpose. Discovery of the tomb as empty is not mentioned in any kerygmatic statement of the passion and resurrection in the NT. Nor is it necessarily implied in references to Jesus' burial (e.g. in I Cor. 15⁴; Rom. 6⁴), which are probably to be taken with the statement of his death as underlining it – 'dead and buried'. Nor is it likely to have been attached to any story of an appearance of the risen Lord as its prelude, or to a sequence of such stories. For these would seem to have been told as self-contained units, and to have been made into a sequence, and a continuation of the passion narrative, only by the evangelists. The story of the empty tomb would also seem to have been a self-contained unit, which the evangelists, apart from Mark, use as a bridge between the death and burial of Jesus on the one hand, and such stories of appearances as they intend to record on the other. What purpose was the story designed to serve when told on its own? This question is especially acute in view of the fact that the testimony of women was so little regarded in Judaism, and the effect of the discovery made by these particular women was bewilderment and fear; whereas the witness to appearances of the risen Lord is mostly that of male apostolic figures, whose hesitation and doubt was overcome. Was the story originally one form of proclaiming the resurrection faith alongside stories of post-resurrection appearances? This question is raised by the problematic ending of Mark's gospel. If Mark 16¹⁻⁸ was intended as a conclusion, then Mark's (the earliest?) version of this story could have been, not as in the other gospels a (necessary) prelude to stories of appearances, but the vehicle – in Mark the only vehicle – of announcing the resurrection. If so, on what principle, and for what purpose, was it brought together with stories of appearances? In the view of some the story emerged into prominence in the tradition only at a later stage, either to counter Jewish charges that the Christian message was based on a fraud, the disciples having removed the body (cf. Matt. 27⁶²–28¹⁵; John 20¹⁻¹³?), or to emphasize against Gentile misunderstanding that the Christian proclamation was not of something purely 'spiritual' in the sense of non-material (see Ellis, pp. 273ff., 'A Special Note on the Empty Tomb').

A further question raised by the story in any form is of what conception of resurrection underlay it that for that to have taken place the grave had to be empty. In what was probably the earliest form of resurrection belief in Judaism, the hope of the martyrs is for the restoration of the earthly body so as to participate in God's kingdom on earth (II Macc. 7¹⁴⁻³⁸; 14⁴⁶). This requires an empty grave, but is clearly not the conception here, as the risen Jesus is not expected to be Lord in a kingdom of God on earth. A later form of resurrection belief is a hybrid of Jewish and Greek thought, where the souls of the righteous go to God as immortal (cf. Wisd. 3^1). This does not require anything other of the body than that it corrupts in the grave (cf. Jubilees 23^{31}, 'Their bones shall rest in the earth, and their spirits shall have much joy'). A third conception is that at resurrection the dead are all given bodies for the purpose of identification at the judgment; but these are only temporary, and in the case of those who pass through the judgment they are transformed into bodies of glory for a heavenly existence (II Baruch 50–51). This conception may lie behind the story of the empty tomb and some of the stories of resurrection appearances. That is, the Lord's body is absent from the tomb because it has become the substance of his new identity as the risen one both with God and with man. (This is not what Paul meant by the 'spiritual body' [I Cor. 15^{44}], or 'the body of glory' [Phil. 3^{21}]). It implies that Jesus' resurrection state was a temporary one and for a limited purpose. In L–A, where Jesus ascends in his risen body (A. 1$^{3-11}$), no reference is made to any further transformation into the body of glory, in which he exists with God and is seen by men in vision (A. 7$^{55-56}$; 9^3).

Luke has been variously judged here to have been solely dependent on Mark, or to have revised with help from Mark, either a non-Markan version (L) which was part of a continuous non-Markan passion narrative (so Easton, pp. 357ff.), or an isolated tradition which also underlies John 20$^{1-10}$ (Leaney, pp. 28ff., Jeremias, *Eucharistic Words*, pp. 149ff.). Judgment on the last is affected by whether v. 12, where the similarities with John are close, is to be read or not. Apart from this verse the scope and sequence of events of both versions are identical. The differences could be explained by (i) the need to improve Mark's vigorous but also rather rough account; (ii) the need to remove the obscurity of a message of future appearance in Galilee and of the women's silence from terror; and (iii) the need to change it from a mysterious announcement of resurrection into a transition to, and basis of, subsequent appearances of the risen Lord in or near Jerusalem. Easton labels the following words and expressions Lukan – *behold, men, stood by* (v. 4), *how* (v. 6), *words* (*rhēmata*, v. 8), *returning, told* (v. 9), *with* (*sun*, v. 10), *words, to them* (*enōpion* = 'in their presence'), *an idle tale* (v. 11). To these could well be added: the repetition in vv. 2 and 3 of the same word *find* in a slightly different sense, a Lukan characteristic; *in dazzling apparel* (v. 4, of an angel, cf. A. 10^{30}); *as they were frightened* (the adjective *emphobos* and the verb *ginesthai* + v. 37, A. 10⁴ in reaction to an angel, A. 24²⁵; Rev. 11¹³); *all, the rest* (v. 9); *the other women* (*hai loipai* = 'the rest, v. 10). There is no compelling reason to see the words translated *prepared* (v. 1) *perplexed* (v. 4) and *remember* (v. 6) as evidence of a non-Markan source, and Easton's judgment (p. 358) that the style of vv. 4–5 – the construction 'it came to pass' followed by the dative of the infinitive and by 'and behold' – 'is too Semitic to be due to Luke', is plainly erroneous, as it is with this construction that Luke revises Mark in 5¹². Luke's version may then be accounted for linguistically as a revision of Mark's.

ಬಬ

In Luke, as in Mark (though not in Matthew), the purpose of the women's journey is to complete by embalming a previously hurried burial. All English translations, however, miss the continuity here by placing a full stop after *the commandment* (23⁵⁶), and beginning a new paragraph at 24¹. Whereas in Mark the two prerequisites of the story – the women's observation of the tomb and their preparation of unguents – are separated by the intervening sabbath, in Luke, by a different time sequence, they are elegantly brought together in *they went to the tomb, taking the spices which they had prepared*. The narrative thus flows on without break in the single sentence, 23⁵⁶ᵇ–24¹, the particles *men . . . de* (= 'on the one hand . . . on the other hand', not translated in RSV) making a contrast between *on the sabbath* and *on the first day of the week*.

on the first day of the week, at early dawn: The time references in Mark 16¹⁻² are typically pleonastic; as elsewhere Luke reduces them to a single statement. *on the first day of the week* occurs only here in Luke, and is taken from Mark 16². To this is added the literary *orthrou* (+ A. 5²¹; John 8²) *batheōs* = 'in the small hours', 'at first light'.

the tomb: Here *to mnēma*, as in the corresponding Mark 16², though in v. 2 *mnēmeion*, as in the corresponding Mark 16³.

2–3
It is necessary to take these two verses together, since they form a single sentence, smoothly constructed around a characteristic Lukan use of the same word in a slightly different sense – they *found* the stone rolled away . . . they did not *find* the body. The conversation in Mark 16³ and the parenthesis in Mark 16⁴, are popular in style; and while they heighten the miracle they heighten also the foolishness of the women in setting out if there was no hope of moving the stone; and in Mark 16⁵⁻⁶ the story takes a strange turn when the women, on entering the tomb, encounter 'a young man sitting on the right

side, dressed in a white robe'; that the tomb is empty is only implied by his words. In Luke the stone, not previously mentioned, is simply assumed (as in John 20^{1}), and the miracle of its having been rolled away (*apokulizein*, as in Mark 16^{3}; Matt. 28^{2}, the only other instances of the word in the NT) is simply stated in passing. The angels are not yet mentioned; what is immediately and explicitly stated as the chief point of the story, and as the basis of all that is to follow, is the absence of the body. Most mss have 'of the Lord Jesus' after *the body*. This designation would be unique in the Gospel, though it is found in A. 1^{21}; 4^{33} in connection with the resurrection. If genuine here it would mark the transition from the earthly to the risen Jesus, 'the Lord' being a title associated with the resurrection (cf. Rom. 10^{9}). It is, however, omitted by the Western text – D a b e ff^{2} l r^{1} – and by RSV and NEB. It is not easy to suggest a reason for its excision, and it is more readily explained as a formal and reverential addition to soften the harshness of *the body*. The reading of a few mss 'of Jesus' would be explicable on the same basis – cf. 23^{52} 'the body of Jesus' with 23^{53} 'it', and 24^{23} 'his body'.

4
While they were perplexed about this: It is by way of the women's perplexity (*aporein*, a classical word = 'to be at a loss', or, more strongly, 'to be in consternation' + A. 25^{20}; Mark 6^{20}; John 13^{22}; II Cor. 4^{8}; Gal. 4^{20}) at the absence of the body, and not, as in Mark, through their entrance into the tomb, that the transition is made to the angelic appearance. It is not clear whether what follows takes place inside or outside the tomb.

behold, two men stood by them in dazzling apparel: The 'young man . . . dressed in a white robe' (Mark 16^{5}) is an enigmatic figure for such an important moment; it is not certain whether he is meant to be an angel. In Matt. 28^{2-5} he is replaced by the official 'angel of the Lord'; here by *two men*, who *stood by* (*ephistanai*, apart from I Thess. 5^{3}; II Tim. $4^{2,\ 6}$ confined to L–A in the NT; in 2^{9}; A. 12^{7} it is used of the (sudden) manifestation of a previously invisible supernatural being). Their apparel, described as *dazzling* (*astraptein* + 17^{24}), makes it likely that they are intended as angels (v. 23 makes it certain; a comparison of A. $10^{3,\ 22}$; 11^{13} with A. 10^{30} shows that a man in a shining garment is for Luke a mode of description of an angel). They speak in unison. Some see here an instance of a concern for twofold witness which they detect throughout Luke's Gospel; but it is the women who are here to be the witnesses, and the duplication of the angels may be a conventional trait to heighten the effect (cf. A. 1^{10}, where the same pair may be intended, and A. $9^{38f.}$ for two men as messengers; John 20^{12} is different, as they have special positions at the head and feet).

5a
as they were frightened and bowed their faces to the ground: In place of the women's

amazement (Mark 16⁵), but perhaps not without reference to their fear (Mark 16⁸), Luke underlines the numinous character of the moment of divine revelation by an elaborate description of their reverential awe. For fear in this sense, cf. 1¹²ᶠ·, ³⁰; 2⁹ᶠ·, and in combination with 'astonishment' Mark 16⁸, cf. 5²⁶. There are various expressions for obeisance in a similar situation, such as 'to bow to the ground' (Gen. 18²), or 'to fall on one's face' (5¹²; 17¹⁶; Josh. 5¹⁴); Luke's *bowed their faces to the ground* is highly distinctive, and appears to be his own creation.

5b–8

The angelic utterance is the crux of the narrative in the synoptics. For here is the voice of the 'interpreting angel', a familiar figure in apocalyptic literature, and it is through his voice, and not, as in the passion narrative, by the use of OT language, that the divine meaning of the event is disclosed. This is done in three (two?) stages.

(i) In all three gospels the women's pursuit (in John 20¹⁵ Mary's pursuit) is referred to as 'seeking', the object of the search being in Mark 'Jesus the Nazarene, the crucified', in Matthew 'Jesus the crucified', in John 'the Lord'. In Luke, where Jesus is nowhere called the 'crucified', the reference is not to him by name, but by means of a general question, which is also a rebuke, '*Why do you seek the living among the dead?*' Their coming at all to embalm, and their distress at the absence of the body, are incompatible with what they should have been expecting as disciples. This incompatibility is expressed almost proverbially; cf. Isa. 8¹⁹, 'Should they consult the dead on behalf of the living?', and the words of Moses and Aaron to Pharaoh in Exod. rabba 5, 'Fool, are the dead to be sought among the living and the living among the dead?' (quoted in SB II, p. 269). There, however, 'the living' means those alive on earth; here it means those alive beyond death. This could be Luke's own formulation in view of his emphasis on resurrection as 'life' (cf. his additions to Mark in 20³⁵, ³⁸), and on Jesus as the one who 'is alive' (v. 23; A. 1³; 3¹⁵; 5²⁰; 25¹⁹). For the thought, cf. II Cor. 13⁴; Heb. 7²⁵; I Peter 3¹⁸; Rev. 1¹⁸.

(ii) The second stage is an explicit announcement by the angels of the resurrection, 'He is not here, but has risen'. This, however, is uncertain in the text. It is absent from most mss of the Western text (see Tasker, *The Greek New Testament*, p. 424). Marcion has 'he is risen'; e has 'he is risen from the dead'. It is omitted by RSV and NEB. A decision here is difficult. It is not easy to see why the words should have been dropped from the text, and they could be explained as a scribal assimilation to Mark 16⁶, or more likely Matt. 28⁶. On the other hand, they are in a different position from Mark's – after the inspection of the tomb, not as an invitation to enter it – and the different word order from Mark, though not from Matthew, makes a neat chiasmus with *Why do you seek the living among the dead?*, which is more likely to have come from Luke than from a scribe. It could be said that a statement of the resurrection is required at this point to prepare for the rehearsal of Jesus' prophecy in v. 7; but it could also be held that the question in v. 5 is by implication such a statement; cf. v. 23, where the resurrection is conveyed by the words 'that he was alive'.

(iii) As in Mark/Matthew the angel's words end with a reminder of a previous prophecy of Jesus, though the differences here are fundamental. In Mark 16^7 the prophecy is that spoken in Mark 14^{28} (omitted by Luke), and it refers to what is still future, viz. that after resurrection Jesus will go before the disciples (i.e. either precede them or lead them) to Galilee, where they will 'see' him, perhaps in his parousia glory. This was quite unsuitable for Luke. It made Galilee the locus of the manifestation of the risen Lord, and of his future action with respect to his disciples. For Luke this is exclusively Jerusalem (v. 33, v. 49; A. 1^4). Also, in Mark, the promised manifestation was such as to reduce the women to silent terror; whereas in Luke the resurrection of Jesus was natural, intelligible and to be received with joy (vv. 25–27, 44–46, 41). Hence the angelic message now becomes an injunction to recall a different prophecy of Jesus, which they can be presumed to have heard as disciples from Galilee. This does not contain any message for others, and it no longer points forward, since it has now been fulfilled without remainder. It is introduced by the formula *Remember how he told you*, which is similar to that in 22^{61}; A. 11^{16}; 20^{35} and in early Christian tradition for citing 'the words of the Lord Jesus'; and it is followed by the corresponding *And they remembered his words*. The form of the prophecy (*how, hōs* = 'in this manner', rather than *hoti* = 'that') is a compound of the previous formal predictions in the Gospel of the passion and resurrection, taken from Mark – *that the Son of man* (cf. 9$^{22, 44}$; 18^{31}) *must be* (cf. 9^{22}) *delivered* (cf. 9^{44}; 18^{32}) *into the hands of sinful men* (cf. 9^{44}) *and be crucified* (cf. Matt. 20^{19}; 26^2), *and on the third day rise* (cf. 9^{22}; 18^{33}). For *sinful* (omitted by D it), cf. Mark 14^{41} (omitted by Luke); it probably means here the Jews, who in A. 2^{38} are exhorted to repent of the crucifixion. These predictions were not accepted at the time of their utterance (9^{45}; 18^{34}), but now the absence of the body of the crucified points to their fulfilment, and they interpret the absence of the body in terms of the resurrection of the crucified one. That is, resurrection to glory and power involves the removal by transformation of the physical body. Easton (p. 358) sees here a combination by Luke of two incompatible traditions from Mark and L; but the words *while he was still in Galilee* are gratuitous as an introduction to the prophecy, and are a tell-tale sign that Luke is solely occupied in revising Mark's text, from which he gets the reference to Galilee, and in removing the obstacle to his own presentation of the resurrection appearances in Jerusalem. By this revision he neutralizes the Markan (and Matthaean) apocalyptic understanding of the resurrection, and makes room for his own narrative to go forward in accordance with a different conception of the relation of the risen Lord to his church and to history.

9

In the other gospels the climax of the story is a message concerning the future in the light of the resurrection, which, however, is not delivered in Mark (16⁸), is presumed to have been delivered in Matthew (28⁷, ¹⁰, ¹⁶), and is stated to have been delivered in John (20¹⁸). Owing to Luke's re-drafting of the angelic utterance in vv. 6–7 there is no such message to be delivered from the Lord here, or in vv. 18–35 (any message about the future is delivered by the Lord himself, vv. 44ff.). But it was natural to Luke's understanding that the events so far – the empty tomb, the angelic announcement that Jesus was alive, and the connection of this with his own words – should be reported to the apostles and their companions, who in ch. 24 and A. 1 constitute a kind of Christian headquarters (cf. vv. 33–35). The women's report thus becomes their common possession (cf. vv. 22f.). *the rest* is a loose term for an unspecified number of men and women, presumably Galilean disciples. In A. 1¹⁵ they number, along with the apostles and the Lord's family, about a hundred and twenty. Together with the eleven they form the nucleus of the future church, and they appear only in Luke in the gospel accounts of the resurrection. This is in anticipation of the story in A. *they told all this . . . to all the rest* exhibits the typical Lukan use of *all*, but in this context it could be a deliberate counter to Mark 16⁸, 'they said nothing to anyone'.

10

The story would reach a satisfactory ending with v. 9, or with v. 9 followed by v. 11, and it is not easy to account for the clumsiness of v. 10, both grammatically, and as an unnecessary repetition, which suggests either that there is a distinction between the eleven (v. 9) and the apostles (v. 10), or that the apostles are the principal recipients of the report. The sentence may be punctuated to produce either (i) 'And they (the women previously mentioned) were Mary Magdalene and Joanna and Mary the mother of James: and the other women with them told this to the apostles' (but it hardly makes sense that the named women did not report), or (ii), 'And they were Mary Magdalene . . . and the other women with them. They told (asyndeton) . . . the apostles'. The variant readings omitting 'they were' or providing 'who' before *told* (so RSV) are attempts to make the sentence grammatical. Its awkwardness may be due to its being a 'seam' joining the incident of the empty tomb, both to the previous passion and burial narratives, and to the narratives of appearances to apostolic figures that are to follow.

Of the group of women disciples from Galilee who have been in attendance at the crucifixion (23⁴⁹), who have witnessed the burial (23⁵⁵), and who could be expected to recall what Jesus had said in Galilee (24⁶), three are now named, somewhat belatedly, in their role of reporting witnesses (cf. Mark 15⁴⁰, 'There were women looking on, among whom were . . .'). Two of these, Mary Magdalene and Mary the mother of James, correspond with two of the three named in Mark 15⁴⁰; 16¹, and with the pair named in Mark 15⁴⁷. If Mary the mother of James in Mark is a cryptic reference to the mother of Jesus (cf. Mark 15⁴⁰, 'Mary the mother of James the younger and Joses' with Mark 6³, 'the son of Mary, brother of James and Joses') Luke does not recognize it to be so, since he includes 'the mother of Jesus' as such among the believing women in A. 1¹⁴. The third woman in Mark, the otherwise unknown Salome (= the mother of the sons of Zebedee?, Matt. 27⁵⁶), becomes in Luke Joanna, presumably the wife of Herod's steward, who is singled out together with Mary Magdalene and Susanna in the group of ministering Galilean women disciples in the special Lukan tradition in 8³. What the number was of *the other women with them* is not stated; but whereas the burial and visit to the tomb were in Mark the concern of two (three?) women, in Matthew of two and in John of one, the reader is here made aware that a considerable group has been involved. This may be to increase by force of numbers the weight of their testimony as women, in this case as the female disciples of Jesus, to whom Luke has drawn attention earlier (8²ᶠ·).

After the mention of the whole body of disciples as having received the women's report (v. 9, preparing for v. 13, vv. 22–23), the apostles are now singled out as its recipients. This accords with Luke's emphasis on the apostles as the core of the church, and on them as pre-eminently witnesses to the resurrection (cf. v. 33; A. 1²¹⁻²⁶; 4³³; 5¹⁷⁻³²).

11

At this juncture the report is met by the apostles with unbelief and ridicule. The verse is plainly editorial. The phraseology is Lukan in *these words* (*ta rhēmata tauta*, cf. A. 5²⁰; 10⁴⁴; 13⁴²), *seemed* (*phainein*, in the intellectual sense only here in the NT), *to them* (*enōpion* = 'in their sight', cf. A. 4¹⁹; 6⁵), *an idle tale* (*lēros* + +, a literary word, in the LXX only IV Macc. 5¹¹), *did not believe* (*apistein*, of disbelieving specific statements + v. 41, A. 28²⁴). Such a reaction is not intended to depreciate the empty tomb in comparison with the appearances, but, as in other references to doubt in the resurrection traditions, to magnify the miracle of divine action by setting it over against human incredulity. It does indicate, however, that the empty tomb, even when interpreted by heavenly messengers, was not regarded as a proof of resurrection. As with the appearances sight has to be quickened by belief. But the picture is somewhat blurred; for it is not clear whether *they did not believe them* means that the apostles thought the women's story was the result of hallucinations, or that they accepted the story but not its implications for belief in the resurrection. Nor is it clear whether the women themselves accepted these implications of their own story.

12

But Peter rose and ran to the tomb; stooping and looking in he saw the linen cloths (lying, some mss, *by themselves*, some mss, *by themselves lying*, some mss, *lying by themselves*, some mss); and *he went home wondering* (or, he went away wondering to himself) *at what had happened.*

John 20$^{3-10}$:
Peter then came out with the other disciple, and they went toward *the tomb.* They both *ran*, but the other disciple outran Peter and reached the tomb first; *and stooping* to look in, *he saw the linen cloths* lying, but he did not go in. Then Simon Peter came, following him, and went into the tomb; he saw the linen cloths lying, and the napkin, which had been on his head, not lying with the linen cloths, but rolled up in a place *by itself* . . . Then the disciples *went back to their homes.*

Verse 12 is read by the majority of texts, including p^{75}. It is omitted by D, the Old Latin mss a b d e l r^1, Marcion, some mss of the Palestinian Syriac, the Arabic Diatessaron and by Eusebius in half of his references. It is put in the margin in RSV and NEB. Its presence or absence makes some difference to ch. 24 as a whole. Without it vv. 1–11 are self-contained, and the empty tomb is connected directly with the women alone, and with the disciples only indirectly. With it the disciples, in the person of Peter, become witnesses to it as well as to the appearances, and a smoother sequence of events is created. Without it there is nothing in the previous narrative for v. 24b to refer to; on the other hand it is in contradiction with 24b (Peter alone, and not 'Some of those who were with us', went to the tomb). This contradiction has been suggested as the reason why the verse was subsequently omitted from the text; but it could be argued that such a clumsy contradiction is more likely to have been the work of a scribe than of Luke himself. The verbal agreements with John (indicated by the italics above) have been given three different explanations.

(i) Luke wrote the verse, and it was later used by John. Against this is that some of the common language is characteristic of John rather than of Luke – *linen cloths* (*othonia*, cf. John 19^{40}), *stoop* (*parakuptein*, cf. John 20^{11}), *he saw* (the historical present, very rare in L–A, comparatively frequent in John); the variant readings in relation to *lying, by themselves* indicate that at some stage Luke's text has been further assimilated to John's. Even in *wondering at what had happened* (*thaumazōn to gegonos*), which could be said to be characteristic of Luke, the evidence suggests that Luke would have been more likely to use the verb 'to wonder' with the preposition *epi* and the dative (as in 2^{33}; 4^{22}; 9^{43}; 20^{26}; A. 3^{12}) than with a direct object in the accusative (as here).

(ii) Luke and John have used a common tradition of the empty tomb story in which disciples (Peter) were connected with the tomb, each doing so in his own way. Luke has combined it with Mark's story, while John has incorporated the beloved disciple into it (so Leaney, pp. 28ff., and others). Against this, apart from the Johannine character of the language referred to above, the verse would be the only evidence for such a common tradition to be found in Luke's version, which is otherwise based on Mark's, and it follows awkwardly after 'an idle tale', giving the impression of something tacked on.

(iii) The verse is a later harmonizing addition to Luke's text, formed largely out of language borrowed from John 20$^{3-10}$, with the object of improving the transition to the narrative of appearances, and of bringing Peter (cf. v. 34) into relation to the tomb (so Brown, *The Gospel according to John*, pp. 1000ff., and others). This is the most likely explanation of the presence of the verse here, and of its clumsiness.

24$^{13-35}$ THE APPEARANCE ON THE WAY TO
AND AT EMMAUS

13 *That very day two of them were going to a village named Emmaus, about seven miles* from Jerusalem,* 14*and talking with each other about all these things that had happened.* 15*While they were talking and discussing together, Jesus himself drew near and went with them.* 16*But their eyes were kept from recognizing him.* 17*And he said to them, 'What is this conversation which you are holding with each other as you walk?' And they stood still, looking sad.* 18*Then one of them, named Cleopas, answered him, 'Are you the only visitor to Jerusalem who does not know the things that have happened there in these days?'* 19*And he said to them, 'What things?' And they said to him, 'Concerning Jesus of Nazareth, who was a prophet mighty in deed and word before God and all the people,* 20*and how our chief priests and rulers delivered him up to be condemned to death, and crucified him.* 21*But we had hoped that he was the one to redeem Israel. Yes, and besides all this, it is now the third day since this happened.* 22*Moreover, some women of our company amazed us. They were at the tomb early in the morning* 23*and did not find his body; and they came back saying that they had even seen a vision of angels, who said that he was alive.* 24*Some of those who were with us went to the tomb, and found it just as the women had said; but him they did not see.'* 25*And he said to them, 'O foolish men, and slow of heart to believe all that the prophets have spoken!* 26*Was it not necessary that the Christ should suffer these things and enter into his glory?'* 27*And beginning with Moses and all the prophets, he interpreted to them in all the scriptures the things concerning himself.*

28*So they drew near to the village to which they were going. He appeared to be going further,* 29*but they constrained him, saying, 'Stay with us, for it is toward evening and the day is now far spent.' So he went in to stay with* them. 30 *When he was at table with them, he took the bread and blessed, and broke it, and gave it to them.* 31 *And their eyes were opened and they recognized him; and he vanished out of their sight.* 32 *They said to each other, 'Did not our hearts burn within us while he talked to us on the road, while he opened to us the scriptures?'* 33 *And they rose that same hour and returned to Jerusalem; and they found the eleven gathered together and those who were with them,* 34 *who said, 'The Lord has risen indeed, and has appeared to Simon!'* 35 *Then they told what had happened on the road, and how he was known to them in the breaking of the bread.*

* Greek *sixty stadia*; some ancient authorities read *a hundred and sixty stadia*

Luke, in contrast to Matthew and John, has no resurrection appearance at the site of the tomb, but, like them, has an appearance to individuals prior to that which constitutes the risen Lord's authoritative commission to the corporate body of disciples (apostles). Since stories of appearances are likely to have been independent of one another in the tradition, and to have lacked any chronological connections, the placing of this story first after the visit to the tomb will have been Luke's decision. It is a natural one, since the appearance to the corporate body, and their commissioning, must clearly come last, and bring any sequence of appearances to an end. This story does not correspond to any of the appearances listed in the traditional formula in I Cor. 15⁵⁻⁷. It contains no reference to the future, nor any message to be delivered to others. It is primarily concerned to establish the theological bases of the resurrection faith for the thought and experience of the church.[c] As with other 'appearance' stories it is complete in itself, with *kai idou* = 'And behold' (not translated in RSV) as a beginning, and with v. 32 as a retrospective conclusion. Only when followed by vv. 33ff. does it become the basis for a further appearance, or does the lateness of the hour present difficulties. In its length, however, in the protracted character of the narrative, in its dramatic quality and its artistry, it is unique. For this reason it proves difficult to categorize. Dibelius classifies it as a legend – without vv. 21b, 22–24 a legend 'in pure form' (*Tradition,*

c 'It is a thoroughly polished literary creation, and embodies the most comprehensive "philosophy of the Resurrection" in the New Testament' (H. Anderson, 'The Easter Witness of the Evangelists', in *The New Testament in Historical and Contemporary Perspective*, ed. H. Anderson and W. Barclay, Oxford 1965, p. 47.

p. 191); so also does Bultmann (*History*, p. 286). But legend, if defined as 'a narrative of a sainted person', hardly covers the theological core of the story, where the risen Lord travels incognito with disciples, to whom he interprets scripture with reference to the suffering and risen messiah. A. Ehrhardt classifies it as myth, i.e. a story concerned with the manifestation of the divine, and in particular as an epiphany.[d] As pointers to this he sees the fact that the disciples' eyes are 'overpowered', that Jesus 'vanishes', and that he is referred to as *autos* = 'he himself' in giving divine instruction. But features generally associated with epiphany, such as a heavenly countenance or supernatural phenomena, are notably absent, and an important characteristic of the story is that, except at the very end, it is entirely human, and at the furthest remove from any vision of the Lord in glory. There is undoubtedly an element in it of the theme of 'entertaining angels unawares' (cf. Heb. 13²), of which OT examples are Gen. 18¹ff., Judg. 13, and a pagan example the legend of Baucis and Philemon, who entertained Jupiter and Minerva.[e] But while this element provides a framework for the story at its beginning, it is not responsible for the greater part of its contents. Grundmann (p. 442) classifies it as a 'Recognition' story. This was a familiar genre in the ancient world, in which characters who have long been separated meet by chance, recognize each other, and then engage in talk (cf. the third-century? Christian work the *Clementine Recognitions*). But here the element of recognition is reduced to a minimum, coinciding with the moment of disappearance, and it does not lead on, as generally in this genre, to reverence, or conversation or instruction, but only to a retrospective reflection on what the Lord had said when still unrecognized. An important element in the story is the dramatic irony whereby the reader knows, as the two travellers do not, that what they tell of the destruction of their hopes is in fact the fulfilment of them, and that the exegete of the OT is the Lord, who is speaking about himself. This is not, however, without a certain artificiality, and the suggestion has been made that originally the story was shorter, and primarily concerned with the presence and knowledge of the Lord in the breaking of the bread, and that Luke expanded it out of his special

---

d 'The Disciples of Emmaus', *NTS* 10, 1963–64, pp. 182–201.

e See A. B. Cook, *Zeus* II.2, Cambridge 1925, p. 1096, for the worship of Zeus the Suppliant as resting on the primitive idea that a stranger appearing suddenly might be a god on his travels.

concern with the OT basis of the gospel.[f] But this latter theme so dominates the story that it is difficult to envisage what an earlier form which had its climax in vv. 30–31 would have looked like, or to establish such on linguistic grounds.[g]

Easton (p. 362), and others, have observed that the story is written with wonderful grace and charm, though he is probably incorrect in putting so much of this down to the author of the source L, from which he thinks Luke obtained it. For of the expressions he cites as evidence of L rather than Luke, the construction of *egeneto* = 'it came to pass' with the articular infinitive (as in v. 15, *While they were talking*, and v. 30, *When he was at table*) is used by Luke in revising Mark at 18[35]; 5[12], and the only other instances in L–A of *engizein eis* for 'to draw near' (v. 15) are in 18[35], 19[29], where he takes it over from Mark. *went with them* (v. 15, *sunporeuesthai*) in its only other occurrences (7[11]; 14[25]) introduces a story, and could well be from Luke's hand. The contrast between rulers and people in v. 20 is characteristic of the Gospel and A.; *glory* (v. 26) in this personal sense is taken over from Mark in 9[26], and is added to Mark in 9[32]; *beginning* (v. 27) is a typically Lukan use of this participle; *blessed* (v. 30) is traditional language (cf. 9[16] from Mark). As for the rest of the language A. R. C. Leaney finds the story 'a treasury of Luke's septuagintal style and vocabulary'.[h] It should be noted, however, that there is also a strong literary flavour, and a high concentration of words that are either absent from the LXX, or are so rare there as hardly to qualify as septuagintal. Of the first are *discussing* (v. 15, *sunzētein*), *slow of heart* (v. 25, *bradeis tē kardiā* = 'slow-witted'), and *vanished* (v. 31, *aphantos*). Of the second are *talking* (v. 15, *homilein* = 'to converse' + A. 20[11]; 24[26]), *conversation* (v. 17, *antiballein* = 'to have an altercation' ++), *looking sad* (v. 17, *skuthrōpos* = 'sullen' + Matt. 6[16]), *foolish* (v. 25, *anoētos*, not elsewhere in the gospels and A.), *interpreted* (v. 27, *diermēneuein* + A. 9[36] and four times in Paul), *appeared to be* (v. 28, *prospoieisthai* ++), *constrained* (v. 29, *parabiazesthai* + A. 16[15]), *is far spent* (v. 29 *kataklinein*, only Luke in the NT), *burn* (v. 32, of

---

f See P. Schubert, 'The Structure and Significance of Luke 24', in *Neutestamentliche Studien für Rudolf Bultmann*, ed. W. Eltester, *BZNW* 21, 1954, pp. 165ff.

g But see Alsup, *Post-Resurrection Appearance Stories*, pp. 190–4, who detects, though tentatively, an original story made up of vv. 13, 15b, 16, 28–31, Luke's redaction being traced in vv. 15a, 17–23, 32, 33–35.

h 'The Resurrection Narratives in Luke XXIV.12–53', *NTS* 2, 1955–56, pp. 110–14.

the heart only here in the NT). The dialogue in vv. 17–27 is in good Greek, but in the narrative, 13–16, 28–31, there is an excessive use of *autos* = 'he', which is Semitic. This may be due to the exigencies of a narrative in which one of the characters cannot be referred to by name since he must remain incognito; but Ehrhardt (*NTS* 10, p. 186) detects here a deliberate emphasis on the authority of the Lord as divine instructor, somewhat after the manner of the Pythagorean school of philosophers with their well-known expression *autos ephā* = 'He (the Master) used to say'. As significant as the undoubted charm of the story is its passion, which is conveyed by a certain vehemence in the language, not always brought out in translation. Thus, the two disciples are forcefully prevented from recognizing Jesus (v. 16); they argue heatedly (v. 17); they are brought to a standstill with glowering faces (v. 17); they ask a rude question (v. 18) and are rudely answered (v. 25); and when he pretends to go further they forcibly restrain him (vv. 28–29); their hearts burn (v. 32).

 app

13–14
Luke begins the story by linking it firmly with the preceding one by (i) *That very day* (a Lukan expression), i.e. the same day as the visit to the tomb, and (ii) *two of them*, i.e. of *all the rest* (v. 9), and not of *the apostles* (vv. 10–11), since the one named (v. 18) is not an apostle; this indicates that v. 9 ends the previous story, and that vv. 10–11 are adjuncts. This then is to be the first of the appearances. That there are two is probably not dictated here by the requirement of two at least for reliable witness (19^{29}); it is so that a conversation, upon which everything hangs, may take place. *were going* is the periphrastic tense of continuous action, and so provides the setting of the whole story, which falls into two unequal parts – the journey and dialogue, and the arrival and meal. No reason is given for the journey. If, as has been suggested, *Stay with us* (v. 29) means 'stay at our home', they would be going home, and would not be Galilean disciples. But that is immaterial. What really sets the stage is their conversation. They converse about *all these things that had happened* (*sumbainein* = 'to take place', a very common classical, Hellenistic and LXX word, but found only eight times in the NT, only here in this Gospel and three times in A.). This not only makes a further link with what has gone before, but also opens the way for its rehearsal, confirmation and interpretation.

a village named Emmaus, about seven miles from Jerusalem: The location is uncertain, as is also the distance, some mss reading 'sixty stades' (the *seven miles* in RSV, a stade being approximately 607 feet), and others reading 'a hundred and sixty stades', i.e. eighteen miles. Emmaus has been identified with el Qubeiheh, seven miles north-west of Jerusalem; but this is based on a report of Crusaders (1099) that there was a fort there called Castellum Emmaus. Excavations have unearthed a first-century village. An alternative identification is with 'Amwas, twenty miles west-north-west of Jerusalem on the road to Jaffa, which is probably the Emmaus mentioned more than once in I Maccabees (e.g. 3⁴⁰), and by Josephus (*BJ* 2.71; as burnt down in the Jewish War, *Ant.* 17.291). It was rebuilt as Nicopolis, and as such was identified with Emmaus here by Eusebius in his Onomasticon. Another suggestion is the modern village of Kaloniye, taken as an equivalent of the Latin *colonia*, and identified with the Ammaous which, according to Josephus (*BJ* 7.217), was a *colonia* of Vespasian. This is four miles west of Jerusalem. Nowhere else in the synoptists is a location fixed by reference to its distance from Jerusalem (cf. John 11¹⁸; II Macc. 11⁵; 12²⁹), and this could be an important point for Luke, for whom Jerusalem is the centre of events connected with the risen Lord and the future church.

15–16
The construction in v. 15 – lit. 'It came to pass during their talking and discussing (and – some mss) Jesus (himself – some mss) drew near' – is used here with some force, since the reader knows that it is the subject of their conversation who now overtakes and joins the two disciples. At this point the story is distinctive among the resurrection traditions in two respects, which are related. (i) Here only the risen Lord enters on the scene in entirely natural circumstances as a man performing normal human actions among men. He does not first decsare himself before giving instructions, and he is not recognized for who he is until the end. (ii) In 'recognition' scenes the characters have generally been separated long enough for them not to be able to recognize each other. This cannot apply here; indeed what they are talking about happened the day before yesterday. So a special reason for non-recognition has to be supplied. Elsewhere this can be some initial difference in the Lord himself, which sets the scene for his self-manifestation as the risen one – he appears despite closed doors (John 20¹⁹, ²⁶), so as to be taken for a ghost (v. 37), or in a form that evokes worship (Matt. 28⁹, ¹⁷). Here, however, he appears as a man on a journey, and yet is not recognized for the man he was. The scene has then to be set by an initial difference in the disciples themselves. This is expressed forcefully by *their eyes were kept from recognizing him*. The verb rendered *kept* is *kratein*, meaning 'to grasp', 'to secure forcibly'. Their eyes were overpowered. The passive (cf. 9⁴⁵; 18³⁴) could intend an unreflective statement of fact, a conclusion drawn from the actual course of events; but it probably intends to denote a mysterious supernatural action of God (here of the risen Lord himself?), who brings it about that they were precluded from recognizing him throughout the journey. It does not refer to lack of spiritual insight on the disciples' part. It is a theological narrative device.

17

The narrative continues to be vivid. On joining them the stranger chooses to enquire the subject of their conversation, knowing that it is that of which he will give the true interpretation. With his question, lit. 'What are the words which . . .?', cf. his later statement (v. 44), 'These are my words which . . .' The conversation has already been described as agitated (v. 15, *discussing* is *sunzētein* = 'to debate'). It is now described as an altercation; *holding* is *antiballein*, which in classical and Hellenistic Greek means 'to throw (weapons) against' or 'in turn', and occasionally 'to compare' (cf. II Macc. 11^{13}, the only other instance in the Greek Bible, 'to weigh the pros and cons'). At the stranger's question they come to a halt (*they stood still*). *looking sad* (v.l. 'are you looking sad?') is the single word *skuthrōpos*, which originally meant 'angry' (Euripides, *Medea* 271); 'sullen' is perhaps the meaning here, since the stranger's question evokes an ill-mannered counter-question.

18

one of them, named Cleopas: The question is not voiced in unison, as often in Luke, but by one of the pair, who is belatedly named. This has been, and remains, a baffling feature, both stylistically and historically. Originally the story could have been of two anonymous persons, one of whom is now given a name, for ease of expression in recording dialogue, or from the novelistic tendency of later tradition to identify anonymous persons. This is improbable, as *one of them* would have sufficed for the purposes of narrative, and a more famous name is likely to have been supplied for witness to the resurrection – e.g. an apostle (cf. v. 10). If, on the other hand, the name of one had been preserved in tradition, thus anchoring the story to history (cf. Mark 15^{21}), why were not the names of both preserved, and mentioned at the beginning of the story? The name Cleopas is Greek, an abbreviation of Cleopatros. It may, or may not, be a Greek equivalent of the Semitic name Clopas, which appears in John 19^{25} as that of the husband of one of the women at the crucifixion. Eusebius (*HE* 3.11), in an account taken from the Memoirs of Hegesippus of the election of Symeon, the son of Clopas, as leader of the church in Jerusalem after the death of James, the Lord's brother, records an oral tradition preserved by Hegesippus that Symeon 'was a cousin – at any rate so it is said – of the Saviour', and mentions that Hegesippus had related that Clopas was Joseph's brother, i.e. Jesus' uncle. On the basis of these statements (of dubious worth) it has been suggested that Luke's story originated in traditions emanating from Jesus' family at a time when there was a possibility that the leadership of the Jerusalem church might devolve permanently on members of that family (cf. the resurrection appearance to James, I Cor. 15^7, which might have been responsible for his assuming the leadership – as in A. 15^{13}; 21^{18}). There has been no lack of suggestions of the identity of Cleopas's companion, the most common, as also the most improbable, being Peter. This provided a historical basis for the isolated statement in

v. 34. Thus, Origen (*Against Celsus* II, 62, 68, *Commentary on John* 1.5, 8) refers without comment to Simon and Clopas as the pair. This was perhaps because he had the reading which referred *who said* (v. 34) to the two returning from Emmaus, and made it possible to identify the appearance to Simon (v. 34) with that at Emmaus.

Are you the only visitor to Jerusalem who does not know?: The question serves to represent the recent events as being of universal notoriety and importance, but the exact sense depends on the meaning to be given to the verb *paroikein*. Normally this meant 'to sojourn', 'to be a visitor'; hence the rendering of RSV here. It implies that in some way the stranger was identified as a foreigner. Bauer (s.v. *paroikein*) suggests a rhetorical sense, 'Are you such a stranger in Jerusalem that . . .?' But the verb could mean 'to dwell', and the sense could be 'Are you the only inhabitant of Jerusalem who has not heard . . .?'

19–24

From this point on there is a double dramatic irony, as not only is the stranger represented as still ignorant of the crucial events of which he has been the subject, but also his companions are unaware that they are talking to him about himself. These events are now rehearsed by the two in unison (the reference to Cleopas is not pursued any further), and by the technique of the flash-back. They are given kerygmatic form, so that, taken together with vv. 26f., they provide a blueprint of what is to be Luke's version of the apostolic message in A. Here that message is distributed between the two participants, the disciples supplying the ingredients up to, but not including, the resurrection, and the stranger supplying the resurrection and the scriptural basis of the whole. To supply this message has been a principal factor in shaping the story as Luke tells it.

19

'*Concerning Jesus of Nazareth . . .*': The events are said to be the things concerning – *ta peri*, a Lukan expression (cf. v. 27; A. 1^3; 13^{29}; 18^{25}; 23$^{11, 15}$), and one used by classical writers for 'the history of' – Jesus of Nazareth. This identification of Jesus by reference to his own town, made here for the benefit of a stranger, is in the Greek *Nazarenos*, which, if the correct reading, could be a sign of a source, as the only other instance of it is in 4^{34} (taken from Mark), and Luke's own word in such formulae is *Nazōraios* (18^{37}; A. 2^{22}; 3^6; 4^{10}; 22^8; 26^9). This is, however, the reading in a considerable number of mss, and *Nazarēnos* could be a scribal assimilation to Mark 16^6. All the elements in the description to follow occur in A., sometimes in apostolic speeches.

a prophet mighty in deed and word before God and all the people: Jesus was (*egeneto* = 'proved to be') a prophet (*anēr prophētēs* = 'a prophetic man'). For *anēr* = 'man' followed by an adjectival noun, cf. 5^8; 17^{12}; A. 1^{16}; 3^{14}; 13^6. For Jesus as a man in kerygmatic formulae, cf. A. 2²²; 17³¹. For him as a prophet, cf. 7¹⁶; 9⁸; A. 3²²; 7³⁷. Here he is said in formal terms to have been a prophet acknowledged as such by God (*enantion* = 'before', confined to L–A in the NT, cf. 1⁶), though it is not indicated how, as well as by the people. In A. 3²²; 7³⁷ Jesus is identified with the prophet like Moses promised in Deut. 18¹⁵, and this could be the force of *mighty in deed and word* (a common expression in Greek literature), as Moses is so described in A. 7²². This designation of Jesus as a prophet is thus not necessarily to be taken as voicing an inadequate pre-resurrection form of belief, which is to be superseded as a result of the resurrection; for expectation of a Mosaic eschatological prophet appears to have been one form of Jewish hope alongside that of a Davidic messiah (see Cullmann, *Christology*, pp. 14ff.).

20

The recital continues – though somewhat awkwardly by a change from *concerning* to *and how* – by a reference to the crucifixion. This is stated in Lukan terms as an act of the Jewish authorities, the *chief priests and rulers* (cf. 23¹³; *our* seems to imply that they think the stranger a non-Jew), who, although they handed Jesus over to the Romans for the condemnation of death (*krima thanatou*, a purely LXX expression, cf. Deut. 21²²), had carried it out themselves (cf. 23²⁵ff.).

21a

But we had hoped that he was the one to redeem Israel: Whether this hope is meant to be confirmed or repudiated in vv. 25–27 depends on the sense to be given to *lutrousthai* = 'to redeem'. In the only other (late) occurrences in the NT the redemption is moral and religious, and the suffering and risen Christ is the author of it (Titus 2¹⁴; I Peter 1¹⁸; cf. Heb. 9¹² for the corresponding noun). *Israel* will then be a religious term for whoever are God's chosen ones. But redemption in 1⁶⁸; 2³⁸ refers to national deliverance, as does 'deliverer' (*lutrōtēs*) applied to Moses in A. 7³⁵. With that sense the disciples' hope would be repudiated in vv. 25–27, and replaced by a different doctrine of messianic deliverance.

21b

Yes, and besides all this, it is now the third day since this happened: The artificial character of the recital now begins to show through. This statement does not follow naturally after v. 21a, except for the reader who knows of the resurrection of Jesus on the third day. A general Jewish belief that after three days the soul ceased to hover over the body, which then began to decompose, would hardly be a sufficient basis for such an observation to be made at this juncture. The kerygma of saving events now gives way to additional pieces of information, which are not strictly necessary to it, but which are attached in order to bring the recital, upon which vv. 25–27 are to be the comment, completely up to date. This artificiality is reflected in the awkwardness of the language. *Yes, and besides all this* renders *alla ge kai* = '(not only this) but also indeed', and *sun pasi toutois*, where *sun* = 'with' is used loosely in the sense of 'on top of'. *it is the third day* renders *agei* followed by 'this third day' in the accusative, which appears to be an impersonal use of this verb (D Latin has *agit* = 'it is a matter of'), though no parallel is cited to this in Greek literature. The translation suggested by Bauer (s.v. *ago*), 'he (Jesus) is spending the third day since . . .' is very harsh.

22–24

The stranger is given further information (*Moreover, alla kai*) in what amounts to a polished summary of vv. 1–11. He is to understand that these events have affected closely a particular group of people, some of whose women (*of our company*, lit. 'from among us') had amazed them (*existanai*, used transitively + A. 8⁹), when, after visiting the tomb *early* (*orthrinos* + +) and finding it empty, they reported a vision of angels (*optasia* + 1²²; A. 26¹⁹; II Cor. 12¹ suggests something less substantial than the two men in v. 4), who affirmed that *he* (*autos*) was alive (there is no hint that the women's report had been dismissed, as in v. 11). 'And also' (*kai*, v. 24, not translated in RSV) *some of those who were with us* (*sun hēmin* = 'attached to us', not, as before, 'from among us') had visited the tomb, confirmed the women's report that it was empty, *but him they did not see*. This last observation is gratuitous without prior knowledge or expectation of Jesus' resurrection. Thus Luke augments the kerygmatic tradition by additional facts, but in a puzzling manner. For v. 24 does not refer back to anything in the previous narrative if v. 12 does not belong to the text, and it contradicts v. 12 if it does. Luke is aware of a tradition of a visit to the tomb subsequent to that of the women, but the form in which he gives it – *some of those who were with us* – does not suggest a common source with John 20³⁻¹⁰. As in v. 7 the kerygma is drawn into the story of the empty tomb, so here the empty tomb is drawn into the kerygma, and that in sufficient detail to provide a solid factual basis for the resurrection faith, which the two disciples are made to come as near affirming as the circumstances allowed.

25

And he said to them: The stranger now responds to this recital, and this is the crux of the story as Luke conceived it. The risen Lord himself (*he, autos, said*) is the authoritative source of the apostolic message to be given in A. (v. 26), and of that message as the content of scripture (v. 27).

'O foolish men, and slow of heart to believe all that the prophets have spoken!': The Lord's understanding is set in contrast with the inability of human intelligence, for all its acquaintance with the facts and its capacity to argue about them, to draw the conclusion of faith. The two are chided with some emotion (O) as stupid (*anoētos*, a common invective in Greek comedy + five times in Paul, cf.

Gal. 3¹), and as mentally slow (*bradus* = 'slow' + James 1¹⁹; *of heart* is in Semitic thought 'in mind'). The construction which follows – *pisteuein* followed by *epi* and the dative – is not used elsewhere by Luke for 'to believe in'. The verb may then be taken absolutely, and the meaning be – 'slow to become believers (i.e. to see the facts aright) on the basis of (*epi*), or with the assistance of, all that the prophets had said'. It is not clear whether this means that the facts of the empty tomb and the angelic vision ought to have sufficed for them to draw the conclusion that Jesus had risen (referring to vv. 22–24), or that they should have been sufficiently conversant with scripture not to have been put off from believing in Jesus' mission by his condemnation, suffering and death (referring to vv. 19–21).

26

The speaker passes from negative rebuke to positive assertion of the truth, which should have been obvious. In doing so he does not refer to himself, nor to something still in process, but summarizes in a general and impersonal doctrinal statement what is now regarded as completed and past.

Was it not necessary?: *edei* (cf. 9²², 'must suffer'). This is not the necessity of fate, but of the divine will.

that the Christ should suffer these things and enter into his glory?: This will be repeated in vv. 44–48 for the disciples' future use, and is so used in A. 17³; 26²³. The christology is nearest to that of I Peter 1¹¹, ²¹; 5¹. *the Christ* now emerges as a title that can be used to cover the whole career of Jesus (contrast A. 2³⁶, where he becomes the Christ by resurrection and exaltation). *suffer these things* expresses Luke's understanding of the cross as 'being done to by others' and as the absence of external power (cf. A. 1³; 3¹⁸; 17³; 26²³; so also in I Peter). *glory* denotes the divine mode of existence, and is connected in the NT with the resurrection as a permanent exaltation to God. Generally glory is predicated of Jesus at his parousia or future coming (cf. 9²⁶; Mark 10³⁷; 13²⁶; Titus 2¹³; I Peter 4¹³; 5¹), but here the eschatology is spatial rather than temporal. By resurrection (exaltation) the Christ has already entered into the heavenly mode of existence, where he is now to be seen (22⁶⁹; A. 1⁹⁻¹¹; 2³³; 7⁵⁵; 22¹¹), and the parousia is not part of the doctrinal summary here, nor in vv. 44ff., nor in A., except somewhat remotely in A. 1¹¹; 3²¹.

27

The statements in vv. 25–26 are now comprehensively reinforced, though not without a certain awkwardness. *beginning with* (*apo* = 'from') *Moses and all the prophets* is loosely expressed if it means 'beginning with the law and going on to the prophets'; and if it means 'taking the law and the prophets as a starting point', it leaves uncertain whether *all the scriptures* denotes them, or includes the rest of the OT. *the things concerning* (*ta peri*) occurs in the NT, apart from Mark

5^{27}, only in L-A ,where it is used of the passion (A. 13^{29}), or, without further specification, of the gospel story as a whole (22^{37}?; A. 18^{25}; 23^{11}; 24^{22}; 28^{31}). Here *the things concerning himself* is bound to be somewhat awkward, as it cannot mean that the stranger so interpreted the OT as to disclose who he was (saying 'This refers to me'), but only as to show it to be teaching the true doctrine of the messiah, or the truth about a third person, Jesus of Nazareth, who had been the subject of the previous conversation. If *the things* included his ministry of deed and word (v. 19) it would be more awkward still, since the unknown stranger could not exhibit knowledge of that without arousing suspicion. It is not said how extensive these *things* were, but an exegesis involving, apparently, a great deal of the OT is scarcely feasible in the course of a single journey. The story now becomes general, and describes not an actual but an ideal situation, in which the risen Lord acts as the source and model of what was to become the church's use of scripture. That the death and resurrection of Christ were 'according to the scriptures' already belongs to the formula in I Cor. 15$^{3f.}$, and NT writings show the application of individual OT passages to the passion, and, though less frequently, to the resurrection. The recurrent *all* here may be another instance of Luke's extravagant use of this word, but his intention may have been to go beyond, or repudiate, the use of a limited number of proof texts, and to anchor Christianity in the OT as a whole, claiming it as a Christian book throughout when properly understood.[i] By the time the story has reached this point it has succeeded in doing what no other single resurrection story was able to do; viz. present in narrative form the whole credal formula: 'Christ died (for our sins) according to the scriptures, and was buried, and was raised the third day according to the scriptures, and appeared.' It has also traced back to the risen Lord himself, both the doctrine of a suffering and exalted messiah, at which the church eventually arrived, and also the scriptural investigation which was to lie behind its interpretation of its message.

28–29

After the dialogue (with the participants standing still, v. 17?) the journey is resumed, and the story moves towards the meal, which is still its climax, and in an earlier form of the story might have been its main point. The language again becomes forceful – there is a strong element of assonance, with the Greek words translated by *going*, *appeared*, *going further* and *constrained* all beginning with the letter *pi*. It also conveys a sense of mystery. *So they* (i.e. all three) *drew near to* (or 'arrived at') *the village to which* (*hou* = 'whither' + 10^1; I Cor. 16^6) *they* (i.e. the two disciples) *were going. He* (*autos*) *appeared to be going further.* This is a weak translation. The verb rendered *appeared* (*prospoieisthai* + +) should be

i See A. Ehrhardt, *NTS* 10, pp. 187ff., and O'Neill, *The Theology of Acts*, p. 95, 'Acts presents a theology in which the Church has abandoned the People and appropriated the Book.'

given its normal meaning of 'to pretend to', 'to make as though'. The Lord deliberately acts in such a way as mysteriously to bring to light an urgent but unconscious need of the disciples. The situation resembles that in Mark 6$^{48f.}$ (omitted by Luke), where, in walking on the sea, Jesus 'meant to pass them by'. At this they *constrained him*; the verb *parabiazesthai* (+ A. 16^{15}) means 'to use force to accomplish something', and even when used metaphorically has a strong sense of compulsion. Their demand is that he stays with them. The verb here, *menein*, could mean 'to remain', and the request could be 'do not leave us'; but it was regularly used for 'to live', 'to dwell' or 'to lodge' (cf. 1^{56}; John 1$^{38f.}$). The request could then be for him to break his journey, and to put up with them (at their house?) at Emmaus. The reason given is also forceful, being the only double time reference in this gospel – *it is towards evening* (*pros hesperan*, a common classical and Hellenistic phrase), *and the day is now far spent* (*klinein* = 'to incline', 'to decline', of the time of day + 9^{12}). That is, it is late afternoon, by which time the day was regarded as almost over. The stranger submits to the demand, but the story moves straightway to the meal.

30

It is pointless to enquire whether this was the midday meal taken late or the evening meal taken early; for it is no ordinary meal when the invited guest automatically and without explanation assumes the role of host. This is evident from his actions and the words used of them. *he took bread and blessed, and broke it, and gave it to them* is the set terminology for grace before meals said by the head of the Jewish household (see Jeremias, *Eucharistic Words*, pp. 109, 174f.). At this preliminary action the eyes of the two are opened to recognize him (*autos*), and the meal does not take place, since at that moment *he* (*autos*) vanishes. This experience is later described by the two themselves as *how he was known to them in the breaking of the bread* (v. 35).

This account poses problems by its cryptic character. Bultmann comments (*History*, p. 291): 'When a meal plays a part in an appearance of the risen Lord in two of the Synoptic Easter stories (Lk. 24$^{30, 41-43.}$; also Acts 1^4? 10$^{41.}$, Jn. 21$^{12f.}$; Mk. 16$^{14.}$) we are led to think "how the coming of the Lord was expected and experienced at the Lord's Supper in the Early Church" and to find the motif of the presentation in that.' Strictly this applies only to the present story, as it is not clear that a meal is involved in vv. 41–43 or in A. 1^4; and in John 21$^{12f.}$ it is an appendix to the story, and Mark 16^{14} is late and apocryphal. Even in the case of the present story the wide consensus of opinion that the setting presupposed is the Christian eucharist, dependent on the Last Supper, and that basically the account is a paradigm of the spiritual truth that the Lord is present and known there, is not as securely based as is often supposed.^{j} The

j For exponents of this view, see Alsup, *Post-Resurrection Appearance Stories*, p. 197 n. 564.

language used is, with minor variations, that used of the Last Supper (22¹⁹ᵃ), as also of the Feeding (9¹⁶), but this extends no further than the traditional wording for the act of saying grace, and there is no trace of anything that could be said to be distinctive of the Last Supper. The comment in v. 35, which is plainly from Luke's hand, raises the question of what he meant by *the breaking of the bread*, an expression which is without parallel in Jewish or Greek usage, and which he alone uses of the practice of the early church (A. 2⁴²; with the verb A. 2⁴⁶; 20⁷, ¹¹). It could be a term for what took place at the Last Supper only if the shorter text (22¹⁹ᵃ) is read there. Jeremias (*Eucharistic Words*, p. 120, n. 3) argues that in A. 2⁴², 'fellowship . . . the breaking of the bread', the former refers to the Agape or fellowship meal, and the latter to the eucharist or ritual meal already separated from it; and he interprets v. 35 as 'He was recognized by them in the course of (*en* = "during") the eucharist'. This is far from convincing, and the opposite has been argued, that the breaking of the bread was a fellowship meal which the first Christians celebrated in their spiritual exaltation (A. 2⁴⁶). Strictly speaking the two cannot have arrived at a recognition of Jesus by being made to recall his actions at the Last Supper, since, except on the unlikely supposition that the unnamed one was an apostle, they had not been present at it. Taking *en* as instrumental, 'through the breaking of the bread', some have fallen back on naturalistic explanations of what it was in the Lord's actions or words which brought about this recognition. One suggestion is that he had a special way of tearing the loaf, or a special form of words in blessing (cf. Jeremias, *Eucharistic Words*, p. 120, n. 3), perhaps at meals with disciples (of which, however, the gospels do not afford instances). Another suggestion is that the reception of the blessed bread restored their wearied mental and spiritual faculties to recognize him (so Leaney, p. 293). This might be held to have some basis in the variant (Western) reading in v. 31, 'When they took the bread from him their eyes were opened'; but this may be to underline that the two events coincided, and not to establish cause and effect. Alsup observes (op. cit., pp. 197f.) that the motif of the meal is subordinate to the motif of recognition, and Luke may have seen in the recognition an inexplicable act brought about by God (or by the risen Lord), as miraculous and supernatural as the original overpowering of their eyes.

31

The recognition does not, as in some resurrection stories, have as its consequence further communication with the Lord, for immediately *he vanished out of their sight*. This is the only such story to terminate with a 'disappearance'. Elsewhere in L–A the Lord either ascends or is parted from the disciples, while in Matthew and John nothing is said on this score, the scenes closing with authoritative words of the Lord. The phraseology here, *aphantos egeneto* = 'he became invisible', is unusual. *aphantos*, a poetical and late prose equivalent for the normal word for 'invisible', *aphanēs*, is not found again in the Greek Bible, and is more at home in Greek mythology, especially for journeys to the underworld – cf. Sophocles, *Oedipus the King* 832, 'May I go from mortal men to be invisible', *Oedipus at Colonus* 1556, of Persephone as the invisible goddess of the underworld (for further references, see Klostermann, p. 238). Used here it is a counterpart to 'he appeared' (*ōphthē*) in the Christian vocabulary of resurrection, 'he made himself visible'. This 'vanishing' of one who had spent so much time with them in substantial form as a man suggests a different conception of the resurrection state of the Lord from other stories, where it is something unusual in his form which prevents his being recognized until he speaks.

32

No effect is recorded of the miraculous disappearance, but only of the recognition, which is the reflection that their hearts had been burning *while he talked to us on the road, while he opened to us the scriptures* (the double clause makes the statement emphatic). Here Luke brings together the two motifs of the story – recognition and scriptural interpretation – and does so in characteristic fashion by using the same word in variant senses. The eyes whose closure had prevented them, not from understanding what had been said, but from knowing who he was who said it, so that he had instructed them incognito, are now miraculously *opened* (v. 31, *dianoigein*) to see who 'he' had been. The result is that they are moved to recall, not how he had *opened* the scriptures (v. 32, *dianoigein* as a semi-technical term for interpretation, cf. A. 17³), which they had understood, but the burning intelligence which had accompanied it (and which should have led them to recognize him earlier?). *burn* in a metaphorical sense is found only here in the NT ,and it is not certain to what it refers. Generally passages such as Ps. 39³; Jer. 20⁹ are cited as parallels, but there the burning of the heart denotes an inner turmoil and distress which cannot be contained. Here *heart* is likely to have the Semitic sense of 'mind', and the burning may be that of a mind set on fire by understanding. Difficulties about the meaning and relevance of the word here appear to have led to strange variant readings in the Western text – *kekalummenē* = 'covered' D, excaecatum = 'blinded' c, optusum = 'obtuse' l, exterminatum = 'destroyed' e, gravatum = 'weighed down' syr.

33–35

In view of what has happened the original purpose of the journey to Emmaus, whatever that may have been, is abandoned, and, despite the lateness of the hour, the pair immediately return to headquarters in Jerusalem (*the eleven gathered together and those who were with them*), and report their experiences of recognizing the Lord in the breaking of the bread, and of being instructed by him on the road. These then cease to be private, and become the common possession of the company of disciples. The vocabulary of vv. 33, 35 is throughout Lukan. But between their arrival and their report, and in place of any reference to how those were received, an emphatic announcement is made to them (*indeed*; *ontōs* = 'for certain') of that of which the company is already in possession, viz. the knowledge that the Lord has been raised, and has appeared to Simon (v. 34). This intercalated verse, and its introduction into the narrative in this manner, are remarkable in several respects. (i) It is very awkwardly attached, being tucked in at the tail end of the Emmaus story – lit. 'they found the eleven gathered together, and those who were with them, saying . . .' (*legontas*, the present participle in the accusative, agreeing with 'the eleven . . . with them'). A variant reading in D and in Origen has the participle in the nominative, and it is the two returning from Emmaus who say *The Lord has risen indeed, and has appeared to Simon!* This might have been an emendation to improve the grammar and sequence of the narrative; but it is more likely an attempt to identify the otherwise unrecorded appearance to Simon (= Peter) with that on the Emmaus road, and by implication to identify Cleopas's unnamed companion with Peter. (ii) The form of the statement is kerygmatic, similar to that at the beginning of the formula in I Cor. 15³⁻⁵ᵃ, 'Christ (here *the Lord*) . . . was raised (perfect tense, here aorist tense) . . . and appeared to Cephas (here Simon).' This is the only instance of a kerygmatic statement of a resurrection appearance standing within a narrative of resurrection appearances, and of a clear correspondence between an item in the list of appearances in I Cor. 15⁵⁻⁷ and anything recorded in the gospels. Whether Luke was aware of the formula in I Cor. 15³⁻⁷ (which Paul says he received from tradition), and excerpted from it the appearance to Peter at the head of the list, or received it as an isolated statement in tradition, is uncertain. Also uncertain is whether he intended by this curious introduction of it here to assert, as does the list, the priority of the appearance to Peter – in the context despite the apparent priority of the appearance on the way to, and at, Emmaus. (iii) It is a reflection of the complex, unsystematic and perhaps fortuitous character of the resurrection traditions in the churches, that by the time of the writing of the gospels only Luke was able to supply any notice of the appearance to Peter, and then only in kerygmatic form. It is one of the riddles of the gospel traditions that, despite the priority of the appearance to Peter in the comparatively early formula in I Cor. 15³⁻⁷, and despite the evident importance of Peter in more than one strand of tradition (e.g. Mark 16⁷; Matt. 16¹⁸ᶠ·; John 20²⁻⁷; 21⁷⁻¹⁹; A. 1¹⁵⁻²¹⁴; Gal. 1¹⁸⁻²¹⁴) no narrative of that appearance survived. On this see W. Marxsen,ᵏ who argues that the appearance to Peter was not only the first, but was constitutive of faith for others, for whom appearances were not the origin of faith as for Peter. See also on 5¹⁻¹¹ for the possibility that that story was originally an account of the appearance of the risen Lord to Peter, which Luke, and possibly the tradition behind him, no longer recognized as such.

---

k *The Resurrection of Jesus of Nazareth*, London and Philadelphia 1970, pp. 82 ff.

³⁶*As they were saying this, Jesus himself stood among them.*★ ³⁷*But they were startled and frightened, and supposed that they saw a spirit.* ³⁸*And he said to them, 'Why are you troubled, and why do questionings rise in your hearts?* ³⁹*See my hands and my feet, that it is I myself; handle me, and see; for a spirit has not flesh and bones as you see that I have.'*† ⁴¹*And while they still disbelieved for joy, and wondered, he said to them, 'Have you anything here to eat?'* ⁴²*They gave him a piece of broiled fish,* ⁴³*and he took it and ate before them.*

⁴⁴*Then he said to them, 'These are my words which I spoke to you, while I was still with you, that everything written about me in the law of Moses and the prophets and the psalms must be fulfilled.'* ⁴⁵*Then he opened their minds to understand the scriptures,* ⁴⁶*and said to them, 'Thus it is written, that the Christ should suffer and on the third day rise from the dead,* ⁴⁷*and that repentance and forgiveness of sins should be preached in his name to all nations,*‡ *beginning from Jerusalem.* ⁴⁸*You are witnesses of these things.* ⁴⁹*And behold, I send the promise of my Father upon you; but stay in the city, until you are clothed with power from on high.'*

⁵⁰*Then he led them out as far as Bethany, and lifting up his hands he blessed them.* ⁵¹*While he blessed them, he parted from them.*§ ⁵²*And they*★★ *returned to Jerusalem with great joy,* ⁵³*and were continually in the temple blessing God.*

★ Other ancient authorities add *and said to them, 'Peace to you!'*

† Other ancient authorities add v. 40, *And when he said this he showed them his hands and his feet*

‡ Or *nations. Beginning from Jerusalem you are witnesses.*

§ Other ancient authorities add *and was carried up into heaven*

★★ Other ancient authorities add *worshipped him and*

This final appearance in the Gospel, like those in Matt. 28¹⁶⁻²⁰ (in Galilee) and John 20¹⁹⁻²³, both establishes the resurrection of Jesus, and points to the future in a commissioning of a group of believers – in

Luke 'the eleven and the rest', in Matthew 'the eleven', in John 'the disciples'. In Luke these two aspects are treated separately and more extensively in (i) an appearance to them (vv. 36–43), and (ii) their instruction and commissioning (vv. 44–49), to which is appended (iii) a parting benediction (vv. 50–53).

(i) *The appearance* (vv. 36–43). This could have stood on its own in a tradition, possibly as the sole resurrection appearance there. In conception and tone it is very different from what has preceded in vv. 13–35. In its present context it can hardly represent the appearance to the twelve in I Cor. 15⁵, as it is to the eleven and their companions, though it might represent that to 'all the apostles' (I Cor. 15⁷), if 'apostles' there means 'the (future) missionaries'. Behind it may lie a tradition common with John 20¹⁹⁻²³, since both have the same sequence of thought – the establishing of identity, to be followed (in vv. 44ff.) by mission and the spirit – though features characteristic of each evangelist make reconstruction of such a common tradition difficult. That it was a common written tradition is likely only if we read v. 36b and v. 40 (see notes). Luke's version is more vividly written than John's. Emphasis is obtained by repeated combination and duplication: *startled and frightened* (v. 37), *hands and feet, handle and see, flesh and bones* (v. 39), *disbelieved and wondered* (v. 41). There are literary refinements in *questionings* (v. 38, *dialogismoi* = 'hostile arguments', as in 2³⁵; 5²²; 6⁸; 9⁴⁶ᶠ·), *rise in your hearts* (v. 38, *anabainein en tē kardiā* = 'to arise in the mind' is without parallel), *to eat* (v. 41, *brōsimos* = 'eatable' ++), *a piece* (v. 42, *optos* ++).

 තත

36

As they were saying this: What is to follow is made continuous with what has preceded, which it confirms by means of an instantaneous appearance. It presumably began with the name 'Jesus' (cf. John 20¹⁹), but this is supplied in RSV; the Greek text has simply *autos* = 'he himself', which is an assimilation to *autos* used throughout vv. 13–35. Likewise, in any oral form of the story those to whom he appears would have been named (cf. John 20¹⁹); here *they* refers to the eleven and the rest, who have already been assembled in vv. 9–10, 33. No location is given, except that it is in Jerusalem (v. 33); that it was the 'upper room' depends on combining John 20¹⁹ with A. 1¹³.

stood among them: This is very abrupt, with no attendant circumstances (contrast John 20¹⁹). The abruptness is relieved in most mss by the continuation with 'and said to them, "Peace to you!"' This, however, is absent from D a b e ff² l r¹, and is omitted by RSV and NEB as an assimilation to John 20^{19, 26}. The effect of the appearance in v. 37 would be more intelligible if the Lord had not already addressed them in this way.

37

they were startled and frightened: The effect of the appearance is terror – *ptoeisthai* + 21⁹ can mean 'startled' but is more likely to mean 'terrified', especially in combination with *emphoboi genomenoi* + v. 5; A. 10⁴; 24²⁵; Rev. 11¹³.

supposed that they saw a spirit: This could mean a spiritual being such as an angel (cf. A. 23^{8f.}; cf. 1¹², where 'troubled' (*tarassein*, v. 38) is used in connection with the appearance of an angel). It is more likely that *pneuma* means 'ghost' here, in the sense of 'phantom' – D and Marcion have *phantasma*, the word used in Mark 6⁴⁹ in the story of the Walking on the Water, with which Luke's story here has some similarities.[1] The use of *pneuma* for ghost would be unique in the NT, and this is the only resurrection appearance in which the form of the risen Lord produces such an impression (contrast vv. 13–35; John 20^{14ff., 19ff.}; 21^{4ff.}; Matt. 28^{9, 16f.}). If the story originally ran more as in John 20^{19ff.}, Luke, or the tradition behind him, may have developed it in this direction, and have made the dominant motif the establishment of the corporeal reality of the risen Lord.

38

The picture here is somewhat blurred, as these questions seem to imply that the Lord has already been recognized, and that doubts have begun to arise (cf. Matt. 28¹⁷). The Lord then proceeds to establish his identity in three stages.

39

See my hands and my feet, that it is I myself: That the risen Lord was to be recognized in this way and not by his face was put down by Wellhausen to a folk belief that the hands and feet could remain the same even when the face changes, and this would connect more closely with v. 39b. But it is more likely that there is a cryptic reference to the marks of nails there, even though no reference has been made to such in the account of the crucifixion, and it is assumed that the reader will know that they were an accompaniment of crucifixion. There is a reference to nails in this connection in John 20²⁵, though only with reference to the hands, again without any mention of them in the crucifixion narrative. That nails were used in this way (though not necessarily in all cases of crucifixion) is shown by the discovery in a first-century ossuary on the Mount of Olives of an ankle bone with the nail still in it.[m] In the Greek *hoti ego eimi autos*

l On this see Alsup, *Post-Resurrection Appearances*, pp. 168ff.

m See H.-W. Kuhn, 'Der Gekreuzigte von Giv'at ha Mivtar' in *Theologia Crucis – Signum Crucis*, ed. C. Andresen and G. Klein, Tübingen 1979, pp. 303–34.

(= *that it is I myself*), *ego eimi* = 'I am' can stand alone to declare the (divine) presence of the Lord (cf. Mark 6^{50}, and see on 21^8); but here it is not declarative but probative, and Luke adds *autos*, which could mean 'it is I myself', or 'I am himself', perhaps in the sense of 'the Master', as in vv. 13–35. The risen Lord carries in hands and feet (permanent?) marks of his being 'the crucified one' (cf. Rev. 5^6). But the establishing of personal identity, which is central in John 20$^{20,\ 24ff.}$, is here preliminary, and passes over into demonstration that this identity involves the physical reality of the risen body.

handle me, and see; for a spirit has not flesh and bones as you see that I have: It is assumed that the disciples have voiced their supposition that they were seeing a ghost. It is now rebutted in the strongest terms that at resurrection he had shed his humanity, and had passed into the sphere of pure spirit. This could be said to counter the docetism of Gnostics, as, apparently, when Ignatius (*Smyrneans* 2–3) quotes (from Luke according to some, from a variant version according to others) a similar statement, 'He genuinely suffered even as he genuinely raised himself. It is not as some believers say, that his passion was a sham. It is they who are a sham. Yes, and their fate will fit their fancies – they will be ghosts and apparitions. For myself, I am convinced and believe that even after his resurrection he was in the flesh. And when he came to Peter and his company he says to them, "Lay hold and handle me and see that I am not a demon without a body." And at once they touched him and believed, being united to his flesh and blood . . . And after his resurrection he ate and drank with them as fleshly, although spiritually united to the Father.' Gnostics, however, were generally concerned to deny the real humanity of Jesus in his earthly life and before his resurrection. The words here may be aimed less at a philosophical dualism which opposed matter and spirit, than at a more vulgar level of belief, which saw resurrection appearances as apparitions from the demon world or the underworld (cf. 16^{27}), and therefore as spectral. It is not clear whether Luke, here or elsewhere, considered Jesus at his resurrection to have entered already into his 'glory' (i.e. heavenly existence, v. 26), or into a temporary state between heaven and earth, which was to give way to an exalted state; or what transformation was involved in resurrection, apart from an ability of the body to appear and disappear. He seems, however, to be emphatic that the risen and exalted Lord remains a man (A. 1^{11}; 17^{31}). This is now demonstrated (cf. A. 1^3 'by many proofs') visibly and tangibly by *flesh and bones*. This was not a standing expression for a human being, like the Semitic 'flesh and blood' (but cf. the addition in some mss of Eph. 5^{30} 'of his flesh and of his bones'). OT parallels have 'bone and flesh' (Gen. 29^{14}; Judg. 9^2; II Sam. 5^1). The closest parallel is in Homer, *Odyssey* 11.219, where it is said of the shades in Hades that 'the sinews no longer have flesh (in the plural, as here in the original hand of ℵ) and bones'. Marcion, Tertullian and Hilary read here simply 'bones', which would correspond with the most literalistic form of Jewish belief that the bones, of which flesh and skin were only the covering, were the essential things, and destruction of these meant the loss of all hope of resurrection. This unusual and realistic description of the human person is not in principle different from what is presupposed in the appearances in vv. 13–35; John 20²⁰⁻²⁷; 21¹⁻¹⁴; Matt. 28⁹, ¹⁷. Unless the resurrection was to a temporary state only, it cannot easily be reconciled with Paul's statement that flesh and blood cannot inherit the kingdom of God, or with his conception of the 'spiritual body', or 'body of glory', which the believer will possess at the resurrection in conformity with the risen and glorified body of the Lord (I Cor. 15⁴²⁻⁵³; Phil. 3²¹). And here the difficulty is how a body of flesh and bones could convey the impression of being a ghost.

Most mss continue here with 'And when he had said this, he showed them his hands and his feet', but it is absent, not only from the texts listed in respect of v. 36b, but also by syr^cur ^sin and Marcion. It comes too late, and somewhat lamely, after v. 39, and is omitted by RSV and NEB as an assimilation to John 20²⁰, with 'feet' for 'side'.

41

And while they still disbelieved for joy: This unique expression punctuates the narrative at this point, and prepares for what follows in vv. 44ff. There is joy at the recognition of the Lord in John 20²⁰, and the theme of unbelief attaches to several stories in the resurrection tradition (cf. v. 11, Matt. 28¹⁷, and John 20²⁴⁻²⁹, where it is given special treatment). Here the two are remarkably combined, and the doubt is caused by, and is dissolved into, the joy and confidence which are to be marks of the early church (v. 52; A. 2⁴⁶; 5⁴¹; 4¹³, ³³). Although no reaction is given to the Lord's further action, the disciples are now ready for the teaching and instructions to follow.

'Have you anything here to eat?': It is not certain whether for Jews eating would be a proof of not being an angel or spirit. It is so in Tobit 12¹⁹, where Raphael says, 'All these days did I appear unto you, and I did neither eat nor drink, but you saw a vision,' but the angels in Gen. 19³ do eat. With a view to further proof of his human and corporeal reality the Lord requests something to eat, as that which flesh and bones require.

42–43

He is given *a piece of broiled fish*, i.e. not the ingredients of a meal, but something that happens to be at hand, and is sufficient for the purposes of demonstration. He eats it in their presence. This is not a meal, and should not be compared with A. 10⁴¹, where communal eating of food by the risen Lord and disciples as a proof of resurrection has become part of the preaching (that refers back to A. 1³⁻⁴), nor with John 21⁹⁻¹³, where the Lord provides food but does not eat. Nor is this eating in the kingdom of God (14¹⁵), which for Luke is still future (22¹⁶, ³⁰), though the curious and widely distributed addition to the text 'and of bee honeycomb' (or, 'honeycomb from a beehive') may have been intended to make it so, if (milk and) honey were regarded as the symbolic food of the promised land (cf. Hippolytus, *Apostolic Tradition* 23), or of paradise (so some Babylonian texts). Nor is it eucharistic, though the addition in some texts, 'he gave it to them', may be an attempt to make it so.

(ii) *The instruction and commissioning* (vv. 44–49)

The story of appearance and recognition is complete in itself, and furnishes a solid foundation for apostolic faith in, and preaching of, the resurrection. Only with some difficulty does it become the basis for the close of the Gospel, and for the transition to its sequel in A., in being followed by instruction and commissioning, as in Matt. 28^{16-20} and John 20^{19-23} (in vv. 13–35 the order of recognition and teaching is reversed). Strictly this instruction is unnecessary after v. 7, vv. 25–27, 32, the contents of which are repeated. The repetition is likely to be due to Luke, and shows his special concerns. What had been said to the women and to the two disciples is now reiterated and expanded so as to become the possession of the whole 'apostolic' company as the basis of their faith and message. It falls into two parts. (i) Verses 44–45 (v. 45 goes with v. 44 and not with v. 46), introduced by *Then he said to them*, are still concerned with the past, and refer back to the angelic message in vv. 6–7 and the exegesis given to the pair in vv. 26–27. (ii) Verses 46–49, with a separate introduction *and* (he) *said to them*, combine past, present and future, and after repeating the messianic doctrine of vv. 25–26 sketch the future mission of the church in terms – Jerusalem, witness, promise, power – which are to recur in A. 1^{4-8}.

44

'*These are my words which I spoke to you*' : Grammar and sense are obscure. There is no main verb, and a literal translation would be 'These my words which I spoke to you being yet with you, that . . .' Creed (p. 300) takes *logoi* = 'words' in the possible sense of 'happenings', and renders 'These events (sc. my death and resurrection) explain the words which I spoke . . .' But the obscurity could have arisen from an intention of Luke to introduce the final words of the Lord, who is the prophet like Moses (A. 3^{22}), by an echo of the opening words of Deuteronomy, 'These the words that Moses spoke to all Israel beyond Jordan . . .'; which words are then made to refer not only forwards, as in Deuteronomy, but also backwards to what Jesus had previously said. They cover two distinct but complementary subjects – that everything about him in scripture has been fulfilled (vv. 44–45), and that scripture teaches the suffering and resurrection of the messiah, and a universal proclamation in his name (vv. 46–47).

while I was still with you: This refers to the period of the earthly ministry as in the past, though it had ceased only two days before, and there is no record in the Gospel of Jesus having so taught during it. It recalls the Lukan form of the angelic message at the tomb (v. 6), 'Remember how he told you, while he was still in Galilee', though there the reference was limited to the previous prophecies of death and resurrection.

everything written about me in the law of Moses and the prophets and the psalms must be fulfilled: That the meaning here is not 'such things in the Old Testament as are written about me', but rather 'the whole of the Old Testament as speaking about me' is suggested by v. 45. For 'the things about me' (*ta peri emou*, here with 'written'), see on v. 27. In comparison with 'Moses and all the prophets' in that verse, the unique expression here shows that the OT canon was not yet closed, or at least not yet known by a single designation. A tripartite division of it appears in the prologue to Ecclesiasticus, where are mentioned, alongside the law and the prophets, 'other books of our fathers' and 'the rest of the books'. Josephus (*Against Apion* 1.40) refers to 'the other four books (sc. Psalms, Proverbs, Ecclesiastes, the Song of Solomon) of praises to God or rules of life for men'. II Macc. 2^{13} mentions 'writings of David' alongside those about kings and prophets. Here *the psalms* may be a Jewish designation of this third group by reference to what was regarded as the most important book in it; or, possibly, the threefold denomination was a liturgical designation of the OT in view of the place of the psalms in worship. Just possibly it was a Christian designation in view of the prominence of the psalms in Christian exegesis – of the passion (see pp. 767f.) and the resurrection (cf. A. 2$^{25ff., 34f.}$; 13$^{33, 35}$).

45

he opened their minds to understand the scriptures: This is repeated from vv. 31, 32, though the verb *dianoigein* = 'to open' is used in yet a third sense, not now of 'eyes' or of 'the scriptures', but of the *mind* (*nous*), a thoroughly Greek word, which is very rare in the LXX (except in the Hellenistic book IV Maccabees), and is otherwise confined in the NT to the Pauline and deutero-Pauline letters, and Rev. 13^{18}; 17^9. Thus the gospel in its widest scope (*everything . . . about me*) is once more, and now for the whole church, established from the whole of the OT, understood as a Christian book. In the person of the Lord this has a twofold authoritative basis, in that the OT is intelligible only in relation to him, and he is the only one able to show this to be so; and his own words have the same authority as the scriptures they interpret.

46

At this juncture a general Christian exegesis of the OT with reference to what has already happened is insufficient, and the instructions in vv. 47–49, introduced afresh so as to enable a return to direct speech after v. 45, apply it to the future. But first the passion (suffering) and the resurrection (the active verb *rise* conveys less the sense of the resurrection as God's act than the passive 'was raised') of the messiah (with whom the risen Jesus now identifies himself, *about me*, v. 44) are once more enunciated as the core of scripture (cf. vv. 26f.). But now is added to it, though not deduced from it, the mission of the church, of which the Lord and the OT together are thus the authors.

47

that repentance and forgiveness of sins should be preached in his name: This, the sole object of the mission (cf. John 20$^{21-23}$, contrast Matt. 28$^{19f.}$), is held to be already contained in scripture. Preaching, generally of the kingdom of God, has previously summarized the activity of Jesus (4^{44}; 8^1), and of the apostles and missionaries under his supervision (9^2; 10^9). It is now to become the principal function of the 'apostolic' company. Its content corresponds with Luke's emphasis on repentance and forgiveness in the teaching and ministry of Jesus, though the actual form of words – *repentance and* (p^{75} ℵ B and others have *eis* = 'with a view to') *forgiveness of sins* has previously been associated with the Baptist (3^3 = Mark 1^4, cf. 1^{77}). Apart from Mark 1^4 this form of words is confined to L–A in the NT, and it governs the presentation of the church's mission in A. Thus to Israel the preaching takes the special form of exhortation to repentance for the act of rejecting Jesus, with a view to receiving forgiveness, the Spirit, and the messianic blessing which God has made available in raising and exalting Jesus (A. 2^{38}; 3^{19}; 5^{31}). Later, as proclaimed by Peter to Gentiles (A. 10^{42}), it takes the form that by his resurrection Jesus has been made universal judge, and that, as the prophets bear witness, forgiveness is available through his name for those who believe in him; and this is connected with God's gift to them of repentance unto life (A. 11^{18}). It is preached also to Gentiles by Paul in the form of a turning from Satan to God to receive remission of sins and a place among the elect (A. 26$^{16-18}$; cf. A. 3^{26}), and is preached by him to Jews and Gentiles in the form of an exhortation to all men to repent in view of the appointment of Jesus through his resurrection to be universal judge (A. 17$^{30f.}$); and Paul's ministry is summarized as 'bearing witness to Jews and Greeks of repentance towards God and faith in our Lord Jesus Christ' (A. 20^{21}), and as announcing to Jews and Gentiles the necessity of repentance and turning to God (A. 26^{20}). In these passages repentance and forgiveness are not connected with any doctrine of the death of Christ as an atonement or sacrifice, but with his resurrection and exaltation to be both judge and gracious messiah. Here the connection is made by *in his name*. This phrase is, apart from Mark 9$^{37,\ 39}$; 13^6, confined to L–A in the NT. It probably means 'as his representatives'. In A. 4$^{17f.}$; 5$^{28,\ 40}$, it is used with a verb of speaking, and should probably be taken here with *preached* rather than with *forgiveness of sins* (in A. 10^{43} forgiveness is 'through' his name).

to all nations: Also traced by the risen Lord to a proper understanding of the

OT is the universal scope of the church's mission. This is found in Mark 13¹⁰, along with bearing witness, in the context of the crisis of the last things. Here it characterizes a continuing historical process, which is thought of in spatial rather than temporal terms (in Matt. 28¹⁸⁻²⁰ the spatial and temporal are combined). It is repeated in more detail in A. 1⁸ ('to the end of the earth'), and is the key to the plan of A. as Luke chose to write it; though he cannot conceal that it was not immediately carried out. It is argued for exegetically on the basis of OT texts in A. 10³⁴⁻⁴³; 13⁴⁰⁻⁴⁶; 15¹⁴⁻¹⁹; 26¹⁷⁻²³; 28²⁸.

beginning from Jerusalem: Another instance of Luke's use of the participle of *archesthai* = 'to begin' (cf. 23⁵; 24²⁷; A. 1²²; 8³⁵; 10³⁷); but it is very clumsy, as, being in the nominative plural, it stands outside the sentence, which is constructed as an accusative and infinitive. There are consequently several variants, and some texts take it with the following words – 'beginning from Jerusalem you will be witnesses' – but that is also very abrupt. That the mission is to proceed from Jerusalem, which is repeated in A. 1⁴, ⁸, is also traced to the OT, but it is not to be found there except in the form that Gentiles will flock to Jerusalem in the eschatological time (Isa. 2²ᶠ·; Mic. 4¹ᶠ·; Zech. 8²⁰ᶠᶠ·). According to Jeremias (*Jesus' Promise to the Nations*) that was Jesus' own view.

48–49

Here are stated the relative parts to be played by the apostolic company and the risen Lord in this universal mission.

48

You are witnesses of these things: There is no verb in the Greek; in the light of A. 1⁸, where it is repeated to the apostles only, 'shall be' is probably to be understood. The characterization of the company as *witnesses*, and their speech and activity as testimony, is almost confined to L-A in the NT. Thus, 'witness' (*martus*), which in Paul is limited to the expression 'God is my witness', in Revelation has the special sense of 'martyr', and in the few instances in the rest of the NT refers to witnesses at a trial (I Peter 5¹ is an exception), is the word regularly used in A. of the apostolic company, including Paul, in their testimony to the gospel facts, and especially to the resurrection (A. 1⁸, ²²; 2³²; 3¹⁵; 5³²; 10³⁹, ⁴¹; 13³¹; 22¹⁵; 26¹⁶). Of the cognate words *marturion* = 'the witness borne' is used only at A. 4³³, *marturia* = 'the act of witnessing' only at A. 22¹⁸, *marturein* = 'to bear witness' at A. 23¹¹, and *diamarturesthai*, which is a synonym for *marturein* (cf. A. 23¹¹) is, apart from instances where it refers to emphatic speech (e.g. I Thess. 4⁶), confined to L-A in the NT (16²⁸; A. 2⁴⁰; 8²⁵; 10⁴²; 18⁵; 20²¹; 23¹¹; 28²³). The vocabulary is legal in origin, and denotes the giving of evidence at a trial, or of testimony to character. Luke's use of it indicates his conception of the Christian message and movement as compelling because based on evident and undeniable fact . In A. 1⁸ the apostles are to be 'my witnesses', i.e. 'my representatives in witnessing' or 'witnesses to me' (cf. in a rather different sense Isa. 43^{10-12}), and that is brought into closer connection with the universal mission. Here they are to be witnesses of *these things*, which in the context means primarily the resurrection of the suffering messiah, and the consequent repentance and forgiveness (cf. A. 1^{22}; $2^{32, 38}$; $3^{15, 19ff.}$; 4^{33}; $5^{31f.}$; 10^{41-43}; 13^{31-39}). But it may also extend to 'the things concerning Jesus of Nazareth' (v. 19), 'the things concerning himself' (v. 27), and 'everything written about me' (v. 44), as in A. $1^{3, 8, 21f.}$; 10^{37-39}; 13^{31}, and to the pre-ordination of these things in scripture, which for Luke is also historical fact. The apostolic missionaries are thus established as the divinely ordained foundation of the Christian faith and the repositories of its tradition, and they stand alongside the OT prophets (A. $1^{21f.}$; 10^{41-43}). Paul is to be drawn into their company on the basis of their testimony as well as his own vision of the exalted Lord (A. 13^{31}; 22^{15}).

49

And behold, I send the promise of my Father upon you: With the dramatic *And behold*, with an emphatic *ego* in the Greek alongside the verb, and the use of the present tense to denote what is future but immediate, the Lord in his final utterance states his own part in the mission. *I send (exapostellein)* is confined to L-A in the NT, apart from Gal. $4^{4, 6}$, where, as in A. 12^{11}; 13^{26}, it means 'to send from heaven' (cf. A. 2^{33-35}; for this with God's spirit, cf. Ps. 104^{30}). The message of the suffering and risen messiah is thus completed by reference, not to his ascension, nor to his parousia, nor to his appointment as saviour or judge, but to his agency with respect to the presence in and with the church of the divine gift and power (defined in A. 1^8, but not here, as the Spirit), which alone will make their witness effective (cf. A. $1^{5, 8}$). The statement is binitarian. Father and Son are engaged in a relation both to each other and to the church. The Son sends that which is the Father's promise; but he does not do this by passing on the power and spirit with which he had been filled for his ministry ($4^{1, 14}$; 5^{17}; 6^{19}), but by way of an exaltation so as to receive it from the Father, and to send it from a heavenly source – so explicitly in A. 2^{33}, where, together with A. $1^{4, 7}$, are the only references in A. to God as 'the Father'. (For the alternation of the Father and the Son as the source of the Spirit, cf. John 14^{26}; 15^{26}). What in A. is expressly designated the Spirit is here called *the promise of my Father*. This, which is repeated in A. 1^4, and is argued for exegetically in A. $2^{33ff., 39}$, is peculiar to Luke (except for Eph. 1^{13}, where, however, the meaning may be 'the Holy Spirit who is a promise of more to come'). The statement cannot have been made in this form in Aramaic or Hebrew, which does not have a word corresponding to the Greek noun *epangelia* = 'promise'. It rests upon a wider conception of the whole OT as a book of promises (cf. A. 7^{17}; $13^{23, 32}$; 26^6), for which Paul may have been largely responsible with his dialectic of law and grace (cf. Rom. 4^9; Gal. 3–4). That the Spirit should be selected from the OT as *the* (special) *promise* of God, which is thus almost a synonym for it, could reflect a judgment that the Spirit had in fact proved the chief agent in the emergence and operation of the church as the fulfilment of God's promises (cf. Gal. 3$^{2-5}$ for the Spirit as the primary possession that marks off the Christian). This judgment may also be seen in Luke's choice of the experience at Pentecost as the beginning of the narrative of the church in A., along with its interpretation by means of a strongly eschatological passage from Joel promising the pouring out of the Spirit on mankind. There is thus created a doctrine unknown in Judaism of the messiah as the dispenser of the Spirit.

stay in the city, until you are clothed with power from on high: *until* does not indicate the length of time; but *stay* (*kathizein* = 'to sit', used in the sense of 'remain' + A. 18^{11}; Mark 14^{32} par.) *in the city*, repeated in A. 1^{4}, implies that it will be short. In fact it is until the next festival. The promise is now further specified as *power* (repeated in A. 1^{8}). This is thoroughly Jewish – 'spirit' and power' belong together, and can form a hendiadys (cf. 1$^{17,\,35}$; 4^{14}; A. 10^{38}; Rom. 1^{4}; 15^{13}) – as is the conception of them as clothing (cf. Judg. 6^{34}; I Chron. 12^{8}; II Chron. 24^{20}; Ps. 92^{1}; Isa. 52^{1}; Ecclus 17^{3}). The choice of power here may also correspond with the presentation of Christianity in A. as a movement which was effective and irresistible because it had its source in God (A. 5$^{38f.}$; so here *from on high*, a common LXX expression), the gift and forceful irruption of whose Spirit (A. 5$^{3,\,9}$; 8$^{29,\,39}$) makes Christians (A. 2$^{1-38}$; 10$^{44-47}$), inspires their intelligent and confident speech (A. 4$^{8,\,31,\,33}$; 5^{32}; 6$^{5,\,10}$; 7^{55}), invests them with divine authority (A. 5$^{3,\,9}$; 8$^{14ff.}$; 15^{28}), and directs their purposeful movements (A. 8^{29}; 10$^{19f.}$; 11$^{24f.}$; 13$^{2-4}$; 16$^{6-7}$; 20$^{22f.}$). The outburst of the Spirit which had marked the events in chs. 1–2 is now to be renewed, though it is not indicated why this must wait upon a previous exaltation of Jesus. The Lord's words thus end on a strong note of expectation, which has to be recreated in A. 1$^{1-8}$.

(iii) *The parting benediction* (vv. 50–53)

This section is problematical in more than one respect. It raises, firstly, the vexed question of how a gospel was to end (cf. the strange endings in Mark 16$^{1-8}$; John 21). It raises here the further question of how a transition was to be made from the story of the earthly but now risen (exalted) Jesus to that of the church of the exalted (risen) Lord, and what measure of overlap there was to be between them. In the background here is also the question of what might have happened to the text as a result of the process (probable, but now hidden), by which an original two-volume work was divided into two separate books for inclusion into different parts of a developing Canon, each now to have its own beginning and ending.

Verse 49 would have provided an impressive ending to the Gospel (cf. Matthew, who concludes with the Lord's words, and John (20 or

21), which does so with a brief summary after them). This would be especially so if Luke judged the fulfilment of the expectation aroused there (including the ascension as belonging with it) to be the matter for a sequel. Verses 50–53 are transitional, and end somewhat lamely as the conclusion of a book. *he parted from them* (*diestē* = 'he withdrew') could be a more reserved form of 'he vanished out of their sight' (v. 31); in continuation of v. 50 it denotes a solemn parting, though not necessarily a final separation. The following words 'and was carried up into heaven' are absent from ℵ (original hand) D a b e ff² j l syrˢⁱⁿ one tradition of the Georgian version, and sometimes Augustine; they are omitted by RSV and NEB. If they are read they make the ending weaker. For if they are a synonym for *he parted from them* they are tautologous, and if not, and the sense is 'he parted from them, and then was carried up into heaven', they make the ascension (indicated as the goal in 9^{51}) take place on the same day as the resurrection appearances, and as an invisible event to be inferred only, and referred to in the barest possible formal statement (cf. Mark 16^{19}, and contrast A. 1^{9-11}). The problem is then why A. begins with an overlap of this conclusion of the Gospel, consisting of a reference back to this ascension, a repetition of the injunctions to await the Spirit as promise and as power to witness to Jesus in a universal mission, and an extended narrative of the ascension in the presence of apostles only, to whom in the meantime there have been resurrection appearances over a period of forty days (A. 1^{1-11}). The absence of 'and was carried up into heaven' has been explained as due to scribal omission aimed at reducing these contradictions between the ending of the Gospel and the beginning of A. On the other hand their lameness could be explained as due to their addition at a later stage to make the Gospel, once it was separated from A., complete in itself.[n] Some have proposed a more massive redaction at this point, suggesting that the vocabulary and ill-written character of A. 1^{1-5} indicate that it is from a later hand, and aimed to provide a beginning to A., as vv. 50–53 aimed to provide an ending to the Gospel, when the two were separated.[o]

---

n See Evans, *Resurrection*, pp. 99ff., for a discussion of attempts to defend the longer reading, and to account for the contradictions by Luke's holding two different conceptions of the resurrection/ascension at the same time.

o For this see P. Menoud, 'Remarques sur les textes de l'ascension dans Luc–Actes' in *Neutestamentliche Studien für R. Bultmann*, ed. Eltester, pp. 158ff. It is criticized by Haenchen, *Acts*, pp. 136ff.

At some time in the night, if the events from v. 27 onwards are continuous, the risen Lord conducts the company on a journey to the vicinity of Bethany (and therefore of the Mount of Olives?, cf. 19^{29}; A. 1^{12}), a place hallowed by his previous retreats there (21^{37}), and perhaps the location of his further appearances over forty days (A. 1^{3-12}). There is then a scene of high priestly blessing. For *lifting up his hands*, cf. Lev. 9^{22} of Aaron's blessing of Israel, and Ecclus 50^{20} of the high-priest Simon's blessing of the whole congregation with the utterance of the divine name (also II Enoch 56^1 for Enoch blessing his sons before his departure to heaven). This need not be pressed to imply a doctrine of Jesus as a priestly messiah, nor of the disciples as constituting the new temple. The blessing is perhaps that reserved for all repentant Israelites at the hands of the messiah (cf. A. 3^{19-26}).

Commentators have often noted the symmetry of the Gospel's beginning and ending at Jerusalem and in the temple ($1^{5ff.}$), but this could be fortuitous. The reaction of the company to the Lord's blessing and departure is to return to Jerusalem ('worshipped him', omitted by the same mss as omit the reference to the ascension, is probably a pious addition), and to be themselves constantly engaged in the temple in *blessing* (the same verb as is used in v. 50) *God*. This somewhat conventional expression (cf. 1^{64}; 2^{20}) is probably intended to point forward to the later attachment of the apostles to the temple (A. 2^{46}; $3^{1f.}$; $5^{20, \ 42}$; 22^{17}). If so, it does not provide a climax, but rather calls for a sequel.

Index of Modern Authors and Editors